Alan Rogers

2006

D0714466

France

Quality camping & caravanning sites

INSPECTED CAMPSITES & SELECTED

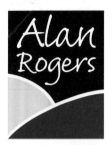

Compiled by: Alan Rogers Guides Ltd

Designed by: Paul Effenberg, Vine Design Ltd

Maps created by Customised Mapping (01769 540044)
contain background data provided by GisDATA Ltd
Maps are © Alan Rogers Guides and Gis DATA Ltd 2005

© Alan Rogers Guides Ltd 2006

Published by: Alan Rogers Guides Ltd,
Spelmonden Old Oast, Goudhurst, Kent TN17 1HE
www.alanrogers.com Tel: 01580 214000

British Library Cataloguing-in-Publication Data:
A catalogue record for this book is available from the
British Library.

ISBN-13 978 0954 52718 1
ISBN-10 0 9545271 8 6

Printed in Great Britain by J H Haynes & Co Ltd

CONTENTS

" ...the campsites included in this book have been chosen entirely on merit, and no payment of any sort is made by them for their inclusion."

Alan Rogers, 1968

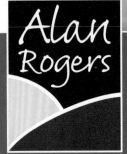

the Alan Rogers approach

IT IS NEARLY 40 YEARS SINCE ALAN ROGERS PUBLISHED THE FIRST CAMPSITE GUIDE THAT BORE HIS NAME. SINCE THEN THE RANGE HAS EXPANDED TO SIX TITLES. WHAT'S MORE, ALAN ROGERS GUIDES HAVE BECOME ESTABLISHED IN HOLLAND TOO: ALL SIX TITLES ARE ALSO PUBLISHED IN THE NETHERLANDS AND STOCKED BY WELL OVER 90% OF ALL DUTCH BOOKSHOPS.

THERE ARE OVER 11,000 CAMPSITES IN FRANCE OF VARYING QUALITY: THIS GUIDE CONTAINS IMPARTIALLY WRITTEN REPORTS ON OVER 580, INCLUDING SOME OF THE VERY FINEST, EACH BEING INDIVIDUALLY INSPECTED AND SELECTED. ALL THE USUAL MAPS AND INDEXES ARE ALSO INCLUDED, DESIGNED TO HELP YOU FIND THE CHOICE OF CAMPSITE THAT'S RIGHT FOR YOU. WE HOPE YOU ENJOY SOME HAPPY AND SAFE TRAVELS – AND SOME PLEASURABLE 'ARMCHAIR TOURING' IN THE MEANTIME!

A question of quality

The criteria we use when inspecting and selecting sites are numerous, but the most important by far is the question of good quality. People want different things from their choice of campsite so we try to include a range of campsite 'styles' to cater for a wide variety of preferences: from those seeking a small peaceful campsite in the heart of the countryside, to visitors looking for an 'all singing, all dancing' site in a popular seaside resort. Those with more specific interests, such as sporting facilities, cultural events or historical attractions, are also catered for.

The size of the site, whether it's part of a campsite chain or privately owned, makes no difference in terms of it being required to meet our exacting standards in respect of its quality and it being 'fit for purpose'. In other words, irrespective of the size of the site, or the number of facilities it offers, we consider and evaluate the welcome, the pitches, the sanitary facilities, the cleanliness, the general maintenance and even the location.

INSPECTED SINCE 1968 & SELECTED

Independent and honest

Whilst the content and scope of the Alan Rogers guides have expanded considerably since the early editions, our selection of campsites still employs exactly the same philosophy and criteria as defined by Alan Rogers in 1968.

'telling it how it is'

Firstly, and most importantly, our selection is based entirely on our own rigorous and independent inspection and selection process. Campsites cannot buy their way into our guides – indeed the extensive Site Report which is written by us, not by the site owner, is provided free of charge so we are free to say what we think and to provide an honest, 'warts and all' description. This is written in plain English and without the use of confusing icons or symbols.

Expert opinions

We rely on our dedicated team of Site Assessors, all of whom are experienced campers, caravanners or motorcaravanners, to visit and recommend sites. Each year they travel some 100,000 miles around Europe inspecting new campsites and re-inspecting the older ones. Our thanks are due to them for their enthusiastic efforts, their diligence and integrity.

We also appreciate the feedback we receive from many of our readers and we always make a point of following up complaints, suggestions or recommendations for possible new sites. Of course we get a few grumbles too – but it really is a few, and those we do receive usually relate to overcrowding or to poor maintenance during the peak school holiday period.

Please bear in mind that although we are interested to hear about any complaints we have no contractual relationship with the campsites featured in our guides and are therefore not in a position to intervene in any dispute between a reader and a campsite.

Alan Rogers 2006 France · Central Europe · Europe · Spain & Portugal · Britain & Ireland · Italy

Highly respected by site owners and readers alike, there is no better guide when it comes to forming an independent view of a campsite's quality. When you need to be confident in your choice of campsite, you need the Alan Rogers Guide.

- ✓ Sites only included on merit
- ✓ Sites cannot pay to be included
- ✓ Independently inspected, rigorously assessed
- ✓ Impartial reviews
- ✓ Nearly 40 years of expertise

INSPECTED CAMPSITES & SELECTED

WRITTEN IN PLAIN ENGLISH, OUR GUIDES ARE EXCEPTIONALLY EASY TO USE, BUT A FEW WORDS OF EXPLANATION REGARDING THE LAYOUT AND CONTENT MAY BE HELPFUL. REGULAR READERS WILL SEE THAT OUR SITE REPORTS ARE GROUPED INTO 19 'TOURIST REGIONS' AND THEN BY THE VARIOUS DÉPARTEMENTS IN EACH OF THESE REGIONS IN NUMERICAL ORDER.

Region

The Site Reports – *Example of an entry*

Site no **Site name**

Postal Address (including département)

A description of the site in which we try to give an idea of its general features – its size, its situation, its strengths and its weaknesses. This section should provide a picture of the site itself with reference to the facilities that are provided and if they impact on its appearance or character. We include details on pitch numbers, electricity (with amperage), hardstandings etc. in this section as pitch design, planning and terracing affects the site's overall appearance. Similarly we continue to include reference to pitches used for caravan holiday homes, chalets, and the like. Importantly at the end of this column we indicate if there are any restrictions, e.g. no tents, naturist sites.

Facilities

Lists more specific information on the site's facilities, as well as certain off site attractions and activities.

Open

Site opening dates.

At a glance

Welcome & Ambience	✓✓✓✓	Location	✓✓✓✓✓
Quality of Pitches	✓✓✓✓✓	Range of Facilities	✓✓✓✓

Our inspectors grade each site out of five, giving a unique indication of certain key criteria that may be important when making your decision.

Directions

Separated from the main text in order that they may be read and assimilated more easily by a navigator en-route. Bear in mind that road improvement schemes can result in some road numbers being altered. Websites like **www.mappy.com** and others give detailed route plans.

GPS: references are provided as we obtain them for satellite navigation systems (in degrees and minutes).

Charges 2006

Reservations

including contact details

Regions and départements

For administrative purposes France is actually divided into 23 official regions covering the 95 départements (similar to our counties). However, these do not always coincide with the needs of tourists. For example the area we think of as the Dordogne is split between two of the official regions. We have, therefore, opted to feature our campsites within unofficial 'tourist regions', and the relevant départements are stated in our introduction to each region with their official number (eg. the département of Manche is number 50) included. We use these département numbers as the first two digits of our campsite numbers, so any campsite in the Manche département will start with the number 50, prefixed with FR.

Indexes

Our three indexes allow you to find sites by site number and name, by region and site name or by the town or village where the site is situated.

Campsite Maps

The maps relate to our tourist regions and will help you to identify the approximate position of each campsite. You will certainly need more detailed maps and we have found the Michelin atlas to be particularly useful.

Facilities

Toilet blocks

We assume that toilet blocks will be equipped with a reasonable amount of British style WCs, washbasins with hot and cold water and hot showers with dividers or curtains, and will have all necessary shelves, hooks, plugs and mirrors. We also assume that there will be an identified chemical toilet disposal point, and that the campsite will provide water and waste water points and bin areas. If not the case, we comment. We continue to mention certain features that some readers find important: washbasins in cubicles, facilities for babies, facilities for those with disabilities and motorcaravan service points. Readers with disabilities are advised to contact the site of their choice to ensure that facilities are appropriate to their needs.

Shop

Basic or fully supplied, and opening dates.

Bars, restaurants, takeaway facilities and entertainment

We try hard to supply opening and closing dates (if other than the campsite opening dates) and to identify if there are discos or other entertainment.

Children's play areas

Fenced and with safety surface (e.g. sand, bark or pea-gravel).

Swimming pools

If particularly special, we cover in detail in our main campsite description but reference is always included under our Facilities listings. Opening dates, charges and levels of supervision are provided where we have been notified. There is a regulation whereby Bermuda shorts may not be worn in swimming pools (for health reasons). It is worth ensuring that you do take 'proper' swimming trunks with you.

Leisure facilities

E.g. playing fields, bicycle hire, organised activities and entertainment.

Dogs

If dogs are not accepted or restrictions apply, we state it here. Check the quick reference list at the back of the guide.

Off site

This briefly covers leisure facilities, tourist attractions, restaurants etc nearby.

At a glance

All Alan Rogers sites have been inspected and selected – they must meet stringent quality criteria. A campsite may have all the boxes ticked when it comes to listing facilities but if it's not inherently a 'good site' then it will not be in the guide.

These 'at a glance' ratings are a unique indication of certain key criteria that may be important when making your decision. Quite deliberately they are subjective and, modesty aside, are based on our inspectors' own expert opinions at the time of their inspection.

Charges

These are the latest provided by the sites. In those few cases where 2005 or 2006 prices are not given, we try to give a general guide.

Reservations

Necessary for high season (roughly mid-July to mid-August) in popular holiday areas (ie beach resorts). You can reserve via our own Alan Rogers Travel Service or through tour operators. Or be wholly independent and contact the campsite(s) of your choice direct, using the phone or e-mail numbers shown in the site reports, but please bear in mind that many sites are closed all winter.

Telephone numbers

All numbers assume that you are phoning from within France. To phone France from outside that country, prefix the number shown with the relevant International Code (00 33) and drop the first 0, shown as (0) in the numbers indicated.

Opening dates

Are those advised to us during the early autumn of the previous year – sites can, and sometimes do, alter these dates before the start of the following season, often for good reasons. If you intend to visit shortly after a published opening date, or shortly before the closing date, it is wise to check that it will actually be open at the time required. Similarly some parks operate a restricted service during the low season, only opening some of their facilities (e.g. swimming pools) during the main season; where we know about this, and have the relevant dates, we indicate it – again if you are at all doubtful it is wise to check.

Some French site owners are very laid back when it comes to opening and closing dates. They may not be fully ready by their stated opening dates – grass and hedges may not all be cut or perhaps only limited sanitary facilities open. At the end of the season they also tend to close down some facilities and generally wind down prior to the closing date. Bear this in mind if you are travelling early or late in the season – it is worth phoning ahead.

The Camping Cheque low season touring system goes some way to addressing this in that participating campsites are encouraged to have all key facilities open and running by the opening date and to remain fully operational until the closing date.

Our Accommodation Section

 Mobile homes ▶ page 403

Over recent years, more and more campsites have added high quality mobile home and chalet accommodation. In response to feedback from many of our readers, and to reflect this evolution in campsites, we have now decided to include a separate section on mobile homes and chalets. If a site offers this accommodation, it is indicated above the site report with a page reference where full details are given. We have chosen a number of sites offering some of the best accommodation available and have included full details of one or two accommodation types at these sites. Please note however that many other campsites listed in this guide may also have a selection of accommodation for rent.

Whether you're an 'old hand' in terms of camping and caravanning or are contemplating your first trip, a regular reader of our Guides or a new 'convert', we wish you well in your travels and hope we have been able to help in some way. We are, of course, also out and about ourselves, visiting sites, talking to owners and readers, and generally checking on standards and new developments.

We wish all our readers thoroughly enjoyable Camping and Caravanning in 2006 – favoured by good weather of course!

THE ALAN ROGERS TEAM

have you visited
 www.alanrogers.com
yet?

INSPECTED CAMPSITES & SELECTED

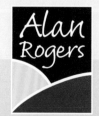 Alan Rogers

Thousands have already, researching their holiday and catching up with the latest news and special offers.

Launched in January 2004 it has fast become the first-stop for countless caravanners, motorhome owners and campers all wanting reliable, impartial and detailed information for their next trip.

It features a fully searchable database of the best campsites in the UK & Ireland, and the rest of Europe: over 2,000 campsites in 26 countries. All are Alan Rogers inspected and selected, allowing you to find the site that's perfect for you, with the reassurance of knowing we've been there first.

REGIONS OF FRANCE

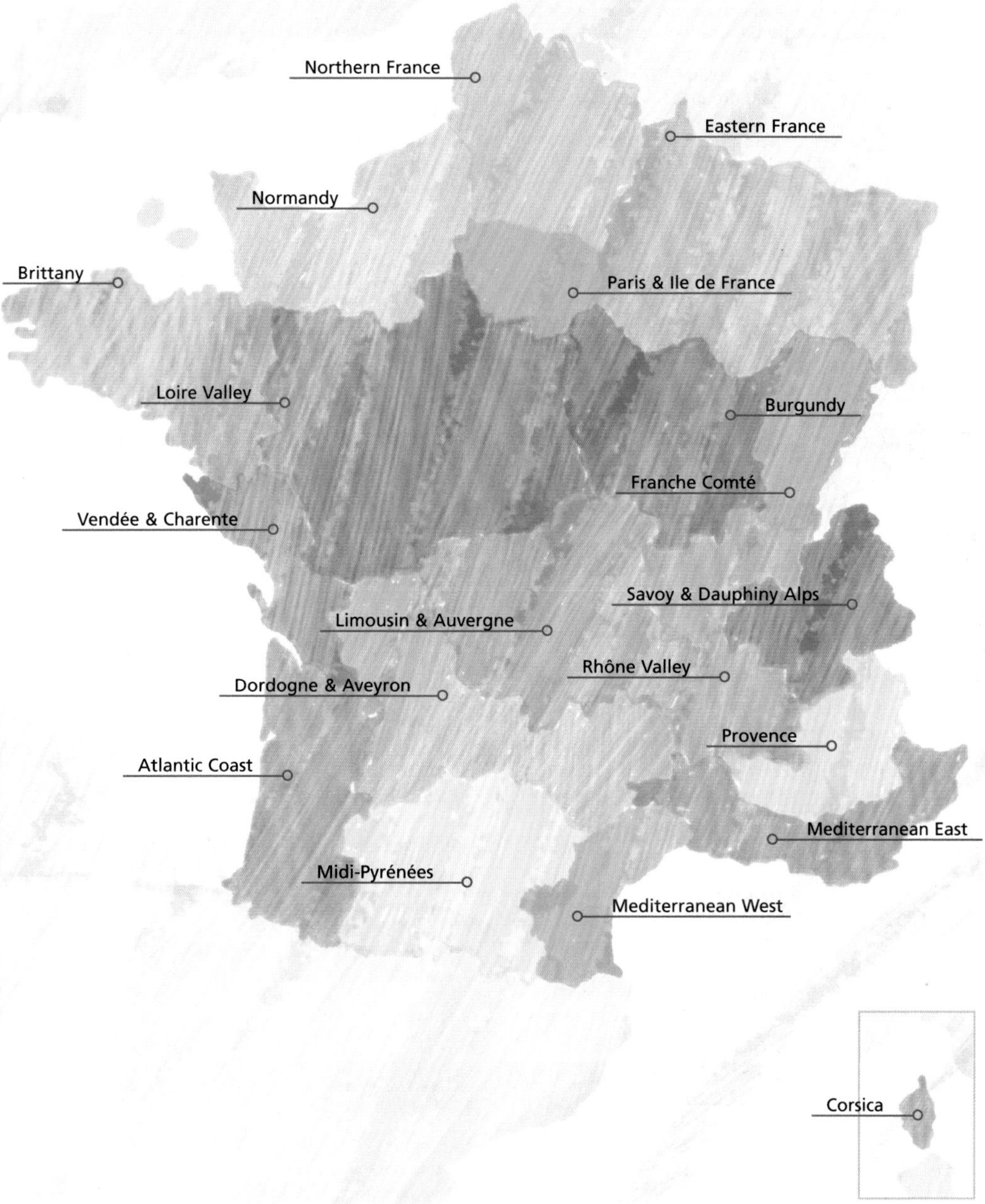
Northern France
Eastern France
Normandy
Brittany
Paris & Ile de France
Loire Valley
Burgundy
Franche Comté
Vendée & Charente
Savoy & Dauphiny Alps
Limousin & Auvergne
Rhône Valley
Dordogne & Aveyron
Provence
Atlantic Coast
Mediterranean East
Midi-Pyrénées
Mediterranean West
Corsica

In 2004 we introduced the first ever Alan Rogers Campsite Awards.

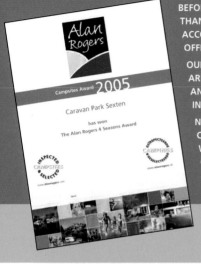

BEFORE MAKING OUR AWARDS, WE CAREFULLY CONSIDER MORE THAN 2000 CAMPSITES FEATURED IN OUR GUIDES, TAKING INTO ACCOUNT COMMENTS FROM OUR SITE ASSESSORS, OUR HEAD OFFICE TEAM, AND, OF COURSE, OUR READERS.

OUR AWARD WINNERS COVER A MASSIVE GEOGRAPHICAL AREA FROM THE IBERIAN PENINSULA TO EASTERN SLOVENIA, AND, IN OUR FIRST YEAR, WE MADE AWARDS TO CAMPSITES IN 11 DIFFERENT COUNTRIES.

NEEDLESS TO SAY, IT'S AN EXTREMELY DIFFICULT TASK TO CHOOSE OUR EVENTUAL WINNERS, BUT WE BELIEVE THAT WE HAVE IDENTIFIED A NUMBER OF CAMPSITES WITH TRULY OUTSTANDING CHARACTERISTICS.

IN EACH CASE, WE HAVE SELECTED AN OUTRIGHT WINNER, ALONG WITH TWO HIGHLY COMMENDED RUNNERS-UP.

Listed below are full details of each of our award categories and our winners for 2005, followed on page 12 by our first ever winners from 2004.

Alan Rogers Progress Award 2005

This award reflects the hard work and commitment undertaken by particular site owners to improve and upgrade their site.

WINNER
Camping Idro Rio Vantone, Italy

RUNNERS-UP
Camping Le Moulin Fort, France

Camping Mas Nou, Spain

Alan Rogers Welcome Award 2005

This award takes account of sites offering a particularly friendly welcome and maintaining a friendly ambience throughout reader's holidays.

WINNER
Camping Coin Tranquille, France

RUNNERS-UP
Woodlands Park Touring Park, Ireland

Camping t'Strandheem, Netherlands

Alan Rogers Active Holiday Award 2005

This award reflects sites in outstanding locations which are ideally suited for active holidays, notably walking or cycling, but which could extend to include such activities as winter sports or water sports

WINNER
Camping Wulfener Hals, Germany

RUNNERS-UP
Camping Ty Naden, France

Ferienparadies Natterer See, Austria

Alan Rogers Motorhome Award 2005

Motor home sales are increasing and this award acknowledges sites which, in our opinion, have made outstanding efforts to welcome motorhome clients.

WINNER
Camping La Barbanne, France

RUNNERS-UP
Camping El Garrofer, Spain

Oxon Hall Touring Park, England

Alan Rogers 4 Seasons Award 2005

This award is made to outstanding sites with extended opening dates and which welcome clients to a uniformly high standard throughout the year.

WINNER
Caravan Park Sexten, Italy

RUNNERS-UP
Brighouse Bay Holiday Park, Scotland

Camping L'Escale, France

Alan Rogers Seaside Award 2005

This award is made for sites which we feel are outstandingly suitable for a really excellent seaside holiday.

WINNER
Camping Union Lido Vacanze, Italy

RUNNERS-UP
Lanternacamp, Croatia

Playa Montroig Camping, Spain

Alan Rogers Country Award 2005

This award contrasts with our former award and acknowledges sites which are attractively located in delightful, rural locations.

WINNER
Camping La Ribeyre, France

RUNNERS-UP
Camping Alte Sagemuhle, Germany
Ruthern Valley Holidays, England

Alan Rogers Rented Accommodation Award 2005

Given the increasing importance of rented accommodation on many campsites, and the inclusion in many Alan Rogers guides, of a rented accommodation section, we feel that it is important to acknowledge sites which have made a particular effort in creating a high quality 'rented accommodation' park.

WINNER
Yelloh! Village Le Club Farret, France

RUNNERS-UP
Centro Vacanze Pra' Delle Torri, Italy
Camping & Bungalow Park Sanguli, Spain

Alan Rogers Unique Site Award 2005

This award acknowledges sites with unique, outstanding features – something which simply cannot be found elsewhere and which is an important attraction of the site.

WINNER
Topcamp Feddet, Denmark

RUNNERS-UP
Camping Mazurski Eden, Poland
Skjerneset Camping, Norway

Alan Rogers Family Site Award 2005

Many sites claim to be child friendly but this award acknowledges the sites we feel to be the very best in this respect.

WINNER
Camping Les Medes, Spain

RUNNERS-UP
Trevornick Holiday Park, England
Camping Breebronne, Netherlands

Alan Rogers Readers' Award 2005

In 2005 we introduced a new award, which we believe to be the most important, our Readers' Award. We simply invited our readers (by means of an on-line poll at www.alanrogers.com) to nominate the site they enjoyed most. The outright winner is a well known and much loved Italian site celebrating its 50th anniversary in 2005:

WINNER
Camping Union Lido Vacanze, Italy

Alan Rogers Special Award 2005

A special award is made to acknowledge sites which we feel have overcome a very significant set-back, and have, not only returned to their former condition, but has added extra amenities and can therefore be fairly considered to be even better than before. In 2005 we acknowledge three sites, all of which have overcome major problems.

Yelloh! Village Le Serignan Plage, France
Camping Arinella Bianca, France
Slavoj Autocamp Litomerice, Czech Republic

In 2004 we introduced the first ever Alan Rogers Campsite Awards.

BEFORE MAKING OUR AWARDS, WE CAREFULLY CONSIDER MORE THAN 2000 CAMPSITES FEATURED IN OUR GUIDES, TAKING INTO ACCOUNT COMMENTS FROM OUR SITE ASSESSORS, OUR HEAD OFFICE TEAM, AND, OF COURSE, OUR READERS.

OUR AWARD WINNERS COVER A MASSIVE GEOGRAPHICAL AREA FROM THE IBERIAN PENINSULA TO EASTERN SLOVENIA, AND, IN OUR FIRST YEAR, WE MADE AWARDS TO CAMPSITES IN 11 DIFFERENT COUNTRIES.

NEEDLESS TO SAY, IT'S AN EXTREMELY DIFFICULT TASK TO CHOOSE OUR EVENTUAL WINNERS, BUT WE BELIEVE THAT WE HAVE IDENTIFIED A NUMBER OF CAMPSITES WITH TRULY OUTSTANDING CHARACTERISTICS.

IN EACH CASE, WE HAVE SELECTED AN OUTRIGHT WINNER, ALONG WITH TWO HIGHLY COMMENDED RUNNERS-UP.

Listed below are full details of each of our award categories and our first ever winners from 2004.

Alan Rogers Progress Award 2004

This award reflects the hard work and commitment undertaken by particular site owners to improve and upgrade their site.

WINNER

Camping und Freizeitpark Lux Oase, Germany

RUNNERS-UP

Trethem Mill Touring Park, England

Camping Les Deux Vallées, France

Alan Rogers Welcome Award 2004

This award takes account of sites offering a particularly friendly welcome and maintaining a friendly ambience throughout reader's holidays.

WINNER

Camping Caravaning Les Pêcheurs, France

RUNNERS-UP

Balatontourist Diana Camping, Hungary

Camping des Abers, France

Alan Rogers Active Holiday Award 2004

This award reflects sites in outstanding locations which are ideally suited for active holidays, notably walking or cycling, but which could extend to include such activities as winter sports or water sports

WINNER

Castel Camping Le Ty Nadan, France

RUNNERS-UP

Camping Menina, Slovenia

River Dart Adventures, England

Alan Rogers Motorhome Award 2004

Motor home sales are increasing and this award acknowledges sites which, in our opinion, have made outstanding efforts to welcome motorhome clients.

WINNER

Camping El Garrofer, Spain

RUNNERS-UP

Castel Camping Sequoia Parc, France

Camping Jungfrau, Switzerland

Alan Rogers 4 Seasons Award 2004

This award is made to outstanding sites with extended opening dates and which welcome clients to a uniformly high standard throughout the year.

WINNER

Camping Caravaning L'Escale, France

RUNNERS-UP

Camping Vilanova Park, Spain

Ferienparadies Natterer See, Austria

Alan Rogers Seaside Award 2004

This award is made for sites which we feel are outstandingly suitable for a really excellent seaside holiday.

WINNER

Camping Union Lido Vacanze, Italy

RUNNERS-UP

Yelloh! Village Le Brasilia, France

Pentewan Sands Holiday Park, England

Alan Rogers Country Award 2004

This award contrasts with our former award and acknowledges sites which are attractively located in delightful, rural locations.

WINNER

Castel Camping Pyrénées Natura, France

RUNNERS-UP

Camping Il Collaccio, Italy

Camping Elbsee, Germany

Alan Rogers Rented Accommodation Award 2004

Given the increasing importance of rented accommodation on many campsites, and the inclusion in many Alan Rogers guides, of a rented accommodation section, we feel that it is important to acknowledge sites which have made a particular effort in creating a high quality 'rented accommodation' park.

WINNER

Camping and Bungalows Sanguli, Spain

RUNNERS-UP

Sunêlia Les Bois du Bardelet, France

Sandy Balls Holiday Centre, England

Alan Rogers Unique Site Award 2004

This award acknowledges sites with unique, outstanding features – something which simply cannot be found elsewhere and which is an important attraction of the site.

WINNER

Bøsøre Strand Ferie Park, Denmark

RUNNERS-UP

Skånes Djurparks Camping, Sweden

Camping De Vechtstreek, Netherlands

Alan Rogers Family Site Award 2004

Many sites claim to be child friendly but this award acknowledges the sites we feel to be the very best in this respect.

WINNER

Woodlands Leisure Park, England

RUNNERS-UP

Camping de Molenhof, Netherlands

Camping Cambrils Park, Spain

Alan Rogers Special Award 2004

A special award is made to acknowledge sites which we feel have overcome a very significant setback, and have, not only returned to their former condition, but has added extra amenities and can therefore be fairly considered to be even better than before.

In 2004 we acknowledged 3 French campsites, all of which have undergone major problems and all of which have made highly impressive recoveries.

Domaine de la Rive, France

Domaine du Colombier, France

Domaine de Gaujac, France

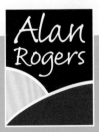

Alan Rogers

service
and value

The Alan Rogers Travel Service was set up to provide a low cost booking service for readers. We can tailor-make a holiday to suit your requirements, giving you maximum choice and flexibility: exactly what we have been offering for some 6 years now.

Alternatively you can opt for one of our Value+ holidays, pocketing a 20% saving off base price in return for accepting various restrictions (see opposite).

And because we organise so many holidays we can offer outstanding Ferry Deals too!

Unbeatable
Ferry Deals

WE ARE ALWAYS NEGOTIATING NEW OFFERS ON CHANNEL CROSSINGS. MAKE SURE YOU ASK US ABOUT OUR FAMOUS DEALS!

- ✓ CARAVANS GO FREE
- ✓ TRAILERS GO FREE
- ✓ MOTORHOMES PRICED AS CARS

SEE PAGES 18-19

At the Alan Rogers Travel Service we're always keen to find the best deals and keenest prices. There are always great savings on offer, and we're constantly negotiating new ferry rates and money-saving offers, so just call us on

0870 405 4055

and ask about the latest deals.

or visit
www.alanrogersdirect.com

THE AIMS OF THE TRAVEL SERVICE ARE SIMPLE.

- To provide convenience - when booking a campsite yourself can be anything but convenient.

- To provide peace of mind - when you need it most.

- To provide a friendly, knowledgeable, efficient service - when this can be hard to find.

- To provide a low cost means of organising your holiday – when prices can be so complicated.

HOW IT WORKS

1 Choose your campsite(s)

2 Choose your dates

3 Choose your ferry crossing

Then just call us for an instant quote

0870 405 4055

or visit
www.alanrogersdirect.com

LET US BOOK YOUR PITCH AND FERRY FOR YOU

For full details request our FREE 2006 CAMPSITE RESERVATION GUIDE

0870 405 4055

Ask about our incredible Ferry Deals:

- ☑ Caravans GO FREE
- ☑ Motorhomes Priced as Cars

Value+ Holidays SAVE 20%

We can book many campsites for you, with complete flexibility: any dates, any duration, any arrival/departure day, any ferry and so on.

But some readers do not necessarily need such choice and would prefer 'off the shelf' convenience and even lower prices. Our **Value+** holidays allow you to reduce your base price by a massive 20%, in return for meeting certain conditions.

We can offer **Value+** holidays at over 50 campsites within our 2006 programme. To qualify for huge savings please understand that your holiday must be...

- + Ferry-inclusive
- + Single site only – no overnight campsite stops
- + Minimum of 7 nights
- + Either 7, 14 or 21 nights duration
- + Booked at least 30 days in advance of travel
- + Subject to availability on each site

See our 2006 Campsite Reservation Guide for details or call us today for a no-obligation quote.

0870 405 4055

Leave The Hassle To Us

- All site fees paid in advance – you won't need to take extra currency with you.

- Your pitch is reserved for you – travel with peace of mind.

- No endless overseas phone calls or correspondence with foreign site owners.

- No need to pay foreign currency deposits and booking fees.

- Take advantage of our expert advice and experience of camping in Europe.

Already Booked Your Ferry?

We're confident that our ferry inclusive booking service offers unbeatable value. However, if you have already booked your ferry then we can still make a pitch-only reservation for you. Your booking must be for a minimum of 10 nights, and since our prices are based on our ferry inclusive service, you need to be aware that a non-ferry booking will always result in somewhat higher prices than if you were to book direct with the site.

You still benefit from:

- Hassle-free booking with no booking fees and foreign currency deposits.

- Comprehensive Travel Pack.

- Peace of mind: site fees paid in advance, with your pitch reserved for you.

ASK FOR A COPY OF OUR 2006
CAMPSITE RESERVATION GUIDE
0870 405 4055

book on-line
and save money

www.alanrogersdirect.com is a website designed to give you everything you need to know when it comes to booking your Alan Rogers inspected and selected campsite, and your low cost ferry.

Our glossy brochure gives you all the info you need but it is only printed once a year. And our friendly, expert reservations team is always happy to help on **0870 405 4055** – but they do go home sometimes!

Visit www.alanrogersdirect.com and you'll find constantly updated information, latest ferry deals, special offers from campsites and much more. And you can visit it at any time of day or night!

alanrogersdirect.com
book on-line and save

Campsite Information
- ☑ Details of all Travel Service campsites - **instantly**
- ☑ Find latest special offers on campsites - **instantly**
- ☑ Check campsite availability - **instantly**

Ferry Information
- ☑ Check ferry availability - **instantly**
- ☑ Find latest ferry deals - **instantly**
- ☑ Book your ferry online - **instantly**
- ☑ Save money - **instantly**

Save Money!
BOOK YOUR CAMPSITE AND FERRY - INSTANTLY

Crossing the Channel

One of the great advantages of booking with the Alan Rogers Travel Service is the tremendous value we offer. Our money-saving Ferry Deals have become legendary: see below. As agents for all the cross-Channel operators we can book all your travel arrangements with the minimum of fuss and at the best possible rates.

Just call us for an instant quote

0870 405 4055

or visit

www.alanrogersdirect.com
Book on-line AND SAVE

Short Sea Routes

Hop across the Channel in the shortest possible time and you can be on your way. We offer all main routes at great prices (when you book a pitch + ferry 'package' through us). And why not take advantage of our Ferry Deals? Caravans and trailers can go **FREE** on Dover – Calais with P&O Ferries.

SPECIAL OFFERS

norfolkline
DOVER - DUNKERQUE FERRIES
Dover – Dunkirk

3 brand new ships will be operational for 2006, offering comfort, speed and efficiency.

Motorhomes **Priced as Cars***   Caravans from **£7** each way**

Travel **any time of day**, (including weekends for motorhomes). Popular times will book up fast, so don't delay to secure your first choice!

Weekends are Friday, Saturday, Sunday in each direction. Offer valid all year.

* Supplements for vehicles over 7m may apply. Please ask for details.
** Offer applies to all dates excluding crossings between 14/7-10/9 2006 (midweek and weekend).

P&O Ferries
Dover – Calais

Caravans **Go FREE***   Motorhomes **Priced as Cars****

* Between 23.30 – 07:15, all year except high season weekends.
** Any length, for off peak crossings all year.

SEAFRANCE
DOVER-CALAIS FERRIES
Dover – Calais

Caravans **Go FREE***   Motorhomes **Priced as Cars****

* Between 23:30 – 07:00, midweek and weekends all year.
** Up to 8m all year.

Longer Sea Routes

Sometimes it pays to take a longer crossing: a more leisurely journey perhaps. Or a chance to enjoy dinner on board ship, followed by a night in a comfortable cabin, awaking refreshed and ready for the onward drive. Either way there are still savings to be had with our super Ferry Deals (when you book a pitch and ferry 'package' through us).

SPECIAL OFFERS

Brittany Ferries

Portsmouth – Caen

Portsmouth – Cherbourg

St Malo – Portsmouth
(low season only)

Plymouth – Roscoff

50% OFF Caravans
Off peak mid-week crossings.
Offer does not apply to certain Plymouth – Roscoff crossings.

P&O Ferries **Hull – Rotterdam/Zeebrugge**

Caravans **Go FREE**   Motorhomes **Priced as Cars**
Any length, Sat/Sun crossings only.
Between 1st May - 31st October 2006.
Bookings must be made by 5th January 2006.

Condorferries   **Poole/Weymouth – St Malo**

Motorhomes Priced As Cars on all crossings direct to
St Malo and via Channel Islands, travelling any day of the week.
Offer excludes high season (26-28/5 and 14/7-23/8 out, 2-4/6 and 21/7-3/9 in).

lst time abroad?

REPARATIONS FOR THAT
FIRST TRIP CAN DE
DAUNTING. BUT DON'T
WORRY - WE'RE WITH
YOU ALL THE WAY.

Don't delay – these offers are strictly subject
to availability and will be first come, first served.

Ferry offers only valid in conjunction with a Camping Cheque or Alan Rogers Travel
Service holiday.

Just call us for an instant quote **0870 405 4055**

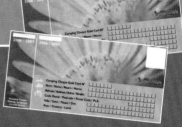

MAP 1

Brittany

Rolling sandy beaches, hidden coves, pretty villages and a picturesque coastline all combine to make Brittany a very popular holiday destination. Full of Celtic culture steeped in myths and legends, Brittany is one of the most distinctive regions of France.

DÉPARTEMENTS: 22 CÔTES D'ARMOR, 29 FINISTÈRE, 35 ILLE-ET-VILAINE, 56 MORBIHAN, 44 LOIRE ATLANTIQUE

MAJOR CITIES: RENNES AND BREST

Brittany's 800 miles of rocky coastline offers numerous bays, busy little fishing villages and broad sandy beaches dotted with charming seaside resorts. The coastline to the north of Brittany is rugged with a maze of rocky coves, while to the south, the shore is flatter with long sandy beaches. Inland you'll find wooded valleys, rolling fields, moors and giant granite boulders, but most impressive is the wealth of prehistoric sites, notably the Carnac standing stones.

Breton culture offers a rich history of menhirs, crosses, cathedrals and castles. Strong Celtic roots provide this region with its own distinctive traditions, evident in the local Breton costume and music, traditional religious festivals and the cuisine, featuring crêpes and cider. Many castles and manor houses, countless chapels and old towns and villages provide evidence of Brittany's eventful history and wealth of traditions. The abbey fortress of Mont-St-Michel on the north coast should not be missed and Concarneau in the south is a lovely walled town enclosed by granite rocks.

Places of interest

Cancale: small fishing port famous for oysters.

Carnac: 3,000 standing stones (menhirs).

Concarneau: fishing port, old walled town.

Dinan: historical walled town.

La Baule: resort with lovely, sandy bay.

Le Croisic: fishing port, Naval museum.

Guérande: historic walled town.

Perros-Guirec: leading resort of the 'Pink Granite Coast'.

Quiberon: boat service to three islands: Belle Ile (largest of the Breton islands), Houat, Hoedic.

Rennes: capital of Brittany, medieval streets; half timbered houses; Brittany Museum.

St Malo: historical walled city, fishing port.

Cuisine of the region

Fish and shellfish are commonplace; traditional *crêperies* abound and welcome visitors with a cup of local cider.

Agneau de pré-salé: leg of lamb from animals pastured in the salt marshes and meadows.

Beurre blanc: sauce for fish dishes made with shallots, wine vinegar and butter.

Cotriade: fish soup with potatoes, onions, garlic and butter.

Crêpes Bretonnes: the thinnest of pancakes with a variety of sweet fillings.

Galette: can be a biscuit, cake or pancake; with sweet or savoury fillings.

Gâteau Breton: rich cake.

Poulet blanc Breton: free-range, quality, white Breton chicken.

FR22010 Camping Les Capucines

Kervourdon, F-22300 Tredrez-Locquémeau (Côtes d'Armor)

A warm welcome awaits at Les Capucines which is quietly situated about a kilometre from the village of Saint Michel with its good, sandy beach and also very near Locquémeau, a pretty fishing village. This attractive, family run site has 100 pitches on flat or slightly sloping ground. All are well marked out by hedges, with mature trees and with more recently planted. There are 70 pitches with electricity, water and drainage, including 10 for larger units. All the amenities are open all season. A good value restaurant/crêperie can be found at Trédrez, others at Saint Michel. A Sites et Paysages member.

Facilities	Directions
Two modern toilet blocks, clean and very well kept, include washbasins mainly in cabins, facilities for babies and disabled people. Laundry. Small shop (bread to order). Takeaway, bar with TV. Swimming and paddling pools. Playground. Tennis. Minigolf. Dogs are not accepted. Off site: Fishing 1 km. Riding 2 km. Beach 1 km.	Turn off main D786 road northeast of St Michel where site is signed, and 1 km. to site.

Charges 2006

Per unit incl. 2 persons	€ 13,50 - € 19,10
incl. electricty (7A) and water	€ 18,00 - € 25,50
extra person	€ 3,70 - € 5,20
child	free - € 3,40

Open

1 May - 11 September.

Reservations

Advised for high season and made for any length with deposit (€ 70). Tel: 02 96 35 72 28. Email: les.capucines@wanadoo.fr

At a glance

Welcome & Ambience	✓✓✓✓✓	Location	✓✓✓✓
Quality of Pitches	✓✓✓✓✓	Range of Facilities	✓✓✓✓

FR22030 Camping Nautic International

Route de Beau-Rivage, F-22530 Caurel (Côtes d'Armor)

This friendly family site is on the northern shore of the Lac de Guerledan. The lake is popular for all manner of watersports and there are some pleasant walks around the shores and through the surrounding Breton countryside and forests. The site is terraced down to the lake shore and offers 100 large pitches, all with electrical connections. A number of 'super pitches' (160-200 sq.m.) are also available. There is an imaginatively designed swimming pool and smaller children's pool, both heated by a wood burning stove (15/5-25/9). Small boats can be launched from the site, and other boating activities are available on the lake. A member of 'Sites et Paysages'.

Facilities	Directions
Washing and drying machines. Small shop (7/7-31/8). Swimming pools. Gym. Giant chess. Play area. Fishing. Tennis. Table tennis. Games room. Mobile homes for rent. Off site: Watersports. Riding. Canal from Nantes to Brest. Seaside 50 minutes by car.	From N164 Rennes – Brest road, turn off between Mur-de-Bretagne and Gouarec to the village of Caurel. Site is well signed from there.

Charges 2006

Per person	€ 3,30 - € 5,00
pitch and vehicle	€ 7,00 - € 9,60
electricity (10A)	€ 4,30

Open

15 May - 25 September.

Reservations

Contact site. Tel: 02 96 28 57 94. Email: contact@campingnautic.fr.st

At a glance

Welcome & Ambience	✓✓✓✓	Location	✓✓✓✓
Quality of Pitches	✓✓✓✓	Range of Facilities	✓✓✓✓

FR22060 Camping Municipal La Hallerais

6 Bourg de Taden, F-22100 Taden (Côtes d'Armor)

As well as being an attractive old medieval town, Dinan is quite a short run from the resorts of the Côte d'Armor. This useful municipal site, open for a long season, is just outside Dinan, beyond and above the little harbour on the Rance estuary. There is a pleasant riverside walk where the site slopes down towards the Rance. The 226 pitches, all with electricity (6A) and most with water and drainaway, are mainly on level, shallow terraces connected by tarmac roads, with trees and hedges giving a park-like atmosphere. This is a clean efficiently run and well organised site.

Facilities	Directions
Three traditional toilet blocks, of good quality and heated in cool weather, have some private cabins with shower and washbasin. Unit for disabled people. Laundry room. Shop. Attractive bar/restaurant with outside terrace and takeaway (all season). Swimming and paddling pools (15/5-30/9). Tennis. Minigolf. Games and TV rooms. Playground. Fishing. Mobile homes for rent. Off site: Bus in Taden, 15 minutes walk. Riding 2 km. Bicycle hire 5 km. Beach 20 km.	Taden is northeast of Dinan. On leaving Dinan on D766, turn right to Taden and site before reaching large bridge and N176 junction. From N176 take Taden/Dinan exit and follow Taden signs to pick up signs for site.

Charges 2005

Per person	€ 3,16 - € 3,77
child (under 7 yrs)	€ 1,33 - € 1,63
pitch incl. electricity	€ 6,90 - € 11,78

Open

15 March - 4 November.

Reservations

Made for high season only (min. 1 week) with deposit (€ 30). Tel: 02 96 39 15 93. Email: camping.la.hallerais@wanadoo.fr

At a glance

Welcome & Ambience	✓✓✓✓	Location	✓✓✓✓
Quality of Pitches	✓✓✓✓	Range of Facilities	✓✓✓✓

FR22020 Camping Fleur de Bretagne

Kerandouaron, F-22110 Rostrenen (Côtes d'Armor)

This small, rural site is British owned and is set in the heart of the Brittany countryside, one kilometre from the small town of Rostrenen. Well kept pitches are laid out in groups of seven or eight and these groups are separated by small trees and shrubs. The site is terraced and slopes gently down to a fishing lake. This site lends itself to a quiet holiday spent with friends and it is particularly suitable for campers using tents.

Facilities

Two well kept toilet blocks provide showers and washbasins, some in cubicles. Facilities for disabled visitors. Small bar which serves snacks and has a terrace overlooking a grassy area where children can play. Bread to order. Small unheated swimming pool. Football field. Boules. Fishing.

Open

All year.

At a glance

Welcome & Ambience	✓✓✓✓	Location	✓✓✓✓
Quality of Pitches	✓✓✓✓	Range of Facilities	✓✓✓

Directions

Rostrenen is in the heart of Brittany, about halfway between St Brieuc and Quimper. From the N164 Loudéac - Carhaix-Plouger road, turn south to Rostrenen and take the D764 Route de Pontivy to the site which is on the southeast edge of the town.

Charges 2005

Per person	€ 3,50 - € 5,00
child (4-13 yrs)	€ 2,00 - € 3,00
pitch	€ 5,00 - € 7,00
electricity	€ 3,50
dog	€ 1,00

Reservations

Made with € 30 deposit; contact site.
Tel: 02 96 29 16 45.
Email: info@fleurdebretagne.com

FR22040 Camping Le Châtelet

Rue des Nouettes, F-22380 St Cast-le-Guildo (Côtes d'Armor)

Carefully developed over the years from a former quarry, Le Châtelet is pleasantly and quietly situated with lovely views over the estuary from many pitches. It is well laid out, mainly in terraces with fairly narrow access roads. There are 216 good-sized pitches separated by hedges, all with electricity and 70 with water and drainage. Some pitches are around a little lake (unfenced) which can be used for fishing. A 'green' walking area is a nice feature around the lower edge of the site and a path leads from the site directly down to a beach (about 200 m. but including steps). Saint Cast, 1 km. away to the centre, has a very long beach with many opportunities for sail-boarding and other watersports. Used by three different tour operators (73 pitches).

Facilities

Four toilet blocks with access at different levels include plentiful washbasins in cabins and small toilets and showers for children. Three small, attractive toilet blocks have been added for the lower terraces. Some facilities may be closed outside July/Aug. Motorcaravan services. Heated swimming pool and paddling pool. Shop for basics, takeaway service, bar lounge and general room with satellite TV and pool table. Games room with table tennis, amusement machines. Small play area. Organised games and activities for all the family in season. Dancing weekly in June, July and Aug. Off site: Bicycle hire, riding and golf within 1.5 km. Beach 200 m.

At a glance

Welcome & Ambience	✓✓✓✓✓	Location	✓✓✓✓✓
Quality of Pitches	✓✓✓✓	Range of Facilities	✓✓✓✓

Directions

Best approach is to turn off D786 road at Matignon towards St Cast; just inside St Cast limits turn left at sign for 'campings' and follow camp signs on C90.

Charges 2006

Per person	€ 4,10 - € 6,10
child (under 7 yrs)	€ 2,80 - € 4,10
pitch	€ 12,10 - € 19,60
electricity (6/10A)	€ 4,20 - € 5,20
animal	€ 2,80 - € 3,80

Reservations

Necessary for July/Aug. and made (min. 1 week) with deposit (€ 60) and booking fee (€ 20).
Tel: 02 96 41 96 33. Email: chateletcp@aol.com

Open

1 May - 11 September.

FR22050 Camping Le Vieux Moulin

14 rue des Moulins, F-22430 Erquy (Côtes d'Armor)

Le Vieux Moulin is a family run site, just two kilometres from the little fishing port of Erquy on Brittany's Emerald Coast on the edge of a pine forest and nature reserve. It is situated about 900 metres from a beach of sand and shingle. Taking its name from the old mill opposite, the site has 173 pitches, 150 with electricity (6/9A) and 30 with electricity, water and drainage. One section of 39 pitches is arranged around a pond. Most pitches are of a fair size in square boxes with trees giving shade. The good, recently extended pool complex includes a paddling pool and water slides and there are plans to add an indoor pool and jacuzzi for 2006. The site is a popular choice with families with younger children with a good play area and a merry-go-round provided for them, yet it becomes quite lively in high season. Evening entertainment is organised and there is a friendly pizzeria. About 60 tour operator pitches add to the holiday atmosphere.

Facilities

Two good quality toilet blocks have mostly British style toilets and plenty of individual washbasins, facilities for disabled people and for babies. A further small block provides toilets and dishwashing only. Washing machines and dryer. Motorcaravan service point. Shop. Smart pizzeria and takeaway. Attractive bar and terrace overlooking the heated pool complex. Two play areas with carousel roundabout. Free tennis, free fitness gym. TV room (with satellite) and games room with table tennis. Bicycle hire. Electric barbecues are not permitted. Off site: Fishing 1.2 km. Golf and riding 7 km. Beach 900 m.

At a glance

| Welcome & Ambience | ✓✓✓✓ | Location | ✓✓✓✓ |
| Quality of Pitches | ✓✓✓✓ | Range of Facilities | ✓✓✓✓✓ |

Directions

Site is 2 km. east of Erquy. Take minor road towards Les Hôpitaux and site is signed from junction of D786 and D34 roads

Charges 2006

Per person	€ 4,50 - € 5,60
child (under 7 yrs)	€ 3,20 - € 4,20
pitch	€ 10,00 - € 13,50
vehicle	€ 4,00 - € 5,00
electricity (6/9A)	€ 4,50 - € 5,00
dog	€ 3,00 - € 4,00

Reservations

Made for min. 1 week. Tel: 02 96 72 34 23. Email: camp.vieux.moulin@wanadoo.fr

Open

30 April - 10 September.

FR22070 Camping Les Plages de Beg-Léguer

Route de La Côte, Beg-Léguer, F-22300 Lannion (Côtes d'Armor)

This site is spacious, tranquil and well managed with an enthusiastic and friendly new owner. It is 400 metres from the sandy beach (with lifeguards in July and August) and is well situated for visits to the resorts of the 'Pink Granite' coast – Trébeurden, Trégastel and Perros Guirec. Walkers will appreciate the long-distance GR34 footpath which passes next to the site. Comprising five hectares, the campsite provides 229 pitches of which 34 are used for mobile homes. There are no tour operators. There is plenty of shade and young hedges are growing to provide separation. Some pitches have sea views. The shop, bar, restaurant and takeaway are all open from Easter and an outdoor, heated swimming pool opens from 1 June. Amenities include a play area, table tennis and trampoline for children and in high season, music, karaoke and magic shows provide entertainment.

Facilities

A very clean toilet block includes private cabins and facilities for disabled visitors. Shop. Bar, restaurant and takeaway. Swimming pool. Play area. Some entertainment in high season. Off site: Beach 400 m.

Open

Easter - 31 October.

At a glance

| Welcome & Ambience | ✓✓✓✓✓ | Location | ✓✓✓✓ |
| Quality of Pitches | ✓✓✓✓ | Range of Facilities | ✓✓✓✓ |

Directions

From the bypass at Lannion take the D65 towards Trébeurden. Turn left, southwest, signed Beg Léguer, then Plages Beg Léguer until signs for site appear.

Charges 2005

Per person	€ 3,00 - € 5,00
child (0-10 yrs)	€ 2,00 - € 4,00
pitch	€ 5,00 - € 7,00
electricity (6/10A)	€ 3,00 - € 4,50
dog	free - € 1,00

Reservations

Contact site. Tel: 02 96 47 25 00. Email: info@campingdesplages.com

FR22080 Yelloh! Village Le Ranolien

Ploumanach, F-22700 Perros Guirec (Côtes d'Armor)

Le Ranolien has been attractively developed around a former Breton farm – everything here is either made from, or placed on or around the often massive pink rocks. The original buildings are sympathetically converted into site facilities and there is an imaginative pool complex with terraces and water toboggans, with water cascading over boulders into smaller pools and a covered, heated pool which can be opened. It is all quite impressive and is overlooked by the bar terrace. The site is on the coast, with beaches and coves within walking distance and there are spectacular views from many pitches. The 560 pitches are of a variety of sizes and types, mostly large and flat but some are quite small. Some are formally arranged in rows with hedge separators, but most are either on open ground or under trees, amongst large boulders. With many holiday caravans and tour operator tents around the site (318 pitches), there are 70 pitches for tourists, all with electricity and some with water and drainage. Reservation is recommended for high season. This site can be noisy in high season and is not for those seeking a calm and peaceful holiday.

Facilities

The main toilet block, heated in cool weather, is supplemented by several other more open type blocks around the site. Washbasins in cabins, mostly British style WCs and good showers. Dishwashing facilities are mainly in the open. Laundry. Motorcaravan service facilities. Supermarket and gift shop (1/5-18/9). Restaurant, crêperie and bar (all open over a long season). Disco some nights in high season. Minigolf. Table tennis. Games room. Play area. Cinema. Gym and steam room. Mobile homes for hire. Off site: Beach 150 m. Beach 300 m. Bicycle hire 1 km. Riding 3 km. Golf 10 km.

Open

2 April - 17 September.

At a glance

Welcome & Ambience	✓✓✓✓	Location	✓✓✓✓✓
Quality of Pitches	✓✓✓✓	Range of Facilities	✓✓✓✓✓

Directions

From Lannion take D788 to Perros Guirec. Follow signs to 'Centre Ville' past main harbour area and then signs to Ploumanach, La Clarté. Pass through village of La Clarté and around sharp left hand bend. Site is immediately on the right.

Charges 2005

Per unit incl. 2 persons and electricity	€ 13,00 - € 29,00
with water and drainage	€ 15,00 - € 37,00
extra person	€ 5,00 - € 7,00
child (2-7 yrs)	free - € 5,00
animal	€ 2,00

Reservations

Contact site. Tel: 02 96 91 65 65.
Email: leranolien@yellohvillage.fr

FR22090 Castel Camping Le Château de Galinée

La Galinée, F-22380 St Cast-le-Guildo (Côtes d'Armor)

Situated a few kilometres back from St Cast and owned and managed by the Vervel family, Galinée is in a parkland setting on level grass with numerous and varied mature trees. It has 273 pitches, all with electricity, water and drainage and separated by many mature shrubs and bushes. The top section is mostly for mobile homes. An attractive pool complex has swimming and paddling pools, two new pools with a water slide and a 'magic stream'. Entertainment is organised during peak season featuring traditional Breton music at times or weekly discos. The gate is locked 23.00-07.00 hrs.

Facilities

The main tiled, modern sanitary block includes washbasins in private cabins, facilities for babies and a good unit for disabled people. Dishwashing under cover. Laundry room. Shop for basics, bar and excellent takeaway menu (both 1/7-30/8). Attractive, heated pool complex (26/5-2/9) with swimming and paddling pools. Three tennis courts. Fishing. Play area and field for ball games. Off site: Golf 3.5 km. Riding 6 km. Beach 6 km.

Open

6 May - 10 September.

At a glance

Welcome & Ambience	✓✓✓✓	Location	✓✓✓✓
Quality of Pitches	✓✓✓✓	Range of Facilities	✓✓✓✓✓

Directions

From D168 Ploubalay-Plancoet road turn onto D786 towards Matignon and St Cast. Site is very well signed 1 km. after leaving Notre Dame de Guildo.

Charges 2006

Per person	€ 3,85 - € 5,80
child (under 7 yrs)	€ 2,30 - € 4,00
pitch incl. water and drainage	€ 8,40 - € 14,00
electricity (10A)	€ 4,70
animal	€ 3,30

Camping Cheques accepted.

Reservations

Made with deposit (€ 31) and fee (€ 15.24); min. 1 week July/Aug. Tel: 02 96 41 10 56.
Email: chateaugalinee@wanadoo.fr

FR22100 Camping L'Abri Côtier

Ville Es Rouxel, F-22680 Etables-sur-Mer (Côtes d'Armor)

L'Abri Côtier is a well-cared-for, family run site 500 metres from a sandy beach. Small and tranquil, it is arranged in two sections separated by a lane. The pitches are marked out on part level, part sloping grass, divided by mature trees and shrubs with some in a charming walled area with a quaint, old-world atmosphere. The second section has an orchard type setting. Tim Lee and his French wife are busy with ideas for this very popular, friendly site and recent improvements include a tarmac entrance and car park. The evening bar forms a good social centre. In total there are 140 pitches, all with electrical connections (long leads useful) and 60 fully serviced. The beach is within walking distance and there are restaurants in the village.

Facilities

Good clean sanitary facilities, heated in low season, include some washbasins in cabins, two units for disabled visitors (shower, washbasin and toilet) and a baby bath/shower. Dishwashing under cover. Laundry room. Well stocked shop, set menu and simple takeaway service. Bar (with TV) and outdoor terrace area. Sheltered, heated swimming pool with paddling pool and outdoor jacuzzi. Playground. Games room with billiards, darts, pinball and table tennis. Some entertainment in peak season. Gates locked at 11 pm. Off site: Restaurants and indoor pool in the village. Riding 1 km. Fishing 2 km. Bicycle hire 4 km. Golf 10 km. Beach 500 m.

Open

6 May - 15 September.

At a glance

Welcome & Ambience	✓✓✓✓	Location	✓✓✓✓
Quality of Pitches	✓✓✓✓	Range of Facilities	✓✓✓✓

Directions

From N12 (Saint Brieuc bypass) take D786 towards St Quay Portrieux. After about 12 km. pass Aire de la Chapelle on the right and take second left on D47 towards Etables sur Mer. Take second right to site at quiet crossroads in about 100 m.

Charges 2005

Per person	€ 4,00 - € 4,50
child (under 7 yrs)	€ 2,50 - € 3,00
pitch	€ 6,00 - € 7,00
serviced pitch	€ 6,50 - € 8,00

Reservations

Advised in season; made with deposit (25%, sterling cheque acceptable). Tel: 02 96 70 61 57. Email: camping.abricotier@wanadoo.fr

FR22110 Camping Les Madières

Le Vau Madec, F-22590 Pordic (Côtes d'Armor)

Les Madières is well placed for exploring the Gaëlo coast with its seaside resorts of St Quay-Portrieux, Binic and Etables-sur-Mer – ports used in the past by fishing schooners and now used by pleasure boats and a few coastal fishing boats. The new young and enthusiastic owners here have already made their mark on this quiet campsite. With plenty of open spaces and set in the countryside, yet near the sea (800 m), it has 83 pitches of which 17 are used for mobile homes. There are no tour operators. The site has an outdoor swimming pool and some entertainment is organised in July and August by the welcoming and helpful owners.

Facilities

Two refurbished toilet blocks include facilities for disabled visitors. Basic provisions are kept all season. Bar, restaurant and takeaway (all season). Swimming pool (1/6-20/9). Some entertainment (high season). Off site: Beach 800 m. Bus service nearby. Riding 2.5 km. Bicycle hire 3 km.

Open

1 April - 31 October.

At a glance

Welcome & Ambience	✓✓✓✓✓	Location	✓✓✓✓
Quality of Pitches	✓✓✓✓	Range of Facilities	✓✓✓

Directions

From St Brieuc ring-road (N12), turn north on D786 signed Paimpol (by the coast). Les Madières is at Pordic, 3 km. from the ring-road. Site is well signed from the D786.

Charges 2005

Per person	€ 4.50
child (0-7 yrs)	€ 2,80
pitch	€ 7,50
electricity (10A)	€ 3,50
dog	€ 1,80

Discounts outside July and August.

Reservations

Contact site. Tel: 02 96 79 02 48. Email: campinglesmadieres@wanadoo.fr

FR22130 Camping de Port l'Epine

Venelle de Pors Garo, F-22660 Trélévern (Côtes d'Armor)

Port L'Epine is a pretty little site in a unique situation on a promontory. There is access to the sea, therefore, on the south side of the site, with views across to Perros Guirec, and just outside the entrance on the north side is a further sandy bay with little boats moored and facing an archipelago of seven small islands. It is charming – you can sail or swim from both sides. However, as an added attraction, the site has its own small heated pool. The area covered by the site is not large but there are 160 grass pitches, all with electricity, which are divided by pretty hedging and trees. Some are used for mobile homes. Access is a little tight in parts. This site is ideal for families with young children (probably not for teenagers). The site is used by tour operators (17 pitches).

Facilities

The original toilet block is well equipped and a second block has been refurbished in modern style, including facilities for disabled visitors. Unusual dishwashing sinks in open air stone units. Shop and bar/restaurant with takeaway facility (both 1/7-31/8). Small heated swimming pool and paddling pool. Fenced play area near the bar/restaurant. Table tennis and video games. Bicycle hire. Site's own beach has rock pools, jetty and slipway for small boats or fishing. Barrier closed 23.00-07.00 hrs. Off site: Riding or golf 15 km. Useful small supermarket up-hill from site. Many coastal paths to enjoy.

Open

1 April - 30 September.

At a glance

| Welcome & Ambience | ✓✓✓✓ | Location | ✓✓✓✓✓ |
| Quality of Pitches | ✓✓✓✓ | Range of Facilities | ✓✓✓✓ |

Directions

From roundabout south of Perros Guirec take D6 towards Tréguier. After passing through Louannec, take left turn at crossroads for Trélévern. Go through village following camp signs – Port L'Epine is clearly marked as distinct from the municipal site. On first arrival, you must park outside in the car park and walk to reception, as there is now a barrier which requires an access code.

Charges 2005

Per pitch incl. 2 persons	
and electricity	€ 14,50 - € 27,50
serviced pitch	€ 2,30
extra person	€ 5,00
child (2-7 yrs)	€ 2,50
animal	€ 2,50

Camping Cheques accepted.

Reservations

Made with deposit (€ 90 or € 45 for stay of less than 3 nights). Tel: 02 96 23 71 94.
Email: camping-de-port-lepine@wanadoo.fr

FR22140 Camping de Port La Chaine

F-22610 Pleubian (Côtes d'Armor)

The Palvadeau family has worked hard to establish Camping de Port La Chaîne as a comfortable, quiet, family site. In a beautiful location on the 'Untamed Peninsula' between Paimpol and Perros Guirec, attractive trees and shrubs provide a balance of sun and shade, edging the central road and the grassy bays or fields which branch off on the gradual decline towards the bay and the sea (a sandy bay with rocks). To the right are mostly French-owned mobile homes, quite discreet, with the left side for independent units. Most of the bays have a slight slope, so those with motorcaravans will need to choose their pitch carefully. More open, level pitches nearer the sea are useful for tents. In all there are 200 pitches with electricity said to be available everywhere (a long lead may be useful). There are good opportunities for walking and cycling, with a way-marked footpath running along the coast to the Sillon du Talbert that juts out into the sea opposite the Island of Bréhat.

Facilities

Two traditional style toilet blocks are comfortable and fully equipped, both now completely renovated. Washbasins in cabins, British and Turkish style toilets. Cabins for families or disabled visitors. Plentiful dishwashing sinks. Laundry sinks with cold water only. Washing machines and dryer. Bar/restaurant with terrace and takeaway (19/6-31/8). Heated swimming pool (22/5-8/9). Play area. Games room. Petanque pitch. Children's entertainer in July/Aug. Beach, fishing and sailing. Off site: Bus 1 km. Village 2 km. for tennis, market, shops and restaurants. Good fishing and diving. Boat launching 1 km. Bicycle hire 2 km. Riding 6 km. Golf 18 km.

At a glance

| Welcome & Ambience | ✓✓✓✓✓ | Location | ✓✓✓✓✓ |
| Quality of Pitches | ✓✓✓✓ | Range of Facilities | ✓✓✓✓ |

Directions

Leave D786 between Lézardrieux and Tréguier to go north to village of Pleubian (about 8 km). Continue on D20 towards Larmor Pleubian and site signed on left, 2 km. from Pleubian.

Charges 2005

Per person	€ 5,40
child (under 7 yrs)	€ 3,40
pitch	€ 9,40
electricity	€ 3,80
dog	€ 2,30

Less 10-20% in low seasons.

Reservations

Contact site. Tel: 02 96 22 92 38.
Email: info@portlachaine.com

Open

1 May - 15 September.

FR22200 Camping Au Bocage du Lac

Rue du Bocage, F-22270 Jugon-les Lacs (Côtes d'Armor)

This well kept former municipal site has been updated over the past few years by the current owners M. and Mme. Riviere. It is on the edge of the village beside a lake, 25 km. from the sea. It offers 181 good size pitches, all with electrical connections, set on gently sloping grass and divided by shrubs and bushes, with mature trees providing shade. Some 40 wooden chalets and mobile homes are intermingled with the touring pitches. On-site facilities include a good pool with children's section and sunbathing patio.

Facilities

Two main sanitary blocks include facilities for disabled visitors, British and Turkish style WCs and some washbasins in cabins. Washing machine. Small shop (1/4-31/10). Bar (1/4-31/10). Swimming pool (15/6-10/9). Table tennis, tennis, football. Play area. Activity programmes July/Aug. Fishing. Bicycle hire. Off site: Supermarket in village (1 km). River 1 km.

Open

1 April - 31 October.

At a glance

Welcome & Ambience	✓✓✓✓✓	Location	✓✓✓✓
Quality of Pitches	✓✓✓✓	Range of Facilities	✓✓✓✓

Directions

From N176 (E401) Lamballe - Dinan road, approx. 15 km. from Lamballe take turning for Jugon-les-Lacs. Site is signed shortly after.

Charges 2005

Per person	€ 3,50 - € 3,90
child (under 7 yrs)	€ 2,35 - € 2,50
pitch	€ 5,50 - € 6,50
electricity (5A)	€ 2,80

Reservations

Contact site. Tel: 02 96 31 60 16.

Camping ★★★ Au Bocage du Lac

AU BOCAGE DU LAC
Hôtel de Plein Air

campingjugon.com

Open from 1st April to 31st October

On the lakeside, for both relaxation and leisure, you will find a wide range of activities : heated pool, water slide, paddling pool, childrens' mini camp, tennis, minigolf, sailing, fishing, walking. One new sanitary block includes private cabins, facilities for babies. WELCOME IN BRITTANY !
22270 Jugon les Lacs
Tél : 02.96.31.60.16
Fax : 02.96.31.75.04

FR22160 Camping Le Neptune

Kerguistin, F-22580 Lanloup (Côtes d'Armor)

Situated on the Côte de Goëlo at Lanloup, Le Neptune offers a peaceful, rural retreat for families. The friendly owners, M. and Mme. Schira, keep the site neat and tidy and there is a regular programme of renovation. There are 84 level, grass pitches (65 for touring units) separated by trimmed hedges providing privacy and all with electricity. There are also 13 mobile homes to rent. A heated swimming pool has a retractable roof so can be open for a long season. Within walking distance is the local village, with a restaurant and shop, and sandy beaches. The site is also a good base for cycling and walking.

Facilities

The modern toilet block is of a good standard, clean and well maintained. Laundry room with washing machine and dryer. No restaurant but good takeaway (all season). Small shop well stocked for basic needs. Bar with indoor and outdoor seating. Heated swimming pool (Easter - end Oct). Petanque. Volleyball. Table tennis, table football. Animation in season. Off site: Tennis 300 m. Fishing and beach 2 km. Golf 4 km. Riding 8 km. Restaurant and shop within walking distance. Beach 2.5 km.

Open

1 April - 31 October.

At a glance

Welcome & Ambience	✓✓✓✓✓	Location	✓✓✓✓✓
Quality of Pitches	✓✓✓✓	Range of Facilities	✓✓✓✓

Directions

From Saint Brieuc (N12) take D786 Paimpol ('par la Côte'). After 28 km. on approaching Lanloup, site is well signed. GPS: N48:42.49 W02:58.00

Charges 2005

Per person	€ 4,50
child (under 7 yrs)	€ 3,00
pitch	€ 7,50
electricity (6A)	€ 3,00
dog	€ 1,70

Camping Cheques accepted.

Reservations

Less 10% in low season. Tel: 02 96 22 33 35. Email: contact@leneptune.com

FR22210 Camping Bellevue

Route de Pléneuf Val-André, F-22430 Erquy (Côtes d'Armor)

Situated a mile from the beaches between Erquy and Pléneuf Val-Andre, Camping Bellevue offers a quiet country retreat with easy access to the cliffs of Cap Fréhel, Sables d'Or and St Cast le Suildo. There are 140 pitches of which 120 are available for touring units, most with electricity (6/10A) and 15 with water and drainage. Children are well catered for at this campsite – there are heated swimming and paddling pools, three play areas and minigolf, petanque and volleyball. Indoor entertainment for all includes theme evenings, Breton dancing and visits to a local cider house. There are numerous walks in the area and a vast range of aquatic sports at nearby Erquy. The site also has 20 mobile homes, chalets and bungalows to rent. A 'Sites et Paysages' member.

Facilities

Two modern, unisex toilet blocks are of a high standard. Some washbasins in cubicles. Facilities for disabled visitors. Dishwashing and laundry facilities. Shop and bar (15/6-10/9). Restaurant and takeaway (12/6-31/8). Swimming and paddling pools (10/6-10/9). Play areas. Pool table. TV room. Table football, video games and library. Minigolf. Petanque. Volleyball. Entertainment and organised activities in high season. Off site: Beach and fishing 2 km. Golf 3 km. Bicycle hire and boat launching 5 km. Riding 6 km.

At a glance

Welcome & Ambience	✓✓✓✓✓	Location	✓✓✓✓
Quality of Pitches	✓✓✓✓	Range of Facilities	✓✓✓✓

Directions

From St Brieuc road take D786 towards Erquy. Site is adjacent to the D786 at St Pabu and is well signed.

Charges 2006

Per person	€ 3,80 - € 4,80
child (7-13 yrs)	€ 3,20 - € 4,20
pitch	€ 14,20 - € 18,00
electricity	€ 3,20 - € 4,50

Reservations

Contact site. Tel: 02 96 72 33 04.
Email: campingbellevue@yahoo.fr

Open

31 March - 30 September.

FR29040 Camping Ar Kleguer

Plage Ste Anne, F-29250 Saint Pol de Leon (Finistère)

Ar Kleguer is located 20 minutes from the Roscoff ferry terminal in the heart of the Pays du Léon in north Finistère. It would suit for long or short stays and is immaculately kept by the Kerbrat family. The site is in two sections – one is in a quiet woodland setting which incorporates a small domestic animal and bird park. The other section is divided into several more open areas at the edge of the sea with spectacular views overlooking the Bay of Morlaix. There are 173 large and well kept pitches, all with 10A electricity connections. Of these, 125 are for touring units. This neat site is decorated with attractive flowers, shrubs and trees and there are tarmac roads. However, the real plus here is the beautiful surroundings and the friendly and helpful owners will advise on how best to enjoy this peaceful part of Brittany.

Facilities

Three modern, tiled toilet blocks are bright and clean. Heated when required, they include facilities for babies, children and disabled visitors. Laundry room and dishwashing. Shop (July/Aug). Bar and takeaway (July/Aug). Good heated pool complex. Table tennis. Pool table. Tennis. Bicycle hire. Animal park. Play area. Activities for children and some entertainment in high season. Beach adjacent with fishing and sailing. Off site: Restaurant at site entrance. Sailing 800 m. Riding 3 km. Golf 5 km.

Open

Easter - 30 September.

At a glance

Welcome & Ambience	✓✓✓✓✓	Location	✓✓✓✓✓
Quality of Pitches	✓✓✓✓✓	Range of Facilities	✓✓✓✓

Directions

From Roscoff take D58 to Morlaix. From Morlaix follow signs to Saint-Pol-de-Léon (centre). In the centre follow white 'campings' signs or Plage de Sainte Marie until 'camping Ar Kleguer' signs appear.

Charges 2005

Per person	€ 3,50 - € 4,40
child (2-7 yrs)	€ 2,00 - € 2,70
pitch	€ 4,60 - € 6,20
car	€ 1,50 - € 1,90
electricity (5A)	€ 3,20

Reservations

Made with deposit (€ 60) and fee (€ 16).
Tel: 20 98 69 18 81.
Email: info@camping-ar-kleguer.com

FR29000 Yelloh! Village Les Mouettes

Mobile homes ▶ page 406

La Grande Grève, F-29660 Carantec (Finistère)

Les Mouettes is less than 15 kilometres from the Roscoff ferry port, so is well situated when heading to or from home. However, it also provides many good facilities for a longer family holiday and for those who do not want to drive too far, the area has plenty to offer with beautiful bays and many places of interest within easy reach. Les Mouettes is a sheltered site on the edge of an attractive bay with access to the sea at the front of the site. In a wooded setting with many attractive trees and shrubs, the 273 pitches include just 70 for touring units, the remainder being taken by tour operators and around 60 site-owned mobile homes and tents (located together at the top of the site). The touring pitches, mostly arranged in hedged areas in the lower areas of the site, are of a good size and all have electricity. The focal point of the site is an impressive heated pool complex comprising a water slide pool and three water slides, 'tropical river', swimming pool, paddling pool, a jacuzzi and a sauna.

Facilities

Three clean unisex sanitary blocks include washbasins in cabins, mainly British toilets and baby bathrooms. Facilities for disabled people. Laundry facilities. Motorcaravan services. Shop (limited hours outside the main season). Takeaway. Centrally located bar overlooking pool complex. Games and TV rooms. Play area. Volleyball, two half-courts for tennis and minigolf (in peak season). Table tennis. Discos and other entertainment organised in main season. American style motorhomes and double axle caravans should phone first. Dogs are not accepted after 26 June. Off site: Fishing 1 km. Golf 2 km. Riding 6 km. Bicycle hire 10 km. Beach 2 km.

At a glance

Welcome & Ambience	✓✓✓✓	Location	✓✓✓✓
Quality of Pitches	✓✓✓✓	Range of Facilities	✓✓✓✓✓

Directions

From D58 Roscoff - Morlaix road, turn to Carantec on D173. Site is approx. 4 km. from here on the outskirts of the village, signed to the left at roundabout immediately after passing supermarket on right.

Charges 2006

Per unit incl. 2 persons, electricity and water	€ 17,00 - € 42,00
extra person	€ 4,00 - € 7,20
child (under 7 yrs)	free - € 4,10
dog	€ 2,50 - € 4,50

Reservations

Write to site with deposit (€ 90) and fee (€ 30). Tel: 02 98 67 02 46. Email: camping@les-mouettes.com

Open

1 May - 10 September.

FR29340 Camping de la Côte des Légendes

Keravezan BP 36, F-29890 Brignogan-Plages (Finistère)

Located just behind a safe, sandy beach on the Bay of Brignogan and adjacent to a Centre Nautique (sailing, windsurfing, kayak), this site is ideal for a family seaside holiday or as a base to discover the history behind the fables of the Côte des Légendes. Visit the nearby preserved fishing village of Meneham, set amongst spectacular random granite outcrops and boulders, and learn of its history of coastal defence from the English. Less than 40 km. from Roscoff ferry port, Brignogan is ideal if you do not want to drive too far in France. This is a quiet site with 147 level pitches arranged in rows and protected by hedges. There are a few mobile homes and chalets for rent but no tour operators. A shop, bar and takeaway are open in high season when activities are arranged for adult and children by the helpful owner (good English is spoken). The beach of fine sand can be reached directly from the site which would suit families with young children looking for a quiet, seaside holiday.

Facilities

The main toilet facilities are at the rear of the site in a large block that provides washbasins in cubicles, baby baths and facilities for disabled visitors. Dishwashing and laundry sinks. Motorcaravan service point. The upper floor provides a games room with views of the sea. Further toilet facilities are at the reception building, also a laundry (2 washing machines and a dryer). Bar, small shop and takeaway (July/Aug). Playground and play field. Table tennis. Off site: Watersports centre adjacent. Village services 700 m. Bicycle hire 1 km. Riding 6 km.

Open

Easter - 1 November.

At a glance

Welcome & Ambience	✓✓✓✓✓	Location	✓✓✓✓✓
Quality of Pitches	✓✓✓✓	Range of Facilities	✓✓✓✓

Directions

From Roscoff take the D58 towards Morlaix and after 6 km. turn right on the D10 towards Plouescat and then Plouguerneau. Turn right on the D770 to Brignogan-Plages. In the main street (Général de Gaulle) go straight on following signs for site and Club Nautique.

Charges 2005

Per unit incl. 2 persons	€ 10,00 - € 12,00
extra person	€ 3,00 - € 3,60
child (1-13 yrs)	€ 2,70 - € 3,60
electricity	€ 2,20 - € 3,60
animal	€ 1,00

Reservations

Advised for high season. Tel: 02 98 83 41 65. Email: camping-cote-des-legendes@wanadoo.fr

FR29130 Camping des Abers

Mobile homes ▶ page 408

Dunes de Sainte Marguerite, F-29870 Landéda (Finistère)

The location of this delightful twelve acre site is beautiful. Almost at the tip of the Sainte Marguerite peninsula on the north-western shores of Brittany, it is on a wide bay formed between the mouths (abers) of two rivers, L'Aber Wrac'h and L'Aber Benoit. With a soft, white sandy beach and rocky outcrops and islands at high tide, the setting is ideal for those with younger children and this quiet, rural area provides a wonderful, tranquil escape from the busier areas of France, even in high season. Camping des Abers is set just back from the beach, the lower pitches sheltered from the wind by high hedges or with panoramic views of the bay from the higher places. There are 180 pitches arranged in distinct areas, many partly shaded and sheltered by mature hedges, trees and flowering shrubs, all planted and carefully tended over 30 years by the Le Cuff family. Landscaping and terracing where appropriate on the different levels avoids any regimentation or crowding. Easily accessed by good internal roads, electricity is available to all (long leads may be needed). Speaking several languages, the family who own and run this site with 'TLC' will make you very welcome.

Facilities

Three toilet blocks (one part of the reception building and all recently refurbished) are very clean, providing washbasins in cubicles and roomy showers (token from reception €0.80). Good facilities for disabled visitors and babies have been added at the reception block. Dishwashing sinks. Fully equipped laundry. Motorcaravan service point. Mini-market stocks essentials (1/6-15/9). Simple takeaway dishes (1/7-31/8). Pizzeria and restaurant next door. Table tennis. Good play area (on sand). Games room. Live music, Breton dancing and Breton cooking classes, and guided walks arranged. Splendid beach reached direct from the site with good bathing (best at high tide), fishing, windsurfing and other watersports. Torch useful. Gates locked 22.30-07.00 hrs. Off site: Miles of superb coastal walks. Tennis close. Riding 10 km. Golf 30 km. The nearby town of L'Aber Wrac'h, a well known yachting centre, has many memorable restaurants.

At a glance

Welcome & Ambience	✓✓✓✓✓	Location	✓✓✓✓✓
Quality of Pitches	✓✓✓✓	Range of Facilities	✓✓✓✓

Directions

From Roscoff (D10, then D13), cross river bridge (L'Aber Wrac'h) to Lannilis. Go through town taking road to Landéda and from there signs for Dunes de Ste Marguerite, 'camping' and des Abers.

Charges 2006

Per person	€ 3,30
child (1-7 yrs)	€ 1,80
pitch	€ 5,70
car	€ 1,50
electricity	€ 2,50
dog	€ 1,70

Less 10% outside 15/6-31/8.
Camping Cheques accepted.

Reservations

Write to site. Tel: 02 98 04 93 35.
Email: camping-des-abers@wanadoo.fr

Open

28 April - 30 September.

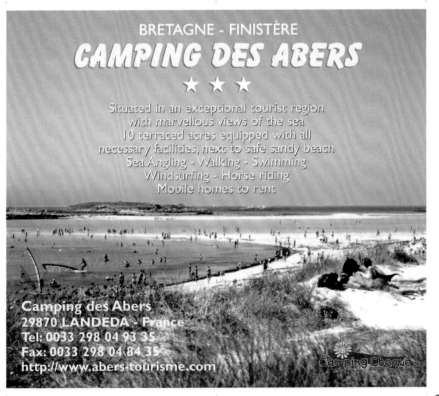

FR29210 Camping Municipal Bois de la Palud

F-29250 Plougoulm (Finistère)

This delightful, small municipal site is on the edge of the little village of Plougoulm, about 10 kilometres southwest of Roscoff. It sits on the brow of a hill with lovely views across the Guillec valley and the sandy bay and estuary to which there is access by footpath. There are 34 reasonably level, numbered pitches grouped in small hedged bays and most have access to 6A electricity (although long leads may be necessary). A small building near the entrance houses reception and toilet facilities. The season is short.

Facilities

All necessary toilet facilities are provided. Play area. Off site: Fishing, bicycle hire, riding and golf, all within 4 km.

Open

15 June - 15 September.

At a glance

| Welcome & Ambience | ✓✓✓ | Location | ✓✓✓✓ |
| Quality of Pitches | ✓✓✓ | Range of Facilities | ✓✓ |

Directions

Leaving Roscoff, follow signs for Morlaix. After 6 km. take D10 (west) signed Plouescat and after 3 km. watch for clear camp signs in village of Plougoulm.

Charges guide

| Per person | € 3,00 |
| pitch incl. electricity | € 7,00 |

No credit cards.

Reservations

Advised in high season. Tel: 02 98 29 81 82. When closed contact the Mairie. Tel: 02 98 29 90 76.

FR29020 Camping Club du Saint Laurent

Kerleven, F-29940 La Forêt-Fouesnant (Finistère)

Saint-Laurent is a well established site, situated on a sheltered wooded slope bordering one of the many attractive little inlets that typify the Brittany coastline. There is direct access from the site to two small sandy bays, which empty at low tide to reveal numerous rock pools (ideal for children to explore), and the site is on the coastal footpath that leads from Kerleven to Concarneau. The 260 pitches are on level terraces, under tall trees. All are of average size (100 sq.m) and divided by hedges and partly shaded, all with electricity connections. Pitches with the best sea views tend to be adjacent to the cliff edge and may not be suitable for families with young children. Access to some places can be a little difficult, but the friendly site owners offer to site any caravan using their own 4 x 4 vehicle. The swimming pool (complete with paddling pool and two water slides) is overlooked by the bar terrace. With organised activities and entertainment in high season, this site is an ideal choice for a lively family holiday, particularly for older children. Around 50% of the pitches are occupied by tour operators or site owned mobile homes.

Facilities

Two sanitary blocks provide combined shower and washbasin cubicles, separate washbasin cubicles, baby changing and facilities for disabled people. Laundry and dishwashing sinks. Washing machines, dryers and ironing. Small shop at reception provides essentials. Bar, snack bar and takeaway. Swimming pools. Gym and sauna. Canoe and boat hire. Basketball, two tennis courts (no charge), and table tennis. Play area. Daily entertainment for adults and children is organised (July/Aug; in English as well as in French), with discos in the bar each evening.

Open

2 May - 9 September.

At a glance

| Welcome & Ambience | ✓✓✓✓✓ | Location | ✓✓✓✓✓ |
| Quality of Pitches | ✓✓✓ | Range of Facilities | ✓✓✓✓✓ |

Directions

From N165 take D70 Concarneau exit. At first roundabout take first exit D44 (Fouesnant). After 2.5 km. turn right at T-junction, follow for 2.5 km, then turn left (Port La Forêt). At roundabout, straight ahead (Port La Forêt) and after 1 km. turn left (site signed here). In 400 m. left turn to site at end of this road. GPS: N47:53.770 W03:57.305

Charges 2005

Per unit incl. 1 or 2 persons	€ 15,00 - € 34,00
extra person	€ 2,50 - € 5,50
child (2-7 yrs)	free - € 3,50

Reservations

Advised for July/Aug (min 7 nights 9/7-20/8). Made with 25% deposit. Tel: 02 98 56 97 65. Email: info@camping-du-saint-laurent.fr

FR29010 Castel Camping Le Ty-Nadan

Mobile homes ⏵ page 406

Route d'Arzano, F-29310 Locunolé (Finistère)

Ty Nadan is a well organised site set amongst wooded countryside along the bank of the River Elle. The 183 pitches for touring units are grassy, many with shade and 152 with 10A electricity. An exciting and varied programme of activities is offered throughout the season – canoeing, rock climbing, mountain biking, aqua-gym, riding or walking – all supervised by qualified staff. A full programme of entertainment for all ages is provided in high season including concerts, Breton evenings with pig roasts, dancing, etc. (be warned, you will be actively encouraged to join in!) The pool complex with its slides and paddling pool is very popular and now has an attractive viewing platform. Super recent additions include a large indoor pool complex and an indoor games area with a climbing wall. Several tour operators use the site (90 pitches). This is a wonderful site for families with children of all ages.

Facilities

Two older, split-level toilet blocks are of fair quality and unusual design, including washbasins in cabins and baby rooms. An impressively equipped newer block provides easier access for disabled people. Dishwashing facilities in two attractive gazebo style units. Washing machines and dryers. Good sized restaurant, takeaway, bar and well stocked shop (all open all season). Crêperie (July/Aug). Heated outdoor pool (17 x 8 m) with water slides and paddling pool. New indoor pool. Small beach on the river (unfenced). Tennis courts, table tennis, pool tables, archery and trampolines. Indoor badminton and rock climbing facility. Exciting adventure play park and new 'Minikids' park for 5-8 yrs. Riding. Bicycle hire. Boat hire. Fishing. Canoe and sea kayaking expeditions. High season entertainment. Paintball. Off site: Beaches 20 minutes by car. Golf 12 km.

At a glance

Welcome & Ambience	✓✓✓✓✓	Location	✓✓✓
Quality of Pitches	✓✓✓✓✓	Range of Facilities	✓✓✓✓✓

Directions

Make for Arzano which is northeast of Quimperlé on the Pontivy road and turn off D22 just west of village at camp sign. Site is approx. 3 km.

Charges 2006

Per person	€ 4,30 - € 8,40
child (under 7 yrs)	€ 1,70 - € 5,20
pitch	€ 8,70 - € 21,00
electricity (10A)	€ 2,60 - € 6,30
dog	€ 1,70 - € 5,80

Less 15-20% outside July/Aug.
Camping Cheques accepted.

Reservations

Made for exact dates with deposit (€ 50) and fee (€ 25). Tel: 02 98 71 75 47.
Email: infos@camping-ty-nadan.fr

Open

1 April - 7 September.

FR29030 Camping du Letty

F-29950 Bénodet (Finistère)

Built around their former farm, the Guyader family have ensured that this excellent and attractive site, with direct beach access, has plenty to offer for all the family. The site on the outskirts of the popular resort of Bénodet spreads over 22 acres with 493 pitches, all for touring units. Groups of four to eight pitches are set in cul-de-sacs with mature hedging and trees to divide each cul-de-sac. Most pitches have electricity, water and drainage. At the attractive floral entrance, former farm buildings provide a host of facilities including an extensively equipped fitness room. There is also a modern, purpose built nightclub and bar providing high quality live entertainment most evenings (situated well away from most pitches to avoid disturbance). Although there is no swimming pool here, the site has direct access to a small sandy beach, and has provided a floating pontoon with a diving platform into the sea (safe bathing depends on the tides).

Facilities

Six well placed toilet blocks are of good quality and include mixed style WCs, washbasins in large cabins and controllable hot showers (charged). One block includes a separate laundry and dog washing enclosures. Four well equipped baby rooms. Separate facility for disabled visitors. Launderette. Hairdressing room. Motorcaravan service points. Well stocked mini-market. Extensive snack bar and takeaway (22/6-30/8). Bar with games room and night club. Library/reading room with four new computer stations. Games lounge with billiard and card tables and entertainment room with satellite TV. Fitness centre (no charge). Saunas, jacuzzi and solarium (all on payment). Table tennis. Two tennis and two squash courts (charged). Boules, volleyball, basketball and archery. Well equipped play area. In July/Aug. entertainment and activities organised for the whole family.

At a glance

Welcome & Ambience	✓✓✓✓✓	Location	✓✓✓✓✓
Quality of Pitches	✓✓✓✓	Range of Facilities	✓✓✓✓✓

Directions

From N165 take D70 Concarneau exit. At first roundabout take D44 to Fouesnant. Turn right at T-junction. After about 2 km. turn left to Fouesnant (still D44). Continue through La Forêt Fouesnant and Fouesnant, picking up signs for Bénodet. Shortly before Benodet at roundabout turn left (signed Le Letty). Turn right at next mini roundabout and site is 500 m. on left.

Charges 2006

Per person	€ 5,00
child (under 7 yrs)	€ 2,50
pitch	€ 9,00
car or motorcaravan	€ 2,00
m/cycle	€ 1,20
electricity (1, 2, 5 or 10A)	€ 1,50 - € 4,00

Reservations

Not made. Tel: 02 98 57 04 69.
Email: reception@campingduletty.com

Open

15 June - 6 September.

FR29100 Camping du Manoir de Pen-ar-Steir

F-29940 La Forêt-Fouesnant (Finistère)

This campsite will appeal to those who prefer a quiet place to stay at any time of the year, away from the noise and bustle of busier sites, even in high season. Situated on terraces up the steep sides of a valley in the grounds of an old Breton house, the site has a picturesque, garden-like quality. Beautifully kept, the entrance is a mass of planted flower displays, with a pond, stream and a small aviary next to the reception, and carefully tended trees and plants throughout the site itself. There are 105 pitches, of which about half are for touring units (the remainder used for mobile homes). Pitches vary in size (80-100 sq.m) and some are accessed by steep slopes, but all are on flat, grassy terraces, with low hedging around them, and all have electricity (3-10A), water and drainage. The main village is easily reached on foot which makes the site an ideal choice for those with motorcaravans or motorbikes.

Facilities

Two sanitary blocks, refurbished to a high standard, include mixed British and Turkish style toilets, cabins with washbasins and showers, baby areas and children's toilets. The small block at rear of the old house contains washing machines and dryers, along with sanitary facilities (including those for disabled people) that are heated for winter use. Children's play area. Tennis court and volleyball. Barrier with card (deposit € 15,24). Off site: Baker 50 m. Village with all amenities 150 m. Golf.

Open

1 February - 15 November.

At a glance

Welcome & Ambience	✓✓✓✓	Location	✓✓✓✓✓
Quality of Pitches	✓✓✓✓	Range of Facilities	✓✓✓

Directions

From N165 take D70 Concarneau exit. At first roundabout take D44 (signed Forêt Fouesnant). Follow to T-junction and turn right on D783. After 2 km. turn left back onto D44 to Forêt Fouesnant. In village take first exit right at roundabout to site 150 m. on left.

Charges guide

Per person	€ 3,76 - € 4,70
child (under 7 yrs)	€ 2,40 - € 3,00
pitch incl. car	€ 6,08 - € 7,60
electricity (3-10A)	€ 2,20 - € 3,10
dog	€ 1,28 - € 1,60

No credit cards. Less 20% outside 1/7-26/8.

Reservations

Write for details. Tel: 02 98 56 97 75.
Email: info@camping-penarsteir.com

FR29050 Castel Camping L'Orangerie de Lanniron Mobile homes ▶ page 407

Château de Lanniron, F-29336 Quimper (Finistère)

L'Orangerie is a beautiful and peaceful, family site in 10 acres of a XVIIth century, 42 acre country estate, formerly the home of the Bishops of Quimper, and attractively set on the banks of the Odet river. It is just to the south of Quimper and about 15 km. from the sea and beaches at Bénodet. The family's five year programme to restore the park, the original canal, fountains, ornamental 'Bassin de Neptune', the boathouse, the gardens and avenues is very well advanced. The original outbuildings have been attractively converted around a walled courtyard. The site has 200 grassy pitches, 146 for touring units. Of three types (varying in size and services), they are on flat ground laid out in rows alongside access roads with shrubs and bushes providing pleasant pitches. All have electricity and 88 have all three services. The restaurant and the gardens are both open to the public and in Spring the rhododendrons and azaleas are magnificent, with lovely walks within the grounds. Used by tour operators (30 pitches). All facilities are available when the site is open.

Facilities

The main heated block in the courtyard has been totally refurbished and is excellent. A second modern block serves the newer pitches at the top of the site and includes facilities for disabled people and babies. Washing machines and dryers. Motorcaravan service point. Shop (15/5-9/9). Gas supplies. Bar, snacks and takeaway, plus restaurant (open daily), reasonably priced with children's menu). Swimming pool (144 sq.m.) with paddling pool. New pool planned for 2006. Small play area. Tennis. Minigolf, attractively set among mature trees. Table tennis. Fishing. Archery. Bicycle hire. General reading, games and billiards rooms. TV/video room. Karaoke. Animation provided including outdoor activities with large room for indoor activities. Off site: Two hypermarkets 1 km. Historic town of Quimper under 3 km. Activities in the area include golf, cycling, walking, fishing, canoeing, surfing and sailing. Beach 15 km.

At a glance

Welcome & Ambience	✓✓✓	Location	✓✓✓✓✓
Quality of Pitches	✓✓✓	Range of Facilities	✓✓✓✓

Directions

From Quimper follow 'Quimper Sud' signs, then 'Toutes Directions' and general camping signs, finally signs for Lanniron.

Charges 2005

Per person	€ 6,20
child (2-10 yrs)	€ 4,00
pitch (100 sq.m.)	€ 15,00
with electricity (10A)	€ 19,00
special pitch (120/150 sq.m.)	
with water and electricity	€ 22,00 - € 24,00
animal	€ 3,50

Less 15% outside July/Aug.
Camping Cheques accepted.

Reservations

Made with deposit (€ 80) and fee (€ 20).
Tel: 02 98 90 62 02. Email: camping@lanniron.com

Open

15 May - 15 September.

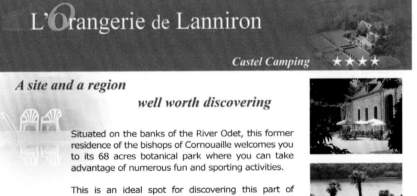

L'Orangerie de Lanniron

Castel Camping ★★★★

A site and a region

well worth discovering

Situated on the banks of the River Odet, this former residence of the bishops of Cornouaille welcomes you to its 68 acres botanical park where you can take advantage of numerous fun and sporting activities.

This is an ideal spot for discovering this part of Brittany, so rich in historical sites, monuments and folklore.

Large pitches and comfortable accommodations

* To get more informations or to book:

www.lanniron.com

camping@lanniron.com

Château de Lanniron 29336 Quimper Cedex
Tél:00.33.(0)2.98.90.62.02 - Fax:00.33.(0)2.98.52.15.56

ADAC 2005

FR29060 Camping Caravaning Le Pil-Koad

Route de Douarnenez, Poullan-sur-Mer, F-29100 Douarnenez (Finistère)

Pil-Koad is an attractive, family run site just back from the sea near Douarnenez in Finistère. It has 190 pitches on fairly flat ground, marked out by separating hedges and of quite good quality, though varying in size and shape. With 100 pitches used for touring units, the site also has a number of mobile homes and chalets. Nearly all pitches have electrical connections and the original trees provide shade in some areas. A large room, the 'Woodpecker Bar', is used for entertainment with discos and cabaret in July/Aug. The gates are closed 10.30 - 07.00 hrs. A variety of beaches is within easy reach, with the coast offering some wonderful scenery and good for walking.

Facilities

Two main toilet blocks in modern style include mainly British style WCs and washbasins mostly in cabins. Laundry facilities. Motorcaravan service point. Gas supplies. Small shop for basics and bar (both 17/6-16/9). Takeaway (24/6-2/9). Heated swimming pool and paddling pool (no Bermuda-style shorts). Tennis court. Table tennis. Minigolf. Volleyball. Fishing. Bicycle hire. Playground. Weekly outings and clubs for children (30/6-30/8) with charge included in tariff. Off site: Restaurants in village 500 m. Riding 4 km. Nearest sandy beach 5 km. Douarnenez 6 km.

Open

20 May - 30 September.

At a glance

Welcome & Ambience	✓✓✓✓	Location	✓✓✓✓
Quality of Pitches	✓✓✓✓✓	Range of Facilities	✓✓✓✓

Directions

Site 500 m. east from the centre of Poullan on D7 road towards Douarnenez. From Douarnenez take circular bypass route towards Audierne; if you see road for Poullan sign at roundabout, take it, otherwise there is camping sign at turning to Poullan from the D765 road.

Charges 2006

Per person	€ 3,00 - € 4,50
child (under 7 yrs)	€ 1,50 - € 3,00
pitch	€ 6,50 - € 15,00
electricity (10A)	€ 3,50
dog	€ 2,00 - € 3,00

Camping Cheques accepted.

Reservations

Made for min. 1 week with 25% deposit and fee (€ 20). Tel: 02 98 74 26 39. Email: info@pil-koad.com

FR29110 Yelloh! Village La Plage

Rue de Men-Meur B.P. 9, F-29730 Le Guilvinec (Finistère)

La Plage is a friendly site located beside a long sandy beach between the fishing town of Le Guilvinec and the watersports beaches of Penmarc'h on the southwest tip of Brittany. It is spacious and surrounded by tall trees, which provide shelter, and is made up of several flat, sandy meadows. The 410 pitches (100 for touring units) are arranged on either side of sandy access roads, mostly not separated but all numbered. There is less shade in the newer areas. Electricity is available on most pitches. Like all beach-side sites, the facilities receive heavy use. There is plenty to occupy one at this friendly site but the bustling fishing harbour at Le Guilvinec and the watersports of Penmarc'h and Pointe de la Torche are within easy travelling distance. Used by tour operators (176 pitches). A 'Yelloh Village' member.

Facilities

Five sanitary blocks are of differing designs but all provide modern, bright facilities including washbasins in cabins, good facilities for children and toilets for disabled people. Laundry facilities. Motorcaravan service point. Shop with gas supplies. Bright, airy well furnished bar, crêperie and takeaway. Heated swimming pool with paddling pool and water slide. Sauna. Play area. TV room. Tennis courts. Volleyball, basketball, minigolf, badminton, petanque, table tennis, giant chess/draughts. Bicycle hire. Beach. Off site: Fishing and watersports near. Riding 5 km. Golf 20 km.

Open

5 May - 9 September, with all facilities.

At a glance

Welcome & Ambience	✓✓✓✓✓	Location	✓✓✓✓✓
Quality of Pitches	✓✓✓	Range of Facilities	✓✓✓✓

Directions

Site is west of Guilvinec. From Pont l'Abbé, take the D785 road towards Penmarc'h. In Plomeur, turn left on D57 signed Guilvinec. On entering Guilvinec fork right signed Port and camping. Follow road along coast to site on left.

Charges 2006

Per unit incl. 2 persons and 5A electricity	€ 16,00 - € 37,00
extra person	€ 4,00 - € 6,00
child (under 10 yrs)	free - € 4,00
electricity (10A)	€ 1,00 - € 1,00
dog	€ 3,00 - € 3,50

Reservations

Advised and accepted until 15/6 with deposit (25%) and fee (€ 19). Tel: 02 98 58 61 90. Email: info@campingsbretagnesud.com

FR29080 Camping Le Panoramic

Route de la Plage-Penker, F-29560 Telgruc-sur-Mer (Finistère)

This medium sized, traditional style site is situated on quite a steep, ten acre hillside, with fine views along the coast. It is well tended and personally run by M. Jacq and his family who all speak good English. The site is in two parts, divided by a fairly quiet road leading to a good beach. The main upper site is where most of the facilities are situated, with the swimming pool, terrace and a playground located with the lower pitches across the road. Some up-and-down walking is therefore necessary, but this is a small price to pay for such pleasant and comfortable surroundings. The 200 pitches are arranged on flat, shady terraces, mostly in small groups with hedges and flowering shrubs and 20 pitches have services for motorcaravans. A good area for lovely coastal footpaths. A 'Sites et Paysages' member.

Facilities

The main site has two well kept toilet blocks with another very good block opened for main season across the road. All three blocks include British and Turkish style WCs, washbasins in cubicles, facilities for disabled people, baby baths, dishwashing, plus washing machines and dryers. Motorcaravan services. Small shop (1/7-31/8). Bar/restaurant with good value takeaway (1/7-31/8). Barbecue area. Heated swimming pool, paddling pool and jacuzzi (all 1/6-15/9). Playground. Games and TV rooms. Sports ground with tennis courts, volleyball. Bicycle hire. Off site: Fishing 700 m. Good sandy beach 700 m. downhill by road, bit less on foot. Riding 6 km. Golf 14 km. Sailing school nearby.

Open

1 June - 15 September.

At a glance

Welcome & Ambience	✓✓✓✓✓	Location	✓✓✓✓
Quality of Pitches	✓✓✓	Range of Facilities	✓✓✓✓

Directions

Site is just south of Telgruc-sur-Mer. On D887 pass through Ste Marie du Ménez Horn. In 11 km. turn left on D208 signed Telgruc-sur-Mer. Continue straight on through the town and site is on right within 1 km. GPS: N48:13.428 W04:22.382

Charges 2006

Per person	€ 5,00
child (under 7 yrs)	€ 3,00
pitch	€ 12,00
electricity (6-10A)	€ 3,10 - € 4,50
water and drainage connection	€ 2,50
dog	€ 1,60

Less 20% outside July/Aug.

Reservations

Made for any period; contact site.
Tel: 02 98 27 78 41.
Email: info@camping-panoramic.com

FR29090 Camping Le Raguenès-Plage

Mobile homes ▶ page 407

19 rue des Iles, Raguenès, F-29920 Névez (Finistère)

Madame Guyader and her family will ensure you receive a warm welcome on arrival at this well kept and pleasant site. Le Raguenès Plage is an attractive and well laid out campsite with many shrubs and trees. The 287 pitches are a good size, flat and grassy, separated by trees and hedges. All have electricity, water and drainage. The site is used by one tour operator (50 pitches), and has 44 mobile homes of its own. A pool complex complete with water toboggan is a key feature and is close to the friendly bar, restaurant, shop and takeaway. From the far end of the campsite a delightful five minute walk along a path and through a cornfield takes you down to a pleasant, sandy beach looking out towards the Ile Verte and the Presqu'île de Raguenès.

Facilities

Two clean, well maintained sanitary blocks include mixed style toilets, washbasins in cabins, baby baths and facilities for disabled visitors. Laundry and dishwashing sinks. Laundry room. Motorcaravan service point. Small shop (from 15/5). Bar and restaurant (from 1/6) with outside terrace and takeaway. Reading and TV room, internet access point. Heated pool with sun terrace and paddling pool. Sauna (charged). Play areas, table tennis, games room and volleyball. Various activities are organised in July/Aug. Currency and traveller's cheques can be exchanged at reception. Off site: Beach, fishing and watersports 300 m. Supermarket 3 km. Riding 4 km.

Open

1 April - 16 October.

At a glance

Welcome & Ambience	✓✓✓✓	Location	✓✓✓✓
Quality of Pitches	✓✓✓✓✓	Range of Facilities	✓✓✓✓

Directions

From N165 take D24 Kerampaou exit. After 3 km. turn right towards Nizon and bear right at church in village following signs to Névez (D77). Continue straight over roundabout through Névez, following signs to Raguenès. Continue for about 3 km. to site entrance on left (take care - entrance is quite small and easy to miss). GPS: N47:47. W03:48

Charges 2005

Per unit incl. 2 persons	€ 15,00 - € 26,00
extra person	€ 3,90 - € 5,50
child (under 7 yrs)	€ 2,20 - € 3,20
electricity (2-10A)	€ 3,00 - € 4,60

Reservations

Advised for high season, min. 7 days preferred for July/Aug. Write with deposit (€ 100).
Tel: 02 98 06 80 69.
Email: info@camping-le-raguenes-plage.com

FR29120 Yelloh! Village le Manoir de Kerlut

F-29740 Plobannalec-Lesconil (Finistère)

Le Manoir de Kerlut is a comfortable site in the grounds of a manor house on a river estuary near Pont l'Abbé. The old 'Manoir' is not open to the public, but is used occasionally for weddings and private functions. The campsite has neat, modern buildings and is laid out on flat grass providing 240 pitches (90 for touring units). All have electricity connections, some also have water and drainage and around ten pitches have hardstanding. One area is rather open with separating hedges planted, the other part being amongst more mature bushes and some trees which provide shade. Site amenities are of good quality. Used by tour operators (18 pitches). A 'Yelloh Village' member.

Facilities

Toilet facilities in two good blocks (each with several rooms, not all open outside July/Aug), include washbasins all in cabins, and facilities for babies and disabled people. Laundry. Small shop. Takeaway. Large modern bar with TV (satellite) and entertainment all season. Bar in the Manoir. Two heated swimming pools, paddling pool and water slide. Sauna, solarium and small gym. Play area. Tennis, volleyball, badminton and petanque. Games room. Bicycle hire. Gates closed 22.30 - 7.30 hrs. Off site: Beach 2 km. Fishing 2 km. Riding 5 km. Golf 15 km.

Open

24 May - 2 September, with all services.

At a glance

Welcome & Ambience	✓✓✓✓	Location	✓✓✓✓
Quality of Pitches	✓✓✓✓✓	Range of Facilities	✓✓✓✓✓

Directions

From Pont l'Abbé, on D785, take D102 road towards Lesconil. Site is signed on the left, shortly after the village of Plobannalec.

Charges 2006

Per unit incl. 2 persons and 5A electricity	€ 15,00 - € 37,00
extra person	€ 4,00 - € 6,00
child (under 7 yrs)	free - € 4,00
electricity (10A)	free - € 1,00
dog	€ 3,00 - € 3,50

Reservations

Write to site with 10% deposit. Tel: 02 98 82 23 89.
Email: info@campingsbretagnesud.com

FR29140 Siblu Camping Domaine de Kerlann

Land Rosted, F-29930 Pont-Aven (Finistère)

Siblu (formerly Haven Europe) have, with careful and imaginative planning, ensured that their mobile homes blend naturally into the environment here. The remaining 20% of around 110 touring pitches (some 80 sq.m, some 120 sq.m) have been left in a more natural situation on rough grass with a small stream flowing through and with some mature trees providing shade. Electricity is available to all pitches. Land drainage is poor due to the park being situated on low lying ground. The 'piece de resistance' of the site is the amazing pool complex comprising three outdoor pools with separate toboggan, attractively landscaped with sunbathing terraces, and an indoor tropical style complex complete with jacuzzi and its own toboggan. Much evening holiday camp style entertainment (with a French flavour) takes place on the bar terrace with its raised stage which overlooks the complex.

Facilities

The main large toilet block on the centre of the mobile home area includes washbasins in cubicles, outside dishwashing and laundry sinks. Good laundry. A second block in the touring section opens in high season. Mini supermarket. French style restaurant, snack restaurant, takeaway and bar. Impressive pool complex including indoor and outdoor pools with lifeguards. Well equipped play areas. All weather multi-sports court, tennis courts, minigolf. Video games room, pool tables and satellite TV in the bar. Three children's clubs for different age groups. Gas barbecues are not permitted. Off site: Pont-Aven with its Gauguin connection, art galleries and museums is well worth visiting. Small ports and villages nearby. Beach 5 km.

Directions

From Tregunc - Pont-Aven road, turn south towards Névez and site is on right.

Charges guide

Per pitch incl. up to 2 persons	
with electricity	€ 13,00 - € 34,00
extra person	€ 3,00 - € 6,00
extra vehicle	€ 1,00 - € 4,00

Reservations

Accepted at any time for min. 4 days; no booking fee. Contact site or Siblu in the UK on 0870 242 7777 for information or reservation. Tel: 02 98 06 01 77. Email: kerlann@siblu.fr

Open

1 April - 29 October.

At a glance

Welcome & Ambience	✓✓✓	Location	✓✓✓
Quality of Pitches	✓✓	Range of Facilities	✓✓✓✓

FR29220 Camping Municipal de Kerisole

Kerisole, F-29390 Scaër (Finistère)

Within walking distance of the pleasant little town of Scaër, Camping Kerisole is an attractive and well kept site, ideal for exploring inland Brittany and yet only 32 km. from the coast. There are 80 mostly level, grass pitches, not hedged, but individually numbered. 28 have electricity connections. At the back of the site is access to a marked woodland footpath, which also has a range of 'assault course' obstacles along the way. Throughout the season the campsite in conjunction with the local council organises walks, local visits and various activities (even how to make genuine Breton crêpes!), many of which are free of charge. With its delightful park-like setting, reasonable charges, and proximity to both town facilities and countryside walks, this site makes an ideal base.

Facilities

Central, clean and tidy sanitary blocks include washbasins in cubicles and separate facilities for men and ladies. Facilities for disabled people. Laundry with free use of washing machine and dryer. Dishwashing sinks. Bread to order and delivered to your pitch. Adjacent play area in large grassy field. Off site: Nearby tennis, basketball and petanque courts, and indoor swimming pool (free entry for campers). Shops, bars and restaurants a few minutes walk away in the centre of Scaër. Beach 25 km.

Open

15 June - 15 September.

At a glance

Welcome & Ambience	✓✓✓✓✓	Location	✓✓✓✓✓
Quality of Pitches	✓✓✓✓✓	Range of Facilities	✓✓✓

Directions

From N165 take D70 to Rosporden, then D782 to Scaër. Drive through town centre, following signs for Faouet, and site is on left at traffic lights on leaving town centre. GPS: N48:01 W003:41

Charges 2005

Per person	€ 1,50 - € 2,30
child (under 7 yrs)	€ 1,60
pitch	€ 2,50 - € 2,80
car	€ 1,60
motorcycle	€ 1,40
electricity (10A)	€ 2,60

No credit cards.

Reservations

Contact site. Tel: 02 98 57 60 91.
Email: mairie@ville-scaer.fr

FR29170 Camping de la Piscine

Kerleya B.P. 12, Beg-Meil, F-29170 Fouesnant (Finistère)

There are many campsites in this area but La Piscine is notable for the care and attention to detail that contributes to the well-being of its visitors. Created by the Caradec family from an apple orchard, the 185 level, grass pitches are of generous size and are separated by an interesting variety of hedges and trees. Water, waste and electricity points are provided, normally one stand between two pitches. The nearby towns of Beg-Meil and Fouesnant, and (a little further) Quimper, are well worth a visit if only to taste the local cider and crêpes which are specialities of the area. A quiet site, set back from the sea, La Piscine will appeal to families looking for good quality without too many on site activities.

Facilities

Two refurbished toilet units of differing design and size include British and Turkish style toilets and washbasins in cabins. Facilities for disabled people. Dishwashing and laundry sinks, washing machines and dryers. Motorcaravan service point. Shop well stocked with basic provisions. Takeaway (high season). New pool complex with attractive swimming pool, three slides, waterfall and jacuzzi. Sauna and solarium. Play area. BMX track. Football pitch, volleyball, half-court tennis and table tennis. TV room. Entertainment organised in high season. Caravan storage. Off site: Bicycle hire, fishing and riding within 4 km. Golf 7 km. Beach 1 km.

Open

15 May - 15 September.

At a glance

Welcome & Ambience	✓✓✓✓	Location	✓✓✓✓
Quality of Pitches	✓✓✓✓✓	Range of Facilities	✓✓✓✓

Directions

Site is 5 km. south of Fouesnant. Turn off N165 expressway at Coat Conq signed Concarnau and Fouesnant. At Fouesnant join D45 signed Beg Meil and shortly turn left on D145 signed Mousterlin. In 1 km. turn left and follow signs to site. GPS: N47:51.941 W04:00.932

Charges 2006

Per person	€ 3,75 - € 5,50
child (under 7 yrs)	€ 1,85 - € 2,75
pitch	€ 7,50 - € 11,00
electricity (3-10A)	€ 3,00 - € 4,40
dog	€ 1,30 - € 2,00

Reservations

Made with deposit (€ 40) and fee (€ 19). Tel: 02 98 56 56 06. Email: contact@campingdelapiscine.com

FR29180 Camping Les Embruns

Rue du Philosophe Alain, Le Pouldu, F-29360 Clohars-Carnoët (Finistère)

This site is unusual in that it is located in the heart of a village, yet is only 250 metres from a sandy cove. It is also close to beautiful countryside and the Carnoët Forest. The entrance with its card operated barrier and wonderful floral displays, is the first indication that this is a well tended and well organised site, and the owners have won numerous regional and national awards for its superb presentation. The 180 pitches (100 occupied by mobile homes) are separated by trees, shrubs and bushes, and most have electricity, water and drainage. There is a covered, heated swimming pool, a circular paddling pool and a water play pool. It is only a short walk to the village centre with all its attractions and services.

Facilities

Two modern sanitary blocks, recently completely renewed, include mainly British style toilets, some washbasins in cubicles, baby baths and good facilities for disabled visitors. New family bathrooms. Washing, drying and ironing facilities. Motorcaravan service point. New mini-market and restaurant open by site entrance. Bar and terrace (1/7-31/8) overlooking a covered, heated swimming pool and paddling pool. Takeaway (20/6-5/9). Large games hall. Play area. Football field, volleyball and minigolf. Communal barbecue area. Daily activities for children and adults organised in July/Aug. Off site: Nearby sea and river fishing and watersports. Bicycle hire 50 m. Beach 250 m. Riding 2 km.

Open

9 April - 17 September.

At a glance

Welcome & Ambience	✓✓✓✓✓	Location	✓✓✓✓✓
Quality of Pitches	✓✓✓✓	Range of Facilities	✓✓✓✓✓

Directions

From N165 take either 'Kervidanou, Quimperlé Ouest' exit or 'Kergostiou, Quimperlé Centre, Clohars Carnoët' exit and follow D16 to Clohars Carnoët. Then take D24 for Le Pouldu and follow site signs in village. GPS: N47:46 W03:32

Charges 2005

Per unit incl. 2 persons	€ 10,50 - € 15,00
fully serviced pitch	€ 14,50 - € 27,00
extra person	€ 3,90 - € 5,10
child (under 7 yrs)	€ 2,50 - € 3,10
electricity on ordinary pitch	€ 3,50

Use of motorcaravan services € 4.

Reservations

Advised for high season. Deposit of € 80. Non-refundable booking fee € 20 (1/7-25/8). Tel: 02 98 39 91 07. Email: camping-les-embruns@wanadoo.fr

FR29160 Camping Les Genets d'Or

Kermerour, Pont Kereon, F-29380 Bannalec (Finistère)

Les Genets d'Or is situated in a country hamlet at the end of a road from Bannalec, 12 km. from Pont-Aven in Finistère. The spacious surroundings offer a safe haven for children and a tranquil environment for adults. The gently sloping, grassy site is edged with mature trees and divided into hedged glades with the odd apple tree providing shade. There are only 52 pitches (46 for tourers), all of a good size - some of over 100 sq.m. - and most pitches have electricity, each glade having a water point. Alan and Judy, the English owners, provide a warm friendly welcome and are justifiably proud of their site which they have improved and keep in pristine condition. A play and picnic area has been added in 2005.

Facilities

The good quality toilet block provides all the necessary amenities and washing facilities, including a shower for disabled campers. Washing machine and dryer. New bar area. Bread delivered in season. Ice pack service. Small library and an indoor room provides snooker and table tennis. Bicycle hire. Caravan storage. Off site: Riding 3 km. Beach 12 km. Village 15 minutes walk with bars, shop, etc.

Open

Easter/1 April - 30 September.

At a glance

Welcome & Ambience	✓✓✓✓✓	Location	✓✓✓✓✓
Quality of Pitches	✓✓✓✓✓	Range of Facilities	✓✓✓✓✓

Directions

Take exit D4 from N165 towards Bannalec. In Bannalec turn right into Rue Lorec (signed Quimperlé) and follow camp signs for 1 km.

Charges 2005

Per person	€ 3,00
child (under 6 yrs)	€ 2,00
pitch	€ 5,50
electricity (6A)	€ 3,00

Less 10% for over 7 nights.

Reservations

Contact site. Tel: 02 98 39 54 35. Email: Enquiries@holidaybrittany.com

41

FR29190 Camping Les Prés Verts

B.P. 62, Kernous-Plage, F-29186 Concarneau Cedex (Finistère)

What sets this family site apart from the many others in this region are its more unusual features - its stylish pool complex with Romanesque style columns and statue, and its plants and flower tubs. The 150 pitches are mostly arranged on long, open, grassy areas either side of main access roads. Specimen trees, shrubs or hedges divide the site into smaller areas. There are a few individual pitches and an area towards the rear of the site where the pitches have sea views. Concarneau is just 2.5 km. and there are many marked coastal walks to enjoy in the area, plus watersports or boat and fishing trips available nearby. A 'Sites et Paysages' member.

Facilities

Two toilet blocks provide unisex WCs, but separate washing facilities for ladies and men. Pre-set hot showers and washbasins in cabins for ladies, both closed 9 pm - 8 am. Some child-size toilets. Dishwashing and laundry sinks, washing machine and dryer. Pizza service twice weekly. Heated swimming pool (1/7-31/8) and paddling pool. Playground (0-5 yrs only). Minigolf (charged). Off site: Path to sandy/rocky beach (300 m.) and coastal path. Riding 1 km. Supermarket 2 km. Bicycle hire 3 km. Golf 5 km.

Open

1 May - 22 September.

At a glance

Welcome & Ambience	✓✓✓✓	Location	✓✓✓✓✓
Quality of Pitches	✓✓✓✓✓	Range of Facilities	✓✓✓

Directions

Turn off C7 road, 2.5 km. north of Concarneau, where site is signed. Take third left after Hotel de l'Océan. GPS: N47:53. W03:56.

Charges 2005

Per unit incl. 2 adults	€ 18,10 - € 22,70
extra adult	€ 5,20 - € 6,50
child (2-7 yrs)	€ 3,40 - € 4,30
dog	€ 1,30 - € 1,60
electricity (2-6A)	€ 3,20 - € 4,90

Reservations

Contact site. Tel: 02 98 97 09 74.
Email: info@presverts.com

FR29240 Camping de Kéranterec

Route de Port la Forêt, F-29940 La Forêt Fouesnant (Finistère)

The area around La Forêt Fouesnant is very much 'picture postcard' Brittany - plenty of enticing crêperies and seafood restaurants, enchanting mediaeval villages and towns and delightful hidden coves. For these and many other reasons, there are plenty of campsites to choose from and Camping de Keranterec is well worth considering. A well established family run site with a very French ambience (unlike some of the neighbouring sites which have a much higher UK presence), Keranterec has 265 grassy pitches in two distinct areas. The upper part of the site is more open and has little shade, and is also largely taken up by private mobile homes. The lower and more mature area is predominantly for tourers, with terraced pitches set in a former orchard (the trees still provide fruit for the cider produced on site, which we can highly recommend!). Some of these pitches have shade from the many trees on this part of the site, and some also overlook the little cove at the rear of the site. Spacious and divided by mature hedging, all have electrical connections (25 m. cable advised) and most also offer water and drainage. At the rear of the site a gate leads to a small beach and the coastal footpath to Concarneau (8 km).

Facilities

Two modern, fully equipped toilet blocks kept very clean include washbasins in cubicles, baby baths and facilities for disabled visitors. Washing machines, dryers and ironing boards. Small shop and bar (15/6-10/9) and takeaway (1/7-31/8). TV room with satellite. Heated swimming pool (1/6-10/9) with paddling pool, jacuzzi and three new water slides. Tennis court, boules, volleyball and basketball, table tennis (some indoors). Play area. In July/Aug. organised daily events and activities for all the family, and a free children's club. Off site: Attractive sandy beach of Kerleven 10 minutes walk. Golf 1 km. Riding 3 km.

Open

8 April - 17 September.

At a glance

Welcome & Ambience	✓✓✓✓	Location	✓✓✓✓✓
Quality of Pitches	✓✓✓✓	Range of Facilities	✓✓✓✓

Directions

From N165 take D70 Concarneau exit. At first roundabout take D44 signed Fouesnant. After 2.5 km. turn right at T-junction, and follow for 2.5 km. and turn left (Port La Forêt - take care, 200 m. before junction a sign implies Port La Forêt is straight on - it isn't). Continue to roundabout and take second exit (straight ahead), signed Port La Forêt. After 1 km. turn left (site signed), then in 400 m. turn left to site on left. GPS: N47:53.930 W03:57.375

Charges 2005

Per person	€ 6,00 - € 8,00
child (under 7 yrs)	€ 3,00 - € 4,00
pitch	€ 7,50 - € 10,00
electricity	€ 4,00
dog	€ 1,90 - € 2,50

No credit cards.

Reservations

Advised in high season and made with deposit (€ 100) and fee (€ 30). Tel: 02 98 56 98 11. Email: info@camping-keranterec.com

FR29310 Camping La Roche Percée

Hent Kerveltrec, Beg-Meil, F-29170 Fouesnant (Finistère)

Close to the beautiful Brittany coastline, La Roche Percée combines a tranquil setting with a friendly and active family environment, only 400 metres from the beach. Under new ownership, there are 123 pitches, of which 80 are for touring units, the rest being for privately owned or site owned mobile homes. Pitches are arranged in cul-de-sacs off a central area and are of a good size, grassy and flat, all with electrical connections (some may require a long lead). All pitches are separated by mature hedging, and some benefit from the shade of the variety of trees planted around the site. The bar terrace overlooks the swimming and paddling pools, and there is a waterslide into the main pool. During high season the owners organise a variety of entertainment activities, including boules, table tennis, pool and darts tournaments, barbecues, and live music in the bar.

Facilities

The clean, tidy central toilet block includes mostly British style toilets, washbasins in cubicles, dishwashing and laundry sinks. Baby bath and changing area. Wheelchair access provided on request. Motorcaravan service point. Small shop, snack bar and bar (open 15/5-15/9, with bread to order outside these dates, which can be flexible if busy.) Swimming pools (all season). Two play areas. Football and volleyball. Large trampoline (parental supervision essential!) Bicycle hire. Off site: Beach 400 m. Sailing school, golf and riding nearby.

Open

2 April - 26 September.

At a glance

Welcome & Ambience	✓✓✓	Location	✓✓✓✓✓
Quality of Pitches	✓✓✓✓	Range of Facilities	✓✓✓

Directions

From N165 take D70 Concarneau exit. At first roundabout take first exit on D44 (signed Fouesnant, Benodet). Following D44, turning right at T-junction, after approx. 2 km. turn left and follow through Forêt Fouesnant. About 2 km. after village are two roundabouts. Go straight over first (smaller) one and turn left at second on D45 to Beg Meil. After 3 km. site is signed on left. Turn left, site entrance just past the Auberge de la Roche Percée.

Charges guide

Per person	€ 3,00 - € 4,50
child (under 7 yrs)	€ 1,50 - € 2,50
pitch	€ 8,50 - € 11,50
electricity (6/10A)	€ 3,00
dog	€ 1,50 - € 2,00

Reservations

Accepted with deposit (€ 77) and booking fee (€ 15.50). Tel: 02 98 94 94 15.
Email: contact@camping-larochepercee.com

FR29250 Camping Bois des Ecureuils

F-29300 Guilligomarc'h (Finistère)

Situated in beautiful countryside between the rivers Scorff and Elle, this two star site provides rural camping for those seeking an ideal base from which to explore southern and central Brittany. The site is set in nine acres of natural woodland and open field with trees providing a leafy backdrop to many of the 40 pitches. There are plans to extend the site in 2006. With a choice of sunny or shady pitches, many pitches have electricity. The British owners provide a wealth of information on places to visit and activities in the area. The tranquillity of this rural setting, combined with the friendly reception, make it ideal for a relaxing rural holiday whilst still only a short drive from southern Brittany's finest beaches.

Facilities	Directions
Small toilet block with showers, washbasins in cubicles, British and Turkish style WCs, dishwashing and laundry facilities. Reception/shop provides basic groceries and bread to order. Play area. Large grass leisure area with boules pitch, table tennis and badminton net. Bicycle and kayak hire. Off site: Beach 17 km.	From south on N165 take D769 road. After 24 km. turn right on D6(E) to Meslan/Arzano. In 700 m. take next left on D6 towards Arzano. After 1 km. turn left onto C2 to Guilligomarch. Site is on left in 1.1 km. GPS: N47:57. W03:25.

Open	Charges 2005	
15 May - 15 September.	Per person	€ 2,80
	pitch incl. electricity (5A)	€ 7,00
	No credit cards.	

At a glance				Reservations
Welcome & Ambience	✓✓✓✓	Location	✓✓✓✓	Made with deposit (€ 15). Tel: 02 98 71 70 98.
Quality of Pitches	✓✓✓✓✓	Range of Facilities	✓✓✓	

FR29280 La Pointe Superbe Camping

Route de St Coulitz, F-29150 Châteaulin (Finistère)

La Pointe, just outside Châteaulin, has been lovingly and impressively brought back to life by its delightful English owners Colin Grewer and Sue Dodds. Châteaulin is a bustling market town, 15 km. from the beach at Pentrez and within easy reach of Quimper, mediaeval Locronan and the Crozon peninsula. This very tranquil site boasts particularly large, grassy pitches in a quiet valley leading down to the River Aulne, which makes up part of the Nantes - Brest canal. The 60 pitches all have electricity with water close by. This small site is well suited to those who like peace and quiet.

Facilities	Directions
The first-class toilet block, kept very clean at all times, has many washbasins in cubicles. Shower cubicles are somewhat small but have full adjustable taps. Facilities for disabled visitors. Baby room. Motorcaravan services. Play area. Table tennis, volleyball. Large activity room. Off site: Châteaulin 700 m. Riding and tennis nearby. Beach 9 km.	Site is just southeast of Châteaulin. From town centre bridge follow signs for St Coulitz/Quimper. Shortly turn left signed St Coulitz. Site is signed at this point.

Open	Charges 2006	
6 March - 31 October.	Per unit incl. 2 persons	€ 14,00
	electricity (10A)	€ 2,60
	No credit cards.	

At a glance				Reservations
Welcome & Ambience	✓✓✓✓	Location	✓✓✓✓	Advised for high season and made with deposit (€ 15). Tel: 02 98 86 51 53. Email: lapointecamping@aol.com
Quality of Pitches	✓✓✓✓✓	Range of Facilities	✓✓✓✓	

FR29350 Sunêlia L'Atlantique

Mousterlin, F-29170 Fouesnant (Finistère)

L'Atlantique is quietly situated just outside Beg-Meil and is a superb site for families and those looking for a beach holiday. The sandy beach faces the Glénan Islands and is a pleasant 400 m. walk away through a nature reserve. The 432 pitches are predominantly used by tour operators with about 70 for independent visitors. Level and grassy, all with electricity, they are separated by an attractive variety of low shrubs, with apple orchards used for cider production also on the site. All the facilities are grouped together at the centre of the site including an innovative play area and excellent pool complex.

Facilities	Directions
Clean, modern, fully equipped toilet blocks include facilities for disabled visitors. Shop. Bar. Snack bar with takeaway meals and pizza. Heated outdoor pool, water complex with slides (all 15/5-12/9). Tennis. TV room. Billiards, table tennis. Minigolf. Sports ground. Play area. Children's club (4-12 yrs) and evening entertainment in July/Aug. Off site: Fishing 300 m. Windsurf hire 1 km. Riding 3 km. Golf 8 km.	From Fouesnant follow directions for Mousterlin for 4.5 km. Site is signed. GPS: N47:51.406 W04:01.258

	Charges 2005	
	Per unit incl. 2 persons	€ 21,00 - € 38,00
	extra person	€ 2,70 - € 7,00
	child (0-10 yrs)	€ 1,30 - € 4,00

Open	Low season reductions.
1 May - 15 September.	Camping Cheques accepted.

At a glance				Reservations
Welcome & Ambience	✓✓✓✓	Location	✓✓✓	Contact site. Tel: 02 98 56 14 44. Email: information@camping-atlantique.fr
Quality of Pitches	✓✓✓	Range of Facilities	✓✓✓✓✓	

FR29290 Yelloh! Village le Grand Large

48 route du Grand Large, Mousterlin, F-29170 Fouesnant (Finistère)

Le Grand Large is a beach-side site situated on the Pointe de Mousterlin in natural surroundings. The site is separated from the beach by the road that follows the coast around the point. It is also protected from the wind by an earth bank with trees and a fence. The beach itself looks over the bay towards the Isles de Glénan. There are 300 pitches with just 54 rather small uneven places used for touring units. Tour operators take 70 pitches and the site itself has tents and mobile homes to rent. The ground is rather sandy in places with some shrubs and mature trees. Electricity is available everywhere (long leads useful) and some pitches have drainage. A small river runs through the site but it is fenced. Benodet (7 km.) and Fouesnant (5 km.) are near in different directions and the sandy beach is just up the steps and across the road. A family site, Le Grand Large would also suit nature lovers in low season as it is next to a large tract of protected land, Marais de Mousterlin, ideal for walking, cycling and birdwatching.

Facilities

Two neat toilet blocks, the largest only opened in high season, include plenty of washbasins in cabins. Two baby baths in the larger block with children's shower and toilet and facilities for disabled people in both blocks. Washing machines, dryers and plenty of laundry and washing up sinks. Bar overlooking the sea with attractive terrace. Crêperie/grill restaurant including takeaway. Swimming pool with paddling pool, water slides in separate pool. Tennis court and multi-sport court for 5-a-side football, badminton, volleyball, handball or basketball. Small play area. TV room and games room with table tennis and billiards. Bicycle hire. Off site: Fishing 100 m. Golf and riding 5 km. Beach 100 m.

At a glance

Welcome & Ambience	✓✓✓✓	Location	✓✓✓✓✓
Quality of Pitches	✓✓	Range of Facilities	✓✓✓✓✓

Directions

Site is 7 km. south of Fouesnant. Turn off N165 expressway at Coat Conq, signed Concarneau and Fouesnant. At Fouesnant take A45 signed Beg Meil, then follow signs to Mousterlin. In Mousterlin turn left and follow camping signs.

Charges 2006

Per unit incl. 2 persons and 5A electricity	€ 16,00 - € 37,00
extra person	€ 4,00 - € 6,00
child (under 10 yrs)	free - € 4,00
electricity (10A)	€ 1,00 - € 1,00
dog	€ 3,00 - € 3,50

Reservations

Made with deposit (€ 45) and non-refundable fee (€ 19). Tel: 02 98 56 04 06.

Open

15 April - 10 September (with all services).

FR35010 Camping Le Bois Coudrais

F-35270 Cuguen (Ille-et-Vilaine)

This gem of a campsite, owned and run by a delightful couple from Jersey, is the kind of small, rural site that is becoming a rarity in France. It has 26 medium to large, well kept, grassy pitches, some divided by young shrubs, others by mature trees. They are spread over three small fields, one of which has an area set aside for ball games and is also home to a group of friendly goats and some chickens – a magnet for children. Electrical connections are possible in most areas. Four attractive gîtes are available, but there are no mobile homes, organised games or music. Claire and Philippe Ybert are intent on keeping their site a peaceful and natural retreat. In the small bar which also serves as reception and restaurant, Claire is happy to prepare and serve a selection of home-made meals. Within a thirty minute drive are the attractions of St Malo, Dinan and Mont St Michel.

Facilities

The toilet block beside the house provides washbasins in cubicles, showers and sinks for dishwashing and laundry, plus facilities for disabled visitors. Bar with meals (May-Sept). Small swimming pool. Play area on grass. Animal enclosure. Table tennis. Bicycle hire. Games field. Internet access. Off site: Shop in village 0.5 km. Combourg 5 km. Fishing 5 km. Golf and riding 15 km. Beach 20 km.

Open

1 May - 30 September.

At a glance

Welcome & Ambience	✓✓✓✓✓	Location	✓✓✓✓✓
Quality of Pitches	✓✓✓✓✓	Range of Facilities	✓✓✓✓

Directions

From St Malo take the D137 (in the direction of Rennes) to Combourg. Follow signs on D83 for Fougères and Mont St Michel. Site is 0.5 km. past Cuguen on the left, well signed. GPS: N48:27.237 W01:39.08

Charges 2005

Per person	€ 2,50
child (0-12 yrs)	€ 2,10
pitch	€ 8,50
electricity	€ 2,00

Reservations

Contact site. Tel: 0033 2 99 73 27. Email: info@vacancebretagne.com

FR35050 Domaine de la Ville Huchet

Route de la Passagère, Quelmer, F-35400 St Malo (Ille-et-Vilaine)

Domaine de la Ville Huchet is a friendly, former municipal site which has been taken over by the owners of FR35020 Les Ormes. It is being progressively overhauled by its new owners and is a useful site on the edge of St Malo, with easy access to the ferry terminal, old town and beaches. Pitches are on level ground set around the old manor house at the centre of the site. Most pitches have electricity connections (6A), and there is shade from mature trees in some areas. Amenities include a small, well-stocked shop and a bar. The large pool is attractively landscaped and has a number of water slides. Some road noise is audible from the St Malo by-pass. Mobile homes for rent.

Facilities

The sanitary blocks are old and undergoing renovation but were clean when we visited. Facilities for disabled visitors. Bar and snack bar. Shop. Aqua park with water slides. Football pitch. Bicycle hire. Animation programme in peak season (including live bands). Play area. Off site: Aquarium 700 m. St Malo (beaches, ferry terminal and old town) 4 km.

Open

1 May - 15 September.

At a glance

Welcome & Ambience	✓✓✓✓	Location	✓✓✓	
Quality of Pitches	✓✓✓	Range of Facilities	✓✓	

Directions

From St Malo take D301 heading south. Join D165 signed Quelmer and the site is well signed (2 km).

Charges 2005

Per person	€ 4,35 - € 4,90
child (1-7 yrs)	€ 2,30 - € 2,55
pitch	€ 10,55 - € 11,75
electricity	€ 3,65 - € 4,10

Reservations

Contact site. Tel: 02 99 73 53 00.
Email: valarie@desormes.com

FR35020 Castel Camping Le Domaine des Ormes

Epiniac, F-35120 Dol-de-Bretagne (Ille-et-Vilaine)

This impressive site is in the northern part of Brittany, about 30 km. from the old town of Saint Malo, in the grounds of the Château des Ormes. In an estate of wooded parkland and lakes it has a pleasant atmosphere, busy in high season but peaceful at other times, with a wide range of facilities. The 800 pitches are divided into a series of different sections, each with its own distinctive character and offering a choice of terrain - flat or gently sloping, wooded or open. Only 150 of the pitches, all with electricity connections, are used for touring units and there is a large variety of other accommodation available. A marvellous 'Aqua Park' with pink stone and palms and a variety of pools, toboggans, waterfalls and jacuzzi is set just above the small lake (with pedaloes and canoes for hire). A pleasant bar and terrace overlook the pools and a grass sunbathing area surrounds them. The original pools are sheltered by the restaurant building, parts of which are developed from the 600 year old water-mill. A particular feature here is an 18 hole golf course, with a practice range, a beginners' 5 hole course and lessons. A restaurant and hotel with pool is part of the complex. The equestrian centre offers a variety of riding options (including lessons and even stabling for your own horse). A popular site with British visitors, some 80% of the pitches are occupied by tour operators and seasonal units and the site is consequently very busy with much organised entertainment.

Facilities

The toilet blocks are of fair standard, including washbasins in cabins and ample facilities for disabled people. Motorcaravan services. Shop, bar, restaurant, pizzeria and takeaway. Games room, bar and disco. Two traditional heated swimming pools and Aqua park. Adventure play area. Golf. Bicycle hire. Fishing. Equestrian centre with riding. Minigolf. Two tennis courts. Sports ground with volleyball, etc. Paintball, Archery. Cricket club.

Open

20 May - 10 September, with all services.

At a glance

Welcome & Ambience	✓✓✓✓	Location	✓✓✓✓
Quality of Pitches	✓✓✓✓	Range of Facilities	✓✓✓✓✓

Directions

Access road leads off main D795 about 7 km. south of Dol-de-Bretagne, north of Combourg.
GPS: N48:29 W01:43

Charges 2005

Per person	€ 6,75 - € 7,50
child (under 7 yrs)	€ 3,90 - € 4,25
pitch incl. vehicle	€ 19,75 - € 21,85
electricity 3/6A	€ 3,85 - € 4,25
water and drainage	€ 1,85 - € 2,15
dog	€ 1,50 - € 1,65

Less 10% outside July/Aug.

Reservations

Made for min. 3 nights; details from site.
Tel: 02 99 73 53 00. Email: info@lesormes.com

FR35000 Camping Le Vieux Chêne

Baguer-Pican, F-35120 Dol-de-Bretagne (Ille-et-Vilaine)

This attractive, family owned site is situated between Saint Malo and Mont Saint Michel. Developed in the grounds of a country farmhouse dating from 1638, its young and enthusiastic owner has created a really pleasant, traditional atmosphere. In spacious, rural surroundings it offers 199 good sized pitches on gently sloping grass, most with 10A electricity, water tap and light. They are separated by bushes and flowers, with mature trees for shade. A very attractive tenting area (without electricity) is in the orchard. There are three lakes in the grounds and centrally located leisure facilities include a restaurant with a terrace overlooking an attractive pool complex. Some entertainment is provided in high season, which is free for children. Used by a Dutch tour operator (10 pitches).

Facilities

Three very good, unisex toilet blocks include washbasins in cabins, a baby room and facilities for disabled people. All have recently been refurbished and can be heated. Small laundry with washing machine, dryer and iron. Motorcaravan services. Shop, takeaway and restaurant (15/5-15/9). Medium sized, heated swimming pool, paddling pool, slides, etc. (15/5-15/9; lifeguard July/Aug). TV room (satellite) and games room. Minigolf. Giant chess. Play area. Riding in July/Aug. Fishing is possible in two of the three lakes. Off site: Supermarket in Dol 3 km. Golf 12 km. Beach 20 km.

Open

1 April - 1 October.

At a glance

Welcome & Ambience	✓✓✓	Location	✓✓✓✓
Quality of Pitches	✓✓✓✓	Range of Facilities	✓✓✓✓

Directions

Site is by the D576 Dol-de-Bretagne - Pontorson road, just east of Baguer-Pican. It can be reached from the new N176 taking exit for Dol-Est and Baguer-Pican.
GPS: N48:32.972 W01:41.03

Charges 2005

Per person	€ 4,00 - € 5,50
child (under 13 yrs)	free - € 3,50
pitch	€ 6,00 - € 16,00
electricity (10A)	€ 4,00
dog	€ 1,50

Reservations

Made with deposit (€ 30) and fee (€; 15).
Tel: 02 99 48 09 55. Email: vieux.chene@wanadoo.fr

FR35040 Camping Le P'tit Bois

Mobile homes ▶ page 408

F-35430 St Jouan des Guerets (Ille-et-Vilaine)

On the outskirts of Saint Malo, this neat, family oriented site is very popular with British visitors, being ideal for one night stops or for longer stays in this interesting area. Le P'tit Bois is a busy site providing 274 large level pitches with around 140 for touring units. In two main areas, either side of the entrance lane, these are divided into groups by mature hedges and trees, separated by shrubs and flowers and with access from tarmac roads. Nearly all have electrical hook-ups and over half have water taps. Behind reception, an attractive, sheltered terraced area around the pools provides a focus during the day along with a bar and snack bar. There are site-owned mobile homes and chalets but this does mean that the facilities are open over a long season (if only for limited hours). There are card operated security gates (with a deposit payable) with parking ouside for new arrivals.

Facilities

Two fully equipped toilet blocks, one in the newer area across the lane, include washbasins in cabins, baby baths and laundry facilities. Simple facilities for disabled people. Motorcaravan service point. Small shop (from 15/5). Bar (all season) with entertainment and discos in July-Aug. Snack bar with takeaway, small bar, TV room (large screen for sports events) and games rooms. Swimming pool with paddling pool and two water slides (from 15/5). Indoor pool with jacuzzi and Turkish bath. Playground and multi-sports court. Tennis court, minigolf, table tennis, and outdoor chess. Charcoal barbecues are not permitted. Off site: Beach 1.5 km. Buses 2 km. Fishing 1.5 km, bicycle hire or riding 5 km, golf 7 km.

Open

16 April - 10 September.

At a glance

Welcome & Ambience	✓✓✓✓✓	Location	✓✓✓✓
Quality of Pitches	✓✓✓✓	Range of Facilities	✓✓✓✓✓

Directions

St Jouan is west off the St Malo - Rennes road (N137) just outside St Malo. Site is signed from the N137 (exit St Jouan on the D4).
GPS: N48:36.579 W01:59.21

Charges 2005

Per person	€ 6,00 - € 8,00
child (under 7 yrs)	€ 3,00 - € 5,00
pitch and car	€ 10,00 - € 20,00
electricity (6A)	€ 4,00
water and drainage (min 7 nights)	€ 4,00
dog	€ 4,00

Reservations

Made on receipt of 25% of total cost, plus fee (€ 30) for July and August. Tel: 02 99 21 14 30.
Email: camping.ptitbois@wanadoo.fr

PARC SAINTE-BRIGITTE
★ ★ ★ ★ N.N.
De Luxe Camping Site

HEATED SWIMMING POOL

Close to the fishing village of LaTurballe and neighbouring beaches. 10 km from the well-known resort of La Baule. The charm of the countryside with the pleasures of the seaside. Sanitary facilities as in a first class hotel. Heated and covered swimming pool (approximately 200 m² water and 200 m² covered terrace around it). The cover can be retracted during warm weather. Children's pool.

campingsaintebrigitte@wanadoo.fr
www.campingsaintebrigitte.com

FR44040 Castel Camping Le Parc Sainte-Brigitte

Domaine de Bréhet, F-44420 La Turballe (Loire-Atlantique)

Le Parc Sainte-Brigitte is a well established site in the attractive grounds of a manor house, three kilometres from the beaches. It is a spacious site with 150 good pitches, 110 with electricity and 25 also with water and drainage. Some are arranged in a circular, park-like setting near the entrance, others are in wooded areas under tall trees and the remainder are on more open grass in an unmarked area near the pool. One can walk around many of the areas of the estate not used for camping, there are farm animals to see and a fishing lake is very popular. This is a quiet place to stay outside the main season, whilst in high season, when it is mainly used by families with its full share of British visitors, it can become very busy. Used by a tour operator (12 pitches).

Facilities

The main toilet block is of good quality, supplemented by second block next to it. Washbasins in cabins, and two bathrooms. Washing machines and dryer (no washing to be hung out on pitches, lines provided). Motorcaravan services. Small shop. Pleasant restaurant/bar with takeaway (both 15/5-15/9). Heated swimming pool with retractable roof and paddling pool (all season). Playground. Bicycle hire. Boules, volleyball, pool and 'baby-foot'. Table tennis. TV room and traditional 'salle de reunion'. Fishing.
Off site: Riding 2 km. Beach 2.5 km. Golf 15 km.

Open

1 April - 1 October.

At a glance

Welcome & Ambience	✓✓✓	Location	✓✓✓✓
Quality of Pitches	✓✓✓✓✓	Range of Facilities	✓✓✓✓

Directions

Entrance is off the busy La Turballe-Guérande D99 road, 3 km. east of La Turballe. A one-way system operates - in one lane, out via another. GPS: N47:20. W02:28.

Charges 2005

Per person	€ 5,50
child (under 7 yrs)	€ 4,50
pitch	€ 6,00
with water and electricity	€ 12,00
car	€ 3,00

No credit cards.

Reservations

Made for any length with exact dates with deposit (€ 64.75) plus fee (€ 15.25). Tel: 02 40 24 88 91. Email: saintebrigitte@wanadoo.fr

FR35060 Camping La Touesse

F-35800 St Lunaire (Ille-et-Vilaine)

This family campsite was purpose built and has been developed since 1987 by Alain Clement who is keen to welcome more British visitors. Set just back from the coast road, 300 metres from a sandy beach, it is in a semi-residential area. It is, nevertheless, an attractive, sheltered site with a range of trees and shrubs. The 142 level, grass pitches in bays have electricity and are accessed by tarmac roads. The plus factor of this site, besides its proximity to Dinard, is the fine sandy sheltered beach. The owners speak English.

Facilities

The central toilet block is well maintained, heated in low season and provides modern facilities. Part of it may be closed outside July/Aug. Baby bath and toilet for disabled people. Two washing machines and a dryer. Motorcaravan service point. Shop for basics (1/4-20/9). Bar/restaurant with TV. Volleyball, table tennis and video games. Sauna.
Off site: Fishing 300 m. Riding 500 m. Bicycle hire 1 km. Golf 4 km. Sandy beach 300 m. Buses 100 m.

Open

1 April - 30 September.

At a glance

Welcome & Ambience	✓✓✓✓	Location	✓✓✓
Quality of Pitches	✓✓✓✓	Range of Facilities	✓✓✓

Directions

From Dinard take D786 coast road towards St Lunaire; watch for site signs to the left.

Charges 2006

Per person	€ 3,80 - € 4,90
child (under 7 yrs)	€ 2,10 - € 2,70
pitch	€ 4,90 - € 6,10
car	€ 2,60 - € 3,10
electricity (5/10A)	€ 3,20 - € 3,50
dog	€ 1,50

No credit cards.

Reservations

Contact site. Tel: 02 99 46 61 13. Email: camping.la.touesse@wanadoo.fr

FR44020 Camping Municipal du Moulin

Route de Nantes, F-44190 Clisson (Loire-Atlantique)

This good value, small site is conveniently located on one of the main north - south routes on the edge of the interesting old town of Clisson. A typical municipal site, it is useful for short stays. There are 47 good sized, marked and level pitches with electricity and divided by hedges and trees giving a good degree of privacy; also an unmarked area for small tents. A barbecue and camp fire area (with free wood) is to the rear of the site above the river where one can fish or canoe (via a steep path). The warden lives on site in high season. The attractive old town is within walking distance.

Facilities	Directions
The fully equipped unisex toilet block includes some washbasins in cabins. Unit for disabled people. Cleaning can be a bit haphazard at times. Bread delivered daily. Table tennis, volleyball, and small playground. No double axle or commercial vehicles. Off site: Supermarket across the road.	Entering Clisson from the north on N 1 49 (Nantes - Poitiers) road, turn right at roundabout after passing Leclerc supermarket on your left. Site access is directly off roundabout.

Open

Easter - mid October.

Charges 2005

Per unit incl. 1 adult and electricity	€ 7,36
extra person	€ 2,45
child (0-7 yrs)	€ 1,64

Reservations

Contact site. Tel: 02 40 54 44 48.

At a glance

Welcome & Ambience	✓✓✓✓	Location	✓✓✓✓
Quality of Pitches	✓✓✓✓	Range of Facilities	✓✓✓

FR44130 Camping L'Hermitage

36 ave du Paradis, F-44290 Guemene-Penfao (Loire-Atlantique)

L'Hermitage is a pretty wooded site set in the Vallée du Don and would be useful for en-route stops or for longer stays. Both Nantes and Rennes are 30 minutes away, La Baule with its beaches is 40 minutes. The enthusiastic staff, even though their English is a little limited, provide a warm welcome and maintain this reasonably priced site to a good standard. There are 110 pitches of which 80 are a good size for touring and camping. Some are formally arranged on open, level grass pitches, whereas others are informal amongst light woodland. Electricity (6A) is available to all (a long lead may be useful).

Facilities	Directions
A clean and well serviced toilet block includes some washbasins in cabins with warm water. Smallish pool, paddling pool and slide, nicely maintained and carefully fenced. Small play area. Table tennis. Petanque. Games room with video games. Off site: Indoor pool opposite. Fishing 500 m. Village 1 km. Riding 2 km.	Exit N137 at Derval (signed Châteaubriant) but take D775 for Redon. Guémené-Penfao is approx. 13 km. Watch for site signs before village centre. Site is in the outskirts in a semi-residential area to the northeast.

Open

1 April - 31 October.

Charges 2005

Per unit incl. 2 adults	€ 8,30 - € 9,90
extra person	€ 2,00 - € 2,90
electricity	€ 2,50

Reservations

Contact site. Tel: 02 40 79 23 48.
Email: contact@campinglhermitage.com

At a glance

Welcome & Ambience	✓✓✓✓✓	Location	✓✓✓
Quality of Pitches	✓✓✓✓	Range of Facilities	✓✓✓

FR44150 Camping La Tabardière

F-44770 La Plaine-sur-Mer (Loire-Atlantique)

Owned and managed by the Barre family, this campsite lies next to the family farm. Pleasant, peaceful and immaculate, this site will suit those who want to enjoy the local coast and towns but return to an 'oasis' for relaxation. It still, however, provides activities and fun for those with energy remaining. The pitches are mostly terraced either side of a narrow valley and care needs to be taken in manoeuvring caravans into position - although the effort is well worth it. Most pitches have access to electricity and water taps are conveniently situated. The site is probably not suitable for wheelchair users. Whilst this is a rural site, its amenities are excellent with pools and a water slide, tennis, boules and a challenging minigolf, plus a friendly bar. A 'Sites et Paysages' member.

Facilities	Directions
Two good, clean toilet blocks are well equipped and include laundry facilities. Motorcaravan service point. Bar. Shop. Snacks and takeaway. Good sized swimming pool, paddling pool and slides (supervised). Playground. Minigolf. Table tennis. Volleyball and basketball. Half size tennis courts. Boules. Overnight area for motorcaravans (€ 9 per night). Off site: Beach 3 km. Sea fishing, golf, riding all 5 km.	Site is well signed, situated inland off the D13 Pornic - La Plaine sur Mer road.

Charges 2005

Per unit incl. 2 persons	€ 12,50 - € 20,00
extra person	€ 3,30 - € 5,50
child (2-10 yrs)	€ 2,50 - € 3,50
dog	€ 2,70
electricity (3/6A)	€ 2,80 - € 4,20

Open

1 April - 30 September.

Reservations

Made with deposit (€ 60) and fee (€ 16).
Tel: 02 40 21 58 83.
Email: info@camping-la-tabardiere.com

At a glance

Welcome & Ambience	✓✓✓✓✓	Location	✓✓✓✓
Quality of Pitches	✓✓✓✓	Range of Facilities	✓✓✓✓✓

FR44090 Camping Château du Deffay

Mobile homes ▶ page 409

B.P. 18 Le Deffay, Ste Reine de Bretagne, F-44160 Pontchâteau (Loire-Atlantique)

A family managed site, Château de Deffay is a refreshing departure from the usual formula in that it is not over organised or supervised and has no tour operator units. The landscape is natural right down to the molehills, and the site blends well with the rural environment of the estate, lake and farmland which surround it. For these reasons it is enjoyed by many. However, with the temptation of free pedaloes and the fairly deep, unfenced lake, parents should ensure that children are supervised. The 142 good sized, fairly level pitches have pleasant views and are either on open grass, on shallow terraces divided by hedges, or informally arranged in a central, slightly sloping wooded area. Most have electricity. The facilities are located within the old courtyard area of the smaller château (that dates from before 1400). The larger château (built 1880) and another lake stand away from this area providing pleasant walking. The reception has been built separately to contain the camping area. Alpine type chalets overlook the lake and fit well with the environment.

Facilities

The main toilet block, housed in a converted barn, is well equipped including washbasins in cabins, provision for disabled people and a baby bathroom. Washing machines, and dryer. Maintenance can be variable and, with the boiler located at one end of the block, hot water can take time to reach the other in low season. Extra facilities are in the courtyard area where the well stocked shop, bar, small restaurant with takeaway and solar heated swimming pool and paddling pool are located (all 15/5-15/9). Play area. TV in the bar, separate room for table tennis. English language animation in season including children's mini club. Torches useful. Off site: Golf and riding 5 km. Close to the Brière Regional Park, the Guérande Peninsula, and La Baule with its magnificent beach (20 km).

At a glance

Welcome & Ambience ✓✓✓✓ Location ✓✓✓✓
Quality of Pitches ✓✓✓✓ Range of Facilities ✓✓✓✓

Directions

Site is signed from D33 Pontchâteau - Herbignac road near Ste Reine. Also signed from the D773 and N165.

Charges 2005

Per person	€ 3,00 - € 4,80
child (2-12 yrs)	€ 2,00 - € 3,20
pitch	€ 7,00 - € 10,75
with electricity (6A)	€ 10,40 - € 14,60
with 3 services	€ 11,90 - € 16,45

Camping Cheques accepted.

Reservations

Accepted with deposit (€ 10 per day) and fee (€ 16).
Tel: 02 40 88 00 57.
Email: campingdudeffay@wanadoo.fr

Open

1 May - 30 September.

FR44170 Camping Les Ajoncs d'Or

Chemin du Rocher, F-44500 La Baule (Loire-Atlantique)

This site is situated in pine woods, 1.5 km. on the inland side of La Baule and its beautiful bay. It can be difficult to find an informal campsite close to an exciting seaside resort that retains its touring and camping identity, but Les Ajoncs d'Or does this. A well maintained, natural woodland setting provides a wide variety of pitch types, some level and bordered with hedges and tall trees to provide shade and many others that maintain the natural characteristics of the woodland. Most pitches have electricity and water nearby and are usually of a larger size. A central building provides a shop and open friendly bar that serve snacks and takeaways. The English speaking Bazillails family (the owners) who live on site will welcome you to their campsite. There are only just over 200 pitches, so large areas of woodland have been retained for quiet and recreational purposes and are safe for children to roam. Enjoy the gentle breezes off the sea that constantly rustle the trees. The family are justifiably proud of their site.

Facilities

Two good quality sanitary blocks are clean and well maintained providing plenty of facilities including a baby room. Washing machines and dryers. Shop and bar (July/Aug). Snack bar (July/Aug). Good size swimming pool and paddling pool (1/6-5/9). Sports and playground areas. Bicycle hire. Reception with security barrier (closed 22.30 - 7.30 hrs). Off site: Everything for an enjoyable holiday can be found in nearby La Baule. Fishing and riding 1.5 km. Golf 3 km. Beach 1.5 km.

Open

1 April - 30 September.

At a glance

Welcome & Ambience	✓✓✓✓✓	Location	✓✓✓✓
Quality of Pitches	✓✓✓✓	Range of Facilities	✓✓✓

Directions

From N171 take exit for La Baule les Pins. Follow signs for 'La Baule Centre', then left at roundabout in front of Champion supermarket and follow site signs.

Charges 2005

Per unit incl. 2 persons	€ 13,50 - € 18,00
with electricity	€ 15,75 - € 21,00
with water and drainage	€ 17,25 - € 23,00
extra person	€ 4,50 - € 6,00
child (2-7 yrs)	€ 2,25 - € 3,00
dog	€ 0,71 - € 0,95

Less 15-25% outside July/Aug.

Reservations

Contact site. Tel: 02 40 60 33 29.
Email: contact@ajoncs.com

FR44100 Sunêlia Le Patisseau

Mobile homes ▶ page 409

29 rue du Patisseau, F-44210 Pornic (Loire-Atlantique)

Le Patisseau is situated in the countryside just a short drive from the fishing village of Pornic. It is a relaxed site with a large number of mobile homes and chalets, which is popular with young families and teenagers. Touring pitches, which all have electrical connections (6A), are divided between the attractive 'forest' area with plenty of shade from mature trees and the more open 'prairie' area. A number of communal barbecues are provided throughout the site, helping to create a sociable atmosphere. A railway line runs along the bottom half of the site with trains two or three times a day, but they do finish at 22.30 hrs and the noise is minimal. The site's spacious restaurant and bar overlook the indoor pool. Outside two waterslides are cleverly concealed amongst the trees. This is a lively site and the Morice family work very hard to maintain a friendly atmosphere.

Facilities

The new toilet block (opened in 2005) can be heated all season and includes washbasins in private cabins, facilities for babies, fully equipped laundry rooms and dishwashing facilities. Additional facilities are part of the indoor pool building. Shop (main season). Bar and restaurant (3/4-12/9). Takeaway (1/7-31/8). Indoor heated pool with sauna, jacuzzi and spa (all season). Outdoor pools with water slides (1/5-12/9). Play area. Volleyball and table tennis. Bicycle hire. Off site: Fishing 1.5 km. Beach 2.5 km. Riding 4 km. Golf 5 km.

Open

8 April - 6 November.

At a glance

Welcome & Ambience	✓✓✓✓✓	Location	✓✓✓✓
Quality of Pitches	✓✓✓	Range of Facilities	✓✓✓✓

Directions

Site signed at roundabout junction of D751 (Pornic - Nantes) road. From the town centre take the Rue du General de Gaulle and then the rue de Nantes, which crosses the D751. At the next roundabout turn left and follow the signs.

Charges 2005

Per unit incl. 2 persons	€ 20,00 - € 30,50
incl. electricity (6A)	€ 24,00 - € 34,50
extra person	€ 5,50 - € 7,50
child (1-7 yrs)	€ 3,00 - € 5,00
animal	€ 5,00

Camping Cheques accepted.

Reservations

Made with deposit (€ 50) and fee (€ 30); contact site by letter, phone or fax. Tel: 02 40 82 10 39.
Email: contact@lepatisseau.com

www.alanrogers.com for latest campsite news

FR44160 Camping Armor-Héol

Route de Guérande, F-44420 Piriac-sur-Mer (Loire-Atlantique)

Situated only 700 metres from Piriac town and the beach, and 14 km. from Guérande, this campsite makes an ideal base for a beach holiday or for touring the beautiful Breton countryside and coastline. With considerable recent investment, the site now offers excellent facilities for visitors of all ages. There are 250 good sized (120 sq.m) level pitches all with 5A electricity. Although site owned mobiles and chalets take 160 pitches, they do not feel intrusive to the camper and caravanner. In 2002 a new facility was completed providing an outdoor swimming pool, a paddling pool and 70 m. of exciting water slides, together with a bar and restaurant with a large terrace. In 2003 a new indoor pool with water movement where you swim and stay stationary was added. This is a friendly site with English speaking reception and good amenities.

Facilities

Two clean and well maintained toilet blocks include washbasins in cabins, baby rooms, family rooms, rooms with shower, basin and toilet. Washing machines and dryers. Super bar and restaurant (1/6-15/9). Most activities are in one part of the site with heated pools and water slides ((1/6-15/9). Multi-sports area, tennis courts, volleyball. Playground. Off site: Beach and town, fishing, boat launching, surfing and bicycle hire 700 m. Golf 2 km. Riding 2 km.

Open

3 April - 26 September.

At a glance

Welcome & Ambience	✓✓✓✓✓	Location	✓✓✓✓
Quality of Pitches	✓✓✓✓	Range of Facilities	✓✓✓✓✓

Directions

From N165 Vannes - Nantes road, take D774 southwest at Guérande. Follow D333 signed Piriac sur Mer. Site is on left 0.5 km. before Piriac sur Mer, 4 km. from Guérande.

Charges 2005

Per unit incl. 2 persons	€ 13,00 - € 29,75
extra person	€ 3,50 - € 7,45
child (under 4 yrs)	€ 2,10 - € 4,60
animal	€ 2,00 - € 4,00
electricity	€ 3,05 - € 3,45

Reservations

Made with deposit (€ 30 per week booked) and fee (€ 20). Tel: 02 40 23 57 80. Email: armor.heol@wanadoo.fr

FR44200 Camping Municipal Saint Clair

F-44530 Guenrouet (Loire-Atlantique)

This is a very well maintained campsite in a lovely position, next to Brest - Nantes canal making it suitable for anyone interested in boating or fishing. There are about 100 pitches of varying sizes, many within a wooded area, and all with electricity (6A). The site would be ideal for an overnight stop or for a longer stay.

Facilities

Three well maintained, modern toilet blocks provide toilets (mixed British and Turkish style), washbasins in cabins and showers. Facilities for disabled visitors. Small play area. Tennis. Petanque. Games room. Off site: Leisure complex with outdoor pool, restaurant and crêperie opposite site. Village with small supermarket and other facilities 500 m.

Open

23 June - 31 August.

At a glance

Welcome & Ambience	✓✓✓✓	Location	✓✓✓✓✓
Quality of Pitches	✓✓✓✓	Range of Facilities	✓✓✓

Directions

On the N165 from Nantes, take D773 signed St Gildas de Bois. At St Gildas, turn right on D2 for Guenrouet. Site is on right after village, just before river.

Charges guide

Per person	€ 2,50 - € 3,50
child (0-10 yrs)	€ 1,50 - € 2,50
pitch	€ 4,00 - € 5,00
electricity	€ 2,60
dog	€ 1,00 - € 1,50

Reservations

Contact site. Tel: 02 40 87 61 52.

FR44190 Camping Le Fief

Mobile homes ▶ page 410

57 chemin du Fief, F-44250 St Brévin-les-Pins (Loire-Atlantique)

If you are a family with young children or lively teenagers, this could be the campsite for you. Le Fief is a well established site only 800 metres from sandy beaches on the southern Brittany coast. It also has its own magnificent 'aqua park' with outdoor and covered swimming pools, paddling pools, slides, river rapids, fountains, jets and more. This a lively site in high season with a variety of entertainment and organised activity for all ages. This ranges from a mini-club for 5-12 year olds, to 'Tonic Days' for adults with aquagym, jogging and sports competitions, and to evening events which include karaoke, themed dinners and cabaret. There are plenty of sporting facilities for active youngsters. The site has 220 pitches for touring units (out of 413). Whilst these all have electricity (5A), they vary in size and many are worn and may be untidy. In addition there are 143 mobile homes and chalets to rent and 55 privately owned units.

Facilities

There is one excellent new toilet block and three others of a lower standard. Washing machines and dryers. Well stocked shop (15/5-15/9). Bar, restaurant and takeaway (15/4-15/9) with terrace overlooking the pool complex. Outdoor pools, etc. (15/5-15/9). Covered pool (all season). Play area. Tennis. Volleyball. Basketball. Pétanque. Table tennis. Archery. Games room. Internet access. Organised entertainment and activities (July/Aug). Off site: Beach 800 m. Bus stop 1 km. Bicycle hire 800 m. Riding 1 km. Golf 15 km. Planète Sauvage safari park.

Open

1 April - 15 October.

At a glance

Welcome & Ambience	✓✓✓✓	Location	✓✓✓✓
Quality of Pitches	✓✓	Range of Facilities	✓✓✓✓

Directions

From the St Nazaire bridge take the fourth exit from the D213 signed St Brévin – L'Océan. Continue over first roundabout and bear right at the second to join Chemin du Fief. The site is on the right, well signed.

Charges 2005

Per pitch incl. 2 persons	€ 12,00 - € 28,00
extra person	€ 3,50 - € 6,50
child (0-7 yrs)	€ 1,75 - € 3,25
electricity	€ 4,00
dog	€ 1,50 - € 4,00

Reservations

Contact site. Tel: 02 40 27 23 86.
Email: camping@lefief.com

FR44180 Camping de la Boutinardière

Rue de la Plage de la Boutinardière, F-44210 Pornic (Loire-Atlantique)

This is truly a holiday site to suit all the family whatever their age. The site has 250 individual good sized pitches, 100-120 sq.m. in size, many bordered by three metre high, well maintained hedges for shade and privacy. All pitches have electricity available. This is a family owned site and English is spoken by the helpful, obliging reception staff. Beside reception is the excellent site shop and across the road is a complex of indoor and outdoor pools and a water slide. Facing the water complex, the bar, restaurant and terraces are also new and serve excellent food. On site there are also sports and entertainment areas. This site is difficult to better in the South Brittany, Loire Atlantique area.

Facilities
Toilet facilities are in three good blocks, one large and centrally situated and two supporting blocks. Quality, maintenance and cleanliness are amongst the best. Washbasins are in cabins. Laundry room. Excellent shop (15/6-15/9). New complex of bar, restaurant, terraces (1/4-22/9). Three heated swimming pools, one indoor, a paddling pool and water slides (15/5-22/9). Games room. Sports and activity area. Playground. Minigolf. Table tennis. Off site: Sandy cove 200 m. Golf, riding, sea fishing, boat trips, sailing and windsurfing, all within 5 km. of site.

Directions
From north or south on D213, take Nantes D751 exit. At roundabout (with McDonalds) take D13 signed Bemarie-eb-Retz. After 4 km. site is signed to right. Note: do NOT exit from D213 at Pomic Ouest or Centre.

Charges 2006

Per unit incl. 2 persons	€ 13,00 - € 30,00

Reservations
Made with deposit (€ 62) and fee (€ 23).
Tel: 02 40 82 05 68. Email: info@laboutinardiere.com

Open
1 April - 30 September.

At a glance

Welcome & Ambience	✓✓✓✓	Location	✓✓✓✓
Quality of Pitches	✓✓✓✓✓	Range of Facilities	✓✓✓✓✓

FR56020 Camping de la Plage

Plage de Kervilaine, F-56470 La Trinité-sur-Mer (Morbihan)

The area of Carnac/La Trinité is popular with holiday makers and the two La Trinité sites of La Plage and La Baie have the great advantage of direct access to a good sandy beach. Both sites are owned by the same family, and each is very well maintained, both having a small (12 m.) heated pool with a slide. The grassy pitches, which have electricity and water (70% with drainage also), are separated by hedges and shrubs and at La Plage there are attractive flower beds. Situated on a low cliff, the terrace with its views across the bay is a very popular place for a meal or a drink. Reception areas are welcoming and friendly with tourist information on display. Both sites have a number of tour operator pitches.

Facilities
Toilet blocks have washbasins in cubicles and facilities for disabled people and small children. Washing machines and dryers. Well stocked shop with bakery. Bar, restaurant, crêperie, takeaway. Swimming pools with new water slides, etc. Good play areas including ball pool. Tennis, basketball, minigolf, table tennis. Large TV screen. Lively entertainment programme in high season for all ages and some evening entertainment in nearby disco. Bicycle hire. Beach. Guided tours on foot or bicycle. Internet access. Small communal barbecue areas (only gas ones permitted on pitches). Not suitable for American motorhomes or twin axle caravans. Off site: The village of La Trinité is 20 minutes walk along the cliff path and 10 minutes (approx) by car. Carnac is a 10-15 minutes drive in the opposite direction.

Directions
Site is signed in different places from the D186 coast road running from La Trinité to Carnac-Plage.

Charges 2006

Per unit incl. 2 persons	€ 16,90 - € 33,70
extra adult	€ 5,00
child (2-18 yrs)	€ 3,00 - € 4,00
electricity (6/10A)	€ 3,00 - € 4,00
dog	free - € 1,20

Reservations
Contact site; when booking it is important to state size of unit in order that appropriate size pitch can be allocated. Tel: 02 97 55 73 28.
Email: camping@camping-plage.com

Open
29 April - 17 September.

At a glance

Welcome & Ambience	✓✓✓✓	Location	✓✓✓✓✓
Quality of Pitches	✓✓✓✓	Range of Facilities	✓✓✓✓

FR56080 Camping Municipal Le Pâtis

3 chemin du Pâtis, F-56130 La Roche Bernard (Morbihan)

This is another of those excellent municipal sites one comes across in France. Situated beside the River Vilaine, just below the very attractive old town of La Roche Bernard and beside the port and marina, it provides 60 level grass, part-hedged pitches in bays of four, with 10A electricity and water. Next door is a sailing school, boats to hire, fishing, tennis, archery, etc. A restaurant and bar are on the quay-side, with others uphill in the town.

Facilities

There are two fully equipped sanitary blocks, one new and very modern, the other fully refurbished. Laundry room behind reception with washing machine and dryer. Small play area. Bicycle hire. Off site: Bicycle hire 500 m. Riding 5 km. Golf 15 km.

Open

Easter/April - 30 September.

At a glance

Welcome & Ambience	✓✓✓✓	Location	✓✓✓✓
Quality of Pitches	✓✓✓✓✓	Range of Facilities	✓✓✓

Directions

Go into town centre and follow signs for the Port around a one-way system and then a sharp turn down hill.

Charges 2005

Per person	€ 3,00
child (under 9 yrs)	€ 1,50
pitch	€ 4,00
vehicle	€ 2,00
animal	€ 1,00
electricity	€ 3,00

No credit cards.

Reservations

Contact site. Tel: 02 99 90 60 13.

FR56040 Camping de Penboch

9 chemin de Penboch, F-56610 Arradon (Morbihan)

Penboch is 200 metres by footpath from the shores of the Golfe du Morbihan with its many islands, where there is plenty to do including watersports, fishing and boat trips. There are also old towns with weekly markets nearby and it is 30 minutes walk to Arradon which has a good range of shops and restaurants. The site, in a peaceful, rural area, is divided into two parts - one in woodland with lots of shade and used mainly for mobile homes and the other main part, across a minor road on more open ground with hedges and young trees. Penboch offers 175 pitches on flat grass, mostly divided into groups; electricity is available on most pitches (6/10A) and there are plenty of water points. British tour operator (12 pitches). A 'Sites et Paysages' member.

Facilities

Three fully equipped toilet blocks, two on the main part of the site (one of which is heated) and one on the annex, include washbasins in cabins. Facilities can be under considerable pressure in peak season. Washing machines and dryers. Motorcaravan service point. Friendly bar with satellite TV, snacks and takeaway, shop with basic food supplies (all 20/5-11/9) and further TV room. Heated swimming pool with water slide, toboggan and children's pool with mushroom fountain (1/5-17/9). Good playground, visible from reception, with interesting play equipment. Games room. Caravan storage. American motorhomes accepted in low season. Off site: Beach and fishing 200 m. Sailing and windsurfing 2 km. Bicycle hire, golf and riding 6 km.

At a glance

Welcome & Ambience	✓✓✓✓	Location	✓✓✓✓✓
Quality of Pitches	✓✓✓✓	Range of Facilities	✓✓✓✓✓

Directions

From N165 at Auray or Vannes, take D101 along northern shores of the Golfe du Morbihan; or leave N165 at D127 signed Ploeren and Arradon. Take turn to Arradon and site is signed.

Charges 2006

Per unit incl. 2 persons	€ 9,95 - € 29,80
extra person	€ 3,00 - € 5,90
child (2-7 yrs)	€ 2,50 - € 4,20
electricity (6/10A)	€ 3,20 - € 4,20
dog	free - € 3,50

Reservations

Advised for high season (min. 7 days 10/7-18/8). Tel: 02 97 44 71 29. Email: camping.penboch@wanadoo.fr

Open

8 April - 23 September.

FR56010 Castel Camping La Grande Métairie

Route des Alignements de Kermario, BP 85, F-56342 Carnac (Morbihan)

La Grande Métairie is a good quality site quietly situated a little back from the sea, close to the impressive rows of the famous 'menhirs' (giant prehistoric standing stones). It has a great deal to offer on site and is lively and busy over a long season. There is a feeling of spaciousness with a wide entrance and access road, with 575 individual pitches (128 for touring units), surrounded by hedges and trees. All have electricity (30 m. cables are needed in parts). Paddocks with ponds are home for ducks, goats and ponies to watch and feed. A super swimming pool complex comprises heated pools, water slides and toboggans, a flowing river, jacuzzi and a covered pool. Services are limited before late May. The site is well known and popular and has many British visitors with 358 pitches taken by several tour operators, plus site-owned mobile homes and many British touring caravanners and campers.

Facilities

Three large toilet blocks are good and well maintained, with washbasins in cabins, and facilities for babies and disabled people. Laundry room in each block. Motorcaravan service points. Shop and boutique. Restaurant, good takeaway. Bar lounge and terrace, and adjoining TV and games rooms. Pool complex with poolside bar and terrace. Two playgrounds and large playing field with football posts. Two tennis courts. Volleyball and basketball. Minigolf. BMX track. Bicycle hire. Table tennis. Fishing (on permit). Pony rides around the site. Outside amphitheatre for musical evenings and barbecues. Organised events daytime and evening. Occasional dances (pitches near these facilities may be noisy late at night - the bar closes at midnight). American motorhomes accepted up to 27 ft. Dogs and other pets only accepted by arrangement. Off site: Riding 1 km. Nearest beach 3 km. by road. Golf 12 km. Local market at Carnac on Wednesdays and Sundays.

At a glance

Welcome & Ambience	✓✓✓✓	Location	✓✓✓✓
Quality of Pitches	✓✓	Range of Facilities	✓✓✓✓✓

Directions

From N165 take Quiberon/Carnac exit onto the D768. After 5 km. turn left on D119 towards Carnac and after 4 km. turn left onto D196 to the site.

Charges 2006

Per person	€ 4,00 - € 7,20
child (under 7 yrs)	€ 3,50 - € 5,40
pitch incl. car	€ 8,00 - € 23,90
6A electricity	€ 2,00 - € 3,50

Less 20% 22/5-29/6 and after 1/9.

Reservations

Made (min. 1 week) with deposit € 120. English is spoken - office open from 2 Jan. Tel: 02 97 52 24 01. Email: info@lagrandemetairie.com

Open

1 April - 9 September (all services from 20/5).

FR56050 Camping de Kervilor

F-56470 La Trinité-sur-Mer (Morbihan)

Kervilor may be a good alternative for those who find the beach-side sites in La Trinité too busy and lively. In a village on the outskirts of the town, it has 230 pitches on flat grass and is attractively landscaped with trees (silver birch) and flowers giving a sense of spaciousness. The 230 pitches are in groups divided by hedges, separated by shrubs and trees and 200 have electricity (6/10A). Around 174 are used for touring units. The site has an inviting, well designed pool complex with swimming and paddling pools, slides and fountains. Activities and entertainment are organised in high season. The pleasant port is only 1.5 km. with sandy beaches within 2 km. Used by tour operators (24 pitches).

Facilities

Two modern toilet blocks are of a good standard with further facilities in an older block by the entrance. They include many washbasins in cabins, facilities for disabled people and babies. Dishwashing under cover. Small laundry. Small shop for basics and takeaway in season. Bar with terrace (28/5-9/9). Pool complex. Play area. Minigolf, pétanque, tennis and volleyball. Table tennis. Bicycle hire. Only charcoal barbecues are permitted. Off site: Town facilities 1.5 km. Fishing or riding 2 km. Bicycle hire 3 km. Golf 12 km. Sandy beach 2 km.

Open

1 May - 10 September.

At a glance

Welcome & Ambience	✓✓✓✓✓	Location	✓✓✓✓✓
Quality of Pitches	✓✓✓✓✓	Range of Facilities	✓✓✓✓

Directions

Site is north of La Trinité-sur-Mer and is signed in the town centre. From Auray take D186 Quiberon road; turn left at camp sign at Kergroix on D186 to La Trinité-sur-Mer, and left again at outskirts of town.

Charges 2005

Per person	€ 4,80
child (under 7 yrs)	€ 3,10
pitch	€ 14,50
electricity	€ 3,20 - € 3,70

Less 25% outside high season.
7 days for the price of 6 outside July/Aug.

Reservations

Made with deposit (€ 46) and fee (€ 18).
Tel: 02 97 55 76 75.
Email: ebideau@camping-kervilor.com

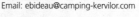

camping **Kervilor**

Near to the port and beaches, Camping de Kervilor will welcome you to its calm, shaded setting - with heated swimming pools, waterslides (including multi-track), spa bath, bar, entertainment tennis court, multi-sport terrain - divertissement room and billards, multi-sport terrain - everything on site. Mobile home rental.

56470 La Trinité sur Mer - Tel. 0297557675 - Fax. 0297558726
www.camping-kervilor.com - ebideau@camping-kervilor.com

© Photo Luc Vignaud

FR56090 Camping Moulin de Kermaux

F-56340 Carnac (Morbihan)

Only 100 metres from the famous Carnac megaliths, Le Moulin de Kermaux is an excellent base from which to see these ancient stones as they portray their ever changing mood, colour and profile. The family run site has 150 pitches, of which 120 have 6-10A electricity, and its compact nature offers a safe environment for parents and children. The 70 pitches for touring units are mostly separated by hedges and mature trees offer welcome shade. Keen walkers and families with young children alike, will enjoy the numerous footpaths in the area. This is a well run, quiet and comfortable site.

Facilities

The fully equipped toilet block has high standards of cleanliness and washbasins in cabins. Toilets are a mix of (mainly) British and (a few) Turkish types. Facilities for disabled visitors. Baby bath. Washing machine and dryer. Motorcaravan service point. Well stocked shop (26/6-31/8). Bar (12/6-31/8) evenings in low season, all day in high season. Swimming and paddling pools. Sauna and jacuzzi. Adventure playground. Volleyball. basketball, minigolf and table tennis. Organised activities in July/Aug. Internet access (July/Aug only). Not suitable for American motorhomes or twin axle caravans. Off site: Fishing, bicycle hire and riding within 2 km. Sandy beaches and rocky coves within 3 km.

At a glance

Welcome & Ambience	✓✓✓✓✓	Location	✓✓✓✓✓
Quality of Pitches	✓✓✓✓	Range of Facilities	✓✓✓✓

Directions

From N165 take Quiberon/Carnac exit on D768. After 5 km. turn left on D119 and then, after 3 km. turn left on D196 (Route de Kerlescan). Site is 1 km.

Charges 2005

Per person	€ 4,00
child (under 7 yrs)	€ 3,00
pitch and car	€ 14,00
electricity 6A	€ 3,00

Less 10-40% outside high season.

Reservations

Contact site. Tel: 02 97 52 15 90.
Email: moulin-de-kermaux@wanadoo.fr

Open

30 March - 15 September.

FR56100 Camping de Moulin Neuf

F-56220 Rochefort-en-Terre (Morbihan)

This quiet family site is in wooded countryside, 600 m. from the small medieval town. Ian and Norma Hetherington have worked hard over the last few years to develop Moulin Neuf into a neat, tidy and organised site. There is provision for 72 pitches (60 for tourers, 44 with 10A electricity) of good size (120 sq.m.) on neat grass, laid out on two levels. The top level, with a limited number of electrical hook-ups, is flat and pitches are divided by young shrubs. The entrance to the site is here and reception is located just beyond the security gate. The lower level is partly sloping but offers mature trees, shade and electricity on all the pitches. Rochefort en Terre itself is a marvellous medieval town, beautifully preserved and only ten minutes walk from the site, with a wealth of art and craft workshops, antique shops and art galleries.

Facilities

The modern heated sanitary block is on the lower level but convenient for both. Facilities are kept very clean and include large, comfortable showers, cabins with washbasins and British and Turkish style WCs. Provision for disabled people. Baby room. Dishwashing area and laundry room with sinks. Washing machine, dryer and washing lines. Bread delivered each morning. Heated swimming pool (1/6-31/8). Tennis court, table tennis, basketball, football area. Two play areas. Off site: Lake within 500 m. with watersports. Shop 600 m. Riding and golf locally. Vannes is a 30 minute drive and the beaches of Golfe du Morbihan.

At a glance

Welcome & Ambience	✓✓✓✓	Location	✓✓✓✓
Quality of Pitches	✓✓✓✓	Range of Facilities	✓✓✓

Directions

From Redon take D775 Vannes road west for 25 km. Branch north on D774 signed Rochefort en Terre. Follow road past the lake on left, in 800 m. Turn left and follow sign to site.

Charges guide

Per person	€ 4,30 - € 5,00
child (under 8 yrs)	€ 2,60 - € 3,50
pitch	€ 7,00 - € 8,00
electricity	€ 4,40

Reservations

Made with deposit (€ 100) and fee (€ 10); contact site for booking form. Tel: 02 97 43 37 52.

Open

15 May - 16 September.

FR56110 Camping Le Moustoir

Route du Moustoir, F-56340 Carnac (Morbihan)

Camping du Moustoir is a friendly, family run site situated about three kilometres inland from the many beaches of the area and close to the famous 'alignments' of standing stones. Pitches are grassy and separated by shrubs and hedges, with several shaded by tall pine trees. There is a popular pool area with slides, a separate swimming pool and a paddling pool with 'mushroom' fountain. The bar and terrace adjoining the pool become the social centre of the site in the evenings. A high season programme includes family entertainment and a daily 'Kid's club' which attracts children of several nationalities. Several small tour operators use the site.

Facilities

The substantial, traditional style toilet block is well maintained and clean (outside peak season some sections may be closed). New motorcaravan service facilities. Shop. Bar and takeaway (from 20/5). Heated swimming pool (21 x 8 m), water slides with landing pool, and paddling pool (from 20/5). Adventure style playground. Tennis. Boules. Volleyball, football and basketball. Table tennis and pool table. 'Kids Club' daily in high season. Barrier deposit € 20. Off site: Easy access to watersports at Carnac Plage. Beach 3 km. Fishing, bicycle hire or riding 2 km. Golf 10 km.

Open

14 May - 29 September.

At a glance

Welcome & Ambience	✓✓✓✓✓	Location	✓✓✓✓
Quality of Pitches	✓✓✓	Range of Facilities	✓✓✓✓

Directions

From N165, take exit to D768 (Carnac and Quiberon). At second crossroads after 5 km. turn left D119) towards Carnac. After 3 km. turn left (oblique turning) after a hotel, and site is 500 m. on your left. GPS: N47:36 W03:03

Charges 2006

Per person (over 2 yrs)	€ 4,40
pitch incl. car	€ 5,00 - € 16,00
electricity	€ 3,20
animal	€ 1,50
Camping Cheques accepted.	

Reservations

Made with deposit (€ 75). Tel: 02 97 52 16 18. Email: info@lemoustoir.com

FR56130 Camping Mané Guernehué

52 rue Mané er Groez, F-56870 Baden (Morbihan)

Located close to the Morbihan Gulf, Mané Guernehué is a smart, modern site offering a variety of pitches. Some are terraced beneath pine trees, others in a former orchard with delightful views of the surrounding countryside. The 377 pitches are generally large, 200 being occupied by mobile homes and chalets. Most pitches have 10A electricity and a few are also equipped with water and drainage. Many are level but others, particularly those in the centre of the site, slope to varying degrees. There are plenty of excellent amenities including a well stocked fishing lake. Used by tour operators (around 146 pitches).

Facilities

Two modern toilet blocks include washbasins in cabins. The maintenance of the blocks does seem to be under some pressure. Facilities for disabled visitors. Washing machines and dryers. Small shop, bar and takeaway. Heated swimming pool, waterslide, jacuzzi and gym. Fishing. Teenagers' room with table tennis, pool, billiards and TV. Play area. Varied entertainment programme in high season, based around a large purpose built hall. Off site: Beach 3 km. Golf 3 km.

Open

8 April - 30 September.

At a glance

Welcome & Ambience	✓✓✓	Location	✓✓✓✓
Quality of Pitches	✓✓✓✓	Range of Facilities	✓✓✓✓✓

Directions

From Auray or Vannes use the D101 to Baden and watch for signs to site.

Charges 2005

Per person	€ 3,10 - € 6,40
child (2-6 yrs)	€ 2,00 - € 4,50
pitch	€ 10,50 - € 18,00
electricity (10A)	€ 4,20
dog	€ 1,60 - € 3,40

Camping Cheques accepted.

Reservations

Advised for high season and made with deposit (€ 70) and fee (€ 20). Tel: 02 97 57 02 06. Email: mane-guernehue@wanadoo.fr

FR56120 Camping Les Iles

La Pointe du Bile, F-56760 Pénestin-sur-Mer (Morbihan)

You will receive a warm and friendly welcome at this family run campsite where the owner, Madame Communal, encourages everyone to make the most of this beautiful region. The 107 pitches are mostly of a reasonable size (although larger caravans and American motorhomes are advised to book) and all have electricity. All services are fully open 14/5-16/9, with a limited service at other times. There is direct access from the site to cliff-top walks and local beaches (you can even walk to small off-shore islands at low tide). Used by one tour operator (26 pitches).

Facilities

The large central toilet block has mostly British style WCs and washbasins in cabins (with hairdryers for ladies). Dishwashing and laundry sinks. Facilities for disabled people and two baby baths. Motorcaravan service point across the road at 'Parc des Iles', the mobile home section of the site. Shop. New bar and restaurant with takeaway overlooking new pool complex (14/5-16/9). Modern multi-sports pitch for football, basketball and volleyball. Tennis court across the road. Bicycle hire. Riding. Full range of activities and entertainment for adults and children in July/Aug. Off site: Windsurfing 500 m. Sailing school 3 km.

Open

1 April - 1 October.

At a glance

Welcome & Ambience	✓✓✓✓	Location	✓✓✓✓✓
Quality of Pitches	✓✓✓✓✓	Range of Facilities	✓✓✓✓✓

Directions

From Pénestin take D201 south, taking a right fork to Pointe du Bile after 2 km. Turn right at crossroads just before beach and site is on left. Take care on arrival - the barrier is fairly close to the entrance, but there is some parking along the road outside.

Charges 2006

Per unit incl. 2 adults	€ 15,00 - € 34,00
extra person (over 7 yrs)	€ 2,30 - € 5,00
child (2-7 yrs)	€ 1,30 - € 2,50
pet	€ 1,50 - € 3,00
electricity (6A)	€ 3,20

Reservations

Made with deposit (€ 100) and fee (€ 20). Tel: 02 99 90 30 24. Email: contact@camping-des-iles.fr

Camping et Parc
DES ILES
La Pointe du Bile
56760 PENESTIN
Tél. 02 99 90 30 24
Fax 02 99 90 44 55
www.camping-des-iles.fr
E mail : contact@camping-des-iles.fr

FR56200 Camping La Ferme de Lann Hoedic

Route du Roaliguen, F-56370 Sarzeau (Morbihan)

Whilst still maintaining the character of 'Camping a la Ferme', the welcoming owners, Mireille and Timothy Prouten have upgraded this site to a good standard, and have attractively landscaped the site with many flowering shrubs and trees. The 108 pitches, all with electricity (10A) are large and mostly level, with maturing trees which are beginning to offer some shade. There are new toilet facilities and an excellent play area. Families are welcome to visit the working farm which produces cereal crops and raises sheep. Located in the countryside on the Rhuys Peninsula, Golfe du Morbihan, it is an ideal base for cycling, walking and water based activities.

Facilities

Two new, high quality toilet blocks with facilities for disabled people and bathing babies. Washing machines and dryers. Playground with modern well designed equipment. Volleyball and petanque. Bread delivery (high season). Ice creams and soft drinks available at reception. Takeaway meals and traditional Breton 'soirées' (high season). Bicycle hire. Off site: Beach or boating 800 m. Fishing 600 m. Riding 2 km. Golf 6 km.

Open

1 April - 31 October.

At a glance

Welcome & Ambience	✓✓✓✓✓	Location	✓✓✓✓
Quality of Pitches	✓✓✓	Range of Facilities	✓✓✓✓

Directions

East of Vannes on the N165, join the D780 in the direction of Sarzeau. Exit D780 at the 'Super U' roundabout south of Sarzeau, following signs for Le Roaliguen. Campsite is signed.

Charges 2005

Per person	€ 4,10
child (under 7 yrs)	€ 2,00
pitch	€ 7,50
electricity	€ 2,60

Camping Cheques accepted.

Reservations

Made with deposit (€ 45). Tel: 02 97 48 01 73. Email: contact@camping-lannhoedic.fr

SOUTHERN BRITTANY

Only 2 hours south of St Malo, discover the beautiful Gulf of Morbihan from our peaceful and spacious 3 star site. 800 meters from sandy beaches, we offer brand new facilities and a warm welcome waiting just for you.

Open from 01/04 to 31/10

Route du Roaliguen   56370 Sarzeau
Tel : +33 297 48 01 73
Fax : +33 297 41 72 87
contact@camping-lannhoedic.fr

The comfort of a 3-star campsite, the charm of a country setting

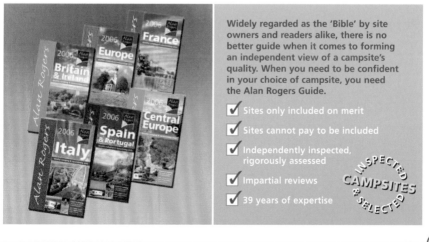

FR56150 Camping du Haras

Aérodrome Vannes-Meucon, F-56250 Vannes-Meucon / Monterblanc (Morbihan)

Close to Vannes and the Golfe du Morbihan in southern Brittany, Le Haras is a small, family run, rural site that is open all year. There are just 50 pitches at the moment, although there are plans to extend the site. With a variety of settings, both open and wooded, the pitches are well kept and of a good size, all with electricity (4-10A) and most with water and drainage. Whilst M. Danard intends keeping the site quiet and in keeping with its rural setting, he provides plenty of activities for lively youngsters, including some organised games and evening parties. There is a good pool with waves, a long slide, fountains and plenty of sunbathing space. Small animals are kept at the animal park on site and there is a riding school nearby. The site is close to a small airfield, where there are opportunities for leisure flights over the Morbihan, Vannes and Carnac areas, all of which are also easily accessible by car. The beaches are 25 km.

Facilities
The single small toilet block is modern and heated in winter. It provides a few washbasins in cabins and controllable showers, plus facilities for babies and a good unit for disabled visitors. Washing machine and dryer. No shop but basics are kept in the bar. Bar with snacks (May - Oct). Swimming pool (1/5-31/10). Play area. Animal park. Table tennis. Trampoline. Minigolf. Bicycle hire. Some organised activities (high season). Off site: Riding 400 m. Fishing 3 km. Golf 25 km. Beach 25 km.

Open
All year.

At a glance
Welcome & Ambience	✓✓✓✓✓	Location	✓✓✓
Quality of Pitches	✓✓✓✓	Range of Facilities	✓✓✓

Directions
From Vannes on the N165 take exit signed Pontivy and airport on the D767. Follow signs for airport and Meucon. Turn right on the D778, continuing to follow signs for airport and yellow campsite signs. GPS: N47:43. W02:43.

Charges 2005
Per person	€ 3,00 - € 4,00
child (0-7 yrs)	€ 2,00 - € 3,00
pitch	€ 3,00 - € 6,00
electricity	€ 2,00 - € 6,00
dog	€ 3,00

Reservations
Contact site. Tel: 02 97 44 66 06.
Email: camping-vannes@wanadoo.fr

FR56160 Camping La Vallée du Ninian

Le Rocher, F-56800 Taupont (Morbihan)

M. and Mme. Joubaud have developed this peaceful family run site in central Brittany from a former farm and they continue to make improvements to ensure that their visitors have an enjoyable holiday. The level site falls into the three areas - the orchard with 32 large, hedged pitches with electricity, the wood with about 13 pitches more suited to tents, and the meadow by the river providing a further 35 pitches delineated by small trees and shrubs, some with electricity. The bar has as its centre-piece a working cider press with which M. Joubaud makes his own 'potion magique'. The adjoining new social area is the venue for song and dance evenings with a Breton flavour and occasional camp fire sing-songs are organised. A new reception and shop have been added at the entrance to the site and bread is freshly cooked on site in a traditional bread oven.

Facilities
A central building houses unisex toilet facilities including washbasins in cubicles, large cubicle with facilities for disabled visitors and laundry area with washing machines, dryer and ironing board. Covered dishwashing area with hot water. Shop selling basic provisions (July/Aug). Small (7 x 12 m) heated swimming pool and new children's pool with slide and fountain. Swings and slides, large trampoline, popular with children. Fishing. Off site: Riding and bicycle hire 4 km. Golf 7 km.

Open
1 May - 30 September.

At a glance
Welcome & Ambience	✓✓✓✓✓	Location	✓✓✓✓
Quality of Pitches	✓✓✓✓✓	Range of Facilities	✓✓✓✓

Directions
From Plo'rmel centre follow signs to Taupont north on the N8. Continue through village of Taupont and turn left (east) signed Vallée du Ninian. Follow road for 3 km. to site on left. From Josselin follow signs for Hellean. Go through village and turn sharp right after the bridge over the river Ninian. Site is 400 m. on the right.

Charges 2005
Per person	€ 3,10
child (under 7 yrs)	€ 2,30
pitch and car	€ 5,00
electricity (3/6A)	€ 1,60 - € 3,10
animal	€ 1,00

Credit cards accepted in July/Aug. only.

Reservations
Contact site. Tel: 02 97 93 53 01.
Email: info@camping-ninian.com

FR56180 Camping Le Cénic

F-56760 Pénestin-sur-Mer (Morbihan)

Le Cénic is attractively set amidst trees and flowers, providing activities for all tastes. An attractive covered aquatic complex has water slides, bridges, rivers and a jacuzzi, whilst the outdoor pool comes complete with water slide, 'magic mushroom' fountain and sunbathing areas. You may fish in the pretty lake or use inflatables, watched by the peacock and the geese and turkeys. Unusually there is also a covered sports hall for ball games. A range of accommodation is on offer from tent and caravan pitches to static caravans and chalets and bungalows to rent. There are 90 pitches with electricity (6A) available. The area has much to offer from the beaches of La Mine d'Or, the harbour at Trébiguier-Pénestin, the Golf du Morbihan with its numerous islands, La Baule with its magnificent beach and the medieval city of Guérande to the unique Brière nature reserve.

Facilities

Fully equipped toilet facilities include laundry and dishwashing sinks. Washing machines and dryers. Bar, restaurant, shop, TV and games room. Indoor and outdoor swimming pools. Play area. Indoor ball area. Fishing.

Open

1 May - 30 September.

At a glance

| Welcome & Ambience | ✓✓ | Location | ✓✓✓ |
| Quality of Pitches | ✓✓✓✓ | Range of Facilities | ✓✓✓✓ |

Directions

Site is 300 m. from the D34, and 1 km. from the town, to the southwest.

Charges 2005

Per person	€ 4,50 - € 6,00
child (under 7 yrs.)	€ 2,00 - € 3,00
pitch	€ 5,00 - € 10,00
electricity	€ 4,00
dog	€ 1,50 - € 2,50

Camping Cheques accepted.

Reservations

Necessary for high season. Tel: 02 99 90 33 14.
Email: info@lecenic.com

MAP 2

A striking area whose beauty lies not only in the landscape. Famed for its seafood and Celtic tradition, certain areas of Normandy remain untouched and wonderfully old fashioned.

DÉPARTEMENTS: 14 CALVADOS, 27 EURE, 50 MANCHE, 61 ORNE, 76 SEINE MARITIME

MAJOR CITIES: CAEN AND ROUEN

Normandy has a rich landscape full of variety. From the wild craggy granite coastline of the northern Cotentin to the long sandy beaches and chalk cliffs of the south. It also boasts a superb coastline including the Cotentin Peninsula, cliffs of the Côte d'Albâtre and the fine beaches and fashionable resorts of the Côte Fleurie. Plus a wealth of quiet villages and unspoilt countryside for leisurely exploration.

The history of Normandy is closely linked with our own. The famous Bayeux Tapestry chronicles the exploits of the Battle of Hastings and there are many museums, exhibitions, sites and monuments, including the Caen Memorial Museum, which commemorate operations that took place during the D-Day Landings of 1944.

Known as the dairy of France you'll also find plenty of fresh fish, rich cream, butter, and fine cheeses such as Camembert and Pont l'Evêque. The many apple orchards are used in producing cider and the well known Calvados, Normandy's apple brandy.

Places of interest

Bayeux: home to the famous tapestry; 15th-18th century houses, cathedral, museums.

Caen: feudal castle, Museum of Normandy, Museum for Peace.

Omaha Beach: D-Day beaches, Landing site monuments, American Cemetery.

Deauville: seaside resort, horse racing centre.

Giverny: home of impressionist painter Claude Monet, Monet Museum.

Honfleur: picturesque port city with old town.

Lisieux: pilgrimage site, shrine of Ste Thérèse.

Mont St Michel: world famous abbey on island.

Rouen: Joan of Arc Museum; Gothic churches, cathedrals, abbey, clock tower.

Cuisine of the region

Andouillette de Vire: small chitterling (tripe) sausage.

Barbue au cidre: brill cooked in cider and Calvados.

Douillons de pommes à la Normande: baked apples in pastry.

Escalope (Vallée d'Auge): veal sautéed and flamed in Calvados and served with cream and apples.

Ficelle Normande: pancake with ham, mushrooms and cheese.

Poulet (Vallée d'Auge): chicken cooked in the same way as Escalope Vallée d'Auge.

Tripes à la Mode de Caen: stewed beef tripe with onions, carrots, leeks, garlic, cider and Calvados.

FR14020 Camping Municipal du Bayeux

Boulevard Eindhoven, F-14400 Bayeux (Calvados)

Whether or not you want to see the tapestry, this site makes a very useful night stop on the way to or from Cherbourg, and in addition it is only a few kilometres from the coast and the landing beaches. Pleasantly laid out with grassy lawns and bushes, its neat, cared for appearance makes a good impression. The 140 pitches are in two areas (many are on hardstanding), and are well marked, generally of good size and with electricity. The site is busy over a long season - early arrival is advised as reservations are not taken. There is a full time site warden from 15/6-15/9, otherwise reception is open from 08.00-10.00 and 17.00-19.00 hrs. There may be some road noise on one side of the site.

Facilities

The two good quality toilet blocks have British and Turkish style WCs, washbasins in cabins in the main block, and units for disabled people. Motorcaravan service point. Laundry room. Takeaway food and snacks. Two children's playgrounds. Volleyball. Reading room with TV. Games room. Off site: Large public indoor swimming pool adjoins site with children's pool and jacuzzi. Large supermarket very close (closes 8 pm). Bicycle hire 1 km. Riding 5 km. Golf or fishing 8 km. Beach 8 km.

Open

1 May - 30 September.

At a glance

Welcome & Ambience	✓✓✓✓	Location	✓✓✓✓
Quality of Pitches	✓✓✓✓	Range of Facilities	✓✓✓

Directions

Site is on the south side of northern ring road (D613) to town, and just west of the junction with the D516 to autoroute. GPS: N49:17.037 W00:41.857

Charges 2006

Per person	€ 3,10
child (under 7 yrs)	€ 1,65
pitch and car	€ 3,83
electricity	€ 3,14 - € 3,08

Less 10% for stay over 5 days.

Reservations

Not made. Tel: 02 31 92 08 43.

FR14030 Castel Camping Le Château de Martragny

F-14740 Martragny (Calvados)

Martragny is an attractive site in a parkland setting adjoining the château and close to D-Day beaches. This is a particularly convenient location for access to the ports of both Caen and Cherbourg, and the site has the facilities and charm to encourage both long stays and stopovers. The pleasant lawns that surround and approach the château take 160 units, with electricity connections for 140. The majority of the pitches are divided by either a small hedge or a couple of trees, only a few not marked out. Bed and breakfast (en-suite) are available in the château all year (reservation essential). Madame de Chassey takes great pride in the site and takes care that the peace and quiet is preserved. This is a perfect place for a quiet relaxing holiday yet only 12 km. from the sea, the wartime landing beaches, the excellent museum at Arromanche, the Bayeux tapestry or the Calvados 'Cider Route'.

Facilities

Two recently modernised sanitary blocks include washbasins in cabins, sinks for dishes and clothes and two baby baths. Disabled people are well catered for. Good laundry. Well stocked shop and takeaway food bar open 15/5-15/9. Bar. Swimming pool (20 x 6 m.) and paddling pool heated in poor weather. Play areas, one new. Tennis courts. Minigolf, games and TV room, table tennis and billiards. Fishing. Bicycle and buggy hire. Off site: Riding 1 km. Beach 15 km. Golf 20 km.

Open

1 May - 15 September.

At a glance

Welcome & Ambience	✓✓✓✓	Location	✓✓✓✓
Quality of Pitches	✓✓✓✓	Range of Facilities	✓✓✓✓

Directions

Site is off N13, 8 km. southeast of Bayeux. Take Martragny exit from dual carriageway. GPS: N49:14.595 W00:36.348

Charges 2005

Per person	€ 4,70
child (under 7 yrs)	€ 2,70
pitch for caravan or motorcaravan	€ 10,60
tent pitch	€ 10,00
electricity (6A)	€ 3,00

Less 15% outside 1/7-31/8.
Camping Cheques accepted.

Reservations

Made for min. 3 nights; deposit and small fee required. Tel: 02 31 80 21 40.
Email: chateau.martragny@wanadoo.fr

FR14060 Camping Les Hautes Coutures

Route de Ouistreham, F-14970 Bénouville (Calvados)

Les Hautes Coutures is a useful site near the Caen-Portsmouth ferry terminal suitable for overnight stays. It is beside the Caen ship canal, 2 km. from the sea (and ferry port) and 10 km. from Caen – the site gates are opened at 6 am. for early ferries and there can be movement on site late into the evening. There are 120 grass touring pitches of 100 sq.m, clearly marked by mature hedges with tarmac roads. All pitches have electrical connections (up to 10A). An area close to the canal is being developed to provide further pitches. There are also around 150 mobile homes on the site. Ouistreham is within walking distance along the canal and the Pegasus Bridge Airborne Division Museum. A pedestrian gate leads on to the towpath (a code is needed for re-entry).

Facilities

Two toilet blocks include showers, washbasins in cabins (warm water only). Facilities can be under pressure at peak times and the hot water supply can be variable. In low season only one block may be open. Dishwashing and laundry facilities with washing machine and dryer. Motorcaravan service point. Small shop keeps basic items. Bar and takeaway. Small heated swimming pool (from June) which is kept locked - ask for access. Small lounge/TV area and games room. Play area on sand. Two tennis courts. Volleyball. Minigolf. Boules. Table tennis. Off site: Beach and riding 2 km. Golf 4 km.

At a glance

Welcome & Ambience	✓✓✓✓	Location	✓✓✓✓
Quality of Pitches	✓✓✓✓	Range of Facilities	✓✓✓✓

Directions

Site is just off the D514 dual-carriageway, north of Benouville. From Caen, follow Ouistreham car ferry signs and take first exit from D514 after Benouville. GPS: N49:15.003 W00:16.396

Charges 2006

Per person	€ 8,00
child (under 7 yrs)	€ 5,50
pitch	€ 8,00
electricity (4/10A)	€ 6,10 - € 8,50

Reservations

Contact site. Tel: 02 31 44 73 08. Email: camping-hautes-coutures@wanadoo.fr

Open

1 April - 30 September.

FR14090 Castel Camping du Brévedent

Le Brévedent, F-14130 Pont-l'Evêque (Calvados)

Le Brévedent is a well established, traditional site with 144 pitches (109 for tourists) set in the grounds of an elegant 18th century hunting pavilion. Level pitches are set around the fishing lake or in the lower gardens, others are in the old orchard. Most have electricity. Reception provides a vast amount of tourist information and organised tours in the main season include a cider farm and a local distillery. The site is used by a tour operator (31 pitches). It is an excellent holiday destination within easy reach of the Channel ports. The church bells ring out every morning at 07.00 hrs, but the otherwise peaceful, friendly environment makes it ideal for mature campers or families with younger children (note the lake is unfenced). Particularly popular are the Sunday countryside rambles and evening talks, the firework displays for Bastille Day and Assumption Day, Saturday eving music sessions and the site's annual music festival in late September.

Facilities

Three toilet blocks of varying ages (one new) include washbasins in cubicles, dishwashing and laundry sinks, and good facilities for babies and disabled people. Good motorcaravan service point. Laundries with washing machines and dryers. Well stocked shop. Baker calls each morning. Small bar in the hunting lodge itself, open each evening (1/5-25/9). Restaurant including snacks and traditional Normandy cuisine (24/5-19/9). Takeaway (1/5-25/9). Clubroom with internet access, TV and library. Swimming and paddling pools (unsupervised) are heated and in separate enclosures (1/5-25/9). Playground in the old walled garden by the restaurant. Table tennis. Minigolf. Boules. Volleyball. Games room with machines and pool table. Fishing is free (but put the fish back). Rowing boats (with lifejackets). Bicycle and buggy hire. Organised activities for children including pony lessons. Dogs are not accepted. Off site: Discounts arranged for riding (1 km), the nearby St Julien golf club and tennis on the local court. Pont L'Evêque 14 km. Château de Betteville with motor museum. Beach 25 km.

At a glance

Welcome & Ambience	✓✓✓✓	Location	✓✓✓✓
Quality of Pitches	✓✓✓✓	Range of Facilities	✓✓✓✓

Directions

From Pont L'Evêque take D579 toward Lisieux for 4 km. then D51 towards Moyaux. At Blangy le Château turn right (still on D51) to Le Brévedent. GPS: N49:13.528 E00:18.342

Charges 2005

Per person	€ 6,00
child 1-6 yrs	€ 3,00
child 7-12 yrs	€ 4,00
pitch	€ 8,00
electricity	€ 3,00
Camping Cheques accepted.	

Reservations

Advised for the main season; contact site. Tel: 02 31 64 72 88. Email: contact@campinglebrevedent.com

Open

1 May - 25 September.

FR14070 Camping de la Vallée

88 rue de la Vallée, F-14510 Houlgate (Calvados)

Camping de la Vallée is an attractive site with good, well maintained facilities. Situated on a grassy hillside overlooking Houlgate, the 373 pitches (98 for touring units) are large and open. Hedges have been planted and all pitches have 4 or 6A electricity. Part of the site is sloping, the rest level, with gravel or tarmac roads. An old farmhouse has been converted to house a good bar and comfortable TV lounge and billiards room. English is spoken in season. Used by tour operators (104 pitches). Very busy in high season, maintenance and cleaning could be variable at that time. There are 150 mobile homes on site and around 40 seasonal units are also taken.

Facilities

Three good toilet blocks include washbasins in cabins, mainly British style toilets, facilities for disabled people and baby bathroom. Dishwashing, laundry with machines, dryers and ironing boards (no washing lines allowed). Motorcaravan services. Shop (from 1/5). Bar. Small snack bar with takeaway in season (from 15/5). Heated swimming pool (15/5-20/9; no shorts). Games room. Playground. Bicycle hire. Volleyball, football field, tennis, petanque and table tennis. Organised entertainment in Jul/Aug. Internet access. Off site: Riding 500 m. Beach, town or fishing 1 km. Championship golf course 2 km.

Open

1 April - 30 September.

At a glance

Welcome & Ambience	✓✓✓✓	Location	✓✓✓✓
Quality of Pitches	✓✓✓✓	Range of Facilities	✓✓✓✓

Directions

From A13 take exit for Cabourg and follow signs for Dives/Houlgate going straight on at roundabout. Go straight on at next roundabout, then four sets of traffic lights. Turn left along seafront. After 1 km. at lights turn right, carry on for 1 km. and over mini-roundabout - look for site sign on right. It is well signed especially from the D513 coast road. GPS: N49:17.644 W00:04.097

Charges 2005

Per unit incl. 2 persons	
and electricity (4A)	€ 21,00 - € 28,00
electricity (6A)	€ 2,00
extra adult	€ 5,00 - € 6,00
child (under 7 yrs)	€ 3,00 - € 4,00

Camping Cheques accepted.

Reservations

Made with deposit and fee. Tel: 02 31 24 40 69. Email: camping.lavallee@wanadoo.fr

CAMPING CARAVANING

LA VALLÉE
★ ★ ★ ★

88, Rue de la Vallée
14510 Houlgate
Tel: 0033 231.24.40.69
Fax: 0033 231.24.42.42

❑ SHOP ❑ BAR ❑ GAMES ROOM
❑ TENNIS ❑ HEATED SWIMMING POOL
❑ CHILDREN'S POOL ❑ ENTERTAINMENT

FR14100 Camping Municipal du Château

3 rue du Val d'Ante, F-14700 Falaise (Calvados)

The location of this site is really quite spectacular, lying in the shadow of the Château de Falaise, in the old part of the town, in the 'coeur de Normandie'. The site itself is small, with only 66 pitches (all with 6A electricity). It has a rather intimate 'up-market' feel about it, rather different from the average municipal site. With good shade, tarmac roads and easy access, whatever this site lacks in size and facilities it makes up for in its situation, close to the town centre, the tennis club and near to the river for fishing. The charges are reasonable and the reception friendly.

Facilities

The sanitary facilities could be insufficient in terms of quantity when the site is full - perhaps it never is and campers we met felt they were adequate. Although dated the quality is good and they are reasonably clean. Unit for disabled visitors (shower room and separate WC). Access to showers closed 22.00-07.30. Motorcaravan service point. Play area. Boules. Table tennis. TV room. Fishing. Off site: Bicycle hire 300 m. Riding 500 m.

Open

1 May - 30 September.

At a glance

Welcome & Ambience	✓✓✓✓	Location	✓✓✓✓
Quality of Pitches	✓✓✓✓	Range of Facilities	✓✓✓

Directions

Site is on western side of town, well signed from the ring road. From N158 heading south take first roundabout into Falaise (site signed), then pass through residential suburb to site. GPS: N48:53.734 W00:12.288

Charges 2006

Per person	€ 3,30
child (3-12 yrs)	€ 2,30
pitch	€ 3,00
electricity	€ 2,50

Reservations

Advised for July/Aug. Tel: 02 31 90 16 55. Email: camping@falaise.fr

FR14160 Camping Bellevue

Route des Dives, F-14640 Villers sur Mer (Calvados)

Bellevue is located just west of Villers-sur-Mer with its sandy beach, and 9.5 km. west of fashionable Deauville. A fairly large site with 249 pitches in total, but including 190 privately owned mobile homes and 20 units for rent, there are only 59 pitches left for tourists. Many of these are on terraces, individual and relatively small with restricted access, so suitable only for smaller units. Double axle caravans will have difficulty and will only be able to access pitches adjacent to the road. There are around half a dozen, further level pitches behind reception mostly used by motorcaravans (unsuitable for American RVs). We have concerns about the water and power supplies which are not on conventional standpipes and posts - water taps are on free floating plastic pipes and electric supplies are French sockets on the end of an electric cable (6A), and are not really suitable for a touring pitch. We hope that the new owners (March 2005) will provide a more correct installation as soon as possible. Whilst sanitary units are modern and well presented, the laundry and some dishwash facilities are in need of total refurbishment. The main complex is arranged around the spacious site entrance and is quite smart. The swimming pool complex has three pools including a paddling pool and a wide sunbathing area, and is well fenced and gated.

Facilities

Two sanitary units provide unisex facilities, all in individual cubicles, with some wide door cubicles for disabled visitors. Baby changing room. Laundry room with washing machine, dryer and a range of sinks for laundry and dishwashing. Swimming pool complex (15/6-15/9). Bar (1/7-15/9). Takeaway van in July/Aug. Boules court. Video games machines. Pool table. Playground. Organised activities in peak season. Off site: Golf 4 km. Riding 2 km. Beach and town 1.5 km.

Open

1 April - 31 October.

Directions

Villers-sur-Mer is about 8 km. west of Deauville. The site is 1.5 km. west of Villers on the D513; be ready to turn right into lane (site signed) at the crest of a hill, where the road bends to the right.
GPS: N49:18.562 W00:1.178

Charges 2005

Per person	€ 6,00
child (0-7 yrs)	€ 3,50
pitch	€ 7,00
electricity	€ 4,00
dog	€ 2,50

Reservations

Made with deposit of € 100, incl. € 16 fee.
Tel: 02 31 87 05 21.
Email: contact@camping-bellevue.com

At a glance

Welcome & Ambience	✓✓✓	Location	✓✓✓
Quality of Pitches	✓✓✓	Range of Facilities	✓✓✓

FR14150 Sunelia Port'land

Chemin du Castel, F-14520 Port en Bessin (Calvados)

Port'land is a new site lying 700 m. to the east of the little resort of Port en Bessin, one of Normandy's busiest fishing ports. A coastal path leads to the little town and the nearest beach (the sandy Omaha Beach is 4 km. away). The 256 pitches are large and grassy. Most offer 10A electricity although there is a separate area for tents (without electricity). The camping area has been imaginatively designed with the creation of a number of distinct zones, some overlooking a series of small fishing ponds, and another radiating out from a central barbecue area. The central building houses reception, the shop, bar and restaurant, as well as a large TV and games room from where there are fine views of the Normandy coast. The heated swimming pool is adjacent and is covered in low season. In peak season a range of entertainment is organised including disco and karaoke evenings, and a range of children's activities. Mobile homes for hire. A member of the Sunelia group.

Facilities

The two sanitary blocks are modern and well maintained. Special disabled facilities. Covered swimming pool and paddling pool. Bar, restaurant, takeaway (all open all season). Multisports pitch. Fishing. Play area. Off site: Nearest beach 4 km. 27 hole Omaha Beach International golf course adjacent. D-Day beaches. Colleville American war Cemetery. Bayeux.

Open

1 April - 6 November.

Directions

Site is clearly signed off the D514 4 km. west of Port en Bessin.

Charges 2005

Per unit incl. 2 persons, electricity	€ 15,50 - € 32,30
extra person	€ 4,80 - € 7,30
child (2-10 yrs)	€ 2,80 - € 4,20
Reductions for stays over 7 nights.	

Reservations

Contact site. Tel: 02 31 51 07 06.
Email: campingportland@wanadoo.fr

At a glance

Welcome & Ambience	✓✓✓✓	Location	✓✓✓✓
Quality of Pitches	✓✓✓✓	Range of Facilities	✓✓✓✓

FR14140 Camping Municipal Pont Farcy

F-14380 Pont Farcy (Calvados)

This well tended, riverside site is in a tranquil location within easy walking distance of the small village, with a warden who lives on site. Reception can also provide maps of local walks and cycle routes. Many activities are available either on-site or at the adjacent 'base plein air'. Swimming is not permitted and the river is well fenced with access gates for anglers. The 60 numbered pitches are on grass, some separated by small hedges, with electricity (5A) available to all (some long leads may be needed). This site is also within easy driving distance of Cherbourg or Caen and is just off the A84 motorway.

Facilities	Directions
A rather stylish modern building houses all the facilities, including some washbasins in cubicles and a suite for disabled campers. First floor 'salle' with dining tables for campers, table tennis and other games (ask the warden). There is a lift from the ground floor. Adventure style playground (5-12 yrs). Off site: Village garage with a small shop, bakery, butcher, post office. Bar/hotel.	Pont-Farcy is about 25 km. due south of St Lo. From A84, exit 39, take D21 south for 1 km. and site is on left at entrance to village. GPS: N48:56.395 W01:02.120

Open

1 April - 30 September.

Charges 2005

Per unit incl. 1 or 2 persons	€ 9,00
extra person	€ 2,15
child (under 7 yrs)	€ 1,00
electricity	€ 1,85

No credit cards.

At a glance

Welcome & Ambience	✓✓✓✓	Location	✓✓✓✓✓
Quality of Pitches	✓✓✓✓	Range of Facilities	✓✓✓✓

Reservations

Contact site. Tel: 02 31 68 32 06.

FR14130 Camping Le Fanal

Rue de Fanal, F-14230 Isigny-sur-Mer (Calvados)

A useful informal spacious site, Le Fanal is on the outskirts of a fairly typical small town. There are 112 pitches, of which 97 are used as touring pitches, all on grass with around 42 electric hook-ups (16A), arranged in several large bays, surrounded by mature trees. Some areas could be a little soft in inclement weather, so the site is not really suitable for American RVs. The small, fenced swimming pool (8 x 4 m) may look like a child's pool, but is in fact between one and two metres deep - only supervised children are permitted (open July and Aug, ask for key). The town is noted for its dairy products, with visits possible to factories producing cheese, butter, cream, and caramels.

Facilities	Directions
The main sanitary unit provides washbasins in cubicles, pre-set hot showers, plus facilities for disabled people. Motorcaravan service point. Dining room with a microwave and soft drink dispensing machines, a lounge with TV, a laundry, plus more toilets and washbasins. Small swimming pool. Playground. Tennis, table tennis, volleyball, boules. Off site: Fishing and boating in the adjacent lake.	Isigny-sur-Mer is just off N13, midway between Cherbourg and Caen, (10 km. east of Carentan). Site is west of town centre off D197A, and is well signed. GPS: N49:19.194 W01:06.589

Open

1 April - 15 October.

Charges guide

Per adult	€ 3,05 - € 3,35
child under 16 yrs (third free)	€ 1,55
pitch incl. electricity	€ 6,10 - € 7,65

No credit cards.

At a glance

Welcome & Ambience	✓✓✓✓	Location	✓✓✓✓
Quality of Pitches	✓✓✓	Range of Facilities	✓✓✓

Reservations

Contact site. Tel: 02 31 21 33 20.
Email: camping@isigny-sur-mer.fr

FR27050 Camping Municipal Saint Paul

2 route de St Paul, F-27480 Lyons-La Foret (Eure)

The village of Lyons-La-Foret, with its medieval covered market and magnificently preserved half-timbered buildings is regarded as one of the most beautiful in France. Within walking distance (900 metres), next to the stadium and public swimming pool, this quiet municipal campsite provides a pleasant respite. The site has 100 level grass, numbered pitches of which 60 are available for tourists. Each has access to electricity (6A), water and drainage. They are separated by hedges or mature trees providing shade. The site is edged by fast-flowing, shallow (unfenced) streams.

Facilities	Directions
Two reasonable toilet blocks include facilities for people with disabilities. These facilities could be stretched in peak season and cleaning may be variable. Washing machine. Drying lines. Play area. Separate tent area. Off site: All facilities in nearby village. Many walking and cycling routes.	Site is to the north of Lyons-La-Foret on the D921 road. GPS: N49:24.185 E01:28.693

Open

1 April - 31 October.

Charges 2005

Per unit incl. 2 persons	€ 15,00
tent pitch incl. 2 persons	€ 13,00
extra person	€ 2,50
animal	€ 1,00

No credit cards.

At a glance

Welcome & Ambience	✓✓✓	Location	✓✓✓✓
Quality of Pitches	✓✓✓✓	Range of Facilities	✓✓✓

Reservations

Contact site. Tel: 02 32 49 42 02.

FR27030 Camping Saint Nicolas

F-27800 Le Bec-Hellouin (Eure)

This lovely site (formerly a municipal site and still run by the same resident wardens) is located on a forested hillside above the interesting and attractive small town of Le Bec-Hellouin. There are 90 marked grassy pitches, 30 used for seasonal units, leaving about 60 for tourists all with 10A hook-ups and some with water taps. There is limited shade from a few mature trees. A rather steep footpath leads down to the town and the imposing Abbey of Bec. This is still a working monastery, which was founded in 1034, at the time of William the Conqueror, and has links to the archbishops of Canterbury. It is well worth a visit. The town itself is quite photogenic, has the usual tourist shops, several bars and restaurants and horse drawn carriage rides. The surrounding area is very popular with artists and photographers and there is a wealth of interesting historical and cultural places to visit.

Facilities

A modern heated unit has good showers, British style WCs, open and cubicled washbasins, and a dishwashing area which overlooks the good playground via an attractive bay window. Extra facilities in the old unit by reception, where you will find the laundry with washing machine and dryer. Reception keeps soft drinks and ices, and the baker calls each morning. Playing field and tennis courts. Off site: Le Bec-Hellouin and its Abbey 1.5 km. Fishing 1.5 km. Riding 2 km. Swimming pool at Brionne, 6 km. Golf 7 km.

Open

1 April - 30 September.

At a glance

Welcome & Ambience	✓✓✓✓	Location	✓✓✓✓
Quality of Pitches	✓✓✓✓	Range of Facilities	✓✓✓

Directions

Le Bec-Hellouin is about 30 km. southwest of Rouen, just off the D130 between Pont Authou and Brionne. Turn east on D39 to Le Bec-Hellouin (site is signed), pass through edge of town and at far end of one-way section, turn left on minor road (site signed). Continue for 1 km. then fork left and carry on to site entrance on right. GPS: N49:14.086 E00:43.519

Charges 2006

Per unit incl. 2 persons	€ 7,55
extra person	€ 2,85
electricity	€ 2,85
No credit cards.	

Reservations

Contact site. Tel: 02 32 44 83 55.

CAMPING SAINT-NICOLAS** N.E.

Association "MON VILLAGE"   27800 Le Bec-Hellouin
Tel 02 32 44 83 55   info@lebec-hellouin.com

FR27020 Camping du Domaine Catinière

Route de Honfleur, F-27210 Fiquefleur-Equainville (Eure)

A peaceful, friendly site, close to the coast, in the countryside yet in the middle of a very long village, this site is achieving a modern look, whilst retaining its original French flavour. There are 42 mobile homes, but there should be around 88 pitches for tourists including a large open field for tents and units not needing electricity. Caravan pitches are separated, some with shade, others are more open and all have electricity. The site is divided by well fenced streams, popular with young anglers. The pretty harbour town of Honfleur less than 5 km. away. A 'Sites et Paysages' member.

Facilities

Toilet facilities include mostly British style WCs, some washbasins in cubicles, and facilities for disabled people and babies (cleaning can be variable). Washing machine and dryer. Reception with shop. Small bar/restaurant with regional dishes and snacks. Heated swimming pool (1/6-31/8). Two playgrounds, trampoline. Table tennis. Boules. Off site: Beuzeville (7 km). Beach 7 km.

Open

7 April - 24 September.

At a glance

Welcome & Ambience	✓✓✓✓	Location	✓✓✓✓
Quality of Pitches	✓✓✓✓	Range of Facilities	✓✓✓✓

Directions

From the Pont de Normandie (toll) take first exit (no. 3, A29) signed Honfleur. At roundabout turn left under motorway (Le Mans. Alencon) on D180. Take second exit on the right after about 2.5 km, on D22 towards Beuzeville. Site is on right after about 1 km. GPS: N49:24.054 E00:18.365

Charges 2006

Per pitch incl. 1 or 2 persons	€ 14,00 - € 17,50
with electricity (4A)	€ 17,50 - € 20,50
extra person	€ 4,00 - € 5,00
Credit cards accepted (minimum of € 70).	

Reservations

Conact site. Tel: 02 32 57 63 51.
Email: info@camping-catiniere.com

FR50000 Camping L'Etang des Haizes

43 rue Cauticotte, F-50250 St Symphorien-le-Valois (Manche)

This is an attractive and very friendly site which has recently added a swimming pool complex with four-lane slides, jacuzzi and a paddling pool. L'Etang des Haizes has 98 good size pitches, of which 60 are for touring units, on fairly level ground and all with electricity (10A). They are set in a mixture of conifers, orchard and shrubbery, with some very attractive slightly smaller pitches overlooking the lake and 38 mobile homes inconspicuously sited. The fenced lake has a small beach (swimming is permitted!), ducks and pedaloes, and offers good coarse fishing for huge carp (we are told!): believe it or not, a turtle can sometimes be seen on a fine day!

Facilities

Two well kept toilet blocks are of modern construction, open plan and unisex. They have British-style toilets, washbasins in cabins and units for disabled people and two new family cabins. Dishwashing under cover, small laundry. Motorcaravan services. Milk, bread and takeaway snacks are available on site (no gas). Snack-bar/Bar with TV and terrace overlooking the lake and pool complex (all 20/5-10/9). Two play areas. Bicycle hire. Table tennis, pool table, petanque and volleyball. Entertainment and activities organised for all ages, including treasure hunts, archery and food tasting (10/7-25/8). Off site: La Haye-du-Puits (1 km) has two supermarkets, good restaurants and a market on Wednesdays. Good sandy beach 10 km. Normandy landing beaches 25 km.

Open

1 April - 15 October.

At a glance

Welcome & Ambience	✓✓✓✓✓	Location	✓✓✓✓
Quality of Pitches	✓✓✓✓	Range of Facilities	✓✓✓✓

Directions

The site is located just north of La Haye du Puits which is on the primary route from Cherbourg to Mont St Michel, St Malo and Rennes, 24 km south of N13 at Valognes and 29 km north of Coutances: leave D900 at roundabout at northern end of by-pass (towards town) and site is signed almost immediately on the right. GPS: N49:18.031 W01:32.729

Charges 2005

pitch	€ 6,00 - € 17,00
Per person over 4yrs	€ 4,00 - € 6,00
electricity (10A)	€ 2,00 - € 4,00
dog	€ 1,00 - € 2,00

Camping Cheques accepted.

Reservations

Made with 25% deposit. Tel: 02 33 46 01 16.
Email: etang.des.haizes@wanadoo.fr

71

FR50030 Castel Camping Le Château de Lez Eaux

Saint Aubin des Préaux, F-50380 Saint Pair-sur-Mer (Manche)

Set in the spacious grounds of a château, Lez Eaux lies in a rural situation just off the main route south, under two hours from Cherbourg. It is a very pleasant location from which to explore this corner of the Cotentin peninsula, with swimming pools on site and beaches nearby. There are 229 pitches of which 113 are tourist pitches all with electricity (5 or 10A) and 70 fully serviced. Most pitches are of a very good size, partly separated by trees and shrubs on either flat or very slightly sloping, grassy ground overlooking Normandy farmland or beside a small lake (with carp and other fish). Although there is a considerable tour-operator presence, these units by no means dominate the site, being generally tucked away in their own areas.

Facilities

Three modern toilet blocks (cleaned continually from early till late by a team of contractors) include British-style toilets, hot showers and washbasins in cabins, good facilities for children and babies, and full provision for disabled people. Shop, small bar, snacks and takeaway (all from 15/5). Small heated swimming pool (12 x 6 m.) and attractive, indoor tropical-style fun pool with slides and a glass roof (from 15/5, no T-shirts or Bermuda style shorts). Adventure play area. Good tennis court. Football, volleyball. Games room with table tennis, and TV room. Bicycle hire. Lake fishing. Torches might help at night. Only one dog per pitch accepted. Off site: Nearest beach is 4 km. St Pair is 4 km. and Granville 7 km. Riding 5 km. Golf 7 km.

At a glance

Welcome & Ambience	✓✓✓✓✓	Location	✓✓✓✓	
Quality of Pitches	✓✓✓✓	Range of Facilities	✓✓✓✓✓	

Directions

Lez-Eaux is just to the west of the D973 about 17 km. northwest of Avranches and 7 km. southeast of Granville. Site is between the two turnings east to St Aubin des Préaux and is well signed. GPS: N48:47.764 W01:31.480

Charges 2006

Per pitch incl. 2 persons	€ 13,50 - € 31,00
extra person	€ 8,50
child (under 7 yrs)	€ 6,50
electricity (5A)	€ 7,00
all services	€ 10,00

Reservations

Advisable for high season and made with 25% deposit. Tel: 02 33 51 66 09. Email: lez.eaux@wanadoo.fr

Open

1 May - 15 September.

FR50050 Camping Le Cormoran

Ravenoville-Plage, F-50480 Sainte-Mère-Eglise (Manche)

Set in a flat and open landscape and only separated from the beach by the coast road, Le Cormoran is ideal for a holiday or short break quite near to Cherbourg (33 km), with the Landing Beaches close by. Holiday mobile homes, many privately owned, take 136 places and include 40 for rent. The remaining 80 pitches for touring units are sheltered from the wind by neat hedges and have 6A electricity available. With a narrow frontage, decorated with flags and a fountain, it is a fairly long site with most of the amenities at the entrance. This is a well run, family managed site with many regular visitors, which gets full in peak season. Those only staying for one night may be asked to pitch on the overflow area adjacent to the main site. A 'Sites et Paysages' member.

Facilities

Four toilet blocks are of varying styles and ages. Washbasins are in cabins. Dishwashing sinks. Washing machine and dryer in three blocks. A new sanitary block serves 15 extra large pitches (150 sq.m.) at the back of the site. Small shop, bar with snacks (all season) and takeaway. Swimming pool (heated 1/5-15/9, unsupervised). Three small play areas. Tennis court. Boules pitch. Entertainment, TV and games room completely renovated in 2005. Bicycle and shrimp net hire. Communal barbecue. Off site: Archery, riding and day trips to the Channel Islands can be organised. Golf 5 km. Utah Beach 5 km. Sports field and storage for up to 60 boats adjacent to the site. Beach 50 m.

Open

1 April - 24 September.

At a glance

Welcome & Ambience	✓✓✓✓	Location	✓✓✓✓	
Quality of Pitches	✓✓✓✓	Range of Facilities	✓✓✓✓	

Directions

From N13 take Ste Mère Eglise exit and in centre of town take road to Ravenoville (6 km), then Ravenoville-Plage (3 km). Just before beach turn right and site is 500 m. GPS: N49:27.960 W01:14.104

Charges 2006

Per unit incl. 1 or 2 persons	€ 16,20 - € 25,00
extra person	€ 4,60 - € 7,00
child (3- 7 yrs)	€ 1,80 - € 2,50
electricity (6A)	€ 3,80
dog	€ 2,80 - € 3,00
Camping Cheques accepted.	

Reservations

Essential for July/Aug. and made with 25% deposit. Tel: 02 33 41 33 94. Email: lecormoran@wanadoo.fr

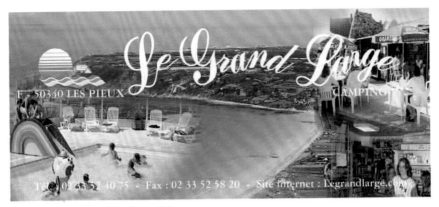

FR50060 Camping Le Grand Large

F-50340 Les Pieux (Manche)

Le Grand Large is a well established, quality family site with direct access to a long sandy beach and within a 20 km. drive of Cherbourg. A neat, tidy site with both touring and mobile home pitches which are divided and separated by hedging, giving an orderly well laid out appearance. At the entrance, alongside the security barrier, stands the modern reception area. Decorating the forecourt are low brick walls with sunken flower beds, the toilet blocks also having their share of flower troughs. To the rear of the site and laid out in the sand-hills is an excellent play area for children, with swings, slides and climbing frame. However, the sandy beach is the big attraction. There are pleasant views across the bay to the tip of the Cherbourg peninsula. A 'Sites et Paysages' member.

Facilities

The two toilet blocks are well maintained, the main one modern and colourful including washbasins in cubicles and some family rooms. WCs are mostly to the outside of the building. Provision for people with disabilities is good. Baby bathroom, dishwashing sinks, laundry area, and motorcaravan services. Shop for basic groceries, bar (all season), snacks (1/7-26/8). Swimming pool and children's pool. Play area. Tennis, table tennis, volleyball and boules. TV room. Animation in July/Aug. Off site: Bicycle hire and riding 5 km. Golf 15 km.

Open

8 April - 17 September.

At a glance

Welcome & Ambience	✓✓✓✓	Location	✓✓✓✓
Quality of Pitches	✓✓✓✓	Range of Facilities	✓✓✓✓✓

Directions

From Cherbourg port take N13 south for approx. 2 km. Branch right on D650 road signed Cartaret. Continue for 18 km to Les Pieux. Take D4 in town and turn left just after supermarket and follow camp signs via D117/517. GPS: N49:29.665 W01:50.544

Charges 2006

Per unit incl. 2 persons	€ 17,00 - € 28,00
extra person	€ 4,00 - € 6,00
child (under 7 yrs)	€ 2,50 - € 3,50
electricity (6A)	€ 4,00

Less 20% in low seasons (excl. electricity).
Camping Cheques accepted.

Reservations

Made with deposit (€ 80). Tel: 02 33 52 40 75. Email: le-grand-large@wanadoo.fr

FR50090 Camping La Gerfleur

Rue Guillaume Le Conquérant, F-50270 Barneville Carteret (Manche)

La Gerfleur is a very pleasant little site with a warm welcome from the owners, a new heated pool, a fishing lake and reasonable sanitary facilities. There are 44 mobile homes, but these are separated from 49 tourist pitches. On grass with small dividing hedges, these all have electricity and some shade from mature trees. A few are in a newly-created, more open area next to the lake, and will need more time to fully mature. The new outdoor, heated pool has a separate circular paddling pool. La Gerfleur makes a good holiday base, being an easy cycle ride from the large sandy beach at Barneville Plage, or from the harbour and the smaller cove at Carteret (both only 1.5 km).

Facilities

Clean facilities include British style WCs, chain operated showers and some washbasins, all in modern cubicles, units for disabled visitors. Washing machine and dryer. Basic motorcaravan service point. Swimming pool. Fishing lake. Small playground. In July and August extra services include a bar, 'frites' and bread supplies. Off site: Barneville town centre 300 m. Beach 1.5 km. Golf 4 km. Riding 7 km.

Open

1 April - 31 October.

At a glance

Welcome & Ambience	✓✓✓✓	Location	✓✓✓✓
Quality of Pitches	✓✓✓✓	Range of Facilities	✓✓✓

Directions

From the north turn off the D904 Barneville-Carteret by-pass, and use the old road to the town. After 1 km. at roundabouts, continue on D903E towards town centre, and site is on the right. GPS: N49:22.974 E01:45.341

Charges guide

Per person	€ 4,30
child (under 13 yrs)	€ 3,00
pitch incl. electricity (6A)	€ 8,70

Reservations

Contact site. Tel: 02 33 04 38 41. Email: alabouriau@aol.com

Beach at 100 m

50330 MAUPERTUS/MER
Tel : 33 (0) 233 549 357
Fax : 33 (0) 233 514 966
Internet : www.anse-du-brick.com
Mail : welcome@anse-du-brick.com   Mobil home and chalets to rent

FR50070 Castel Camping Caravaning L'Anse du Brick

Route du Val de Saire, F-50330 Maupertus-sur-Mer (Manche)

A friendly, family site, L'Anse du Brick overlooks a picturesque bay on the northern tip of the Cotentin peninsula, eight kilometres east of Cherbourg Port. This quality site makes a pleasant night halt, or an ideal longer stay destination for those not wishing to travel too far. Its pleasing location offers direct access to a small sandy beach, also to a woodland walk where only the noise of a cascading stream disturbs the peace. Beyond the site lie miles of walking tracks through the gorse-covered hills which, together with a stark rock face, cluster around the site and make it a sheltered sun-trap. This is a mature, terraced site with magnificent sea and hill views from certain pitches. Tarmac roads lead to the 117 touring pitches (all with 10A electricity) which are level, separated and mostly well shaded by the many trees, bushes and shrubs.

Facilities

Two sanitary blocks, although not ultra-modern, are kept spotlessly clean and are well maintained. British-style toilets, washbasins mainly in cubicles and push-button showers, provision for disabled visitors, laundry and dishwashing areas, motorcaravan service point. Heated swimming pool complex (1/5-15/9). Shop (1/4-30/9). Restaurant and popular bar/ pizzeria (1/5-10/9). Tennis court. Play area. Organised entertainment in season. Mini-club for children (6-12 yrs). Bicycle and kayak hire. Off site: Fishing 100 m. Riding 4 km. Golf 10 km. Gourmet restaurant outside campsite gates.

Open

1 April - 30 September.

At a glance

Welcome & Ambience	✓✓✓✓✓	Location	✓✓✓✓
Quality of Pitches	✓✓✓	Range of Facilities	✓✓✓✓

Directions

From Cherbourg port follow directions for Caen and Rennes. After the third roundabout, take slip road to right and under road towards Bretteville-en-Saire (D116). From southeast on N13 at first (Auchan) roundabout, take slip road to right towards Tourlaville (N13 car ferry - route for Poids Lourds), ahead at next roundabout then turn right at third lights onto D116 to Bretteville. Continue for 7 km. and site is signed to right. GPS: N49:40.044 W01:29.293

Charges 2006

Per person	€ 4,00 - € 6,00
child (3-12 yrs)	€ 3,00 - € 4,00
pitch	€ 5,40 - € 14,40
dog	€ 1,90 - € 2,10
electricity (10A)	€ 4,00

Camping Cheques accepted.

Reservations

Advised for July/Aug. Tel: 02 33 54 33 57.
Email: welcome@anse-du-brick.com

Camping Haliotis

Located at 5mn from Mont-Saint-Michel along a river
NORMANDIE

Tel : +33(0)2 33 68 11 59   Fax : +33(0)2 33 58 95 36
info@camping-haliotis-mont-saint-michel.com

SITES & PAYSAGES de FRANCE

Camping Qualité

FR50100 Camping Municipal Le Pont-Roulland

F-50370 Brécey (Manche)

Comfortable and good value, this little site is set in an old orchard of apple and cherry trees and is ideal for a relaxing short break, perhaps before heading further south or west. Various possible outings include Villedieu-les-Poêles (14 km.), Avranches (16 km.) and Mont St Michel (30 km). The 50 numbered tourist pitches are on lush grass, with electric hook-ups (6A) for all, although some may need long leads. The entire site has a slight slope, so motorcaravans will probably need levelling blocks. There is good site lighting and tarmac roads. Although off-ground barbecues are allowed on the pitch, a large communal barbecue is provided in a traditional style 'storehouse'. The guardienne lives on site and reception is open 9.00-22.00 (July/Aug), 17.00-22.00 (low season) – just choose your pitch and pay later if she is not around. The usual small country town hustle and bustle and swimming pool noise during the day gives way to quiet nights after 8 pm.

Facilities

A traditional Normandy stone building houses toilet facilities with modern fittings including British-style toilets, spacious hot showers, some basins in cubicles, dishwashing and laundry sinks, and a washing machine, but no dedicated facilities for disabled visitors. Table tennis. Playground for young children. Off site: Town centre and shops 1 km. Reception issues vouchers for free admission to adjacent municipal swimming pool (June 16.30-19.00, July/Aug 14.00-19.00) and tennis (balls and rackets for hire). Small park with free paddling pool also adjacent. River fishing nearby. Golf 18 km. Beaches 25 km.

Open

1 April - 30 September.

At a glance

Welcome & Ambience	✓✓✓✓	Location	✓✓✓✓
Quality of Pitches	✓✓✓✓	Range of Facilities	✓✓✓

Directions

Brécey is 16 km. east of Avranches. Site is 1 km. east of town centre just off D911. Turn south on D79 towards Les Cresnays (site signed). Site entrance is adjacent to the swimming pool, off a public car park. GPS: N48:43.366 W01:09.154

Charges 2005

Per person	€ 2,35
child (under 7 yrs)	€ 1,20
pitch	€ 2,20
electricity	€ 2,00
dog	€ 0,45

No credit cards.

Reservations

Contact site. Tel: 02 33 48 60 60.
Email: contact@tourisme-brecey.com

FR50080 Camping Haliotis

Chemin des Soupirs, F-50170 Pontorson (Manche)

The Duchesne family have achieved a remarkable transformation of this former municipal site. Situated on the edge of the little town of Pontorson and next to the river Couesnon, Camping Haliotis is within walking, cycling and canoeing distance of Le Mont Saint-Michel. The site has 154 pitches, including 110 for touring units. Most pitches have electricity. A swimming pool with a jacuzzi has been built and there is now a sauna and solarium. There are plans for a covered pool in 2006. The large, comfortable reception area has been developed to incorporate a bar and restaurant. A 'Sites et Paysages' member.

Facilities

Very clean, renovated and well-equipped wash block. Bar and restaurant. No shop or takeaway on site, facilities available in nearby town. Swimming pool with jacuzzi, separate paddling pool. Sauna and solarium. Good fenced play area. Large games room. Free tennis court. Bicycle hire. Free fishing in the River Couesnon. Off site: Local services in Pontorson within walking distance. Riding 5 km. Golf 18 km. Beach 30 km.

Open

1 April - 10 November.

At a glance

Welcome & Ambience	✓✓✓✓✓	Location	✓✓✓✓✓
Quality of Pitches	✓✓✓✓✓	Range of Facilities	✓✓✓✓

Directions

Site is 300 m. from the town centre, west of D976, alongside the river, and is well signed from the town. GPS: N48:33.424 W01:30.67

Charges 2005

Per person	€ 4,20 - € 5,00
child (under 7 yrs)	€ 1,95 - € 2,50
pitch	€ 4,00 - € 4,50
electricity	€ 2,50 - € 3,00
dog	€ 0,50

No credit cards. Camping Cheques accepted.

Reservations

Contact site. Tel: 02 33 68 11 59.
Email: info@camping-haliotis-mont-saint-michel.com

FR50110 Camping Saint Michel

35 route du Mont Saint Michel, F-50220 Courtils (Manche)

This delightful site is owned and run by an enthusiastic young couple, the Duchesnes. It is located in a peaceful, rural setting, yet is only 8 km. from busy tourist attraction of Mont St Michel. From the new restaurant and its terrace overlooking the pool, the site slopes gently down to a small enclosure of farm animals that are kept to entertain children and adults alike. Meet Nestor and Napoléon, the donkeys, Linotte the pony and Dédé and Dedette, the Vietnamese potbellied pigs, as well as miniature goats, sheep, chickens and ducks. The site has 100 pitches which include 36 for touring units and 25 for mobile homes and chalets to rent. Electricity connections (6A) are available and many attractive trees and shrubs provide shade to the pitches. It is M. and Mme. Duschesne's intention to maintain a quiet and peaceful site, hence there are no discos or organised clubs.

Facilities

The modern, well maintained toilet block has washbasins in cubicles and showers. Separate laundry. Facilities for disabled visitors in the new reception building. All is of an excellent standard. Motorcaravan service point. Shop. Bar (1/4-30/9). Restaurant (15/6-10/9). Heated swimming pool (1/5-30/9). Animal farm. Play area. Games room. Bicycle hire. Off site: Fishing 2 km. Riding 3 km.

Open

15 March - 15 October.

At a glance

Welcome & Ambience	✓✓✓✓	Location	✓✓✓
Quality of Pitches	✓✓✓	Range of Facilities	✓✓✓

Directions

From St Malo take the N137 south and join the N176 east to Pontorson where it becomes the N175. In about 20 km. turn northwest on D43 signed Courtils. Site is through the village on the left. GPS: N48:37.657 W01:24.96

Charges 2005

Per person	€ 3,00 - € 5,00
child (0-7 yrs)	€ 1,50 - € 2,00
pitch incl. car	€ 4,00 - € 4,50
electricity (6A)	€ 2,60
dog	€ 1,00

Reservations

Made with deposit (€8 - €15); contact site. Tel: 02 33 70 96 90. Email: info@campingsaintmichel.com

FR50120 Camping Caravaning Aux Pommiers

28 route du Mont St Michel, F-50170 Beauvoir-Mont (Manche)

This is a small, narrow campsite on a busy road. The feel is somewhat rural and basic, although it is situated near to Mont St Michel. If your reason for visiting this area is to see the Mont, then Aux Pommiers would be satisfactory for one or two nights. M. Bigrel, the owner complete with droopy French moustache, maintains the site well. There are 107 pitches, some used for mobile homes and chalets leaving 78 for touring units. Electricity is available on around half. Amenities include a small pool with two slides and a bar with takeaway snacks.

Facilities

One modern, central toilet block provides British style toilets, showers and washbasins in cubicles. Washing machine and dryer in separate building. Small shop. Bar and takeaway (all 1/4-10/9). Small heated swimming pool (15/6-10/9). Minigolf. Play area (on gravel). Small games room. Off site: Fishing 300 m. Riding and bicycle hire 2 km.

Open

20 March - 13 November.

At a glance

Welcome & Ambience	✓✓	Location	✓✓✓
Quality of Pitches	✓✓✓✓	Range of Facilities	✓✓✓

Directions

From Ponterson take D976 north towards Mont St Michel. The campsite is 5 km. well signed on the right.

Charges 2005

Per person	€ 2,75 - € 4,20
child (2-10 yrs)	€ 1,75 - € 2,00
pitch	€ 5,00
electricity	€ 2,00
dog	€ 1,20 - € 2,10

Reservations

Contact site. Tel: 02 33 60 11 36. Email: pommiers@aol.com

FR61010 Camping Municipal La Campière

Bvd. du Docteur Dentu, F-61120 Vimoutiers (Orne)

This small, well kept site is situated in a valley to the north of the town, which is on both the Normandy Cheese and Cider routes. Indeed the town is famous for its cheese and has a Camembert Museum, five minutes walk away in the town centre. The 40 pitches here are flat and grassy, separated by laurel hedging and laid out amongst attractive and well maintained flower and shrub beds. There is some shade around the perimeter and all pitches have electricity.

Facilities
The single central sanitary block is clean and heated, providing open washbasins, good sized, well designed showers, children's toilets and a bathroom for disabled visitors. Dishwashing and laundry facilities under cover. Off site: No shop but a large supermarket is 300 m. Tennis courts and a park are adjacent. Water sports facilities or riding 2 km.

Open
March - October.

At a glance
Welcome & Ambience	✓✓✓✓	Location	✓✓✓✓
Quality of Pitches	✓✓✓✓	Range of Facilities	✓✓✓

Directions
Site is on northern edge of town, signed from main Lisieux-Argentan road next to large sports complex. GPS: N48:55.954 E00:11.805

Charges 2005
Per person	€ 2,30 - € 2,75
child (under 10 yrs)	€ 1,34 - € 1,60
pitch	€ 1,63 - € 1,95
extra car	€ 1,63 - € 1,95
animal	€ 0,92 - € 1,10
electricity	€ 1,63 - € 1,95

Reductions for 7th and subsequent days.

Reservations
Not normally necessary. Tel: 02 33 39 18 86. Email: mairie.vimoutiers@wanadoo.fr

FR61040 Camping Municipal du Champ Passais

F-61700 Domfront (Orne)

Situated on the edge of the old fortified town of Domfront, this small site has 34 individual pitches on a series of level terraces and a separate open grassy area for tents. The nine pitches nearest the entrance are all hardstandings separated by grass and are supplied with a 10A electricity connection. Grass pitches on the lower levels, divided by well tended shrubs and hedges, have a 5A electricity connection and most have water and waste water points. The site is lovingly cared for by an energetic lady warden who keeps everything immaculate and is justifiably proud of the amazing entries in her visitors book.

Facilities
Excellent sanitary facilities, housed in a modern building, include British-style toilets, some washbasins in cubicles, facilities for disabled people, dishwashing and laundry sinks plus a washing machine. No separate chemical waste disposal point, but a notice tells visitors where to empty toilet cassettes. Motorcaravan service point planned. Boules. Play area. Double axle caravans are not accepted under any circumstances; American RVs can be accommodated. Off site: Sports centre adjacent to site. Supermarket, with cheap fuel 800 m. Fishing 1 km.

Open
1 April - 30 September.

At a glance
Welcome & Ambience	✓✓✓✓✓	Location	✓✓✓✓✓
Quality of Pitches	✓✓✓✓✓	Range of Facilities	✓✓✓

Directions
Domfront is on the N176 Alençon-Mont St Michel road and the site is just off this road to the south of the town; it is signed to the right as you climb the hill towards the town centre - or the left as you leave town heading west. GPS: N48:35.491 W00:39.146

Charges 2006
Per unit incl. 1 person	€ 3,70
extra person	€ 2,00
child (under 10 yrs)	€ 1,00
electricity (10A)	€ 3,00
dog	€ 0,60

No credit cards.

Reservations
Not normally necessary. Tel: 02 33 37 37 66. Email: mairie@domfront.com

FR76040 Camping La Source

Petit Appeville, F-76550 Hautot-sur-Mer (Seine-Maritime)

This friendly, attractive, site is just four kilometres from Dieppe and is useful for those using the Newhaven - Dieppe ferry crossing either as a one-night stop-over or for a few days' break before heading on further. The 120 pitches are flat and there is some shade; the site is quietly located in a valley with the only disturbance the occasional passing train. A fast-flowing small river runs along one border (not protected for young children), with opportunities for fishing (including eels), rowing or canoeing. There are hardstandings for motorcaravans and electricity is available. The site is well lit and stays open for late night ferries, although such arrivals are fairly rare and disturbance is minimal.

Facilities

A good, clean single toilet block (men to the left, ladies to the right) includes washbasins in cubicles and mainly British style WCs. Well equipped en-suite unit for disabled people but the unmade gravel roads may cause problems. Dishwashing under cover and laundry. Small bar and terrace (15/3-15/10). Small play field. TV room and room for young people with table tennis and amusement machines. Volleyball, basketball and badminton. Fishing. Bicycle hire. Off site: Riding 2 km. Beach 3 km. Golf 4 km.

Open

15 March - 15 October.

At a glance

Welcome & Ambience	✓✓✓✓	Location	✓✓✓
Quality of Pitches	✓✓✓	Range of Facilities	✓✓✓

Directions

From ferry terminal, follow main exit road (town centre should be avoided) to roundabout and turn west on D925 signposted first Dieppe and then Fécamp. At foot of long descent at traffic lights in Petit Appeville turn left (site is signed). From west, turn right (signed D153 St Aubin and site). Just after passing railway station, turn left under bridge and ahead on narrow road. Site is on left in short distance. GPS: N49:53.925 E01:03.398

Charges 2005

Per person	€ 4,00
child (under 7 yrs)	€ 3,00
caravan	€ 7,00
tent	€ 5,00
car	€ 1,00
motorcaravan	€ 8,00
Camping Cheques accepted.	

Reservations

Write to site Tel: 02 35 84 27 04.

FR76090 Camping Municipal d'Etennemare

Hameau d'Etennemare, F-76460 St Valery-en-Caux (Seine-Maritime)

This comfortable, neat municipal site is two kilometres from the harbour and town, 30 km. west of Dieppe. Quietly located, it has 116 pitches of which 49 are available for touring units. The grassy pitches are all on a slight slope, all with electricity (6A), water and drain, but there is very little shade. Reception is open all day in July and August, but in low season is closed 12.00-15.00 hrs daily and all day Wednesdays: there is a card operated security barrier. The site is close to the municipal sports complex with tennis and football field, and there are shops and restaurants in the bustling town and a Casino, pools and plenty of entertainment along the sea-front.

Facilities

Two modern, clean and well maintained sanitary buildings are side by side, one containing showers and the other, more recently refitted, has toilets, both open and cubicled washbasins and facilities for disabled people. Both blocks can be heated in winter. Dishwashing and laundry sinks. Washing machines. Small shop (July/Aug). Playground. Table tennis Off site: Hypermarket 1.5 km. Harbour and beach (pebbles) 2 km.

Open

All year.

At a glance

Welcome & Ambience	✓✓✓✓	Location	✓✓✓✓
Quality of Pitches	✓✓✓✓	Range of Facilities	✓✓✓

Directions

From Dieppe keep to D925 Fécamp road by-passing town (not D925 through town), at third roundabout turn right on D925E towards town and Leclerc hypermarket. From Fécamp turn left on D925E as before. Take first right almost immediately, signed to campsite which is on left in about 1 km. GPS: N49:51.515 E00:42.279

Charges 2005

Per unit incl. 2 adults and electricity	€ 13,40
extra person	€ 2,75
child (under 10 yrs)	€ 1,75

Reservations

Essential for July/Aug; contact site. Tel: 02 35 97 15 79.

FR76110 Camping Municipal Les Boucaniers

Rue Pierre Mendès France, F-76470 Le Tréport (Seine-Maritime)

This large, good quality, municipal site has an attractive entrance and some floral displays, tarmac roads and site lighting. The 300 pitches are on level grass, some with dividing hedges, and a variety of trees to provide a little shade. There are 22 good quality wooden chalets for rent, and some privately owned mobile homes, which leaves around 262 pitches for tourists, all with electric hook-ups (6A). A small unit acts as shop, bar and takeaway and operates all season, the baker calls daily in high season, and every day except Monday in low season. The town centre is within walking distance with a choice of many good seafood restaurants.

Facilities

Three well equipped sanitary blocks (one can be heated) provide mainly British style WCs, washbasins in cubicles, pre-set hot showers, with facilities for small children and disabled persons in one block. Multi-sport court. Minigolf. Boules. Off site: Tennis, football and gymnasium nearby. Fishing, golf and beach 2 km. Riding 3 km. Markets at Le Tréport (Mon and Sat) and at Eu (Fri).

Open

Easter weekend - 30 September.

At a glance

Welcome & Ambience	✓✓✓✓	Location	✓✓✓✓
Quality of Pitches	✓✓✓✓	Range of Facilities	✓✓✓

Directions

Site is just north of the D925 Abbeville - Dieppe road; take D1915 towards Le Tréport town centre, (from Dieppe, at second roundabout) and at first set of traffic lights on a multi-way junction, turn right into Rue Pierre Mendès-France. Site is on that corner and the entrance is immediately on right (not signed from main road). GPS: N50:03.463 E01:23.322

Charges 2005

Per person	€ 2,70 - € 2,85
child (2-10 yrs)	€ 1,56 - € 1,65
pitch	€ 2,61 - € 2,75
with electricity	€ 6,30 - € 6,65

Reservations

Contact site. Tel: 02 35 86 35 47.
Email: ville.le.treport@wanadoo.fr

FR76100 Camping Municipal Cany-Barville

F-76450 Cany-Barville (Seine-Maritime)

This good quality site, first opened in 1997 next to the municipal sports stadium, has a floral entrance and tarmac roads. Of the 100 individual hedged pitches 75 are available for tourists. There are around 40 concrete hardstandings (awnings can be a problem) and the remainder are on grass: all are fully serviced with water, drain and electric hook-ups (10A). Shade from recently-planted specimen trees is still very limited. Cany-Barville is a bustling small town with a traditional Normandy market on Monday mornings. There is a Château and an Eco-museum (1/4-30/10), and the Durdent valley has numerous other châteaux, mills, churches and 'colombiers'.

Facilities

The modern, centrally located, sanitary unit can be heated and has British-style toilets, controllable showers and washbasins in cubicles. Dishwashing and laundry sinks. Copious hot water. Separate suites for disabled people. Drive-over motorcaravan service point with chemical disposal facility. Table tennis, volleyball, boules. Games room with pin-ball machine and ski-simulator. Off site: Bakery, restaurants 600 m. Supermarket 1 km. Sailing and windsurfing centre 2 km. Beach 10 km.

Open

1 April - 1 October.

At a glance

Welcome & Ambience	✓✓✓✓	Location	✓✓✓✓
Quality of Pitches	✓✓✓✓	Range of Facilities	✓✓✓

Directions

Cany-Barville is 20 km. east of Fécamp on D925 to Dieppe. From traffic lights on eastern side of town turn south on D268 towards Yvetot. Go under railway arch and site is 600 m. from town centre on right, just after sports stadium. GPS: N49:46.990 E00:38.546

Charges 2005

Per person	€ 2,80
child (under 14 yrs)	€ 1,15
pitch	€ 1,85 - € 2,80
electricity (10A)	€ 2,80
animal	€ 0,95

Reservations

Advisable in July and August. Tel: 02 35 97 70 37.

FR76120 Camping Municipal Veulettes-sur-Mer

8 rue de Greenock, F-76450 Veulettes-sur-Mer (Seine-Maritime)

A good value, well kept municipal site in an attractive little coastal town, just 500 m. from the beach and all town services. There are 116 marked pitches on open level grass, 40 of which are seasonal pitches, which leaves 76 pitches for tourists, all with electric hook-ups, water and waste water drain. Reception keeps soft drinks and ices during July/August. Also on site is an attractive 'salle' with a library and TV, a games area with electronic game, table tennis, babyfoot and further toilet facilities.

Facilities

Three good modern sanitary units in traditional style buildings are of varying ages (one can be heated). These provide pre-set hot showers, washbasins in cubicles, and facilities for disabled people in the smallest unit on the far side of the site. Laundry room. Playground. Boules. TV, library and table tennis. Off site: Public park with tennis courts and large playground, beach (pebble), watersports centre and all shops and services are within 500 m.

Open

1 April - 31 October.

At a glance

Welcome & Ambience	✓✓✓✓	Location	✓✓✓✓
Quality of Pitches	✓✓✓✓	Range of Facilities	✓✓✓

Directions

Veulettes-sur-Mer is on the coast approx. 45 km. west of Dieppe. Site is central in town, lying about 500 m. back from the main promenade (signed).
GPS: N49:50.967 E00:35.791

Charges 2005

per person	€ 2,60
child (4-10 yrs)	€ 1,30
pitch	€ 2,25
car	€ 1,05
electricity (10A)	€ 2,60
animal	€ 0,50

Reservations

Contact site. Tel: 02 35 97 53 44.

FR76130 Camping de la Forêt

Rue Mainberthe, F-76480 Jumieges (Seine-Maritime)

This is a pretty family site with a friendly laid back atmosphere. It is located just 10 km. from the A13 Paris - Caen autoroute, and is best accessed by ferry across the River Seine. The great abbey at Jumieges was founded in 654 by St Philibert, rebuilt by the Normans and consecrated in the presence of William the Conqueror – well worth a visit! The site was formerly a municipal and has recently been taken on by the Joret family. The 111 grassy pitches (94 for tourers) are attractively located in woodland. Many pitches have some shade and all have 10A electrical connections. There is a separate area for tents. A good range of shops, cafes, restaurants etc. can be found in Jumieges, just 600 m. away. The site organises some activities in high season and these include treasure hunts and guided walks.

Facilities

Two toilet blocks, both of modern construction and maintained to a good standard with British toilets, some basins in cubicles and pre-set showers. Baby room. Facilities for disabled visitors. Washing and drying machines. Shop. Baker calls daily and pizzas are available on Friday and Saturday evenings 18.30 hrs. Small swimming pool and children's pool (heated 15/6-15/9). Playground. Boules court. Games room with TV. Cycle hire. Motorcaravan service point. Chalets and mobile homes to let.
Off site: Village 600 m.

Open

2 April - 30 October.

At a glance

Welcome & Ambience	✓✓✓✓	Location	✓✓✓✓
Quality of Pitches	✓✓✓✓	Range of Facilities	✓✓✓✓

Directions

Jumieges is 10 km. north of the A13 autoroute (Bourg-Achard exit). Take D313 towards Caudebec-en-Caux. Then, either take the ferry across the Seine (toll) from Heurtauville to Jumieges, or continue over the Pont de Brotonne and back on D982 to Jumieges. Site is clearly signed. GPS: N49:26.092 E00:49.738

Charges 2005

Per unit incl. 2 persons	€ 14,00 - € 16,00
extra person	€ 3,60 - € 4,00
electricity	€ 2,70

Reduced charges in low season.
Camping Cheques accepted.

Reservations

Contact site. Tel: 02 35 37 93 43.
Email: info@campinglaforet.com

MAP 3

Northern France, with its lush countryside and market towns, is much more than just a stop off en-route to or from the ports. The peaceful rural unspoilt charms of the region provide a real breath of fresh air.

NORD/PAS DE CALAIS: 59 NORD, 62 PAS-DE-CALAIS
MAJOR CITY: LILLE

PICARDY: 02 AISNE, 60 OISE, 80 SOMME
MAJOR CITY: AMIENS

This is a region where centuries of invaders have left their mark. At Vimy Ridge near Arras, World War One trenches have been preserved intact, a most poignant sight. Elsewhere almost every village between Arras and Amiens has its memorial. It is also the birthplace of Gothic architecture with six cathedrals, including Laon, Beauvais and Amiens, arguably the grandest in France.

The area however is predominately rural. Inland and south are long vistas of rolling farmland broken by little rivers and well scattered with pockets of forest woodland. The coastline is characterised by sandy beaches, shifting dunes and ports. It is a quiet and sparsely populated area with peaceful villages and churches that provide evidence of the glorious achievements of French Gothic architecture. Boulogne is home to Nausicaa, the world's largest sea-life centre and from Cap Griz-Nez you may be able to see the White Cliffs of Dover. There are also many huge hypermarkets where you may stock up on wine, beer and cheese.

Places of interest

Amiens: Notre Dame cathedral, monument to 1918 Battle of the Somme.

Chantilly: Château of Chantilly with a 17th century stable with a 'live' Horse museum.

Compiègne: Seven miles east of the town is Clairière de l'Armistice. The railway coach here is a replica of the one in which the 1918 Armistice was signed and in which Hitler received the French surrender in 1942.

Laon: 12th century cathedral, WW1 trenches, Vauclair Abbey.

Marquenterre: one of Europe's most important bird sanctuaries.

Cuisine of the region

Carbonnade de Boeuf à la Flamande: braised beef with beer, onions and bacon.

Caudière (Chaudière, Caudrée): versions of fish and potato soup.

Ficelles Picardes: ham pancakes with mushroom sauce.

Flamiche aux poireaux: puff pastry tart with cream and leeks.

Hochepot: a thick Flemish soup with virtually everything in it but the kitchen sink.

Soupe courquignoise: soup with white wine, fish, moules, leeks and Gruyère cheese.

Tarte aux Maroilles: a hot creamy tart based on Maroilles cheese.

Waterzooï: a cross between soup and stew, usually of fish or chicken.

FR02000 Camping Caravaning du Vivier aux Carpes

10 rue Charles Voyeux, F-02790 Seraucourt-le-Grand (Aisne)

Vivier aux Carpes is a small quiet site, close to the A26, two hours from Calais, so it is ideal for an overnight stop but is also worthy of a longer stay. A neat, purpose designed site is imaginatively set out taking full benefit of large ponds which are well stocked for fishing. There is also abundant wild life. The 60 well spaced pitches, are at least 100 sq.m. on flat grass with dividing hedges. The 45 for touring units all have electricity (6A), some also with water points, and there are special pitches for motorcaravans. This peaceful site has a comfortable feel and is close to the village centre. The enthusiastic owners and the manager speak excellent English and are keen to welcome British visitors. Although there is no restaurant on site, good and reasonable hotels are close. The cathedral cities of St Quentin, Reims, Amiens and Laon are close, Disneyland just over an hour away, Compiegne and the WW1 battlefields are near and Paris easily reached by train (1 hr 15 mins from St Quentin). This site is good for couples or fishing enthusiasts.

Facilities

The spacious, clean toilet block has separate, heated facilities for disabled visitors, which are made available to other campers in the winter months. Laundry facilities. Motorcaravan service point (fresh water for large vans is charged). Above the toilet block is a large TV/games room with table tennis and snooker. Small play area. Bicycle hire. Petanque. Fishing (about € 5.50 p/day). Gates close 22.00 hrs, office open 09.00-21.30. Rallies welcome. Off site: Village has post office, doctor, chemist and small supermarket. Riding 500 m. Golf 12 km.

Open

1 March - 30 October.

At a glance

| Welcome & Ambience | ✓✓✓✓ | Location | ✓✓✓✓ |
| Quality of Pitches | ✓✓✓✓ | Range of Facilities | ✓✓✓ |

Directions

Leave A26 (Calais - Reims) road at exit 11 and take D1 left towards Soissons for 4 km. Take D8 and on entering Essigny-la-Grand (4 km.) turn sharp right on D72 signed Seraucourt-le-Grand (5 km). Site is clearly signed - it is in the centre of the village. GPS: N49:46.915 E03:12.850

Charges 2006

Per unit incl. 2 persons and electricity	€ 16,50
extra person	€ 3,50
child (under 10 yrs)	€ 2,50
pet	€ 0,60

Monthly, weekly or weekend rates available. Discounts for students with tents. No credit cards.

Reservations

Advised for peak season. Tel: 03 23 60 50 10. Email: camping.du.vivier@wanadoo.fr

FR02030 Caravaning La Croix du Vieux Pont

F-02290 Berny-Riviere (Aisne)

Attractively located on the banks of the River Aisne, La Croix du Vieux Pont is a very smart, modern site offering a high standard of facilities. Many pitches are occupied by mobile homes and tour operator tents, but there are 52 pleasant touring pitches, some on the banks of the Aisne. The 34 hectare site is maintained to a high standard with some excellent amenities, notably four heated swimming pools, one indoors with a waterslide and jacuzzi. There are two tennis courts, an amusement arcade and volleyball court. At the heart of the site is a well-stocked fishing lake which is also used for pedaloes and canoes.

Facilities

The six toilet blocks are modern and kept very clean, with washbasins in cabins and free hot showers. Washing and drying machines. Facilities for disabled visitors. Large supermarket. Bar, takeaway and good value restaurant (most amenities 1/4-30/9). Swimming pool complex (covered pool 1/4-30/10, outdoor 1/5-30/9). Play area. Fishing. Bicycle hire. Coach trips organised on a regular basis to Paris, Parc Asterix and Disneyland. Appartments to let. Dogs are not accepted. Off site: Riding 100 m. Golf 30 km.

Open

8 April - 31 October.

At a glance

| Welcome & Ambience | ✓✓✓✓ | Location | ✓✓✓✓ |
| Quality of Pitches | ✓✓✓✓✓ | Range of Facilities | ✓✓✓✓✓ |

Directions

From Compiegne take N31 towards Soissons. At Vic-sur-Aisne turn right, towards Berny-Riviere and site is on right after 400 m. GPS: N49:24.292 E03:07.704

Charges 2005

| Oer unit incl. 2 persons and electricity | € 19,00 - € 21,50 |
| incl. 4 persons | € 27,00 - € 29,50 |

Camping Cheques accepted.

Reservations

Essential for high season and made with deposit (€ 40). Tel: 03 23 55 50 02. Email: info@la-croix-du-vieux-pont.com

FR02060 Camping Municipal Guignicourt

14 bis rue Godins, F-02190 Guignicourt (Aisne)

This very pleasant little municipal site has 100 pitches, 50 for long stay units and 50 for tourists. These two sections are separated by the main facilities on a higher terrace. Pitches are generally large and level, although you might need an extra long electricity lead for some, but there are few dividing hedges. Pitches along the river bank have most shade, with a few specimen trees providing a little shade to some of the more open pitches. The town is quite attractive and is worthy of an evening stroll. At the junction of the N44 and D925, 7 km. west of the town, is the Chemin des Dames, Monument des Chars d'Assaut - a memorial to the WW1 tank campaign at Berry-au-Bac, with two remarkably well preserved tanks. Further to the west is the Caverne du Dragon, a former stone quarry which sheltered troops during the 1914-18 conflict, which is now a museum depicting everyday life on the front line. You may notice a low level hum from the nearby Generale Sucrière factory, a major industry of the town, but you may also hear the site's nightingales.

Facilities

The modern sanitary unit has British and Turkish style toilets, washbasins (cold only except for the one in a cubicle), push-button hot showers, dishwashing and laundry sinks. Bar (1/4-30/9). Playground. Tennis and boules courts. Fishing. Off site: The town has all services including a supermarket and bank. Golf 3km. Beach 15 km.

Open

1 April - 30 September.

At a glance

| Welcome & Ambience | ✓✓✓✓ | Location | ✓✓✓✓ |
| Quality of Pitches | ✓✓✓✓ | Range of Facilities | ✓✓✓ |

Directions

Guignicourt is about 20 km. north of Reims, just east of the A26, junction 14. The site is well signed from D925 in the village. GPS: N49:25.922 E03:58.223

Charges guide

Per adult	€ 2,00
child (2-10 yrs)	€ 1,20
pitch incl. electricity (6/10A)	€ 7,80 - € 15,60
animal	€ 1,00

Reservations

Contact site. Tel: 03 23 79 74 58.
Email: camping.guignicourt@free.fr

FR59010 Camping Caravaning La Chaumière

529 Langhemast Straete, F-59285 Buysscheure (Nord)

This is a very friendly, pleasant site, tucked away in the département du Nord with a strong Flanders influence, well worth considering for those using the local Channel crossings. There is a real welcome here and the owners, Guy and Bernadette, are much liked by the regular British visitors. Set just behind the village of Buysscheure (with a shop and two cafés), the site has just 22 individual pitches separated by young trees and bushes. With 16 for touring units, mostly quite large and with some slope, they are on grass with a gravel hardstanding area for the car. Access from narrow site roads can sometimes be difficult. Each pair of pitches shares a brick-built unit, decorated with flowers, incorporating a light, electricity connections, water points and rubbish container. A small, fenced fishing lake contains some large carp (seen!) and the ducks will help you eat your baguettes. A bonus is that Bernadette works for the local vet and can arrange all the documentation for British visitors' pets. English is spoken.

Facilities

Although modern, the unisex toilet facilities are simple and small in number, with two WCs, one shower and one washbasin cabin. Facilities provided for disabled visitors may also be used (a toilet and separate washbasin/shower room). Dishwashing room. Laundry room. Motorcaravan services. Very basic chemical disposal. Bar (daily) and restaurant (weekends only, all day, all season). Dog exercise area - with jumps etc. Small heated pool planned. Off site: Interesting local market (Monday) at Bergues. St Omer is an interesting old town. This is a popular area for cycling. Shop and café/restaurants in the village. Beach 30 km.

Open

1 April - 31 October.

At a glance

| Welcome & Ambience | ✓✓✓✓✓ | Location | ✓✓✓✓ |
| Quality of Pitches | ✓✓✓ | Range of Facilities | ✓✓✓✓ |

Directions

From Calais take N43 towards St Omer for 25 km. Just beyond Nordausques take D221 left to Watten. In Watten turn left for the centre, then right onto D26 towards Cassel. Soon after Lederzeele the site is signed to the right (just before railway bridge). On reaching Buysscheure turn left and then right from where the site is signed again. Single track road to site (1 km.) with bend.

Charges guide

Per unit incl. 2 persons and electricity	€ 14,00
extra person	€ 7,00
child (under 7 yrs)	€ 3,50
dog	€ 1,00

No credit cards.

Reservations

Contact site. Tel: 03 28 43 03 57.
Email: camping.LaChaumiere@wanadoo.fr

FR62060 Caravaning L'Orée du Bois

Chemin Blanc, F-62180 Rang-du-Fliers (Pas-de-Calais)

This fairly peaceful but extensive campsite is in a natural woodland setting, and only 3 km. from a large sandy beach. From reception you pass through a corner of the mobile home (privately owned) section, then through an area of natural, preserved woodland which separates the touring area. This has 80 individual, touring pitches, all with shade and electric hook-ups. On sandy grass which can be slightly undulating, most are separated by hedges and bushes, but the emphasis is on 'nature'. Also on the touring site are 67 wooden camping lodges. A separate clearing in the woodland is reserved for tents, and useful for cyclists or backpackers is 'Camp Sherpa' comprising eight 2-berth wooden tents. A modern sanitary unit is central in the touring area, with a second smaller unit in the mobile homes area, useful when walking between your pitch and the bar/brasserie with takeaway, tennis courts, pétanque etc. Berck Plage is only 3 km. and has a magnificent sandy beach and promenade, with extensive free parking areas, with many bays for disabled motorists. Indeed the site and the area are well suited to disabled visitors of all ages.

Facilities

Modern facilities with open and cubicle washbasins, controllable hot showers, a laundry with washing machines and dryer, and good facilities for disabled persons (with low level dishwashing and laundry sinks), small children and babies. Note: water for the toilets is obtained from a borehole, and has a slight brownish colour. Basic motorcaravan service point by reception, with a full service area located close to the nearby Intermarché. Bar/brasserie (30/3-20/10). Animation and dancing in July/Aug. Multi-court tennis. Several playgrounds. The woodland area conceals a football field, volleyball, a fitness trail, a course for quads and all terrain bikes, and a fishing lake. Off site: Small supermarket adjacent, large Intermarché complex 700 m. Sports centre at Berck-Plage. Also close by is Le Parc de Bagatelle, the largest amusement park in northern France. Beach 3 km. Cycle hire 2 km. Riding 1.5 km. Boat launching 3 km. Golf 8 km. Market in Berck-Plage Tues/Wed/Thurs/Sat/Sun, and in Rang du Fliers Thursday.

Open

30 March - 20 October.

At a glance

Welcome & Ambience	✓✓✓✓	Location	✓✓✓✓
Quality of Pitches	✓✓✓	Range of Facilities	✓✓✓✓

Directions

Rang du Fliers is just east of Berck Plage and about 15 km. south of Le Touquet. From Berck Plage take D917 east to roundabout by Intermarché supermarket, turn left (north) at next roundabout (site signed), site entrance is 500 m. on left. From A16 exit 25, follow D917 towards Berck Plage. After four roundabouts, a railway crossing, and two more roundabouts, turn right at the seventh roundabout (site signed), site entrance is 500 m. on left. GPS: N50:25.024 E01:36.694

Charges 2005

Per unit incl. 2 persons	
and electricity	€ 15,00 - € 21,00
extra person	€ 4,00 - € 5,50
child (3-7 yrs)	€ 3,00 - € 3,50
animal	€ 2,00

Discounts for stays of 14 days.
Barrier card deposit € 50.

Reservations

Essential for July/Aug, and advisable at other times. Made with deposit of 25% of total fees. Tel: 03 21 84 28 51. Email: oree.du.bois@wanadoo.fr

FR59050 Camp Municipal du Clair de Lune

Route de Mons, F-59600 Maubeuge (Nord)

This is an attractive site convenient for a night-stop or for longer stays close to the RN2 road. It is a neat and tidy municipal site with 92 marked pitches of fair size. Mainly on level ground and separated by trim hedges, most have electrical connections (6 or 10A) and some have hardstanding. A variety of broadleaf trees provides shade when needed. When inspected, reception staff were friendly and helpful. Although there are few amenities on the site, the interesting town centre of Maubeuge itself is only about 1 km.

Facilities

Two circular sanitary blocks provide good modern facilities. Dishwashing sinks under cover and washing machines. The block used in winter can be heated. Motorcaravan service point. Small adventure-style playground. Fishing. Off site: Riding and bicycle hire 2 km. Golf 2.5 km.

Open

All year.

At a glance

Welcome & Ambience	✓✓✓✓	Location	✓✓✓✓
Quality of Pitches	✓✓✓✓	Range of Facilities	✓✓✓

Directions

Site is on the RN2 road (known as the N6 in Belgium) north of the town, on the right going towards Mons.

Charges guide

Per person	€ 3,05
child (4-7 yrs)	€ 2,15
pitch	€ 3,05
electricity (3/10A)	€ 4,15 - € 5,03
dog	free

Reservations

Not normally made or necessary, but if in doubt telephone site. Tel: 03 27 62 25 48.

FR62050 Camping Caravaning St Louis

Rue Leulène, F-62610 Autingues par Ardres (Pas-de-Calais)

Convenient for the ferry port at Calais, this is a peaceful little site with 84 pitches. Many are taken by privately owned holiday homes, but there are around 25 pitches for tourists. In a garden-like setting, they are individual and grassy with some shade. Electricity hook-ups are available for all. In high season the site is usually full by 17.00 hrs, so arrive early.

Facilities

Rather old but clean and tidy unisex toilet facilities which provide showers on payment (€ 1 token) and washbasins mostly in cubicles. Facilities for disabled people. Baby room. Dishwashing and laundry sinks, washing machine. Motorcaravan service point free to campers (€ 4 for non-residents). Snack bar and takeaway open all season. Playground. Games room with table football, table tennis. Off site: Beach 20 km.

Open

1 April - 31 October.

At a glance

Welcome & Ambience	✓✓✓	Location	✓✓✓✓
Quality of Pitches	✓✓✓✓	Range of Facilities	✓✓✓

Directions

From Calais take N43 towards St Omer for 15 km, and just east of Ardres, turn south on D224, where site is signed.

Charges 2005

Per unit incl. 2 persons and electricity	€ 17,00
extra person	€ 3,00
child (2-7 yrs)	€ 1,50
tent pitch inlc 2 persons	€ 10,00

Reservations

Advised for high season. Tel: 03 21 35 46 83. Email: domirine@aol.com

FR62010 Castel Camping Caravaning La Bien-Assise

D231, F-62340 Guines (Pas-de-Calais)

A mature and well developed site, the history of La Bien-Assise goes back to the 1500s. The château, farm and mill now form the focal point for this popular campsite which is under new ownership. The farm buildings house the facilities and pool complex, with the entrance to a more formal and excellent restaurant, 'La Ferme Gourmande' in the mellow farmyard opposite the dovecote. There are 220 grass pitches mainly set among mature trees with others on a newer field. Connected by gravel roads and of a good size (up to 300 sq.m), shrubs and bushes divide most of the pitches. The site's position, 15 minutes from Calais, the Channel Tunnel exit 6 km. and 20 minutes from Boulogne, make it a good stopping point en-route north or south, but it is well worth a longer stay. Reception opens for long hours to meet the needs of those crossing the Channel and the site can have heavy usage at times (when maintenance can be variable). Used by tour operators (50 pitches).

Facilities

Three well equipped toilet blocks provide many washbasins in cabins, mostly British style WCs and provision for babies, laundry and dishwashing. The main block is in four sections, two unisex. Motorcaravan service point. Shop. Restaurant. Bar/grill and takeaway (evenings from 1/5). TV room. Pool complex (11/5-20/9) with a fun pool/toboggan, covered paddling pool and outdoor pool with sliding roof to suit all weather conditions. Play areas. Minigolf. Tennis court. Bicycle hire. Off site: Local market and walks from the site. Fishing 8 km. Riding 10 km. Beach 9 km.

Open

25 April - 20 September.

At a glance

Welcome & Ambience	✓✓✓✓	Location	✓✓✓✓
Quality of Pitches	✓✓✓✓	Range of Facilities	✓✓✓✓

Directions

From the ferry or the tunnel follow signs for A16 Boulogne. Take exit 40 (Frethun, Gare TGV) and take the RD215 towards Frethun. At the first roundabout take the third exit for Guines. Pass under the TGV. In Frethun take the RD246 towards Guines and St Tricat and at roundabout take exit for Guines. Pass through St Tricat and Hames Boucres, and in Guines follow signs for site turning right towards Marquise for 120 m.

Charges 2006

Per adult	€ 3,40 - € 5,40
child (under 9 yrs)	€ 2,00 - € 4,00
pitch	€ 8,00 - € 14,00
electricity (6A)	€ 3,00 - € 4,00
dog	€ 1,00 - € 2,00
Less 10% in low seasons	

Reservations

Advised for July/Aug. or if arriving late in the evening. Made for any length with deposit (€ 39) and fee (€ 7.62) for stays 5 days or more. Tel: 03 21 35 20 77. Email: castel@bien-assise.com

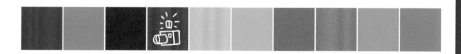

FR62030 Camping Château du Gandspette

F-62910 Eperlecques (Pas-de-Calais)

This friendly, comfortable, family run site is in the grounds of the Château du Gandspette. It is conveniently situated for the channel ports and tunnel, providing useful overnight accommodation and a range of facilities for a longer stay. The 17th century building adjacent to the château now houses an attractive bar/restaurant. A gravel road gives access to three different camping areas and a central open space. There are 170 pitches (100 or 150 sq.m), of which 55 are taken by semi-permanent French holiday caravans which intermix with some of the touring pitches giving a real French ambience. All pitches have electricity and are delineated by trees and some hedging. Mature trees form the perimeter of the site, through which there is access to woodland walks. Used by tour operators (10 pitches), and there are also 8 site owned rental mobile homes. A 'Sites et Paysages' member.

Facilities

A partially renovated sanitary block provides satisfactory facilities with a mixture of open and cubicled washbasins in the older part of the site. The newer area is now served by a stylish modern unit which also contains facilities for disabled people and a baby changing area. Covered dishwashing sinks. Washing machines and dryers. Good motorcaravan service point. Bar, grill restaurant and takeaway (all 15/5-15/9). Two swimming pools, one large and one smaller (15/5-30/9). Adventure style playground, and play field. Tennis, petanque and a children's room with table tennis and electronic games. Entertainment is organised in season. Off site: Fishing 3 km. Riding and golf 5 km. Beach 30 km. Bicycle hire 9 km. Small supermarket in village 1 km. Market Watten (Friday) and St Omer (Saturday). The WW2 'Blockhaus' nearby is worthy of a visit, as is La Coupole at St Omer which also dates from WW2 and is equally fascinating.

At a glance

Welcome & Ambience	✓✓✓✓	Location	✓✓✓✓
Quality of Pitches	✓✓✓✓	Range of Facilities	✓✓✓✓

Directions

From Calais follow N43 towards St Omer for 25 km. Southeast of Nordausques take D221 (east) and follow camp signs for 5-6 km. From St Omer follow N43 to roundabout at junction with D600. Turn right onto D600 towards Dunkirk and after 5 km. turn left on D221. Site is 1.5 km. on right.
GPS: N50:49.137 E02:10.740

Charges 2006

Per unit incl. 2 persons	€ 16,00 - € 22,00
extra person (over 6 yrs)	€ 5,00 - € 6,00
electricity (6A)	€ 4,00
child (3-6yrs)	€ 3,00 - € 4,00
animal	€ 1,00

Camping Cheques accepted.

Reservations

Necessary for July/Aug - write to site.
Tel: 03 21 93 43 93.
Email: contact@chateau-gandspette.com

Open

1 April - 30 September.

FR80090 Camping Caravaning Le Val d'Authie

20 route de Vercourt, F-80120 Villers-sur-Authie (Somme)

In a village location, this well organised site is fairly close to several beaches, but also has its own excellent pool complex, small restaurant and bar. The owner has carefully controlled the size of the site, leaving space for a leisure area. An indoor pool is planned for 2006. There are 170 pitches in total, but with many holiday homes and chalets, there are only 60 for touring units. These are on grass, some are divided by small hedges, with 3 or 6A electric hook-ups, and 15 have full services. Ideas for excursions include the 15/16th century chapel and hospice and the Aviation Museum at Rue, a pottery at nearby Roussent, a flour mill at Maintenay, and the steam railway which runs from Le Crotoy to Cayeux-sur-Mer around the Baie de Somme. A 'Sites et Paysages' member.

Facilities

Good modern toilet facilities include some shower and washbasin units, washbasins in cubicles, and limited facilities for disabled people and babies. Facilities may be under pressure in high season and a reader reports poor cleaning at that time. Ice pack service. Shop for basics (not in October). Bar/restaurant serving good value meals (1/5-15/9; hours vary according to season). Swimming pool with small jacuzzi and paddling pool (1/5-15/9, with lifeguards in July/Aug). Indoor pool planned. Good playground for small children, club room with TV, and weekend entertainment in season (discos may be noisy until late). Multi-court, beach volleyball, football, boules and tennis court (all free). Fitness trail and running track, mountain bike circuit, and plenty of good paths for evening strolls.

Open

1 April - 31 October.

At a glance

Welcome & Ambience	✓✓✓✓	Location	✓✓✓✓
Quality of Pitches	✓✓✓✓	Range of Facilities	✓✓✓✓

Directions

Villers-sur-Authie is about 25 km. NNW of Abbéville. From A16 junction 24 take N1 to Vron, then left on D175 to Villers-sur-Authie. Alternatively use D85 from Rue, or D485 from Nampont St Martin. Site is at southern end of village at junction of minor road (easy to miss if coming from Nampont).
GPS: N50:18.815 E01:41.729

Charges 2006

Per person	€ 6,00
child (under 7 yrs)	€ 3,00
pitch	€ 5,50
electricity (4-10A)	€ 4,00 - € 8,00
animal	€ 1,50

Camping Cheques accepted.

Reservations

Advisable for high season, peak weekends and B.Hs.
Tel: 03 22 29 92 47. Email: camping@valdauthie.fr

FR80040 Camping Le Royon

1271 route de Quend, F-80120 Fort-Mahon-Plage (Somme)

This busy family run site, some two kilometres from the sea, has 300 pitches of which 100 are used for touring units. Of either 95 or 120 sq.m, the marked and numbered pitches are divided by hedges and arranged either side of access roads. Electricity (6A) and water points are available to all. The site is well lit, fenced and guarded at night (€ 30 deposit for barrier card). Entertainment is organised for adults and children in July/Aug. The site is close to the Baie de l'Authie which is an area noted for migrating birds.

Facilities

Four toilet blocks provide mostly unisex facilities with British or Turkish style WCs and some washbasins in cubicles. Units for disabled people. Baby baths. Dishwashing and laundry sinks under cover. Small shop (all season). Mobile takeaway calls each evening in July/Aug. Friendly clubroom and bar sells bread and has the usual games machines. Attractive, heated, covered pool (16 x 8 m; 1/5-10/9) with open air children's pool and sun terrace. Playground. Table tennis, multi-court, tennis court and boules. Bicycle hire. Off site: Fishing, riding or golf within 1 km. Windsurfing, sailing, sand yachting, canoeing, swimming, climbing and shooting nearby. Cinema, disco and casino near.

At a glance

Welcome & Ambience	√√√	Location	√√√√
Quality of Pitches	√√√	Range of Facilities	√√√√

Directions

Site is on outskirts of Fort Mahon Plage, on D32 from Quend which is on the D940 Berck - Le Tréport road. GPS: N50:19.98 E01:34.811

Charges 2005

Per pitch 95 sq.m. incl. caravan, car, water tap, electricity (6A) and 3 persons	€ 17,00 - € 26,00

Reservations

Essential for July/Aug; made with deposit (€ 40 p/week) and fee (€ 10). Tel: 03 22 23 40 30. Email: info@campingleroyon.com

Open

7 March - 1 November.

17 € PRIVILEGE CAMPING TICKET 17 €

Present this Privilege Camping Ticket at reception and you will only pay 17 Euros per night for a pitch with electricity up to 3 people

Offer valid for year 2006, except in July and August

SUGGESTED BY AIROTEL CAMPING LE ROYON
Camping Qualité Picardie**** - 1271 Route de Quend - 80120 Fort-Mahon Plage
Tel: (33)3 22 23 40 30 - Fax (33)3 22 23 65 15 - www.campingleroyon.com

FR80030 Camping du Port de Plaisance

Route de Paris, F-80200 Péronne (Somme)

Run by a non-profit making association under the auspices of the Chamber of Commerce, this is a good quality site. Formerly a municipal site, it is informally laid out beside the Canal du Nord on the outskirts of the small town of Peronne, on the river Somme. The associations with the Great War are strong and the WW1 battlefields and cemeteries are numerous in this area. Only some two or three hours drive from the Channel ports and Tunnel, Peronne is convenient for overnight stops en-route to or from further south or east. The site itself is attractive, being surrounded by trees, with 90 marked pitches (87 have 6/10A electricity hook-up) of varying shapes and sizes on mainly level grass, some being seasonal.

Facilities

The modernised toilet block is kept spotlessly clean, well maintained and heated in winter. Excellent provision for people with disabilities. Laundry area with washing machine and dryer. Motorcaravan service point. New reception building includes a small shop (1/5-31/8), bar and TV room (bread orders are taken). Attractive swimming pool (June-Sept). Play area. Fishing. Off site: Bicycle hire 2 km. Riding 10 km.

Open

1 March - 31 October.

At a glance

Welcome & Ambience	√√√√	Location	√√√√
Quality of Pitches	√√√√	Range of Facilities	√√√√

Directions

From north on the A1 autoroute, take exit 14 and follow N17 south to Peronne. Take signs for town centre and continue through looking for camp signs. Pass over river Somme and Canal du Nord and site is on right just past garage at Porte du Plaisance (2 km. from town centre). Alternatively use exit 13. From south use exit 13 and RN29 to Villers Carbonnel to pick up the N17 going north. Look for signs on left after traffic lights. GPS: N49:55.078 E02:55.975

Charges 2005

Per unit incl. 1-3 persons	€ 13,10 - € 19,50
extra person	€ 3,30 - € 4,20
electricity (6/10A)	€ 4,00 - € 5,95

Reservations

May be necessary in main season; contact site. Tel: 03 22 84 19 31. Email: contact@camping-plaisance.com

Camping le Château de Drancourt

Camping le Château de Drancourt - BP 80022, 80230 St. Valéry-sur-Somme
Tel.: (33) 3 22 26 93 45 - Fax: (33) 3 22 26 85 87 - E-mail: chateau.drancourt@wanadoo.fr
www.chateau-drancourt.com

FR80010 Castel Camping Le Château de Drancourt

B.P. 22, F-80230 St Valéry-sur-Somme (Somme)

A popular, busy and lively holiday site within easy distance of Channel ports, between Boulogne and Dieppe, Domaine de Drancourt is in four sections. The original section has 100 marked and numbered, grassy pitches of good size, with good shade. An extension taking some 90 units is in light woodland and two newer touring sections are on flat or gently sloping meadow, with little shade as yet. There are 356 pitches in total, of which 220 are occupied by several tour operators. The site also has 30 units for rent which leaves 80 pitches for touring units. Electricity is available in all areas. It can be dusty around the reception buildings and château in dry weather. The pools and toilet blocks can become stretched at times in peak season. English is spoken. The site is run personally by the energetic owner and his staff.

Facilities

Three modern, well equipped toilet blocks include washbasins in cubicles, family bathrooms and facilities for disabled visitors. Laundry and dishwashing sinks, washing machines and dryers. Drainage difficulties can still cause occasional problems. Shop, restaurant and takeaway (from 25/3; closed Tuesday in low season). Bar in château, new large first floor bar and pool-side bar with karaoke in season. Three TV rooms, one for children. Disco (free entry). Games room with table tennis. Two heated swimming pools, one indoor (from 25/3) and one open air with water slide and heated paddling pool. Tennis court, golf practise range and minigolf. Bicycle hire. Pony riding in season (stables 15 km). Fishing (free). Off site: Beach 14 km.

Open

Easter - 31 October.

At a glance

Welcome & Ambience	✓✓✓✓	Location	✓✓✓✓
Quality of Pitches	✓✓✓✓	Range of Facilities	✓✓✓✓

Directions

Site is 2.5 km. south of St Valéry and is signed from the D940 Berck - Le Tréport road. Turn south on the D48 Estreboeuf road and turn immediately left to Drancourt and the site. GPS: N50:09.228 E01:38.156

Charges 2005

Per unit incl. 2 persons	€ 19,90 - € 29,80
extra person	€ 6,40
child (under 5 yrs)	€ 4,60
electricity (6A)	€ 3,20
dog	free

Reservations

Advised for the main season and made for any length, with deposit for longer stays.
Tel: 03 22 26 93 45.
Email: chateau.drancourt@wanadoo.fr

FR80080 Camping Municipal Le Bois des Pêcheurs

Route de Forges Les Eaux, F-80290 Poix-de-Picardie (Somme)

The municipal site at Poix-de-Picardie is excellent for a one night stop, or even a few days to explore the region. The 135 pitches are on level, neatly mown grass, either individual or in hedged bays of four. The pitches at one end are often occupied by long stay or holiday groups, but there are up to 125 pitches available for tourists, all with electricity (10A). The city of Amiens (28 km.) is worth visiting for its famous cathedral and quayside market (Thursday and Saturday) in the old, restored St Leu quarter.

Facilities

The well maintained, central toilet block includes pushbutton showers, and some washbasins in cubicles. Washing machine and dryer. Small playground. Bicycle hire. Volleyball, boules and table tennis. TV room. Caravan storage. Off site: Supermarket 200 m. Fishing 1 km. Shops, services and swimming pool in Poix de Picardie 1.5 km.

Open

1 April - 30 September.

At a glance

Welcome & Ambience	✓✓✓✓	Location	✓✓✓✓
Quality of Pitches	✓✓✓✓	Range of Facilities	✓✓✓

Directions

The town is 27 km. south west of Amiens just off the N29. Site is southwest of the town on the D919 road, and is signed from the D901 Grandvilliers road. GPS: N49:46.588 E01:58.479

Charges 2005

Per unit incl. 1 or 2 adults	€ 11,00
electricity	€ 3,80
No credit cards.	

Reservations

Write for details. Tel: 03 22 90 11 71.
Email: camping@ville-poix-de-picardie.fr

www.fermedesaulnes.com

FR80070 Camping La Ferme des Aulnes

Mobile homes ▶ page 411

1 rue du Marais, Fresne-sur-Authie, F-80120 Nampont-St Martin (Somme)

This peaceful site has been developed on the grassy meadows of a small, 17th century farm on the edge of the village of Fresne and is lovingly cared for by its enthusiastic owner and his hard-working team. Restored outbuildings house reception and the site's facilities, arranged around a central, landscaped courtyard that now boasts a fine heated swimming pool. Of the 120 pitches, 55 are available for touring units, with most of the remainder occupied by or for sale to private owners for holiday mobile homes. All tourist pitches have electricity (6A) and are fairly level. Many are individual and divided by shrubs and young trees, others are on an open, slightly sloping, grassy area.

Facilities

Sanitary fittings are smart, modern and well maintained, including washbasins in cubicles with a large cubicle for disabled people. Facilities are unisex but there are four new individual cabins for ladies. Dishwashing and laundry sinks. Small shop with local produce and necessities (all season - as are all other facilities). Piano bar and restaurant. TV room. Swimming pool (16x9 m; heated and with cover for cooler weather). Fitness room. Aquagym and Balneo therapy. Playground for small children. Beach volleyball, table tennis, boules and archery. Off site: Fishing is possible in the river 50 m. from the site. Golf 3 km. Riding 8 km.

Open

1 April - early November.

At a glance

Welcome & Ambience	✓✓✓✓✓	Location	✓✓✓✓✓
Quality of Pitches	✓✓✓✓	Range of Facilities	✓✓✓✓

Directions

At Nampont St Martin (on the N1 between Montreuil and Abbeville) turn west off the N1 on the D485 (site is signed), towards Villers-sur-Authie. Site is on right after about 3 km. in village of Fresne.
GPS: N50:20.157 E01:42.740

Charges 2006

Per person	€ 7,00
child (under 7 yrs)	€ 4,00
pitch	€ 6,00
dog	€ 4,00
electricity (6A)	€ 5,00 - € 10,00

Camping Cheques accepted.

Reservations

Contact site for details. Tel: 03 22 29 22 69.
Email: contact@fermedesaulnes.com

TO BOOK CALL **0870 405 4055**
or **www.alanrogersdirect.com**
A TRAVEL SERVICE SITE

FR80100 Camping Parc des Cygnes

111 rue de Montières, F-80080 Amiens (Somme)

Formerly Camping de L'Ecluse, this is now a new 3.2 hectare site which has been completely levelled and attractively landscaped. Bushes and shrubs divide the site into areas and it is planned to plant some 20 mature trees to provide some shade. The 145 pitches are all dedicated to the touring trade, with plans for just a handful of mobile homes for rent. All the pitches are grassed with plenty of space on the tarmac roads in front of them for motorcaravans to park in wet conditions. There are 42 pitches with electricity (6/16A), water and drainage and further water points throughout the rest of the site. The enthusiastic manager is working very hard to make sure everything is fully up and running for 2005 – and is planning a pool for 2006! The site is just a few minutes from the N1, the A16 Paris - Calais motorway and the A29/A26 route to Rouen and the south, so it is useful as a stop-over about 50 km. from the ports. Amiens itself is an attractive cathedral city where you can eat out on the waterfront of the 'Venice of the North' or take a boat trip around the 'floating gardens' of 'Les Hortillonnages'.

Facilities

Two identical toilet blocks (one open only when site is busy) with separate toilet facilities but unisex shower and washbasin area. Dishwashing and laundry sinks under cover. Everything is smart and clean with hot and cold water throughout. Facilities for disabled people. The reception building also houses toilets, showers and washbasins (heated when necessary). Laundry room with washing machine, dryer and ironing. Small shop (1/4-15/9). Bar and takeaway (1/5 – 15/9; weekends only in low season). Games and TV room, also used for occasional music events in high season. Bicycle hire. Fishing. Off site: Golf and riding 5 km. Beaches 70 km.

Open

1 April - 31 October.

At a glance

Welcome & Ambience	✓✓✓✓✓	Location	✓✓✓✓
Quality of Pitches	✓✓✓✓	Range of Facilities	✓✓✓

Directions

Site is signed on all approaches to Amiens. From A16, leave at exit 20. Take the Rocade Nord (northern bypass) to exit 40, follow signs for Amiens Longpré and at roundabout take second exit to Parc de Loisirs and then right to campsite (signs all the way). GPS: N49:55.255 E02:15.53

Charges guide

Per person	€ 5,40
child (0-7 yrs)	€ 4,40
pitch	€ 6,10 - € 8,90
car	€ 2,90
electricity	€ 3,10
dog	€ 1,60

Low season price for 2 persons and pitch € 13.

Reservations

Made for min. 2 nights with deposit (€ 25) and fee (€ 15.10). Tel: 03 22 43 29 28. Email: camping.amiens@wanadoo.fr

FR80120 Camping les Aubépines

Saint-Firmin, F-80550 Le Crotoy (Somme)

This peaceful, family-run site is on the edge of the Parc Ornithologique du Marquenterre and is just 1 km. from a beach on the Baie de Somme, a river estuary famous for its resident population of seals. It is an attractively laid out site which has a relaxed and very French feel and should appeal to those seeking a quiet holiday close to nature. There are 196 pitches, although around 100 are occupied by privately-owned mobile homes with a few available for rent. Consequently there are just 76 touring pitches scattered throughout the site. All on level ground, they are of a reasonable to good size, separated by hedges and trees and with water taps and electricity (3-10A) close by. For 2005 there is to be an elegant swimming pool with a paddling pool and sunbathing area – a bar is part of future plans.

Facilities

Two unisex toilet blocks are fairly basic but are kept clean and in good order. British style toilets (seatless), washbasins in cubicles, push-button showers and some larger cubicles with shower and basin. Baby bath and tiny toilet. Facilities for disabled visitors are minimal (no grab-rails) Redevelopment of the older block is planned. Dishwashing sinks. Laundry room. Small shop. Table tennis and other indoor games. Morning club for younger children, afternoon activities for older ones and some evening family events (all in high season). Small play area. Bicycle hire. Off site: Riding adjacent. Beaches: tidal estuary 1 km; open sea 10 km. Nautical base 500 m. Golf 10 km. Tennis 3 km. Fishing 2 km. Bird sanctuary 3 km.

Open

1 April - 1 November.

At a glance

Welcome & Ambience	✓✓✓✓	Location	✓✓✓✓
Quality of Pitches	✓✓✓✓	Range of Facilities	✓✓✓

Directions

Le Crotoy is on the D940 Berck - Le Tréport road. At roundabout for town, take D4 to St Firmin, turning right at next roundabout. Immediately after sign for village, turn left (site signed) to site which is on right in about 500 m. GPS: N50:15.004 E01:36.747

Charges 2006

Per unit incl. 2 persons	€ 19,00 - € 23,00
incl. 3A electricity	€ 19,00 - € 23,00
extra person	€ 4,30 - € 4,70
child (2-7 yrs)	€ 3,30 - € 3,60
electricity 6/10A	€ 5,00 - € 5,00
pet	€ 1,50 - € 1,50

Less 10% in low season.

Reservations

Made for min. 6 days with deposit (€ 50). Tel: 03 22 27 01 34. Email: contact@camping-lesaubepines.com

Camping le Val de Trie ***

Situated at only 1 hour from Calais (A16)
Ideal spot for first or last night or longer stay
12 km from the coast

Quiet and relaxing
Swimming pools
Fishing pond

Cottages to rent.
Seven days stay, six days to pay
(outside July /August).

Moyenneville   Tel: 00 33 (0)3 22 31 48 88   www.camping-levaldetrie.fr
raphael@camping-levaldetrie.fr

FR80060 Camping Le Val de Trie

Mobile homes ▶ page 410

Bouillancourt-sous-Miannay, F-80870 Moyenneville (Somme)

Le Val de Trie is a natural countryside site in a woodland location, near a small village. It is maturing into a well managed site with modern facilities. The 100 numbered, grassy pitches are of a good size, divided by hedges and shrubs with mature trees providing good shade in most areas, and all have electricity (6A) and water. Access roads are gravel (the site is possibly not suitable for the largest motorcaravans). There are good walks around the area and a notice board keeps campers up to date with local market, shopping and activity news. The site has a friendly, relaxed atmosphere and English is spoken. Very much off the beaten track, it can be very quiet in April, June, September and October. If you visit at these times and there is no-one on site, just choose a pitch or call at the farm to book in. There are a few Dutch tour operator tents (5).

Facilities

The two sanitary buildings are well maintained and cleaned, and include washbasins in cubicles, units for disabled people, babies and children, plus laundry and dishwashing facilities (and a microwave to warm babies' food). Washing machine and dryer. Basic motorcaravan services. An extended shop (from 1/4) provides basic necessities, farm produce and wine, bread can be ordered each evening and butcher visits twice weekly in season. Bar with TV (English or French) (1/4-31/10), snack-bar with takeaway (29/4-10/9). There is a terrace and (in high season) a children's club. Pleasant, heated small swimming pool (open 29/4-10/9), fenced with large paddling pool and jacuzzi. Table tennis, boules and volleyball. Fishing lake (free). Bicycle hire. Children's play areas and small animal enclosure. Off site: Riding 2 km. Golf 10 km. Beach 12 km.

At a glance

Welcome & Ambience	✓✓✓✓	Location	✓✓✓✓✓
Quality of Pitches	✓✓✓✓	Range of Facilities	✓✓✓✓

Directions

From exit 2 on A28 near Abbeville take D925 to Miannay and turn left on D86 to Bouillancourt sous Miannay: site is signed in village
GPS: N50:05.038 E01:42.779

Charges 2005

Per unit incl. 2 persons	€ 12,00 - € 17,60
with electricity	€ 15,00 - € 21,00
extra person	€ 2,90 - € 4,40
child (under 7 yrs)	€ 1,90 - € 2,80
dog	€ 0,80 - € 1,30

Camping Cheques accepted.

Reservations

Made with dates, plus deposit (€ 50; no fee for AR readers). Tel: 03 22 31 48 88.
Email: raphael@camping-levaldetrie.fr

Open

1 April - 1 November.

MAP 3

With its tree lined boulevards, museums, art galleries, the Arc de Triomphe and of course the famous Eiffel Tower, this cosmopolitan city has plenty to offer. Less than 30 miles from the heart of the capital, a fun-packed trip to Disneyland Paris is also within reach

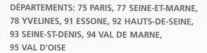

DÉPARTEMENTS: 75 PARIS, 77 SEINE-ET-MARNE, 78 YVELINES, 91 ESSONE, 92 HAUTS-DE-SEINE, 93 SEINE-ST-DENIS, 94 VAL DE MARNE, 95 VAL D'OISE

MAJOR CITIES: PARIS, VERSAILLES, IVRY, MELUN, NANTERRE, BOBIGNY, CRETEIL AND PONTOISE.

One of the most chic and culturally rewarding cities in the world, Paris has something for everyone. The list of things to do is virtually endless and could easily fill many holidays - window shopping, the Eiffel Tower, Notre Dame, Montmartre, trips on the Seine, pavement cafés and the Moulin Rouge, the list goes on.

As a peaceful retreat, you can relax and enjoy the lush scenery of surrounding hills and secret woodlands of the Ile de France. Square bell towers in gentle valleys, white silos on endless plains of wheat; soft and harmonious landscapes painted and praised by La Fontaine, Corot and all the landscape painters. Paris is surrounded by forests, Fontainebleau, Compiègne, Saint-Germain-en-Laye and majestic châteaux such as Fontainbleau and Vaux-le-Vicomte.

Disneyland Resort Paris provides a great day out for all the family with two fantastic theme parks with over 70 attractions and shows to choose from. On the outskirts of Paris is Parc Asterix. with one of Europe's most impressive roller-coasters.

Places of interest

Fontainebleau: château and national museum, history of Napoléon from 1804-1815.

Malmaison: château and national museum.

Meaux: agricultural centre, Gothic cathedral, chapter house and palace.

Paris: obviously! The list of places is too extensive to include here.

St Germain-en-Laye: château, Gallo-roman and Merovingian archeological museum.

Sèvres: ceramics museum.

Thoiry: château and Parc Zoologique, 450-hectare park with gardens and African reserve containing 800 animals.

Versailles: Royal Castle, Royal Apartments, Hall of Mirrors, Royal Opera and French History Museum.

Cuisine of the region

Although without a specific cuisine of its own, Paris and Ile de France offer a wide selection of dishes from all the regions of France. Paris also has a wide choice of foreign restaurants, such as Vietnamese and North African.

FR75020 Camping du Bois de Boulogne

2 allée du Bord de l'eau, F-75016 Paris (Paris)

A busy site and the nearest to the city, this site is set in a wooded area between the Seine and the Bois de Boulogne. One can reach the Champs Elysees in 10-15 minutes by car or, from April to October, there is a shuttle bus running every half hour from the site to the Metro station. The site is quite extensive but nevertheless becomes very full with international visitors of all ages. There are 510 pitches (including mobile homes and a few chalets) of which 280 are marked, with electricity (10A), water, drainage and TV aerial connections. At the entrance is a functional, modern reception building (open 24 hrs) with a card operated barrier system. The site has undergone a huge improvement and re-development programme including the refurbishment of all toilet blocks. Reservations are made but if not booked, arrive early in season (in the morning). Note: you are in a major city environment - take care of valuables.

Facilities

All toilet blocks have British and Turkish style WCs, washbasins in cubicles and showers with divider and seat with hot water throughout. All these facilities suffer from heavy use in season. Washing machines and dryers. Motorcaravan service point. Mini-market. Bar and restaurant (1/4-15/10). Bar open 7 am. - midnight at most times and until 2 am. in peak season. Pizza bar and takeaway service. Playground. Information service. Off site: Organised excursions (July/Aug). Fishing 1 km. Bicycle hire 2 km. Ticket sales for Disneyland, Asterix Parc, etc.

Open

All year.

At a glance

Welcome & Ambience	✓✓✓	Location	✓✓✓✓
Quality of Pitches	✓✓✓✓	Range of Facilities	✓✓✓

Directions

Site is on east side of Seine between the river and the Bois de Boulogne, just north of the Pont de Suresnes. Easiest approach is from Port Maillot, watch for traffic lights at site entrance. Follow signs closely and use a good map.

Charges guide

Per unit incl. 2 persons with electricity, water and drainage	€ 18,50 - € 24,50
	€ 22,50 - € 31,70
tent incl. 2 persons	€ 11,00 - € 15,40
extra adult	€ 4,40 - € 6,20
child (under 7 yrs)	€ 2,20 - € 3,00
dog	€ 2,00 - € 2,50

Reservations

Contact site. Tel: 01 45 24 30 00.
Email: camping-boulogne@stereau.fr

FR77040 Caravaning des 4 Vents

F-77610 Crévecoeur-en-Brie (Seine-et-Marne)

This peaceful, pleasant site has been owned and run by the same family for over 35 years and is within easy reach of Disneyland (just 16 km. by road). There are around 200 pitches, with many permanent or seasonal units, however, there are 130 spacious grassy pitches for tourists, well separated by good hedges, all with 6A electricity and most with a water tap. The whole site is well landscaped with flowers and trees everywhere. This is a great family site with pool and games facilities located at the top end of the site so that campers are not disturbed. Crevecoeur-en-Brie celebrates the 'feast of small villages' on 21/22 June each year. Central Paris is just a 40 minute train ride from the nearest railway station (8 km).

Facilities

Three modern sanitary units provide an adequate number of British style WCs, washbasins (mainly in cubicles) and pushbutton showers. Facilities for disabled people. Washing machine and dryer. Good motorcaravan service point. In high season (July/Aug) an excellent mobile snack bar and pizzeria is on site and is open from 16.00-23.00, and a baker is there from 07.30-11.00. Well fenced, circular swimming pool (16 m. diameter; June to Sept). Excellent playground, a large games room with table tennis and table football, volleyball court, a billiard hall and a boules court. Off site: La Houssaye (1 km) has a grocer, bakery and post office. Fontenay (5 km) has a supermarket and all other services.

At a glance

Welcome & Ambience	✓✓✓✓	Location	✓✓✓✓
Quality of Pitches	✓✓✓✓✓	Range of Facilities	✓✓✓✓

Directions

Crèvecoeur is just off the D231 between the A4 exit 13 and Provins. From north, after passing a large obelisk turn right in 3 km, and from south 19 km. after junction with N4, turn left at signs to village and follow signs to site. Site is on western side of village. GPS: N48:45.044 E02:53.775

Charges 2006

Per unit incl. 2 persons and electricity	€ 22,00
extra person (over 5 yrs)	€ 5,00

Reservations

Essential for July/Aug. Tel: 01 64 07 41 11.
Email: f.george@free.fr

Open

1 March - 15 November.

FR77090 Camping Les Etangs Fleuris

Route Couture, F-77131 Touquin (Seine-et-Marne)

This is a pleasant, peaceful site which is near enough to both Paris (50 km.) and Disneyland (23 km.) to provide a practical alternative to the busier sites nearer the centre. It has a very French feel despite the presence of a fair number of tour operator mobile homes, since these occupy their own areas round the periphery. The touring pitches are grouped on the level ground around the attractive lakes which are home to some sizeable carp as well as being restocked daily with trout (fishing € 5 for half a day). The life of the site centres round a smart bar/function room which doubles as reception and a shop, as well as the lakes and an attractive, irregularly shaped pool. There are 60 touring pitches, all with electricity (10A) and water, separated by hedges and with plenty of shade from the mature trees.

Facilities

The fairly basic toilet has British-style toilets, push-button showers, and open washbasins (with dividers and hooks) for men but mainly in cubicles for ladies. Cleaning could be a bit hit-and-miss at busy times for the hardworking owner. No facilities for disabled visitors. A second heated block among the mobile homes is only opened in cold weather or when the site is very busy. Washing machine and dryer. Very limited shop (bread and basics) in bar (both all season). Heated pool with paddling section (15/5-15/9). A trailer on site provides takeaway meals and snacks (15/5-15/9). Off site: Riding 5 km. Golf 15 km.

Open

1 April - 15 October.

At a glance

Welcome & Ambience	✓✓✓✓	Location	✓✓✓✓
Quality of Pitches	✓✓✓✓	Range of Facilities	✓✓✓

Directions

Touquin is off the D231, 21 km. from exit 13 of the A4 motorway and 30 km. northeast of Provins. From D231 follow signs for Touquin, then Etangs Fleuris and site which is 2.5 km. west of the village along a single-track road with passing places.
GPS: N48:43.867 E03:02.845

Charges 2006

Per person	€ 7,00 - € 8,00
child (0-9 yrs)	€ 3,50 - € 4,00
Camping Cheques accepted.	

Reservations

Contact site. Tel: 01 64 04 16 36.
Email: contact@etangs-fleuris.com

FR77020 Camping Le Chêne Gris

Mobile homes ▶ page 411

24 place de la Gare de Faremoutiers, F-77515 Pommeuse (Seine-et-Marne)

This site is currently being developed by its new Dutch owners and when we visited in July 2005, work was very much behind schedule. The impressive new building which will house reception on the ground floor and an airy restaurant/bar plus a takeaway will clearly be of high quality. Terraces will look out onto the heated leisure pool complex and an adventure-type play area for over-fives, whilst the play area for under-fives is at the side of the bar with picture windows overlooking it. Of the 190 pitches, 134 are touring pitches, the rest (higher up the hill on which the site is built) being occupied by mobile homes and tents of a Dutch tour operator. Presently awaiting modernisation (new electricity hook-ups (6A) and new tarmac access roads) they are in terraces and are generally large and hedged: all have a water tap.

Facilities

Modern, well equipped toilet block with push-button showers, washbasins in cubicles and a dishwashing and laundry area under cover (hot and cold water to all basins and sinks). Facilities for disabled visitors (although grab-rail only for WC and shower seemed to be set too high). Children's area with toilets and baby bath but showers at adult height! Washing machine and dryer. Bar, restaurant and takeaway (all season). Off site: Shops, bars and restaurants within walking distance. Fishing and riding 2 km. Site is next to a railway station with trains to Paris (45 minutes). Disneyland is 20 km.

Open

23 April - 1 November.

At a glance

Welcome & Ambience	✓✓	Location	✓✓✓
Quality of Pitches	✓✓	Range of Facilities	✓✓✓✓

Directions

Pommeuse is 55 km. east of Paris. From A4 motorway at exit 16 take N34 towards Coulommiers. In 10 km. turn south for 2 km. on D25 to Pommeuse; campsite is on right after level-crossing. Site is also signed from the south on the D402 Guignes - Coulommiers road, taking the D25 to Faremoutiers.
GPS: N48:48.514 E02:59.530

Charges 2005

Per unit incl. 2 persons, electricity	€ 29,00 - € 35,00
extra person	€ 2,00 - € 3,50
child (3-11 yrs)	€ 2,00 - € 3,00
animal	€ 2,50

Reservations

Contact site. Tel: 01 64 04 21 80.
Email: lechenegris@wanadoo.fr

FR77030 Camping International de Jablines

Base de Loisirs, F-77450 Jablines (Seine-et-Marne)

Redesigned in 1997, Jablines replaces an older site in an upmarket, modern style which, with the accompanying leisure facilities of the adjacent 'Espace Loisirs', provides an interesting, if a little impersonal alternative to other sites in the region. The whole complex close to the Marne has been developed around old gravel workings. Man-made lakes provide marvellous water activities - dinghy sailing, windsurfing, canoeing, fishing and supervised bathing, plus a large equestrian centre. In season the activities at the leisure complex are supplemented by a bar/restaurant and a range of very French style group activities. The 'Great Lake' as it is called, is said to have the largest beach on the Ile-de-France! The site itself provides 150 pitches, of which 132 are for touring units. Most are of a good size with gravel hardstanding and grass, accessed by tarmac roads and clearly marked by fencing panels and newly planted shrubs. All have 10A electrical connections, 60 with water and waste connections also.

Facilities

Two identical toilet blocks, heated in cool weather, are solidly built and well equipped. They include push-button showers, some washbasins in cubicles, indoor dishwashing and laundry facilities with washing machine and dryer. Motorcaravan service (charged). Shop (all season). Play area. Bar/restaurant adjacent at leisure centre/lake complex along with a range of watersports including 'water cable ski', riding activities, tennis and minigolf. Whilst staying on the campsite, admission to the leisure complex is free. Internet point. Ticket sales for Disneyland and Asterix. Off site: Golf 24 km.

Open

25 March - 30 October.

At a glance

| Welcome & Ambience | ✓✓✓✓ | Location | ✓✓✓✓ |
| Quality of Pitches | ✓✓✓✓ | Range of Facilities | ✓✓✓✓ |

Directions

From A4 Paris - Rouen turn north on A104 west of Disneyland. Take exit 8 on D404 Meaux/Base de Loisirs Jablines. From the A1 going south, follow signs for Marne-la-Vallée and Disneyland immediately after Charles de Gaulle airport using the A104. Take exit 6A Clay-Souilly on N3 (Meaux). After 6 km. turn south on D404 and follow signs. At park entry keep left for campsite. GPS: N48:54.817 E02:44.051

Charges 2005

Per standard pitch incl.	
2 persons and 10A electricity	€ 19,00 - € 22,00
luxury pitch	€ 21,00 - € 24,00
extra person	€ 4,50 - € 5,50
child (under 12 yrs)	€ 3,00 - € 4,00
dog	€ 1,50

Camping Cheques accepted.

Reservations

Essential for July/Aug. and made with booking form from site and 30% deposit. Tel: 01 60 26 09 37. Email: welcome@camping-jablines.com

FR77070 Camping La Belle Etoile

Quai Joffre, La Rochette, F-77000 Melun (Seine-et-Marne)

Ideally situated for visiting Fontainebleau and Paris, and alongside the River Seine, this site has an overall mature and neat appearance, although the approach road along the banks of the river is somewhat off putting with several industrial plants. Continue past this point and you discover that La Belle Etoile enjoys a pleasant position with pitches to the fore of the site within view of the barges which continually pass up and down the Seine. This is a friendly, family run site with English speaking owners who are pleasant and helpful. The 170 touring pitches, with electricity connections (6/10A), are on grass and laid out between the many shrubs and trees. There are ten units for hire.

Facilities

The toilet blocks are not new but they are kept very clean and the water is very hot. Laundry room. Baby bath. Facilities for disabled visitors (shower, washbasin and WC). Motorcaravan service point. Small bar, snacks and shop with limited stock (28/6-30/8). Takeaway (1/5-15/9). Swimming pool (1/5-15/9). Play area. Fishing. Bicycle hire. Tickets for Disney and Vaux le Vicomte are sold by the site. Off site: Fontainebleau is a short drive away and Paris easily accessible by train. Golf 15 km.

Open

1 April - 22 October.

At a glance

Welcome & Ambience	✓✓✓✓	Location	✓✓✓	
Quality of Pitches	✓✓✓	Range of Facilities	✓✓✓	

Directions

Travelling north on N6 Fontainebleau - Melun road, on entering La Rochette, pass Total petrol station on left and turn immediately right into Ave de la Seine. Continue to end of road and turn left at river, site on left in approx. 500 m. GPS: N48:31.501 E02:40.164

Charges 2006

Per person	€ 4,90 - € 5,40
child (0-11 yrs)	€ 2,20 - € 3,40
pitch	€ 5,00 - € 5,40
electricity (6A)	€ 3,20 - € 3,30

Camping Cheques accepted.

Reservations

Made for a min. 3 nights. Tel: 01 64 39 48 12. Email: info@campinglabelleetoile.com

Camping La Belle Etoile
- Familycampsite
- Many playfacilities
- Hirefacilities:
  - Tent bungalows with toilet and shower
  - Mobil homes and chalets

GPS. 48,52578/2,66911 (lat / long)
E-mail: info@campinglabelleetoile.com
Internet: www.campinglabelleetoile.com
Tel: ++33(0) 1 64 39 48 12
Fax: ++33(0) 1 64 37 25 55

We accept Camping-Cheque

FR78040 Camping Municipal de l'Etang d'Or

Route du Château d'Eau, F-78120 Rambouillet (Yvelines)

This is a pleasant site in a peaceful forest location, with good tarmac access roads, site lighting and 190 touring pitches of varying size and surfaces. Some of the pitches are divided by hedges, others are more open and sunny. All have electricity, 83 also have water and drainage, with a few hardstandings. Campers get a discount brochure for local sites or activities (e.g. the municipal swimming pool, animal park, bowling and billiards, bicycle hire), and a special permit for the fishing lake. There are many good cycle and footpaths in the area. It is possible to visit Paris by rail and Rambouillet itself is an interesting town, with Chartres and Versailles within reach.

Facilities

Two heated sanitary buildings include British and Turkish style WCs, washbasins (some in cubicles), dishwashing and laundry sinks, plus basic facilities for baby changing and for disabled persons. Facilities could be a little stretched during the high season. Washing machine and dryer. One block is closed in winter. Motorcaravan service point (€1.29). Café/bar and small shop. Good playground. Off site: Large supermarket at southern end of the town.

Open

All year, excl. 18 Dec - 29 Jan..

At a glance

Welcome & Ambience	✓✓✓	Location	✓✓✓✓	
Quality of Pitches	✓✓✓	Range of Facilities	✓✓✓✓	

Directions

Rambouillet is 52 km. southwest of Paris. Site is southeast of town: from N10 southbound take Rambouillet/Les Eveuses exit, northbound take Rambouillet centre exit, loop round and rejoin N10 southbound, taking next exit. Pass under N10, following signs for site. GPS: N48:37.623 E01:50.727

Charges 2005

Per person	€ 3,90 - € 4,30
child (2-10 yrs)	€ 2,70 - € 3,00
pitch incl. electricity (6-10A)	€ 7,30 - € 8,70

Camping Cheques accepted.

Reservations

Contact site for details. Tel: 01 30 41 07 34. Email: rambouillet.tourisme@wanadoo.fr

FR78050 Camping Le Val de Seine

Base de Loisirs, chemin du Rouillard, F-78480 Verneuil-sur-Seine (Yvelines)

This is an excellent little site located in a large leisure and country park on the western outskirts of Paris. It has been completely refurbished to high standards and offers a pleasant alternative to the busier sites closer to Paris for those wishing to visit the city. Trains and RER services from nearby stations take you there in less than half an hour and even on to Disneyland. Versailles is easily reached by motorway. The site has 87 pitches in two sections, one end for campers (mainly groups) with its own toilet block, the other for caravans and tents. Here there are 37 level pitches each with electricity (6A), water and drainage. Campers here have free access to the huge country park (800 m. from site) which has three large lakes, one with a beach for swimming, others for sailing and pedalo hire. There are miles of paths and cycle tracks and many other activities.

Facilities

Two modern toilet blocks (not unisex) have British-style toilets, controllable showers and some washbasins in cubicles. Facilities for disabled visitors. Excellent dishwashing provision. Small block (low-level toilets, basins and showers) for children plus baby room. Washing machines and dryers, also motorcaravan service point. Reception sells bread (to order) and basic supplies. Country park with lakes, fishing, sailing, 9-hole practice golf (free), many other sports facilities, a self-service restaurant and brasserie serving beer and cold drinks. Also (not free) bicycle hire, tennis courts, 18 hole minigolf. Off site: Riding adjacent. Golf 7 km.

Open

1 April - 30 September.

At a glance

Welcome & Ambience	✓✓✓	Location	✓✓✓✓
Quality of Pitches	✓✓✓	Range of Facilities	✓✓✓✓

Directions

From A13 take exit 8 (Meulan-les Mureaux) and follow signs for 'Base de Loisirs du Val de Seine'. Go through Les Mureaux and bear right on D154 towards Verneuil. At roundabout turn left (signed 'Base de Loisirs') to site. GPS: N48:59.762 E01:57.548

Charges 2005

Per person (4 yrs and over)	€ 3,00 - € 4,00
pitch	€ 3,50 - € 5,00
car	€ 2,50
electricity	€ 4,00
pet	€ 1,50 - € 2,00

Reservations

Contact site. Tel: 01 39 28 16 20.
Email: sce-client@valdeseine78.com

FR78010 Camping Caravaning International

1 rue Johnson, F-78600 Maisons-Laffitte (Yvelines)

This busy site on the banks of the Seine is convenient for Paris – you can walk to the RER station and be in the centre in 20 minutes. The third, more open in style is only used in July/August. The facilities are clean and well maintained but with the volume of visitors, constant supervision is necessary. Provision for people with disabilities. Laundry and a short drive away. Maisons-Laffitte is a pleasant suburb with a château, a racecourse and some large training stables. The site has multilingual and friendly reception staff and occupies a grassy, tree covered area bordering the river. There are 351 pitches, 66 occupied by mobile homes and 90 used by tour operators, plus two areas dedicated to tents. Most pitches are separated by hedges, are of a good size with some overlooking the Seine (unfenced access), and all 195 touring pitches have electricity hook-ups (6A). The roads leading to the site are a little narrow so large vehicles need to take care. Being so close to Paris this site is consistently busy. Train noise can be expected.

Facilities

There are three sanitary blocks, two insulated for winter use. The third, more open in style is only used in July/August. The facilities are clean and well maintained but with the volume of visitors, constant supervision is necessary. Provision for people with disabilities. Laundry and dishwashing areas. Motorcaravan service point. Self-service shop. Restaurant/bar with takeaway food and pizzeria. TV room, table tennis, football area. Internet point. SNCF representative on site each morning 15/6-15/8 for travel advice. Off site: Sports complex adjoins the site. Riding 500 m. Bicycle hire 5 km.

Open

1 April - 31 October.

At a glance

Welcome & Ambience	✓✓✓✓	Location	✓✓✓✓
Quality of Pitches	✓✓✓	Range of Facilities	✓✓✓✓

Directions

Site is best approached from A13 or A15 autoroute. From A13 take exit 7 (Poissy) and follow D153 to Poissy, the D308 to Maisons-Laffitte, then site signs on right before town centre. From A15 exit 7 take D184 towards St Germain, after 11 km. turn left on D308 to Maisons-Laffitte and follow site signs as above. From A1 take the A86, then at exit 2 (for Bezons) take D308 to Maisons-Laffitte and follow signs to site on left. GPS: N48:56.394 E02:08.740

Charges 2005

Per unit incl. 2 persons	€ 19,50 - € 22,50
electricity	€ 2,50
tent incl. 2 persons	€ 11,00 - € 12,00
extra adult	€ 5,10 - € 5,70
child (5-10 yrs)	€ 2,40 - € 2,80
animal	€ 2,50

Reservations

Advisable for July/Aug. and made with deposit (€ 10). Tel: 01 39 12 21 91.
Email: ci.mlaffitte@wanadoo.fr

FR78060 Huttopia Versailles

F-78000 Versailles (Yvelines)

This is a new site and a member of Huttopia, a group of campsites set up to combine a 'back to nature' outlook with a good range of modern amenities. We plan to carry out a full inspection in 2006. Huttopia Versailles is located within a dense forest but is just 20 minutes by train from the Eiffel Tower! There are 180 shady pitches, some more than 120 sq.m. in size and some specially designated for motorcaravans. An imaginative range of rented accommodation is available here including 'roulottes', an adaptation of gypsy caravans.

Facilities

Sanitary building including a family shower room. Special bivouacs set up for cooking and washing up. Restaurant with takeaway food. Bar. Games room. Swimming and paddling pool. Shop. Playground, table tennis, children's club. Off site: Versailles and its château. Hiking. Cycling trails. Golf. Paris 20 minutes by RER express train from Versailles.

Open

1 April - 31 October.

Directions

From the front of the chateau of Versailles take the Avenue de Paris and the site is signed after 2 km.

Charges 2005

Per person	€ 5,50 - € 6,00
child (2-7 yrs)	€ 2,50 - € 3,00
pitch	€ 8,00 - € 18,00
electricity	€ 3,60

Reservations

Contact site. Tel: 01 39 51 73 61.

FR91010 Camping Caravaning Le Beau Village

1 voie des Prés, F-91700 Villiers-sur-Orge (Essonne)

This is a pleasant, typically French campsite just 25 km. south of Paris and conveniently located at the centre of a triangle formed by the A6 motorway, the N20/A10 to Orleans and the N104 east/west link road 'La Francilienne'. Half of its 100 pitches are occupied on a seasonal basis by Parisians; the remainder are touring pitches, all hedged and with 10A electricity. Trees provide some shade. The site is on the bank of the Orge river with fishing possible, but access is available only to occupants of the seasonal pitches, unless one of these is vacant (as when we visited). Reception, in a traditionally-styled building, also has a pleasant little bar, a games room with internet access and an attractive terrace with wooden tables, benches, thatched canopies and a stone-built barbecue. Opposite is a fenced adventure-type play area The RER station is just 700 m. away and trains take you to the centre of Paris in 20 minutes.

Facilities

The main toilet block is fairly modern with controllable showers and some washbasins in cabins. A second (older) block has adequate facilities for disabled visitors, the third (in a 'portacabin') has a washing machine and dryer and a very tired unit for children. All three blocks can be heated. Small bar. Games room with internet access (charge). Play area (3-12 yrs). Free loan of canoes (launching arranged by campsite owner). Off site: Tennis and football adjacent. Shops and restaurants nearby. Golf and riding 2 km. River beach and sailing 3 km. Boat launching 4 km.

Open

All year.

At a glance

Welcome & Ambience	✓✓✓✓	Location	✓✓✓
Quality of Pitches	✓✓✓	Range of Facilities	✓✓✓

Directions

From N20 at Ballainvillers take exit for La Ville du Bois on D35 southeast to Villiers-sur-Orge. In the village at foot of hill, turn right on Voie des Prés along river bank to site on left (signed). From A6 leave at exit 6 (Savigny-sur-Orge) and turn west. Follow signs for Quartier Latin then D25 to Villiers-sur-Orge. Turn left after river and as above. From A10 turn east on N104. From N104 take N20 north, then as above.

Charges 2005

Per person	€ 4,50
child (0-7 yrs)	€ 2,25
pitch	€ 5,50
electricity	€ 3,50
animal	€ 2,00

Reservations

Contact site. Tel: 01 60 16 17 86.
Email: le-beau-village@wanadoo.fr

FR91020 Le Parc des Roches

La Petite Beauce, F-91530 Saint-Chéron (Essonne)

This large site with 400 pitches occupying a wooded hill-top is principally dedicated to providing Parisians with somewhere to escape from city life, but also offers 80 touring pitches on gently sloping ground near the entrance. These are reasonably well tended and all have 5A electricity. This is a convenient location for a night's break if travelling north or south on the N20. A large heated swimming pool has a lifeguard at busy times and has plenty of space for sunbathing (but no loungers!) The bar/restaurant is pleasant and offers basic food at reasonable prices. The nearby village of St Chéron has shops and supermarkets and an RER station (50 minutes to Paris).

Facilities

The main toilet block is modern and provides pre-set showers, washbasins in cabins (warm water only), covered dishwashing and laundry facilities. Several separate toilets, washbasins in cubicles and showers (with detachable shower-heads) for disabled visitors. An older adjacent block is more basic with open style washbasins. Both blocks appeared to be kept clean and can be heated when necessary. Swimming pool (1/6-15/9). Bar/restaurant and takeaway (15/6-15/9) also sells some basic provisions. Table tennis. Tennis. Football goals. Volleyball and basketball. Play area (in residential part of site).

Open

15 April - 1 November.

At a glance

| Welcome & Ambience | ✓✓✓ | Location | ✓✓✓ |
| Quality of Pitches | ✓✓✓ | Range of Facilities | ✓✓✓ |

Directions

From the N20, 5 km. south of junction with N104 (La Francilienne) turn west at Arpajon on D97. At roundabout turn south on D116 signed St Chéron and Dourdan. In St Chéron at first traffic lights turn left past railway station and then left on D132 for 3 km. to la Petite Beauce. After hamlet turn left to campsite. GPS: N48:32.717 E002:08.22

Charges 2005

Per person	€ 6,40
child (0-18 yrs)	€ 3,75 - € 4,90
pitch incl. car	€ 7,40
electricity	€ 2,55
dog	€ 1,70

Train station 3 km. (Paris, Versailles). Fishing 6 km. Riding 10 km. Golf 15 km.

Reservations

Contact site. Tel: 01 64 56 65 50. Email: contact@parcdesroches.com

FR94000 Camping du Tremblay

Boulevard des Alliés, F-94507 Champigny-sur-Marne (Val-de-Marne)

This is a very useful site for those wishing to visit Paris and is also convenient for Disneyland Paris as there is a bus service from the campsite gates to the Metro RER station serving both destinations. It is also close to the A4 motorway which is free as far as Disneyland. The site is on flat land beside the River Marne with 450 pitches, 76 of which are occupied by mobile homes and chalets to rent. The 220 touring pitches are on gravel and are separated by hedges. All have electricity (10A) but water has to be fetched from the toilet blocks except for the 32 serviced pitches which have taps and waste water points. There is also a large area of grass pitches for camping where there are water points but no electricity. It is very much a short-stay site but seems well run.

Facilities

The three toilet blocks are old-fashioned and lacking in any refinements, but they are apparently cleaned three times a day and this process seemed fairly thorough. Toilets are mainly segregated with many Turkish-style but some British and with the occasional seat! One block had unisex toilets which are seat-less British style. Showers are pre-set and washbasins in cubicles with warm and cold water. Facilities for disabled visitors (some en-suite) are fairly basic and there are no grab rails. Dishwashing sinks mainly under cover. Laundry sinks not recommended! Washing machines and dryers. Small, well stocked shop, bar and snack bar (15/3-15/10). Fishing.

Open

All year.

At a glance

| Welcome & Ambience | ✓✓✓ | Location | ✓✓✓✓ |
| Quality of Pitches | ✓✓✓ | Range of Facilities | ✓✓✓ |

Directions

From A4 take exit 5 onto D45 south (towards Champigny). At lights, turn right on N303 towards St Maur. At next lights continue ahead (now N4 to Vincennes) and immediately turn right at next lights onto Boulevard de Polangis. As you approach (but before you reach) the motorway flyover, turn right along Boulevard des Allies. Site entrance is on the left (passing under motorway). There are signs for Camping IDF at most points if you can spot them! It is suggested that you check your route back to the motorway before you leave if heading east. GPS: N48:49.777 E02:28.624

Charges guide

Per unit incl. 2 persons	€ 15,60 - € 21,10
incl. electricity	€ 17,90 - € 23,90
incl. water and drainage	€ 18,90 - € 25,80
extra person	€ 4,10 - € 5,50
child (0-7 yrs)	€ 2,40 - € 2,90
pet	€ 2,00 - € 2,50

Reservations

Made with deposit and € 12 fee. Tel: 01 43 97 43 97. Email: receptcc@stereau.fr

FR95000 Parc de Séjour de L'Etang

10 chemin des Bellevues, F-95690 Nesles-la-Vallée (Val-d'Oise)

Parc de Sejour de L'Etang is small, informal site 33 km. northwest of Paris. It is situated on the southern outskirts of the village of Nesles-la-Vallée in a pretty, tree-lined river valley not far from L'Isle-Adam, which is a popular destination for Parisians at weekends. Many of the 165 pitches are occupied by seasonal caravans but there are 65 large, flat pitches available for touring units of which 25 have electricity (3/9A). The site is informally arranged around a duck pond with many trees to provide shelter and shade and semi-tame rabbits competing with the ducks for food and attention. Chantilly, Parc Asterix and Disneyland are easily reached by car. By far the best way to visit Paris is by train from Valmondois, 5 minutes away via the D15 road (trains every half hour, journey time about 50 minutes).

Facilities

The main, central toilet block (heated in cooler weather) is a plain substantial building including washbasins in rather small cubicles and, in separate rooms, rather older style British and Turkish WCs. Covered dishwashing and laundry sinks. Washing machine. Smaller, much older unit includes fairly basic facilities for disabled people. Good playground, volleyball and basketball areas, and under cover play barn with table tennis. Off site: Village and restaurant within walking distance. Fishing permits for the river available in village. Riding 500 m, golf 7 km.

Open

1 March - 15 November.

At a glance

Welcome & Ambience	✓✓✓✓	Location	✓✓✓✓
Quality of Pitches	✓✓✓✓	Range of Facilities	✓✓✓

Directions

From A15 exit 10 take D915 to Pontoise, avoiding town centre, then D27 to Beauvais which joins the D927 and then D79 to Nesles-la-Vallée. Site is on left as you leave village on D64. From N1 or A16 (exit 11) take the D922 southwest towards L'Isle Adam, and then D64 northwest to Nesles la Vallée. Site is on the right as you enter the village. GPS: N49:07.647 E02:11.047

Charges 2005

Per person	€ 4,00
child (1-6 yrs)	€ 3,00
pitch	€ 4,00
with electricity (3/9A)	€ 7,15 - € 8,10
animal	€ 1,00

No credit cards.

Reservations

Contact site. Tel: 01 34 70 62 89.
Email: brehinier1@hotmail.com

FR60010 Camping Campix

B.P. 37, F-60340 St Leu-d'Esserent (Oise)

This informal site has been unusually developed in a former sandstone quarry on the outskirts of the small town. The quarry walls provide very different boundaries to most of the site, giving it a sheltered, peaceful environment and trees have grown to soften the slopes. Not a neat, manicured site, the 160 pitches are arranged in small groups on the different levels with stone and gravel access roads (some fairly steep and possibly muddy in poor weather). Electricity (6A) is available to about 140 pitches. Torches are advised. There are very many secluded corners mostly for smaller units and tents and plenty of space for children to explore (parents must supervise – some areas, although fenced, could be dangerous). Recent additions include an outdoor swimming pool and paddling pool with a grassy recreation area. A footpath leads from the site to the town where there are shops and restaurants. The site is well placed for visiting several local places of interest and the friendly, English speaking owner will advise. These include Chantilly, the Asterix Park and the Mer de Sable, a Western theme amusements park, both 20 km. Disneyland is 70 km. It is also possible to visit Paris by train (information at reception).

Facilities

At the entrance to the site a large building houses reception and two clean, heated sanitary units - one for tourers, the other usually reserved for groups. Two suites for disabled people double as baby rooms. Laundry facilities with washing machine and dryer. At quieter times only one unit is opened but facilities may be congested at peak times. Motorcaravan service facilities. Bread and milk delivered daily. Pizza and other Italian food delivery service in the evenings. New swimming pool for 2006. Off site: Fishing 1 or 5 km, riding or golf 5 km.

Open

7 March - 30 November.

At a glance

Welcome & Ambience	✓✓✓	Location	✓✓✓
Quality of Pitches	✓✓✓	Range of Facilities	✓✓✓

Directions

St Leu-d'Esserent is 11 km. west of Senlis, 5 km. northwest of Chantilly. From the north on the A1 autoroute take the Senlis exit, from Paris the Chantilly exit. Site is north of the town off the D12 towards Cramoisy, and is signed in the village. GPS: N49:13.509 E02:25.638

Charges 2006

Per unit	€ 3,50 - € 5,00
person	€ 3,00 - € 5,00
child (under 9 yrs)	€ 2,00 - € 3,00
small tent	€ 2,50 - € 4,00
electricity	€ 2,50 - € 3,50
dog	€ 1,00 - € 2,00

Reservations

Advisable for July/Aug. Tel: 03 44 56 08 48.
Email: campixfr@aol.com

MAP 4

Home to the Champagne region, the varied landscapes of Eastern France include dense forests, vineyards and winding rivers. The whole area is dotted with fascinating ancient churches and castles, towns and villages.

EASTERN FRANCE IS DEFINED AS:
CHAMPAGNE-ARDENNE: 08 ARDENNES, 51 MARNE, 10 AUBE, 52 HAUTE-MARNE. LORRAINE VOSGES: 54 MEURTHE-ET-MOSELLE, 55 MEUSE, 57 MOSELLE, 88 VOSGES. ALSACE: 67 BAS-RHIN, 68 HAUT-RHIN

Situated on the flatlands of Champagne are the most northerly vineyards in France where special processing turns the light, dry wine into 'le Champagne' and names such as Moet et Chandon and Veuve Clicquot spring to mind. Nowhere else in the world are you allowed to make sparkling wine and call it champagne. Travelling further east you come across the spa towns such as Vittel, Bains-les-Bains and Plombières and the birth place of St Joan of Arc at Domrémy.

Today you can descend from the mountains into the Alsace vineyards and fairy tale wine villages. The 'Route des Vins' follows the vineyards along the Rhine valley from Mulhouse to Colmar and north almost to Strasbourg. Alsace and Lorraine have been frequently fought over and today there are many poignant reminders of the turbulent past. You'll find noticeable German influence in architecture, cuisine and language. There are also numerous little wine towns, medieval villages and a host of ruined castles stretching along the north eastern margins of the Vosges.

Places of interest

Épernay: home of champagne production.

Le Linge: trenches including rusty barbed wire have been left as they were.

Reims: 13th century Gothic cathedral.

Riquewihr: traditional town, fortifications and medieval houses.

Verdun: hill forts such as Fort de Vaux and Fort de Douaumont, large military cemetery at Douaumont.

Cuisine of the region

Quiche Lorraine: made only in the classical manner with cream, eggs and bacon.

Potage Lorraine: potato, leek and onion soup.

Tarte (aux mirabelles): golden plum tart. Also made with other fruits.

Tarte à l'oignon Alsacienne: onion and cream tart.

FR08010 Camping Municipal du Mont Olympe

Rue des Paquis, F-08000 Charleville-Mezieres (Ardennes)

Attractively situated alongside the Meuse River, within easy walking distance across a footbridge to the centre of the pleasant large town, this site was completely rebuilt in 2001/2, just a short distance from the old one. It now offers excellent facilities, with 128 grass pitches, all with electricity (10A), water and waste water connections. There are 66 from 108 to 219 sq.m. in asize, 48 up to 106 sq.m. and 12 smaller pitches designed especially for motorcaravans.

Facilities

Three heated buildings provide first class showers, private cabins, baby rooms and facilities for the disabled, plus inside dishwashing (including one for the disabled) and a well-equipped laundry room. Motorcaravan service point. Children's play area and paddling pool. TV and games room. Off site: Municipal pool next door. Boat trips on the river. Attractive town centre close by.

Open

1 April - 15 October.

At a glance

Welcome & Ambience	✓✓✓	Location		✓✓✓✓✓
Quality of Pitches	✓✓✓✓	Range of Facilities		✓✓✓

Directions

Site is north of Charleville on the island of Montcy St Pierre and is signed from the city centre 'Mont Olympe'. From the north D988/D1 follow the river, over the bridge, then immediately left. From the southeast (A203/N51/N43) take 'centre' exit, head for 'Gare' then follow Avenue Forest north and sharp left after the bridge. The entrance is about 150 metres further on from where the old site was situated.

Charges guide

Per person	€ 4,10
child (5-17yrs)	€ 2,80
pitch and vehicle	€ 4,50 - € 5,50
dog	€ 1,35
electricity (6/10A)	€ 2,50 - € 3,50
motorcaravan overnight	€ 10,00

Reservations

Contact site. Tel: 03 24 33 23 60.

FR08040 Camping La Samaritaine

F-08240 Buzancy (Ardennes)

What a surprise and a pleasure it was to arrive at such a delightful new site in the heart of the Ardennes. It is peacefully situated just outside the village beside a stream, although there may be some high season noise from the nearby lake where you can swim or fish. Flowers decorate the entrance and bushes and saplings have been planted to separate the pitches, although there is not much shade at present. The 101 numbered touring pitches all have electricity (10A) and are on level grass off hard access roads. They vary in size up to 130 sq.m. 55 have water and waste water, and there are attractive small wooden containers for waste. There are also 10 mobile homes and 9 chalets for rent on the site.

Facilities

A modern building houses the usual sanitary facilities, with private cabins, baby bath, washing machine and dryer, inside dishwashing and facilities for the disabled. A large recreation room houses some games and there are tables to sit at. Table tennis is under cover. Bread is delivered daily. A few essentials are kept in reception. Snack bar/takeaway (mid-May - end-Sept). High season accompanied walks and entertainment programme. Motorcaravan Service Point and an "Aire Exterieur" are beside the entrance road to the site. Off site: Just along from the site towards the lake is the volleyball court and boules, whilst at the lake is some play equipment 'under adult supervision only'. Lake swimming is supervised only at certain times (2 metres deep), with a paddling area up to 1.2 metres depth. Restaurant in village.

At a glance

Welcome & Ambience	✓✓✓✓	Location		✓✓✓✓
Quality of Pitches	✓✓✓✓	Range of Facilities		✓✓✓✓

Directions

The village of Buzancy is about 22 km. east of Vouziers on the RD947 towards Stenay and Montmédy. The site is just over 1.5km. from the centre of the village down a small road, and is well signed. GPS: N49:25.584 E04:56.406

Charges 2006

Per person	€ 3,00 - € 4,00
child (under 10 yrs)	€ 2,00 - € 3,00
pitch	€ 4,50 - € 5,00
water and waste water	€ 2,00
electricity (10A)	€ 3,50
animal	€ 1,50 - € 2,50

Reservations

Contact site. Tel: 03 24 30 08 88.
Email: info@campinglasamaritaine.com

Open

14 April - 30 September.

FR10010 Camping Municipal de Troyes

1 rue de Roger Salengro, F-10150 Pont-Sainte-Marie (Aube)

This municipal campsite, within the Troyes city boundary and about 4 km. from the centre, has been taken over by two young enthusiastic managers who are turning it into an attractive place to stay. There are 110 level grassy pitches (6 with hardstanding), all for tourers, about equally shaded and open. All have electrical connections (5A), and there are plenty of water taps. Being on one of the main routes from Luxembourg to the southwest of France, and on the main route from Calais to the Mediterranean, Troyes makes a good night stop. It is also a delightful city, with a marvellous mediaeval centre and interesting museums, and is well worth a longer stay. In addition, not far from the site is the biggest centre in Europe for factory shops and cut-price designer outlets, run by the same company that has seven such centres in Great Britain.

Facilities

Two modern toilet blocks contain British style WCs, washbasins and pre-set showers. Facilities for disabled people. Motorcaravan services. Washing machines and dryer. Shop for basics (all season). Gas supplies. Restaurant, snack bar and takeaway (15/6-15/9). TV room. Games room. Playground. Minigolf. Table tennis. Volleyball. Boules. Bicycle hire. Off site: Bus to Troyes centre 50 m. Supermarket 100 m. Other shops, restaurants, bars, ATM 300 m. Riding 8 km.

Open

1 April - 15 October.

At a glance

Welcome & Ambience	✓✓✓✓	Location	✓✓✓✓
Quality of Pitches	✓✓✓✓	Range of Facilities	✓✓✓

Directions

From the north, leave the A26 at exit 22 (Charmont). Turn right (southwest) on the D15 towards Troyes. In about 4 km., turn left (south) at the roundabout on N77 towards Troyes. After another 6 km. pass over the ring road, continuing towards the town centre. At about 2 km. more the road swings left and then right. Shortly afterwards you should see the large sign for the campsite on the right. From the centre of Troyes, follow the road north, signed St Dizier and/or Nancy. In 2 or 3 km., the large campsite sign will be on the left.

Charges 2005

Per person	€ 4,10
child (2-11 yrs)	€ 2,70
pitch	€ 5,60
electricity	€ 2,70

Reservations

Contact site. Tel: 03 25 81 02 64.
Email: info@troyescamping.net

FR51020 Camping Municipal en Champagne

Rue de Plaisance, F-51000 Châlons-en Champagne (Marne)

The location of Châlons, south of Reims and near both the A4 and A26 autoroutes, about 200 miles from Calais and Boulogne, make this an ideal stopover. It is also ideally situated for exploring this famous region in the plain of the River Marne and its historical connections. This site on the southern edge of town is an example of a good municipal site. The wide entrance with its well tended appearance of neatly mown grass and flower beds sets the tone for the rest of the site. Ninety-five of the 148 pitches, accessed from tarmac roads, are on a gravel base with the rest on grass. The majority have electricity (10A). The generously sized gravel pitches are separated by hedges and 48 of these are multi-serviced. Trees abound although there is no shade in some parts. The newest area of pitches overlooks the small lake.

Facilities

Two toilet blocks, one behind reception which can be heated, the other at the far end of the site. These facilities are of varying standards due to an ongoing programme of refurbishment. Some washbasins in cabins, baby room and hairdressing station, facilities for disabled visitors including some special pitches adjacent, plus a washing machine and dryer and dishwashing room. Numerous refuse bins enclosed by wooden palings which enhance the general appearance of the site. Bread to order. Bar, snack bar and takeaway (1/6-31/9 evenings plus lunchtime July/Aug). Gas supplies. Games and TV rooms. Playground. Mini golf, tennis, table tennis, volleyball, boules and place for mini-football. Motorcaravan Service Point. Off site: Fishing (free for campers) nearby. Bus stop at site entrance. Town has number of notable buildings, churches and half timbered houses.

At a glance

Welcome & Ambience	✓✓✓✓	Location	✓✓✓✓
Quality of Pitches	✓✓✓✓	Range of Facilities	✓✓✓✓

Directions

From the north on the A4, take La Veuve exit (27) onto the N44 which by-passes the town. Leave at last exit signed St Memmie and follow camping signs. From the south on A26, take exit 18 onto N77 and head towards town. Site is well signed 'Camping', and is south of town centre on the D60. GPS: N48:56.156 E04:22.994

Charges 2005

Per person	€ 4,60
child (under 7 yrs)	€ 1,75
pitch	€ 4,60
vehicle	€ 3,05
electricity	€ 3,05

Reservations

Write to site. Tel: 03 26 68 38 00.
Email: camping.mairie.chalons@wanadoo.fr

Open

1 April - 31 October.

FR52030 Camping Lac de la Liez

Peigney, F-52200 Langres (Haute-Marne)

Managed by the enthusiastic Baude family, this newly renovated lakeside site is near the city of Langres. With its old ramparts and ancient city centre, Langres was elected one of the 50 most historic cities in France. Situated only 10 minutes from the A5, Camping Lac de la Liez provides an ideal spot for an overnight stop en-route to the south of France. There is also a lot on offer for a longer stay, including the lake and an impressive indoor pool complex, with a sauna. The site provides 131 fully serviced pitches, some with panoramic views of the lake. The 200 hectare lake has a sandy beach for play and swimming, a play area and a small harbour where boats and pedaloes may be hired. Access to the lake from the campsite is down steps and across what is quite a fast road (in total 150 m).

Facilities

Two new toilet blocks have all facilities in cabins. Facilities for disabled people and babies. Laundry facilities. Motorcaravan services. Shop, bar and restaurant (with takeaway food). Indoor pool complex with spa and sauna. Heated outdoor pool (1/6-30/9). Games room. Playground. Extensive games area and tennis court (free in low season). Off site: Lake with beach and boat hire. Bicycle hire and cycle tracks around the lake. Fishing 100 m. Riding 5 km. Golf 40 km.

Open

1 April - 1 November.

At a glance

Welcome & Ambience	✓✓✓✓	Location	✓✓✓✓
Quality of Pitches	✓✓✓✓	Range of Facilities	✓✓✓✓✓

Directions

From Langres take the N19 towards Vesoul. After approximately 3 km. turn right, straight after the large river bridge, then follow site signs. GPS: N47:52.44 E05:22.628

Charges 2005

Per person	€ 4,50 - € 6,00
child (2-12 yrs)	€ 3,00 - € 4,00
pitch	€ 6,00 - € 8,00
electricity	€ 3,00 - € 4,00
dog	€ 2,00

Camping Cheques accepted.

Reservations

Made with deposit of 25% and fee (€ 6). Tel: 03 25 90 27 79. Email: campingliez@free.fr

FR52040 Camping de la Croix d'Arles

RN 74, F-52200 Bourg-Langres (Haute-Marne)

This quiet site is only 8 km. south of the interesting town of Langres, but is also ideally situated for exploring the lakes, rivers, canal, paths and cycle tracks of the region. There are 100 pitches, of which 81 are for tourers. Most of the facilities are near the site entrance, as is a flat grassy area mostly used by caravans and motorcaravans. There are electrical points and water taps, but no pitch markings and no shade. Further into the site is a wooded area where there are groups of numbered pitches with lots of shade (leads for electricity of up to 40 m. could be needed). Further on is an area without electricity supply. A tour operator uses the site, and in high season their couriers run activities for all campers.

Facilities

Two modern toilet blocks contain British style WCs, washbasins (some in cabins) and controllable showers. Facilities for disabled people. Baby room. Laundry. Shop for basics (all season). Restaurant, bar, snack bar and takeaway (1/4 - 31/10). Games rooms. Swimming and paddling pools (15/5-15/9). Playground. Table tennis. Boules. Off site: Town 2 km. Fishing 8 km. Riding 10 km. Bicycle hire 5 km.

Open

15 March - 31 October.

At a glance

Welcome & Ambience	✓✓✓✓	Location	✓✓✓
Quality of Pitches	✓✓✓✓	Range of Facilities	✓✓✓✓

Directions

From the north, take the N74 from Langres (towards Dijon). After 8 km. site entrance is on the right. From the south, turning left from the N74 into the site is forbidden. Go 2 km. north, take right hand slip road towards trading estate (also to the A31), pass under N74, then left to rejoin the N74 going south.

Charges 2005

Per person	€ 2,50 - € 4,00
pitch	€ 5,00 - € 6,00

Reservations

Contact site. Tel: 03 25 88 24 02. Email: croix.arles@wanadoo.fr

La Forge de Sainte-Marie
www.laforgedesaintemarie.com +33 (0) 3 25 94 42 00
New PDF brochure ▶ : e-mail
info@laforgedesaintemarie.com

Mobile homes ▶ page 413

FR52020 Castel Camping La Forge de Sainte Marie

F-52230 Thonnance-les-Moulins (Haute-Marne)

The département of Haute-Marne is situated between the better known areas of Champagne and the Vosges. It is a sleepy land of rolling hills, forests and farmland. In the heart of this lies Thonnance-les-Moulins, twelve kilometres east of Joinville and the north – south N67 main road between St Dizier and Chaumont. This most attractive campsite has been created from the remains of old forge buildings and their surroundings in this secluded valley. As soon as one enters through the arched gateway, one is impressed by the setting. A picturesque bridge links the upper part of the site with a lower road going to the section near the river. Opposite reception, another old building has been skilfully converted into gites for letting. Grass pitches, 165 for touring units, are of a very generous size on terraces amongst the trees or in more open areas. Electricity (6A) and water are available and 120 pitches are fully serviced. There is much of interest in the area - Joan d'Arc and General de Gaulle lived near and it is not too far to the Champagne vineyards and cellars at Reims. Nigloland for the children is within range and Joinville is worth exploring. It is also possible to visit the largest man-made lake in Europe at Giffaumont-Champaubert. There are also 30 mobile homes and chalets, and 22 tour operator units on site. The enthusiastic British and Dutch managers are determined to make a success of the site.

Facilities

There are two modern sanitary blocks which do come under pressure at peak times and in high season. However, additional facilities are available at reception or in the pool complex. Shop and excellent restaurant and bar with terrace. Splendid heated indoor pool with a smaller one for children (all open 29/4-15/9). Four children's play areas imaginatively placed around the site. Level open grass area for football and volleyball. Bicycle hire. Free fishing. Games room. Internet terminal. Organized games for children in high season. Varied programme for adults including a farm visit by tractor with a barbecue, music, dancing and excursions. Organised golfing holidays arranged.
Off site: Riding 15 km. Golf 45 km. A visit to Grand (20 km.) with its Gallo-Roman amphitheatre and mosaic is a must.

At a glance

Welcome & Ambience	✓✓✓✓	Location	✓✓✓✓
Quality of Pitches	✓✓✓✓	Range of Facilities	✓✓✓✓✓

Directions

Site is about 12 km. southeast of Joinville between Poissons and Germay on road D427. The site entrance may be a little tight for large units. GPS: N48:24.392 E05:16.270

Charges 2006

Per pitch incl. 2 persons and electricity	€ 18,00 - € 29,00
extra person	€ 3,50 - € 7,00
child (2-9 yrs)	€ 1,75 - € 3,50
animal	€ 1,00 - € 1,00

Less 20% outside July/Aug.
Camping Cheques accepted.

Reservations

Contact site for details. Tel: 03 25 94 42 00.
Email: la.forge.de.sainte.marie@wanadoo.fr

Open

29 April - 15 September.

FR54000 Camping Le Brabois

Avenue Paul Muller, F-54600 Villers-les-Nancy (Meurthe-et-Moselle)

This former municipal site, within the Nancy city boundary and 5 km. from the centre, was taken over by the Campeole group in 1998. Situated within a forest area, there is shade in most parts and, although the site is on a slight slope, the 185 good-sized, numbered and separated pitches are level. Of these, 160 pitches have electrical connections (5/15A) and 30 also have water and drainage. Being on one of the main routes from Luxembourg to the south of France, Le Brabois makes a good night stop. However, Nancy is a delightful city in the heart of Lorraine and well worth a longer stay, not only for the interesting 18th century Place Stanislas (pedestrianised) and 11th century city centre, but for the many other attractions of the area. The British manager has a wide range of tourist literature, publishes a monthly English newsletter and is pleased to help plan visits and day trips. Horse racing takes place every two weeks at the Nancy race track next to the campsite, and good wine is produced nearby.

Facilities

Six sanitary blocks spread around the site are old and due for refurbishment over the next few years. They have a mix of British and Turkish style WCs and some washbasins in cubicles. One block can be heated in cool weather. Two units for disabled visitors. Washing machine and dryer. Motorcaravan service point. Small shop (all season). Bread to order. Restaurant incorporating bar and small shop (15/6-31/8). Small library for book exchange. Playground for young children. Area for ball games and table tennis under cover. Off site: Restaurants and shops about 1 km. Excellent walks and cycle rides. Buses to Nancy every 15 minutes.

Open

1 April - 15 October.

At a glance

Welcome & Ambience	✓✓✓✓	Location	✓✓✓✓
Quality of Pitches	✓✓✓✓	Range of Facilities	✓✓✓✓

Directions

Take exit 2b 'Brabois' from autoroute A33, continue for about 500 m. to 'Quick' restaurant on left. Turn left here, pass the racetrack to T-junction, turn right and after about 400 m. turn right on to site entrance road.

Charges 2005

Per unit incl. 2 persons	€ 11,00 - € 12,90
extra person	€ 4,00 - € 5,00
child (2-5 yrs)	free - € 3,30
electricity	€ 3,90
hiker	€ 6,00 - € 7,10
dog	€ 2,50 - € 2,60

Credit cards minimum € 15.
Barrier card deposit € 20.

Reservations

Advised for July but site say no-one is turned away.
Tel: 03 83 27 18 28.
Email: campeoles.brabois@wanadoo.fr

FR54010 Camping de Villey-le-Sec

34 rue de La Gare, F-54840 Villey-le-Sec (Meurthe-et-Moselle)

Being not far from the motorway from Luxembourg to the Mediterranean, this neat campsite is a popular overnight stop, but the area is worth a longer stay. Toul, with its 2000 years of history and Vauban fortifications, is well worth a visit. Villey-le-Sec itself has its own fortifications, part of the defensive system built along France's frontiers after the 1870 war, and a long distance cycling track passes less than 2 km. from the campsite. The site, right on a bank of the Moselle river, has 64 level grassy marked touring pitches, with electricity (6A) and plenty of water taps. There are also individual water taps and waste water drainage for 8 of these pitches. Another area without electricity accommodates 11 tents. Just outside the site is an overnight stopping place for motorcaravans.

Facilities

Two modern toilet blocks (one heated) contain British style WCs, washbasins in cabins and controllable showers. Facilities for disabled people and babies. Motorcaravan services. Washing machine and dryer. Gas supplies. Shop. Bar/restaurant. Snack bar and takeaway. Games room. Playground. Playing field. Table tennis. Boules. Fishing. Off site: Riding 2 km. Rock climbing 4 km. Golf 15 km.

Open

1 April - 30 September.

At a glance

Welcome & Ambience	✓✓✓✓	Location	✓✓✓✓
Quality of Pitches	✓✓✓✓	Range of Facilities	✓✓✓✓

Directions

Villey-le-Sec is about 20 km. east of Nancy, and 7 km. east of Toul. From Toul take the road east (towards Nancy), crossing the bridge over the Moselle, Just after going under the A31 motorway, turn right on the D909 to Villey-le-Sec. From there follow signs to site, turning left after crossing the old railway line.

Charges 2005

Per person	€ 2,60
child (0-7 yrs)	€ 1,60
pitch	€ 4,10 - € 4,90
electricity (6A)	€ 2,70
animal	€ 1,60

Reservations

Contact site. Tel: 03 83 63 64 28.
Email: info@campingvilleylesec.com

FR55010 Camping Les Breuils

Allée des Breuils, F-55100 Verdun (Meuse)

Thousands of soldiers of many nations are buried in the cemeteries around this famous town and the city is justly proud of its determined First World War resistance. Les Breuils is a neat site beside a small fishing lake and close to the famous town and Citadel. It provides 166 flat pitches of varying sizes on two levels (144 for touring units), many with shade. Separated by trees or hedges, they are beside the lake and 120 offer the possibility of electricity connection (6A) although long leads will be necessary for some. The overall appearance of this busy site is attractive.

Facilities

Sanitary facilities, in two blocks, are a mixture of old and new, the newer parts being of a better standard, including washbasins in cabins for ladies, washing machines and dryers, facilities for the disabled and babies. Conveniently sited among the pitches are sets of four dishwashing sinks under pitched roofs (cold water only; hot water at the blocks). Cleaning and maintenance variable. Motorcaravan services. Small shop, (1/5-30/9) selling wines and essentials, reception has various local guide books for sale (1/5-31/8). Restaurant serves breakfast, evening and lunchtime snacks and takeaway (Mid June-31/8), bar (Eves 1/5-30/9). Swimming pool (200 sq.m.) and children's pool (1/6-31/8). Large fenced play area on gravel. New multi-sports complex (football, volleyball, basketball). Off site: Bicycle hire and town centre 1 km. Riding 5 km. The 'Citadelle Souterraine' is well worth a visit and is within walking distance of the site.

Directions

The RN3 forms a sort of ring road round the north of the town. Site is signed from this on the west side of the town (500 m. to site). GPS: N49:09.222 E05:21.938

Charges 2005

Per person	€ 5,00
child (under 10 yrs)	€ 3,00
caravan or motorcaravan	€ 4,20
double axle caravan	€ 15,00
tent	€ 2,80
electricity (6A)	€ 3,80

Discounts for low season and longer stays.
Double axle caravans € 15 per night.
Credit cards accepted for minimum of € 15.

Reservations

Advised for high season. Tel: 03 29 86 15 31.
Email: contact@camping-lesbreuils.com

Open

1 April - 30 September.

At a glance

Welcome & Ambience	✓✓✓	Location	✓✓✓
Quality of Pitches	✓✓✓✓	Range of Facilities	✓✓✓✓

FR67030 Camping Caravaning du Ried

Route de Rhinau, F-67860 Boofzheim (Bas-Rhin)

The area between the main road from Strasbourg to Colmar and the river Rhine is usually bypassed by those who are exploring Alsace or passing through to Switzerland and Italy. However, if looking for a night stop or a different base in the region, Camping du Ried could well fit the bill. Situated on the edge of a small, picturesque village, it has 100 tourist pitches (with 5A electricity) amongst the 120 rental and 55 private static caravans. Most of these are under tall trees, on grass and separated by hedges. One might think that this is just another reasonable campsite until one sees the excellent pool complex just inside the site entrance which has an attractive outdoor pool for use in July and August and a heated indoor one open from May to September. There is also a lake and small beach on site. We found this a pleasant site with very friendly management who would like to welcome more British visitors, although no English is spoken.

Facilities

The main, heated toilet block is quite a large building and was refurbished in 2002. It is well tiled and has all the usual facilities including those for disabled people. Washing machines and dryer. Additional small units by lake or reception. Bar/restaurant (weekends 1/4-30/6 and 1/9-30/9, daily 1/7-31/8). Splendid outdoor and heated indoor (1/5-30/9) pools (bracelets must be worn). These also have toilets and showers. Motorcaravan service point. Playground. Boules. Minigolf. Canoeing. High season animation for children and daily programme including a variety of excursions, guided canoe trips and competitions. Library. Archery. Fitness trail around lake. Volleyball. Fishing. Off site: Large supermarket outside gates (with ATM, fuel station and car wash). Markets at Benfeld Mondays and Selestat Tuesdays. Bicycle hire 1 km. Riding 4 km. Golf 18 km.

Directions

Leave N83 Strasbourg - Colmar road at Benfeld and go east on D5 to Boofzheim. Site is 500 m. beyond village towards Rhinau. GPS: N48:19.753 E07:41.640

Charges 2006

Per unit incl. 2 persons	€ 13,00 - € 17,50
extra person	€ 3,00 - € 5,50
hiker	€ 7,00 - € 9,00
animal	€ 3,00
electricity (5A)	€ 5,00

Security barrier card deposit €30.
Discount for longer stays.

Reservations

Made with deposit and fee; contact site.
Tel: 03 88 74 68 27. Email: info@camping-ried.com

Open

1 April - 30 September.

At a glance

Welcome & Ambience	✓✓✓✓	Location	✓✓✓
Quality of Pitches	✓✓✓✓	Range of Facilities	✓✓✓✓

FR57050 Camping Municipal de Metz-Plage

Allée de Metz-Plage, F-57000 Metz (Moselle)

As this site is just a short way from the autoroute exit and within easy walking distance for the city centre, it could make a useful night stop if travelling from Luxembourg to Nancy or for a longer stay if exploring the area. By the Moselle river, the 151 pitches are on level grass, most are under shade from tall trees and 73 have electricity (10A) and water connections. Tent pitches are on the river banks.

Facilities
The two sanitary blocks, one newer than the other, are acceptable if not luxurious. Baby room. Laundry and dishwashing sinks. Shop. Bar, restaurant and takeaway. 3 pitches for over night stops for motorcaravans. Off site: Fishing nearby. Riding 5 km. Golf 8 km.

Open
5 May - 23 September.

At a glance
Welcome & Ambience	✓✓✓✓	Location	✓✓✓✓✓
Quality of Pitches	✓✓✓✓	Range of Facilities	✓✓✓

Directions
From autoroute take Metz-Nord - Pontiffray exit (no. 33) and follow camp signs

Charges 2005
Per person	€ 2,40
child (4-10 yrs)	€ 1,20
pitch incl. electricity	€ 4,40 - € 6,40
tent and vehicle	€ 2,40

Reservations
Not possible. Tel: 03 87 68 26 48.
Email: campingmetz@mairie-metz.fr

FR67010 Camping l'Oasis

3 rue du Frohret, F-67110 Oberbronn (Bas-Rhin)

This is an attractively situated, inexpensive site, set amidst the mountains and forests of northern Alsace, not far from the German border. There are good views over the valley to one side and the pretty village with trees sheltering the other. The circular internal road has pitches around the outside (120 for touring units, 30 for seasonal units), as well as space in the centre where there is also a children's playground. The solar-heated pool is of excellent quality. A 'Centre de Vacances' was added for 2004, with a covered pool, sauna and fitness room.

Facilities
The first well appointed toilet block, heated in cool weather, has some washbasins in cabins for ladies, washing machines and dryers, a baby room and facilities for disabled people. The second block is unisex and small. Small shop. General room with table football and air hockey. Swimming pool and children's pool (July/Aug). Indoor pool next to site. Playground. Tennis court. Off site: Riding 700 m. Supermarket in the village 1 km. Fishing 3 km. Fitness circuit in the nearby forest.

Open
14 March - 13 November.

At a glance
Welcome & Ambience	✓✓✓✓	Location	✓✓✓✓
Quality of Pitches	✓✓✓✓	Range of Facilities	✓✓✓✓

Directions
Travel northwest from Haguenau on N62 for 20 km. South of Niederbronn turn left on D28 to Oberbronn-Zinswiller - site is signed. From A4 use exit 42 to Sarreguemines, then Haguenau and as above.

Charges 2006
Per person	€ 3,70
child (under 7)	€ 2,20
pitch incl. vehicle	€ 4,20
electricity	€ 3,90

Less 5% outside 1/7-31/8. No credit cards.

Reservations
Advised for high season. Write with precise dates; no deposit required. Tel: 03 88 09 71 96.
Email: oasis.oberbronn@laregie.fr

FR67050 Camping Municipal Wasselonne

Route de Romanswiller, F-67310 Wasselonne (Bas-Rhin)

A good quality municipal site with a resident warden, the facilities here include a well stocked small shop, a crêperie in season and the added bonus of free admission to the superb indoor heated swimming pool which is adjacent to the site. There are 70 tourist pitches and around 30 seasonal units, on grass with a slight slope and all with electricity hook-ups (5/10A). Four new rental chalets are in a separate fenced area. A full programme of events is offered in the town by the Tourist Office, including welcome evenings, guided tours, concerts, musical festivals, food tasting evenings. This could be an excellent base from which to visit Strasbourg.

Facilities
The single, large, and well maintained sanitary unit behind reception has unisex facilities with ample sized showers and washbasins in cubicles. Laundry room with washing machine and dryer and covered dishwashing sinks. No specific facilities for disabled visitors but the rooms are spacious and should be accessible to many. Motorcaravan service point. Off site: Heated swimming pool, hotel with restaurant, tennis courts, plus an athletics stadium are all adjacent to the site. Supermarket 500 m.

At a glance
Welcome & Ambience	✓✓✓✓	Location	✓✓✓✓
Quality of Pitches	✓✓✓✓	Range of Facilities	✓✓✓✓

Directions
Wasselonne is 25 km. west of Strasbourg. Site lies southwest of town centre on D224 towards Romanswiller, and is well signed.
GPS: N48:38.264 E07:25.907

Charges guide
Per unit incl. 1 person	€ 7,30
extra person	€ 3,30
electricity	€ 2,10 - € 3,50

Reservations
Possible, contact site for details. Tel: 03 88 87 00 08.

Open
15 April - 15 October.

FR68070 Camping Les Sources

Route des Crêtes, F-68700 Wattwiller (Haut-Rhin)

Wattwiller is just off the N83 Alsace 'Route du Vins – Route des Crêtes', tucked away in the forest hills beyond the vineyards, but not far from them, in the popular region of the Vosges. Camping Les Sources occupies a very steep slope above the village under a covering of tall trees. Of the 362 pitches, 106 are occupied by mobile home pitches for rent and 14 by seasonal units, leaving 242 for touring units. All these pitches have electricity (5A) and most are on terraces of gravel hardstanding. The trees mean that the site is very shady, so it can be rather gloomy in overcast or wet weather. A narrow hard road meanders between pitches and is very steep in places making it difficult for large units, although staff will assist with a tractor if required. Les Sources would suit those who are fit (there is much up and down walking) and wish to enjoy the quiet, secluded location although there would appear to be plenty on offer during high season. The site issues a map for walking in the area and a sheet in English with places to visit, and staff will be pleased to give further information.

Facilities

Three old toilet blocks are spread around the site and are fully equipped, but cleaning and maintenance is variable. No provision for disabled visitors who would find the steep roads too difficult. Washing machines and dryers. Shop. Good restaurant. Two swimming pools, one outdoor (July/Aug. only) and another heated and covered (all season). Arena for horse riding activities. Tennis court, table tennis, minigolf and volleyball. Entertainment area. Play area. Games room. Internet point. Organised programme with walking, games and creative activities (July and August).

Open

1 April - 30 September.

At a glance

Welcome & Ambience	✓✓✓	Location	✓✓✓
Quality of Pitches	✓✓✓	Range of Facilities	✓✓✓✓

Directions

From N66 Thann - Mulhouse road, go north to Cernay and continue through Uffholtz to Wattwiller. Turn left at roundabout on southern edge of village, left again and follow D5 for 2 km. uphill to site. GPS: N47:50.046 E07:09.939

Charges 2005

Per unit incl. 2 persons	€ 15,00 - € 22,00
extra person	€ 5,50 - € 7,00
child (1-7 yrs)	€ 4,00 - € 5,00
electricity (5A)	€ 3,90

Less 15-20% in low seasons. Barrier card deposit € 10. Pool wristband deposit € 2. Camping Cheques accepted.

Reservations

Made with deposit (€ 80) and fee (€ 14 July and August only). Tel: 03 89 75 44 94. Email: camping.les.sources@wanadoo.fr

FR68080 Camping Clair Vacances

Route de Herrlisheim, F-68127 St Croix-en-Plaine (Haut-Rhin)

Alsace is a popular and picturesque area of lovely villages, large vineyards, mountains and forests, and is also on the route taken by many heading for Switzerland or Italy. Clair Vacances, opened in 1997, and extended in 2003 is a very neat, tidy and pretty site with 130 level pitches of generous size which are numbered and most are separated by trees and shrubs. All have electricity connections (8-13A) and 10 are fully serviced with water and drainage. The site has been imaginatively laid out with the pitches reached from hard access roads. This is a quiet family site. The friendly couple who own and run it will be pleased to advise on the attractions of the area. The site is 1 km. from the A35 exit, not far from Colmar.

Facilities

Two excellent, modern toilet blocks include washbasins in cabins, well equipped baby rooms and good facilities for disabled visitors. Laundry and dishwashing facilities. Shop with limited supplies. Swimming pool and children's pool with large sunbathing area. Playground. Table tennis. Volleyball. Community room. Archery in high season. Dogs are not accepted in July/Aug. Camping Gaz stocked. Off site: Colmar with restaurants and shops is not far away.

Open

Week before Easter - 15 October.

At a glance

Welcome & Ambience	✓✓✓✓	Location	✓✓✓✓
Quality of Pitches	✓✓✓✓	Range of Facilities	✓✓✓✓

Directions

Site is signed from exit 27 of the A35 south of Colmar on the Herrlisheim road (D1). GPS: N48:00.957 E07:20.989

Charges 2005

Per unit incl. 2 adults and electricity	€ 15,00 - € 19,00
extra adult	€ 3,00 - € 5,00
child (under 7 yrs)	€ 1,50 - € 3,00

Reservations

Made with deposit of € 50 and € 14 fee per week. Tel: 03 89 49 27 28. Email: clairvacances@wanadoo.fr

FR68030 Camping Municipal Masevaux

3 rue du Stade, F-68290 Masevaux (Haut-Rhin)

Masevaux is a pleasant little town in the Haut-Rhin département of Alsace, just to the north of the A36 Belfort - Mulhouse motorway. The municipal camping site is situated in a quiet edge of town next to the sporting complex which has a good indoor pool and other sporting opportunities. The pretty flower decked entrance promises a neat, excellent site and one is not disappointed. The neatly mown 120 pitches for tourists are on level grass, of reasonable size, marked by trees and hedges, and all have electricity (3/6A). Most are well shaded by a variety of trees and have good views of the surrounding hills. The attractive town is a short walk.

Facilities	Directions
A modern, well designed and well equipped sanitary block has most washbasins in private cabins. Baby room. Laundry and covered dishwashing area. Baker calls in high season. TV room, small library, Boules. Play area. Tennis courts (extra charge), volleyball, table tennis. Off site: Supermarket, restaurants and indoor pool near. Fishing.	From D466 in Masevaux follow signs for Belfort and then 'Camping Complexe Sportif'. GPS: N47:46.677 E06:59.462

Open

1 March - 31 October.

Charges 2005

Per person	€ 2,65
pitch	€ 2,65
electricity (3/6A)	€ 2,65 - € 5,00

Reservations

Contact site. Tel: 03 89 82 42 29.
Email: camping-masevaux@tv-com.net

At a glance

Welcome & Ambience	✓✓✓✓	Location	✓✓✓✓
Quality of Pitches	✓✓✓✓	Range of Facilities	✓✓✓

FR68040 Camping Municipal Les Trois Châteaux

10 rue du Bassin, F-68420 Eguisheim (Haut-Rhin)

The village of Eguisheim is on the Alsace 'Rue du Vin' to the west of Colmar. The three châteaux from which the site gets its name are clearly visible on the distant hills. About 400 m. from the village, Les Trois Châteaux is busy and popular. Flowers, shrubs and a variety of trees, along with the well tended grass areas make this a very pleasant place. The 121 pitches, 115 with electricity (6A), are either on a slight slope or a terrace, and are marked and numbered, most with good shade. Around 80% of pitches now have some gravel hardstandings, most of irregular shape and size. The facilities of the fascinating village of Eguisheim are close and the site is well located for exploring this delightful part of Alsace.

Facilities	Directions
The single sanitary block has hot showers and warm water only to washbasins. Some washbasins in cubicles and facilities for disabled people. Playground. Caravans over 7 m. and/or 1 ton in weight are not accepted. Motorcaravan service point. Off site: Fishing 3 km.	Eguisheim is just off the N83 and the site is well signed in the village.

Open

1 April - 30 September.

Charges 2005

Per person	€ 3,50
pitch	€ 3,70
electricity (6A)	€ 3,40

No credit cards.

Reservations

Not made - arrive early in season.
Tel: 03 89 23 19 39.

At a glance

Welcome & Ambience	✓✓✓✓	Location	✓✓✓✓
Quality of Pitches	✓✓✓✓	Range of Facilities	✓✓✓

FR68060 Camping Intercommunal Riquewihr

Route des Vins, F-68340 Riquewihr (Haut-Rhin)

Surrounded by vineyards and minutes from the delightful village of Riquewihr, this is a well run site which has earned its good reputation. Situated in the heart of the Alsace wine region the site covers three hectares with views across the open countryside. Immediately to the right of the security barrier stands a modern, part-timbered building housing reception and information area. Close by is a small summer house and both are heavily garlanded with flowers. The 161 spacious individual grass pitches, many with shade and divided by hedging, have electrical connections (6A).

Facilities	Directions
There are three sanitary blocks, one of a more modern design. Facilities include private cabins with basins, good nursery room and excellent facilities for disabled people. Motorcaravan service point. Campers' room with tables and chairs. Shop for basic necessities, drinks and papers (from 1/5). Off site: Children's play area and sports field adjacent. Fishing 3 km. Bicycle hire 5 km.	From N83 north of Colmar take D4 westwards to Bennwihr. Turn north on D18 for 2 km. towards Ribeauvillé. Site is signed off roundabout at southern end of Riquewihr bypass. Do not enter village. GPS: N48:09.731 E07:19.014

Open

1 April - 31 December.

Charges guide

Per person	€ 3,35 - € 3,70
pitch	€ 3,60 - € 4,00
electricity	€ 4,10
use of motorcaravan services	€ 5,30

Reservations

Not accepted. Tel: 03 89 47 90 08.
Email: camping.riquewihr@tiscali.fr

At a glance

Welcome & Ambience	✓✓✓✓	Location	✓✓✓✓
Quality of Pitches	✓✓✓✓	Range of Facilities	✓✓✓

FR68050 Camping Municipal Pierre de Coubertin

23 rue de Landau, F-68150 Ribeauvillé (Haut-Rhin)

The fascinating medieval town of Ribeauvillé on the Alsace Wine Route is within walking distance of this attractive, quietly located site. Popular and well run, the site has 226 tourist pitches, all with electricity hook-ups (2/ 6A) and some separated by shrubs or railings. There are tarmac or gravel access roads. This is a site solely for tourists – there are no mobile homes or seasonal units here. The small shop is open daily for most of the season (hours vary) and this provides bread, basic supplies and some wines. Only breathable groundsheets are permitted.

Facilities

Large, centrally located heated block provides modern facilities with washbasins in cubicles. Baby changing facilities. Large laundry and dishwashing rooms with a generous supply of sinks. A smaller, unit at the far end of the site is opened for July/Aug. Very good facilities for disabled campers at both units. Recycling. Excellent adventure style playground with a rubber base. Tennis court. Two boules pitches. Table tennis. TV room. Off site: Outdoor pool (June-Aug) with reduced price tickets for campers available from reception. Nearby sports complex with indoor pool (all year). Worth a visit is Ferme l'Hirondelle at Ribeauvillé Gare which makes its own cheese, farm shop for milk, cheese, butter, yoghurt, and regional products, and the children can visit the animals whilst you relax on the shady terrace of the bar/restaurant.

At a glance

Welcome & Ambience	✓✓✓✓	Location	✓✓✓✓✓
Quality of Pitches	✓✓✓✓	Range of Facilities	✓✓✓

Directions

Ribeauvillé is about 13 km. southwest of Sèlestat. Site is well signed, turn north off D106 at traffic lights by large car park, east of town centre.
GPS: N48:11.697 E07:20.198

Charges 2005

Per person	€ 3,80
child (0-7 yrs)	€ 1,90
pitch	€ 4,00
electricity	€ 2,50 - € 4,00

Reservations

Not made - arrive early in season.
Tel: 03 89 73 66 71.
Email: camping.ribeauville@wanadoo.fr

Open

15 March - 15 November.

FR68090 Camping Le Schlossberg

Rue du Bourbach, F-68820 Kruth (Haut-Rhin)

The attractive village of Kruth lies in a valley in the southern part of the hills and forests of the Vosges in excellent walking country. A leisure lake (reservoir) is 2.5 km. to the north and the area is also popular for hang-gliding. In between the lake and the village lies this spacious, well run campsite. There are 160 touring pitches. Fewer than a quarter have shade, but all are of good size, grassy, level or only slightly sloping, with 2A or 6A electricity supply (Europlug), and there are plenty of water taps. In July/August a club for children is organised, plus other regular activities and entertainment. Signed walks start from the entrance road to the site, and there is pleasant cycling both from the site and around the lake.

Facilities

Two modern toilet blocks (one heated) contain British style WCs, washbasins in cabins, controllable and pre-set showers, facilities for disabled people and babies. Washing machines, dryers and washing lines. Shop for basics. Gas supplies. Bar. Snack bar and takeaway (July/Aug). Small play area. Table tennis. Volleyball. Boules. Off site: In Kruth (1.5 km.) - shops, restaurants and bars, bicycle hire, bus stop. River fishing 300 m. At the lake (1 km.) - bathing, boating, sailing, canoeing, pedaloes, fishing. Riding 7 km.

Open

Easter - 30 September.

At a glance

Welcome & Ambience	✓✓✓✓	Location	✓✓✓✓
Quality of Pitches	✓✓✓✓	Range of Facilities	✓✓✓

Directions

Kruth is ESE of Remiremont and WNW of Mulhouse. Shortest way from Remiremont is via the D417 to St Amé, then the D43 almost to Cornimont, then Kruth. The last 15 km. this way are steep and winding, so you might prefer to take the N66 from Remiremont to Fellering, then go north to Kruth. Site is north of the village, signed. From Mulhouse, take the N66 to Fellering.

Charges 2005

Per person	€ 3,80
child (2-10 yrs)	€ 2,10
pitch	€ 3,60
electricity (2/6A)	€ 3,00
dog	free

Reservations

Made with fee (€ 10); contact site.
Tel: 03 89 82 26 76. Email: contact@schlossberg.fr

1

FR88040 Camping Club du Lac de Bouzey

Mobile homes ▶ page 413

19 rue du Lac, F-88390 Sanchey (Vosges)

Camping-Club Lac de Bouzey is eight kilometres west of Épinal, overlooking the lake, at the beginning of the Vosges Massif. It is well placed for exploring the hills, valleys, lakes and waterfalls of the south of Alsace Lorraine. The word 'Club' has been added to the name to indicate the number of activities organised in high season. The 125 individual 100sqm. back-to-back grass pitches are arranged on either side of tarmac roads with electricity (6-10A). 100 are fully serviced. They are on a gentle slope, divided by trees or beech hedging, under a cover of tall, silver birch trees and some overlook the 130 hectare lake. Units can be close together when the site is busy. The lake has a number of sandy beaches. Many water sports may be enjoyed, from pedaloes to canoes, windsurfing and sailing. The large, imposing building at the entrance to the site houses a restaurant and bar with terraces overlooking the lake. Two bars by the lake would indicate that the lake-side is popular with the public in summer but the camping area is quiet, separated by a road and well back and above the main entrance. An 'all year' site, there is lots going on for teenagers. English is spoken. A 'Sites et Paysages' member.

Facilities

The central sanitary block, partly below ground level, includes a baby room and one for disabled people (although there is up and down hill walking on the site). In winter a small, heated section in the main building with toilet, washbasin and shower is used. Good laundry and dishwashing facilities. Motorcaravan service point. Well stocked shop. Bar and restaurant. Heated swimming pool (1/5-30/9) of an original shape and backed by two sunbathing terraces. Fishing, riding, volleyball, games room, archery and bicycle hire on site. Internet access. Below ground, under the restaurant, is a sound-proof room for cinema shows and discos for those staying on site only. Staff escort young people back to their pitch at the end of the evening. High season programme of activities for all ages, including excursions, entertainment, sports and a mini-club. Off site: Golf 8 km.

At a glance

| Welcome & Ambience | ✓✓✓✓ | Location | ✓✓✓✓ |
| Quality of Pitches | ✓✓✓ | Range of Facilities | ✓✓✓✓✓ |

Directions

Site is 8 km. west of Épinal on D460 and is signed from some parts of Épinal. Follow signs for Lac de Bouzey and Sanchey. GPS: N48:10.015 E06:21.594

Charges 2005

Per unit incl. 2 adults	€ 15,00 - € 23,00
extra person	€ 5,00 - € 7,00
child (4-10 yrs)	free - € 5,00
electricity (6-10A)	€ 4,00 - € 5,00
dog	free - € 3,00

Camping Cheques accepted.

Reservations

Made with deposit (€ 12 per day booked) and fee (€ 25). Tel: 03 29 82 49 41. Email: camping.lac.de.bouzey@wanadoo.fr

Open

All year.

FR88060 Camping La Vologne

Rue Retournermer, F-88400 Xonrupt-Longemer (Vosges)

Lac de Longemer, in the heart of the Vosges massif, lies south of Xonrupt-Longemer. There are busy campsites at the lakeside but this site, a short walk from the southern end of the lake, is more suited to those wanting a quiet, simple, inexpensive campsite with good basic facilities. It is also well placed for the signed walks in the hills around the lake, with direct access to some of them. There are 103 grassy pitches of which 99 are for tourers, all with electricity (2/5A) although long leads would be required in some places. They lie either side of the river Vologne, which is about four metres wide where it runs through the site and can be fished for trout. The pitches on the far side of the river from reception have the most shade; until the trees mature the others will be in the open.

Facilities

Two modern toilet blocks contain 12 British and 4 Turkish style WCs, washbasins (some in cabins) and pre-set showers. Facilities for disabled people, children and babies. Motorcaravan services. Washing machines and dryer. Shop for basics (July/Aug). Gas supplies. Games and TV room. Table football. Playground. Playing field. Table tennis. Boules. Trampoline. Volleyball. Badminton. Off site: Beach, windsurfing, sailing, canoe hire 700 m. Restaurant and bar 1 km. ATM 5 km. Xonrupt-Longemer for shops 7 km. Bicycle hire 10 km. Riding 10 km.

Open

1 May - 15 September.

At a glance

| Welcome & Ambience | ✓✓✓✓ | Location | ✓✓✓✓ |
| Quality of Pitches | ✓✓✓ | Range of Facilities | ✓✓✓ |

Directions

Xonrupt Longemer is just east of Gerardmer, and 46 km. west of Colmar, on the D470. Take the D67 or the D67A, which run southeast from Xonrupt near the edges of Lac de Longemer. Just after the junction of these two roads, site is on the right.

Charges 2005

Per person	€ 2,70 - € 2,90
child (0-7 yrs)	€ 1,30 - € 1,45
pitch	€ 2,90 - € 3,20
electricity (2/5A)	€ 2,30 - € 3,50
dog	€ 1,00

Reservations

Contact site. Tel: 03 29 60 87 23. Email: paulette@lavologne.com

FR88080 Camping Domaine des Bans

Rue James Wiese, F-88430 Corcieux (Vosges)

Corcieux is in the heart of the Vosges mountains, near the lakeside resort of Gerardmer, the Alsace 'Route de Vin' and on the edge of the Ballons des Vosges National Park. Domaine des Bans is a large, busy campsite with 630 pitches in a country setting, where there are plenty of opportunities to be active. There is a very high percentage of static and tour operator units, but room for about 80 tourist units. Pitches (with electricity, water and drainage), numbered and separated by hedges, vary in size with some on low terraces. There is good shade. Some pitches are tucked away in quiet areas with others nearer to where activities take place. New pool complex. The older swimming pool is partly covered and is surrounded by a sun terrace with snack bar. Domaine des Bans is not really a site for short stays, but is a base for exploring the varied and interesting countryside, Haut Koenigsbourg Castle with Colmar, Épinal and Strasbourg within range for day trips.

Facilities

Three functional toilet blocks are spread around the site. Some washbasins are in cabins. Shop (30/5-30/9). Bar (1/6-15/9). Restaurant (1/5-15/9). Takeaway (30/4-15/9). Swimming pools (outdoor 1/6-15/9, indoor 1/5-15/9). Playground and open area for ball games. Tennis, table tennis, badminton, minigolf, volleyball and archery. Bicycle hire. Riding. Lakes for fishing and boating. High season entertainment programme including discos (sound-proof underground room), theatre performances and other live music. 'Goats Castle' with about two dozen goats provides interest for children. Off site: Smaller restaurant just outside the site boundary with others a short distance away in the village.

At a glance

Welcome & Ambience	✓✓✓✓	Location	✓✓✓✓
Quality of Pitches	✓✓✓	Range of Facilities	✓✓✓✓

Directions

From D8 St Dié - Gerardmer road, turn west on D60 just north of Gerbepal to Corcieux. GPS: N48:10.142 E06:52.817

Charges 2005

Per person	€ 5,00 - € 7,00
child (3-7 yrs)	free - € 7,00
pitch incl. electricity	€ 15,00 - € 33,00

Reservations

Advised in high season and made with 25% deposit and € 30 fee. Tel: 03 29 51 64 67. Email: les-bans@domaine-des-bans.com

Open

26 April - 30 September.

FR88090 Base de Loisirs du Lac de la Moselotte

Les Amias – B.P. 34, F-88290 Saulxures-sur-Moselotte (Vosges)

This neat, well run, spacious lakeside site, part of a leisure village complex, has 75 generously sized, grassy and individual hedged pitches. All have electrical hook-ups (10A) and 25 of these are multi-serviced with electricity, water and waste water drainage. The many trees are not yet mature enough to provide more than a little shade. The site is fully fenced with a security barrier and a key for the pedestrian gates (to site and lakeside) issued by the friendly and helpful reception staff. All facilities are modern and well maintained. The adjacent 'base de loisirs' has a wide variety of activities on offer, and the surrounding area is very good for walking and cycling.

Facilities

The heated modern toilet block is light and airy with controllable hot showers, some washbasins in cubicles and good facilities for babies and disabled campers. Washing machines and tumble dryers. Shop for basic supplies (July/Aug); bread can be ordered at reception all year. Bar/snack bar and terrace (all season). Bicycle hire. Play area. Outdoor skittle alley. 30 chalets for rent. Off site: The town is an easy level walk and has all services, including a tourist office. The 'base de loisirs' has a lake (supervised swimming July/Aug), a sandy beach and large grass area, a climbing wall, fishing, archery and hire of pedalos, canoes and kayaks. Signposted walks. Close to the site is 'La Voie Verte' - 56 km. of former railway line now used for cycling, roller skating and walking. Other attractions in the region include the Route des Vins in summer, and skiing in winter.

At a glance

Welcome & Ambience	✓✓✓✓✓	Location	✓✓✓✓
Quality of Pitches	✓✓✓✓	Range of Facilities	✓✓✓✓

Directions

Saulxures-sur-Moselotte is about 20 km. east of Remiremont. From Remiremont take D417 east to St Ame, then turn right (east) on D43 towards La Bresse for 10.5 km. Turn left into Saulxures (site is signed), and site entrance is on right after 0.5 km. by lake. GPS: N47:57.164 E06:45.127

Charges 2005

Per person	€ 4,00 - € 5,00
child (4-10 yrs)	€ 2,40 - € 3,00
pitch	€ 4,00 - € 5,00
electricity	€ 5,00 - € 6,00
animal	€ 1,00

Reservations

Contact site. Tel: 03 29 24 56 56. Email: lac-moselotte@ville-saulxures-mtte.fr

Open

All year.

FR88120 Camping Le Clos de la Chaume

21 rue d'Alsace, F-88430 Corcieux (Vosges)

Corcieux is in the heart of the 'Ballons des Vosges' and this site would make a good base to explore the area. Within walking distance of the town and on level ground with a small stream adjacent, it is very pleasant. The friendly family owners live on site and do their best to ensure campers have an enjoyable relaxing stay. There are 100 level grassy pitches of varying sizes, with some holiday homes (private and rental) leaving 70 pitches for tourists. All have electricity hook-ups (6/10A) and some are divided by shrubs and trees. Access roads are sandy and large units or American RVs should telephone first to check pitch availability. The site boasts an attractive, well fenced, small swimming pool and an excellent small adventure style playground. The site has some excellent and informative leaflets (available in several languages) which give details of walks and mountain biking routes in the surrounding countryside.

Facilities

Two units provide well maintained facilities including a laundry with washing machines and dryers, a dual purpose family/disabled room and dishwashing sinks. Good motorcaravan service point. Recycling. Reception keeps basic supplies during July/August. Campingaz stocked. Swimming pool (13 x 7m, June-Sept). Games room with table football and a pool table. Table tennis, boules and volleyball. Off site: Bicycle hire 800 m. in the town. Riding 2 km. Fishing 3 or 10 km. Golf 30 km. Corcieux market on Mondays.

Open

29 April - 17 September.

At a glance

Welcome & Ambience	✓✓✓✓	Location	✓✓✓✓
Quality of Pitches	✓✓✓✓	Range of Facilities	✓✓✓✓

Directions

Corcieux is about 17 km. south-south-west of St Dié des Vosges. Site is on D60, east of town centre, by the town boundary sign.
GPS: N48:10.094 E06:53.401

Charges 2006

Per unit incl. 2 persons	€ 11,20
extra person	€ 3,20
child (0-7 yrs)	€ 1,70
electricity	€ 2,80
animal	€ 1,20

Reservations

Made with deposit (€ 5 per day. Tel: 03 29 50 76 76. Email: info@camping-closdelachaume.com

---

FR88130 Camping La Vanne de Pierre

Mobile homes  page 414

5 rue du camping, F-88100 St Dié-des-Vosges (Vosges)

La Vanne de Pierre is a neat and attractive site with 118 pitches, many of which are individual with good well trimmed hedges giving plenty of privacy. There are 9 chalets and mobile homes (for rent) and a few seasonal units, leaving around 105 tourist pitches, all multi-serviced with water, drain and electricity hook-up (6/10A). The reception building has been recently refitted and provides a well stocked small shop plus a restaurant/bar with a takeaway facility (all operating all year but opening hours may vary). A small L-shaped outdoor swimming pool (max. depth 1.5 m) is well fenced and a programme of children's entertainment is arranged in July and August. The city centre is an easy 2 km. cycle ride or a level walk alongside the river. A 'Sites et Paysages' member.

Facilities

The main unit is a modern, heated and well tiled building with good facilities including washbasins in cubicles. Three family rooms each with WC, basin, and shower and two similar units fully equipped for disabled campers. Dishwashing room. Laundry room with washing machine and dryer. A second unit, slightly older in style, towards the far end of the site, is opened for July/Aug. Small shop. Bar/restaurant and takeaway. Swimming pool (1/4-30/9, weather permitting). Internet terminal in reception. Campingaz stocked. Bicycle hire. Off site: Golf course, tennis courts (indoor and outdoor), archery, riding all within 1 km. Fishing on nearby river. Places to visit include the St Dié Cathedral, Museum Pierre-No'l, Liberty Tower. Two large supermarkets (Cora and LeClerc) on town outskirts have 2.5 m. height barriers. The Intermarché on N420 (Rue d'Alsace) within the town does not.

At a glance

Welcome & Ambience	✓✓✓✓	Location	✓✓✓✓
Quality of Pitches	✓✓✓✓	Range of Facilities	✓✓✓✓

Directions

St Dié is south east of Nancy. Site is east of town centre on the north bank of the river Meurthe and just south of the D82 to Nayemont les Fosses. Site is well signed from most routes around the town.
GPS: N48:17.160 E06:58.199

Charges 2005

Per unit incl. 2 persons	€ 15,00 - € 20,00
extra person	€ 4,00 - € 6,00
child (4-10 yrs)	free - € 4,00
electricity	€ 4,00 - € 5,00

Camping Cheques accepted.

Reservations

Contact site. Tel: 03 29 56 23 56. Email: vannedepierre@wanadoo.fr

Open

All year.

MAP 5

It's not only the fine beaches that make this holiday region so appealing. Sleepy fishing harbours, historic ports and charming towns all create a great holiday atmosphere.

WE HAVE EXERCISED A LITTLE TOURISM LICENSE WITH THIS AREA TAKING ONE DÉPARTEMENT FROM THE OFFICIAL WESTERN LOIRE REGION, 85 VENDÉE, AND ONE FROM THE POITOU-CHARENTES REGION, 17 CHARENTE-MARITIME

With a sunshine record to rival the south of France, the Vendée and Charente regions are among the most popular areas in France. Running alongside the coastal area stretching down from La Rochelle past Rochefort to Royan, it boasts gently shelving sandy beaches, warm shallow waters and fragrant pine forests. Explore the coasts for traditional fishing villages or head inland for fields of sunflowers and unspoilt rural villages.

The Vendée was the centre of the counter-revolutionary movement between 1793 and 1799 and a 'son et lumière' held at Le Puy-du-Fou tells the whole story. Les Sables d'Olonne is its main resort renowned for its excellent sandy beach. The area between the Vendée and Charente, the Marais Poitevin, is one of the most unusual in France – a vast tract of marshland with a thousand or more tree-lined canals and slow moving streams. The port of La Rochelle, with massive medieval towers, buzzes with life and the island of Ré is popular with those seeking beaches and small, quiet ports.

Places of interest

Marais Poitevin: marshes known as the 'Green Venice'.

Angoulême: Hill-top town surrouded by ramparts, cathedral, Renaissance château.

La Rochelle: port, Porte de la Grosse Horloge (clock gate), Museum of the New World.

Le Puy-du-Fou: 15th-16th century castle, sound and light show involving over 700 participants.

Les Sables d'Olonne: fishing port and seaside resort.

Noirmoutier: linked to the mainland by a 3 mile bridge.

Saint Savin: 17th century abbey, mural painting.

Cuisine of the region

Fish predominates, both fresh water (eel, trout, pike), sea water (shrimps, mussels, oysters). Light fruity wines from Haut-Poitou, Deux-Sèvres and Charente, and Cognac and Pineau des Charentes – an aperitif of grape juice and Cognac.

Cagouilles: snails from Charentes.

Chaudrée: ragout of fish cooked in white wine, shallots and butter.

Mouclade: mussels cooked in wine, egg and cream, served with Pineau des Charentes.

Soupe de moules à la Rochelaise: soup of various fish, mussels, saffron, garlic, tomatoes, onions and red wine.

Sourdons: cockles from the Charentes.

FR17010 Camping Bois Soleil

Mobile homes ▶ page 416

2 avenue de Suzac, F-17110 St Georges-de-Didonne (Charente-Maritime)

Close to the sea and the resort of St Georges, Bois Soleil is a fairly large site in three separate parts, with 165 serviced pitches for touring units and a few for tents. All touring pitches are hedged, and have electricity, with water and a drain between every two. There are a few pitches with lockable gates for late night entry and exit. The main part, 'Les Pins', is mature and attractive with ornamental trees and shrubs providing shade. Opposite is 'La Mer' which has direct access to the beach. It has some areas with rather less shade and a raised central area for tents. The sandy beach here is a wide public one, sheltered from the Atlantic breakers although the sea goes out some way at low tide. The third part of the site, 'La Forêt', is for static holiday homes. The areas are well tended with the named pitches (not numbered) cleared and raked between clients and with an all-in charge including electricity and water. This lively site offers something for everyone, whether they like a beach-side spot or a traditional pitch, plenty of activities or the quiet life – it is best to book for the area you prefer. It can be full mid-June - late August.

Facilities

Each area is served by one large sanitary block, supplemented by smaller blocks providing toilets only. Another heated block is near reception. Well designed and appointed buildings, cleaned twice daily, they include washbasins in cubicles, facilities for disabled people (WC, basin and shower) and for babies. Launderette. Nursery for babies. Supermarket, bakery (July/Aug) and beach shop. Restaurant and bar by pool. Excellent takeaway (from April). Heated swimming pool. 'Parc des Jeux' with tennis, table tennis, bicycle hire, boules and children's playground. TV room and library. Comprehensive tourist information and entertainment office. Internet terminal. Charcoal barbecues are not permitted but gas ones can be hired by the evening. Pets are not accepted. Off site: Fishing and riding within 500 m. Golf 20 km.

Open

1 April - 31 October.

At a glance

Welcome & Ambience	✓✓✓✓✓	Location	✓✓✓✓✓
Quality of Pitches	✓✓✓✓✓	Range of Facilities	✓✓✓✓✓

Directions

From Royan centre take coast road (D25) along the sea-front of St Georges-de-Didonne towards Meschers. Site is signed at roundabout at end of the main beach.

Charges 2006

Per unit incl. 2 persons, and 6A electricity	€ 19,00 - € 32,50
3 persons	€ 22,00 - € 32,50
tent incl. 2 persons	€ 14,00 - € 28,00
extra person	€ 3,50 - € 6,50
child (3-7 yrs)	€ 1,50 - € 4,50
electricity (10A)	€ 3,30 - € 5,00

Less 20% outside July/Aug.
Camping Cheques accepted.

Reservations

Made with 25% deposit and € 26 fee.
Tel: 05 46 05 05 94.
Email: camping.bois.soleil@wanadoo.fr

FR17020 Airotel Le Puits de L'Auture

151 avenue de La Grande-Côte, F-17420 St Palais-sur-Mer (Charente-Maritime)

This popular region has a very sunny climate and Le Puits de l'Auture is well situated with the sea outside the gates, just across the road, and a long sandy beach starting 400 m. away. It is situated at the start of a pleasant coastal development down to Royan and beyond. The flower beds at the entrance to the site, with the shop and overnight parking opposite reception, welcome you in. Of the 400 numbered pitches, 240 are for touring units, all these being level and having electricity (6A). A fair number are separated by bushes with some trees giving shade and all have access to water and drainage. Mobile homes occupy the rest of the site, a few used by a tour operator. Considering its close proximity to the beach and its popularity, there is a remarkably calm and relaxed atmosphere and the site is well worth considering.

Facilities

Well maintained toilet blocks are more than adequate for the number of visitors. Most WCs are British type and all washbasins are in cabins, showers are adjustable and hot water is plentiful. Baby baths and showers, and full facilities for disabled people. Washing machines and ample sinks for dishwashing and laundry. Well stocked shop (1/5-30/9). Takeaway and bar (1/6-15/9). Swimming pool complex with sunbathing areas (most attractive with banana plants making a backdrop with a difference). Volleyball. Table tennis. Games room. Play area. Bicycle hire. Barbecues are only allowed in a special area. Dogs are not accepted. Off site: Riding and golf 800 m. Several restaurants nearby specialise in sea food.

Open

1 May - 30 September.

At a glance

Welcome & Ambience	✓✓✓✓	Location	✓✓✓✓✓
Quality of Pitches	✓✓✓✓	Range of Facilities	✓✓✓✓

Directions

Site is on the coast, 2 km. from St Palais and 8 km. from Royan. From Royan take D25 past St Palais following signs for La Palmyre. At two lane junction system turn back left signed Grande Côte and St Palais and site is 800 m.

Charges 2005

Per unit incl. 2 persons	€ 16,00 - € 31,00
with 6A electricity	€ 20,00 - € 35,00
with 10A electricity	€ 23,00 - € 39,00
with water and drainage	€ 30,00 - € 43,00
extra person (over 3 yrs)	€ 5,00 - € 7,00

Reservations

Made for min. 5 days with deposit and fee.
Tel: 05 46 23 20 31.
Email: camping-lauture@wanadoo.fr

Bois Soleil

Camping ★★★★
Charente-Maritime

urrounded by pine trees and a sandy beach on the Atlantic
oast, with one direct access to the beach, Bois Soleil
roposes to you many attractions like tennis, tabletennis,
hildren playgrounds and entertainment.
hops, take-away and snack-bar with big TV screen.

Les pieds dans l'eau
www.lespiedsdansleau.com

Camping mague

Camping Qualité

Spring and Summer 2006

2, avenue de Suzac - 17110 ST GEORGES DE DIDONNE
Tel: 0033 546 05 05 94 - Fax: 0033 546 06 27 43
www.bois-soleil.com / e-mail: camping.bois.soleil@wanadoo.fr

FR17040 Camping International Bonne Anse Plage

La Palmyre, F-17570 Les Mathes (Charente-Maritime)

On the edge of the Forêt de la Coubre, just beyond the popular resort of La Palmyre, Bonne Anse has a lovely setting amongst pine trees, just a short stroll from an extensive tidal inlet. It is a spacious, gently undulating site, carefully designed to provide 865 level, marked pitches, of which 460 are for touring units, all with electricity. Most are shaded by the pines, the ones nearer the sea less so (these are rather more sandy). The site's amenities are centred around the entrance and reception building and include a restaurant and bar with a spacious outdoor terrace and an impressive pool complex. This forms the social focus of the site and overlooks the boules area with the pool complex opposite. English and Dutch are spoken and rallies welcomed with visit programmes organised. Used by tour operators (35 pitches). With plenty to do for the active, the site is perhaps a little impersonal.

Facilities

Seven sanitary blocks include some washbasins in cabins, British style toilets with a few Turkish, hot and cold showers. Facilities for disabled visitors and babies. Washing up and laundry sinks under cover. Launderette. Motorcaravan service point. Shopping centre (all season) includes a supermarket, excellent delicatessen and takeaway, crêperie, shops for bread and pastries, holiday goods and papers, plus visiting traders' stalls (wines, seafood, etc) in high season. Restaurant and bar (20/6-30/8). Takeaway (19/5-5/9). Splendid, lively swimming pool complex with heated pool (35 x 25 m), three water toboggans and a water slide. Playground, large video games room, TV (satellite), minigolf and table tennis. Enclosed area with an all-weather surface for football, volleyball or basketball. Trampolines. Direct access to cycle tracks (bicycle hire available) that avoid the main road. Entertainment in season. Internet access. Only gas barbecues are permitted. Dogs are not accepted. Off site: Fishing and riding 1 km. Golf 5 km. Facilities for watersports and tennis nearby. Supervised, safe beaches 500 m. Fitness track.

Directions

Leave A10 autoroute at Saintes and head for Royan (N150). In Royan take signs for La Palmyre (D25). At La Palmyre roundabout follow signs for Ronce-les-Bains and site is 1 km. on the left.

Charges 2005

Per unit incl. 2 persons	€ 31,00
extra person (over 1 yr)	€ 8,50
electricity (5A)	€ 6,00

Reservations

Min. 5 days - phone, fax or write for details.
Tel: 05 46 22 40 90. Email: Bonne.Anse@wanadoo.fr

Open

24 May - 4 September.

At a glance

Welcome & Ambience	✓✓✓✓	Location	✓✓✓✓
Quality of Pitches	✓✓✓	Range of Facilities	✓✓✓✓✓

FR17070 Camping Les Gros Joncs

850 route de Ponthezieres, Les Sables Vignier, F-17190 St Georges d'Oleron (Charente-Maritime)

Situated on the west coast of the holiday island of Ile d'Oléron, Les Gros Joncs is owned and run by the Cavel family. The have strived to keep the site up to date and of high quality. The restaurant and takeaway are of a standard unusual in a campsite. The shop with its own bakery and patisserie stocks a wide range of foods, drinks and everyday essentials. There are 50 or so touring pitches of a good size (some extra large) and providing a choice between full sun and varying degrees of shade. All have water and electricity (10A) to hand. A short stroll through a small wood and sand dunes to a rock pool area is enjoyed by children, while at a distance of some 800 m. is a sandy beach suitable for swimming. The site has a heated pool with hydrotherapy and beauty treatments available. Slides and other attractions, including an indoor pool are planned for the future. Much attention has been given to the needs of disabled visitors including chalets sleeping six persons where space and equipment is specially adapted.

Facilities

Toilet facilities are of traditional design, kept very clean and very adequate in number. Washing machines, dryers and laundry rooms. Motorcaravan services. Well stocked shop with bakery (1/4-15/9). Bar with TV, restaurant and snack bar with takeaway (all 1/4-15/9). Swimming pool (1/4- 15/9) with hydrotherapy and beauty treatments. Bicycle hire. Children's club (1/7-15/9). WiFi internet access. Barbecues are not allowed. Off site: Bus service from Chéray. Fishing 2 km. Riding 6 km. Golf 8 km. Beach 200 or 400 m.

Open

All year.

At a glance

Welcome & Ambience	✓✓✓✓✓	Location	✓✓✓✓
Quality of Pitches	✓✓✓✓	Range of Facilities	✓✓✓✓

Directions

Cross the viaduct onto the Ile d'Oléron and take the D734 (signed St George d'Oléron) At the traffic lights in Chéray turn left and follow the signs for camping and Sable Vignier. Shortly there are site signs to indicate the direction of Les Gros Joncs.

Charges 2005

Per unit incl. 2 persons	€ 13,10 - € 35,80
incl. 3 persons	€ 15,20 - € 35,80
extra person	€ 5,00 - € 10,00
child (0-7 yrs)	€ 2,10 - € 6,10
electricity	€ 2,60

Reservations

Contact site. Tel: 05 46 76 52.
Email: camping.gros.joncs@wanadoo.fr

FR17050 Camping L'Orée du Bois

225 route de la Bouverie, La Fouasse, F-17570 Les Mathes (Charente-Maritime)

L'Orée du Bois has 388 pitches of about 100 sq.m. in a very spacious, pinewood setting. There are 150 for touring units, mainly scattered amongst the permanent chalets and tents. They include 40 large pitches with hardstanding and individual sanitary facilities (built in small, neat blocks of four and containing your own shower, toilet, washbasin and dishwashing sink). The pitches are on flat, fairly sandy ground, separated by trees, shrubs and growing hedges and all have electrical connections (6A). The forest pines offer some shade. Sandy beaches (with lifeguards in season) are fairly near, plus opportunities for walking, riding or cycling in the 10,000 hectare Forêt de la Coubre. A very lively site in high season, suitable for all age groups, it can be noisy but is tranquil in low season with large, spacious pitches. Used by several tour operators.

Facilities

Four attractively designed, main toilet blocks have good fittings, including some washbasins in cabins. Three blocks have laundry rooms, dishwashing under cover and fully equipped units for disabled people. Well stocked shop. Excellent bar, restaurant, crêperie and takeaway service. Large swimming pools, including water slide and paddling pool (proper swimming trunks, not shorts). Two play areas. Tennis court, boules, volleyball, table tennis, football and basketball areas. Games room and TV lounge (with satellite). Bicycle hire. Twice weekly discos and free, all day children's entertainment organised in July/Aug. Internet access. Barbecues allowed in special areas. Off site: Riding 300 m. Fishing 4 km. Golf 20 km.

Open

6 May - 30 September.

At a glance

Welcome & Ambience	✓✓✓✓	Location		✓✓✓
Quality of Pitches		✓✓✓	Range of Facilities	✓✓✓✓

Directions

From north follow D14 La Tremblade road. At roundabout just before Arvert turn onto D268 signed Les Mathes and La Palmyre. Site is on right in Fouasse. From the south, at Royan take D25 towards La Palmyre and in the town turn north to Les Mathes. At first roundabout in Les Mathes follow sign for Fouasse and La Tremblade. Site is on left after 2 km.

Charges 2005

Per unit incl. 2 persons	€ 16,00 - € 31,00
with private sanitary facility	€ 23,00 - € 39,00
extra person (over 3 yrs)	€ 6,00
animal	€ 3,50

Min. stay 7 days in high season.
Camping Cheques accepted.

Reservations

Made with 30% deposit plus fee (€ 21); min. 7 days in high season. Tel: 05 46 22 42 43.
Email: info@camping-oree-du-bois.fr

FR17060 Airotel Oléron

Domaine de Montravail, F-17480 Le Château Oléron (Charente-Maritime)

The site is on the outskirts of Le Château d'Oléron, shortly after leaving the bridge joining Ile d'Oléron to the mainland. The entrance appears to be in a residential area but the site itself is surrounded by paddocks and backs onto the Marais. With the horses, stables and indoor riding school on one side of the approach and the geese and ducks on the other it has a rural feeling. The many peacocks add novelty, and noise! This is a mature site with about 270 pitches of medium to large size, with varying degrees of shade provided by an attractive selection of trees and ornamental shrubs. It is well laid out with the touring pitches (130) and mobile homes each in several separate groups. Most touring pitches have electricity (10A) and four have their own water and waste as well. There is an attractive swimming pool complex and a range of other sporting facilities, with a full entertainment programme in high season. This family run site offers a friendly, attentive, laid-back atmosphere in which to enjoy campsite life – especially equestrian activities – and the exploration of the island with its fine sandy beaches on the Atlantic coast and the miles of flat tracks for walking, cycling or horse riding.

Facilities

Two toilet blocks are well maintained and clean with toilets of both styles, and washbasins in cabins. Washing machines plus laundry and dishwashing sinks at each block. Motorcaravan service point. Fridge hire. Well stocked shop with pleasant staff. Bar, restaurant and takeaway (15/6-15/9). TV and games room. Internet access in reception. Heated swimming and paddling pools. Two tennis courts. Table tennis and play area. Bicycle hire. Riding (hard hats can be supplied, but best to take your own).

Open

15 April - 30 September.

At a glance

Welcome & Ambience	✓✓✓✓	Location		✓✓✓✓
Quality of Pitches		✓✓✓✓	Range of Facilities	✓✓✓✓

Directions

Immediately after the viaduct turn right onto the D734 to Le Château and follow camp signs at junctions.

Charges 2005

Per unit incl. 2 persons	€ 13,00 - € 21,00
extra person	€ 4,00 - € 6,00
electricity (8A)	€ 3,80
dog	€ 2,40

Reservations

Made for exact dates (min. about one week in Aug.) with deposit (€71,65) and booking fee (€19,82). Tel: 05 46 47 61 82.
Email: info@camping-airotel-oleron.com

FR17080 Camping Le Royan

10 rue des Bleuets, F-17200 Royan (Charente-Maritime)

Camping Le Royan is a well established family site located close to the popular resort of Royan and its beaches. There are 186 grassy pitches here, of which around 100 are available for touring. These are of a good size and generally offer electrical connections. Some pitches may suffer from road noise from the nearby Royan by-pass. The site has tarmac access roads and well maintained toilet blocks. The swimming pool is particularly attractive with a number of features including a jacuzzi and a number of slides. A lively entertainment programme is organised in peak season, as well as a children's club.

Facilities

Two sanitary buildings with facilities for disabled people. Snack bar and pizzeria. Shop. Swimming pool with waterslides and other features. Paddling pool. Games room. Playground, Table tennis. Volleyball. Bicycle hire. Children's club. Entertainment. Mobile homes and chalets for rent. Off site: Nearest beach 2.5 km. Royan centre 2 km.

Open

1 April - 10 October.

At a glance

Welcome & Ambience	✓✓✓✓	Location	✓✓✓
Quality of Pitches	✓✓✓✓	Range of Facilities	✓✓✓✓

Directions

Site is close to the Royan by-pass to the northwest of the town heading towards La Palmyre, well signed.

Charges 2005

Per pitch incl. 3 people and electricity	€ 21,50 - € 30,50
extra person	€ 3,50 - € 6,00
baby (under 2 yrs)	free

Reservations

Contact site. Tel: 05 46 39 09 06.
Email: camping.le.royan@wanadoo.fr

Camping Le Royan

Located in parkland at on the edge of Royan, this quality site offers you a warm welcome in a family friendly setting. Only 2.5 km away from beautiful sandy beaches, Camping Le Royan offers you high quality chalets and mobile homes during the whole season. There are 100 grassy pitches reserved for caravans and tents. The site's heated pool complex is open from 1st May

Camping Le Royon • 10 Rue Des Bleuets • 17200 Des Bleuets
Tel.: 05 46 39 09 06 • fax: 05 46 38 12 05
Email: camping.le.royan@wanadoo.fr • www.le-royan.com

FR17110 Camping Caravaning Monplaisir

Route de la Palmyre, F-17570 Les Mathes – La Palmyre (Charente-Maritime)

Monplaisir provides a small, quiet haven in an area with some very hectic campsites. It is ideal for couples or families with young children. The site is quite close to the town set back from the road, and the entrance leads through an avenue of trees, past the owners home to a well kept, garden-like site with many varieties of trees and shrubs. There are 114 level, marked pitches and all but 9 have electricity. On 14 there are caravans for rent and a modern building attached to the site provides flats for rent. There is no shop, bar or restaurant but it is a happy, friendly site with visitors who return year after year.

Facilities

The toilet block has good facilities including some washbasins in cabins and excellent facilities for disabled people. Laundry and dishwashing sinks outside, but under cover. Washing machine and dryer. Ice pack service in reception. Bread delivered daily. TV, games room and library. Heated swimming pool and paddling pool (early May - 30/9). Small play area. Minigolf adjacent (owned by the site). Winter caravan storage. Off site: Fishing 500 m. Riding 1 km. Golf 5 km. Supermarket short walk.

Open

1 April - 1 October.

At a glance

Welcome & Ambience	✓✓✓✓	Location	✓✓✓✓
Quality of Pitches	✓✓✓✓	Range of Facilities	✓✓✓

Directions

Follow the D25 to La Palmyre and, in the town, turn north to Les Mathes. At roundabout turn right to town centre and site is on left. From north on the D14 La Tremblade road turn onto D268 signed Les Mathes and Palmyre at roundabout just before Arvert. Keep straight on to Les Mathes when the road becomes D141 and turn left (north) at roundabout. Site is 600 m. on left.

Charges guide

Per unit incl. 2 persons	€ 16,00
incl. 3 persons	€ 18,00
extra person	€ 4,50
baby under 2 yrs	€ 2,00
electricity	€ 3,00
Less 20% outside July/Aug.	

Reservations

Made with deposit and fee, min. stay 4 nights.
Tel: 05 46 22 50 31.

FR17030 Camping Le Bois Roland

82 route Royan - Saujon, F-17600 Medis (Charente-Maritime)

This site is in an urban area on a busy N-road but, nevertheless, has some unique features. Over the past 30 years, the owner, has planted a very large number of tree varieties on his site to mark and separate the pitches. Now mature, the trees give some shade. Royan, with all its noise and sophistication and well used beaches, is only 5 km. The site has 88 pitches for touring units, mainly between 80-90 sq.m. All have electricity (some may need long leads). The majority of pitches are of good size and to return after a day in Royan may well be worth the drive. The family run a bar and provide simple takeaway food in July and August. The village of Medis, with a variety of shops, is a 600 metre walk.

Facilities

Two modernised toilet blocks contain a mixture of Turkish and British style toilets (no seats and no paper). Modern showers. Baby room. Facilities for disabled campers. Laundry room. Play area. Off site: Buses pass the gate. Riding 1 km. Fishing 4 km. Bicycle hire 5 km. Beach 5 km.

Open

23 April - 30 September.

At a glance

Welcome & Ambience	✓✓✓	Location	✓✓✓
Quality of Pitches	✓✓✓✓	Range of Facilities	✓✓✓

Directions

Site is clearly signed on the west side of the N150 road, 600 m. north of the village of Medis (the N150 runs between Saujon and Royan).

Charges 2005

Per unit incl. 2 persons	€ 14,00 - € 17,00
extra person	€ 4,50
electricity (5A)	€ 4,00

Reservations

Contact site. Tel: 00 33 05 46 05.
Email: boisnoland@wanadoo.fr

FR17140 Castel Camping Sequoia Parc

Mobile homes ▶ page 414

La Josephtrie, F-17320 St Just-Luzac (Charente-Maritime)

Approached by an impressive avenue of flowers, shrubs and trees, Séquoia Parc is a Castel site set in the grounds of La Josephtrie, a striking château with beautifully restored outbuildings and a spacious courtyard. There is a stork's nest on the site. The site itself is designed to a high specification with reception in a large, light and airy room retaining its original beams and leading to the courtyard area where you find the bar and restaurant. The pitches are 140 sq.m. in size with 6A electricity connections and separated by young shrubs. The pool complex with water slides, large paddling pool and sunbathing area is impressive. The site has some 300 mobile homes and chalets, of which 125 are used by tour operators. This is a popular site with a children's club and entertainment throughout the season and reservation is necessary in high season. A 'Yelloh Village' member.

Facilities

Three luxurious toilet blocks, maintained to a high standard, include units with washbasin and shower, dishwashing sinks, facilities for disabled visitors and baby baths. New laundry. Motorcaravan service point. Gas supplies. Large new supermarket. Restaurant/bar and takeaway. Impressive swimming pool complex with paddling pool. Tennis, volleyball, football field. Games and TV rooms. Bicycle hire. Pony trekking. Organised entertainment all season.

Open

13 May - 10 September, with all services.

At a glance

Welcome & Ambience	✓✓✓✓	Location	✓✓✓✓
Quality of Pitches	✓✓✓✓✓	Range of Facilities	✓✓✓✓✓

Directions

Site is 5 km. southeast of Marennes. From Rochefort take D733 south for 12 km. Turn west on D123 to Ile d'Oléron. Continue for 12 km. and turn southeast on D728 towards Saintes. Site clearly signed, in 1 km. on the left. GPS: N45:48.699 W01:03.637

Charges 2006

Per unit incl. 2 persons	
and electricity	€ 15,00 - € 37,00
extra person	€ 6,00 - € 8,00
child (3-7 yrs)	€ 3,00 - € 5,00
dog	€ 5,00
Camping Cheques accepted.	

Reservations

Made with 25% deposit and € 30 booking fee.
Tel: 05 46 85 55 55. Email: sequoia.parc@wanadoo.fr

FR17150 Camping Municipal du Château Benon

F-17170 Benon (Charente-Maritime)

Benon was once the capital of this area and had strong English connections, its castle being built in 1096, although now all that remains is a single round tower. However, the mayor and villagers are still anxious to welcome English visitors and local information is provided in reception (part of the toilet block). The municipal campsite is beautifully kept, with open and shady areas and is ideal for those wanting a peaceful stay, and to stroll or cycle through the fields and woods which surround Benon. There are 70 pitches on neat grass, 40 with 10A electricity, although many are sloping or uneven. This is a pretty, quiet site where visitors are made welcome.

Facilities

The reasonably modern toilet block is fully equipped, with hot water always available and facilities for disabled visitors. Tennis court. Reception may only be open in the mornings. Off site: Auberge, general shop and post office in village, 250 m. La Rochelle is within easy reach (25 minutes). Riding 5 km. Fishing or bicycle hire 7 km. Golf 13 km.

Open

1 May - 30 September.

At a glance

Welcome & Ambience	✓✓✓✓	Location	✓✓✓✓
Quality of Pitches	✓✓✓✓	Range of Facilities	✓✓✓

Directions

Benon is 28 km. east of La Rochelle on the N11. Turn south at 'Relais de Benon', Benon 2 km. and site in centre of village.

Charges 2006

Per person	€ 2,70
child (under 11 yrs)	€ 1,60
pitch incl. electricity	€ 3,80

No credit cards.

Reservations

Advised for 14/7-15/8; contact the Mairie.
Tel: 05 46 01 61 48. Email: mairie-benon@smic17.fr

FR17160 Camping Le Clos Fleuri

8 impasse du Clos Fleuri, F-17600 Médis (Charente-Maritime)

Camping Le Clos Fleuri really does live up to its name. The profusion of different trees and, in the more open area, the lawns and flower beds give this small site a very rural atmosphere. There is always a warm welcome from the Devais family who created the site in 1974. The 125 touring pitches are mostly of generous size (a little uneven in places), varying in the amount of shade they receive (from full sun to well shaded) and 110 have electrical connections. The bar/restaurant is a converted barn with stone walls and a high timbered ceiling – a very convivial venue for gatherings and evening entertainment. The surrounding countryside is very pleasant with crops of sunflowers, wheat and maize, while beaches of all sorts are within easy reach. All in all the Clos Fleuri combines a great deal of charm, beauty and friendliness with a location from which the attractions of the Charente Maritime may be discovered.

Facilities

Toilet facilities are in two blocks which are kept scrupulously clean. One block is segregated male and female, the other is unisex with each unit in its own cubicle. Facility for disabled visitors with shower, basin and separate WC. Baby baths, washing machines and dryers. Attractive small pool. Sauna. Good shop (1/7-15/9). Restaurant (1/7-31/8) and bar (1/7-15/9). In high season there are twice weekly 'soirées' and boules and archery competitions. Minigolf. Small football pitch. Off site: Shops in Médis 2 km.

Open

1 June - 18 September..

At a glance

Welcome & Ambience	✓✓✓✓✓	Location	✓✓✓✓
Quality of Pitches	✓✓✓✓	Range of Facilities	✓✓✓✓

Directions

Médis is on the N150 from Saintes, halfway between Saujon and Royan. Drive into village. Site is signed to south at various points in Médis and is about 2 km. outside the village. GPS: N45:37.782 W00:56.768

Charges 2005

Per pitch incl. 2 adults	€ 23,50
extra person	€ 7,20
child (2-7 yrs)	€ 5,00
electricity (5/10A)	€ 4,10 - € 5,30

Less 25% in June and Sept.

Reservations

Essential for high season and made with deposit (€ 100) and fee (€ 20). Tel: 05 46 05 62 17. Email: clos-fleuri@wanadoo.fr

FR17200 Camping Municipal Au Fil de l'Eau

6 rue de Courbiac, F-17100 Saintes (Charente-Maritime)

Saintes is a 2,000 year old Gallo-Roman city, well worth a couple of days to visit the Cathedral, the Abbey, the Arch of Germanicus, the Amphitheatre and several museums, all within walking distance of the site (reception can provide a city map). Do take a stroll through the well tended, very pretty public gardens by the riverside. This pleasant site is well run as a franchise from the local municipality and has 214 mostly shady and generally grassy level pitches, with 132 electric hook-ups, and six mobile homes for rent.

Facilities

The main toilet block is a large and modern building, with two smaller older units opened at peak times. Washbasins in cubicles. Facilities for disabled people are in a unit by the laundry building. Motorcaravan service point. Shop. Bar. Restaurant and takeaway (July/Aug). TV room. Boules. Minigolf. Small playground. Off site: The adjacent open air swimming pool is free for campers (23/6-10/9).

Open

1 April - 30 October.

At a glance

Welcome & Ambience	✓✓✓✓	Location	✓✓✓✓
Quality of Pitches	✓✓✓	Range of Facilities	✓✓✓

Directions

From east and northeast follow signs for town centre, turning right after crossing river. To avoid centre and from all other directions, use bypass following signs for N137 La Rochelle to large roundabout at northern end and turn right signed town centre. Turn left at next roundabout and follow signs to site.

Charges 2005

Per person	€ 4,30
pitch incl. electricity (5A)	€ 8,80

Reservations

Not generally required. Tel: 05 46 93 08 00.
Email: info@campingsaintes.com

FR17190 Le Logis du Breuil

F-17570 St Augustin-sur-Mer (Charente-Maritime)

The first impression on arrival at this impressive campsite is space. Between the site buildings and pool, and the camping area is a 200 m. expanse of farm pasture where (on different areas) cattle graze and children play. The camping areas themselves are set among rows of mature and shady trees which give a very restful, dappled effect to the grassy pitches. The 320 pitches (250 with electricity) are very large and have direct access to wide, unpaved alleys, which lead on to the few tarmac roads around the site. The campsite amenities are centred around the reception area and pool complex. The area around the site is very pleasant agricultural land and the beaches of the Atlantic coast are nearby, as are the oyster and the mussel beds of Marennes and La Tremblade. The Gagnard family started the campsite about 25 years ago and obviously takes great pride in what it has now become a peaceful, friendly and very pleasant site from which to explore a delightful holiday area. A 'Sites et Paysages' member.

Facilities

Four very well maintained toilet blocks are well spaced around the camping area. Laundry facilities. Swimming pools. Shop, bar and snacks and takeaway (franchised) are well run. No evening entertainment. Play area. Indoor area providing archery, pool and table tennis. Bicycle hire. Tennis and basketball. Excursions organised. Internet access. Off site: A 50 minute walk through the forest from the site leads to the sea near St. Palais sur Mer.

Open

1 May - 30 September.

At a glance

Welcome & Ambience	✓✓✓✓✓	Location	✓✓✓✓✓
Quality of Pitches	✓✓✓✓✓	Range of Facilities	✓✓✓✓✓

Directions

Approaching Royan follow signs to St Palais sur Mer, bypassing Royan centre. Continue straight on past first set of lights and two roundabouts. At second set of lights turn right towards St Augustin. Site is approx. 2 km. on left, just before the village centre. GPS: N45:40.463 W01:05.768

Charges 2005

Per unit incl. 2 adults	€ 13,60 - € 16,30
with 3A electricity	€ 16,95 - € 19,90
extra person	€ 3,70 - € 5,00

Reservations

Advised for high season and made with deposit (€ 46) and booking fee (€ 8). Tel: 05 46 23 23 45.
Email: camping.Logis-du-Breuil@wanadoo.fr

123

FR17220 Camping La Brande

Route des Huitres, F-17480 Le Château-d'Oléron (Charente-Maritime)

A good quality site, run and maintained to the highest standard, La Brande offers an ideal holiday environment on the delightful Ile d'Oléron, famed for its oysters. La Brande is situated on the oyster route and close to a sandy beach. The Barcat family ensure that their visitors not only enjoy quality facilities, but Gerard Barcat offers guided bicycle tours and canoe trips. This way you discover the nature, oyster farming, vineyards and history of Oléron, which is joined to the mainland by a 3 km. bridge. Pitches here are generous and mostly separated by hedges and trees, the greater number for touring outfits. All are on level grassy terrain and have electricity hook-ups, some are fully serviced. A feature of this site is the heated swimming pool which can be covered under a sliding roof in cool weather and is open all season. The many activities during the high season, plus the natural surroundings, make this an ideal choice for families.

Facilities

Three heated, bright and clean sanitary blocks have spacious, well equipped showers and washbasins (mainly in cabins). Baby bath/changing area. Excellent facilities for people with disabilities (separate large shower, washbasin and WC). Laundry room with hot water and sinks, plus washing machine and dryers. Drive over motorcaravan service point. Restaurant/takeaway and bar in July/Aug. Shop with basics in low season, but well stocked in main season. Play area on grass. Football field, tennis, minigolf, fishing and archery. Bicycle hire. Canoe hire. Internet access. Off site: Beach 300 m.

Open

15 March - 15 November.

At a glance

Welcome & Ambience	✓✓✓✓	Location	✓✓✓✓
Quality of Pitches	✓✓✓✓	Range of Facilities	✓✓✓✓✓

Directions

After crossing bridge to L'Ile d'Oléron turn right towards Le Château d'Oléron. Continue through village and follow sign for Route des Huitres. Site is on left after 3 km.

Charges 2005

Per unit incl. 2 persons	€ 16,00 - € 26,00
large 125 sq.m. pitch	€ 16,00 - € 33,00
extra person	€ 5,00 - € 7,50
electricity (6-10A)	€ 3,20
dog	€ 2,50

Camping Cheques accepted.

Reservations

Advised in high season and made with 25% deposit and € 16 fee. Tel: 05 46 47 62 37.
Email: info@camping-labrande.com

FR17170 Domaine des Charmilles

St Laurent de la Prée, F-17450 Fouras (Charente-Maritime)

Fouras is a relatively little known resort situated between La Rochelle and Rochefort which retains much of the charm missing from larger, more heavily commercialised resorts in the area. Les Charmilles is located about a mile from the town centre. It is very easily accessed from the main La Rochelle to Rochefort road (N137). There are 270 large pitches, of which only 60 are touring pitches. The remainder are occupied by mobile homes, chalets and tour operators. All touring pitches have electricity (10A) and many have water and drainage. Ten are specially for disabled visitors. Roughly a third are well shaded, with the remainder in a sunnier, more open setting. The latter area is also away from the busy road which runs past the front of the site. A variety of entertainment is provided in high season which can mean that the site is noisy until at least midnight. Recent improvements include the attractive refurbishment of the bar and restaurant, the upgrading of the main pool with extra slides and a new pool with sliding doors. These changes have created a high quality focal point for the site.

Facilities

Three modern toilet blocks provide most washbasins in cubicles and facilities for babies and disabled people. Washing machines and dryers. Small shop (1/6-15/9). Bar and takeaway (15/5-15/9). Restaurant (1/6-15/9). Heated swimming pools, water slides and large sunbathing terrace (15/5-30/9). Sauna. Jacuzzi. Good playground. Minigolf, table tennis and multisports court. Bicycle hire. Entertainment. Minibus service to the beach in July/Aug. Charcoal barbecues are not permitted. Off site: Fishing 3 km. Golf 5 km. Riding 15 km.

Open

1 April - 25 September.

At a glance

Welcome & Ambience	✓✓✓✓	Location	✓✓✓
Quality of Pitches	✓✓✓✓	Range of Facilities	✓✓✓✓

Directions

Leave N137 at exit for Fouras and St Laurent de la Prée, joining D937 towards Fouras. Site is on left in about 800 m.

Charges 2006

Per pitch incl. 2 adults	€ 15,00 - € 30,00
extra person	€ 6,00
child (under 5 yrs)	€ 4,00
electricity	€ 4,00
animal	€ 5,00 - € 6,00

Reservations

Necessary for high season with deposit and fee. Tel: 05 46 84 00 05. Email: charmilles17@wanadoo.fr

La BRANDE

Alain Barcat and his team welcomes you at La Brande - an open air hotel, camping and caravan site. Situated 1,5 miles outside of Château d'Oléron on la route des huîtres nearby the seaside, you will discover the peace of the country and the pleasures of the sea...

Route des Huitres • 17480 Le Château d'Oléron
Tél. +33 (0)5 46 47 62 37
Fax +33 (0)5 46 47 71 70
info@camping-labrande.com
www.camping-labrande.com

FR17230 Camping de L'Océan

Mobile homes ▶ page 415

La Passe, La Couarde-sur-Mer, F-17670 Ile de Ré (Charente-Maritime)

L'Océan lies close to the centre of the Ile de Ré, just 50 m. from a sandy beach. There are 338 pitches here with around 200 for touring units, the remainder occupied by mobile homes and chalets. The camping area is well shaded and pitches are of a reasonable size, most with electricity (10A) and 60 with water and drainage. Pride of place goes to the large heated swimming pool which is surrounded by an attractive sunbathing terrace. Bicycle hire is popular here as the island offers over 100 km. of interesting cycle routes. There is a pleasant bar/restaurant with a terrace overlooking the pool. In peak season a range of entertainment is organised including disco evenings. Future plans include a new toilet block, internet access in the bar and an indoor pool.

Facilities

The recently renovated toilet blocks are modern and well maintained with facilities for disabled visitors and a dog shower. Motorcaravan services. Shop. Bar/restaurant and takeaway (all season). Swimming pool. Riding. Bicycle hire. Tennis court. Fishing pond adjacent. Basketball. Play area. Minigolf (free). Helicopter rides, sub-aqua diving and pony riding (high season). Entertainment in high season. Charcoal barbecues are not permitted. Off site: South facing beach 50 m. La Couarde (nearest restaurants, shops etc.) 2.5 km. Golf 5 km.

Open

3 April - 24 September.

At a glance

Welcome & Ambience ✓✓✓✓ Location ✓✓✓✓
Quality of Pitches ✓✓✓✓ Range of Facilities ✓✓✓✓

Directions

After crossing the toll bridge onto the island, join D735 which runs along the north side of the island until you pass La Couarde. The site is 2.5 km. beyond the village (in the direction of Ars en Re).

Charges guide

Per unit incl. 2 persons	€ 14,00 - € 35,00
extra person	€ 4,00 - € 8,80
electricity	€ 5,00
dog	€ 1,70 - € 4,20

Camping Cheques accepted.

Reservations

Contact site. Tel: 05 46 29 87 70.
Email: campingdelocean@wanadoo.fr

17670 - La Couarde sur Mer
Tél. 05 46 29 87 70
Fax. 05 46 29 92 13
E.mail : campingdelocean@wanadoo.fr
site : campingocean.com

CAMPING CARAVANING INTERNATIONAL

125

FR17210 Sunêlia Interlude

Plage de Gros Jonc, F-17580 Le Bois-Plage-en-Ré (Charente-Maritime)

The island of Ré, which is no more than 30 km. long and 5 km. wide, lies off the coast at La Rochelle and is reached by a toll bridge. It is a paradise for cyclists, walkers and those who wish to commune with nature. Camping Interlude enjoys a pleasant location with access to an excellent beach. A popular site even in low season, (may become very crowded with overstretched facilities in high season), it has 387 pitches, 136 of which are for touring units. Pitches are sand based, vary in size from 80-120 sq.m. and are mostly divided by hedges on part undulating, sandy terrain. Many are placed to the left of the site in a pine forest setting, others mingle with the tour operators and mobile homes. Choosing a shady pitch is not a problem for there are many trees. Interlude makes an ideal base for exploring the island of Ré and for those planning an early holiday, the facilities on site are all operational from the beginning of April. It is a suitable site for all ages, with plenty of recreational pursuits to keep families happy, both on and off the site.

Facilities

Two modern, clean and well equipped sanitary blocks provide washbasins in cabins and some shower units suitable for families with twin washbasins. The building of a new toilet block should be ready. Baby room, child size toilets, en suite facilities for disabled visitors, laundry sinks, washing machines and dryers, plus dishwashing areas. Motorcaravan service point. Restaurant/bar and shop (all season). Bread baked on premises. Two swimming pools, one outdoor and one inside. Play area. Volleyball, boules. Organised events and entertainment for young and old. Games/TV room. Tennis courts. Bicycle hire. Communal barbecues. Multi-sport area.

Open

9 April - 2 November.

At a glance

Welcome & Ambience	✓✓✓✓	Location	✓✓✓✓✓
Quality of Pitches	✓✓✓✓	Range of Facilities	✓✓✓✓

Directions

After crossing the toll bridge to the Ile de Ré follow sign for Le Bois Plage. Turn left at first roundabout and continue straight on at next two, then left at fourth roundabout where site is signed. GPS: N46:10.440 W01:22.701

Charges 2005

Per pitch incl. 1 adult:	
100 sq.m. incl. electricity	€ 17,50 - € 28,50
120 sq.m. water and drainage	€ 22,00 - € 32,50
140 sq.m. water and drainage	€ 22,00 - € 35,50
extra person	€ 4,00 - € 10,50
pet	€ 4,00 - € 8,00

Camping Cheques accepted.

Reservations

Advisable all season. Tel: 05 46 09 18 22. Email: infos@interlude.fr

FR17270 Camping L'Anse des Pins

Chemin du Râteau - Domino, F-17190 St Georges d'Oleron (Charente-Maritime)

Rock pools, sand dunes and spectacular sun sets, with sea views from many of the pitches, help to make this site attractive to those seeking an away from it all holiday in a quiet part of the holiday island of the Ile d'Oléron. The campsite is arranged in three areas, some parts having good shade from tall trees and shrubs, but with a fair proportion in full sun. There are 350 pitches including 188 for touring units, the remainder used for mobile homes. Electricity connections are available (3-10A) and 22 pitches also have water and drainage. The leisure facilities are to one side of the site and are of a high standard. They include a good tennis court and a complex of outdoor pools (unheated) which, together with a children's play area are open all season. There is a bar and snack bar with takeaway and a small shop open from May. Activities are organised for all (games, competitions, swimming lessons) with some evening entertainment in high season. Out of season facilities are limited and the nearest village (Domino) is about 2.5 km. away where one can visit the daily market or hire a bike. Mobile home numbers at this site increase each year.

Facilities

The two main toilet blocks (together with two small blocks for high season use) provide adequate facilities with mainly British style toilets. Showers and washbasins in cabins provide warm water, cleaned regularly. Washing machines, dryers and ironing table. Gas supplies. Bar. Shop with limited takeaway and snack bar. Swimming and paddling pools (all season). Some organised activities in high season (1/7- 31/8). Seven boules courts. Table tennis tables in purpose built area. No TV room (poor reception). Barbecues are not permitted except in a communal area. Off site: Beach 50 m. Bicycle hire 1 km. Riding 10 km. Bus service in St Georges 5 km.

Open

April - September.

At a glance

Welcome & Ambience	✓✓	Location	✓✓✓✓
Quality of Pitches	✓✓✓	Range of Facilities	✓✓✓✓

Directions

Cross the bridge onto Ile d'Oléron and follow the D734 towards St Dennis. In the village of Chéray, turn left at traffic lights (signed Camping). Stay on this road to Domino, avoiding any side roads to Domino. Follow green (small) signs to Rex and L'Anse des Pins Camping. The roads are narrow. GPS: N45:58.226 W01:23.213

Charges 2005

Per unit incl. 2 persons	€ 16,00 - € 28,00
extra person	€ 6,00 - € 7,00
child (0-4 yrs)	€ 3,00 - € 4,00
electricity	€ 2,50 - € 4,00
animal	€ 5,00

Reservations

Contact site. Tel: 05 46 76 55 97. Email: camping-lansdedespins@wanadoo.fr

FR17260 Camping Le Cormoran

Route de Radia, Ars en Ré, F-17590 Ile de Ré (Charente-Maritime)

Situated just outside Ars en Ré and within 500 metres of a sandy beach, Le Cormoran offers a quiet rural holiday for families with young children. The swimming pool is the focal point – it is covered during April and May and is heated throughout the season. The pitches vary in size and are a mixture of sand and grass. All have electricity but long leads may be necessary. The site's restaurant and bar overlook the pool and are open during the season apart from Mondays and Tuesdays until June. Basic provisions are stocked in the bar. There are the usual shops in Ars, which is some 800 m. away. Le Cormoran is close to the local oyster beds. The sister site, Camping La Plage, is about 3 km. away and concentrates mainly on its 148 mobile homes. There are 44 pitches for touring units but the facilities for them are old fashioned and in need of modernisation and better maintenance.

Facilities

Unisex toilet facilities are in two blocks with toilets (British and Turkish style), showers and washbasins mainly in cabins. Good provision for the disabled visitors. Dishwashing facilities are under cover. Laundry room with two washing machines and a dryer. Good motorcaravan service point. Bar, restaurant and takeaway meals. Swimming pool (covered in low season). Fitness centre. Tennis. Volleyball. Games room. Play area. Entertainment programme in high season. Bicycle hire. Off site: Nearest beach 500 m. Ars-en-Ré 800 m. (buses, shops, restaurants etc). Fishing 500 m. Slipway for launching small boats 1 km. Riding 3 km. Golf 10 km.

At a glance

Welcome & Ambience	✓✓✓	Location	✓✓✓
Quality of Pitches	✓✓	Range of Facilities	✓✓✓

Directions

Cross the toll bridge from La Rochelle onto the Ile de Ré and continue on D735 to Ars en Ré from where site is well signed.

Charges 2005

Per unit incl. 2 persons	€ 16,00 - € 23,00
extra person	€ 5,30 - € 10,30
child (0-9 yrs)	€ 3,20 - € 10,30
electricity (10A)	€ 4,90
animal	€ 2,60 - € 5,30

Reservations

Contact site. Tel: 05 46 29 46 04.
Email: info@cormoran.com

Open

1 April - 30 September.

127

FR17300 Camping Au Petit Port de l'Houmeau

F-17137 L'Houmeau (Charente-Maritime)

Au Petit Port de l'Houmeau is a pretty site which makes a good base for exploring the Charente Maritime coast. Its proximity to the fascinating town of La Rochelle is an important bonus. This is a quiet, rural site on the edge of the small seaside village of l'Houmeau. The friendly English speaking owners ensure high standards of maintenance. Pitches are clustered in little groups of four or five and are of a good size, and are all equipped with 5A electrical connections. Virtually all offer some degree of shade. Although well managed, the site is delightfully free of signs announcing rules and regulations. That said, larger motorcaravans may have difficulty finding a suitable pitch. There are relatively few amenities here, but the village shops, bars and a good restaurant are very close by.

Facilities

Two well maintained toilet blocks. Washing machines and dryers. Snack bar (July/Aug). Internet point. Bicycle hire. Play area. 'Moules/frites' evenings in high season. Mobile homes and chalets for rent (all year). Off site: Beach 800 m. Hourly bus to La Rochelle from village centre. Shops, bars, restaurant.

Open

31 March - 31 October.

At a glance

Welcome & Ambience	✓✓✓✓✓	Location	✓✓✓✓✓
Quality of Pitches	✓✓✓✓	Range of Facilities	✓✓✓

Directions

From the northbound N137 dual-carriageway (La Rochelle bypass), leave at Lagord exit, then immediately follow signs to L'Houmeau. Upon reaching L'Houmeau (5 minutes), site is well signed.

Charges 2005

Per unit incl. 2 persons	€ 12,00 - € 15,00
extra person	€ 3,00 - € 4,00
child (0-10 yrs)	€ 1,80 - € 2,50
electricity (5/10A)	€ 3,20 - € 4,00
pet	€ 1,90

Reservations

Contact site. Tel: 05 46 50 90 82.
Email: info@aupetitport.com

FR85040 Castel Camping Caravaning La Garangeoire

St Julien-des-Landes, F-85150 La Mothe-Achard (Vendée)

La Garangeoire is one of a relatively small number of seriously good sites in the Vendée, situated some 15 km. inland near the village of St Julien des Landes. One of its more memorable qualities is the view of the château through the gates as you drive in. Imaginative use has been made of the old Noirmoutiers 'main road' which passes through the centre of the site and now forms a delightful, quaint thorough-fare, nicknamed the Champs Elysées. Providing a village like atmosphere, it is busy at most times with the facilities opening directly off it. The site is set in the 200 ha. of parkland surrounding the small château of La Garangeoire. The peaceful fields and woods, where campers may walk, include three lakes, one of which is used for fishing and boating (life jackets supplied from reception). With a spacious, relaxed atmosphere, the main camping areas are arranged on either side of the old road, edged with mature trees. The 300 pitches, each with a name not a number and individually hedged, are especially large (most 150-200 sq.m.) and are well spaced. Most have electricity (12A), some water and drainage also. The site is popular with tour operators (144 pitches).

Facilities

Ample sanitary facilities are of good standard, well situated for all areas. One excellent block has facilities for babies and disabled people. All have washbasins in cabins. Good laundry facilities. Motorcaravan service point. Good shop. Full restaurant, takeaway and a separate crêperie with bars and attractive courtyard terrace overlooking the swimming pool complex (from 1/5) with water slides, fountains and a children's pool. Large play field with play equipment for children's activities, whether organised or not. Games room. Two tennis courts. Bicycle hire. Table tennis, crazy golf, archery and volleyball. Riding in July/Aug. Fishing and boating. Off site: Beaches 15 km.

Open

5 April - 24 September.

At a glance

Welcome & Ambience	✓✓✓✓✓	Location	✓✓✓✓✓
Quality of Pitches	✓✓✓✓✓	Range of Facilities	✓✓✓✓✓

Directions

Site is signed from St Julien; the entrance is to the east off the D21 road, 2.5 km. north of St Julian-des-Landes.

Charges 2005

Per unit incl. 2 persons	€ 14,00 - € 27,00
with electricity	€ 17,00 - € 31,00
with services	€ 18,50 - € 34,50
extra person	€ 4,50 - € 6,50
child (under 10 yrs)	€ 2,50 - € 3,20
dog	€ 3,00
Camping Cheques accepted.	

Reservations

Made for min. 7 days with deposit (€ 61) and fee (€ 22.87). Tel: 02 51 46 65 39.
Email: garangeoire@wanadoo.fr

FR85260 Village de la Guyonnière

La Guyonnière, F-85150 St Julien-des-Landes (Vendée)

La Guyonnière is a spacious, rural site, away from the hectic coast. It is popular for many reasons, the main ones being the free and easy atmosphere and its reasonable pricing. It is Dutch owned but English is spoken and all visitors are made very welcome. It is a farm type site with five different fields, each being reasonably level and each having a toilet block albeit the fifth block is a mobile 'portacabin' style construction (a new sanitary block is planned). The 183 pitches have a mix of sun and shade. They are very large (the few smaller ones are cheaper) and are separated by a tree and a few bushes. All have access to electricity connections. Bar/restaurant facilities are housed in the original farm buildings attractively converted. Entertainment is provided in the bar on high season evenings. A perfect place for families, with large play areas on sand and grass, and paddling pond with shower. Being in the country, it is a haven for cyclists and walkers, with many signed routes from the site. A pleasant 500 m. walk takes you to the Jaunay lake where fishing is possible (permits from the village), canoeing (lifejackets from reception) and pedaloes to hire. There are no tour operators and, needless to say, no road noise.

Facilities

Toilet blocks are modern, functional and central for each area. Most cubicles are quite small but they serve their purpose and were very clean when we visited; however, perhaps not adequate in high season. Washbasins are in cubicles. Limited provision for babies and disabled visitors. Dishwashing and laundry sinks at each block. Shop (1/5-15/9; order bread from reception outside these dates). Bar with TV and pool table and pleasant restaurant (1/5-15/9). Pizzeria with takeaway. Small swimming pool, new heated pool with jacuzzi and slide, very attractive and can be covered in cool weather. Paddling pool. Play areas, sand pit. Table tennis, volleyball, tennis and football fields. Bicycle hire. Car wash. Off site: Riding 3 km. Golf 8 km. Beaches 10 km.

At a glance

Welcome & Ambience	✓✓✓✓✓	Location	✓✓✓✓✓
Quality of Pitches	✓✓✓✓✓	Range of Facilities	✓✓✓✓

Directions

Site is off the D12 road (La Mothe Achard - St Gilles Croix de Vie), approx. 4 km. west of St Julien-des-Landes. It is signed about 1 km. from the main road.

Charges 2005

Per unit incl. 2 persons	
and electricity	€ 13,50 - € 28,00
extra person	€ 4,00 - € 5,00
child (3-9 yrs)	€ 2,50 - € 3,00
animal	€ 2,50

Less 10-20% outside high season.

Reservations

Made with 25% deposit. Tel: 02 51 46 62 59. Email: info@laguyonniere.com

Open

1 May - 30 October.

FR85090 Camping L'Abri des Pins

Route de Notre-Dame-de-Monts, F-85160 St Jean-de-Monts (Vendée)

L'Abri des Pins is situated on the outskirts of the pleasant, modern resort of St Jean-de-Monts and is separated from the sea and long sandy beach by a strip of pinewood. From the back entrance of the site, it is a pleasant 15 minute walk to the beach. Bathing is said to be safer here than on most of the beaches on this coast, but is nevertheless supervised in July/August. The site has 218 pitches, 78 of which are for touring units, with 30 larger than average with electricity, water and drainage. Electricity is also available to the other pitches which are around 100 sq.m, fully marked out with dividing hedges and quite shady. Many pitches are occupied by privately owned mobile homes, but there are no tour operators on the site. Throughout the season, visitors may use the facilities at Les Places Dorées (under the same family ownership) across the road.

Facilities

The two sanitary blocks have been modernised and include washbasins in cabins, laundry and dishwashing sinks. Good small shop and bar/restaurant on the far side of the site provides good quality, value for money meals, both to eat in and take away (all 1/7-31/8). Outdoor, heated swimming pool and water slide, plus small pool for children, with decked sunbathing area (1/6-15/9; no Bermuda style shorts). Daily children's club, football, petanque, aqua aerobics. Off site: Supermarket 10 minutes walk. Many restaurants nearby. Walking, cycling and fishing within 1 km. Riding 2 km. Golf 5 km. Beach 700 m.

Open

1 June - 15 September.

At a glance

Welcome & Ambience	✓✓✓✓	Location	✓✓✓✓
Quality of Pitches	✓✓✓✓	Range of Facilities	✓✓✓✓

Directions

Site is 4 km. from the town centre on St Jean-de-Monts - Notre Dame-de Monts/Noirmoutiers road (D38), on left heading north, just after Camping les Amiaux. GPS: N46:48.562 W02:06.540

Charges 2005

Per unit incl. 3 persons and electricity	€ 21,50 - € 31,50
extra person	€ 3,50 - € 5,00
child (under 5 yrs)	€ 2,50 - € 3,50
dog	free - € 3,00
Deposit required for armband for access to pool and site (high season only).	

Reservations

Advised for high season; min. stay 12 nights between 14/7-15/8. Made with deposit (€ 92) and fee (€ 23). Tel: 02 51 58 83 86. Email: abridespins@aol.com

FR85280 Camping Les Places Dorées

Route de Notre-Dame-de-Monts, F-85160 St Jean-de-Monts (Vendée)

Les Places Dorées is owned by the same family as L'Abri des Pins (FR85090) which is just across the road. It is a much newer site, but maturing trees are gradually beginning to offer some shade. The site has a range of facilities, including a pool complex, but one of the main reasons for visiting the Vendée is for its beaches and the closest beach to Les Places Dorées is a pleasant 15 minute walk away. The site has 245 grassy pitches, the quietest being towards the back of the site. Each is separated, all have electricity and some are also equipped with water and drainage. One small Dutch tour operator is on site. In low season the site is quiet but it can be noisy in high season with the bar and disco closing late.

Facilities

Three modern toilet blocks include washbasins in cubicles. Facilities for disabled visitors. Laundry and dishwashing sinks. Washing machines and dryers. Swimming pool complex with water slides, jacuzzi area and waterfall. In high season the site becomes quite lively with plenty of organised entertainment, most based around the bar/restaurant area. High season children's club at L'Abri des Pins, also organised activities for adults (petanque tournaments, aqua-aerobics, etc). Facilities at L'Abri des Pins may be used - well stocked shop (July/Aug), tennis court, fitness room, pools and a games room. Off site: Fishing 500 m. Riding 2 km. Golf 5 km. Beach 700 m.

Open

1 June - 1 September.

At a glance

Welcome & Ambience	✓✓✓✓	Location	✓✓✓✓
Quality of Pitches	✓✓✓✓	Range of Facilities	✓✓✓✓

Directions

Site is 4 km. north of St Jean de Monts on the D38 St Jean de Monts - Notre Dames de Monts road on the right hand side, almost opposite L'Abri des Pins. GPS: N46:48.690 W02:06.685

Charges 2005

Per pitch incl. 3 persons and electricity	€ 21,50 - € 31,50
extra person	€ 3,50 - € 5,00
child	€ 2,50 - € 3,50
dog	free - € 3,00

Reservations

Advised for high season; min. stay 12 nights between 14/7-15/8. Tel: 02 51 59 02 93. Email: abridespins@aol.com

FR85020 Camping du Jard

123 Mal de Lattre de Tassigny, F-85360 La Tranche-sur-Mer (Vendée)

Camping du Jard is a well maintained site situated between La Rochelle and Les Sables d'Olonne. First impressions on booking in are good, with a friendly welcome from M. Marton or his staff and each new arrival being personally shown to their pitch. The 350 pitches are level and grassy, hedged on two sides by bushes. The smallest are 100 sq.m. (the majority larger) and most are equipped with electricity, half with water and drainage. It is a comparatively new site, but the large variety of trees is beginning to provide a little shade. An impressive pool complex has a toboggan, paddling pool and an indoor pool with jacuzzi. The site is 700 m. from a sandy beach with many shops and restaurants nearby. The site is used by British tour operators (150 pitches).

Facilities

Three toilet blocks, well designed and maintained, are light and airy with excellent facilities for babies and disabled people and most washbasins in cabins. Washing machines and dryer. Dishwashing and laundry sinks. Small shop for basics (1/6-10/9), restaurant and bar (both 25/5-10/9). Heated swimming pool with toboggan and paddling pool, plus good heated indoor pool with jacuzzi (no Bermuda-style shorts in the pools). Sauna, solarium and fitness room with instructors. Tennis court, minigolf, table tennis. Bicycle hire. Play area, games room and TV room. Card operated barrier with outside parking. American motorhomes are not accepted. Dogs allowed with papers.

Open

25 May - 15 September.

At a glance

Welcome & Ambience	✓✓✓✓	Location	✓✓✓✓
Quality of Pitches	✓✓✓✓	Range of Facilities	✓✓✓✓✓

Directions

Site is east of La Tranche-sur-Mer on the D46. From D747 (La Roche-sur-Yon to La Tranche) follow signs for La Faute-sur-mer along the new bypass. Take exit for La Grière and then turn east to site.

Charges 2005

Per pitch incl. 2 persons and electricity (10A)	€ 20,70 - € 27,60
extra person	€ 3,90 - € 5,10
child (under 5 yrs)	€ 2,70 - € 3,60

Reservations

Advisable for July/Aug. (min. 1 week, Sat.- Sat.) with deposit (€ 100). Tel: 02 51 27 43 79. Email: info@campingdujard.fr

---

FR85080 Hotellerie de Plein Air La Puerta del Sol

Les Borderies, Chemin de Hommeaux, F-85270 St Hilaire-de-Riez (Vendée)

La Puerta del Sol is a good quality campsite a short distance away from the busy coast. It is suitable not only for families with teenage children to entertain, but also for those seeking a more peaceful and relaxing holiday. There are 216 pitches, of which 158 are used for touring units. Pitches are level with dividing hedges and many receive shade from the mature trees on the site. Each pitch is fully serviced with water, waste water point and electricity. A self-service restaurant and takeaway with reasonably priced food overlooks the pool and terrace. In July/Aug. a range of activities is provided for adults and children, including a children's club, aqua aerobics, swimming lessons, tournaments and games, with evening entertainment in the bar. There is one small French tour operator on site (20 pitches).

Facilities

Three well maintained toilet blocks of identical design have a mix of Turkish and British style WCs, washbasins in cabins and baby baths. Dishwashing and laundry sinks. Laundry with washing machines and irons. Fully equipped rooms for disabled visitors. Small shop (1/7-31/8). Bar (15/5-15/9). Self-service restaurant and takeaway (1/7-31/8). Swimming pool, new slide and paddling pool (15/5-15/9; no Bermuda style shorts). Play area. Tennis court. Bicycle hire. Volleyball, table tennis and video games. American motorhomes are accepted in limited numbers with reservation.
Off site: Riding, fishing and golf within 5 km. Nearest sandy beach 5 km. St Jean de Monts 7 km.

Open

1 May - 15 September.

At a glance

Welcome & Ambience	✓✓✓✓	Location	✓✓✓✓
Quality of Pitches	✓✓✓✓	Range of Facilities	✓✓✓✓

Directions

From Le Pissot (7 km. north of St Gilles Croix-de-Vie on D38) take the D59 towards Le Perrier. Site is 2 km. along this road on the right down a short side road. A large sign for the site is 200 m. before the turn with another on the left directly opposite the turning.

Charges 2005

Per unit incl. up to 2 persons and services	€ 17,00 - € 27,00
extra person	€ 5,00 - € 6,50
child (under 5 yrs)	free - € 4,00
animal	€ 3,50

Reservations

Advised for high season and made for any period with deposit (€ 138) and fee (€ 30.49). Tel: 02 51 49 10 10. Email: puerta-del-sol@wanadoo.fr

FR85070 Camping Les Biches

Route de Notre-Dame-de-Riez, F-85270 St Hilaire-de-Riez (Vendée)

Les Biches is a popular site 4 km. from the sea. Set in a pinewood, nearly everywhere has shade. There are 434 pitches with around 60 for touring units. The large, spacious pitches are mostly hedged and on fairly sandy ground, all with electricity, water and drainage. The majority for tents and caravans are in the far part of the campsite, although a few others are scattered through the rest of the site. A very attractive pool complex is near the entrance, overlooked by the bar and terraces. Useful for families with children, it is popular with British tour operators (65%) and tends to be busy and active all season.

Facilities

The four sanitary blocks are clean and well maintained, with pre-set showers. Some washbasins are in cabins. Washing machines and dryers. Facilities for disabled visitors. Shop (all season) with ice service. Large bar (all season). Restaurant and crêperie (1/6-10/9). Takeaway (20/5-10/9). Two heated swimming pools, water slide, jacuzzi and indoor pool. Tennis. Volleyball, table tennis and minigolf. Games room with amusement machines. Large adventure type playground. Bicycle hire. Disco. TV room. Off site: Private fishing lake 1.5 km. Beach 4 km. Riding 4.5 km. Golf 6 km.

At a glance

| Welcome & Ambience | ✓✓✓✓ | Location | ✓✓✓✓ |
| Quality of Pitches | ✓✓✓✓ | Range of Facilities | ✓✓✓✓✓ |

Directions

Site is about 2 km. north of St Hilaire, close to and well signed from the main D38 road.

Charges 2005

Per unit incl. 3 persons	€ 38,00
with electricity	€ 42,00
extra person	€ 7,00

Less 30% May, June and Sept.

Reservations

Contact site. Tel: 02 51 54 38 82.
Email: campingdesbiches@wanadoo.fr

Open

15 May - 15 September.

FR85120 Siblu Camping Le Bois Masson

149 rue des Sables, F-85160 St Jean-de-Monts (Vendée)

Le Bois Masson is a large, lively site with modern buildings and facilities in the seaside resort of St Jean-de-Monts. As with other sites here, the long, sandy beach is a few minutes away by car, reached through a pinewood. This site, popular with tour operators, offers 500 good sized pitches, all with electricity. Most are occupied by mobile homes. Pitches are of sandy grass, mostly separated by hedges, with medium sized trees providing some shade. There are some pitches with water and drainage and an area kept for those who prefer a quieter pitch. There is plenty of on-site entertainment over a long season. The pool complex is impressive and includes a large outdoor pool, a paddling pool, a slide and, for cooler weather, an indoor pool, with sliding doors to the outside. A jacuzzi, sauna and fitness room are also provided together with many other sports. Very busy in high season, this is not a site for those seeking somewhere quiet, but there is plenty to do for those perhaps with older children.

Facilities

Four sanitary blocks of excellent design provide modern showers with mixer taps, washbasins in cabins and British style WCs. Facilities for disabled visitors and babies. Dishwashing room (with dishwashers). Laundry. Comprehensive amenities housed in modern buildings fronting on to the road: good supermarket, large, lively bar with entertainment room above, overlooking the pools, restaurant and a crêperie. Many activities including tennis, volleyball, table tennis and bicycle hire. Gas barbecues only are permitted. Mobile homes and rooms to rent. Off site: Riding, golf, squash, watersports near.

At a glance

| Welcome & Ambience | ✓✓✓✓✓ | Location | ✓✓✓✓ |
| Quality of Pitches | ✓✓✓✓ | Range of Facilities | ✓✓✓✓✓ |

Directions

From the roundabout at the southeast end of the St Jean-de-Monts bypass road, turn into town following signs to 'Centre Ville' and site, which is on the right after 400 m.

Charges guide

| Per pitch incl. 2 persons and electricity | € 13,00 - € 34,00 |

Reservations

Contact site or Siblu in the UK. Tel 0870 242 777. Site tel: 02 51 58 62 62.
Email: boisdormant@siblu.fr

Open

19 March - 23 September.

www.**alanrogers**.com for latest campsite news

FR85150 Camping La Yole

Mobile homes ▶ page 415

Chemin des Bosses, Orouet, F-85160 St Jean-de-Monts (Vendée)

La Yole is an attractive and well run site, two kilometres from a sandy beach (by road). It offers 278 pitches, the majority of which are occupied by tour operators and mobile homes to rent. There are 100 touring pitches, most with shade and separated by bushes and trees. The newer area at the rear of the site is more open, although the bushes are growing well. All the pitches are of at least 100 sq.m. and have electricity (10A), water and drainage. An inviting pool complex is surrounded by a paved sunbathing area and overlooked by the terrace of the bar and restaurant. Entertainment is organised here in high season. The pool complex includes an attractive, irregularly shaped outdoor pool, a paddling pool, slide and an indoor heated pool with a jacuzzi. This is a friendly, popular site with welcoming owners. A 'Sites et Paysages' member.

Facilities

Two toilet blocks of older design, one refurbished, include washbasins in cabins, units for disabled people and baby baths, all kept very clean. The third block in the newer part of the site is very modern with baby room. Laundry with washing machine, dryer and iron. Well stocked shop. Bar, restaurant and takeaway (18/5-10/9). Outdoor pool with slide and paddling pool. Indoor heated pool with jacuzzi. Play area on sand. Large field for ball games. Club room. Tennis. Table tennis, pool and video games. Organised entertainment in high season. Only gas barbecues are permitted. Off site: Bus service 2 km. Bicycle hire 2 km. Riding 3 km. Fishing, golf and watersports 6 km. at St Jean. Beach 2 km.

Open

7 April - 29 September.

At a glance

Welcome & Ambience	✓✓✓✓✓	Location	✓✓✓✓
Quality of Pitches	✓✓✓✓	Range of Facilities	✓✓✓✓✓

Directions

Signed off the D38, 6 km. south of St Jean de Monts in the village of Orouet.

Charges 2006

Per unit incl. 2 persons	
and electricity	€ 16,00 - € 29,00
extra person	€ 3,65 - € 5,90
child (2-9 yrs)	€ 2,05 - € 4,30
baby (0-2 yrs)	free - € 3,25
dog	€ 4,00 - € 5,00

Camping Cheques accepted.

Reservations

Advised, particularly for June, July and Aug.
Tel: 02 51 58 67 17. Email: contact@la-yole.com

FR85140 Camping Naturiste Le Colombier

F-85210 St Martin-Lars-en-St Hermine (Vendée)

A countryside site for naturists near La Roche sur Yon, this site is almost akin to 'Camping a la Ferme', but with the benefit of good facilities. It provides around 160 pitches in seven very natural fields on different levels linked by informal tracks. There are level, terraced areas for caravans and a feeling of spaciousness with pitches around the edges of fields, unmarked and with electricity (up to 16A) available at various strategic points. Sheep may be watched in a central enclosure in one field. Mellow old farm buildings are pleasing and the bar/restaurant is in a converted barn. For nature lovers the site's 125 acres provide many walks throughout the attractive, wooded valley and around the lake. Children are also well catered for with some unusual activities helped by volunteers. The local area is interesting, with antique 'Bocage Vendéen' and sculpture featuring prominently, and provides a very different view from the hectic coastal Vendée. English is spoken by the Dutch owner and staff.

Facilities

Fully equipped modern toilet blocks (one new) are good, providing some showers in cubicles. Dishwashing sinks. Motorcaravan service point. Grocer/baker calls daily. Bar/restaurant with 'a la carte' and full menu (order before 1 pm), home baked bread and pizzas. Heated swimming pool. Fishing. Volleyball, boules and table tennis. Playground. Pony and trap rides around the woods and one day a week the bread oven is lit and children can make their own bread. Ghost tours in the woods, sledging on artificial ski slope (all main season only). E-mail facilities. Off site: Shop 1 km.

Open

1 April - 30 October.

At a glance

Welcome & Ambience	✓✓✓✓	Location	✓✓✓✓✓	
Quality of Pitches	✓✓✓✓	Range of Facilities	✓✓✓✓	

Directions

From N148, La Roche sur Yon - Niort road, at St Hermine, turn onto D8 eastward for 4 km. Turn left on D10 to St Martin-Lars where there are signs to the site.

Charges guide

Per person	€ 7,20
child (4-9 yrs)	€ 3,20
child (10-16 yrs)	€ 4,50
electricity	€ 2,90
animal	€ 3,20

Reservations

Not considered necessary. Tel: 02 51 27 83 84. Email: lecolombier.nat@wanadoo.fr

FR85130 Camping Pong

Rue du Stade, F-85220 Landevieille (Vendée)

A comfortable family run site, Camping Pong is in a rural situation on the edge of a neat village, 12 km. southeast of St Gilles-Croix-de-Vie, and 5 km. from the coast at Brétignolles. It has 229 pitches with 187 used for touring units, the remainder for mobile homes and chalets. All have electricity connections (4/6A) and are of a good size with some larger ones costing a little more. The redeveloped entrance and reception area provides an efficient welcome and the bar, restaurant, function room, games room, gym and shop have all recently been rebuilt. The original part of the site around the small, lightly fenced fishing lake (there are warning signs) has a mixture of mature trees, whereas, in the newer areas trees and shrubs are developing well. An attractive pool area includes a delightful paddling pool with many fascinating features for children and a pretty patio area overlooked by the bar. There are no tour operator pitches.

Facilities

Four modern, unisex sanitary blocks provide toilets of mixed styles and some washbasins in cabins. Facilities for disabled people, separate baby room, dishwashing under cover and laundry room. Shop, takeaway, bar and restaurant (15/6-15/9). Swimming pools including heated pool with jacuzzi, toboggan and paddling pool (from 15/5). Small gym, TV lounge and games room. Bicycle hire. Fishing. Exciting fenced play area and regular children's club. Off site: Tennis 200 m. Large Lac du Jaunay 2.5 km. (canoeing and pedaloes). Golf or riding 5 km. Nearest beach 5 km. Lac d'Apremont and its château 14 km.

Open

1 April - 30 September.

At a glance

Welcome & Ambience	✓✓✓✓	Location	✓✓✓✓	
Quality of Pitches	✓✓✓✓	Range of Facilities	✓✓✓✓	

Directions

Site is on the edge of Landevieille and is signed from both the D32 (Challons-Les Sables d'Olonne) and D12 (La Mothe Achard-St Gilles Croix de Vie) roads.

Charges 2005

Per unit incl. 2 persons	€ 12,00 - € 18,00
extra person	€ 3,00 - € 4,50
child (under 5 yrs)	€ 2,25 - € 3,30
electricity 4-6A	€ 3,00 - € 4,00
water and drainage	€ 1,50
dog	€ 1,75 - € 2,00

Reservations

Made with dates of arrival and departure, plus deposit and fee. Tel: 02 51 22 92 63. Email: info@lepong.com

FR85210 Camping Les Ecureuils

Route des Goffineaux, F-85520 Jard-sur-Mer (Vendée)

Les Ecureuils is a wooded site in a quieter part of the southern Vendée. It is undoubtedly one of the prettiest sites on this stretch of coast, with an elegant reception area, attractive vegetation and large pitches separated by low hedges with plenty of shade. Of the 261 pitches, some 128 are for touring units, each with water and drainage, as well as easy access to 10A electricity. The town of Jard is rated among the most pleasant and least hectic of Vendée towns. The harbour is home to some fishing boats and rather more pleasure craft, and has a public slipway for those bringing their own boats. This site is very popular with tour operators (103 pitches). And in case you are curious, yes there are squirrels on site, including red ones!

Facilities

Two toilet blocks, well equipped and kept very clean, include baby baths, and laundry rooms. Small shop (bread baked on site). New snack-bar. Takeaway service (pre-order 1/6-15/9). Snacks and ice-creams available from the friendly bar. Good sized L-shaped swimming pool and separate paddling pool (30/5-15/9). Indoor pool and fitness centre (all season). Two play areas for different age groups. Modern play area. Minigolf, table tennis and a pool table. Club for children (5-10 yrs) daily in July/Aug. Bicycle hire. Only gas barbecues are allowed. Dogs are not accepted. Internet access. Off site: Nearest beach 400 m. Fishing 400 m. Many places to eat at nearby marina or in town which has good supermarket and weekly market.

Open

1 April - 30 September.

At a glance

Welcome & Ambience	✓✓✓✓✓	Location	✓✓✓✓
Quality of Pitches	✓✓✓✓	Range of Facilities	✓✓✓✓

Directions

Jard-sur-Mer is on the D21 road between Talmont St Hilaire and Longeville sur Mer. Site is well signed from the main road - caravanners will need to follow these signs to avoid tight bends and narrow roads. GPS: N46:24.683 W01:35.382

Charges 2005

Per person	€ 6,50
child (0-4 yrs)	€ 2,00
child (5-9 yrs)	€ 4,50
per pitch with water and drainage	€ 11,50
with electricity (10A)	€ 15,50

Less 10% outside 30/6-1/9.

Reservations

Advised for July/Aug. Tel: 02 51 33 42 74.
Email: camping-ecureuils@wanadoo.fr

FR85200 Camping La Petite Boulogne

12 rue du Stade, F-85670 St Etienne-du-Bois (Vendée)

Set in countryside 24 km. northwest of La Roche sur Yon, St Etienne-du-Bois is a quiet village, well away from the hustle and bustle of the big Vendée resorts. This delightful campsite, owned by the local council, has 40 grassy pitches (most slightly sloping), all with electricity, water and drainage. Pitches are marked by low hedges giving the site an open and sunny aspect. Although the site is inland, it is only 20 km. to the coast with its large sandy beaches, but there are also many attractions and places to visit inland in the Vendée, and this excellent value municipal site provides a great base from which to explore the whole region.

Facilities

The modern, heated toilet block includes some washbasins in cabins. Laundry and dishwashing sinks. Room for disabled people with toilet and shower. Washing machine and dryer. Reception sells bread and a few other essentials. Small unheated pool (June - Aug). TV room. Table tennis. Small play area. Two free tennis courts. Bicycle hire. Daily events in area listed in reception and occasional animation organised in high season, introducing the region and its produce. Charcoal barbecues are only permitted in the communal area. Off site: Open-air, heated pool nearby. Bar and restaurant both few minutes walk away in village. Fishing possible in the nearby Petite Boulogne river. Volleyball and petanque at local sports centre (300 m.). Supermarket 8 km. at Legé. Beach 30 km.

Open

1 May - 31 October.

At a glance

Welcome & Ambience	✓✓✓✓✓	Location	✓✓✓✓	
Quality of Pitches	✓✓✓✓	Range of Facilities	✓✓✓	

Directions

From Legé take D978 south towards Palluau for 7 km. then turn left on D94 towards St Etienne-du-Bois. Go straight through village and, as you come out the other side, cross a small bridge over the river. Site is 50 m. further on, on the right.

Charges 2005

Per unit incl. 2 persons	€ 12,00
extra person	€ 3,00
child (under 7 yrs)	€ 2,00
dog	€ 2,00
electricity (6A)	€ 2,60
No credit cards.	

Reservations

Made with deposit (€ 31). Tel: 02 51 34 54 51. Email: la.petite.boulogne@wanadoo.fr

FR85250 Camping Caravaning Le Littoral

Le Porteau, F-85440 Talmont-Saint-Hilaire (Vendée)

Le Littoral is a quality site maintained to a high standard and fully modernised over recent years by the Boursin family. It is situated on the southern Vendée coast between the ports and beaches of Les Sables d'Olonne and Bourgenay – to which a complimentary bus service runs in high season. Although the site's 483 pitches are mainly used for mobile homes and chalets for hire, there are just 33 touring pitches which are hedged and of a good size. They are interspersed with the mobile homes and all have water, electricity and drainage. A very attractive feature of the site is the three-in-one heated outdoor pool complex together with an indoor heated pool. The restaurant is open daily and introduces frequent themed evenings. Lots of entertainment and activities for all ages is organised in high season and excursions are organised to many places of interest. There is direct access from the site to a spectacular cove with wonderful sea views. A well fenced headland walk leads to a sandy bathing beach which can also be reached using the free minibus service.

Facilities

Four modern sanitary blocks have both British and Turkish style WCs, showers and washbasins in cubicles. Baby rooms in the ladies' sections. Facilities for disabled visitors. Washing machines and dryers. Fridge hire. Well stocked shop (all season). Bar (Easter - 10/9). Restaurant and takeaway (15/5-3/9). Pizzeria and crêperie (high season). Indoor pool (3/4-30/9). Outdoor pool complex with slides (15/5-10/9). Bicycle hire. Multisport pitches. Tennis (charge). Large, well planned play area. Games room. organised activities, entertainment and excursions. Free minibus to beach. Off site: Bus passes site gate. Beach 3 km. (rocky cove 200 m.) Fishing (sea) 200 m. Riding 500 m. Golf 1.5 km.

Open

1 April - 30 September.

At a glance

Welcome & Ambience	✓✓✓✓	Location	✓✓✓✓✓	
Quality of Pitches	✓✓✓✓✓	Range of Facilities	✓✓✓✓✓	

Directions

From D949 Les Sables - Talmont road, take the D4 south to Port Bourgenay. Turn onto the D129 westward and site is on left in 300 m. GPS: N46:27.098 W01:42.121

Charges 2005

Per unit incl. 2 persons	€ 17,00 - € 30,00
extra person	€ 4,00 - € 6,00
child (0-12 yrs)	€ 2,20 - € 3,50
animal	€ 2,20 - € 3,50

Reservations

Made with deposit (€ 76) and fee (24). Tel: 02 51 22 04 64. Email: info@campinglelittoral.fr

FR85300 Camping La Grand' Métairie

Mobile homes ▶ page 416

8 rue de la Vineuse en Plaine, F-85440 St Hilaire la Forêt (Vendée)

Just five kilometres from the super sandy beach at Jard sur Mer, La Grand' Métairie offers many of the amenities of its seaside counterparts, but with the important advantage of being on the edge of a delightful, sleepy village, otherwise untouched by tourism. It is a busy well run site with a programme of lively entertainment in high season. The site has 180 pitches (69 for touring units), all with electricity, water and drainage. The pitches as yet have little shade but are all separated by small trees and bushes and are reasonable in size.

Facilities

Two modern toilet blocks are kept very clean and include washbasins mainly in cabins. Units for disabled people. Washing machines and dryers. Fridge hire. Basic provisions available on site, with useful village store just 100 m. from the gate. Smart bar/restaurant (all 1/5-10/9). Attractive, kidney-shaped heated pool, indoor pool, jacuzzi and paddling pool. Tennis, minigolf (free in low season). Visiting hairdressing. Internet access. Not suitable for American motorhomes. Off site: Riding and fishing within 5 km.

Open

1 April - 30 September.

At a glance

Welcome & Ambience	✓✓✓✓✓	Location		✓✓✓✓
Quality of Pitches	✓✓✓✓	Range of Facilities		✓✓✓✓

Directions

Site is in centre of St Hilaire la Forêt. From Les Sables d'Olonne take D949 (La Rochelle) towards Talmont St Hilaire and Luçon. 7 km. after Talmont turn right on D70 to St Hilaire la Forêt. Site is on the left before village centre. GPS: N46:26.907 W01:31.580

Charges 2005

Per unit incl. 2 persons and electricity (6A)	€ 28,00 - € 26,00
extra person	€ 6,00 - € 8,00
child (2-5 yrs)	€ 4,00

Reservations

Advised for high season with 25% deposit and fee (€ 25). Tel: 02 51 33 32 38.
Email: grand-metairie@wanadoo.fr

FR85270 Chadotel Camping L'Oceano d'Or

58 rue Georges Clémenceau, B.P. 12, F-85520 Jard-sur-Mer (Vendée)

This site should appeal to families with children of all ages. It is very lively in high season but appears to be well managed, with a full programme of activities (it can therefore be noisy, sometimes late at night). The site is only 999 metres from the excellent beach. There are 430 flat, grass and sand pitches of which 40% are occupied by tour operators and mobile homes. The 260 for touring units, all with electricity, are quite large (about 100 sq.m.). Some are separated by high hedges, others are more open with low bushes between them. A modern complex at the entrance houses all the facilities. There are shops, bars and restaurants, and a weekly market in the pleasant little town of Jard-sur-Mer.

Facilities

Four modern, unisex toilet blocks include washbasins all in cabins, plenty of dishwashing and laundry sinks and washing machines and dryers. Small shop (1/6-10/9). Bar and snack bar (both 1/6-10/9, but limited hours outside high season). Swimming pool (15/5-15/9) with 3 water slides, 2 waterfalls and children's pool. Walled (three sides) play area with lots of recently refurbished equipment. Tennis, table tennis, volleyball, pétanque and minigolf. Electric barbecues are not allowed. Internet access. Off site: Golf, riding, karting and numerous other activities within 15 km. Excellent beach within walking distance.

At a glance

Welcome & Ambience	✓✓✓	Location		✓✓✓✓✓
Quality of Pitches	✓✓✓✓	Range of Facilities		✓✓✓✓✓

Directions

Site is on the D21 Talmont St Hilaire - Longeville sur Mer, just east of the turning to the town centre.

Charges 2006

Per pitch incl. 2 adults	€ 14,50 - € 23,50
with electricity (6A)	€ 19,00 - € 28,00
extra person	€ 3,80 - € 5,80

Reservations

Necessary for high season with deposit (€ 40) and fee (€ 25). Central reservations: Siege Social - Centrale de Reservation, BP 12, 85520 Jard-sur-Mer.
Tel: 02 51 33 05 05. Email: chadotel@wanadoo.fr

Open

1 April - 24 September.

137

FR85320 Camping Caravaning Val de Vie

Rue du Stade, F-85190 Maché (Vendée)

Opened in 1999, Val de Vie is a small, good quality site run with enthusiasm and dedication by its English owners on the outskirts of a rural village back from the coast. There are currently 52 pitches for touring units (42 with electricity; 4, 6 or 10A) that vary in size from 80-137 sq.m. on mostly level grass with newly planted hedging. There will be 12 new touring pitches for 2006 (including 9 'super pitches' which must be booked for high season). The ground can become very hard so steel pegs are advised. The pitches are arranged in circular fashion around the toilet block which, with reception, is built in local style with attractive, red tiled roofs. The owners, Peter and Shelagh McClearns, want you to experience real French village life and culture and encourage you to enjoy the local amenities. If you are looking for a beach, the Vendée coast is 20 km.

Facilities

The toilet block provides excellent, modern facilities including some washbasins in cabins, baby bath, facilities for disabled people, dishwashing and laundry sinks, and washing machine. Reception also offers wine, beer, soft drinks and ice cream. Small play area for young children. Heated swimming pool (from mid May). Bicycle hire. Not suitable for American motorhomes. Off site: Tennis courts, shops, bar, tabac, etc. all within walking distance. Lake d'Apremont (300 m.) and Aprement itself with Renaissance château are 4 km. Vendée coast 20 km.

Open

1 May - 30 September.

At a glance

Welcome & Ambience	✓✓✓✓✓	Location	✓✓✓✓✓
Quality of Pitches	✓✓✓✓	Range of Facilities	✓✓✓

Directions

From La Roche sur Yon take the D948 northwest. At the end of the Aizenay bypass continue for 2 km; cross the River Vie and take the next left (D40). The site is signed in the village.

Charges 2006

Per unit incl. 2 persons	€ 14,40 - € 18,00
extra person	€ 3,40 - € 4,25
child (under 10 yrs)	€ 2,56 - € 3,20
electricity (4-10A)	€ 2,90 - € 3,50
dog	€ 1,60 - € 2,00

Less 20% in low season (excl. electricity).

Reservations

Contact site. Tel: 02 51 60 21 02.
Email: campingvaldevie@aol.com

FR85310 Chadotel Camping la Trévillière

Rue de Bellevue, F-85470 Bretignolles-sur-Mer (Vendée)

A member of the Chadotel group, La Trévillière has a pleasant semi-rural setting on the edge of the little resort town of Bretignolles. Although just 2 km. from the nearest beach and less than 5 km. from the Plage des Dunes (one of southern Vendée's best beaches), La Trévillière has a more 'laid-back' feel than many other sites in the area, particularly in low season. After a new extension, there are now 203 pitches, all with easy access to electricity and water. The original area provides either level or slightly sloping pitches separated by hedges or low bushes and there is a mix of shady or more open positions. The new area has no shade as yet from newly planted trees and bushes. The site has around 50 mobile homes and chalets and is used by three small tour operators, but it remains very much a camping and caravanning site. There is a heated swimming pool with water slide, a small paddling pool and a large sunbathing terrace with plenty of loungers. Overlooking the pool is the building housing the bar and reception. In early season the site is very quiet, becoming much livelier in July and August when there is a good range of morning activities for children, afternoon events for families and evening entertainment for all.

Facilities

Three modern, clean toilet blocks include washbasins in cubicles, a unit for disabled people and baby room with bath, shower and toilet. Washing machines and dryers. Bar (limited opening in low season). Small independently operated shop and snack bar with takeaway (20/6-8/9). New restaurant. Heated outdoor pool (15/5-15/9) with slide and paddling pool. Play area. Minigolf, table tennis. Charcoal barbecues are not allowed. Off site: Bus service in the town. Fishing 3 km. Riding 5 km. Golf 10 km. Karting, water sports and water parks are all within easy reach. Beach 2 km.

Open

1 April - 25 September.

At a glance

Welcome & Ambience	✓✓✓✓	Location	✓✓✓✓
Quality of Pitches	✓✓✓✓	Range of Facilities	✓✓✓✓

Directions

Bretignolles is on the D38 Noirmoutier - Les Sables d'Olonne coast road. From the north, after St Gilles go through Bretignolles-La Sauzaie (take left fork) and before reaching Bretignolles itself turn left (sign for site) on sharp right hand bend, heading for water tower. Site is on right in 800 m. From south, after centre of Bretignolles, turn right (sign 'Ecoles') and then left (signs for sports centre and site). Site is signed to left after stadium.

Charges 2005

Per pitch incl. 2 adults	€ 12,00 - € 22,50
with electricity	€ 16,50 - € 27,00
extra person	€ 5,70
child (under 5 yrs)	€ 3,70
animal	€ 2,80

Reservations

Necessary for high season with deposit and fee. Central reservations: Siege Social - Centrale de Reservation, BP 12, 85520 Jard sur Mer. Tel: 02 51 33 05 05. Fax: 02 51 33 94 04. E-mail: chadotel@wanadoo.fr.

FR85330 Camping Naturiste Cap Natur'

Mobile homes ▶ page 418

151 avenue de la Faye, F-85270 St Hilaire-de-Riez (Vendée)

Situated on the northern outskirts of the busy resort of St Hilaire-de-Riez, and only about 2 km. from the nearest beach (6 km. from the nearest official naturist beach beside Plage des 60 Bornes) this family campsite for naturists is in an area of undulating sand dunes and pine trees. The 140 touring pitches nestle among the dunes and trees and offer a wide choice to suit most tastes, including the possibility of electrical connections (10A), although in some cases long leads are needed. Despite the undulating terrain, some pitches are quite level and thus suitable for motorcaravans. The modern facilities are excellent and include both open air and indoor pools, and a jacuzzi. Around the pool is an ample paved sunbathing area, including a stepped 'solarium'. The whole of the indoor complex is a designated no-smoking area. In season a regular Saturday evening 'soirée' is held with a set Vendéen meal, wine and entertainment. There is an air of peace and quiet about this site which contrasts with the somewhat frenzied activity which pervades many of the resorts in this popular tourist area, with a friendly, warm welcome from the family that own it. A number of apartments, tents and mobile homes are on site.

Facilities

Sanitary facilities are basic, but clean, consisting of two indoor (heated) and one outdoor (but roofed) block. Both blocks have open plan hot showers, British style WCs, washbasins, baby baths and children's toilets. Small shop (with takeaway pizzas) and restaurant (menu includes some local specialities), good sized bar, with TV, pool tables and various indoor table games. Indoor and outdoor swimming pools. Fitness classes in high season. Massage room. Play area on soft sand. Volleyball. Torches useful. Bicycle hire. Not suitable for American motorhomes. Off site: Beach 2 km. Fishing 5 km. Naturist beach 6 km. Golf, riding and boat launching 10 km.

Open

1 April - 1 November.

At a glance

Welcome & Ambience	✓✓✓✓	Location	✓✓✓✓
Quality of Pitches	✓✓✓✓	Range of Facilities	✓✓✓✓

Directions

Site is on the north side of St Hilaire-de-Riez. From Le Pissot roundabout go south on the D38, follow signs for St Hilaire at first roundabout you come to (first exit off roundabout), then at second roundabout (garage) turn right signed 'Les Plages'. At third Y-shaped junction turn right again signed 'Parée Prèneau' (also site sign here). The site is 2 km. along this road on the left.

Charges 2005

Per unit incl. 2 adults	€ 14,50 - € 27,50
extra person	€ 2,50 - € 6,70
child (under 13 yrs)	€ 1,60 - € 5,00
electricity (10A)	€ 4,20

Camping Cheques accepted.

Reservations

Advised in high season and for French holidays. Made with 25% deposit and booking fee (€ 27.44). Single male visitors are not accepted.
Tel: 02 51 60 11 66. Email: info@cap-natur.com

FR85350 Camping Caravaning La Ningle

Chemin des Roselières 66, F-85270 St Hilaire-de-Riez (Vendée)

Camping La Ningle is well situated to explore the beautiful port of St Gilles-Croix-de-Vie, with its abundance of restaurants (where seafood is served direct from the morning's catch) and pedestrianised shopping area with a variety of individual boutiques. You are guaranteed to receive a warm welcome at this site from M. et Mme. Guibert, who have established a very pleasant campsite with a friendly, family atmosphere. There are 155 pitches, 80 available for touring units. All have electricity (6A) and a limited number are fully serviced (electricity, water and drainage). Pitches are spacious with dividing hedges and all have some shade. The nearest beach is a 500 m. walk through a pine forest, but there are also three small swimming pools on site.

Facilities

Two regularly cleaned toilet blocks include some washbasins in cubicles. Well equipped toilet/shower room for disabled people and large family shower room in the main block. Laundry and dishwashing facilities. Washing machines and dryer. Bread available July/Aug. Takeaway three evenings per week. Bar (July/Aug) with entertainment twice a week in high season. Main swimming pool, larger children's pool, paddling pool and water slide. Small fitness suite with range of equipment (no instructor, but free). Tennis court. Games field with volleyball and table tennis. Games room with pinball and arcade machines. Small lake for fishing (free). Children's activities (July/Aug), and regular petanque and tennis competitions. Off site: Small supermarket and takeaway 200 m.

Open

15 May - 10 September.

At a glance

Welcome & Ambience	✓✓✓✓✓	Location	✓✓✓✓
Quality of Pitches	✓✓✓✓	Range of Facilities	✓✓✓✓

Directions

Driving south on D38 St Jean de Monts - St Gilles road, turn right at L'Oasis hotel/restaurant in Orouet (6 km. outside St Jean de Monts), signed Les Mouettes. After 1.5 km. you come to a roundabout. Turn left here signed St Hilaire de Riez. After passing two campsites (Les Ecureuils and Bois Tordu) take next left turn, signed La Ningle. Site is approx. 150 m. on the left.

Charges 2005

Per pitch incl. 2 persons	€ 14,30 - € 20,50
with 6A electricity	€ 16,50 - € 23,50
with 10A electricity	€ 18,60 - € 25,80
extra person	€ 3,00 - € 4,20
child (under 7 yrs)	€ 1,60 - € 2,60
dog	€ 1,85

No credit cards.

Reservations

Made with deposit (€ 77.50) and fee (€ 15.25).
Tel: 02 51 54 07 11.
Email: campingdelaningle@wanadoo.fr

FR85360 Camping La Forêt

190 chemin de la Rive, F-85160 St Jean-de-Monts (Vendée)

Camping La Forêt has been owned by M. and Mme. Jolivet for the past few years and they work hard to provide a small, quality site. Well run and attractive, with a friendly, family atmosphere, it provides just 61 pitches with 50 for touring units. Of 100 sq.m. in size, the pitches are surrounded by mature hedges and have water and electricity. Over 50 species of trees are planted on the site, providing shade to every pitch. There is one tour operator on the site (13 pitches), but their presence is in not intrusive and the site has a quiet and relaxed atmosphere, ideal for couples or families with young children.

Facilities

The central toilet block is kept very clean and includes washbasins in cubicles. Baby bath. Facilities for disabled people. Washing machine. Motorcaravan waste tanks can be emptied on request. Basic provisions sold in reception, including fresh bread. Takeaway all season. Small, but inviting swimming pool (15/5-15/9). Play area. Table tennis. Bicycle hire. Only gas and electric barbecues allowed. Not suitable for American motorhomes. Off site: Local beach 400 m. along forest path. Network of cycle paths.

Open

15 May - 28 September.

At a glance

Welcome & Ambience	✓✓✓✓✓	Location	✓✓✓✓
Quality of Pitches	✓✓✓✓	Range of Facilities	✓✓✓✓

Directions

Site is 5.5 km. from town centre, just off the D38. Follow D38 out of St Jean de Monts, towards Notre Dame de Monts. After 5.5 km. turn left at sign for site and 'Plage de Pont d'Yeu'. Follow road and site is on left in about 100 m.

Charges 2005

Per pitch incl. 2 persons	€ 16,00 - € 24,50
extra person	€ 3,50 - € 4,50
electricity (6A)	€ 3,80
No credit cards.	

Reservations

Advised and made with € 34 deposit; min. 15 nights 2/7-19/8. Tel: 02 51 58 84 63.
Email: camping-la-foret@wanadoo.fr

FR85370 Camping Les Mancellières

Route de Longeville-sur-Mer, F-85440 Avrillé (Vendée)

This is a family run site on the edge of the small town of Avrillé, on the road between La Rochelle and Noirmoutiers, yet only a short drive from some of the delightful beaches of the southern Vendée. It is a simple, traditional and well-established site with 130 pitches (73 touring pitches), most with a mixture of sun and shade, but some very shaded. The fact that the snack bar is not licensed might appeal to those who prefer a simple life! Organised events include a weekly outdoor disco and competitions.

Facilities

The two sanitary blocks are kept clean, with mainly British style WCs, washbasins (some in cubicles). Baby bath. Unit for disabled visitors. Washing machine. Small shop and snack bar July/Aug. Swimming pool and slide (until 15/9). Jacuzzi planned. Play area and sports area. Off site: Tennis 800 m. Sea 5 km. Riding 7 km. Golf 10 km.

Open

1 May - 30 September.

At a glance

Welcome & Ambience	✓✓✓✓	Location	✓✓✓✓
Quality of Pitches	✓✓✓✓	Range of Facilities	✓✓✓✓

Directions

Avrillé is on the D949 Les Sables d'Olonne - Luçon road, 23 km. from Les Sables. Site is about 1 km. south of the town, on D105 to Longeville-sur-Mer.

Charges 2005

Per unit incl. 2 persons	€ 10,36 - € 14,80
extra person	€ 3,50
child (under 7 yrs)	€ 3,00
electricity (6A)	€ 3,50

Reservations

Advised for high season. Tel: 02 51 90 35 97.
Email: camping.mancellieres@tiscali.fr

FR85390 Camping des Batardières

F-85440 St Hilaire-la-Forêt (Vendée)

Camping des Batardières is a haven of tranquillity on the edge of an unspoilt village, yet just 5 km. from the sea. It is an attractive, unsophisticated little site, lovingly maintained by its owners for the past 23 years. Many visitors return year after year. There are 75 good-sized pitches (a few up to 130 sq.m.) and all are available for touring units (there are no mobile homes and no tour operators!) All have easy access to water and electricity (6A, or 2A for tents). Otherwise there are few facilities on site.

Facilities

The central sanitary block is kept very clean and visitors are encouraged to keep it that way. Some washbasins in cubicles for ladies. Dishwashing and laundry facilities, including a washing machine and a dryer. TV room, table tennis and a tennis court. Play area and a huge field for games, kite-flying etc. Not suitable for American motorhomes. Off site: Village shop and bar 200 m.

Open

27 June - 2 September.

At a glance

Welcome & Ambience	✓✓✓✓	Location	✓✓✓✓✓
Quality of Pitches	✓✓✓✓✓	Range of Facilities	✓✓✓

Directions

Site is on edge of St Hilaire-la-Forêt. From Les Sables d'Olonne take D949 (la Rochelle) road towards Talmont St Hilaire and Luçon. 7 km. after Talmont turn right on D70 to St Hilaire-la-Forêt and site is signed to the right as you approach the village.

Charges guide

Per unit incl. 2 persons	€ 19,00
with electricity	€ 22,00
extra person	€ 3,00
child (under 5 yrs)	€ 2,00

Reservations

Contact site. Tel: 02 51 33 33 85.

FR85400 Camping Bois Soleil

Mobile homes ▶ page 418

Chemin des Barres, F-85340 Olonne-sur-Mer (Vendée)

This site has a very French feel, the majority of the population when we visited seeming to be French. It is a traditionally laid out site with 199 marked pitches, separated by hedges, on flat or gently sloping ground. There are just two tour operators and a scattering of mobile homes and chalets, leaving some 87 pitches available for tourers and tents. All have electricity (6A, French style sockets) and water points adjacent and many also have waste water pipes. The main buildings house a small reception and tourist information room as well as the bar and attached shop. There is an excellent swimming pool complex with sunbathing areas, swimming and paddling pools two water slides and an impressive flume, plus an indoor pool. In July and August a range of daily activities is organised for adults and children.

Facilities

The two well equipped and maintained toilet blocks have copious hot water, mainly British style toilets, with washbasins in cubicles in the new block. This block is locked overnight, but basic toilet facilities are provided. Two washing machines. Shop (July/Aug. only) with 'eat in' or takeaway service; bread (and cooked chicken) must be ordered the previous day. Bar (28/6-31/8). Indoor and outdoor pools. Sandy play area (caged), trampoline and table tennis. Bicycle hire. Barbecues are not permitted. Off site: Bus service in Olonne sur Mer. Riding 400 m. Fishing and golf 3 km. Beaches are just 2.5 km. The thriving resort of Les Sables d'Olonne is 5 km. along the coast.

At a glance

Welcome & Ambience	✓✓✓✓	Location	✓✓✓
Quality of Pitches	✓✓✓	Range of Facilities	✓✓✓✓

Directions

Site is off the D80 coast road between the towns of Olonne-sur-Mer and Brem-sur-Mer, clearly signed on the inland side.

Charges 2005

Per unit incl. 2 persons	€ 15,00 - € 21,50
with electricity	€ 18,00 - € 24,50
extra person	€ 2,60 - € 3,70
child (under 7 yrs)	€ 2,10 - € 2,70

Reservations

Advised for July/Aug. and made with 25% deposit and fee in July/Aug of € 18. Tel: 02 51 33 11 97. Email: camping.boissoleil@wanadoo.fr

Open

5 April - 28 September.

Camping Bois Soleil★★★★

94, Chemin des Barres - 85340 Olonne sur Mer
T. +33 (0) 251 33 11 97 - F. +33 (0) 251 33 14 85
camping.boissoleil@wanadoo.fr - www.campingboisoleil.com

FR85420 Camping 'Bel

Rue du Bottereau, F-85360 La Tranche-sur-Mer (Vendée)

Camping Bel's owner, M. Guicau, who has a very dry sense of humour, takes an individual approach. The first priority is the contentment of the children, who receive various small gifts during their stay. The site is popular with a large proportion of returning French clients, despite the large presence of British tour operators (130 pitches). The 70 touring pitches are on level, sandy grass. They are separated by hedges with some mature trees giving shade. All of the pitches have electrical connections (10A). It is only 150 m. from a good sandy beach and in the seaside town of La Tranche sur Mer with all amenities within walking distance. This is a good site for a family beach holiday.

Facilities

Two modern toilet blocks have washbasins in cabins, very good baby units and facilities for disabled visitors. Shop with basic provisions. Bar. Heated outdoor pool with jacuzzi. Plenty of entertainment for children aged 6-14 yrs (July/Aug). Table tennis. Fitness area. Tennis and badminton. Pets are not accepted. Not suitable for American motorhomes or twin axle caravans. Off site: Bicycle hire 100 m. Supermarket with fuel 200 m. Fishing 150 m. Watersports 150 m. Riding 5 km.

At a glance

Welcome & Ambience	✓✓✓✓✓	Location	✓✓✓✓
Quality of Pitches	✓✓✓✓	Range of Facilities	✓✓✓✓✓

Directions

Follow signs from the roundabout on the La Tranche bypass, near 'Super U' supermarket onto avenue General de Gaulle. Turn left after 50 m. onto rue du Bottereau. Site is on right after 100 m.

Charges 2006

Per unit with 2 persons and water	€ 21,00
with electricity (6A)	€ 25,00
extra person	€ 4,50

Reservations

Contact site. Tel: 02 51 30 47 39.

Open

27 May - 3 September with all services.

FR85450 Camping Les Roses

Rue des Roses, F-85100 Les Sables d'Olonne (Vendée)

Les Roses has an urban location, with the town centre and the lovely beach just a short walk away. It has an informal air with the 210 pitches arranged interestingly on a knoll. Mature trees give good shade to some areas of the site. There are 107 touring pitches of varying size, many being more suitable for tents than caravans. All pitches have access to electricity, although long cables may be needed. In high season caravanners might find access to the site tricky at times due to overloaded town centre traffic systems. The site has 103 mobile homes and chalets, but no tour operators.

Facilities	Directions
Three well maintained toilet blocks have washbasins in cubicles, unit for disabled visitors, baby room, washing machines and dryers. Simple bar and takeaway (15/5-15/9). Simple shop. Small heated, outdoor pool with slide (1/5-30/9). Play area. Bicycle hire. Off site: Beach 500 m.	Site is signed from the D949 Les Sables to La Rochelle road, north of the 'Géant Casino' roundabout. Turn south at minor junction.

Charges 2005	
Per pitch incl. 2 persons	€ 14,50 - € 23,00
with electricity	€ 19,00 - € 27,50
extra person	€ 5,70

Open

1 April - 31 October.

Reservations	
Contact site. Tel: 02 51 33 05 05. Email: info@chadotel.com	

At a glance

Welcome & Ambience	✓✓✓	Location	✓✓✓✓
Quality of Pitches	✓✓✓	Range of Facilities	✓✓✓

FR85240 Camping Caravaning Jarny-Ocean

Le Bouil, F-85560 Longeville-sur-Mer (Vendée)

Jarny Ocean is the sort of the site the French love – wooded (though less so than before the storms of Dec. 99) and with many pitches separated by thick hedges giving plenty of privacy. There are other areas, however, which are more open and with plenty of sun. There are 303 large, grassy pitches on level ground, of which 200 are for touring units, around 25% well shaded. All have electrical connections (6/10A) and about 30 also with water and drainaway. A beach is within easy walking distance (800 m.) or a beach with lifeguards (and parking) is 4 km. English is spoken.

Facilities	Directions
Five toilet blocks of differing ages have a mix of British and Turkish style WCs. Small shop for basics in July/Aug, but bread, croissants, etc. can be ordered from reception all season. Takeaway in the Centre de Vacances that shares the site (from 1/5). Bar (weekends in low season). Heated swimming pool (1/5 -15/9). Large central play area. Table tennis. Tennis (free in low season). Bicycle hire. Volleyball and basketball. Off site: Bars, restaurants and minigolf are a short walk. Riding or fishing 4 km. Golf 20 km.	From D21 Talmont - Longeville road, soon after Jard, pass through St Vincent and very shortly the site is signed towards the coast (before Longeville). Turn left in village of Le Bouil (site signed) and site is on left in 800 m. GPS: N46:24.812 W01:31.249

Charges guide	
Per unit incl. 2 adults	€ 9,25 - € 20,00
with 6A electricity	€ 11,00 - € 22,80
with water and drainage	€ 12,70 - € 24,40
extra person	€ 2,05 - € 3,20

Open

1 May - 30 September.

Reservations	
Made with deposit (€ 45.73) and fee (€ 15.24). Tel: 02 51 33 42 21. Email: jarny-ocean@wanadoo.fr	

At a glance

Welcome & Ambience	✓✓✓	Location	✓✓✓✓
Quality of Pitches	✓✓✓	Range of Facilities	✓✓✓

FR85510 Camping Le Bois Joli

2 rue de Châteauneuf, F-85710 Bois de Céné (Vendée)

This site is a hidden gem in a small village away from the hustle and bustle of the seaside resorts. Suitable for people looking for a quiet holiday, it is still within driving distance of the Vendée coast (20 km). A warm welcome is given by the English speaking Malard family, who make every effort to make your stay enjoyable. On site is a small lake with free fishing and a large sports field (with a 'portacabin' style toilet block). The site also has a small swimming pool. There are 130 pitches of which 90 are for touring units. All pitches have 6A electricity. An extra 60 pitches and a new toilet block are planned.

Facilities	Directions
Three toilet blocks – old, but with modem, bright tiles and very clean. All are unisex with some washbasins in cubicles, some controllable showers, two baby baths, two washing machines. Bar with evening entertainment. Takeaway (1/7-31/8). Good play area. Table tennis. Tennis. Petanque. Bicycle hire. Off site: Supermarket and bus service in the village (two minutes walk). Riding 5 km. Beach 18 km.	From Challans take D58 to Bois de Céné (10 km). Turn left at first road junction and site is on right.

Charges 2005	
Per pitch incl. 2 persons	€ 9,30 - € 13,60
with electricity (6A)	€ 11,05 - € 16,40
extra person	€ 2,70 - € 3,75

Reservations	
Contact site. Tel: 02 51 68 20 05. Email: campingboisjoli@free.fr	

Open

1 April - 25 September.

At a glance

Welcome & Ambience	✓✓✓✓✓	Location	✓✓✓✓
Quality of Pitches	✓✓✓✓	Range of Facilities	✓✓✓✓

FR85480 Camping Caravaning Le Chaponnet

Rue du Chaponnet N-16, F-85470 Brem-sur-Mer (Vendée)

This well established family run site is within five minutes walk of Brem village centre and 1.5 km. from a long sandy beach. The 100 touring pitches are level with varying amounts of grass, some with shade from mature trees. All pitches are separated by tall hedges and serviced by tarmac or gravel roads and there are frequent water and electricity points. A warm welcome is given at the large reception area. Tour operators have mobile homes and tents on 70 pitches and there are 70 privately owned mobile homes and chalets. The swimming pool complex has indoor (heated) and outdoor pools with jacuzzi, water slides and a children's pool, together with a sauna and fitness centre. It is overlooked by the spacious bar and snack bar. Entertainment is provided for all ages by day and three or four musical evenings a week provide family fun rather than teenage activities.

Facilities

The six sanitary blocks are modern light and airy, well maintained and cleaned and evenly spread throughout the site. Washbasins are in cubicles, some showers and basins have controllable water temperature and there are good facilities for babies and disabled people. Washing machines, dryers and ironing boards. Bar, snack bar and takeaway (1/6-6/9). No shop but bread and croissants available at the bar. Good play area with plenty of space for ball games. Table tennis, tennis and bicycle hire. Indoor games room. Off site: Village shops and restaurants are five minutes walk away. Beach 1.5 km. Fishing 5 km. Golf 12 km. Riding 10 km.

At a glance

Welcome & Ambience	✓✓✓✓	Location	✓✓✓
Quality of Pitches	✓✓✓	Range of Facilities	✓✓✓✓

Directions

Brem is on the D38 St Gilles - Les Sables d'Olonne road. Site is clearly signed, just off the one-way system in the centre of the village.

Charges guide

Per unit incl. 3 persons	€ 16,40 - € 25,20
with electricity	€ 20,00 - € 28,70
extra person	€ 3,10 - € 4,60
child (under 5 yrs)	€ 2,10 - € 3,10
dog	€ 1,60

Reservations

Contact site. Tel: 02 51 90 55 56.
Email: chaponnet@free.fr

Open

1 May - 15 September.

FR85440 Camping Les Brunelles

Le Bouil, F-85560 Longeville-sur-Mer (Vendée)

This is a well managed site with good facilities and a varied programme of high season entertainment for all the family. The owner, M. Guinard is justifiably proud of his campsite. The leaflet given to all visitors on arrival (together with a bottle of wine) explains in detail the workings of the campsite and the standards of behaviour expected. In mid July the site was very busy but there was an atmosphere of well ordered calm. M. Guinard believes that if the children are happy and occupied then the parents are also happy. This approach certainly seems to work. This has to be one of the cleanest and neatest sites on the Vendée. The 60 touring pitches are all level on sandy grass and separated by hedges, away from most of the mobile homes on site. There is a mixture of sunny and shaded pitches and all have easy access to electricity (6A). Water points are not so frequent. A good supervised sandy beach is just 900 m. away. The village of St Vincent sur Jard (2 km.) has shops, bars and restaurants and the pleasant seaside town of Jard sur Mer with its market is just 4 km.

Facilities

Four old but well maintained and modernised toilet blocks have British and Turkish style toilets, washbasins both open style and in cabins, plenty of sinks for dishwashing and laundry, five washing machines, two dryers and ironing. Shop (from 8/4-28/9). Takeaway and large modern, airy bar (15/6-10/9) with games area overlooks the impressive pool complex. New covered pool with jacuzzi (all season). Outdoor pool with slides and paddling pools (15/5-15/9), both pools are heated but unsupervised. Fenced area for football, volleyball and basketball. Table tennis. Tennis. Bicycle hire. Off site: Golf, riding, karting and numerous other activities within 15 km.

Open

8 April - 23 September.

At a glance

Welcome & Ambience	✓✓✓✓	Location	✓✓✓
Quality of Pitches	✓✓✓	Range of Facilities	✓✓✓✓✓

Directions

From the D21 Talmont - Longueville road, between St Vincent and Longueville, site is well signed south from the main road towards the coast. Turn left in village of Le Bouil (site signed) and site is 800 m. on left. GPS: N46:24.798 W01:31.388

Charges 2006

Per unit incl. 2 persons	€ 15,00 - € 28,00
with electricity	€ 18,00 - € 33,00
extra person	€ 5,00
child (under 5 yrs)	free - € 5,00
animal	€ 3,00 - € 4,00

Camping Cheques accepted.

Reservations

Made with 25% deposit and € 20 fee.
Tel: 02 51 33 50 75.
Email: camping@les-brunelles.com

www.alanrogers.com for latest campsite news

FR85430 Camping Club La Bolée d'Air

Route de Longeville, F-85520 St Vincent sur Jard (Vendée)

This is a well managed site with good facilities and a varied programme of high season entertainment. The 120 touring pitches are level and well grassed on sandy soil. Many are around the perimeter of the site and are separated by trimmed hedges giving good privacy but little shade. Long electricity cables may be required. The main road runs along one side of the site and may cause traffic noise at some times, although when we visited in July there did not appear to be a problem. A good, sandy, supervised beach is just 900 m. away. The site is used by two small tour operators.

Facilities

Three modernised, unisex toilet blocks provide washbasins in cabins. Washing machines and dryers. Shop and takeaway (1/6-31/8). Bar (1/5-30/9). Heated indoor pool, outdoor pool (1/6-30/9) with slide, jacuzzi and paddling pool. Tennis. Minigolf. Bicycle hire. Table tennis. Good multi-sport all-weather terrain. Off site: Bus service in the town. Karting and many other activities within 1.5 km. Riding 4 km. Fishing 10 km. Beach 900 m. Village 1.5 km.

Open

2 April - 25 September.

At a glance

Welcome & Ambience	✓✓✓✓	Location	✓✓✓✓
Quality of Pitches	✓✓✓✓	Range of Facilities	✓✓✓✓

Directions

Site is just off the D21 Les Sables La Franche road, just east of St Vincent-sur-Jard and is well signed from the main road.

Charges 2005

Per unit with 2 persons and car	€ 12,00 - € 22,50
with electricity	€ 16,50 - € 27,00
extra person	€ 5,70
child (under 5 yrs)	€ 3,70
animal	€ 2,80

Reservations

Made with deposit (€ 40 p/week), fee (€ 25) and cancellation insurance. Tel: 02 51 90 36 05. Email: info@chadotel.com

FR85570 Camping Caravaning Le Pomme de Pin

Rue Vincent Auriol, F-85520 Jard-sur-Mer (Vendée)

This family run site, set amongst the pine trees, is just 150 metres from a sandy beach in a quiet residential area and within easy reach of the town of Jard with its lively weekly market and fishing harbour. It specialises in mobile homes (over 140) but there are ten small touring pitches. These are well shaded as the site has a cover of the pine trees from which it gets its name. The compact, attractively laid out swimming pool is overlooked by a bar and its sun terrace. There is a good entertainment programme for all ages in high season.

Facilities

Three unisex toilet blocks provide washbasins in cabins (warm water only) and preset showers. Simple facilities only for babies and disabled visitors. Washing machines and dryer. Bar, restaurant, takeaway (1/6-30/9). Small well-stocked shop (15/6-30/9). Play area and outdoor table tennis table. Charcoal barbecues are not permitted. Off site: Sailing school, water sports, minigolf, tennis and beaches all within 2 km.

Open

1 April - 30 September.

At a glance

Welcome & Ambience	✓✓✓✓	Location	✓✓✓
Quality of Pitches	✓✓✓	Range of Facilities	✓✓✓

Directions

From the D21 (Talmont - Longueville) road, site is signed to the south.

Charges guide

Per unit incl. 2 persons	€ 14,50 - € 22,00
with electricity	€ 18,00 - € 26,00
extra person	€ 5,40
child (under 5 yrs)	€ 3,50

Reservations

Contact site. Tel: 02 51 33 43 85. Email: info@pommedepin.net

FR85520 Camping Domaine des Renardières

13 chemin du Chêne Vert, F-85270 Notre-Dame-de-Riez (Vendée)

Just seven kilometres from the busy coastal strip with its many large, multi-activity campsites, Domaine des Renardières is an oasis of calm in the traditional French manner. Converted from the family farm in 1970 by the present owner's father, the site consists of three fields with varying amounts of shade and two further open fields in full sun. The visitors are 65% French, many of whom, together with British visitors, return year after year. The 100 touring pitches are well grassed and level; torches and long cables are advisable. Mme. Raffin's benevolent authority is to be seen everywhere. There is an abundance of flowers and plants, the facilities are scrupulously maintained and all arriving clients are provided with a set of campsite rules which are also explained at the regular Monday Aperitif welcome meeting. A doctor calls twice a day in high season and Mme. Raffin is highly qualified in first aid. The welfare of her clients is of paramount importance to her. The site is very well organised with a soft touch.

Facilities

The new unisex toilet block has private wash cubicles, baby changing room and a bathroom for disabled visitors. Showers are closed at night except for one cold shower. Dishwashing under cover. Washing machine and dryer. Small shop, takeaway, air-conditioned bar with TV, video games and pool (all 1/7-27/8). Small outdoor pool attractively laid out (1/5-4/9). Play area. Only gas barbecues are permitted. Motorhome service point. Not suitable for American motorhomes. Off site: Fishing 700 m. Bicycle hire 6 km. St Hilaire de Riez (7 km) has shops, bars, restaurants and all entertainments as well as a good sandy beach. Riding 9 km. Golf 11 km.

Open

1 May - 4 September.

At a glance

Welcome & Ambience	✓✓✓✓✓	Location	✓✓✓✓
Quality of Pitches	✓✓✓	Range of Facilities	✓✓✓✓

Directions

Site is well signed from the centre of the village of Notre Dame de Riez.

Charges 2006

Per unit incl. 2 persons	€ 14,50
with electricity (6A)	€ 17,50
extra person	€ 3,50
child (under 5 yrs)	€ 2,50
dog	€ 1,50 - € 3,00

Less 10-20% outside 15/7-21/8. No credit cards.

Reservations

Made with deposit and € 10 fee.
Tel: 02 51 55 14 17. Email: caroline.raffin@free.fr

FR85550 Camping Le Port de Moricq

Le Port de Moricq, F-85750 Angles (Vendée)

Nestling amongst the marshes, this site was bought in 2002 by Mme. Louche who is slowly but surely exerting her influence in carrying out improvements to the facilities. The 20 touring pitches are level and grassy and spread amongst the mobile homes. There is little shade but hedges divide the pitches all of which have easy access to water and electricity (10/16A). Outside high season the site is very quiet but in July and August there is a children's club twice a day and a varied evening entertainment programme. Fishing is possible in the canal near the site. It is 2 km. from Angles and 7 km. from the beach at La Plage des Conches. Used by two Dutch tour operators.

Facilities

One traditional style, well maintained toilet block (a second is planned), has Turkish and British style toilets, washbasins in cubicles and open plan, a unit for disabled visitors. Dishwashing and laundry sinks under cover. Washing machine and dryer. Bar (15/3-15/10), Restaurant and takeaway (15/6-15/10). Heated, covered outdoor pool (15/6-30/9). TV and games room with cable TV. Playground. Multi-sports pitch. Bicycle hire. Off site: Fishing nearby. Beaches, golf and riding all within 15 km.

Open

15 March - 15 September.

At a glance

Welcome & Ambience	✓✓✓	Location	✓✓✓✓
Quality of Pitches	✓✓✓	Range of Facilities	✓✓✓

Directions

Site is signed from roundabout on the D747 (La Roche-sur-Yon - La Tranche), 7 km. south of the junction with D949 (Les Sables - Luçon) road.

Charges 2006

Per unit incl. 2 persons	€ 14,40 - € 19,50
with electricity	€ 16,40 - € 23,60
extra person	€ 4,60 - € 5,10
child under 4 yrs	€ 4,10 - € 4,60
dog	€ 3,10 - € 3,60

Reservations

Made with deposit (€ 80) and fee (€ 15).
Tel: 02 51 28 95 21.
Email: infos@camping-port-de-moricq.com

FR85530 Camping La Parée Préneau

23 avenue de la Parée Préneau, F-85270 St Hilaire-de-Riez (Vendée)

This site was founded in 1968 by the grandfather of the present owner. It has been gradually and thoughtfully expanded to its present size (206 pitches). Of these, 150 are touring pitches of varying shapes and sizes, interestingly arranged. Mature trees proliferate to give varying amounts of shade to the undulating site, although the pitches are level. All have electricity (6A) and many also have water and drainage. The calm atmosphere is enhanced by the absence of tour operators. All amenities are very clean and well maintained. The cosy welcoming bar overlooks the pool area. The friendly welcome in campsite reception is indicative of the caring attitude of those running the site.

Facilities

The two sanitary blocks are modern and include washbasins (some in cubicles), facilities for babies and disabled visitors. WCs are a mixture of British, seatless and Turkish, all thoroughly cleaned twice a day. Laundry and dishwashing sinks, washing machine and dryer. No restaurant or shop but bread, milk and other essentials are available. Mobile takeaway vendors call in high season. Heated indoor and outdoor swimming pools with jacuzzi and paddling pool surrounded by wide sun terrace. Large play area with football, volleyball/basketball pitch. Table tennis (indoor). Bicycle hire. Not suitable for American motorhomes or twin axle caravans. Off site: Beach 1 km. Riding 3 km. Shops, bars, restaurants 5 km. Fishing, golf and sailing 7 km.

Open

15 May - 8 September.

At a glance

Welcome & Ambience	✓✓✓✓	Location	✓✓✓✓
Quality of Pitches	✓✓✓✓	Range of Facilities	✓✓✓

Directions

From large roundabout on D38 just north of St Hilaire-de-Riez, turn south signed St Hilaire for 400 m. Take first exit at next roundabout signed Les Plages and after another 400 m. continue straight on at junction. Site is on left after 3 km.

Charges 2005

Per unit incl. 2 persons	€ 14,00 - € 18,50
with electricity	€ 16,10 - € 20,60
extra person	€ 3,60 - € 4,40
child (under 5 yrs)	€ 2,20 - € 2,60
dog	€ 1,50 - € 2,00

Reservations

Made with deposit (€ 35) and fee (€ 15). Tel: 02 51 54 33 84. Email: camplapareepreneau@wanadoo.fr

FR85590 Camping Plein Sud

246 route de Notre-Dame-de-Monts, F-85160 St Jean-de-Monts (Vendée)

Plein Sud is a small welcoming site with 110 grassy pitches, many with adequate shade and separated by hedges. All are of about 100 sq.m. and have electricity (4/6A), water and drainage. There is one main drive through the site and site owned and private mobile homes are mostly positioned nearer the entrance. Touring pitches are situated further from the main road and bar area and are more pleasantly peaceful. The pool is inviting with a small children's pool and fountain alongside. Only 800 m. away is the beautiful long stretch of safe sandy beach, which is accessed via a pleasant walk through pines and sand dunes. In high season there is a security guard and gate. There are no tour operators.

Facilities

Two modern, clean sanitary blocks provide washbasins in cabins. One block has a baby room. Dishwashing facilities. Washing machines and dryers. Small bar with TV and terrace. Heated pool (no Bermuda style shorts). Play area with volleyball and table tennis. Bread and milk can be ordered daily at reception. Outside caterers provide regular takeaways. Bicycle hire. Daily pony and trap rides for young children (free). Children's entertainment organised in high season. Off site: Small supermarket, bar and restaurants within 500 m. Fishing 1 km. Riding 2 km. Golf 3 km. Beach 800 m.

Open

1 May - 15 September.

At a glance

Welcome & Ambience	✓✓✓✓	Location	✓✓✓✓
Quality of Pitches	✓✓✓✓	Range of Facilities	✓✓✓✓

Directions

Site is about 3 km. north of St Jean de Monts on the D38, Route de Notre Dame de Monts, on the right almost opposite Camping L'Abri des Pins.

Charges 2005

Per unit incl. 3 persons	€ 12,00 - € 23,00
incl. 4A electricity	€ 15,00 - € 25,00
incl. water and drainage	€ 18,00 - € 28,00
extra person	€ 2,50 - € 5,00
child (2-5 yrs)	free - € 3,00
dog	free - € 2,00

Reservations

Made with deposit (€ 53) and fee (€ 23). Tel: 02 51 59 10 40. Email: camping-pleinsud@club-internet.fr

FR85660 Camping Le Pont Rouge

Rue Clemenceau, F-85220 St Révérend (Vendée)

This small, tranquil site is situated down a short tree-lined country lane just 600 metres from a small village. Suitable for people who prefer to be away from the frenzy of activity at the nearby coastal resorts. Owned and run by a young, enthusiastic, English-speaking and a very friendly couple, Mr and Mme Pousse, who make great efforts for an enjoyable stay. The pitches are grassy, varied in shape and size with most located near mature trees giving ample shade and separated by tall hedges, some flowering, ensuring peace and privacy. The 13 mobile-homes, most with timber terraces, are situated, with some touring pitches, in an open sunny aspect. All pitches have electricity but long leads may be required on some. Ample water points are situated close to all pitches.

Facilities

Two toilet blocks, one within the main reception building with bright modern tiles has segregated showers, toilets, and wash cubicles. The second new block has segregated showers and wash cubicles with a unisex toilet section and includes a washing machine, and washing and ironing facilities. All very clean. Two play area - one with swings, slides and adventure frames set on a sandy base and one near new toilet block set on grass. Small sports field at rear of site. Small, neat, fenced-off pool complex (renovated during 2005 and now with a large mural around it) at rear of reception with separate children's pool and slide. Bicycle hire. Basic provisions available in reception. Off site: Shops, restaurant and bakery in village - 600 m. Country walks, cycling. Golf and riding nearby.

At a glance

Welcome & Ambience	✓✓✓✓	Location	✓✓✓✓✓
Quality of Pitches	✓✓✓✓✓	Range of Facilities	✓✓✓

Directions

From the D6 Aizenay to St Gilles-Croie-de-Vie turn north onto D94 signed St Révérend about 4 km. west of Coëx. Site is on left after 400 m., just before the village.

Charges 2005

Per unit incl. 2 persons	€ 13,30 - € 15,30
with electricity	€ 15,60 - € 17,90
extra person	€ 3,35 - € 3,80
child (under 8 yrs)	€ 2,40 - € 2,80
animal	€ 1,90 - € 2,20

Reservations

SiteTextReservations Tel: 02 51 54 68 50.
Email: camping.pontrouge@wanadoo.fr

Open

1 April - 31 October.

FR85610 Camping Les Aventuriers de la Calypso

Route de Notre-Dame-de-Monts, Les Tonnelles, F-85160 St Jean-de-Monts (Vendée)

This site is ideally situated within 700 metres of the beautiful, sandy Vendée beaches and close to St Jean de Monts (4 km.) with its wide variety of shops and restaurants. Although there are 253 pitches, only a limited number are for touring units, and these are situated amongst the site's own mobile homes (there are no tour operators here). The pitches are level, grassy and of good size, and are either in the open or shade, with hedges providing privacy. All have electricity (3-10A) and some have water and drainage. The site is neatly maintained with an attractive pool complex and amenities. There is a good variety of entertainment for all ages during the high season. A useful complex with facilities is 150 metres from the site which includes a pizzeria, supermarket and a popular seafood shop.

Facilities

The modern sanitary block is fully equipped including facilities for babies and disabled campers. A 'portacabin' style block has WCs, showers and washbasins. Both are very clean and well maintained. Laundry. Bar with restaurant area (high season). Very small shop with basic supplies. Games area. Tennis court. Bicycle hire. Entertainment in July and August. Off site: Commercial centre 150 m. Nearest beach 700 m. Notre Dame de Monts 3 km. St Jean de Monts 4 km. Numerous cycle routes.

At a glance

Welcome & Ambience	✓✓✓	Location	✓✓✓✓
Quality of Pitches	✓✓✓	Range of Facilities	✓✓✓✓

Directions

Site is on the D38 St Jean de Monts - Notre Dame de Monts road, at the Les Tonnelles roundabout.

Charges 2005

Per unit incl. 2 persons	€ 21,00 - € 23,00
extra person	€ 5,00
child (under 5 yrs)	€ 2,50
electricity	€ 2,50 - € 4,00

Reservations

Made with deposit (€ 100) and fee (€ 15).
Tel: 02 515 608 78.

Open

1 April - 30 September.

147

FR85680 Camping Le Pin Parasol

Lac du Jaunay, F-85220 La Chapelle-Hermier (Vendée)

Tucked away in the Vendée interior, not far from St Gilles-Croix-de-Vie and 15 minutes drive from the beach, this site enjoys a pleasant rural setting away from the bustle of the coast. Originally a farm, it is partly set on a slight hillside running down towards the Lac du Jaunay, and there are good views over wooded shores from the pool terrace. There is lakeside access and pedaloes, canoes, etc. are available. The enthusiastic family owners are very hands-on and their dynamism is evident. Facilities are of a high standard, most notably the pool area with its well constructed new indoor pool and the adjacent large, modern bar/restaurant. There are over 200 pitches with around 100 used for touring units and the remainder used for mobile homes and chalets to rent. Of a good size, the pitches are mostly fairly open with some shade. Electricity connections are available.

Facilities

Fully equipped toilet blocks include facilities for babies and disabled visitors. Washing machines and dryers. Shop. Restaurant/bar with terrace. Takeaway. Pool complex with swimming pool and slides. Indoor pool. Lake 50 m. with fishing, boating, canoeing, etc. Play area. Multi-sports pitch. Table tennis. Boules. Bicycle hire. Entertainment in high season. Off site: Tennis, golf and riding within 5 km. Beach 15 minutes by car.

Open

15 May - 15 September.

At a glance

Welcome & Ambience	✓✓✓✓	Location	✓✓✓✓
Quality of Pitches	✓✓✓	Range of Facilities	✓✓✓✓

Directions

Site is signed to the south of the D42 Challans - La Chapelle Hermier road, east of the junction with the D40. It is signed from Landevieille.

Charges 2005

Per unit incl. 2 persons	€ 9,50 - € 22,00
extra person	€ 4,50
child (0-10 yrs)	€ 3,00
electricity (6/10A)	€ 3,50 - € 4,00
animal	€ 2,70

Reservations

Made with 25% deposit and fee (€ 50). Tel: 02 51 34 64 72.

FR85620 Camping Le Caravan'ile

B.P. 4, La Guérinière, F-85680 Ile de Noirmoutier (Vendée)

This well appointed, 8.5 hectare, family run site is reached by crossing the bridge on the D38 to the pretty island of Noirmoutier. It is also accessible via the causeway (Le Gois) at low tide. Not far from the town centre, with an adjoining sandy beach, the site offers indoor and outdoor swimming pools, a popular sauna, jacuzzi and mini gym and a variety of entertainment in high season to suit all ages. The level touring pitches are mainly situated near the beach (shielded by the sand dune) and all have electricity. Some also have a water point, but no dividing hedges or shade. A few are situated on a ridge with sea views to the front and rear. Camping Le Caravan'ile has a very French ambience, with no tour operators.

Facilities

Three immaculately clean sanitary blocks, each with showers, British toilets, some enclosed wash cabins and facilities for disabled people. Hot showers only available 0800-1200 and 1700-2100 hrs. Laundry. Dishwashing. Heated indoor and outdoor swimming pools, paddling pools and flume. Fitness room, sauna and jacuzzi. Bar/takeaway (July/August). Games and sports area. Electronic games room. Organised entertainment in July/August. Off site: Bar, restaurant, ATM, small supermarket and minigolf, all 500 m. Riding, cycling, windsurfing, aquarium, water theme park and salt marshes within close proximity.

Open

1 March - 15 November.

At a glance

Welcome & Ambience	✓✓✓✓	Location	✓✓✓✓✓
Quality of Pitches	✓✓✓	Range of Facilities	✓✓✓✓

Directions

Take D38 road from the mainland, crossing bridge to Ile de Noirmoutier. Site is at the roundabout at La Guérinière, on the left.

Charges guide

Per unit incl. 2 persons	€ 9,10 - € 17,20
incl. 5A electricity	€ 11,10 - € 20,30
extra person	€ 2,70 - € 4,20
child (2-7 yrs)	€ 1,70 - € 2,70
animal	€ 1,60 - € 2,60

Reservations

Contact site. Tel: 02 51 39 50 29. Email: contact@caravanile.com

FR85690 Campings Moncalm & Atlantique

BP 19, F-85750 Angles (Vendée)

Moncalm and Atlantique are sister sites owned by the Atlantique Pellerin Vacances group. The majority of the pitches on these sites are occupied by mobile homes and chalets, mostly to rent. However, there is a small number of touring pitches too. The sites are on either side of a quiet road and lie 300 m. from the village centre. The sandy beaches at La Tranche sur Mer are 7 km. distant and a free shuttle bus runs there in high season. An impressive range of amenities is on offer, including a large covered pool on Moncalm, and an open-air pool at Atlantique, both with waterslides. A lively entertainment programme is organised in high season, including regular discos and competitions.

Facilities

Shop. Bar. Takeaway. Covered pool (Moncalm), open air pool (Atlantique) and water slides. Sauna, jacuzzi and gym. Tennis. Basketball. Play area. Games room. Football pitch. Minigolf. Children's club. Entertainment programme. Shuttle bus to beach. Off site: Nearest beach 7 km. Angles village centre (restaurants, shops, etc.) 300 m.

Open

9 April - 24 September.

At a glance

Welcome & Ambience	✓✓✓✓	Location	✓✓✓
Quality of Pitches	✓✓✓	Range of Facilities	✓✓✓✓

Directions

Angles can be found close to the D747 La Tranche-sur-Mer - La Roche sur Yon road, 7 km north of La Tranche. The sites are close to the village centre and are clearly indicated.

Charges 2005

Per unit incl. 2 persons	€ 15,00 - € 23,00
serviced pitch	€ 17,00 - € 26,00
dog	€ 2,50
from to	

Reservations

Contact APV group. Tel: 02 51 97 55 50.
Email: camping-apv@wanadoo.fr

Loire Valley

With over one hundred of France's finest châteaux, this is a region to inspire the imagination. The Loire valley is a charming region of lush countryside, fields of sunflowers, rolling vineyards and of course the great river itself.

OUR TOURIST REGIONS INCLUDES ALL THE LOIRE VALLEY: 18 CHER, 28 EURE-ET-LOIR, 36 INDRE, 37 INDRE-ET-LOIRE, 41 LOIR-ET-CHER, 45 LOIRET. FROM WESTERN LOIRE: 49 MAINE-ET-LOIRE, 53 MAYENNE, 72 SARTHE. AND FROM POITOU-CHARENTES: 79 DEUX SÈVRES, 86 VIENNE

For centuries the Loire valley was frequented by French royalty and the great river winds its way past some of France's most magnificent châteaux: Amboise, Azay-le-Rideau, Chenonceau, with its famous arches that span the river and appear to 'float' on the water, and the fairytale Ussé with myriad magical turrets are just some of the highlights.

Known as the Garden of France, the Loire's mild climate and fertile landscape of soft green valleys, lush vineyards and fields of flowers makes it a favourite with the visitors. Renowned for its wines, with hundreds to choose from, all are produced from vineyards stretching along the main course of the River Loire. Imposing abbeys, troglodyte caves, tiny Romanesque churches, woodland areas such as the Sologne and sleepy, picturesque villages reward exploration. Cities like Blois and Tours are elegant with fine architecture and museums and Paris is only one hour by TGV. One of the oldest towns of Loire valley is Saumur. Its old quarter, grouped around the riverbank beneath the imposing château, is particularly pleasant to wander around.

Places of interest

Amboise: château, Leonardo da Vinci museum

Beauregard: château with Delft tiled floors

Blois: château with architecture from Middle Ages to Neo-Classical periods

Chambord: Renaissance château

Chartres: cathedral with stained glass windows

Chinon: old town, Joan of Arc museum

Loches: old town, château and its fortifications

Orléans: Holy Cross cathedral, house of Joan of Arc

Tours: Renaissance and Neo-Classical mansions, cathedral of St Gatien,

Vendôme: Tour St Martin, La Trinité

Villandry: famous renaissance gardens

Cuisine of the region

Wild duck, pheasant, hare, deer, and quail are classics and fresh water fish such as salmon, perch and trout are favourite. Specialities include rillettes, andouillettes, tripes, mushrooms and the regional cheeses of Trappiste d'Entrammes and Cremet d'Angers, Petit Sable and Ardoises d'Angers cookies

Bourdaines: apples stuffed with jam and baked

Tarte a la citrouille: pumpkin tart

Tarte Tatin: upside down tart of caramelised apples and pastry

FR28110 Camping Municipal de Bonneval

Bois de Chievre, F-28800 Bonneval (Eure-et-Loir)

On the outskirts of Bonneval and within walking distance of the centre, this municipal site offers good facilities in peaceful surroundings. The site has thick cover from trees in most parts with some pitches entirely hidden for those who like lots of privacy. Nearly all the pitches are marked out on grass in clearings, some on a slope, but the majority fairly flat. Of the 130 pitches, 120 have 6A electricity, some hardstanding. The site has no bar, restaurant or shop, but all are available in Bonneval itself or, when open, in the municipal swimming pool and tennis complex adjacent (reduced rates for campers). Caravans with double axles or more than 5.6 m. are not accepted.

Facilities

Sanitary facilities consist of one large block, plus three smaller units without showers. The large block has mostly chain operated hot showers, some washbasins in cubicles and facilities for disabled people. Laundry room with washing machine and ironing facilities. Motorcaravan services. Large TV room. Playground. Bicycle hire. Fishing. Boules. Off site: Swimming pool and tennis adjacent.

Open

1 April - 31 December.

At a glance

Welcome & Ambience	✓✓✓✓	Location	✓✓✓✓
Quality of Pitches	✓✓✓✓	Range of Facilities	✓✓✓✓

Directions

Site signed from Bonneval town centre on N10 from Châteaudun to Chartres (on Rte de Vouvray). GPS: N48:10.244 E01:23.169

Charges guide

Per person	€ 2,80
child (2-7 yrs)	€ 1,50
pitch	€ 3,00
electricity	€ 3,00 - € 4,00

No credit cards.

Reservations

Contact site. Tel: 02 37 47 54 01.
Email: camping.bonneval@wanadoo.fr

FR28120 Camping Municipal du Pré de l'Eglise

Avenue du Pré de l'Eglise, F-28380 St Remy-sur-Avre (Eure-et-Loir)

This neatly kept, useful little site has only 45 pitches, but is quite popular as a short stay or transit site with many nationalities as it lies just off the main N12 cross country route. The pitches are on level grass and divided by hedges, with 10A electric hook-ups, and are arranged around a circular access road, with some shade from specimen trees. The guardian lives adjacent to site entrance.

Facilities

The sanitary unit, in the older style, is adequate and includes facilities for disabled people. Dishwashing and laundry sinks are under cover. Washing lines. Salle with TV. No double axle caravans are accepted. Off site: Supermarket 2 km. in the direction of Nonancourt.

Open

1 April - 30 September.

At a glance

Welcome & Ambience	✓✓✓✓	Location	✓✓✓✓
Quality of Pitches	✓✓✓✓	Range of Facilities	✓✓✓

Directions

St Remy-sur-Avre is 9 km. west of Dreux on N12 and site is signed from N12 at traffic lights. Turn towards town centre and almost immediately turn right, then following signs turn left, and then left again. Site is on right with parking space outside the barrier. GPS: N48:45.822 E01:14.209

Charges guide

Per person	€ 2,46
pitch incl. electricity	€ 5.83 - € 11,27

Reservations

Contact site. Tel: 02 37 48 93 87.

FR36050 Camping Municipal Les Vieux Chênes

F-36310 Chaillac (Indre-et-Loire)

A delightful site on the outskirts of an attractive village, this is another little gem - a small site within walking distance of the centre. The 40 grass pitches, all with electricity (16A), are generous in size, slightly sloping, with hedging and some mature trees. The well manicured appearance and relaxed atmosphere add to the attraction of this peaceful environment. The adjacent lake is for fishing only, although there is access to a larger lake just 1 km. away where varied watersports - swimming, windsurfing, canoeing and pedaloes - can be enjoyed. The small water toboggan is free of charge. A warden lives on the site.

Facilities

Heated sanitary facilities are insulated for winter use and include washbasins in private cabins. Limited facilities for disabled campers. Washing machine. Winter caravan storage. Off site: Tennis club adjacent. Fishing 25 m. Shops 200 m. Watersports 1 km.

Open

All year.

At a glance

Welcome & Ambience	✓✓✓✓	Location	✓✓✓✓
Quality of Pitches	✓✓✓✓	Range of Facilities	✓✓✓

Directions

From the north leave A20, south of Argenton sur Creuse, take D1 to St Benoit (16 km.) and then west to Chaillac on D36 (8.5 km.). From the south leave A20 at exit 21, take D10 to St Benoit, then D36 as before. Go through the village and turn left by the Mairie. GPS: N46:25.921 E01:17.735

Charges 2005

Per person	€ 1,65
pitch incl. electricity	€ 3,80 - € 5,40

No credit cards.

Reservations

Not made. Tel: 02 54 25 61 39.

FR37010 Camping de la Mignardière

22 avenue des Aubépines, F-37510 Ballan-Miré (Indre-et-Loire)

Southwest of the city of Tours, this site is within easy reach of several of the Loire châteaux, notably Azay-le-Rideau. In addition, there are many varied sports amenities on the site or very close by. The site has 177 numbered pitches of which 139 are for touring units, all with electricity (6/10A) and 37 with drainage and water. The pitches are of a good size on rather uneven grass with limestone gravel paths (which are rather 'sticky' when wet). The site's facilities are supplemented by a small 'parc de loisirs' just across the road which provides a bar and refreshments, pony rides, minigolf, small cars, playground and other amusements. The barrier gates (coded access) are closed 22.30 - 07.30 hrs. Reservation is essential here for most of July/August.

Facilities

Two toilet blocks, one new near the site entrance, the other totally refurbished, include washbasins in private cabins, a unit for disabled people, baby bath and laundry facilities. Motorcaravan service point. Shop (15/5-15/9). Takeaway (1/7-31/8). Two large, heated swimming pools (15/5-15/9). Good tennis court. Table tennis. Bicycle hire. Off site: Attractive lake catering particularly for windsurfing 300 m. (boards can be hired or use your own) and family fitness run. Fishing 500 m. Riding 1 km. Golf 3 km. Tours centre 8 km.

Open

10 April - 25 September.

At a glance

Welcome & Ambience ✓✓✓✓✓ Location ✓✓✓✓
Quality of Pitches ✓✓✓✓ Range of Facilities ✓✓✓✓

Directions

From A10 autoroute take exit 24 and D751 towards Chinon. Turn right after 5 km. at Campanile Hotel following signs to site. From Tours take D751 towards Chinon.

Charges 2006

Per unit incl. 2 persons with electricity, water and drainage	€ 14,00 - € 20,00
	€ 20,00 - € 27,50
extra person	€ 4,00 - € 5,00
child (2-10 yrs)	€ 2,60 - € 3,00

Camping Cheques accepted.

Reservations

Made for any length with 30% deposit (min. € 40). Tel: 02 47 73 31 00. Email: info@mignardiere.com

FR37030 Camping Le Moulin Fort

F-37150 Francueil-Chenonceaux (Indre-et-Loire)

Camping Le Moulin Fort is a tranquil, riverside site that has been redeveloped by British owners, John and Sarah Scarratt. The 137 pitches are enhanced by a variety of trees and shrubs offering some shade and 110 pitches have electricity (6A). The attractive (unheated) swimming pool is accessed by a timber walkway over the mill race from the snack bar terrace adjacent to the restored mill building. The picturesque château of Chenonceaux is little more than 1 km. along the Cher river and many of the Loire châteaux are within easy reach, particularly Amboise and its famous Leonardo de Vinci museum. Although not intrusive there is some noise from the railway line across the river and a few trains run at night. The site is more suitable for couples and families with young children, although the river is unfenced.

Facilities

Two toilet blocks with all the usual amenities of a good standard, including washbasins in cubicles and baby baths. Shop (1/4-30/9). Bar, restaurant and takeaway (all 15/5-30/9). Swimming pool (15/5-30/9). Minigolf. Games room and TV. Small library. Regular family entertainment including wine tasting, quiz evenings, activities for children and light-hearted games tournaments. Motorcaravan service point. Fishing. Bicycle and canoe hire. Off site: Riding 12 km. Golf 20 km.

Open

1 April - 30 September.

At a glance

Welcome & Ambience ✓✓✓✓ Location ✓✓✓✓✓
Quality of Pitches ✓✓✓✓ Range of Facilities ✓✓✓✓

Directions

Site is well signed from the N76 Tours - Vierzon road. From the D40 Tours - Chenonceaux road, go through the village and after 2 km. turn right on D80 to cross the river at Chisseaux. Site is on left just after the bridge. GPS: N47:19.637 E01:05.358

Charges 2006

Per unit incl. 2 persons	€ 9,00 - € 20,00
extra adult	€ 3,00 - € 5,00
child (4-12 yrs)	€ 2,00 - € 4,00
electricity (6A)	€ 4,00
dog	€ 2,00 - € 3,00

Reservations

Advised for high season and for large units at any time; contact site. Tel: 02 47 23 86 22. Email: lemoulinfort@wanadoo.fr

FR37050 Camping Caravanning La Citadelle

Avenue Aristide Briand, F-37600 Loches en Touraine (Indre-et-Loire)

A pleasant, well maintained site, La Citadelle is within walking distance of Loches, noted for its perfect architecture and its glorious history, at the same time offering a rural atmosphere in the site itself. Most of the 128 level, good-sized touring pitches (all with 10A electricity and 42 fully serviced) offer some shade from trees. The most recent addition is an on-site outdoor pool with paddling pool (solar heated). Loches, its château and dungeons, is 500 m. A free bus/little train runs from the campsite to the centre of Loches during the summer. A 'Sites et Paysages' member.

Facilities

Three sanitary blocks provide British and Turkish style WCs, washbasins (mostly in cabins) and showers. Dishwashing and laundry sinks. Laundry facilities and a motorcaravan service area at the block nearest reception. Two excellent baby units and provision for disabled people. Play equipment for children. Boules, volleyball and games room. Small bar and snack bar (15/6-13/9). Internet access and TV. Off site: Riding 3 km. Supermarket 3 km; market on Wednesday and Saturday mornings. Golf 7 km.

Open

19 March - 19 October.

At a glance

Welcome & Ambience	✓✓✓✓	Location	✓✓✓✓✓
Quality of Pitches	✓✓✓✓✓	Range of Facilities	✓✓✓✓

Directions

The easiest approach is from the south. From any direction take the town bypass (RN143) and leave via the roundabout at the southern end (by LeClerc supermarket). Site is well signed towards the town centre on the right in 800 m. Do not enter the town centre. GPS: N47:07.382 E01:00.134

Charges 2005

Per pitch incl. 2 adults	€ 13,30 - € 23,50
extra person	€ 3,90 - € 4,80
electricity (10A)	€ 3,60

Camping Cheques accepted.

Reservations

Advised in July/Aug. Tel: 02 47 59 05 91.
Email: camping@lacitadelle.com

FR37060 Camping L'Arada Parc

Mobile homes ▶ page 419

Rue de la Baratière, F-37360 Sonzay (Indre-et-Loire)

A good, well maintained site in a quiet location, Camping L'Arada Parc is a popular base from which to visit the numerous châteaux in this beautiful part of France. The 81 grass pitches all have electricity and 22 have water and drainage. The clearly marked pitches, some slightly sloping, are separated by maturing trees and shrubs that will, in time, provide some shade. An attractive, heated pool is on a pleasant terrace beside the restaurant and campers can enjoy their meal or a drink overlooking the pool. Entertainment, themed evenings and activities for children are organised in July/August. This is a new site with modern facilities which is developing well. A 'Sites et Paysages' member.

Facilities

Two modern toilet blocks provide unisex toilets, showers and washbasins in cubicles. Excellent baby room, Facilities for disabled visitors (wheelchair users may the gravel in front of the lower block difficult). Laundry with washing machine, dryer and ironing board. Shop, bar, restaurant and takeaway (27/3-31/10). Swimming pool (no shorts; 1/5-13/9). Play area, covered games area. Boules, volleyball, badminton and table tennis. TV room. Bicycle hire. Off site: Riding 7 km. Fishing 9 km. Golf 12 km.

Open

1 April - 1 November.

At a glance

Welcome & Ambience	✓✓✓✓✓	Location	✓✓✓✓
Quality of Pitches	✓✓✓✓	Range of Facilities	✓✓✓✓✓

Directions

Sonzay is northwest of Tours. From the N138 Le Mans - Tours or the A28 take the exit for Neuillé-Pont-Pierre onto the D766 towards Sonzay then follow camping signs.

Charges 2006

Per unit incl. 2 persons	€ 15,00 - € 17,50
extra person	€ 3,50 - € 4,50
child (2-10 yrs)	€ 2,75 - € 3,50
electricity (10A)	€ 3,50
animal	€ 1,50

Camping Cheques accepted.

Reservations

Made with deposit (30%); contact site.
Tel: 02 47 24 72 69. Email: laradaparc@free.fr

FR37070 Camping de L'Ile Auger

Quai Danton, F-37500 Chinon (Indre-et-Loire)

This is a well-placed site for exploring the old medieval town of Chinon and its impressive castle that was a home of England's Henry II and includes a museum to Joan of Arc. Alongside the River Vienne, it is a five minute walk over the main bridge to the town centre. The 277 pitches are numbered but not separated, with electricity (4/8/12A). A number are shaded by tall trees. A warden lives on site.

Facilities

Six toilet blocks around the site have mostly British style WCs. A very good new block is next to the office building. Washing up sinks. Barrier locked 22.00 - 07.00 hrs. Motorcaravan service point. Playground, table tennis and boules court. Off site: Tennis. Indoor and outdoor swimming pools nearby. Bicycle hire 1 km. Shop 1 km. Fishing 3 km.

Open

15 March - 15 October.

Directions

From Chinon town cross the river and turn right at the end of the bridge. The campsite entrance is about 100 m. on the right. GPS: N47:09.827 E00:14.121

Charges 2005

Per person	€ 1,85
pitch	€ 4,20
child (under 7)	€ 1,23
electricity (4-12A)	€ 1,85 - € 3,20

No credit cards.

Reservations

Contact site or the Mairie. Tel: 02 47 93 53 00.

At a glance

Welcome & Ambience	✓✓✓✓	Location	✓✓✓✓✓
Quality of Pitches	✓✓✓✓	Range of Facilities	✓✓✓

FR37090 Camping du Château de La Rolandière

F-37220 Trogues (Indre-et-Loire)

This is a charming little site set in the grounds of a château which has the appearance of a Queen Anne style dolls house. There are 30 medium sized, flat pitches, some gently sloping front to rear, and all separated by neat hedges. All but four have 10A electricity and water taps nearby and the parkland trees give shade. The château and adjoining buildings contain rooms to let and a swimming pool (14 x 6m.) and paddling pool pool serve them and the campsite. An 18-hole minigolf meanders through the parkland and there is an area set aside for ball games, swings and slides for younger children. Sabine Toulemonde and her husband, who bought the château in 2002, offer a very warm welcome. Situated on the D760 road between Ille Bouchard and St Maure-de-Touraine, the site is 5 km. west of the A10, convenient for an overnight break or for longer stays to explore the châteaux at Chinon, Loches or Azay-le-Rideau and the villages of Richelieu and Crissay-sur-Manse.

Facilities

The refurbished French style toilet block provides showers, washbasins, dishwashing and laundry areas around central British style WCs with a separate provision for disabled visitors. There is a single washbasin cabin in both the male and female units. Washing machine and dryer available via reception. Bar with terrace and snacks/takeaway. Small shop in reception for basic provisions (July/Aug). Swimming pool (15/5-30/9). Minigolf. Play area. Bicycle hire. Off site: Fishing 1 km. to River Vienne. Restaurant 5 km. adjacent to A10 junction. Full range of shops and commercial facilities in St Maure 8 km. Interesting excursions to gardens, grottos. In nearby Azay-le-Rideau visit the wicker craftsmen's workshops.

At a glance

Welcome & Ambience	✓✓✓✓✓	Location	✓✓✓✓
Quality of Pitches	✓✓✓✓	Range of Facilities	✓✓✓✓

Directions

The site is 5 km. west from junction 25 on A10 at St Maure-de-Touraine on the D760 towards Chinon. The entrance is clearly signed and marked by a model of the château. GPS: N47:06.460 E00:30.631

Charges 2005

Per person	€ 5,00 - € 6,00
child	€ 2,50 - € 3,00
pitch	€ 7,00 - € 8,50
electricity	€ 3,50

No credit cards.

Reservations

Contact site. Tel: 02 47 58 53 71. Email: contact@larolandiere.com

Open

15 April - 30 September.

FR37110 Camping Municipal Au Bord du Cher

RN 76, F-37270 Veretz (Indre-et-Loire)

This is an inexpensive, well laid out site on the banks of the River Cher with views through tall elm trees to the Château of Veretz. Monsieur Menard and his wife live in a caravan on site during the season and are always pleased to welcome British tourists. With 64 pitches, most divided by small hedges and all with at least 6A electricity, the site is just outside the town of Veretz where shops, restaurants, bars, etc. can be found. A wooden chalet houses reception and plenty of tourist information, with notice boards giving weather forecasts, etc. In addition, the manager is always willing to offer information and advice about where to go and what to see in the area. Of particular interest for railway enthusiasts are restored steam trains and track in the area. River trips are possible in the replica of a boat used to carry goods (mainly wine) on the river until the '20s. English is spoken.

Facilities

Large, modern sanitary block includes British and Turkish style WCs, dishwashing under cover, laundry and washing machine. Motorcaravan service point. Takeaway with covered area to sit and eat (from mid-June). Communal barbecue. Playground. Table tennis. Not suitable for American motorhomes. Off site: Baker 700 m. Tennis 1 km. Riding 3 km. Outdoor swimming pool (July/Aug) 4 km. Bicycle hire 12 km. Bus service from Tours station to Bleré passes site entrance. Fishing nearby.

At a glance

| Welcome & Ambience | ✓✓✓✓ | Location | ✓✓✓✓ |
| Quality of Pitches | ✓✓✓ | Range of Facilities | ✓✓✓ |

Directions

Site is at Veretz, via the N76 road, 10 km. southeast of Tours (much better than the municipal at St Avertin en-route).

Charges guide

Per person	€ 2,00
child (under 7 yrs)	€ 1,00
pitch	€ 3,50 - € 6,00
electricity	€ 2,60 - € 4,60

No credit cards.

Reservations

Contact site. Tel: 02 47 50 50 48.

Open

22 May - 26 September.

FR37140 Huttopia Rillé

F-37340 Rillé (Indre-et-Loire)

Rillé is a new site and a member of Huttopia, a group of campsites set up to combine a 'back to nature' outlook with a good range of modern amenities. This site has been recommended by our agent and we plan to include it in a future inspection programme. Rillé is located north of the Loire and lies on the banks of the Lac de Rillé, an important bird sanctuary. There are 120 large pitches, most of which are well shaded and many offer electrical connections (6/10A). Vehicle access to the camping area is limited to arrivals and departures and otherwise a separate parking area must be used. A special area has been designated for motorcaravans. An imaginative range of rented accommodation is available including 'roulottes', an adaptation of gypsy caravans.

Facilities

Sanitary building including a family shower room. Special bivouacs set up for cooking and washing up. Lakeside restaurant with takeaway food. Bar. Games room. Watersports. Swimming pool. Playground, Table tennis, Tennis. Children's club. Motorcaravan service point. Off site: Ornithological excursions. Steam train around the lake. Hiking. Cycling trails. Fishing. Watersports on the lake. Golf. Châteaux of the Loire.

Open

25 June - 30 October.

Directions

Rillé can be found around 30 km. north of Langeais on the D57. The lake and site are north of the village.

Charges 2005

Per person	€ 4,50 - € 4,70
child (2-7 yrs)	€ 3,00 - € 3,20
pitch	€ 3,50 - € 14,00
electricity (6A)	€ 3,60

Reservations

Contact site.

FR37120 Castel Camping Parc de Fierbois

Ste Catherine de Fierbois, F-37800 St Maure-de-Touraine (Indre-et-Loire)

Parc de Fierbois has an impressive entrance and a tree lined driveway – all rather beautiful and grand. Set among 250 acres of lakes and forest in the heart of the Loire Valley, the site itself is a lively family holiday site with a super pool complex and a sandy beach on the shores of the lake. In all, there are 320 pitches including 100 for touring units, the remainder being used by tour operators and for chalets and mobile homes. There are 80 touring pitches, mostly level and separated by low hedging or small trees, with water, drainage and electricity hook-ups (2-8A). The other pitches are small or medium in size, many unmarked and some sloping and in the shade. There is plenty here to occupy and entertain children and this site would be good for family holidays. English is spoken in reception.

Facilities

Three toilet blocks provide British style WCs, hot showers and washbasins in cubicles. Baby room. Dishwashing under cover. Washing machines and dryers. Motorcaravan service point. Shop. Bar. Restaurant. Takeaway. Pizzas. Indoor heated swimming pool. Water park complex with pools, long slides, paddling pool, etc. and grass sunbathing areas. New indoor entertainment and games bar with paved terrace overlooking the pools. Tennis. Volleyball. Badminton. Football pitch. Petanque area. Minigolf. Bicycle hire. Go-karts, electric cars and red London buses on a small circuit. TV and video room (French and English). Fishing. Pedaloes and canoeing in July/Aug. Entertainment programme in July/Aug. Off site: Riding 10 km. Golf 30 km.

At a glance

Welcome & Ambience	✓✓✓	Location	✓✓✓✓
Quality of Pitches	✓✓✓	Range of Facilities	✓✓✓✓

Directions

Travelling south on N10 from Tours, go through Montbazon and continue towards Ste Maure and Chatellerault. Site is signed about 16 km. outside Montbazon near the village of Ste Catherine. Turn off main road and follow signs to site. From A10 autoroute use Ste Maure exit and turn north up N10.

Charges 2006

Per unit incl. 2 persons	€ 16,00 - € 35,00
extra person	€ 6,00
electricity	€ 4,00

Reservations

Made with 25% deposit and fee (€ 15). Tel: 02 47 65 43 35. Email: parc.fierbois@wanadoo.fr

Open

15 May - 15 September.

FR41010 Le Parc du Val de Loire

Route de Fleuray, F-41150 Mesland (Loir-et-Cher)

Between Blois and Tours, quietly situated among vineyards away from the main roads and towns, this site is nevertheless centrally placed for visits to the châteaux; Chaumont, Amboise and Blois (21 km.) are the nearest in that order. There are 232 touring pitches of reasonable size, either in light woodland marked by trees or on open meadow with separators. All the pitches have electricity (6A) and 100 of them also have water and drainage. Sports and competitions are organised in July/Aug. with a weekly disco and dance for adults and opportunities for wine tasting are arranged weekly. There are local walks and bike rides on marked paths (free maps available). New, experienced owners have recently taken over the site.

Facilities

Two original toilet blocks of varying ages are clean and acceptable. Units for disabled visitors, baby bathrooms and laundry facilities. Motorcaravan services. Large shop with bakery (July/Aug. only). Bar next to the pools. Restaurant, snack service, pizzeria and takeaway (July/Aug). TV room and large recreation room. Three swimming pools, the two smaller ones can be heated, one with popular water slide (the newest 200 sq.m.). Tennis and tennis training wall. Good playgrounds with skate board facilities. Bicycle hire. Table tennis. Minigolf. Football pitch. Volleyball, badminton and basketball. Barbecue area. Off site: Fishing 2 km. Golf 4 km. Riding 10 km. Nearby – balloon and helicopter flights over the Loire valley.

Open

1 April - 15 October.

At a glance

Welcome & Ambience	✓✓✓✓	Location	✓✓✓✓
Quality of Pitches	✓✓✓	Range of Facilities	✓✓✓

Directions

From the A10 exit 18 (Château-Renault, Amboise) take D31 south to Autrèche (2 km). Turn left on D55 for 3.5 km. In Darne-Marie Les Bois turn left and almost immediately right onto D43 to Mesland. Follow signs to site. Alternatively, if approaching from the south, site is well signed from Onzain. GPS: N47:30.601 E01:06.286

Charges 2005

Per pitch incl. 2 persons	€ 10,00 - € 21,70
large pitch (150 sq.m.)	
with water and drainage	€ 13,80 - € 27,30
extra person	€ 2,00 - € 5,60
child (2-7 yrs)	€ 1,50 - € 3,20
electricity 6-10A	€ 3,80
animal	€ 2,20

Reservations

Made for min. 4 days with deposit (25%) and fee (€ 20). only in high season Tel: 02 54 70 27 18. Email: parc.du.val.de.loire@wanadoo.fr

FR41020 Castel Camping Château La Grenouillière

Mobile homes ▶ page 419

F-41500 Suèvres (Loir-et-Cher)

Château de la Grenouillière is a comfortable site with good amenities on the N152 midway between Orléans and Tours. It is well situated for visiting many of the Loire châteaux and there are enough attractions on site and locally to make it suitable for a longer stay holiday. It is set in a 28-acre park and the 260 pitches (including 130 for tour operators and mobile homes) are in three distinct areas. The majority are in a well wooded area, with about 60 in the old orchard and the remainder in open meadow, although all pitches are separated by hedges. There is one water point for every four pitches and only 10 lack an electric hook-up (5A). Additionally, there are 14 'grand confort' pitches with a separate luxury sanitary block in the outbuildings of the château itself. A weekly trip to Paris, a canoe-kayak trip, wine cellar and cheese tasting visits, musical evenings and children's entertainment are organised in high season.

Facilities

Three sanitary blocks, one for each area, are modern and well appointed, including some washbasins in cabins. Washing machines and dryers in a small laundry. Shop. Bar. Pizzeria and pizza takeaway. Restaurant and Chicken Grill takeaway (1/6-5/9). Swimming complex of four pools (one covered) and a water slide. Tennis, squash, table tennis, pool, baby foot and video games. Internet point. Bicycle and canoe hire (July/Aug). Guided tours organised once a week. Off site: Fishing, riding, and aqua sports 5 km. Golf 10 km. Suèvres 3 km.

Open

1 May - 5 September.

At a glance

Welcome & Ambience	✓✓✓✓	Location	✓✓✓✓
Quality of Pitches	✓✓✓✓	Range of Facilities	✓✓✓✓✓

Directions

Site is between Suevres and Mer on north side of N152 and is well signed.

Charges guide

Per unit incl. 2 persons	€ 18,50 - € 28,00
with 5A electricity	€ 22,50 - € 32,00
with full services	€ 26,00 - € 40,00
extra person	€ 5,00 - € 6,50
child (under 7 yrs)	€ 3,00 - € 4,50
dog	€ 3,00 - € 4,00

Less 10% during middle season, and 35% during low season.

Reservations

Made with deposit (€ 90) and fee (€ 20). Tel: 02 54 87 80 37. Email: la.grenouillere@wanadoo.fr

FR41030 Yelloh! Village Le Parc des Alicourts

Domaine des Alicourts, F-41300 Pierrefitte-sur-Sauldre (Loir-et-Cher)

A secluded holiday village set in the heart of the forest and with many sporting facilities, Parc des Alicourts is midway between Orléans and Bourges, to the east of the A71. There are 490 pitches, 150 for touring and the remainder occupied by mobile homes and chalets. All pitches have electricity (6A) and good provision for water, and most are 150 sq.m. (min. 100 sq.m.). Locations vary from wooded to more open areas, thus giving a choice of amount of shade. All facilities are open all season and the leisure amenities are exceptional. Competitions are organised for adults as well as children and, in high season organised activities include a club for children with an entertainer twice a day, a disco once a week and a dance for adults. An inviting water complex (all season) includes two swimming pools, a pool with wave machine and beach area, and a spa, not forgetting three water slides.

Facilities

Three modern sanitary blocks include some washbasins in cabins and baby bathrooms. Washing machines and dryers. Excellent facilities for disabled visitors in one block (but with shallow step to reach them). Motorcaravan services. Shop with good range of produce (the nearest good-sized town is some distance). Restaurant with reasonable prices, plus takeaway in a pleasant bar with terrace. Water complex. 7 hectare lake with fishing, bathing, canoes, pedaloes and play area. Nine hole golf course (very popular). Well equipped play area. Football pitch, volleyball, tennis, minigolf, table tennis, boules. Roller skating/skateboard area (bring your own equipment). Bicycle hire with cyclo-cross and mountain bikes and a way-marked path for walking and cycling. Internet access.

Open

Mid May - 7 September.

At a glance

Welcome & Ambience	✓✓✓✓	Location	✓✓✓✓
Quality of Pitches	✓✓✓	Range of Facilities	✓✓✓✓✓

Directions

From A71, take Lamotte Beuvron exit (no 3) or from N20 Orléans to Vierzon (which runs parallel with the A71) turn left on to D923 towards Aubigny. After 14 km, turn right at camping sign on to D24E. Site is clearly marked from there in about 4 km. GPS: N47:32.639 E02:11.516

Charges 2005

Per unit incl. 2 persons and electricity	€ 15,00 - € 38,00
extra person	€ 6,00 - € 8,50
child (7-17 yrs)	€ 4,00 - € 6,50
child (1-6 yrs)	free - € 5,50
dog	€ 7,00

Reductions for low season longer stays.

Reservations

Made for min. 7 days for July/Aug. only, with 25% deposit. Tel: 02 54 88 63 34. Email: parcdesalicourts@wanadoo.fr

FR41070 Camping Caravanning La Grande Tortue

Mobile homes ▶ page 420

3 route de Pontlevoy, F-41120 Candé-sur-Beuvron (Loir-et-Cher)

This is a pleasant, shady site that has been developed in the surroundings of an old forest. It provides 169 touring pitches the majority of which are more than 100 sq.m. 150 have 10A electricity and the remainder are fully serviced. The family owners continue to develop the site with a new multi-sports court already created. During July and August, they organise a comprehensive programme of trips including wine/cheese tastings, canoeing and horse riding excursions. The site is used by tour operators. This site is well placed for visiting the châteaux of the Loire or the cities of Orléans and Tours.

Facilities

Three sanitary blocks offer British style WCs, washbasins in cabins and push-button showers. Laundry with deep sinks, washing machine, dryer and ironing board. Shop selling provisions. Terraced bar and restaurant with reasonably priced food and drink (15/4-15/9). Swimming pool and two shallower pools for children (1/5-30/9). Trampolines, a ball crawl with slide and climbing wall, bouncy inflatable, table tennis. New multi-sport court. Off site: Walking and cycling. Bicycle hire 1 km. Fishing 500 m. Golf 10 km. Riding 12 km.

Open

9 April - 30 September.

At a glance

Welcome & Ambience	✓✓✓	Location	✓✓✓✓
Quality of Pitches	✓✓✓	Range of Facilities	✓✓✓✓

Directions

Site is just outside Candé-sur-Beuvron on the D751, midway between Amboise and Blois. From Amboise, turn right just before entering Candé, then immediately left into the campsite (well signed from the road). GPS: N47:29.389 E01:15.515

Charges 2005

Per unit incl. 2 persons	€ 13,50 - € 21,50
incl. electricity	€ 17,50 - € 25,00
extra adult	€ 4,60 - € 6,00
child (3-9 yrs)	€ 3,30 - € 4,30
animal	€ 3,00

Camping Cheques accepted.

Reservations

Necessary in July and August. Tel: 02 54 44 15 20. Email: grandetortue@libertysurf.fr

Camping Caravaning International ★★★★

La Grande Tortue

3, route de Pontlevoy
41120 CANDÉ-sur-BEUVRON
Tel: 0033 254 44 15 20 - Fax: 0033 254 44 19 45
Website: www.la-grande-tortue.com

159

FR41040 Camping Château des Marais

27 rue de Chambord, F-41500 Muides-sur-Loire (Loir-et-Cher)

The Château des Marais campsite is well situated to visit the chateau at Chambord (its park is impressive) and the other châteaux in the 'Vallée des Rois'. The site, providing 133 large touring pitches, all with electricity (6/10A), water and drainage and with ample shade, is situated in the oak and hornbeam woods of its own small château. An excellent swimming complex offers pools and two flumes. English is spoken and the reception from the enthusiastic owners and the staff is very welcoming. In high season, canoe trips on the Loire are popular; campers are taken by coach to Muides-sur-Loire and are collected three hours later at Blois. Used by tour operators (90 pitches). A 'Sites et Paysages' member.

Facilities

Four modern, purpose built sanitary blocks have good facilities including some large showers and washbasins en-suite. Washing machine. Motorcaravan service point. Shop and takeaway. Bar/restaurant with large terrace. Swimming complex with heated and unheated pools, water slide and cover for cooler weather. TV room. Bicycle hire. Fishing pond. Excursions by coach to Paris, an entertainment programme and canoe trips organised in high season. Internet access. Off site: Riding 5 km. Golf 12 km. Village of Muides sur Loire, with a variety of small shops, etc. five minutes walk.

Open

15 May - 15 September.

At a glance

Welcome & Ambience	✓✓✓✓	Location	✓✓✓✓
Quality of Pitches	✓✓✓✓	Range of Facilities	✓✓✓✓✓

Directions

From A10 autoroute take exit 16 to Mer, then cross the Loire to join the D951 and follow signs. Site is signed off D103 to southwest of village. 600 m. from junction with the D112.
GPS: N47:39.948 E01:31.726

Charges 2005

Per pitch incl. 2 persons	€ 22,00 - € 30,00
extra person	€ 6,00
child (under 5 yrs)	€ 4,00
electricity (6/10A)	€ 4,00 - € 6,00
dog	€ 4,00

Credit cards accepted for amounts over € 80.

Reservations

Advised July/Aug. Tel: 02 54 87 05 42.
Email: chateau.des.marais@wanadoo.fr

FR41060 Camping de Dugny

CD45 (La Cabinette), F-41150 Onzain (Loir-et-Cher)

This well organised campsite started life as an 'a la ferme' back in 1976. Since then it has grown into an eight hectare camping site surrounded by many acres of wonderfully quiet farmland. Still under the same ownership, it now opens all year round. There are 300 pitches, with mobile homes (privately owned and to rent) leaving 190 tourist pitches. Generously sized, they are partially separated, some with shade and others open. All but 30 have electricity (10A), water and drainage. This is a site for active people, both young and older. Play areas and sports fields includes equipment for youngsters, minigolf, a trampoline, football and basketball. A marquee provides entertainment for children aged up to 12 years and a large barn offers undercover table tennis. Adult and children's quad bikes can be hired or you can take a flight in a microlight from the site landing strip. Most activities take place away from the camping area to guard a quiet atmosphere. Coach trips to chateaux, wine cellars and other places of interest are arranged in July and August or when numbers are adequate.

Facilities

Three sanitary units include some washbasins in cubicles and provision for disabled people. Dishwashing and laundry sinks. Bread, ices, soft drinks and gas are stocked. Small restaurant and takeaway, with barbecue evenings organised on the terrace. Heated outdoor swimming pool complex with two pools (one with slides) and paddling pool. Large play areas for 4-12 year olds. Minigolf, table tennis, volleyball, basketball and a pétanque court. Internet point. Pony and horse riding around the farmland. Microlight flights. Pedaloes and row boats for hire. Varied activity programme including children's disco, boules and table tennis tournaments and camp-fire evenings. Off site: Local markets at Onzain, Montrichard, Blois and Amboise. A little train takes guests to a nearby wine cave, and a local farm that produces goats cheese.

Open

All year.

At a glance

Welcome & Ambience	✓✓✓✓	Location	✓✓✓✓
Quality of Pitches	✓✓✓	Range of Facilities	✓✓✓✓✓

Directions

Onzain is southwest of Blois (15 km.) and on the opposite side of the river from Chaumont-sur-Loire. Take N152 Blois to Tours road, turn right onto D1 signed Onzain. Site is signed after the railway bridge. Turn right onto D58, then left onto D45. Keep following signs.

Charges 2005

Per person	€ 6,00 - € 12,00
child (5-14 yrs)	€ 4,00 - € 7,00
child (under 5)	free
pitch	€ 4,00 - € 8,00
electricity	€ 5,00

Camping Cheques accepted.

Reservations

Not normally required, but made with 25% deposit. Tel: 02 54 20 70 66.
Email: info@camping-de-dugny.fr

FR41090 Camping Municipal de la Varenne

F-41210 Neung-sur-Beuvron (Loir-et-Cher)

This is a particularly well organised site in a peaceful location, yet within easy walking distance of the town centre. It is a good economic base for visiting Orléans, Blois or the Chateaux of the Loire. The site has a slight slope but most of the 69 grass touring pitches are fairly level, all with electricity (10A). Some pitches are individual, others in bays of four, and some for tents amongst the trees. There is good shade in most areas. At the rear of the site is a large open field which slopes down to the small river - a very popular place with the children on hot days. Each evening the warden visits every pitch to take the bread order, which is available from reception at 08.00 next morning. Four mobile homes are for rent.

Facilities

An excellent, clean and well equipped modern building includes spacious showers, baby changing facilities, a suite for disabled people, and a washing machine. A second unit at the rear of the reception building has additional good facilities. Freezer for ice blocks. Motorcaravan service point. Playground. Volleyball. Two tennis courts. Table tennis. Bicycle hire. River fishing adjacent to site. Off site: The town has all services including restaurants, bars, supermarket.

Open

Easter - 30 September.

At a glance

Welcome & Ambience	✓✓✓✓	Location	✓✓✓✓
Quality of Pitches	✓✓✓✓	Range of Facilities	✓✓✓✓

Directions

Neung-sur-Beuvron is about 40 km. east of Blois, and is 2 km. west of the 0922 about 22 km. north of Romarantin-Lanthenay. Site is 1 km. northeast of town centre (well signed).
GPS: N47:32.293 E01:48.905

Charges 2005

Per person	€ 1,90
child (5-16 yrs)	€ 1,00
pitch	€ 2,50
electricity	€ 2,30

Reservations

Contact site. Tel: 02 54 83 68 52.
Email: camping.lavarenne@wanadoo.fr

FR41100 Camping Les Saules

D102 route de Contres, F-41700 Cheverny (Loir-et-Cher)

Set in the heart of the châteaux region, this site had been allowed to run down and was eventually closed, but has recently been revitalised and re-opened by a local family. The tastefully renovated traditional reception buildings in their lakeside setting give a very pleasant welcome. There are 166 good size, level pitches with 159 available for touring units. All have shade from the many trees on the site, 150 have electrical connections (a few will require leads longer than 25 m.), and there are ample water taps. Cheverny is considered to have the best interior and furnishings of all the châteaux in the Loire region, and many others are within easy reach.

Facilities

Two sanitary blocks with modern toilets showers, washbasins in cubicles and facilities for disabled visitors. Dishwashing and laundry sinks. Washing machine. The older block is due to be refurbished for 2005. Motorcaravan service point. Gas supplies. Shop selling local produce. Restaurant. Bar. Snack bar and takeaway. Swimming and paddling pools. TV/social room with toys, board games, books. Two play areas. Large grass area for ball games. Minigolf (free), Table tennis. Fishing. Bicycle hire. Off site: Golf 3 km. Riding 3 km.

At a glance

Welcome & Ambience	✓✓✓✓✓	Location	✓✓✓✓
Quality of Pitches	✓✓✓✓	Range of Facilities	✓✓✓✓

Directions

From Cheverny take D102 south towards Contres. Site is on the right after about 2 km.

Charges 2006

Per unit incl. 2 persons	€ 15,00 - € 25,00
extra person	€ 4,50
child (4-10 yrs)	€ 2,00
electricity	€ 3,50 - € 7,00

Reservations

Can be made at any time with 25% deposit.
Tel: 02 54 79 90 01.
Email: contact@camping-cheverny.com

Open

1 April - 16 October.

Les Bois du Bardelet ★★★★
LOIRE VALLEY
With the family card:
Canoeing, Archery Tennis, Heated Indoor Swimming Pool, Mini-golf, Fishing. Visit Paris Wednesday in high season. Evenings with entertainment.
www.bardelet.com

Sunêlia open style

Club Vacances

FR45010 Sunêlia Les Bois du Bardelet

Mobile homes ▶ page 420

Route de Bourges, Poilly, F-45500 Gien (Loiret)

This attractive, lively family site, in a rural setting, is well situated for exploring the less well known eastern part of the Loire Valley. A lake and pool complex have been attractively landscaped in 12 hectares of former farmland, blending old and new with natural wooded areas and more open field areas with rural views. Bois du Bardelet provides 260 pitches with around 140 for touring units. All are larger than 100 sq.m. and have electricity, with some fully serviced. The communal areas are based on attractively converted former farm buildings with a wide range of leisure facilities. A family club card can be purchased to make use of the many activities on a daily basis (some high season only). Various activities and excursions are organised, the most popular being to Paris, which can be pre-booked.

Facilities

Three sanitary blocks (only one open outside 15/6-31/8) include washbasins in cabins and facilities for people with disabilities and babies. Washing machines. Shop (1/4-15/9). Pleasant terraced bar. Snack bar, takeaway and restaurant (1/4-15/9) and pizzeria. Three swimming pools, one outside for serious swimmers (1/5-31/8), one indoor children's pool, both free, and another indoor pool, heated and needing the club card. Aqua gym, fitness and jacuzzi room. New pool and games area for children. Archery. Lake for canoeing and fishing. Tennis, minigolf, boules and table tennis. Bicycle hire. Internet access. Off site: Supermarket 5 km. Riding 7 km. Golf 25 km. Walking and cycling routes of different lengths are available at reception. Given 5 km.

Open

1 April - 30 September.

At a glance

| Welcome & Ambience | ✓✓✓✓✓ | Location | ✓✓✓✓ |
| Quality of Pitches | ✓✓✓✓ | Range of Facilities | ✓✓✓✓✓ |

Directions

From Gien take D940 towards Bourges. After 5 km. turn right (signed) and right again to cross the road and follow signs to site. From Argent sur Sauldre take D940 towards Gien and site is signed to right after approx. 15 km. (narrow road). The entrance is about 200 yd. past what looks like the first opening to the site. GPS: N47:38.497 E02:36.891

Charges 2005

Per unit incl. 2 persons	€ 24,00
electricity	€ 5,40
extra person (over 2 yrs)	€ 5,90
animal	€ 4,00
family leisure card (per week)	€ 38,00 - € 48,00

Less 15-25% in low seasons (20-40% for over 60s). Camping Cheques accepted.

Reservations

Made with deposit (€ 54) and fee (€ 30). Tel: 02 38 67 47 39. Email: contact@bardelet.com

FR49030 Camping Caroline

F-49800 Brain-sur-l'Authion (Maine-et-Loire)

Camping Caroline is an attractive former municipal site, lying on the edge of the little village of Brain sur l'Authion at the heart of the Anjou. This is a relaxing site with 120 large grassy pitches, mostly with reasonable shade and electricity. There are several leisure amenities at the site entrance, notably a heated pool and snack bar. The River Authion is 200 m. away and is popular with anglers. This isa useful base for visiting the vineyards of the Anjou which are all around. Member Escapades Terre Océane group.

Facilities

The two sanitary blocks are of very different designs but are clean and well maintained. Facilities for disabled visitors. Heated swimming pool and paddling pool. Snack bar. Play area. Children's club in peak season. Mobile homes for hire. Off site: Tennis. Fishing (charge applies). Boating. Multisports pitch. Walking and cycle trails. Boat trips.

Open

26 March - 1 October.

At a glance

| Welcome & Ambience | ✓✓✓ | Location | ✓✓✓✓ |
| Quality of Pitches | ✓✓✓✓ | Range of Facilities | ✓✓✓ |

Directions

From Angers take the N147 towards Saumur and then the D113 to the south of the village of Brain sur l'Authion. Site is clearly signed from the village.

Charges 2005

Per person	€ 3,00 - € 3,50
child (0-7 yrs)	€ 2,00 - € 2,50
pitch incl. electricity (6A)	€ 11,00 - € 13,00

Reservations

Advised for high season. Tel: 05 46 55 10 01. Email: info@campingterreoceane.com

FR49000 Camping du Lac de Maine

Avenue du Lac de Maine, F-49000 Angers (Maine-et-Loire)

Situated in the heart of the Anjou region, the Lac de Maine campsite has the advantage of being at the southern end of the Parc de Loisirs du Lac de Maine which is a leisure area with all sorts of activities. Most of the level 141 touring pitches are part grass and part gravel hardstanding, with the remainder being all gravel. All have water, drain and electricity (6/10A). The main park entrance has a height restriction of 3.2 m, although there is an alternative gate for higher vehicles. The adjacent 100 acre lake has a sandy beach for swimmers, windsurfing, sailing and pedaloes available, while the parkland provides tennis courts and a nature reserve. This is a useful site, open for a long season and only five minutes from the centre of Angers. With wide access roads, it is also suitable for American RVs.

Facilities

Two sanitary blocks, one which can be heated and includes some washbasins in cubicles. British style WCs (no seats). Facilities for babies and visitors with disabilities. Washing machines. Excellent motorcaravan service point. Reception stocks gas. Restaurant/bar (both early June - mid Sept). Heated L-shaped swimming pool. Volleyball. Pétanque. Bicycle hire. Playground. Internet point. Barrier card deposit € 20. Off site: Lake beach 0.5 km. Fishing 1 km. Riding 3 km. Golf 5 km.

Open

25 March - 10 October.

At a glance

Welcome & Ambience	✓✓✓✓	Location	✓✓✓✓✓
Quality of Pitches	✓✓✓✓	Range of Facilities	✓✓✓✓

Directions

Leave N23 (Angers ring road) at signs for Quartier de Maine and Lac de Maine. Follow signs for Pruniers and Bouchemaine. Site is on the D111 and is well signed. Site also signed from centre of Angers (5 km).

Charges 2005

Per unit incl. 2 persons	€ 10,70 - € 14,90
extra person	€ 2,10
child (under 13 yrs)	€ 1,35
electricity (10A)	€ 3,10
animal	€ 1,50

Camping Cheques accepted.

Reservations

Advised for July/Aug. and made with deposit (€ 8 per night of stay) and fee (€ 6). Tel: 02 41 73 05 03. Email: camping@lacdemaine.fr

FR49010 Castel Camping L'Etang de la Brèche

Route Nationale 152, 5 Impasse de la Breche, F-49730 Varennes-sur-Loire (Maine-et-Loire)

The Saint Cast family have developed L'Etang de la Brèche with loving care and attention on a 25 hectare estate four kilometres northeast of Saumur on the edge of the Loire behind the dykes. It is a peaceful base from which to explore the famous châteaux, abbeys, wine cellars, mushroom caves and Troglodyte villages in this region. The site provides 201 large, level pitches with shade from mixed tall trees and bushes, facing central, less shaded grass areas used for recreation. There are electrical connections to all pitches (in some cases a long cable may be required due to the size of the pitches), with water and drainaway on 63 of them. The restaurant, also open to the public, blends well with the existing architecture and, together with the bar area and terrace, provides a social base and is probably one of the reasons why the site is popular with British visitors. The swimming complex includes three pools: one with a removable cover, one outdoor, and a lovely pool for toddlers. The site includes a small lake (used for fishing) and wooded area ensuring a quiet, relaxed and rural atmosphere and making L'Étang de la Brèche a comfortable holiday base for couples and families. Used by tour operators (85 pitches).

Facilities

Three toilet blocks, modernised to good standards, include facilities for babies with two units for people with disabilities. Washing up sinks and laundry. Shop and epicerie. Restaurant, pizzeria and takeaway. Three heated pools. Tennis, basketball, minigolf and a field for football. Bicycle hire. General room, games and TV rooms. Internet point. Well organised, varied sporting and entertainment programme (10/7-25/8). Child minding is arranged in afternoons. Torch useful. Off site: Riding 2 km. Golf 8 km.

Open

15 May - 15 September.

At a glance

Welcome & Ambience	✓✓✓✓✓	Location	✓✓✓✓
Quality of Pitches	✓✓✓✓	Range of Facilities	✓✓✓✓✓

Directions

Site is 100 m. north off the main N152, about 4 km. northeast of Saumur on the north bank of the Loire.

Charges 2006

Per unit incl. 2 persons	€ 18,00 - € 30,00
extra person	€ 5,00 - € 7,00
child (4-10 yrs)	€ 3,00 - € 3,50
electricity (10A)	free - € 3,00
water and drainage	€ 2,50

7th night free in low season.

Reservations

Made for min. 7 nights in high season (3 days in low season) with deposit and fee. Tel: 02 41 51 22 92. Email: mail@etang-breche.com

FR49060 Camping Parc de Montsabert

Montsabert, F-49320 Coutures (Maine-et-Loire)

Owned and run by a friendly Dutch family who are continually looking to improve it, this extensive campsite has a rural atmosphere in the shadow of Montsabert château, from where visiting peacocks happily roam in the spacious surroundings. The main features are the heated swimming pool (with cover) and the adjoining refurbished, rustic style restaurant. There are 82 large, well marked touring pitches, divided by hedges and all with water tap, drain and electricity (5/10A). Picnic tables are provided in the shade near the entrance with a communal barbecue area. Partially wooded by impressive redwood trees, this site offers the peace of the countryside and yet easy access to both Saumur and Angers. It is an ideal base for exploring, whether by foot, bicycle or car. The site is used by two tour operators (30 pitches).

Facilities

The main central toilet block can be heated and has washbasins and bidets in cabins and a baby room. Washing machines and dryer. A second block serves the pool and another unit provides more WCs. Shop (15/6-30/8). Restaurant and takeaway (both 15/6-15/9). Bar (1/6-15/9). Large 25 m. heated swimming pool which can be covered (20/5-12/9; no Bermuda style shorts) and separate paddling pool. Sports hall, minigolf, volley and basketball, table tennis and tennis. Play area. Bicycle hire. Entertainment programme in high season. Barrier key deposit (€ 10). Off site: Windsurfing, canoeing and sailing near. Fishing and golf 5 km. Riding 8 km.

Open

30 April - 16 September.

At a glance

Welcome & Ambience	✓✓✓✓✓	Location	✓✓✓✓
Quality of Pitches	✓✓✓✓✓	Range of Facilities	✓✓✓✓✓

Directions

From Le Mans going towards Angers, take exit 12 (Seiches-sur-Loire). Turn left on D74 signed Bauné, Château Montgeoffroy and Mazé. In Mazé take the D55 towards St Maturin-sur-Loire. Pass the bridge and follow signs for 'Parc de Montsabert', L'Européen and Coutures.

Charges 2006

Per pitch incl. 2 persons	€ 15,30 - € 23,80
extra person	€ 4,50
child (1-10 yrs)	€ 3,00
electricity (5/10A)	€ 2,95 - € 4,10
dog	€ 3,10

Reservations

Made with 30% deposit and fee (€ 10).
Tel: 02 41 57 91 63.
Email: camping@parcdemontsabert.com

FR49020 Camping de Chantepie

St Hilaire-St Florent, F-49400 Saumur (Maine-et-Loire)

The drive along the winding road bordered by apple orchards and vineyards is well rewarded on arriving at the colourful, floral entrance to Camping de Chantepie. A friendly greeting awaits at the attractive reception office which is set beside a tastefully restored farmhouse. The site is owned by a charitable organisation which provides employment for local disabled people. Linked by gravel roads (which can be dusty), the 150 grass pitches are level and spacious, with some new larger ones for long units (state a preference when booking). Most pitches have electricity (5/10A) and are separated by low hedges of flowers and trees which offer some shade. The panoramic views over the Loire from the pitches on the terraced perimeter of the meadow are stunning and from here a footpath leads to the river valley. Leisure activities for all ages are catered for in July/Aug. by the Chantepie Club, including wine tastings, excursions and canoeing. This is a good site for families. A 'Sites et Paysages' member.

Facilities

The toilet block is very clean and the provision of facilities is adequate with washbasins in cubicles, new showers (men and women separately) and facilities for disabled visitors. Well stocked shop. Bar, terraced café and takeaway (from 19/5). Covered and heated pool, outdoor pool and paddling pool protected from the wind by a stone wall. Play area with wide variety of apparatus. Terraced minigolf. Volleyball, TV, video games and table tennis. Pony rides. Bicycle and mountain bike hire. Off site: Fishing 200 m. Golf 2 km. Riding 6 km.

Open

14 May - 10 September.

At a glance

Welcome & Ambience	✓✓✓✓✓	Location	✓✓✓✓
Quality of Pitches	✓✓✓	Range of Facilities	✓✓✓✓✓

Directions

From Saumur take D751 signed Gennes. Turn right at roundabout in St Hilaire-St Florent and continue until you reach Le Poitrinea and campsite sign, then turn left. Continue for about 3 km. and then turn right into road leading to site.

Charges 2005

Per unit incl. 2 persons	€ 15,00 - € 24,00
extra person	€ 4,50 - € 6,00
child (0-10 yrs)	€ 3,00 - € 3,50
electricity	€ 3,00
dog	€ 2,00

Reservations

Made with € 11 fee. Tel: 02 41 67 95 34.
Email: info@campingchantepie.com

FR49040 Camping de l'Etang

Mobile homes ▶ page 421

Route de St Mathurin, F-49320 Brissac (Maine-et-Loire)

Originally the farm of the Château de Brissac (yet only 24 km. from the lovely town of Angers), this rural campsite retains the tranquillity and ambience of bygone days and added the necessary comforts expected by today's campers. The 150 level touring pitches have pleasant views across the countryside. Separated and numbered, some have shade and all have electricity with water and drainage nearby. A small bridge crosses the river Aubance which runs through the site and there are two lakes where fisherman can enjoy free fishing. The site has its own vineyard and the wine produced can be purchased on the campsite and is highly recommended. Tour operators use 18 pitches. A 'Sites et Paysages' member.

Facilities

Three well maintained toilet blocks provide all the usual facilities. Laundry room with washing machines and dryers. Excellent baby room. Disabled visitors are well catered for. Motorcaravan service point. The adapted farmhouse houses reception, small shop and takeaway (from 19/5). Across the courtyard is a bar/restaurant serving crêpes, salads, etc (evenings form 15/6, all day 1/7-31/8). Swimming pool (heated and covered) and paddling pool. Fishing. Play area. Bicycle hire. Wide variety of evening entertainment in high season. Off site: The adjacent Parc de Loisirs is a paradise for young children with many activities including boating, pedaloes, pony rides, miniature train, water slide, bouncy castle and swings (free entry for campers). Golf and riding 10 km.

At a glance

Welcome & Ambience	✓✓✓✓✓	Location	✓✓✓✓	
Quality of Pitches	✓✓✓✓	Range of Facilities	✓✓✓✓	

Directions

Take D748 south from Angers. Follow signs to Brissac-Quincé but do not enter the town, proceed to site along D55 (well signed) in direction of St Mathurin.

Charges 2005

Per unit incl. 2 persons	€ 15,00 - € 24,00
extra person	€ 4,50 - € 6,00
child (0-10 yrs)	€ 3,00 - € 3,50
electricity	€ 3,00
dog	€ 2,00

Reservations

Contact site. Tel: 02 41 91 70 61.
Email: info@campingetang.com

Open

15 May - 15 September.

FR49090 Camping l'Isle Verte

Avenue de la Loire, F-49730 Montsoreau (Maine-et-Loire)

This friendly, natural site, with pitches overlooking the Loire, is just 100 metres from the centre of Montsoreau, an ideal starting point to visit the western Loire area. Most of the 88 shaded, level and good-sized tourist pitches are separated by low hedges but grass tends to be rather sparse during dry spells. All have electricity (16A). Fishermen are particularly well catered for here, there being an area to store equipment and live bait (permits are available in Saumur). Attractions within walking distance of the campsite include the château, Troglodyte (mushroom caves and restaurant), both just 500 metres, wine tasting in the cellars nearby, and a Sunday market in the town. Excellent English is spoken in the reception and bar.

Facilities

A single building provides separate male and female toilets. Washbasins, some in cabins, and showers are unisex. Separate facilities for disabled campers. Baby room. Laundry room with deep sinks, washing machine and dryer. Dishwashing area under cover at the front of the building. Motorcaravan service point. Bar and snack bar (1/5-30/9). Swimming and paddling pools (15/5-30/9). Small play area. Table tennis, volleyball and boules. Bicycle hire (June - August or by special request). Fishing. Off site: Golf 6 km. Riding 15 km.

Open

1 April - 30 September.

At a glance

Welcome & Ambience	✓✓✓✓	Location	✓✓✓✓
Quality of Pitches	✓✓✓	Range of Facilities	✓✓✓✓

Directions

Take D947 from Saumur to Montsoreau and site is clearly signed on left along the road into town.
GPS: N47:13.092 E00:03.159

Charges 2005

Per unit incl. 1 or 2 persons	€ 12,50 - € 16,00
extra adult	€ 3,00
child (2-10 yrs)	€ 2,00
electricity	€ 3,00

Motorcaravan services € 6 (free if camping).
Camping Cheques accepted.

Reservations

Advised for July/Aug. with 25% fee and booking fee.
Tel: 02 41 51 76 60. Email: isleverte@wanadoo.fr

FR49080 Camping Ile d'Offard

Rue de Verden, Ile d'Offard, F-49400 Saumur (Maine-et-Loire)

Situated on an island between the banks of the Loire and within walking distance of the centre of Saumur, this site is useful as an overnight stop en-route south or as a short-term base from which to visit the numerous châteaux in the region. The 224 touring pitches are at present on grass at the far end or hardstanding nearer the entrance. Some 34 pitches are occupied by tour operators and caravan holiday homes and these can be intrusive in some areas. Pitches have access to electricity hook-ups (6-10A). The adjacent municipal swimming pools and minigolf (open in July/Aug) are free for campers. The site owners have started an extensive redevelopment plan, some of which may be comppleted in time for the 2006 season.

Facilities

Three sanitary blocks, one heated in winter, include provision for disabled visitors. Toilet facilities in all blocks are unisex. Block one has a well equipped laundry. The other blocks are only open in high season. Restaurant and bar (early May - late Sept) with takeaway. Internet access. Table tennis, volleyball. Play area. Some activities with a children's club, wine tastings, etc. in high season. Off site: Thursday market 500 m. Saturday morning market 2 km. Riding 5 km. Fishing in the Loire (permits from Saumur).

Open

1 March - 31 October.

At a glance

Welcome & Ambience	✓✓✓	Location	✓✓✓
Quality of Pitches	✓✓✓	Range of Facilities	✓✓✓

Directions

From the north and A85 exit 3, take N147 south towards Saumur. After 2.5 km. turn left (where the N147 bears right) and follow old road directly towards river and town centre. Cross the first bridge onto the island and take first left. Site is straight on at the end of the road. Approaching from the south through the town is not recommended.
GPS: N47:15.457 W00:03.660

Charges 2005

Per unit incl. 2 adults	€ 14,50 - € 19,50
extra person	€ 4,00
child (2-10 yrs)	€ 2,00
electricity	€ 3,00

Motorcaravan service point
€ 4.50 - € 7.50 (free to campers).
Camping Cheques accepted.

Reservations

Advised for July/Aug. with 25% deposit plus charge for registration. Tel: 02 41 40 30 00.
Email: iledoffard@wanadoo.fr

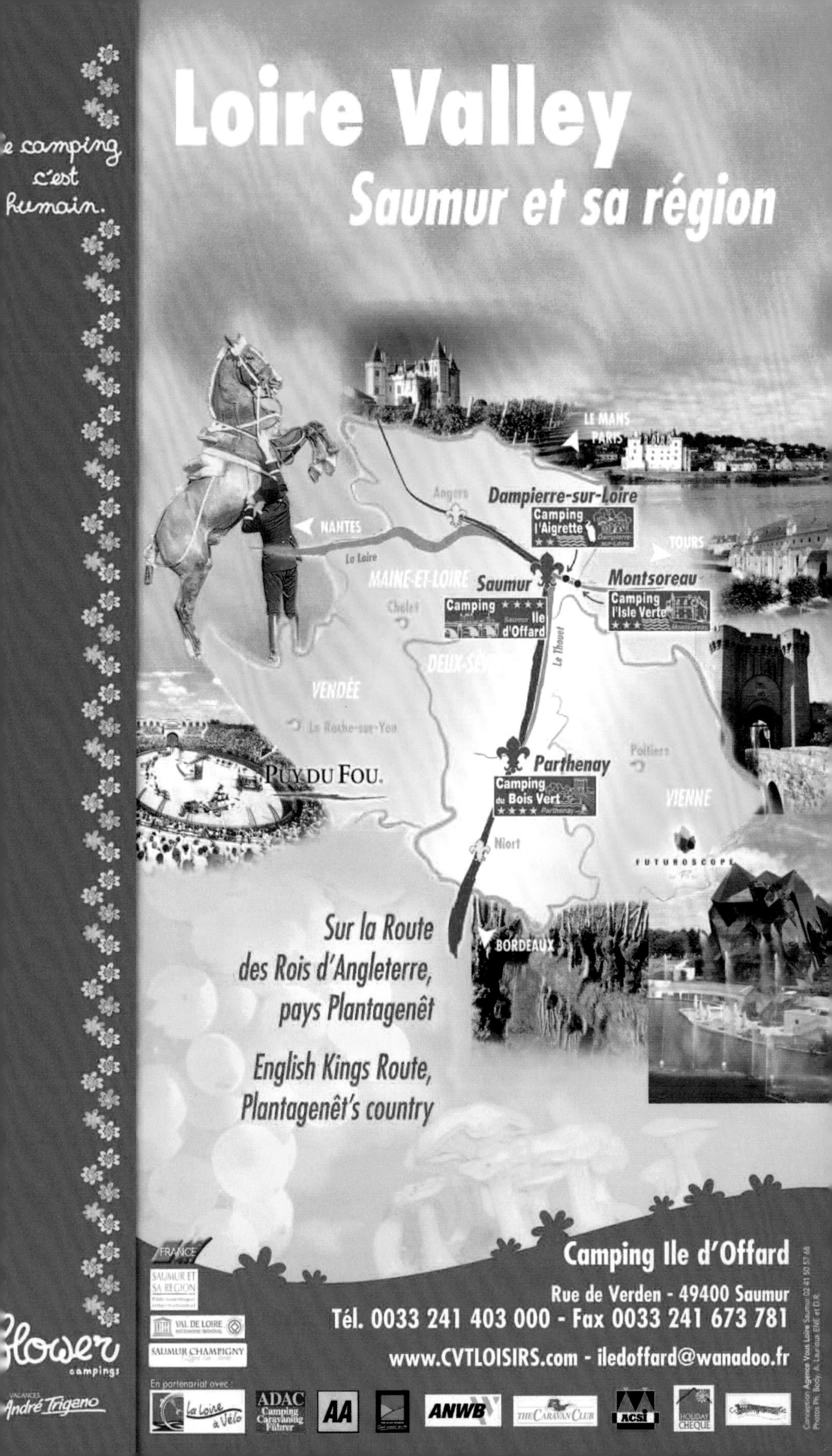

Loire Valley
Saumur et sa région
e camping
c'est
humain.
LE MANS
PARIS
Angers
Dampierre-sur-Loire
Camping
l'Aigrette
Dampierre-sur-Loire
NANTES
TOURS
La Loire
MAINE-ET-LOIRE
Saumur
Montsoreau
Camping
l'Isle Verte
Montsoreau
Cholet
Camping
Ile
d'Offard
Saumur
Le Thouet
VENDÉE
La Roche-sur-Yon
PUY DU FOU.
Parthenay
Poitiers
Camping
du Bois Vert
Parthenay
VIENNE
Niort
FUTUROSCOPE
BORDEAUX
Sur la Route
des Rois d'Angleterre,
pays Plantagenêt
English Kings Route,
Plantagenêt's country
Camping Ile d'Offard
Rue de Verden - 49400 Saumur
Tél. 0033 241 403 000 - Fax 0033 241 673 781
www.CVTLOISIRS.com - iledoffard@wanadoo.fr
FRANCE
SAUMUR ET SA REGION
VAL DE LOIRE
SAUMUR CHAMPIGNY
flower
campings
André Trigano
En partenariat avec :
La Loire à Vélo
ADAC
Camping
Caravaning
Führer
AA
ANWB
THE CARAVAN CLUB
ACSI
HOLIDAY CHEQUE
Conception Agence Vous Loire Saumur 02 41 50 57 68
Photos Ph. Body, A. Lauriaux ENE et D.R.

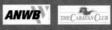

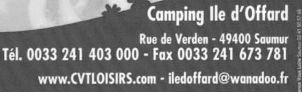

FR49070 Camping Caravaning la Vallée des Vignes

La Croix Patron, F-49700 Concourson-sur-Layon (Maine-et-Loire)

The enthusiasm of the English owners here comes across instantly in the warm welcome received by their guests. The attention to detail in all they do and the improvements they have made shows how keen they are to make this site prosper. The site entrance with flowers, vines and wine press welcomes visitors –even the dog has a wine barrel for a kennel! Bordering the Layon river, the 54 good sized touring pitches are reasonably level and fully serviced (10A electricity, water tap and drain). Five pitches have a hardstanding for cars. Attractions include a newly enclosed bar and restaurant with folding doors to open in good weather, a generously sized sun terrace surrounding the pool and high season activities for children and adults. These include wine tasting, a hog roast (or similar) followed by competitions and treasure hunts. The site is also an ideal base for visiting the châteaux of the Loire and the many caves and vineyards in the area.

Facilities
The toilet block includes washbasins in cabins, with dishwashing facilities at either end, under cover. Baby room. facilities for disabled visitors. Washing machine and dryer. Bar (from 15/5 or on request) serving meals, snacks and takeaway (from 15/5). Swimming and paddling pools (from 15/5). Playground, games area and small football pitch. Minigolf, volleyball, basketball, table tennis. Internet access. Fishing possible from 2005. Caravan storage. Off site: Zoo and rose gardens at Doué-la-Fontaine. Grand Parc Puy du Fou.

Open
15 March - 20 October.

At a glance
Welcome & Ambience	✓✓✓✓✓	Location	✓✓✓✓✓
Quality of Pitches	✓✓✓✓	Range of Facilities	✓✓✓✓

Directions
Site signed off D960 Doué - Vihiers road, just west of Concourson-sur-Layon.

Charges 2006
Per unit incl. 2 persons	€ 15,00 - € 20,00
extra person	€ 3,50 - € 4,50
child (2-12 yrs)	€ 2,00 - € 2,50
electricity (10A)	€ 3,00
dog	€ 2,50

Special offers available.

Reservations
Contact site. Tel: 02 41 59 86 35.
Email: Campingvdv@wanadoo.fr

FR72030 Castel Camping Le Château de Chanteloup

F-72460 Sillé-le-Philippe (Sarthe)

A peaceful, pleasant site with a certain rural charm, 15 kilometres from Le Mans, Chanteloup is situated in the park of a 19th century château in the heart of the Sarthe countryside. There are 148 pitches, some along the edge of the woods, many on the lawn and completely open, and a few overlooking the lake, so the degree of shade varies. The pitches are open and all have electricity although long leads will be required in some instances. This lack of regimentation enhances the atmosphere and feeling of spaciousness in the grounds surrounding the old château. Tours of the grounds and the village by pony and cart can be arranged.

Facilities
Sanitary facilities in the château outbuildings are a long way from some pitches and cleaning and maintenance can be variable. Washbasins are in cabins. Dishwashing and laundry sinks, and washing machine under cover. Small shop. Pleasant bar (31/5-6/9) with terrace in the château with breakfast, lunch and dinner served (all 10/6-22/8). Swimming pool (fenced). Play area (parental supervision essential). Games room, tennis, volleyball, table tennis. Mountain bike hire. Organised activities in high season Off site: Riding 7 km. Golf 14 km. Free use of tennis club in Le Mans (tennis, squash and badminton).

Open
1 June - 8 September.

At a glance
Welcome & Ambience	✓✓✓✓	Location	✓✓✓✓
Quality of Pitches	✓✓✓	Range of Facilities	✓✓✓✓

Directions
Site is 15 km. northeast of Le Mans. From autoroute take exit 23 and follow signs for Le Mans and Tours, then Le Mans and Savigne l'Evèque. Site is halfway between Bonnétable and Savigne l'Evèque (road is narrow) on western edge of Sille-le-Phillippe village. GPS: N48:06.281 E00:20.424

Charges 2006
Per person	€ 5,50 - € 8,50
child (under 7 yrs)	€ 3,00
pitch	€ 8,00 - € 13,00
electricity	€ 3,00

Less 10% outside 24/6-20/8.
Charges are higher during the 24 hr race week at Le Mans.

Reservations
No minimum length. Tel: 02 43 27 51 07.
Email: chanteloup.souffront@wanadoo.fr

FR72020 Camping Municipal du Lac

Rue du Lac, F-72120 St Calais (Sarthe)

St Calais is a small town 37 km. east of Le Mans. Camping du Lac has 59 marked pitches, most separated by hedges and all with electricity (3/6A), water and drain. A separate area is for tents. Pizzas are sold on Saturday evenings and in high season there are theme evenings (crêpes or pizzas with guitar music), walks, competitions, children's activities, and communal meals (campers take own food and dance to music). Reception is welcoming, the value is excellent and this would make a good night stop or base for visiting the Le Mans 24 hour race. There is some road noise.

Facilities

Two sanitary blocks provide some washbasins in private cabins. Washing machine in larger block. Bread and croissants (to order), post cards and T-shirts available at reception. Two small play areas. Off site: Swimming pool adjacent. Local supermarket just a short walk.

Open

1 April - 15 October.

At a glance

Welcome & Ambience	√√√√	Location	√√√√
Quality of Pitches	√√√√	Range of Facilities	√√√

Directions

Well signed from N157, site is beside lake north of the town, near the station. Follow signs for 'Camping Plan d'eau'.

Charges 2005

Per person	€ 2,50
child (under 10 yrs)	€ 1,20 - € 2,50
pitch	€ 2,20
electricity (3/6A)	€ 1,65 - € 2,55
hiker/cyclist's tent	€ 1,00

Reservations

Made with deposit (€ 15.24). Tel: 02 43 35 04 81.

FR72060 Camping Municipal du Val de Sarthe

Rue de l'Abreuvoir, F-72170 Beaumont sur Sarthe (Sarthe)

This delightful, inexpensive riverside site is conveniently located just a short walk from the pretty little town and its shops and services. The 73 level, grassy individual pitches are large, divided by growing hedges and all have electricity (5A). Some of the pitches including those along the river's edge may require a longer cable. An excellent activity area provides swings and other children's play equipment, boules pitches, tennis, netball, and a fitness trail. Those intending to stay longer than one night require a barrier card (refundable deposit). Reception opens 08.00 - 22.00 daily in high season, 10.00 - 20.00 in low season. The barrier opens at 07.00.

Facilities

The central sanitary unit is accessed by a flight of steps although there is a long and fairly steep ramp for disabled people. Modern and well looked after facilities include some washbasins in cubicles and spacious showers. Dishwashing and laundry sinks, washing machine. Motorcaravan service point. Bread and croissants to order and soft drinks available from reception. Activity area. River fishing. Room for campers' use (July/Aug). Double axle caravans are not accepted. Off site: Sports centre with outdoor pool, tennis and minigolf. Riding 10 km. Bicycle hire 15 km. Golf 25 km.

Open

1 May - 30 September.

At a glance

Welcome & Ambience	√√√√	Location	√√√√
Quality of Pitches	√√√√	Range of Facilities	√√√

Directions

Site is well signed from approach roads and from the town centre. GPS: N48:13.533 E00:08.069

Charges guide

Per person	€ 1,57
child (under 7 yrs)	€ 0,78
pitch	€ 1,23
electricity	€ 2,06
dog	€ 0,32

Barrier card deposit € 30.
Credit cards accepted, minimum amount € 20.

Reservations

Not normally necessary. Tel: 02 43 97 01 93.
Email: beaumont.sur.sarthe@wanadoo.fr

FR79020 Camping de Courte Vallée

F-79600 Airvault (Deux-Sèvres)

A warm welcome is given to all visitors (85% of whom are British) with a glass of wine and a friendly chat from the English owners. This very attractive site, within walking distance of Airvault, has 65 pitches on level grass amongst trees and shrubs, all with electricity (8A). The owners have spent lots of time and work improving what was already a well laid out site, and have recently added several hardstanding pitches and four 'super' pitches. This is an ideal location for a short stay or as a base for touring the Poitou-Charentes region and the Loire valley. Nearby are Puy du Fou, Fontevraud Abbey, Doué la Fontaine zoo and the châteaux of Saumur and Oiron. From this peaceful site you can wander into the picturesque medieval town or venture further afield to enjoy one of the excellent local restaurants.

Facilities

A modern unisex block has spacious cubicles for showers and washbasins, and shower and WC cubicles for disabled visitors, all kept to a very high standard of cleanliness. Dishwashing area under cover. Washing machine and dryers. Reception sells 'frites', drinks, ice cream and wine. Internet access. Swimming pool. Boules. Table tennis. Play area. Caravan storage. Wine tasting events and barbecues. Off site: The historic town of Airvault (the birthplace of Voltaire) with good facilities is a 10-15 minute walk. Fishing 300 m. Riding 8 km.

Open

8 April - 30 September.

At a glance

Welcome & Ambience	✓✓✓✓✓	Location	✓✓✓✓
Quality of Pitches	✓✓✓✓	Range of Facilities	✓✓✓✓

Directions

From D938 (Parthenay-Thouars) take D725 Airvault. On approaching village turn left over bridge. At T-junction at top of hill turn sharp left, take second exit at roundabout and left at junction to site on left. Site is well signed from Airvault. Caravans are not allowed in the village. GPS: N46:49.937 W00:08.909

Charges 2005

Per person	€ 6,00 - € 7,00
child (under 7 yrs)	€ 2,00 - € 4,00
pitch	€ 9,00 - € 11,00
incl. electricty and car on pitch	€ 11,00 - € 13,00
electricity (8A)	€ 4,00
animal	free - € 2,50

No credit cards.

Reservations

Advised for July/August. Tel: 05 49 64 70 65.
Email: camping@caravanningfrance.com

FR79040 Camping de la Venise Verte

178, route des Bords de Sèvre, F-79510 Coulon (Deux-Sèvres)

This family run site on the edge of the Sevre Nortaise and the Marais Poitevin is ideal for short or long stays. With canoe and cycle hire on site you have no excuse for not exploring the local area. In the Deux Sevres, the 'department of discovery', so named because it has two rivers named Sevre, the Noirtaise and Nantaise, the Venise Verte provides an excellent site. The flat pitches are of a good size with electricity, water and drainage and with some shade. To try a real local flavour walk into Coulon and taste, and then perhaps buy, some 'Pissenlit', dandelion liqueur. You should drink it from a frozen glass and ice cold – it has a unique flavour. Also explore the Marais on foot or by boat or perhaps visit La Rochelle less than an hour away, with its museums, harbour and quayside restaurants. A 'Sites et Paysages' member.

Facilities

Modern, heated toilet facilities are of a high standard with free showers. Washing machine and dryer. Motorcaravan services. Restaurant/bar. Heated swimming pool (high season) Bicycle and canoe hire. Boules area. Off site: Coulon 1.0 km. and boat trips in the Marais. Ideal for walking, cycling or canoeing.

Open

1 April - 30 October.

At a glance

Welcome & Ambience	✓✓✓✓	Location	✓✓✓✓
Quality of Pitches	✓✓✓✓	Range of Facilities	✓✓✓✓

Directions

From Niort take N11 towards La Rochelle. Turn on the D3 towards Sansais and then north on the D1 towards Coulon. At traffic lights head towards 'centre ville' (Coulon) at mini-roundabout turn slightly right. Follow the Sevre Noirtaise for about 1.5 km. to site on the right just before blue bridge.

Charges 2006

Per unit incl. 2 persons and electricity	€ 15,00 - € 20,00
extra person	€ 3,50 - € 5,00
child (3-5 yrs)	€ 1,50 - € 1,90
dog	€ 2,00

Reservations

Advised for high season. Tel: 05 49 35 90 36.
Email: accueil@camping-laveniseverte.com

FR79050 Camping du Bois Vert

14 rue Boisseau, Le Tallud, F-79200 Parthenay (Deux-Sèvres)

Recommended by our agent, we hope to include a full report on this popular campsite in a future inspection programme. Le Bois Vert is located in the southern Loire Valley within the historical town of Parthenay. The site lies on the banks of the River Thouet and also has access to a lake. There are 90 grassy pitches, most of which have electricity. There is an attractive range of amenities and a swimming pool is planned for 2006.

Facilities

Sanitary building. Playground. Canoeing. Table tennis. Games room. Mobile homes for rent. Off site: Easy access to the mediaeval town of Parthenay. Shops, bars, restaurants nearby. Fishing, walking, cycle trails. Golf.

Open

1 April - 30 September.

See advertisement on page 165.

Directions

Follow signs to La Roche-sur-Yon from the centre of Parthenay. Site is well signed.

Charges 2005

Per unit incl. 2 persons	€ 12,50 - € 16,50
extra person	€ 4,00 - € 4,60
child (2-10 yrs)	€ 2,00
electricity	€ 3,00

Camping Cheques accepted.

Reservations

Contact site. Tel: 05 49 64 78 43.
Email: bois-vert@wanadoo.fr

FR86030 Camping Le Relais du Miel

Mobile homes ▶ page 421

Route d'Antran, F-86100 Châtellerault (Vienne)

With very easy access from the A10 and N10 roads, in the northern outskirts of Châtellerault, this site is being developed in the 10 acre grounds of a grand house dating from Napoleonic times. It is surrounded by majestic old trees beside the River Vienne. Twin barns form two sides of a courtyard behind the house, one of which has already been converted very stylishly into reception, a high ceilinged function and games room, and a bar. Beams taken from the original ceiling now form part of the bar top and act as arm rests. There is also an orchard and stone gateposts leading onto ground, previously the home farm, that now forms 80 large, flat pitches. Divided by trees and bushes, now maturing well and some providing shade, all the pitches have electricity (10A) and water, 15 with drainage. You may fish on the river bank with access through a gate in the walled grounds. Mobile homes and apartments to rent.

Facilities

Excellent toilet facilities include washbasins in cabins, facilities for disabled people, a washing machine and dryer. Basic essentials and gas are kept. Bar and restaurant serving good value meals. Pizzas to order (from local pizzeria). Takeaway. Small snack bar with outdoor tables, sheltered by canopy, open in evenings 1/7-31/8. Swimming and paddling pools (15 x 7 m). Playground. First class tennis courts. Volleyball, basketball. Bicycle hire. Boules and games room with electronic games, pool and table tennis. Observatory with telescope. Internet access. Torch useful. Off site: Supermarket 400 m. Riding 5 km. Golf 11 km. Futuroscope 16 km.

At a glance

Welcome & Ambience	✓✓✓✓✓	Location	✓✓✓✓
Quality of Pitches	✓✓✓✓	Range of Facilities	✓✓✓✓✓

Directions

Take exit no. 26 from the A10 autoroute (Châtellerault-Nord) and site is signed just off the roundabout. From the N10 follow signs for Antran north of the town.

Charges guide

Per unit incl. 2 persons, electricity	€ 19,00 - € 21,00
extra person over 5 yrs	€ 3,00 - € 5,00
extra tent	€ 3,00 - € 5,00

Less 15% for 1 week, 20% for 2 weeks.

Reservations

Made with 10% deposit. Tel: 05 49 02 06 27.
Email: camping@lerelaisdumiel.com

Open

15 May - 2 September.

FR86010 Castel Camping Le Petit Trianon

Saint Ustre, 1 rue du Moulin de St Ustre, F-86220 Ingrandes-sur-Vienne (Vienne)

A family owned site for many years, quaint and rustic are words that spring to mind on arrival here. Situated between Tours, Poitiers and Futuroscope, the approach to Le Petit Trianon is through a grand, narrow, gateway leading onto a slightly sloping meadow surrounded by trees in front of the château, plus a newer, large, more open field with a woodland area between. The 99 spacious, open but marked pitches are arranged to leave plenty of free space and there is shade in parts. All have electricity (13A). Reception is housed in the 18th century château which was once a hunting lodge. The pool area is located on the sunny side of a rather picturesque castled facade in which is a large, very cool reading room. This is an attractive campsite with many well tended plants around the site. Futuroscope at Poitiers is well worth at least a day's visit (if you stay for the after dusk laser, firework and fountain show, remember your late night entry code for the site gate).

Facilities

The original toilet unit is dated but immaculate. It includes washbasins in cabins, some washbasin and shower units, baby baths, laundry with washing machines and dryer, and sinks for dishwashing. Smaller blocks serve the newer parts of the site and one contains facilities for disabled people. Motorcaravan service point. Shop with essentials, bread to order. Takeaway. Heated swimming pool and paddling pools. Playground. Table tennis. Minigolf. Badminton, croquet, volleyball and boules. TV room with satellite, books and games. Bicycle hire. Local wine and cognac tastings on site and organised excursions. Internet access. Caravan storage. Off site: Restaurant (menu displayed on site) 50 m. Fishing 3 km. Riding 15 km.

Open

20 May - 20 September.

At a glance

Welcome & Ambience	✓✓✓✓✓	Location	✓✓✓✓
Quality of Pitches	✓✓✓	Range of Facilities	✓✓✓✓

Directions

Ingrandes is signed from the N10 north of the town, which is between Dangé and Châtellerault. From autoroute A10 take exit 26 for Châtellerault-Nord and at roundabout follow signs for Tours to Ingrandes where site is signed.

Charges 2006

Per person	€ 7,00
child (0-6 yrs)	€ 1,10 - € 3,50
pitch incl. car	€ 8,00 - € 10,90
electricity (5/10A)	€ 4,10 - € 4,50
dog	€ 2,10

Less 10-20% for longer stays.

Reservations

Made with 25% deposit and fee (€ 12.50); min. 5 days in July/Aug. Tel: 05 49 02 61 47. Email: chateau@petit-trianon.fr

FR86080 Camping Caravaning Les Peupliers

F-86700 Couhé (Vienne)

Family owned and run since 1968, Les Peupliers is located in a valley south of Poitiers. The site is arranged on the banks of a river (unfenced), the 160 pitches on both sides or around a fishing lake. On level grass, most are separated and all have 16A electricity, while 50 are fully serviced. There is a good pool complex (open until midnight) that includes impressive water slides and new toboggans, a heated main pool, a paddling pool and a lagoon with two slides for younger children (under 10 yrs), jacuzzi, plus water games. There is a local market for every day of the week (Chaunay, Lezay, Civray, Gencay, Rouillé or Vivonne). Nearby Vaux has an ostrich farm, and at Romagne there is 'La Vallée des Singes' with 25 species of monkey, ape and gorilla. There is some noise from the N10 which runs fairly close to the site.

Facilities

The three toilet blocks of varying ages are in Mediterranean style, with washbasins in cubicles and facilities for babies and disabled people. Dishwashing and laundry sinks. Washing machines and dryers. The newest block is in regular use, with the other two opened as the season progresses. TV and fridge rental. Small, well stocked shop. Snack bar, restaurant and bar with covered terrace and entertainment in peak season. Swimming pool complex. Playgrounds. Fishing lake. Minigolf. Table tennis, football, volleyball and boules court. Motorcaravan service point. Off site: Tennis 800 m. Bicycle hire 1 km. Riding 5 km.

Open

2 May - 30 September. Chalets for hire all year.

At a glance

Welcome & Ambience	✓✓✓✓	Location	✓✓✓
Quality of Pitches	✓✓✓✓	Range of Facilities	✓✓✓✓✓

Directions

Couhé is about 30 km. south of Poitiers on the N10. From the north, follow the signs for Couhé town centre and the campsite, which is a short distance from the slip road on the right. From the south, take 2nd Couhé exit from N10 and site entrance is oppsite end of slip road. GPS: N46:18.706 E00:10.670

Charges 2005

Per person	€ 6,00
child (2-10 yrs)	€ 3,50
pitch	€ 8,50
electricity	€ 3,50
electricity, water and drainage	€ 5,00

Less 30% in low season.
Credit cards accepted (min € 50).
Camping Cheques accepted.

Reservations

Contact site. Tel: 05 49 59 21 16. Email: info@lespeupliers.fr

Open all year. Panoramic view over the Futuroscope situated at 2 kms.
Heated swimming pool, pond, snack, bar, restaurant. Chalets for hire.

86130 St-Georges-les-Baillargeaux
Tel/Fax: 0033 549 52 47 52
www.camping-le-futuriste.fr

FR86040 Camping Le Futuriste

Mobile homes ▶ page 422

F-86130 St Georges-les-Baillargeaux (Vienne)

On raised ground with panoramic views over the strikingly modern buildings and night-time bright lights that comprise the popular attraction of Futuroscope, Le Futuriste is a neat, modern site, open all year. It is ideal for a short stay to visit the park which is only 1.5 km. away (tickets can be bought at the site) but it is equally good for longer stays to see the region. With a busy atmosphere, there are early departures and late arrivals. Reception is open 08.00-22.00 hrs. There are 118 individual, flat, grassy pitches divided by young trees and shrubs which are beginning to provide some shelter for this elevated and otherwise rather open site (possibly windy). 82 pitches have electricity (6A) and a further 30 have electricity, water, waste water and sewage connections. All are accessed via neat, level and firmly rolled gravel roads. Of course, the area has other attractions and details are available from the enthusiastic young couple who run the site. Note: it is best to see the first evening show at Futuroscope otherwise you will find yourself locked out of the site - the gates are closed at 23.30 hrs.

Facilities

Excellent, very clean sanitary facilities are housed in two modern blocks which are insulated and can be heated in cool weather. The facilities in the newest block are unisex. and include some washbasins in cabins and facilities for disabled people. Dishwashing and laundry sinks. Washing machine and dryer. Small shop (1/5-30/9) provides essentials (order bread the night before). New bar/restaurant. Snack bar and takeaway. Two heated outdoor pools, one with a slide and paddling pool (1/5-30/9). Games room. TV. Volleyball, boules and table tennis. Free fishing in lake on site. Youth groups are not accepted. Off site: Bicycle hire 500 m. Golf 5 km. Riding 10 km. Hypermarket and ATM 600 m.

Open

All year.

At a glance

Welcome & Ambience	✓✓✓✓	Location	✓✓✓✓
Quality of Pitches	✓✓✓✓	Range of Facilities	✓✓✓✓

Directions

From either A10 autoroute or the N10, take Futuroscope exit. Site is located east of both roads, off the D20 to St Georges-Les-Baillargeaux. From all directions follow signs to St Georges. The site is on the hill; turn by the water tower and site is on the left. GPS: N46:39.928 E00:23.668

Charges 2005

Per pitch incl. 1-3 persons	€ 13,10 - € 18,00
extra person	€ 1,70 - € 2,40
electricity	€ 2,40 - € 3,30
animal	€ 1,65

Camping Cheques accepted.

Reservations

Phone bookings accepted for min. 2 nights. Made with 50% deposit and fee (€ 15).
Tel: 05 49 52 47 52.
Email: camping-le-futuriste@wanadoo.fr

173

FR86090 Camping du Parc de Saint Cyr

Mobile homes ▶ page 422

F-86130 Saint Cyr (Vienne)

This well organised, five hectare campsite is part of a 300 hectare leisure park, based around a large lake with sailing and associated sports, and an area for swimming (supervised July/Aug). Land-based activities include tennis, two half-courts, table tennis, fishing, badminton, pétanque, beach volleyball, TV room, and a well equipped fitness suite, all of which are free of charge. In high season there are extra free activities including a kids club, beach club, archery and an entertainment programme. Also in high season but charged for are sailing school, aquatic toboggan, windsurfing, canoe, kayak and water bikes. Campers can also use the 9 and 18 hole golf courses (with 20% discount for the 18 hole). The campsite has around 185 tourist pitches, 10 mobile homes and 3 'yurts' (canvas and wooden tents) for rent. The marked and generally separated pitches are all fully serviced with electricity (10A), water and drainage.

Facilities

The main toilet block is modern and is supplemented for peak season by a second, recently refitted unit, which should prove adequate for demand, although they do attract some use by day-trippers to the leisure facilities. They include washbasins in cubicles, dishwashing and laundry sinks, washing machines and dryers, and facilities for babies and disabled persons. Shop, restaurant and takeaway (April - Sept). Playground on the beach. Bicycle hire. Barrier locked 22.00-07.00 hrs (€ 10 deposit for card). Off site: Riding 200 m. Golf 800 m. ATM 5 km.

Open

1 April - 30 September.

At a glance

Welcome & Ambience	✓✓✓✓	Location	✓✓✓✓
Quality of Pitches	✓✓✓✓	Range of Facilities	✓✓✓✓✓

Directions

Saint Cyr is approx. midway between Châtellerault and Poitiers. Site is signed to the east of the N10 at Beaumont along the D82 towards Bonneuil-Matours, and is part of the Parc de Loisirs de Saint Cyr.

Charges 2005

Per person	€ 2,50 - € 5,00
child (1-7 yrs)	€ 1,50 - € 2,00
pitch incl. electricity, water and drainage	€ 6,00 - € 12,00
animal	free - € 1,50

Reservations

Advisable for high season, made with 30% deposit and fee (€ 8). Tel: 05 49 62 57 22. Email: contact@parcdesaintcyr.com

MAP 8

Burgundy is a wonderfully evocative region offering breathtaking châteaux and cathedrals, rolling hills and heady mountain views, vineyards and superlative cuisine, not to mention of course, a wide variety of world renowned wines.

DÉPARTEMENTS: 21 CÔTE D'OR, 58 NIÈVRE, 71 SAÔNE-ET-LOIRE, 89 YONNE

MAJOR CITY: DIJON

In the rich heartland of France, Burgundy was once a powerful independent state and important religious centre. Its golden age is reflected in the area's magnificent art and architecture: the grand palaces and art collections of Dijon, the great pilgrimage church of Vézelay, the Cistercian Abbaye de Fontenay and the evocative abbey remains at Cluny, once the most powerful monastery in Europe.

However Burgundy is best known for its wine, including some of the world's finest, notably from the great vineyards of the Côte d'Or and Chablis, and also for its sublime cuisine. You'll also notice how driving through the country villages is like reading a wine merchant's list with plenty of opportunities for tasting and choosing your wine.

The area is criss-crossed by navigable waterways and includes the Parc Régional du Morvan; good walking country amidst lush, rolling wooded landscape.

Places of interest

Autun: 12th century St Lazare cathedral

Beaune: medieval town; Museum of Burgundy Wine

Cluny: Europe's largest Benedictine abbey

Dijon: Palace of the Dukes, Fine Arts Museum, Burgundian Folklore Museum.

Fontenay: Fontenay Abbey and Cloister

Joigny: medieval town

Mâcon: Maison des Vins (wine centre)

Paray-le-Monial: Romanesque basilica, pilgrimage centre

Sens: historic buildings, museum with fine Gallo-Roman collections

Vézelay: fortified medieval hillside

Cuisine of the region

Many dishes are wine based, including *Poulet au Meursault* and *Coq au Chambertin*. Dijon is known for its *pain d'épice* (spiced honey-cake) and spicy mustard

Boeuf Bourguignon: braised beef simmered in a red wine-based sauce

Garbure: heavy soup, a mixture of pork, cabbage, beans and sausages

Gougère: cheese pastry based on Gruyère

Jambon persillé: parsley-flavoured ham, served cold in jelly

Matelote: fresh-water fish soup, usually based on a red wine sauce

Meurette: red wine-based sauce with small onions, used with fish or poached egg dishes

FR21010 Camping Municipal Louis Rigoly

Esplanade St Vorles, F-21400 Châtillon-sur-Seine (Côte d'Or)

This well kept, small, hillside municipal site has 52 touring pitches. Mainly individual and separated, they are on fairly flat grass, all with electricity with mature trees providing shelter. Adjoining the site is the municipal pool complex with both indoor and outdoor pools (free in July and August). There is no shop, but the town is close. The site, which has much transit trade, can become full by evening in season.

Facilities	Directions
The main toilet block at the lower end of the site is satisfactory. A smaller heated unit behind reception contains facilities for babies, a washing machine and dryer. Facilities for disabled visitors provided in a separate block. Snack bar July/Aug. Baker calls every morning (except Tuesday). Play area. Boules. Volleyball. Motorcaravan service point. Internet access. Off site: Fishing or bicycle hire 1 km. Riding 4 km.	On northeast outskirts of town; site is signed from centre (steep hills approaching site, narrow roads).

Open

1 April - 30 September.

At a glance

Welcome & Ambience	✓✓✓✓	Location	✓✓✓✓
Quality of Pitches	✓✓✓	Range of Facilities	✓✓✓

Charges 2005

Per person	€ 3,00
child (under 7 yrs)	€ 1,30
pitch incl. vehicle	€ 4,20
electricity (4/6A)	€ 2,15 - € 4,30

No credit cards.

Reservations

Not officially made, but if you write shortly before your visit, they will reserve until 7 p.m. Tel: 03 80 91 03 05.
Email: tourism-chatillon-sur-seine@wanadoo.fr

FR21020 Camping Municipal Les Cent Vignes

10 rue Auguste Dubois, F-21200 Beaune (Côte d'Or)

The Côte de Beaune, situated southeast of the Côte d'Or, produces some of the very best French wines. Beaune is also a city of art and has a charm all of its own and there are several 'caves' in the town just waiting to be visited. Les Cents Vignes is a very well kept site offering 116 individual pitches of good size, separated from each other by neat beech hedges high enough to keep a fair amount of privacy. Over half of the pitches are on grass, ostensibly for tents, the remainder on hardstandings with electricity for caravans. A popular site, within walking distance of the town centre, Les Cent Vignes becomes full mid-June to early Sept. but with many short-stay campers there are departures each day.

Facilities	Directions
Two modern, fully equipped and well constructed, sanitary blocks, one of which can be heated, should be large enough. Nearly all washbasins are in cabins. Dishwashing and laundry sinks. Washing machines. Shop, restaurant with takeaway (all 1/4-15/10). Playground. Sports area. TV room. Off site: Bicycle hire 1 km. Centre of Beaune 1 km.	From autoroute exit 24 follow signs for Beaune centre on D2 road, camping signs to site in approx. 1 km. Well signed from other routes.

Open

15 March - 31 October.

At a glance

Welcome & Ambience	✓✓✓✓	Location	✓✓✓✓✓
Quality of Pitches	✓✓✓✓	Range of Facilities	✓✓✓✓

Charges 2005

Per person	€ 3,35
child (2-7 yrs)	€ 1,60
pitch	€ 4,20
electricity (6A)	€ 3,20

Reservations

Made before 30 May without deposit. Tel: 03 80 22 03 91.

FR21030 Camping Municipal Les Premier Pres

Route de Bouilland, F-21420 Savigny-les-Beaune (Côte d'Or)

This popular site is ideally located for visiting the Burgundy vineyards, for use as a transit site or for spending time in the town of Beaune. During the high season it is full every evening, so it is best to arrive by 4 pm. The 90 level pitches are numbered, with electric hook-ups and room for an awning. If reception is closed when you arrive, you find a pitch and report later, otherwise 'Madame' will allocate a place. Whilst the famed wine region alone attracts many visitors, Beaune, its capital, is unrivalled in its richness of art from times gone by. Narrow streets and squares are garlanded with flowers, pavement cafés are crammed with tourists and overlooking the scene is the glistening Hotel Dieu.

Facilities	Directions
Well kept sanitary facilities are housed in a modern building behind reception. Table tennis. Motorcaravan service point. Torch useful. Staff are pleasant and ice can be purchased. Off site: Sunday market in the village 1 km. Beaune 7 km.	From A6 autoroute take exit 24 signed Beaune and Savigny-lès-Beaune onto D2. Turn right towards Savigny-lès-Beaune (3 km) and follow signs to site.

Open

1 May - 30 September.

At a glance

Welcome & Ambience	✓✓✓✓	Location	✓✓✓✓
Quality of Pitches	✓✓✓✓	Range of Facilities	✓✓✓

Charges 2005

Per person	€ 2,05
pitch incl. electricity	€ 6,30

No credit cards.

Reservations

Not accepted. Tel: 03 80 26 15 06.

FR21040 Camping de l'Etang de Fouché

Rue du 8 Mai 1945, F-21230 Arnay le Duc (Côte d'Or)

Useful as an overnight stop en-route to or from the Mediterranean or indeed for longer stays, this quite large but peaceful, lakeside site has good facilities and the added advantage of being open all year. It can be very busy during the school holidays, and is probably better visited outside the main season. There are 190 good sized pitches, on fairly level grass and all with 10A electricity (some with water). This part of Burgundy is popular and Arnay le Duc itself is an attractive little town with an interesting history and renowned for its gastronomy, with many hotels and restaurants. The pitches, many hedged, offer a choice of shade or more open aspect. In July/August there are regular activities for children and adults.

Facilities

At the time of the inspection, only two of the four sanitary blocks were open. They are reasonably modern and well maintained, including some British style WCs, washbasins in cabins, facilities for disabled visitors. Washing machines and dishwashing under cover. Shop (with bread), bar, restaurant, takeaway (all 15 May to 15 Sep). TV/games room. Boules. Table tennis. Playground. Off site: Site is within 800m of the town centre, which has tennis courts, shops etc. At the supervised lakeside beach next to the site - small playground, water slides, pedaloes, canoes, soft drinks.

Open

15 April - 15 October.

At a glance

| Welcome & Ambience | ✓✓✓✓ | Location | ✓✓✓✓ |
| Quality of Pitches | ✓✓✓✓✓ | Range of Facilities | ✓✓✓✓ |

Directions

Site is on east side of town (well signed), 15 km. from A6 autoroute (exit at péage de Pouilly en Auxois).

Charges 2005

Per unit incl. 2 persons	€ 9,30 - € 13,60
extra person	€ 2,80 - € 3,90
child (under 7 yrs)	€ 1,40 - € 2,00
electricity	€ 3,30
animal	€ 1,50

Reservations

Advised for Jul/Aug; contact site. Reservation fee € 10, deposit € 30. Tel: 03 80 90 02 23.
Email: info@campingfouche.com

FR21000 Camping Lac de Panthier

F-21320 Vandenesse-en-Auxois (Côte d'Or)

An attractively situated lakeside site in Burgundy countryside, Camping Lac de Panthier is divided into two distinct campsites. The first, smaller section houses the reception, shop, restaurant and other similar facilities. The second, larger area is 200 m. along the lakeside road and is where the site activities take place and the pool can be found. The 207 pitches (157 for touring units) all have electricity connections and are mostly on level grass, although in parts there are shallow terraces. The most obvious attraction here is the proximity to the lake with its many watersports facilities. The site's restaurant has panoramic views over the lake. Used by tour operators.

Facilities

Four unisex toilet blocks (two for each site) also provide for babies and disabled people. Shop, bar and restaurant (all season). Games room. TV room. Swimming pool, children's pool and water-slide (15/5-15/9). Indoor pool, sauna and fitness equipment. Fishing. Riding. Bicycle and canoe hire. Watersports. Entertainment and activities organised in high season include wine tasting, dances, karaoke and clubs for children and teenagers. Off site: Boat excursions from Pouilly en Auxois (8 km). Riding and golf 10 km. Dijon, Autun and Beaune are also within easy reach. Bus to Dijon and Poilly-en-Auxois 300 m.

Open

8 April - 15 October.

At a glance

| Welcome & Ambience | ✓✓✓✓ | Location | ✓✓✓✓ |
| Quality of Pitches | ✓✓✓✓ | Range of Facilities | ✓✓✓✓ |

Directions

From the A6 join the A38 and immediately exit at junction 24. Take N81 towards Arnay Le Duc (back over the A6), then almost immediately turn left on D977 for 5 km. Fork left again for Vandenesse en Auxois. Continue through village on D977 for 2.5 km, turn left again and site is on left.

Charges 2005

Per pitch incl. 2 persons	€ 11,80 - € 19,40
electricity	€ 4,00
extra adult	€ 3,80 - € 6,20
child (2-7 yrs)	€ 1,90 - € 3,20
dog	€ 2,50

Camping Cheques accepted.

Reservations

Contact site. Tel: 03 80 49 21 94.
Email: info@lac-de-panthier.com

FR21050 Camping La Grappe d'Or

2 route de Volnay, F-21190 Meursault (Côte d'Or)

Meursault, the capital of the great white wines of Burgundy, is southwest of Beaune and La Grappe d'Or offers terraced pitches overlooking acres of vineyards. Most of the 125 pitches are flat, of varying sizes, and some have shade from mature trees. They all have electrical connections. There is an outdoor pool and flume and, during July and August, aqua gym and other water activities are organised. A second part of the site is located 100 m. towards the village in the grounds of the owners' house. Here there are caravan holiday homes for rent as well as those used by tour operators. This is a reasonable site from which to enjoy some of the cycle/walking tours around the local vineyards.

Facilities

Sanitary facilities are in three blocks with some washbasins in cabins. Child/baby room, facilities for visitors with disabilities, laundry and undercover dishwashing sinks. Shop, bar, restaurant, takeaway and swimming pool (all 1/5 - 30/9, pool heated 15/6-15/9). Play area, volleyball, tennis courts. Bicycle hire. Off site: Golf or riding 7 km. Indoor swimming pool 7 km. Fishing 8 km. Beaune 9 km.

Open

1 April - 15 October.

At a glance

Welcome & Ambience	✓✓✓✓	Location	✓✓✓✓	
Quality of Pitches	✓✓✓	Range of Facilities	✓✓✓✓	

Directions

Site is north of Meursault. Take N74 from Beaune and follow the sign for Meursault; campsite is well signed from the town.

Charges 2006

Per unit incl. 2 persons	€ 12,50
extra person	€ 3,00
electricity	€ 3,50

Camping Cheques accepted.

Reservations

Made with € 25 deposit plus € 5 fee.
Tel: 03 80 21 22 48.
Email: info@camping-meusauet.com

FR21060 Camping Les Bouleaux

F-21200 Vignoles (Côte d'Or)

Camping Les Bouleaux is an excellent little campsite located at Vignolles, northeast of Beaune. There are just 46 pitches, all with an electrical connection (3-6A, long leads may be required on some pitches). The large flat pitches are attractively laid out and most are separated by hedges and trees giving some shade. Monsieur Rossignal takes great pride in his campsite, keeping the grounds and facilities exceptionally clean and tidy, and by planting bright flowers near the reception. The nearest shops are 3 km.

Facilities

An older unisex building provides Turkish style WCs, while the adjacent modern block houses British style WCs (no paper). Washbasins in cabins or communal; push-button controllable showers, excellent facilities for visitors with disabilities. No shop, but wine and basic groceries can be bought at reception. Gas exchange. Off site: Bicycle hire, fishing or golf 3 km. Riding 6 km. Beaune 3 km.

Open

All year.

At a glance

Welcome & Ambience	✓✓✓✓✓	Location	✓✓✓✓	
Quality of Pitches	✓✓✓✓✓	Range of Facilities	✓✓✓	

Directions

Leave A6 at junction 24.1 south of Beaune. Turn right at roundabout, straight on at traffic lights (centre lane), then right at next roundabout. Cross autoroute and follow campsite signs.

Charges guide

Per person	€ 3,30
pitch incl. car	€ 4,00
electricity (3/6A)	€ 2,00 - € 4,10

No credit cards.

Reservations

Not usually required, but phone during July and August to confirm availability. Tel: 03 80 22 26 88.

FR21070 Camping Municipal Les Grèbes

F-21330 Marcenay (Côte d'Or)

This attractive, peacefully located and very spacious lakeside site has 90 level, grassy pitches all with electricity hook-ups. They are arranged in small clearings with dividing shrubs and hedges. The stylish reception building has a small shop and a snack bar with drinks. The site has access via pedestrian gates onto the lakeside path, there is a small beach and marked swimming area and one can use non-powered boats or fish. The nearby Haut Fourneau is worth a visit.

Facilities

Two good quality modern sanitary units. The main one can be heated, the second at the rear of the site is open only for peak season. Both provide washbasins in cubicles and spacious hot showers. Good units for disabled people. Baby changing. Washing machine, dryer and iron. Motorcaravan service point. Shop. Snack bar. TV room. Small pool for children. Canoe hire. Playground. Internet access.

Open

1 April - 15 October.

At a glance

Welcome & Ambience	✓✓✓✓	Location	✓✓✓✓	
Quality of Pitches	✓✓✓✓	Range of Facilities	✓✓✓	

Directions

Marcenay is about 35 km. east of Tonnerre and 14 km. west of Chatillon-sur-Seine, just north of the D965 road joining these towns. Site is signed from Marcenay. GPS: N47:52.195 E04:24.276

Charges 2005

Per person	€ 2,50
pitch and car or motorcaravan	€ 4,60
electricity (6A)	€ 2,90

Reductions for stays over 15 days.

Reservations

Advised for July/Aug. No deposit required.
Tel: 03 80 81 61 72. Email: marcenay@club-internet.fr

FR21080 Camping des Sources

Avenue des Sources, F-21590 Santenay (Côte d'Or)

Santenay lies in the heart of the Côte de Beaune, a region justly renowned for its wine and châteaux, and within easy reach of Beaune itself. If you need to relax or recover after a day's sightseeing or 'dégustation', it also has a casino and a spa. For the more energetic it is alongside a long distance track for cycling, rollerskating and walking, from which start a number of shorter circular routes. This relatively new site is next to the village sports and leisure area, with direct access to the supervised heated swimming pool and paddling pool (free to campers 1/6 - 31/8). There are 110 comfortable level grassy touring pitches. All have electrical connections (6A) and a water tap is never far.

Facilities

The modern toilet block contains British style WCs, washbasins and pre-set showers. Facilities for disabled people. Motorcaravan services. Washing machine and dryer. Gas supplies. Shop. Bar, restaurant, snack bar and takeaway (15/5-15/9). Games room. Internet terminal. Playground. Playing field. Table tennis. Minigolf. Boules. Skittles. Off site: Just outside site – tennis courts, skateboarding area. Casino and ATM 300 m. Spa 400 m. Santenay 1.5 km. has shops, restaurants, bars and a bus stop. Bicycle hire 1.5 km. Riding 2 km. Fishing, boat launching 4 km.

Open

15 April - 1 November.

At a glance

Welcome & Ambience	✓✓✓✓	Location	✓✓✓✓
Quality of Pitches	✓✓✓✓	Range of Facilities	✓✓✓✓

Directions

Santenay is about 18 km. southwest of Beaune. From Beaune take the N74 (towards Autun and Montceau-les-Mines). After about 2 km., at roundabout, continue on the N74. After a further 11 km., pass under the N6 and in a further 3 km. turn right into Santenay. Site is signed from the village. GPS: N46:54.26 E04:41.06

Charges 2005

Per unit incl. 2 persons	€ 11,50
extra person	€ 3,00
child (0-7 yrs)	€ 1,40
electricity	€ 3,50
animal	€ 1,00

Reservations

Contact site. Tel: 03 80 20 66 55.
Email: info@campingsantenay.com

FR58010 Camping des Bains

Mobile homes ▶ page 423

15 avenue Jean Mermoz, F-58360 St Honoré-les-Bains (Nièvre)

You are assured of a warm welcome at this attractive family run site, which is well situated for exploring the Morvan area in the heart of Burgundy. This is an area of rolling countryside, woods, rivers and country villages, ideal for walking or cycling. The spacious 130 level grassed pitches (all with 6A electricity) are mostly separated by hedges with a large variety of mature trees offering shade. Next to the camping is the 'thermal spa' where there are opportunities to 'take the waters' for a three day session or a full blown cure of three weeks! Details are found at reception. There is an excellent restaurant almost opposite the campsite entrance. A 'Sites et Paysages' member.

Facilities

The two main sanitary units have mostly British style WCs, washbasins in separate cabins and ample hot showers (one block may be closed in low season). Dishwashing sinks, baby bath, laundry. Facilities for disabled people. Traditional family bar also provides food and a takeaway service. Small swimming pool (12 x 12 m) with a separate slide and new paddling pool (15/6-10/10). Excellent play area and two small streams for children to fish. Table tennis. Minigolf. Games room. Entertainment weekly for children in July/Aug. Large screen and projector for TV and DVDs. Internet access. Off site: Bicycle hire or riding 500 m. Fishing 5 km. Canal-side cycle route runs for 50 km. from Vandenesse (6 km). Casino in village.

At a glance

Welcome & Ambience	✓✓✓✓	Location	✓✓✓✓
Quality of Pitches	✓✓✓✓	Range of Facilities	✓✓✓✓

Directions

From Nevers, travel east on D978; turn right onto D985 towards St Honoré-les-Bains, from where site is signed 'Camping des Bains', on entering town. Care is needed at narrow site entrance.

Charges 2005

Per unit incl. 2 persons	€ 15,50
extra person	€ 4,50
child (2-7 yrs)	€ 2,85
electricity (6A)	€ 3,20
dog	€ 1,50

Reservations

Contact site for details. Tel: 03 86 30 73 44.
Email: camping-les-bains@wanadoo.fr

Open

1 April - 10 October.

179

FR58030 Castel Camping Manoir de Bezolle

F-58110 St Pereuse-en-Morvan (Nièvre)

Manoir de Bezolle is well situated to explore the Morvan Natural Park and the Nivernais area. It has been attractively landscaped to provide a number of different areas, some giving pleasant views over the surrounding countryside. The 95 touring pitches of good size are on level grass with shade, some with terracing and 50 have access to electricity (10A). There are two small lakes, stocked with many fish for anglers. This site is good for families, with a range of activities provided for them.

Facilities

Two main toilet blocks (opened as needed) provide washbasins in cabins, mostly British style WCs, bath, provision for disabled visitors and a baby bath. A fibreglass unit contains two tiny family WC/basin/shower suites for rent. A smaller, older block is by the pools. Laundry. Motorcaravan services. Shop. Bar and restaurant. Pizza and takeaway (main season only). Internet point. Two swimming pools with sunbathing terrace (1/6-15/9). Pony rides (June-Sept). Table tennis, minigolf and boules. Mini zoo. Fishing. Animation is organised in season.

Open

15 May - 15 September.

At a glance

Welcome & Ambience	✓✓✓✓	Location	✓✓✓✓
Quality of Pitches	✓✓✓✓	Range of Facilities	✓✓✓✓

Directions

Site is between Nevers and Autun (mid-way between Châtillon-en-Bazois and Château-Chinon), just north of the D978 by small village of St Péreuse-en-Morvan.

Charges 2005

Per pitch incl. 2 persons	€ 20,00 - € 27,00
extra person	€ 5,00 - € 6,00
child (3-7 yrs)	€ 3,00 - € 4,00
electricity (10A)	free - € 3,00
animal	€ 2,00

Camping Cheques accepted.

Reservations

Made with deposit (about € 50) and fee (about € 16). Tel: 03 86 84 42 55. Email: info@bezolle.com

FR58060 Domaine Naturiste de la Gagère

F-58170 Luzy (Nièvre)

At this spacious, attractive, well equipped campsite, you will receive a really good welcome from the enthusiastic founders of Naturocamp. It lies near the southern end of the Morvan Regional Natural Park, surrounded by wooded hills, but within easy reach of attractions such as the European Community sponsored Museum of Celtic History, and Kagyu Ling, the largest Buddhist temple in Europe. There are 120 good sized level grassy pitches, some shaded, some open, of which 105 are available for tourers. Many are arranged around three sides of rectangles between hedges, leaving a good grass area for relaxation and play. There is an electricity supply to 84 pitches, 6 of which are fully serviced, but some will need leads of up to 40 m. There are plenty of water points. In high season there are organised activities and entertainment (some of which relate to the customs and culture of the Morvan), and a children's club meets twice per week.

Facilities

Three modern unisex heated toilet blocks contain British style WCs, washbasins and pre-set showers. En-suite facilities for disabled people. Baby changing room. Motorcaravan services. Washing machine, dryer and ironing board. Shop for basics (31/5-15/9). Bar (all season). Restaurant with snack bar and takeaway (1/5-15/9). Satellite TV. Two heated swimming pools (one all season, the other 15/5-15/9). Sauna and health suite. Three playgrounds. Table tennis. Volleyball. Boules. Bicycle hire. Only gas barbecues are permitted (available for hire). Off site: Luzy 10 km. with supermarket, shops, restaurants, bars, takeaway, ATM and bus stop. Fishing 5 km. Riding 10 km.

Open

1 April - 1 October.

At a glance

Welcome & Ambience	✓✓✓✓✓	Location	✓✓✓
Quality of Pitches	✓✓✓✓	Range of Facilities	✓✓✓✓

Directions

Luzy is 34 km. southwest of Autun, on the N81. Travel northeast from Luzy towards Autun. After about 6 km. the campsite is signed to the right. Site is then reached by 3 km. of winding road, narrow in parts, with passing places.

Charges 2005

Per person	€ 5,00
child (0-12 yrs)	€ 3,00
pitch	€ 13,00
incl. electricity	€ 15,50 - € 20,00
animal	€ 3,50

Less 10-30% outside July/Aug. Admin. Fee for stays of 3 nights or less (€ 5).

Reservations

Made with deposit (40%) and fee (€ 10). Tel: 03 86 30 48 11. Email: info@la-gagere.com

FR58050 Airotel Château de Chigy

Chigy, F-58170 Tazilly (Nièvre)

This very spacious site (20 ha. for pitches and another 50 ha. of fields, lakes and woods) lies just at the southern tip of the Morvan Regional Natural Park, within easy reach of the European Community sponsored Museum of Celtic History, Kagyu Ling, the largest Buddhist temple in Europe, and other places well worth visiting. As you enter the site, you first see the well maintained château, which houses the reception and apartments for rent. Most of the facilities are nearby, and behind are 54 good sized, shaded pitches, with electricity and water supply near. Behind them is a large woodland area with paths, next to which are 100 or so more pitches, some of up to 150 sq.m. Some are level, some are terraced, some are slightly sloping, some are bumpy, all are open. All have electrical connections and there are enough water taps. Fishing is possible in the lakes. In high season there are organised activities and entertainment, and a children's club meets twice a week.

Facilities

Two modern toilet blocks contain British style WCs, washbasins in cubicles, and showers (some pre-set, some controllable). A 'portacabin' style unit has 4 small cubicles, each containing toilet, washbasin and shower, which can be hired as private facilities in July/August. Facilities for disabled people and babies. Washing machine and dryer. Gas supplies. Shop for basics. Attractive oak-beamed bar, restaurant and takeaway (July/Aug). Two outdoor swimming pools, one incorporating a paddling pool (15/5-30/9). Swimming in lake. Games room. TV room. Playground. Minigolf. Boules. Table tennis. Table football. Playing field. Off site: Luzy (4 km.) with supermarket, shops, restaurants, bars, takeaway, ATM and bus stop. Riding 9 km.

Open

29 April - 30 September.

At a glance

Welcome & Ambience	✓✓✓✓	Location	✓✓✓✓
Quality of Pitches	✓✓✓	Range of Facilities	✓✓✓✓

Directions

From Luzy (34 km. southwest of Autun via the N81) take the D973 towards Bourbon Lancy. After about 4 km. the site is signed to the left.

Charges 2005

Per person	€ 4,65 - € 6,90
child (2-7 yrs)	free - € 3,45
pitch	€ 5,85 - € 8,55
electricity	€ 3,50
dog	€ 1,50

Reductions during certain periods, for age 55+, and for longer stays.

Reservations

Made with deposit (€ 173; (includes € 8 cancellation insurance). Tel: 03 86 30 10 80.
Email: reception@chateaudechigy.com.fr

FR71060 Camping Caravaning Château de Montrouant

F-71800 Gibles (Saône-et-Loire)

This is a small, pretty site beside a lake in the grounds of an imposing chateau, located in a steep valley in the rolling Charolais hills. There is ample shade from the many mature trees and the 45 pitches (12 used by tour operators) are on reasonably flat grassy terraces, mainly separated by small hedges. All have electrical connections. The overall appearance is attractive with some pitches overlooking the lake and some next to a field where ponies graze. This site is probably best for smaller units as the access roads are very steep and not in very good condition; caravans (and motorcaravans) are towed off site if required. The enthusiastic owner organises several unusual and interesting activities during the main season, including stone masonry, model boat building, walks, wine tours, etc. Good fishing is possible in the site's lakes and is a feature of the site. Regrettably the season here is short and the site becomes quickly full mid-July - mid-Aug. and is very popular with the Dutch. The best times could be from late June - mid July or the second half of August. Motorcaravan owners should always check in advance as there may not be a suitable pitch. Used by a Dutch tour operator.

Facilities

The sanitary facilities, not too well designed and with maintenance that can be variable, are housed in a part of the château. They include washbasins in cabins. Dishwashing sinks. Washing machine and dryer. Basic supplies available at reception. Very small open-air bar/restaurant /takeaway for evening barbecues (only open certain evenings). Swimming pool (1/6-10/9) with secluded sunbathing area, has been sympathetically landscaped. Half-court tennis. Fishing. Pony riding. Free bicycle loan. Torches useful. Off site: The village of Gibles, with shops, restaurant, etc. is 2 km. Riding 10 km.

Open

1 June - 4 September.

At a glance

Welcome & Ambience	✓✓✓✓	Location	✓✓✓✓
Quality of Pitches	✓✓✓	Range of Facilities	✓✓✓✓

Directions

Site is to the west of Mâcon and can be reached from the A6 (Macon Sud) via the N79 to Charolles (approx. 55 km). Take exit for Trivy - Dompierre-les-Ormes and D41 towards Montneland and Gibles.

Charges 2005

Per person	€ 5,20
child (under 7 yrs)	€ 3,50
pitch	€ 4,70
vehicle	€ 4,70
electricity (6A)	€ 4,70
dog	€ 3,00

Special weekly charges. 10% reduction outside 1/7 - 31/8. Camping Cheques accepted.

Reservations

Essential for high season (8/7-25/8) and made with 25% deposit. Tel: 03 85 84 54 30.

FR71010 Camping Municipal Mâcon

RN 6, F-71000 Mâcon (Saône-et-Loire)

Always useful and well cared for, this site is worth considering as a stopover or for longer stays as it is close to the main route south. The 250 good sized pitches, 190 with 6 A electricity and 60 with fresh and waste water points, are on mown, flat grass, accessed by tarmac roads. There is a generally bright and cheerful ambience. A central play area is divided, part with a rubber base for toddlers and part with adventure equipment for 7-15 year-olds. The bar/restaurant is open all year and seems to be a favourite haunt for the locals at lunchtime. Gates are closed 22.00 - 06.30 hrs. but large units note, the security barrier has a 3.8 m. height restriction so watch those top boxes and air-conditioners!

Facilities

Sanitary facilities in three modernised, well maintained units, are fully equipped with British and Turkish style WCs, and washbasins in cubicles. A fourth modern block is next to the heated pool (for campers only, 15/5-15/9). Facilities for disabled visitors. Washing machine and dryer. Excellent motorcaravan service point. Shop/tabac. Bar. Takeaway and restaurant. Playground. Off site: Centre of Mâcon 3 km.

Open

15 March - 31 October.

\At a glance

Welcome & Ambience	✓✓✓✓	Location	✓✓✓✓
Quality of Pitches	✓✓✓✓	Range of Facilities	✓✓✓✓

Directions

Site is on northern outskirts of Mâcon on main the N6, 3 km. from the town centre (just south of the A40 autoroute junction).

Charges 2005

Per unit incl. 2 persons	€ 11,60
with electricity (5A)	€ 14,10
tent pitch incl. 2 persons	€ 9,90
extra person	€ 3,10
child (under 7 yrs)	€ 1,65

Reservations

Not normally required. Tel: 03 85 38 16 22.

FR71020 Le Village des Meuniers

Mobile homes ▶ page 423

F-71520 Dompierre-les-Ormes (Saône-et-Loire)

In a tranquil setting with panoramic views, the neat appearance of the reception building sets the tone for the rest of this attractive site.The main part has 113 terraced, grass pitches, some with hardstanding, are all fairly level, each with electricity and ample water points. Of these, 75 also have waste water outlets. A second section, used only in high season contains 16 standard pitches. All pitches enjoy stunning views of the surrounding countryside - the Beaujolais, the Maconnais, the Charollais and the Clunysois. An extensive sunbathing area surrounds the attractively designed pool complex. This is a superb site, tastefully landscaped, with a high standard of cleanliness in all areas. As hedges and trees mature they will offer more shade. This is an area well worth visiting, with attractive scenery, interesting history, excellent wines and food. Used by tour operators (12 pitches) and 15 chalets to rent.

Facilities

Sanitary facilities mainly in an unusual, purpose designed hexagonal block, with modern fittings, of high standard. Smaller unit in the lower area of the site. Motorcaravan service point in car park. Café (high season). Bar, shop and takeaway. Swimming pool complex with three heated pools and toboggan run (1/6-31/8). Children's activities organised in high season. Football. Minigolf. Internet access. Off site: Village 500 m. for all services (banks and some shops, closed Sun/Mon). Fishing 1.5 km. Riding 10 km.

Open

1 May - 30 September.

At a glance

Welcome & Ambience	✓✓✓✓	Location	✓✓✓✓
Quality of Pitches	✓✓✓✓✓	Range of Facilities	✓✓✓✓

Directions

Town is 35 km. west of Macon. Follow N79/E62 (Charolles, Paray, Digoin) road and turn south onto D41 to Dompierre-les-Ormes (3 km). Site is clearly signed through village.

Charges 2006

Per person	€ 4,50 - € 7,50
child (2-13)	€ 3,00 - € 4,50
pitch	€ 6,00 - € 9,00
electricity	€ 3,00 - € 4,50
dog	€ 1,50

Reservations

Advised for July/Aug. Tel: 03 85 50 36 60.
Email: levillagedesmeuniers@wanadoo.fr

www.alanrogers.com for latest campsite news

FR71030 Camping Municipal Saint Vital

Rue des Griottons, F-71250 Cluny (Saône-et-Loire)

Close to this attractive small town (300 metres walk) and adjacent to the municipal swimming pool (free for campers), this site has 174 pitches. On gently sloping grass, with some small hedges and shade in parts, electricity is available (long leads may be needed). Some rail noise is noticeable during the day but we are assured that trains do not run 23.30-07.00 hrs. The town has the world famous abbey, the National Stud farm, and don't miss the Cheese Tower for the best views of Cluny. The really excellent traffic free cycle path from Cluny to Givry is highly recommended.

Facilities

Two sanitary buildings provide British and Turkish style WCs, some washbasins in cubicles and controllable showers (no dividers). Washing machine and dryer. Off site: Fishing and bicycle hire 100 m. Rding 1 km. Wine routes, chateaux.

Open

1 May - 30 September.

At a glance

Welcome & Ambience	✓✓✓✓	Location	✓✓✓✓
Quality of Pitches	✓✓✓✓	Range of Facilities	✓✓✓

Directions

Site is east of town, by the D15 road towards Azé and Blanot.

Charges guide

Per person	€ 3,35
pitch and vehicle	€ 4,10
electricity	€ 2,66

Reservations

Advised for high season. Tel: 03 85 59 08 34. Email: cluny-camping@wanadoo.fr

FR71050 Camping Moulin de Collonge

F-71390 St Boil (Saône-et-Loire)

This well run, family site offers an 'away from it all' situation surrounded by sloping vineyards and golden wheat fields. It has an instant appeal for those seeking a quiet, relaxing environment. There are 57 level pitches, most with electrical hook-ups although long cables may be required. Hanging flower arrangements are in abundance and, like the shrubs and grounds, are constantly attended. Beyond the stream that borders the site are a pool, patio and a pizzeria (also open to the public all year). A lake has been created for leisure activities. The 'Voie Vert', a 117 km. track for cycling or walking starts nearby.

Facilities

Toilet facilities in a converted barn are tastefully decorated and well kept. Some washbasins are in cubicles. Washing machine and dryer under cover. Freezer for campers' use. Bread is delivered at 8.30 each morning. Shop (1/6 - 3/9). Pizzeria/snack bar (1/7 - 31/8). Swimming pool covered by plastic dome - some of the walls can be opened in good weather. Playgrounds. Bicycle hire. Table tennis. Fishing. Pony trekking. Off site: Riding 4 km. Chateaux, wine route.

Open

15 March - 30 September.

At a glance

Welcome & Ambience	✓✓✓✓	Location	✓✓✓✓
Quality of Pitches	✓✓✓	Range of Facilities	✓✓✓✓

Directions

From Chalon-sur-Saône travel 9 km. west on the N80. Turn south on D981 through Buxy (6 km). Continue south for 7 km. to Saint-Boil and site is signed at south end of the village.

Charges 2006

Per person	€ 4,50 - € 5,50
pitch incl. car	€ 5,50 - € 8,00
electricity	€ 3,00 - € 3,50
Less 20% outside July/Aug.	
Camping Cheques accepted.	

Reservations

Accepted - contact site. Tel: 03 85 44 00 32. Email: millofcollonge@wanadoo.fr

FR71110 Camping du Lac

Le Fourneau, F-71430 Palinges (Saône-et-Loire)

Camping du Lac is special and it is all due to Monsieur Labille, its owner. He thinks of the campsite as his home and every visitor as his guest, the central amenity block is spotlessly clean and the site is adjacent to a lake with a beach and safe bathing. Monsieur Labille provides tables and chairs for tent campers and freezes bottles of water for cyclists to take away (free of charge). Guests can also use the washing machine and fridge free of charge. If you want visit a specific place, then Monsieur knows exactly where you should go. There are 47 good sized touring pitches, each with a small hardstanding. All but 8 of the pitches have two 10A electricity connections, and 24 have water and waste points.

Facilities

The central sanitary block provides showers, washbasins in cubicles, facilities for campers with disabilities and two family rooms. Washing machine and fridge. Bread and croissants to order. Boules. Play area. TV room. Sports field, lake beach and swimming adjacent. Bicycle and pedalo hire in July/Aug. Motorcaravan service point. Riding 200 m. Palinges within walking distance.

Open

1 April - 15 October.

At a glance

Welcome & Ambience	✓✓✓✓✓	Location	✓✓✓✓✓
Quality of Pitches	✓✓✓✓✓	Range of Facilities	✓✓✓✓

Directions

Palinges is midway between Montceau les Mines and Paray le Monial. From Montceau take N70, then turn left on D92 to Palinges. Follow campsite signs. Also well signed from D985 Toulon - Charolles road.

Charges 2005

Per unit incl. 2 persons with electricity	€ 15,50
extra person	€ 2,00
child (0-10 yrs)	€ 1,00
dog	€ 1,50
No credit cards.	

Reservations

Advised in July and August. Tel: 03 85 88 14 49.

FR71080 Camping de L'Etang Neuf

L'Etang Neuf, F-71760 Issy-l'Évêque (Saône-et-Loire)

This quiet and tranquil campsite overlooking a lake, with a forest on one side and a view of the 19th century Château de Montrifaut on another, is a real countryside haven for relaxation. Separated by low hedges, there are 61 clearly marked grass pitches with 6A electricity connections and a small hardstanding area on which to park a car. Some young trees offer a little shade. A separate area is set aside for tents. Visitors come here to relax and enjoy the surroundings and there is no organised entertainment but a play area, fenced swimming and paddling pools and plenty of space will keep children happily amused. Many walks and mountain bike trails start from the site and free maps to explore the area are provided by the friendly manager, Marc Pille.

Facilities

Two very clean sanitary blocks include British and Turkish style WCs and washbasins in cabins. Dishwashing and laundry sinks. Washing machine, ironing board and baby room. Separate shower and toilet rooms for disabled people are in the lower block. Motorcaravan service point. Bar/restaurant. Bread and croissants to order. Boules pitch. TV and games room. Table tennis. Volleyball. Internet access. Off site: Minigolf just outside the site entrance. Riding 500 m. Nearest shop 1 km. in Issy l'Éveque.

Open

28 April - 16 September.

At a glance

Welcome & Ambience	✓✓✓✓	Location	✓✓✓✓
Quality of Pitches	✓✓✓✓	Range of Facilities	✓✓✓✓

Directions

From D973 (Luzy - Bourbon-Lancy) turn left onto the D25 (just west of Luzy) and continue for about 12 km. Turn right on D42 in centre of Issy l'Évêque, signed to campsite. The road narrows slightly as you approach the site entrance on the right.

Charges 2005

Per unit incl. 2 persons	€ 16,00 - € 17,00
with electricity	€ 16,00 - € 20,00
extra person	€ 3,00 - € 4,50
child (3-8 yrs)	€ 2,00 - € 3,00
Camping Cheques accepted.	

Reservations

Advised for July and August. Made with deposit (€ 75) and fee (€ 10). Tel: 03 85 24 96 05. Email: info@camping-etang-neuf.com

FR71090 Camping Intercommunal du Lac de Saint Point

F-71520 St Point (Saône-et-Loire)

On the banks of the lake, this site is managed by a young husband and wife team. It would make a convenient overnight stop, but its location on the lake may influence you to stay longer. The area is renowned for its wine and cheese as well as Roman churches, abbeys and châteaux. The site has 35 reasonably level, serviced touring pitches, mostly separated by low hedges, and 46 tent pitches on a sloping and partly terraced field behind. On-site activities include swimming in the lake (lifeguard on duty during July and August), with pedaloes for hire and fishing.

Facilities

Two sanitary blocks, one adjoining the reception and the other towards the back of the site up a slope, provide all the usual facilities and a washing machine. Shower and toilet/washbasin in separate cabins for campers with disabilities. Bar and snacks (1/6-30/9). Play area. Volleyball, basketball and badminton. Table tennis. Games room. Boules pitch. Mountain bike hire. Off site: Nearest shop 300 m. Tennis 4 km. Organised walks. Riding 5 km.

Open

1 April - 31 October.

At a glance

Welcome & Ambience	✓✓✓	Location	✓✓
Quality of Pitches	✓✓	Range of Facilities	✓✓✓✓

Directions

Leave A6 at junction 29 and take the N79 as far as the Cluny exit. Bear left and follow the signs to Saint-Point; site is on the outskirts of the village.

Charges 2005

Per unit incl. 2 adults, 2 children	€ 11,50
with electricity	€ 14,50 - € 17,00
extra person	€ 2,00
extra child (up to 7 yrs)	€ 1,50
No credit cards.	

Reservations

Advised in July/August. For reservations contact Les Chalets Decouverts: 04 73 19 11 11. Email: camping.stpoint@wanadoo.fr

Camping du lac de Saint Point Lamartine

Very comfortable campsite
Near Beaujolais and Mâconnais vineyards,
Cluny (romanesque abbey)
An excellent location by a lake
Quiet, shady, family atmosphere
Bathing, fishing, hiking, Mountain biking,
playground, sportsground, games room, snack-bar
Chalets for hire
For reservations please contact Chalets Decouverts: 0033 (0) 4 73 19 11 11
Open 1st April - 31st October
Le Lac, 71520 Saint-Point
Tel: 0033 385 50 52 31 - Fax: 0033 385 50 51 92
E-mail: camping.stpoint@wanadoo.fr
http://perso.wanadoo.fr/camping.stpoint

Southern Burgundy

184

FR71070 Castel Camping Château de l'Epervière

F-71240 Gigny-sur-Saône (Saône-et-Loire)

Peacefully situated on the edge of the little village of Gigny-sur-Saône, yet within easy distance of the A6 autoroute, this site nestles in a natural woodland area near the Saône river (subject to flooding in winter months). With 135 pitches, nearly all with 10A electricity, the site is in two fairly distinct areas. The original part has semi-hedged pitches on part-level ground with plenty of shade from mature trees, close to the château and fishing lake - you may need earplugs in the mornings because of the ducks! The centre of the second area has a more open aspect, with large hedged pitches and mature trees offering shade around the periphery and central open grass area. A partly fenced road across the lake connects the two areas of the site (care is needed with children). The managers, Gert-Jan and Francois, and their team enthusiastically organise a range of activities for visitors that includes wine tastings in the cellars of the château and a Kids' Club in July/Aug. Used by tour operators (60 pitches). A member of 'Les Castels' group.

Facilities

Two well equipped toilet blocks, one beside the château and a newer one on the lower section include washbasins in cabins, dishwashing and laundry areas under cover. Washing machine and dryer. Shop providing bread and basic provisions (1/5-30/9). Tastefully refurbished restaurant in the château with a distinctly French menu (1/4-30/9). Second restaurant with more basic menu and takeaway service. A converted barn houses an attractive bar, large screen TV and games room. Unheated swimming pool (1/5-30/9), with many sun loungers, partly enclosed by old stone walls protecting it from the wind, plus a smaller indoor heated pool with jacuzzi, sauna and paddling pool. Well equipped play area. Outdoor paddling pool. Bicycle hire. Off site: Riding 15 km. Golf 20 km.

Open

1 April - 30 September.

At a glance

Welcome & Ambience	✓✓✓✓✓	Location	✓✓✓✓
Quality of Pitches	✓✓✓✓	Range of Facilities	✓✓✓✓✓

Directions

From N6 between Châlon-sur-Saône and Tournus, turn east on D18 (just north of Sennecey-le-Grand) and follow site signs for 6.5 km. From A6, exit Châlon-Sud from the north, or Tournus from the south.

Charges 2006

Per person	€ 5,40 - € 6,90
child (under 7 yrs)	€ 3,30 - € 4,80
pitch	€ 7,90 - € 10,20
dog	€ 2,20 - € 2,90
electricity	€ 2,20 - € 2,90

Camping Cheques accepted.

Reservations

Contact site. Tel: 03 85 94 16 90.
Email: domaine-de-leperviere@wanadoo.fr

Domaine du Château de l'Epervière

LES CASTELS — Camping Qualité

WELCOME IN THE HEART OF BURGUNDY

Domaine du Chateau de l'Epervière   71240 Gigny sur Saône
Tél : 03 85 94 16 90   Fax : 03 85 94 16 97
www.domaine-epervière.com   E-mail : domaine-de-leperviere@wanadoo.fr

FR71120 Camping La Heronnière

Lac de Laives, F-71240 Laives (Saône-et-Loire)

Camping la Herronière is a quiet relaxing site on the edge of a leisure lake in pleasant rolling woodland countryside. The 90 touring pitches are good sized, grassy and level. About half have shade, with electrical connections for 81 and there are plenty of water points. A pleasant walk, reached directly from the campsite, runs along the edge of the lake. The site is within easy reach of Châlon-sur-Saône, Tournus and the Chalonnais vineyards and wine route. Cluny and the former industrial towns of Le Creusot and Montceau-les-Mines are each about 40 km. away. The Voie Verte, a 117 km. long linear cycling route, is 15 km. to the west.

Facilities

The modern sanitary block provides toilets, showers, washbasins, dishwashing and laundry sinks, and facilities for campers with disabilities. Baby rooms. Washing machine. Snack bar near pool with hot food (June - Aug). Covered area with tables and chairs just outside reception, from which bread, drinks, ice cream, basic provisions and French breakfast can be obtained. Heated outdoor pool. Volleyball. Table tennis. Boules. Bicycle hire. Fishing. Marquee with TV and board games. Playground. Off site: Popular, guarded part of the lake for swimming with grass area and beach, bar and restaurant 300 m. Also at the lake - exercise circuit, canoeing, windsurfing and pedaloes. Golf 15 km. Riding 10 km. Cluny's world famous abbey, museums at Châlon, Le Creusot and Montceau-les-Mines. Shops, etc., at Laives 4 km.

At a glance

Welcome & Ambience	✓✓✓✓	Location	✓✓✓✓
Quality of Pitches	✓✓✓✓	Range of Facilities	✓✓✓✓

Directions

Leave N6 road (Châlon-sur-Saône - Mâcon) at Sennecy-le-Grand (about 18 km. south of the centre of Châlon), taking D18 west to Laives (4 km.). Site is signed from Laives, 4 km. to the northwest, initially along the D18.

Charges 2005

Per person	€ 4,00
child (0-7 yrs)	€ 2,80
pitch incl. car	€ 4,50
electricity (6A)	€ 3,80
animal	€ 1,50

No credit cards. Camping Cheques accepted.

Reservations

Advisable in July and August. Tel: 03 85 44 98 85. Email: camping.laives@wanadoo.fr

Open

1 May - 15 September.

FR89060 Camping Les Ceriselles

Route de Vincelottes, F-89290 Vincelles (Yonne)

A distinctive, modern site, Les Ceriselles was created in 1998 on land adjacent to the Canal du Nivernais and is owned by a group of communities. A very level site, it has 84 pitches on grass, all with electricity and 37 with full services. A covered terrace houses a small snack bar with a good range of snacks, takeaway and drinks. Staff live on site and the gates are locked 22.00 - 07.00 hrs. Cars are parked on the secure on-site car park and not on the pitches. Double axle caravans are not accepted. This good value site is just off the popular N6 route and ideal for exploring the Yonne valley and Auxerre region.

Facilities

Four small heated toilet blocks each provide 1 WC, 2 washbasins in cubicles and 2 showers per sex, with a unit for disabled visitors in block one (nearest reception). Chemical toilet disposal is via screw cap joints on the fully serviced pitches at present. Snack bar (all season, hours vary acc. to demand). Playground. Bicycle hire. Fishing. Boules. Off site: Supermarket and restaurant within walking distance. Cycle path along canal for 8 km. in either direction.

Open

1 April - 30 October.

At a glance

Welcome & Ambience	✓✓✓✓	Location	✓✓✓✓
Quality of Pitches	✓✓✓✓	Range of Facilities	✓✓✓

Directions

Vincelles is about 10 km. south of Auxerre. From the A6 take 'Auxerre Sud' exit and follow N65 towards Auxerre. After 4 km. turn south on N6 towards Avallon and after 10 km. turn left on D38. Site entrance is on left just before canal. GPS: N47:42.407 E03:38.134

Charges 2006

Per person	€ 3,00
child (2-7 yrs)	€ 1,50
pitch	€ 5,00 - € 8,00
electricity	€ 1,80
animal	€ 1,00

Reductions for longer stays.

Reservations

Contact site. Tel: 03 86 42 39 39. Email: lesceriselles@wanadoo.fr

MAP 9

Located to the south of Alsace, the historic province of Franche Comté boasts a varied landscape ranging from flat plains to dense woodlands, rugged dramatic mountains and limestone valleys.

DÉPARTEMENTS: 25 DOUBS, 39 JURA, 70 HAUTE-SAÔNE, 90 TRE. DE BELFORT

MAJOR CITY: BESANÇON

Franche Comté is really made up of two regions. The high valley of the Saône is wide, gently rolling farmland with a certain rustic simplicity, while the Jura mountains are more rugged with dense forests, sheer cliffs, craggy limestone escarpments and torrents of clear, sparkling water gushing through deep gorges. It is for this thrilling scenery that Franche Comté is best known. Nature lovers can climb, bike and hike in the mountains or explore the hills honeycombed with over 4,000 caves.
The streams and lakes provide world-class fishing. The spa towns of Salins les Bains and Besançon offer relaxation and a chance to 'take the waters'.

The region has a rich architectural heritage dating from many different periods, including medieval abbeys and châteaux and a poignant chapel in memory of the war. Roman remains, fortresses perched on cliff tops and elegant spa towns can all be explored at leisure. The region's position, bordering Switzerland and close to Germany, is reflected in its culture and also the great diversity of architectural style in the many fine buildings.

Places of interest

Arbois: Pasteur Family Home and Museum, Museum of Wine and Wine Growing

Belfort: sandstone lion sculpted by Bartholdi; Memorial and Museum of the French Resistance

Besançon: citadel with good views over the city

Champlitte: Museum of Folk Art

Dole: lovely old town, Louis Pasteur's birthplace

Gray: Baron Martin Museum

Luxeuil-les-Bains: Tour des Echevins Museum

Ornans: Gustave Courbet birthplace, museum

Ronchamp: Chapel of Notre-Dame du Haut de Ronchamp designed by Le Corbusier

Salins-les-Bains: Salt mines and tunnels

Sochaux: Peugeot Museum

Cuisine of the region

Freshwater fish such as trout, grayling, pike and perch are local specialities. The region has a rare wine known as *vin de paille* as well as *vin jaune* (deep yellow and very dry) and *vin du jura*, Jura wine.

Brési: water-thin slices of dried beef; many local hams

Gougére: hot cheese pastry based on the local *Comté* cheese

Jésus de Morteau: fat pork sausage smoked over pine and juniper

Kirsch: cherry flavoured liqueur

Pontarlier: aniseed liqueur

Poulet au vin jaune: chicken, cream and *morilles* cooked in *vin jaune*

FR25000 Castel Camping Le Val de Bonnal

Bonnal, F-25680 Rougemont (Doubs)

This is an impressive, well managed site in a large country estate, harmoniously designed in keeping with the surrounding countryside, well away from main roads and other intrusions. Having said that, the site itself is very busy, with a wide range of activities and amenities. The 350 pitches, all of a good size and with electricity (5A), are separated by a mixture of trees and bushes, carefully landscaped. Some of the newer pitches are less secluded, but the ambience generally is peaceful despite the size of the site (300 pitches in a large area) and its deserved popularity. The main attraction must be the variety of watersports on the three large lakes and nearby river which include swimming, pedaloes, and fishing as well as water skiing, windsurfing and canoeing. In fact, the range of activities available in high season is almost inexhaustible, not to say exhausting! Used by tour operators (150 pitches).

Facilities

Five clean toilet blocks include washbasins in cabins. Separate washing up blocks. Washing machines, ironing boards and sinks for laundry. Riverside restaurant, snack bar/takeaway, bar and terrace, shop (all 20/5-8/9), sympathetically converted from former farm buildings. New swimming pool complex features water slides. Well equipped play areas. Range of sport facilities including table tennis, boules, bicycle hire, and water sports, etc. Fishing on the river and lake. Off site: Golf 6 km. Day trips to Switzerland.

Open

4 May - 4 September.

At a glance

Welcome & Ambience	✓✓✓✓	Location	✓✓✓✓
Quality of Pitches	✓✓✓✓	Range of Facilities	✓✓✓✓✓

Directions

From Vesoul take D9 towards Villersexel. After approx. 20 km. turn right in the village of Esprels at sign for Val de Bonnal. Follow for 3.5 km. and site is on the left. From autoroute A36 take exit for Baume-les-Dames; go north on D50, then D486 to Rougemont and follow signs to site. GPS: N47:30.211 E06:21.116

Charges 2005

Per pitch with electricity, incl. 2 persons	€ 27,00 - € 32,00
extra person	€ 8,00
child (3-8yrs)	€ 2,00

Less 20% outside July/Aug.

Reservations

Only made for pitches with electricity.
Tel: 03 81 86 90 87.
Email: val-de-bonnal@wanadoo.fr

FR25030 Camping du Bois de Reveuge

F-25680 Huanne (Doubs)

As Bois de Reveuge was only opened in 1992, it still has a new look about it, in as much as there is little shade yet from the young trees. Being on a hillside, the pitches are on terraces with good views across the surrounding countryside and leading down to two lakes which may be used for fishing and canoeing. The site also has private use of a ten hectare lake set in a park 10 km. away where there are swimming and boating opportunities. Tall trees have been left standing at the top of the hill. 190 pitches available for tourers have a water supply as well as electricity and some are extra large (150 - 180 sq.m). There is a good solar heated swimming pool which can be covered in cool weather and another pool with four water slides. Several supervisors are in attendance during the summer.

Facilities

Four modern sanitary blocks are nicely spaced around the site and have British and Turkish style WCs and washbasins mainly in cabins. Kiosk for basic food supplies (open all season) and restaurant/pizzeria with terrace (1/6-3/9). Swimming pools. Four play areas. High season 'baby club' with a large tent for wet weather, large video screen and some music and other entertainment for adults. Bowling alley. Shooting range. Pony club. Groups may request activities such as orienteering. A package deal includes the use of canoes as well as archery, fishing, bicycle hire and pedaloes.

Open

23 April - 17 September.

At a glance

Welcome & Ambience	✓✓✓✓	Location	✓✓✓✓
Quality of Pitches	✓✓✓	Range of Facilities	✓✓✓✓

Directions

Site is well signed from the D50. From A36 autoroute south of the site, take exit for Baume-les-Dames and head north on D50 towards Villersexel for about 7 km. to camp signs GPS: N47:26.472 E06:20.352

Charges 2005

Per unit incl. 2 persons	€ 17,00 - € 35,00
extra person	€ 3,00 - € 6,00
child (2-5 yrs)	€ 2,00 - € 4,00
animal	€ 2,00

Camping Cheques accepted.

Reservations

Made with 30% deposit and fee (€ 20).
Tel: 03 81 84 38 60.
Email: info@campingduboisdereveuge.com

FR25050 Camping Municipal de Saint Point-Lac

8 rue du Port, F-25160 St Point-Lac (Doubs)

A good example of a municipal campsite in which the village takes a pride, this site is on the banks of a small lake with views to the distant hills. The 84 level, numbered pitches are on grass and 60 have electricity (16A). It is worth making a detour from the Pontarlier - Vallorbe road or for a longer stay. The village shop and restaurant are an easy 200 m. walk from the site entrance.

Facilities

Good central sanitary block has British style WCs and free hot water. Hot snacks and takeaway in high season (July/Aug). Fishing. Off site: Bicycle hire 5 km.

Open

1 May - 30 September.

At a glance

Welcome & Ambience	✓✓✓	Location	✓✓✓✓
Quality of Pitches	✓✓✓	Range of Facilities	✓✓✓

Directions

From north, take D437 south of Pontarlier and keep on west side of the lake to the second village (Saint Point-Lac); from south exit N57 at Les Hopitaux-Neufs and turn west to lake. GPS: N46:48.709 E06:18.186

Charges 2006

Per pitch incl. 2 persons	€ 5,30 - € 9,60
with electricity	€ 12,20 - € 13,80
extra person	€ 2,00 - € 2,50
child (4-10 yrs)	€ 1,00 - € 1,25

Reservations

Made with deposit (€ 45) and fee (€ 7.60). Contact site from 1 May, or the Mairie in writing only (postal address as above). Tel: 03 81 69 61 64. Email: camping-saintpointlac@wanadoo.fr

FR39010 Camping La Plage Blanche

3 rue de la Plage, F-39380 Ounans (Jura)

Situated in open countryside, along the banks of the River Loue, this site has 220 good sized, marked pitches on level ground, 194 of which are for touring and all have electricity (6A). Trees provide both fully shaded and semi-shaded pitches. Approximately a kilometre of riverside and beach provides the ideal setting for children to swim and play safely in the gently flowing, shallow water – inflatables are popular and there is a canoe/kayak base. The site also has a swimming pool and paddling pool.

Facilities

Modern, well kept sanitary facilities in three unusual blocks include separate washing cabins. Dishwashing facilities are in blocks of 8 sinks. Launderette. Motorcaravan service area. Bar/restaurant with terrace (1/5-30/9). Shop (15/6-30/9). Pizzeria and takeaway (all season). TV room. Library. Swimming pool and children's pool. Play area. River fishing. A new fishing lake is planned for 2006. Table tennis. Entertainment and activities in July and August. Internet access. Off site: Bicycle hire 200 m. Riding 700 m. Golf, paragliding and hang-gliding 10 km.

Open

1 April - 15 October.

At a glance

Welcome & Ambience	✓✓✓✓	Location	✓✓✓✓
Quality of Pitches	✓✓✓✓	Range of Facilities	✓✓✓✓

Directions

Ounans is 20 km. southeast of Dole. From autoroute 36 from Besançon, take Dole exit and then D405 to Parcey. After Parcey take N5 to Mont Sous Vaudrey (8 km) then D472 towards Pontarlier to Ounans from where site is signed. From autoroute A9 take Dole exit and follow signs for N5, Poligny and Lons le Saunier. From Parcey follow directions above. GPS: N47:00.177 E05:39.823

Charges 2005

Per person	€ 5,10
child (1-7 yrs)	€ 3,20
pitch	€ 6,50
electricity	€ 3,20
dog	€ 1,00

Camping Cheques accepted.

Reservations

Made with fee (€ 10). Tel: 03 84 37 69 63. Email: reservation@la-plage-blanche.com

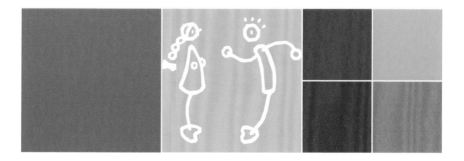

FR39030 Camping Domaine de Chalain

F-39130 Doucier (Jura)

Doucier lies east of Lons-le-Saunier among the wooded hills of the Jura and rather away from the main routes. This large, park-like site (804 pitches) is on the edge of the Lac de Chalain surrounded on three sides by woods and some cliffs. Large areas are left for sports and recreation. The lake shelves gently at the edge but then becomes deep quite suddenly. Day visitors can be very numerous during fine weekends. The site also has an attractive, well equipped pool complex. The site is divided into two parts, one (nearer the lake) with larger pitches (costing more). You should find room in the other part, but for July and August, it is better to reserve to make sure. There are 476 touring pitches, all with electricity (7A) but with little shade. 46 also have water and drainage. Used by tour operators (250 pitches).

Facilities

Nine sanitary blocks, improved over the years, include washbasins with warm water (all in cabins). Showers are in separate blocks. One block can be heated with facilities for babies and disabled people. Washing machines. Several shops (15/5-15/9). Restaurant. Bar. Takeaway and snacks (20/6-31/8) and a community room. New pool complex with heated indoor pool, outdoor pools with slide, sauna and spa. Four children's playgrounds. Large area for football. Open-air theatre. Fishing. Tennis (free outside 2/7-26/8). Minigolf. Pedalo and bicycle hire. Large merry-go-round and cinema (charged). Table tennis, volleyball, basketball, boules, skateboard area, outdoor chess, rock climbing, archery, aquagym. TV room. Disco, entertainment and organised activities. Animals and birds in enclosures. Dogs are not permitted on the lake beach. Maximum accepted length of caravan or motorcaravan is 6.5m. Off site: Signposted walk starts at edge of site. Riding 2 km. Golf 25 km.

Directions

Site can only be approached via Doucier: from Switzerland via N5 (from Geneva), then the N78 and D39; from other directions via Lons-le-Saunier or Champagnole. GPS: N46:39.849 E05:48.848

Charges 2005

Per unit incl. 3 persons acc. to location and services	€ 19,60 - € 33,40
extra adult	€ 6,22 - € 7,95
child (4-15 yrs)	€ 3,96 - € 4,90
electricity	€ 2,65
dog	€ 2,65

10% discount for couples over 60 staying more than 6 nights in low season.

Reservations

Made for min. 7 days with 30% deposit (min. € 60). Sat.-Sat. only in high season. Tel: 03 84 25 78 78. Email: chalain@chalain.com

Open

1 May - 20 September.

At a glance

Welcome & Ambience	✓✓✓✓✓	Location	✓✓✓✓✓
Quality of Pitches	✓✓✓✓	Range of Facilities	✓✓✓✓✓

FR39040 Sunêlia La Pergola

1 rue des Vernois, F-39130 Marigny (Jura)

Close to the Swiss border and overlooking the sparkling waters of Lac de Chalain, La Pergola is a neat, tidy and terraced site set amongst the rolling hills of the Jura. Awaiting discovery as it is not on the main tourist routes, La Pergola is very well appointed, with 350 pitches, mainly on gravel and separated by small bushes, and all with electricity, water and drainage. 127 are available for touring. Arranged on numerous terraces, connected by steep steps, some have shade and the higher ones have good views over the lake. A tall fence protects the site from the public footpath that separates the site from the lakeside but there are frequent access gates. The entrance is very attractive and the work that Mme. Gicquaire puts into the preparation of the flower-beds is very evident. The bar/restaurant terrace is beautiful, featuring grape vines for welcome shade and a colourful array of spectacular flowers leading on to a landscaped waterfall area next to the three swimming pools and entertainment area. English is spoken. Used by tour operators (123 pitches).

Facilities

The latest sanitary block serving the lower pitches is well appointed with private cabins. Slightly older blocks serve the other terraces. Visitors with disabilities are advised to select a lower terrace where special facilities are provided. Washing machines and dryers. Shop (1/6-18/9). Bar. Restaurant. Pizzeria/takeaway. Pool complex, two pools heated. Good play areas and children's club. Table tennis, archery, boules and volleyball. Windsurfing, pedaloes, canoes and small boats for hire. Organised programme in high season includes cycle tours, keep fit sessions and evening entertainment with disco twice weekly. Internet access. Off site: Hang-gliding 2 km. Riding 3 km.

Open

15 May - 18 September.

At a glance

Welcome & Ambience	✓✓✓✓	Location	✓✓✓✓
Quality of Pitches	✓✓✓✓	Range of Facilities	✓✓✓✓✓

Directions

Site is 2.5 km. north of Doucier on Lake Chalain road D27. It is signposted from Marigny. GPS: N46:40.621 E05:46.851

Charges 2005

Per unit incl. 2 persons and electricity	€ 20,00 - € 36,00
extra person	€ 4,40 - € 6,50
child (2-7 yrs)	free - € 5,50
animal	€ 4,00

Various special offers available. Camping Cheques accepted.

Reservations

Made with deposit (25%) and fee (€ 30). Tel: 03 84 25 70 03. Email: contact@lapergola.com

FR39050 Camping Fayolan

B.P. 52, F-39130 Clairvaux-les-Lacs (Jura)

This modern site, backed by wooded hills, is situated on the shores of Le Petit Lac about a mile from the town of Clairvaux-les-Lacs amid the lakes and forests of the Jura. Here one can relax, enjoy the peaceful countryside, explore the interesting villages, historic towns and museums of the area by car or cycle or take to the water where you can swim, windsurf and canoe. The neat, tidy site is in two parts, with pitches from 80-100 sq.m. either on terraces overlooking the lake or on the flatter area near the shore. There are electrical connections (6A) for those who want them and 200 pitches have electricity, water, drainage and sewage connections. The upper part has little shade until the young trees grow but there is some on the lower section. Used by tour operators (130 pitches).

Facilities

Four modern toilet units spread around the site have warm water from push-button taps in washbasins and showers and hot water in sinks. Baby room. Washing and drying machines. Ironing facilities. Shop. Restaurant. Bar. Snack bar/pizzeria and takeaway. Two good attractive swimming pools (heated from mid-May) and a smaller one for children (trunks, not shorts). Playground. Organised activities include archery, a fitness trail, walks, games, competitions, children's club and dancing. Fishing. Entertainment. Internet access. Off site: Bicycle hire 800 m. Riding 4 km.

Open

10 May - 15 September.

At a glance

Welcome & Ambience	✓✓✓✓	Location	✓✓✓✓
Quality of Pitches	✓✓✓✓	Range of Facilities	✓✓✓✓✓

Directions

Clairvaux-les-Lacs is on the N78 between Lons-le-Saunier and Morez. In Clairvaux follow signs for 'Lacs Campings' and Fayolan.
GPS: N46:33.866 E05:45.367

Charges 2005

Per unit incl. 2 persons	
and electricity	€ 15,00 - € 29,00
extra person	€ 5,00 - € 6,50
child (3-11 yrs)	€ 2,00 - € 5,00
serviced pitch	€ 4,00
animal	€ 3,00 - € 3,50

Reservations

Made with 30% deposit and € 16 fee (from 16/7-15/8). Tel: 03 84 25 26 19.
Email: reservatio@rsl39.com

FR39060 Camping La Marjorie

640 boulevard de l'Europe, F-39000 Lons-le-Saunier (Jura)

La Marjorie is a spacious site set on the outskirts of the spa town of Lons-le-Saunier. It is a former municipal site with 200 level pitches, of which 185 are available for tourists. Mainly on hardstanding they are separated by well trimmed hedges interspersed with tall trees which gives privacy plus a little shade at some part of the day. Bordering one area of the site are open fields and woodlands. There are 130 pitches with electricity (6/10A) and 37 are fully serviced. The site is 2.5 km. from the centre of the town which is the capital town of the Jura region. There is a bicycle path from the site into town and a mountain bike track behind the site. English is spoken.

Facilities

Three well maintained toilet blocks, two modern and heated, have individual cubicles with washbasins and large showers. Baby baths, good facilities for disabled people, washing and ironing. Motorcaravan service point (charge). Small shop (15/6-31/8). Small bar with takeaway meals (all 15/6-31/8). TV room, table tennis, small play area, boules pitch, volleyball and football field. Archery, canoeing and riding can be arranged (fee). Off site: Local swimming pool 200 m. Bus stop 400 m. Restaurants 500 m. Bicycle hire 1.5 km. Fishing 3 km. Riding 5 km. Golf 6 km. Caves and waterfalls 17 km.

Open

1 April - 15 October.

At a glance

Welcome & Ambience	✓✓✓✓	Location	✓✓✓✓
Quality of Pitches	✓✓✓✓	Range of Facilities	✓✓✓✓

Directions

Site is off the N83 Lons-le-Saunier - Besancon road. Approaching Lons on the D52 or the N78 or D471, site is signed from the first roundabout on the outskirts of the town. When approaching from Bescancon on N83, follow signs for Club Nautique on outskirts of Lons - this takes you under the N83 to the site. Just before the entrance, be aware of traffic from the right. GPS: N46:41.053 E05:34.096

Charges 2005

Per unit incl. 2 persons	
with electricity (6A)	€ 11,90 - € 14,50
tent pitch incl. 2 persons	€ 13,70 - € 16,95
extra person	€ 10,00 - € 12,90
child (under 10 yrs)	€ 2,80 - € 3,70
dog	€ 1,50 - € 2,20
	€ 1,00

7% reduction for stays of 7-19 nights.
15% reduction for stays over 19 nights.

Reservations

Made with deposit (25%) and fee (€ 15).
Tel: 03 84 24 26 94.
Email: info@camping-marjorie.com

FR39080 Camping du Domaine de l'Epinette

15 rue de l'Epinette, F-39130 Chatillon (Jura)

This quiet site has the same owners as FR39040, but is more recently established and less than half the size. It is set in charming wooded countryside on land sloping down to the river Ain, which here is shallow and slow moving. There are 150 grassy pitches, of which 8 are occupied by a Dutch tour operator and 126 (including 4 with hardstanding) are available for touring units. These are arranged on terraces and separated by hedges and young bushes and trees, about half being shaded and half in the open. The number of slightly sloping and level pitches is about equal. Nearly all have electricity nearby, although some long leads might be needed. There is an attractive swimming pool, paddling pool and surrounds. An activity club for children takes place in July/August. Guided canoe trips on the river start and finish at the campsite.

Facilities

Two modern toilet blocks provide some Turkish toilets, showers and washbasins (some in cubicles). Unit for disabled visitors. Baby bath. Dishwashing and laundry sinks, all with warm or hot and cold water. Washing machine and dryer. Small shop for basics in reception. Snack bar and takeaway (evenings). A new reception, bar, TV room and larger shop were built in 2005. Playground. Table tennis under marquee. Boules. Direct access to river for swimming and canoeing (at your own risk). Off site: Riding 6 km. Golf 25 km. Shops, etc. in Dorcier 6 km.

Open

Mid-June - mid-September.

At a glance

Welcome & Ambience	✓✓✓✓	Location	✓✓✓✓✓
Quality of Pitches	✓✓✓✓	Range of Facilities	✓✓✓✓

Directions

From Lons-le-Saunier take D471 eastwards towards Champagnole. After about 8 km. fork right onto the D39 towards Doucier. After about 11 km. at Chatillon turn right onto D151 south towards Blye. Site is less than 2 km. on the left.

Charges 2005

Per unit incl. 2 persons and electricity	€ 16,00 - € 26,50
extra person	€ 2,00 - € 4,00
child (2-7 yrs)	free - € 2,50
animal	€ 2,00

Less 10% for 10 days or longer.
Camping Cheques accepted.

Reservations

Made with 25% deposit and € 30 fee for high season bookings. Tel: 03 84 25 71 44.
Email: info@domaine-epinette.com

FR39100 Camping Trélachaume

Lac de Vouglans, F-39260 Maisod (Jura)

This spacious campsite is situated in an attractive part of the Jura. From just outside the entrance, a path leads down to a sandy bathing beach on the edge of a large leisure lake, the Lac de Vouglans. Alternatively, you can take your canoe, boat, or fishing tackle by car and use the good road to the same spot. The site has 180 pitches of varying sizes up to large, of which 153 are for touring units. Of these, 85 (the ones with the most shade) have electrical connections (6A; nearly all French sockets). Some long leads will be needed in places. There is no restaurant or bar, etc. on the site, but a good bar with snacks and a takeaway operates 20 metres from the site entrance (1/6-31/8). In high season there are organised events and activities, many of them in the municipal 'salle des fêtes' on the edge of the site, which the owners take over for this period.

Facilities

Three modern toilet blocks contain British style WCs, washbasins and pre-set showers. En-suite facilities for disabled people. Baby bathing room. Washing machine, spin dryer and ironing board. Shop for basics (1/6-31/8). Gas supplies. Paddling pool (20/6-31/8). Playground. Table tennis. Volleyball. Boules. Bicycle hire. Only gas barbecues are permitted (available for hire). Off site: Bathing, boating, canoeing, sailing and fishing 1 km. Bus stop 2 km. Riding 3 km.

Open

29 April - 10 September.

At a glance

Welcome & Ambience	✓✓✓	Location	✓✓✓✓
Quality of Pitches	✓✓✓	Range of Facilities	✓✓✓

Directions

From Lons-le-Saunier, follow signs for Orgelet. On outskirts of Lons-le-Saunier, caravans and lorries must go straight on, southeast on the N78. Eventually they rejoin the D52 south to Orgelet. At Orgelet, take D470 going east, signed St Claude; immediately after Pont de la Pyle turn right to Maisod. Site is signed from there. From the south on the A404- when the motorway ends, continue north towards Orgelet and Lons-le-Saunier on the D31, D436, D27, and D470. Just before Charchilla go left on D301 to Maisod.

Charges 2005

Per unit incl. 2 persons	€ 11,50 - € 12,80
extra person (over 4 yrs)	€ 3,10
electricity	€ 2,70
dog	€ 1,50

Reservations

Contact site. Tel: 03 84 42 03 26.
Email: info@camping-trelachaume.com

FR39090 Camping Les Bords de Loue

Chemin du val d'Amour, F-39100 Parcey (Jura)

This spacious (10 ha) campsite, on a bank of the river Loue, enables canoeing, boating and fishing to be enjoyed direct from the site. It is also at the western end of the Val d'Amour, where the attractive countryside and villages make for pleasant walking and cycling. The site has 284 numbered grass pitches, of which 216 are for tourers. Some are undulating and/or slightly sloping, and only a few have shade. All have electricity (6A), some requiring long leads. Some of the pitches at the western end of the site would involve walks of over 100 m. to the nearest water tap. In July/August there are organised events and activities, including pony rides.

Facilities

Three modern toilet blocks contain British style WCs, washbasins in cabins and pre-set showers. Facilities for disabled people. Motorcaravan services. Washing machines and dryers. Gas supplies. Bar (all season). Snack bar and takeaway (July/Aug). Satellite TV. Swimming pool and paddling pool (1/5-1/9). Playground. Tennis (free outside July/Aug). Archery. Volleyball. Boules. Off site: Parcey 1 km. with shops, bar, ATM. Golf 1.5 km. Riding 4 km. Bicycle hire 7 km.

Open

15 April - 10 September.

At a glance

Welcome & Ambience	✓✓✓	Location	✓✓✓✓
Quality of Pitches	✓✓✓	Range of Facilities	✓✓✓✓

Directions

Parcey is 8 km. south of the centre of Dole, via the D405 (towards Lons-le-Saunier and Poligny). Site is on the north bank of the river Loue, signed from Parcey. From the north, leave the A39 at exit 6 (Dole). Go southwest for about 1 km. on the N75 (Beaune and Châlon-sur-Saône). At roundabout, turn left (southeast) onto the N5 to Parcey.

Charges 2005

Per person	€ 3,90
child (0-7 yrs)	€ 2,00
pitch	€ 4,50
electricity (6A)	€ 2,20
dog	€ 1,20

Reservations

Contact site. Tel: 03 84 71 03 82.
Email: contact@jura-camping.com

FR39110 Camping Le Moulin

Patornay, F-39130 Clairvaux-les-Lacs (Jura)

Patornay is a pleasant village, just by the river Ain where it starts to widen on its way to the Lac de Vouglans. This well equipped, 5 hectare campsite lies right on the river bank, with direct access for boating, canoeing and fishing. Of the 160 touring pitches, 120 are between well trimmed hedges and trees, with electricity and water taps very near. The other 40 are in a more natural area, where there is no electricity and water taps are a bit further apart. There is plenty to occupy campers on the site, but the countryside, its villages and other attractions are also well worth exploring on foot, by bicycle or by car. In July/August the site arranges activities and events for children and for all.

Facilities

Two modern unisex heated toilet blocks contain British style WCs, washbasins in cabins and pre-set showers. En-suite facilities for disabled people. Baby room. Motorcaravan services. Washing machines and dryers. Shop for basics. Bar, snack bar, takeaway and terrace (29/5-31/8). Satellite TV. Internet terminal. Games room. Swimming pool with slides and flume, paddling pool (29/5-31/8). Playground. Playing and football field. Table tennis. Volleyball. Boules. Off site: Pont-de-Poitte (200 m.) with supermarket, shops, restaurants, bars, takeaway, ATM, bus stop. Bicycle hire 1 km. Riding 4 km. Sailing 10 km. Golf 17 km.

Open

20 May - 17 September.

At a glance

Welcome & Ambience	✓✓✓✓	Location	✓✓✓✓
Quality of Pitches	✓✓✓✓	Range of Facilities	✓✓✓✓

Directions

From north or west, from Lons-le-Saunier, take the N78 in a southeasterly direction towards Pont-de-Poitte. After about 17 km. at Pont-de-Poitte, cross the bridge over the River Ain, towards Clairvaux-les-Lacs. After 100 m., turn left at site sign and immediately take the left fork.

Charges 2005

Per person	€ 4,00 - € 5,00
child (4-10 yrs)	€ 2,40 - € 3,00
pitch	€ 4,00 - € 5,00
electricity (10A)	€ 5,00 - € 6,00

Reservations

Contact site. Tel: 03 84 48 31 21.
Email: contact@camping-moulin.com

FR39120 Camping Beauregard

F-39130 Mesnois (Jura)

There are many good sites in the Jura, and Camping Beauregard is one that has been recommended by our French agent. The site can be found in rolling country, 500 metres from the River Ain. There are 192 pitches here, most with electrical connections, as well as a range of mobile homes and chalets. We plan to undertake a detailed inspection of this site in 2006.

Facilities	Directions
Sanitary building with special facilities for disabled visitors. Restaurant specialising in local cuisine. Bar. Swimming and paddling pools. Games room. Playground, Table tennis. Volleyball. Off site: Hiking and cycling trails. River Ain (fishing and swimming) 500 m. Riding.	From Lons-le-Saunier head south on the N78. Mesnois is signed to the left (D151) in the hamlet of Thuron, shortly after passing Nogna (and before reaching Pont de Poitte).

Open

1 April - 30 September.

Reservations

Contact site. Tel: 03 84 48 32 51.

Charges 2005

Per unit incl. 2 persons	€ 20,00
extra person	€ 3,60
child (2-8 yrs)	€ 2,20
electricity	€ 2,60
Less 20% in low season.	

FR70020 Camping International du Lac Vesoul

F-70000 Vesoul (Haute-Saône)

This is one of the better examples of a municipal site and is part of a leisure park around a large lake. A five kilometre path has been created around the lake for jogging, walking and cycling and there is a large open space for ball games or sunbathing, along with a good children's playground and bar/restaurant. A map at the entrance shows the water areas for swimming, boating and windsurfing. Watersports are organised by the Club Nautique Haut-Saonois Vesoul and there is also tennis, table tennis, archery, basketball and night-time carp fishing. The campsite does not have direct access to the lake as it is separated by a security fence, but access is possible at the site entrance. There are 160 good sized, level, grass pitches, all with electricity. Access is from hard roads and pitches are separated by shrubs. There is a large hard area in the centre of the site brightened by flowers and young trees.

Facilities	Directions
Three good quality toilet blocks, one heated, are well spaced around the site. They have a mix of British and Turkish style WCs and free, pre-mixed warm water from push-button taps in the washbasins and showers. Baby room. Facilities for disabled visitors. Washing machines and dryers.	On road D457 to west of Vesoul on route to Besançon, well signed around the town. GPS: N47:37.812 E06:07.70

Open

1 March - 31 October.

At a glance

Welcome & Ambience	✓✓✓✓	Location	✓✓✓✓
Quality of Pitches	✓✓✓✓	Range of Facilities	✓✓✓

Charges guide

Per person	€ 3,00
child (under 7 yrs)	€ 1,30
pitch with electricity (10A)	€ 5,10
vehicle	€ 2,10
No credit cards.	

Reservations

Contact site. Tel: 03 84 76 22 86.

FR90000 Camping L'Etang des Forges

11 rue Béthouart, F-90000 Belfort (Tre.-de-Belfort)

Belfort (known as the City of the Lion) is a historic fortified town with much history. The region is well endowed with footpaths and cycle trails and this site would make a good base for a longer stay. There are also opportunities for ballooning and hang-gliding. Although 178 pitches are marked out, this very spacious site only uses 90 of them, and you should always be able to find room here. The pitches are all on level, mostly open ground divided by low bushes. A few trees around one end give a little shade to some pitches and there are electricity hook-ups (6A) to all pitches and a good supply of water taps. The reception building also contains a small shop and cafe.

Facilities	Directions
A single modern sanitary building (heated in cool weather) provides washbasins in cubicles, a suite for disabled people, dishwashing and laundry sinks, a washing machine and dryer. Motorcaravan service point. Outdoor swimming pool. Volleyball. Table tennis. Small playground. TV Room. Shop and cafe (1/7-31/8). Internet terminal. Off site: Large supermarket is on edge of town on the Mulhouse road.	Site is northeast of town centre towards Offemont, adjacent to the lake and sports facilities (well signed). GPS: N47:39.200 E06:51.866

Open

14 April - 30 September.

At a glance

Welcome & Ambience	✓✓✓✓	Location	✓✓✓✓✓
Quality of Pitches	✓✓✓✓	Range of Facilities	✓✓✓✓

Charges 2005

Per person	€ 3,40 - € 3,80
child (4-9 yrs)	€ 2,50 - € 3,10
pitch	€ 8,00 - € 8,50
electricity	€ 3,00
animal	€ 1,00 - € 1,50

Reservations

Not usually necessary. Tel: 03 84 22 54 92.
Email: contact@campings-belfort.com

MAP 9

Deep valleys dividing mountain slopes, covered in lush alpine pastures and evergreen woods - this is the Savoy Alps bordering Switzerland. Further south you'll come across the Dauphiné Alps which, although they can appear harsh and forbidding, offer spectacular scenery.

DÉPARTEMENTS: 38 ISÈRE, 73 SAVOIE, 74 HAUTE-SAVOIE

MAJOR CITY: GRENOBLE

Lying between the Rhône Valley and the Alpine borders with Switzerland and Italy are the old provinces of Savoie and Dauphiné. This is an area of enormous granite outcrops, deeply riven by spectacular glacier hewn and river etched valleys. One of the world's leading winter playgrounds there is also a range of outdoor activities in the summer. Despite development, great care has been taken to blend the old with the new and many traditional villages still retain their charm and historical interest. For many, it is an opportunity to escape the crowds and enjoy some clean air, unusual wildlife, stunning views, hidden lakes and sometimes isolated villages in spectacular mountain settings.

From Chambéry, north to the shores of Lac Léman (Lake Geneva) are many towns and villages that, since Roman times, have attracted visitors to take the waters. Aix-les-Bains, Evian and Annecy were three major lakeside spa resorts of the Victorians; while Chamonix and Grenoble attracted the 19th century travellers who pioneered modern skiing and 'alpinism'. To the north is the region of Chartreuse famous for its monastery and liqueur!

Places of interest

Aix-les-Bains: spa resort on the Lac du Bourget, boat excursions to the Royal Abbey of Hautecombe

Albertville: 1992 Winter Olympics, museum, now has an active night-life!

Annecy: canal-filled lakeside town, 12th century château, old quarter

Bourg-St-Maurice: centre of Savoie café society

Chambéry: old quarter, Dukes of Savoie château, Savoie museum.

Chamonix: site of first Winter Olympics in 1924, world capital of mountain climbing

Evian-les-Bains: spa and casino on Lake Geneva

Grenoble: University city, Fort de la Bastille

Cuisine of the region

Plat gratiné applies to a wide variety of dishes; in the Alps this means cooked in breadcrumbs.

Farcement (Farçon Savoyard): potatoes baked with cream, eggs, bacon, dried pears and prunes

Féra: a freshwater lake fish

Fondue: hot melted cheese and white wine

Gratin Dauphinois: potato dish with cream, cheese and garlic

Gratin Savoyard: another potato dish with cheese and butter

Lavaret: a freshwater lake fish, like salmon

Longeole: a country sausage

Lotte: a burbot, not unlike an eel

Tartiflette: potato, bacon, onions and Reblochon cheese

FR38120 Camping du Bontemps

F-38150 Vernioz (Isère)

This spacious, attractive and well cared for site is enhanced by a wide variety of coniferous and deciduous trees planted by the dedicated owner nearly 30 years ago. The 200 large, level and grassy pitches are arranged in groups, partly separated by neat hedges, all with water and electricity. Seven pitches are used for mobile homes and chalets and a group at the back is used by weekenders. The shop, bar/restaurant and landscaped swimming pool are near the entrance. The large sports area and excellent activity hall are off to one side minimising noise problems. There is a field and stable for horses, a small river and fishing lake next to the site. This is an excellent site for both short and long stays.

Facilities

The excellent two main toilet blocks contain all the necessary facilities. Motorcaravan service points. Shop. Bar/restaurant (all season). Swimming pools (June - 30 Sept). Play areas. Minigolf. Table tennis. Tennis. Badminton. Archery. Riding. Activities (high season). Off site: Vernioz 2 km. Bicycle hire 7 km. Golf 20 km.

Open

1 April - 30 September.

At a glance

Welcome & Ambience	✓✓✓✓✓	Location	✓✓✓✓
Quality of Pitches	✓✓✓✓	Range of Facilities	✓✓✓✓

Directions

Exit A7 south of Lyons at junction 11. Continue south for about 7 km. on the N7. Just north of Auberives turn left on D37 and follow campsite signs for 7 km. GPS: N45:25.485 E04:55.729

Charges 2006

Per person	€ 5,00
child (under 7 yrs)	€ 2,50
pitch incl. electricity	€ 9,00 - € 11,50

Reservations

Essential in high season. Tel: 04 74 57 83 52. Email: info@campinglebontemps.com

FR38010 Le Coin Tranquille

F-38490 Les Abrets (Isère)

Set in the Dauphiny countryside north of Grenoble, Le Coin Tranquille is truly a 'quiet corner', especially outside school holiday times, although it is still popular with families in high season. Les Abrets is well placed for visits to the Savoie regions and the Alps. It is an attractive and well maintained site of 192 grass pitches (160 for touring units), all with electricity. They are separated by well maintained hedges of hydrangea, flowering shrubs and a range of trees to make a lovely environment doubly enhanced by the rural aspect and marvellous views across to the mountains. This is a popular, family run site with friendly staff (English spoken) that makes a wonderful base for exploring the area, especially in low season. Used by a tour operator (17 pitches). A 'Sites et Paysages' member.

Facilities

The central large sanitary block is of good quality, heated in low season. Washbasins in cabins, facilities for children and disabled people and a laundry room. Two other blocks on either edge of the site. Busy shop. Excellent restaurant, open all year (closed two days weekly in low season). Swimming pool and paddling pool (15/5-30/9). Play area. TV/video room, games room and quiet reading room. Supervised games for children and weekly entertainment for adults including live music (not discos) mid-May - end-August. Bicycle hire. Off site: Riding 6 km. Fishing 8 km. Golf 25 km. Les Abrets 2 km.

Open

26 March - 31 October.

At a glance

Welcome & Ambience	✓✓✓✓✓	Location	✓✓✓✓
Quality of Pitches	✓✓✓✓✓	Range of Facilities	✓✓✓✓

Directions

Site is east of Les Abrets. From the roundabout in the centre of town take N6 towards Chambery, turning left in just under 2 km. (signed Camping). Follow signs along lane for just over 1 km. and entrance is on right. GPS: N45:32.482 E05:36.489

Charges 2006

Per pitch incl. 2 persons	€ 14,50 - € 26,50
extra person	€ 4,00 - € 6,50
child (2-7 yrs)	€ 2,50 - € 4,50
electricity (2/6A)	€ 1,30 - € 3,00
Camping Cheques accepted.	

Reservations

Write with deposit (€ 134) and fee (€ 16). Tel: 04 76 32 13 48. Email: contact@coin-tranquille.com

Le Coin Tranquille - 38490 Les Abrets   www.coin-tranquille.com

FR38050 Camping Caravaning Le Temps Libre

F-38150 Bouge-Chambalud (Isère)

You will receive a warm welcome at this spacious, family run site which is close to the A7 motorway, between Lyon and Valence, making it ideal for an overnight stay. It would also make a base to discover this interesting region – discover the rolling countryside, vineyards, orchards and picturesque villages. There are 199 pitches, with 90 available for tourers, the mobile homes and seasonal pitches being in a separate section. The medium to large, party sloping, grassy pitches are mostly separated by high hedges and trees giving privacy and some shade. All have 9A electricity and water close by. Most are in cul-de-sacs, in groups of eight and a few have tricky access. There is a large hardstanding area with electricity for motorcaravans and overnight stays. The site has a large pool complex and sunbathing area comprising a swimming pool plus three other pools with toboggans to suit all ages (no Bermuda style shorts). There is a large area adjacent for youngsters to let off steam. A 'Sites et Paysages' member.

Facilities

Three toilet blocks, two (both refurbished) for tourers, one near the entrance and one in the centre by the pool. Motorcaravan service point. Good shop (1/5-31/8), bar/restaurant and takeaway (all 1/7-31/8). Swimming pools. Two playgrounds. Club/TV room. Football pitch. Volleyball. Boules. 3 tennis courts (free). Fishing. Minigolf. Organised activities for all ages and pony cart rides (July and Aug). Internet access. Off site: Golf and riding 10 km.

Open

1 April - 30 September.

At a glance

Welcome & Ambience	✓✓✓✓	Location	✓✓✓✓
Quality of Pitches	✓✓✓	Range of Facilities	✓✓✓✓

Directions

From A7 motorway take exit 12 (Chanas) or from the N7 take D510 east towards Grenoble for about 7 km. to Bougé Chambalud. Turn right in the village (site signed) and entrance is a few hundred metres.

Charges 2006

Per unit incl. 2 persons	€ 14,00 - € 20,00
extra person	€ 4,00 - € 6,50
child (2-4 yrs)	€ 1,50 - € 3,00
electricity (9A)	€ 4,00

Camping Cheques accepted.

Reservations

Contact site. Tel: 04 74 84 04 09.
Email: camping.temps-libre@libertysurf.fr

FR38090 Camping Caravaning Belle Roche

F-38930 Lalley (Isère)

Belle Roche, a good, spacious, family run site, has extremely pleasant mountain views all round and is convenient for an overnight stop, or even a longer stay. The level site is only a few years old, so is rather open at present with very little shade, but it is nonetheless neat and well maintained throughout. There are 57 large, slightly uneven and slightly sloping pitches, many part grass with a gravel hardstanding, partially delineated by shrubs and young trees. Rock pegs are necessary. All have 10A electricity (long leads may be necessary) and there are ample water points. This is a good base from which to explore the Vercors National Park ánd for enjoying this scenic but relatively unknown Trièves part of the Isère.

Facilities

Two modern, well equipped and clean toilet blocks provide some washbasins in private cabins. Facilities for disabled visitors. Good motorcaravan service point. Bar/TV room and terrace serving simple, good value meals (all season). Bread from reception. Swimming pool (19 x 12 m; mid-May-Sept.) with large sunbathing area and sun beds. Large play area. Off site: Shop 400 m. Bicycle hire 8 km. Riding 15 km.

Open

1 April - 15 October.

At a glance

Welcome & Ambience	✓✓✓✓	Location	✓✓✓✓
Quality of Pitches	✓✓✓✓	Range of Facilities	✓✓✓✓

Directions

Follow N75 south from Grenoble (65 km.) turn left onto D66, signed Lalley, Mens and campsite, and then follow camping signs through the village. GPS: N44:45.295 E05:40.736

Charges 2005

Per unit incl. 2 persons	€ 11,50 - € 14,50
extra person	€ 3,00
child (0-7 yrs)	€ 1,50
electricity (10A)	€ 3,20

Reservations

Advised for July/Aug (25% deposit).
Tel: 04 76 34 75 33. Email: gildapatt@aol.com

(197)

FR38070 Camping L'Oursière

F-38250 Villard de Lans (Isère)

This friendly, family run site is ideally situated within easy walking distance of the attractive summer and winter resort of Villard de Lans which provides a very wide range of activities. It is ideal for those who prefer a peaceful site in a more natural setting. The good sized grass and stone pitches are slightly uneven but have magnificent views over the surrounding mountains. There are 186 marked pitches, 155 for touring and most have electricity (6/10A). A variety of trees offer some shade. Rock pegs are essential. Because the town of Villard de Lans offers so much entertainment, little is organised on site. There are good shops, bars, restaurants, a bank, swimming pool complex, ice skating rink (last two open most of the year) and a gambling casino. There are many marked walks and bike rides (on and off road) around the town, several starting from the site. This is an excellent value for money base for those seeking a relaxing or active holiday, both summer and winter.

Facilities

Four heated and clean toilet blocks, partly refurbished, each with all the necessary facilities including washing machine, dryer, ski store and drying room. Facilities for disabled visitors. Motorcaravan service point. A single building houses the reception, bar (July/Aug), cosy lounge with open fireplace, TV room, several games rooms, ski store and drying room. Snack bar (July/Aug). Internet access. Play area. Boules. Volleyball. Trout fishing. Off site: Bus service to Autrans and Grenoble plus excursions. Free bus service to ski resorts (winter). Supermarket 1 km. Bicycle hire 1 km. Riding 2 km. Golf 5 km.

Open

All year excl. October and November.

At a glance

Welcome & Ambience	✓✓✓✓	Location	✓✓✓✓
Quality of Pitches	✓✓✓	Range of Facilities	✓✓✓

Directions

From autoroute A48, northwest of Grenoble, take exit 13 (going south) or 3A (going north). Follow N532 to Sassenage, turn west at a roundabout on D531. The road climbs to Villard de Lans (about 25 km). On entering Villard de Lans, fork left signed Villard Centre and site is shortly on the left. Entrance closed 12.00 – 16.00 in low season. This is the only recommended route for caravans and motorcaravans. GPS: N45:4.655 E05:33.37

Charges 2005

Per unit incl. 2 persons	€ 12,25 - € 13,75
extra person	€ 3,55 - € 4,05
child (5-10 yrs)	€ 3,00 - € 3,50
electricity	€ 3,00 - € 6,00

Reservations

Advised for high season with deposit (€ 7 per night) and fee (€ 8). Tel: 04 76 95 14 77.
Email: info@camping-oursiere.fr

FR38040 Camping La Rencontre du Soleil

Route de l'Alpe d'Huez, F-38520 Bourg-d'Oisans (Isère)

This part of the Isère is an attractive and popular region with some exceptional scenery for which this site proves a good base from which to explore. Pleasant, friendly and family run, it nestles between two impressive mountain ranges, at the base of France's largest National Park, Le Parc des Ecrins with its external snows and abundance of rare and protected plants. Explore the many hidden villages and the breathtaking mountain passes close by. Bourg d'Oisans lies in the Romanche valley 725 m. above sea level surrounded by high mountains. This is a real sun trap and gets very hot in summer. The area is a regular staging point for the Tour de France and the Alpe d'Huez road past the campsite, with its 21 hairpin bends is revered by serious cyclists as it is often used as the 'king of the mountain' stage. This compact site, only 2 km. from Bourg d'Oisans has 73 level, hedged pitches, most of average size, with mature trees offering good shade (43 for touring). Electricity is available (2, 6 or 10A). Rock pegs are advised. Canoeing, rafting, riding and many other activities are possible nearby. The site is used by a tour operator (20 pitches). A 'Sites et Paysages' member.

Facilities

A large heated toilet block provides all the usual amenities, all of high quality and extremely clean and well maintained, but no facilities for disabled people. Washing machine and dryer. Motorcaravan service point. Bread to order. Restaurant and takeaway (all season). Sitting room with TV and children's play room adjoining. Small, sheltered swimming pool (all season). Play area. Programme of activities in high season includes walking, mountain biking and a mini-club for children. Off site: Supermarket 1 km. towards Bourg d'Oisans. Fishing 5 km. Bicycle hire and riding 2 km. Canoeing, rafting, riding, hiking, climbing and many other activities nearby. Cable car at Alpe d'Huez. Some skiing normally possible until mid-July at Les Deux Alpes (16 km).

At a glance

Welcome & Ambience	✓✓✓✓✓	Location	✓✓✓✓
Quality of Pitches	✓✓✓	Range of Facilities	✓✓✓✓

Directions

Leave Bourg d'Oisans on the N91 towards Briancon. Shortly after crossing the river, on a sharp right hand bend, turn left on D211 signed Alpe d'Huez. Site is on left just beyond Camping la Piscine. Entrance is on a sharp bend - take care.
GPS: N45:03.940 E06:02.381

Charges 2006

Per unit incl. 2 persons	€ 14,70 - € 24,00
extra person	€ 4,95 - € 6,00
child (2-5 yrs)	€ 3,35 - € 4,50
electricity (2/10A)	€ 3,00 - € 4,20
Camping Cheques accepted.	

Reservations

Advised in high season with 25% deposit and fee (€ 15.25) Tel: 04 76 79 12 22.
Email: rencontre.soleil@wanadoo.fr

Open

11 May - 15 September.

FR38080 Camping Caravaning Au Joyeux Réveil

Le Château, F-38880 Autrans (Isère)

The small town of Autrans is set on a plateau, 1,050 m. high, in the Vercors region. Here the days can be very hot and sunny and the nights quite chilly. The well organised site is run by a very friendly family (English is spoken). It is ideally situated for any of the activities that this wonderful area has to offer: from walking, mountain biking and pot-holing in summer to downhill and cross-country skiing in winter, it is all there for you in magnificent scenery. The site is on the outskirts of the town, set below a ski jump and short lift. The 111 pitches (80 for touring) are mainly on grass, reasonably level with small trees giving only a little shade. All have electricity connections and are in a sunny location with fantastic views over the surrounding wooded mountains. There is a new swimming pool area with a separate paddling pool and two other pools with river and slide. The D531 and the D106 look a little daunting on the map and do involve a stiff climb but they are good roads with no difficult bends. A 'Sites et Paysages' member.

Facilities

The new toilet block is very well appointed, with under-floor heating and all the expected facilities. Another new building houses a bar with terrace, snack bar/takeaway (July and August). New pool area with two pools, toboggan for children, sunbathing area and a separate paddling pool. Small play area and large chess table. TV room. Internet point. Off site: Autrans with a few shops, restaurants, bars and a bank 500 m. Villard de Lans, supermarket, shops, restaurants, bars, ice rink and many other activities 16 km. Short ski lift is near the site and a shuttle bus runs regularly (in winter) to the longer runs (5 km). Fishing, bicycle hire or riding 300 m. Marked walks. Bus to Villard de Lans and Grenoble several times a day.

Open

1 December - 31 March and 1 May - 30 September.

At a glance

Welcome & Ambience	✓✓✓✓✓	Location	✓✓✓✓
Quality of Pitches	✓✓✓	Range of Facilities	✓✓✓✓

Directions

Exit autoroute A48, northwest of Grenoble at junction 13 (going south) or 3A (going north). Follow N532 to Sassenage, turn west at a roundabout onto D531 to Lans en Vercors. At a roundabout turn right on D106 signed Autrans. On entering Autrans turn right at roundabout (site signed) and very shortly right again. Site is on your left. This is the only route recommended for caravans and motorcaravans. GPS: N45:10.515 E05:32.87

Charges 2005

Per unit incl. 1 or 2 persons	€ 16,00 - € 25,00
extra person	€ 5,00
child (under 6 yrs)	€ 3,50
electricity (2-10A)	€ 2,00 - € 4,60

Winter prices - apply to site.
Camping Cheques accepted.

Reservations

Write to site with € 50 deposit and € 10 fee.
Tel: 04 76 95 33 44.
Email: camping-au-joyeux-reveil@wanadoo.fr

FR38100 Camping Belledonne

Rochetaillée, F-38520 Bourg-d'Oisans (Isère)

This extremely neat and spacious site, takes its name from the nearby Belledonne mountain range, and one of the six valleys of the Oisans area. All are impressive, but there is something rather magnificent about the views surrounding this site; furthermore it enjoys sunshine for most of the day. Access roads throughout are tarmac and each of the 180 grassy pitches, 148 for touring, are not only level and well drained, but also generously sized, with electricity (3/6A). There is some road noise from a few pitches. The site is divided into six areas, each named after one of the local valleys. Beech hedges and abundant mature trees provide ample privacy and shade. A cosy bar/restaurant and terrace (open all season) is next to an attractive pool complex, comprising two swimming pools, one paddling pool and sunbathing space surrounded by well tended gardens and grass spaces. In July and August the site becomes quite lively with a daily programme of organised activities. All in all this is a friendly and well run site (English spoken), suitable for relaxing or as a base for exploring this famous mountain area. Take to the hills for the sights and scents of the many rare and protected wild flowers. A 'Sites et Paysages' member.

Facilities

Two sanitary blocks include washbasins in cabins, a mixture of British and Turkish style toilets, washing up sinks, laundry, baby changing rooms and facilities for disabled visitors. Shop. Bar/restaurant and takeaway (all open all season). TV and games room. Swimming and paddling pools. Tennis. Table tennis. Volleyball. Good play area and a large grass meadow with comprehensive fitness course. Bicycle hire (July/Aug). Off site: Allemont, shops 2 km. Interesting town of Bourg d'Oisans, shops, bars, restaurants, banks and supermarket (market on Saturdays) 8 km. Riding and fishing nearby. Hiking, mountain biking, white water rafting, canoeing, bungee jumping, paragliding and much more.

Open

20 May - 9 September.

At a glance

Welcome & Ambience	✓✓✓✓	Location	✓✓✓✓
Quality of Pitches	✓✓✓✓	Range of Facilities	✓✓✓✓✓

Directions

The site is 8 km. west of Bourg d'Oisans. From Grenoble take N85 to Vizille and then N91 towards Bourg d'Oisans. In Rochetaillée branch left (site signed) onto D526, signed Allemont and site is approx. 250 m. on right. GPS: N45:06.854 E06:00.459

Charges 2005

Per pitch incl. 2 persons	€ 15,10 - € 22,40
incl. 3 persons	€ 17,90 - € 26,20
extra person	€ 4,00 - € 5,80
child (under 7 yrs)	€ 2,80 - € 3,80
electricity (3-6A)	€ 2,80 - € 3,90
dog	€ 1,10

Camping Cheques accepted.

Reservations

Made with € 15 fee; contact site.
Tel: 04 76 80 07 18. Email: belledon@club-internet.fr

FR38110 Camping Le Champ du Moulin

Bourg d'Arud, F-38520 Venosc (Isère)

With steep-sided mountains on all sides, Le Champ du Moulin nestles comfortably on the floor of the narrow Vénéon valley. Even though the bustling town of Le Bourg d'Oisans is only a 15 minute drive away, this peaceful campsite is enjoyed by visitors in both winter and summer. It is a good base for skiing and for exploring this beautiful region. A telecabin near the entrance transports visitors to Les 2 Alpes. This renowned resort lies out of sight over a sharp rise and offers miles of ski runs in winter and extensive glacier skiing and mountain hiking in summer. Watching over the site is the more traditional village of Venosc which clings to the hillside a short walk away. Its church, narrow streets, old buildings and notable craft shops are a delightful alternative to the more recently developed glitzy ski towns. On site, generous stone and grass pitches are part-shaded by large trees and all have electricity (up to 10A). Rock pegs are essential. When the mountain snows start to melt in late May/early June, the river beside the site changes from its winter trickle to an impressive torrent. Parents with small children need to be especially vigilant. On the edge of the Ecrins National Park, this is a peaceful location with stunning mountain scenery and miles of marked cycling and walking trails. It is an ideal site for active outdoor families rather than those seeking late-night revelry. A 'Sites et Paysages' member.

Facilities

A heated toilet block (undergoing refurbishment) is welcome and clothes soon dry on the racks provided. Baby room and spacious facilities for disabled people. Laundry. Motorcaravan service point. Chalet restaurant/bar with very good home cooking at easy-on-the-pocket prices. Small shop sharing reception with bread each morning. Play area. TV room. Computer room with internet access. Fishing. Off site: Municipal heated outdoor pools and flume next door open in summer, together with a playground, tennis courts and tree-top adventure park. White water rafting, canoeing, paragliding, bungee jumping, hill walking and off-road biking available nearby. Discounted ski passes. Riding 0.5 km, golf 3 km. (both summer only).

Open

15 December - 30 April and 1 June - 15 Se.

At a glance

Welcome & Ambience	✓✓✓	Location	✓✓✓✓
Quality of Pitches	✓✓✓	Range of Facilities	✓✓✓

Directions

From the Grenoble direction, pass through Bourg d'Oisans on the N91 following signs for Briancon. After 3 km. turn right at sharp left hand bend onto the D530 signed Venosc. In 8 km. along the twisting valley road, pass the telecabin station on the left. Site is on right in 400 m. GPS: N44:59.182 E06:7208

Charges 2005

Per unit incl. 1 or 2 persons	€ 13,00 - € 18,00
extra person	€ 3,80 - € 4,60
child (3-7 yrs)	€ 2,30 - € 2,80
electricity (3/6/10A)	€ 2,50 - € 8,00
dog	€ 0,50 - € 1,00

Less 10% for 14 nights, 15% for 21 nights. Special ski arrangements.

Reservations

Made with deposit (and high season € 15 booking fee). Tel: 04 76 80 07 38. Email: christian.avallet@wanadoo.fr

FR38140 Camping Le Colporteur

Le Mas du Plan, F-38521 Bourg-d'Oisans (Isère)

At over 700 metres above sea level, Bourg d'Oisans is in the largest national park in France. It is surrounded by high mountains making it a real suntrap and can be very hot in summer. The area is revered by serious cyclists as several mountain roads close by are regularly used by the Tour de France. This is an ideal base for exploring this scenic region with its abundance of wild flowers, old villages and rushing waterfalls; by car, on foot or by bike. The site is within a few minutes level walk of the attractive small market town with its many shops, banks, bars and restaurants, making this an ideal spot for motorcaravanners. The owners have recently put in much effort to improve this attractive site. There are 150 level grassy pitches, 130 for touring, mostly separated by hedging and a variety of mature trees that offer some shade. All pitches have 15A electricity and rock pegs are advised. Although there is no pool on the site, campers are given free entry to the adjacent municipal pool. In July and August the attractive bar/restaurant is the focal point for evening activities.

Facilities

Large well equipped, modern, airy toilet block has all the necessary facilities including washbasins in cabins, a baby room and a spacious en-suite room for disabled campers. Games room. Boules. Table tennis. Volleyball. Small play area. Organised family activities (July/Aug). Off site: Shops, bars, restaurants in town and supermarket 500 m. Cycling, mountain biking, hiking, rafting, canoeing, rock climbing, horse riding, hang-gliding, Parc des Ecrins, cable cars (July/August) and many mountain passes. Bus services.

Open

1 May – 30 September.

At a glance

Welcome & Ambience	✓✓✓✓	Location	✓✓✓✓✓
Quality of Pitches	✓✓✓✓	Range of Facilities	✓✓✓

Directions

Site is in the centre of Bourg d'Oisans. From the direction of Grenoble follow the N91 into the town and shortly after the road bears left in the town centre and just beyond a petrol station, turn right (site signed). Follow signs to campsite, a few hundred metres. GPS: N45:03.156 E06:02.13

Charges 2005

Per unit incl. 2 persons	€ 20,00
extra person	€ 5,00
child (5-10 yrs)	€ 2,90
child (0-5 yrs)	€ 1,80
electricity	€ 3,60

Reservations

Advised in high season and made for min. 8 days with deposit and fee. Tel: 04 76 79 11 44. Email: info@camping-colporteur.com

FR73020 Camping Caravaneige Le Versoyen

Route des Arcs, F-73700 Bourg-St Maurice (Savoie)

Bourg-St-Maurice is on a small, level plain at an altitude of 830 m. on the River Isère, surrounded by high, often snow-capped mountains. For many years a winter ski resort, it now caters for visitors all year round. The Parc National de la Vanoise is nearby, along with a wealth of interesting places. Le Versoyen itself attracts visitors all year round (except for a month when they close). The site's 205 unseparated, flat pitches (180 for touring) are marked by numbers on the tarmac roads and all have electrical connections (4/6A). Most are on grass but some are on tarmac hardstanding making them ideal for use by motorcaravans or in winter. Trees typically seen at this altitude give shade in some parts, although most pitches have almost none. Duckboards are provided for snow and wet weather. This is a good base for winter skiing, summer walking, climbing, rafting or canoeing, or for car excursions.

Facilities

Two acceptable toilet blocks can be heated, although the provision may be hard pressed in high season. British and Turkish style WCs. Laundry. Motorcaravan service facilities. Heated restroom with TV. Small bar with takeaway in summer. Free shuttle in high season to funicular railway. Off site: Fishing or bicycle hire 200 m. Riding 1 km. Golf 15 km. Commercial centre (500 m.) with a variety of shops. Tennis and swimming pool 500 m. (free for campers during July/Aug). Bourg-st-Maurice 1.5 km. Les Arcs (15 minutes by funicular railway) with ski lifts, to wonderful mountain tracks for bikes and ramblers (15 km). Cross country ski track (up to 30 km. in winter) just behind site.

Directions

Site is 1.5 km. east of Bourg-St-Maurice on the CD119 Les Arcs road. GPS: N45:37.324 E06:47.010

Charges 2006

Per unit incl. 2 persons	€ 10,20 - € 15,60
extra person	€ 3,60 - € 5,55
child (7-13 yrs)	€ 3,40 - € 4,85
electricity (4-12A)	€ 4,30 - € 7,55
dog	€ 1,00

Reservations

Write to site with deposit (€ 30) and fee (€ 10).
Tel: 04 79 07 03 45. Email: leversoyen@wanadoo.fr

Open

All year excl. 7 Nov. - 4 Dec. and 2 - 25 May.

At a glance

| Welcome & Ambience | ✓✓✓✓ | Location | ✓✓✓✓ |
| Quality of Pitches | ✓✓✓✓ | Range of Facilities | ✓✓✓ |

FR73030 Camping Les Lanchettes

 Mobile homes ▶ page 424

F-73210 Peisey-Nancroix (Savoie)

This site is in the beautiful Vanoise National Park and at 1,470 m. is one of the highest campsites in this guide. There is a steep climb to the site, not recommended for underpowered units, although the spectacular scenery is well worth the effort. A natural, terraced site, it has 90 good size, reasonably level and well drained, grassy/stony pitches, with 80 used for touring units, 70 having electricity. Because it is very cold in winter and quite cold on some spring and autumn evenings (warm bedding necessary) there are no outside taps. In winter about 30 of the pitches at the bottom of the site are unused as they become part of a cross-country ski run. For those who love mountains, wonderful scenery, flora and fauna and for those wanting a walking/biking summer holiday, from novice to expert, this is the site for you. In winter it is ideal for the serious skier being close to the famous resort of Les Arcs (via free bus service and cable car). A 'Sites et Paysages' member.

Facilities

Comprehensive facilities are all in the basement of the house, very cosy in winter. The large, open entrances are closed during cold weather and when the evenings are cold allowing the building to be heated. Motorcaravan service point. Restaurant with takeaway (July/Aug. and mid Dec-mid April). Playground. Club/TV room. Large tent/marquee used in bad weather for a meeting place and as a dormitory by those with small tents. In winter a small bus (free) runs to all the hotels, bars, ski tows etc. and calls at the campsite. A wide range of footpaths and mountain bike rides is available in the valley and mountains around. Some chair lifts carry bikes up to the walking/bike tracks high up in the mountains; the descent is breathtaking. The roads around are ideal for the serious road cyclist. Off site: Accompanied walks (one free) in the National Park. Riding next to site. Village of Peisey-Nancroix with a few restaurants, bars and shops 3 km. Les Arcs winter sports centre 6 km. Outdoor swimming pool and bicycle hire 6 km. Golf and indoor pool 8 km.

Directions

From Albertville take N90 towards Bourg-St-Maurice, through Moutiers and Aime and 9 km. further turn right on D87, signed Landry and Peisey-Nancroix. Follow road down and then up a reasonably wide, steep, winding hill (with hairpin bends) for 10 km. Pass through Peisey-Nancroix and Nancroix; site is on right about 1 km. beyond Nancroix. GPS: N45:31.882 E06:46.536

Charges 2006

Per unit incl. 2 persons	€ 11,60 - € 13,10
extra person	€ 4,00 - € 4,40
child (2-7 yrs)	€ 2,30 - € 2,50
electricity (3-10A)	€ 3,00 - € 7,30
dog	€ 1,00 - € 1,20

Camping Cheques accepted.

Reservations

Made with 25% deposit and fee (€ 10).
Tel: 04 79 07 93 07. Email: lanchettes@free.fr

Open

15 December - 15 October.

At a glance

| Welcome & Ambience | ✓✓✓✓ | Location | ✓✓✓✓ |
| Quality of Pitches | ✓✓✓✓ | Range of Facilities | ✓✓✓ |

FR73040 Camping Municipal Le Savoy

Avenue du Parc, F-73190 Challes-les-Eaux (Savoie)

This attractive, well run and easily accessible municipal site is surrounded by mountains and only a few hundred metres from the centre of the spa town of Challes-les-Eaux. There are 100 level pitches, mostly for touring and 91 with electricity (5A). Some are separated by beech hedges and mature trees offer some shade. There are 12 pitches with hardstanding for motorcaravans, 47 part hardstanding super pitches with water, drain and 10A electricity with the remainder on grass. Rock pegs are advised for hardstanding areas. This site is a very good base for touring this scenic region and makes an ideal stop over for those on route to the Fréjus Tunnel and Italy.

Facilities

Two modern, very clean and well equipped toilet blocks with all the necessary facilities although they may be stretched in high season. Facilities for disabled visitors. Most of the facilities are near the entrance but there is also a small toilet block in the middle of the site. Bar, snacks and a meal every Friday (15/6-30/8). Good sized playground. Boules, table tennis and table football. Off site: Adjacent is a small park with a small lake for swimming and the municipal tennis and volleyball courts. Challes-les-Eaux, with shops, banks, bars, restaurants, spar, casino and minigolf, a few hundred metres. Interesting old town of Chambery 6 km. Fréjus Tunnel 96 km. and Bardonecchia (Italy) 110 km.

Open

1 May - 30 September.

At a glance

| Welcome & Ambience | ✓✓✓ | Location | ✓✓✓✓ |
| Quality of Pitches | ✓✓✓✓ | Range of Facilities | ✓✓✓ |

Directions

Leave autoroute A43 at exit 20 and head towards Challes-les-Eaux. Site is on the N6 at the northern edge of the town, just before a small park and lake. Turn right at traffic lights, site well signed. GPS: N45:33.094 E05:59.036

Charges 2005

per person	€ 3,10
child (0-12 yrs)	€ 1,30
pitch	€ 3,55 - € 4,00
electricity	€ 2,50
electricity, water and drain	€ 5,05

Reservations

Made with deposit (€ 30.5) and fee (€ 10,70). Tel: 04 79 72 97 31. Email: camping73challes-les-eaux@wanadoo.fr

FR74060 Camping La Colombière

St Julien-en-Genevois, F-74160 Neydens (Haute-Savoie)

La Colombière, a family owned site, is on the edge of the small residential village of Neydens, a few minutes from the A40 autoroute and only a short drive from Geneva. It is an attractive site with only 107 pitches (72 for touring), all reasonably level and separated by fruit trees, flowering shrubs and hedges. There are views to the east and west of the mountain ridges. M. Bussat owns a small vineyard close to the site, has the wine made in Switzerland and sells it by the glass or bottle in the restaurant (a very nice rosé). One of France's long-distance footpaths (GR65) passes close to the site. The village of Neydens is the first stage for pilgrims from Northern Europe on the pilgrim route to Santiago de Compostella on their way to cross the Pyrénées at St Pied de Port. The site has a dormitory with eight beds for pilgrims or for anyone else who may need a bed, for example, motorcyclists or a family en-route south. Neydens makes a good base for visiting Geneva and the region around the lake. It is a very pleasant, friendly site where you may drop in for a night stop – and stay for several days! English is spoken. A 'Sites et Paysages' member.

Facilities

Three good sanitary blocks (one can be heated) include all the necessary facilities and units for disabled people. Motorcaravan service point. Fridge hire. Gas supplies. Very good bar/restaurant (all season) and terrace overlooking the heated pool (15/5-15/9). Low season organised visits of discovery, in high season one daily event including visits to Geneva, organised mountain walks and guided cycle tours (bicycle hire on site). Archery, volleyball and boules competitions. Playground. French country music evenings. Off site: Fishing 2 km. Riding 3 km. Golf 6 km. Tennis (reduced price). St Julien-en-Genevois (5 km) has many bars, restaurants, shops and supermarkets. Switzerland 3 km. Geneva with its magnificent old town, Lake Geneva and beautiful surrounding area with many walks and cycle rides.

At a glance

| Welcome & Ambience | ✓✓✓✓✓ | Location | ✓✓✓✓ |
| Quality of Pitches | ✓✓✓✓ | Range of Facilities | ✓✓✓✓ |

Directions

Take exit 13 from A40 autoroute south of Geneva, and then N201 towards Annecy. After 2 km. turn left into village of Neydens and follow campsite signs to site in just over 1 km. GPS: N46:07.213 E06:06.323

Charges 2006

Per unit incl. 2 persons	€ 15,00 - € 24,00
extra person	€ 3,50 - € 5,50
child (2-7 yrs)	€ 3,00 - € 4,00
electricity (5/6A)	€ 4,00
dog	€ 2,00
Camping Cheques accepted.	

Reservations

Made with fee (€ 12). Less 3% for 11th and subsequent days. Tel: 04 50 35 13 14. Email: la.colombiere@wanadoo.fr

Open

1 April - 30 September.

FR74030 Camping Belvédère

8 route du Semnoz, F-74000 Annecy (Haute-Savoie)

Annecy is a very interesting town in a beautiful setting at the head of the lake of the same name. The old centre has historical interest and is intersected by flower decked canals with many restaurants and shops to visit. There is much to see and do in this region in both summer and winter, with Geneva, Chamonix and the high Alps close by. Le Belvédère, as its name implies, overlooks the lake and some of the pitches have stunning views over the lake to the mountains beyond. This municipal site is the nearest campsite to the town which can be reached in 15 minutes by a quiet, but steep footpath. There are 120 good sized pitches with electricity (10A). Of these 80 with part hardstanding are fully serviced with water and a drain and there are 50 grass pitches for tents (rock pegs essential). Space may be limited if the site is busy. One small area is reserved for groups. Tall pines and a steep hillside to the west provide a backdrop to the site and a variety of trees provide decoration and some shade. This site is ideally placed for visiting Annecy but it is not suitable for large units.

Facilities

Three modern toilet blocks, two recently refurbished to a high standard, are situated around the site and were very clean. One is heated in cold weather, with a washroom for visitors with disabilities. Laundry facilities. Small shop, bar and restaurant (June-Aug). Large games/wet weather room. Good playground. Swimming is possible in the lake and municipal pool. Bicycle hire. Communal area for barbecues. Sporting activities can be booked from the site. Bus to Annecy in July/Aug. Off site: Boat launching 600 m. Lakeside beach 800 m. Swimming pool 800 m. Many other activities on and around Lake Annecy. Boat trips. Lakeside cycle track. Hang-gliding and canyoning.

Open

4 April - 10 October.

At a glance

Welcome & Ambience	✓✓✓✓	Location	✓✓✓✓
Quality of Pitches	✓✓✓✓	Range of Facilities	✓✓✓✓

Directions

Leave A41 at Annecy Sud and take N508 towards Albertville and drive around the town. Just after some traffic lights descend a hill looking for 'H' and 'Silence' signs for the hospital. Very soon after, on left hand bend, turn right up the hill, signed Le Semnoz. Keep right at the fork. Take care at next junction – do not take right hand road signed Belvédère (this leads down a very steep and narrow hill. Turn left, signed Camping Belvédère, to site shortly on right.

Charges guide

Per unit incl. 2 persons	€ 13,80 - € 17,80
tent/car incl. 2 persons	€ 10,00 - € 13,30
extra person	€ 3,90 - € 4,70
child (2-10 yrs)	€ 2,40 - € 2,80
electricity (10A)	€ 2,50

Reservations

Necessary for July/Aug. - write with 30% deposit to Mairie d'Annecy, B.P. 2305, 74011 Annecy Cedex. Tel. 04 50 33 87 96. Email: camping@ville-annecy.fr

FR74040 Camp de la Ravoire

Bout-du-Lac, route de la Ravoire, F-74210 Doussard (Haute-Savoie)

De la Ravoire is a high quality site, some 800 metres from Lake Annecy, noted for its neat and tidy appearance and the quietness of its location in this popular tourist region. The 112 numbered and level pitches are on well mown grass with some shade and separated by small shrubs and some hedging. The 90 pitches for touring units (21 with water and drain) have electricity connections. Those looking for a quiet campsite in this most attractive region without the 'animation' programmes that so many French sites feel are necessary will find this a peaceful base although disco noise from a site by the lake may drift across under some weather conditions. Take to the back roads and explore the ancient villages and wonderful countryside. Used by a tour operator (18 pitches).

Facilities

The very good central toilet block includes washbasins in cabins, facilities for disabled people, and a laundry room with washing machines, dryers and irons. Bar and snack bar with takeaway. Shop. Outdoor pool with separate water slide and paddling pool. All open all season. Good play area. Sports areas. Off site: Fishing, boat launching, bicycle hire 1 km. Riding 6 km. Golf 8 km. Good restaurant on the lakeside where the camp road leaves the main road, with others near, plus shops in Doussard village and Annecy. Cycle track (20 km) almost to Annecy passes close by. Canyoning and hang-gliding close. Boat trips on the lake.

Open

15 May - 15 September.

At a glance

Welcome & Ambience	✓✓✓✓✓	Location	✓✓✓✓
Quality of Pitches	✓✓✓✓	Range of Facilities	✓✓✓✓

Directions

Site is signed from the N508 Annecy - Albertville road, just north of Bout-du-Lac. About 2 km. south of the traffic lights in Brédannaz turn right (west, site signed) and then very shortly left. Site is on left in about 1 km. GPS: N45:48.147 E06:12.579

Charges 2006

Per unit incl. 2 adults and electricity (5A)	€ 28,60
with water and drainage	€ 31,60 - € 32,40
extra person	€ 5,90
child (0-15 yrs)	€ 2,70 - € 3,90
electricity (10/15A)	€ 2,10 - € 3,20

Less 20% outside July/Aug. Camping Cheques accepted.

Reservations

Essential for July/Aug; made for min. 10 days with deposit (€ 130-150). Tel. 04 50 44 37 80. Email: info@camping-la-ravoire.fr

203

FR74010 Camping Les Deux Glaciers

Route des Tissiéres, Les Bossons, F-74400 Chamonix (Haute-Savoie)

A pleasant and well kept, naturally laid out, small mountain site for summer and winter use. Les Deux Glaciers lies at the foot of two glaciers and is close to the well known ski resort of Chamonix. This is a magnificent region, the summer flowers, walking, bike rides and winter skiing are almost beyond description. Explore the high mountain passes in the area and visit Italy (Courmeveur 21 km) and Switzerland (Martigny 48 km). The site has 135 individual pitches on terraces, 110 for touring, levelled out of quite steeply rising ground, with electricity (2-10A) available for 100 pitches. Rock pegs are advised. It is pleasantly laid out with different trees and seasonal floral displays. Access may be difficult for large outfits. There are magnificent views of Mont Blanc Range and the Aiguille-de-Midi. With a good position and adequate amenities, the site becomes full for much of July/Aug. The temperature drops as soon as the sun sets and it can be quite cold at night. There is significant road noise. Reservations are not taken in summer, so arrive early.

Facilities

Two small, clean sanitary blocks, both heated in cool weather, have dated facilities. At least half the washbasins are in cabins. Facilities for disabled visitors, although the site is not ideal for those with walking difficulties. Washing machine and drying room. Restaurant/takeaway (all year). Mobile traders call in season. General room (for winter use only). Table tennis. Small play area. WiFi. Off site: Village shop 500 m. Fishing, bicycle hire or riding within 2 km. Golf 4 km. Chamonix, swimming, hang-gliding, cable cars, ski lifts, funicular railway all within 3 km. Walks and bike rides. Bus to Chamonix and other villages all season. Fantastic skiing in winter.

Open

All year.

At a glance

Welcome & Ambience	✓✓✓	Location	✓✓✓✓✓
Quality of Pitches	✓✓✓	Range of Facilities	✓✓✓

Directions

From west turn right off main Geneva - Chamonix road (N205) at second exit for Les Bossons ; site is on right in a few hundred metres. From east turn right at sign for Les Bossons, then left at T-junction and pass under the main road; site is on the right in few hundred metres.

Charges 2005

Per unit incl. 2 persons	€ 12,70
extra person	€ 4,80
child (7-13 yrs)	€ 4,00
child (0-7 yrs)	€ 2,40
electricity (2-10A; higher in winter)	€ 2,30 - € 6,70

Reservations

Not made for summer. Tel: 04 50 53 15 84.
Email: glaciers@clubinternet.fr

FR74070 Camping Caravaning L'Escale

F-74450 Le Grand-Bornand (Haute-Savoie)

You are assured a good welcome from the Baur family at this beautifully maintained, picturesque site. Situated at the foot of the Aravis mountain range, beside the picture postcard ski resort of Le Grand-Bornand, L'Escale has wonderful views, is surrounded by fields of flowers in summer and is clearly popular. The 149 fairly sunny pitches (142 for touring) are of average size, clearly marked with a part grass, part gravel surface and separated by trees and shrubs. All have electricity and 86 pitches are fully serviced. Rock pegs are essential. The village (200 m.) has all the facilities of a major resort with ongoing activity for summer or winter holidays. In summer a variety of well signed footpaths and cycle tracks provide forest or mountain excursions of all degrees of difficulty. In winter the area provides superb facilities for down-hill and cross-country skiing and après-ski entertainment. La Maison du Patrimoine is a must to visit.

Facilities

The very good toilet blocks (heated when cold) have all the necessary facilities. Two chalet buildings provide further facilities. Large drying room with sinks, dryer and washing machines. Separate room for skis and boots. Superb new complex with interconnected indoor (all season) and outdoor pools and paddling pools (10/6-31/8). Bar and restaurant (all season). Play area. Tennis and table tennis. Torches essential (no street lighting). Off site: The village (5 minutes walk) has shops, bars, restaurants, municipal pool complex, archery, paragliding, hang-gliding, 150 km. of signed walks. Activities are organised for children and adults. Ice skating and ice hockey in winter. Bicycle hire 200 m. Riding and golf 3 km.

Open

1 December - 23 April and 20 May - 24 September.

At a glance

Welcome & Ambience	✓✓✓✓	Location	✓✓✓✓✓
Quality of Pitches	✓✓✓✓	Range of Facilities	✓✓✓✓✓

Directions

Probably the best access is via Annecy following the D16 and D909 roads towards La Clusaz. Shortly before La Clusaz, at St Jean-de-Sixt, turn left at roundabout on D4 signed Le Grand Bornand. Just before entering village turn right signed Vallée de Bouchet and camping. Site is just over 1 km. at a roundabout on right. GPS: N45:56.412 E06:25.695

Charges 2006

Per unit incl. 2 persons	€ 17,50 - € 22,00
extra person	€ 4,00 - € 5,60
electricity (2-10A)	€ 3,80 - € 8,40
animal	€ 2,30

Camping Cheques accepted.

Reservations

Made with deposit (€ 71) and fee (€ 10).
Tel: 04 50 02 20 69.
Email: contact@campinglescale.com

FR74100 Village Camping Europa

1444 route Albertville, F-74410 St Jorioz (Haute-Savoie)

You will receive a friendly welcome at this quality, family run site. The flowers, shrubs and trees (giving some shade) are lovely and everything is kept neat and tidy. There are 210 medium to large size pitches (110 for touring) on level stony grass. Rock pegs are advised. All pitches have electricity (6A) close by and 18 have water and drainage. The static units are separated from the touring section by high hedges giving the impression that you are on a small site. There may be some noise from the adjacent main road. Europa should suit those families who like to make their own entertainment although there are some activities for children and a weekly soirée (high season) and a pool complex with slides, jacuzzi, cascade and paddling pool. This is a good base from which to tour the Lake Annecy area with its beautiful old villages and the fantastic countryside of the region.

Facilities

Two very good toilet blocks, recently modernised to a high standard, have all the necessary facilities including some large cubicles with both showers and washbasins. Motorcaravan service point. Good bar and restaurant (1/6-31/8). Swimming pool complex (entry bracelet € 2). Volleyball. Basketball. Football. Bicycle hire. Internet access. Mini-club. Some musical evenings. Off site: Fishing 300 m. Boat launching 500 m. Lakeside beach 2 km. Riding 3 km. Golf 8 km. Lakeside bike ride. Lake Annecy and all its activities. Canyoning and hang-gliding nearby. Boat trips.

Open

6 May - 12 September.

At a glance

Welcome & Ambience	✓✓✓✓	Location	✓✓✓✓
Quality of Pitches	✓✓✓✓	Range of Facilities	✓✓✓✓

Directions

From Annecy take N508 signed Albertville. Site is well signed on the right on leaving Saint-Jorioz.

Charges 2005

Per unit incl. 2 persons and electricity	€ 18,00 - € 29,50
serviced pitch	€ 21,30 - € 32,80
extra person	€ 3,70 - € 5,70
child (2-6 yrs)	€ 2,50 - € 4,50
dog	€ 2,00 - € 2,20

Reservations

Made with deposit (30%) and fee (€ 16). Tel: 04 50 68 51 01. Email: info@camping-europa.com

Village Camping EUROPA

Charming site, 400 meters from the lake of Annecy – 1 heated swiming pool, 1 water complex (with 5 water slides, waterfalls, children's games, jacuzzi, lagoon) – Restaurant with specialities of the Savoy region Quality installations – Chalets and mobile homes to let – Bikes for hire – Situated next to a cycling track.

Village Camping EUROPA
1444, route d'Albertville 74 410 ST – JORIOZ
Tel. 33 (0) 4 50 68 51 01 Fax. 33 (0) 4 50 68 55 20
E-mail : info@camping-europa.com
www.camping-europa.com

FR74110 Camping Le Taillefer

1530 route de Chaparon, F-74210 Doussard (Haute-Savoie)

This excellent, small site is family run and friendly. It is only 1.5 km. from Lake Annecy, yet it offers a quiet, very relaxing and beautiful environment all at a very good price. The views over the lakeside mountains are stunning. This site is terraced and abounds with attractive flowers, shrubs and small trees. It only has 32 average to good sized, grassy, level and sunny pitches, 28 with electricity (6A). Those at the bottom of the site are reserved for tents. In high season the site is quiet as there are no organised events, although there are plenty on and around the lake close by.

Facilities

The modern toilet block with very good separate facilities for ladies and men is near reception. Facilities for disabled visitors. Very small shop selling bread, drinks and ices etc. Small bar in high season. Playground. Small club/TV room. Torches needed (no site lighting). Off site: Nearby village of Doussard has several shops. Lake Annecy with beaches 2 km. Golf 8 km. Riding 7 km.

Open

1 May - 30 September.

At a glance

Welcome & Ambience	✓✓✓✓	Location	✓✓✓✓
Quality of Pitches	✓✓✓✓	Range of Facilities	✓✓✓

Directions

From Annecy take N508 signed Albertville. At traffic lights in Brédannaz turn right and then immediately left for 1.5 km. and site is on the left. Do not turn in by reception (this is a dead end) – wait in road until directions are received. GPS: N45:48.141 E06:12.339

Charges 2006

Per unit incl. 2 persons	€ 12,00 - € 14,00
extra person	€ 3,00 - € 3,20
electricity (6A)	€ 3,40

Reservations

Made with € 30 booking fee. Tel: 04 50 44 30 30. Email: info@campingletaillefer.com

FR74090 Camping Le Plan du Fernuy

Route des Confins, F-74220 La Clusaz (Haute-Savoie)

The pretty little village of La Clusaz is 32 km. east of Annecy at 1,200 m. above sea level and in the heart of the Savoie Alps. Le Plan du Fernuy, 2 km. east of the village lies just to the north of the Avaris mountain range in a peaceful, scenic location. The wild flowers in early summer are a joy to behold. The neat and open site has separate summer and winter seasons. It has 80 pitches, 58 for tourists. All of reasonable size and with electricity, and 22 fully serviced, the pitches are stony with some grass. Arranged in rows on either side of hard access roads, there are good mountain views but little shade. Rock pegs are essential. The site's crowning glory is an excellent indoor heated pool with large windows looking out on to the mountains and sunbeds beside them. This is a good site for ski-ing in winter (with access to a ski-tow from the campsite and a free bus to other centres). In summer it is a good base for walking and cycling with other sporting opportunities nearby. The pleasant owners speak good English.

Facilities

The large apartment building at the entrance houses very good sanitary provision on the ground floor and is heated in cool weather. Some washbasins in cabins. Baby room. Facilities for disabled visitors. Separate rooms for dishwashing and laundry with washing machine and dryer. Drying room for ski clothing and boots, etc. Motorcaravan service point. Small shop and bar provides snacks, takeaway, basic food supplies. Video games and a TV room. Heated indoor pool and paddling pool. Skiing from site and ski excursions organised. Off site: Shops and restaurants in village 2 km. Riding 800 m. Golf, bicycle hire and fishing 1.5 km.

Open

4 June - 4 September and 18 December - 24 April.

At a glance

Welcome & Ambience	✓✓✓✓	Location	✓✓✓✓
Quality of Pitches	✓✓✓✓	Range of Facilities	✓✓✓✓

Directions

From Annecy take D909 to La Clusaz and at roundabout turn towards Les Confins. Site is on right after 2 km. (well signed). It is best to avoid using D909 from Flumat particularly with caravans or motorhomes. GPS: N45:54.567 E06:27.114

Charges 2005

Per pitch incl. 2 persons	€ 16,50 - € 20,00
with electricity (4-13A)	€ 20,00 - € 27,00
extra person	€ 5,50
child (2-7 yrs)	€ 4,00
animal	€ 2,00

Winter prices are higher and may be quoted per week only.

Reservations

Advised for mid-July - mid-Aug. and winter.
Tel: 04 50 02 44 75. Email: info@plandufernuy.com

FR74130 Camping de la Plage

304 rue de la Garenne, F-74500 Amphion-les-Bains (Haute-Savoie)

This very good, family run site is small, quiet and friendly. It has a very long season and is only a few hundred metres from Lake Geneva and the village of Amphion making it an excellent centre to relax and explore this wonderful region. Madame Frossard loves gardening and the site does her credit with its flowers, trees, hedges and beautifully mown grass. The 53 pitches, only a few used by mobile homes, are level, medium to large and separated by trees. They all have water points, drains and electricity. In addition to the very small pool on the site, there is a super centre in the adjacent park (with a large pool, paddling pool, diving pool, wave pool and a giant slide), plus an excellent playground and plenty of space to enjoy. The site does not accept large units or double-axle caravans.

Facilities

The ample facilities are comprehensive and first class, with fully controllable showers, washbasins in cabins, facilities for children and disabled people, sinks for dishwashing and laundry. One block is heated off season. Washing machine, dryer and iron. Small bar and takeaway (high season). Small heated swimming pool, covered in cool weather. Sauna. Small playground for young children. Table tennis, boules. TV room. Well equipped exercise room with superb play area for young children. Wifi. Off site: Lake Geneva with beaches, restaurants, snack bars, fishing and many water sports. Ferry service around lake incl. Geneva and Lausanne. Small shops, restaurants and supermarket within walking distance in village. Hypermarket 1 km. Golf 3 km.

Open

All year excl. 2 November - 24 December.

At a glance

Welcome & Ambience	✓✓✓✓✓	Location	✓✓✓✓✓
Quality of Pitches	✓✓✓✓	Range of Facilities	✓✓✓✓

Directions

Site is between Thonon les Bains and Evian les Bains. Turn north off the N5 at Amphion les Bains (at roundabout with statue and fountains) and follow site signs - site is a few hundred metres on the right. GPS: N46:23.589 E06:31.958

Charges 2005

Per unit incl. 2 persons	€ 16,00 - € 21,00
extra person	€ 6,00 - € 6,10
child (under 8 yrs)	€ 3,00

Reductions for long stay in low season.

Reservations

Essential in high season and made with 25% deposit and € 11 booking fee. Tel: 04 50 70 00 46. Email: info@camping-dela-plage.com

FR74140 Camping Les Dômes de Miage

197 route des Contamines, F-74170 St Gervais-les-Bains (Haute-Savoie)

Saint Gervais is a pleasant spa town, 22 km. west of Chamonix-Mont Blanc and this site is 2 km. to the south on just about the only level land available by the road into the mountains. On its 3 hectares (7.5 acres) are 150 reasonably sized flat grassy pitches, about half with shade. The 75 or so nearest the reception block have individual electricity points (3, 6 or 10A). The remainder are on terraced ground, and are used for tents. There are few water taps and some pitches are up to 80 m. from one. The region is good for walking and there is a bus service into Saint Gervais, from where there is a frequent shuttle bus to its spa and a tramway to the Mont Blanc range. There is also good public transport between the town and Chamonix.

Facilities

Two centrally placed sanitary blocks, one heated, with WCs, washbasins (H&C) and showers together in cubicles, a suite for disabled visitors and baby room. Dishwashing sinks (H&C), laundry sinks (mostly H&C), washing machines and dryer. Motorcaravan service point. Small shop area in reception for basics, wine, ice cream and gaz. Social and TV room with library and ironing board. Excellent playground. Playing field with table tennis, volleyball, basketball basket, goal net. Off site: Fishing 100 m. Bicycle hire 1 km. Riding 8 km. Shops, and outdoor swimming pool in St Gervais.

Open

13 May - 15 September.

At a glance

Welcome & Ambience	✓✓✓✓	Location	✓✓✓✓
Quality of Pitches	✓✓✓✓	Range of Facilities	✓✓✓

Directions

From St Gervais take D902 towards Les Contamines and site is on left after 2 km.

Charges 2005

Per unit incl. 1 or 2 persons	€ 14,00 - € 19,00
extra person	€ 2,50 - € 3,50
child (2-10 yrs)	€ 2,00 - € 3,00
electricity (3/6A0	€ 2,90 - € 3,90
dog	€ 2,00

Camping Cheques accepted.

Reservations

Made with deposit (€ 50) and booking fee (€ 10, includes cancellation insurance). Tel: 04 50 93 45 96. Email: info@camping-mont-blanc.com

FR74150 Camping de la Mer de Glace

200 chemin de la Bagna, Les Praz, F-74400 Chamonix (Haute-Savoie)

This attractive site is convenient for Chamonix but is in a tranquil setting away from its hustle and bustle. Set in a large level clearing, with a view of the Mont Blanc range, it has been kept as natural as possible without a pool, restaurant, bar or disco, etc. and is well suited to those looking for quiet and relaxation. For those more interested in exercise, the area is rich in trails for walking and mountain biking, and many pass near the site. The buildings are of typical regional timber construction, decorated with traditional painted flower designs. Inside, they have modern facilities and are well maintained and clean. There are 150 pitches of varying sizes, of which 75 have electricity connections (3, 6 or 9A) and are suitable for caravans and camper vans. The others are usually allocated for tents. There are sufficient water points.

Facilities

Three sanitary blocks, all unisex: one with toilets (some Turkish), one with washbasins (some in cubicles) and baby room, one with showers. Facilities for disabled visitors. Dishwashing and laundry sinks (H&C). Two washing machines and a dryer. Motorcaravan service point (not WC tank). Bread can be ordered for the following morning. Pizza van twice weekly in July/Aug. Meeting room and snack room. Small playground for young children. Free internet and WiFi access. Off site: Fishing and golf 500 m. Bicycle hire 1 km. Riding 5 km. Shops, etc. 700 m. in Les Praz or 1.5 km. in Chamonix. Indoor and outdoor swimming pools in Chamonix 1.5 km.

Open

28 April - 1 October.

At a glance

Welcome & Ambience	✓✓✓✓	Location	✓✓✓✓
Quality of Pitches	✓✓✓✓	Range of Facilities	✓✓✓

Directions

From Chamonix take N506 northeast towards Les Praz. After about 1 km. site is signed to the right. NOTE: the first two signs direct you under a 2.4 m. high bridge. It is best to wait until you reach a small roundabout at the entrance to Les Praz, turn right there and follow the signs.

Charges 2006

Per person	€ 5,40 - € 6,20
child (0-3 yrs)	free
pitch	€ 5,10 - € 7,00
electricity (3A)	€ 2,80

Reservations

Not made. Tel: 04 50 53 44 03. Email: info@chamonix-camping.com

207

FR74160 Camping l'Ile des Barrats

185 chemin de l'Ile des Barrat, F-74400 Chamonix (Haute-Savoie)

A delightful neat and tidy, small and tranquil site, l'Ile de Barrats is run by the third generation of a very friendly family who speak good English. It is within easy walking distance of the beautiful town of Chamonix. It is surrounded by magnificent mountains with views over the Mont Blanc range. In summer the mountain flowers are second to none. There are several cable cars and chair lifts close by which operate during the summer high season giving access to Alpine walks ranging from the casual stroll to the full mountain hike.There are 53 slightly sloping, grassy pitches all for touring mostly separated by small hedges and a variety of trees offering some shade. All have electricity (5/10A) and 32 have water and a drain. No twin axle caravans.

Facilities

A modern and very clean toilet block offers all the necessary facilities, including those for disabled visitors. Covered picnic area with table and benches, ideal for those with small tents. Ice pack service. Motorcaravan service point. Store room for those leaving tents and other equipment on site whilst in the mountains. Daily visits from a mobile shop in July/Aug. No organised activities on site. Off site: Baker 500 m. Chamonix (800 m level walk)..

At a glance

Welcome & Ambience	✓✓✓✓✓	Location	✓✓✓✓✓	
Quality of Pitches	✓✓✓✓	Range of Facilities	✓✓✓	

Directions

On entering Chamonix on the main road from Geneva, turn left at first roundabout after turn for Mont Blanc Tunnel. Turn left at next roundabout and the site is on the right. GPS: N45:54.855 E06:51.689

Charges guide

Per person	€ 5,40
pitch incl. electricity	€ 10,10

Reservations

Contact site. Tel: 04 50 53 51 44.

Open

1 May - 3 October.

FR74170 Camping Moulin Dollay

206 rue du Moulin Dollay, F-74570 Groisy (Haute-Savoie)

This spacious site with only 30 pitches, all for touring, is a gem for those seeking a peaceful site in a parkland setting alongside a rushing stream. It is an ideal base for touring the interesting Haute Savoie by car or bicycle, or on foot. Nestling between Annecy (15 km.) and Geneva (35 km.) you will discover beautiful countryside with its mountains, waterfalls, woods, birds, animals and flowers. The friendly and enthusiastic owner has worked hard to develop this site to a high quality over the last few years and in 2004 it was voted the campsite with the best floral display in the region. The large to very large, level, grass pitches are partially separated by hedges and trees provide some shade. All pitches have electricity and 15 also have sole use of a tap and a drain. Rock pegs are recommended. The small adjacent river is ideal for fishing and paddling and has a picturesque track alongside suitable for walking and biking.

Facilities

The spacious modern toilet block (heated when necessary) has well appointed and very clean facilities, including those for disabled visitors and a baby room with heater. Washing machine and dryer. Motorcaravan service point. The attractive reception building serves as a bar and meeting place with a TV corner. Very large open play and sports area with swings, slides, volleyball and table tennis. River fishing. Off site: Shops, restaurants, bank and supermarkets at Groisy 1 km. Many marked walks and bike rides to suit all abilities. Riding 4 km. Golf 6 km.

At a glance

Welcome & Ambience	✓✓✓✓✓	Location	✓✓✓✓	
Quality of Pitches	✓✓✓✓✓	Range of Facilities	✓✓✓	

Directions

Site is 12 km. north of Annecy. Heading north on the N203 Annecy - Bonneville road, turn left on the D2d road at Groisy le Plot. Cross the river and go under road bridge and turn right and then left, following site signs. GPS: N46:00.146 E06:11.45

Charges 2005

Per unit incl. 2 persons	€ 13,00 - € 15,00
extra person	€ 4,00
electricity	€ 3,00

Reservations

Advised in high season. Tel: 04 50 68 00 31.

Open

1 May - 30 September.

MAP 10

Endless shimmering beaches, huge sand dunes, watersports aplenty, fragrant pine forests, the fine wines of Bordeaux, and the chic city of Biarritz: it's easy to see the allure of the Atlantic Coast.

THE COASTAL DÉPARTEMENTS OF THE OFFICIAL REGION OF AQUITAINE, STRETCHING FROM BORDEAUX IN THE NORTH TO THE PYRÉNÉES AND THE SPANISH BORDER ARE INCLUDED IN OUR 'TOURIST' REGION: 33 GIRONDE, 40 LANDES, 64 PYRÉNÉES ATLANTIQUES

The Atlantic Coast stretches north from Biarritz to Arcachon. The most notable features are the uninterrupted line of vast sandy beaches, over 100 miles long, and the endless pine woods in the hinterland - this is Europe's largest man-made forest. There are also many lakes to see, ideal for watersports activities.

The département of the Gironde covers the area from the Bassin d'Arcachon, famed for its oysters and Europe's highest sand dune, to the Gironde estuary and Bordeaux. The vineyards of Bordeaux are world famous and especially well known for their Médoc, Sauternes, and St Emilion wines.

The Pays Basque area in the southwest corner is much influenced by Spain. The most famous Basque towns are Biarritz, Bayonne and the picturesque old port of St-Jean-de-Luz. Further inland and nearer the Pyrénées is the attractive town of St-Jean-Pied-de-Port on the pilgrims' route to northern Spain and Santiago de Compostela, close to the forest of Iraty with its lakes and ski runs.

Places of interest

Bayonne: old streets and fortifications; Basque Museum

Bordeaux: 14,000 piece Bohemian glass chandelier in foyer of the Grand Theatre, 29 acre Esplanade des Quinconces

Pau: famous motor racing circuit on (closed) public highway; stadium for the Basque game of *pelota*

St Emilion: visit the castle ramparts or drink premier cru St Emilion at pavement cafés

St Jean-de-Luz: seaside resort and fishing village

St Jean-Pied-de-Port: ancient city with citadel, bright Basque houses in steep streets

Cuisine of the region

Seafood is popular, local specialities include carp stuffed with foie gras and mullet in red wine

Chorizos: spicy sausages

Chou farci: stuffed cabbage, sometimes *aux marrons* (with chestnuts)

Foie Gras: specially prepared livers of geese and ducks, seasoned and stuffed with truffles

Gâteau Basque: shallow custard pastry with fillings

Jambon de Bayonne: raw ham, cured in salt and sliced paper thin

Lamproie: eel-like fish with leeks, onions and red Bordeaux wine

FR33010 Camping de la Dune

Route de Biscarrosse, F-33115 La Pyla-sur-Mer (Gironde)

La Dune is an informal and friendly site, with a range of amenities. From its situation at the foot of the enormous dune (the highest in Europe) you can reach the beach either by climbing over the dune – a ladder leading directly from the site goes up nearly to the top – or by driving round. The 325 marked pitches, some sloping, some terraced but level, vary considerably in size but all are hedged with shade from pine trees. Nearly half are caravan pitches with electricity and water. Some of the site roads are quite narrow and parts are quite sandy. English is spoken. This is a busy site with good security. There are no tour operators.

Facilities

Modern sanitary blocks include one small one and one that can be heated in cool weather and has been refurbished to make roomy showers and washbasins en-suite. WCs are of British and Turkish types, many washbasins are in private cabins. Some blocks may be closed at night. Motorcaravan service point. Small supermarket. Pleasant little bar and restaurant with takeaway - (opens June, all other facilities are all season). Medium-size swimming pool. Playground with mini-club. Open-air theatre, sports and tournaments organised July-end Aug. Purpose built barbecue (only gas individual ones are allowed). Fridges for hire. Off site: Riding 2 km. Fishing 3 km. Golf 10 km.

Open

1 May - 30 September.

At a glance

Welcome & Ambience	✓✓✓✓	Location	✓✓✓✓
Quality of Pitches	✓✓✓✓	Range of Facilities	✓✓✓✓

Directions

The D259, signed from the N250 to Biscarrosse and Dune du Pilat, just before La Teste, avoids Pyla-sur-Mer. At end of new road turn left at roundabout onto D218 coast road. La Dune is the second site on the right.

Charges 2005

Per pitch incl. 2 persons	€ 12,50 - € 24,50
with electricity	€ 15,50 - € 27,00
extra person	€ 4,00 - € 8,00
child (under 10 yrs)	€ 2,50 - € 5,00
dog	€ 2,50 - € 3,50

Reservations

Made with deposit (€ 100). Tel: 05 56 22 72 17.
Email: reception@campingedeladune.fr

FR33020 Camping Caravaning Fontaine-Vieille

4 boulevard du Colonel Wurtz, F-33510 Andernos-les-Bains (Gironde)

Fontaine Vieille is a large, traditional site that has been operating for over 50 years. The site stretches along the eastern edge of the Bassin d'Arcachon under light woodland in the residential area of the small town of Andernos. Popular with the French, it has nearly 700 individual pitches, of which 520 are touring pitches (about 400 with electricity). On flat, grassy or sandy ground, they are marked by stones in the ground or young trees. A beach runs alongside the tidal 'Bassin' which can be used for boating when the tide is in. When it is out, there is sand and mud but it is claimed that swimming in the channels is still possible. A full range of entertainment is organised in high season.

Facilities

Seven sanitary blocks of rather unusual design provide an adequate number of hot showers, plus facilities for people with disabilities and children. Shop (1/6-15/9). Bar with terrace and takeaway (all season). Restaurant (1/6-15/9). Swimming pool complex. Four tennis courts. TV room. Two play areas for little ones and adventure area for older children. Minigolf. Boats, sailboards for hire. Sports organised in high season. Communal barbecue areas (only gas may be used on pitches). Off site: Golf 3 km. Riding 5 km. Town shops near.

Open

1 April - 30 September.

At a glance

Welcome & Ambience	✓✓✓✓	Location	✓✓✓✓
Quality of Pitches	✓✓✓	Range of Facilities	✓✓✓✓

Directions

Turn off D3 at southern end of Andernos towards Bassin at campsite sign.

Charges 2006

Per unit incl. 2 persons	€ 13,30 - € 20,40
with electricity (5A)	€ 16,30 - € 24,50
extra person	€ 3,10 - € 5,10
child (2-7 yrs)	€ 1,50 - € 2,50
animal	€ 2,00 - € 3,00

Reservations

Made for any length with deposit (€ 80) and fee (€ 20). Tel: 05 56 82 01 67.
Email: contact@fontaine-vieille.com

FR33040 Camping La Pinède

F-33260 Cazaux La Teste de Buch (Gironde)

La Pinede is a popular family site with an attractive forest setting, close to the Dune de Pyla. The site is also just 3 km. from the very large Lac de Cazaux with many watersport activities. It also has direct access to a river with mooring opportunities. This site has been recommended by our French agent and we plan to conduct a full inspection in 2006. There are 200 pitches here, mostly well shaded and with electricity.

Facilities

Sanitary buildings. Restaurant, bar and takeaway food. Shop. Swimming pool. Games room. Playground. Table tennis. Volleyball. Canoe hire. Mobile homes for rent. Off site: Hiking and cycling trails through the Landes forest. Lac de Cazaux (fishing and watersports) 3 km. Nearest beach 7 km.

Open

1 May - 30 September.

Directions

From Arcachon head south towards Cazaux on the D112. Site is located north of the village.

Charges 2005

Per person	€ 3,50 - € 4,50
child (1-6 yrs)	€ 2,50 - € 3,50
pitch	€ 7,00 - € 12,00
electricity	€ 3,00 - € 4,50

Reservations

Contact site. Tel: 05 56 22 23 24. Email: info@campinglapinede.net

FR33030 Camping Club Arcachon

5 allée Galarie, BP476, F-33312 Arcachon (Gironde)

The Arcachon basin with all its bustle and activity is an ideal base for those seeking an 'out and about' holiday. Watersports, paragliding, sailing, tennis tournaments, climbing the biggest sand dune in Europe, and not forgetting such gastronomic delights as oysters and mussels, are readily available. The Camping Club of Arcachon enjoys a situation well back from the hustle and bustle, where nights are quiet and facilities are of a high standard. Those with caravans, motorcaravans or tents all have their own area of the site. The latter have pitches of varying sizes on neatly formed terraces. In total there are 250 pitches, with 150 for touring units. Electricity connections (6/10A) are available. The site enjoys good security with day and night time 'guardians'. The site restaurant is well thought of, and in season the outdoor pool with its water slide is open all day. Reception staff speak English.

Facilities

Three sanitary blocks provide toilets of mainly British pattern, hot showers and washbasins in cabins. Motorcaravan service point. Dishwashing and laundry facilities under cover. Washing machines and dryers (tokens at reception). Fridge hire. Shop (15/5-15/9). Bar, restaurant, snack bar and takeaway (April - Oct). Swimming pool (1/6-30/9). Bicycle hire. Play area. Games room. Club for children (15/6-15/9). Entertainment for all age groups (15/6-15/9). Barbecues are only permitted in communal areas. Off site: Beach 1.8 km. Arcachon 2-3 km. Riding 1 km. Golf 2 km.

Open

All year.

At a glance

Welcome & Ambience	✓✓✓✓	Location	✓✓✓✓
Quality of Pitches	✓✓✓✓	Range of Facilities	✓✓✓✓

Directions

Approaching Arcachon on a new bypass (from Bordeaux area) take exit for 'Hopital Jean Hameau'. Cross over the bypass following signs for the hospital, then signs for Abatilles. At next roundabout follow signs for 'Camping'. Take care as the route travels through suburban housing.
GPS: N44:09.078 W01:10.445

Charges 2005

Per person	€ 3,00 - € 6,00
child (4-10 yrs)	€ 1,00
pitch	€ 5,00 - € 15,00
electricity	€ 4,00
animal	€ 2,00 - € 3,00

Reservations

Made with deposit (20%) and fee (€ 25).
Tel: 05 56 83 24 15.
Email: info@camping-arcachon.com

FR33080 Domaine de la Barbanne

Route de Montagne, F-33330 St Emilion (Gironde)

La Barbanne is a pleasant, friendly, family-owned site in the heart of the Bordeaux wine region, only 2.5 km. from the famous town of St Emilion. With 174 pitches, of which only 10 per cent carry mobile homes, the owners created a carefully maintained, well equipped site. The original parts of the site bordering the lake have mature trees, good shade and pleasant surroundings, whilst in the newer area the trees have yet to provide full shade and it can be hot in summer. The pitches are all large, level and grassy with dividing hedges and electricity connections (long leads may be necessary). Twelve pitches for motorcaravans have a tarmac hardstanding surrounded by grass. La Barbanne has an attractive entrance and reception area with ample space for parking or turning. The site owners run a free minibus service twice a day to St Emilion and also organise excursions in July and August to local places of interest, including Bordeaux. A 'Sites et Paysages' member.

Facilities

Two modern, fully equipped toilet blocks provide washbasins mostly in private cabins. Visitors with disabilities are well catered for. Motorcaravan service point. Small, well stocked shop. Bar with terrace, takeaway and restaurant (1/6-20/9). Two swimming pools with sun beds, one heated with cork-screw water slide (15/4-22/9). Fully enclosed play area with seats for parents and an organised children's club (from 1/7). Evening entertainment (from 1/7). Tennis, boules, volleyball, table tennis and minigolf. The lake provides superb free fishing, pedaloes, canoes and lakeside walks. Bicycle hire. Off site: St Emilion and shops 2.5 km. Riding 8 km.

Open

1 April - 22 September.

At a glance

Welcome & Ambience	✓✓✓✓✓	Location	✓✓✓✓✓
Quality of Pitches	✓✓✓✓	Range of Facilities	✓✓✓✓✓

Directions

From St Emilion take D122 north for 2.5 km. From Lussac take D122 south 2 km. past Montage. Turn east at site sign and it is on left after 400 m. Caravans and motorhomes are forbidden through the village of St Emilion. They must approach the site by taking the D243 from Libourne or from Castillon on the D936 via D130/D243.
GPS: N44:54.997 W0:08.513

Charges 2005

Per unit incl. 1 or 2 persons	€ 14,00 - € 21,50
extra person	€ 4,00 - € 6,80
child (0-7 yrs)	€ 2,50 - € 5,60
pet	free - € 2,00
Camping Cheques accepted.	

Reservations

Made for min. 4 days. Tel: 05 57 24 75 80.
Email: barbanne@wanadoo.fr

FR33050 Camping Les Ourmes

Avenue du Lac, F-33990 Hourtin (Gironde)

Located only 500 metres from the largest fresh water lake in France, only 10 minutes drive from the beach and with its own pool, this is essentially a holiday site. Of the 270 pitches, 240 are for tourers, marked but in most cases not actually separated, and arranged amongst tall pines and other trees which give good shade. All have electricity connections. The site's amenities are arranged around a pleasant courtyard at the entrance where an evening entertainment programme is organised in season. This site has a busy, cosmopolitan feel, with visitors of many different nationalities.

Facilities

Three recently refurbished toilet blocks are of a good standard including some washbasins in cabins. Washing machine in each block and dryer, with hot water taps for washing up. Small shop (1/6-31/8). Bar/restaurant (1/7-31/8). Swimming and paddling pools (1/5-15/9). Separate large leisure area with play area, volleyball and basketball. TV, games rooms. Boules. Off site: Watersports and fishing on the lake, bicycle hire, tennis and riding within 500 m.

Open

1 April - 30 September.

At a glance

Welcome & Ambience	✓✓✓✓	Location	✓✓✓✓
Quality of Pitches	✓✓✓	Range of Facilities	✓✓✓✓

Directions

Follow Route du Port (Ave du Lac) from the town centre and site is signed on left. GPS: N45:10.926 W01:04.566

Charges 2005

Per unit incl. 2 persons	€ 11,00 - € 18,50
incl. electricity	€ 14,00 - € 21,50
extra person (over 2 yrs)	€ 1,80 - € 3,00
dog	€ 1,20 - € 1,50

No credit cards.

Reservations

Necessary in high season. Tel: 05 56 09 12 76. Email: lesourmes@free.fr

CAMPING CARAVANING ★★★★

Le Pressoir

Petit Palais
33570 LUSSAC
SAINT-ÉMILION

Tél. 05 57 69 73 25
Fax 05 57 69 77 36

www.campinglepressoir.com
camping.le.pressoir@wanadoo.fr

Discover a region, quiet and open, in the middle of an abundant nature with its wordwide wellknown vineyards

SPECIAL PRICE from 6 € a pers. based on a 2 pers. stay outside season

FR33090 Camping Le Pressoir

Petit Palais et Cornemps, F-33570 Lussac (Gironde)

Buried in the famous wine producing countryside of the Lussac, Pomerol and St Emilion area north of Bordeaux, Le Pressoir is surrounded by fields of vines. The manicured entrance featuring attractive trees, shrubs and flowers, together with preserved equipment from its former role as a wine farm, welcomes one to the site. The 100 large pitches are arranged on either side of a gravel road leading up a slight hill. Most are shaded by attractive trees, but almost all are sloping. They are over 100 sq.m. and equipped with electricity (blue EC plugs) and interspersed with five Trigano type tents for hire. The old barn has been converted into a stylish bar and a really charming, separate restaurant. A quiet, family site, Le Pressoir provides a comfortable base for a holiday in this area famous for good food and wine.

Facilities

Fully equipped toilet facilities (no paper) in purpose built block near the farmhouse include hair and make-up area for ladies, facilities for disabled visitors, and washing machine. Bar and restaurant (all season). Swimming pool (15/5-15/9, no Bermuda shorts). Playground with timber equipment. Petanque, volleyball and table tennis. Gates locked 22.00 - 08.00 hrs. Off site: Tennis nearby. Fishing 5 km. Riding and bicycle hire 10 km.

Open

25 March - 1 October.

At a glance

Welcome & Ambience	✓✓✓✓	Location	✓✓✓✓
Quality of Pitches	✓✓✓	Range of Facilities	✓✓✓

Directions

From N89 turn at St Médard de Guizières towards Lussac on the D21. From Castillon-la-Bataille south of the site on the D936 Libourne - Bergerac road take D17 north towards St Médard and Lussac. Where D17 forks left to Lussac at Roques, go straight on via the D21 through Petit Palais. Site is signed from the D21. GPS: N44:59.824 W0:03.801

Charges 2006

Per person	€ 6,25
child (2-6 yrs)	€ 4,00
pitch	€ 7,00
with 6A electricity	€ 10,00

Camping Cheques accepted.

Reservations

Contact site. Tel: 05 57 69 73 25. Email: camping.le.pressoir@wanadoo.fr

FR33110 Airotel Camping de la Côte d'Argent

Mobile homes ▶ page 424

F-33990 Hourtin-Plage (Gironde)

Spread over 20 hectares of undulating sand-based terrain and in the midst of a pine forest, this large site is well placed and well equipped for leisurely family holidays. It also makes an ideal base for walkers and cyclists, with over 100 km. of cycle lanes leading through the Medoc countryside. Hourtin-Plage is a pleasant invigorating resort on the Atlantic coast and a popular location for watersports enthusiasts, or those who prefer spending their days on the beach. More appealing though may be to stay on site, for Côte d'Argent's top attraction is its pool complex with wooden bridges connecting the pools and islands, on which there are sunbathing patios and play areas. There is also an indoor heated pool. There are 550 touring pitches which are not clearly defined and in the trees, some on soft sand-based ground. The site is well organised and ideal for children. Entertainment takes place at the bar near the entrance (until 12.30). Extensive development plans include a new bar, restaurant and supermarket. There are 48 hardstandings for motorcaravans outside the site, providing a cheap stop-over, but with no access to the site facilities.

Facilities
Five very clean sanitary blocks of various ages (two new in 2005) include provision for disabled visitors. Plenty of laundry machines. Motorcaravan service points. Large supermarket, restaurant, takeaway and pizzeria bar. New supermarket, bar, restaurant and hotel are planned for 2006. Four outdoor pools with slides and flumes. Indoor pool. Massage. Astronomy once a week. Two tennis courts. Pool tables. Four play areas. Mini-club and organised entertainment in season. Fishing. Riding. Bicycle hire. Internet access. ATM on site. Charcoal barbecues are not permitted. Off site: Path to the beach 300 m. Golf 30 km.

Open
13 May - 18 September.

At a glance
Welcome & Ambience	✓✓✓✓	Location		✓✓✓✓
Quality of Pitches	✓✓✓	Range of Facilities		✓✓✓✓✓

Directions
Turn off D101 Hourtin-Soulac road 3 km. north of Hourtin. Then join D101E signed Hourtin-Plage. Site is 300 m. from the beach.
GPS: N45:13.381 W01:09.868

Charges 2006
Per unit incl. 2 persons	
and electricity	€ 25,00 - € 39,00
tent incl. 2 persons	€ 15,00 - € 29,00
extra person	€ 3,00 - € 6,00
child (2-10 yrs)	€ 2,00 - € 5,00
electricity (6A)	€ 4,00
dog	€ 2,00 - € 5,00

Camping Cheques accepted.

Reservations
Necessary for July/August. Tel: 05 56 09 10 25.
Email: info@camping-cote-dargent.com

FR33120 Camping La Cigale

Route de Lège, F-33740 Arès (Gironde)

La Cigale is an attractive little site with charm and ambience where the owners extend a very warm welcome. Small and beautifully maintained, it is set amid pine trees and M. Pallet's floral displays. The 95 level, grassy pitches, most with electricity and of 100 sq.m. in size, are divided by hedges and flower borders. The majority of the pitches have shade from the pine trees. There are two small swimming pools in a pleasant setting and under the ample shade of a large plane tree, where drinks, meals and snacks are served on the bar terrace. This is an exceptional area for cycling, with designated routes. Across the bay lies bustling Arcachon and the enormous Dune de Pilat, easily reached by ferry from Cap Ferret. Used by tour operators (18%).

Facilities
The central, flower-bedecked, unisex toilet block includes a family room with two showers, facilities for disabled visitors and a laundry with a washing machine and dryer. All is meticulously maintained. Motorcaravan services. Simple shop. Bar terrace with meals and snacks. Pizza takeaway at front of the site (all 17/6-10/9). Two small swimming pools (15/5-7/9). Small play area. Full-time entertainers for children and adults in July/Aug. Free donkey cart rides every Sunday. Off site: Site is convenient for a wide choice of beaches. Village centre 800 m. Fishing or riding 1 km.

Open
29 April - 2 October.

At a glance
Welcome & Ambience	✓✓✓✓✓	Location		✓✓✓✓
Quality of Pitches	✓✓✓✓✓	Range of Facilities		✓✓✓✓

Directions
Leave Bordeaux ring road at exit 10 (D213) or exit 11 (D106) and continue on good roads direct to Arès. Turn into Arès following road to church square. Turn right following signs for Lège/Cap Ferret. Site is 800 m. on left. GPS: N44:46.366 W01:08.537

Charges guide
Per unit incl. 1 or 2 persons	€ 16,50 - € 22,80
extra person	€ 4,20 - € 4,80
child (7 yrs)	€ 2,60 - € 2,80
electricity (4/6A)	€ 4,80

Reservations
Advised for July/Aug. and made with deposit (€ 79) and fee (€ 16). Tel: 05 56 60 22 59.
Email: campinglacigaleares@wanadoo.fr

FR33130 Yelloh! Village Les Grands Pins

Plage Nord, F-33680 Lacanau-Océan (Gironde)

This Atlantic coast holiday site with direct access to a fine sandy beach, is on undulating terrain amongst tall pine trees. A large site, it provides 600 pitches, with 130 mobile homes to rent, leaving around 470 pitches of varying sizes for touring units. The site is well served by tarmac access roads, and although not noticeably divided, one half of the site is a traffic free zone (except for arrival or departure day, caravans are placed on the pitch, with separate areas outside the zone for car parking). There is a good number of tent pitches, those in the centre of the site having some of the best views, and especially useful for tenters are safety deposit and fridge boxes which are available for rent. The large sandy beach is a 350 m. stroll from the gate at the back of the site.

Facilities

Four toilet blocks, three of which are new (one heated) include washbasins in cubicles, dishwashing and laundry sinks, a dog and wetsuit washing area, baby room and facilities for disabled people (not all units are open in low season). Well equipped launderette. Motorcaravan services. Good sized supermarket, surf boutique. Bar, restaurant and snack bar with takeaway. Heated swimming pool (20 x 10 m, all season, with lifeguard in July/Aug) with large paved sunbathing surround. Jacuzzi. Free fitness activities (aqua gym, etc). Games room. Fitness suite. Tennis (charge in July/Aug). Two playgrounds. New adventure playground. Bicycle hire. Organised activities for children, teenagers and adults all season. Entrance barrier with keypad access. Only gas barbecues are permitted. Off site: Fishing, golf, riding and bicycle hire 5 km.

Open

23 April - 24 September.

At a glance

Welcome & Ambience ✓✓✓✓✓   Location ✓✓✓✓✓
Quality of Pitches ✓✓✓✓   Range of Facilities ✓✓✓✓✓

Directions

From Bordeaux take N125/D6 west to Lacanau, continue on D6 to Lacanau Ocean. At second roundabout, take second exit: Plage Nord and follow signs to camps sites. Les Grand Pins is signed to the right at the far end of the road. If approaching from northern France you could use the ferry from Royan to Le Verdon. GPS: N45:00.664 W01:11.602

Charges 2005

Per unit incl. 2 persons and electricity	€ 15,00 - € 35,00
extra person	€ 3,00 - € 9,00
child (2-12 yrs)	free - € 6,00
dog	€ 3,00 - € 4,00

Reservations

Essential for high season, made with deposit and fee. Discounts for early booking. Tel: 05 56 03 20 77. Email: reception@lesgrandspins.com

FR33140 Camping Le Grand Pré

Route de Casteljaloux, F-33430 Bazas (Gironde)

In a rural position, this is a site where the owners stated philosophy of tranquillity in nature is realised. There are only 30 grass pitches at present, which are separated by flowering shrubs and bushes, but there are plans to expand and four pitches are now occupied by mobile homes. All have electricity hook-ups (6-16A), water and drainage. Reception facilities and a bar are in a very tastefully converted old barn, where you may have breakfast or collect bread if ordered the day before. There is a traffic free footpath direct from the site to the town, which we can recommend. The fortified town is notable for the magnificent Cathedral (illuminated at night), the annual festival of the Bazardais cattle, the bonfires of St Jean, and the weekly Saturday market, and is on the Pilgrim Route to Santiago de Compostella. A new cycle path runs from Bazas to the Atlantic coast (on 80 km. of old railway track). Reservation is advisable for July and August.

Facilities

The single, high quality toilet block may not be adequate for demand, but we are told more units will be built. It includes open and cubicle washbasins, washing machine and dryer, dishwashing and laundry sinks, an excellent baby room, and full facilities for disabled persons. Motorcaravan service point. Unusual swimming pool and paddling pool. Sunbathing area. Small playground. Volleyball, boules. Library with some English books. B&B nearby at the Château. By prior arrangement touring motorcaravans may park overnight here (with electricity) when the site is closed. Off site: Shops, bars, restaurants, gas supplies available in Bazas, 1.5 km.

At a glance

Welcome & Ambience ✓✓✓✓✓   Location ✓✓✓✓
Quality of Pitches ✓✓✓✓   Range of Facilities ✓✓✓✓

Directions

Bazas is around 55 km. southeast of Bordeaux, and 15 km. south of Langon. From Bazas centre take the D655 east towards Casteljaloux, and the site entrance is about 1 km. on your right (well signed).

Charges 2005

Per unit incl. 1 or 2 persons	€ 7,88 - € 18,85
incl. 3 persons	€ 9,48 - € 22,00
electricity (6-16A)	€ 3,20 - € 4,74
extra person over 10 yrs	€ 2,37 - € 3,93
dog	free - € 3,00

Discounts for longer stays.

Reservations

Advisable for July and August.
Tel: 05 56 65 13 17. Email: legrandpre@wanadoo.fr

Open

1 April - 30 September.

FR33150 Camping Municipal Les Gabarreys

Route de la Rivière, F-33250 Pauillac (Gironde)

An attractive, small site with well tended flower beds, Les Gabarreys is surrounded by the many vineyards of the Médoc region (reception can provide a good map). An excellent site, it has 59 pitches, 41 with hardstanding for caravans or motorcaravans (so pegging out awnings could be a problem), 14 grass pitches for tents and 6 mobile homes, all with electric hook-ups, some may require long leads). The 'Maison du Tourisme et du Vin' should be your first port of call, the surrounding area is well supplied with wine caves, and being fairly level you could perhaps cycle to some of them. The site is popular with the grape pickers in September, but the warden always keeps some pitches for tourists.

Facilities

Two immaculate toilet blocks provide open and cubicle washbasins and excellent facilities for disabled people. Motorcaravan services. General room with satellite TV, fridge-freezer and a small library. Minigolf (free). Volleyball.

Open

3 April - 9 October.

Reservations

Advisable for July, August and September.
Tel: 05 56 59 10 03.
Email: camping.les.gabarreys@wanadoo.fr

At a glance

| Welcome & Ambience | √√√√ | Location | √√√√ |
| Quality of Pitches | √√√ | Range of Facilities | √√√ |

Directions

Pauillac lies on the western side of the Gironde estuary, NNW of Bordeaux. From Bordeaux take the D1 to St Laurent, then the D206 to Pauillac. At roundabout turn right to Pauillac Guais, then straight ahead at next roundabout and turn right just before the Maison du Tourisme. Site is 800 m. on the left. Alternatively if approaching from the north, you could use the ferry from Royan to Le Verdon, or Blaye to Lamarque (cheaper). GPS: N45:11.098 W00:45.524

Charges 2005

Per unit incl. 1 person	€ 7,90 - € 8,40
incl. 2 persons	€ 11,60 - € 12,60
extra person	€ 3,80 - € 4,20
child (2-7 yrs)	€ 2,80 - € 2,90
dog	€ 1,60 - € 1,80
electricity (5/10A)	€ 3,70 - € 5,00

FR33160 Euronat

F-33590 Grayan et l'Hopital (Gironde)

Euronat is really a large naturist town with extensive facilities, a Thalassotherapy centre and direct access to the beach. There are various 'villages' surrounding the commercial centre of this 335 hectare site. The caravan and camping sites are in two areas separate from the villages of privately owned chalets and mobile homes. Unfortunately many trees were lost in the storms of 1999 and, despite planting, it will take some time before the levels of shade on the site return to the previous cover. However, there is a sense of openness and many other plants are now flourishing. A variety of fair sized fairly flat pitches, includes some suitable for large American-style motorhomes. The 'town centre' is superb with two supermarkets, an organic supermarket, cash-point, butcher, fish shop, bakery (baking on the premises) where freshly squeezed orange juice is available every morning, several restaurants including fish, Chinese, brasserie, pizzeria/crêperie and a large takeaway with a good selection of hot and cold dishes and desserts which you can eat in the 'square' at picnic tables. The beach is of fine sand, 1.5 km. in length, with a special area for dogs. It is cleaned daily and there are two lifeguard stations. A bicycle is suggested as the easiest means of travelling round the 'town'. The large, modern and airy Thalassotherapy centre where a range of treatments may be found is supervised by a doctor. Many site owned mobile homes, caravans, chalet and tents are on site. English is spoken.

Facilities

The large number of sanitary blocks include British style WCs (and a few Turkish style) and communal hot showers. All blocks are well maintained with some heated in low season. Facilities for people with disabilities. Many dishwashing and laundry sinks (cold water). Launderette. Basic service point for motorcaravans. Range of shops and restaurants. New swimming pool with flumes and children's pool. Many activities and workshops (in main season) including archery, pony club, horse riding, tennis, petanque, volleyball, table tennis, special activities for children, handicrafts. Three TV rooms, video and games centre. Library. Large multi-purpose hall used for dances, film nights, music evenings, sports activities. Barbecues are not permitted.

At a glance

| Welcome & Ambience | √√√√ | Location | √√√√ |
| Quality of Pitches | √√√√ | Range of Facilities | √√√√ |

Directions

From Bordeaux ring road take exit 7, then RN215 to Lesparre and Vensac, then follow (large) signed route.

Charges 2005

Per unit incl. 2 persons, fully serviced pitch	€ 20,00 - € 39,50
tent pitch incl. 2 persons	€ 15,00 - € 32,50
extra person	€ 3,00 - € 6,00
animal	€ 3,00

Camping Cheques accepted.

Reservations

Made with deposit (25%) and fee (€ 28). Tel: 05 56 09 33 33. Email: info@euronat.fr

Open

23 march - 3 November.

FR33240 Camping Airotel de L'Océan

F-33680 Lacanau (Gironde)

Its location on the Atlantic coast, only 600 metres from a lovely sandy beach makes this site extremely popular. Set in 10 hectares of wooded sand dunes, the site offers the total holiday experience with 550 pitches (including about 80 for tour operators) set amongst pine trees with areas for peace and quiet and areas for those who want to be on top of it all. Some pitches are quite spacious, some level and others requiring blocks. At the time of our visit everywhere was very dry and there was very little grass. There is a large swimming pool complex, a bar and disco (in a soundproof building). Lacanau-Océan has many weekend visitors from Bordeaux and is popular for surfing. There is a surf school in high season.

Facilities

Six toilet blocks provide spacious facilities including washbasins in cabins, a room for disabled visitors in each block (although the site is quite hilly in places), baby rooms, washing machines and dishwashing. Motorcaravan service point. Supermarket. Bar, restaurant and takeaway. Large leisure pool complex. Various sports facilities. Fitness gym. TV and games rooms. Internet access. Bicycle hire. Barbecue area. Off site: Beach 600 m. Shops 1 km. Many cycle routes through the woods.

Open

9 April - 25 September.

At a glance

Welcome & Ambience	✓✓✓	Location	✓✓✓✓
Quality of Pitches	✓✓✓	Range of Facilities	✓✓✓✓✓

Directions

From Bordeaux take D106 then onto D3 to Royan and through the wooded areas of the Atlantic coast. At Lacanau join D6 to Lacanau Ocean. At roundabout before village turn right and site is 800 m. on the right. GPS: N45:00.511 W01:11.544

Charges 2005

Per unit incl. 2 persons	€ 16,50 - € 26,50
with electricity	€ 16,50 - € 29,50
extra person	€ 4,50 - € 7,50
child (under 10 yrs)	free - € 4,00
dog	€ 2,50 - € 4,00

Reservations

Made with 25% deposit and € 28 fee.
Tel: 05 56 03 24 45.
Email: airotel.lacanau@wanadoo.fr

FR33210 Sunêlia La Pointe du Medoc

Route de la Pointe de Grave, F-33123 Le Verdon-sur-Mer (Gironde)

La Pointe du Medoc, part of the Sunelia group, was established four years ago close to the tip of the Medoc peninsula and it benefits from some excellent, modern amenities. This site has 267 pitches, with around half taken by mobile homes or chalets. It is situated roughly equi-distant between the sandy Atlantic beach (accessed by a pleasant walk through the forest opposite the site) and that of the Gironde estuary, both around 1 km. away. Pitches are generally large (100–150 sq.m). Some are in full sun (the site lost many trees in the great storm of 1999) but those towards the rear of the site offer much more shade. All are equipped with electricity (6A), and many have water and drainage. A large office has recently been converted to provide a library with internet access and a full size billiard table. A little used railway line passes by the front of the site, as well as the main road to Le Verdon. The site is well located for excursions to the Medoc chateaux or marshland.

Facilities

Two modern toilet blocks are maintained to a high standard, with good hot showers and washbasins in private cabins. Pleasant bar and restaurant with takeaway. Heated swimming pool with small waterfalls, split-level paddling pool. Massage room. Beach volleyball. Minigolf. Multi-sport terrain. Bicycle hire. Communal barbecue area. Wide range of organised entertainment and imaginative children's club (ages 4-11) throughout the season. Small farm and children's garden. Activities for teenagers in July and August. Off site: Sea fishing 1 km. Riding 5 km.

Open

9 April - 30 September.

At a glance

Welcome & Ambience	✓✓✓✓	Location	✓✓✓✓
Quality of Pitches	✓✓✓✓	Range of Facilities	✓✓✓✓✓

Directions

Site is on the RN215 just south of Le Verdon and can be accessed either from the south (Bordeaux or the Blaye ferry), or from the north using the regular Royan – Pointe de Grave car ferry.

Charges 2005

Per unit incl. 1 or 2 persons	€ 13,00 - € 20,00
with electricity	€ 16,00 - € 24,00
with water and drainage	€ 18,00 - € 26,00
extra person (over 1 yr)	€ 3,00 - € 6,00
dog	€ 5,00

Reservations

Essential for high season – contact site.
Tel: 05 56 73 39 99.
Email: info@camping-lapointedumedoc.com

FR33220 Sunêlia Le Petit Nice

Route de Biscarosse, F-33115 Pyla-sur-Mer (Gironde)

Le Petit Nice is a traditional seaside site, just south of the great Dune de Pyla (Europe's largest sand dune, and a genuinely remarkable sight). It is a friendly, if relatively unsophisticated, site with direct (steep) access to an excellent sandy beach. The 225 pitches are for the most part terraced, descending towards the sea. Many are quite small, with larger pitches generally occupied by mobile homes. For this reason it is likely to appeal more to campers and those with smaller motorcaravans and caravans. Most pitches are shaded by pine trees but those closest to the sea are unshaded. Unusually, the site also has a private hang-gliding and paragliding take-off strip (very popular activities here).

Facilities

Two refurbished toilet blocks include washbasins in cubicles, baby rooms and facilities for disabled people. New, very smart bar/restaurant. Well stocked shop. Games room. Attractive swimming pool with small slide, children's pool and jacuzzi. Good fenced play area. Tennis, table tennis and boules court.

Open

7 April - 30 September.

At a glance

Welcome & Ambience	✓✓✓	Location	✓✓✓✓✓
Quality of Pitches	✓✓	Range of Facilities	✓✓✓✓

Directions

The site is on the D218 (Arcachon – Biscarosse) south of the Dune de Pyla and is the fifth site you pass after the Dune. GPS: N44:34.339 W01:13.255

Charges 2005

Per pitch incl. 2 persons	€ 14,00 - € 28,00
with electricity (6A)	€ 17,00 - € 32,00
extra person	€ 4,00 - € 7,00
child (2-12 yrs)	€ 2,00 - € 6,00

Camping Cheques accepted.

Reservations

Essential in high season. Tel: 05 56 22 74 03.
Email: camping.petit.nice@wanadoo.fr

FR33310 Yelloh! Village Le Panorama

Grand Dune du Pyla, route de Biscarrosse, F-33260 Pyla-sur-Mer (Gironde)

Many campsites set amongst pine trees have a rather untidy look, but Panorama is different. Here the entrance is very inviting with well tended flower beds and a pleasant, airy reception. From the entrance there is a steep climb up to the pitches, passing the swimming pool and play area. The touring pitches are a mix of those suitable for caravans and motorcaravans and those suitable only for tents. They are set on terraces amongst the tall pines outnumbering the pitches used for mobile homes and most have electricity (3-10A). Access to the toilet blocks may involve a steep climb (the site is probably not suitable for people with disabilities). There are many activities and entertainments organised in high season, even classical concerts. All potentially noisy activities – pool, play areas, shop, discos, concerts, bar and takeaway – are grouped on the entrance side of the dune, away from the pitches. A track leads down to the beach with a staircase and right next door is Europe's largest dune, the Dune de Pyla, a favourite with parascenders. The area is a maze of off road cycle tracks. A Yelloh Village member.

Facilities
Seven toilet blocks (progressively being renovated) are clean and well maintained with free hot showers, baby rooms and facilities for disabled people. Fridge hire. Laundry facilities. Motorcaravan service point. Bar/restaurant with panoramic view of the ocean. Attractive pool area with three heated swimming pools and jacuzzi (1/5-30/9). Adjacent play area. Tennis. Minigolf and table tennis. Paragliding. Sub-aqua diving. Organised entertainment in high season for all ages. Off site: Riding and golf 10 km.

Open
1 May - 30 September.

At a glance
Welcome & Ambience	✓✓✓✓✓	Location	✓✓✓✓✓
Quality of Pitches	✓✓✓✓	Range of Facilities	✓✓✓✓

Directions
From the N250, just before La Teste, take D259 signed Biscarrosse and Dune de Pilate. At roundabout at end of road turn left (south) on D218 coast road signed Biscarrosse and Dune de Pyla. Site is 4 km. on the right.

Charges 2005
Per person	€ 3,50 - € 8,00
child (under 12 yrs)	€ 1,50 - € 2,50
pitch	€ 8,00 - € 17,00
electricity (3-10A)	€ 3,00 - € 5,00
animal	€ 3,00 - € 5,00

Reservations
Made with deposit (€ 120) and fee (€ 30); min. 10 days in high season. Tel: 05 56 22 10 44. Email: mail@camping-panorama.com

FR33320 Camping Talaris Vacances

Route de l'Océan, F-33680 Lacanau (Gironde)

This is a typically French campsite where the owner is anxious to welcome more British visitors. It is located near a large lake and just 6 km. from the Atlantic coast at Lacanau Océan, so there are opportunities for swimming in either lake or sea, for surfing, water-skiing or sailing. There are plenty of cycle tracks and horse riding is available nearby. On site, there is plenty going on for youngsters – the many activities take place in front of the bar, restaurant and swimming pool area, so it is probably not the place for parents to relax! However, the part of the campsite allocated to the 150 tourist pitches is amongst mature trees (mainly oak, silver birch and the inevitable pines) at the far end of the site, so is surprisingly peaceful and relaxed (depending, of course, on one's neighbours!) Some 100 mobile homes and chalets are available for rent, grouped in another part of the site. A 'Sites et Paysages' member.

Facilities
Two similar almost identical toilet blocks, one serving mainly the area occupied by tour operators providing activity holidays for young people, but the one in the camping/caravanning area is adequate, with pre-set showers, washbasins in cubicles and solar heating used for water. Dishwashing and laundry sinks under cover. Washing machines and dryers. Baby room and facilities for disabled people. Shop (July/Aug). Bar/restaurant and takeaway with covered terrace (1/5-13/9). Swimming pools (1/5-13/9). Off site: Lake 1 km. Riding 1 km. Golf 3 km. Beach 6 km.

Open
1 May - 17 September.

At a glance
Welcome & Ambience	✓✓✓✓	Location	✓✓✓
Quality of Pitches	✓✓✓	Range of Facilities	✓✓✓✓

Directions
From Bordeaux, take N125/D6 west to Lacanau and continue on D6 towards Lacanau Océan. Site is on right in about 7 km. GPS: N45:00.288 W01:06.443

Charges 2005
Per unit incl. 2 persons	€ 16,25 - € 26,50
extra person	€ 3,00 - € 5,50
child (4-10 yrs)	free - € 3,30
animal	€ 2,50 - € 3,00
electricity (6A)	€ 3,00

Reservations
Contact site. Tel: 05 56 03 04 15. Email: talarisvacances@free.fr

FR40020 Camping Les Chênes

Bois de Boulogne, F-40100 Dax (Landes)

Dax is not a place that springs at once to mind as a holiday town but, as well as being a 'spa', it promotes a comprehensive programme of events and shows during the summer season. Les Chênes is a well established site, popular with the French themselves and situated on the edge of town amongst parkland (also near the river) and close to the spa for the thermal treatments. The 183 touring pitches are of two types, some large and traditional with hedges, water and electricity connections, and others more informal, set amongst tall pines with electricity if required. This is a reliable, well run site, with a little of something for everyone, but probably most popular for adults taking the 'treatments'.

Facilities

Two very different toilet blocks, one new and very modern with heating, washbasins in cubicles, facilities for disabled people and babies and young children. The older block has been refurbished. Laundry room. Ample laundry and dishwashing sinks. Reasonably well stocked shop also providing takeaway food (1/4-28/10). Unusual and attractive swimming and paddling pools (6/5-16/9). Good play area. Large field for ball games, table tennis and boules pitch. Bicycle hire. Mini-club for children (July/Aug). Occasional special evenings for adults with meals and dancing. Charcoal barbecues are not permitted. Off site: Restaurant opposite site entrance. Fishing 100 m. Riding and golf 300 m. Beaches 28 km.

Open

1 April - 28 October.

At a glance

Welcome & Ambience	✓✓✓✓	Location	✓✓✓
Quality of Pitches	✓✓✓✓	Range of Facilities	✓✓✓

Directions

Site is west of town on south side of river, signed after main river bridge and at many junctions in town - Bois de Boulogne (1.5 km). In very wet weather the access road to the site may be flooded (but not the site). GPS: N43:42.721 W01:04.385

Charges 2005

Per unit incl. 1 or 2 persons and electricity (5A)	€ 13,00 - € 15,60
with water and drainage	€ 15,50 - € 18,20
extra person	€ 5,00
child (0-12 yrs)	€ 3,00
animal	€ 1,00

Reservations

Made with deposit (€ 46.50) and fee (€ 7.50); contact site. Tel: 05 58 90 05 53. Email: camping-chenes@wanadoo.fr

FR40040 Camping Village La Paillotte

F-40140 Azur (Landes)

La Paillotte, in the Landes area of southwest France, is a site with a character of its own. The campsite buildings (reception, shop, restaurant, even sanitary blocks) are all Tahitian in style, circular and constructed from local woods with the typical straw roof (and layer of waterproof material underneath). Some are now being replaced but still in character. It lies right beside the Soustons lake, 1.5 km. from Azur village, and has its own sandy beach. This is particularly suitable for young children because the lake is shallow and slopes extremely gradually. For boating the site has a small private harbour where you can keep your own non-powered boat (of shallow draught). All 310 pitches at La Paillotte are marked, individual ones and are mostly shady with shrubs and trees planted. The 132 pitches for touring units vary in price according to size, position and whether they are equipped with electricity, water, etc. La Paillotte is an unusual site with its own atmosphere which appeals to many regular clients. Used by tour operators (45 pitches).

Facilities

Circular rustic-style toilet blocks are rather different from the usual campsite amenities, but are modern and fully tiled. They include individual washbasins, partly enclosed, some toilets and basins en-suite and separate 'mini' facilities for children. Outside washing-up sinks. Washing machines and dryers. Motorcaravan service points. Shop (1/6-29/9). Good restaurant with pleasant terrace overlooking the lake, bar, takeaway (all 13/4-26/9). Swimming pool complex (13/4-26/9). Sports, games and activities organised for children and adults. 'Mini-club' room, with 'mini' equipment. TV room, library. Fishing. Bicycle hire. Table tennis. Sailing, rowing boats and pedaloes for hire. Torches useful. No dogs are accepted. Off site: Riding 5 km. Golf 10 km. Atlantic beaches 10 km.

Open

April - September.

At a glance

Welcome & Ambience	✓✓✓✓	Location	✓✓✓✓✓
Quality of Pitches	✓✓✓✓	Range of Facilities	✓✓✓✓✓

Directions

Coming from the north along N10, turn west on D150 at Magescq. From south go via Soustons. In Azur turn left before church (site signed).
GPS: N43:47.229 W01:18.570

Charges 2006

Per unit incl. 2 persons
with 10A electricity	€ 15,00 - € 35,00
with electricity and water	€ 17,00 - € 37,00
pitch by the lake	€ 20,00 - € 43,00
extra person (over 4 yrs)	€ 3,00 - € 7,00

Reservations

Advised for high season; made for Sat. to Sat. only 2/7-27/8, with deposit (€ 38.11 per week) and fee (€ 25). Tel: 05 58 48 12 12. Email: info@paillotte.com

FR40030 Les Pins du Soleil

Départementale 459, F-40990 St Paul-lès-Dax (Landes)

This site will appeal to families, particularly those with younger children, or those who prefer to be some way back from the coast within easy reach of shops, cultural activities, etc. and well placed for touring the area. Dax is a busy spa town with many attractions – Les Pins du Soleil is actually at St Paul lès Dax, some 3 km. from Dax itself. The site has 145 good sized pitches, 99 for touring units of which 59 have electricity and drainage. Although new, the site benefits from being developed in light woodland so there is a fair amount of shade from the many small trees. A range of excursions is possible by bus to St Sebastian, Lourdes, etc. and the nearby Calicéo aquatic centre is recommended. English is spoken.

Facilities

Modern sanitary facilities include facilities for babies, disabled visitors and laundry. Small supermarket. Bar. Takeaway (2/6-15/9). Attractive, medium sized swimming pool with café (both 2/6-15/9). Playground and children's mini-club in high season. Volleyball. Table tennis. Bicycle hire. Off site: Fishing 1 km. Riding 3 km. Bus to the thermal baths.

Open

2 April - 29 October.

At a glance

Welcome & Ambience	✓✓✓✓	Location	✓✓✓
Quality of Pitches	✓✓✓	Range of Facilities	✓✓✓✓

Directions

Approaching from west on N124, avoid bypass and follow signs for Dax and St Paul. Almost immediately turn right at roundabout onto D459 and follow signs. Site is a little further along on the left. It is also well signed from the town centre, north of the river. GPS: N43:43.224 W01:05.64

Charges 2005

Per unit incl. 2 persons with electricity, water and drainage	€ 8,00 - € 17,00
	€ 15,00 - € 23,00
extra person	€ 6,00
child (4-10 yrs)	€ 3,50
animal	€ 2,00

Less for stays over 21 nights.
Camping Cheques accepted.

Reservations

Made with deposit (€ 35) and fee (€ 6).
Tel: 05 58 91 37 91. Email: pinsoleil@aol.com

FR40050 Sunêlia Le Col-Vert

Lac de Leon, F-40560 Vielle-St Girons (Landes)

This extensive but natural site edges a nature reserve and stretches along the shore of the Lac de Léon, a conservation area, for one kilometre on a narrow frontage. This makes it particularly suitable for those who want to practise water sports such as sailing and windsurfing. Bathing is also possible as the lake bed shelves gently making it easy for children. The site has a supervised beach in July and August, sail-boarding courses are arranged in high season and there are some boats and boards for hire. There are some 800 pitches in total, the 380 pitches for touring units being flat and covered by light pinewood, most with good shade and many along the lake side. They are of around 100 sq.m, only partly separated and some 120 have water and electricity points. Activities are organised in season: children's games, tournaments, etc. by day and dancing or shows in the evenings. Used by tour operators (80 pitches).

Facilities

Of the four toilet blocks, one is heated in low season. Mostly British WCs, washbasins in cabins. Dishwashing sinks (mainly cold water but with hot tap to draw from). Washing machines, dryer and dishwasher. Very good facilities for disabled people. Motorcaravan services. Shops (8/4-10/9). Good bar/restaurant by the lake (open to all). Simple takeaway. Two pools (all season and supervised), one open air with whirlpool and one covered and heated. Sunbathing areas. Playground. TV room, table tennis (6 tables in covered building). Games room. Two sports areas with boules, tennis and volleyball. Fitness centre and sauna. Two jogging tracks. Safety deposit boxes. An overall charge is made for the leisure activities but this excludes certain facilities, e.g. riding, bicycle hire, sauna, tennis, minigolf. Fishing (lessons for children). Riding. Sailing school (15/6-15/9). Several areas for barbecues. Off site: Walking and cycle ways in the forest. Atlantic beaches 5 km. Golf 10 km.

At a glance

Welcome & Ambience	✓✓✓✓	Location	✓✓✓✓✓
Quality of Pitches	✓✓✓✓	Range of Facilities	✓✓✓✓✓

Directions

Site is off D652 Mimizan-Léon road, 4 km. south of crossroads with D42 at St Girons. Road to lake and site is signed at Veille. GPS: N43:54.190 W01:18.631

Charges 2005

Per unit incl. 2 persons acc. to season and location	€ 11,00 - € 43,50
extra person	€ 2,00 - € 6,00
child (3-13 yrs)	€ 1,50 - € 5,00
electricity (3/10A)	€ 3,70 - € 5,00
dog	€ 1,00 - € 4,00

Camping Cheques accepted.

Reservations

€ 46 deposit per week booked and € 30 fee.
Tel: 05 58 42 94 06. Email: contact@colvert.com

Open

8 April - 24 September.

FR40100 Camping du Domaine de la Rive

Mobile homes ▶ page 425

Route de Bordeaux, F-40600 Biscarosse (Landes)

Set in pine woods, La Rive has a superb beach-side location on Lac de Sanguinet. It provides mostly level, numbered and clearly defined pitches of 100 sq.m. all with electricity connections (6A). The swimming pool complex is wonderful, with various pools linked by water channels and bridges, the four-slide pool having a wide staircase to the top to speed up enjoyment. There is also a jacuzzi, paddling pool and two large, unusually shaped swimming pools, all surrounded by paved sunbathing areas and decorated with palm trees. An indoor pool is heated and open all season. The latest addition is a super children's aqua park with various games, etc. The beach is excellent, shelving gently to provide safe bathing for all ages. There are windsurfers and small craft can be launched from the site's slipway. This is a friendly site with a good mix of nationalities.

Facilities

Five modern, very good quality toilet blocks have washbasins in cabins and mainly British style toilets. Visitors with disabilities well catered for in three blocks. Baby baths. We found the facilities very clean. Motorcaravan service point. Well stocked shop with gas (1/5-15/9). Bar serving snacks and takeaway. Games room adjoining. Restaurant with reasonably priced family meals (1/5-10/9). Swimming pool complex, supervised July/Aug (outdoor pools 1/5-15/9). Play area. Two tennis courts. Bicycle hire. Hand-ball or basketball court, table tennis, boules, archery and football. Fishing. Water skiing. Watersports equipment may be hired and tournaments in various sports are arranged in June-Aug. Skateboard park. Trampolines with safety harness. Play area. Discos and karaoke evenings organised outside bar with stage and tiered seating. Mini-club for children twice daily. Charcoal barbecues not permitted on pitches (central area available). Caravan storage. Off site: Riding 5 km. Golf 10 km.

At a glance

Welcome & Ambience	✓✓✓✓	Location	✓✓✓✓
Quality of Pitches	✓✓✓	Range of Facilities	✓✓✓✓✓

Directions

Take D652 from Sanguinet to Biscarrosse and site is signed on the right in about 6 km.
GPS: N44:27.607 W01:07.808

Charges 2005

Per pitch incl. 2 persons and electricity	€ 20,00 - € 36,00
with water and drainage	€ 23,00 - € 39,00
extra person	€ 3,40 - € 6,60
child (3-10 yrs)	€ 2,30 - € 5,00
boat	€ 5,00 - € 6,00
dog	€ 2,10 - € 4,00

Camping Cheques accepted.

Reservations

Advised for July/Aug. and made with deposit (€ 100).
Tel: 05 58 78 12 33.
Email: info@camping-de-la-rive.fr

Open

1 April - 30 September.

FR40110 Camping Caravaning Sen Yan

Le Village Tropical, F-40170 Mézos (Landes)

This exotic family site is about 12 km. from the Atlantic coast in the Landes forest area, set just outside the village. There are 310 pitches marked with hedges, 190 with electricity, and with ample water points. Some mobile homes and tour operator pitches are in a separate 'village'. The reception, bar and pool area is almost tropical with the luxuriant greenery of its banana trees, palm trees, tropical flowers and its straw sunshades. Activities and evening entertainment include a disco twice weekly in high season.

Facilities

Three toilet blocks with good quality fittings have showers and washbasins in cabins and some British style WCs. The newest block is especially suitable for low season visitors with a special section for babies, plus facilities for disabled people. Shop (from 15/6). Bar, restaurant and snacks (1/7-31/8). Outdoor swimming pools (1/7-30/8). Heated indoor pool(1/6-15/9). Archery. Practice golf. Bicycle hire. Only gas barbecues are permitted. Off site: Fishing 500 m. Riding 6 km. Beach 12 km.

Open

1 June - 15 September.

At a glance

Welcome & Ambience	✓✓✓✓	Location	✓✓✓✓
Quality of Pitches	✓✓✓✓	Range of Facilities	✓✓✓✓✓

Directions

From N10 take exit 14 (Onesse-Laharie), then the D38 Bias/Mimizan road. After 13 km. turn south to Mézos from where site is signed.
GPS: N44:04.337 W01:09.38

Charges 2006

Per person	€ 5,00 - € 6,00
child (under 7 yrs)	free - € 5,00
pitch with 6A electricity	€ 24,00 - € 34,00

Reservations

Made with deposit (€ 84) and fee (€ 26).
Tel: 05 58 42 60 05. Email: reception@sen-yan.com

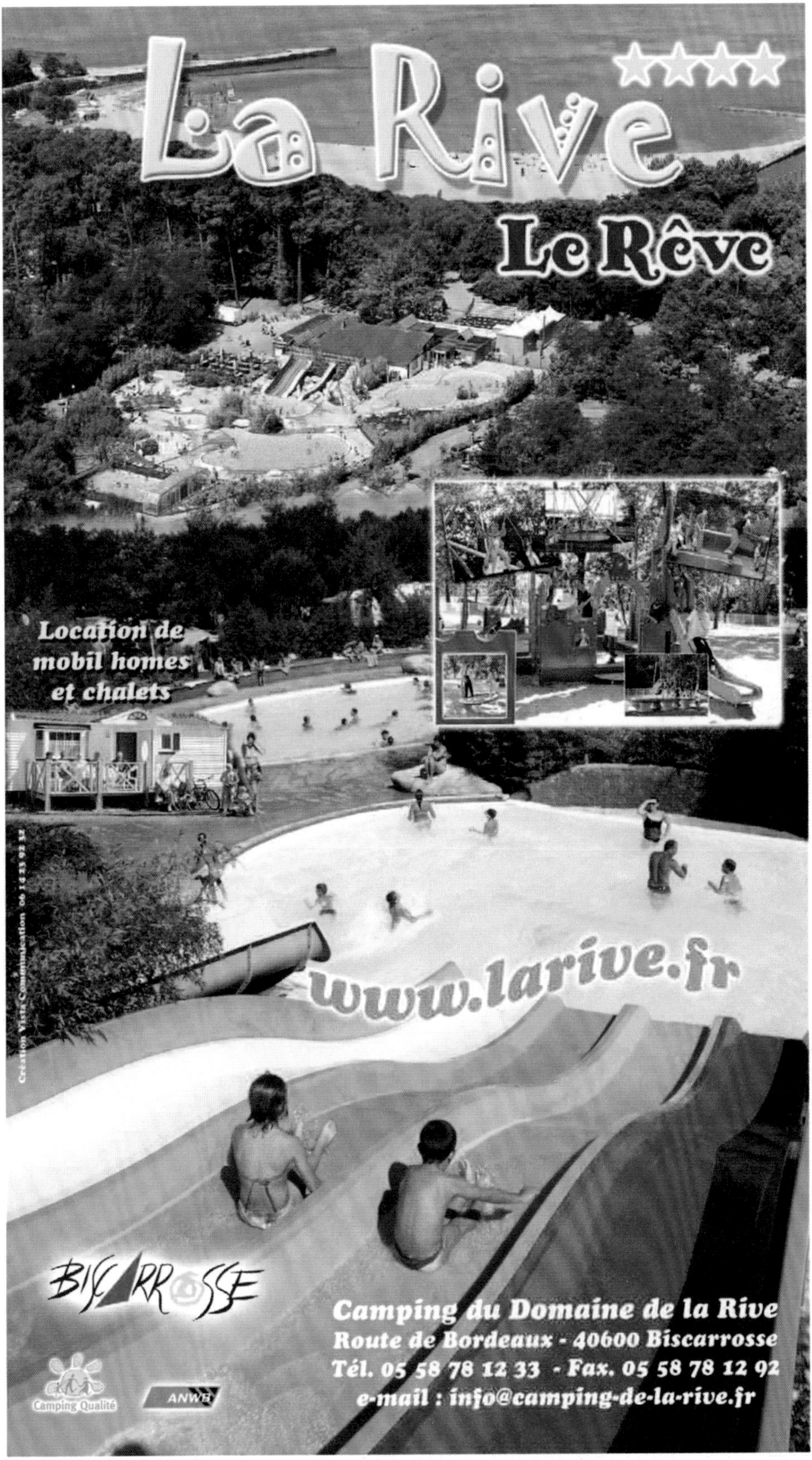

La Rive ★★★★
Le Rêve
Location de mobil homes et chalets
www.larive.fr
Création Vista Communication 06 14 25 92 32
BISCARROSSE
Camping Qualité
ANWB
Camping du Domaine de la Rive
Route de Bordeaux - 40600 Biscarrosse
Tél. 05 58 78 12 33 - Fax. 05 58 78 12 92
e-mail : info@camping-de-la-rive.fr

FR40060 Camping Eurosol

Route de la Plage, F-40560 Vielle-St Girons (Landes)

The sandy beach 700 metres from Eurosol has supervised bathing in high season. The site also has its own swimming pool with paved sunbathing areas which are planted with palm trees giving quite a tropical feel. The site itself is on undulating ground amongst mature pine trees giving good shade and the pitches on the slopes are mainly only suitable for tents. The 417 pitches for touring units are numbered (although with nothing to separate them, there is little privacy) and 209 have electricity with 120 fully serviced (86 with mobile homes). A family site with entertainers who speak many languages, many games and tournaments are organised, for example a beach volleyball competition which is held each evening in front of the bar.

Facilities

There are four main toilet blocks all refurbished to include washbasins in cabins. Two smaller blocks have facilities for babies and disabled people. Motorcaravan service point. Fridge rental. Well stocked shop (8/5-18/9). Bar (8/5-18/9), restaurant and takeaway (1/7-31/8). Raised deck area and a stage for live shows (mainly performed by the very versatile staff) arranged in July/Aug. and finishing by midnight. Outdoor swimming pool (8/5-18/9). Tennis. Multi-sport court for basketball, handball and football. Bicycle hire. Charcoal barbecues are not permitted. Off site: Riding school opposite. Fishing 700 m.

Open

13 May - 16 September.

At a glance

Welcome & Ambience	✓✓✓✓	Location	✓✓✓✓
Quality of Pitches	✓✓✓	Range of Facilities	✓✓✓✓✓

Directions

Turn off D652 at St Girons on D42 towards St Girons-Plage. Site is on left before coming to beach (4.5 km).
GPS: N43:57.100 W01:21.087

Charges 2005

Per unit incl.1 or 2 persons	€ 11,00 - € 24,00
with electricity	€ 13,50 - € 28,50
with water and drainage	€ 13,50 - € 31,50
extra person (over 4 years)	€ 4,00
dog	€ 2,50

Reservations

Made for min. 1 week with deposit (€ 95) and fee (€ 25). Tel: 05 58 47 90 14.
Email: contact@camping-eurosol.com

FR40070 Camping Lous Seurrots

Contis Plage, F-40170 St Julien-en-Born (Landes)

Lous Seurrots is only a short 300 metre walk from the beach and parts of the site have views across the estuary. There are 610 pitches, mainly in pine woods on sandy undulating ground. They are numbered but only roughly marked out, most have good shade and over 80% have electrical hook-ups. The site's pool complex is in a superb setting of palm trees and flower beds and the paved sunbathing areas have wonderful views out to the estuary and the sea. For all its size, Lous Seurrots is a family site with the emphasis on peace and tranquillity (no discos). Used by tour operators.

Facilities

Six well kept, modern toilet blocks cope very well and include some washbasins in cabins, and some showers with washbasins. Baby rooms and good facilities for disabled people. Numerous laundry and dishwashing sinks and washing machines. Motorcaravan service point. Large well stocked shop (1/6-15/9). Bar, takeaway and restaurant (15/5-15/9). Swimming pool complex (15/5-30/9), four pools and a jacuzzi with keep fit classes held every morning in July/Aug. Tennis, table tennis, archery, volleyball and minigolf. Canoeing. Bicycle hire. Fishing. Mini-club for younger children. Evening entertainment twice weekly in high season in open-air auditorium. Only gas barbecues are permitted. Off site: Riding 3 km.

At a glance

Welcome & Ambience	✓✓✓✓	Location	✓✓✓✓
Quality of Pitches	✓✓✓	Range of Facilities	✓✓✓✓✓

Directions

Turn off D652 on D41 (15 km. south of Mimizan) to Contis-Plage and site is on left as you reach it.
GPS: N44:05.347 W01:18.990

Charges 2005

Per unit incl. 2 persons	€ 11,00 - € 30,00
extra person	€ 4,00 - € 6,00
child (3-7 yrs)	free - € 4,00
electricity (6A)	€ 4,00
animal	€ 3,00

Reservations

Made with deposit (€ 46) and fee (€ 18.29).
Tel: 05 58 42 85 82. Email: info@lous-seurrots.com

Open

1 April - 30 September.

FR40080 Airotel Club Marina – Landes

Rue Marina, F-40200 Thinigan (Landes)

If ever a campsite could be said to have two separate identities, then Club Marina-Landes is surely the one. In early and late season it is quiet, with the pace of life in low gear – come July and until 1 September, all the facilities are open and there is fun for all the family with the chance that family members will only meet together at meal times. Activities include discos, play groups for children, specially trained staff to entertain teenagers and concerts for more mature campers. There is swimming, tennis, a fitness room, minigolf and volleyball, and much more, not to mention the superb beach nearby. A nightly curfew ensures that all have a good night's sleep. Staff are pleased to see you and helpful. The site has 445 touring pitches (277 with 10A electricity) and 128 mobile homes and chalets for rent. The pitches are on firm grass, most with good size hedges and they are large (mostly 120 sq.m. or larger). Well maintained and clean, this would be a very good choice for a family holiday.

Facilities

Four toilet blocks are opened as required by the numbers on site. Well maintained and well equipped, there are hot and cold showers and many washbasins in cabins. Facilities for babies, children and disabled visitors. Laundry facilities. Motorcaravan services. Fridge hire. Shop with bread baked on the premises (all season). Bar and restaurant (all season). Snack bar, pizzas and takeaway (1/7-31/8). Covered pool (all season). Outdoor pool (2/7-31/8). Minigolf. Table tennis. Tennis. Volleyball and basketball. Bicycle hire. Play area. Internet access. Entertainment and organised activities (high season). Only gas or electric barbecues are permitted. Off site: Excellent beach and fishing 500 m. Bus service 1 km. Large supermarket in Mimizan 8 km. Riding 1 km. Golf 7 km.

At a glance

Welcome & Ambience	✓✓✓✓	Location	✓✓✓✓✓
Quality of Pitches	✓✓✓✓	Range of Facilities	✓✓✓✓✓

Directions

From Mimizan head for Mimizan Plage, sometimes signed just 'Plage' until dual carriageway after some 5 km. Turn left at Marina-Landes small sign and follow signs to site.

Charges 2005

Per unit incl. 3 persons	€ 14,00 - € 35,00
incl. electricity	€ 17,00 - € 38,00
extra person (over 3 yrs)	€ 3,00 - € 6,00
dog	€ 2,00 - € 4,00

Reservations

Made with 25% deposit and € 31 fee; contact site for full details. Tel: 05 58 09 12 66. Email: contact@clubmarina.com

Open

12 May - 18 September.

FR40120 Domaine Naturiste Arnaoutchot

F-40560 Vielle-St Girons (Landes)

'Arna' is a large naturist site with extensive facilities and direct access to a beach. Even with 500 pitches, its layout in the form of a number of sections, each with its own character, make it quite relaxing and very natural. These sections amongst the trees and bushes of the Landes provide a variety of reasonably sized pitches, most with electricity (3/6A), although the hilly terrain means that only a limited number are flat enough for motorcaravans. The centrally located amenities are extensive and of excellent quality. The site has the advantage of direct access to a large, sandy naturist beach, although access from some parts of the site may involve a walk of perhaps 600-700 metres. The 'Arna Club' provides more than 40 activities and workshops (in the main season). There are chalets, mobile homes, caravans and tents for rent. The site is used by a tour operator (20 pitches). Member 'France 4 Naturisme'. English, Dutch and German spoken at reception.

Facilities

Sanitary facilities include the usual naturist site type of blocks with communal hot showers and also a number of tiny blocks with one hot shower, WC and washbasin each in an individual cabin. All blocks have been upgraded to provide fully tiled, modern facilities, one block is heated in low season. Laundry. Motorcaravan service point. Large supermarket and range of other shops. Bar/restaurant, pizzeria and tapita (fish) bar (opening dates subject to demand). Pizza delivery to pitches or to telephone point on beach. Heated indoor swimming pool with solarium, whirlpool and slide. Outdoor pool and terraced sunbathing area. Spa centre with sauna, steam, whirlpool and massage treatments. Arna Club (main season) including archery, golf practise, tennis, petanque, swimming, rambling, cycling, handicrafts, excursions and special activities for children. TV, video and games rooms. Cinema. Library. Hairdresser and chiropodist. Cash point. Internet point. Bicycle hire. Fishing on site. Torches useful. Gas and electric barbecues are permitted. American motorhomes not accepted. Off site: Riding or golf 5 km.

At a glance

Welcome & Ambience	✓✓✓✓	Location	✓✓✓✓
Quality of Pitches	✓✓✓	Range of Facilities	✓✓✓✓✓

Directions

Site is signed off the D652 road at Vielle-Saint-Girons. Follow D328 for 3-4 km. GPS: N43:54.449 W01:21.866

Charges 2005

Per unit incl. 1 person	€ 9,90 - € 32,90
extra person (over 3 yrs)	€ 2,00 - € 6,80
electricity (3/6A)	€ 3,60 - € 5,10
animal	€ 1,20 - € 3,00

Special offers available.
Camping Cheques accepted.

Reservations

Made with 25% deposit and fee (€ 30). Tel: 05 58 49 11 11. Email: contact@arna.com

Open

1 April - 25 September.

FR40200 Yelloh! Village Le Sylvamar

Avenue de l'Océan, F-40530 Labenne Océan (Landes)

Camping Village Sylvamar is less than a kilometre from the long sandy beach of Labenne Ocean. The large, light and airy reception area is very welcoming. The 500 pitches (320 for touring units) are level, numbered and mostly separated by low hedges. All have electricity (10A), many also have water and waste water points and there is welcoming shade. The swimming pool complex is absolutely superb, set in a sunny location. There are pools of various sizes with a very large one for paddling. The four toboggans are very popular. There is a fast flowing channel that youngsters find very exciting, sailing down in the inflatable boats and rubber rings provided. There is ample room for sunbathing and all is overlooked by the bar/restaurant and its terrace. A Yelloh! Village member.

Facilities

Four modern toilet blocks with good quality fittings have washbasins in cabins, and facilities for babies and disabled visitors. Washing machines at each block. Small shop on site but a large supermarket is only 500 m. Bar/restaurant (all season) sells bread and takeaway and has a good menu for adults and children. Play area for young children. Mini-club in July/Aug. with painting, games etc. Fitness centre. Tennis. Bicycle hire. Table tennis. Badminton. Library with comfortable seating. Extensive entertainment programme for all ages, incl. evening shows in the outdoor amphitheatre from folklore, cabaret, concerts to karaoke. Fridge hire. Barbecues are not permitted (communal ones provided). Internet access (July/Aug. only).

At a glance

Welcome & Ambience	✓✓✓✓	Location	✓✓✓✓
Quality of Pitches	✓✓✓✓	Range of Facilities	✓✓✓✓✓

Directions

Labenne is on the N10. In Labenne, head west on D126 signed Labenne Océan and site is on right in 4 km. GPS: N43:35.72 W01:27.383

Charges 2006

Per unit incl. 2 persons, electricity	€ 16,00 - € 36,00
extra person (over 7 yrs)	€ 3,00 - € 7,00
dog	free - € 4,00

Reservations

Made with deposit (€ 130), fee (€ 30) and cancellation insurance (€ 16). Tel: 05 59 45 75 16. Email: camping@sylvamar.fr

Open

17 April - 25 September.

FR40130 Camping de la Côte

F-40660 Messanges (Landes)

A peaceful family site, surrounded by pine forests near the beaches of the Landes, this site has large, level pitches edged with newly planted trees and shrubs. A number of the 104 touring pitches are set among trees that provide shade; all have electricity and 9 have water and drainage. The beach and dunes are 20 minutes walk. M. and Mme. Moresmau are proud of the site which is very well maintained. It is a happy site where the owners are always about creating the family atmosphere that is a hallmark of many small sites in this guide. Although it does not have the full range of facilities, such as a pool, it fills a niche for quiet, family holidays in an area where there are many brasher, more active options.

Facilities

Two modern toilet blocks are of excellent quality and very well maintained. Washbasins in cabins, a baby room and provision for disabled people. Washing machines and dryer. Motorcaravan service point. Reception sells a few basic supplies and gas (1/7-31/8). Takeaway (July/Aug). Play area. Boules. Off site: Fishing or riding within 1 km. Bicycle hire 1.5 km. Golf 2 km. Vieux-Boucau near.

Open

1 April - 30 September.

At a glance

Welcome & Ambience	✓✓✓✓✓	Location	✓✓✓✓
Quality of Pitches	✓✓✓✓	Range of Facilities	✓✓✓

Directions

Site is signed off the D652, 1.5 km. north of Vieux-Boucau, 2.5 km. south of Messanges. GPS: N43:48.021 W01:23.50

Charges 2005

Per unit incl. 2 persons	€ 8,60 - € 13,40
extra person	€ 2,30 - € 3,20
child (under 7 yrs)	€ 1,60 - € 2,20
electricity (6/10A)	€ 3,30 - € 4,10
water and drainage	€ 2,00 - € 3,30

Reservations

Advised and made with deposit (€ 60). Tel: 05 58 48 94 94. Email: info@campinglacote.com

FR40140 Camping Caravaning Lou P'tit Poun

Mobile homes ▶ page 425

110 avenue du Quartier Neuf, F-40390 St Martin de Seignanx (Landes)

The manicured grounds surrounding Lou P'tit Poun give it a well kept appearance, a theme carried out throughout this very pleasing site. It is only after arriving at the car park that you feel confident it is not a private estate. Beyond this point the site unfolds to reveal an abundance of thoughtfully positioned shrubs and trees. Behind a central sloping flower bed lies the open plan reception area. The avenues around the site are wide and the 168 pitches are spacious. All have electricity (6/10A), 30 are fully serviced and some are separated by low hedges. The jovial owners not only make their guests welcome, but extend their enthusiasm to organising weekly entertainment for young and old during high season. A 'Sites et Paysages' member.

Facilities

Two unisex sanitary blocks, maintained to a high standard and kept clean, include washbasins in cabins, a baby bath and provision for disabled people. Dishwashing sinks and laundry facilities with washing machine and dryer. Motorcaravan service point. Café, bread and ices (1/7-31/8). Swimming pool (1/6-15/9) Play area. Games room, TV. Half court tennis. Table tennis. Bicycle hire. Caravan storage. Off site: Bayonne 6 km. Fishing or riding 7 km. Golf 10 km. Sandy beaches of Basque coast ten minute drive.

Open

1 June - 15 September.

At a glance

Welcome & Ambience	✓✓✓✓✓	Location	✓✓✓✓
Quality of Pitches	✓✓✓✓✓	Range of Facilities	✓✓✓✓

Directions

Leave A63 at exit 6 and join N117 in the direction of Pau. Site is signed at Leclerc supermarket. Continue on N117 for 5.5 km. and site is then clearly signed on right. GPS: N43:31.451 W01:24.730

Charges 2006

Per pitch incl. 1 or 2 persons	€ 10,40 - € 23,50
with 4A electricity	€ 13,50 - € 27,00
with water and drainage	€ 20,50 - € 31,50
extra person	€ 5,10 - € 6,50
child (under 7 yrs)	€ 2,10 - € 4,30
pet	€ 3,10 - € 4,10

Reservations

Made with deposit (25%) and fee (€ 20). Tel: 05 59 56 55 79. Email: contact@louptitpoun.com

FR40160 Camping Les Vignes

Mobile homes ▶ page 427

Route de la Plage du Cap de L'Homy, F-40170 Lit-et-Mixe (Landes)

Les Vignes is a large holiday site close to the Atlantic coast with 450 pitches, of which 262 are occupied by a mix of mobile homes, bungalows and tents, most of which are for rent. The 188 tourist pitches are relatively level on a sandy base, all serviced with electricity (10A) and water, some with waste water drains. The site's amenities, including a supermarket, restaurant and bar, are located at the entrance to the site. The rather stylish swimming pool complex includes a six lane water slide. A wide range of activities is provided and during July and August a great variety of entertainment options for both adults and children, some of which take place in the new entertainment 'Big Top'.

Facilities

Four virtually identical sanitary units (not all open in low season) provide combined washbasin and shower cubicles, washing machines and dryers, facilities for babies and disabled people. Large supermarket (15/6-10/9). Restaurant and bar (15/6-10/9). Takeaway (July/Aug). Pool complex (1/6-15/9). Tennis. Golf driving range. Minigolf. Volleyball, basketball. Pétanque. Kids club and playground. Bicycle hire. Internet access. Off site: Golf course, canoeing, kayaking, surfing, riding. Many cycle tracks.

Open

1 June - 15 September.

At a glance

Welcome & Ambience	✓✓✓✓✓	Location	✓✓✓✓
Quality of Pitches	✓✓✓✓	Range of Facilities	✓✓✓✓

Directions

Lit-et-Mixe is on the D652 20 km. south of Mimizan. Turn west on D88 1 km. south of town towards Cap de l'Homy for 1.5 km. where site entrance is on left. GPS: N44:01.375 W01:16.787

Charges 2005

Per pitch incl. 2 persons, electricity and water	€ 14,50 - € 45,00
extra person	€ 4,00 - € 6,00
child (under 5 yrs)	€ 2,00 - € 4,00

Reservations

Advisable for high season, made with deposit and fee. Tel: 05 58 42 85 60. Email: contact@les-vignes.com

Les Vignes ★★★★ Grand Confort

AIROTEL CAMPING CARAVANING
Route de la plage du Cap de l'Homy
40170 LIT-ET-MIXE
Tél : 05 58 42 85 60 Fax : 05 58 42 74 36
www.les-vignes.com
E-mail : contact@les-vignes.com

Aquatic space with slides, lagoon and exotic gardens. Multisport ground, mini-golf, play area, game of bowls. July and August :managerial staff : sport and activities, Miniclub, evening parties, Television. Nearby : cycle track, surf, Canoeing kayaking and Horse riding.

Accommodation : canvas bungalows, Mobil-homes, chalets and Apartments "luxury"

Open from 01/06 to 15/09

FR40170 Siblu Camping La Réserve

Gastés, F-40160 Parentis-en-Born (Landes)

La Resérve is owned and run by Siblu (formerly Haven Europe). It is a large site set in a pinewood. It has access to a large lake with a beach and small harbour and the Atlantic beaches are fairly near (20 km). The lake shelves very gradually so is good fun for children and there are good facilities for windsurfing and sailing; powered boats for water ski-ing are also permitted here. The 700 numbered pitches (200 for touring) are of above average size (mostly 120 sq.m.) set on mainly flat ground and marked by stones in the ground. Most have electricity. A variety of entertainment, sports and activities are organised in the Haven Europe tradition, often in and around the super pool complex.

Facilities

Five toilet blocks, with en-suite facilities in one, include washbasins in cabins. Washing machines. When visited they were in some need of care and maintenance - this is being addressed. Supermarket. Restaurant and large bar with entertainment all season. Pool complex with water slides, paddling pools, etc. (lifeguards on duty). Children's club. Two tennis courts (floodlit in the evening), minigolf, table tennis and volleyball. Boat hire, windsurfing courses and water ski-ing. TV room. Amusements. Fishing. Bicycle hire. Dogs are not accepted. Off site: Beaches 20 km.

Open

29 April - 23 September.

At a glance

Welcome & Ambience	✓✓✓✓	Location	✓✓✓✓
Quality of Pitches	✓✓✓	Range of Facilities	✓✓✓✓✓

Directions

Turn west off D652 Gastes - Mimizan road on southern outskirts of Gastes by campsite sign, then 3 km. to site. GPS: N44:18.801 W01:10.140

Charges 2005

Per pitch incl. 2 persons	€ 12,00 - € 54,00
with electricity	€ 14,00 - € 39,00
extra person	€ 3,00 - € 6,00

Reservations

Accepted at any time for min. 4 days; no booking fee. Contact site or Siblu in the UK on 0870 998 2288 for information or reservation. Site tel: 05 58 09 74 79. Email: lareserve@siblu.fr

FR40180 Camping Le Vieux Port

Mobile homes ▶ page 427

Plage sud, F-40660 Messanges (Landes)

The area to the north of Bayonne is heavily forested and a number of very large campsites are attractively located close to the superb Atlantic beaches. Le Vieux Port is probably the largest and certainly one of the most impressive of these. A well established destination appealing particularly to families with teenage children, this lively site has no fewer than 1,406 open pitches of mixed size, most with electrical hook-ups (6/8A) and some with water and drainage. Sprawling beneath the pines, the camping area is well shaded and pitches are generally of a good size, attractively grouped around the toilet blocks. There are many tour operators here and well over a third of the site is taken up with mobile homes (private, site owned and tour operator) and another 400 pitches are used for tour operator tents. The heated pool complex is exceptional boasting five outdoor pools, one a heated pool for children, and three large water slides. There is also a heated indoor pool. At the back of the site a path leads across the dunes to a good beach (500 m). A little train also trundles to the beach on a fairly regular basis in high season (small charge). All in all, this is a lively site with a great deal to offer an active family.

Facilities

Nine well appointed toilet blocks are all of modern design and well maintained. Facilities for disabled people. Motorcaravan service point. Good shopping facilities, include a well stocked supermarket and various smaller shops in high season. Several restaurants (including takeaway) and three new bars (all open all season). Large pool complex (no Bermuda shorts) including new covered pool and Polynesian themed bar. Three tennis courts, two football pitches, a multi-sport pitch, minigolf etc. Bicycle hire. Well run and popular riding centre. Large animation team organises a wide range of activities in high season including discos and karaoke evenings. Only communal barbecues are allowed. Off site: Fishing 1 km. Golf 8 km.

Open

1 April - 30 September.

At a glance

Welcome & Ambience	✓✓✓	Location	✓✓✓✓✓
Quality of Pitches	✓✓✓	Range of Facilities	✓✓✓✓✓

Directions

Leave RN10 at Magescq exit heading for Soustons. Pass through Soustons following signs for Vieux-Boucau. Bypass this town and site is clearly signed to the left at second roundabout.
GPS: N43:47.863 W01:23.959

Charges 2006

Per unit incl. 2 persons	€ 12,00 - € 35,00
extra person	€ 3,50 - € 6,00
child (under 10 yrs)	€ 2,50 - € 4,00
electricity (6/8A)	€ 4,00 - € 6,50
animal	€ 2,00 - € 3,50

Camping Cheques accepted.

Reservations

Essential in high season. Tel: 01 72 03 91 60.
Email: contact@levieuxport.com

FR40190 Le Saint Martin Airotel Camping

Mobile homes ▶ page 428

Avenue de l'Océan, F-40660 Moliets-Plage (Landes)

A family site aimed mainly at couples and young families, Airotel St Martin is a welcome change to most of the sites in this area in that it has only a small number of mobile homes (77) compared to the number of touring pitches (583). First impressions are of a neat, tidy, well cared for site and the direct access to the beach is an added bonus. The pitches are mainly typically French in style with low hedges separating them plus some shade. There is also a 'free and easy' area under tall trees. Electric hook ups are 11-15A and a number of pitches also have water and drainage. Entertainment in high season is low key (with the emphasis on quiet nights) – daytime competitions and a 'mini-club' and the occasional evening entertainment, well away from the pitches and with no discos or karaoke.

Facilities
Six toilet blocks of a high standard have washbasins in cabins, large showers, baby rooms and facilities for disabled visitors. Motorcaravan service point. Washing machines and dryers. Fridge rental. Very good supermarket and various bars, restaurants and takeaways are at the entrance (Easter - 31/10). Attractive indoor pool, jacuzzi and sauna (open all season, charged for in July/Aug). Large outdoor pool area with pools, jacuzzi and paddling pool (June - 15/9). Multi sports pitch. Small play area. Internet access. Only electric barbecues are permitted. Off site: Special tariffs available at local golf course 700 m. Tennis 700 m. Riding 7 km.

At a glance
Welcome & Ambience	✓✓✓✓	Location	✓✓✓✓✓
Quality of Pitches	✓✓✓✓	Range of Facilities	✓✓✓✓

Directions
From the N10 take D142 to Lèon, then D652 to Moliets-et-Mar. Follow signs to Moliets-Plage, site is well signed. GPS: N43:51.145 W01:23.239

Charges 2006
Per unit incl. 1 or 2 adults, 1 child	€ 17,50 - € 27,00
with electricity	€ 21,00 - € 30,00
with services	€ 22,50 - € 38,50
extra person	€ 3,20 - € 5,50

Prices are for reserved pitches.

Reservations
Contact site. Tel: 05 58 48 52 30.
Email: contact@camping-saint-martin.fr

Open
Easter - 31 October.

FR40220 Camping Les Acacias

Route d'Azur, Quartier Delest, F-40660 Messanges (Landes)

Close to the Atlantic beaches of Les Landes, this small family run site is quiet and peaceful. There are 79 large, generally flat touring pitches separated by trees and shrubs, with chalets and mobile homes ranged unobtrusively on two sides of the site. There are also some seasonal caravans. All the touring pitches have electricity (5/10A) but water is only available at the toilet block. Pitches are easily accessed by tarmac internal roads. M and Mme Dourthe are constantly improving the site and the facilities and services show the care taken in design. This site is a suitable centre for a quiet family holiday or for exploring the coast and forests of Les Landes on foot or by bicycle.

Facilities
One modern, clean and well designed toilet block with British style toilets, washbasins (some in cabins), showers (one a family shower). Facilities for disabled people. Washing machines, dryer and ironing board. Motorcaravan services. Fridge hire. Shop (15/6-15/9). Takeaway (high season). Games room. Small play area. Football. Volleyball. Table tennis. Boules. Bicycle hire. Off site: Bus service 1 km. Beach and fishing 2 km. Riding 1.5 km. Golf 4 km.

Open
25 March - 25 October.

At a glance
Welcome & Ambience	✓✓✓	Location	✓✓✓✓
Quality of Pitches	✓✓✓✓	Range of Facilities	✓✓✓

Directions
Site is signed off the D652, turning inland (east) 2 km north of Vieux-Boucau; 2 km south of Messanges.

Charges 2006
Per unit incl. 1 or 2 persons	€ 8,50 - € 13,00
extra person	€ 2,60 - € 3,30
child (0-7 yrs)	€ 1,80 - € 2,20
electricity	€ 2,60 - € 4,00
animal	€ 0,80 - € 1,80

Reservations
Advised in high season. Tel: 00 33 (0) 55 84.
Email: lesacacias@lesacacias.com

FR64010 Europ Camping

Ascarat, F-64220 St Jean-Pied-de-Port (Pyrénées-Atlantiques)

Europ Camping is a neat and orderly, family run site with wonderful views of the vine-covered closer hills and the distant high Pyrénées. The 111 pitches (90 for touring units) are clearly marked and separated by shrubs and all have electricity (6A), water and drainage. The area is good for walking or mountain biking and there is rafting on a local river. The site is only 20 km. from the forest of Iraty with its lakes and ski-runs, and the Spanish border on the route de St Jacques-de-Compostelle, is 8 km.

Facilities

The central, modern and well appointed toilet block includes washbasins in cubicles and facilities for disabled visitors. Two washing machines, dryer. Laundry and dishwashing sinks (with excellent supply of hot water) outside, but all under cover. Motorcaravan service point. Small shop. Bar/restaurant with reasonably priced meal of the day and takeaway. Swimming pool with paddling pool and sauna. Play area. Volleyball and petanque. Barbecue area. Off site: Tennis near. Fishing 200 m. Bicycle hire 2 km. St Jean-Pied-de-Port 2 km. Riding 10 km.

Open

Easter - 30 September.

At a glance

Welcome & Ambience	✓✓✓✓	Location	✓✓✓✓
Quality of Pitches	✓✓✓✓	Range of Facilities	✓✓✓✓

Directions

Site is 2 km. northwest of St Jean-Pied-de-Port in the hamlet of Ascarat and is signed from the D918 Bayonne road. GPS: N43:10.370 W01:15.239

Charges guide

Per person	€ 5,40
child (under 7 yrs)	€ 2,70
pitch and car	€ 7,50
electricity (6A)	€ 3,80
dog	€ 2,00

Reservations

Made in writing with 30% deposit and € 21.34 fee. Tel: 05 59 37 12 78.

FR64070 Castel Camping Le Ruisseau des Pyrénées

Route d'Arbonne, F-64210 Bidart (Pyrénées-Atlantiques)

This pleasant, busy site, just behind the coast, is about 2 km. from Bidart and 2.5 km. from a sandy beach. It has two swimming pools – one 1,100 sq.m. pool complex with slides on the main site and an indoor heated pool on the newer area opposite. There is also a little lake, where fishing is possible, in the area at the bottom of the site which has a very pleasant open aspect and now includes a large play area. Pitches on the main campsite are individual, marked and of a good size, either on flat terraces or around the lake. The terrain is wooded so the great majority of them have some shade. There are 330 here with a further 110 on a second area where shade has developed and which has its own good toilet block. Electrical connections are available throughout. Animation is provided in the main season, with organised day-time sports and evening entertainment nightly in season. The site is popular with tour operators and the site has a number of its own mobile homes.

Facilities

Toilet facilities (unisex) consist of two main blocks and some extra smaller units. With washbasins in cabins, they are regularly refurbished and maintained. Washing machines. Shop. Large self-service restaurant with takeaway and separate bar with terraces, and TV (all 15/5-12/9). Outdoor swimming pools and indoor pool (15/5-12/9). Sauna. Large play area. Two tennis courts (free outside July/Aug). Volleyball, table tennis. Fitness track. TV and games rooms. Minigolf. Fitness room. Bicycle hire. Crazy golf. Fishing. Motorhome service point. Internet access. Off site: Riding and golf 2 km.

Open

20 May - 17 September.

At a glance

Welcome & Ambience	✓✓✓✓	Location	✓✓✓✓
Quality of Pitches	✓✓✓✓	Range of Facilities	✓✓✓✓✓

Directions

Site is east of Bidart on a minor road towards Arbonne. From A63 autoroute take Biarritz exit (4), turn towards St Jean-de-Luz and Bidart on N10. After Intermarche turn left at roundabout and follow signs to site. GPS: N43:26.207 W01:34.068

Charges 2006

Per unit incl. 2 persons	€ 15,00 - € 28,00
extra person	€ 5,00 - € 6,50
child (under 7 yrs)	€ 2,50 - € 3,50
electricity	€ 3,00 - € 4,00
dog	free - € 2,00

Reservations

Made for exact dates, for min. a week or so in main season, with deposit (€ 53.36), fee (€ 9.45) and cancellation insurance (€ 2.74). Tel: 05 59 41 94 50. Email: francoise.dumont3@wanadoo.fr

2

FR64080 Camping Les Tamaris Plage

Quartier Acotz, F-64500 St Jean-de-Luz (Pyrénées-Atlantiques)

This is a small, pleasant and well kept site. It is situated well outside the town but just across the road from a sandy beach with 79 numbered pitches, 45 with electricity, including some mobile homes and bungalows. They are of very good size and separated by hedges, on slightly sloping ground with some shade. It becomes full for nearly all July and August with families on long stays, so reservation then is advisable. There is no shop, but bread is available daily across the road.

Facilities

Single toilet block of superb quality and unusual design and should be ample provision for the site. Washbasins and showers in private cabins, mainly British style WCs, dishwashing sinks, facilities for disabled people and washing machine. New covered terrace with views of the sea. TV room for adults and children's room with TV and games. Playground. Not suitable for American motorhomes or twin axle caravans. Off site: Fishing 30 m. Bicycle hire or golf 4 km. Riding 7 km.

Open

1 April - 30 September.

At a glance

Welcome & Ambience	✓✓✓✓	Location	✓✓✓✓✓
Quality of Pitches	✓✓✓✓	Range of Facilities	✓✓✓

Directions

Proceed south on N10 and 1.5 km. after Guethary take first road on right (before access to the motorway and Carrefour centre commercial) and follow camp signs. GPS: N43:25.077 W01:37.429

Charges 2005

Per unit (100 sq.m. pitch) incl. 2 persons, electricity (5A)	€ 23,10 - € 30,50
tent pitch (80 sq.m.)	€ 18,20 - € 25,40
extra person (over 2 yrs)	€ 4,00 - € 6,00
dog	€ 3,00

Reservations

Made with 20% deposit and fee (€ 18.30). Tel: 05 59 26 55 90. Email: tamaris1@clubinternet.fr

FR64210 Camping Municipal Chibaou-Berria

F-64500 St Jean-de-Luz (Pyrénées-Atlantiques)

The first impression of this large site beside the beach is one of neatness. From the entrance, tarmac roads lead to spacious pitches which are divided by hedges with plenty of room for awnings. Pitches to the left hand side beyond reception are placed at different levels, whilst those to the right have a sea view. There are 202 pitches in all, all with electrical hook-ups. There is direct access to the beach for surfing and wind-surfing. Nearby are discos, tennis courts and often Basque folk festivities or Corridas with Landes cows.

Facilities

Toilet facilities, spotlessly clean when visited, include some showers with washbasins and individual wash cabins. Toilets are a mix of British and Turkish style. Dishwashing sinks in open position. Laundry facilities including washing machines and ironing room. There are only a few spaces suitable for motorhomes. Unsuitable for American motorhomes and twin axle caravans. The approach road is very narrow.

Open

1 June - 15 September.

At a glance

Welcome & Ambience	✓✓✓✓	Location	✓✓✓✓✓
Quality of Pitches	✓✓✓✓	Range of Facilities	✓✓✓

Directions

From A63 autoroute (St Jean de Luz Nord) take N10 towards Bayonne, then take second left signed Acotz Campings. Site signed in about 1 km. (the first left at Carrefour has a low bridge). From north, 1.5 km. after Geutherey on N10 take right at Carrefour supermarket, signed 'Plages'. GPS: N43:24.546 W01:38.174

Charges 2005

Per person	€ 5,25
child (under 13 yrs)	€ 3,20
pitch incl. electricity	€ 8,55

Reservations

Contact site. Tel: 05 59 26 11 94.

FR64230 Camping Municipal de Mosqueros

F-64270 Salies de Béarn (Pyrénées-Atlantiques)

In scenic surroundings convenient for the A64, this 3 star municipal site is worthy of its grading and is attractively located in a parkland situation 1 km. from the pretty little town of Salies de Béarn. It has an immaculate appearance, welcoming wardens and very clean facilities. Tarmac roads lead from the entrance barrier (locked at night), past reception to spacious, numbered pitches. Most have electricity (10A), many have water taps and all are separated by tall shrubs and hedges giving privacy. Salies de Béarn, with its old houses overhanging the river and its thermal baths, is only minutes away.

Facilities

The fully equipped toilet block is in a central position and maintained to a high standard. Dishwashing and laundry area with sinks, washing machine, dryer and iron. TV and recreation room. Off site: Swimming pool (special rates for campers) and tennis court adjacent. Golf and riding 2 km.

Open

15 March - 31 October.

At a glance

Welcome & Ambience	✓✓✓✓	Location	✓✓✓✓
Quality of Pitches	✓✓✓✓	Range of Facilities	✓✓✓

Directions

Site is well signed in the town and is on the D17 Bayonne road, west of the town. GPS: N43:28.51 W00:56.282

Charges 2005

Per person	€ 2,60
child (1-7 yrs)	€ 1,60
pitch incl. electricity	€ 5,25 - € 7,85

Reservations

Advisable for July/Aug. Contact site. Tel: 05 59 38 12 94.

FR64040 Camping des Gaves

F-64440 Laruns (Pyrénées-Atlantiques)

Des Gaves is a clean, small and well managed site, open all year, with very friendly owners and staff. It is set high in Pyrennean walking country on one of the routes to Spain. Laruns is only 25 km. from the Spanish border. There are 101 pitches including 50 level touring pitches of which 38 are fully serviced, numbered and separated (the remainder are used for seasonal units). The river runs alongside the site (well fenced) and fishing is possible. The busy little tourist town of Laruns is only a short walk. There are also five delightful wooden chalets to rent.

Facilities
The very clean toilet block has been refurbished and has modern fittings. Washbasins for ladies in curtained cubicles. Laundry room. No shop but baker calls daily (July/Aug). Small bar with TV, pool and video games (July/Aug). Larger bar with table tennis tables. Play area. Boules. Volleyball. Fishing. Off site: Bicycle hire 800 m.

Open
All year.

At a glance
Welcome & Ambience	✓✓✓✓	Location	✓✓✓✓
Quality of Pitches	✓✓✓	Range of Facilities	✓✓✓

Directions
Take N134 from Pau towards Olorons and branch left on D934 at Gan. Follow to Laruns and just after town, turn left following signs to site.
GPS: N42:58.929 W00:25.057

Charges 2005
Per person	€ 2,90 - € 3,70
child (under 10 yrs)	€ 1,83 - € 2,40
pitch incl. electricity (3-10A)	€ 6,92 - € 16,84

Reservations
Advised for July/Aug. and winter sports season.
Tel: 05 59 05 32 37.
Email: campingdesgaves@wanadoo.fr

FR64060 Camping Le Pavillon Royal

Avenue du Prince de Galles, F-64210 Bidart (Pyrénées-Atlantiques)

Le Pavillon Royal has an excellent situation on raised ground overlooking the sea, with good views along the coast to the south and to the north coast of Spain beyond. Beneath the site – and only a very short walk down - stretches a wide sandy beach where the Atlantic rollers provide ideal conditions for surfing. A central, marked-out section of the beach is supervised by lifeguards (from mid-June). There is also a section with rocks and pools. Alternatively there is a large swimming pool and sunbathing area on site. The site is divided up into 303 marked, level pitches, many of a good size. About 50 are reserved for tents and are only accessible on foot. The remainder are connected by asphalt roads. All have electricity and most are serviced with water and drainage. Much of the campsite is in full sun, although the area for tents is shaded. Reservation in high season is advisable.

Facilities
There are separate blocks for toilets and washing facilities, all of good quality. Mainly British style WCs, washbasins in cabins, baby baths and a good unit for disabled people. Washing facilities are closed at night except for two single night units. Washing machines and dryers. Motorcaravan services. Well stocked shop (including gas). Restaurant with takeaway (from 1/6). Swimming and paddling pools. Sauna. Playground. TV room and games room, also used for films. Fishing. Surf school. Dogs are not accepted. Off site: Riding 1 km. Bicycle hire 3 km. Sailing 5 km.

At a glance
Welcome & Ambience	✓✓✓✓	Location	✓✓✓✓✓
Quality of Pitches	✓✓✓✓✓	Range of Facilities	✓✓✓✓

Directions
From A63 exit 4, take the N10 south towards Bidart. At roundabout after the 'Intermarché' supermarket turn right (signed for Biarritz). After 600 m. turn left at campsite sign. GPS: N43:27.275 W01:34.562

Charges 2005
Per unit incl. 2 persons, electricity and water	€ 24,00 - € 39,50
tent pitch incl. 1 or 2 persons	€ 17,50 - € 29,50
child (over 4 yrs)	€ 6,00 - € 7,50

Reservations
Made for exact dates with deposit and fee.
Tel: 05 59 23 00 54. Email: info@pavillon-royal.com

Open
15 May - 25 September.

Le Pavillon Royal camping caravaning ★★★★ NN

64210 BIDART
Tél: 05.59.23.00.54
Website: www.pavillon-royal.com
E-mail: info@pavillon-royal.com

1 Right by a sandy beach with direct access

1 On the outskirts of Biarritz

1 Very peaceful situation

1 Sanitary installations of really exceptional quality

235

FR64150 Airotel Residence des Pins

Avenue de Biarritz, F-64210 Bidart (Pyrénées-Atlantiques)

This is a very pleasant, reasonably priced site which will appeal greatly to couples and young families. Set on a fairly gentle hillside, the top level has reception, bar restaurant and behind reception there are some of the pitches, all reasonably level. Slightly lower are the paddling and swimming pools in a sunny location with sun-beds. Next comes the well stocked shop, tennis courts and the rest of the pitches. The pitches are all set under tall trees, some slightly sloping and separated by hydrangea hedges. There are some electric hook-ups (10A, long leads required). There is a varied entertainment programme in July and Aug. There is a little day-time road noise but it is not intrusive. The site is not suitable for American motorhomes. It is used by tour operators and there are mobile homes around the outer edges of the site. Buses pass the gate.

Facilities

The two toilet blocks have washbasins in cabins, also washbasins and showers together. Washing machines, dryers and ironing boards and full facilities for disabled people. Drive over motorcaravan service point. Shop and bar open all season, restaurant and takeaway (20/6-15/9). Pool open all season. Games room. Table tennis. Tennis (charged in July/Aug). Play area (3-8 yrs). Bicycle hire. Off site: Lake 600 m. with fishing (no licence required). Golf 1 km. Riding 1 km. Beach with lifeguard 600 m.

Open

14 May - 30 September.

At a glance

Welcome & Ambience	✓✓✓✓	Location	✓✓✓✓
Quality of Pitches	✓✓✓✓	Range of Facilities	✓✓✓

Directions

Heading south on the A63 towards Spain, take exit J4 onto the N10 towards Bidart. At the roundabout straight after Intermarche turn right towards Biarritz. The site is on the right after 1 km.
GPS: N43:27.185 W01:34.425

Charges 2005

Per unit incl. 2 persons	€ 15,30 - € 23,50
extra person (over 2 yrs)	€ 3,10 - € 5,60
electricity	€ 3,10 - € 4,90
dog	free - € 2,30

Camping Cheques accepted.

Reservations

Contact site. Tel: 05 59 23 00 29.
Email: lespins@free.fr

FR64140 Sunêlia Berrua

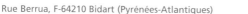

Mobile homes ▶ page 429

Rue Berrua, F-64210 Bidart (Pyrénées-Atlantiques)

Berrua, set only 1 km. from the sea, is an ideal location for visiting the beaches here in southwest France. A neat and tidy site, it has 270 level pitches (120 for touring units) set amongst trees. Most have electricity (6A) and some are fully serviced. The focal point of the site is an excellent new swimming pool complex with several pools, slides and paddling pools which is surrounded by sun-beds for sunbathing. Activities and entertainment for both adults and children are organised in high season, for example guided walks, dances, sporting competitions, bingo and karaoke. A member of the Sunêlia group.

Facilities

Toilet facilities are good (unisex) consisting of two blocks with washbasins in cabins, baby rooms, facilities for disabled visitors, washing machines and dishwashing sinks (cold water only). Motorcaravan service point. Shop (July/Aug). Bar/restaurant and takeaway (15/4-15/9). New pool complex. Games room. Play area (3-10 yrs only). Bicycle hire. Archery. Boules. Off site: Fishing 1 km. Golf and riding 3 km. Beach 1 km.

Open

6 April - 5 October.

At a glance

Welcome & Ambience	✓✓✓✓	Location	✓✓✓✓
Quality of Pitches	✓✓✓✓	Range of Facilities	✓✓✓✓✓

Directions

From A63 exit 4, take N10 south towards Bidart. At roundabout after the 'Intermarché' supermarket, turn left. Bear right then take next right (site signed).
GPS: N43:26.293 W01:34.942

Charges 2005

Per unit incl. 2 persons	€ 16,10 - € 26,40
extra person	€ 3,20 - € 5,70
child (2-10 yrs)	€ 2,30 - € 3,50
electricity (6A)	€ 2,90 - € 4,50
animal	free - € 3,10

Camping Cheques accepted.

Reservations

Contact site. Tel: 05 59 54 96 66.
Email: contact@berrua.com

Camping Caravaning Du Col D'Ibardin

Open 01 April – 30 September
Swimming pool ● Tennis ● Bar ● Children's Pool and Club
Launderette ● Hot Water ● Snacks ● Playground ● Bicycle Hire
● Little farm with animals for children
● Mobil-homes to rent

Tel: (0033) (0)559.54.31.21
Fax: (0033) (0)559.54.62.28
Site: www.col-ibardin.com
E-mail: Info@col-ibardin.com
64122 URRUGNE
PAYS BASQUE

FR64110 Camping du Col d'Ibardin

Mobile homes ▶ page 428

F-64122 Urrugne (Pyrénées-Atlantiques)

This family owned site at the foot of the Basque Pyrénées is highly recommended and deserves praise. It is well run with emphasis on personal attention, the friendly family and their staff ensuring that all are made welcome and is attractively set in the middle of an oak wood. Behind the forecourt, with its brightly coloured shrubs and modern reception area, various roadways lead to the 178 pitches. These are individual, spacious and enjoy the benefit of the shade (if preferred a more open aspect can be found). There are electricity hook-ups (4/10A) and adequate water points. From this site you can enjoy the mountain scenery, be on the beach at Socoa within minutes or cross the border into Spain about 14 km. down the road.

Facilities

Two toilet blocks, one rebuilt to a high specification, are kept very clean. WC for disabled people. Dishwashing facilities in separate open areas. Laundry unit with washing machine and dryer. Motorcaravan service point. Small shop selling basic food and gas, with orders taken for bread (1/7-31/8). Catering and takeaway service in July/Aug. Bar and occasional evening entertainment which includes Flamenco dancing. Swimming pool and paddling pool. Children's playground and club with adult supervision. Tennis courts, boules, table tennis, video games. Bicycle hire. A multi-purpose sports area is planned. Not suitable for American motorhomes. Off site: Shopping centre 5 km. Riding 2 km. Fishing 5 km. Golf 7 km.

Open

1 April - 30 September.

At a glance

Welcome & Ambience	✓✓✓✓	Location	✓✓✓✓
Quality of Pitches	✓✓✓✓	Range of Facilities	✓✓✓✓

Directions

Leave A63 autoroute at St Jean-de-Luz sud, exit no. 2 and join the RN10 in the direction of Urrugne. Turn left at roundabout (signed Col d'Ibardin) on the D4 and site is on right after 5 km. Do not turn off to the Col itself, but carry on towards Ascain. GPS: N43:20.035 W01:41.077

Charges 2005

Per unit incl. 2 persons	€ 12,00 - € 21,50
extra person	€ 2,60 - € 5,00
child (2-7 yrs)	€ 1,60 - € 3,00
electricity (4/10A)	€ 2,75 - € 5,50
animal	€ 1,00 - € 1,60

Reservations

Are accepted - contact site. Tel: 05 59 54 31 21. Email: info@col-ibardin.com

2

Dordogne & Aveyron

MAP 11

The Dordogne is a historical region of great beauty, full of pretty golden-stoned villages and ancient castles. Home to delicacies such as foie gras, truffles and walnuts, plus Roquefort cheese and Cognac, it is one of the gastronomic centres of France.

TO FORM 'THE DORDOGNE' WE HAVE USED DÉPARTEMENTS FROM THESE OFFICIAL REGIONS: FROM AQUITAINE: 24 DORDOGNE AND 47 LOT-ET-GARONNE, FROM MIDI-PYRÉNÉES: 12 AVEYRON, 46 LOT, FROM POITOU-CHARENTES: 16 CHARENTE

The Dordogne's history goes back many thousands of years when man lived in the caves of Périgord and left cave paintings at sites such as Les Eyzies and Lascaux. Aquitaine was ruled by the English for 300 years following the marriage of Eleanor of Aquitaine to Henry Plantagenet, who became King of England in 1154.

The villages and castles of the area bear evidence of the resulting conflict between the French and English, and today add charm and character to the countryside. Monpazier is the best example of the 'bastides' (fortified towns) and is set in a diverse region of mountains, vineyards, and fertile river valleys. The rolling grasslands and dense forests include the beautiful valleys of the Dordogne and Vézère.

South of the cultivated fields and cliff-side villages beside the river Lot lie the higher, stony lands of the Quercy Causse and the rocky gorges of the Rivers Aveyron and Tarn. Centred around Millau, there are tortuous gorges and valleys, spectacular rivers, underground caves and grottes, and thickly forested mountains.

238

Places of interest

Agen: rich agricultural area, famous for its prunes.

Angoulême: Hill-top town surrouded by ramparts, cathedral, Renaissance château.

Cognac: the most celebrated *eau de vie* in the world, cellars, Valois Castle.

Cordes: medieval walled hilltop village.

Monflanquin: well preserved fortified village.

Rocamadour: cliffside medieval pilgrimage site.

Saint Cirq-La Popie: medieval village perched on a cliff.

Sarlat: Saturday market.

Cuisine of the region

Local specialities include the fish dishes: carp stuffed with foie gras, mullet in red wine and *besugo* (sea bream), plus *cagouilles* (snails from Charentes).

Cassoulet: a hearty stew of duck, sausages and beans.

Cèpes: fine, delicate mushrooms; sometimes dried.

Chou farci: stuffed cabbage, sometimes aux marrons (with chestnuts).

Confit de Canard (d'oie): preserved duck meat.

Foie Gras: specially prepared livers of geese and ducks, seasoned and stuffed with truffles.

Magret de canard: duck breast fillets.

Mouclade: mussels cooked in wine, egg yolks and cream, served with Pineau des Charentes.

FR12010 Castel Camping Le Val de Cantobre

Mobile homes ▶ page 429

F-12230 Nant-d'Aveyron (Aveyron)

This very pleasant terraced site has been imaginatively and tastefully developed by the Dupond family over a 25 year period. In particular, the magnificent carved features in the bar create a delightful ambience, complemented by a recently built terrace. True, the ground is hard in summer but reception staff supply robust nails if your awning pegs prove a problem. Most of the 200 pitches (all with electricity and water) are peaceful, generous in size and blessed with views of the valley. The pools have a new surround, bedecked by flowers and crowned by a large urn which dispenses water into the paddling pool. But it is the activity programme that is unique at Val de Cantobre, supervised by qualified instructors in July and August, some arranged by the owners and some at a fair distance from the site. Passive recreationists appreciate the scenery, especially Cantobre, a medieval village that clings to a cliff in view of the site. Nature lovers will be delighted to see the vultures wheeling in the Tarn gorge alongside more humble rural residents. Butterflies in profusion, orchids, huge edible snails, glow worms, families of beavers and the natterjack toad all live here. It is easy to see why - the place is magnificent. Although tour operators occupy around 40% of the pitches, the terrace design provides some peace and privacy, especially on the upper levels and a warm welcome awaits from the Dupond family.

Facilities

The impressive, fully equipped toilet block is beautifully appointed with a huge indoor dishwashing area. Laundry. Fridge hire. Shop, although small, offers a wide variety of provisions; including many regional specialities (comparing well with local shops and markets). Attractive bar, restaurant, pizzeria and takeaway facility (some fairly steep up and down walking from furthest pitches to some facilities). Three adjoining swimming pools. Minigolf. Table tennis. Play area. Around 15 types of activity including river rafting, white water canoeing, rock climbing or jumps from Millau's hill tops on twin seater steerable parachutes. All weather sports pitch. Torch useful. Off site: Fishing 4 km. Riding 15 km. Bicycle hire 25 km.

At a glance

Welcome & Ambience	✓✓✓✓✓	Location	✓✓✓✓✓
Quality of Pitches	✓✓✓✓	Range of Facilities	✓✓✓✓

Directions

Site is 4 km. north of Nant, on D991 road to Millau. From Millau direction take D991 signed Gorge du Dourbie.

Charges 2006

Per unit incl. 2 persons and 4A electricity	€ 19,00 - € 31,50
extra person (4 yrs and over)	€ 4,00 - € 7,00
dog	free - € 3,00

Camping Cheques accepted.

Reservations

Made for any length with 25% deposit, fee (€ 25) and optional cancellation insurance. Tel: 05 65 58 43 00. Email: info@valdecantobre.com

Open

6 May - 10 September, with all facilities.

Wake up to fresh croissants delivered to your doorstep every morning !

LES CASTELS ★★★★

Castel-Camping Val de Cantobre ★★★★
www.valdecantobre.com

Camping Cheque

239

FR12000 Camping Caravaning de Peyrelade

Route des Gorges du Tarn, F-12640 Rivière-sur-Tarn (Aveyron)

Situated at the foot of the Tarn gorges on the banks of the river, this attractive site is dominated by the ruins of the Château de Peyrelade. Bathing from the pebble beach is safe and the water is clean. The 130 touring pitches are terraced, level and shady with 6A electricity hook-ups (long leads may be required for the riverside pitches) and nearby water points. The site is ideally placed for visiting the Tarn, Jonte and Dourbie gorges, and centres for rafting and canoeing are a short drive up the river. Other nearby attractions include the Caves of Aven Armand, the Chaos de Montpellier, Roquefort (of cheese fame) and the pleasant town of Millau. Many of the roads along and between the Gorges are breathtaking for passengers, but worrying for drivers who won't like looking down!

Facilities

The two toilet blocks have been refurbished. Young children are catered for, also people with disabilities. Washing machines and dryer. Bar, restaurant, pizzeria and takeaway (all from 1/6). Paddling pool and attractively designed swimming pool (proper swimming trunks, no shorts). Good playground. Games room and mini-club. Fishing. Off site: Bicycle hire 100 m. Riding 3 km. Facilities in the adjacent leisure centre can be booked at reception at reduced charges. Millau nearby with hypermarket, shops and night markets but note road to/from Millau can be jammed at peak hours.

Open

15 May - 15 September.

At a glance

Welcome & Ambience	✓✓✓✓	Location	✓✓✓✓
Quality of Pitches	✓✓✓	Range of Facilities	✓✓✓✓

Directions

Take autoroute A75 to exit 44-1 Aguessac then onto D907 (follow Gorges du Tarn signs). Site is 2 km. past Rivière sur Tarn, on the right - the access road is quite steep.

Charges 2006

Per unit incl. 2 persons	€ 14,00 - € 22,00
extra person	€ 3,50 - € 5,00
child (under 5 yrs)	€ 2,00 - € 3,00
electricity (6A)	€ 3,00
dog	€ 2,00

Reservations

Made with deposit (€ 84) and fee (€ 16).
Tel: 05 65 62 62 54.
Email: campingpeyrelade@wanadoo.fr

FR12040 Castel Camping Les Tours

F-12460 St Amans-des-Cots (Aveyron)

This is an impressive campsite set in beautiful countryside very close to the Truyère Gorges, Upper Lot valley and the Aubrac Plateau. Efficiently run, it is situated on the shores of the Lac de la Selves. There are 275 pitches of around 100 sq.m. with 6A electrical connections, some bordering the lake, the rest terraced and hedged with views of the lake. About 100 pitches also have individual water points. The site has a spacious feel, enhanced by the thoughtfully planned terraced layout and it is well kept and very clean. The owner and his staff are friendly and helpful. Used by tour operators (70 pitches). There is some up and down walking to the facilities, especially from the upper terraces.

Facilities

Four good toilet blocks including two excellent new ones, one of an unusual round design, are fully equipped including individual washing cubicles and are more than adequate for number of campers. Attractive central complex housing the amenities. Restaurant, bar. Swimming pools (650 and 40 sq.m.). Shop (with gas), Takeaway. Play area. Volleyball, tennis courts, football area and table tennis under cover. Varied programme of daytime and evening activities, with mini-club, archery and tree climbing (all supervised). Lake activities include canoeing, pedaloes, windsurfing, water ski-ing and provision for launching small boats. Internet terminal. Off site: Riding and golf 8 km.

Open

20 May - 9 September.

At a glance

Welcome & Ambience	✓✓✓✓	Location	✓✓✓✓✓
Quality of Pitches	✓✓✓✓	Range of Facilities	✓✓✓✓✓

Directions

Take the D34 from Entraygues-sur-Truyère to St Amans-des-Cots (14 km). In St Amans take the D97 to Colombez and then D599 to Lac de la Selves (site signed and is 5 km. from St Amans). Alternatively, from autoroute A75, take St Flour exit and follow D921 south for 41 km. Go 1.5 km. past Lacalm and turn right on D34 signed St Amans-des-Cots. Follow signs for 23 km.

Charges guide

Per unit incl. 2 persons	€ 20,80 - € 26,50
extra person	€ 4,40 - € 5,50
child (under 7 yrs)	€ 3,00 - € 3,80
electricity	€ 2,40 - € 3,00
Camping Cheques accepted.	

Reservations

Advised for July/Aug; contact site.
Tel: 05 65 44 88 10.
Email: camping-les-tours@wanadoo.fr

FR12050 Camping Les Terrasses du Lac

Route du Vibal, F-12290 Pont-de-Salars (Aveyron)

At an altitude of some 700 m. on the plateau of Le Lévézou, this outlying site enjoys attractive views over Lac de Pont de Salars. The site seems largely undiscovered by the British, perhaps as it is only open for a short season. A terraced site, it provides 180 good sized, level pitches, 130 for touring, with or without shade, all with electricity. Some pitches have good views over the lake which has direct access from the site at two places – one for pedestrians and swimmers, the other for cars and trailers for launching small boats. This site is well placed for excursions into the Gorges du Tarn, Caves du Roquefort and nearby historic towns and villages. Although there are good facilities for disabled visitors, the terracing on the site may prove difficult.

Facilities

Four toilet blocks of varying ages include some washbasins in private cabins, plus dishwashing areas under cover and laundry facilities. Fridge hire. Shop. Large bar/restaurant with a lively French ambience serving full meals in high season and snacks at other times, with takeaway (all 1/7-31/8). Heated swimming pool (200 sq.m.) and children's pool (1/6-30/9). Solarium. Playground. Volleyball, pétanque, table tennis, billiards. Games and TV rooms. Entertainment and activities organised in high season. Barbecue area. Off site: Tennis 3 km. Riding 5 km. Golf 20 km.

Open

1 April - 30 September.

At a glance

Welcome & Ambience	✓✓✓✓✓	Location	✓✓✓✓
Quality of Pitches	✓✓✓✓	Range of Facilities	✓✓✓✓

Directions

Using D911 Millau - Rodez road, turn north at Pont de Salars towards the lake on the D523. Follow camp signs. Ignore first site and continue following lake until Les Terraces (approx. 5 km).
GPS: N44:18.281 E02:44.098

Charges 2005

Per pitch incl. 2 persons	€ 11,00 - € 19,90
extra person	€ 3,50 - € 4,50
child (2-7 yrs)	€ 3,20 - € 3,50
electricity (6A)	€ 3,60
dog	€ 1,25

Reservations

American motorhomes and twin axle caravans must reserve. Made with deposit (€ 84) and fee (€ 16). Tel: 05 65 46 88 18.
Email: campinglesterrasses@wanadoo.fr

FR12060 Camping Beau Rivage

Lac de Pareloup, route de Vernhes, F-12410 Salles-Curan (Aveyron)

This small, family run, immaculate site has a wonderful position alongside the beatutiful Lac de Paraloup. It has been carefully landscaped to maximize the views over the lake and surrounding hills. There are 80 level, grassy pitches (60 for touring) attractively arranged on terraces. They are separated by neat hedges and a variety of small trees which only offer a little shade. All have electricity (6A). A wide range of watersports is available on the lake (mostly in July and August) and many family activities are organised both on and off site in high season. This is an excellent site for all the family to spend an active holiday or to unwind peacefully. It is also an ideal base for exploring the surrounding countryside with its many picturesque towns and villages with their markets, museums and châteaux. There are many marked walks and cycle rides including a ride around the lake (24 km). On arrival at the site, park outside and go to reception. The site entrance is narrow and quite steep and tractor assistance is available. Once on site access to pitches is easy. Good English is spoken.

Facilities

Two modern, well equipped and very clean toilets blocks provide all the necessary facilities, including those for disabled visitors and a baby room. Washing machines. Cosy bar and snack bar, terrace with takeaway meals (July/Aug) overlooking the pool. Small shop (July/Aug). Swimming pool. Games rooms. TV room. Pool table, baby foot and table tennis. Beach volleyball. Small play area. Fishing, boating and bathing in the lake. Very small boat ramp. Off site: Several bars and restaurants close by. Old town of Salles Curan (4 km) with shops, bars, restaurants, banks. Boat ramp 200 m. and wide range of watercraft for hire on the lake nearby (mostly July/Aug). Bicycle hire 2 km. Tennis 3 km. Riding 3 km. Golf 35 km. Canoeing, rafting, paragliding, caving, windsurfing and walking in the trees.

At a glance

Welcome & Ambience	✓✓✓✓	Location	✓✓✓✓✓
Quality of Pitches	✓✓✓✓	Range of Facilities	✓✓✓✓

Directions

From the D911 Rodez - Millau road turn south on D993 signed Salles Curan. In about 7 km, just after crossing a bridge over the lake, turn right on D243 (site signed). The entrance is on the right in just over 1 km. Park outside gate.

Charges 2005

Per unit incl. 2 persons	€ 11,50 - € 14,00
extra person	€ 3,00 - € 6,00
child (2-7 yrs)	free - € 4,00
electricity (6A)	€ 2,00 - € 3,00
animal	€ 1,50 - € 3,00

Reservations

Advised for high season and made with deposit (25%) and fee (€ 20). Tel: 05 65 46 33 32. Email: camping-beau-rivage@wanadoo.fr

Open

1 May - 30 September.

FR12070 Camping La Grange de Monteillac

F-12310 Sévérac-l'Eglise (Aveyron)

La Grange de Monteillac is a modern, well equipped site in the beautiful, well preserved small village of Sévérac L'Église. A spacious site, it provides 105 individual pitches, 70 for touring, on gently sloping grass, separated by flowering shrubs and mostly young trees offering little shade. All pitches have electricity (6A, long leads may be required), and 24 have water and waste water connections. There are 35 chalets, mobile homes and tents for rent in separate areas. The friendly owner will advise about the many interesting activities in the region. An evening stroll around this delightful village is a must, and Sévérac Le Château (21 km), Rodez (28 km), and many other attractive old towns and villages with their châteaux, museums and weekly markets should satisfy all shopping, sightseeing and cultural needs.

Facilities

The toilet block central to the touring area is modern, spacious and clean, with all washbasins in cubicles. Facilities for babies and disabled people. Dishwashing and laundry sinks. Washing machine and dryer. Shop at reception (1/7-31/8). Poolside restaurant/snack-bar serving pizzas, grills etc. and takeaway (1/7-31/8). Music or groups feature in the bar (July-Aug). Two swimming pools with toilets and changing rooms below (1/6-15/9). Pool/bar/restaurant/music room some way from touring area. Large well equipped playground plus plenty of grassy space for ball games. Organised activities include children's club, bicycle hire and archery lessons. Off site: Fishing 1 km. Shops in village 3 km. Riding 9 km. Golf 25 km. Many marked walks and bicycle rides, canoeing, rafting, canyoning, rock climbing and hang gliding.

At a glance

Welcome & Ambience	✓✓✓	Location	✓✓✓✓
Quality of Pitches	✓✓✓✓	Range of Facilities	✓✓✓✓

Directions

Site is on the edge of Sévérac L'Église village, just off N88 Rodez - Sévérac Le Château road. From A75 use exit 42. At Sévérac L'Église turn south onto D28, site is signed. Site entrance is very shortly on left. GPS: N44:21.911 E02:51.086

Charges 2005

Per unit incl. 2 persons and electricity	€ 21,50
extra person	€ 3,80
child (under 7 yrs)	€ 2,50
dog	€ 1,30

Less 30% outside July/Aug.

Reservations

Advised for high season. Deposit 25% plus fee € 18. Tel: 05 65 70 21 00. Email: info@la-grange-de-monteillac.com

Open

1 May - 15 September.

GORGES DU TARN • MILLAU • AVEYRON
Avenue de l'Aigoual - 12100 MILLAU - France
Tél. 00 33 (0)5 65 61 01 07 • Fax 00 33 (0)5 65 59 03 56

www.campinglesrivages.com
e-mail : campinglesrivages@wanadoo.fr

FR12020 Camping Caravaning Les Rivages

Mobile homes ⏵ page 431

Avenue de l'Aigoual, route de Nant, F-12100 Millau (Aveyron)

Les Rivages is a large site on the outskirts of the town. It is well organised and well situated, being close to the high limestone Causses and the dramatic gorges of the Tarn and Dourbie, the latter of which runs past the back of the site. Smaller pitches, used for tents and small units, abut a pleasant riverside space suitable for sunbathing, fishing or picnics. Most of the 314 pitches are large, 100 sq.m. or more, and well shaded. A newer part of the site (on the right as you enter) has less shade but pitches are larger. All pitches have electricity (6A), and 100 have water and drainage. The site offers a very wide range of sporting activities close to 30 in all (see facilities). Millau is a bustling and pleasant town. Don't miss the night markets, but don't eat before you get there – there are thousands of things to taste, many of them grilled or spit roasted. The gates are shut 10 pm - 8 am, with night-watchman.

Facilities

Four well kept modern toilet blocks have all necessary facilities. Special block for children with baby baths, small showers and toilets, as well as ironing facilities. Shop for most essentials (1/6-15/9). Terrace restaurant and bar overlooking a good-sized main swimming pool and children's pool (from 10/5). Play area. Much evening entertainment, largely for children, along with child-minding and a mini-club. Tennis (indoor and outdoor). Squash (can be viewed from the bar). Table tennis. Floodlit petanque. Many river activities, walking, bird watching and fishing. Off site: Rafting and canoeing arranged. Bicycle hire 1 km. Riding 10 km. Hypermarket in Millau.

At a glance

Welcome & Ambience	✓✓✓✓	Location	✓✓✓✓
Quality of Pitches	✓✓✓✓	Range of Facilities	✓✓✓✓

Directions

From Millau, take D991 road south towards Nant. Site is about 400 m. on the right.

Charges 2006

Per pitch incl. 2 persons	
and electricity	€ 16,00 - € 24,50
with water and drainage	€ 18,00 - € 26,50
extra person (over 3 yrs)	€ 4,50
pet	€ 3,00

Reservations

Advisable for July/Aug. with deposit (€ 61) and fee (€ 15,24). Tel: 05 65 61 01 07.
Email: campinglesrivages@wanadoo.fr

Open

15 March - 15 October.

FR12080 Camping Club Les Genêts

Lac de Pareloup, F-12410 Salles-Curan (Aveyron)

This family run site is on the shores of Lac de Pareloup and offers both family holiday and watersports facilities. The 162 pitches include 102 grassy, mostly individual pitches for touring units. These are in two areas, one on each side of the entrance lane, and are divided by hedges, shrubs and trees. Most have electricity (6A) and many also have water and waste water drain. The site slopes gently down to the beach and lake with facilities for all watersports including waterskiing. A full animation and activities programme is organised in high season, and there is much to see and do in this very attractive corner of Aveyron. The site is not suitable for American style motorhomes. Used by tour operators (25 pitches). A 'Sites et Paysages' member.

Facilities

Two main sanitary units include washbasins in cubicles and a suite for disabled people. Refurbishment of the older unit is planned, whilst the other unit is new. Baby room. Dishwashing and laundry sinks. Laundry room. Very well stocked shop. Bar and restaurant. Snack bar serving pizzas and other snacks in main season. Swimming pool and spa pool (both from 1/6; unsupervised). Playground. Minigolf, volleyball and boules. Bicycle hire. Red Indian style tee-pees. Hire of pedaloes, windsurfers and kayaks. Fishing licences available.

Open

31 May - 11 September.

At a glance

| Welcome & Ambience | ✓✓✓✓ | Location | ✓✓✓✓✓ |
| Quality of Pitches | ✓✓✓✓ | Range of Facilities | ✓✓✓✓✓ |

Directions

From Salles-Curan take D577 for about 4 km. and turn right into a narrow lane immediately after a sharp right hand bend. Site is signed at junction.

Charges 2005

Per unit incl. 1 or 2 persons	
and 6A electricity	€ 11,00 - € 28,00
lakeside pitch	€ 11,00 - € 36,00
extra person	€ 4,00 - € 6,00
child (under 2 yrs)	free
pet	€ 3,00 - € 4,00

Refundable deposits for barrier card € 20 and for pool bracelet € 8 per person.

Reservations

Advised for July/Aug. and made with deposit (€ 155) and fee (€ 29). Tel: 05 65 46 35 34.
Email: contact@camping-les-genets.fr

FR12120 Camping du Rouergue

Avenue de Fondiès, F-12200 Villefranche-de-Rouergue (Aveyron)

A spacious and well appointed site in the Vallée de L'Aveyron, Camping du Rouergue is adjacent to the municipal sports facilities. Run by the Rouergue Tourisme Service, the managers are friendly and welcoming. The site has 98 grassy individual pitches of varying sizes, served by tarmac roads, and all serviced with electricity (16A), water and drain. Some pitches are shady. There are reduced rates for campers at the municipal swimming pool and shops and restaurants are within walking distance along the riverside foot and cycle path. Villefranche-de-Rouergue is one of the larger Bastide towns of the region and is on the pilgrim route to Santiago de Compostela. The site is also ideally placed for exploring the many other historical bastides of the Rouergue and Aveyron.

Facilities

The modern spacious sanitary unit includes washbasins in cubicles. Facilities for babies and disabled persons. Dishwashing and laundry sinks. Washing machine. With two identical sections to the block, only one is open during low season. Motorcaravan service point outside campsite entrance. Small bar (June-Oct). TV room. Well equipped playground. Bicycle hire. Off site: Fishing 1 km. Riding 5 km.

Open

15 April - 15 October.

At a glance

| Welcome & Ambience | ✓✓✓✓✓ | Location | ✓✓✓✓ |
| Quality of Pitches | ✓✓✓✓ | Range of Facilities | ✓✓✓ |

Directions

Villefranche de Rouergue is about midway between Cahors and Rodez. Site is 1 km. southwest of town on D47 towards Monteils, follow signs from D911 to campsite and 'Stade'.

Charges 2006

Per pitch incl. 2 persons	€ 10,50 - € 13,50
extra person (over 10 yrs)	€ 2,30
child (4-10 yrs)	€ 1,50
electricity	€ 2,50

Reservations

Advisable for high season, made with 20% deposit. Tel: 05 65 45 16 24.
Email: campingrouergue@wanadoo.fr

FR12160 Camping Caravaning Les Peupliers

Mobile homes ▶ page 432

Route des Gorges du Tarn, F-12640 Rivière-sur-Tarn (Aveyron)

Les Peupliers is a friendly, family site on the banks of the Tarn river. Most of the good-sized pitches have shade, and all have electricity, water and a waste water point. It is possible to swim in the river and there is a landing place for canoes. The site has its own canoes (to rent).In a lovely, sunny situation on the site is a swimming pool with a paddling pool, sun beds and a new slide, all protected by a beautifully clipped hedge and with a super view to the surrounding hills and the Château du Peyrelade perched above the village. Some English is spoken. A treat for us at dusk was to watch beavers playing on the river bank.

Facilities

Large, light and airy toilet facilities are a good provision with adjustable showers, washbasins in cubicles and mainly British style WCs. Good baby facilities with baths, showers and WCs. Facilities for disabled visitors. Washing machines. Shop (1/6-30/9). Bar with TV. Internet point. Snack bar and takeaway (1/5-30/9). Swimming pool (from 1/5). Games and competitions organised in July/Aug. Fishing. Volleyball. Football. Badminton. Play area. Weekly dances organised in July/Aug. Canoe hire. Off site: Village with shops and restaurant 300 m. Riding 0.5 km. Bicycle hire 2 km. Golf 25 km.

Open

1 April - 30 September.

At a glance

Welcome & Ambience	✓✓✓✓	Location	✓✓✓✓
Quality of Pitches	✓✓✓✓	Range of Facilities	✓✓✓✓

Directions

Heading south from Clermont Ferrand to Millau on the A75 autoroute take exit 44-1 signed Aguessac/Gorges du Tarn. In Aguessac follow signs to Riviere sur Tarn (5 km.) and site is clearly indicated. GPS: N44:11.061 E03:07.402

Charges 2005

Per unit incl. 2 persons	€ 10,00 - € 17,00
extra person	€ 5,00 - € 7,00
child (under 7 yrs)	€ 2,00 - € 3,00
electricity (6A)	€ 3,00
dog	€ 1,50

Camping Cheques accepted.

Reservations

Made with deposit (€ 125) and fee (€ 25).
Tel: 05 65 59 85 17.
Email: lespeupliers12640@wanadoo.fr

245

FR12150 Camping Marmotel

Mobile homes ▶ page 430

F-12130 St Geniez-d'Olt (Aveyron)

The road into Marmotel passes various industrial buildings and is a little off-putting – persevere, as they are soon left behind. The campsite itself is a mixture of old and new. The old part provides many pitches with lots of shade and separated by hedges. The new area is sunny until the trees grow. These pitches each have a private sanitary unit, with shower, WC, washbasin and dishwashing. New and very well designed, they are reasonably priced for such luxury. All the pitches have electricity (10A). A lovely restaurant has a wide terrace with views of the hills and overlooking the heated swimming and paddling pools. These have fountains, a toboggan and sun beds either on grass or the tiled surrounds. The Lot river runs alongside the site where you can fish or canoe. A 'Sites et Paysages' member.

Facilities

Good sanitary facilities include baby baths and facilities for disabled visitors. Shower cubicles are a little small. Washing machines. Bar/restaurant and takeaway (all season). Swimming pools. Small play area. Multi-sports area. Entertainment for all ages in July/Aug. including a disco below the bar, cinema screen, karaoke, dances and a mini club for 4-12 yr olds. Bicycle hire. Fishing. Canoeing. Off site: Large supermarket 500 m. Riding 10 km. Bicycle tours and canoe trips on the Lot and rafting on the Tarn.

Open

10 May - 10 September.

At a glance

Welcome & Ambience	✓✓✓✓	Location	✓✓✓✓
Quality of Pitches	✓✓✓✓	Range of Facilities	✓✓✓✓✓

Directions

Heading south on autoroute 75 (free) take exit 41 and follow signs for St Geniez d'Olt. Site is at western end of village. Site is signed onto D19 to Prades d'Aubrac, then 500 m. on left.

Charges 2005

Per unit incl. 1 or 2 persons, 10A electricity	€ 17,00 - € 28,80
extra person	€ 2,90 - € 5,40
child under 4 yrs	€ 1,00 - € 3,10

Less 30% outside July/Aug.
Camping Cheques accepted.

Reservations

Made with deposit (€ 100) and fee (€ 16).
Tel: 05 65 70 46 51. Email: info@marmotel.com

Marmotel
Camping-Village

"VERY COMFORTABLE, VERY NATURAL."
5 ha in the Lot Valley, by the riverside. 180 pitches, 42 of which have individual toilet. Chalets and Mobile homes for hire. 350 sqm swimming pools, waterslides, tennis, animations, kids club, bar, restaurant.
Open 10/05 – 10/09 2006
www.marmotel.com

FR12190 Camping Les Calquières

17 avenue Jean Moulin, F-12150 Sévérac le Château (Aveyron)

This site is ideally situated, as it is only 3 km. from the free A75 autoroute and makes an excellent short stay for those on route to the south. It would also be a good base for those wishing to visit the nearby Cévennes National Park with its beautiful and rugged scenery. This quiet, neat, family run site nestles below the old village and medieval château and close to the lower part of the town, all within easy walking distance of the site. There are spectacular views from the Château, floodlit at night. There are 97 good sized, level, grassy pitches mostly separated by a variety of hedges with maturing trees providing some shade. All have electricity (6A).

Facilities

Two good toilet blocks, one built in 2003 to a very high standard. They contain all the necessary facilities, including those for disabled visitors, and were very clean when visited. Off site: Adjacent municipal swimming pool (July/Aug) and tennis courts, both free to campers. Lower part of Sévérac le Château (1 km) with a small range of shops, restaurants and bank. Old, upper part of the town, with the Château other shops etc, is a similar walking distance but involves a good climb. Riding 1 km. Fishing 800 m.

Open

1 April - 30 September.

At a glance

Welcome & Ambience	✓✓✓✓	Location	✓✓✓✓
Quality of Pitches	✓✓✓	Range of Facilities	✓✓✓

Directions

From A75 take exit 42 and at roundabout take N9 signed Sévérac le Château. Shortly turn hard right (N88) and at crossroads go straight on, signed Centre Ville and Gare. At station roundabout turn left and follow road beside the railway line through the town. Turn left at camp sign and immediately left again. Site shortly on the right. GPS: N44:19.100 E03:3.833

Charges 2005

Per unit incl. 2 persons	€ 11,20 - € 13,10
extra person	€ 3,00 - € 3,50
child (0-7 yrs)	€ 2,00
electricity (6A)	€ 2,50

Reservations

Not needed. Tel: 05 65 47 64 82.

FR12170 Sunêlia Le Caussanel

Lac de Pareloup, F-12290 Canet de Salars (Aveyron)

This large, extremely spacious site on the banks of Lac de Pareloup is greatly improved. It is ideal, in low season, for those seeking a tranquil holiday in a beautiful region of France or in high season, for those seeking an active holiday. It has 235 large, fairly level, grassy pitches, with 143 for touring. Most have 6A electricity (a few have 10A) but very long leads may be necessary, and 33 have water and a drain. The pitches are defined by a tree or boulder in each corner and offer little privacy but many have wonderful views over the lake. Most pitches have little shade with only a few having good shade. The site has a new swimming pool, a pool with slides and a large paddling pool. The adjacent lake offers a large area, 1 km. long, for swimming and watersports. One tour operator takes 20 pitches.

Facilities

Five modern toilet blocks have all the necessary facilities. Motorcaravan service point (€ 3) at entrance. Shop. Bar. Restaurant and takeaway (July/Aug). Swimming pool and paddling pool (from June). New pool complex. Very large play area. Boules. Tennis. Football. Volleyball. Large room for table tennis. TV room and clubhouse. Extensive programme of family events (July/Aug). Fishing. Bicycle hire (July/Aug). Motor boat launching. Various water sports (July/Aug) and swimming in adjacent lake. Internet access. Off site: Cycle and footpaths around the lake (24 km). Shops, banks, restaurants, etc. 8 km. Riding 10 km. Golf 30 km. Canoeing, rafting, paragliding caving and windsurfing.

At a glance

Welcome & Ambience	✓✓✓✓	Location	✓✓✓✓
Quality of Pitches	✓✓✓✓	Range of Facilities	✓✓✓✓✓

Directions

From D911 Rodez - Millau, east of Pont de Sellars, turn south on D993 (Salles-Curan). In 6 km. turn right on D538 signed Le Caussanel. Very shortly turn left to site. GPS: N44:12.877 E02:45.995

Charges 2005

Per unit incl. 2 persons	€ 13,20 - € 23,50
extra person	€ 4,40 - € 6,00
electricity	€ 3,10

Camping Cheques accepted.

Reservations

Made with deposit (25%) and fee (€ 15).
Tel: 05 65 46 85 19. Email: info@lecaussanel.com

Open

29 April - 2 September.

FR16040 Camping Devezeau

F-16230 St Angeau (Charente)

Set in the gently rolling Charente countryside, close to the N10 and on the pilgrim route to Santiago de Compostella, Camping Devezeau is open all year and provides a pleasant stopping place on the way to and from the south. For those looking for a longer stay it is situated close to the old towns of Angoulême and La Rochefoucauld. The site has recently (2004) been taken over by British owners who are working hard to upgrade what is already an attractive site. There are just 39 pitches (34 for touring units) mainly on grass and separated by immature shrubs, although there are four hardstandings for motorcaravans. Most have electricity. The swimming pool is an added attraction for such a small site.

Facilities

The toilet block in a converted barn provides single sex facilities, facilities for disabled people, laundry and dishwashing sinks, and a washing machine. Gas supplies. Swimming pool (12 x 12 m; 1/5-30/9). Play area. Off site: Shop and bar in village 1.5 km. Fishing 2 km.

Open

All year.

At a glance

Welcome & Ambience	✓✓✓✓✓	Location	✓✓✓✓✓
Quality of Pitches	✓✓✓✓	Range of Facilities	✓✓✓

Directions

From north on N10 take exit for Mansle. Turn left (east) at lights on D6 for St Angeau. After 9 km. turn south onto D15 (Tourriers). Take first left after 300 m. and site is 150 m. From south on N10 take exit for Tourriers/St Angeau. Follow signs to St Angeau on D15. Site is signed to right after about 10 km.

Charges 2005

Per unit incl. 2 persons	€ 10,00 - € 17,00
extra person	€ 4,00 - € 6,00
electricity	€ 2,00 - € 5,00

Reservations

Advised for July/Aug. Tel: 05 45 39 21 29.
Email: info@campingdevezeau.com

247

FR16020 Castel Camping Les Gorges du Chambon

Eymouthiers, F-16220 Montbron (Charente)

A welcoming and friendly, family site in pretty, rolling Périgord Vert countryside, Gorges du Chambon is arranged around a restored Charente farmhouse and its outbuildings. It provides an attractive, spacious setting with 140 large, marked pitches of which 90 are for touring units. All have electrical connections (6A) and 4 have water and drainage. On gently sloping grass and enjoying extensive views over the countryside, the pitches are arranged in two circular groups with a sanitary block at the centre of each. The pitches for mobile homes and tour operator tents are not obtrusive. The site is in an area noted for nature trails and bird watching, and information boards abound. It also offers canoe hire on the river and a footpath has been created to the river with two beaches where swimming is possible. A converted barn provides an interesting gallery arrangement in the restaurant/bar. The site owners are very helpful and there is even a herb garden for use by campers.

Facilities

Traditional style, unisex blocks include washbasins in private cabins, facilities for disabled people, a baby bath, laundry sinks, washing machine and tumble dryer, and good dishwashing rooms. Small shop stocks basics and bread can be ordered the day before. Bar and restaurant (May - Sept; good food, well priced). Takeaway including pizzas (all season). Swimming pool (18 x 7 m) and children's pool. Children's play area. Games room, TV and table tennis. Tennis, archery and minigolf, bicycle and canoe hire. Animation is organised in July/Aug. including a children's club, youth disco and teenagers' corner. Dogs and other animals are not accepted. Off site: Private fishing (free) 6 km; with licence 200 m. Golf 6 km. Riding 10 km. Sailing 20 km. Visits are organised to local producers and day trips (low season).

At a glance

Welcome & Ambience	✓✓✓✓✓	Location	✓✓✓✓
Quality of Pitches	✓✓✓✓	Range of Facilities	✓✓✓✓

Directions

From N141 Angoulême - Limoges road at Rochefoucauld take D6 to Montbron village. Follow D6 in direction of Piegut-Pluviers and site is signed to the north on D163 just as you enter Tricherie.
GPS: N45:39.588 E0:33.460

Charges 2006

Per person	€ 3,75 - € 6,50
child (1-7 yrs)	€ 1,50 - € 3,25
pitch	€ 5,35 - € 7,90
vehicle	€ 1,50 - € 2,10
electricity (6A)	€ 3,20

Camping Cheques accepted.

Reservations

Necessary for July/Aug; contact site quoting Alan Rogers. Tel: 05 45 70 71 70.
Email: gorges.chambon@wanadoo.fr

Open

1 April - 31 October.

FR16050 Camping Municipal de Cognac

Boulevard de Châtenay, route de Ste-Sévère, F-16100 Cognac (Charente)

If you are a lover of brandy this area is a must, with abundant vineyards and little roadside chalets offering tastings of Pineau (a Cognac based aperitif) and a vast range of Cognacs. This municipal site by the Charente river is convenient as a night stop or longer stay to visit the area, and for sleeping off the effects of the 'tastings' – you probably won't even notice the slight noise from the nearby road! The 168 large touring pitches, all with electricity (5/6A), are neatly laid out and separated by shrubs and trees. A few mobile homes are positioned along one boundary. The famous Cognac Houses (Pineau, Hennessy, Hine, Martell, Remy Martin, etc.) and the Cognac Museum may be visited. There is public transport to the town centre (daily July/Aug; Saturdays only at other times).

Facilities

Two fairly modern toilet blocks (access by steps) have mixed British and Turkish style WCs, including children's toilets, washbasins in cabins, and a washing machine. Separate ground level facilities for disabled visitors. Motorcaravan services. Small swimming pool on site (municipal pool nearby). Shop, snack bar, takeaway and entertainment (15/6-15/9). Fishing. Volleyball. Table tennis. Play area. Off site: Bicycle hire 2 km. Riverside walks. Restaurants, bars and shops in the town (2.3 km). Golf 5 km. Riding 6 km.

Open

1 May - 15 October.

At a glance

Welcome & Ambience	✓✓✓✓	Location	✓✓✓✓
Quality of Pitches	✓✓✓✓	Range of Facilities	✓✓✓

Directions

Site is signed from N141 Saintes - Angoulême road following signs for town centre. It is to the north of the town beside the river on the D24 to Boutiers and Ste-Sévère. GPS: N45:42.544 W00:18.759

Charges 2005

Per pitch incl. 2 persons	€ 6,00 - € 10,90
extra person	€ 3,00 - € 3,30
Less for stays over 3 days.	

Reservations

Contact site in season; out of season contact Communauté de Communs de Cognac, 50 Avenue Paul Firino Martell, 16100 Cognac (05 45 36 64 30). Site tel: 05 45 32 13 32.
Email: info@campingdecgnac.com

FR16060 Camping Marco de Bignac

Lieudit 'Les Sablons', F-16170 Bignac (Charente)

The small village of Bignac is set in peaceful countryside not too far from the N10 road, north of Angoulême. This mature, British owned site is arranged along one side of an attractive lake on a level, grassy meadow. The 85 large touring pitches are marked at each corner by a tree so there is shade, and electricity (3/6A) is available to most. At the far end of the site is a hedged swimming pool and plenty of grassy space for ball games. The lake shores are home to ducks and the lake itself is used for fishing and small boats. There is much of historical interest within easy reach and the owners have prepared maps of suitable walks, cycle rides and visits which may be found at reception. There is a bar, snack bar and restaurant with tables outside and views across the lake. The bar and restaurant are also popular with the locals, and the cooking is done by the family. This site is popular with British visitors and is a peaceful, relaxing location for couples or young families. There is no noisy entertainment and all the activities are free of charge. Rallies are welcome and programmes can be provided.

Facilities

Two traditional style toilet blocks have functional facilities all in cabins opening from the outside. British style WCs. Dishwashing or laundry sinks at either end of each block. Washing machine. Bar and snack bar (1/6-31/8; closed Mon. until high season). Small shop and baker calls daily (high season). Swimming pool (15/6-31/8, unsupervised). Football field, badminton, tennis, table tennis, pedaloes, minigolf, boules (boules provided) and fishing, all free. Library. Play area. Pets corner. Special evenings, outings and competitions organised in high season. A torch may be useful. Off site: Local markets. Riding 5 km. Golf 25 km.

Open

15 May - 15 September.

At a glance

Welcome & Ambience	✓✓✓✓	Location	✓✓✓✓✓
Quality of Pitches	✓✓✓✓	Range of Facilities	✓✓✓✓

Directions

From N10 south of Poitiers, 14 km. north of Angoulême, take D11 west to Vars and Basse. Where you turn right onto D117 to Bignac. Site is signed at several junctions and in village (Camping Bignac). GPS: N45:47.850 E00:03.831

Charges 2006

Per pitch incl. 2 persons	€ 13,00 - € 19,00
extra person	€ 3,00 - € 5,00
child (2-7 yrs)	free - € 2,50
electricity (3/6A)	€ 2,50 - € 4,00

Reservations

Made with deposit (€ 50 per week).
Tel: 05 45 21 78 41.
Email: camping.marcodebignac@wanadoo.fr

FR16030 Camping Municipal Le Champion

F-16230 Mansle (Charente)

Le Champion is a convenient stop-over from the N10 or a good base to explore the northern Charente area. Beside the Charente river, the site has a cool, relaxing atmosphere created by its attractive location and the 'hippodrome' provides open grassy space on the other side. The site, with 116 average sized and separated touring pitches, is mostly open with little shade. All pitches have electricity (10A) and 15 have water points. Groups are welcome and there is a dedicated area with a second toilet block at the back of the site for groups of more than ten caravans. A privately owned restaurant is at the site entrance, attractively canopied for 'al fresco' eating and another outlet sells snacks. Information on opportunities for cycling, walking, canoeing or fishing is available from reception with several guides and maps of suggested routes for sale. There is some road noise from the N10.

Facilities

The main modern sanitary block is well maintained and provides some washbasins in cabins and facilities for disabled people. Dishwashing and laundry areas and a small washing machine. An additional smaller, older block is in the tenting area at the rear of the site. Motorcaravan service point at entrance. Minigolf. Volleyball. Basketball. Petanque. English spoken. Off site: Restaurant and snacks outside site. Town with its Roman bridge. Tourist office 500 m. Swimming pool in town (discount for campers), recreation area next to the site.

Open

15 May - 15 September.

At a glance

Welcome & Ambience	✓✓✓✓	Location	✓✓✓✓
Quality of Pitches	✓✓✓✓	Range of Facilities	✓✓✓

Directions

From N10, 30 km. north of Angoulême, take exit for Mansle. From the north, site is on left after 1.5 km. just before the bridge over the river. From the south, follow signs for Centre Ville, continue past town centre and church, and site is on right, immediately after crossing river. Site is well signed from all directions. GPS: N45:52.692 E00:10.891

Charges 2005

Per person	€ 2,10
child (under 7 yrs)	€ 1,10
pitch incl. car	€ 6,20 - € 10,50
electricity	€ 2,50

Reservations

Bookings accepted without deposit, although not usually necessary. In low season phone (0)5.45.22.20.43. Tel: 05 45 20 31 41. Email: ot.pays-manslois@wanadoo.fr

An arboresque 2 hectare campsite situated on the banks of the river 'Charente'. 120 flat sites separated by small hedges. Mobile homes to rent.

Open from 15 May to 15* September.*

Leisure : Children's park, fishing, mini-golf, snack-bar, restaurant, canoe/kayak base near-by.

★ ★ ★

Camping Municipal " Le Champion "

Rue de Watlington 16230 Mansle - mairie.mansle@wanadoo.fr
Tel: (+33) 05.45.20.31.41 or 05.45.22.20.43 - Fax: (+33) 05.45.22.86.30

Château **Le Verdoyer** ★★★★
Castel
Camping – Caravaning
Dordogne – France

Located at the heart of Perigord Vert. Entertainment throughout the season, particularly for children to 13 years. Restaurant with regional specialities.
Mobile homes, chalets and apartments for rent

LES CASTELS ★★★★

F 24470 Champs Romain
Tél. 00 33 5 53 56 94 64   Fax. 00 33 5 53 56 38 70
www.verdoyer.fr   E mail : chateau@verdoyer.fr

FR24010 Castel Camping Château Le Verdoyer

Mobile homes ▶ page 432

Champs Romain, F-24470 St Pardoux (Dordogne)

Le Verdoyer has been developed in the park of a restored château and is owned by a Dutch family. We particularly like this site for its beautiful buildings and lovely surroundings. It is situated in the lesser known area of the Dordogne sometimes referred to as the Périgord Vert, with its green forests and small lakes. The 26 hectare estate has three such lakes, two for fishing (one in front of the château) and one with a sandy beach and safe swimming area. There are 135 marked touring pitches of a good size, level, terraced and hedged. With a choice of wooded area or open field, all have electricity (5/10A) and most share a water supply between four pitches. There is a pool complex and in high season activities are organised for children (5-13 yrs) but there is definitely no disco! The courtyard area between reception and the bar is home to evening activities, and provides a pleasant place to enjoy drinks and relax. The château itself has rooms to let and its excellent lakeside restaurant is also open to the public. This site is particularly well adapted fopr those with disabilities, with two fully adapted chalets, wheelchair access to all facilities and even a lift into the pool.

Facilities

Three very well appointed toilet blocks include washbasins in cabins, excellent facilities for disabled people and baby baths. Serviced launderette. Motorcaravan service point. Fridge rental. Multi-purpose shop with gas. Bar (with snacks and takeaway) and restaurant, both open all season. Good value bistro serving meals (July/Aug). Two pools (25 x 10 m. and 10 x 7 m; the smaller one can be covered in low season), slide (36 m.) and paddling pool. Play areas. All-weather tennis court. Volleyball, basketball and badminton. Table tennis. Minigolf. Bicycle hire (tennis and bicycles free in low season). Small library. Off site: Riding 3 km.

Open

16 April - 15 October.

At a glance

Welcome & Ambience	✓✓✓✓✓	Location	✓✓✓✓
Quality of Pitches	✓✓✓✓	Range of Facilities	✓✓✓✓✓

Directions

Site is 2 km. from the Limoges (N21) - Chalus (D6bis-D85) - Nontron road, 20 km. south of Chalus and is well signed from the main road. Site is on the D96 about 4 km. north of village of Champs Romain.

Charges 2005

Per unit incl. 2 persons
and electricity	€ 18,00 - € 29,00
full services	free - € 4,50
extra person	€ 5,00 - € 6,00
child (under 4 yrs)	free
dog	free - € 4,60

Between 9/7-20/8 stay 14 nights, pay for twelve. Camping Cheques accepted.

Reservations

Write to site. Tel: 05 53 56 94 64.
Email: chateau@verdoyer.fr

251

FR24030 Camping Les Périères

Route Ste Nathalène, F-24203 Sarlat (Dordogne)

Les Périères is a good quality small site set on an attractive hillside within walking distance of the beautiful medieval town of Sarlat. The 100 pitches are arranged on wide terraces around the semi-circle of a fairly steep valley, overlooking a central leisure area that includes indoor and outdoor swimming pools and two tennis courts. The pitches are of a very good size, all equipped with electricity (6A), individual water and drainage points and many have dappled shade from the numerous walnut trees on the site (the walnuts can be bought in the campsite shop). Reservations are advised for high season, when the site becomes busy. The site has a refreshingly spacious and open feel, quite free from overcrowding, even at busy times.

Facilities

The toilet blocks of varying styles and sizes should be quite sufficient, including washbasins in cabins, facilities for disabled visitors, a good baby bathroom in one block and washing machines and dryers. Motorcaravan service point. Small shop. Pleasant bar. Small snack bar/takeaway (July/August). Outdoor swimming pool (no shorts) and paddling pool and heated indoor spa pool and sauna (all season). Two tennis courts. Table tennis (indoors and out), football pitch and fitness track with exercise halts. Stone cottages to rent. No electric barbecues allowed.
Off site: Bicycle hire 1 km, fishing 5 km, riding or golf 7 km.

Open

Easter - 30 September.

At a glance

Welcome & Ambience	✓✓✓✓	Location	✓✓✓✓✓
Quality of Pitches	✓✓✓✓	Range of Facilities	✓✓✓✓

Directions

Site is on the east side of Sarlat, on the D47 to Ste Nathalene. (Negotiating Sarlat town centre is best done outside of peak hours).

Charges 2005

Per unit incl. 2 persons	€ 18,20 - € 24,60
with electricity	€ 22,00 - € 28,50
extra person	€ 6,10
child (under 7 yrs)	€ 4,00

Credit cards accepted with 2% fee.

Reservations

Advised for high season and made for min. 1 week with deposit (€ 80 per week) and fee (€ 15 - July-August only). Tel: 05 53 59 05 84.
Email: les-perieres@wanadoo.fr

FR24040 Castel Camping Le Moulin du Roch

Route des Eyzies - Le Roch, D47, F-24200 Sarlat (Dordogne)

Le Moulin du Roch is set on natural sloping woodland in the grounds of a former water mill and the Dutreux family have worked hard to ensure that it is an attractive and well run family campsite, fully deserving of its place in the Castels and Camping chain. Only 10 km. from the charming medieval town of Sarlat and 52 km. from Pèrigueux – the capital town of the Périgord region – this campsite is well situated for exploring the natural, historical, cultural and gastronomic riches of the Dordogne. The site has 199 pitches, of which 104 are for touring units. Pitches are mostly flat (some slope slightly) and grassy, and all have electricity (6A). Pitches on the upper levels have plenty of shade, whilst those on the lower level near the amenities and the fishing lake are more open. Entertainment and activities are organised from June to September, with something for everyone from craft workshops and sports tournaments to canoeing and caving for the more adventurous. An excellent multi-lingual children's club runs in July and August. Walking and mountain biking lead from the site through surrounding woodland.

Facilities

Three modern toilet blocks provide clean and well maintained facilities. Washing machines and dryers. Shop (all season) stocks a good range of groceries and fresh food, and is very reasonably priced. Bar with terrace (1/6-31/8). Takeaway (2/5-16/9). Superb restaurant (13/5-9/9, closed Mondays). Attractive swimming pool, paddling pool and sun terrace with loungers (all season). Fishing lake (carp and roach - no charge), tennis, table tennis, boules area, volleyball pitch, playground, discos twice weekly in high season. Dogs and other animals are not accepted.
Off site: Supermarkets, banks, etc. at Sarlat 10 km. Bicycle hire and riding 10 km. Golf 15 km.

At a glance

Welcome & Ambience	✓✓✓✓✓	Location	✓✓✓✓
Quality of Pitches	✓✓✓✓	Range of Facilities	✓✓✓✓✓

Directions

Site is 10 km. west of Sarlat la Canéda, on south side of D47 Sarlat - Les Eyzies road.

Charges 2006

Per pitch incl. 2 persons	€ 14,00 - € 26,00
with electricity	€ 18,00 - € 30,00
with full services	€ 22,00 - € 34,00
extra person	€ 3,50 - € 7,80
child (4-9 yrs)	free - € 2,80

Camping Cheques accepted.

Reservations

Essential from June - August, with deposit (20%) and fee (€ 9 in low season, € 19.50 in July/Aug). Tel: 05 53 59 20 27.
Email: moulin.du.roch@wanadoo.fr

Open

29 April - 16 September.

FR24060 Camping Le Paradis

St Léon-sur-Vézère, F-24290 Montignac (Dordogne)

Le Paradis is a well maintained riverside site, halfway between Les Eyzies and Montignac. Well situated for exploring places of interest in the Dordogne region, the site is very well kept and laid out with mature shrubs and bushes of different types. It has 200 individual pitches of good size on flat grass, divided by trees and shrubs (146 for touring units). All have electricity, water and drainage, and there are some special pitches for motorcaravans. At the far end of the site, steps down to the Vézère river give access for canoe launching and swimming. The site welcomes a good quota of Dutch and British visitors, many through a tour operator. Organised games, competitions and evening events are aimed at maintaining a true French flavour. English is spoken. This is a site of real quality, which we thoroughly recommend.

Facilities

Two unisex toilet blocks are of outstanding quality and fully equipped. They can be heated, have baby baths and toilets, extensive laundry facilities and even outside showers for swimmers. Well stocked shop (with gas). Restaurant with extensive choice of menu with good takeaway service. Very good pool complex heated in low season, with a large deep pool, a smaller shallower one, plus a paddling pool. Two tennis courts. Football, BMX track, volleyball, table tennis and pool activities. Multisport court. Canoe hire. Fishing. Bicycle hire. Quad bike and horse riding excursions. Playground. Off site: Riding 2 km. Various trips organised to surrounding area.

At a glance

Welcome & Ambience	✓✓✓✓	Location	✓✓✓✓
Quality of Pitches	✓✓✓✓	Range of Facilities	✓✓✓✓

Directions

Site is 12 km. north of Les Eyzies and 3 km. south of St Léon-sur-Vézère, on the east side of the D706.

Charges 2005

Per person	€ 4,80 - € 7,10
child (3-12 yrs)	€ 3,70 - € 5,30
pitch	€ 7,60 - € 11,00
electricity (6A)	€ 3,00

Low season reductions. 10% discount for pensioners in low season. Camping Cheques accepted.

Reservations

Made for any length with deposit (€ 80) and fee (€ 20). Tel: 05 53 50 72 64. Email: le-paradis@perigord.com

Open

1 April - 25 October.

FR24090 Camping Soleil Plage

Mobile homes ▶ page 433

Caudon par Montfort, Vitrac, F-24200 Sarlat (Dordogne)

This spacious site is in one of the most attractive sections of the Dordogne valley, right on the riverside. The site has a total of 199 pitches, divided into three sections, of which around 94 are available for touring units. The smallest section surrounds the main reception and other facilities, which are housed in a renovated Périgordine farmhouse, whilst the largest section of the site is about 250 m. from the reception and pool areas, and offers river bathing from a sizeable pebble bank. All pitches are bounded by hedges and are of good size, and in the larger section there are a few bigger pitches for large families. Most pitches have some shade, all have electricity (6A) and many have water and a drain. Various activities are organised during high season including walks and sports tournaments, and daily canoe hire is available from the site. Once a week there is a 'soirée' usually involving a barbecue or paella, with band and lots of free wine - worth catching! The site is becoming increasingly popular and reservation is advisable. Used by UK tour operators (50 pitches). English and Dutch are spoken.

Facilities

Toilet facilities are in two modern unisex blocks. Washing machines. Motorcaravan service point. Pleasant bar with extensive and good value takeaway menu, refurbished restaurant serving excellent Périgourdine menus, and well stocked shop (all 12/5-15/9). Very impressive swimming pool complex includes main pool, paddling pool, spa pool and two water slides. Tennis court, devilish minigolf, table tennis, volleyball and football pitches. TV room. Playground. Fishing. Canoe and kayak hire. Bicycle hire. Currency exchange. Off site: Golf 1 km. Riding 5 km.

Open

1 April - 30 September.

At a glance

Welcome & Ambience	✓✓✓✓✓	Location	✓✓✓✓
Quality of Pitches	✓✓✓✓✓	Range of Facilities	✓✓✓✓

Directions

Site is 8 km. south of Sarlat. From A20 take exit 55 (Souillac) towards Sarlat. Follow the D703 to Carsac and on to Montfort. at Montfort castle turn left for 2 km. down to the river. From Bergerac, at Vitrac-port, turn right to Golf de Rochebois and right again at the T-junction down to the river.

Charges 2006

Per person	€ 4,20 - € 6,80
child (2-9 yrs)	€ 2,50 - € 3,90
pitch	€ 6,00 - € 11,30
with electricity	€ 9,30 - € 14,80
with full services	€ 12,00 - € 23,00

Reservations

Made for exact dates: min. 1 week with deposit (€ 65) and fee (€ 35); send for booking form. Tel: 05 53 28 33 33. Email: info@soleilplage.fr

FR24140 Camping Bel Ombrage

F-24250 St Cybranet (Dordogne)

Bel Ombrage is a quiet, well maintained site located in a pretty location by the little River Céou, with a pebble beach onto a backwater that is safe and clean for bathing. The site has a good pool complex, but otherwise there are few on site facilities. The 180 well shaded, grass pitches are flat and of a good size, marked out by trees and bushes and all with electricity. The quiet and tranquil setting makes the site particularly popular with couples. Bel Ombrage is very close to Domme and Castelnaud and would make an ideal and inexpensive base for visiting the southern Dordogne area. It is a short walk to the village of St Cybranet, with bar, restaurant and a small well stocked supermarket, and a short drive takes you to the beautifully restored village of Daglan.

Facilities

Two modern toilet blocks are kept spotlessly clean, with facilities for disabled visitors and babies. Laundry facilities. Bread van calls each morning. Large swimming pool with sun terrace, children's pool and paddling pool (soft drinks and ice-creams sold in high season). Play area. Games room. Fishing. Excursions can be booked at reception. Off site: Pizzeria next door. Tennis and canoeing close. Riding and bicycle hire 3 km. Golf 6 km. More shops at Cénac.

Open

1 June - 5 September.

At a glance

Welcome & Ambience	✓✓✓	Location	✓✓✓✓
Quality of Pitches	✓✓✓✓✓	Range of Facilities	✓✓✓

Directions

Site is about 14 km. south of Sarlat, on the east side of the D57 Castelnaud-la-Chapelle - St Cybranet road, about 1 km. north of the junction with the D50.

Charges guide

Per person	€ 5,00
child (under 7 yrs)	€ 3,00
pitch	€ 6,60
electricity (10A)	€ 3,50
No credit cards.	

Reservations

Write to site. Tel: 05 53 28 34 14.
Email: belombrage@wanadoo.fr

FR24080 Camping Caravaning Le Moulin de David   Mobile homes ▶ page 433

Gaugeac, F-24540 Monpazier (Dordogne)

Owned and run by a French family who continually seek to improve it, this pleasant and attractive site is one for those who enjoy peace, away from the hustle and bustle of the main Dordogne attractions, yet sufficiently close for them to be accessible. Set in a 14 hectare wooded valley, it has 160 pitches split into two sections; 102 are available for touring vans – 33 below the central reception complex in a shaded situation, and 69 above on partly terraced ground with varying degrees of shade. All pitches have electricity (3-10A). Spacing is good and there is no crowding. The site has been attractively planted with a pleasing variety of shrubs and trees, and combined with the small stream that runs through the centre of the site they create a beautiful and tranquil setting. There is a delightful wooded walk via a long distance footpath (GR 36) to Château Biron, about 2-3 km. distance. A 'Sites et Paysages' member.

Facilities

All three toilet blocks are good, including washbasins in cabins, facilities for disabled visitors and babies in each. Adequate dishwashing and laundry sinks. Laundry room. Good shop. Bar/restaurant with shaded patio and takeaway. Swimming pool and children's paddling pool, plus freshwater pool with waterslide. Play area. Boules, half-court tennis, table tennis, volleyball, basketball, trampolining and football area. Library. Bicycle hire. Events, games and canoe trips organised (1/7-31/8). Off site: Small supermarket and cash point in Monpazier 2.5 km.

Open

14 May - 10 September.

At a glance

Welcome & Ambience	✓✓✓✓	Location	✓✓✓✓
Quality of Pitches	✓✓✓✓✓	Range of Facilities	✓✓✓✓

Directions

From Monpazier take the D2 Villeréal road. Take third turning left (after about 2 km), signed to Moulin de David and 'Gaugeac Mairie'. Site is about 500 m. along this road on the left.

Charges 2006

Per person (over 2 yrs)	€ 3,80 - € 6,80
normal pitch	€ 5,25 - € 9,85
large pitch incl. water and drainage	€ 8,20 - € 12,70
extra child's tent	€ 1,40 - € 3,35
electricity (3/10A)	€ 3,45 - € 5,85
animal	€ 1,50 - € 2,90
Camping Cheques accepted.	

Reservations

Advisable for Jul/Aug, with deposit (€ 65 per week reserved) and fee (€ 19) for stays between 26/6 and 21/8). Tel: 05 53 22 65 25.
Email: info@moulin-de-david.com

FR24070 Camping Lestaubière

Pont St Mamet, F-24140 Douville (Dordogne)

Set just off the main N21 road near Pont St Mamet, mid-way between Bergerac and Perigueux, this quiet and charming campsite is well situated for exploring the western side of the Dordogne and the Bergerac vineyards. There are 104 large pitches (150 sq.m). Most are on fairly flat, shaded wooded ground at the top of the site, some on more sloping open meadow with views across the valley and others on flat ground beside the lake. Pitches are marked and all have electrical connections (4/10A), some requiring long leads. The swimming pool and small lake with diving platform and beach encourage longer stays. A pleasant, shaded patio terrace under vines and maples leads to a general room with a bar and a separate room for young people with amusement machines (July/Aug). There are many British and Dutch visitors, but no tour operators. Good English is spoken by the friendly Dutch owners.

Facilities

Three toilet blocks, one brand new, include some washbasins in private cabins in the larger blocks. Baby baths and large family shower room. Facilities for disabled visitors. Ample dishwashing and laundry sinks. Washing machine and dryers. Small shop. Bar. Library. Swimming pool (unsupervised) and paddling pool. Excellent adventure style play area. Volleyball. Boules. Fishing. Children's club and organised activities in July/Aug. Off site: Tennis 500 m.

Open

1 May - 1 October.

At a glance

Welcome & Ambience	✓✓✓✓✓	Location	✓✓✓✓
Quality of Pitches	✓✓✓✓	Range of Facilities	✓✓✓✓

Directions

Site is 19 km. north east of Bergerac. From N21 Bergerac - Perigueux road take the exit for Pont St Mamet. The site is 500 m. north of the village, on the eastern side of the road, and is well signed. After you turn off the main road at this point the site entrance is almost immediately on you left.

Charges 2005

Per person	€ 4,60 - € 5,50
child (under 7)	€ 2,80 - € 3,30
pitch	€ 5,60 - € 8,00
electricity (4/10A)	€ 2,70 - € 4,00
animal	€ 0,75

Reservations

Advised for July and August. No deposit and booking fee. Tel: 05 53 82 98 15. Email: lestaubiere@cs.com

FR24100 Sunêlia Le Moulinal

F-24540 Biron (Dordogne)

A rural, lakeside site with extensive wooded grounds, Le Moulinal offers activities to occupy children and adults of all ages. Of the 280 grassy pitches, only around 62 are available for touring units, and these are spread amongst the site's own mobile homes, chalets and a small number of British tour operator tents. All pitches are flat, grassy and have electricity (6A), but vary considerably in size from 75 sq.m. to 100 sq.m. The five-acre lake has a sandy beach and is suitable for boating (canoe hire available), swimming and fishing. Ambitious, well organised animation is run throughout the season including craft activities, children's club (age 5+), pony rides, children's shows, walking and cycling tours, night time wildlife rambles and regular evening entertainment in July and August.

Facilities

Toilet facilities, built to harmonise with the surroundings, include British and Turkish style toilets (most in one block), some washbasins in cabins, and dishwashing sinks. Facilities for disabled people and babies. Laundry with washing machines and dryers. Motorcaravan service point. Excellent restaurant serving regional meals. Bar serving snacks and light meals. Snack bar/takeaway. Large, heated swimming pool with jacuzzi and children's pool. Rustic play area on grass. Multisport court, ping pong tables, boules, volleyball, tennis, football, basketball, archery, roller skating track. Mountain bike hire. All facilities open all season. Off site: Riding and climbing 5 km, potholing 10 km. Bastide towns of Monpazier, Villeréal and Monflanquin 15 km.

Open

1 April - 16 September.

At a glance

Welcome & Ambience	✓✓✓✓	Location	✓✓✓
Quality of Pitches	✓✓✓	Range of Facilities	✓✓✓✓✓

Directions

Site is 53 km. southeast of Bergerac. From D104 Villeréal - Monpazier road take the D53/D150 south to Lacapelle Biron. Just before Lacapelle Biron turn right onto the D255 towards Dévillac, (site is well signed here), and site is 1.5 km. along on the left. GPS: N44:35.988 E00:52.249

Charges 2005

Per pitch incl. 2 persons and electricity	€ 17,00 - € 35,00
with electricity, water and drainage	€ 20,00 - € 42,00
pitch near lake with electricity	€ 18,00 - € 38,00
extra person	€ 4,00 - € 9,00
child (2-7 yrs)	free - € 8,00
animal	€ 5,00

Reservations

Made with deposit (€ 92) and booking fee (€ 30 - high season only). Tel: 05 53 40 84 60. Email: lemoulinal@perigord.com

FR24150 Camping Les Deux Vallées

F-24220 Vézac (Dordogne)

This site is enviably situated almost under the shadow of Beynac castle in the heart of the Dordogne. There are 95 flat marked touring pitches, most of a good size, some large, and with electricity (6/10A). There is plenty of shade and the general feel is of unspoilt but well managed woodland. There is a small fishing lake on site, and it is only a short distance to the Dordogne river for bathing or canoeing. The site is being steadily upgraded by its Dutch owners who provide a warm and friendly welcome. English is spoken. This site would be ideal for those wanting a quiet and relatively inexpensive base from which to visit the Dordogne, particularly in low season, as the site has the advantage of being open all year.

Facilities

The main unisex toilet block is modern and very clean, and gives an ample provision, with good access for disabled people. A second smaller recently refurbished block can be heated for off-season use. Shop and bar/restaurant (both 1/6-30/9) serving good value snacks and more ambitious meals to take away, eat inside or on the terrace. Good sized pool (1.6 m. deep) and children's pool (from mid May). Bicycle hire. Volleyball, basketball, small minigolf, boules area, table tennis, table football. Quiz nights, painting lessons and barbecues are a regular feature in the main season. Facilities may open earlier than stated if demand is sufficient. Off site: Riding 2 km. Golf 8 km.

Open

All year.

At a glance

Welcome & Ambience	✓✓✓✓	Location	✓✓✓✓
Quality of Pitches	✓✓✓	Range of Facilities	✓✓✓✓

Directions

Site is on the northwest side of the D57 Beynac-et-Cazenac - Sarlat road, about 8 km. from Sarlat and 2 km. from Beynac. From Beynac follow D57, pass under railway bridge and then take second turning left (by a bus shelter, small site sign). Follow road around and take first turn left over a small bridge. Turn immediately left and site is about 200 m. ahead. From Sarlat the turn off the D57 will be on your right, just past a detached stone house.

Charges 2005

Per person	€ 3,00 - € 5,00
child (3-7 yrs)	€ 2,00 - € 5,00
pitch	€ 4,00 - € 6,50
electricity (6A)	€ 3,00
animal	€ 0,60 - € 1,00

Reservations

Advised for July/Aug. and made with deposit (€ 100) and fee (€ 15). Tel: 05 53 29 53 55. Email: les2v@perigord.com

FR24160 Camping Le Grand Dague

Atur, F-24750 Périgueux (Dordogne)

Le Grand Dague is a good quality site only a few miles from Périgueux and yet in an extremely rural and tranquil setting. Built on a hillside, the site is clean, attractive and very spacious and 68 of the 93 pitches are for touring units. The pitches are only slightly sloping but those with disabilities might find the interconnecting roads quite steep. There is a large field at the top of the site (with electricity) which can accommodate large motorhomes. All pitches have electricity (6A), and are divided by tall, mature hedging. Several large, open grassy areas provide plenty of space for youngsters and games, and along with a range of equipment in the play area make this an ideal site for young families. The Dutch owners have a passion for motorcycling, the 'Harley Davidson' themed campsite bar bearing witness to this! There are no tour operators.

Facilities

Excellent sanitary facilities are housed in a centrally located unit, part of which is heated for use in colder months. Mostly unisex facilities which include washbasins in cubicles, a baby room and facilities for people with disabilities. Dishwashing and laundry sinks. Small shop for essentials (15/6-30/9). Bar and attractive restaurant with appetising menu and takeaway (both from June). Swimming pool, water slide and paddling pool (from early May). Football, volleyball, badminton, petanque, minigolf and table tennis. Play area. Fishing. Off site: Paintball outside gate. Riding 5 km. Bicycle hire 8 km. Golf 10 km.

Open

1 May - 30 September.

At a glance

Welcome & Ambience	✓✓✓✓	Location	✓✓✓✓
Quality of Pitches	✓✓✓✓	Range of Facilities	✓✓✓✓

Directions

From the Bordeaux - Brive inner ring road in Périgueux take the D2 south, signed Atur, at roundabout 200 m. east of the N21 to Bergerac. Campsite is signed. Turn east at roundabout just before entering village (site signed) and follow signs along this road for 3 km. to site. GPS: N45:08.880 E00:46.657

Charges 2005

Per person	€ 4,25 - € 6,25
child (0-7 yrs)	€ 2,75 - € 4,00
pitch	€ 4,95 - € 8,00
electricity (6A)	€ 3,50
animal	€ 1,75

Reservations

Advised for high season and made with deposit (€ 136) and fee (€ 23). Tel: 05 53 04 21 01. Email: info@legranddague.fr

FR24170 Camping Le Port de Limeuil

F-24480 Allés-sur-Dordogne (Dordogne)

At the confluence of Dordogne and Vézère rivers, opposite the picturesque village of Limieul, this delightful family site exudes a peaceful and relaxed ambience. There are 90 marked, grassy, flat and numbered pitches, some very spacious and all with electricity connections (5A). The buildings are in traditional Périgourdine style and surrounded with flowers and shrubs - it is a very pretty site - and the young French owners have been steadily developing the facilities. A sports area on a large open grassy space between the river bank and the main camping area adds to the feeling of space, and provides an additional recreation and picnic area (there are additional unmarked pitches for tents and camper vans along the bank here). This is an ideal location for visiting the west central part of the Dordogne département, and is recommended for long stays. It is used fairly unobtrusively by a tour operator.

Facilities

Two clean, modern toilet blocks provide excellent facilities. Bar/restaurant with snacks and takeaway (all 20/5-5/9). Small shop. Swimming pool with jacuzzi, paddling pool and children's slide (1/5- 30 /9). Badminton, football, boules and volleyball. Mountain bike hire. Canoe hire - launched from the site's own pebble beach. Off site: The pretty medieval village of Limeuil 200 m. Riding 1 km. Golf 10 km.

Open

1 May - 30 September.

At a glance

Welcome & Ambience	✓✓✓✓✓	Location	✓✓✓✓
Quality of Pitches	✓✓✓✓	Range of Facilities	✓✓✓✓

Directions

Site is about 7 km. south of Le Bugue. From D51/D31E Le Buisson to Le Bugue road turn west onto D51 towards Limeuil. Just before you cross the bridge into the village of Limeuil, turn left (site signed here), across another bridge. Site is about 100 m. along this road on the right.
GPS: N44:52.878 E00:53.444

Charges 2006

Per pitch incl. 2 persons	€ 14,00 - € 24,90
extra person	€ 4,50 - € 5,50
child (under 10 yrs)	€ 2,50 - € 3,50
electricity (5A)	€ 2,50 - € 3,50
dog	€ 1,40 - € 2,00

Reservations

Advised for mid July - end August.
Tel: 05 53 63 29 76. Email: didierbonvallet@aol.com

FR24180 Camping Caravaning Saint Avit Loisirs

Le Bugue, F-24260 St Avit-de-Vialard (Dordogne)

Although Saint Avit Loisirs is set in the middle of rolling countryside, far from the hustle and bustle of the main tourist areas of the Dordogne, the facilities are first class, providing virtually everything you could possibly want without the need to leave the site. This makes it ideal for families with children of all ages. The site is divided into two sections. One smaller part is dedicated to chalets and mobile homes, whilst the main section of the site contains 199 flat and mainly grassy pitches, all a minimum of 100 sq.m and with electricity (6A), arranged in cul-de-sacs off a main access road. Tour operator tents and mobile homes (with lots of British visitors) occupy around half the pitches, leaving 99 for touring units. Three modern unisex toilet blocks provide high quality facilities, but could possibly become overstretched (particularly laundry and dishwashing sinks) in high season. The café, shop and bar open onto a large terrace with pergola and hanging baskets, which overlooks the excellent pool complex. In high season a variety of activities and entertainments are organised - tournaments of all sorts, aqua gym, bingo and even weekly films in English.

Facilities

Clean and modern toilet blocks include washbasins in cabins. Well stocked shop, bar, restaurant, good-value cafeteria and takeaway are housed in a traditional-style stone building. Outdoor swimming pool (200 sq.m), children's pool, water slide, 'crazy river' and heated indoor pool with jacuzzi and adjacent fitness room. Disco behind bar, sound-proofed. Table tennis. Floodlit minigolf and boules area and dirt bike track. Good quality tennis court, volleyball and extensive play area. Canoe trips on the Dordogne and other sporting activities organised. Good walks direct from the site. Off site: Sarlat and Perigeux within range for markets and hypermarkets.

Open

3 April - 25 September.

At a glance

Welcome & Ambience	✓✓✓✓	Location	✓✓✓
Quality of Pitches	✓✓✓✓	Range of Facilities	✓✓✓✓✓

Directions

Site is 6 km. north of Le Bugue. From D710 Le Bugue - Perigueux road, turn west on C201 (about 2.5 km. from Le Bugue), toward St Avit de Vialard. Follow road around and through hamlet of St Avit, bearing right - site is about 1.5 km. past here, on the right. Note: the road to St Avit is narrow and bumpy in places. GPS: N44:57.082 E00:50.825

Charges 2006

Per person	€ 3,70 - € 8,60
child (under 4 yrs)	free
pitch	€ 5,80 - € 12,50
with electricity	€ 9,50 - € 17,10
with water and drainage	€ 12,10 - € 20,40
dog	€ 2,10 - € 4,20

Reservations

Made with deposit (€ 46 per week) and fee (€ 15). Tel: 05 53 02 64 00.
Email: contact@saint-avit-loisirs.com

FR24110 Camping Caravaning Aqua Viva

Route Sarlac - Souillac, Carsac-Aillac, F-24200 Sarlat (Dordogne)

This shaded woodland site is ideally situated for visits to Rocamadour and Padirac, as well as the many places of interest in the Dordogne region, including the medieval town of Sarlat, only 7 km. away. The site is divided into two sections, separated by a small access road. Pitches are flat, mainly on grass, divided by shrubs, and vary from average to large. Many have shade from the numerous trees. All have electricity. Organised activities, children's clubs and entertainments run throughout the season, making this site popular with families, especially those with pre-teen and younger teenage children. English is spoken. The site attracts a good mixture of nationalities, resulting in a very 'international' ambience.

Facilities
Each part of the site has a central, modern toilet block, with facilities for disabled people, laundry and baby areas. Bar and restaurant/takeaway with terrace. Shop selling good range of groceries. Heated swimming pool and children's pool. Small fishing lake. High quality minigolf. Half tennis court, ping pong tables, volleyball and badminton nets. Good under 7's play park. Floodlit boules pitch and multi-sports court. Bicycle hire. Off site: Aerial woodland assault course 500 m. Riding and golf 5 km.

Open
14 April - 25 September.

At a glance
Welcome & Ambience	✓✓✓✓✓	Location	✓✓✓✓
Quality of Pitches	✓✓✓✓	Range of Facilities	✓✓✓✓✓

Directions
Site is 7 km. from Sarlat on the south of the D704A road from Sarlat to Souillac. Coming from Souillac, the access road to the site is just around a left hand bend, and is not easy to see, but if you miss the turning there is a roundabout a kilometre or so further on where you can turn around easily.

Charges 2005
Per person	€ 3,90 - € 6,50
child (2-7 yrs)	€ 2,60 - € 4,70
pitch	€ 4,80 - € 9,50
electricity (6/10A)	€ 3,50

Reservations
Made with 50% deposit and € 15 fee (fee charged 18/6-3/9). Tel: 05 53 31 46 00. Email: aqua-viva@perigord.com

Carsac - 24200 SARLAT
France

Tél. 00 33 (0)5 53 31 46 00
Fax 00 33 (0)5 53 29 36 37

Internet : www.aquaviva.fr
E-mail : aqua-viva@perigord.com

CAMPING - CARAVANING
BUNGALOWPARC - LOISIRS

FR24360 Camping Le Mondou

F-24370 St Julien de Lampon (Dordogne)

This quiet and peaceful site mid-way between Sarlat and Souillac is ideally situated for visiting a wide range of attractions in the Dordogne and Lot departments. It is set amongst countryside at the edge of the small village of St Julien, and only 2 km. from the Dordogne river. The 62 grassy pitches are of medium to large size, divided by shrubs, and with some shade from a wide variety of trees. All have electricity (6A). The friendly and helpful owners, John and Lia, organise regular evening entertainment during high season, and work hard to ensure that everyone enjoys their stay at Le Mondou.

Facilities
Two sanitary blocks provide basic facilities, including facilities for disabled visitors, baby baths, washing machine, ironing board and iron. Terrace bar and snack bar with reasonably priced menu. Large swimming pool with sun terrace and children's paddling pool. Rustic style play area and large playing field. Boules pitch, volleyball/badminton net. Off site: Bar, restaurant and small shop in the village of St Julien-de-Lampon about 1 km. away.

Open
1 April - 15 October.

At a glance
Welcome & Ambience	✓✓✓✓	Location	✓✓✓✓
Quality of Pitches	✓✓✓	Range of Facilities	✓✓✓

Directions
Site is 12 km. southwest of Souillac. From the D703 (Sarlat - Souillac) turn south across the river at Rouffillac, signed St Julien-de-Lampon. On entering village of St Julien turn left on D50, signed Mareuil and Le Roc. Follow road (it is narrow in one or two places), and just at end of village site is signed at a right turn. Follow for 500 m. to site on the right.

Charges 2005
Per person	€ 4,25
child (under 7 yrs)	€ 2,00
pitch incl. electricity	€ 6,75

Reservations
Advised for July and August with € 50 deposit per week reserved. Tel: 05 53 29 70 37. Email: lemondou@camping-dordogne.info

FR24230 Camping Le Moulin de Paulhiac

F-24520 Daglan (Dordogne)

Daglan is a very pretty well restored village that is becoming something of a tourist centre for this quieter area of the Dordogne. It is very close to Domme and La Roque-Gajeac and is in an ideal location for visiting the southern attractions of the region. You will be guaranteed a friendly welcome from the Armagnac family, who are justifiably proud of their well-kept and attractive site, built in the grounds surrounding an old mill. The 150 numbered pitches (98 for touring) are separated by hedges and shrubs, all have electricity, with water and waste water connections if required (supplement payable), and there is plenty of shade. Many pitches are next to a stream that runs through the site, and joins the River Ceou along its far edge. A tent field slopes gently down to the river, which is quite shallow and used for bathing. This site will appeal especially to families with younger children. Used by a tour operator (44 pitches).

Facilities
Two clean toilet blocks provide modern facilities, including those for disabled visitors. Well-stocked site shop - you can buy the owner's home-grown walnuts (delicious!). Good value restaurant and takeaway. Modern heated pool complex (no Bermuda style shorts) with a main pool, heated and covered by a sliding roof in low season, children's pool, a further small pool and two slides with landing pool. Volleyball, table tennis, badminton and boules. Bicycle hire. Canoe trips are organised on the Dordogne. Regular evening activities organised. Children's club in high season.

Open
15 May - 15 September.

At a glance
Welcome & Ambience	✓✓✓✓	Location	✓✓✓✓
Quality of Pitches	✓✓✓✓	Range of Facilities	✓✓✓✓

Directions
Site is about 17 km. south of Sarlat, and is on the east side of the D57, about 5 km. north of the village of Daglan.

Charges 2005
Per person	€ 6,20
child under 10 yrs	€ 4,55
child under 2 yrs	€ 2,40
pitch	€ 9,00
electricity (6-10A)	€ 3,35 - € 4,00
water and drainage	€ 2,30

Special offers in low season.

Reservations
Made for any length with deposit (€ 72) and booking fee (€ 8). Tel: 05 53 28 20 88. Email: Francis.Armagnac@wanadoo.fr

FR24240 Camping Les Bo-Bains

F-24150 Badefols-sur-Dordogne (Dordogne)

Offering a limited number of touring pitches, but a good range of facilities and activities, Les Bo-Bains is a well kept site in an attractive location alongside the Dordogne river. The flat, grassy and good sized pitches are all set along the river bank, with beautiful views across the Dordogne. Pitches are divided by hedges, shrubs and bushes of different varieties, and have plenty of shade. All pitches have electricity, with water taps and drainaway points between each pair. Canoeing can be arranged from reception and there are places to launch one's own small craft. The site welcomes a good quota of French and Dutch clients, but not many British as yet. Mobile homes and chalets are available to rent.

Facilities
The two main toilet blocks are of good quality with baby rooms and laundry facilities. Small shop. Bar (open all season) and restaurant with a choice of menu and good takeaway service (15/5-15/9). Swimming pool complex with a main pool (18 x 9 m), another shallower one (5 x 5 m), plus three slides and landing pool (14 x 7 m). Several small play areas. TV room. Multi-gym. Small football field. Minigolf, archery, boules, trampoline, volleyball, badminton, table tennis and basketball courts. Games, competitions, evening events and children's club organised daily during high season. Quad bike and bicycle hire. Tennis. Riding. Canoeing excursions. Off site: The small village of Badefols is within easy walking distance, and has a restaurant, bar, tobacconist and an historic château.

At a glance
Welcome & Ambience	✓✓✓	Location	✓✓✓✓
Quality of Pitches	✓✓✓✓✓	Range of Facilities	✓✓✓✓✓

Directions
Site is on the D29 Bergerac - Sarlat road, about 4 km. east of Lalinde, on the north side of the road.

Charges 2005
Per pitch incl. 2 persons and electricity (5A)	€ 16,00 - € 28,00
extra person over 4 yrs	€ 3,00 - € 7,50
animal	free - € 3,00

Reservations
Advised for July and August. Made for any length with deposit (30% - minimum € 45) and booking fee (€ 16). Tel: 05 53 73 52 52. Email: info@bo-bains.com

Open
15 April - 30 September.

FR24250 Camping les Tourterelles

F-24390 Tourtoirac (Dordogne)

This is a well maintained, Dutch owned site with its own equestrian centre that will appeal to lovers of the countryside, in an area that is ideal for walking or horse riding, yet is within easy reach of Pèrigueux and the better known sights of the Dordogne. The adjacent riding stables with 30 horses is run by the owner's daughter Angélique. The horses have been selected to be ideal for the local terrain, and to be safe and dependable. There are 125 pitches in total, but the site has some chalets, bungalows and mobile homes which leaves around 88 grassy pitches for tourists. These are on several different levels most with good shade from mature trees, and all have electricity hook-ups (6A). In low season the site can organise tours to local walnut farms, dairies etc. Rallies are welcome and themed programmes can be arranged.

Facilities

Three good, fully equipped toilet blocks include Facilities for disabled visitors and a baby unit. Laundry. Bread can be ordered. Bar/restaurant serving good value meals, with takeaway. Freezer pack service. Swimming pool (20 x 10 m.) and paddling pool. Riding. Tennis. Volleyball. Badminton. Table tennis. Children's club and comprehensive activity and entertainment programme in main season. Off site: Shop at Tourtoirac 1 km. Supermarket at Hautefort 6 km. Fishing 1 km. Bicycle hire 6 km.

Open

16 April - 30 September.

At a glance

Welcome & Ambience	✓✓✓✓	Location	✓✓✓✓
Quality of Pitches	✓✓✓✓	Range of Facilities	✓✓✓✓

Directions

From Limoges take D704 south to St Yrieux (70 km. south), Lanouaille and Cherveix-Cubas. In Cherveix-Cubas turn right (west) onto D5 to Tourtoirac. From Pèrigueux, take D5 east to Tourtoirac. Turn north onto D67 in village (site signed) and fork left on D73 towards Coulaures; site is on left in 1 km. GPS: N45:16.833 E01:02.913

Charges 2005

Per person	€ 3,80
child (under 10 yrs)	€ 3,20
pitch	€ 8,85 - € 10,75
electricity	€ 3,50
animal	€ 3,50

Low season discounts for over 55's.
No credit cards.

Reservations

Advised for July/Aug. Tel: 05 53 51 11 17.
Email: les-tourterelles@tiscali.fr

FR24280 Camping de Barnabé

Rue des Bains, F-24750 Perigueux (Dordogne)

The only site in Pèrigueux itself, Barnabé is a memorable site in a unique setting. A distinctive 1936 Art Deco style building houses the reception, bar, restaurant and games room, complete with an attractive terrace overlooking the River L'Isle, in the style of the old 'Cafe de Paris'. The bar has its own Wurlitzer juke box, and you will find pool tables, pinball and table football in the old ballroom. This site (created by the present owner's father in 1953) has 56 touring pitches, hedged and shaded by mature trees, all with electricity (4/6A). Twelve pitches also have water and drainage. Pitches are in four areas, with 42 pitches on one side of the river. The other 14 are in an annex on the opposite side and use a separate entrance (you are given a map). Pedestrian access between the two parts of the site is provided by an old fashioned, passenger operated ferry boat, which is a delightful way to cross the river. The entrance and access roads are a little narrow, and larger units will need to take great care. The ground may be rather firm for tent pegs and occasionally floods in winter.

Facilities

Six sanitary buildings around the site (one on the far side of the river). Not modern, but functional, simple and clean with spacious shower cubicles. Unisex facilities, with both British and Turkish style toilets (no paper). One heated block is open in winter. Bar (1/4-15/10). Fishing. Off site: Pèrigueux centre 2 km. Golf 7 km. Riding 10 km.

Open

All year.

At a glance

Welcome & Ambience	✓✓✓	Location	✓✓✓✓
Quality of Pitches	✓✓✓✓	Range of Facilities	✓✓✓

Directions

Approaching from the east of town, at N2089 and N221 roundabout, take exit for Pèrigueux 'centre ville'. After about 3 km. turn right at traffic lights at town boundary. From the west side follow signs for 'Brive', cross the river, and after 1.5 km. turn left at lights mentioned above. Site is signed to the right after 400 m. Site is also signed at the lights and from the town centre. GPS: N45:11.207 E00.44.515

Charges 2005

Per person	€ 3,50
child (under 7 yrs)	€ 2,20
pitch	€ 5,00 - € 5,40
electricity (4/6A)	€ 2,80 - € 2,95
dog	€ 1,00

Less 10-15% for longer stays in low season.

Reservations

Contact site for details. Tel: 05 53 53 41 45.
Email: contact@barnabe-perigord.com

FR24310 Camping Caravaning La Bouquerie

Mobile homes ▶ page 434

F-24590 St Geniès-en-Périgord (Dordogne)

La Bouquerie is a well maintained site, situated within easy reach of the main road network in the Dordogne, but without any associated traffic noise. The main complex is based around some beautifully restored traditional buildings. It includes a shop, and a bar and restaurant overlooking the pool complex, with a large outdoor terrace for fine weather. The excellent restaurant menu is varied and reasonably priced. Of the 165 pitches, 61 are used for touring units and these are of varying size (80-120 sq.m.), flat and grassy, some with shade, and all with electrical connections (5A). The rest of the pitches are taken up by site owned mobile homes and a UK tour operator. In high season the site offers sporting activities (aqua-gym, archery, canoeing, walks etc) as well as a children's club. La Bouquerie is ideally situated for exploring the Périgord region, and has something to offer families with children of all ages.

Facilities

Three unisex toilet blocks contain a mixture of new and older facilities, but are all extremely clean and well maintained. Two blocks provide facilities for disabled visitors and baby rooms. Separate covered laundry area with washing machines and covered drying lines. Shop (15/5-15/9) for bread, milk, papers and groceries, as well as takeaway food. Bar and restaurant (both 15/5-15/9). Pool complex (all season) with paddling pool, large shallow pool (heated) and large deep pool, with loungers provided. Carp fishing in lake on site. Bicycle hire. Riding. Off site: Shops and restaurants, etc. in the nearby village of St Geniès.

At a glance

Welcome & Ambience	✓✓✓✓	Location	✓✓✓✓
Quality of Pitches	✓✓✓	Range of Facilities	✓✓✓

Directions

Site is signed on east side of the D704 Sarlat - Montignac road (on the east side of the road), about 500 m. north of junction with D64 St Geniès road. Turn off D704 at campsite sign and take first left turn signed La Bouquerie - site is straight ahead.

Charges 2006

Per person	€ 4,60 - € 6,50
child (under 7 yrs)	€ 3,20 - € 4,50
pitch incl. electricity	€ 9,30 - € 12,00

Reservations

Advised for high season. Tel: 05 53 28 98 22. Email: labouquerie@wanadoo.fr

Open

15 April - 23 September.

CAMPING CARAVANING ★★★★

LA BOUQUERIE

Tel : +33(0)5 53 28 98 22
Fax : +33(0)5 53 29 19 75
E-mail : labouquerie@wanadoo.fr
Website : www.labouquerie.com

FR24290 Camping Le Moulin du Bleufond

Avenue Aristide Briand, F-24290 Montignac (Dordogne)

Built on flat ground around a 17th century mill, this converted and improved former municipal site has its own pool as well as adjacent town facilities. The 84 pitches (66 for tourers) are divided by mature hedges, all have electricity and most have some shade. Pitches vary considerably in size (70-100 sq.m). The small town of Montignac is only 5 minutes walk. The town is at the head of what is to become a World Heritage site - the Vezère valley - which has some of the planet's most important prehistoric caves. The site is separated from the river by a fairly quiet road, but there is a sizeable bank for fishing.

Facilities

Modern, clean sanitary facilities are well cared for by the energetic owners and can be heated if required. Bread and a few essentials available at reception. Bar, snack bar and terrace restaurant (all season). Heated swimming pool (140 sq.m) and paddling pool. Games room with giant TV screen. Canoe trips and bicycle hire can be arranged. Musical evenings weekly in high season. Off site: Shops, supermarkets, bars and a range of interesting restaurants.

Open

1 April - 15 October.

At a glance

Welcome & Ambience	✓✓✓✓	Location	✓✓✓✓✓
Quality of Pitches	✓✓✓✓	Range of Facilities	✓✓✓✓

Directions

Site is just south of Montignac town centre, on the D65 to Sergeac. Just after you cross the stone bridge on the one way system in the centre of the town turn sharp right (allow for a wide sweep!) The site is 750 m. on the left.

Charges 2005

Per person	€ 3,45 - € 4,60
child (2-8 yrs)	€ 2,06 - € 2,75
pitch incl. electricity (10A)	€ 7,20 - € 8,60

Reservations

Advised for July/Aug with 30% deposit (no booking fee). Tel: 05 53 51 83 95. Email: le.moulin.du.bleufond@wanadoo.fr

FR24320 Camping Les Peneyrals

Mobile homes ▶ page 434

Le Poujol, F-24590 St Crépin-Carlucet (Dordogne)

Within easy reach of all the attractions of the Périgord region, M. and Mme. Havel have created an attractive and friendly family campsite at Les Peneyrals. Set on a wooded hillside, with flowers in abundance (thanks to the dedication of Mme. Havel's mother), the site has 199 pitches, of which 87 are available for touring units. The pitches at the bottom of the hill tend to be quieter as they are further from the main facilities, but are all level and grassy (some on terraces), with electricity (5/10A), and most have some shade. An attractive bar and restaurant with terrace overlook the excellent pool complex and sunbathing areas. At the bottom of the campsite is a small fishing lake with carp (no charge to fish), and in July and August, activities are organised including archery, various sports tournaments, aqua gym, discos and a children's club. The site is used fairly unobtrusively by a UK tour operator (67 pitches).

Facilities
Two modern, unisex toilet blocks provide good quality facilities, including provision for babies and disabled visitors. Motorcaravan service point. Good value shop, restaurant and takeaway. Pool complex with two large pools (one heated), paddling pool and four water slides with splash pool. Bicycle hire. Minigolf, tennis court (charged). Football. Badminton, volleyball and table tennis. Play area. Games room, TV room and small library. Off site: Supermarkets, banks, etc. in Sarlat (11 km).

Open
13 May - 16 September.

At a glance
Welcome & Ambience	✓✓✓✓	Location	✓✓✓✓
Quality of Pitches	✓✓✓✓	Range of Facilities	✓✓✓✓✓

Directions
Site is 11 km. north of Sarlat. From D704 Sarlat - Montignac road turn east on D60 towards Salignac-Eyvigues. After 4 km. turn south on D56 towards St Crépin-Carlucet. Site is about 500 m. along this road on the right.

Charges 2006
Per person	€ 4,60 - € 7,30
child (under 7 yrs)	free - € 4,80
electricity (5/10A)	€ 2,00 - € 3,60
dog	€ 1,30 - € 2,00

Reservations
Advised for July/Aug. with € 72 deposit (and € 18 booking fee in high season).
Tel: 05 53 28 85 71.

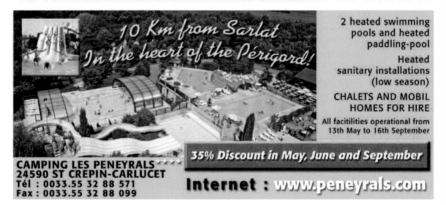

FR24300 Camping La Rivière Fleurie

St Aulaye de Breuilh, F-24230 St Antoine de Breuilh (Dordogne)

This quiet and pleasant campsite is close to the vineyards of Pomerol and St Emilion, and not far from the extensive shopping of St Foy la Grande and Bergerac. The 60 pitches are all spacious, divided by shrubs, and maturing trees are beginning to provide shade on many. All pitches have electricity (4/10A) There are no tour operators, but 12 pitches are used for site owned mobile homes, and there are also studio apartments to let throughout the year. The site has a tranquil and peaceful ambience, suitable for anyone looking for a quiet and relaxing holiday.

Facilities
Sanitary facilities are plentiful and modern (no toilet paper). Bar and terrace restaurant serving a range of basic meals. Swimming pool (100 sq.m) and toddlers' pool. Football, volleyball, table tennis, table football and TV room. Weekly 'soirées' where the owners host an evening of French food and entertainment. Canoe trips arranged. Off site: Municipal tennis court adjacent (free to campers). Fishing 100 m. Riding 4 km. Bicycle hire 8 km.

Open
1 April - 30 September.

At a glance
Welcome & Ambience	✓✓✓✓	Location	✓✓✓✓
Quality of Pitches	✓✓✓✓	Range of Facilities	✓✓✓✓

Directions
Site is in the hamlet of St Aulaye, 3 km. south of the D936 (Bordeaux - Bergerac). Site is signed off the D936 down local roads, at 6 km. east of Lamothe-Montravel, and at the western end of St Antoine de Breuilh. Follow 'camping' signs.
GPS: N44:49.743 E00:07.343

Charges 2005
Per unit incl. 2 persons	€ 13,00 - € 16,00
extra person	€ 4,00 - € 5,00
electricity	€ 2,90 - € 4,00

Reservations
Advised for July/Aug. Deposit of 30% (sterling cheques accepted as deposit). Tel: 05 53 24 82 80.
Email: info@la-riviere-fleurie.com

263

Dordogne & Aveyron

FR24340 Camping Le Val de la Marquise

F-24260 Campagne (Dordogne)

This well kept little campsite, set between the tourist centres of Le Bugue and Les Eyzies, is in an ideal situation from which to explore the châteaux and prehistoric sites of the Perigord region. The 104 pitches (88 for touring) are flat, grassy and all of a good size. The pitches are divided by shrubs, and some have shade from mature trees, whilst others are more open. Most have electricity (15A). Reception stocks a range of basic groceries including bread and croissants made freshly on site every morning. Weekly entertainment and excursions are organised in high season, but the site retains a relaxed peaceful air and is an ideal retreat after a busy day of sightseeing in the area.

Facilities

The central, very clean toilet block provides first-rate facilities, including controllable showers, washbasins in cubicles and a baby bath. A smaller block near reception houses good facilities for disabled visitors (no ramp but only a half inch step into the building) and washing and drying machines. Good quality bar (1/6-15/10) and snack bar/takeaway (1/7-30/8) with terrace. Swimming pool and paddling pool. Small fishing lake (free). Chalets and mobile homes to rent. Off site: Bars and restaurants in the village of Campagne 500 m. Supermarket in Le Bugue 5 km.

Open

1 April - 30 October.

At a glance

Welcome & Ambience	✓✓✓✓	Location	✓✓✓✓
Quality of Pitches	✓✓✓✓	Range of Facilities	✓✓✓

Directions

Site is 28 km. west of Sarlat, and 5 km. southeast of Le Bugue. Take D703/D706 Le Bugue - Les Eyzies road. At village of Campagne take D35 heading southeast towards St Cyprien (there is a peculiar 'Y' junction where the 3 roads meet). Site is about 500 m. along the D35 on the right.

Charges 2006

Per person	€ 3,10 - € 4,40
child (2-10 yrs)	€ 2,10 - € 3,00
pitch	€ 4,90 - € 7,00
electricity (15A)	€ 3,00
animal	€ 1,20 - € 1,80

Reservations

Advised for July/Aug. with deposit (€ 40 per week). Tel: 05 53 54 74 10. Email: val-marquise@wanadoo.fr

camping ★★★

"An exceptional situation in the heart of Périgord Noir - Dordogne"

Camping le Val de la Marquise - 24260 Campagne - France

val-marquise@wanadoo.fr www.levaldelamarquise.com   tél. : +33(0)5 53 54 74 10   fax : +33(0)5 53 54 00 70

FR24350 Camping RCN Le Moulin de la Pique

F-24170 Belvès (Dordogne)

Set in the grounds of converted former mill and iron foundry, this impressive and well managed site offers something for every member of the family. The 135 touring pitches are flat, grassy and extremely spacious (most well over 100 sq.m.) and most have electricity (6A), water and drainage. Some pitches border the lake which can be used for both fishing and boating. The 11th century fortified town of Belvès is only 2 km. away and the campsite is well located for access to the many other attractions of the Dordogne valley. Daily entertainment and activities are organised and there is even a 'fossil field', where children can become amateur archaeologists, digging for genuine fossils. Discounted golf, canoeing, bike hire and riding can be arranged through reception. Used by two UK tour operators.

Facilities

Three modern toilet blocks provide good quality unisex facilities. Baby baths and changing. Facilities for disabled visitors. Dishwashing and laundry sinks. Washing and drying machines. Bar and restaurant, snack bar and shop (open all season), Swimming pool (heated), paddling pool, four water slides, 'lazy river' with terrace. Playing field, football field. Volleyball. Table tennis. Tennis. Boules. Minigolf. Various play areas. TV and games room. Toddler's playroom. Library. Internet access. Mobile homes to rent. Off site: Bars, restaurants and shops in the village of Belvès 2 km.

At a glance

Welcome & Ambience	✓✓✓✓	Location	✓✓✓✓
Quality of Pitches	✓✓✓✓✓	Range of Facilities	✓✓✓✓✓

Directions

Site is 35 km. southwest of Sarlat on the east side of the D710, about 7 km south of Siorac-en-Périgord.

Charges 2005

Per pitch incl. up to 6 persons and electricity, water	€ 22,50 - € 45,50
pet	€ 4,00

Reservations

Advised for July/Aug. with 50% deposit. Tel: 05 53 29 01 15. Email: info@rcn-lemoulindelapique.fr

Open

15 April - 7 October.

FR24420 Camping Les Valades

D703, F-24220 Coux-et-Bigaroque (Dordogne)

Once in a while we come across small but beautifully kept campsites which seem to have been a well kept secret, and Les Valades certainly fits the bill. From the moment you arrive you can see that the owners, M. and Mme. Berger, take enormous pride in the appearance of their campsite, with an abundance of well tended flowers and shrubs everywhere you look. Set on a hillside overlooking countryside between the Dordogne and Vezère rivers, each of the 49 touring pitches is surrounded by variety of flowers, shrubs and trees. Pitches are flat and grassy, mostly on terraces, all with electricity (10A), and most with individual water and drainage as well. At the bottom of the hill, well away from the main camping area, is the swimming pool, alongside a good sized lake for carp fishing, swimming or canoeing (free canoe hire). There are also a few well shaded 'woodland' camping pitches down here too.

Facilities

The central toilet block provides clean and modern facilities, including those for disabled people. British style toilets (with paper), washbasins in cubicles, pre-set hot showers. Washing machine. The main reception building also houses the bar and snack bar (both July/Aug), with a terrace overlooking the valley. Swimming pool with sun terrace and paddling pool (all season). Mobile homes and chalets to rent. Off site: Small shop, bar, restaurant in Coux-et-Bigaroque 5 km. Supermarket at Le Bugue 10 km. Riding and bicycle hire 5 km. Golf 6 km.

Open

1 April - 15 October.

At a glance

Welcome & Ambience	✓✓✓✓	Location	✓✓✓
Quality of Pitches	✓✓✓✓	Range of Facilities	✓✓✓

Directions

Site is signed down a turning on west side of the D703 Le Bugue - Siorac-en-Perigord road, about 3.5 km. north of the village of Coux-et-Bigaroque. Turn off the D703 and site is 1.5 km. along on the right.

Charges 2005

Per person	€ 4,50
child (0-7 yrs)	€ 3,30
pitch	€ 6,00
electricity (10A)	€ 3,00
dog	€ 2,20

No credit cards.

Reservations

Accepted with booking fee (€ 15) and deposit of € 5 per day reserved. Tel: 05 53 29 14 27. Email: camping.valades@wanadoo.fr

FR24330 Camping de l'Etang Bleu

F-24340 Vieux-Mareuil (Dordogne)

Set halfway between the historic towns of Perigueux and Angoulême, this is a tranquil countryside site in a mature woodland setting. It is run by enthusiastic British owners Mark and Jo Finch, who really are 'Living The Dream' as described in a BBC documentary about their site. 151 of the 169 pitches are available to touring units, with the remainder taken up by site owned mobile homes for rent. The pitches are of a good size, flat and grassy, with mature hedging and trees providing privacy and plenty of shade. All pitches have water and 90 have electricity (10/16A). At the bottom of the site is a fishing lake stocked with carp (permit required), and various woodland walks start from the campsite grounds. The bright and cheerful 'bistro bar' provides good value food and drinks, and becomes a focal point for evening socialising on site. This site is ideal for couples or families with young children who are looking for a quiet and relaxing holiday away from the hustle and bustle of the busiest tourist areas, but still within reach of some of the area's major towns.

Facilities

The modern, clean and well maintained toilet block provides British style toilets, washbasins, showers, facilities for babies and disabled people. Laundry. Dishwashing facilities. Small playground with paddling pool. Swimming pool (20m x 10m) with sun terrace and loungers. Pleasant bar with terrace (all season) and restaurant with 'bistro' food (1/6-30/9) and additional poolside bar. Takeaway (1/6-30/9). Small shop (items not stocked can be ordered on request). Table tennis, boules, volleyball and badminton. Canoe and bicycle hire. Various entertainments, sporting activities and excursions organised in high season. Off site: Restaurant 'Auberge de L'Etang Bleu' adjacent to campsite, small supermarket, post office etc. in Mareuil (7 km).

Open

Easter/1 April -18 October.

At a glance

Welcome & Ambience	✓✓✓✓	Location	✓✓✓
Quality of Pitches	✓✓✓✓	Range of Facilities	✓✓✓✓

Directions

From Angoulême take D939 south, from Perigueux take D939 north. From either direction after about 45 km. the village of Vieux Mareuil is signed on north side of the road. Turn here on D93, and follow narrow road through the village. Just after leaving village site is signed on right, just past Auberge de L'Etang Bleu. Turn right here and follow signs down long gravel drive to site entrance.

Charges 2005

Per person	€ 3,75 - € 5,50
child (2-7 yrs)	€ 1,25 - € 2,00
pitch and car	€ 5,00 - € 9,25
with electricity and water	€ 7,75 - € 11,50
pet	€ 3,00

Reductions for over 60's and stays of 14 nights or more all season if reserved in advance.

Reservations

Advisable for high season. Tel: 05 53 60 92 70. Email: marc@letangbleu.com

FR24440 Camping Les Acacias

Bourg de la Canéda, F-24200 Sarlat la Canéda (Dordogne)

Only 2.5 kilometres from the historic medieval town centre of Sarlat, and yet surrounded by peaceful countryside, this campsite is well suited to those seeking a relaxing and peaceful site within easy reach of the major attractions of the Dordogne. The 110 grassy pitches are mostly flat, divided by hedges or trees, with plenty of shade, and all have electricity (6A). The small but welcoming bar and terrace are the focal point for daily events and entertainment during high season, with activities for both adults and children. A bus service 50 metres from the campsite entrance runs six times daily into Sarlat centre.

Facilities

Two toilet blocks provide clean and comfortable showers, washbasins in cabins, British style toilets, facilities for disabled people, baby bath and children's shower, toilet and washbasin. Laundry facilities. Bar serving snacks and takeaway food (May – Sept). Bread to order from reception (no shop, but large supermarket only 1.5 km). Swimming pool and paddling pool (10/5 – 20/9), with sun loungers and parasols. Volleyball. Football. Table tennis. Play area. Bicycle hire. Canoe excursions arranged from site.
Off site: Supermarket, bar/restaurant, pizza takeaway all 1.5 km. River fishing 3 km.

Open

1 April - 30 September.

At a glance

| Welcome & Ambience | ✓✓✓✓ | Location | ✓✓✓✓ |
| Quality of Pitches | ✓✓✓✓ | Range of Facilities | ✓✓✓ |

Directions

From Sarlat follow directions for Souillac and Cahors. Pass under an impressive stone railway viaduct, then take the second turn right, signed La Canéda. Follow this road until a small sports field and stadium on your left, and bear right here into the village of La Canéda. Site is signed about 500 m. along on the right.

Charges 2005

Per unit incl. 2 persons	€ 10,40 - € 13,00
extra person	€ 3,20 - € 4,00
child (0-7 yrs)	€ 1,60 - € 2,00
electricity	€ 2,50
dog	€ 0,50

Reservations

Advised for July/August and made with deposit (€ 50) and fee (€ 8). Tel: 05 53 31 08 50.

FR46030 Camping Les Pins

F-46350 Payrac-en-Quercy (Lot)

Set amongst four hectares of beautiful pine forest, Camping Les Pins is well situated for exploring the historical and natural splendours of the Dordogne region, as well as being a convenient overnight stop when heading north or south. There are 125 clearly marked, level pitches (100 sq.m), of which 75 are for touring units. The pitches are well marked and separated by small shrubs or hedges. Many have shade from the abundant pine trees and all have 6A electricity connections. There is a bar and a good value restaurant with a terrace overlooking the pool area. The friendly and welcoming owners are keen to encourage visitors to explore the region and have negotiated reductions for their guests when visiting certain local attractions.

Facilities

Three toilet blocks, two recently modernised, are well maintained and include washbasins in cabins and good baby bath facilities. Dishwashing and laundry sinks, washing machines and dryers (with plenty of drying lines). Motorcaravan service point. Shop with limited range of basics (1/6-31/8). Bar/restaurant and takeaway (1/6-31/8). Swimming pool (15 x 17 m.), three water slides and smaller paddling pool (15/5-15/9). Tennis court. Table tennis, pétanque and volleyball. TV and library. Some entertainment in season, including weekly family discos. Walking routes starting from the site. English and Dutch are spoken.
Off site: Fishing 7 km. Riding 10 km.

At a glance

| Welcome & Ambience | ✓✓✓✓ | Location | ✓✓✓✓ |
| Quality of Pitches | ✓✓✓✓ | Range of Facilities | ✓✓✓✓ |

Directions

Site entrance is 16 km. from Souflas on western side of the N20 just south of the village of Payrac-en-Quercy.

Charges 2006

Per person	€ 3,75 - € 6,30
child (under 7 yrs)	€ 1,50 - € 4,20
pitch	€ 5,50 - € 9,00
with electricity	€ 8,50 - € 12,00

Special low season family price.

Reservations

Made for min. 1 week with deposit (25%) plus fee (€ 15.24). Tel: 05 65 37 96 32.
Email: info@les-pins-camping.com

Open

8 April - 15 September.

FR46010 Castel Camping La Paille Basse

Mobile homes ▶ page 435

F-46200 Souillac-sur-Dordogne (Lot)

Set in a rural location some eight kilometres from Souillac, this family owned, high quality site is easily accessible from the N20 and well placed to take advantage of excursions into the Dordogne. It is part of a large domain of 80 hectares, which is available to campers for walks and recreation. The site is quite high up and there are excellent views over the surrounding countryside. The 250 pitches are in two main areas - one is level in cleared woodland with good shade, and the other on grass in open ground without shade. Numbered and marked, the pitches are a minimum 100 sq.m. and often considerably more. All have electricity (3/6A) with about 80 also equipped with water and drainage. A wide range of activities and entertainment are organised in season (animation was of a very high standard when we stayed). For good reason, the site can get very busy in high season and is popular with tour operators (25%), but there is more space available from mid August.

Facilities

Three main toilet blocks all have modern equipment and are kept very clean. Laundry facilities. Shop for essentials. Good restaurant, bar with terrace and takeaway. Crêperie. Good pool complex, with main swimming pool (25 x 10 m), a smaller one (10 x 6 m), paddling pool (unheated) and water slides. Sun terrace with loungers. Sound-proofed disco room (three times weekly in season). TV rooms (with satellite). Cinema room below the pool area. Tennis (charged), football, volleyball and table tennis. Play area. Off site: Golf 4 km.

Open

15 May - 15 September.

At a glance

Welcome & Ambience	✓✓✓✓	Location	✓✓✓✓
Quality of Pitches	✓✓✓✓	Range of Facilities	✓✓✓✓

Directions

From Souillac take D15 and then D62 roads leading northwest towards Salignac-Eyvignes and after 6 km. turn right at camp sign and follow steep and narrow approach road for 2 km.

Charges 2006

Per person	€ 5,40 - € 6,70
child (under 7 yrs)	€ 3,80 - € 4,70
pitch	€ 7,80 - € 9,80
incl. water and drainage	€ 9,80 - € 11,80
dog	€ 4,00

Less 20% outside 15/6-1/9.
Camping Cheques accepted.

Reservations

Advised mid-July - mid-Aug. and made for min. 1 week with deposit and booking fee.
Tel: 05 65 37 85 48. Email: paille.basse@wanadoo.fr

FR46040 Camping Moulin de Laborde

F-46700 Montcabrier (Lot)

Based around a converted 17th century watermill, Moulin de Laborde has been created by the Van Bonnel family to provide a tranquil and uncommercialised campsite for the whole family to enjoy. Bordered by woods, hills and a small river, there are 90 flat and grassy pitches, all of at least 100 sq.m. and with electricity (6A). A variety of pretty shrubs and trees divide the pitches and provide a moderate amount of shade. A gate at the back of the site leads walkers onto a 'Grand Randonée' footpath which passes through the village of Montcabrier, 1 km. away. A small lake with rafts and rowing boats, and an adventure-type play area with rope bridges and 'death slide' will keep children amused, whilst parents can relax in the charming courtyard area which houses the bar and restaurant.

Facilities

The centrally located and very clean toilet block has well designed showers and washbasins in cabins. Covered area provides sinks for dishwashing and laundry. Unit for disabled people. Washing machine and dryer. Shop stocks basics and gas (all season). Small bar, restaurant and takeaway. Swimming pool with sunbathing area and paddling pool (1/5-15/9). Play area. Small lake for recreation with free rafts and rowing boats. Fishing in the river. Volleyball and badminton nets. Boules pitch. Covered recreation area and table tennis. Mountain bike hire. Rock climbing and archery lessons. Live music one evening a week (more in high season). Dogs are not accepted. Off site: Riding 5 km. Golf 8 km. Tennis nearby and canoeing on the Lot. The Château of Bonaquil 6 km. Fumel 12 km.

Directions

Site is on the north side of the D673 Fumel - Gourdon road about 1 km. northeast of the turn to village of Montcabrier.

Charges 2005

Per person	€ 5,80
child (under 7 yrs)	€ 3,30
pitch	€ 8,00
electricity (6A)	€ 2,60

Less 30% outside July/August. No credit cards.

Reservations

Accepted with deposit (€ 7.50 per night booked). Tel: 05 65 24 62 06. Email: moulindelaborde@wanadoo.fr

Open

29 April - 15 September.

At a glance

Welcome & Ambience	✓✓✓✓	Location	✓✓✓✓
Quality of Pitches	✓✓✓✓	Range of Facilities	✓✓✓

FR46050 Camping Le Rêve

F-46300 Le Vigan (Lot)

Le Rêve is a very peaceful site situated in the heart of rolling countryside where the Perigord runs into Quercy. You are assured of a warm reception from the van Iersels, a Dutch couple who have been providing a friendly and hospitable welcome to their clients for the past 17 years. The 56 flat and grassy touring pitches are all of good size, with access to electricity (6A) and divided by shrubs. A few of the pitches are situated at the edge of the forest and provide plenty of shade. Plenty of large grassy areas give lots of space for children to play and make this site particularly suitable for young families.

Facilities

The modern toilet block includes an enclosed area for cooler weather. Washbasins in cabins, special cubicles for disabled people and a baby room. Washing machine and dryers. Small shop for basics (bread, milk etc.), pleasant bar, restaurant and takeaway (all open all season). Small, clean, solar heated swimming pool and large paddling pool with 'mushroom' fountain. Play area. Boules. Table tennis and volleyball. Off site: Riding 2 km. Fishing 5 km. Golf 20 km.

Open

25 April - 15 September.

At a glance

Welcome & Ambience	✓✓✓✓	Location	✓✓✓
Quality of Pitches	✓✓✓✓	Range of Facilities	✓✓✓

Directions

From N20 Souillac - Cahors road turn west onto the D673 3 km. south of Payrac. After 2 km. site is signed down small lane on west side of the road. Turn here, and follow signs for another 2.5 km. to site.

Charges 2006

Per person	€ 4,20
child (under 7 yrs)	€ 2,60
pitch	€ 6,25
electricity (6A)	€ 2,60
dog	€ 0,75

Less 20-30% outside July/Aug. No credit cards.

Reservations

Advised for high season and made for any length with deposit (€ 70) and fee (€ 5). Tel: 05 65 41 25 20. Email: info@campinglereve.com

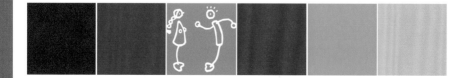

FR46110 Camping du Port

F-46600 Creysse (Lot)

Set off the beaten track this small, unassuming riverside campsite provides an unusual combination of peace and tranquillity alongside a range of sporting activities to occupy even the most adventurous of people. Pitches are mostly flat, and of a large size (100m^2+), with plenty of shade from the abundant trees, but no dividing hedges or fences. 70 of the 92 touring pitches have electricity (4/6A). The far side of the site slopes down to the picturesque Dordogne river, providing a launching area for canoes, and a small gravel 'beach'. The campsite owner runs daily activities including canoeing, caving, climbing, canyoning, cycling, walking and woodland assault course through the trees, all under qualified supervision. High season entertainment includes regular paella, 'moules and frites' and barbecue evenings, live musical entertainment and open air cinema screenings (July/Aug). Despite all these activities the campsite retains a very rural 'a la ferme' ambience, and is ideal for anyone seeking a restful time away from the hustle and bustle of the larger sites along the Dordogne. A torch would be useful.

Facilities

Central toilet block contains a mix of older and more modern facilities, which are maybe a little basic, but are well cleaned, and would appear more than adequate for the number of pitches. Toilets are mostly British style, washbasins (cold water only) both open and in cubicles, showers pre-set pushbutton type. Dishwashing and laundry sinks, washing machine. Small shop with reasonable range of groceries, bread, camping gas etc (15/6-15/9). Open bar and terrace (15/6-15/9), small snack bar/takeaway (July-Aug). Attractive swimming pool with sun terrace (no paddling pool). Mobile homes to rent.
Off site: Bar/restaurant in the pretty medieval village of Creysse, about 500 yds away, providing a varied menu.

At a glance

| Welcome & Ambience | ✓✓✓ | Location | ✓✓✓ |
| Quality of Pitches | ✓✓✓✓ | Range of Facilities | ✓✓✓✓ |

Directions

Site is about 15 km. east of Souillac. From the village of Martel on the D703 take the D23 south to Creysse. The site is signed on the left just before you enter the village.

Charges 2005

Per person	€ 3,90
child under 7 yrs	€ 2,90
pitch with electricity	€ 6,90
animal	€ 0,50

Reservations

Not required. Tel: 05 65 32 20 82.
Email: contact@campingduport.com

Open

1 May - 30 September.

FR46150 Camping La Truffière

F-46330 St Cirq-Lapopie (Lot)

Set in 4 hectares of mature oak woodland, only 2.5 km from the cliff top village of St Cirq-Lapopie, La Truffière is well suited to those seeking a peaceful countryside holiday amongst the stunning natural scenery of the 'Parc naturel régional des Causses de Quercy'. The 80 terraced touring pitches are of varying sizes, and a mixture of grass and gravel (larger units should reserve pitches in advance). All pitches have electricity (6A) and most have shade from the abundant trees. There are various walks and mountain bike trails in the area, and you can hire bikes on site. In high season the campsite owners organise a range of activities including guided walks, château visits, sports tournaments and a daily children's entertainment (not always in English). Due to the woodland nature of the campsite, barbecues are not permitted on individual pitches, but there are three communal barbecue areas around the site.

Facilities

Two clean and modern toilet blocks (one heated in low season) provide a full range of facilities including those for disabled visitors. Motorcaravan service point. Fridge hire. Bar/restaurant (1/6-31/8) with terrace overlooking swimming pool and playing field. Snack bar (15/5-15/9). Swimming pool and paddling pool with sun terrace and loungers (May – Sept). Small shop with essentials (open all season). Large playing field for volleyball, basketball and football. Adventure style play area. Table tennis. Trampolines. Boules pitches. English spoken. Off site: Small shop in village, hypermarkets 36 km. in Cahors. Riding 3 km. Fishing (in the River Lot) 3 km.

Open

1 April - 15 September.

At a glance

| Welcome & Ambience | ✓✓✓✓ | Location | ✓✓✓ |
| Quality of Pitches | ✓✓✓ | Range of Facilities | ✓✓✓ |

Directions

From D911 Cahors - Rodez road, turn north on the D42 at village of Concots (signed towards St Cirq-Lapopie). Site is about 5 km. along this road on the right. Approaching from the north on the D42 via St Cirq-Lapopie is not recommended due to an extremely tight left hand turn at the edge of the village.

Charges 2006

Per person	€ 5,00
child (0-7 yrs)	€ 3,00
pitch	€ 5,00
electricity	€ 3,00
dog	€ 1,50

Less 10% outside July/Aug. Credit cards only accepted 1/6-15/8. Camping Cheques accepted.

Reservations

Advisable in high season and made with fee (€ 11.50). Tel: 05 65 30 20 22.
Email: Contact@camping-truffiere.com

FR47030 Camping Le Château de Fonrives

Rives, F-47210 Villeréal (Lot-et-Garonne)

This is a very pleasant Dordogne site set in pretty part-farmed, part-wooded countryside, close to the delightful old town of Villeréal. The neat, orderly site is a mixture of hazelnut orchards, woodland with lake, château (mostly 16th century) and camping areas. An attractive avenue leads to the barns adjacent to the château which have been tastefully converted (the restaurant particularly so). There are 200 pitches, 160 for touring units, all of good size (100-150 sq.m.) and with electricity (4, 6 or 10A). Pitches near the woodland receive moderate shade, but elsewhere there is light shade from hedges and young trees. Former barns have been converted to provide a good quality restaurant with covered terrace and large, airy bar with an open terrace overlooking the outdoor pool. The lake can be used for fishing or boating.

Facilities

Two main sanitary units are clean and adequate including washbasins in well appointed cabins and some private bathrooms (for hire by the week). Facilities for children and babies. Laundry rooms. Motorcaravan services. Shop. Elegant restaurant, plus snacks and takeaway meals (all 10/6-10/9). Bar with disco area and terrace (15/5-15/9). Covered swimming pool (April-Oct) and outdoor pool with water slides and paddling pool (15/5-15/9; no Bermuda style shorts). Play areas. Small field for volleyball and football. Reading room. Minigolf. Tennis. Bicycle hire. Activities organised in season, including excursions and walks. Caravan storage. Off site: Riding 8 km.

At a glance

Welcome & Ambience	✓✓✓✓	Location	✓✓✓✓
Quality of Pitches	✓✓✓✓	Range of Facilities	✓✓✓✓

Directions

Site is about 2 km. northwest of Villeréal, on west side of the D14/D207 Bergerac - Villaréal road.

Charges guide

Per unit incl. 2 persons	€ 16,00 - € 23,00
extra person	€ 4,00
child (under 7 yrs)	€ 2,00
electricity 4-10A	€ 3,00 - € 5,50

Reservations

Advisable for July/Aug. with deposit (€ 77) and fee (€ 20). Tel: 05 53 36 63 38. Email: chateau.de.fonrives@wanadoo.fr

Open

4 May - 14 September.

FR47100 Camping Municipal Tonneins

F-47400 Tonneins (Lot-et-Garonne)

Close to the River Garonne, this small site has a rather formal charm with neat flower beds, well mown lawns and a generally extremely well cared for appearance. With a small reception, the Gardien based on site and a security barrier, it only has 32 pitches plus a meadow for additional camping. All with electricity (15A), the pitches are of a reasonable size, separated by small trees which provide a little shade. The site is on the southern outskirts of the town with a fair choice of shops, restaurants, etc, and only a 15 minute drive from the charming old riverside town of Port Ste Marie. There is some road and rail noise at times. This is a good stopping off point or base from which to explore the local area.

Facilities

Sanitary facilities provide British style WCs, washbasins in cabins and dishwashing sinks (H&C) under cover. Purpose built and roomy but of fairly old design, they are adequate rather than luxurious. Washing machine. No proper chemical disposal point. Under cover area with fridge and freezer and tables and chairs. Small play area. Torch useful. Off site: 1.5 km to Tonneins town centre.

Open

1 June - 30 September.

At a glance

Welcome & Ambience	✓✓✓✓	Location	✓✓✓✓
Quality of Pitches	✓✓✓✓✓	Range of Facilities	✓✓✓

Directions

Take either exit 5 from autoroute to Marmande then the N113 south or exit 6 to Aiguillon (avoid town) and follow N113 north. Site on west side of the N113 just south of Tonneins.

Charges 2005

Per pitch incl. 1 person	€ 5,50
incl. 2 persons	€ 7,50
extra person	€ 2,50
electricity	€ 3,00
No credit cards.	

Reservations

Contact site. Tel: 05 53 79 02 28.

270

FR47010 Camping Caravaning Moulin du Périé

Mobile homes ▶ page 435

F-47500 Sauveterre-la-Lemance (Lot-et-Garonne)

Set in a quiet area and surrounded by woodlands this peaceful little site is well away from much of the tourist bustle. Its 125 grass pitches, divided by mixed trees and bushes, are reasonably sized and extremely well kept, as indeed is the entire site. All pitches have electricity (6A) and most enjoy good shade, with a wide variety of trees and shrubs. The picturesque old mill buildings, adorned with flowers and creepers, now house the bar and restaurant where the food is to be recommended, as is the owner's extensive knowledge of wine that he is pleased to share with visitors. The attractive front courtyard is complemented by an equally pleasant terrace at the rear. Two small, clean swimming pools overlook a shallow, spring water lake, ideal for inflatable boats and paddling, and bordering the lake, a large grass field is popular for games. A quiet, friendly site with regular visitors - reservation is advised for July/Aug. A 'Sites et Paysages' member.

Facilities

Two clean, modern and well maintained toilet blocks include facilities for disabled visitors. Motorcaravan service point. Fridge, cot, barbecue and chemical toilet hire (book in advance). Shop for essentials (with gas). Bar/reception and restaurant (including takeaway). Two small swimming pools (no Bermuda-style shorts). Football and volleyball. Boules, table tennis, outdoor chess. Playground and trampoline. Small, indoor play area. Bicycle hire. In season various activities are arranged; including canoeing, riding, wine tasting visits, sight seeing trips plus weekly barbecues and gastronomic meals. Winter caravan storage.
Off site: Fishing 1 km. Small supermarket in village and larger stores in Fumel.

Open

23 April - 20 September.

At a glance

Welcome & Ambience	✓✓✓✓	Location	✓✓✓
Quality of Pitches	✓✓✓✓	Range of Facilities	✓✓✓

Directions

From D710 Fumel - Périgueux road, turn southeast into village of Sauveterre-le-Lemance across the railway line. Continue straight through village and turn left (northeast) at far end on C201 minor road signed to campsite, Château Sauveterre and Loubejec. Continue straight along this road and site is 3 km. on the right.

Charges 2005

Per unit incl. 2 persons	€ 12,40 - € 20,85
with electricity	€ 16,10 - € 24,55
extra person	€ 4,00 - € 6,20
child (under 7 yrs)	€ 1,70 - € 3,30
animal	€ 2,05 - € 3,90

Camping Cheques accepted.

Reservations

Advised for July/Aug. and made with deposit (€ 140) and fee (€ 20). Tel: 05 53 40 67 26.
Email: moulinduperie@wanadoo.fr

(271)

FR47050 Camping Moulin de Campech

F-47160 Villefranche-de-Queyran (Lot-et-Garonne)

This site is run by Sue and George Thomas along with Sue's parents, Dot and Bob Dunn. A cheery welcome and a free drink await you along with a determination to ensure that you enjoy your stay. At the entrance to the site, a trout lake with graceful weeping willows feeds under the restored mill house which is home to the owners as well as housing the bar and restaurant. Enjoy the fare produced by Sue on the lakeside terrace as the trout jump (fresh trout is a menu option). The river continues through one side of the site. Children will need supervision around the lake and at the pool which is on an elevated area above the mill house. The 60 large-sized pitches are mostly divided by hedges, with electricity available (2/6A, long leads may be necessary in places, but can be borrowed free of charge).

Facilities

The single, rather ordinary toilet unit has modern fittings, mainly British and Turkish style WCs, some washbasins in cubicles with hot water, and open washbasins. Covered dishwashing and laundry sinks (H&C). Washing machines and tumble dryer. Bar and restaurant. Terraced swimming pool. Open grassy area for games. Table tennis. Board games, boules and English library. Barbecue and gourmet nights organised in high season. Fishing (discounted rate for campers - no permit required). Torch useful.
Off site: Watersports, bicycle hire, golf (discounted rate for campers) or riding 10 km. Markets every day in villages and towns around the region.

At a glance

Welcome & Ambience	✓✓✓✓	Location	✓✓✓✓
Quality of Pitches	✓✓✓✓	Range of Facilities	✓✓✓

Directions

Take A10 south to Bordeaux. Join A62 for Toulouse and take exit 6 for Damazan. Follow D8 to Mont de Marsan, at Cap du Bosc turn right onto D11 for Casteljaloux. The site is 5 km. on the right and signed.

Charges 2005

Per person	€ 3,60 - € 5,10
child (under 7 yrs)	€ 2,70 - € 3,60
pitch	€ 7,00 - € 8,75
electricity (2/6A)	€ 2,30 - € 3,80
dog	€ 2,40

Reservations

Advised for July/Aug, with 10% or 1 night's deposit. Tel: 05 53 88 72 43. Email: campech@wanadoo.fr

Open

24 March - 23 October.

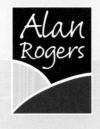

MAP 12

These two quiet and deeply rural provinces are right in the centre of France and are surrounded by the tourist regions of the Loire Valley, the Dordogne and the Auvergne. Unknown to many, it is often 'forgotten territory' but by some it's considered close to paradise.

WE HAVE COMBINED TWO OFFICIAL REGIONS: LIMOUSIN WITH DÉPARTEMENTS 19 CORRÈZE, 23 CREUSE, 87 HAUTE-VIENNE; AND AUVERGNE, 03 ALLIER, 15 CANTAL 43 HAUTE-LOIRE, 63 PUY-DE-DÔME. ALSO INCLUDED IS 48 LOZÈRE, PART OF THE OFFICAL REGION OF LANGUEDOC-ROUSSILLON

This is the home of Limoges porcelain and Aubosson tapestry, of exceptional Romanesque and Gothic churches and fairytale Renaissance châteaux. Limousin is an unspoilt, thinly populated region on the western side of the Massif Central. With hills and gorges and lush green meadows, numerous ancient village churches dot the landscape as well as more imposing abbey churches and fortresses. The many lakes and rivers of the Limousin provide endless possibilities for canoeing, sailing, wind-surfing and other watersports. To the south, fortified cities cling to mountain sides, home to many religious events and legends.

The Auvergne, set in the heart of the Massif Central, was formed by a series of volcanic eruptions and is a dramatic region of awe-inspiring non-active volcanoes, lakes, sparkling rivers, green valleys and forests. There are also numerous underground streams that have carved out extensive and fantastic cave systems, for which the region is famous. It is a wonderful destination for nature lovers, those who enjoy active outdoor pursuits or for people who want to relax at spa resorts.

Places of interest

Aubusson: long tradition of tapestry making, Hotel de Ville tapestry collections.

Clermont-Ferrand: old city centre, 11th and 12th century Notre Dame du Port Basilica, 13th century cathedral; known as *ville noire* for its houses built in local black volcanic rock.

Limoges: porcelain, enamel and faience work, château, church of St Michel-de-Lions, cathedral of St Etienne.

Vichy: spa, natural spring park.

Cuisine of the region

Limousin is known for a thick soup called *bréjaude* and its beef, which is extremely tender and full of flavour. Local specialties in the Auvergne include ham and andouille sausages, stuffed cabbage, and bacon with lentil and *cèpes* (mushrooms). Le Puy is famed for its lentils and *Vereine du Velay* – yellow and green liqueurs made from over 30 mountain plants.

Aligot: purée of potatoes with Tomme de Cantal cheese, cream, garlic and butter.

Friand Sanflorin: pork meat and herbs in pastry.

Jambon d'Auvergne: a tasty mountain ham.

Perdrix à l'Auvergnate: partridge stewed in white wine.

Potée Auvergnate: a stew of vegetables, cabbage, pork and sausage.

FR03010 Camping de la Filature

Ile de Nieres, F-03450 Ebreuil (Allier)

Near the spa town of Vichy and beside a fine fly fishing river that borders the Massif Central region, this site makes a good base to explore the Auvergne including the nearby river gorges, medieval châteaux and extinct volcanoes. Developed on the site of a spinning mill, this rural setting is home to peacocks (including some white ones). There are 80 spacious, grassy pitches, most with shade from mature trees and many directly on the river bank. In summer the river is clean, shallow and pleasant to play in. There is a deeper swimming area 500 m. away. Most pitches have electricity (3/6A). The area is ideal for walking and cycling, especially mountain biking and touring by car on the quiet country roads. Bird watching and wild flowers are additional attractions. You will receive a warm welcome from the English owners (their superb takeaways are very popular).

Facilities

Very clean sanitary facilities are in individual cubicles in pleasantly decorated buildings. Fully equipped, they include mostly British type toilets, a bathroom and a room for disabled visitors. Washing machine and ironing facilities. Small shop for essentials (1/5-30/9). Baker calls. Bar (1/6-30/9). Excellent takeaway (1/6-30/9). Barbecues and pizza nights organised in high season. River bathing and fishing. Play area. Bicycle hire. Minigolf. Off site: Riding, canoeing and tennis nearby. Ébreuil with shops and restaurants 1 km. Parc des Volcans and Vulcania attraction.

Open

31 March - 1 October.

At a glance

Welcome & Ambience	✓✓✓✓✓	Location	✓✓✓
Quality of Pitches	✓✓✓✓	Range of Facilities	✓✓✓

Directions

Site is well signed from exit 12 of A71 autoroute to Clermont Ferrand in the direction of Ébreuil. It is about 6 km. from the A71 and 1 km. west of Ébreuil beside the river on the D915 towards the Chouvigny gorges. GPS: N46:06.526 E03:04.403

Charges 2005

Per unit incl. 2 persons	€ 15,00
extra person	€ 5,00
child (under 16 yrs)	€ 2,50
electricity (3/6A)	€ 3,00 - € 6,00

Discounts in low season.

Reservations

Made with deposit (€ 30 per week of stay or full amount if stay costs less). Tel: 04 70 90 72 01. Email: camping.filature@libertysurf.fr

Don't wait to die to go to heaven, come to: ★★★★

CAMPING DE LA FILATURE DE LA SIOULE

03450 EBREUIL, FRANCE

See us on website www.campingfilature.com

- Very clean facilities and a bathroom
- Really hot water ● Excellent take away with pizza and barbecue evenings in high season ● Bar and terrace
- Low season bargains for long stays
- Children up to 16 charged child rate
- Near to exit 12 of A71 for stopover or long stay

Tel: 0033 (0)4 70 90 72 01 Fax: 0033 (0)4 70 90 79 48
E-mail: camping.filature@libertysurf.fr

FR03170 Camping Municipal Dompierre

F-03290 Dompierre-sur-Besbre (Allier)

This immaculate and attractive site has 68 level, partly shaded, individually hedged, grassy pitches, all with easy access. It is located next to the municipal sports fields and is ideal for motorcaravans being within easy walking distance of the town centre and supermarket (700 m). There are 70 pitches, some very large, with only a few long stay units, leaving about 65 for tourists; 60 have electricity (10A) and most have full service facilities. The warden is very proud of his efficiently run, value for money site and its award-winning floral displays.

Facilities

Two recently modernised, heated toilet blocks are kept very clean and with all the necessary facilities including provision for disabled visitors. Some washbasins in curtained cubicles for ladies. Dishwashing and laundry sinks plus a washing machine. Excellent motorcaravan service point. Off site: The small town has shops, several restaurants. Tennis and a swimming pool close by. Fishing. Cycle tracks and footpaths. Le Pal theme park and zoo 8 km.

Open

15 May - 15 September.

At a glance

Welcome & Ambience	✓✓✓✓✓	Location	✓✓✓✓
Quality of Pitches	✓✓✓✓	Range of Facilities	✓✓✓

Directions

Dompierre is 35 km. east of Moulins. Leave N79 at eastern end of Dompierre bypass and turn southwest on N2079 towards the town. The entrance to the sports complex and campsite is on the left beyond the junction with the D55 before the river bridge and town centre. GPS: N46:31.052 E03:41.24

Charges 2005

Per person	€ 1,90
child (5-14 yrs)	€ 1,10
pitch	€ 1,60 - € 1,90
electricity	€ 1,80

Reservations

Advised for high season. Tel: 04 70 34 55 57.

FR03020 Camping Château de Chazeuil

F-03150 Varennes-sur-Allier (Allier)

This spacious site is set in the attractive parkland surrounding a château. Here you will be surrounded by beautiful plants, flowers and bird song (if you are lucky, you will hear the nightingale). The 60 large, marked pitches are laid out on a well maintained lawn and all have electricity (although long leads may be necessary). Mature trees provide some pitches with shade. Although the entrance is adjacent to the main N7, traffic noise should be no problem as the site is set up a long drive. A one-way road system operates to ensure a safe exit from the site. The site provides a pleasant night's stop or short stay. There are walks from the campsite and the surrounding area has several interesting towns such as Vichy and St Pourçain with its vineyards. Many châteaux, churches and museums are also in the area.

Facilities

The modern sanitary block provides washbasins and showers in cabins, a washing machine and dishwashing and laundry sinks. It is maintained to a satisfactory level. Very pleasant unheated swimming pool and sunbathing area. Play area. Table tennis. Reading/information room. Off site: Shops, restaurants, etc. in Varennes 2 km. Fishing and canoeing in River Allier 2 km. Marked walks and cycle rides.

Open

15 April - 15 October.

At a glance

Welcome & Ambience	✓✓✓✓	Location	✓✓✓
Quality of Pitches	✓✓✓✓	Range of Facilities	✓✓✓

Directions

Site is 25 km. south of Moulins and just north of Varennes on the eastern side of the main N7. The entrance is at the traffic lights at the D46 turning for St Pourçain.

Charges 2005

Per person	€ 4,50
child (under 7 yrs)	€ 2,75
pitch incl. car	€ 9,00
animal	€ 1,00
electricity (6A)	€ 2,75

Reservations

Made for min. 3 days with € 32 deposit.
Tel: 04 70 45 00 10.
Email: camping-de-chazeuil@ifrance.com

FR03050 Camping Caravaning La Petite Valette

Sazeret, F-03390 Montmarault (Allier)

Originally a working farm, La Petite Valette has been transformed by its hard working Dutch and German owners into a very attractive and peaceful, secluded campsite. There are 55 level grassy pitches of good size, many with rural views, each with an electricity point (6A). They are separated by flowering bushes and trees giving some shade and privacy, and many have pleasant, rural views. A small lake in one of the lower fields is stocked with fish for anglers. Ponies and small livestock (rabbits, chickens and ducks) keep the farm feeling alive. The restaurant tables are in a cottage garden overflowing with flowers providing a tranquil atmosphere. The countryside is ideal for cycling and there are many interesting old villages nearby. The lane to the site is narrow making access difficult for large units.

Facilities

Toilet facilities are housed in original outbuildings, each block having very good quality, modern fittings. A large separate room has full facilities for disabled people, families and babies. Laundry. Bread can be ordered. Meals and snacks served in the farmhouse restaurant (to order only). Takeaway service. Small swimming and paddling pools, with sunbathing areas. Good fenced play area with seating. Table tennis in one of the barns, mountain bike hire and organised activities in July/Aug. Off site: Tennis, riding and sailing in the area. Small town of Montmarault 6 km. for shopping needs.

Open

1 April - 30 October.

At a glance

Welcome & Ambience	✓✓✓✓	Location	✓✓✓
Quality of Pitches	✓✓✓✓	Range of Facilities	✓✓✓✓

Directions

Leave A71 autoroute at exit 11. At first roundabout take the D46 signed St Pourcain. Turn left at next roundabout onto D945 signed Deux-Chaises and La Valette. After 2.5 km. turn left at site sign (La Valette) and follow narrow lanes to site (just under 2 km). GPS: N46:32.568 E02:59.581

Charges 2005

Per person	€ 3,95 - € 4,95
child (0-8 yrs)	€ 2,90 - € 3,85
pitch	€ 6,05 - € 7,50
electricity (6A)	€ 2,85
dog	€ 1,68
Surcharge for one night stay motorcaravan	€ 4,00

For one night stay 1/7-31/8, plus 10%.

Reservations

Essential for July/Aug. and made with 50% deposit.
Tel: 04 70 07 64 57.
Email: la.petite.valette@wanadoo.fr

FR15030 Camping Caravaning Le Val Saint Jean

F-15200 Mauriac (Cantal)

La Val Saint-Jean is part of a typical, newly developed 'Centre de Loisirs' which the French do so well, set beside a lake in the heart of the département of Cantal. The campsite is situated at a height of 700 m. and provides 100 generously sized touring pitches (with 10A electricity), terraced with good views and organised for the maximum of privacy, on a hill above the lake. The site is well planned so that you are never far from a sanitary block and it has an impressive number of good quality facilities. Most of the activities are situated by the lake where you can use all the facilities of the leisure club (high season) including cycling, canoeing, kayaking and pedaloes. The lake has a sandy beach and an area for swimming. There is a large swimming pool, plus one for children on the campsite with sunbathing areas (free to campers). Both the pool and the lake have lifeguards most of the time in high season and they can get very busy in the main season. This less well known region is well worth exploring and the local gastronomy can be experienced in the village of Mauriac with its attractive architecture typical of the area.

Facilities

The two toilet blocks (4 and 6 years old) are well equipped with hot water throughout, providing some washbasins in cabins, dishwashing sinks and a laundry room with washing machine and dryer. Facilities for people with disabilities. Limited shop. Bar, snack bar and restaurant (all May - Sept). Swimming and paddling pools (1/6-15/9). Play area, playing field and table tennis. Watersports. Fishing. Activities organised for children (8-16 yrs) in July/Aug. Off site: Nine-hole golf course next to site. Mauriac village 600 m. Riding 2 km.

Open

1 May - 18 September.

At a glance

Welcome & Ambience	✓✓✓✓	Location	✓✓✓✓✓
Quality of Pitches	✓✓✓✓	Range of Facilities	✓✓✓✓

Directions

From Clermont-Ferrand take RN89 towards Bordeaux, then D922 towards Bort-les-Orgues and Mauriac. Site is well signed in Mauriac.
GPS: N45:13.120 E02:18.953

Charges 2005

Per unit incl. 2 persons	€ 10,00 - € 17,00
extra person	€ 4,00 - € 5,00
child (under 10 yrs)	free - € 2,50
dog	€ 1,50
electricity (10A)	€ 3,50

Reservations

Contact site. Tel: 04 71 67 31 13.
Email: info@camping-massifcentral.com

FR19060 Castel Camping Domaine de Mialaret

Route d'Egletons, F-19160 Neuvic (Corrèze)

Mialaret is 4 km. from the village of Neuvic and only 6 km. from the Dordogne river. It is set in the grounds of a 19th century château, now a hotel and restaurant with a good reputation for fresh lobster and with a special evening menu for campers. Most pitches are set in a sunny, gently sloping meadow type situation. Some are level and separated by small bushes, most have some shade and 6A electricity. In low season there are cooking courses with the chefs of the hotel, also at that time of the year the owner has time to take customers on a conducted tour of the estate in his 4x4 vehicle. Entertainment in high season is quite low key with a mini club, some games, tournaments or an evening sing-along around a campfire, also musical evenings by both professionals and of the do-it-yourself type. Ten pitches are used by a tour operator.

Facilities

Three refurbished sanitary blocks give an adequate provision, one heated. Washbasins in cabins and adjustable showers, baby baths, facilities for disabled people, washing machines and dishwashing sinks. Motorcaravan service point. Shop at reception with bread daily. Bar with snacks and takeaway. Dinner at the hotel at special rate for campers. Play areas. Tennis. Table tennis. Fishing. Volleyball, football. Bicycle hire. The original swimming pool, an example of art-deco design, is virtually a national monument. Unfortunately no paddling pool but a swimming pool is planned. Off site: Village with shops and lake 4 km. Golf 4 km. Canoeing, cycling and riding trips organised.

Open

1 May - 31 October.

At a glance

Welcome & Ambience	✓✓✓	Location	✓✓✓✓
Quality of Pitches	✓✓✓	Range of Facilities	✓✓✓✓

Directions

From Clermont-Ferrand take N89 (or the new A89) southwest and, at Ussel, take D962 to Neuvic. In Neuvic take D982 signed Egletons and shortly turn right (D991) signed Egletons and La Mialaret. Site is within 4 km. on right. Note: the D991 Egleton - Neuvic road is only suitable for cars and small motorcaravans.

Charges 2006

Per person	€ 5,50 - € 6,50
child (2-8 yrs)	free - € 3,00
pitch	€ 5,50 - € 7,50
electricity	€ 3,00 - € 3,50
dog	free

Camping Cheques accepted.

Reservations

Contact site. Tel: 05 55 46 02 50.
Email: info@lemialaret.com

FR19070 Camping Château de Gibanel

St Martial Entrayguis, F-19400 Argentat (Corrèze)

This slightly terraced campsite is located in a beautiful estate, dominated by the 16th century château, on the banks of a very clean lake in this lesser known part of the Dordogne valley. Boats of up to 10 hp can be used on the lake for watersports and fishing. The very friendly family (English spoken) has ensured that everything is of a very high standard. Nearly all of the 250 grassy pitches are used for touring units. All have electricity (6A) and they are separated by a variety of mature trees giving varying amounts of shade. Some have an ideal position alongside the lake. Many of the trees have low branches making access to most pitches rather difficult for large motorcaravans. The attractive bar, restaurant and disco in the château is set well away from the pitches and the swimming pool and good sized paddling pool, with large sunbathing terrace, are alongside the spacious and well equipped play area.

Facilities

Four modern, spacious and very clean toilet blocks include many large cubicles with a shower and washbasin making them ideal for families. Washing machine and dryer. Small shop for basics (all season). Bar, restaurant and takeaway (July/Aug). Wide range of family activities in July/Aug, including weekly dance evenings, folklore events, watersports, walking and cycling, Bicycle hire (July/Aug). TV room, Table tennis. Boules. Volleyball. Bus stop on site in July/Aug. Off site: Argentat with its interesting old town, shops, restaurants etc. 5 km.

Open

1 June - 9 September.

At a glance

Welcome & Ambience	✓✓✓✓✓	Location	✓✓✓✓
Quality of Pitches	✓✓✓✓	Range of Facilities	✓✓✓✓

Directions

Site is 5 km. northeast of Argentat. Take D18, signed Eggletons, and after 4 km, alongside the lake, fork right at site sign. Follow lane down to site. GPS: N45:06.650 E01:57.536

Charges 2005

Per person	€ 4,80
child (under 7 yrs)	€ 2,40
pitch	€ 5,80
electricity	€ 3,00
dog	€ 1,50

Reservations

Essential in high season. Tel: 05 55 28 10 11. Email: contact@camping-gibanel.com

FR19080 Camping Le Vianon

F-19160 Palisse (Corrèze)

You will receive a very warm welcome from the new Dutch owners of this spacious and peaceful site and they speak excellent English. The site is tucked away in the lesser known, very beautiful Corrèze region yet it is only a few kilometres from the river Dordogne. This region is reputed to have the purest air in France. The grassy, slightly sloping pitches are of a good size in a natural woodland setting with tall trees offering shade, and all have 6A electricity. The bar, restaurant and terrace overlook the swimming pool and sunbathing area and are open all season. One speciality is the fresh bread and croissants, etc. baked on site each morning. Activities are arranged for all the family when there are enough participants, but these do not continue too late in the evening. As an added attraction they are developing a small farm for the children including a pony, a donkey, a goat, some chickens and some rabbits.

Facilities

Two modern toilet blocks with all the necessary facilities. There are plans for further refurbishment. En-suite unit and special pitches for disabled visitors. Bar. Restaurant and takeaway. Shop. No dedicated motorcaravan service point but arrangements can be made. Boules. Table tennis. Volleyball. Play area plus plenty of other space for children to play. Bicycle hire. Lake fishing. Off site: Neuvic (9 km) is a small town with a range of shops, restaurants and a bank. Large lake near Neuvic with a good range of water sports and area for swimming. Many old towns and villages with markets and museums including Bort les Orgues, Mauriac, Tulle, Egletons and Château de Val, Canoeing in the Dordogne (30 minutes). Riding and golf course at Neuvic. Large range of marked walks and cycle rides (some guided).

At a glance

Welcome & Ambience	✓✓✓✓✓	Location	✓✓✓✓
Quality of Pitches	✓✓✓✓	Range of Facilities	✓✓✓✓

Directions

Leave A89 southwest of Ussel and take N89 towards Egletons. In about 7 km, just before Combressol, turn left on D47 signed Palisse and Camping le Vianon. Site entrance is on the left in 7 km. GPS: N45:25.607 E02:12.350

Charges 2005

Per person	€ 3,90 - € 5,70
child (3-9 yrs)	free - € 3,50
pitch	€ 4,20 - € 7,10
electricity (6A)	€ 3,50
dog	free - € 2,00

Special rates for long stays.

Reservations

Contact site. Tel: 05 55 95 87 22. Email: camping.vianon@wanadoo.fr

Open

12 April - 12 October.

2

FR19090 Camping Le Vaurette

Monceaux-sur-Dordogne, F-19400 Argentat (Corrèze)

The Audureau family has spent over 30 years developing this beautiful campsite from an old farm. The ancient barn at the far end of the site houses the bar and a large TV room (large screen) and the terrace overlooks the good sized and attractive, but unheated, swimming and paddling pools (all season). The well stocked shop and takeaway are near reception. There are 120 large, gently sloping grass pitches, 118 for touring. Separated by a large variety of beautiful trees and shrubs offering varying amounts of shade, all have 6A electricity and many have good views over the river Dordogne as the pitches nearest the river are slightly terraced. The owners are trying to run an active campsite for all the family whilst maintaining an air of tranquillity. You are assured of a warm welcome here, as excellent English and Dutch is spoken.

Facilities

Two very clean and modern toilet blocks offer all the expected facilities, including facilities for disabled people. Further facilities are near the bar and pool. Motorcaravan service point. Shop and takeaway (July/Aug). Football. Volleyball. Badminton. Boules. Table tennis. Tennis (free in low season). Fishing. Accompanied canoe trips, walks and mountain bike rides from site. Wide range of organised activities for all the family (July and Aug) but no late night discos etc. Off site: River Dordogne. Argentat (9 km.) with a good range of shops, banks etc and a water sports centre. Riding 15 km. Many marked walks and mountain bike rides close by.

At a glance

Welcome & Ambience	✓✓✓✓✓	Location	✓✓✓✓
Quality of Pitches	✓✓✓✓	Range of Facilities	✓✓✓✓

Directions

Leave Argentat on the D12 heading southwest, signed Beaulieu. Site is 9 km. on the left. GPS: N45:02.739 E01:50.058

Charges 2006

Per unit incl. 2 persons	€ 14,00 - € 20,00
extra person (over 2 yrs)	€ 3,10 - € 4,80
electricity (6A)	€ 3,00
dog	€ 1,50 - € 2,50

Reservations

Made with fee (€ 10) for middle and high season plus deposit (€ 6 per day). Tel: 05 55 28 09 67. Email: info@vaurette.com

Open

1 May - 21 September.

Camping ★★★★ Le Vaurette

Vallée de la Dordogne
19400 Argentat

Tél. +33 5 55 28 09 67   Fax +33 5 55 28 81 14   camping.le.vaurette@wanadoo.fr

FR19050 Camping La Rivière

Route du Camping Louis Madrias, F-19270 Donzenac (Corrèze)

The Corrèze is not nearly as well known as the Dordogne to the immediate south, but it is, in fact, a beautiful area deserving of more attention. Donzenac itself is an attractive small town with a variety of shops, restaurants, etc. This former municipal site is situated on the outskirts, somewhat less than a mile from the centre (an uphill walk). The site is small and neat with 77 fairly large pitches on level grass, the majority with electricity (10A). A variety of trees and shrubs give some shade. The site is next door to the town tennis courts and swimming pool (July/Aug. only; free to campers).

Facilities

Modernised sanitary facilities are very good and include a laundry room with washing machine and microwave. Baker calls at site in July/Aug. Table tennis, boules and minigolf. Fishing. Double axle caravans are not accepted. Off site: Riding 4 km. Golf 10 km.

Open

1 May - 30 September.

At a glance

Welcome & Ambience	✓✓✓✓	Location	✓✓✓✓
Quality of Pitches	✓✓✓	Range of Facilities	✓✓✓

Directions

At roundabout at southern end of Donzenac (D920) turn southwest onto D170 signed Ussac and La Rivière, Entrance to site is shortly on the right. GPS: N45:13.126 E01:31.122

Charges 2005

Per person	€ 4,10 - € 4,50
child (4-14 yrs)	€ 2,10 - € 2,50
pitch	€ 4,70
electricity (10A)	€ 2,60
dog	€ 1,00

Reservations

Probably unnecessary, but if in doubt phone. Tel: 05 55 85 63 95.

Centre of France

Château de Poinsouze

★★★★

New Family Campsite. Calm & Nature. Exceptional fully enclosed sanitary facilities.
Heated swimming pool. Chalets & mobil-homes for hire. Gites all year long.
Route de la Châtre 23600 Boussac-Bourg - Tel: 0033 555 65 02 21 - Fax: 0033 555 65 86 49
info.camping-de.poinsouze@wanadoo.fr / www.camping-de-poinsouze.com

---

FR23010 Castel Camping Le Château de Poinsouze Mobile homes ▶ page 436

Route de la Châtre, B.P. 12, F-23600 Boussac-Bourg (Creuse)

Le Château de Poinsouze is a well established site with pitches arranged on the open, gently sloping, grassy park to one side of the Château's main drive – a beautiful plane tree avenue. It is a well designed, high quality site. The 145 touring pitches, some with lake frontage, all have electricity (6-25A), water, waste water and 66 have sewage connections. The Château (not open to the public) lies across the lake from the site. Exceptionally well restored outbuildings on the opposite side of the drive house a new restaurant serving superb cuisine, other facilities and the pool area. The site has a friendly family atmosphere, there are organised activities in main season including dances, children's games and crafts, family triathlons, and there are marked walks around the park and woods. All facilities are open all season, though times may vary. This is a top class site with a formula which should ensure a stress-free, enjoyable family holiday. Boussac (2.5 km) has a market every Thursday morning. The massive 12/15th century fortress, Château de Boussac, is open daily all year.

Facilities

The high quality, double glazed sanitary unit is entered via a large utility area equipped with dishwashing and laundry sinks, foot-pedal operated taps, sinks accessible for wheelchair users, drinks machine and two smaller rooms with washing machines, dryer and ironing. Four spacious rooms are very well equipped including some washbasins in cubicles, baby baths, changing mats and child's WC, and two suites for disabled people. Good motorcaravan service point. Well stocked shop. Takeaway. Comfortable bar with games, internet access, TV and library room above. New restaurant. Well fenced, heated swimming pool with slide, children's pool (children wear colour coded bracelets, deposit required). Fenced playground designed with safety in mind. Table tennis, petanque, pool table and table football games. Bicycle hire. Free fishing in the lake (if you put the fish back); boats and lifejackets can be hired. Football, volleyball, basketball, badminton and other games. Dogs are not accepted in high season (9/7-19/8).

At a glance

Welcome & Ambience	✓✓✓✓✓	Location	✓✓✓✓✓
Quality of Pitches	✓✓✓✓	Range of Facilities	✓✓✓✓

Directions

Site entrance is 2.5 km. north of Boussac on D917 (towards La Châtre). GPS: N46:22.356 E02:12.157

Charges 2005

Per pitch incl. 2 persons with electricity (6A), water, and waste water	€ 12,00 - € 19,00
with 10A electricity	€ 18,00 - € 26,00
and sewage connection	€ 23,00 - € 28,00
extra person	€ 3,00 - € 5,50
child (2-7 yrs)	€ 2,00 - € 4,50
electricity 10-25A	€ 2,50 - € 5,00

Camping Cheques accepted.

Reservations

Advisable during July/Aug; made with 25% deposit and € 15 fee. Tel: 05 55 65 02 21. Email: info.camping-de.poinsouze@wanadoo.fr

Open

13 May - 18 September.

FR19100 Sunêlia Au Soleil d'Oc

Monceaux-sur-Dordogne, F-19400 Argentat (Corrèze)

Set amongst a variety of tall trees on the banks of the river Dordogne, this attractive site should appeal to lovers of water and other sports, particularly in July and August when the site organises many activities for all the family. The 120 large, level, grass pitches, 60 for tourists, all with 6A electricity, are mostly separated by neatly trimmed shrubs and hedges. They are set out on two levels; the lower level nearer the river, with fewer static pitches, being some distance from the toilet facilities and sports area. The shop, bar, restaurant and swimming pool are near the entrance and just across the little road is the large sports area. This will be a lively site in July and August. It is not recommended for very large outfits due to the narrow, winding site roads and hedges.

Facilities

Two unisex toilet blocks on the upper level of the site offer all the facilities one would expect. Shop, bar, restaurant and takeaway (mid June – Sept). Swimming pool and small sunbathing area (June – Sept). Bathing in the river Dordogne. Fridge hire. Full entertainment programme of family activities including children's club (July/Aug). Canoe hire and organised trips from site. Fishing, volleyball, football, table tennis, pool table and electronic games. Bicycle hire. Guided walks and bike rides. Off site: River Dordogne. Argentat (4 km) with a good range of shops, banks etc and water sports centre. Riding 15 km.

Open

Easter - 1 November.

At a glance

Welcome & Ambience	✓✓✓	Location	✓✓✓✓
Quality of Pitches	✓✓✓✓	Range of Facilities	✓✓✓✓

Directions

Leave Argentat on the D12 heading southwest, signed Beaulieu. In 3.5 km. turn left across a single track bridge spanning the river Dordogne (camping signed). Immediately turn left and site entrance is a few hundred metres on the left.
GPS: N45:04.514 E01:55.025

Charges 2005

Per unit incl. 2 persons	€ 12,50 - € 19,80
extra person	€ 3,00 - € 5,80
child (2-7 yrs)	free - € 3,90
dog	free - € 2,00
Camping Cheques accepted.	

Reservations

Contact site. Tel: 05 55 28 84 84.
Email: info@dordogne-soleil.com

FR43020 Camping du Puy-en-Velay

Avenue d'Aiguilhe, F-43000 Le Puy-en-Velay (Haute-Loire)

This urban site is within ten minutes walk of the town with its very interesting old centre and is well worth the trip. The Office de Tourisme is in Place du Clauzel, next to the Mairie. The site has a warden who speaks good English and lives on site. Tarmac roads lead to 80 marked pitches with electricity, including 5 with water and drainage. A motorcaravan service point is adjacent - apply to reception for a key, or for an overnight stop (reception opens 08.00 - 21.00 hrs). Access is good and early arrival is advised. Twin axle caravans are not accepted. The site may become noisy in high season.

Facilities

The main sanitary unit includes some washbasins in cubicles. Facilities for disabled persons. An older and more basic unit at the rear of the site is only used in peak season. The facilities may be stretched in high season. Motorcaravan service point. Table tennis, boules, volleyball and badminton. Off site: Indoor pool and tennis adjacent. Baker and small supermarket 5 minutes walk. Golf 4 km. Riding 5 km.

Open

Mid-April - 1 October.

At a glance

Welcome & Ambience	✓✓✓✓	Location	✓✓✓✓
Quality of Pitches	✓✓✓	Range of Facilities	✓✓✓

Directions

Site is northwest of the town centre, close to where N102 crosses the River Borne, and the Rocher St Michel d'Aiguilhe (a church on a rocky pinnacle). Site is well signed from around the town. A large blue 'Aire de Service' sign is at the entrance.

Charges guide

Per unit incl. 2 persons	€ 8,75
extra person	€ 2,64
electricity	€ 2,95
No credit cards.	

Reservations

Contact site for details. Tel: 04 71 09 55 09.

FR43030 Camping du Vaubarlet

Vaubarlet, F-43600 Sainte-Sigolène (Haute-Loire)

This peacefully located, spacious riverside family site has 131 marked, level, grassy and open pitches, with only those around the perimeter having shade and all having electricity (6A). With 102 pitches for tourists, the remainder are occupied by site owned tents or mobile homes. Those who really like to get away from it all can use a small 'wild camping' area on the opposite side of the river with its own very basic facilities. This area is reached either by footbridge or a separate road access. The main site is separated from the river (unfenced) by a large field used for sports activities. Tourist attractions in and around the region include a textile museum in Sainte Sigolène, an 'escargot' farm in nearby Grazac, the stunning scenery, chateaux and churches of the Haute-Loire, and the annual medieval festival in Le Puy each September. A 'Sites et Paysages' member.

Facilities

Two good and very clean toilet blocks (one new) have some washbasins in cubicles for ladies, baby room, laundry with washing machine and dryer and dishwashing sinks. Two new family bathrooms (WC, basin, shower) behind the bar, are also suitable for disabled people. Small shop (bread to order). Takeaway and bar (all season). Attractive swimming pool with children's pool. Bicycle hire. Table tennis, boules, volleyball and plenty of space for ball games. Playground. Organised activities in main season include camp fire and music evenings, canoe lessons for children, pony riding and mini-motorbike motocross (possibly noisy). Trout fishing (licences available). Birdwatching, walking. Barbecues on loan. Off site: Two supermarkets and other shops in Ste Sigolène 6 km. Riding 15 km. Three golf courses around 30 km. Many walks and cycle tracks from site.

At a glance

Welcome & Ambience	✓✓✓✓	Location	✓✓✓
Quality of Pitches	✓✓✓✓	Range of Facilities	✓✓✓✓

Directions

Site is 6 km. southwest of Ste Sigolène on the D43 signed Grazac. Keep left by river bridge, site signed. Site shortly on right.
GPS: N45:12.936 E04:12.766

Charges 2005

Per unit incl. 2 persons	€ 16,00
extra person	€ 3,00
child (2-7 yrs)	€ 2,00
electricity	€ 3,00
pet	€ 1,00

Less 15% outside July/Aug.
Camping Cheques accepted.

Reservations

Advised for high season and made with 25% deposit and fee (€ 19.82). Tel: 04 71 66 64 95.
Email: camping@vaubarlet.com

Open

1 May - 30 September.

FR48000 Camping Caravaning Le Champ d'Ayres

Route de la Brèze, F-48150 Meyrueis (Lozère)

The road to Meyrueis is not for the faint-hearted, although we managed in quite a large motorhome with only a few stretches being a little on the narrow side. Le Champ d'Ayres is a traditionally French style site with a modern feel to it, set in the heart of the Cevennes. Very neat, tidy and well kept, it is run by a young family with young families in mind (teenagers might be bored). The site is slightly sloping with 70 grass pitches, the majority hedged with well trimmed bushes and most with some shade. All have electricity (6/10A) but may require long leads. The area is surrounded by mountains and gorges but the river Jonte is not a canoeing river (a trip to the Tarn would be needed). The Gorges de Jonte has an observatory from which vultures can be observed flying the thermals. Being very central there are many attractions in the area - wild horses have been introduced on the causses a few miles to the north, the observatory at the top of Mt Aigoual is well worth a visit and there are many caves in the region.

Facilities

The central toilet block, kept very clean, includes mainly British style WCs and some washbasins in cabins. Family sized shower room, room with facilities for disabled visitors and baby room. Laundry and dishwashing sinks. Washing machine and dryer. Reception incorporates a small bar (15/6-15/9) which also sells ices and bread. Takeaway (15/6-15/9). Swimming and paddling pools (20/5-15/9). Play area on grass (5-10 yrs), small games room, table tennis, basketball, netball and a boules pitch. In July/Aug activities are arranged for children, also paella evenings with music and activities such as walking and caving. Off site: The pretty small town of Meyrueis has many good shops and restaurants. Fishing 100 m. Riding 300 m. Bicycle hire 500 m.

At a glance

Welcome & Ambience	✓✓✓✓✓	Location	✓✓✓✓
Quality of Pitches	✓✓✓✓	Range of Facilities	✓✓✓✓

Directions

From N9 at Aquessac (5 km. north of Millau) take D907 signed Gorge du Tarn. At Rozier turn right on D996 signed Meyrueis and Gorges de la Jonte. In Meyrueis follow signs for Château d'Ayres and campsite signs. Site is 500 m east of the town.
GPS: N44:10.860 E03:26.135

Charges 2006

Per unit incl. 2 persons	€ 12,00 - € 18,00
extra person	€ 2,50 - € 4,00
child (under 7 yrs)	€ 1,60 - € 2,50
electricity (6A)	€ 3,00

Reservations

Contact site. Tel: 04 66 45 60 51.
Email: campinglechampdayres@wanadoo.fr

Open

8 April - 23 September.

FR48020 Camping de Capelan

F-48150 Meyrueis (Lozère)

The Lozère is one of France's least populated departments but offers some truly spectacular, rugged scenery, wonderful flora and fauna and many old towns and villages. The little town of Meyrueis, accessible from the campsite via a riverside walk, marks the start of the Gorges de la Jonte, with the better known Gorges du Tarn running a little to the north. Le Capelan is a friendly family site with English and Dutch spoken. It has 120 grassy pitches strung out alongside the river, most with some shade and all with electrical connections (6/10A). Around 40 pitches are used for mobile homes. The site has direct river access and trout fishing is popular. Although there are special facilities, the site is not ideal for disabled visitors. A 'Sites et Paysages' member.

Facilities

Two very good toilet blocks are of recent construction and well maintained. Facilities for disabled visitors (but see above). Three bathrooms (bath, shower, basin and WC) for rent. Small shop (from 1/6). Spacious bar (from 1/6) with satellite TV, internet access, pool table. Takeaway (from 1/7). Swimming and paddling pools with sunbathing terrace (from 1/6), accessible only via 60 steps. Multi-sports terrain. Play area. Range of leisure activities including supervised rock climbing. Fishing. Communal barbecue area; only gas and electric barbecues permitted on site. Off site: Town centre with shops, restaurants, banks, etc. 1 km. Bicycle hire 1 km. Riding 3 km. Canoeing. The Cévennes national park with innumerable walking and cycling opportunities. Several excellent caves. Vulture visitor centre.

At a glance

Welcome & Ambience	✓✓✓✓	Location	✓✓✓✓
Quality of Pitches	✓✓✓	Range of Facilities	✓✓✓✓

Directions

From Paris on the A75 take exit 44-1 Aguessac-le Rozier towards Meyrueis. The site is 1 km. west of Meyrueis on the D996, the road to La Jonte. It is well signed from the centre of the town. GPS: N44:11.150 E03:25.193

Charges 2006

Per unit incl. 2 persons and electricity	€ 12,50 - € 18,00
extra person	€ 2,30 - € 3,90
child (under 7 years)	€ 1,60 - € 2,60

Camping Cheques accepted.

Reservations

Contact site. Tel: 04 66 45 60 50.
Email: camping.le.capelan@wanadoo.fr

Open

29 April - 16 September.

FR48060 Camping Les Terrasses du Lac de Naussac

Lac de Naussac, F-48300 Langogne (Lozère)

The Lac de Naussac is the largest in the Lozère and this site has direct access to the lake. With friendly, family owners, this very spacious campsite and hotel complex is set out on the side of a steep hill at nearly 1,000 m. altitude (nights can be cold). There are 180 good size grassy, gently sloping pitches, often with part hardstanding (165 for touring). All have 6A electricity and many have panoramic views over the lake and surrounding hills. There are many small trees on site offering some shade on a few of the pitches. There is a small pool and various other leisure amenities, with plenty of room for children to play, although the facilities are widely spaced around this hilly site. The lake offers a wide range of water based activities, notably sailing and fishing. This is superb walking and bike riding country and the long distance Stevenson trail passes close by at Langogne.

Facilities

The three toilet blocks are modern and well maintained. Very small shop (1/5-30/9). Good value restaurant (1/4-30/9). Small swimming pool (1/6-30/9). Lively 'animation' programme in peak season including children's club but no discos. Play area. Communal barbecue area. Bicycle hire. Gas and electric barbecues only. Off site: Disco 300 m. All kinds of water sports with equipment for hire on lake. Bike hire on lake of 30 km. Langogne (shops, restaurants, Stevenson trail etc.) 2 km. 9 hole golf course 3 km. Riding 3 km.

Open

15 April - 30 September.

At a glance

Welcome & Ambience	✓✓✓	Location	✓✓✓✓
Quality of Pitches	✓✓✓	Range of Facilities	✓✓✓✓

Directions

Leave the N88 (Le Puy - Mende) road just southwest of Langogne. Turn on D26 towards Lac de Naussac, pass by the village of Naussac and follow signs to site. Stop in the parking area beside the lake and just before the hotel, reception inside the hotel. GPS: N44:44.042 E03:50.130

Charges 2006

Per pitch incl. 2 persons	€ 12,50 - € 13,50
extra person	€ 3,50
child (2-6 yrs)	€ 1,50
electricity	€ 2,50
dog	€ 1,00

Camping Cheques accepted.

Reservations

Contact site. Tel: 04 66 69 29 62.
Email: naussac@club-internet.fr

FR63030 Camping Caravaning de l'Europe

Mobile homes ▶ page 436

Route de Jassal, F-63790 Murol (Puy-de-Dôme)

L'Europe is a pleasant site on the edge of the little town of Murol, best known perhaps for its fine 13th century castle. The site is 800 m. from the Lac de Chambon which boasts a sandy beach and range of water sports. There are 219 pitches at L'Europe, many of which are occupied by mobile homes. Pitches are generally of a good size and offer reasonable shade. This is quite a lively site in peak season with a busy animation programme including evening entertainment. The bar/restaurant overlooks the pool and is the site's focal point and entertainment centre. The surrounding area offers very many superb walking and cycling opportunites, and the site organises a number of popular excursions.

Facilities
Bar, restaurant and takeaway food. Swimming and paddling pools. Water slide. Tennis. Archery, Play area. Organised activities and entertainment. Internet access and WiFi. Off site: Lakeside beach 800 m. Murol centre 600 m. Riding. Watersports.

Open
27 May - 3 September.

At a glance
Welcome & Ambience	✓✓✓✓	Location	✓✓✓
Quality of Pitches	✓✓✓	Range of Facilities	✓✓✓✓

Directions
Leave A75 autoroute at the St Nectaire exit (no. 6) and follow signs to Murol. The site is clearly signed upon arrival at Murol.

Charges 2006
Per unit incl. 1 adult	€ 11,00 - € 16,00
extra person (over 5 yrs)	€ 3,20 - € 5,30
child	€ 2,60 - € 4,35
electricity	€ 4,70 - € 5,60
dog	€ 1,80

Reservations
Contact site. Tel: 04 73 39 76 66.
Email: europe.camping@wanadoo.fr

FR63040 Château Camping La Grange Fort

Les Pradeaux, F-63500 Issoire (Puy-de-Dôme)

This site has good, modern facilities, yet is oozing with character. It is very popular with the Dutch. The 15th century castle is impressive, more British in style than the usual French château and it is open for tours twice a week. The new reception is well stocked with tourist information and an internet access point. The restaurant in the castle, originally the kitchen and dining hall, has great atmosphere and offers a simple daily menu. The cosy bar still has the old stable stalls and hay racks. The 120 pitches (90 for touring units) are of average size, mostly on grass but with some crushed stone hardstandings, and connected by rather narrow roads and with limited play space for children. Some of the smaller pitches are in sunny fields around the castle, others in bays with hedges and trees. All have 6A electrical hook-ups. There are pleasant walks in the extensive grounds and beyond. You are assured a warm welcome at this Dutch owned site.

Facilities
Two sanitary blocks have been completely rebuilt. Both ladies and men have baby rooms, the men's also has facilities for disabled visitors and a 'hydra shower'. Dog shower. Laundry room. Reception has a few groceries (bread to order). Restaurant (1/5-15/9), bar (15/6-15/9) and rebuilt takeaway (1/5-15/9). Small indoor pool with sliding glass doors, sauna and massage table (15/4-15/10). Two outdoor pools (15/6-1/10) with grass sunbathing areas. Play area and games room. Internet access. Tennis, minigolf, table tennis, volleyball, football field and boules. Organised activities in season include archery, canoeing, riding and cycling (horses and bikes provided). Torches are useful. Off site: Fishing 250 m. Riding 8 km. Good touring area with magnificent scenery. The Parc des Volcans and the Vulcania exhibition are a must.

At a glance
Welcome & Ambience	✓✓✓✓✓	Location	✓✓✓✓
Quality of Pitches	✓✓✓	Range of Facilities	✓✓✓✓

Directions
From A75 autoroute take exit 13 at Issoire. Travel east on D996 to Parentignat and in village turn right (D999) and after 200 m. right again on D34 signed Nonette. Site is 3 km. up the D34.

Charges 2005
Per person	€ 3,85 - € 5,25
child (under 7 yrs)	€ 2,60 - € 3,00
pitch	€ 4,90 - € 9,50
dog	€ 3,00

Camping Cheques accepted.

Reservations
Contact site for details. Tel: 04 73 71 02 43.
Email: chateau@lagrangefort.com

Open
10 April - 15 October.

FR63050 Sunêlia La Ribeyre

Jassat, F-63790 Murol (Puy-de-Dôme)

This very charming site with fantastic views over the wooded mountains is about a kilometre from the centre of Murol, dominated by its ancient château. The friendly Pommier family, originally farmers, have put much personal effort in constructing the site, its buildings and the pool and they have plans to build a large aqua-park for 2006. Many young trees have been planted to add to those already on site and a man-made lake at one end provides facilities for water sports. There is a picturesque reception area, with a fountain and prize winning floral decorations. The site now provides 400 level, grassy pitches, of which 260 have electricity (6A) and 110 have individual electricity, water and drainage. Although not normally advertised, there are 10A outlets for those who ask. The surrounding area has some superb scenery, from mountains rising to over 6,000 ft, to steep valleys, lakes and caverns. This site is a superb centre, only five or six kilometres from St Nectaire, about ten kilometres from Besse and about twenty kilometres from Le Mont Dore, which is a starting point for the Puy de Sancy, the highest peak in the area. This is a wonderful area for walking and cycling. Visit in May or June for fields of beautiful wild flowers and in September for the autumn colours.

Facilities

Six excellent, very clean modern toilet blocks provide British and Turkish style WCs and some washbasins in cubicles. Washing machines and dryers. Snack bar in peak season (1/6-1/9). Heated swimming pool 200 sq.m.(1/5-1/9). TV and games room. Tennis, volleyball and fishing. New play area. Small campsite lake provides swimming, canoeing and surf boarding (lifeguard in July/Aug). Off site: Riding 300 m. Bicycle hire 1 km. Further shops and restaurants and a large Wednesday market (high season) at Murol, 1 km. Fishing, boating and sailing at Lac Chambon 3 km.

Open

1 May - 15 September.

At a glance

Welcome & Ambience	✓✓✓✓✓	Location	✓✓✓✓
Quality of Pitches	✓✓✓✓	Range of Facilities	✓✓✓✓

Directions

From A75 autoroute, take exit 6, signed St Nectaire and carry on to Murol. Several sites are signed as you go into the town. Turn left up a hill and then, opposite Syndicat d'Initiative, turn right. La Ribeyre is the second site on the left, just after the entrance to Jassat and is well marked on left.
GPS: N45:33.770 E02:56.377

Charges 2005

Per unit incl. 2 persons	€ 13,15 - € 18,60
incl. services	€ 19,55 - € 26,00
extra person	€ 3,85 - € 5,10
child (under 5 yrs)	€ 2,85 - € 3,95
electricity (6A)	€ 3,80 - € 4,35

No credit cards. Camping Cheques accepted.

Reservations

Contact site. Tel: 04 73 88 64 29.
Email: laribeyre@free.fr

FR63090 Camping Les Domes

Les Quatre Routes de Nébouzat, F-63210 Nébouzat (Puy-de-Dôme)

A friendly welcome awaits at this attractive, compact, well cared for site which is run by a family of enthusiastic caravanners. A popular site, it is ideally situated for exploring the beautiful region around the Puy de Dôme. The site has 65 small to medium sized pitches, 50 with 10A electricity, separated by trees and hedges and most are available for touring. Some pitches have a level, paved area ideal for caravans and motorcaravans. Rock pegs are advised. The attractive reception area comprising the office, a small shop for essentials (high season only) and a meeting room has lots of local information and interesting artefacts. An added small attraction is a heated, covered swimming pool, which can be opened in good weather. There are many interesting old villages in the area (Orcival 8 km) and châteaux (Château de Corde 4 km).

Facilities

A well appointed central toilet block is kept very clean, but there are no special facilities for disabled visitors. Basic shop (baker calls). Breakfast, snacks and chips. Boules, pool table, table football, table tennis, giant chess and drafts. Small play area. TV and games room. Off site: Fishing 100 m. Restaurant 200 m. Nebouzat 1.3 km (shops etc). Riding 6 km. Hang gliding and parascending 8 km (Puy de Dôme). New Vulcania exhibition 15 minutes drive. Watersports 9 km. Golf 10 km. Clermond Ferrand with its interesting old town and hypermarkets (18 km). Many marked walks and cycle routes.

At a glance

Welcome & Ambience	✓✓✓✓✓	Location	✓✓✓✓
Quality of Pitches	✓✓✓	Range of Facilities	✓✓✓

Directions

Site is 18 km. southwest of Clermont Ferrand and is well signed from the roundabout at the junction of the N89 and the D941A. It is a few hundred metres from the roundabout along the D216 towards Orcival. GPS: N45:43.537 E02:53.403

Charges 2005

Per unit incl. 2 persons	€ 9,50
extra person	€ 6,00
child (under 5 yrs)	€ 3,00
electricity (10A)	€ 4,00

Reservations

Advised in high season and made with deposit of 3 night's fees. Tel: 04 73 87 14 06.

Open

9 April - 15 September.

FR63060 Camping Le Clos Auroy

Rue de la Narse, F-63670 Orcet (Puy-de-Dôme)

You are assured a friendly welcome at Le Clos Auroy. It is a very well maintained and popular site, 300 metres from Orcet, a typical Auvergne village just south of Clermont Ferrand. Being close (3 km) to the A75, and open all year, it makes an excellent stopping off point on the journey north and south but you may be tempted to stay longer. The 90 good size pitches are on level grass, separated by very high, neatly trimmed conifer hedges, offering lots of privacy but not much shade. All have electricity (5/10A) and 25 are fully serviced. In winter only 20 pitches are available. Access is easy for large units.

Facilities

Two modern, high quality, very clean sanitary units include washbasins in cubicles. Dishwashing and laundry sinks. Washing machine and dryer. A smaller, heated unit at reception is used mainly for the winter season, when it is heated. Chemical disposal is at the motorcaravan service point, close to the site entrance (a long walk from some pitches). Small shop and takeaway (both 1/7-15/9). Heated pool complex with pool, jacuzzi, large play pool for children (15/5-30/9) and terrace next to the bar (15/5-30/9). Playground. Tennis. Children's activities. Off site: Riverside walk just outside gate. Village with shops and three wine 'caves' 300 m. Fishing and canoeing 500 m. Parc des Volcans with fantastic scenery, walking and cycling.

At a glance

Welcome & Ambience	✓✓✓✓	Location	✓✓✓✓
Quality of Pitches	✓✓✓✓	Range of Facilities	✓✓✓✓

Directions

From A75 take exit 4 or 5 towards Orcet and follow campsite signs. It is just before the village. GPS: N45:42.030 E03:10.154

Charges 2005

Per unit incl. 2 persons	€ 16,00
extra person	€ 4,00
child (1-7 yrs)	€ 2,75
electricity (5/10A)	€ 2,90 - € 4,40
animal	€ 1,50

Less for longer stays in low season. No credit cards.

Reservations

Advised for July/August with a fee of € 15.
Tel: 04 73 84 26 97. Email: info@campingclub.info

Open

All year.

FR63140 Camping Les Loges

F-63340 Nonette (Puy-de-Dôme)

This is a pleasant, spacious, rural site bordering the River Allier. There are 126 good sized, level, grassy pitches offering plenty of shade, 100 for touring and all with 6A electricity. This site would suit those seeking a quieter holiday without too much organised activity. The river is ideal for bathing and canoeing and there are many walks and bike rides in the area. It is also well placed to explore the beautiful Auvergne countryside, the extinct volcanoes and the many attractive old towns and villages.

Facilities

The two modern toilet blocks contain all the usual facilities. Heated swimming pool. Small shop (July/Aug). Bar (June-Aug). TV room. Simple takeaway menu (all season). Heated swimming pool with slide and paddling pool (June-Sept). Volleyball. Table tennis. Play areas and play room. River fishing and bathing. Sunday evening dances in high season. Canoe trips arranged from site. Off site: Walking and cycling routes. Riding 10 km. Small village of Nonette 3 km. Small range of shops at Saint Germain 5 km. Larger range of shops, restaurants etc. in Issoire 13 km. Parc des Volcans, Volcania Exhibition.

Open

Easter - 8 October.

At a glance

Welcome & Ambience	✓✓✓✓	Location	✓✓✓✓
Quality of Pitches	✓✓✓✓	Range of Facilities	✓✓✓✓

Directions

From A75 take exit 17 (south of Issoire) and turn left (D214) signed Le Breuil and Jumeaux. Bypass Le Breuil and turn left (D123) signed Nonette. After crossing the river turn left and then immediately very hard left - take care (site signed). Entrance is 1 km. down this lane.

Charges 2005

Per person	€ 3,30 - € 4,35
child (0-7 yrs)	€ 2,10 - € 3,00
pitch	€ 4,40 - € 6,90
electricity	€ 3,35
dog	free - € 1,50

Reservations

Made with 30% deposit and € 8 fee.
Tel: 04 73 71 65 82.
Email: les.loges.nonette@wanadoo.fr

2

FR63080 Camping Le Moulin de Serre

D73, vallée de la Burande, F-63690 Singles (Puy-de-Dôme)

Rather off the beaten track, this very spacious and well maintained site is set in a beautiful wooded valley beside the Burande river where one can pan for gold. It offers a good base for those seeking a quiet relaxing holiday in this lesser known area of the Auvergne. The 90 large pitches (55 for touring) are separated by a variety of trees and hedges giving good shade. A few pitches have hardstanding and all have electricity (3-10A), although long leads may be necessary. Access around the site is easy but the narrow lanes leading to it are twisting which might prove difficult for larger units.

Facilities

Two well appointed very clean toilet blocks with one block heated in spring, the latter having excellent facilities for disabled people and babies. Swimming pool with terrace (8/6-28/9). Takeaway and bar/restaurant (July/Aug). Bread (high season). Washing machine and dryer. Motorcaravan service point. Very large play area with new equipment and activity chalet. Football, table tennis. Canoe hire in high season. Daily programme of organised activities (July/Aug). Off site: Small lake for water sports 2 km. Château de Val 20 km. Spa town of La Bourboule 25 km. Barrage de Bort les Orgues offers watersports. Many marked walks and cycle tracks. Riding.

At a glance

Welcome & Ambience	✓✓✓✓	Location	✓✓✓
Quality of Pitches	✓✓✓✓✓	Range of Facilities	✓✓✓✓

Directions

Site is about 25 km. southwest of La Bourboule. Turn west off the D922 just south of Tauves at site sign. Follow site signs along the D29 and then the D73 for about 10 km. GPS: N45:32.584 E02:32.557

Charges 2005

Per unit incl. 2 persons	€ 10,95 - € 14,60
extra person	€ 2,90 - € 3,90
child (under 10 yrs)	€ 1,95 - € 2,65
electricity (3-10A)	€ 2,90 - € 4,50

Reservations

Advised in high season. Tel: 04 73 21 16 06. Email: moulin-de-serre@wanadoo.fr

Open

14 April - 17 September.

FR63070 Camping Le Pré Bas

Lac Chambon, F-63790 Murol (Puy-de-Dôme)

In the heart of the Parc des Volcans d'Auvergne, beside the beautiful Lac Chambon with its clear, clean water, Le Pré Bas is especially suitable for families and those seeking the watersports opportunities that the lake provides. Level, grassy pitches are divided up by mature hedging and trees and, with 63 mobile homes for rent, around 120 pitches are available for tourists, all with electricity (6A). A gate leads to the lakeside, where in the high season there is windsurfing, pedaloes, canoes and fishing, and 50 m. away is a beach with supervised bathing and a snack bar. The site has a new pool complex with heated swimming pools (one covered), a large slide and a paddling pool. The cable car ride up to the Puy de Sancy, the highest peak in the area, provides superb views offering excellent opportunity for trekking and mountain bike rides. Superb scenery abounds, wooded mountains rising to over 6,000 feet, flower filled valleys and deep blue lakes.

Facilities

One large, refurbished central toilet building plus four smaller units spread around site include washbasins in cubicles, facilities for disabled guests and dishwashing sinks. Laundry with sinks, washing machines, dryers and ironing facilities, and baby room. Motorcaravan service point. Snack bar with a small terrace (10/6-10/9 and some weekends in low season). Well fenced pool complex (20/5-10/9) has three pools of different depths (lifeguard in July/Aug). Watersports and fishing in lake. Games room with table tennis, table football, pool, etc, large 'salle' with giant TV screen and library. Adventure style playground alongside a football/basketball pitch. Organised activities (late June-early Sept) include local visits, guided walks, riding, archery and climbing. Off site: Within a short stroll, beside the lake, are several bars, restaurants and shops. Murol 4 km. St Nectaire is famous for its cheese. Puy de Dome, hang gliding, and the new Vulcania Exhibition make good days out.

At a glance

Welcome & Ambience	✓✓✓✓✓	Location	✓✓✓✓
Quality of Pitches	✓✓✓	Range of Facilities	✓✓✓✓

Directions

Leave A75 autoroute at exit 6 and take D978 signed St Nectaire and Murol, then the D996. Site is located on the left of the D996, 3 km, west of Murol towards Mont Dore, at the far end of Lac Chambon. GPS: N45:34.513 E02:54.854

Charges 2005

Per pitch incl. 2 persons	€ 12,40 - € 19,50
extra person	€ 3,70 - € 5,00
child (5-10 yrs)	€ 2,40 - € 5,00
electricity (6A)	€ 4,10 - € 4,40
animal	free

Reservations

Essential for high season, made with € 39 p/week deposit. Tel: 04 73 88 63 04. Email: prebas@campingauvergne.com

Open

1 May - 30 September.

FR63120 Camping Indigo Royat

Route de Gravenoire, F-63130 Royat (Puy-de-Dôme)

This is a spacious, well tended and attractive site sitting high on a hillside on the outskirts of Clermont Ferrand, but close to the beautiful Auvergne countryside. It has nearly 200 terraced pitches on part hardstanding. There are 150 available for touring units, all with 6/10A electricity (long leads may be needed). The pitches are informally arranged in groups, with each group widely separated by attractive trees and shrubs. The bar overlooks the irregularly shaped swimming pool, paddling pool, sunbathing area, tennis courts and play areas. Although very peaceful off season, it could be lively in July and August. This site would be ideal for those who would like a taste of both the town and the countryside.

Facilities

Five well appointed toilet blocks are placed around the site, some heated off season. They have all the usual amenities but it could be a long walk from some pitches. Small shop. Bar and takeaway. Internet point. Attractive swimming and paddling pools with sunbathing area. Two tennis courts. Boules. Table tennis. Bicycle hire. Two grassy play areas. Organised entertainment in the high season. Off site: Royat 20 minutes walk but bus available every 30 minutes. Clermont Ferrand, Puy de Dôme, Parc des Volcans, Volcania exhibition.

Open

8 April - 28 October.

At a glance

Welcome & Ambience	✓✓✓✓	Location	✓✓✓
Quality of Pitches	✓✓✓✓	Range of Facilities	✓✓✓✓

Directions

From A75 exit 2, just south of Clermont Ferrand follow signs for Bordeaux (D799). At third roundabout take third exit (D3) signed Beaumont. In about 800 m. take left hand lane and turn left (D777) signed Beaumont. At T-junction (traffic lights) turn left (N89) signed Ceyrat. Turn right up the hill (D767) signed Royat. At T-junction turn right (D941C) signed Royat and Puy de Dôme. At top of hill turn left (D5, Route de Gravenoire) signed Royat Indigo. Entrance is 800 m. on the right (mini roundabout). Do NOT turn hard right into the houses (narrow roads) but take the second right into the campsite. GPS: N45:45.526 E03:03.308

Charges 2005

Per person	€ 4,00 - € 4,20
child (2-7 yrs)	€ 2,30 - € 2,50
pitch	€ 4,50 - € 11,00
electricity (6/10A)	€ 4,10 - € 5,60
dog	€ 2,00

Reservations

Made with deposit (€ 5 per day) plus fee of € 15 (high season). Tel: 04 73 35 97 05.
Email: royat@camping-indigo.com

2

FR87020 Castel Camping Le Château de Leychoisier

Domaine de Leychoisier, 1 route de Leychoisier, F-87270 Bonnac-la-Côte (Haute-Vienne)

You will receive a warm welcome at this beautiful, family run 15th century château site. It offers peace and quiet in superb surroundings. Explore the grounds and walk down to the four hectare lake. It is ideally situated for short or long stays being only 2 km. from the A20/N20 and 10 km. north of Limoges. The large and grassy pitches are in a parkland setting with many magnificent mature trees offering a fair amount of shade. Of the 90 pitches, 85 are for touring, 80 have 10A electricity and many have a tap, although long leads and hoses may be necessary. The lake provides free fishing, boating, canoeing and a marked off area for swimming.

Facilities

The toilet block is in the outbuildings of the château. Very clean, but perhaps cramped at busy times. Some washbasins in private cabins with good provision for disabled visitors. Washing machine. Basic food provisions (all season). Attractive restaurant with good menu (from 20/6). Bar, TV room and snack bar. Small swimming pool with large grass sunbathing area (proper swimming trunks, no shorts). Lake. Play area. Bicycle hire, table tennis, tennis and boules courts (both in need of repair when we visited), volleyball and bar billiards. Torch useful. Winter caravan storage. Off site: Mini-market 2 km. supermarket 5 km. Riding 7 km. Golf 20 km. Limoges, noted for its pottery.

Open

15 April - 20 September.

At a glance

Welcome & Ambience	✓✓✓✓✓	Location	✓✓✓✓
Quality of Pitches	✓✓✓✓	Range of Facilities	✓✓✓✓

Directions

From A20 take exit 27 (west) signed Bonnac-La-Côte. Site is well signed from the autoroute (2 km). GPS: N45:55.958 E01:17.404

Charges 2006

Per person	€ 6,00 - € 7,00
child (under 7 yrs)	€ 4,00 - € 4,80
pitch	€ 8,00 - € 9,00
electricity	€ 4,00
dog	€ 0,80

No credit cards.

Reservations

Made with deposit (€ 15.24) and fee (€ 12.20), although short reservations accepted without charge in low season. Tel: 05 55 39 93 43. Email: contact@leychoisier.com

MAP 13

With such a rich and varied landscape, the Rhône Valley offers a spectacular region of craggy gorges and scented hills, ideal for life at a leisurely pace - easy to do when there are so many stunning views to take in.

Rhône Valley

DÉPARTEMENTS: 01 AIN, 07 ARDÈCHE, 26 DRÔME, 42 LOIRE, 69 RHÔNE

MAJOR CITY: LYON

The region's 2,000 year history as a cultural crossroads has blessed the area with a rich blend of customs, architecture and sights of interest. The city of Lyon was developed by the Romans as a trading centre, and was once the capital. It is now the second largest city of France. The Place de la Terreur in the centre of the city is where the guillotine was placed during the French revolution – until it wore out through over-use. Not far from Lyon lies the Dombes, the land of a thousand lakes, and the medieval village of Pérouges and Roman ruins of Vienne.

The Rhône valley holds areas of great interest and natural beauty. From the sun-baked Drôme, with its ever-changing landscapes and the isolated mountains of the Vercors to the deep gorges and high plateaux of the Ardèche, studded with prehistoric caves and lush valleys filled with orchards; and encompassing the vineyards of the Beaujolais and the Rhône Valley. For the energetic there are cycling, horse riding and even white water rafting opportunities, while for the more leisurely inclined, the remote areas are a haven for bird watching and walking.

Places of interest

Beaujolais: vineyards and golden-stone villages.

Bourg-en-Bresse: church of Notre-Dame, craft shops, museum of Ain.

Dombes: lakes, ornithological park.

Lyon: Gallo-Roman artifacts, Renaissance quarter, historical Fabric Museum, silk museum.

Pérouges: medieval village, Galette de Pérouges.

St Etienne: museum of Modern Art.

Vallon-Pont d'Arc: base from which to visit Gorges de l'Ardèche; canoe and rafting centre.

Vienne: Gothic style cathedral, 6th century church St Pierre.

Cuisine of the region

The poultry, cheese, freshwater fish and mushrooms are superb. Local wines include Beaujolais, Côte Rotie, St Julien, Condrieu, Tain-Hermitage, Chiroubles and Julienas.

Bresse (Poulet, Poularde, Volaille de): the best French poultry, fed on corn and when killed bathed in milk; flesh is white and delicate.

Gras-double: ox tripe, served with onions.

Poulet au vinaigre: chicken, shallots, tomatoes, white wine, wine vinegar and a cream sauce.

Poulet demi-deuil (half-mourning): called this because of thin slices of truffle placed under the chicken breast.

Rosette: a large pork sausage.

Sabodet: Lyonnais sausage of pig's head, pork and beef, served hot.

FR01030 Camping Les Ripettes

Chavannes-sur-Reyssouze, F-01190 Pont de Vaux (Ain)

Recently taken over by an enthusiastic and hardworking English couple, this spacious site is situated in quiet, flat countryside near the pleasant small town of Pont-de-Vaux. It would make a useful stop on the way to or from the south of France, but would also serve as a centre to explore the interesting surrounding area. The historic towns of Macon and Tournus are each about 20 km. away, and Bourg-en-Bresse and the vineyards of Beaujolais, Maconnais and Chalonnais are all within 40 km. The 2.5 hectare (6 acre) site has 54 large (over 100 sq.m. to 400 sq.m.) level grassy pitches, 51 of which are available to tourists. Nearly all are separated by hedges and about half are shaded by the many trees on the site. All but two have electrical connections (10A), and there are ample water points.

Facilities

Two small sanitary blocks contain toilets, five enlarged showers (one smaller), washbasins in cubicles and a suite for disabled visitors. Dishwashing sinks. Washing machine and double sink for washing clothes. If the site became full there could be queues for these facilities. No shop, but wine, ice cream and meat for barbecues can be bought at reception, where bread can be ordered. Two swimming pools (one 11 x 5 m, the other 7 m. diameter). Small play area and sandpit. Areas for ball games, volleyball, badminton, table tennis, boules (free loan of equipment). Free loan of board games and books. Bicycle hire. Off site: Riding 2 km. Fishing 4 km. Golf 15 km. Restaurant 1 km. Shops, etc., in Pont-de-Vaux 4 km.

Open

Easter - 31 October (October reservations only).

At a glance

Welcome & Ambience	✓✓✓✓	Location	✓✓✓✓
Quality of Pitches	✓✓✓✓✓	Range of Facilities	✓✓✓

Directions

Leave N6 at Fleurville (18 km. north of Macon, 14 km. south of Tournus). Go east on the D933A to Pont-de-Vaux (5 km). Take D2 east towards St Trivier-de-Courtes. After about 3 km. look for a water tower on the right. Turn left just after this, and left again at next junction (100 m). Site entrance is 300 m. ahead on the left.

Charges 2005

Per person	€ 3,50
child (0-10 yrs)	€ 2,50
pitch	€ 6,00
electricity (10A)	€ 2,50
No credit cards.	

Reservations

Can be made at any time, with deposit but no fee.
Tel: 03 85 30 66 58.
Email: info@camping-les-ripettes.com

FR01040 Camping Lac du Lit du Roi

La Tuillière, F-01300 Massignieu-de-Rives (Ain)

This attractive and well cared for, family run site is ideal for those seeking an active holiday in peaceful setting (English and Dutch are spoken). It has a commanding position beside a beautiful lake which forms part of the River Rhône waterway giving direct access to the much larger Lac du Bourget. This superb, picturesque area offers wonderful opportunities for exploration by foot, bicycle, car and boat. Take time to sample the wines and other local produce on offer. Of the 120 pitches, 90 are available for touring, all being close to the lake and many having wonderful views over the lake and the wooded hills beyond. The slightly sloping grassy pitches are set on low terraces and are partly separated by hedging and a variety of trees give some shade. All have 10A electricity and water points are nearby. In July and August a few social events are organised, suitable for all the family, but this site is best suited for those not requiring a programme of organised activities.

Facilities

Two modern toilet blocks offer all the necessary facilities including washbasins in cabins and provision for disabled visitors. Baby room. Washing machines. Motorcaravan service point. Bar and snack bar with terrace. Bread and croissants to order (all season). Small heated swimming pool and sunbathing area overlooking lake (all season). Tennis. Volleyball. Table tennis. Large unfenced, well appointed play area beside the lake. Grassy beach with pedaloes, canoes surf bikes for hire. Bicycle hire. Lake fishing. Under cover winter caravan storage. Off site: Shops, restaurants, bank and supermarkets at Belley. 8 km. Lac du Bourget (watersports, boat hire and tours). Large nature reserve. Many marked cycle tracks and walks (maps available). Extensive water way for exploration. Small marina and boat ramp close by. Golf 8 km. Riding 15 km.

At a glance

Welcome & Ambience	✓✓✓✓	Location	✓✓✓✓✓
Quality of Pitches	✓✓✓✓	Range of Facilities	✓✓✓✓

Directions

Site is about 8 km. east of Belley. Turn east off the N504 at roundabout (Champion supermarket) on D992 signed Culoz and Seyssel. After 4 km. turn right over river bridge on D37 signed Massignieu. Follow signs to site (2 km).
GPS: N45:46.122 E05:46.92

Charges 2005

Per unit incl. 2 persons	€ 17,00 - € 22,00
extra person	€ 5,00 - € 6,00
child (0-7 yrs)	€ 3,00 - € 4,00
electricity	€ 3,00
animal	€ 3,50

Reservations

Advised for high season (20% deposit).
Tel: 04 79 42 12 03. Email: acamp@wanadoo.fr

Open

16 April - 2 October.

FR01010 Camping La Plaine Tonique

Base de Plein Air, F-01340 Montrevel-en-Bresse (Ain)

This site belongs to a syndicate of several local villages. It is a very well maintained, large site with 560 marked and numbered pitches, all with 10A electricity. The majority are of a good size, hedged and on flat grass, with reasonable shade in most parts. Although large, the site is spacious and certainly does not feel so as it is broken up into smaller sections by trees and hedges. The site is on the edge of a large, 320-acre lake with its own beach and adjacent public beach. A variety of watersports is available, including sailing, windsurfing, swimming, canoeing and, on other parts of the lake, water-skiing and fishing. Campers may bring their own boats, but not motor boats. A separate area of the site is used by Dutch tour operators (100 pitches).

Facilities

Sanitary facilities are in eleven blocks, with most now renovated to a very high standard. They include some washbasins in cabins, baby rooms and washing machines. Motorcaravan service point. Restaurant, bar (all season) and shop (July/Aug) are next to the site. 'Aquatonic' centre with five pools (reduced charge for campers). Watersports and fishing. Minigolf and several tennis courts. Adventure play area on beach. Games and TV rooms. Archery, bicycle hire and roller skating area. Off site: Montrevel town 300 m. walk. Riding 2 km.

Open

14 April - 28 September.

At a glance

Welcome & Ambience	✓✓✓	Location	✓✓✓✓
Quality of Pitches	✓✓✓✓	Range of Facilities	✓✓✓✓

Directions

Site is 20 km. north of Bourg-en-Bresse and 25 km. east of Macon. Montrevel is on the D975; site is signed in town centre towards Etrez on D28.

Charges 2005

Per person	€ 2,60 - € 4,50
child (3-7 yrs)	€ 1,40 - € 2,30
pitch incl. electricity	€ 6,90 - € 11,00
pet	€ 1,40 - € 1,90

Reservations

Required mid July - end Aug; write with 25% deposit. Tel: 04 74 30 80 52. Email: plaine.tonique@wanadoo.fr

FR07120 Camping Nature Parc L'Ardéchois

Mobile homes ▶ page 437

Route touristique des Gorges, F-07150 Vallon-Pont-d'Arc (Ardèche)

This very high quality, family run site is within walking distance of Vallon-Pont-d'Arc. It borders the River Ardèche and canoe trips are run, professionally, direct from the site. This campsite is ideal for families with younger children seeking an active holiday. The facilities are comprehensive and of an extremely high standard, particularly the central toilet block. Of the 244 pitches, there are 197 for tourers, separated by trees and individual shrubs. All have electrical connections and 125 have full services. The focal point of the site is the bar and restaurant (good menus), with terrace and stage overlooking the attractive heated pool, large paddling pool and sunbathing terrace. There is a well thought out play area plus plenty of other space for the youngsters to play on the site and along the river. Activities are organised throughout the season; these are family based - no discos. Patrols at night ensure a good night's sleep. Access to the site is easy and suitable for large outfits.

Facilities

Two well equipped toilet blocks, one superb with 'everything' working automatically. Facilities are of the highest standard, very clean and include good facilities for babies, those with disabilities, washing up and laundry. Four private bathrooms to hire. Washing machines. Well stocked shop. Swimming pool and paddling pool (no Bermuda shorts). Football, volleyball, tennis and table tennis. Very good play area. Internet access point. Organised activities, canoe trips. Only gas barbecues are permitted. Communal barbecue area. Off site: Canoeing, rafting, walking, riding, mountain biking, golf, rock climbing, bowling, wine tasting and dining. Vallon-Pont-d'Arc 800 m.

At a glance

Welcome & Ambience	✓✓✓✓✓	Location		✓✓✓✓
Quality of Pitches	✓✓✓✓	Range of Facilities	✓✓✓✓✓	

Directions

From Vallon-Pont-d'Arc (western end of the Ardèche Gorge) at a roundabout go east on the D290. Site entrance is shortly on the right.
GPS: N44:23.873 E04:23.929

Charges 2006

Per pitch incl. 2 persons	€ 24,00 - € 39,00
140 sq.m. pitch with services	€ 29,50 - € 46,00
extra person	€ 5,50 - € 7,50
electricity	€ 4,20

Reservations

Made with deposit (€ 95) and fee (€ 35).
Tel: 04 75 88 06 63. Email: ardecamp@bigfoot.com

Open

Easter - 30 September.

FR01020 Camping de l'Ile Chambod

F-01250 Hautecourt (Ain)

This small site has recently been redeveloped by its enthusiastic English-speaking owners. It provides two modern toilet blocks, a swimming pool and small café. The 110 grassy pitches (about 100 sq m.) are separated by low hedges and most have some shade. They all have access to water points and electricity (5/10A) although some may need long leads. A lakeside beach is only 300 m. (charged for in high season), offering simple watersports and minigolf. There is plenty to see in the region and Bourg-en-Bresse offers a wealth of shops, restaurants, museums, etc.

Facilities

Two modern toilet blocks include some washbasins in cabins, dishwashing, laundry and vegetable preparation sinks. Washing machine and dryer. Both blocks have facilities suitable for disabled visitors and one has a baby room. Bread available to order. Small shop and takeaway (June, July and Aug). Small play area. Activities organised in high season for children up to 12 years.

Open

1 May - 30 September.

At a glance

Welcome & Ambience	✓✓✓✓	Location		✓✓✓✓
Quality of Pitches	✓✓✓	Range of Facilities	✓✓✓	

Directions

Site is about 23 km. southeast of Bourg-en-Bresse via the D979. It is well signed from the crossroads in Hautecourt, and is a further 4 km. down the lane.

Charges 2005

Per person	€ 4,50
child (up to 12 yrs)	€ 3,00
pitch incl. vehicle	€ 5,50
electricity 5-10A	€ 2,50 - € 3,50
No credit cards.	

Reservations

Advised for July/Aug. Tel: 04 74 37 25 41.
Email: camping.chambod@free.fr

FR07020 Camping Caravaning L'Ardéchois

Le Chambon, Gluiras, F-07190 St Sauveur-de-Montagut (Ardèche)

This attractive site is quite a way off the beaten track and the approach road is winding and narrow in places. However, it is worth the effort, to find in such a spectacular setting, a hillside site offering a wide range of amenities. There are 106 pitches (83 for touring) laid out on steep terraces, of varying sizes and many separated by trees and plants. Some are alongside the small, fast-flowing stream, while the rest (60%) are on higher, sloping ground nearer the restaurant/bar and pool. All 83 touring pitches have electricity (10A). The main site access roads are tarmac but are quite steep and larger units may find access to some terraces difficult. The amenities have been created by the careful conversion of old buildings which provide modern facilities in an attractive style (all from Easter). The friendly Dutch owners have developed an extensive excursion programme for exploring this attractive area on foot or by car. There are two entrances to the site so, on arrival, park outside on the road and go to reception on foot. A 'Sites et Paysages' member.

Facilities

Two good sanitary blocks provide washbasins in private cabins, baths and showers for babies and facilities for people with disabilities. Dishwashing and laundry rooms. Motorcaravan service point. Shop, bar/restaurant and takeaway (1/5-25/9). New restaurant planned. Swimming pool (heated in low season; no Bermuda style shorts; 1/5-25/9) with adjacent bar, snack bar and terrace, plus a paddling pool for children. TV room. Table tennis. Volleyball. Bicycle hire, archery and fishing. Comprehensive entertainment programme. Off site: Canyoning, climbing, river walking and canoeing trips organised.

Open

Easter - 31 October.

At a glance

Welcome & Ambience	✓✓✓✓	Location	✓✓✓
Quality of Pitches	✓✓✓✓	Range of Facilities	✓✓✓✓

Directions

From Valence take N86 south for 12 km. At La Voulte-sur-Rhône turn right onto D120 to St Sauveur de Montagut (site well signed), then take D102 towards Mézilhac for 8 km. to site.

Charges 2005

Per unit incl. 2 persons	€ 19,00 - € 25,50
extra person	€ 4,00 - € 5,50
child (0-3 yrs)	free
animal	€ 3,00 - € 4,00

Low season price for over 55s.
Camping Cheques accepted.

Reservations

Write with deposit (€ 69) and fee (€ 23); min. 10 days 6/7-24/8. Tel: 04 75 66 61 87. Email: ardechois.camping@wanadoo.fr

FR07030 Yelloh! Village Soleil Vivarais

Sampzon, F-07120 Ruoms (Ardèche)

A large, lively, high quality site bordering the River Ardèche, complete with beach, Soleil Vivarais offers much to visitors, particularly families with children. A popular feature is the 'barrage' with its canoe ramp, used by children with rubber boats more than canoeists, and providing an invigorating shower for bathers. Water is shallow in high season, but swimming is best in one of the pools. Of the 350 pitches, 88 generously sized, level pitches are for tourers, all with 10A electricity. Rock pegs are advised. Many are shaded and 30 have full services. During the day the proximity of the swimming pools to the terraces of the bar and restaurant make it a pleasantly social area. In the evening the purpose built stage, with professional lighting and sound system, provides an ideal platform for a regular family entertainment programme, mostly mimed musical shows. A new section beyond the beach houses good quality chalets, and a very attractive new pool complex, which all may use. Used by tour operators (52 pitches).

Facilities

Four modern, very clean and well equipped toilet blocks. Baby and child room. Facilities for people with disabilities. Washing machines and dryers. Motorcaravan service area. Small supermarket. Bright, modern bar/restaurant complex which in addition to takeaways and pizzas (cooked in a wood burning oven), caters for a range of appetites and budgets (all open all season). Heated main pool and paddling pool (no Bermuda style shorts). Water polo, aqua-aerobics, pool games. Tennis (charged). Basketball and volleyball. Fishing. Boules, table tennis and archery. Extensive animation programme for all ages in June, July and August. Off site: Riding 2 km. Golf 10 km. Activities nearby, many with qualified instruction and supervision, include mountain biking, walking, canoeing, rafting, climbing and caving. Get off the beaten track and explore the many old towns and villages in magnificent surroundings.

At a glance

Welcome & Ambience	✓✓✓✓	Location	✓✓✓✓✓
Quality of Pitches	✓✓✓✓	Range of Facilities	✓✓✓✓✓

Directions

From Le Teil, just west of Montélimar, turn off the N86 and take the N102 westwards through Villeneuve-de-Berg. Disregard the first sign for Vallon-Pont-d'Arc and continue for about 5 km. on N102 before turning left on D103, toward Vogüé, then left on D579 and through Ruoms. Still on the D579, follow Vallon-Pont-d'Arc signs towards Sampzon. Turn right over river bridge controlled by lights.

Charges 2006

Per unit incl. 2 persons and electricity	€ 16,00 - € 41,00
extra person	€ 4,50 - € 7,80
child (1-10 yrs)	€ 0,00 - € 6,50
pet	free - € 4,00

Reservations

Made by fax and credit card or write to site with 25% deposit (and € 30 fee in July/August). Tel: 04 75 39 67 56. Email: info@soleil-vivarais.com

Open

8 April - 16 September.

FR07050 Sunêlia Le Ranc Davaine

St Alban-Auriolles, F-07120 Ruoms (Ardèche)

Le Ranc Davaine is a quite large, busy, family oriented site set in two areas separated by a reasonably quiet road. The larger area provides all the entertainment facilities and most of the 430 pitches. The 113 touring pitches are mostly scattered between static caravan and tour operator pitches and are on fairly flat, rather stony ground under a variety of trees giving much needed shade. All are supplied with electricity (6/10A), some needing very long leads which may cross tarmac roads. Rock pegs are advised. The lower part is beside the river (unfenced). Sunbathing areas surround the pool complex, overlooked by the terrace of the restaurant, providing very pleasant surroundings, especially attractive with evening floodlighting. A lively entertainment programme (July/Aug) is aimed at young children and teenagers. The site is popular with tour operators (113 pitches) and there are 170 mobile homes. It can get very busy for much of the season.

Facilities

Five fully equipped toilet blocks include full facilities for disabled visitors. Dishwashing and laundry sinks, washing machines, dryers and irons. Large shop catering for most needs. Cash point. Internet point in reception. Bar/restaurant serving good range of meals. Pizzeria and takeaway (all open all season). Attractive large, irregularly shaped swimming pool, covered pool (heated), supplemented by two small square pools and a large slide (all open all season, no shirts or Bermuda style shorts). Play area. Tennis, table tennis, basketball, football, archery and minigolf. Fishing. Extensive programme of sports in the pools, clubs for youngsters and teenagers, many other organised activities. Discos in closed, air-conditioned room (until 3 am four times a week in high season). Off site: Canoe hire nearby for excursions down the River Ardèche. Rafting. Bicycle hire 2 km. Riding 6 km. Karting.

At a glance

Welcome & Ambience	✓✓✓✓	Location	✓✓✓✓
Quality of Pitches	✓✓✓	Range of Facilities	✓✓✓✓✓

Directions

From Ruoms go south on the D111. Just before Grospierres turn right onto D246, cross the river bridge (2.5 m. width restriction) and then left on D208 towards Chandolas and site. GPS: N44:24.848 E04:16.374

Charges 2005

Per unit incl. 2 persons	€ 20,00 - € 35,00
with electricity	€ 25,00 - € 39,00
extra person	€ 6,20 - € 9,30
child (2-13 yrs)	€ 3,60 - € 9,30
animal	€ 4,65
Camping Cheques accepted.	

Reservations

Made with deposit (€ 100) and fee (€ 30). Tel: 04 75 39 60 55. Email: camping.ranc.davaine@wanadoo.fr

Open

23 March - 14 September.

FR07070 Camping Les Ranchisses

Route de Rocher, F-07110 Largentière (Ardèche)

Combining farming, wine-making, running an Auberge and a friendly family campsite is no simple task, but the Chevalier family seem to manage it quite effortlessly. Well run and with the emphasis on personal attention, this is a highly recommended site. In a somewhat lesser known area of the Ardèche, the site has developed from an original 'camping á la ferme' into a very well equipped modern campsite. There are 165 good-sized, level, grassy pitches, 88 for tourists with electricity (10A) which include 42 multi-serviced pitches (electricity, water, waste water). The pitches are in two distinct areas - the original site which is well shaded, and the lower part which is more open with less shade, serviced by tarmac and gravel access roads. The site runs parallel to the road and there may be background traffic noise in some areas. There is a small lake (unfenced) connected to the river, providing opportunities for bathing, fishing or canoeing (free life jackets) with one part of the bathing area quite safe for youngsters. The site's own Auberge is set in the original 1824 building that once used to house silk worms. It serves meals and takeaway food at lunch-time and evenings (all season) either inside the cave-like restaurant or outside on the attractive, shaded terrace.

Facilities

Two modern, comprehensively equipped toilet buildings include washbasins in cubicles, dishwashing and laundry sinks and facilities for babies and disabled persons. It is an excellent provision, kept immaculate. Laundry in separate building. Motorcaravan service point. Small shop, takeaway and bar with terrace (all season). Excellent pool complex with two large pools (both heated all season) and paddling pool. Adventure style playground. Organised amusements for children in high season. Tennis court. Minigolf. Table tennis. Boules. Canoeing. Off site: Canoe and kayaking arranged from the site each Monday and Wednesday (mid -June - end Aug). Medieval village of Largentière (1.5 km.) with Tuesday market and medieval festival in July. Take to the back roads to see the real Ardèche and don't miss the wonderful old villages of Balazuc and Labaume.

At a glance

Welcome & Ambience	✓✓✓✓	Location	✓✓✓✓
Quality of Pitches	✓✓✓✓	Range of Facilities	✓✓✓✓✓

Directions

Largentière is southwest of Aubenas and is best approached using the D104. After 16 km. just beyond Uzer at a roundabout turn northwest on the D5. After 5 km. at far end of Largentière, fork left downhill signed Valgorge. Site is on left in about 1.8 km.

Charges 2006

Per unit incl. 2 persons	€ 24,00 - € 34,00
serviced pitch	€ 26,50 - € 36,00
extra person (over 1 yr)	€ 4,50 - € 7,00
dog	€ 3,00
Camping Cheques accepted.	

Reservations

Made with 30% deposit plus booking/insurance fee (€ 15). Tel: 04 75 88 31 97. Email: reception@lesranchisses.fr

Open

14 April - 30 September.

FR07110 Domaine Le Pommier

RN102, F-07170 Villeneuve-de-Berg (Ardèche)

Domaine Le Pommier is an extremely spacious Dutch owned site of 10 hectares in 32 hectares of wooded grounds. It has first class facilities, including the most up-to-date toilet blocks, a very good bar/restaurant and one of the best swimming and paddling pool complexes we have seen – ideal for all the family. The site is steeply terraced (a tractor is available for assistance) and has wonderful views over the Ardèche mountains and beyond. There are 400 pitches with 275 for tourists. They are grassy/stony, of good size and well spaced. Separated by young trees and hedges, some have little or no shade. All have access to electricity and water is close by. The site is not recommended for large units.

Facilities

Four excellent toilet blocks, one with under-floor heating, provide all the necessary facilities. Comprehensive shop. Bar/restaurant. Heated pool complex with water slides, a flowing 'river', several good, unusual paddling pools and a conventional pool for serious swimming. Everything opens from the end of April. Boules, football, minigolf, badminton, games in the woods, table tennis, archery, water polo, tug of war, volleyball, tennis etc. Sound proof disco. Very extensive programme of events on and off site. Off season excursions to vineyards, wine tasting, museums, nougat factory and old villages. Also bridge classes and water colour classes. Off site: Villeneuve de Berg 1.5 km. River Ardèche 12 km. Potholing, rock climbing, canoeing, canyoning, mountain biking, walking or riding. Touring the many old villages and the superb scenery of the Ardèche Gorge and mountains.

At a glance

Welcome & Ambience	✓✓✓✓	Location	✓✓✓✓
Quality of Pitches	✓✓✓	Range of Facilities	✓✓✓✓✓

Directions

Site is west of Montélimar on the N102. The entrance is adjacent to the roundabout at the eastern end of the Villeneuve-de-Berg bypass.
GPS: N44:34.350 E04:30.669

Charges guide

Per unit incl. 2 persons	€ 14,00 - € 29,00
extra person over 4 yrs	€ 4,00 - € 6,50
electricity	€ 4,00
dog	free - € 4,00

Max. 6 persons per pitch. Special offers for longer stays in low season.

Reservations

Made with 30% deposit and fee (€ 23).
Tel: 04 75 94 82 81.
Email: info@campinglepommier.com

Open

1 May - 30 September.

Rhône Valley

295

FR07080 RCN La Bastide en Ardèche

RD111, route d'Alès, Sampzon, F-07120 Ruoms (Ardèche)

Though more expensive than some, this site is maintained to a high standard and this is evident as soon as you drive in, with its neat and tidy appearance and flowers everywhere. On driving down to your pitch, it seems that there are many mobile homes. Actually there are only 46 mobile homes, 25 small chalets plus another 16 pitches used by a tour operator, which out of 300 pitches is really not many. Once past these, the site opens up to reveal pleasant, good sized pitches, all with some shade and bordered by flowering trees and bushes. All have electricity, the basic pitches with 3A, and 86 fully serviced ones with 5A. Security patrols ensure quiet nights. Canoe trips are arranged down the Gorge d'Ardèche and in mid-June each year a large section of the river bank next to the site is cleared of boulders and sand put down - just the job for children.

Facilities

Two toilet blocks, the newest with very high quality fittings including washbasins in cubicles, a baby room and facilities for disabled people. The older block is only open in high season and has mainly Turkish style WCs, plus showers, etc. Shop. Attractive restaurant, pizzeria and bar (mid June to end Aug). Heated swimming pool with pleasant sunbathing area. Play area. Table tennis, boules, volleyball, football, basketball and tennis courts. Fishing. Games and competitions are organised in July/Aug. plus discos in a soundproof cellar. Doctor calls daily (July/Aug) and hairdresser weekly (July/Aug). Only gas barbecues are permitted. Off site: Riding and bicycle hire 3 km. Golf 6 km. Watersports on the nearby River Ardèche. The small town of Ruoms is 4 km. Vallon-Pont-d'Arc 7 km. The old villages of Balazuc, Labaume and Largentière.

At a glance

Welcome & Ambience	✓✓✓✓✓	Location	✓✓✓✓
Quality of Pitches	✓✓✓✓	Range of Facilities	✓✓✓✓✓

Directions

Going south from Ruoms on the D579, after 2.5 km. at roundabout, turn right on D111 signed Alès. Cross river bridge and site is 200 m. on the left. GPS: N44:25.375 E04:19.297

Charges 2006

Per unit incl. 2 persons	€ 20,00 - € 43,50
incl. 3-6 persons	€ 25,50 - € 48,50
dog	€ 4,00

Reservations

Made with deposit (€ 110) and booking fee (€ 40). Tel: 04 75 39 64 72. Email: info@rcn-labastideenardeche.fr

Open

1 April - 25 November.

FR07090 Castel Camping Le Domaine des Plantas

F-07360 Les Ollières-sur-Eyrieux (Ardèche)

A good quality site in a spectacular setting on the steep banks of the Eyrieux river, Domaine des Plantas offers an attractive alternative to those in the more popular southern parts of the Ardèche. The Eyrieux valley is less well known, but arguably just as attractive as those further south and a good deal less crowded, particularly in the main season. Perhaps the only drawback to this site is the narrow twisting 3 km. approach road which, although by no means frightening, may present something of a challenge to those with large outfits - however, the helpful owners have an ingenious convoy system designed to assist campers on departure. There is a sandy beach beside the quite fast-flowing, but fairly shallow, river (used for bathing) and a swimming pool and paddling pool with tiled surrounds for sunbathing. The old, original buildings house the reception, restaurant and bar. The terrace provides a stunning viewpoint. The 162 pitches (90 for touring) are steeply terraced and shaded. They have electricity connections (10A, long leads may be needed). Much up and down walking is required making this site unsuitable for those with walking difficulties.

Facilities

Two excellent toilet blocks (one can be heated) are very well equipped. There are some facilities which will certainly please the very young. Dishwashing and laundry sinks. Washing machine. Motorcaravan service point. Small shop (bread to order). Bar, restaurant and disco. Heated kidney shaped swimming pool and paddling pool. Adventure play area beside river. High season animation for children organised six days a week, and discos for 14-18 year olds held in cellar twice weekly (strictly no alcohol). Many activities and excursions are possible, arranged according to campers' motivations. Only gas and electric barbecues are allowed. Off site: Riding 15 km. Mountain biking, canoeing, canyoning, riding and walking. A wonderful area for touring.

Open

29 April - 9 September.

At a glance

Welcome & Ambience	✓✓✓✓	Location	✓✓✓✓
Quality of Pitches	✓✓✓✓	Range of Facilities	✓✓✓✓

Directions

From A7 take exit 15 (Valence Sud). Immediately after the péage turn right to Valence centre, then follow signs to Montélimar via the N7 for 7 km. Turn right towards Charmes sur Rhône, thence to Beauchastel. On leaving Beauchastel follow signs to Ollieres sur Eyrieux. In the village cross the river and follow campsite signs (3 km). GPS: N44:48.520 E04:38.125

Charges 2005

Per unit incl. 2 persons and electricity	€ 19,00 - € 29,00
extra person over 4 yrs	€ 4,00 - € 7,00
animal	free - € 3,00

Camping Cheques accepted.

Reservations

Made with deposit (€ 110) and fee (€ 20). Tel: 04 75 66 21 53. Email: plantas.ardeche@wanadoo.fr

FR07130 Camping Les Coudoulets

Pradons, F-07120 Ruoms (Ardèche)

For those who prefer a more intimate, peaceful campsite beside the river Ardèche, only a short distance away from the main centre, then this well cared for site is for you. It is run by a very enthusiastic and friendly family who has developed this site from their farm. They have a small vineyard and their wine is on sale in the bar; we fully recommend it. There are 125 good sized, grassy and well shaded pitches, separated by trees and shrubs. There are 112 for touring, all with 6A electricity. Organised events in July/August for all the family include the occasional evening event such as barbecues and musical evenings (no discos). There is an area for bathing in the river and it is an ideal spot for canoeists, etc.

Facilities

The very good, clean, recently refurbished toilet block has all the necessary facilities including excellent facilities for disabled people. Motorcaravan service point. Bar with TV and terrace (May - Sept) also selling bread, ices and drinks. Snacks in July/Aug. Butcher calls three times a week in high season. Small heated swimming pool and paddling pool (May - Sept). Fishing, football, volleyball and table tennis. Off site: Shop 300 m. Ruoms with range of shops 4 km. Canyoning and rafting etc on the river Ardèche. Tennis or riding 2 km. Accompanied walks, canoe trips and visits to a wine cellar from site.

Open

1 May - 12 September.

At a glance

Welcome & Ambience	✓✓✓✓✓	Location	✓✓✓✓
Quality of Pitches	✓✓✓✓	Range of Facilities	✓✓✓✓

Directions

Leave Montélimar going west on N102 towards Aubenas. Shortly after passing Villeneuve de Berg turn left on D103 towards Vogüé for 5 km. Turn left on D579 towards Ruoms and site is on right in approx. 10 km. on entering the village of Pradons. GPS: N44:28.598 E04:21.514

Charges 2005

Per unit incl. 2 persons	€ 13,00 - € 20,00
extra person	€ 3,50 - € 4,20
child (under 7 yrs)	€ 3,00 - € 3,70
electricity (6A)	€ 3,60
dog	free - € 2,00

Reservations

Made with deposit (€ 70) but no booking fee. Max. 6 persons and 1 car per pitch. Tel: 04 75 93 94 95. Email: camping@coudoulets.com

FR07140 Camping Les Lavandes

Le Village, F-07170 Darbres (Ardèche)

Although slightly less sophisticated than some others in the region, this site should appeal to those seeking the real France for a pleasant family holiday. Situated to the northeast of Aubenas, in a quieter part of this region, Les Lavandes is surrounded by magnificent countryside, vineyards and orchards. A ride along the panoramic road to Mirabel is a must. The enthusiastic French owners, who speak good English, run a site that appeals to all nationalities. The 70 pitches (58 for touring) are arranged on low terraces separated by a variety of trees and shrubs that give welcome shade in summer. Visit at the end of May to see the campsite trees laden with luscious cherries. There is no problem with electricity, most pitches having 6A but a few have 10A. Water taps are not so abundant. Traditional buildings house the reception (full of tourist information including a touch screen), shop, restaurant, takeaway and cosy bar offering excellent views over the swimming pool to the village (just a stroll away) and hillside beyond. Organised activities include wine tasting, shows, musical evenings and children's games.

Facilities

The recently refurbished facilities are comprehensive and well maintained. Excellent room with facilities for disabled people and a baby room. Washing machine. Small shop (1/7-31/8). Cosy bar and terrace (1/6-31/8). Restaurant (1/7-31/8). Takeaway (14.4-31.8). Swimming pool and paddling pool surrounded by paved sunbathing area with larger grass area adjacent, all with super views. Two small play areas for younger children. Table tennis, table football and pool table. Electric barbecues are not permitted. Off site: Fishing 1 km. Bicycle hire 3 km. Tennis 5 km. Canoeing, walking, cycling, riding and carting nearby. Caves, troglodyte villages, historical villages, interesting geological formations and museums. Wonderful area for birds (Golden Orioles and Bonellis eagle).

At a glance

Welcome & Ambience	✓✓✓✓	Location	✓✓✓✓
Quality of Pitches	✓✓✓✓	Range of Facilities	✓✓✓

Directions

You are advised to approach the site from the south. From Montélimar take the N102 towards Aubenas. After passing through Villeneuve, in Lavilledieu, turn right at traffic lights on D224 to Darbres (10 km). In the village of Darbres turn very sharp left by the post office (care needed) and follow signs to site.

Charges 2005

Per unit incl. 2 persons	€ 11,00 - € 16,00
extra person	€ 2,80 - € 3,50
child under 8 yrs	€ 1,00 - € 2,60
electricity	€ 3,50
dog	€ 1,50 - € 2,50

Reservations

Made with deposit (€ 85) and fee (€ 15). Tel: 04 75 94 20 65. Email: sarl.leslavandes@online.fr

Open

15 April - 15 September.

FR07150 Camping Domaine de Gil

Mobile homes ▶ page 437

Route de Vals-les-Bains, Ucel, F-07200 Aubenas (Ardèche)

This very attractive and well organised, smaller site in a less busy part of the Ardèche should appeal to couples and families with younger children. The 80, good sized, level pitches, 43 for touring, are surrounded by a variety of trees offering plenty of shade. All have 5A electricity with European type connectors. The focal point of the site is formed by the very attractive swimming pool, paddling pool and large sunbathing area, with the bar, restaurant and well appointed children's play areas all adjacent. A spacious sports area and shady picnic/play area are alongside the river Ardèche - an ideal spot to cool off on a hot day. You will receive a warm welcome from the enthusiastic and friendly, new Dutch owners (who speak excellent English).

Facilities

All the excellent facilities are in a single, cheerful, modern block adjacent to the pool. Most washbasins are in cabins. Plenty of dishwashing and laundry sinks plus a washing machine and iron. Motorcaravan service point. Small shop for basics. Bar/restaurant and takeaway (from June). Swimming pool and paddling pool, heated all season (proper swimming trunks only). Two play areas. Volleyball, boules, minigolf, football, tennis court. Canoeing, boating and fishing in the river. Some organised activities in high season. In July/Aug. only gas and electric barbecues are permitted. Off site: Shops, etc. at Vals-les-Bain 1.5 km. Interesting old town with larger range of shops, restaurants and bars 3 km. Organised canoe trips and canyoning on the river Ardèche. Bicycle hire and riding 4 km.

Open

14 April - 17 September.

At a glance

Welcome & Ambience	✓✓✓✓✓	Location	✓✓✓✓
Quality of Pitches	✓✓✓✓	Range of Facilities	✓✓✓✓

Directions

Site is just north of Aubenas at Ucel. Coming from the southeast on N102, just after passing through a tunnel, turn right at roundabout (signed Privas) and cross the river Ardèche into Pont d'Ucel. Shortly bear right and at roundabout, take last exit (signed Ucel). Shortly turn left (narrow road, signed Ucel D18) and then right (Ucel D578B). Site is about 2 km. on the left. GPS: N44:38.558 E04:22.775

Charges 2006

Per unit incl. 2 persons	€ 14,00 - € 27,50
extra person	€ 3,50 - € 5,50
child (under 9 yrs)	free - € 4,00
electricity	€ 3,80
animal	€ 2,00 - € 3,50

Reservations

Made with deposit (€ 120) and fee (€ 15). Tel: 04 75 94 63 63. Email: info@domaine-de-gil.com

FR07170 Ludocamping

F-07170 Lussas (Ardèche)

Ludocamping is set amongst the magnificent scenery of the Auzon valley, a delight for nature lovers particularly in early season when the many wild flowers and cherry trees are at their best. There are numerous birds including eagles and the elusive golden oriole, heard but seldom seen. A ride through Darbres and Mirabel has breathtaking views. This site, run by a very friendly Dutch family (excellent English is spoken) should appeal to couples of all ages and young families. The emphasis is on a quiet family campsite whilst offering a really wide range of activities. From mid-July – early August, only families with children under 14 yrs are accepted which allows the activities to be focussed on this age group – an unusual and interesting idea. The 160 grassy pitches, all for touring, are in two separate areas. Those in the upper section are large super pitches (approx 160 sq.m.) with wonderful views of the surrounding hills but little shade. Those in the lower area, closer to the small river, are well spaced, set naturally amongst the trees and have good shade. All have electricity, most 5A but some 10A. There is an attractive swimming pool (heated all season), good sized paddling pool and large sunbathing area.

Facilities

Four very clean, good quality toilet blocks, two in each area, offering all the necessary facilities. Bar (all season), takeaway (from 1/5) and terrace area overlooking the valley. Play area. Volleyball. Table tennis. Very large recreational area next to the river. Paddling area in river and separate deeper area. Fishing, Bike hire. Excellent club for over 6/7 yr olds offering a very wide range of activities such as biking, climbing, carting, canoeing and canyoning. Off season club for older children, same as for the younger children plus abseiling and bungee jumping etc. Off season club for seniors with large range of excursions in the campsite coach. Only gas and electric barbecues allowed. Off site: Small village of Lussas (a few shops, restaurant and bar) 600 m. Riding 6 km. Gliding, hang-gliding, canoeing and speed boating arranged. Old villages, with their markets, museums etc, caves, mountains, river gorges, caves, wine tasting.

Open

1 April - 15 October.

At a glance

Welcome & Ambience	✓✓✓✓✓	Location	✓✓✓✓
Quality of Pitches	✓✓✓✓	Range of Facilities	✓✓✓✓

Directions

From Montélimar take the N102 west towards Aubenas, pass around Villeneuve and at the traffic lights in Lavilledieu turn right onto the D224 towards Lussas. The site entrance is on the right just before the village (approx 4 km. from N102). GPS: N44:36.299 E04:28.247

Charges 2005

Per unit incl. 2 persons	€ 11,00 - € 22,00
extra person	€ 2,50 - € 6,00
child (0-7 yrs)	free - € 3,00
electricity (6A)	€ 3,00
dog	€ 1,00 - € 1,50

Special long stay, low season offers.
No credit cards.

Reservations

Contact site. Note: from 13/7-8/8 only children under 14 yrs allowed. Tel: 04 75 94 21 22. Email: info@ludocamping.com

FR07200 Camping L'Oasis

St Peliet Chaleat, F-07370 Eclassan (Ardèche)

This is a small but spacious, steeply terraced and rural site in a lesser known area of the northern Ardèche. Immaculately kept, it is run by the enthusiastic and friendly Faure family (English is spoken). The level, grassy pitches are very large, well spaced and most have good views. There are 63 pitches with 45 for touring, some on shady terraces with shrubs and trees and others being more open and sunny. All have 3/6A electricity, some have individual tap and drain. Due to the very steep site roads, this site is unsuitable for large outfits or for those with walking difficulties. Caravans and trailers are taken by tractor onto the pitches. There are many walks and cycle routes, some starting from the site.

Facilities

Two very clean, modern toilet blocks offer excellent facilities, including washbasins in cabins, some showers and toilets with washbasins, and two baths. Facilities for disabled visitors (but see above). Shop (closed Monday). Bar/restaurant (all season) offering basic menu and takeaway. Swimming pool (heated May - mid Sept). Internet point. Very large play area and playground alongside a small stream. Badminton. Minigolf. Bicycle hire (brought to site). Family entertainment (no discos). Only gas and electric barbecues permitted (available for rent). Off site: Eclassan, baker butcher and grocer 4 km. Ardoix 7 km. by road, only 20 minutes on foot. Riding 4 km. Golf 15 km.

Open

15 April - 30 September.

At a glance

Welcome & Ambience	✓✓✓✓✓	Location	✓✓✓
Quality of Pitches	✓✓✓✓✓	Range of Facilities	✓✓✓✓

Directions

From A7 autoroute south of Lyons take exit 12 (from north) or exit 13 (from south). Cross the Rhône and take N86 to Sarras. In town turn west on D6, signed St Jeure. Follow winding road up hill for 8 km. Turn right just before quarry (site signed) and site is 4 km. along narrow lane. You must park at entrance and ring for assistance. Tractors take caravans to and from pitch as the site road is very steep. GPS: N45:10.756 E04:44.374

Charges 2005

Per pitch incl. 2 persons	€ 11,00 - € 17,50
extra person	€ 3,70
electricity (6A)	€ 3,50

Reservations

Advised for high season (min. 7 nights) with deposit (€ 40 per week). Tel: 04 75 34 56 23. Email: oasis.camp@wanadoo.fr

camping
L'OASIS ★★★

Ardèche Nature
Heated swimming-pool
Mobilehome & chalet to rent

Le petit Chaléat 07370 Eclassan
Tél. : +33(0)4 75 34 56 23
www.oasisardeche.com
e-mail : oasis.camp@wanadoo.fr

FR07190 Camping Le Chambourlas

F-07360 Les Ollières sur Eyrieux (Ardèche)

Tucked away up a steep and winding country road in a beautiful setting, in the hills above Privas, this small, neat and tidy family owned site (Dutch and English spoken) is popular with Dutch visitors. The 75 grassy, slightly sloping pitches (72 for touring) are set on low terraces and separated by an interesting variety of trees. All have 10A electricity and excellent views over the wooded hills. There is a wide range of family orientated activities, especially in July and August, but these do not extend late into the night. Although there are special facilities, this is not an ideal site for those walking difficulties. It is not ideal for very large units due to the narrow and steep roads in the vicinity.

Facilities

One modern toilet block with all the necessary facilities including those for disabled visitors. Bar, restaurant and takeaway (all 15/5-28/8). Small shop (July/Aug). Swimming pool (15/4-30/9). Play area. Volleyball. Table tennis. Boules. Good range of activities, some in low season, No discos. River fishing. Off site: Many walks and bike rides. Excursions. Village of les Ollières sur Eyrieux 6 km.

Open

1 April - 1 October.

At a glance

Welcome & Ambience	✓✓✓	Location	✓✓✓
Quality of Pitches	✓✓✓✓	Range of Facilities	✓✓✓✓

Directions

In Privas take D2 road north, signed Le Cheylard. Follow road as it bears left and right, then over two river bridges. Site entrance is on the right 12 km. after traffic lights. Take care – this is a fairly tortuous climb. GPS: N44:46.870 E04:37.016

Charges 2006

Per unit incl. 2 persons	€ 15,00 - € 28,00
extra person	€ 4,50 - € 5,50
Camping Cheques accepted.	

Reservations

Made with deposit (€ 100) and fee (€ 15). Tel: 04 75 66 24 31. Email: info@chambourlas.com

FR07210 Camping L'Albanou

Quartier Pampelonne, F-07000 St Julien-en-St Alban (Ardèche)

This small neat site is enthusiastically run by the welcoming Pougalan family (English spoken). Within 15 minutes of the A7 autoroute, this is an ideal base for those seeking a short stay, but you may well be tempted to stay longer. It is situated in the beautiful northern Ardèche region with its many old villages, markets and museums – well worth exploring. The site's 60 large, level and easily accessible pitches (59 for touring) are in groups separated by tall hedges, all with electricity (6A). An attractive modern building houses the reception and a small bar with a terrace. Snacks are available to order. In high season a few games are organised for younger children but the emphasis here is on a quiet and peaceful site.

Facilities

One central toilet block, recently refurbished to a very high standard, has all the necessary facilities including those for disabled visitors. Small shop (all season) with basic essentials and bread to order. Small bar and snack takeaway (all season). Good sized swimming pool and paddling pool (mid May - mid Sept). Motorcaravan service point. Only gas or electric barbecues are permitted. Off site: St Julien (shop, bar/restaurant) 2 km. Pouzin with shops, bars, restaurants, banks 4 km. Supermarket 5 km. Fishing 300 m. Bicycle hire 10 km. Riding 15 km.

Open

28 April - 22 September.

At a glance

Welcome & Ambience	✓✓✓✓✓	Location	✓✓✓✓
Quality of Pitches	✓✓✓✓	Range of Facilities	✓✓✓

Directions

From A7 autoroute take exit 16 for Loriol and head west across the Rhône to Le Pouzin. At roundabout take N104, signed Aubenas, and follow the road up the hill. Turn left in about 4 km. just before St Julien. Follow signs to site. GPS: N44:45.435 E04:42.722

Charges 2005

Per unit incl. 2 persons	€ 13,00 - € 15,00
extra person	€ 3,50 - € 4,00
child (0-7 yrs)	€ 2,50 - € 3,00
electricity (6A)	€ 3,50
animal	€ 2,00

Reservations

Advised for high season; contact site.
Tel: 04 75 66 00 97.
Email: camping:albanou@wanadoo.fr

FR07220 Camping Le Merle Roux

Le Roux Est, F-07210 Baix (Ardèche)

This extremely spacious, popular site in the northern part of the Ardèche is owned by an enthusiastic Dutch family. It is ideal for those looking for an active holiday based around the campsite. It has a very good swimming pool complex and a large but cosy bar/restaurant and terrace offering an excellent menu and takeaway service. There are 180 irregularly shaped pitches with 130 for touring, set out on steep terraces. Most have wide ranging views and some shade from a variety of small trees, all have 6A electricity and many have water and drain. The steep roads and terracing may make access difficult for larger and under-powered units on some pitches. Rock pegs are essential. In July and August there is an extensive programme of activities for all the family and in low season some activities are organised including excursions. Explore the Rhône valley with its many famous vineyards, old towns and villages. Cross the Rhône to visit the very interesting large town of Montélimar (nougat, good shops and hypermarkets) and the beautiful Drôme region. This site is very popular with Dutch visitors.

Facilities

Two main toilet blocks, one recently refurbished, and three much smaller blocks without showers. These offer all necessary modern facilities including washbasins in cabins, facilities for babies and for those with disabilities, although they are a long distance from some pitches. Bar/restaurant with meals and takeaways (all season). Pizza van calls. Well stocked shop (all season). Excellent unheated pool complex with separate paddling pool, pool with toboggans and two swimming pools. Boules court. Table tennis. Basketball. Play area. Only gas barbecues are permitted. Off site: Pouzin with its shops, bars, restaurants, banks and supermarket 5 km. Other small villages of Baix, Braine and Chomerac close by. Tennis 1 km. Fishing 1.5 km. Bicycle hire 10 km. Riding 15 km.

At a glance

Welcome & Ambience	✓✓✓✓	Location	✓✓✓
Quality of Pitches	✓✓✓	Range of Facilities	✓✓✓✓✓

Directions

Leave the A7 autoroute at exit 16 for Loriol and go west across the River Rhône to Le Pouzin. At roundabout take N86 (south). After crossing a river and just before the railway crossing turn right on D22a (site signed). In 500 m. turn left and follow road to site (about 2 km).
GPS: N44:42.313 E04:44.284

Charges 2005

Per unit incl. 2 persons	€ 13,00 - € 23,00
extra person	€ 2,50 - € 4,00
child (2-7 yrs)	€ 1,25 - € 2,25
electricity (6/10A)	€ 3,00
dog	€ 0,90 - € 1,50

Reservations

Contact site. Tel: 04 75 85 84 12.
Email: lemerleroux@hotmail.com

Open

1 April - 31 October.

FR26030 Sunêlia Le Grand Lierne

B.P. 8, F-26120 Chabeuil (Drôme)

In addition to its obvious attraction as an overnight stop, fairly convenient for the A7 autoroute, this site provides a pleasant base to explore this little known area between the Ardèche and the Vercors mountains and the Côte du Rhône wine area. It has 161 marked, stony pitches, 76 for touring units, mainly separated by developing hedges or oak trees. Many have good shade, some are on flat ground and all have electricity (6/10A). A more open area exists for those who prefer less shade and a view of the mountains, but this area contains many mobile homes. Used by tour operators (30%).

Facilities

Two sanitary blocks include washbasins in cabins, facilities for disabled people and a small WC for children. Dishwashing under cover. Washing machines (powder provided), dryers and outdoor lines by the blocks. Motorcaravan services. Shop/restaurant and terrace (1/7-31/8). Bar/takeaway (1/5-8/9). Fridge rental. Excellent swimming pool complex with three pools, one very small open all season and covered and heated in low season (other pools 15/5-31/8; no Bermuda shorts). Paddling pool and 50 m. water slide. Playgrounds and trampoline. Mini-tennis, minigolf, table tennis, volleyball, archery and football field. Bicycle hire. Library. Extensive entertainment programme for all the family, including excursions (from the end of May). Only gas and electric barbecues are permitted. Dogs and other pets are not accepted in high season (8/7-18/8). Caravan storage. Off site: Golf 3 km. Bicycle hire 4.5 km. Fishing 5 km. Riding 7 km. Canoe/kayak near. Vercors mountains. Chabeuil 5 km.

Directions

Site signed in Chabeuil about 11 km. east of Valence (18 km. from autoroute). It is best to approach Chabeuil from the south side of Valence via the Valence ring road, thence onto the D68 to Chabeuil itself. Site is off the D125 to Charpey, 5 km. from Chabeuil, but well signed.
GPS: N44:54.951 E05:03.907

Charges 2006

Per unit incl. 2 adults	€ 16,70 - € 29,60
extra person	€ 7,10 - € 8,30
child (2-7 yrs)	€ 3,60 - € 6,00
electricity (6/10A)	€ 4,30 - € 5,70
animal	€ 4,00

Camping Cheques accepted.

Reservations

Accepted with 25% deposit and fee (€ 30).
Tel: 04 75 59 83 14. Email: contact@grandlierne.com

Open

28 April - 10 September, with all services.

At a glance

Welcome & Ambience	✓✓✓	Location	✓✓✓
Quality of Pitches	✓✓✓	Range of Facilities	✓✓✓

FR26040 Camping Le Couspeau

F-26460 Le Poët Célard (Drôme)

As one approaches this site a magnificent landscape of mountains and valleys unfolds and the overall impression is one of beauty and tranquillity. The site has 127 pitches with 87 for touring. Access to the 62 touring pitches on the older section of the site (all with 6A electricity) is reasonably easy, although levelling blocks may be handy as some of the terraced pitches are slightly sloping. Mature trees provide shade and there are adequate water points around the site. The 25 pitches on the new lower section of the site are very large (150 sq.m) and all have electricity, water and a drain. They are separated by small hedges and some small trees but have little shade. Access is via a steep road but tractor assistance is available. Rock pegs are advised. The site has a good restaurant/bar and a terrace with panoramic views. In July and August on one evening each week there is live music, on another a themed meal. Those seeking to unwind and relax should appreciate the delightful scenery and setting of this medium sized site. The most direct approach to the site is via a steep road, and with several hairpin bends to negotiate, care is required (underpowered units not advised). For many people the views are reward enough, for others there is an alternative, easier route (see below).

Facilities

Three sanitary blocks, two in the old section and one in the new, are kept very clean. Laundry and dishwashing sinks, washing machines and dryer. Facilities for disabled campers (on the older section), but the site is not ideal due to steep roads and steps. Well stocked shop (15/6-30/9). Restaurant/bar and takeaway (15/6-30/9). Main pool (1/6-30/9) and smaller, covered one (1/5-30/9 and heated in low seasons) plus a toddlers' pool. Play area and organised activities for children in high season. Tennis, table tennis and volleyball. Guided hill walks and cycle trips. Manual and electric bicycle hire. Rafting, canoe trips (on the River Drôme), riding and paragliding arranged. Off site: Riding and fishing 5 km. Canoeing, rafting and paragliding. Ideal area for the serious cyclist, mountain biker and hiker. Medieval towns and villages, markets and châteaux. Crest, Po't-Laval. Vercors mountains.

Open

1 May - 14 September.

At a glance

Welcome & Ambience	✓✓✓	Location	✓✓✓✓
Quality of Pitches	✓✓✓✓	Range of Facilities	✓✓✓✓

Directions

From A7 autoroute take exit 16 and D104 to Crest. At traffic lights, on the Crest bypass, turn hard right on D538 south towards Bourdeaux. Shortly before Bourdeaux turn right over small river bridge onto D328B, signed Le Poët Célard. After climbing for about 1.5 km, at T-junction, turn right on D328 and just before Le Poët Célard turn left onto D328A. Site is up the hill on the left, well signed. Alternatively, continue through to Bourdeaux, in the direction of Dieuleft and follow signs for site (this is 6 km. further but it is easier). GPS: N44:35.744 E05:06.680

Charges guide

Per unit incl. 2 persons	€ 13,00 - € 23,00
extra person	€ 4,00 - € 6,00
child (under 7 yrs)	free - € 4,00
electricity (6A)	€ 3,00

Camping Cheques accepted.

Reservations

Advised for July/Aug. and made with deposit (€ 80) and fee (€ 20). Tel: 04 75 53 30 14.
Email: info@couspeau.com

FR26080 Camping Le Gallo Romain

Route du Col de Tourniol, F-26300 Barbières (Drôme)

Surrounded by wooded hills and mountains, this spacious site with new, enthusiastic Dutch owners, makes a good base from which to unwind and explore the spectacular Vercors mountains. It is quiet and peaceful, in an attractive location with pitches set on terraces that descend to a babbling stream. The 80 level and grassy pitches, 66 for touring, are separated by mature trees and shrubs, most with some shade and 6A electricity (long leads may be needed). The area is ideal for walking or mountain biking with many tracks in the hills, or for wild flower, bird or butterfly enthusiasts. A good bar/restaurant has a terrace overlooking the pool and the mountains beyond. English and Dutch are spoken.

Facilities
Two toilet blocks, although not new, are kept very clean, with all the necessary facilities including for disabled visitors. Small shop. Bar/restaurant. Swimming and paddling pools. Games room with large screen TV, pool table, table tennis. Volleyball. Small play area. All facilities open all season. Off site: A few shops at Barbières 1 km. Romans and Chabeuil with shops, banks, etc. 14 km. Riding and golf 6 km.

Open
1 April - 30 October.

At a glance
Welcome & Ambience ✓✓✓✓✓   Location ✓✓✓✓
Quality of Pitches ✓✓✓✓   Range of Facilities ✓✓✓✓

Directions
Leave A49/E713 autoroute at exit 7 (Romans-sur-Isère) and turn south on D149, following signs to Col de Tourniol. Barbières is approx. 12 km. along this road. Drive carefully through narrow streets in the village; the site is about 1 km. beyond the village on the right. GPS: N44:56.669 E05:09.099

Charges 2006
Per person	€ 4,00
child (under 7 yrs)	€ 3,00
pitch	€ 14,00
electricity (6A)	€ 2,70
dog	€ 1,80

Credit cards accepted with small fee.

Reservations
Advised for high season; made for exact dates with deposit and fee. Tel: 04 75 47 44 07. Email: info@legalloromain.net

FR26090 Camping Les Truffières

Lieu-dit Nachony, F-26230 Grignan (Drôme)

This is a delightful small site in a rural setting within walking distance of the picturesque ancient village of Grignan with wonderful views and providing peace and tranquillity. The 85 good sized pitches are level and fairly stony with 79 for touring units. Shaded by oak trees and separated by rosemary or laurel hedging, water, waste water and refuse disposal are close at hand and each pitch has electricity (10A). The Croze family is most welcoming and achieves high standards of cleanliness and order while maintaining a friendly and relaxed atmosphere. The Drôme is one of the most beautiful regions of France; vineyards, olive orchards, lavender, sunflowers, wild flowers and fruit orchards abound. Many old towns and villages, reading like a wine list, with their restaurants, shops, museums, wine tasting and local markets, are close at hand. Vaison la Romaine, a Roman town, and Nyons, the olive capital of France, are two of the most famous.

Facilities
The good, main toilet block provides all the necessary facilities. Extra facilities by the pool are opened when needed. Dishwashing and laundry facilities under cover. Washing machine and ironing board. Snack bar and takeaway with limited menu at mid-day and evening in congenial atmosphere (June - Sept). Swimming pool and smaller pool for children (no Bermuda shorts). Volleyball, table tennis and boules. Little in the way of on site entertainment but many off site activities can be booked. Dogs are not accepted.

Open
20 April - 1 October.

At a glance
Welcome & Ambience ✓✓✓✓✓   Location ✓✓✓✓
Quality of Pitches ✓✓✓✓   Range of Facilities ✓✓✓

Directions
From N7 (or A7 autoroute exit 18) south of Montélimar, take D133 (changes to D541) signed Grignan. After 9 km, just before entering Grignan, take D71 towards Charamet and site is shortly on the left. GPS: N44:24.714 E04:53.433

Charges 2005
Per unit incl. 2 persons	€ 13,50 - € 16,00
extra person	€ 4,70
child (under 7 yrs)	€ 3,20
electricity (10A)	€ 4,70

No credit cards.

Reservations
Contact site. Tel: 04 75 46 93 62. Email: info@lestruffieres.com

www.alanrogers.com for latest campsite news

FR26120 Gervanne Camping

Mobile homes ▶ page 438

Bellevue, F-26400 Mirabel et Blacons (Drôme)

This spacious, riverside family run site with 177 pitches, 167 for touring, is divided into two sections. The newer section is adjacent to the bar, restaurant, superb swimming pool, jacuzzi and the large sunbathing terrace from which there are mountain views. The newer pitches are of average size with some shade and are separated by a few small shrubs and trees. The older section is close to the river and on the other side of the road, but is connected to the newer section by an underpass. It is less formally laid out and mature trees offer plenty of shade. All pitches, in both sections, have easy access to electricity (4 or 6A) and there are water points around the site. This interesting historic area on the edge of the Vercors National Park offers opportunities for walking, cycling and other outdoor activities. The pretty hillside villages sit amongst vineyards and fields of lavender and sunflowers.

Facilities

Each section has a well appointed, very clean toilet block with the majority of washbasins in cabins, and a baby room in each with bath, shower and changing facilities and some cabins now with showers and washbasins. Washing machine, tumble dryer, sinks for laundry and dishwashing. Large en-suite unit for disabled people. Bar/restaurant (1/6-15/9) with simple menu, takeaway service and internet terminal. Swimming pool. Small play area, table tennis and boules. Bicycle hire. Only electric and gas barbecues are allowed. Motorcaravan service point. Off site: Supermarket next door. Fishing, canoeing and bathing in the River Drôme adjacent. Riding 5 km. Golf 13 km.

Open

1 April - 1 November.

At a glance

Welcome & Ambience	✓✓✓✓	Location	✓✓✓✓
Quality of Pitches	✓✓✓✓	Range of Facilities	✓✓✓✓

Directions

Site is about 22 km. east of exit 16 (D104 to Crest) on the A7 autoroute. After Crest follow signs to Die for about 6 km. and then turn left (D164A) and cross the river into Mirabel et Blacons, turn left at roundabout and follow signs to campsite.
GPS: N44:42.666 E05:05.409

Charges 2006

Per unit incl. 2 adults	€ 12,10 - € 17,20
extra person	€ 3,40 - € 5,10
child (up to 7 yrs)	€ 1,70 - € 2,60
dog	€ 1,60 - € 2,00
electricity (4/6A)	€ 2,60 - € 3,20

Reservations

Required mid July - end August; write with deposit of € 60 and € 10 fee. Tel: 04 75 40 00 20.
Email: info@gervanne-camping.com

FR26130 Camping L'Hirondelle

Bois de St Ferreol, F-26410 Menglon (Drôme)

This natural, spacious and peaceful site is run by a very friendly family and you are assured a good welcome. It lies in a beautiful valley, south of the Vercors mountains and the Vercors National Park, beside the River Bez, a tributary of the River Drôme which is also close by. It is close to the interesting and ancient small town of Die, the home of the famous Clairette de Die - a sparkling wine mentioned in dispatches by the Romans around 40 AD. In natural openings in woodland, the 100 large to very large pitches all have electricity (3/6A) and are stony and slightly bumpy (rock pegs advised). There are 64 for touring units. If you are lucky you may see red squirrels and beavers and, in June there is a wide variety of flowers including several types of orchids. Although this site is not manicured like some others, the large pitches, separated from others by a wide variety of trees, the 1.5 km. of river bank on one side and the large open campsite field on the other, give both privacy and plenty of space. It is a very good site for couples and young families, to explore this beautiful part of France, partake in the local sporting activities and yet completely unwind and enjoy the views and the beautiful sunset over the mountains. A 'Sites et Paysages' member.

Facilities

Two large toilet blocks offer all the necessary facilities. Very good bar/restaurant with good menus and takeaway (all season). Small range of supplies, including bread, on sale from the bar. Traditional rectangular swimming pool, plus new excellent pool complex with small slide, paddling pool, jacuzzi and a section that flows like a river (1/5 -17/9). Ample room to play and paddle in the river. Playground. Club/TV room. Internet access. Fishing. Football, boules, volleyball, archery. Organised events for young children and adults (animateurs speaking French, Dutch and English). Advice on sporting activities, etc, in the region and bookings made. Occasional evening events. Off site: Riding and bicycle hire 3 km. Canoeing, kayaking, climbing, rambling, mountain biking and cycling over the steep local passes.

At a glance

Welcome & Ambience	✓✓✓	Location	✓✓✓✓
Quality of Pitches	✓✓✓	Range of Facilities	✓✓✓✓

Directions

From Die follow D93 southwards and after 5 km, at Pont de Quart, turn left on D539 signed Châtillon. After approx. 4 km. turn right on D140, signed Menglon. Site entrance is shortly on the right just after crossing a small river.
GPS: N44:40.885 E05:26.846

Charges 2005

Per pitch incl. 2 persons	€ 16,20 - € 22,55
extra person	€ 4,85 - € 6,80
child (2-10 yrs)	€ 3,30 - € 5,65
electricity (3-6A)	€ 3,10 - € 4,20

Camping Cheques accepted.

Reservations

Made with 30% deposit and fee (€ 18.50).
Tel: 04 75 21 82 08.
Email: contact@campinghirondelle.com

Open

28 April - 17 September.

FR26110 Les 4 Saisons Camping de Grâne

Route de Roche-sur-Grâne, F-26400 Grâne (Drôme)

This small, terraced site, open all year, nestles in the hillsides of the lower Drôme valley. With its 80 pitches (73 for touring units), it provides mainly overnight accommodation but it is worth a longer stay. The modern main building houses reception on the top floor, with other facilities below, and provides commanding views across the valley towards Crest and the Vercors. The pitches are level and stony, of variable size, cut out of the hillside and reached by a one-way system on tarmac roads. All pitches have electricity (6/16A), some with water and drain. This is an excellent base for exploring the Drôme valley and the Vercors mountains.

Facilities

A short flight of steps to a lower level leads to the good sanitary facilities that are heated in low season and include roomy showers, washbasins in cabins. Dishwashing and laundry facilities, two washing machines. Baby room. En-suite facilities for disabled visitors (but site is very sloping and not suitable for wheelchairs). Bar, TV room and snacks (15/4-15/9). Small swimming pool (1/6-15/9). Play area. Bicycle hire arranged. Off site: Village nearby with shops catering for most needs. Fishing 1 km. Riding 3 km.

Open

All year.

At a glance

Welcome & Ambience	✓✓✓✓	Location	✓✓✓✓
Quality of Pitches	✓✓✓✓	Range of Facilities	✓✓✓

Directions

From A7 exit 17, or the N7 at Loriol, take the D104 towards Crest. After 8 km. in Grâne take D113 south. Site is on left about 600 m. beyond the village. GPS: N44:43.622 E04:55.618

Charges 2005

Per unit incl. 2 persons	€ 9,50 - € 11,50
extra person	€ 3,00 - € 5,00
child (0-10 yrs)	€ 2,00 - € 4,00
electricity	€ 4,00
dog	€ 3,00

Reservations

Advised for July/Aug; contact site.
Tel: 04 75 62 64 17.
Email: camping.4saisons@wanadoo.fr

FR42010 Camping Municipal de Charlieu

Rue Riottier, F-42190 Charlieu (Loire)

Charlieu is a very attractive little town, well worth a visit, and the well cared for municipal site here would make a good base for exploring the area. The 100 pitches (30 occupied by seasonal units), all have electricity (6-10A). The pitches are reasonably large and well spaced, on level grass. Most are separated by trim hedges but with little shade. There are few facilities on the site as the small, historic town is within about five minutes walk. A card from reception gives free entry to the municipal swimming pool adjacent to the site, plus discounts for the cinema, museums and attractions plus other activities in and around the town.

Facilities

The clean toilet block should be adequate, except perhaps in high season. It has British and Turkish style WCs, facilities for disabled visitors, dishwashing and laundry facilities. Simple snacks and takeaways available. Bicycle hire. Volleyball, boules. Playground. Fishing. Off site: Swimming pool adjacent.

Open

1 May - 30 September.

At a glance

Welcome & Ambience	✓✓✓✓	Location	✓✓✓
Quality of Pitches	✓✓✓	Range of Facilities	✓✓✓

Directions

Charlieu is 20 km. northeast of Roanne. From Pouilly, on the D482, take D487 to Charlieu (5.5 km). The campsite is southeast of the town next to a sports stadium and is signed from the town centre. GPS: N46:09.517 E04:10.844

Charges 2005

Per person	€ 2,15 - € 2,65
child	€ 1,25 - € 1,55
pitch	€ 1,95 - € 3,20

Reservations

Made without fee; contact site. Tel: 04 77 69 01 70.
Email: camp-charlieu@voila.fr

FR69020 Camping Municipal La Grappe Fleurie

La Lie, F-69820 Fleurie (Rhône)

With easy access from both the A6 autoroute and the N6, this site is ideally situated for night stops or indeed for longer stays to explore the vineyards and historic attractions of the Beaujolais region. Virtually surrounded by vineyards, but within walking distance (less than 1 km.) of the pretty village of Fleurie, this is an immaculate small site, with 85 separated touring pitches. All are grassed and fairly level with the benefit of individual access to water, drainage and electrical connections (10A). Baker calls 07.30 hrs - 08.30 hrs. Wine tasting twice per week in high season. Only gas or electric barbecues are allowed. Restaurant and shopping facilities are available in the village.

Facilities
Sanitary facilities in two blocks have British and Turkish style toilets and very satisfactory shower and washing facilities (showers closed 22.00-07.00 hrs). Facilities for disabled visitors. Two cold showers are provided for those wishing to cool down in summer. Washing machine and tumble dryer. Outdoor swimming pool (15m by 7m). Small playground. Table tennis, tennis and volleyball Off site: Fishing 10 km. Fleurie 600 m.

Open
End of March - End of October.

At a glance
Welcome & Ambience	✓✓✓✓	Location	✓✓✓✓
Quality of Pitches	✓✓✓✓	Range of Facilities	✓✓✓✓

Directions
From N6 at Le Maison Blanche/Romanech-Thorins, take D32 to village of Fleurie from where site is signed.

Charges 2005
Per unit incl. 2 persons and electricity	€ 12,50 - € 14,00
tent pitch incl. 2 persons and electricity	€ 11.50
extra person	€ 4,00 - € 5,00
child (5-10 yrs)	€ 2,50 - € 3,00

Reservations
Advised in high season. Tel: 04 74 69 80 07.
Email: camping@fleurie.org

FR69030 Camping Les Portes du Beaujolais

Chemin des Grandes Levées, F-69480 Anse (Rhône)

Being just off the main motorway south to the Mediterranean, this campsite would make a good overnight stop. Also the good public transport from Anse means that it could be used as a base for visiting Lyon. However, despite some noise from the motorway and the main line railway, there is much more to it than that. The well run site has good facilities and modern buildings of traditional design and materials. Its 150 formal pitches are shady, level, numbered and marked, with neatly trimmed grass and hedges, and electrical connections (6A). There are 20 fully serviced pitches (water tap, waste water and drain). At the same time space has been left for those who prefer to pitch in more simple and open surroundings, and other areas have been left for play or just for plants and trees. Just outside the gate the Azergues river passes on its last 200 m. to the Saône, where there are fishing and other water activities. On the other side of the site a narrow gauge railway and its train follow a longer route to a large artificial lake which is planned for 2006. In July/August activities are organised by trained staff.

Facilities
Two modern toilet blocks contain British style WCs, washbasins in cabins and pre-set showers. Facilities for disabled people. Baby changing room. Motorcaravan services. Washing machines. Shop (all season). Gas supplies. Bar, restaurant and takeaway (1/6-15/9). Games room. Internet terminal. Swimming pool and paddling pool (1/5-30/9) Playground. Playing field. Tennis. Minigolf. Boules. Giant chess/draughts. Free loan of barbecues. Off site: Anse 1 km. with supermarket, shops, restaurants, bars, takeaway, ATM, bus stop. Narrow gauge railway at exit. Fishing 200 m. Boat launching 500 m. Bicycle hire 1 km. Riding 1.5 km. Sailing 1.5 km. Golf 2 km.

Open
1 March - 31 October.

At a glance
Welcome & Ambience	✓✓✓✓✓	Location	✓✓✓✓
Quality of Pitches	✓✓✓✓	Range of Facilities	✓✓✓✓

Directions
Anse is on the N6, 6 km. south of the centre of Villefranche-sur-Saône and 21 km. north of Lyon. Site is signed from the northern and southern ends of the village, but from the southern end there is a height limit of 3.1 m.

Charges 2005
Per unit incl. 2 persons and electricity	€ 16,90 - € 18,67
incl. services	€ 18,45 - € 21,63
extra person	€ 4,33 - € 4,80
child (2-7 yrs)	€ 3,38
animal	€ 3,17

Reservations
Contact site. Tel: 04 74 67 12 87.
Email: campingbeaujolais@wanadoo.fr

FR69010 Camping International Porte de Lyon

Porte de Lyon, F-69570 Dardilly (Rhône)

Camping International is a modern overnight site just off the A6 autoroute. Kept busy with overnight trade, reception and the café (in main season) open until quite late. There are 194 separate numbered plots. 150 have electricity (10A), water and waste water drainage. Those for caravans are mostly on hardstandings on a slight slope, with another small grassy part, while those for tents are on a flatter area of grass. A very large commercial centre has been developed just outside the site, with eight hotels, restaurants, a supermarket, petrol station, etc. There is some road noise. Lyon is a very attractive city, especially noted for the excellence of its food, and well worth a visit. A bus stop for the centre (8 km.) is nearby (timetables in reception).

Facilities

Three heated sanitary blocks have free hot water (solar heated) and washbasins in cabins. Dishwashing and laundry sinks. Baby changing facilities and washing machines. Motorcaravan service point. Unheated swimming and paddling pools (15/6-31/8, supervised and free). Playground. TV room. Games room. Reading room (books and local information). Table tennis. Boules. Volleyball. Picnic and barbecue area.

Open

All year.

At a glance

Welcome & Ambience	✓✓✓✓	Location	✓✓✓✓
Quality of Pitches	✓✓✓	Range of Facilities	✓✓✓

Directions

Travelling south, do not take new A46 motorway around Lyon, but continue on A6 autoroute and take exit marked 'Limonest, Dardilly, Porte de Lyon' about 8 km. north of the Lyon tunnel; at once turn left for Porte de Lyon. Porte de Lyon is well signed from most directions.

Charges 2005

Per person	€ 2,98
child (7-15 yrs)	€ 2,40
motorcaravan or 1 axle caravan	€ 8,20
caravan, 2 axle	€ 16,80
tent	€ 6,30
electricity (higher in winter)	€ 3,00 - € 4,60

Reservations

Made if you write, but there is usually space.
Tel: 04 78 35 64 55.
Email: camping.lyon@mairie-lyon.fr

MAP 14

Provence

This is a corner of France that evokes dreamy images of lazy afternoons amongst sleepy village squares, sunny vineyards and beautiful lavender fields basking under the dazzling blue of the sky.

ONLY THE DÉPARTEMENTS FROM THE MOUNTAINOUS REGION OF PROVENCE HAVE BEEN INCLUDED IN THIS SECTION: 04 ALPES-DE-HAUTE-PROVENCE, 05 HAUTES-ALPES, 84 VAUCLUSE

Provence is a region of magical light, bleached landscapes, olive groves, herb-scented garrigue, vineyards and Roman and medieval antiquities. The river valleys provide natural routes through the mountain barrier. Roman monuments can be seen at Orange, and Vaison-la-Romaine, where a 2,000 year old bridge is still in use. Avignon was the site of the papal court and the Palais des Papes at Avignon is a spectacular construction.

The Hautes-Alpes will reward with stunning vistas, peace and quiet. Briançon is the highest town in Europe and many of the high passes are not for the faint-hearted. The Vaucluse, where in the late spring the southern slopes of the Montagne du Luberon are a mass of colour with wild flowers. The extinct volcanic cone of Mont Ventoux provides dramatic views. The scents, the colours and an amazing intensity of light have encouraged artists and writers to settle amidst the sleepy villages, with narrow streets and ancient dwellings topped with sun-baked terracotta tiles, where the air is fragrant with the perfume of wild herbs and lavender.

Places of interest

Avignon: ramparts, old city, Papal Palace, old palace, Calvet museum.

Mont Ventoux: near Carpentras, one of the best known stages of the classic Tour de France annual cycle race.

Orange: Roman city, gateway to the Midi, Colline St Europe.

St Vaison la Romaine: Roman city, the French Pompei.

Cuisine of the region

Influenced by the Savoie area to the north and the Côte d'Azur to the south, with emphasis on herbs and garlic, and fish. The wine region is mainly known for its dry, fruity rosé wines: Bandol, Bellet, Palette, Cassis. Red wines include Côtes du Rhône and Châteauneuf-du-Pape.

Aigo Bouido: garlic and sage soup with bread (or eggs and cheese).

Farcement (Farçon Savoyard): potatoes baked with cream, eggs, bacon, dried pears and prunes.

Pissaladière: Provencal bread dough with onions, anchovies, olives.

Ratatouille: aubergines, courgettes, onions, garlic, red peppers and tomatoes in olive oil.

Tartiflette: potato, bacon, onions and Reblochon cheese.

FR04100 Camping International

Mobile homes ▶ page 439

Route Napoleon, F-04120 Castellane (Alpes-de Haute-Provence)

Camping International has very friendly, English speaking owners and is a reasonably priced, less commercialised site situated in some of the most dramatic scenery in France with good views. The 274 pitches, 130 good sized ones for touring, are clearly marked, separated by trees and small hedges, and all have electricity and water. The bar/restaurant overlooks the swimming pool with its sunbathing area set in a sunny location, and all have fantastic views. In high season English speaking young people entertain children (3-8 years) and teenagers. On some evenings the teenagers are taken to the woods for campfire 'sing-alongs' which can go on till the early hours without disturbing the rest of the site. There are guided walks into the surrounding hills in the nearby Gorges du Verdon - a very popular excursion, particularly in high season. The weather in the hills here is very pleasant without the excessive heat of the coast. Access is good for larger units.

Facilities

Several small toilet blocks are of an older design with small cubicles and, although they are quite basic, the showers are fully controllable (these blocks are due to be replaced soon). One newer block has modern facilities, including those for disabled visitors, but this is not open early and late in the season. Washing machines, dryer and irons and a baby room. Chemical disposal at motorcaravan service point. Fridge hire. Shop. Restaurant/takeaway. Swimming pool (all 1/5-30/9). Club/TV room. Children's animation and occasional evening entertainment in July/Aug. Play area. Volleyball, football and boules pitches. Internet access. Off site: Riding 800 m. Castellane (1.5 km) is a very attractive little town with a superb river, canyon and rapids, ideal for canoeing, rafting and canyoning etc. Good area for walking and biking. Boat launching 5 km.

At a glance

Welcome & Ambience	✓✓✓✓	Location	✓✓✓✓
Quality of Pitches	✓✓✓✓	Range of Facilities	✓✓✓✓

Directions

Site is 1 km. north of Castellane on the N85 'Route Napoleon'.

Charges 2005

Per unit incl. 2 persons	€ 13,00 - € 21,00
extra person	€ 3,00 - € 5,00
electricity (6A)	€ 3,00 - € 5,00
dog	€ 2,00 - € 3,00

Camping Cheques accepted.

Reservations

Necessary for July/Aug. and made with deposit (€ 45), no booking fee for Alan Rogers customers, so mention the guide while booking.
Tel: 04 92 83 66 67.
Email: info@camping-international.fr

Open

1 April - 30 September

FR04020 Castel Camping Le Camp du Verdon

Mobile homes ▶ page 439

Domaine du Verdon, F-04120 Castellane (Alpes-de Haute-Provence)

Close to the 'Route des Alpes' and the Gorges du Verdon, this is a very popular holiday area, the gorge, canoeing and rafting being the main attractions, ideal for active families. Two heated swimming pools and numerous on-site activities during high season help to keep non-canoeists here. Du Verdon is a large level site, part meadow, part wooded, with 500 partly shaded, rather stony pitches (350 for tourists). Numbered and separated by bushes, they vary in size, have 6A electricity, and 120 also have water and waste water. They are mostly separate from the mobile homes (63) and pitches used by tour operators (110). Some overlook the unfenced river Verdon, so watch the children. One can walk to Castellane without using the main road. Dances and discos in July and August suit all age groups - the latest finishing time is around 11 pm. (after that time patrols make sure that the site is quiet). The site is popular and very busy in July and August.

Facilities

The toilet blocks have been refurbished with British style WCs and up-to-date equipment. One block has facilities for disabled visitors. Washing machines and irons. Motorcaravan service and car wash points. Popular restaurant with terrace and bar including room with log fire for cooler evenings. Large well stocked shop. Pizzeria/crêperie. Takeaway (open twice daily). Two heated swimming pools and new paddling pool with 'mushroom' style fountain (all open all season). Entertainers provide games and competitions for all (July and August). Playgrounds. Minigolf, table tennis, archery, basketball and volleyball. Organised walks. Bicycle hire. Riding. Small fishing lake. ATM. Off site: Castellane and the Verdon Gorge 1 km. Riding 2 km. Boat launching 4.5 km. Golf 20 km. River Verdon and many water sports.

At a glance

Welcome & Ambience	✓✓✓	Location	✓✓✓✓✓
Quality of Pitches	✓✓✓✓	Range of Facilities	✓✓✓✓

Directions

From Castellane take D952 westwards towards Gorges du Verdon and Moustiers. Site is 1 km. on left.

Charges 2005

Per unit incl. 1 or 2 persons	€ 17,00 - € 26,00
with 6A electricity	€ 21,00 - € 33,00
dog	€ 2,50

Camping Cheques accepted.

Reservations

Made for any length with deposit (€ 80 - € 110 depending on pitch) and fee (€ 20).
Tel: 04 92 83 61 29.
Email: contact@camp-du-verdon.com

Open

15 May - 15 September.

Camping International
Route Napoléon
04120 Castellane
Tél : +33 492 836 667
Fax : +33 492 837 767
www.campinginternational.fr

Castel Camping Caravaning
Domaine du Verdon
04120 Castellane
Tél : +33 492 836 129
Fax : +33 492 836 937
www.camp-du-verdon.com

Provence
Castellane
Canyon du Verdon

3 SEASONS ELITE

Camping Cheque

LES CASTELS N°209

FR04030 Camping Moulin de Ventre

Niozelles, F-04300 Forcalquier (Alpes-de Haute-Provence)

This is a friendly, English speaking, family run site in the heart of Haute-Provence, near Forcalquier, a bustling small French market town. Attractively located beside a small lake and 28 acres of wooded, hilly land, which is available for walking. Herbs of Provence can be found growing wild and flowers, birds and butterflies abound – a nature lovers delight. The 124 level, grassy pitches for tourists are separated by a variety of trees and small shrubs, 114 of them having electricity (6A; long leads may be necessary). Some pitches are particularly attractive, bordering a small stream. The site is well situated to visit Mont Ventoux, the Luberon National Park, the Gorges du Verdon and a wide range of ancient hill villages with their markets and museums etc. A 'Sites et Paysages' member.

Facilities

The toilet block, recently refurbished, provides very good, clean facilities including washbasins in cabins and facilities for disabled people. Baby bath. Washing and drying machines. Fridge hire. Bread and a few essentials on sale. Bar/restaurant with waiter service, takeaway meals (all season) and themed evenings (high season). Pizzeria. Large and small swimming pools with large shallow area (15/5-15/9). Playground. Fishing and boules. Some activities organised in high season. No discos. Only electric or gas barbecues are permitted. Off site: Shops, local market, doctor, tennis 2 km. Supermarket, chemist, riding, bicycle hire 5 km. Golf 20 km. Walking, cycling.

Open

2 April - 30 September.

At a glance

Welcome & Ambience	✓✓✓✓	Location	✓✓✓✓✓
Quality of Pitches	✓✓✓✓	Range of Facilities	✓✓✓✓

Directions

From A51 motorway take exit 19 (Brillanne). Turn right on N96 then turn left on N100 (westwards signed Forcalquier) for about 3 km. Site is signed on left, just after a bridge 3 km. southeast of Niozelles.

Charges guide

Per unit incl. 2 persons	€ 20,00
incl. electricity	€ 25,00
extra person	€ 5,50
child (0-4 yrs)	€ 3,00
dog	€ 3,00

No credit cards. Camping Cheques accepted.

Reservations

Advisable for July/Aug with 30% deposit and fee (€ 23). Tel: 04 92 78 63 31.
Email: moulindeventre@free.fr

Haute-Provence
Camping Lac du
Moulin de Ventre
04300 Niozelles
Tel: 0033 492 78 63 31
Fax: 0033 492 79 86 92
www.moulindeventre.com
Restaurant open from
15/04/05 to 15/09/05

FR04010 Sunêlia Hippocampe

Mobile homes ▶ page 438

Route de Napoléon, F-04290 Volonne (Alpes-de Haute-Provence)

Hippocampe is a friendly, 'all action' lakeside site situated in a beautiful area of France. The perfumes of thyme, lavender and wild herbs are everywhere and the higher hills of Haute Provence are not too far away. There are 447 level, numbered pitches (243 for touring units), medium to very large (130 sq.m) in size. All have electricity (10A) and 220 have water and drainage, most are separated by bushes and cherry trees. Some of the best pitches border the lake. The restaurant, bar, takeaway and shop have all been completely renewed (2004). This is a family run site with families in mind, with games, aerobics, competitions, entertainment and shows, plus a daily club for younger family members in July/August. A soundproof underground disco is set well away from the pitches and is very popular with teenage customers. Staff tour the site at night ensuring a good night's sleep. The site is, however, much quieter in low season and, with its good discounts, is the time for those who do not want or need entertaining. The Gorges du Verdon is a sight not to be missed and rafting, paragliding or canoe trips can be booked from the site's own tourist information office. Being on the lower slopes of the hills of Haute-Provence, the surrounding area is good for walking and mountain biking. This is a very good site for an active or restful holiday and is suitable for outfits of all sizes. Used by tour operators (20 pitches). English is spoken.

Facilities

Toilet blocks vary from old to modern, all with good facilities that include washbasins in cabins. They are very clean. Washing machines. Motorcaravan service point. Fridge rental. Bread from reception (from 28/4). Shop and bar (all season). Restaurant, pizzeria and barbecue chicken shop (all 29/4-10/9). Large, attractive pool complex (all season) with two pools of differing sizes and depths, heated in early and late seasons. Tennis (free outside 3/7- 21/8). Fishing, canoeing, boules. Many sports facilities to choose from, some with free instruction, including archery (high season). Charcoal barbecues are not permitted. Off site: Bicycle hire 2 km. Riding 6 km. Village of Volonne 600 m. Monuments, ancient churches, museums, markets, festivals and vineyards.

At a glance

Welcome & Ambience	✓✓✓✓✓	Location	✓✓✓✓
Quality of Pitches	✓✓✓✓✓	Range of Facilities	✓✓✓✓✓

Directions

Approaching from the north turn off N85 across river bridge to Volonne, then right to site. From the south right on D4, 1 km. before Château Arnoux.

Charges 2005

Per unit with 2 persons:	
simple pitch:	€ 13,00 - € 27,00
with electricity	€ 16,00 - € 32,00
with water/drainage	€ 16,00 - € 39,00
extra person (over 4 yrs)	€ 3,00 - € 6,50

Special low season offers.
Camping Cheques accepted.

Reservations

Made with deposit (€ 50 - € 95) and fee (€ 25).
Tel: 04 92 33 50 00.
Email: camping@l-hippocampe.com

Open

8 April - 30 September.

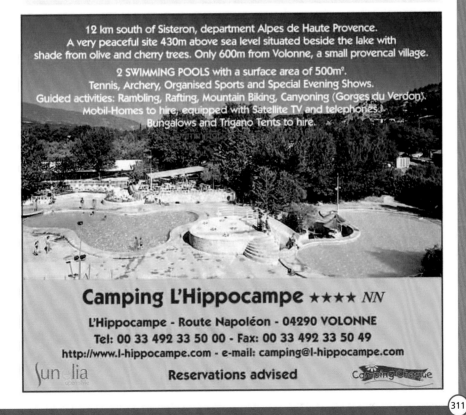

FR04080 Camping Caravaning L'Etoile des Neiges

F-04140 Montclar (Alpes-de Haute-Provence)

This attractive, family run site near the mountain village and ski resort of St Jean Montclar is open most of the year so is suitable for both summer and winter holidays. This beautiful alpine region offers all the usual alpine activities. Being at an altitude of 1,300 m. the nights can get quite cool even in summer. The 121 shady pitches, with 80 for touring, are laid out in terraces and separated by small shrubs and alpine trees. All pitches are close to electricity and water points. An attractive bar and restaurant overlooks the two swimming pools, with the shallow pool having a water slide ideal for children. The site has no shop as the local shops are only a few minutes walk away. Although situated in the southern high Alps, the site can be reached without climbing any stiff gradients. A 'Sites et Paysages' member.

Facilities

The central toilet block, heated in winter, includes washbasins in cabins. Separate room containing facilities for disabled visitors. Two washing machines. Motorcaravan service point. Bar/restaurant. Swimming pool (all amenities open 27/5-9/9). Tennis, table tennis and boules. Two play areas. Rafting and walking organised in July/Aug. Off site: Shops in village a few minutes walk. Bicycle hire and riding in village. Fishing 1.5 km. Watersports and beach at Lac Serre Ponçon 7 km.

Open

15 May - 30 September.

At a glance

Welcome & Ambience	✓✓✓✓✓	Location	✓✓✓✓
Quality of Pitches	✓✓✓✓	Range of Facilities	✓✓✓✓

Directions

Site is 35 km. south of Gap via the D900B. Beyond Serre Ponçon, turn right onto D900 signed Selonnet and St Jean Montclar. On entering St Jean Montclar turn left, go past the chalets and shops and then fork right to the campsite which is on the left. The roads to the site (at 1,300 m.) are steep and can be snowy and icy in winter.

Charges 2005

Per unit incl. 2 persons	€ 12,50 - € 21,00
extra person	€ 4,00 - € 5,00
child (2-5 yrs)	€ 2,50 - € 3,00
electricity (6A)	€ 3,00 - € 4,00
dog	€ 1,50

Camping Cheques accepted.

Reservations

Advised for July/Aug. Deposit of 30% plus € 15 fee.
Tel: 04 92 35 01 29.
Email: contact@etoile-des-neiges.com

FR04060 Camping Caravaning Le Haut-Verdon

RD 908, F-04370 Villars-Colmars (Alpes-de Haute-Provence)

For those seeking a quiet, family site set in most spectacular scenery, Camping Le Haut-Verdon is ideal. It is on the banks of the Verdon, an excellent trout river, which then flows through the spectacular gorge. Surrounded by the majestic peaks of the Alpes-de-Haute-Provence, it is on the doorstep of the Mercantour National Park. Set amongst the pines, the 87 pitches are mostly on the large size but are rather stony. With 73 for touring units, all have electricity (6/10A) but some will require long leads. There is a small village near, and the town of St André is 23 km. English is spoken.

Facilities

The main toilet block, recently refurbished, is heated and includes bidets and washbasins in cabins. Most WCs are British style. Washing machines and irons, dishwashing and laundry sinks. Freezer for ice packs and room for tenters when inclement weather strikes. Motorcaravan service point. Small shop has fresh food. Bar/restaurant and takeaway. Barbecue areas (portable ones banned). Heated swimming and paddling pools (from 1 June). Small play area. Volleyball. Basketball. Giant chess. Boules. Skittle alley. Table tennis. Excellent tennis. TV room. Entertainers organise games and competitions. Fishing. Off site: Bicycle hire and riding 10 km.

Open

1 May - 30 September.

At a glance

Welcome & Ambience	✓✓✓✓✓	Location	✓✓✓✓✓
Quality of Pitches	✓✓✓✓	Range of Facilities	✓✓✓✓✓

Directions

Follow D955 north from St André les Alpes towards Colmar. After about 11 km. the road number changes to D908. Site is on right at the southern edge of Villars-Colmars. Caravans are not advised to use the D908 from Annot or the Col d'Allos from Barcelonnette.

Charges 2005

Per person over 6 yrs	€ 3,00 - € 4,00
child (2-6 yrs)	€ 1,50 - € 2,50
pitch	€ 7,00 - € 12,00
dog	€ 1,00 - € 2,00
electriicty	€ 3,00 - € 4,00

Camping Cheques accepted.

Reservations

Made with deposit (30%) and fee (€ 15.24).
Tel: 04 92 83 40 09.
Email: campinglehautverdon@wanadoo.fr

FR04120 Camping Indigo - Forcalquier

Route de Sigonce, F-04300 Forcalquier (Alpes-de Haute-Provence)

Since this site has acquired new ownership a large modernisation programme has been put in effect. Camping Indigo offers an excellent base for visiting Forcalquier, a 15th century fortified hill town, with its ancient buildings and the Monday market (which has the reputation of being the best in Haute Provence). Although this is an urban site, there are extensive views over the surrounding countryside where there are some excellent walks. The new owners (part of the Indigo group) have arranged for local guides to lead tours of the historic town and areas. The site is secure, with an electronic barrier (card deposit required) and there is no entry between 22.30 and 07.00. The swimming pool is heated to 30°C! The pitches are on grass and are of good size, all with electricity. There are 10 pitches with private water and waste water disposal.

Facilities

The two toilet blocks are undergoing reconstruction - the reconstructed disabled block is excellent and sets the standard for the other two blocks. Showers and wash basins are in cubicles. They are all cleaned twice a day and signed for (rather like British supermarkets). All shops, banks etc. available in town centre, some 200 m. walk. There is a bar, snack bar and take away (1/7-30/9). Play area and paddling pool.

Open

29 March - 1 November.

At a glance

Welcome & Ambience ✓✓✓✓✓ Location ✓✓✓✓✓
Quality of Pitches ✓✓✓✓ Range of Facilities ✓✓✓✓

Directions

From the town centre, follow 'Digne - Sisteron' for 400 metres, turning sharp left at the petrol station, then first right and the site is 200 metres on the right. It is well signed from town.

Charges 2005

Per person	€ 4,50 - € 4,70
child (2-7 yrs)	€ 3,00 - € 3,20
pitch	€ 3,50 - € 10,00
animal	€ 2,00

Reservations

Contact site. Tel: 04 92 75 27 94.
Email: forcalquier@camping-indigo.com

FR05000 Camping des Princes d'Orange

F-05700 Orpierre (Hautes-Alpes)

This attractive, terraced site, set on a hillside above the village, has been gradually and thoughtfully developed by its owners over 20 years. Their genuine, friendly welcome means many families return year upon year, bringing in turn new generations. Divided into five terraces, each with its own toilet block, all its 120 generously sized pitches (96 for tourists) enjoy good shade from trees and wicker canopies and have electricity. In high season one terrace is reserved as a 1-star camping area for young people (no reservations needed). Renowned as a serious rock climbing venue, Orpierre also has an enchanting maze of medieval streets and houses, a walk through is to be recommended – almost like a trip back through the centuries. Whether you choose to drive, climb, walk or cycle there is plenty of wonderful scenery to discover in the immediate vicinity, whilst not far away, exhilarating hang gliding and parascending can be enjoyed. For those seeking to 'get away from it all' in an area of outstanding natural beauty, there can be few more tranquil sites. There can be no doubt that you will be made most welcome.

Facilities

Six toilet blocks with mostly British style WCs and washbasins in cubicles are extremely clean and accessible from all levels. Baby bath. Dishwashing and laundry sinks. Laundry facilities near reception. Bread available from bar each morning (other basics from village). Bar (1/7-31/8)with reasonably priced takeaway service. Heated swimming pool (20 x 10 m), paddling pool (15/6-15/9). Children's play area including small trampoline with safety net. Table tennis, boules and games room. Fridge hire. Only gas barbecues are permitted. Off site: Orpierre with a few shops and bicycle hire 500 m. Fishing 7 km. Nearest shopping centre Laragne 12 km. Riding 19 km. Hang gliding, parascending. Gorges de Guil.

At a glance

Welcome & Ambience	✓✓✓✓✓	Location	✓✓✓✓✓
Quality of Pitches	✓✓✓✓	Range of Facilities	✓✓✓✓

Directions

Turn off N75 road at Eyguians onto D30 – site is signed on left at crossroads in centre Orpierre village.

Charges 2006

Per unit incl. 2 persons	€ 19,50
incl. 3 persons	€ 21,00
extra person	€ 4,00
child (under 7 yrs)	€ 3,00
electricity	€ 3,00

Less 25% in low season. No credit cards.

Reservations

Essential for 14/7-20/8 (min. 14 days) and made with deposit (€ 84) and fee (€ 9). Tel: 04 92 66 22 53. Email: campingorpierre@wanadoo.fr

Open

1 April - 25 October.

FR05030 Camping Les Six Stations

Pont du Fossé, F-05260 St Jean-St Nicolas (Hautes-Alpes)

This is a small, rural, unsophisticated site, run by a very friendly family, lying in the beautiful Drac Noir valley. Level, grassy pitches are set in wooded glades with views of the surrounding mountains but with good shade. The 70 pitches, 48 for touring, all have electricity but very long leads may be necessary. Although the roads to the site offer no problems, the trees and narrow roads around the site makes access to some pitches difficult for large outfits. Some activities are organised in July and August for all the family and walks are arranged to see the marmots and mountain goats.

Facilities

One modern toilet block, heated in winter, with all the usual facilities. Bar (June - Aug). Takeaway (June - Aug). Small swimming pool (June - Aug). Walks and children's activities. Off site: Bicycle hire 1 km. Ski du fond 3 km. Riding 5 km. Restaurant outside gate.

Open

All year.

At a glance

Welcome & Ambience	✓✓✓✓	Location	✓✓✓✓
Quality of Pitches	✓✓✓	Range of Facilities	✓✓✓✓

Directions

Site is northeast of Gap. From N85 take D944 east and continue to Pont du Fossé. Site is on right 1 km. beyond the village. GPS: N44:40.235 E06:14.441

Charges guide

Per pitch incl. 2 persons	€ 12,50
extra person	€ 3,00
electricity (2/4A)	€ 2,50

Reservations

Advised in high season with 25% deposit.
Tel: 04 92 55 91 95. Email: les.6.stations@wanadoo.fr

FR84050 Camping Caravaning La Sorguette

Route d'Apt, F-84800 L'Isle sur la Sorgue (Vaucluse)

This popular, well organised site is well placed, 1.5 km. from Isle sur la Sorgue. You will receive a warm welcome from the English speaking staff. Arranged in groups of four, the 164 medium sized level pitches (124 for touring) all have electricity (4-10A). Each group is separated by tall hedges and most have a little shade during the day. In high season a few competitions are organised (boules or volleyball), plus some children's entertainment, but this is quite low key. Running alongside the site (fenced with a gate), the river Sorgue is only 6 km. from its source in the mountains at Fontaine de Vaucluse. It is still very clear and used for canoeing, swimming or fishing. Isle sur la Sorgue is a very attractive small town; the river forms small canals and waterways, interspersed with a number of water wheels. There are many bars and restaurants, some with seating overlooking the water which has a cooling effect in summer. The markets on Thursday and Sunday (free shuttle bus) fill the old streets, and brightly coloured pottery, table covers, fruit and vegetables make it a photographer's paradise. Many interesting towns and villages, Avignon, Gordes and Orange should not be missed.

Facilities

Three well placed, clean and well maintained toilet blocks include some washbasins in cubicles for ladies, mainly British style WCs and dishwashing and laundry sinks. Two blocks have washing machines, dryer, ironing boards and clothes lines. Units for disabled people at all three. Baby room. Motorcaravan service point. Fridge hire. Shop and bar with snacks (1/7-25/8) set well away from the pitches, outside the entrance which ensures that the occasional entertainment in July/Aug does not disturb campers. Play area, volleyball, half-court tennis and basketball. Canoe and bicycle hire. Internet access. Off site: Indoor/outdoor swimming pools (preferential rates) 2 km. Fishing and riding 5 km. Walking and cycling circuits. Canoeing on River Sorgue.

At a glance

Welcome & Ambience	✓✓✓✓✓	Location	✓✓✓✓
Quality of Pitches	✓✓✓	Range of Facilities	✓✓✓

Directions

Site is 1.5 km. east of L'Isle sur la Sorgue on the N100 towards Apt. It is well signed from the town. GPS: N43:54.893 E05:04.655

Charges 2005

Per unit incl. 2 persons	€ 15,40 - € 19,20
extra person (over 7 yrs)	€ 5,20 - € 6,60
child (1-6 yrs)	€ 2,60 - € 3,30
electricity (4/10A)	€ 3,50 - € 4,60
animal	€ 2,10 - € 2,60

Reservations

Made for a minimum of 1 week with deposit (€ 60), fee (€ 20) and cancellation insurance (€ 7.50). Tel: 04 90 38 05 71. Email: sorguette@wanadoo.fr

Open

15 March - 15 October.

FR84070 Camping Club International Carpe Diem

Route de St Marcellin, B.P. 68, F-84110 Vaison-la-Romaine (Vaucluse)

Perhaps Carpe Diem is a shade pretentious with its Greek statues and amphitheatre surround to its main pool. A developing site, it is only a few years old and will no doubt mellow as the trees and shrubs grow and old and new blend together. It is a good site for active families seeking all day entertainment and the situation is quite impressive with magnificent views over one of the most beautiful parts of France, yet only 800 m. from the village of Vaison-la-Romaine. There are 232 pitches with 152 small to medium sized, grass touring pitches all with electricity and many with some degree of shade. A new terraced area has mobile homes, chalets and unshaded touring pitches. The main pool is impressive with its tiered seating, plants, etc. It is used as a theatre for evening entertainment. A simple square pool is near the play area with grass surrounds.

Facilities

The central toilet block – with fountain – provides mainly British and a few Turkish style toilets, washbasins in cabins and showers with an unusual cupboard for clothes. Dishwashing and laundry sinks. Small editions of everything are provided for children. Washing machine. Extra facilities are behind the main pool. Motorcaravan service point. Reception provides a small shop (25/3-1/11). Bar (3/6-2/9) near the main pool and pizzeria (14/4-30/9). TV room. Swimming pools (3/4-21/10). Play area. Minigolf, archery (cross-bow), volleyball, football and basketball. Mountain bike hire. Mini-club. Extensive entertainment programme and off site activities in high season. There is a charge for participation in sports and entertainment. Barbecues for hire. Off site: Fishing 1 km. Riding 2 km. Golf 20 km. Organised canoeing, riding, climbing, walking, mountain biking. Vaison la Romaine (800 m) with its magnificent Roman ruins, shops, restaurants, market and excellent wine.

At a glance

Welcome & Ambience	✓✓✓✓	Location	✓✓✓✓
Quality of Pitches	✓✓✓✓	Range of Facilities	✓✓✓✓✓

Directions

Leave Vaison-la-Romaine on D938 heading south towards Carpentras. 1 km. beyond the 'Super U' roundabout turn left on D151, signed St Marcellin. Site entrance is on the left immediately after the junction. GPS: N44:14.064 E05:05.381

Charges 2006

Per pitch incl. 1-3 persons	€ 16,00 - € 27,00
extra person	€ 4,00 - € 6,00
child (2-10 yrs)	€ 2,50 - € 5,00
electricity (6/10A)	€ 3,20 - € 4,70
dog	€ 2,00 - € 2,50

Camping Cheques accepted.

Reservations

Made with deposit and fee (€ 77). Tel: 04 90 36 02 02. Email: contact@camping-carpe-diem.com

Open

25 March - 1 November.

FR84060 Camping l'Ayguette

CD 86 Faucon, F-84110 Vaison-la-Romaine (Vaucluse)

Set in the beautiful region of north Provence, surrounded by vineyards and wooded hills, this spacious campsite is ideal for rest and relaxation. It also makes an ideal base for touring this very interesting region. The 99 slightly sloping pitches, all for touring, are widely spaced out on terraces amongst pine and oak trees giving plenty of dappled shade and privacy. All have 10A electricity, although some long leads may be necessary. Rock pegs are essential. Only a few pitches are suitable for large units. The nature of the site means that some pitches are a considerable distance from the amenities which may not be ideal for those with walking difficulties. The reception building houses a bar, snack bar, small shop and terrace. Close by is an attractive swimming pool (heated all season) and sunbathing area. There is some low key entertainment once a week and some children's activities in July and August, but the emphasis is on a quiet and peaceful site. This region is famous for its wines. Visit the many medieval towns and perched villages with their markets and châteaux.

Facilities

Two modern and well equipped toilet blocks, one heated and one recently refurbished to a high standard including hair dryers, soap dispensers and hand dryers. Washbasins in cabins. En-suite room for disabled campers or families with young children. Washing machines. Heated swimming pool with sun terrace (all season). Bar, snack bar and takeaway (July/Aug). Small shop selling essentials with international newspapers and bread to order. Table tennis, darts, pool table and table football. Volleyball. Badminton. Playground. Occasional low key entertainment in high season and some activities for children. Only gas and electric barbecues are allowed. Off site: No public transport. Faucon with bar and restaurant. The Roman town of Vaison la Romaine with shops, banks, bar/restaurants, market and supermarkets 4 km. Nyons with shops bar/restaurants market and museums 15 km. Mont Ventoux 35 km. Fishing and bicycle hire 5 km. Riding 7 km.

At a glance

Welcome & Ambience	✓✓✓✓	Location	✓✓✓✓
Quality of Pitches	✓✓✓✓	Range of Facilities	✓✓✓

Directions

From Vaison la Romaine take the D938 towards Nyons. Shortly turn right on D71, signed St Romain-en-Viennois. Drive through village and then turn right on D86. Site is well signed, on the right. GPS: N44:15.732 E05:07.748

Charges 2005

Per unit incl. 1 or 2 persons	€ 11,00 - € 17,40
incl. electricity	€ 13,50 - € 19,90
extra person	€ 3,50 - € 5,00
child (2-11 yrs)	€ 2,00 - € 3,00
dog	free - € 1,50

Long stay reductions off season.

Reservations

Advised for high season; made with deposit (€ 48) and fee (€ 12). Tel: 04 90 46 40 35. Email: info@ayguette.com

Open

15 April - 30 September.

FR84080 Camping Caravaning La Simioune

F-84500 Bollène (Vaucluse)

This unsophisticated, rural site is a peaceful base especially for those who love horses and it is open all year. Well off the beaten track and set amongst tall pines on sandy, undulating ground, it is bordered on one side by a vineyard. However, please don't go to La Simioune if you prefer a regimented site with neat lawns and flower beds or lots of entertainment. This is actually a riding school with local children coming for lessons. Campers can also hire horses by the hour, although the favourite seems to be the day-long guided trek with a river crossing and picnic lunch (all at reasonable prices). The 80 unmarked and uneven pitches, many used for long stay caravans, are of varying size and shape, most with electricity. Long leads and rock pegs are needed. An area of woodland is set aside for those with tents who prefer a natural environment. The area has many lovely medieval villages and vineyards. Some (not all!) will visit the crocodile farm down by the River Rhône. The site is not recommended for large units.

Facilities

The basic toilet block is quite old but kept clean. Small room for babies with child's WC. Complete room for disabled people although the site itself will be difficult for wheelchairs and those with walking difficulties due to the sandy and undulating terrain. Laundry and dishwashing sinks with two hot taps to draw from and a washing machine. Small bar serves simple meals mid June to mid Sept. Takeaway to order all year. Small unheated swimming and paddling pool (June - Sept). Excellent riding (30 horses) in a large area next to the site. Table tennis, boules, volley-ball. Central barbecue area (individual ones not permitted). Off site: Tennis, fishing, walking and canoeing nearby. Shops and restaurants at Bollène 5 km.

Open

All year.

At a glance

Welcome & Ambience	✓✓✓	Location	✓✓✓
Quality of Pitches	✓✓✓	Range of Facilities	✓✓✓

Directions

From A7 take exit 19 (at Bollène). At first roundabout take third exit signed Suze la Rousse (site signed). Just after traffic lights and before river turn left, site signed (Rue Alphonse Daudet) and follow signs for approx. 5 km. (the last section is up a windy, narrow and bumpy road). GPS: N44:17.811 E04:47.245

Charges 2005

Per person	€ 3,40
child (under 7 yrs)	€ 1,50
pitch	€ 3,00 - € 3,10
electricity (6A)	€ 2,30
animal	€ 1,50

No credit cards.
15% reduction off season (15/9-15/6).

Reservations

Recommended in high season with 20% depostit and € 10 fee. Tel: 04 90 30 44 62. Email: la-simioune@wanadoo.fr

FR84090 Camping du Pont d'Avignon

Ile de la Barthelasse, F-84000 Avignon (Vaucluse)

This is a city site, yet it is in a quiet location and only a short walk or ferry ride from the town. With its island situation, a few pitches have views of the Pope's palace which is floodlit at night. There are 300 level pitches, some on grass and some with hardstanding. 118 with electricity (10A). All have some shade but those with electricity are well shaded. A good play area, tennis courts and volleyball pitch are in the centre of the site separating the tent pitches on one side and the electric pitches on the other. Many pitches are separated by hedges. The restaurant, bar and terrace overlook the attractive pool. The site, although close to the historic centre of Avignon, has a very rural feel, due no doubt to the many flowering trees and shrubs and the fact it is on an island. English is spoken at reception.

Facilities

Toilet blocks are placed around the periphery of the site and kept very clean and well maintained. Mainly British style toilets, roomy showers and all washbasins in cubicles. Dishwashing and laundry sinks. Three washing machines and a dryer. One block has full facilities for disabled visitors. Motorcaravan service point. Well stocked shop (1/4-30/9). Bar/restaurant and takeaway (1/4-30/9). Swimming pool and paddling pool (15/5-15/9). Play area with new climbing frame. Tennis (free). Volleyball. Bicycle hire (July/Aug). Internet access.

Open

20 March - 29 October.

At a glance

| Welcome & Ambience | ✓✓✓✓ | Location | ✓✓✓✓✓ |
| Quality of Pitches | ✓✓✓✓ | Range of Facilities | ✓✓✓✓ |

Directions

Site is on the Ile de la Barthelasse in the middle of the river Rhône, to the west of the city, almost opposite the famous bridge. It is well signed from the many roads into Avignon but the ring road has some very complex junctions. It is accessed from Pont Daladier towards Villeneuve les Avignon. Just after crossing the first section of the river fork right, site signed. Site is about 1 km. on the right.
GPS: N43:57.092 E04:48.116

Charges 2005

Per unit incl. 2 persons	€ 12,00 - € 32,50
extra person	€ 2,80 - € 4,10
child (3-12 yrs)	free - € 4,10
electricity	€ 2,50 - € 3,00
dog	€ 0,85 - € 2,10

Camping Cheques accepted.

Reservations

Essential for July/Aug. Tel: 04 90 80 63 50.
Email: info@camping-avignon.com

FR84110 Camping Les Verguettes

Route de Carpentras, F-84570 Villes-sur-Auzon (Vaucluse)

Friendly and family run, this small campsite is surrounded by fields and vineyards and should appeal to those seeking a more relaxed holiday. It is probably not the ideal site for active youngsters. It lies on the outskirts of the village of Villes-sur-Auzon and at the foot of Mont Ventoux and the Nesque Gorge (1 km). Of the 89 pitches 81 are for touring. They are on the small side and are arranged in groups of six either side of the campsite road and are attractively laid out, separated by a variety of trees and shrubs. They all have electrical connections (5A but a few with 10A) but long leads may be necessary. Close to the attractive swimming pool are the bar and small outside restaurant which offers a simple menu - a pleasant place to relax after a day sightseeing.

Facilities

Two toilet blocks, one near the entrance and other at the far end of the site. The buildings are old but have been refurbished to a high standard and one is heated in low season. Motorcaravan service point. Bar (all season). Small outside restaurant (1/5-15/9) with simple menu and takeaway. Small swimming pool. Tennis. Minigolf. Boules. Table tennis, table football and small games/TV room. Internet point. Off site: Wine tasting, walking, cycling. Mont Ventoux, Nesque Gorge 1 km. Carpentras 10 km.

Open

1 April - 15 October.

At a glance

| Welcome & Ambience | ✓✓✓✓ | Location | ✓✓✓✓ |
| Quality of Pitches | ✓✓✓✓ | Range of Facilities | ✓✓✓✓ |

Directions

Leave A7 autoroute at exit 22 just south of Orange and take D950 to Carpentras. Then take D942 east, signed Sault and Mazan. Site is about 10 km. on the right just after a roundabout on entering village of Villes-sur-Auzon.

Charges 2005

Per unit incl. 2 persons	€ 16,40 - € 18,80
incl. electricity	€ 18,90 - € 21,90
extra person	€ 4,50 - € 5,50
child (0-7 yrs)	€ 2,30 - € 2,80
water and drainage	€ 2,30 - € 2,80
animal	€ 2,10 - € 2,50

Camping Cheques accepted.

Reservations

Made with deposit (€ 16) and booking fee (€ 23). Tel: 04 90 61 88 18.
Email: info@provence-camping.com

FR84100 Camping Le Soleil de Provence

Route de Nyons, F-84110 St Romain en Viennois (Vaucluse)

The views from this spacious, well organised, family run site must take some beating. The 360 degree panorama includes Mont Ventoux, the surrounding hills and the vineyards of northern Provence. It offers an excellent base from which to explore this very interesting area. Within a few kilometres one can find old towns such as Nyons, the olive capital of France, Orange and Avignon. The countryside is full of vineyards, lavender and sunflowers and the mountains offer a challenge to walkers and cyclists. The site has been developed to a high standard. The 162 pitches are of average size, with 140 for touring. They are separated by hedges and a variety of young trees offering only a little shade. They are all supplied with 10A electricity and there are a good number of water points. The excellent pool, surrounded by a sunbathing terrace, and overlooked by the bar, is an unusual shape with an island in the centre. Although there is no paddling pool one end of the pool is very shallow. There is some organised entertainment in July and August but the emphasis is on a quiet and peaceful environment and is an ideal site for relaxing and unwinding.

Facilities

Two modern toilet blocks, heated early and late season, are very well appointed and include washbasins in cabins, facilities for disabled visitors and a baby changing room. Dishwashing and laundry sinks, washing machine, dryer and facilities for ironing. Motorcaravan service point. Small shop for bread, etc, open on demand. Bar and snack bar open all season. Swimming pool. Small play area. Volleyball, table tennis and boules. Off site: Tennis 1 km. Vaison la Romaine 4 km. Rafting, hiking, cycling and mountain biking 4 km. Bicycle hire 5 km. Fishing 15 km.

Open

15 March - 31 October.

At a glance

| Welcome & Ambience | ✓✓✓✓ | Location | ✓✓✓✓✓ |
| Quality of Pitches | ✓✓✓✓ | Range of Facilities | ✓✓✓ |

Directions

Site is 4 km. north of Vaison la Romaine on the D938 road to Nyons. Turn right, signed St Romain-en-Viennois (site signed) and take first left to site. GPS: N44:16.141 E05:06.358

Charges 2005

Per person	€ 3,50 - € 5,50
child (0-7 yrs)	€ 2,50 - € 3,00
pitch	€ 2,50 - € 3,00
car	€ 2,50 - € 3,00
electricity (10A)	€ 2,50

No credit cards.

Reservations

Advised for July/Aug. Tel: 04 90 46 46 00. Email: info@camping-soleil-de-provence.fr

---

FR84020 Domaine Naturiste de Bélézy

Mobile homes ▶ page 440

F-84410 Bédoin (Vaucluse)

At the foot of Mt Ventoux, surrounded by beautiful scenery, Bélézy is an excellent naturist site with many amenities and activities and the ambience is relaxed and comfortable. The 238 marked pitches are set amongst many varieties of trees and shrubs. Electricity points (12A) are plentiful but long leads are necessary. The emphasis is on informality and concern for the environment and during high season cars are banned from the camping area (supervised parking nearby). So far as naturism is concerned, the emphasis is on personal choice (and weather conditions!), the only stipulation being the requirement for complete nudity in the pools and pool area. An area of natural parkland with an orchard, fishpond and woodland (complete with red squirrels), has tennis courts, swimming pools and paddling pool. The largest pool is for swimming and relaxation (you may enjoy a musical serenade) and the smaller pool (heated 26/3-2/10) is used for watersports and aquarobics. Near the pool area is the smart restaurant, with terrace, and the mellow old Mas (Provençal farmhouse) that houses many of the activities and amenities. There is a hydrotherapy centre to tone up and revitalise. Member 'France 4 Naturisme'.

Facilities

Sanitary blocks are a little different. The newer ones are of a standard type and excellent quality, with free hot showers in cubicles and washbasins in cabins. One block, recently refurbished, has heating in low season. Another has a superb children's section. In the same area the adult block has hot showers in the open air, screened by stone dividers. Well stocked shop (26/3-30/9). Restaurant provides excellent food and takeaway meals at affordable prices. Two swimming pools and a paddling pool. Sauna. Two tennis courts. Boules and table tennis. Adventure play area. Activities include painting, pottery and language lessons (not in July/Aug). Archery. Music (bring your instrument). Guided walks. Children's club. Library and information centre. Disco. Hydrotherapy centre (1/4-30/9) - including steam baths, massage and seaweed packs, osteopathy, Chinese medicine (including acupuncture) and Bach therapies. Barbecues are prohibited but there is a central barbecue area. Pets are not accepted. Off site: Bédoin 1 km.

At a glance

| Welcome & Ambience | ✓✓✓✓✓ | Location | ✓✓✓✓ |
| Quality of Pitches | ✓✓✓✓ | Range of Facilities | ✓✓✓✓✓ |

Directions

From A7 autoroute or RN7 at Orange, take D950 southeast to Carpentras, then northeast via D974 to Bédoin. Site is signed in Bédoin, being about 1.5 km. northeast of the village. GPS: N44:08.011 E05:11.247

Charges 2005

Per unit incl. 2 persons	€ 18,50 - € 32,50
extra person	€ 5,00 - € 8,00
child (3-8 yrs)	€ 4,00 - € 7,50
large pitch	€ 5,00 - € 8,00
pitch with water, drainage and sink	€ 5,20
electricity (12A)	€ 4,20

Various offers and reductions outside high season. Camping Cheques accepted.

Reservations

Write with deposit (25%) and fee (€ 30). Tel: 04 90 65 60 18. Email: info@belezy.com

Open

21 March - 2 October.

MAP 15

Rolling fields of yellow sunflowers, the Armagnac vineyards and crumbling, ancient stone buildings amidst the sleepy villages make this colourful region popular with those who enjoy good food, good wine and a taste of the good life.

Midi-Pyrénées

DÉPARTEMENTS: 09 ARIÈGE, 31 HAUTE-GARONNE, 32 GERS, 65 HAUTES-PYRÉNÉES, 81 TARN, 82 TARN-ET GARONNE. WE HAVE LEFT OUT THE DÉPARTEMENTS OF AVEYRON (12) AND LOT (46), WHICH ARE IN OUR DORDOGNE/AVEYRON REGION

Still a relatively unknown region, the Midi-Pyrénées is the largest region of France, extending from the Dordogne in the north to the Spanish border. It is blessed by radiant sunshine and a fascinating range of scenery. High chalk plateaux, majestic peaks, tiny hidden valleys and small fortified sleepy villages, which seem to have changed little since the Middle Ages, contrast with the high-tech, industrial and vibrant university city of Toulouse.

Lourdes is one of the most visited pilgrimage sites in the world. Toulouse-Lautrec, the artist, was born at Albi, the capital of the département of Tarn. Much of the town is built of pink brick which seems to glow when seen from a distance. In the east, the little town of Foix, with its maze of steep, winding streets, is a convenient centre from which to explore the prehistoric caves at Niaux and the Aladdin's Cave of duty-free gift shops in the independent state of Andorra. The Canal du Midi that links Bordeaux to the Mediterranean was commissioned by Louis XIV in 1666 and is still in working order.

Places of interest

Albi: birthplace and Museum of Toulouse-Lautrec, imposing Ste Cécile cathedral with 15th century fresco of 'The Last Judgement'.

Auch: capital of ancient Gascony, boasts a fine statue of d'Artágnan.

Collonges-la-Rouge: picturesque village of Medieval and Renaissance style mansions and manors.

Conques: 11th century Ste Foy Romanesque church.

Cordes: medieval walled hilltop village.

Foix: 11th/12th century towers on rocky peak above town; 14th century cathedral.

Lourdes: famous pilgrimage site where Ste Bernadette is said to have spoken to the Virgin Mary in a grotto and known for the miracles said to have been performed there.

Cuisine of the region

Food is rich and strongly seasoned, making generous use of garlic and goose fat, and there are some excellent regional wines. Seafood such as oysters, salt-water fish, or piballes from the Adour river are popular.

Cassoulet: stew of duck, sausages and beans.

Confit de Canard (d'oie): preserved duck meat.

Grattons (Graisserons): a mélange of small pieces of rendered down duck, goose and pork fat.

Magret de canard: duck breast fillets

Poule au pot: chicken simmered with vegetables.

Ouillat (Ouliat): Pyrénées soup: onions, tomatoes, goose fat and garlic.

Tourtière Landaise: a sweet of Agen prunes, apples and Armagnac.

FR09020 Camping L'Arize

Mobile homes ▶ page 440

Lieu-dit Bourtol, F-09240 La Bastide-de-Sérou (Ariège)

You will receive a warm welcome from Dominique and Brigitte at this friendly little family site and Brigitte speaks excellent English. The site sits in a delightful, tranquil valley among the foothills of the Pyrénées and is just east of the interesting village of La Bastide de Sérou beside the River Arize (good trout fishing). The river is fenced for the safety of children on the site, but may be accessed just outside the gate. Deer and wild boar are common in this area and may be sighted in quieter periods. The owners have built this site from ground level over the last few years and have put much love and care into its development. The 70 large pitches are neatly laid out on level grass within the spacious site. All have 3/6A electricity (French type sockets) and are separated into bays by hedges and young trees. An extension to the site for 2006 will add 24 large, fully serviced pitches and further small toilet block. Discounts have been negotiated for several of the local attractions (details are provided in the comprehensive pack provided on arrival - in your own language). This is a comfortable and relaxing base for touring this beautiful part of the Pyrénées with easy access to the medieval town of Foix and even Andorra for duty-free shopping.

Facilities

The central sanitary block (unheated) includes washbasins in cabins and good facilities for babies and disabled people. Laundry room with dryer. Dishwashing under cover. Chemical disposal (into a large holding tank - the organic sewage system is incompatible with chemicals). Motorcaravan service point. Small swimming pool with paved sunbathing area. Entertainment in high season, weekly barbecues and welcome drinks on Sundays. Fishing, riding and bicycle hire on site. Off site: Golf 5 km. Several restaurants and shops within a few minute's drive. The nearest restaurant is located at the national stud for the famous Merens horses just 200 m. away and will deliver takeaway meals to your pitch.

At a glance

Welcome & Ambience	✓✓✓✓✓	Location	✓✓✓✓
Quality of Pitches	✓✓✓✓	Range of Facilities	✓✓✓✓

Directions

Site is southeast of the village La Bastide-de-Sérou. Take the D15 towards Nescus and site is on right after about 1 km. GPS: N43:00.109 E01:26.723

Charges 2006

Per pitch incl. 2 persons	
and electricity	€ 16,40 - € 23,70
extra person	€ 4,00 - € 5,20
child (0-7 yrs)	€ 3,00 - € 3,60
dog	€ 1,00 - € 1,50

Discounts for longer stays in mid and low season.

Reservations

Made with 25% deposit and fee (€ 18). Tel: 05 61 65 81 51. Email: camparize@aol.com

Open

10 March - 6 November.

FR09080 Camping du Lac

RN 20, F-09000 Foix (Ariège)

Du Lac is a traditional, urban lakeside site just 3 km. north of the very pretty town of Foix. There is both road and rail noise (the site is alongside the old N20) but there is space to manoeuvre at the entrance. The site is informally divided into four areas, one for mobile homes. The other areas are generally flat or slightly sloping and some shade can be found under mature trees. There are 135 pitches, most with electricity (8/13A). Access to the lake is through a gate which is locked at night and the fence is secure. Children will need supervision in this area. The lake is owned by a separate company but campers have free use of the attractive area. Here you will find canoeing and pedaloes, along with fishing, or just picnics and barbecues with a small bar operating. The lake is not for swimming as there is a fair amount of forbidding green weed but there is a clear area for canoes. Groups of young people and backpackers are accepted. The site is good for visiting Foix and exploring the local area.

Facilities

Four unisex sanitary blocks are of different designs. Two older stone and concrete blocks to the rear of the site are supplemented by two slightly newer wooden ones with more modern fittings. However, none was very clean when we visited and facilities are cramped. One of the little blocks contains a washing machine, excellent facilities for disabled campers and a well equipped baby room. Reception sells basic goods but no fresh food. Snack bar and bar/drinks stall close to the pool. Small swimming pool and separate paddling pool. Play areas around the site and another by the lake. Watersports, fishing and canoe instruction (hire charges apply). TV room, electronic games. Tennis court and boules pitch. Some animation in high season. Torches are necessary. Off site: Cycling and walking tours, riding, golf or even white water rafting.

At a glance

Welcome & Ambience	✓✓✓	Location	✓✓✓
Quality of Pitches	✓✓✓	Range of Facilities	✓✓✓

Directions

From the north leave the N20 at exit 10 and take the old road towards the town. Site is well signed on the left, 3 km. north of the town centre (avoid new bypass and tunnel). GPS: N42:59.366 E01:36.942

Charges 2005

Per unit incl. 2 persons	
and electricity	€ 13,00 - € 35,00
extra person	€ 2,00 - € 5,00
dog	€ 0,50 - € 1,50

Camping Cheques accepted.

Reservations

Advised for July/Aug. Tel: 05 61 65 11 58. Email: camping-du-lac@wanadoo.fr

Open

All year.

FR09050 Camping Municipal La Prade

F-09110 Sorgeat (Ariège)

Superbly situated high up on the mountainside overlooking the valley this site has magnificent views, with the river 300 m. distant and a lake at 2 km. A small site, it provides just 40 pitches on terraces, some of which are occupied by long stay units. Well supervised, with the warden present at varying times, the site is kept very clean. A small stream tinkles through the edge of the site and the hills towering above it reverberate with the sounds of goat bells. This is a most reasonably priced campsite.

Facilities

The original, rather small sanitary block has only two showers and two WCs in each half. However, a second block has now been added and standards are very high. Hot water is provided for dishwashing. Good facilities for the disabled. Washing machine. Small play area. Off site: Fishing 0.5 km. Riding and bicycle hire 5 km.

Open

All year.

At a glance

| Welcome & Ambience | ✓✓✓ | Location | ✓✓✓✓ |
| Quality of Pitches | ✓✓✓✓ | Range of Facilities | ✓✓✓ |

Directions

From Ax-les-Thermes take D613 towards Quillan for 4 km. Turn on D52 and continue for 1 km. Bear left at first junction up through Sorgeat village to site. GPS: N42:43.974 E01:51.234

Charges 2005

Per person	€ 2,90
pitch	€ 1,60 - € 1,80
electricity (5/10A)	€ 2,70 - € 5,20

Reservations

Advised for high season. Tel: 05 61 64 36 34.
Email: meciriesotseat@wanadoo.fr

FR09060 Camping Le Pré Lombard

F-09400 Tarascon-sur-Ariege (Ariège)

Didier Mioni, the manager here follows the town motto S'y passos, y demoros – 'if you wish to come here, you will stay here' in his aim to ensure your satisfaction on his site. This busy, good value site is located beside the attractive river Ariége on the outskirts of the town. There are around 180 level, grassy, numbered pitches with shade provided by a variety of trees. At the rear of the site are 60 site-owned chalets and mobile homes. Electricity (10A) is available to all. A gate in the fence provides access to the river bank for fishing (licences required). Open for a long season, it is an excellent choice for early or late breaks, or as a stop-over en-route to the winter sun destinations in Spain. This region of Ariège is in the foothills of the Pyrénées and 45 km. from Andorra. At Tarascon itself you can go underground at the Parc Pyrénéen de l'Art Préhistorique to view prehistoric rock paintings, or the really adventurous can take to the air for paragliding, hangliding, or microlighting.

Facilities

Five sanitary units of varying age, design and size (not all open in low season). Mostly British WCs, open and cubicled washbasins. Facilities for disabled people. Laundry. Excellent motorcaravan service point. Bar and takeaway (open according to demand). Shop Good restaurant with entertainment and dancing (15/5-15/9). Fenced, unsupervised heated swimming pool (15/5-15/9). Separate playgrounds for toddlers and older children. Video games machines, table tennis, table football, boules. Fishing. Internet access. TV. Full programme of entertainment for families in main season. Activity programmes for small groups all year (ski-ing and husky rides in winter, family walking in summer). Off site: Supermarket 300 m. Town 800 m. Riding 5 km. Golf 15 km. Skiing 20 km.

At a glance

| Welcome & Ambience | ✓✓✓✓ | Location | ✓✓✓✓ |
| Quality of Pitches | ✓✓✓✓ | Range of Facilities | ✓✓✓✓ |

Directions

Site is 800 m. south of the town centre adjacent to the river. From north, turn off main N20 into the town centre and there are prominent signs. From south (Andorra) site signed at roundabout on town approach. GPS: N42:50.391 E01:36.720

Charges 2005

Per unit incl. 2 adults and 6A electricity	€ 18,00 - € 25,00
extra person	€ 5,00 - € 8,00
child under 4 yrs	free

Camping Cheques accepted.

Reservations

Advised for high season. Tel: 05 61 05 61 94.
Email: leprelombard@wanadoo.fr

Open

28 January - 15 November.

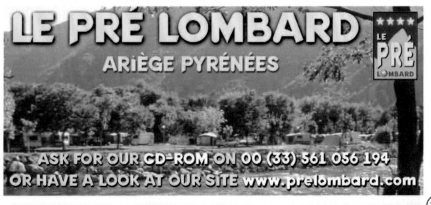
321

FR09090 Naturist Camping Millfleurs

Le Tuilier Gudas, F-09120 Varilhes (Ariège)

Millfleurs is a peaceful naturist site in a secluded location for mature naturists. Owned by a Dutch couple, Gert and Annie Kos who provide a warm welcome and speak excellent English, it really is camping at a relaxed and sublime level. It is so peaceful with some 70 acres of woods and meadows to explore providing guided naturist walks in total privacy. Annie has found 16 different types of orchids and keeps a picture record in the 'salle de reunion'. The long gravel drive leads to a traditional farmhouse housing the campsite office. The site has 40 large flat pitches (26 with 4/8A electricity) on well spaced terraces, but there are also very secluded pitches in wooded areas with shade, or you can pitch a tent in the meadows if you prefer. Long leads are required if you decide to pitch off the terraces. There are few of the normal camping leisure facilities here and the site is definitely aimed at the more mature naturist camper. Transport is required as there is no bus service. Explore the nearby mediaeval town of Foix with its stunning castle towering over the busy centre, and investigate the history of the Cathares and the region with its underground rivers and caves. With its temperate climate, the Foix valley is a prime area for growing the grapes for the white wine used in the production of the famous Cava.

Facilities

An excellent central unisex toilet block, well thought out, includes great facilities for disabled campers, inside and outside showers and cheerful flowers and potted plants. Bread available to order in high season. Guests dine together in the 'salle de reunion' within the farmhouse two nights a week (Sat/Wed) or you just relax and meet friends for a drink. Refrigerator with drinks operated on an honesty system. Petanque court and guide book for walks and cycle rides in local area. Torches essential at night. Pick ups from airports and stations can be arranged. Off site: The coast is approximately 1.5 hours.

Open

1 April - 15 October.

At a glance

Welcome & Ambience	✓✓✓✓	Location	✓✓✓✓
Quality of Pitches	✓✓✓✓	Range of Facilities	✓✓✓

Directions

One can find the site very easily from the village of Varilhes which is 8 km. south of Pamiers on D624 (parallel to N20). Take D13 for Dalou and Gudas cross railway and N20. The site is 2 km. past Gudas, pass small road to left and site drive is further on right. An alternative route for larger units is via the D1 from Foix (avoiding the tunnel), after 7 km. turn left onto D13 and site is 3 km. on left. GPS: N42:59.566 E01:40.731

Charges 2005

Per person (all ages)	€ 4,30 - € 5,10
pitch	€ 4,30 - € 5,10
electricity	€ 2,50
No credit cards.	

Reservations

Not necessary. Tel: 05 61 60 77 56.
Email: ag.kos@wanadoo.fr

FR32060 Yelloh! Village le Lac des Trois Vallées

F-32700 Lectoure (Gers)

Lac des Trois Vallées is a large 40 hectare lively, busy site with many facilities. It is set in the Gers countryside in the heart of Gascony, a land of fortified villages wine and 'foie gras', near the town of Lectoure which was once the main seat of the Counts of Armagnac and is now a spa town. The site with its attractive ivy covered reception complete with water features, is popular with those who like activities and entertainment. It is, in fact, a large holiday complex and good for families with teenagers. The emphasis is on water sports and you can choose between the activities on the lakes or the excellent new pool complex. Lake activities range from water sports, to fishing, and to swimming with the diving platforms or four water chutes, plus one lake for dogs only. There is a large safe paddling area. The impressive pool complex has pleasant paved areas for sunbathing. There are two restaurants, one under canvas beside the pool and one by the lake, and three bars including 'The Pub'. There are some steep inclines from the lakeside to the pitches. Of the 500 pitches, over 300 are for touring units on shaded or open ground, all with electricity. Used by tour operators (100 pitches). A Yelloh Village member.

Facilities

Eight sanitary blocks, one of ultra-modern design, the rest refurbished, and open air baby baths. As this is a busy site they receive heavy use but when we visited all was in order. Launderette. Motorcaravan service point. Mini-market. Two restaurants and three bars (hours vary according to season). Snack bar by the lake plus a drinks kiosk. Swimming pool complex with paddling pools and jacuzzis. Lake complex with slides and diving platforms (open to the public). Lifeguards supervise both areas in season. Watersports and fishing. Tennis and mountain biking (bicycles to hire), with cabaret, shows at the large lakeside amphitheatre and craft activities for all ages. Disco and cinema and children's 'Tepee Club'. Woods and fields for walking. Light aircraft flights. Caravan storage. Off site: Golf 10 km. Riding 20 km.

At a glance

Welcome & Ambience	✓✓✓✓	Location	✓✓✓✓
Quality of Pitches	✓✓✓✓	Range of Facilities	✓✓✓✓

Directions

Site well signed 2 km. outside Lectoure to the south, off the N21.

Charges guide

Per unit incl. 2 persons and electricity	€ 15,00 - € 38,00
with electricity and water	€ 17,00 - € 40,00
extra person	€ 4,00 - € 7,50
dog	free - € 2,70

Many special rates available for couples, families, etc. and low season discounts

Reservations

Made with deposit (€ 81) and non-refundable fee (€ 22,87). Tel: 05 62 68 82 33.
Email: lac.des.trois.vallees@wanadoo.fr

Open

15 May - 12 September with all facilities.

Le Camp de Florence - 32480 La Romieu

Sun * Comfort * Nature * Water

The Gers - A region waiting to be discovered, an unspoilt landscape of rolling hills, sunflowers and historic fortified villages and castles. Peace, tranquillity, the home of Armagnac, Fois Gras and Magret de Canard. A four star camping / caravanning site with bungalows, mobil-homes and Trigano tents for hire.

Tel: 0033 562 28 15 58 - Fax: 0033 562 28 20 04
E-mail: info@lecampdeflorence.com - www.lecampdeflorence.com

FR32010 Le Camp de Florence

Mobile homes ▶ page 441

Route Astaffort, F-32480 La Romieu (Gers)

Camp de Florence is an attractive site on the edge of an historic village in pleasantly undulating Gers countryside. It is run by the Mynsbergen family who are Dutch (although Susan is English) and they have sympathetically converted the old farmhouse buildings to provide facilities for the site. The 183 pitches (95 for tourers) are all over 100 sq.m. Terraced where necessary, all have electricity, 10 are on hardstanding and 25 are fully serviced. They are arranged around a large field (full of sunflowers when we visited) with rural views, giving a feeling of spaciousness. The 13th century village of La Romieu is on the Santiago de Compostela pilgrim route and the collegiate church, visible from the site, is well worth a visit (the views are magnificent from the top of the tower), as is the local arboretum, the biggest collection of trees in the Midi-Pyrénées. The Pyrénées are a two hour drive, the Atlantic coast a similar distance. There are 20 tour operator pitches.

Facilities

Two unisex toilet blocks include some washbasins in cabins. Washing machine and dryer. Motorcaravan services. Good upstairs, air-conditioned restaurant, also open to the public, serves a range of food, including local specialities (1/5-30/9, closed Weds, with a barbecue instead). Takeaway. Bread on site in season. Swimming pool area with jacuzzi, central island and protected children's pool (all open to the public in the afternoons). Adventure play area, games area and pets area. Games room, tennis, table tennis, volleyball and petanque. Bicycle hire. Video shows, discos, picnics, animation and musical evenings and excursions organised. Internet access. Off site: Shop 500 m. in village. Fishing 5 km. Riding 10 km. Walking tours, excursions and wine tasting arranged.

Open

1 April - 8 October.

At a glance

Welcome & Ambience	✓✓✓✓✓	Location	✓✓✓✓
Quality of Pitches	✓✓✓✓	Range of Facilities	✓✓✓✓✓

Directions

Site is signed from D931 Agen - Condom road. Small units can turn left at Ligardes (signed) and follow D36 for 1 km. and take right turn for La Romieu (signed). Otherwise continue until outskirts of Condom and take D41 left to La Romieu and pass through village to site. GPS: N43:58.975 E00:30.091

Charges 2006

Per unit incl. 2 persons	
and electricity	€ 15,00 - € 28,00
extra person	€ 3,50 - € 6,60
child (4-9 yrs)	€ 2,60 - € 4,60
water and drainage	free - € 3,00
dog (max 2)	€ 1,50 - € 2,10

Special prices for groups, rallies, etc.
Camping Cheques accepted.

Reservations

Write or phone for information (English spoken). Tel: 05 62 28 15 58.
Email: info@campdeflorence.com

FR32030 Camping La Plage de Verduzan

Rue du Lac, F-32410 Castera Verduzan (Gers)

This is a pleasant site situated 500 metres from the small village of Castera-Verduzan where there are restaurants, bars, shops, a casino and thermal baths. The site is on the shores of a small lake and access to its sandy beach is free for site customers. Here there is a water slide, pedaloes and a small sailing school. The 56 touring pitches at the site are on level grass, hedged with bushes and ornamental trees and all have electricity hook-up (3/10A). There are also a few mobile homes to rent.

Facilities

The two toilet blocks are mainly unisex with washbasins in cabins, adjustable, roomy showers and mixed laundry and dishwashing sinks with one hot tap to draw from. Washing machine and ironing board. Chemical disposal. Facilities for disabled people. New play area and motorcaravan service point planned. Small bar which also serves snacks and provides low key entertainment, games and competitions (open July/Aug). Table tennis. Fishing from the far side of the lake. Off site: Village shops and restaurants. Golf 25 km. Riding 5 km.

At a glance

Welcome & Ambience	✓✓✓✓	Location	✓✓✓✓
Quality of Pitches	✓✓✓✓	Range of Facilities	✓✓✓

Directions

Castera-Verduzen is on the D930, 20 km. south of Condom. Site is on south side of village and well signed. GPS: N43:48.485 E00:25.848

Charges 2006

Per unit incl. 2 persons	€ 13,00 - € 18,50
extra person	€ 3,00 - € 5,00
child (3-7 yrs)	€ 2,50 - € 2,80
electricity (6A)	€ 1,50

Reservations

Contact site. Tel: 05 62 68 12 23. Email: contact@camping-verduzan.com

Open

10 April - 30 September.

FR32080 Camping Le Talouch

F-32810 Roquelaure (Gers)

Although enjoying an 'away-from-it-all' location Auch, the region's capital, is 10 km. drive from this family run site, which takes its name from the small Talouch river. The entrance, off the D148 road, is fronted by a parking area with reception to the right and the bar and restaurant facing. Beyond this point lies the top half of the touring area with generous pitches of at least 120 sq.m. located between mature trees and divided by hedges, some with chalets. There are 118 pitches, with electricity (4A). The rear half of the site has unshaded pitches in a more open aspect, and chalets have been built on the hillside to one side of the site.

Facilities

There are two immaculate toilet blocks, the larger refurbished building offering modern units with a clean appearance. The smaller block is of a more modern and unusual style, situated to rear of site. Baby bathroom/shower which can be used by people with disabilities. Small shop selling basic foodstuffs and snacks (1/5-30/9). Two swimming pools and new pool with 'jetstream'. Bicycle hire. Two play areas, volleyball, tennis, basketball and 9 hole golf course. Organised entertainment in high season.

Open

1 April - 30 September.

At a glance

Welcome & Ambience	✓✓✓✓	Location	✓✓✓✓
Quality of Pitches	✓✓✓✓	Range of Facilities	✓✓✓✓

Directions

From Auch take N21 for 8.5 km. north and turn west onto D272 to village of Roquelaure. Then follow signs to site 2 km. south of village on D148.

Charges 2006

Per unit incl. 2 adults	€ 14,00 - € 22,05
with electricity	€ 15,90 - € 29,15
extra person	€ 4,15 - € 6,65
child (3-7 yrs)	€ 3,40 - € 5,40
animal	€ 1,50 - € 2,20

Discounts for longer stays.
Camping Cheques accepted.

Reservations

Advisable for July/Aug. Tel: 05 62 65 52 43. Email: info@camping-talouch.com

FR31000 Camping Le Moulin

F-31220 Martres-Tolosane (Haute-Garonne)

Le Moulin is a family campsite located close to the interesting mediaeval village of Martres-Tolosane. The site lies on the bank of the River Garonne, with a mill stream to its other side. It is a longstanding member of 'Sites et Paysages de France' and has been recommended by our French agent. We plan to undertake a full inspection in 2006. Le Moulin has 89 pitches all of which offer electrical connections (6A or 10A). The pitches are grassy and of a good size, mostly with good shade. A number of very large (150 sq.m.) 'super' pitches are also available. The site boasts a friendly bar and has a large swimming pool. During the high season, an activity and entertainment programme is on offer, including a children's club and evening entertainment. Mobile homes and chalets for rent. A 'Sites et Paysages' member.

Facilities
Bar. Snackbar and takeaway food. Small shop (bread delivery). Swimming and paddling pools. Tennis. Fishing. Volleyball. BMX track. Playground. Games room. Entertainment and activity programme. Children's club. Library. Off site: Tourist 'train' between the site and the village, Martres Tolosane 1.5 km. Toulouse 60 km. Walking trails and cycle routes.

Open
15 April - 30 September.

Directions
From the A64 motorway (Toulouse - Tarbes) take exit 21 and follow signs to Martres-Tolosane. Site is well signed from the village.

Charges 2005

Per person	€ 5,00
child (under 7 ys)	€ 2,50
pitch	€ 6,00 - € 9,00
electricity (6A)	€ 3,00

Less 20% outside July and August.

Reservations
Advised for high season; contact site.
Tel: 05 61 98 86 40.
Email: info@campinglemoulin.com

FR65010 Domaine Naturiste L'Eglantière

Aries-Espenan, F-65230 Castelnau-Magnoac (Haute-Pyrénées)

This pretty site is situated in the valley between the Pyrénées and the plain, within easy reach of Lourdes and the mountains. Alongside a small, fast flowing river, in wooded surroundings it comprises 12 hectares for camping and caravanning, with a further 32 for walking and relaxing in the woods and fields. The river is said to be suitable for swimming and canoeing, with fishing nearby. The 83 traditional pitches are of mixed size on fairly level grass, the older ones secluded and separated by a variety of tall trees and bushes, the newer ones more open, with a natural tenting area across the river (28+ pitches). The traditional pitches have 10A electrical connections (long lead for some). The site has is an attractive, central, medium sized swimming pool with sunbathing areas both on paving and grass, and a children's pool, overlooked by the attractive style clubhouse and terrace. A small health centre (massage, sauna) is being developed in the old farmhouse. A range of studios, mobile homes, chalets and tents is on site. Used by a tour operator (six pitches). Member of 'France 4 Naturisme'.

Facilities
Two main sanitary blocks at each end of the site are in typically naturist style, providing under cover, open plan, controllable hot showers, and sinks for washing up. A small centrally located sanitary block has individual cubicles. Shop (July-Aug). Clubhouse with bar (all season), small restaurant (June-Sept), pizzeria and takeaway (July-Aug), internet access and indoor soundproofed activities/disco area, play room for younger children and table tennis for older ones. Swimming pool (all season). Play area and children's animation in season. Volleyball, badminton, table tennis, petanque and archery. Activities on the river. Canoe and mountain bike hire. Trekking and cross country cycling. Barbecues are officially forbidden. Torches useful. Off site: Restaurants in the nearby village.

At a glance

Welcome & Ambience	✓✓✓✓	Location	✓✓✓
Quality of Pitches	✓✓✓	Range of Facilities	✓✓✓

Directions
From Auch take D929 south towards Lannemezan. After Castelnau-Magnoac continue past aerodrome and turn onto the D9 towards Monleon-Magnoac. Take the first left towards Ariès-Espénan and follow site signs. GPS: N43:15.829 E00:31.252

Charges 2005

Per pitch incl. 2 persons	€ 11,00 - € 31,50
extra person	€ 2,00 - € 5,80
child (3-8 yrs)	free - € 4,40
animal	€ 2,20 - € 3,90
electricity (10A)	€ 4,80

Camping Cheques accepted.

Reservations
Made with deposit (25%) and fee (€ 27.44).
Tel: 05 62 39 88 00. Email: info@leglantiere.com

Open
Easter - October.

FR65020 Sunêlia Les Trois Vallées

Avenue des Pyrénées, F-65400 Argelès-Gazost (Haute-Pyrénées)

This is a large and ever-expanding site on the valley road from Lourdes into the Pyrénées. It has a rather unprepossessing entrance and pitches near the road suffer from noise (this may be reduced a little with the opening of a new by-pass) but at the back, open fields allow views of surrounding mountains on all sides. Amenities include an indoor pool, two jacuzzis and an enormous play area that seems to have everything! The site now has 483 flat, grassy pitches of which 200 are for tourers; they are marked out and of reasonable size, all with 3 or 6A electricity. Some fully serviced pitches are also available. The proximity to the road is at least advantageous for touring the area, being by a roundabout with Lourdes one way, Luz-St-Sauveur and mountains another way, and the dramatic Pyrénées Corniche Col d'Aubisque going off to the west. Argelès-Gazost is an attractive town with excellent restaurants and cultural interests. The site is popular with young people and could be quite lively at times.

Facilities

The two unisex toilet blocks are a little dated but include facilities for disabled people and a good laundry room. Cleaning can be variable and facilities could be under pressure at peak times. Bread available on site. Bar/disco. Café and takeaway. Swimming pool complex (from 15/5) with paddling pool and two water slides. TV room. Good playground. Volleyball, football, boules and archery. Entertainment in high season. Off site: Supermarket across the road. Bicycle hire 50 m. Fishing 500 m. Riding 3 km. Nearby is 'La Voie Verte' - a 17 km. traffic-free cycle path from Lourdes south to Soulom.

Open

1 April - 30 September.

At a glance

Welcome & Ambience	✓✓✓	Location	✓✓✓
Quality of Pitches	✓✓✓	Range of Facilities	✓✓✓✓✓

Directions

Argelès-Gazost is 13 km. south of Lourdes. From Lourdes take the new N21 (Voie rapide) south and leave at the third exit. Site entrance is directly off the next roundabout. GPS: N43:00.726 W00:05.871

Charges 2005

Per unit incl. 2 persons	€ 11,00 - € 22,00
incl. 3A electricity	€ 14,00 - € 25,00
incl. 6A electricity	€ 16,50 - € 27,50
extra person	€ 4,50 - € 7,00
child (2-12 yrs)	€ 2,50 - € 6,00
Camping Cheques accepted.	

Reservations

Advised for July/Aug. and made with deposit (€ 70) and fee (€ 30). Tel: 05 62 90 35 47. Email: 3-vallees@wanadoo.fr

---

FR65030 Airotel Pyrénées

46 avenue de Baseue, F-65120 Esquieze-Sere (Haute-Pyrénées)

Airotel Pyrénées is a small site in the heart of the Pyrénées. It is located on the main road into the mountains, south from Argelès-Gazost and surrounded by the high peaks (some pitches will have daytime road noise). There are 163 level pitches, with 85 for touring units, all with electricity and 90 fully serviced. They are on terraced ground and separated by bushes. Lighting runs through the site and across some pitches. The layout of the pitches with the mobile homes can give a rather crowded feel. In high season a programme of activities and tournaments is arranged, from walking and mountain bike trips to rafting. There are tour operator pitches.

Facilities

Two toilet blocks, both fairly modern and well appointed, include washbasins in cubicles, mixed British and Turkish style WCs and can be heated. The block adjoining the indoor pool and sauna has full facilities for disabled people, also doubling as a baby room. Indoor dishwashing and laundry sinks. Bottled water is advised for drinking and cooking. Motorcaravan service point. Small, quite limited shop (1/7-31/8) but bread available 15/5-15/9. Outdoor pool (15/6-15/9). Indoor pool, new balneotherapy pool, sauna and fitness room (1/12-30/9). Pool with water slides. Practice climbing wall, half court tennis, boules and table tennis. Small playground. Off site: Skiing 10 km.

Open

All year, excl. 1 October - 30 November.

At a glance

Welcome & Ambience	✓✓✓	Location	✓✓✓✓
Quality of Pitches	✓✓✓	Range of Facilities	✓✓✓✓

Directions

Take N21 (Voie rapide) south from Lourdes past Argelès-Gazost towards Luz-St-Sauveur. The site is on left at Esquièze-Sere, just before Luz-St-Sauveur. Site is on left immediately after Camping International. GPS: N42:52.749 W00:00.610

Charges 2005

Per pitch incl. 2 persons	€ 15,50 - € 21,00
extra person	€ 5,00
child (2-7 yrs)	€ 3,00
electricity (3/10A)	€ 3,00 - € 6,20
dog	€ 1,50

Reservations

Advised for most periods and made with deposit (€ 50) and fee (€ 25). Tel: 05 62 92 89 18. Email: airotel.pyrenees@wanadoo.fr

FR65040 Camping International

F-65120 Luz St Saveur (Haute-Pyrénées)

Located in a valley in the foothills of the Pyrénées, Camping International is an attractive, family run site with 180 pitches, most of which are on the fairly level lower section. Around 40 pitches (more suitable for tents) are on terraces on the mountainside at the back of the site, all accessed by tarmac roads and with stunning views. However some fairly steep up and down walking will be necessary. With only 30 privately owned and 4 rental mobile homes, there are 146 marked, grassy pitches for tourists all with electricity hook-ups (2/ 6A), many divided by hedges and some with a little shade. Most of the amenities are grouped around the reception area along the front of the site and include a well stocked shop, snack bar and takeaway, bar, the heated swimming pool with paddling pool, water toboggan and jacuzzi, and excellent children's playgrounds. All this should make for a more peaceful camping area, particularly as the buildings help to shield the pitches from any road noise.

Facilities

Two main sanitary buildings, one by reception and one more central on the site, provide a good supply of conventional facilities including some large shower and washbasin cubicles, and an excellent dual purpose room with facilities for babies and disabled campers. Three small units are on the high terraces, each with 2 toilets, 2 washbasins, and 2 showers. One block is heated during the winter months. Shop. Snack bar and takeaway. Heated swimming pool. All amenities 1/6-30/9. Bar (20/6-10/9). Half court tennis. Table tennis. Boules. Minigolf. Volleyball. Badminton. Playground. Organised activities and entertainment in main season. Off site: Paragliding school near Barèges or take the cable car to the Pic du Midi observatory or ski slopes. Fishing 0.5 km. Bicycle hire 1 km. Riding 7 km. Golf 30 km.

At a glance

Welcome & Ambience	✓✓✓✓	Location	✓✓✓✓
Quality of Pitches	✓✓✓✓	Range of Facilities	✓✓✓✓

Directions

From Lourdes take new N21 (Voie rapide) south, pass Argeles Gazost continuing towards Luz St Sauveur on D921. Site is on left at Esquièze-Sere (just before Luz), proceed carefully, site entrance is well signed but could be congested at peak times.
GPS: N42:52.961 W00:00.806

Charges 2005

Per unit incl. 1 or 2 persons	€ 16,30
incl. 3 persons	€ 19,20
extra person	€ 4,54
child (0-7 yrs)	€ 3,10
electricity	€ 1,85 - € 4,90

Reservations

Contact site. Tel: 05 62 92 82 02.
Email: reception@international-camping.fr

Open

1 June - 30 Sept; 15 December - 15 April.

FR65060 Castel Camping Pyrénées Natura

Route du Lac, F-65400 Estaing (Haute-Pyrénées)

Pyrénées Natura, at an altitude of 1,000 metres, on the edge of the National Park is the perfect site for lovers of nature. Eagles and vultures soar above the site and a small open air observatory with seats and binoculars is provided. The Ruysschaert family's aim is that you go home from a holiday here feeling at peace with the world, having hopefully learned something about the flora and fauna of the High Pyrénées. Groups are taken walking in the mountains to see the varied flora and fauna (there are even a few bears but they are seen very rarely). The 60 pitches (46 for tourists), all with electricity, are in a large, level, open and sunny field. Around 75 varieties of trees and shrubs have been planted – not too many to spoil the view though, which can only be described as fantastic. The reception and bar are in a traditional style stone building with tiled floors and an open staircase. The small shop in the old water mill is quite unique. Stocking a variety of produce, including wine, it is left unmanned and open all day and you pay at reception - very trusting, but they have not been let down yet. The last weekend in May is when the local shepherds take their flocks up to the high pastures. Campers help by walking up with them and then helping to separate the different flocks. Returning to the site by bus, with a good old sing-song with the shepherds, the site provides food for everyone. That sounds like a trip worth making.

Facilities

First class toilet facilities with high quality fittings include a cubicle for children, full facilities for disabled visitors and, in the same large room, baby bath, shower and changing mat. Dishwashing and laundry sinks. Washing machine and airers (no lines allowed). Motorcaravan service point. Small shop. Small takeaway (15/5-15/9). Small bar (15/5-15/9) and lounge area. Lounge, library and Satellite TV (mainly used for videos of the National Park). Sauna and solarium (free between 12.00-17.00, otherwise € 5). Excellent music room. Play area for the very young. Small 'beach-like' area beside river. Table tennis, boules and giant chess. Weekly evening meal in May, June and Sept. Internet access. Off site: Village has two restaurants.

Open

1 May - 20 September.

At a glance

Welcome & Ambience	✓✓✓✓✓	Location	✓✓✓✓✓
Quality of Pitches	✓✓✓✓✓	Range of Facilities	✓✓✓✓

Directions

From Lourdes take new N21 (Voie rapide) south towards Argelès-Gazost. Leave at exit 2 and follow old road, signed N2021/D21 into Argelès. Approaching town follow signs for Col d'Aubisque onto D918 towards Aucun. Continue for 8 km. and turn left on D13 to Bun. After Bun cross the river and right on D103 to site (5.5 km). Narrow road with few passing places. GPS: N42:56.451 W00:10.631

Charges 2005

Per unit incl. 2 persons and electricity (3A)	€ 14,50 - € 22,00
extra person	€ 4,00
child (under 8 yrs)	€ 2,50
Less in low season.	

Reservations

Made with deposit (€55). Tel: 05 62 97 45 44.
Email: info@camping-pyrenees-natura.com

FR65070 Camping Caravaning Le Rioumajou

Bousrisp, F-65170 St Lary Soulan (Haute-Pyrénées)

Located in the heart of the Aure valley, adjacent to a fast flowing unfenced river, and with views to the surrounding mountains and countryside, Le Rioumajou is a good base from which to explore this part of the Hautes-Pyrénées. There are 240 pitches, with a mix of rental and private caravans and bengali tents (55), leaving around 185 pitches for tourists. They are generally separated, varying in size, some shady and some more open, and all with electricity hook-ups (2-10A), and ten are all weather pitches. A good cycle track runs alongside the main road in both directions from the site and one can walk to the town along the river bank. Nearby is the Réserve Naturel du Néouvielle National Park, and the Spanish border via the Aragnouet - Bielsa tunnel, and the tourist village of Saint-Lary Soulan is 2 km.

Facilities

Three attractive, fairly modern toilet blocks (only one open and heated in low season and facilities can be stretched). One block (at the far end of the site) has all Turkish style toilets. Some washbasins in cabins, controllable hot showers including some spacious twin units. Lights are on a time delay switch. Laundry with large drying room. One block (not open in winter) has a room for children with toilets, baby bath and shower, changing surfaces and basins. Facilities for disabled visitors (access by key). Small shop for essentials, bar/takeaway (all July/Aug). Well fenced, outdoor heated swimming pool with lifeguard in main season (10 x 25m; June-Sept). Sauna and jacuzzi. Good adventure style playground. TV room. Communal barbecue. Entertainment (July/Aug). Off site: Shops, cinema, night club, ice rink, ski lifts, rafting and canyoning all within 2 km.

At a glance

Welcome & Ambience	✓✓✓	Location	✓✓✓✓✓
Quality of Pitches	✓✓✓✓	Range of Facilities	✓✓✓✓

Directions

From Lannemezan take the D929 south, pass through Arreau, and continue for about 10 km. After passing through Guchen and Guchan, site is on right before Bourisp. GPS: N42:52.296 E00:20.384

Charges 2005

Per person	€ 4,95 - € 6,95
child (4-10 yrs)	€ 3,15 - € 3,45
electricity (2-10A)	€ 3,00 - € 6,00
animal	€ 1,00
No credit cards.	

Reservations

Advisable for high season. Tel: 05 62 39 48 32. Email: lerioumajou@wanadoo.fr

Open

All year.

FR65080 Camping du Lavedan

Lau-Balagnas, F-65400 Argelès-Gazost (Haute-Pyrénées)

Camping du Lavedan is an old established and very French site set in the Argelès Gazost valley south of the Lourdes. It is beside the main road so there is some daytime road noise. The 105 touring pitches are set very close together on grass with some shade and all have electricity (2-10A). The area is fine for walking, biking, rafting and, of course, winter skiing. There is a swimming pool which can be covered in inclement weather and a twice weekly event is organised in July/Aug and weekly in June.

Facilities

The toilet block, though quite old with some Turkish style toilets is acceptable. Showers are quite small, but some washbasins are in cabins. Baby shower and bath. Facilities for disabled visitors. Dishwashing sinks under cover with hot tap to draw from. Washing machines and dryer in separate small block which is heated in winter. Restaurant/takeaway/terrace (1/5-15/9). Bar with TV (all year). No shop but bread delivery daily (1/5-15/9). Swimming pool (with cover), paddling pool and sun beds. Excellent play area. Internet access (July/Aug). Boules and table tennis. Off site: Fishing or bicycle hire 1 km. Supermarket or rafting 2 km. Riding 5 km. Golf 15 km. Nearby is 'La Voie Verte' - a 17 km. traffic-free cycle path from Lourdes south to Soulom.

Open

All year.

At a glance

Welcome & Ambience	✓✓✓✓	Location	✓✓✓
Quality of Pitches	✓✓✓	Range of Facilities	✓✓✓✓

Directions

Lau-Balagnas is 15 km. south of Lourdes and 2 km. south of Argelès-Gazost. From Lourdes take the new N21 (Voie rapide) south. Leave at exit 3 (Argelès Gazost) and take the old road signed N2021, D921 or D21 towards Luz St Sauveur for 2 km. to Lau Balagnas. Site is on right on the southern edge of town. GPS: N42:59.293 W00:05.340

Charges 2005

Per unit incl. 2 persons	€ 13,50 - € 17,50
incl. 3 persons	€ 17,50 - € 21,00
extra person	€ 4,00 - € 6,00
child (2-7 yrs)	€ 3,00 - € 4,50
electricity (2A)	€ 2,00 - € 6,00
dog	€ 2,00
Camping Cheques accepted.	

Reservations

Contact site. Tel: 05 62 97 18 84. Email: contact@lavedan.com

FR65090 Camping Soleil du Pibeste

Mobile homes ▶ page 441

16 avenue du Lavedan, F-65400 Agos Vidalos (Haute-Pyrénées)

Soleil du Pibeste is a quiet rural site with well tended grass and flower beds. It has 23 mobile homes to rent and 67 pitches for tourers. All pitches have electricity (3-15A) and there is some shade. The Dusserm family welcomes all arrivals with a drink and are clearly determined to ensure you have a good stay. They are particularly keen on developing eco-tourism in the Pyrénées. At times some domestic matters could perhaps have a little more attention. It is a perfect site for the active as many activities are organised from the site – from gentle ones like painting and Tai Chi exercise classes to walking, rafting, climbing, parasailing, riding and, of course, in the winter, skiing. There is no shop but the supermarket is only 5 km. and ordered bread is delivered to your door daily. The swimming pool is on a terrace above the pitches with sun beds, a paddling pool and waterfall and the most magnificent view of the mountains. The same wonderful view can be enjoyed whilst doing the washing up. A new by-pass should eliminate most of the road noise.

Facilities

Two heated toilet blocks have washbasins in cabins and large showers. Cleaning can be variable. Baby room. Facilities for disabled visitors (key). Washing machine and dryer. Motorcaravan service point. Bar with piano and internet access, which also serves snacks. Adjoining room for playing cards or reading. Swimming and paddling pools. Small play area. Boules, archery, basketball and volleyball. Table tennis. Bicycle hire. Tai Chi and other relaxation classes. Off site: Fishing 800 m. Golf 10 km. Rafting 2 km. Skiing 2 km.

Open

1 May - 30 September.

At a glance

Welcome & Ambience	✓✓✓✓	Location	✓✓✓✓
Quality of Pitches	✓✓✓	Range of Facilities	✓✓✓✓

Directions

Agos Vidalos is on the N21, 5 km. south of Lourdes. Leave express-way at second exit, signed Agos Vidalos and continue to site on the right in a short distance. GPS: N43:02.134 W00:04.256

Charges 2005

Per unit incl. 2 persons and 3A electricity	€ 15,00 - € 20,00
extra person	€ 3,00 - € 4,00
6A electricity	€ 3,00
animal	€ 2,00

Reservations

Made with 25% deposit and € 26 fee.
Tel: 05 62 97 53 23. Email: info@campingpibeste.com

FR65100 Camping Le Moulin Du Monge

Avenue Jean Moulin, F-65100 Lourdes (Haute-Pyrénées)

A well organised, family run site with a friendly welcome, Moulin de Monge has a convenient location allowing easy access into the city of Lourdes which is just 3 kilometres away. Inevitably there will be some traffic noise from the N21, but with a bus stop just outside the gate you will not need to take your own vehicle into the centre of this busy pilgrimage town. A railway line also passes close to the site. This attractive garden-like site has 57 grassy pitches in several different areas and on different levels. Some are in a level orchard area and these are closest to the main road. A few pitches are on a little woodland knoll behind reception, with the remainder on a higher level at the back of the site beyond the swimming pool. All have electricity hook-ups (2 to 6A). There are also 10 rental units on site.

Facilities

The main unit has all facilities with some washbasins in cubicles. A smaller unit close to the pool has additional facilities, a washing machine and dryer, a sauna, and can be heated. No facilities for disabled campers. Motorcaravan service point. Well stocked shop with fresh produce and gifts. Well fenced, heated swimming pool (14m x 6 m.) with removable sliding cover (15/4-15/10) and paddling pool. Games/TV room. Barbecue and terrace. Table tennis. Sauna. Boules. Playground and trampolines. Off site: Good transport links to the city centre with its famous grotto and all shops and services. Fishing 3 km. Golf 4 km. Bicycle hire 0.5 km.

Open

15 March - 15 October.

At a glance

Welcome & Ambience	✓✓✓✓	Location	✓✓✓
Quality of Pitches	✓✓✓✓	Range of Facilities	✓✓✓✓

Directions

Site is just off the N21 on northern outskirts of Lourdes. From south and town centre follow N21 towards Tarbes and turn right shortly after passing a large shopping centre and a set of traffic lights. Approaching from north on N21, 2 km. south of Adé, be ready to take slip lane (in centre of road), before turning left into Ave. Jean Moulin. Site entrance almost immediately on left. GPS: N43:06.931 W00:01.895

Charges 2005

Per unit incl. 2 persons incl. electricity (2-6A)	€ 12,80 € 14,80 - € 16,80
extra person	€ 4,20
child (0-7 yrs)	€ 2,75

Reservations

Contact site. Tel: 05 62 94 28 15.
Email: camping.moulin.monge@wanadoo.fr

FR81020 Camping Le Moulin de Julien

F-81170 Cordes-sur-Ciel (Tarn)

Close to the picturesque fortified old town of Cordes-sur-Ciel, in a secluded valley location in the heart of the Tarn region, this traditional style site has 130 spacious pitches. The grass pitches are arranged around a fishing lake with good shade in some areas and all with electricity hook-ups (5A). The area has magnificent scenery to enjoy and the fortified towns of the region to discover, including medieval Cordes (1 km). This site is full of character with a charming, friendly owner.

Facilities

Two rather elegant, well maintained sanitary buildings provide open and curtained washbasins, a washing machine, plus facilities for disabled people. Swimming pool (1/6-30/9) and water slide (July/Aug). Minigolf, table tennis, TV room and boules. Fishing. Off site: Shops, bars and restaurants within 1 km. Bicycle hire 3 km.

Open

1 May - 30 September.

At a glance

| Welcome & Ambience | ✓✓✓✓ | Location | ✓✓✓✓✓ |
| Quality of Pitches | ✓✓✓✓ | Range of Facilities | ✓✓✓✓ |

Directions

Cordes is 25 km. northwest of Albi. From D600 just east of Cordes take D922 south, and within 0.5 km. the site is signed at a minor road junction to your left.

Charges guide

Per unit incl. 2 persons	€ 13,60 - € 17,00
incl. 3 persons	€ 16,80 - € 21,00
extra person	€ 4,80 - € 6,00
electricity (5A)	€ 3,50

Reservations

Contact site for details. Tel: 05 63 56 11 10.

FR81030 Camping Municipal de Gourjade

Route de Roquecourbe, F-81100 Castres (Tarn)

Camping de Gourjade is a family run site set in a country park which belongs to the town of Castres. It has the river running along one side and the country park on the other. There are 100 level pitches (88 for tourers), all with electricity (6A) and separated by well trimmed hedges, and some with shade. Those nearest the river are sloping and can be soft. There is a small swimming pool on site. The adjoining country park has everything - larger indoor and outdoor swimming pools with slides etc, minigolf, table tennis, a miniature railway and a 9-hole golf course.

Facilities

The two unisex toilet blocks have adjustable showers, facilities for disabled visitors and baby changing. Maintenance and cleaning are variable. Washing machine and dryer. Drive over motorcaravan emptying point. Very limited shop, with bread daily (hours vary in low season). Attractive restaurant (all season but closed Monday and Tuesday). Small swimming pool. Bicycles kept at reception for the free use of campers. Barrier card deposit €15 (main season). Off site: Country park adjacent. Supermarket 1 km.

Open

1 April - 30 October.

At a glance

| Welcome & Ambience | ✓✓✓✓ | Location | ✓✓✓✓ |
| Quality of Pitches | ✓✓✓ | Range of Facilities | ✓✓✓✓ |

Directions

Castres is 42 km. south of Albi. Site entrance is off the D89 in the Parc de Gourjade north of the town. Do no enter the old city centre. The ringroad is an anticlockwise one-way system. Follow signs to Roquecourbe until roundabout with supermarket, then signs to 'Rive droite' and camping. After 1 km. turn left at T-junction to park entrance in 300 m. on the left. GPS: N43:37.240 E02:15.247

Charges 2005

Per person	€ 2,00 - € 3,00
pitch and vehicle	€ 7,50 - € 12,50
electricity	€ 2,50

Reservations

Made with 20% deposit. Tel: 05 63 59 33 51.
Email: contact@campingdegourjade.com

FR81040 Camp Municipal des Auzerals

Route de Grazac, F-81800 Rabastens (Tarn)

Camping des Auzerals is a small, reasonably priced site with 38 pitches. These are arranged near the lake where fishing is possible and there are walks from the site (leaflets from the tourist information office in the town). This is a perfect site for couples seeking peace and quiet, especially in May, June and Sept. All the pitches are on grass, hedged with neat bushes and all with water, drainage and electricity. The local swimming pool is adjacent and the village is only 2.5 km. There is no shop but a baker calls in July/Aug. This is an unspoilt region of the Tarn within easy reach of Albi and Montauben.

Facilities

The sanitary block is basic but very clean, with mainly Turkish style WCs, good adjustable showers and some washbasins in cubicles. Dishwashing and laundry sinks with hot water. Washing machine. Freezer available in the telephone room. Baker calls. Off site: Village 2.5 km.

Open

1 May - 30 September.

At a glance

| Welcome & Ambience | ✓✓✓✓ | Location | ✓✓✓✓ |
| Quality of Pitches | ✓✓✓✓ | Range of Facilities | ✓✓✓ |

Directions

Site is northeast of Toulouse. Heading south leave A20 at exit 66 and take D930 south. This road changes to the D630 in 23 km. Follow until sign for Albi on D988. Rabastens is 8 km. and site is signed to left on entry to village.

Charges 2005

Per unit incl. 2 persons	€ 7,00 - € 8,00
incl. electricity	€ 8,40 - € 9,50
extra person	€ 2,50 - € 3,00

Reservations

Contact site. Tel: 05 63 33 70 36.

FR81100 Camping de La Rigole

Route de Barrage, F-81540 Les Cammazes (Tarn)

A very pleasant, traditional style site in a countryside location, De la Rigole is partly wooded, and with a friendly reception. Indeed during July/August all new arrivals for the week are greeted with a 'reception' on Sunday morning, and there are organised activities for all guests. The site has 64 pitches which include 9 privately owned mobile homes and 13 mobile homes and chalets for rent. These are well separated from the tourist area. The site is on a slight slope, so most of the 43 individual tourist pitches are on small terraces. All have electricity hook-ups (4-13A) and many have quite deep shade. There is a small bar with a television and a snack bar which offers cooked chicken, pizza and chips, etc. One evening each week in main season the site organises a special meal with regional dishes. The oval swimming pool (120 sq.m.) is well fenced with an electric lock on the gate to prevent access by unaccompanied small children. Small children are well catered for here with playgrounds for both tiny tots and under 7s, and a delightful children's farm with goats, rabbits and chickens. Note: this site is totally unsuitable for American RVs.

Facilities
The fairly modern toilet block is bright and cheerful with push-button showers, washbasins in cubicles, baby bath and changing deck, and facilities for disabled campers. Dishwashing and laundry sinks are in an older block nearby. Extra facilities are by the entrance to the pool, together with washing machines and dryer. Small shop. Bar. Takeaway. Swimming pool. All amenities open 15/4-15/10. Table tennis. Badminton. Volleyball. Boules. Small animal farm. Off site: The site provides a useful little booklet, mostly in French, which should answer most of your questions about the area and the site. Lac des Cammazes with its dam is just 400 metres, and Lac de St Ferréol (5 km.) has a large sandy beach. Fishing 0.4 km. Riding 1.5 km.

At a glance
Welcome & Ambience	√√√√	Location	√√√√
Quality of Pitches	√√√√	Range of Facilities	√√√√

Directions
Les Cammazes is about 25 km. northeast of Castelnaudary, and 10 km. southeast of Revel. From Revel take D629 to Cammazes, continue on D629 through village and after about 1 km. turn left towards the Barrage (site is signed) and site entrance is 200 m. on the right. GPS: N43:24.472 E02:05.196

Charges 2005
Per unit incl. 2 persons	€ 14,00
incl. electricity	€ 16,50
extra person	€ 4,30
child (0-7 yrs)	€ 2,50
animal	€ 1,00

Reservations
Contact site. Tel: 05 63 73 28 99. Email: mary@campingdlr.com

Open
15 April - 15 October.

FR81110 Camping Saint Martin

F-81540 Soréze (Tarn)

This is a pleasant, little traditional style site within easy walking distance of the centre of the historic town of Sorèze with its Abbey school and programme of summer festivals and events. There are 48 individual tourist pitches with 10A electricity and six wooden chalets for rent. The pitches are all on grass, some divided by newly planted hedging and there are some mature trees for shade. Six pitches are reserved for motorcaravans, although these are rather compact. A small swimming pool is well fenced and gated. Reception has a small bar and snack bar and can also provide basic supplies including drinks, sweets, speciality foods and snacks. However, you are only 100 metres from the town centre shops. Camping Saint Martin is under the same ownership as Camping de la Rigole and shares the same telephone and fax numbers for bookings (remember to state which site you want).

Facilities
The single sanitary unit is well built, clean and tidy and provides seated WCs with paper seat cover dispensers, some washbasins in cubicles for ladies. Facilities for disabled visitors. Covered dishwashing and laundry sinks plus a washing machine. Small shop. Bar with TV. Snack bar. Swimming pool. All amenities open 15/6-15/9. Table tennis. Boules. Volleyball net. Communal barbecue. Small playground. Entertainment in high season. Dogs and other animals are not accepted. Off site: Municipal leisure and sports facilities including tennis courts adjacent.

At a glance
Welcome & Ambience	√√√√	Location	√√√√
Quality of Pitches	√√√	Range of Facilities	√√√

Directions
Sorèze is on the D85 about 25 km. southwest of Castres, 5 km. east of Revel. The site is well signed within the town and is adjacent to the fire station. GPS: N43:27.271 E02:04.175

Charges 2005
Per unit incl. 2 persons	€ 14,00
incl. electricity	€ 16,50
extra person	€ 4,30
child (0-7 yrs)	€ 2,50

Reservations
Contact site (see above). Tel: 05 63 73 28 99. Email: mary@campingsaintmartin.com

Open
15 June - 15 September.

FR81060 Camping Les Clots

Mobile homes ▶ page 442

F-81190 Mirandol-Bourgnounac (Tarn)

Les Clots is a very rural, simple site in the heart of the countryside with 48 touring pitches and 15 used for chalets and caravans for rent. The 2.5 km. road from the nearest village of Mirandol is quite narrow. Set around an old farmhouse, the outbuildings have been sympathetically converted giving the site lots of character. Carved out of a steep hillside, terraces take from 1 to 10 units. Nearly all the pitches have electricity. A few, mainly for tents, are set well away from others giving lots of seclusion. Being amongst trees there is enough shade. A quiet site with no entertainment at all – the noisiest things we heard were the owls. A river borders the site but it is quite a walk down the hillside to it.

Facilities

Toilet blocks are quite basic but have everything needed and are kept very clean. Baby bath. Facilities for disabled visitors. Washing machines. Bar in the barn with lots of character (July/Aug). Shop with basic provisions incl. bread (July/Aug). Simple swimming and paddling pools (1/7-30/9). Minigolf. Fishing. Site is not suitable for American style motorhomes.

Open

1 May - 1 October.

At a glance

| Welcome & Ambience | ✓✓✓✓ | Location | ✓✓✓✓ |
| Quality of Pitches | ✓✓✓✓ | Range of Facilities | ✓✓✓ |

Directions

Heading south on N88 from Rodez, just before reaching Carmaux turn right onto the D905 towards Mirandol. The site is 5.5 km. north of Mirandol.

Charges 2006

per unit incl. 3 persons	€ 19,00 - € 22,00
extra person	€ 4,50 - € 4,60
electricity (6A)	€ 2,70 - € 2,80
Low season reductions.	

Reservations

Contact site. Tel: 05 63 76 92 78.
Email: campclots@wanadoo.fr

FR81070 Camping Indigo Rieu Montagné

F-81320 Nages (Tarn)

Rieu Montagné is a delightful site in the heart of the Haut Languedoc Regional park. The site is a member of the Indigo group and lies close to the Lac du Laouzas where a range of sporting activities can be enjoyed. There are 118 touring pitches, mostly on broad terraces with reasonable shade, all with electricity and 47 fully serviced. A heated pool overlooks the lake and In high season there is a varied entertainment programme, and guided walks. Most leisure facilities are available at the lakeside complex, a five minute walk from the site. This site is on a fairly steep slope.

Facilities

The two toilet blocks, comprehensively refitted in 2005, provide mostly British style toilets, washbasins in cubicles and facilities for disabled people and babies. Laundry. Shop with basic provisions (July/Aug). Bar and snack bar with takeaway. Swimming pool (18/6-18/9). Entertainment programme (high season). Chalets, tents and mobile homes to let (53). Off site: Lakeside leisure complex.

Open

18 June - 18 September.

At a glance

| Welcome & Ambience | ✓✓✓ | Location | ✓✓✓✓ |
| Quality of Pitches | ✓✓✓ | Range of Facilities | ✓✓✓✓ |

Directions

From Albi take D999 east towards St Affrique, and 11 km. after Albon turn sharp right on D607 to Lacaune. At T-junction just before town turn left on D622 for 6.5 km. Turn right on D62 through Nages and 2 km. south of town turn left over bridge on D162. Take first left. GPS: N43:38.877 E02:46.888

Charges 2005

Per person	€ 4,50 - € 4,80
child (2-7 yrs)	€ 3,00 - € 3,20
pitch incl. electricity (6/10A)	€ 7,60 - € 22,60

Reservations

Advised for high season. Tel: 05 63 37 24 71.
Email: rieumontagne@camping-indigo.com

FR82010 Camping Les Trois Cantons

F-82140 St Antonin-Noble-Val (Tarn-et-Garonne)

With only 100 pitches set among trees that give dappled shade, Les Trois Cantons is a very friendly site. The pitches are level pitches and all have electricity. The site's pool is covered and heated in early and late season, with activities organised there in July and August. There are also walks, archery and boules, plus wine tastings and a weekly dance. It is however, primarily a site for nature lovers with peaceful nights and walks and mountain bike rides from the site. When the trees are bare early in the season, there could be a little road noise when the wind is in a certain direction.

Facilities

The two toilet blocks, both refurbished, include British and Turkish style WCs, quite large showers, and facilities for disabled visitors. Limited shop (bread daily). Bar serving snacks and takeaways (all season). Play area. Tennis court. Volleyball. Boules. Off site: Riding 4 km, fishing 7 km.

Open

15 April - 30 September.

At a glance

| Welcome & Ambience | ✓✓✓✓ | Location | ✓✓✓ |
| Quality of Pitches | ✓✓✓ | Range of Facilities | ✓✓✓✓ |

Directions

From A20 or N20 at Caussade, take D926 (Caylus, Septfonds). Site signed to right 5 km. after Septfonds. Avoid D5 towards St Antonin (5 km. of narrow road).

Charges 2006

Per pitch and 2 people	€ 14,00 - € 18,75
extra person	€ 4,20 € 5,30
electricity (2/5A)	€ 2,00 - € 6,50
Camping Cheques accepted.	

Reservations

Contact site. Tel: 05 63 31 98 57.
Email: info@3cantons.fr

MAP 15 & 16

Languedoc and Roussillon form part of the Massif Central. With its huge sandy beaches the mountainous Languedoc region is renowned for its long sunshine records, and the pretty coastal villages of Roussillon are at their most beautiful at sunset erupting in a riot of colour.

THIS SECTION COVERS THE SOUTH WEST COASTAL REGION OF THE MEDITERRANEAN, DÉPARTEMENTS: 11 AUDE, 30 GARD, 34 HÉRAULT, 66 PYRÉNÉES-ORIENTALES.

Once an independent duchy, the ancient land of Languedoc combines two distinct regions: the vineyards of the Corbières and Minervois and the coastal plain stretching from the Rhône to the Spanish border. Much of the region is rugged and unspoilt, offering opportunities for walking and climbing.

There is ample evidence of the dramatic past. Ruins of the former Cathar castles can be seen throughout the region. The walled city of Carcassonne with its towers, dungeons, moats and drawbridges is one of the most impressive examples of medieval France.

Today, Languedoc and Roussillon are wine and agricultural regions. Languedoc, with considerable success, is now a producer of much of the nation's better value wines. But above all, vast hot sandy beaches and long hours of sunshine make this a paradise for beach enthusiasts. La Grande Motte, Cap d'Agde and Canet, are all being promoted as an alternative to the more famous Mediterranean stretches of the Côte d'Azur.

Places of interest

Aigues-Mortes: medieval city.

Béziers: wine capital of the region, St Nazaire cathedral, Canal du Midi.

Carcassonne: largest medieval walled city in Europe.

Limoux: medieval town, Notre Dame de Marseilla Basilica, St Martin church.

Montpellier: universities, Roman sites; Gothic cathedral.

Nîmes: Roman remains, Pont du Gard.

Perpignan: Kings Palace; Catalan characteristics, old fortress.

Pézenas: Molière's home.

Villeneuve-lès-Avignon: Royal City and residence of popes in 14th century.

Cuisine of the region

Cooking is Provençal, characterised by garlic and olive oil with sausages and smoked hams. Fish is popular along the coast. Wines include Corbières, Minervois, Banyuls and Muscat.

Aïgo Bouido: garlic soup.

Boles de picoulat: small balls of chopped-up beef and pork, garlic and eggs.

Bouillinade: a type of *bouillabaisse* with potatoes, oil, garlic and onions.

Boutifare: a sausage-shaped pudding of bacon and herbs.

Cargolade: snails, stewed in wine.

Ouillade: heavy soup of *boutifare* leeks, carrots, and potatoes..

Touron: a pastry of almonds, pistachio nuts and fruit.

FR11020 Camping Aux Hamacs

Route des Cabanes, F-11560 Fleury (Aude)

If you are looking for sun, sea and sand, Aux Hamacs is a good venue. It is situated adjacent to the Aude river with the attractive village of Fleury nearby and a good beach less than 2 km. away. It is also well located for exploring Cathar country with its amazing hill top castles and attractions such as the Canal du Midi. The site is well away from the frenzy associated with some of the resorts in this region but near enough to visit for an evening out. With 253 large pitches, there are 190 for touring with 6A electricity and a few fully serviced (10A electricity plus water and waste water). The remaining pitches are used for a range of chalets and mobile homes to rent. This is a peaceful site but without much shade, although there is a relaxing pool open in July and August and an interesting range of activities.

Facilities

One fully equipped new toilet block is opened for the main season. A small older one which can be heated is open all season (with plans to rebuild). All facilities are unisex. Baby room and facilities for disabled visitors (key). Washing machine. Shop, bar, restaurant and takeaway (all fully operational July and August). Swimming pool (July/Aug). Play areas. Activities and entertainment (high season).

Open

20 March - 30 September.

At a glance

Welcome & Ambience	✓✓✓✓	Location	✓✓✓
Quality of Pitches	✓✓✓	Range of Facilities	✓✓✓

Directions

From A9 autoroute take exit 36 Beziers Ouest. Follow directions for Lespignan, Fleury and Les Cabanas de Fleury (D718). Site is on right before village. It is possible to approach from Vendras and Valras Plage by bridge just a little up river from Grau de Vendras.

Charges 2006

Per unit incl. 2 persons, electricity	€ 14,30 - € 23,70
extra person	€ 3,50 - € 5,30
child (2-7 yrs)	free - € 3,10
dog	free - € 4,20

Reservations

Made with € 20 non-refundable booking fee. Tel: 04 68 33 22 22. Email: info@campingauxhamacs.com

FR11040 Camping Le Martinet Rouge

F-11390 Brousses et Villaret (Aude)

Le Martinet Rouge provides a peaceful retreat in the Aude countryside to the north of Carcassonne. It is a small site where the owners have been working hard to improve the facilities. The most striking features of the site are the massive granite boulders (outcrops of smooth rock from the last ice age). The site offers 50 pitches for touring units, all with electricity (3/6A), in two contrasting areas - one is well secluded with irregularly shaped, fairly level, large pitches amongst a variety of trees and shrubs, while the other is on a landscaped gentle hill with mature trees. Pitch quality suffers in hot weather. The pool is attractively landscaped using the original boulders. This is a useful situation from which to visit Carcassonne or to follow the Cathare trail, or visit the Canal du Midi.

Facilities

Four sanitary blocks of various ages, including a good modern unit, have washbasins and showers in cabins, facilities for disabled visitors, baby bathroom and dishwashing and laundry facilities. Swimming pool (15/6-15/9, no Bermuda style shorts). Small shop (no others locally). Bar with terrace and large screen TV (1/7-15/9). Franchised snack bar (1/7-31/8). Barbecue area. Fitness room. Croquet, volleyball, half court tennis, table tennis and a small play area. Internet access in reception. Off site: Visit the paper mill in the village. Tennis, riding and fishing quite close.

Open

1 April - 15 October.

At a glance

Welcome & Ambience	✓✓✓	Location	✓✓✓
Quality of Pitches	✓✓	Range of Facilities	✓✓✓

Directions

Site is just south of Brousses-et-Villaret, approx. 20 km. northwest of Carcassonne. It is best approached from the D118 Carcassonne - Mazamet road. Turn onto D103 15 km. north of Carcassonne to Brousses-et-Villaret. On western outskirts of village turn south to site (signed) in 50 m. GPS: N43:20.350 E02:15.127

Charges 2005

Per pitch incl. 2 persons	€ 10,00 - € 12,50
with electricity	€ 12,50 - € 15,00
extra person	free - € 1,00
child (0-12 yrs)	€ 2,00 - € 3,10
animal	free - € 1,50
No credit cards.	

Reservations

Made with deposit of € 30. Tel: 04 68 26 51 98.

FR11060 Yelloh! Village Domaine d'Arnauteille

Mobile homes ► page 442

F-11250 Montclar (Aude)

Enjoying some beautiful and varied views, this rather unusual site is ideally situated for exploring, by foot or car, the little known Aude Département, the area of the Cathars and for visiting the walled city of Carcassonne (10 minutes drive). However, access could be difficult for large, twin axle vans. The site itself is set in 115 hectares of farmland and is on hilly ground with the original pitches on gently sloping, lightly wooded land and newer ones of good size with water, drainage and electricity (5/10A), semi-terraced and partly hedged. The facilities are quite spread out with the swimming pool complex, in the style of a Roman amphitheatre, set in a hollow basin surrounded by fine views and some mobile homes. The reception building is vast; originally a farm building, with a newer top floor being converted to apartments. This is a developing site so be aware of on-going building work. Some very steep up and down walking between the pitches and facilities is unavoidable. A 'Sites et Paysages' member.

Facilities
The main sanitary block is a distinctive feature, rebuilt to a good standard with a Roman theme. Three other smaller blocks are located at various points. Washbasins in cabins, laundry, facilities for disabled people and a baby bath. Motorcaravan service point and gas. Small shop (15/5-30/9 - the site is a little out of the way). Restaurant in converted stable block, takeaway (15/5-30/9). Swimming pool complex with four pools including children's pool. Boules. Play area. Table tennis. Riding (1/7-31/8). Day trips. Library with internet access and games room with satellite TV. Off site: Fishing 3 km. Bicycle hire 8 km. Golf 10 km.

Open
7 April - 25 September.

At a glance
Welcome & Ambience	✓✓✓✓	Location	✓✓✓✓
Quality of Pitches	✓✓✓✓	Range of Facilities	✓✓✓✓

Directions
Using D118 from Carcassonne, bypass the village of Rouffiac d'Aude, then to a small section of dual carriageway. Before the end of this, turn right to Montclar up narrow road (with passing places) for 2.5 km. Site is signed very sharp left and up hill before the village. GPS: N43:07.636 E02:15.571

Charges 2005
Per pitch incl. 2 persons	€ 13,50 - € 25,00
with 6A electricity	€ 17,00 - € 29,00
incl. water and drainage	€ 20,00 - € 33,00
extra person	€ 4,00 - € 6,80
child (under 7 yrs)	€ 2,50 - € 5,00

Camping Cheques accepted.

Reservations
Made with deposit (25%) and fee (€ 29). Tel: 04 68 26 84 53. Email: Arnauteille@mnet.fr

Domaine d'Arnauteille ★★★★
11250 *Montclar (close to Carcassonne)*
Tel: 0033 468 26 84 53 - Fax: 0033 468 26 91 10
Arnauteille@mnet.fr - www.arnauteille.com
New waterpark with 4 pools in a Greek-Roman style.

FR11030 Camping Municipal La Pinède

Avenue Gaston Bonheur, F-11200 Lézignan-Corbières (Aude)

Within walking distance of the little town and only 35 km. from Narbonne Plage, La Pinède is laid out in terraces on a hillside. The 86 individual, level pitches vary in size and are divided mainly by trees and shrubs with 6A electricity (some 17 for mobile homes and chalets). Outside the gates are a municipal swimming pool (July/Aug), a disco, restaurant and tennis courts. Generally better than many municipal sites in season - it is uncomplicated and peaceful.

Facilities
Three sanitary blocks of good quality are fully equipped and recently refurbished. Not all blocks are opened outside high season. Washing machine. Small shop with gas. Pleasant bar also providing hot food that can be eaten on the terrace (all July/Aug). Torches are necessary. Caravan storage. Off site: Bicycle hire or riding 2 km. Fishing 4 km.

Open
1 March - 30 October.

At a glance
Welcome & Ambience	✓✓✓✓	Location	✓✓✓✓
Quality of Pitches	✓✓✓✓	Range of Facilities	✓✓✓

Directions
Access is directly off the main N113 on west side of Lézignan-Corbières. From A61 (to avoid low bridge) exit at Carcassonne or Narbonne onto N113 and follow to site.

Charges 2006
Per person	€ 3,20 - € 4,30
pitch	€ 5,80 - € 7,50

No credit cards.

Reservations
Advisable in season. Tel: 04 68 27 05 08. Email: reception@campinglapinede.fr

3

FR11110 Camping Val d'Aleth

F-11580 Alet les Bains (Aude)

In the gateway to the upper Aude valley and open all year round, this popular small site is run by Christopher and Christine Cranmer who offer a warm welcome and personal service. The mellow medieval walls of Alet les Bains form one boundary of the site, while on the other and popular with anglers, is the River Aude (fenced for safety). Beyond this is the D118 and a railway which produces noise at times. The 37 mainly small, numbered pitches, around half of which are on hardstandings, all have electricity hook-ups (4-10A) and are separated by hedges and mature trees which give shade. Medieval Alet is a spa town with a thermal pool where the French take 'the cure'. The past life of the old city can be traced through its narrow streets, interesting buildings and the remains of an abbey and cathedral. The town has all services, including three restaurants and a Casino (a remnant of old aristocratic days). The site owners are keen to assist, with books, guides and walking maps available on loan along with brochures (in English) of attractions in the area. Bed and breakfast is also available.

Facilities
There are plans to replace the current unsophisticated toilet block which is just adequate and temporary facilities will be in place until the work is complete. Laundry sinks and washing machine under cover, very basic dishwashing in the open. Reception has small stocks of essential goods, drinks, wine and beer, and the use of a freezer. Small play area. Mountain bike hire. Off site: White water sports nearby. The area is very popular with walkers and mountain-bikers. Bus and train services to Carcassonne and Quillan. Some shops and restaurants in town, full range at Limoux (10 km. north).

Open
All year.

At a glance

Welcome & Ambience	✓✓✓	Location	✓✓✓✓
Quality of Pitches	✓✓✓	Range of Facilities	✓✓

Directions
From Carcassonne take D118 south for 32 km. Ignore first sign to Alet (to avoid narrow stone bridge) and after crossing the river, turn into town. Site is 800 m. on the left (signed). GPS: N42:59.682 E02:15.333

Charges 2005

Per unit incl. 2 persons	€ 11,00
extra person	€ 3,10
child (under 8 yrs)	€ 1,90
dog	€ 1,20
electricity (4A)	€ 2,50

No credit cards.

Reservations
Contact site. Tel: 04 68 69 90 40.
Email: camping@valdaleth.com

FR11140 Domaine La Royale

F-11600 Villardonnel (Aude)

Not a typical French campsite, Domaine La Royale can only be described as small. There are only 10 touring pitches, all slightly sloping and 6 with electricity connections (10A). From most pitches there are fantastic views south to the Aude valley and the distant, snow-capped Pyrenees. There is plenty of room here to spread out on the well kept grass with some shade available. The entrance porch of the house acts as reception and John and his Portuguese wife will help choose places to visit. This place would be ideal for complete relaxation, although for some it could be a little remote. There is no shop, although the baker calls in high season and a small village shop is 2.5 km. They hope to open a bistro, planning consents permitting, as John is a trained chef.

Facilities
Toilets and showers are in the farm buildings. Here also, dishwashing sinks, washing machine and free use of a freezer. Play area for very young children and field for ball games, although older children may soon get bored. Patio area for drinks. Bicycle hire. Gite for rent. Off site: Carcassonne 17 km. Fishing 11 km. Golf 17 km.

Open
May - September.

At a glance

Welcome & Ambience	✓✓✓✓	Location	✓✓✓✓✓
Quality of Pitches	✓✓✓✓	Range of Facilities	✓✓✓

Directions
Site is between villages of Villardonnel (15 km. north of Carcassonne) and Salsigne. From north on D118 Castres - Caracassonne road turn left onto D73 signed Salsigne (about 22 km. south of Castres). After 3.6 km. turn right (opposite farm) and site is 2 km. From the south the route on the D111 is very narrow Villardonnel. Site is 2 km. to the left in about 6 km. GPS: N43:20.292 E02:19.598

Charges 2006

Per person	€ 7,00
electricity	€ 3,00
dog	€ 2,00

Reservations
Contact site. Tel: 04 68 77 51 13.
Email: info@laroyale.net

Chaussée de Mandirac, F-11100 Narbonne (Aude)

Being some six kilometres inland from the beaches of Narbonne and Gruissan, this site benefits from a somewhat less hectic situation than others in the popular seaside environs of Narbonne. The site itself is, however, quite lively with plenty to amuse and entertain the younger generation while, at the same time, offering facilities for the whole family. A purchase of a club card is required in July and August to use the children's club, gym, sauna, tennis, minigolf, billiards etc. (€ 27 per family for your entire stay). A very large, purpose built entertainment centre is under construction. There are 250 pitches in total, 150 for touring units, many in a circular layout of very good size, most with electricity (6A), including a few 'grand confort', and they benefit from a reasonable amount of shade, mostly from 2 metre high hedges. There are also a number of mobile homes and chalets to rent. This could be a very useful site offering many possibilities to meet a variety of needs, on-site entertainment (including an evening on Cathare history), and easy access to popular beaches. Nearby Gruissan is a fascinating village with its wooden houses on stilts, beaches, ruined castle, port and salt beds. Narbonne has Roman remains and inland Cathare castles are to be found perched on rugged hill tops.

Facilities

Four sanitary buildings, three refurbished to high standards, include washbasins in cabins, some British WCs, baby baths, laundry and dishwashing sinks, and washing machines. Shop and 'Auberge' restaurant (open all season). Takeaway (limited in low season). Bar. Small lounge, amusements (July and Aug). Landscaped heated pool with slides and islands (open 1 May). The original pool and a children's pool is open for high season. Adventure play area. Minigolf. Mountain bike hire. Three tennis courts. Volleyball. Sauna and gym. Children's activities, sports organised and adult entertainment in high season. Off site: Riding. Windsurfing/sailing school 300 m. Gruissan's beach 10 minutes by car. Lagoon for boating and fishing can be reached via footpath (about 200 m).

Open

24 March - 31 October.

At a glance

Welcome & Ambience	✓✓✓	Location	✓✓✓✓
Quality of Pitches	✓✓✓✓	Range of Facilities	✓✓✓✓✓

Directions

From A9 take exit 38 (Narbonne Sud) and go round roundabout to last exit taking you back over the autoroute (site signed from here). Follow signs to La Nautique and then Mandirac and site (total 6 km. from autoroute). Also signed from Narbonne centre.

Charges 2005

Per pitch incl. 1 or 2 persons	€ 13,10 - € 19,50
incl. electricity	€ 16,00 - € 24,80
with water and waste water	€ 20,60 - € 28,80
extra person	€ 3,80 - € 5,25
child (2-7 yrs)	€ 2,20 - € 3,40
animal	€ 1,45 - € 2,40
Camping Cheques accepted.	

Reservations

Made with deposit (€ 100) and fee (€ 22).
Tel: 04 68 49 03 72. Email: info@lesmimosas.com

Camping La Nautique

11100 Narbonne - Languedoc Roussillon - France
Tel (+33) 04 68 90 48 19 - Fax (+33) 04 68 90 73 39
info@campinglanautique.com - www.campinglanautique.com

English spoken

from 1/2 till 25/6 and from 1/9 till 25/11 the Camping Card will be accepted

CC

2 miles from exit N°38 (A9)

Open from 1/2 till 25/11

Every pitch is at least 130 m² and has **PRIVATE SANITARY FACILITIES** with toilet, shower and washbasin. The swimmingpool with waterslide, the bar and restaurant will be open from 01-05 till 30-09. Situated next to a large lake, ideal for Windsurfers. Tennis, crazy-golf, football, beach-volley etc. are free of charge. Mobile-home rental. Dogs are permitted. Entertainment for all ages from Easter till the beginning of October.

FR11080 Camping La Nautique

La Nautique, F-11100 Narbonne (Aude)

This extremely spacious site is situated on the Etang de Bages, where flat water combined with strong winds make it one of the best windsurfing areas in France and is owned and run by a very welcoming Dutch family. The site is fenced off from the water for the protection of children and windsurfers can have a key for the gate (with deposit) that leads to launching points on the lake. La Nautique has 390 huge, level pitches (a small one is 130 sq.m), including a good number used for site owned mobile homes and chalets and 30 tour operator pitches. The wide range of evergreens, flowering shrubs and trees on site give a pleasant feel and each pitch is separated by hedges making some quite private and providing shade. All have electricity (10A) and water. The difference between this and other sites is that each pitch has an individual toilet cabin. Various entertainment is organised for adults and children in July/Aug, plus a sports club for supervised surfing, sailing, rafting, walking and canoeing (some activities are charged for). The unspoilt surrounding countryside is excellent for walking or cycling and locally there is horse riding and fishing. English is spoken in reception by the very welcoming Schutjes family. This site caters for families with children including teenagers (in fact they say 8 months to 86 years!)

Facilities

Each individual cabin has a toilet, shower and washbasin (key deposit) and, as each pitch empties, the facilities are cleaned in readiness for the next. Special pitches for disabled people with facilities with a new toilet block for them. Two fully equipped laundry areas. Shop at entrance with reasonable stock. Bar/restaurant with splendid new terrace (evenings only May and Sept) plus large TV. Takeaway. All 1/5 - 15/9. Snack bar 1/7 - 31/8. Swimming pools (solar heated), water slide and paddling pool, and poolside bar (1/7-31/8). New play areas and active children's club. Tennis, table tennis, basketball, volleyball, football, minigolf and boules. Teenagers' disco organised in high season. Recreation area with TV for youngsters. Internet connection. Only electric barbecues are permitted. Torch useful. Off site: Large sandy beaches at Gruissan (10 km) and Narbonne Plage (15 km). Narbonne 4 km.

At a glance

Welcome & Ambience ✓✓✓✓✓ Location ✓✓✓✓
Quality of Pitches ✓✓✓✓ Range of Facilities ✓✓✓✓✓

Directions

From A9 take exit 38 (Narbonne Sud). Go round roundabout to last exit and follow signs for La Nautique and site, then further site signs to site on right in 3 km.

Charges 2006

Per unit incl. electricity, water and sanitary unit	€ 8,50 - € 20,00
person	€ 4,20 - € 6,00
child (1-7 yrs)	€ 2,20 - € 4,50
dog or cat	€ 1,50 - € 3,50

Reservations

Made with deposit (€ 130) and fee (€ 20).
Tel: 04 68 90 48 19.
Email: info@campinglanautique.com

Open

15 February - 15 November.

FR30000 Camping Domaine de Gaujac

Boisset et Gaujac, F-30140 Anduze (Gard)

This large, woodland holiday site is enthusiastically run by the energetic and friendly Holley family (English is spoken). The 293 level pitches are well shaded and include 175 for touring. 153 have electricity (4-6A) and 22 serviced pitches have electricity (4-10A),water and drainage. Access to some areas can be difficult for larger units due to narrow winding access roads, trees and hedges. Larger units should ask for lower numbered pitches (1-148) where access is a little easier. In high season this region is dry and hot, thus grass quickly wears off many pitches leaving just a sandy base. There are 12 special hardstanding pitches for motorcaravans near the entrance. The site has a new covered animation area and courtyard terrace. The extensive and lively programme of activities in the main season includes a children's club, plus cabaret, karaoke, disco, buffet parties and even cinema shows. Just across the lane is the river with a small beach where one can swim, boat or fish.

Facilities

New heated toilet blocks include washbasins in cubicles, special children's low level equipment and good facilities for disabled visitors. Dishwashing and laundry sinks, washing machines, dryer and ironing facilities. Motorcaravan service point. Well stocked shop (2/6-27/8). Newsagent. Takeaway/crêperie (15/4-15/9). Bar and restaurant (15/4-15/9, on demand at other times). Fenced heated swimming and paddling pool complex new for 2006 (all season with lifeguard 5/7-15/8). Playground plus sports field for football, volleyball etc. Two tennis courts (free off season). Minigolf. Only gas and electric barbecues are permitted. Off site: Fishing 70 m. Bicycle hire 5 km. Riding and golf 8 km. Mining museum at Alès, steam trains run between Anduze and St Jean-du-Gard, a music museum at Anduze, and a number of spectacular caverns and grottoes. River beach 70 km. Many marked walks and bicycle rides.

At a glance

Welcome & Ambience	✓✓✓✓✓	Location	✓✓✓✓
Quality of Pitches	✓✓✓	Range of Facilities	✓✓✓✓

Directions

From Alès take N110 towards Montpellier. At St Christol-les-Alès fork right on D910 towards Anduze and in Bagard, at roundabout, turn left on D246 to Boisset et Gaujac. Follow signs to site in 5 km. GPS: N44:02.148 E04:01.455

Charges 2006

Per unit incl. 2 persons	€ 14,00 - € 22,00
extra person	€ 4,00 - € 4,70
child (2-7 yrs)	€ 2,90 - € 3,90
dog	free - € 2,50
electricity (4-10A)	€ 3,00 - € 3,50

Credit cards accepted in high season only. Camping Cheques accepted.

Reservations

Necessary in high season and made with deposit (€ 110) and fee (€ 20). Tel: 04 66 61 80 65. Email: gravieres@club-internet.fr

Open

1 April - 30 September.

FR30040 Camping Mas de Mourgues

Gallician, F-30600 Vauvert (Gard)

This is an English-owned campsite on the edge of the Petite Camargue region, popular with those who choose not to use the autoroutes. It can be hot here, the Mistral can blow and you may have some road noise, but having said all that, the previous owners and the present owners, the Foster family, have created quite a rural idyll. Originally a vineyard on stony ground, some of the vines are now used to mark the pitches, although many other varieties of trees and shrubs have been planted, including tamaris, eucalyptus, olives (they produce their own oil) and myrtle plain. This creates quite a unique environment for this area. The reception building and toilet blocks are also unusual, looking rather like air raid shelters, but they are effective in the climate. The central pool is welcome and the 'al fresco' bar with a barbecue one evening each week, and a Sunday boules competition complete the relaxed atmosphere of this small site. There are 80 pitches with 70 for touring and 62 with 10A electricity. Bird-watching is popular – climb to the bird-watching viewpoint and check what has been seen in the 'wildlife book'. This is a wine-growing area, so take a ride in the horse-drawn 'caleche' to visit the local vineyard.

Facilities

Two small toilet blocks provide for all needs. Facilities for disabled visitors. Washing machine. Motorcaravan service point. Pizza van on site allows for simple meals. Reception keeps essentials and bottled water. Bread to order (evening before). Communal barbecue but gas or electric ones are allowed. Apartments. mobile homes and tents to rent. Off site: Fishing 2 km. (licence not required). Riding 8 km. Golf 20 km. Bicycle hire and boat launching 25 km. Beach 27 km.

Open

1 April - 30 September.

At a glance

Welcome & Ambience	✓✓✓✓	Location	✓✓✓✓
Quality of Pitches	✓✓✓✓	Range of Facilities	✓✓✓✓

Directions

Leave A9 autoroute at exit 26 (Gallargues) and follow signs for Vauvert. At Vauvert take N572 towards Arles and St Gilles. Site is on left after 4 km. at crossroads for Gallician.

Charges 2006

Per unit incl. 2 persons	€ 11,00 - € 13,00
extra person	€ 3,00 - € 4,00
child (0-10 yrs)	€ 1,50 - € 2,00
electricity	€ 2,50
dog	€ 2,00 - € 3,00

Reservations

Made with non-returnable 25% deposit. Tel: 04 66 73 30 88. Email: info@masdemourgues.com

FR30020 Yelloh! Village La Petite Camargue

B.P. 21, F-30220 Aigues-Mortes (Gard)

This is a large, impressive site (553 pitches) with a huge swimming pool complex and other amenities to match, conveniently situated beside one of the main routes across the famous Camargue. Its position alongside this busy road is an advantage for access but could perhaps be a drawback in terms of traffic, although when we stayed overnight in season it was virtually silent. It offers a variety of good sized pitches, regularly laid out and with varying amounts of shade. There are 70 touring pitches (with 6 or 10A electricity) interspersed amongst more than 300 mobile homes and 145 tour operator pitches. The main activity area, situated between the pitches and the road, is attractively designed and provides a wide range of facilities, including the pool area and shops, almost like a village centre. The site is conveniently situated for visiting the Camargue and not far from the sea, beaches and other sport facilities and activities. It also provides a range of on site entertainment with a good activity programme. English is spoken at this well run, busy site. A Yelloh Village member.

Facilities

Three toilet blocks provide modern facilities including many combined showers and washbasins. Laundry facilities. Motorcaravan service point. Range of shops, bar/restaurant with pizzeria and takeaway. Hairdresser and beauty centre. L-shaped swimming pool complex. Play area, and children's club. Riding at adjoining large stables. Volleyball, basketball, tennis and table tennis. Bicycle hire. Quad bikes. Disco. Off site: Fishing 3 km, golf 8 km. Nearest beach 3.5 km, with free bus service July/Aug.

Open

24 April - 19 September (with all services).

At a glance

Welcome & Ambience	✓✓✓✓	Location	✓✓✓✓
Quality of Pitches	✓✓✓✓	Range of Facilities	✓✓✓✓

Directions

From autoroute A9 take exit 26 (Gallargues) towards Le Grau-du-Roi. Continue past Aigues-Mortes on the D62 and site is 2 km. on the right, just before large roundabout for La Grand-Motte and Le Grau-du-Roi junction. Site is approx. 18 km. from exit 26.

Charges guide

Per unit incl. 1 or 2 persons and electricity	€ 15,00 - € 38,00
extra person	€ 5,50 - € 7,50

Reservations

Made with 25% deposit. Tel: 04 66 53 98 98.
Email: petite.camargue@yellohvillage.com

FR30030 Camping Abri de Camargue

320 route du Phare de l'Espiguette, Port Camargue, F-30240 Le Grau-du-Roi (Gard)

This pleasant site has an attractive pool area overlooked by the bar and its outdoor tables on a pleasant sheltered terrace. The larger outdoor pool has surrounds for sunbathing and the smaller indoor one is heated. With 277 level pitches, there are 139 for touring units, mainly of 100 sq.m (there are also smaller ones). Electricity and water are available on most, and the pitches are well maintained and shaded, with trees and flowering shrubs quite luxuriant in parts. Recent additions include an air-conditioned cinema room and a club for children in high season. A summer fair is within walking distance which can be noisy until quite late. English is spoken. In July and August arrivals are not registered until after 4pm.

Facilities

Two well appointed toilet blocks, include washbasins in cubicles, dishwashing and laundry sinks. Facilities for handicapped. Convenient motorcaravan service point. Shop. Bar with TV, restaurant and takeaway with reasonably priced food (all open when site is open). Heated indoor pool and outdoor pool. New cinema room. Entertainment programme. Play area of the highest quality (one of few with a rubber EU standard safety base). Volleyball. Table tennis. Children's club. Petanque. Off site: Tennis 800 m. Riding and bicycle hire 1 km. Fishing 2 km. Golf 5 km. The nearest beach at Port Camargue is 900 m. and the one at L'Espiguette is 4 km. (in high season a free bus passes the gate to L'Espiguette). Boat or surfboard hire nearby.

Open

1 April - 30 September.

At a glance

Welcome & Ambience	✓✓✓✓	Location	✓✓✓✓
Quality of Pitches	✓✓✓✓✓	Range of Facilities	✓✓✓✓✓

Directions

From the A9 autoroute, 38 km. from Montelimar and 44 km. from Nimes take exit for Monpellier Est (Palavas) or for Gallargues. From Le Grau-du-Roi bypass follow signs for 'Port Camargue' and 'Campings' just northeast of Grau-du-Roi then 'Rive gauche' signs towards Phare l'Espiguette over roundabout and site is on right opposite Tobbogan Park. GPS: N43:31.350 E04:08.947

Charges 2005

Per unit incl. 1 or 2 persons	€ 24,00 - € 47,00
incl. 3-5 persons	€ 28,00 - € 49,00
extra person or extra car	€ 6,00 - € 9,00
pet	€ 6,00
Campsite access card deposit of € 15.	

Reservations

Advised for high season (1/7-31/8) when made for min. 1 week with € 33 fee. Tel: 04 66 51 54 83.
Email: contact@abridecamargue.fr

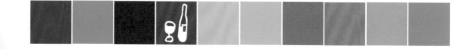

FR30060 Camping Domaine des Fumades

Les Fumades, F-30500 Allègre (Gard)

Domaine des Fumades is a pleasant, busy site with a friendly atmosphere near the thermal springs at Allègre. Reception at the site is a joy to behold. Set in an attractive courtyard, within the farmhouse, it has a central fountain and masses of tubs and baskets of colourful flowers. The entrance as a whole has a very tropical feel with its banana plants and palm trees. The 230 pitches, 80 for touring, are large and level, all with 4A electricity. A variety of trees add privacy and welcome shade. Three pleasantly landscaped swimming pools have ample sunbathing space and bridges and new jacuzzis. This is a good area for walking, cycling, riding, climbing and fishing. Used by tour operators (80 pitches).

Facilities

Two well appointed sanitary blocks. Some washbasins in cabins, baby baths and facilities for disabled people. These facilities are well maintained but, when we visited, were not very clean and one had no hot water. Well stocked shop. Bar, enlarged restaurant, snack bar and takeaway. Two designated barbecue areas. Swimming pools. Large, well equipped playground. Games room, tennis, volleyball, table tennis and boules. Entertainment programme, designed to appeal to families. Off site: Riding 2 km.

Open

15 May - 5 September.

At a glance

Welcome & Ambience	✓✓✓	Location	✓✓✓✓
Quality of Pitches	✓✓✓	Range of Facilities	✓✓✓✓

Directions

From Alès take D16 through Salindres, continue towards Allègre, until signs for Fumades (and thermal springs) on the right.

Charges 2005

Per unit incl. 2 persons	€ 13,70 - € 26,50
with electricity (4A)	€ 16,30 - € 30,60
extra person	€ 2,75 - € 7,15
child (under 7 yrs)	€ 1,60 - € 3,50
pet	€ 2,00

Reservations

Made with deposit (€ 140) and fee (€ 25).
Tel: 04 66 24 80 78.
Email: domaine.des.fumades@wanadoo.fr

FR30070 Castel Camping Le Château de Boisson

Boisson, F-30500 Allegre-Les Fumades (Gard)

Château de Boisson is a quiet family site within easy reach of the Cévennes, Ardèche or Provence. It is set in the grounds of the château, beside the small medieval village of Boisson. Reception at the entrance is new, light and cool, built from the stone in the local style so it blends beautifully with the rest of the buildings. The site is hilly so the pitches are on two levels, many of which slope slightly and all have 5A electricity. Five have personal cabins that provide a WC, washbasin and shower. Rock pegs are essential. Trees provide some shade. The large attractive swimming pool with a toboggan and paddling pool is at the castle in a sunny location and there is also an indoor pool (all season) of excellent quality. The restaurant in the castle is cool and elegant with tables also available outside on the shady terrace.

Facilities

The two toilet blocks, one near the castle, are very clean and well maintained with washbasins in cabins. Washing machines at both blocks, baby bath and shower, facilities for disabled visitors. Small shop. Very good restaurant, bar and snacks. Internet point. Play area. Indoor and outdoor pools (all season). Tennis, boule, volleyball and basketball. Animation in July and Aug. Dogs are not accepted. Barbecues are not allowed. Apartments to rent in the castle.

Open

Easter - 30 September.

At a glance

Welcome & Ambience	✓✓✓✓	Location	✓✓✓✓
Quality of Pitches	✓✓✓✓	Range of Facilities	✓✓✓✓✓

Directions

From Alès take D16 northeast towards Salindres and Auzon. Just after Auzon turn right across river and immediately left, signed Barjac. Turn right and site is signed. This is the only route into the site for trailers and motorcaravans. Do not drive through Boissons.

Charges 2005

Per unit incl. 2 persons	€ 15,00 - € 31,00
with water and drainage	€ 17,00 - € 34,00
extra person	€ 4,00 - € 6,00
child (under 5 yrs)	€ 2,00 - € 3,00

Reservations

Made with deposit and fee. Tel: 04 66 24 82 21.
Email: reception@chateaudeboisson.com

3

FR30100 Camping Naturiste de la Sablière

Domaine de la Sablière, St Privat de Champclos, F-30430 Barjac (Gard)

Spectacularly situated in the Cèze Gorges, this naturist site with a surprising 497 pitches, 240 for touring, tucked away within its wild terrain offers a wide variety of facilities, all within a really peaceful, wooded and dramatic setting. The pitches themselves are mainly on flat stony terraces, attractively situated among a variety of trees and shrubs (some with low overhang). Many are of a good size and have electricity (6/10A), very long leads may be needed. An excellent pool complex (dynamited out of the hill and built in local style) provides a new children's pool area and two large pools, one of which can be covered by a sliding dome, sunbathing terraces, saunas and a bar. Nudity is obligatory around the pool complex. This is a family run and orientated site and the owner, Gaby Cespedes, provides a personal touch that is unusual in a large site. This no doubt contributes to the relaxed, informal atmosphere and first time naturists would find this a gentle introduction to naturism. You must expect some fairly steep walking between pitches and facilities, those with walking difficulties may not find this site appropriate, although there is a minibus shuttle service in July and August. Member France 4 Naturisme.

Facilities

Six good unisex sanitary blocks (most have recently been refurbished) have excellent free hot showers in typical open plan, naturist style, washbasins (cold water), baby baths and facilities for people with disabilities. Dishwashing and laundry sinks. Laundry. Supermarket with a very wide range of goods. Excellent open air, covered restaurant (1/4-22/9) with good value waiter service meals and a takeaway. Swimming pool complex (all season). Bar (1/4-22/9) with TV room and disco. Small café/crêperie. Varied activities include walking, climbing, swimming, canoeing, fitness trail, fishing (permit required), archery, tennis, minigolf and volleyball, book binding, pottery, yoga etc. Entertainment for adults and children (mid June - end Aug). Mobile homes, caravans, chalet and tents to rent. Torch useful. Gas and electric barbecues only. Off site: Barjac with its Antiques Fair at Easter and mid-August. Alès, Chemin de Fer des Cèvennes. Bicycle hire 8 km. Riding 10 km. Golf 12 km.

At a glance

Welcome & Ambience	✓✓✓✓✓	Location	✓✓✓✓
Quality of Pitches	✓✓✓	Range of Facilities	✓✓✓✓✓

Directions

From Barjac take D901 east for 3 km. Turn right at site sign just before St Privat-de-Champclos and follow site signs along a winding country lane to site entrance in approx. 4 km.
GPS: N44:16.021 E04:21.125

Charges 2005

Per pitch incl. 2 persons	€ 11,40 - € 28,90
incl. electricity	€ 15,15 - € 32,55
extra person	€ 3,45 - € 6,49
child (under 8 yrs)	free - € 5,79
dog	€ 1,00 - € 2,50

Camping Cheques accepted.

Reservations

Made with deposit (25%) and fee (€ 30).
Tel: 04 66 24 51 16.
Email: contact@villagesabliere.com

Open

1 April - 1 October.

FR30110 Camping du Mas de Rey

Arpaillargues, F-30700 Uzès (Gard)

A warm welcome from the English speaking Maire family is guaranteed at this small, unsophisticated 70 pitch site. Most of the large (150 sq.m) pitches are separated by bushes, many are shaded and all have 10A electricity. Due to the wonderful climate, grass can at times be hard to find. The reception, bar, restaurant and shop are in the same large airy building. Reception has a wealth of tourist information and they are always willing to give advice on the numerous things to see and do in the area. The owners say the wine festivals in early August at Châteauneuf du Pape and at Uzès in mid Aug. are festivals not to be missed.

Facilities

Two well maintained unisex toilet blocks, one quite new with facilities for disabled visitors, baby room and en-suite family cubicles. Dishwashing and laundry sinks. Washing machine and iron. Shop (high season only but bread to order all season). Bar serves a simple 'menu of the day' most evenings (1/7-31/8). Small circular swimming and paddling pools (1/5-15/10, closed lunch-times). Off site: Riding 5 km, golf or fishing 3 km. and canoeing 10 km. Nîmes, Avignon and the Pont du Gard all near.

Open

10 April - 15 October.

At a glance

Welcome & Ambience	✓✓✓✓	Location	✓✓✓✓
Quality of Pitches	✓✓✓	Range of Facilities	✓✓✓✓

Directions

From D981 in Uzès take the D982 westwards signed Arpaillargues, Anduze, Sommieres, Moussac. Site is 3 km. on the left, well signed.

Charges guide

Per unit incl. 2 persons	€ 16,00
extra person	€ 4,30
child (under 7yrs)	€ 2,60
electricity	€ 3,00
animal	€ 1,60

Less 10-20% outside July/Aug. Special senior tariff in low season. Credit cards accepted in July/Aug only.

Reservations

Made with deposit (€ 46) and fee (€ 62).
Tel: 04 66 22 18 27. Email: masderey@hvtour.fr

FR30080 Camping Le Mas de Reilhe

Crespian, F-30260 Quissac (Gard)

This is a comfortable family site nestling in a valley with 95 pitches (76 for tourers). From here you can explore the Cevennes gorges, enjoy the Mediterranean beaches, visit the Petite Camargue or Nîmes with its Roman remains from le Mas de Reilhe. All but the highest pitches have electricity (some of the upper ones may require long leads). The large lower pitches are separated by tall poplar trees and hedges, close to the main facilities and may experience some road noise. The large terraced pitches on the hillside are scattered under mature pine trees, some with good views, and are more suited to tents and trailer tents but with their own modern sanitary facilities. The entertainment in July and August is for the children with just the occasional competition for adults. The heated swimming pool is in a sunny position and overlooked by the attractive bar/restaurant. There are no shops in the village, the nearest being at the medieval city of Sommières 10 km. away (and well worth a visit). A 'Sites et Paysages' member.

Facilities
Good toilet facilities with washbasins in cabins and pre-set showers. Dishwashing and laundry sinks. Washing machine. Reception with limited shop (bread can be ordered). Bar, takeaway and restaurant. Small play area on grass. Table tennis. Volleyball. Pentaque. Heated swimming pool (8/4-24/9). Internet access. Off site: Tennis 0.5 km. Fishing 3 km. Riding 5 km. Bicycle hire 10 km. Golf 25 km. The sea and the gorges are approx 30 km. and Nîmes 25 km.

Open
8 April - 24 September.

At a glance
Welcome & Ambience	✓✓✓✓	Location	✓✓✓✓
Quality of Pitches	✓✓✓✓	Range of Facilities	✓✓✓✓

Directions
From the A9 take exit 'Nimes ouest' signed Alès, then onto the D999 towards Le Vigan. The site is on the N110 just north of the junction with the D999 at the southern end of the village of Crespian. GPS: N43:52.727 E04:05.813

Charges 2006
Per unit incl. 2 persons	€ 13,00 - € 19,00
extra person	€ 3,40 - € 5,20
child (2-6 yrs)	€ 1,80 - € 3,00
electricity (6/10A)	€ 3,30 - € 4,00
Camping Cheques accepted.	

Reservations
Made with deposit (25% of total) and fee (€ 18). Tel: 04 66 77 82 12. Email: info@camping-mas-de-reilhe.fr

LE MAS DE REILHE ★★★★

Camping Caravaning

" Situated between the Cevennes Mountains and the Mediterranean sea, a small charming & shaded camp site in the sun ". Mobil-homes, chalets and bungalows A. Trigano to rent.

- Heated swimming-pool (14/5-25/9)
- Restaurant, pizzeria & takeaway (1/6-15/9)
- Animations for children (July - August)

Tél : 0033 466 77 82 12 - Fax : 0033 466 80 26 50
E-mail : info@camping-mas-de-reilhe.fr
Website : www.camping-mas-de-reilhe.fr

FR30120 Camping Campeole Ile des Papes

Barrage de Villeneuve, F-30400 Villeneuve-lez-Avignon (Gard)

Now ten years old, Camping Ile des Papes is a large, open and very well equipped site near Avignon with an extensive swimming pool area and a fishing lake with beautiful mature gardens. The railway is quite near but noise is not too intrusive. The 450 pitches are of a good size on level grass and all have electricity, 150 taken by mobile homes or chalets. Avignon and its Palace and museums is 8 km. away.

Facilities
Toilet blocks of very good quality include baby rooms. Dishwashing and laundry sinks. Washing machines. Motorcaravan services. Well stocked shop (limited hours in low seasons). Bar and restaurant. Two large swimming pools and one for children. Play area. Lake for fishing. Archery, tennis, table tennis, volleyball, minigolf and basketball (all free). Bicycle hire. Games and competitions for all ages in high season. Off site: Riding 3 km.

Open
25 March - 20 October.

At a glance
Welcome & Ambience	✓✓✓✓	Location	✓✓✓
Quality of Pitches	✓✓✓	Range of Facilities	✓✓✓✓

Directions
Take N100 Nîmes road out of Avignon towards Bagnoles-sur-Cèze and turn right after crossing the Rhône. Turn left along the bank (Roquemaure D980). After 6 km. turn right on D228 Barrage de Villeneuve and site is 1 km. GPS: N43:59.631 E04:49.081

Charges 2006
Per unit incl. 2 persons	€ 16,00 - € 23,00
extra person	€ 4,50 - € 6,30
electricity (6A)	€ 3,90
Various special offers.	

Reservations
Made with deposit (25%) and fee (€ 23). Tel: 04 90 15 15 90. Email: ile.papes@wanadoo.fr

FR30160 Camping Caravaning Le Boucanet

B.P. 206, F-30240 Le Grau-du-Roi (Gard)

On the beach between Grande Motte and Le Grau-du-Roi, this is a sunny site with only a little shade. Many trees have been planted and are growing but as yet most are not tall enough to give much shade. As to be expected, the 458 pitches are sandy but level. The 317 for touring units are separated by small bushes, most with electricity (6A). Plenty of flowers decorate the site and the pleasant restaurant (open lunchtimes and evenings) overlooks the large pool (heated at beginning and end of season). An excellent shopping arcade provides groceries, fruit, newspapers, a butcher and cooked meats, rotisserie and pizzas. In July and August organised activities include games, competitions, gymnastics, water polo, jogging and volleyball for adults. There is access to the river for fishing and horse riding on the white horses of the Camargue is to be found within a few kilometres.

Facilities

The toilet blocks are convenient for the pitches providing washbasins in cubicles and some British style toilets in two blocks, the remainder Turkish style (about 70%). Some washbasins in cabins. Facilities for disabled people at two blocks. Baby rooms. Dishwashing and laundry sinks have warm water. Washing machines, dryers, irons and fridge hire. Motorcaravan service point. Range of shops. Restaurant (1/5). Takeaway (June to end Aug). Bar with snacks. Large swimming pool and paddling pool. Play area on sand and miniclub in July/Aug. Table tennis, tennis. Bicycle hire. Dogs are not accepted. Off site: Riding 500 m. Golf 1.5 km. Shops, restaurants and bars within 3 km.

Open

15 April - 1 October.

At a glance

Welcome & Ambience	✓✓✓	Location	✓✓✓✓
Quality of Pitches	✓✓✓	Range of Facilities	✓✓✓✓✓

Directions

Site is between La Grand Motte and Le Grau-du-Roi on the D255 coastal road, on the seaward side of the road.

Charges 2005

Per unit incl. 2 persons	€ 17,00 - € 31,00
with electricity	€ 20,50 - € 34,50
pitch on first row of beach, plus	€ 5,00 - € 6,00
extra person	€ 6,00 - € 9,00
child (under 7 yrs)	€ 4,50 - € 7,50
Camping Cheques accepted.	

Reservations

Necessary for July/Aug. and made with 25% deposit and booking fee (€ 25); by money order or credit card only. Tel: 04 66 51 41 48. Email: contact@campingboucanet.fr

CAMPINGS
FranceLoc

Domaine du Boucanet

Pitches, mobile homes, heated indoor pool, many sports and leisure activities during the season on this family site ideal for relaxation!

B.P. 206
30240 Le Grau du Roi
Tél. 0033(0)4 66 51 41 48
Fax. 0033(0)4 66 51 41 87
www.campings-franceloc.com

Méditerranée

FR30170 Camping La Sousta

Avenue du Pont du Gard, F-30210 Remoulins (Gard)

With a long season, La Sousta is a former municipal site set under tall trees and with a ten minute walk of the famous Pont du Gard, a World Heritage site. The 300 pitches (including 60 mobile homes to rent) are mainly level and numbered, but are not very clearly defined. The reception office provides plenty of tourist information and coach trips are organised in high season to various places of interest. A large swimming pool set in a sunny location has surrounding grassy areas for sunbathing. A footpath leads to a private beach on the river.

Facilities

The four toilet blocks are quite basic but give clean facilities with mainly British style WCs, baby bath and showers, and facilities for disabled people. Washing machines and dryer. Bar. Snack bar and takeaway. Swimming and paddling pools. Play areas. Bicycle hire. Weekly disco in July/Aug. Entertainment and canoes trips organised.

Open

1 March - 31 October.

At a glance

Welcome & Ambience	✓✓✓	Location	✓✓✓✓
Quality of Pitches	✓✓✓	Range of Facilities	✓✓✓

Directions

Site is signed from the centre of Remoulins. From N100 follow signs for Beaucaire and Nimes, then site signs. Site is beside the D981, just before Pont du Gard.

Charges 2006

Per unit incl. 2 persons	€ 11,60 - € 19,00
incl. electricity	€ 15,80 - € 22,20
extra person (over 7 yrs)	€ 3,00 - € 6,30

Reservations

Contact site. Tel: 04 66 37 12 80. Email: info@lasousta.com

FR30140 Camping La Soubeyranne

Route de Beaucaire, F-30210 Remoulins (Gard)

Recently acquired by the group France Location, this site is well positioned for visiting the Pont du Gard, Nîmes and Uzès, famed for their Roman connections. It is approached by a short tree-lined avenue which leads to reception. The 200 pitches offer extremely generous amounts of shade and keeping the 4.5 hectares watered involves over 5 km. of hose pipe. Pitches are large, level, numbered and separated, with 170 having 6A electricity connections. An animation programme (July/Aug) is aimed mainly at young children (teenagers may find the site rather quiet). Whilst quiet in some respects, train noise both by day and night can be an irritant.

Facilities

Two well appointed, unisex toilet blocks are basic but clean give more than adequate facilities and include washbasins in cubicles. Motorcaravan service point. Fridges for hire. Small shop selling basics. Restaurant, bar and takeaway (all from 15/6). Heated swimming pool complex (1/5-30/9) with 20 x 10 m. pool and smaller toddlers' pool (unsupervised), and partly shaded. Play area, including trampoline, table tennis, boules, tennis and volleyball. Bicycle hire. Off site: Fishing 1 km. Remoulins 1.5 km.

Open

25 March - 23 September.

At a glance

Welcome & Ambience	✓✓✓	Location	✓✓✓
Quality of Pitches	✓✓✓	Range of Facilities	✓✓✓✓

Directions

From Uzès take D981 to Remoulins, turn right at lights over river bridge, left at roundabout, then left (signed D986 Beaucaire). Site is 1.5 km. further on left. GPS: N43:55.582 E04:33.866

Charges 2006

Per unit incl. 2 persons	€ 5,50 - € 21,00
electricity	€ 3,40
extra person	€ 4,50 - € 6,50
child (under 7 yrs)	€ 2,50 - € 4,00
animal	€ 4,15

Reservations

Contact site for details. Tel: 04 66 37 03 21.
Email: soubeyranne@wanadoo.fr

FR30180 Camping Mas de la Cam

Route de St Andre de Valborgne, F-30270 St Jean-du-Gard (Gard)

Camping Mas de la Cam is rather an unusual site for France in that all the pitches are used for touring units. It is a very pleasant and spacious site with well trimmed grass and hedges and a profusion of flowers and shrubs. Lying alongside the small Gardon river, the banks have been left free of pitches giving neat grass for sunbathing and some trees for shade, whilst children can amuse themselves in the water (no good for canoes). Slightly sloping, the 200 medium to large pitches are on level terraces, some with varying amounts of shade and all with electricity (6A). A quiet, family site; you are assured of a good welcome here. There is no evening entertainment and just a few, low key daytime competitions in July and August. Entrance is via a narrow unfenced bridge, but wide enough for large outfits.

Facilities

High quality toilet blocks provide washbasins in cabins, adjustable showers in large cubicles, a baby bath and facilities for disabled visitors. Washing machines. Relaxing bar/restaurant and terrace. Small shop with bread (to order). Attractive large swimming and paddling pools. Huge play and sports areas, including new multisports court. Club room used in low season for bridge, in high season as a games room. Fishing. Off site: St Jean-de-Gard 3 km. Bus to the village twice a day. Riding 5 km. Bicycle hire 15 km.

At a glance

Welcome & Ambience	✓✓✓✓	Location	✓✓✓✓
Quality of Pitches	✓✓✓✓	Range of Facilities	✓✓✓✓✓

Directions

Site is 3 km. northwest of St Jean-du-Gard in the direction of St André de Valborgne on the D907, site is signed, fork left and descend across narrow bridge to site. Site entrance is not accessible from the north.

Charges 2005

Per unit incl. 2 persons	€ 13,00 - € 19,50
with electricity	€ 16,00 - € 23,00
extra person	€ 3,20 - € 4,50

Reservations

Made with deposit (€ 100) and fee (€ 15).
Tel: 04 66 85 12 02. Email: camping@masdelacam.fr

Open

28 April - 20 September.

3

FR30190 Camping International des Gorges du Gardon

Chemin de la Barque Vieille, F-30210 Vers-Pont-du-Gard (Gard)

Probably the main attraction in the Gardon area of France is the Pont du Gard, an amazing Roman aqueduct built around 50AD. There are, however, other attractions worthy of a visit, such as the medieval village of Castillon-du-Gard perched on a rocky peak with narrow cobbled streets, and Collias at the bottom of the gorge from where you can hire canoes. It provides 200 level, mostly good-sized pitches, 180 for touring. Many are on stony terraces in a woodland setting offering good shade while others are more open, all with electricity (10-15A). Rock pegs are essential. There is direct access to the river where swimming is permitted, although in summer the water level may be a little low. Unsupervised heated attractive swimming pool and paddling pool provide an alternative. The owners, Joseph and Sylvie Gonzales speak a little English, and visitors will always receive a warm and friendly welcome from them. Joseph previously owned a restaurant and we highly recommend his site restaurant. Tourist information is in the reception (open all day) and Sylvie will share her local knowledge if you need any additional help.

Facilities
Two toilet blocks provide unisex facilities: showers, washbasins (some in cabins), and toilets. Facilities for disabled visitors in building nearest reception. Baby room. Washing machine, dishwashing and laundry sinks. Bar and good restaurant (table service and takeaway). Heated swimming and paddling pools (unsupervised). Play areas. Table tennis. Games room and TV. Family entertainment during July/Aug. Off site: Canoeing arranged from site.

Open
15 March - 31 October.

At a glance
Welcome & Ambience	✓✓✓✓✓	Location	✓✓✓✓	
Quality of Pitches	✓✓✓✓	Range of Facilities	✓✓✓✓	

Directions
Exit A9 at Remoulins, then take D981 towards Uzès. About 4 km. after Remoulins, just after the junction for the Pont du Gard, turn left site signed and follow signs to site (a few hundred metres).

Charges 2005
Per unit incl. 2 persons	€ 12,50 - € 16,50
extra person	€ 3,50 - € 6,00
child (under 7 yrs)	€ 2,50 - € 3,00
electricity	€ 3,00

Reservations
Advisable during July and August.
Tel: 04 66 22 81 81.
Email: camping.international@wanadoo.fr

Camping International Les Gorges du Gardon

30210 vers pont du gard / tel. 33 466 228 181 - fax. 33 466 229 012
www.le-camping-international.com   camping.international@wanadoo.fr

FR34020 Camping Le Garden

44 place des Tamaris, F-34280 La Grande Motte (Hérault)

Le Garden is a mature site, situated 300 m. back from a fine sandy beach and with all the choice of sports, entertainment and other facilities of the popular holiday resort of La Grand Motte. With space for 86 caravans and 118 mobile homes, the 100 sq.m. pitches are hedged with good shade on sandy grass base. All have electricity (6A), water and waste water drains. The fine sandy beach and port are only 300 m. away, with a shopping complex, bar and restaurant next to site.

Facilities
Three well situated toilet blocks, smartly refurbished in Mediterranean colours, include washbasins in cabins and baby bath. Dishwashing and laundry sinks. Washing machines. Unit for disabled people. Shop, restaurant, bar and takeaway service (from 15/5). Swimming pool and paddling pool (from 15/5). Play area. Table tennis. Off site: Tennis courts and riding club nearby.

Open
1 March - 31 October.

At a glance
Welcome & Ambience	✓✓✓✓	Location	✓✓✓✓	
Quality of Pitches	✓✓✓✓	Range of Facilities	✓✓✓✓✓	

Directions
Entering La Grand Motte from D62 dual-carriageway, keep right following signs for 'campings' and petite Motte. Turn right at traffic lights by Office de Tourism and right again by the Bar Le Garden and site is on the right. GPS: N43:33.793 E04:04.367

Charges 2005
Per unit incl. 1-3 persons	€ 26,00
with electricity, water and drainage	€ 36,00
extra person	€ 8,00
Bracelet required for pool € 10.	

Reservations
Not made. Tel: 04 67 56 50 09.

FR34030 Camping International Le Napoléon

Avenue de la Méditérranée, F-34450 Vias-Plage (Hérault)

Le Napoléon is a smaller, family run site situated in the village of Vias Plage bordering the Mediterranean. The town of Vias itself is set further back from the sea, in the wine-growing area of the Midi, an area which includes the Camargue, Béziers and popular modern resorts such as Cap d'Agde. The single street that leads to Vias Plage is hectic to say the least in season, but once through the security barrier and entrance to Le Napoléon, the contrast is marked - tranquillity, yet still only a few yards from the beach and other attractions. Not that the site itself lacks vibrancy, with its Californian style pool, amphitheatre for entertainment and other new facilities, but thoughtful planning and design ensure that the camping area is quiet. With good shade from many tall trees, the 240 mainly hedged pitches (105 with hire units) vary in size from 80-100 sq.m. and most have electricity connections. No British tour operators.

Facilities
Three sanitary blocks are of a reasonable standard and were well maintained when seen in peak season. They include washbasins in cabins, baby bath, laundry and facilities for disabled people. Motorcaravan services. Fridges for hire. Well stocked supermarket. Bar. Restaurant/pizzeria. Heated swimming pool with lively piped music. Gym/fitness room. Sauna (on payment) and sun room. Bicycle hire. Tennis, archery, volleyball, basketball, boules. New TV and young people rooms. Children's club. Amphitheatre and wide range of free entertainment until midnight. Site-owned disco outside campsite (Easter-Sept). Off site: Shops, restaurants, and laundry etc. immediately adjacent. Fishing nearby. Riding 1 km. Golf 5 km.

At a glance
Welcome & Ambience	✓✓✓✓	Location	✓✓✓✓
Quality of Pitches	✓✓✓✓	Range of Facilities	✓✓✓✓

Directions
From autoroute take exit for Vias. From town, take D137 towards Vias Plage. Site is on the right near the beach; watch carefully for turning between restaurant and shops. GPS: N43:17.508 E03:24.991

Charges 2005
Per unit incl. 2 persons and electricity	€ 14,00 - € 37,00
extra person (over 4 yrs)	€ 5,00 - € 6,00
electricity (10A)	€ 1,50 - € 2,00
dog	€ 3,00 - € 4,00

Reservations
Taken from 1 Jan. with 30% deposit and fee € 26 incl. cancellation insurance. Tel: 04 67 01 07 80. Email: reception@camping-napoleon.fr

Open
7 April - 30 September.

FR34040 Camping Lou Village

B.P. 30, chemin des Montilles, F-34350 Valras-Plage (Hérault)

Valras is perhaps smarter and is certainly larger than nearby Vias and it has a good number of campsites. Lou Village is a well kept, family owned site with direct access to a sandy beach. A busy site with lots of facilities and quite competitive prices, it does becomes crowded in high season as this is a popular area. The central 'village' area is a veritable hive of holiday activity, with several attractively designed pools and water slides, bars, pizzeria, restaurant and a purpose built stage for the site's extensive entertainment programme. With straw parasols and palm trees, it is an attractive, clean area with a pleasant ambience. There are 580 pitches (200 with mobile homes), 100 with electricity (10A). There is good shade with grass pitches furthest from the beach, partly separated by tall trees whereas nearer the beach the pitches are smaller, sandy and separated by bushes and bamboo hedges. There is lots to do off the site and the history of the Languedoc to discover. English is spoken.

Facilities
Four modern, well sited toilet blocks, all recently refurbished, have reasonable facilities. Mixture of Turkish and British style WCs, showers with no separator and half the washbasins in cabins. Facilities for disabled visitors and babies. Dishwashing and laundry sinks at each block. For a beach site, maintenance seems quite satisfactory. Supermarket, bakery, bazaar and, in high season, a boutique for gifts. Bar and restaurant with ample seating. Takeaway. Swimming pools (one heated), water slides and paddling pool. Playground, children's club and football field. Tennis. Volleyball. Minigolf. Bicycle hire. Sailing and windsurfing. Varied entertainment programme. Gate to beach closes at 21.00. Off site: Riding 500 m. Jet skiing. Paragliding on beach. Canoe kayaking and river fishing 1 km. Golf 12 km.

Open
End April - 10 September.

At a glance
Welcome & Ambience	✓✓✓✓	Location	✓✓✓✓✓
Quality of Pitches	✓✓✓✓	Range of Facilities	✓✓✓✓✓

Directions
Site is south of Béziers. From autoroute, take Béziers-Ouest exit for Valras Plage and continue for about 14 km. Follow 'Casino' signs and site is 1 km. south of centre of Valras Plage in the direction of Vendres. Site is signed to the left at the end of Valras Plage and the start of Vendres Plage.

Charges 2005
Per unit incl. 2 persons and electricity	€ 19,50 - € 35,90
extra person	€ 4,00 - € 6,30
child (under 7 yrs)	free - € 3,20
dog	€ 3,00 - € 4,00
Pool complex bracelet € 5.50 (once only payment).	

Reservations
Made with deposit (€ 183) and fee (€ 30). Tel: 04 67 37 33 79. Email: info@louvillage.com

FR34070 Yelloh! Village Le Sérignan Plage

Mobile homes ▶ page 443

Le Sérignan Plage, F-34410 Sérignan (Hérault)

A large, friendly, family-orientated site with direct access to superb sandy beaches, including a naturist beach, Sérignan Plage exudes a strongly individualistic style which we find very attractive. However, those who look for 'manicured' sites may be less impressed, as its proximity to the beach makes it difficult to keep things neat and tidy. With some 450 mainly good sized, level touring pitches, including some (with little shade) actually alongside the beach, coupled with perhaps the most comprehensive amenities we've come across, the hugely enthusiastic owners, Jean-Guy and Katy Amat continually surprise us with new ideas and developments. New for 2004 was a superb 1,800 sq.m. 'Spa Water Fitness centre' with more new pools, a fitness centre and jacuzzi. The amenities are just too extensive to describe in detail, but they include a pool complex, with slides surrounded by large grassy sunbathing areas and another indoor pool. Perhaps the most remarkable aspect is the cluster of attractive buildings which form the 'heart' of this site with courtyards housing attractive bars, a smart restaurant, shops, takeaway, a stage for entertainment, disco, etc. – all very attractive and with a very special ambience.

Facilities

Nine unisex toilet blocks. The older circular ones with a mix of British and Turkish style WCs are nearest the sea and central 'village' area, seasonal units and mobile homes, etc. and thus take most of the wear and tear. The touring area, furthest from the sea has three modern blocks of individual design. Well planned with good facilities, these include large controllable hot showers with basin and WC en-suite, baby rooms, facilities for disabled people. Washing machines. At peak times maintenance can be a little variable. Well stocked supermarket, bakery, newsagent, ATM and market stalls. Central launderette. Hairdresser. Bars, restaurant and takeaway (all 7/4-10/9). Much animation for children and evening entertainment. Roof-top bar (9 pm - 1 am). - ask for a 'Cucaracha'! Soundproof disco. Heated indoor pool and outdoor pool complex (also heated) with lifeguards in the main season and an ID card system (April - Sept). Sporting activities. Bicycle hire. Off site: Riding 2 km. Golf 10 km. Bicycle hire. Sailing and windsurfing school on beach (lifeguard in high season).

Directions

From A9 exit 35 (Béziers Est) follow signs for Sérignan on D64 (9 km). Don't go into Sérignan, but take sign for Sérignan Plage for 4 km. At small multi sign (blue) turn right on single carriageway. At T-junction turn left over small road bridge and after left hand bend, site is 100 m. after Sérignan Plage Nature.

Charges 2006

Per unit incl. 1 or 2 persons and 5A electricity	€ 19,00 - € 42,00
extra person	€ 6,00 - € 6,50
pet	€ 3,00

Low season offers. Discounts in low season for children under 7 yrs. Camping Cheques accepted.

Reservations

Made from 1 Feb. with deposit (25%) and fee (€ 30). Tel: 04 67 32 35 33. Email: info@leserignanplage.com

Open

6 April - 24 September.

At a glance

Welcome & Ambience	✓✓✓✓	Location	✓✓✓✓✓
Quality of Pitches	✓✓✓✓	Range of Facilities	✓✓✓✓✓

FR34080 Camping Le Sérignan Plage Nature

F-34410 Sérignan (Hérault)

Benefiting from many improvements over the past few years, Sérignan Plage Nature is a distinctly characterful family-orientated site right beside a superb sandy naturist beach. At present it has some 260 good sized touring pitches, on level grass and with plenty of shade except on those right beside the beach. A friendly bar and restaurant are housed in the Romanesque style buildings which form the 'heart' of the site, including the setting for evening entertainment. In recent years the site has been developed by Jean-Guy and Katy Amat, but was originally owned by Jean-Guy's father, who retains an interest and who has been the mastermind behind the award-winning environmentally friendly irrigation system which serves both this site and Camping Sérignan Plage whose extensive facilities are also available to visitors here. Jean-Guy and Katy have some very ambitious plans for both their sites, which may involve significant developments on Sérignan Plage Nature, including a new 'aqua-village'. These developments will probably take a couple of years to complete, so it may be worth checking out the latest state of play before you visit. Member 'France 4 Naturisme'.

Facilities

The toilet blocks of differing design have all been refurbished, and all offer modern facilities with some washbasins in cabins and both British and Turkish style WCs. All is clean and well maintained. Dishwashing under cover. Washing machines. Supermarket, market for fresh fruit and vegetables, newsagent/souvenir shop and ice cream kiosk. Small bar-café. Evening entertainment. Children's disco. Off site: Riding 2 km.

Open

6 April - 24 September.

At a glance

Welcome & Ambience	✓✓✓✓	Location	✓✓✓✓✓
Quality of Pitches	✓✓✓✓	Range of Facilities	✓✓✓✓

Directions

From A9 exit 35 (Béziers Est) follow signs for Sérignan on D64 (9 km). Prior to Sérignan, take road to Sérignan Plage. At small multi sign (blue) turn right onto one-way single carriageway (poorly surfaced) for 500 m. At T-junction turn left over small bridge and site is 75 m. on right immediately after left hand bend (not the first, but the second naturist site).

Charges 2006

Per unit incl. 1 or 2 persons and electricity	€ 17,00 - € 38,00
extra person	€ 5,50 - € 6,50

Camping Cheques accepted.

Reservations

Made from 1 Feb. Tel: 04 67 32 09 61. Email: info@leserignannature.com

Le Sérignan Plage

The magic of the Mediterranean

Imagine – hot sunshine, blue sea, vineyards, olive and eucalyptus trees, alongside a sandy beach – what a setting for a campsite – not just any campsite either !

With three pool areas, one with four toboggans surrounded by sun bathing areas, an indoor pool for baby swimmers plus a magnificent landscaped, Romanesque spa-complex with half Olympic size pool and a superb range of hydro-massage baths to let you unwind and re-charge after the stresses of work.

And that's not all – two attractive restaurants, including the atmospheric "Villa" in its romantic Roman setting beside the spa, three bars, a mini-club and entertainment for all ages, all add up to a fantastic opportunity to enjoy a genuinely unique holiday experience.

Le Sérignan-Plage – F-34410 SERIGNAN
Tel: 00 33 467 32 35 33 – Fax: 00 33 467 32 26 36
info@leserignanplage.com – www.leserignanplage.com

FR34050 Camping Naturiste Le Mas de Lignières

Cesseras-en-Minervois, F-34210 Olonzac (Hérault)

A naturist site hidden in the hills of the Minervois, this is a delightful find, only 3 km. from the medieval town of Minerve with its Cathar connections. Parts of this site enjoy some marvellous views to the Pyrénées, the Corbières and the coast at Narbonne. We recommend that you watch at least one wonderful sunrise over the Pyrénées. The owners Jeanne and Gilles, offer a warm welcome and promote a most enjoyable family atmosphere. The site provides 50 large (200 sq.m.) pitches, all with electricity (6A), and 25 with water and waste water connections. Mainly level grass, they are separated by mature hedges that give considerable privacy. Some smaller pitches (100 sq.m.) are available for tents, with cars parked elsewhere. There is natural shade and a variety of fauna and flora including four types of orchid. Within the confines of the seven hectare site there are some good walks with superb views and, although the camping area is actually quite small, the very large pitches create a very relaxing ambience and a nice introduction to naturist camping. If you ask nicely, Gilles may take you out in his Landrover (he's a bit of an expert on all things natural) to places you would never find otherwise.

Facilities

The pleasant, clean toilet block has open washbasins and semi-open showers. Dishwashing and laundry sinks. En-suite facilities for disabled people. Washing machine. Simple shop for essentials and local specialities. Bread can be ordered (15/6 -15/9). Bar and snack bar (15/7-15/8). Swimming pool with sliding cover for use in early and late season. Paddling pool. Comfortable room for general use with TV, library and tourist information and separate provision for young people. Playground. Tennis, volleyball and boules (all free). Torch useful. Only gas barbecues are permitted. Off site: Sailing, riding and canoeing nearby – Lac de Jouarres. Canal du Midi.

Open

1 April - 2 October.

At a glance

Welcome & Ambience	/////	Location	/////
Quality of Pitches	////	Range of Facilities	////

Directions

From A61 autoroute take Lézignan-Corbières exit, through town via the D611 to Homps, then on D910 to Olonzac. Go through village following the signs to Minerve (D10). Follow road for approx. 4 km. taking left hand turn to Cesseras (D168). At Cesseras follow signs to Fauzan for approx another 4 km. Site is signed to the right where there is a climb up a winding road, which is a little narrow in places.

Charges 2005

Per pitch incl. 2 persons and electricity (6A), water and drainage	€ 24,50
smaller pitch excl. electricity	€ 18,00
extra person	€ 4,00
child (2-7 yrs)	€ 2,80
dog	€ 1,50

Less for longer booked stays.

Reservations

Made until 25/6 with deposit (25%) and fee (€ 10). Tel: 04 68 91 24 86. Email: lemas1@tiscali.fr

FR34060 Hotel de Plein Air L'Oliveraie

Chemin de Bedarieux, F-34480 Laurens (Hérault)

Situated at the foot of the Cevennes, L'Oliveraie has many attractive features and is open all year. Don't assume that the extensive range of sport and recreation available here means that it is all hectic activity – in fact it is surprisingly peaceful. Most of the 116 hedged pitches are large (up to 150 sq.m. in some parts) and all have electrical connections (6/10A). Arranged in rows on two levels, those on the higher level are older and have more shade from mature trees (mainly olives). The ground is stony. The large leisure area is slightly apart from the pitches on the lower area, overlooked by the bar. The old village of Laurens is well worth visiting and is walkable through the vineyards. The area is the home of Faugeres wines (AOC). A 'Sites et Paysages' member.

Facilities

Smart modern toilet block on the higher terrace includes washbasins in cabins, baby bathroom Covered dishwashing and washing machine. A good clean provision. Smaller second block on lower level is open for high season. All perfectly adequate and clean when seen in high season. Small, well stocked shop. Bar/restaurant serving pizzas, salads, etc. Indoor bar, also used for films and activities for younger children (all 1/7-31/8). Good sized pool and children's pool (1/6-30/9). Tennis court and tennis practice wall. Volleyball, basketball, minigolf. Bicycle hire. Good play area for under 13s. Barbecue area. Good facilities for archery - quite a feature of the site. Off site: Local shops at Laurens 1 km. Gorges d'Heric and the Cirques de Navacelles well worth visiting.

At a glance

Welcome & Ambience	////	Location	////
Quality of Pitches	////	Range of Facilities	////

Directions

Site is signed 2 km. north of Laurens off the D909 (Béziers-Bédarieux) road.
GPS: N43:32.080 E03:11.235

Charges 2005

Per unit incl. 1 or 2 persons	€ 9,00 - € 23,60
extra person	€ 5,00
electricity (6-10A)	€ 3,20 - € 6,60
dog	free - € 2,00

Special rates for longer stays.

Reservations

Contact site. Tel: 04 67 90 24 36. Email: oliveraie@free.fr

Open

All year.

FR34100 Camping Le Mas du Padre

4 chemin du Mas du Padre, F-34540 Balaruc-les-Bains (Hérault)

The Durand family took over this site a few years ago and have made many alterations and improvements. Madame Durand speaks excellent English. It is a small site, just 2.5 km. from Balaruc-Les-Bains, near the Lake of Thau and is unusually situated in a residential area that has obviously developed around it over the years. Its 116 secluded pitches of varying sizes are enclosed by hedges and mature trees, some on a very gentle slope and 98 have electricity (6/10A). From the top of the site there are views towards Sete. The site is peaceful and popular with the French who love its simplicity, although a large commercial centre is just 500 m. Beaches and many local attractions are close, but if you decide to stay here it would be advisable to have transport. The road from the site to Sete passes some rather unsightly factory works – don't be put off.

Facilities

Two modern neat, fully equipped toilet blocks include baby changing area, facilities for disabled campers, dishwashing and laundry sinks, and washing machines. Reception sells basic provisions, gas and bread (to order in low season). Two small circular pools including one for children (13/5-16/9). Tennis half-court, table tennis, boules courts, mini-adventure playground. Sports programme including tournaments, aqua-aerobics, animation for children, along with a weekly dance when a temporary bar is organised (all in high season). Torch useful. Off site: Fishing or riding 2 km. Golf 20 km. Bus service to the historic city of Balaruc-Les-Bains from just outside the site.

Open

1 April - 24 September.

At a glance

Welcome & Ambience	✓✓✓✓	Location	✓✓✓
Quality of Pitches	✓✓✓✓	Range of Facilities	✓✓✓✓

Directions

From A9 take exit for Sete and follow N800 to Balaruc le Vieux, at the first roundabout follow Sete/Balaruc les Bains (D2). Pass the centre commercial (Carrefour on the left). At second roundabout again follow Balaruc les Bains/Sete. After 50 m take right for Balaruc les Bains and immediately left across the road you have just left and back down it (50 m) to go immediately right, and follow Chemin du Mas du Padre site on left well hidden.
GPS: N43:27.325 E03:41.280

Charges 2005

Per unit incl. 2 persons and electricity	€ 13,10 - € 32,90
extra person (over 13 yrs)	€ 2,80 - € 4,10
child	€ 1,45 - € 3,05
1 person, 60 sq.m. pitch	€ 7,80 - € 16,30
dog	€ 0,95 - € 1,95

Reservations

Advised for high season only. Tel: 04 67 48 53 41. Email: contact@mas-du-padre.com

FR34090 Camping Caravaning Domaine de la Yole

B.P. 23, F-34350 Valras-Plage (Hérault)

A busy happy holiday village with over 1,100 pitches could seem a little daunting. We expected things to be a little hectic when we arrived on a busy day in mid-August. However, the multi-lingual reception was calm and people were enjoying themselves. There are 590 pitches for touring units, the remainder taken by mobile homes and a few tour operator pitches. Most pitches are of a good size, all are level, hedged and have electricity, water and waste water points and, very importantly for this area, they all have shade. The extensive pool area is attractive with lots of sunbathing areas and the impressive activities are located in a central area. A shopping area provides a supermarket, outdoor vegetable stall, butchers, wine shop (take your own bottles for really good wines on draught), boutique and a takeaway, very much like a village market. The beach, a long stretch of beautiful sand, is 500 m. and here is trampolining, paragliding and jet-skis. This is a busy site with something for all the family. English is spoken.

Facilities

Eight well maintained toilet blocks include some showers and washbasins en-suite, mostly British style WCs and many washbasins in cubicles. One/two blocks have extra large cubicles with everything including a baby bath can be used by families or disabled visitors. All have dishwashing and laundry sinks. Central laundry with washing machines and dryers. Motorcaravan service point (the only chemical disposal point is here, a long walk from many pitches). Refrigerators for hire. Shops. Good restaurant with huge terrace and amphitheatre for daily entertainment (in season). Two large pools and paddling pool, all supervised by lifeguard. All facilities open when site open. Two half size tennis courts (free) and two full size. Multi-sports court. Large play areas with amusements such as moto-track and daily children's club, minigolf, table tennis, boules, volleyball and basketball. Doctor calls daily in high season. Internet access. Off site: Fishing or riding 1 km. Beach 500m, path from site.

At a glance

Welcome & Ambience	✓✓✓✓	Location	✓✓✓✓
Quality of Pitches	✓✓✓✓	Range of Facilities	✓✓✓✓✓

Directions

From A9 autoroute take Beziers Ouest exit for Valras Plage (13-14 km) and follow Casino signs. Site is on left, just after sign for Vendres Plage.

Charges 2006

Per unit incl. 2 adults	€ 16,85 - € 34,90
extra person	€ 5,35 - € 5,90
child 7-16 yrs	free - € 3,50
child under 7 yrs	free - € 1,80
dog	free - € 3,30

Reservations

Made with deposit (€ 90 or € 130) and, in high season, a fee (€ 25); contact site for form.
Tel: 04 67 37 33 87. Email: layole34@aol.com

Open

29 April - 23 September.

3

FR34110 Yelloh! Village Le Club Farret

F-34450 Vias-Plage (Hérault)

This superb site of excellent quality has been developed by the Giner family with love and care over the last 40 years. Well maintained and with welcoming, helpful staff (English spoken), everywhere is neat and tidy - quite outstanding and impressive. It is a large site but even though it was very busy when we visited, the atmosphere seemed very relaxed and not too frantic. There are 756 pitches, with 370 for touring units and only 14% for tour operators, which do not overwhelm at all. The good-sized, level pitches are on grass and sand, with 6A electricity. There is some shade and many trees and shrubs provide a green environment. The mobile home areas are very smart, and have been attractively landscaped, with an African or Balinese themes. The large heated pool has lots of sunbathing room. The safe beach is alongside the site so some pitches have sea views. There is a wide range of evening entertainment and the extensive list of activities includes an unusual art programme offering pottery, silk painting, mosaics and water colours. If you wish you can try your hand at catamaran sailing or windsurfing - free of charge for one hour. The restaurant is high above the pool with views of the sea. Everything is open all season, so a visit in the quiet months of May, June or September doesn't mean less facilities. There is a policy of no advance booking for the touring pitches - they say that they rarely turn anyone away and will accept a phone call the day before arrival to give details of availability. A Yelloh Village member.

Facilities

Seven very clean toilet blocks provide excellent facilities with British style toilets (one or two Turkish in the older blocks). Large showers, many with washbasin. Children's toilets, baby rooms and showers in the guise of a clown. Full facilities in large rooms for disabled customers. Washing machines. Dog shower at the block nearest the beach. Toilets are open all night but the showers are closed. Well stocked supermarket. Hairdresser. Bars with pizzas and snacks to takeaway. Restaurant. Swimming pool complex with lifeguard all season (heated both early and late in the season). Play areas. Mini-club (5-10 yrs). Teenagers' club (11-15 yrs). Tennis, table tennis, archery, volleyball, football and a full programme of games. Multisports court. Bicycle hire. Off site: Riding 1 km. Golf 5 km. Sailing and windsurfing on beach.

Directions

Site is south of Vias at Vias Plage. From N112 (Beziers - Agde) take D137 signed Vias Plage. Site is signed on the left. GPS: N43:17.462 E03:25.147

Charges 2005

Per unit incl. 1 or 2 persons	€ 15,00 - € 42,00
extra person	€ 6,00
extra tent	€ 3,00
pet	€ 3,00

Reservations

Not accepted. Tel: 04 67 21 64 45.
Email: farret@wanadoo.fr

Open

Easter - 24 September.

At a glance

Welcome & Ambience	✓✓✓✓✓	Location	✓✓✓✓✓
Quality of Pitches	✓✓✓✓✓	Range of Facilities	✓✓✓✓✓

FR34130 Camping Le Neptune

Route du Grau, F-34300 Agde (Hérault)

Camping Neptune is a rare find in this area of 'all singing, all dancing' campsites. This small, family run site with only 165 pitches makes a delightful change. There are also a few mobile homes. The Fray family are very welcoming and, even though it is in a busy area, it is a little oasis of calm, very suited to couples and young families. Placed along the D32 to Grau d'Agde which is beside the river Herault, there may be a little daytime road noise. The pitches are mostly separated by flowering bushes, with some shade and most have 6A electricity. The swimming pool is in a sunny position with sun beds and overlooked by the bar. The only entertainment is in high season and is a twice weekly mini-club for children. The beach and the small resort of Grau d'Agde are 1.5 km. and Aqualand 5 km.

Facilities

The large toilet block provides roomy pre-set showers, washbasins in cabins and mainly British style WCs, plus three cold showers for really hot weather. An extra new small block is at the top of the site. Laundry and dishwashing sinks. Two washing machines and dryer. Small shop. Bar (both 15/5-30/9). Swimming pool heated in cool weather, bracelets required (€ 8 deposit, main season). Table tennis and field for sports. Boat mooring facility on the River Herault across the road. Not all breeds of dog are accepted and only one is allowed. Barbecues are not permitted. Off site: Beach 1.5 km. Golf and riding 1.5 km.

Open

1 April - 30 September.

Directions

From A9 autoroute exit 34, follow N312 for Agde which joins the N112. After crossing bridge over Herault river, take exit for Grau d'Agde/Rochelongu, turn left at roundabout at top of exit road over road bridge, left at next roundabout by Hyper U, straight over at next roundabout, down towards the river. Left at next roundabout signed Grau d'Agde/Les Berges de l'Herault on D32 which runs parallel to the River Herault. Watch carefully for site entrance on left. GPS: N43:17.882 E03:27.377

Charges 2005

Per unit incl. 2 persons	€ 16,00 - € 23,00
with electricity	€ 17,00 - € 25,90
extra person	€ 4,50 - € 5,30
child (under 7 yrs)	€ 2,25 - € 2,65
Camping Cheques accepted.	

Reservations

Necessary for July and August. Tel: 04 67 94 23 94.
Email: info@campingleneptune.com

At a glance

Welcome & Ambience	✓✓✓✓	Location	✓✓✓✓✓
Quality of Pitches	✓✓✓✓✓	Range of Facilities	✓✓✓✓

FR34140 Siblu Camping La Carabasse

Route de Farinette, F-34450 Vias-sur-Mer (Hérault)

La Carabasse, a Siblu (formerly Haven) holiday park, is on the outskirts of Vias Plage, a popular place with lots of shops and restaurants. The site has everything you could need with two good pools, bars and a restaurant. Very much orientated to British visitors, there are many activities and entertainment for families and teenagers. There are 950 pitches in total, 50 for touring, with many mobile homes and a good number of tour operator pitches. The touring pitches are set amongst tall poplar and birch trees on level hard ground, all have electricity and partial shade. Some have private sanitary facilities. The wonderful Mediterranean beaches are close and La Carabasse has its own beach club. It is a lively busy site in high season, and Vias Plage itself can also be quite hectic. There is a range of facilities for children and teenagers. Football coaching from U.F.A. qualified staff, for two hours a day, five days a week, can be booked or you can learn snorkelling, life saving or body-boarding and become a 'wave rider'!

Facilities

Two of the toilet blocks are modern and fully equipped. With an older block used in high season. Some pitches have their own private sanitary cabin providing a WC and shower (extra charge). Bars, restaurant and swimming pools. Beach club for windsurfing and pedaloes. Wealth of daytime activities (some charged) from golf lessons to aqua-aerobics and tennis tournaments. Children's clubs. Evening entertainment. Off site: Trips on the Canal du Midi. Vias town with twice weekly market. Modern resort of Cap d'Agde nearby with Aqualand and golf course (18 holes).

At a glance

Welcome & Ambience	✓✓✓✓	Location	✓✓✓✓
Quality of Pitches	✓✓✓	Range of Facilities	✓✓✓✓✓

Directions

Site is south of Vias. From N112 (Agde - Beziers) road turn right at signs for Vias-Plage (D137) and site on the left.

Charges guide

Per pitch incl. up to 6 persons and electricity	€ 11,00 - € 37,00
with private sanitary cabin	€ 12,00 - € 43,00

Reservations

Accepted at any time for min. 4 days; no fee.
Tel: 04 67 21 59 90. Email: reservations@lacarabasse.fr

Open

15 April - 19 September.

FR34160 Yelloh! Village Charlemagne

F-34340 Marseillan Plage (Hérault)

Charlemagne is under the same family ownership as Nouvelle Floride and is across the road from it, 200 metres from the beach. It boasts a large range of amenities including a large supermarket, fast food, bar, restaurant and disco. Facing the main street, these are open to the public and are consequently well stocked, well equipped and open for the whole season. The site is traditionally laid out under the shade of tall trees providing 480 level pitches. Of these 270 are available for touring units, neatly hedged and all with electricity (6A) and water. Access to the beach is by a footpath past Nouvelle Floride but the site also has a super pool complex complete with 'Niagara Falls'. This is a site which caters for all ages.

Facilities

Four toilet blocks, two modern of good quality with washbasins in cabins, dishwashing under cover, laundry sinks and washing machine. The two more traditional blocks have some Turkish style toilets. Motorcaravan service point. Shops, bar/cafe, restaurant, takeaway and disco, all open all season. Pool complex (all season). Good play area. Mini-club (May-Sept). Entertainment.

Open

1 April - 24 September.

At a glance

Welcome & Ambience	✓✓✓✓	Location	✓✓✓✓
Quality of Pitches	✓✓✓✓	Range of Facilities	✓✓✓✓✓

Directions

From A9 exit 34, follow N314 to Agde then take the N112 towards Sete and watch for signs to Marseillan Plage from where site is well signed.

Charges 2005

Per unit incl. 1-2 persons, water and electricity	€ 15,00 - € 43,00
extra person (over 1 yr)	€ 5,00 - € 8,50

Camping Cheques accepted.

Reservations

Made with deposit (€ 120) and fee (€ 30) for July and August. Tel: 04 67 21 92 49.
Email: info@charlemagne-camping.com

FR34150 Yelloh! Village Nouvelle Floride

F-34340 Marseillan Plage (Hérault)

Marseillan Plage is a small, busy resort just east of Cap d'Adge and La Nouvelle Floride enjoys a super position immediately beside a long gently shelving sandy beach. It is a good quality site, very traditional in style and set under tall trees with neat hedges to separate the 520 pitches (370 for tourers). These are on sandy soil and all have water and electricity (6A). Some of the pitches in the newer area (across a small lane) and the hardstanding pitches near the beach have little shade as yet. There are a number of mobile homes but the site is mainly for tourers. Amenities and facilities are generally of excellent quality and include a strikingly attractive bar area overlooking the beach with a raised stage for entertainment. Alongside the play area is a multi-purpose ball court and fitness centre, also on sand with robust machines with the idea of keeping Mum and Dad fit whilst still keeping an eye on the children. Essentially a 'holiday site', there is an extensive programme of entertainment and activities catering for all ages, and a good heated pool complex complete with water slides and whirlpools. However, the main attraction for most will almost certainly be the direct access to a fine beach. The gates on the beach entrance are locked at 9 pm. for security. This is a well run, family run site with lots to offer and aimed at families.

Facilities

The four toilet blocks are impressive, including two with a number of en-suite showers and washbasins, otherwise washbasins all in cabins. Baby rooms, excellent facilities for disabled visitors and even a dog shower. The showers and washing up areas are closed between 23.00-07.00 hrs. Motorcaravan service point. Bar and restaurant. Shop all season, plus a range of shops at Charlemagne across the road. Pool complex with slides, jacuzzi, paddling pools, etc (all season). Play area, fitness centre and multi-purpose ball court. Water sports. Table tennis. Weekly films (DVD) and variety of organised games, competitions, dances and discos. Mini-club in school holidays. Bicycle hire. Off site: Riding and bicycle hire 500 m. Golf 5 km.

At a glance

| Welcome & Ambience | ✓✓✓✓ | Location | ✓✓✓✓✓ |
| Quality of Pitches | ✓✓✓✓ | Range of Facilities | ✓✓✓✓✓ |

Directions

From A9 autoroute exit 34, follow N312 to Agde then take N112 towards Sete. Watch for signs to Marseillan Plage from where site is well signed. GPS: N43:18.522 E03:32.501

Charges 2005

Per unit incl. 2 persons, water and electricity	€ 15,00 - € 43,00
incl. 3 persons	€ 20,00 - € 43,00
extra person (over 1 yr)	€ 5,00 - € 8,50
animal	€ 3,00 - € 3,50

Reservations

Made with deposit (€ 120) and fee (€ 30) for July and August. Tel: 04 67 21 94 49.
Email: info@nouvelle-floride.com

Open

19 March - 24 September.

FR34170 Camping Caravaning Les Mimosas

Port Cassafières, F-34420 Portiragnes Plage (Hérault)

Les Mimosas is quite a large site with 400 pitches – 200 for touring units, the remainder for mobile homes – in a rural situation. The level, grassy pitches are of average size, separated and numbered, all with 6A electricity (long leads may be required), some have good shade others have less. The pool area, a real feature of the site, includes a most impressive wave pool, various toboggans, a large swimming pool and a paddling pool (seven pools in all) with lots of free sun beds. Many day trips and excursions are arranged all season, from canoeing to visiting castles. Portiragnes Plage is about 2 km. and it can be reached by cycle tracks. The Canal du Midi runs along the edge of the site (no access), providing another easy cycle ride. This is a friendly, family run site with families in mind.

Facilities

Two modern unisex toilet blocks with washbasins both open and in cabins, baby rooms, children's toilets and very good facilities for disabled people (the whole site is wheelchair friendly). Both blocks provide family-sized en-suite facilities on payment. Dishwashing and laundry sinks. Washing machines and dryers. Motorcaravan service point. Fridge hire. Large well-stocked shop (bread baked daily all season). Bar with snacks all season, restaurant (from 1/6). Swimming pool complex (early June) with lifeguards all season. Play area. Boules. Gym with instructor and sauna (charged). Supervised multi-sports court. Bicycle hire. Barbecues are not permitted. Off site: Fishing and riding 1 km. Portiragnes Plage with beach bars and restaurants 2 km. Golf 10 km.

Open

20 May - 9 September.

At a glance

| Welcome & Ambience | ✓✓✓✓ | Location | ✓✓✓✓ |
| Quality of Pitches | ✓✓✓✓✓ | Range of Facilities | ✓✓✓✓✓ |

Directions

From A9 autoroute exit 35 (Bezieres Est) take N112 south towards Serignan (1 km). At large roundabout follow signs for Cap d'Agde but watch carefully for D37 Portiragnes (1-2 km) and follow signs for Portiragnes Plage. Site is well signed before Portiragnes Plage (5 km). GPS: N43:17.492 E03:22.409

Charges 2005

Per unit incl. 2 persons	€ 22,00 - € 29,00
with electricity	€ 25,00 - € 33,00
private sanitary unit	€ 7,50 - € 8,50
extra person	€ 4,50 - € 7,00
child (under 4 yrs)	free - € 3,50
animal	free - € 5,50

Reservations

Necessary for July/Aug. Tel: 04 67 90 92 92.
Email: les.mimosas.portiragnes@wanadoo.fr

FR34180 Camping La Borio de Roque

Route de la Salvetat, F-34220 St Pons de Thomières (Hérault)

La Borio de Roque is a peaceful site set in a very rural location hidden in a wooded valley 4 km. from St Pons. It lies at the end of a 1.5 km. track (rough in places) but it is well worth the effort and is set around a lovely restored farmhouse with the outbuildings made into four very attractive gites. The 25 large, individually shaped, terraced pitches have 10A electricity and some shade. Some are very private which the owners will escort you to. When the site was developed, many different varieties of trees were planted which has created a unique environment quite unusual in a French site. Children are encouraged to help with feeding and grooming the goats, sheep and horses. There are numerous walks and tracks for mountain bikes from the site and your Dutch hosts will be only too happy to advise on routes. St Pons (4 km.) is an attractive small town with bars, restaurants and a museum. La Borio is especially suited to couples and young families - not a site for teenagers who like lots of entertainment.

Facilities

The toilet block provides adjustable, roomy showers and washbasins en-suite. Baby bath. Dishwashing and laundry sinks. Adequate chemical disposal. Free use of large freezer. Bread is available all season and ices. Local wine and home produced goat's cheese, honey and cherry jam are for sale. A set menu is cooked four times weekly (to order) in high season and eaten with the family in the bar/barn. This is a very popular event and well subscribed. Swimming pool (from 1/6) and small lake for fishing. Small play area on grass. Barbecue areas. The site is not suitable for American motorhomes. Off site: Bicycle hire 5 km. Golf and riding 20 km. Beach 50 km.

Open

1 May - 30 September.

At a glance

Welcome & Ambience	✓✓✓✓✓	Location	✓✓✓✓
Quality of Pitches	✓✓✓✓✓	Range of Facilities	✓✓✓✓

Directions

St Pons de Thomières is on the N112 northwest of Bezieres. Site is 4.5 km. north of the town on the D907 signed Salvatat, on the right on a bend; then 1.5 km. on a rough track (signed). GPS: N43:30.656 E02:44.789

Charges 2005

Per person	€ 3,25 - € 4,00
child (under 7 yrs)	€ 2,25 - € 3,00
pitch	€ 7,50 - € 8,50
electricity	€ 2,75 - € 3,00
vehicle	€ 1,85 - € 2,00

No credit cards.

Reservations

Necessary for the main season and made with booking fee (€ 16). Tel: 04 67 97 10 97. Email: info@borioderoque.com

FR34190 Camping Caravaning Les Champs Blancs

Route de Rochelongue, F-34300 Agde (Hérault)

Les Champs Blancs is set in high trees, 2 km. from Agde and 2 km. from the sea in a shady environment. The 169 touring pitches, on level, sandy grass, are bordered with bushes with plenty of trees and greenery. All have 10A electricity and 60 have private sanitary cabins. Separate areas for mobile homes. The pool area has been augmented by a super irregular pool, with toboggans, cascade, jacuzzi, bridges and palms with plenty of space for sun beds but retaining the original pool and paddling pool. Games, shows and competitions are arranged in July and August. There are tennis courts and other leisure facilities in the area nearest the road, bordered by trees to deaden possible road noise.

Facilities

Two toilet blocks have been refurbished to provide showers and washbasins together, plus British style WCs. Unit for disabled visitors. Dishwashing and laundry sinks. Washing machines and dryers. 60 en-suite private cabins containing WC, shower and washbasin with an outside sink for dishes. Motor caravan service point. Well stocked shop in high season; only bread available in low season. Bar (from 1 June). Restaurant and bakery (20/6-15/9). Swimming complex (from 8 April depending on weather). Good play area, minigolf, table tennis, tennis, basketball and volleyball. Multicourt. Off site: Riding 1 km. Golf 1.5 km. Beach 2 km.

Open

8 April - 30 September.

At a glance

Welcome & Ambience	✓✓✓✓✓	Location	✓✓✓
Quality of Pitches	✓✓✓✓	Range of Facilities	✓✓✓✓✓

Directions

From A9 autoroute exit 34, follow N312 for Adge which joins the N112 Beziers - Sete road, after crossing bridge over the Herault river take first turning signed Rochelongue and turn right, next left and next left (signed Adge) i.e. round 3 sides of a square. Site on left before you cross another bridge back over the N112. GPS: N43:17.821 E03:28.528

Charges 2005

Per pitch incl. 2 persons	€ 18,00 - € 38,00
with individual sanitary facilities	€ 20,00 - € 45,00
incl. 4 persons	€ 24,00 - € 47,00
with individual sanitary facilities	€ 25,00 - € 53,00
extra person	€ 5,00 - € 10,00
dog	€ 2,00

Bracelet required for pool complex € 5. Camping Cheques accepted.

Reservations

Necessary for July and August. Made with deposit of € 155 and fee of € 25 (deducted from balance). Tel: 04 67 94 23 42. Email: champs.blancs@wanadoo.fr

FR34200 Camping Club Californie Plage

Côte Ouest, F-34450 Vias-Plage (Hérault)

With the benefit of direct access to a sandy cove, with a few, much sought-after pitches overlooking the sea, this is a fairly typical holiday-style campsite with a range of good quality facilities. These include a covered pool on the site and a superb tropical swimming pool complex with the inevitable toboggans, etc., and even a naturist swimming pool situated across the road from the Californie Plage site in the grounds of its sister site. Both sites are located away from Vias Plage, on the Côte Ouest and thereby enjoy a degree of tranquillity in this bustling resort area. The site is traditionally laid out, with mobile homes to one side of the central road and touring pitches to the other. Pitches are mostly of 100 sq.m with shade from tall trees, although those close to the beach are slightly smaller with less shade. All are mainly on level sandy ground, separated by low hedging with electricity connections and in most parts there is a fair amount of shade from tall poplars.

Facilities

Sanitary facilities are of a generally good standard, in three traditional blocks which have been fully refurbished in recent years. Washbasins in cabins, baby rooms, facilities for disabled visitors. Laundry with washing machines and dryer. Shop. Bars. Traditional comfortable restaurant with takeaway. Beach café serving tapas and fish dishes. Covered pool on site (1/4-30/10). Range of pools on sister site across the road (1/7-31/8; code supplied). Tennis court. Bicycle hire. Games room. Play area. Sports nets. Archery. Extensive entertainment programme and children's activities in July/Aug. Off site: Minigolf 2 km. Riding 3 km. Golf 9 km.

Open

Easter - 30 October.

At a glance

Welcome & Ambience ✓✓✓✓✓ Location ✓✓✓✓
Quality of Pitches ✓✓✓✓ Range of Facilities ✓✓✓✓✓

Directions

From N112 Beziers-Agde road take D137 Vias Plage turn. Watch for signs to 'Cote Ouest' and follow campsite signs thereafter.

Charges 2005

Per unit incl. 1 or 2 persons and 6A electricity	€ 16,00 - € 32,00
extra person (4 yrs and over)	€ 3,00 - € 5,00
extra tent	€ 1,60 - € 3,40
10A electricity	€ 3,00
animal	€ 2,00 - € 4,60

Reservations

Made with deposit (€ 102) and fee (€ 23). Before 30 March reservation fee. Tel: 04 67 21 64 69. Email: californie.plage@wanadoo.fr

FR34210 Camping Les Berges du Canal

Promenade les Vernets, F-34420 Villeneuve-les-Béziers (Hérault)

Although most campers or caravanners will be aware of the Canal du Midi, there are surprisingly few campsites which provide an opportunity to enjoy the rather special ambience for which this famous waterway is renowned, so we were really pleased to discover this delightful campsite right alongside the canal at Villeneuve-les-Beziers. Its situation is such that not only can one savour the ambience of the canal, but it is within a few minutes drive of the beaches at Serignan Plage, Vias or Valras, the old city of Beziers, the famous resort of Cap d'Agde, or you can even cycle along the tow-path to the beach at Portiragnes-Plage (10 km). The village of Villeneuve-les-Beziers itself, with shops, restaurants and market is just a few minutes walk along the towpath, access road and over the canal bridge. The campsite has 75 level pitches on sandy grass of average size, mostly with 10A electrical connections (some occupied by mobile homes) in a peaceful and shady situation, separated from the canal only by an access road. There is a pleasant swimming pool complex, one of the two pools being fitted with a jacuzzi-style facility, but there are no big slides or toboggans thereby ensuring that it is relatively peaceful.

Facilities

A fully equipped toilet block has mainly British-style WCs and some Turkish style, and some washbasins in cabins. Facilities for disabled visitors (with key) and children. Beauty therapist visits weekly. Washing machine, laundry and dishwashing sinks, etc. Motorcaravan service point. Two swimming pools. Bar/snack-bar (serving breakfast too). Small restaurant attached to site. Evening entertainment during high season. Off site: Attractive old village centre of Villeneuve-les-Beziers. Beach at Portiragnes Plage. Riding 5km. Canal du Midi.

Open

15 April - 15 September.

At a glance

Welcome & Ambience ✓✓✓✓✓ Location ✓✓✓✓✓
Quality of Pitches ✓✓✓✓ Range of Facilities ✓✓✓✓

Directions

From A9 take exit 35, follow signs for Agde and at first roundabout take N112 (direction Beziers) turning. Then take first left onto D37 signed Villeneve-les-Beziers and Valras Plage. Pass traffic lights, then left at roundabout and follow site signs (take care at junction beside bridge).

Charges 2005

Per unit incl. 2 persons	€ 16,00 - € 23,00
with electricity	€ 16,00 - € 23,00
extra person	€ 2,50 - € 4,50
animal	€ 3,00

Reservations

Contact site. Tel: 04 67 39 36 09. Email: contact@lesbergesducanal.com

FR34220 Camping La Creole

74 avenue des Campings, F-34340 Marseillan-Plage (Hérault)

This is a surprisingly tranquil, well cared for small campsite almost in the middle of this bustling resort that will appeal especially to those seeking a rather less frenetic ambience than that which typifies many sites in this area. Essentially a family orientated site, it offers around 110 good-sized, level grass pitches, all with 6A electricity connections, and mostly with shade from tall poplars and other trees and shrubs. It also benefits from direct access to an extensive sandy beach and the fact that there is no swimming pool or bar actually contributes to the tranquillity and may even be seen as an advantage for families with younger children. The beach will be the main attraction here no doubt, and the town's extensive range of bars, restaurants and shops are all within a couple of minutes walk.

Facilities	Directions
Toilet facilities are housed in a traditional building, modernised inside to provide perfectly adequate, if not particularly luxurious, facilities including some washbasins in private cabins, a baby room and dog shower. Small play area. Table tennis. In high season beach games, dances, sangria evenings etc, are organised, all aimed particularly towards families. Barbecue area. Bicycle hire. Off site: Local market day Tuesday. Riding 1 km.	From autoroute A9 take exit 34 on N312 towards Agde, then N112 towards Sete keeping a look-out for signs to Marseillan Plage off this road. Site is well signed in Marseillan Plage. GPS: N43:18.765 E03:32.779

Open

1 April - 8 October.

At a glance

Welcome & Ambience	✓✓✓✓	Location	✓✓✓✓✓
Quality of Pitches	✓✓✓✓✓	Range of Facilities	✓✓✓

Charges 2006

Per unit incl. 2 persons	€ 13,00 - € 24,50
extra person	€ 2,50 - € 4,50
electricity	€ 2,70

Reservations

Made with deposit (€ 84) and fee (€ 16). Essential for high season. Tel: 04 67 21 92 69. Email: campinglacreole@wanadoo.fr

CAMPING ★★★
LA CREOLE
Direct access to the beach
Located in the Heart of Marseillan-Plage
Mobile home to rent
Low prices in low season
Open from 2/04 to 10/10
74 avenue des campings
34340 Marseillan-Plage
Tel : +33 (0)4 67 21 92 69
Fax : +33 (0)4 67 26 58 16
campinglacreole@wanadoo.fr
www.campinglacreole.com

FR34230 Sunêlia Le Plein Air des Chênes

Route de Castelnau, RD 112, F-34830 Clapiers (Hérault)

Situated just outside the village of Clapiers, only about 5 km. from the exciting and interesting city of Montpellier, yet merely 15 km. from the beach, this is one of those few sites which really does seem to try to provide something for everyone, especially perhaps for those who prefer to spend their holidays without ever leaving the campsite! There are 130 touring pitches (some large with their own individual toilet cabin), plus around chalets, bungalows and mobile homes to rent; all in a nicely shaded terraced setting. The site boasts an amazing landscaped pool complex, with multi-lane toboggan, four pools and surrounding facilities such as bars, restaurants, etc., which is very impressive if you like that sort of thing. It is also open to the public and obviously very popular and noisy.

Facilities	Directions
Three well equipped modern toilet blocks of circular design provide washbasins in cabins and facilities for disabled people. Three washing machines. Shop (07-08). Restaurant open to the public (all year), bar and pool side bar and café (06-09). Takeaway (06-09). Swimming pools (1/6- 12/9). 4 tennis courts. Multi-sports court. Play area. Mini-club and range of evening entertainment in main season. Off site: Golf 10 km. Beaches 15 km. Fishing 15 km.	Site is north of Montpellier, 8 km. from the A9. Take exit 28 on N113 towards Montpellier passing Vendargues, leaving N113 and crossing the N110 (which joins the N 113) to follow D65 for Clapiers north of Montpellier. Follow signs for village then site.

Open

All year.

At a glance

Welcome & Ambience	✓✓✓✓	Location	✓✓✓✓
Quality of Pitches	✓✓✓✓	Range of Facilities	✓✓✓✓✓

Charges 2005

Per unit incl. 2 persons and electricity	€ 23,00 - € 37,00
extra person	free - € 6,50
child (3-10 yrs)	free - € 3,50

Camping Cheques accepted.

Reservations

Made with booking fee (€ 28); contact site. Tel: 04 67 02 02 53. Email: pleinairdeschenes@free.fr

FR34240 Camping Le Castellas

Route Nationale 112, F-34200 Sète (Hérault)

You would expect a campsite situated beside the main road which runs alongside the beach and with a railway line behind to be noisy, whereas in fact once you are within the confines of this site it is surprisingly peaceful offering everything you could want. It is conveniently situated directly across the road from a superb sandy beach, with the Etang du Thau behind, yet it's within a short drive of Sète, Marseillan Plage or Agde. It is a large site but is very well organised. In total there are 994 pitches with 307 used for mobile homes or chalets. The pitches are mainly large and hedged on sandy ground with 6A electricity with some smaller ones at the far end without electricity. All are accessed by hard roads with a variety of shade - the sorts of shrubs that will grow by the sea. A large pool, without noisy toboggans and a sports area have been developed at the back of the site under pine trees, along with a restaurant and bar, all of which appear to be very well managed. Because of its situation security has to be tight, and so it is. There is an obvious emphasis on entertainment with all ages being provided for, although families with younger children are likely to be the most appreciative.

Facilities

Nine toilet blocks of a standard design, fully equipped, some with en-suite showers and basins mainly operate on a unisex basis. Dishwashing sinks. Laundry. Provision for disabled people. Fridge hire. Large supermarket and range of smaller shops and café open to public as well. Restaurant, bars and snack bars. Swimming pool with lifeguards. All open when site is open. Tennis. Multi-sports court. Sports field. Play area and bouncy castles. Hairdresser. Masseurs. Internet bus. ATM. Wide range of entertainment. Site Paper in English for high season. Off site: Bus for Sete daily in July/Aug.

At a glance

Welcome & Ambience	✓✓✓✓	Location	✓✓✓✓
Quality of Pitches	✓✓✓✓	Range of Facilities	✓✓✓✓✓

Directions

Site is beside the RN112 which links Marseillan Plage and Sete (nearer to Marseillian Plage). This road can get very busy indeed in main season.
GPS: N43:20.431 E03:34.949

Charges 2006

Per unit incl. electricity (6A)	€ 20,00 - € 35,00
extra person	€ 4,00 - € 8,00
extra car	€ 2,00 - € 5,00
dog	€ 4,00

Reservations

Advised for July and August and made with booking fee (€ 25) and 30% deposit. Tel: 04 67 51 63 00. Email: camping.lecastellas@wanadoo.fr

Open

1 May - 20 September.

FR34250 Camping des Sources

F-34700 Soubes (Hérault)

This is a 'real' campsite tucked into the side of a small valley with views of the mountains, yet very easily accessed from the A75 autoroute. It has a rural feel with some up and down walking but all your needs will be met. The pitches vary in size and are tucked into bays catering for small or large tents, motorhomes and caravans. All are level with some grass (metal tent pegs could be useful) and with 6A electricity provided. A natural spring water pool is large enough for children to splash around in, whilst another is ideal to cool your drinks if you are travelling light (the water is drinkable). You can also clamber down to the river and cool off there or simply relax. For children it is a marvellous natural playground, although there is also a play area on site. The owner is very proud of his site and happy to provide information and advice on the wide range of activities available, ranging from walking, climbing, riding, sailing, trout fishing and potholing to bird watching and botanic walks. Yet the site is less than an hours drive from the Mediterranean coast.

Facilities

The central traditionally built toilet block is fully equipped including some washbasins in cabins and a washing machine. Simple snack bar. Small pool fed by spring water. Play area. Table tennis. Communal barbecues. Dogs are not accepted. Off site: Village of Soubes 10 minute walk across the river with shop, bar/restaurant etc. Lodeve 5 km. Montpellier and Mediterranean within one hours drive. On route of the Cirque de Navacelles.

Open

1 May - 15 September.

At a glance

Welcome & Ambience	✓✓✓✓	Location	✓✓✓✓
Quality of Pitches	✓✓✓✓	Range of Facilities	✓✓✓

Directions

Site is 3 km. north of Lodève. Soubes is signed from A75, exit 52. Take first right towards Fozieres and follow site signs (approx. 1 km).

Charges 2005

Per unit incl. 2 persons	€ 13,50 - € 14,00
extra person	€ 4,50
child (under 7 yrs)	€ 3,00
electricity	€ 2,50

Reservations

Contact site. Tel: 04 67 44 32 02. Email: jlsources@wanadoo.fr

FR34260 Camping Beau Rivage

F-34140 Mèze (Hérault)

Beau Rivage is situated on the inland shore of the 4.5 km. by 19.5 km. Etang du Thau. This inland salt lake, lying parallel to the Mediterranean and separated by a very narrow strip of land, is well know for its oyster beds. It also popular for fishing, diving and watersports. The campsite on the edge of the town is within easy walking distance in the direction of Sète. The site has 150 level, sandy-grass pitches all with 6A electricity, plus 35 with mobile homes. The main features of the site are a pleasant pool and paddling pool with a bar and snack restaurant for the high season. Sete is well worth visiting with colourful houses overlooking its many canals, its fish market and 'water jousting', a feature of the town.

Facilities

One fully equipped small toilet block is open all season and a larger block for the main season. Baby bath. Facilities for disabled people. Washing machine. Motorcaravan service point. Bar providing snacks and simple takeaway food (July/Aug). Heated swimming and paddling pools (all season). Play area. Volleyball. Activities in July and August. Communal barbecues. Off site: Restaurant 300 m. Supermarket 200 m. Beach 500 m. All facilities of the town within easy walking distance. Tennis and bicycle hire 1 km.

Open

9 April - 24 September.

At a glance

Welcome & Ambience	✓✓✓	Location	✓✓✓
Quality of Pitches	✓✓✓	Range of Facilities	✓✓✓✓

Directions

From A9 autoroute take exit 33 for Sete. Follow RN113 for Poussan, Bouzigues and Mèze. Continue for 5 km. to outskirts of Mèze and site is on left just after a petrol station. The entrance is between the petrol station and a pottery (not too easy to see).

Charges 2006

Per unit incl. 2 persons	€ 17,00 - € 32,00
extra person	€ 4,00 - € 7,00
child (0-4 yrs)	free
dog	€ 3,00

Reservations

Made with 25% deposit and booking fee (€ 20). Tel: 04 67 43 81 48. Email: reception@camping-beaurivage.fr

FR66000 Camping Caravaning de Pujol

Route du Tamariguer, F-66700 Argelès-sur-Mer (Pyrénées-Orientales)

Le Pujol is a very attractive, pretty and well cared for site which has been thoughtfully designed. Argelès is a busy tourist area and in high season it doesn't matter which of the 50 or so sites you are on, there are various loud open air discos and activities which may impinge on the wrong side of midnight for a while. It is however possible to avoid the standard hectic seaside sites in otherwise attractive Argelès, and Pujol may represent the best chance of doing so. There are 310 numbered pitches, all larger than 100 sq.m. on flat grass, nearly all with electrical connections (6A). They include some 90 privately owned British mobile homes and 10 site owned for letting. The site's pride and joy is a delightful pool complex with semi-tropical shrubs and fountains. Care is taken to ensure that the bar is a family bar rather than one overrun by youngsters, who are catered for in an attractively covered meeting area opposite which also houses animation and dances. The site is very close to an interesting fortress and only 2 km. from the fast N114, via which the pretty ports of Collioure and Port-Vendres are a short distance to the south. There is some road noise near the entrance to the site.

Facilities

Well kept fully equipped toilet blocks include a smart shower block. Baby bath. Washing machines. Small supermarket (1/6-15/9). Good terraced restaurant and friendly family bar (1/6-15/9). Fairly large L-shaped swimming pool, children's pool, and spa pool (1/6-15/9). Table tennis, small multi-gym, volleyball, boules and minigolf. Playground. Games room. Only gas or electric barbecues are permitted. Off site: Riding 500 m. Fishing, bicycle hire 1 km. Argelès Plage and quiet resort of Racou short distance.

Open

1 June - 15 September.

At a glance

Welcome & Ambience	✓✓✓✓	Location	✓✓✓✓
Quality of Pitches	✓✓✓✓✓	Range of Facilities	✓✓✓✓

Directions

Perpignan-Nord exit from autoroute, follow the N114 from Perpignan and use exit 10 for Argelès, Cross first roundabout onto Chemin de Neguebous (avoiding town). Turn left at second roundabout and site is 200 m. on right opposite Tour de Pujol.

Charges 2005

Per pitch incl. 2 adults	€ 21,00
with electricity	€ 24,00
extra person	€ 5,00
child (under 3 yrs)	€ 2,50

Less 20% in June and Sept. No credit cards.

Reservations

Made with € 100 deposit. Tel: 04 68 81 00 25.

3

FR66030 Camping Cala Gogo

La Vigie, F-66750 St Cyprien-Plage (Pyrénées-Orientales)

This is an excellent large and well organised site (sister site to FR66040, Le Soleil) and it is agreeably situated by a superb sandy beach where there is a beach bar and boats can be launched. The 450 pitches for touring units are on flat ground and around 100 sq.m. with some 50 odd chalets or mobile homes to let. They are fully marked out on level grass with easy access, electrical connections (6A) everywhere and some shade. The site has a most impressive pool complex carefully laid out with palm trees in ample sunbathing areas. The large bar complex becomes very busy in season and dancing or entertainment is arranged on some evenings on a large stage recently built alongside the bar. A large Aquapark, reputed to be amongst the best in southern France, is nearby. Used by tour operators (148 pitches). An interesting feature of the site is the provision of special beach buggies for the handicapped.

Facilities

All four toilet blocks are of a high standard, fully equipped including British and Turkish style toilets and washbasins in cabins. Good supermarket, small shopping mall and wine boutique. Sophisticated restaurant with excellent cuisine and service, plus a self-service restaurant with simple menu and takeaway. Bar and small bar by the beach in high season. Disco. TV. Three adult pools plus one for children, water-jets, jacuzzi and waterfall. Play area and remote control cars for children. Tennis, table tennis and a playground. Programme of events and sports organised in season. Torches useful. Off site: Fishing, riding, bicycle hire and golf within 5 km. Boat excursions and courses in skin-diving, windsurfing or sailing nearby.

At a glance

Welcome & Ambience	✓✓✓✓✓	Location	✓✓✓✓✓
Quality of Pitches	✓✓✓✓✓	Range of Facilities	✓✓✓✓✓

Directions

Using D81 (southward) avoid St Cyprien Plage and continue towards Argeles. Turn right at roundabout signed Le Port and Aquapark and pick up site signs. Site is just past the Aquapark.

Charges 2006

Per person (over 5 yrs)	€ 8,00
pitch	€ 1,80
electricity (6A)	€ 3,20
dog	€ 3,60

Reservations

Made for Sat. to Sat. and necessary for Jul/Aug, with deposit (€ 81.70) and fee (€ 18.30).
Tel: 04 68 21 07 12.
Email: camping.calagogo@wanadoo.fr

Open

13 May - 23 September.

FR66040 Camping Le Soleil

Route du Littoral, F-66702 Argelès-sur-Mer (Pyrénées-Orientales)

Le Soleil (sister site to Cala Gogo, FR66030), with direct access to the sandy beach, is a busy, popular, family owned site which has grown in the last few years. A large site, more like a small village, it has over 800 individual numbered pitches of ample size, with over 200 used by tour operators, over 70 occupied by mobile homes and around 550 used for touring units. On sandy/grassy ground and with a mixture of trees and shrubs providing some shade, electricity connections (6A) are provided in all areas. Access for caravans sometimes needs care on the narrow access roads. The site has a wide range of amenities, including an impressive pool complex. Spain and the Pyrénées are near enough for excursions. English is spoken and there is a comprehensive reservation system (advised for most of July/Aug) with all facilities open when the site is open.

Facilities

Seven toilet blocks of the type with external access to individual units should give good coverage with showers in four of them. Some now offer family cabins with washbasins and showers with unusually two additional pressure water outlets at waist level in each. Washing machines. Supermarket, general shop, press, tabac and restaurant for sit down or takeaway food is centrally situated. ATM machine. Internet connection. Bar with disco (July/Aug) and beach bar. California type swimming pool complex and entertainment area. Adventure playground. TV room. Tennis. Riding in high season (charge). Dogs are not accepted. Off site: Fishing and mooring boats on the adjacent river. Golf 5 km.

At a glance

Welcome & Ambience	✓✓✓✓	Location	✓✓✓✓✓
Quality of Pitches	✓✓✓✓	Range of Facilities	✓✓✓✓✓

Directions

Site is at north end of the beach about 1 km. from Argelès-Plage village.

Charges 2006

Per person (over 5 yrs)	€ 8,00
pitch	€ 12,10
electricity (6A)	€ 3,20

Less 20% outside July/Aug.
Swimming pool deposit € 15.24 per pitch.

Reservations

Made from Sat or Wed (min. 1 week) with deposit (30%) and booking fee (€ 18.30).
Tel: 04 68 81 14 48.
Email: camping.lesoleil@wanadoo.fr

Open

13 May - 23 September.

FR66050 Camping Le Haras

Domaine Sant Galdric, F-66690 Palau del Vidre (Pyrénées-Orientales)

A distinctly 'French' style site, Le Haras is situated midway between the coast (about 8 km.) and the Pyrénées on the edge of a village, in quiet countryside removed from the bustle of the coastal resorts. Under the same family management as Ma Prairie at Canet Village (nr. 66020), it is a comfortable site popular with British visitors. Le Haras has some 75 individual pitches all with electricity, 18 also with water and drainage, arranged informally in bays of four, in the grounds of an old hunting lodge (designed by Gustave Violet on the lines of a small Italianate palace). A marvellous mixture of trees, shrubs and flowers provides colour and shade. Some of the access roads may be a little narrow for large units. There is an attractive pool complex with a bar and a courtyard area beside the restaurant (developed in the old stables, with an excellent chef) and large function room, often used for weddings, with an Italian feel. Rail noise is possible from the line that runs beside the site, although this is screened by large trees.

Facilities

Unusually designed toilet block, fully equipped with mixed British and Turkish toilets, supplemented by a smart new block. It is planned to renovate and heat the smaller block near the pool. Covered dishwashing and laundry sinks. Washing machines. Fridge hire. Bar. Restaurant, also open to the public (all year, but not every day). Takeaway. Swimming and paddling pools (1/5-15/9). Play area. Charcoal barbecues are not permitted. Internet access. Off site: Three bakers in the village, two butchers and a general stores. Beaches 10 minutes drive. Fishing 500 m. Riding 2 km. Bicycle hire 6 km. Golf 7 km.

Open

20 March - 20 October.

At a glance

Welcome & Ambience	✓✓✓✓	Location	✓✓✓✓
Quality of Pitches	✓✓✓✓	Range of Facilities	✓✓✓✓

Directions

To avoid possible heavy traffic around Perpignan leave autoroute at exit 43 (Le Boulou) and follow D618 in the direction of Argelés for approx. 13 km. Take left turn for Palau-del-Vidre (D11) as you bypass St André. Bear right through village still on D11 in direction of Elne. As you leave village, site is on right, entrance just before railway bridge.

Charges 2005

Per pitch incl. two persons	€ 14,00 - € 22,00
extra person	€ 3,00 - € 5,00
child (under 7 yrs)	free - € 3,50
electricity (5A)	€ 3,80
dog	€ 3,00

Camping Cheques accepted.

Reservations

Necessary for July and August and made with € 100 deposit and € 16 booking fee.
Tel: 04 68 22 14 50. Email: haras8@wanadoo.fr

FR66020 Camping Caravaning Ma Prairie

Route de St Nazaire, F-66140 Canet-en-Roussillon (Pyrénées-Orientales)

The Gil family provide a warm welcome immediately as you arrive at the very pretty ivy covered reception area, which boasts an impressive international collection of hats/helmets and uniform caps. Ma Prairie is an excellent site set 3 km. back from the sandy Canet beaches. It has an excellent pool complex over looked by a large air conditioned bar situated across a small road from the camping area. There are 260 pitches of around 100 sq.m. on flat grassy ground, separated by various trees and bushes which provide shade (possible road noise). Most have electricity, with water and drainage on 35. The Gils have produced another superb touch in their restaurant which is very much a family affair down to mother's cushion designs and grandfather's paintings on the wall. The area of the old restaurant is now used for children's entertainment. Organised wine tastings are held once a week in high season. Used by tour operators (40 pitches). There is a lively family atmosphere. A 'Sites et Paysages' member.

Facilities

Three toilet blocks, fully equipped, include washbasins in cabins with dividers. Baby bath. Washing machines and dryers. Dishwashing and laundry sinks. Extra provision near reception. Shop for basics only, covered snack bar and takeaway. Large air-conditioned bar and restaurant. Large adult pool (10 x 22 m), splendid children's pool. Play area. Tennis. Bicycle hire. Volleyball. Satellite TV, table tennis, billiards and amusement machines. Dancing about three times weekly and busy daily animation programme in season. Caravan storage. Off site: Riding 600 m. Golf 6 km. Canet Village within walking distance with all amenities. Bus/tram services to the busy modern resort of Canet Plage.

Open

5 May - 25 September.

At a glance

Welcome & Ambience	✓✓✓✓	Location	✓✓✓
Quality of Pitches	✓✓✓✓	Range of Facilities	✓✓✓✓

Directions

Leave autoroute A9 at Perpignan North towards Barcares. Site access is from the D11 Perpignan road (exit 5) close to the junction with D617 in Canet-Village. Go under bridge, right at roundabout the left to site.

Charges 2006

Per unit with 2 persons	€ 17,00 - € 28,00
extra person	€ 3,00 - € 6,00
child (4-9 yrs)	€ 2,30 - € 4,00
child under 4 yrs	free - € 3,00
electricity (10A)	€ 4,00
water and drainage	€ 5,00

Camping Cheques accepted.

Reservations

Made for any length with deposit (€ 61) and fee (€ 12.20). Tel: 04 68 73 26 17.
Email: ma.prairie@wanadoo.fr

FR66010 Camping L'Etoile d'Or

Route de Taxo á la Mer, F-66701 Argelès-sur-Mer (Pyrénées-Orientales)

L'Etoile d'Or is a large, family site in the popular resort of Argelès sur Mer (home to more campsites than any other town in France!). This site has been recommended by our French agent and we plan to undertake a full inspection in 2006. L'Etoile d'Or is located 2.5 km from Argelès' sandy beach and 30 minutes drive from the Spanish border. This is a well equipped site with a large swimming pool and extensive shopping and catering amenities including a bar/restaurant. There are 428 pitches all of which offer electrical connections (to 13A). The camping area is well shaded and pitches are generally of a good size. A lively entertainment activity programme is organised here including a children's club and evening entertainment.

Facilities

Bar, restaurant and takeaway. Supermarket. Swimming pool with water slides, aqua gym and children's pool. Tennis. Playground. Games room. Entertainment and activity programme. Excursion programme. Children's club. Mobile homes for rent. Off site: Nearest beach 2.5 km. Sailing, diving.

Open

15 March - 30 September.

Directions

From the A9 motorway (heading south) take the Perpignan Sud exit and follow signs to Argelès sur Mer on the N114. Take exit 10 signed Taxo d'Avall and Taxo d'Amont, then Plages Nord and St Cyprien. Site is 1 km. further down this road.

Charges 2005

Per unit incl. 2 persons	€ 19,00 - € 25,00
extra person	€ 6,00 - € 8,00
child (0-4 yrs)	€ 3,00 - € 4,00
electricity (4A)	€ 4,00

Reservations

Contact site. Tel: 04 68 81 04 34.
Email: info@aletoiledor.com

Your stay at L'ETOILE D'OR will be pleasant and comfortable in the shade of mimosa, oak, pine and fir

Route de Taxo à la Mer - 66701 ARGELES-SUR-MER cedex
+33 (0)4 68 81 04 34 - FAX +33 (0)4 68 81 57 05
www.aletoiledor.com - E-mail : info@aletoiledor.com

FR66070 Yelloh! Village Le Brasilia

Mobile homes ▶ page 444

B.P. 204, F-66141 Canet-en-Roussillon (Pyrénées-Orientales)

An impressive family site beside the beach, well managed. It is pretty, neat and well kept with an amazingly wide range of facilities and activities, and though it is a large site it does not seem so. There are 826 neatly hedged pitches all with electricity varying in size from 100 to 150 sq.m. Some of the longer pitches are suitable for two families together. With a range of shade from mature pines and flowering shrubs, less on pitches near the beach, there are neat access roads (sometimes narrow for large units) and many flowering shrubs. Over 100 of the pitches have mobile homes or chalets to rent. The sandy beach here is busy, with a beach club (you can hire windsurfing boards) and a naturist section is on the beach to the west of the site. There is also a large California type pool, with sunbathing areas bounded by an attractive mosaic wall and bar. The village area of the site provides bars, a busy restaurant, entertainment (including a night club) and a range of shops. In fact you do not need to stir from the site which is almost a resort in itself also providing a cash dispenser, exchange facilities, telephone, post office, gas supplies and even weather forecasts. It does have a nice, lively atmosphere but is orderly and well run - very good for a site with beach access. They seem to have thought of everything, including an escort to your pitch and advice on the best way to site your unit. A 'Yelloh Village' member.

Facilities
Ten modern sanitary blocks are very well equipped and maintained, with British style WCs (some Turkish) and washbasins in cabins. Some very modern and impressive with good facilities for children and for disabled people. All have dishwashing and laundry sinks. Laundry room with washing machines and dryers. Special refuse areas. Hairdressing salon. Bars and restaurant. Swimming pool with life guards (heated and free). Children's play areas. Sports field for football and a smaller games pitch (with 'Astroturf'). Tennis courts. Sporting activities such as aqua gym, aerobics, football, etc. Library, games and video room. Internet café. Daily entertainment programme for young and old. Bicycle hire. Fishing. Special dog walking area, cleaned daily. Torches useful. English is spoken. Off site: Riding 5 km. Golf 12 km. Canet Plage with its long esplanade edging the beach.

At a glance
Welcome & Ambience	✓✓✓✓✓	Location	✓✓✓✓✓
Quality of Pitches	✓✓✓✓✓	Range of Facilities	✓✓✓✓✓

Directions
From A9 motorway take exit 41 (Perpignan Centre/Rivesalts) follow signs for Le Barcarès/Canet on D83 for 10 km, then signs for Canet (D81). Arriving at first Canet roundabout, make a full turn back on yourself (direction Sainte-Marie) and watch for Brasila sign almost immediately on right and follow.

Charges 2005
Per unit incl. 2 persons and electricity (6A)	€ 15,00 - € 41,00
extra person	€ 4,60 - € 7,80
child (1-4 yrs)	free - € 4,00
extra electricity (10A)	€ 1,50
dog	€ 2,00 - € 4,00

Reservations
Advised for July/Aug. Tel: 04 68 80 23 82.
Email: camping-le-brasilia@wanadoo.fr

Open
29 April - 30 September.

FR66110 Camping Le Dauphin

Route de Taxo-d'Avall, F-66701 Argelès-sur-Mer (Pyrénées-Orientales)

Near Taxo in the quieter, northern part of Argelès (a somewhat frenzied resort in season), this family owned site on flat, grassy parkland with plenty of tall trees enjoys good views of the Pyrénées from the terrace area surrounding its excellent complex of swimming pools. There are 310 level, grassy well shaded pitches, all with 10A electricity and some with individual sanitary units; however some 150 pitches are taken by mobile homes and chalets either privately owned or for rent. Tour operators use 70 of the pitches. Although located some 1.5 km. from the town and beach, there is a regular connecting 'road train' service to and fro throughout the day and evening up to midnight.

Facilities
A central sanitary block, although mature, provides all essential facilities including washbasins en-suite. One third of the pitches have their own fully equipped individual sanitary unit. Shops, bar/restaurant, pizzeria with takeaway (all 1/6-15/9). Pool complex (small charge). play area. Tennis courts, minigolf, table tennis, multi-sport court, sports ground and games room. Entertainment programme in high season. Torches useful in some areas. Off site: Riding 1 km. Fishing 2 km.

Open
20 May - 24 September.

At a glance
Welcome & Ambience	✓✓✓✓	Location	✓✓✓✓
Quality of Pitches	✓✓✓✓✓	Range of Facilities	✓✓✓✓

Directions
Site is on north side of Argelès. From autoroute take exit Perpignan-Nord for Argelès and follow directions for Plage-Nord and Taxo d'Avall (similarly from the N114).

Charges 2006
Per unit incl. 2 adults	€ 18,00 - € 24,50
with electricity	€ 20,00 - € 28,50
extra person	€ 4,00 - € 6,00
child (under 5 yrs)	free - € 5,00
water and drainage	€ 3,00 - € 4,00

Reservations
Made with deposit (€ 77) and booking fee (€ 16).
Tel: 04 68 81 17 54.
Email: info@campingledauphin.com

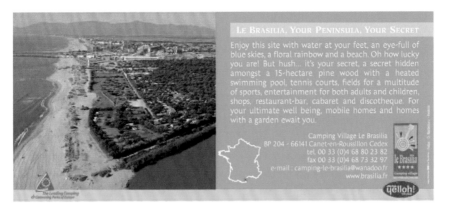
FR66130 Hotel de Plein Air L'Eau Vive

Chemin de St Saturnin, F-66820 Vernet-les-Bains (Pyrénées-Orientales)

Enjoying dramatic views of the towering Pic du Canigou, this small site is 1.5 km. from the centre of the spa town of Vernet-les-Bains in the Pyrénées. It is approached via a twisting road through a residential area. The 77 tourist pitches, all with electricity (4/10A) and 45 with water and drain, are on a slight slope, part hedged and some terraced, with a separate tent field. Most pitches have some shade. Although there is no swimming pool as such, the site has a very attractive, more or less natural pool (created by circulating running water from the nearby stream) that even provides a small beach with water slide (high season). There is a central floating safety line across the pool but parents should keep an eye on children as there is no supervision or safety fence. Access to the bubbling mountain stream is possible. Well situated for touring this area of the Pyrénées and with very comfortable amenities, this small site quickly becomes fully booked in season and reservation is essential. English is spoken by the welcoming Dutch owners who will arrange walks, canoe and rafting trips or even 4x4 excursions up Mont Canigou.

Facilities

First class toilet facilities in two modern blocks include washbasins in cabins, dishwashing under cover and facilities for disabled people. Washing machine in each block. Bread can be ordered in main season. Bar/reception with pool table, amusement machine, library, etc. Attractive open air (but under cover) snack bar with simple food and takeaway (1/6-30/9). A 'meal of the day' can be ordered in advance (good value) Play area. Natural pool for children. Sports field. Basketball. Bicycle hire. Off site: Fishing 200 m. Swimming pool and thermal centre in village 1 km. The nearby medieval, walled town of Ville Franche de Conflent, the Grottes des Canalettes and Fort Libena with its many steps are well worth visiting. Organised rafting, canoeing, and hydrospeed trips.

Open

All year excl. 12 November - 15 December.

At a glance

Welcome & Ambience	✓✓✓✓✓	Location	✓✓✓✓✓
Quality of Pitches	✓✓✓✓	Range of Facilities	✓✓✓✓

Directions

Following the N116 to Andorra, 6 km. after Prades, take turning at Villefranche de Conflent for Vernet-les-Bains. Continue up hill for 5 km. and keep right avoiding town centre. Turn right over bridge towards Sahorre. Immediately, at one end of small block of shops, turn right into Ave de Saturnin and follow for about 1 km. past houses to more open area and site is signed.

Charges 2005

Per unit incl. up to 3 persons	€ 11,00 - € 19,00
incl. electricity	€ 13,00 - € 22,00
extra person (over 4 yrs)	€ 1,50 - € 2,50
animal	€ 2,50

Discounts for weekly stays. Credit cards accepted 15/6-15/9 only. Camping Cheques accepted.

Reservations

Made with deposit (20%), € 15 fee (high season only) and cancellation insurance (details from site). Tel: 04 68 05 54 14. Email: leauv@club-internet.fr

3

FR66180 Mas Llinas Camping

F-66160 Le Boulou (Pyrénées-Orientales)

The highest terraces on this campsite have commanding views over the valley and to the surrounding mountains. On the nearby slopes are vineyards and lower in the valley large quantities of geraniums are grown professionally. The roads up to the level, terraced, hillside pitches (100) are paved to make access easy, with good places to choose from. Some are larger, some grassy and a few hedged for privacy, many with outstanding views and lovely trees (5/10A electricity is available). The ground is stony and may be difficult for tents. This is a simple, peaceful and well maintained site with a relaxed feel and helpful, friendly owners. The beautiful original old farmhouse is situated near the top of the property. The reception is near the bar/café that serves a very limited range of snacks and some local produce, including the wine of the region. Explore the region of the Roussillon wines, historic sites including the military fortress as it would have been in the time of Louis XVI, or just enjoy the peace and quiet.

Facilities

Two unisex toilet blocks, one clean and modern, the other rather small, basic and cramped. Full range of facilities for disabled campers. Washing machine. Motorcaravan services. Limited bar/café (mid June to end Sept). Bread and croissants (July/Aug). Small swimming pool (mid May - Oct. depending on weather). Volleyball. Table tennis. Games room. Electronic games. Torches necessary. Riding. Bicycle hire. Only gas barbecues are permitted. Off site: VTT with guide. Fishing 5 km. Golf 25 km. The site is close to the border and its associated shopping opportunities.

Open

1 March - 30 November.

At a glance

Welcome & Ambience	✓✓✓✓	Location	✓✓✓✓
Quality of Pitches	✓✓✓✓	Range of Facilities	✓✓✓✓

Directions

Le Boulou is about 26 km. from the eastern side of the Spanish border. Travel south from Perpignan on the A9/E15 or N9 to Le Boulou (approx. 30 km). Site is well signed from town and is on the northern outskirts, approached through a light commercial area of town. Follow road uphill through countryside for about 2 km. If crossing the Spanish border at Le Perthus expect long delays particularly off the autoroute as the road travels through the extremely busy and narrow main street where shoppers fight for border bargains. GPS: N42:32.50 E02:50.05

Charges 2005

Per person	€ 4,00 - € 4,70
child (under 10 yrs)	€ 2,50 - € 2,60
pitch	€ 4,50 - € 6,00
electricity (5/10A)	€ 3,00 - € 4,00
animal	€ 2,00

Less 10% for 7 days, 20% for 14 days, in low season.

Reservations

Contact site. Tel: 04 68 83 25 46.
Email: info@camping-mas-llinas.com

FR66170 Camping Mar I Sol

Route de la Plage, F-66440 Torreilles (Pyrénées-Orientales)

Good quality sites with direct access to the beach are hard to find and Mar i Sol is a useful option. It is a fairly large site with 377 pitches with a significant number of mobile homes but with 170 available for touring units. These are sandy grass pitches of good size with some shade and connected by hardcore roads. All have electricity (10A). The owners have renovated the pool area and continue with other improvements adding an 'Institut Balnea' or beauty centre where you can enjoy a sauna, Turkish or spa bath. This is essentially a 'holiday' site with all the popular facilities and an extensive entertainment programme, fitness courses and children's club throughout the main season.

Facilities

Three fully equipped toilet blocks of the same design include mixed British and Turkish toilets, some washbasins in cabins, baby bath and covered dishwashing and laundry sinks. Washing machine in each block. Small supermarket. Bar. TV. Restaurant and takeaway. Heated swimming pool, water slide and children's pool. All facilities open all season. Play area. Tennis court (charged). Table tennis. Archery. Fitness room. Beauty centre. Football and volleyball. Side gate with access to path across semi-dunes to sandy beach (lifeguards in main season). Watersport activities possible. Off site: Sea fishing and water sports on beach. Horse riding and mini golf 0.5 km. Microlites and karting 1.5 km. Bicycle hire 2 km. Golf 10 km. Diving and water skiing 4 km.

At a glance

Welcome & Ambience	✓✓✓✓✓	Location	✓✓✓✓✓
Quality of Pitches	✓✓✓✓	Range of Facilities	✓✓✓✓✓

Directions

From A9 take exit 41(Perpignan Nord) towards Le Barcarès for 9 km then south on D81 towards Canet for 3 km. before turning to Torreilles Plage. Site is signed. GPS: N42:47.059 E03:01.974

Charges 2005

Per unit incl. 2 persons and electricity (10A)	€ 21,00 - € 34,30
extra person (over 6 yrs)	€ 5,30 - € 6,80
child (under 6 yrs)	free - € 3,50
dog	€ 5,90

Reservations

Necessary for July/Aug. and made with deposit (€ 75) and booking fee (€ 26.5). Tel: 04 68 28 04 07.
Email: marisol@camping-marisol.com

Open

1 April - 30 September.

FR66200 Camping Les Marsouins

Avenue de la Retirada, F-66702 Argelès-sur-Mer (Pyrénées-Orientales)

Les Marsouins is a large site situated on the beach road out of Argelès. Of the 587 pitches, 150 are taken by mobile homes. Those for touring units are of a good size on level, mown grass divided by hedging. There is a degree of shade from some tall trees and electricity (5A) is available to all. An outdoor entertainment area is located at the entrance beside the bar and restaurant (for high season entertainment) but the lagoon style heated pool and paddling pool (no water slides) are tucked away to one side of the site with ample space for sunbathing on the lawns surrounding it. The site is well situated for easy access to the good sandy beach, with activities like windsurfing and sea kayaking possible (free 15/5-30/9). English is spoken.

Facilities

Four fully equipped toilet blocks provide facilities for the handicapped and there are dishwashing and laundry sinks, washing machine and iron. Motorcaravan service point. Shop (26/5-8/9). Bar and self-service restaurant (16/6-5/9) near entrance. Takeaway (1/4-30/9). Mini-market (8/6-7/9). Heated swimming pool (identity bracelet required; 15/04-29/9). Large play area. Children's club with free organised activities (24/6-1/9). Tennis, volleyball, table tennis. Range of evening entertainment (30/5-30/8). Off site: Beach 800 m. Riding next door. Boat launching 2 km. Golf 7 km.

Open

9 April - 30 September.

At a glance

Welcome & Ambience	✓✓✓✓	Location	✓✓✓✓
Quality of Pitches	✓✓✓✓✓	Range of Facilities	✓✓✓✓✓

Directions

Take the Perpignan sud exit from A9 autoroute. Follow signs for Argelès (RN114) exit junction 10 and follow Pujols at roundabout then Plage Nord at next roundabout. Site is 1.5 km. on left.
GPS: N42:33.827 E03:02.044

Charges 2005

Per unit incl. 2 persons	
and 5A electricity	€ 12,00 - € 24,50
with water and drainage	€ 13,50 - € 26,00
extra person (over 5 yrs)	€ 4,00 - € 5,50
dog	free

Reservations

Made with booking fee (€ 15). Tel: 04 68 81 14 81. Email: marsouin@campmed.com

FR66190 Sunêlia Les Tropiques

Boulevard de la Méditerranée, F-66440 Torreilles-Plage (Pyrénées-Orientales)

Les Tropiques makes a pleasant holiday venue, only 400 metres from a sandy beach and also boasting two pools. There are 450 pitches with 200 given over to mobile homes and chalets. Pleasant pine and palm trees with other Mediterranean vegetation give shade and provides an attractive environment. Activities are provided for all including a large range of sports, caberets and shows but an identity bracelet for entry to the site is obligatory in high season (small payment required).

Facilities

Modern, fully equipped sanitary facilities include provision for disabled visitors. Launderette. Shop, bar and restaurant with takeaway and pizzeria (all 1/5-30/9). Heated pool open all season, another pool (15/5-30/9) and a paddling pool. Tennis, table tennis, football, volleyball and pétanque. Archery (1/7-31/8). TV and billiards room. Play area. Disco (every evening) and club for 6-12 year olds in July/Aug. Bicycle hire (15/6-15/9). Off site: Minigolf 300 m. Windsurf board hire and sea fishing 400 m. Riding 400 m. Microlites and karting 1.5 km. Diving and water-skiing 4 km.Golf 15 km.

Open

9 April - 8 October.

At a glance

Welcome & Ambience	✓✓✓✓	Location	✓✓✓✓
Quality of Pitches	✓✓✓✓	Range of Facilities	✓✓✓✓✓

Directions

From autoroute A9 take exit for Perpignan Nord and follow D83 towards Le Barcarès for 9 km. Take D81 south towards Canet for 3 km. before turning left at roundabout for Torreilles Plage. Site is the last but one on the left.

Charges 2005

Per unit incl. 2 persons	
with electricity	€ 17,00 - € 33,00
extra person	€ 3,70 - € 7,50
child (0-13 yrs)	€ 2,50 - € 5,50
animal	€ 4,00

Camping Cheques accepted.

Reservations

Made with € 120 deposit and € 30 booking fee. Tel: 04 68 28 05 09.
Email: camping.tropiques@wanadoo.fr

3

FR66220 Camping du Stade

Avenue du 8 Mai 1945, F-66702 Argelès-sur-Mer (Pyrénées-Orientales)

Quieter and more peaceful family orientated sites are about as rare as hen's teeth in this immediate area, so we were pleasantly surprised to discover one in a pleasant shady setting midway between the village and the beach resort – less than 1 km. from both. The 180 good sized pitches, (most with electricity) are in green surroundings with plenty of shade. This traditionally French campsite, could be a quiet haven for those who want to relax at the end of the day without the distraction of a noisy pool and bar, but who want to be close to all the various attractions offered by this resort.

Facilities

With so much within easy walking distance the site itself has few facilities, but it does have two good quality, part modern, part traditional, well-maintained toilet blocks with good sized showers, washbasins in cabins, etc. Unit for disabled people, facilities for babies, covered dishwashing area and washing machine. Snack-bar and takeaway (high season only). Adventure-style play area. Table tennis. Off site: Beach, shops, bars and restaurants all within walking distance.

Open

1 April - 30 September.

At a glance

Welcome & Ambience	✓✓✓✓	Location	✓✓✓✓
Quality of Pitches	✓✓✓✓	Range of Facilities	✓✓✓

Directions

From A9 exit 42 (Perpignan Sud) take N114 towards Argelès. Take exit 10 for Pujols and Argles, then follow signs towards Centre Plage. At first roundabout go straight on (Ave Molliere). At next (small) roundabout turn left and site is immediately on your left.

Charges 2005

Per unit incl. 2 adults	€ 13,20 - € 18,50
with electricity	€ 16,50 - € 22,00
extra person	€ 3,40 - € 4,90
child	€ 2,20 - € 3,15
dog	€ 1,50 - € 2,00

Reservations

Contact site. Tel: 04 68 81 04 40.
Email: info@campingdustade.com

FR66210 Chadotel Camping Le Roussillon

Chemin de la Mer, F-66750 Saint Cyprien (Pyrénées-Orientales)

This a comfortable site, although perhaps somewhat lacking in character. It is part of the Chadotel Group and has a quiet situation on the edge of St Cyprien village, some 2 km. from the beach. A bus service runs in the main season. The site benefits from having a good sized, traditionally shaped swimming pool, with the added attraction for children of a water slide, and plenty of sunbathing areas for adults. There are 166 pitches in total with a number taken by our tour operators and the rest for mobile homes available to rent but there are 25 well-kept, grassy and level touring pitches. Of a good size, they all have 16A electrical connections.

Facilities

Two toilet blocks (one older but refurbished, one more modern) provide modern facilities including a baby bath, laundry and facilities for disabled visitors. Bar/snack-bar with entertainment in season. Play area on grass.

Open

1 April - 24 September.

At a glance

Welcome & Ambience	✓✓✓✓	Location	✓✓✓
Quality of Pitches	✓✓✓✓	Range of Facilities	✓✓✓✓

Directions

Via the D81 southwards, do not go into St Cyprien Plage, but follow signs towards Argelès. At roundabout ('Aqualand' signed to the left) turn right towards St Cyprien village. Bear right and site is indicated by large Chadotel sign on the right hand side of this road.

Charges 2006

Per pitch incl. 2 adults	€ 14,50 - € 23,50
incl. electricity	€ 19,00 - € 28,00
extra person	€ 3,80 - € 5,80
child (under 2 yrs)	free

Reservations

Contact Chadotel Central Reservations, B.P. 12 85520 Jard-sur-Mer. Tel: 02 51 33 05 05. Site tel: 04 68 21 06 45. Email: info@chadotel.com

FR66230 Camping Caravaning Le Romarin

Route de Sorède, chemin des Vignes, F-66702 Argelès-sur-Mer (Pyrénées-Orientales)

In an area dominated by 'all-singing, all-dancing' holiday sites, we were pleased to discover almost by accident this charming little gem of a site tucked away some 2 km. behind the busy resort of Argelès. Essentially a site for families with younger children, or for adults seeking peace and quiet, it provides some 110 good sized touring pitches, all with electricity (6-10A) set among pine, eucalyptus, oak and mimosas. Ideal for exploring this area, especially the Albères range of Pyreneen mountains and the ancient city of Perpignan, it is nevertheless within easy reach of shops, a supermarket (2 km.) and all the attractions of Argelès, both village and Plage.

Facilities

One good large toilet block (half traditional style, half modern) provides a mix of British and Turkish WCs, showers, washbasins in cabins, dishwashing and laundry sinks and washing machine. Snack bar (mid June - end Sept). Swimming pool (mid June - mid Sept). Play area. Table tennis. Some traditional (local) family entertainment in high season. Off site: Riding and bicycle hire 2 km. Fishing 4 km. Golf 8 km.

Open

15 May - 30 September.

At a glance

| Welcome & Ambience | ✓✓✓✓ | Location | ✓✓✓✓ |
| Quality of Pitches | ✓✓✓✓ | Range of Facilities | ✓✓✓✓ |

Directions

From autoroute A9 take exit 42 (Perpignan Sud) on N114 towards Argelès for 25 km. to exit 11a. At roundabout follow directions to St Andre for 300 m. Watch carefully for left turn (with site sign), almost back on yourself. Road is fairly narrow and unnumbered. After approx. 2 km. at T junction turn left on to D11. After a short distance take third left (site signed) and follow lane to site.

Charges 2005

Per unit incl. 2 persons	€ 11,00 - € 14,00
extra person	€ 3,00 - € 4,00
child (2-5 yrs)	free - € 2,00
electricity	€ 2,00 - € 3,50
dog	€ 2,00 - € 3,00

Reservations

Made with 25% deposit. Tel: 04 68 81 02 63.
Email: camping.romarin@libertysurf.fr

FR66240 Chadotel Camping Le Trivoly

Route des Plages, F-66440 Torreilles-Plage (Pyrénées-Orientales)

The popularity of Torreilles derives mainly from its huge sandy beach and for off-site nightlife, shopping, etc. but for smarter resorts one really needs to visit Le Barcares or Canet a few kilometres distance in either direction. Le Trivoly (part of the French Chadotel Group) is about 500 m. gentle stroll from the beach, in a fairly tranquil setting. It has 170 good size, well shaded and hedged pitches with electricity and 100 mobile homes. It perhaps offers a rather more peaceful situation than do the other sites here.

Facilities

Four toilet blocks, although not new, provide modern facilities, including washbasins in (rather small) cabins, and were all clean and well cared for when we visited. Small shop (June- mid Sept). Snack-restaurant and takeaway (June-mid Sept). Reasonably sized pool with water slide and paddling pool. Play area. Bicycle hire. Table tennis. Basketball. Entertainment programme in high season. Off site: Centre Commercial 300 m.

Open

1 April - 24 September.

At a glance

| Welcome & Ambience | ✓✓✓✓ | Location | ✓✓✓✓ |
| Quality of Pitches | ✓✓✓✓ | Range of Facilities | ✓✓✓✓ |

Directions

From autoroute A9 take exit 42 (Perpignan Nord) towards Le Barcarès for 9 km, then turn south onto the D81 towards Canet. After 3 km. turn left at roundabout, signed Torreilles Plage. Site is on left, after about 500 m.

Charges 2005

Per unit incl. 2 persons	€ 12,00 - € 23,00
with electricity (6A)	€ 16,50 - € 27,50
extra person	€ 5,70
child (under 13 yrs)	€ 3,70
animal	€ 2,80

Reservations

Contact Chadotel Central Reservations, B.P. 12, 85520 Jard-sur-Mer. Tel: 02 51 33 05 05.
Site tel: 04 68 28 20 28. Email: info@chadotel.com

MAP 15 & 16

Mediterranean East

Bathed in sunshine from early spring to late autumn, surrounded by stunning scenery, cosmopolitan towns and superb sandy beaches, no wonder this is one of France's most sought-after destinations.

THIS SECTION COVERS THE EASTERN COASTAL REGION OF THE MEDITERRANEAN. WE INCLUDE TWO DÉPARTEMENTS FROM THE OFFICIAL REGION OF PROVENCE AND THE REGION OF CÔTE D'AZUR: 13 BOUCHES-DU-RHÔNE, 83 VAR, 06 ALPES-MARITIME

The glittering Côte d'Azur, perhaps better known as the French Riviera, is a beautiful stretch of coast studded with sophisticated towns such as the famous Monte Carlo, Nice, and Cannes, not forgetting the other famous and arguably the most glamorous resort of St Tropez. With its vast expanses of golden sandy beaches and long lazy hours of sunshine, this is a paradise for sun worshippers and beach enthusiasts. It's a spectacular coast of rugged coves, sweeping beaches and warm seas.

The quaint harbours and fishing villages have become chic destinations, now full of pleasure yachts, harbour-side cafés and crowded summertime beaches. Further up in the hills are quieter tiny medieval villages with winding streets and white-walled houses with terracotta roofs, which have attracted artists for many years. In St Paul-de-Vence visitors browse through shops and galleries set on narrow winding cobblestone streets and inland Grasse is the perfume capital of the world, surrounded by the Provencal lavender fields and shady olive groves which pervade the air with a magical scent at certain times of the year.

Places of interest

Aix-en-Provence: old town with 17th-18th century character, Paul Cézanne and Tapestry museums.

Cannes: popular for conventions and festivals, Cannes Film Festival, la Croisette, old city.

Monte Carlo: main city of Monaco, casinos, gardens, Napoleon Museum. motorsport circuit.

Cuisine of the region

Aigo Bouido: garlic and sage soup.

Bouillabaisse: fish soup.

Rouille: an orange coloured sauce with peppers, garlic and saffron.

Bourride: a creamy fish soup.

Pissaladière: Provençal bread dough with onions, anchovies and olives.

Pistou (Soupe au): vegetable soup bound with *pommade*.

Pommade: a thick paste of garlic, basil, cheese and olive oil.

Ratatouille: aubergines, courgettes, onions, garlic, red peppers and tomatoes in olive oil.

Salade Niçoise: tomatoes, beans, potatoes, black olives, anchovy, lettuce, olive oil and tuna fish.

FR06100 Camping Les Pinèdes

Route du Pont de Pierre, F-06480 La Colle-sur-Loup (Alpes-Maritimes)

Les Pinèdes is seven kilometres inland from the busy coast, located at the centre of all the attractions of the Côte d'Azur, yet far enough away to be peaceful retreat at the end of a busy day sightseeing. In a terraced situation on a wooded hillside where olives and vines used to grow the site, has been in the hands of the welcoming Dugauguez family for the past 30 years. All the level pitches have electricity (3-10A), most also with water and are separated by low bushes. Due to the nature of the terrain there are no facilities for wheelchair users. The owners are keen to attract wildlife to the site and there are many varieties of birds and the odd fox to be seen. Two donkeys are an added attraction. For three weeks from the end of May into June, the evenings are alive with fireflies lighting up the site. The restaurant at the site entrance has an excellent reputation. The owner is very interested in all the local art galleries and will advise on where all the famous painters have paintings hung. There are many typical Provencal villages in close proximity not to mention the towns of Grasse, Menton, Monaco and Antibes, and all are well worth a visit - the family will be only too pleased to give advice. A 'Sites et Paysages' member.

Facilities

Two clean and well maintained toilet blocks have mainly British and a few Turkish style toilets and large shower cubicles. One block has been refurbished, the other is due to be soon. All the usual facilities for dishwashing and laundry etc and a baby room. Shop and bakery. Bar, restaurant and takeaway. Swimming pool. Two small play areas. Field for volleyball, basketball, football and archery. Boule pitch. Entertainment is organised for young and old in July/Aug. Weekly walks in the surrounding hills June - September (with light breakfast carried by the donkeys). Off site: Fishing in Loup river 50 m. Village 1 km. with tennis court, riding school, leisure park with keep fit course and antiques quarter.

At a glance

Welcome & Ambience	✓✓✓✓✓	Location	✓✓✓✓✓
Quality of Pitches	✓✓✓✓✓	Range of Facilities	✓✓✓✓✓

Directions

From A8 take D2 towards Vence. At Colle sur Loup roundabout take D6 signed Grasse, site on right in approx. 3 km. at large sign after the restaurant entrance.

Charges 2006

Per tent incl. 2 persons	€ 14,40 - € 19,00
caravan or motorcaravan	€ 16,60 - € 25,00
extra person	€ 3,90 - € 4,90
child (under 5 yrs)	€ 2,00 - € 3,10
dog	€ 1,70 - € 2,20
electricity (3-10A)	€ 3,10 - € 4,40

Reservations

Necessary for July/Aug. and made with 25% deposit and fee (€ 18.29). Tel: 04 93 32 98 94. Email: camplespinedes06@aol.com

Open

15 March - 30 September.

FR06050 Camping La Vieille Ferme

296 boulevard des Groules, F-06270 Villeneuve-Loubet-Plage (Alpes-Maritimes)

Open all year, in a popular resort area, La Vieille Ferme is a family owned site with good facilities. It provides 131 level gravel-based pitches, 106 with electricity, water and waste water connections and the majority separated by hedges. Some are only small, simple pitches for little tents. There is also a fully serviced pitch on tarmac for motorhomes. There are special winter rates for long stays with quite a few long stay units on site. The entrance to the site is very colourful with well tended flower beds. English is spoken at reception and the whole place has a very friendly feel to it. A one kilometre walk beside the road towards Antibes brings you to the railway station, giving access to all the towns along the coast and to the beach.

Facilities

Three modern, well kept toilet blocks (two heated in winter) provide washbasins all in cabins, children's toilets, baby room and two units for disabled people. Motorcaravan service point. Dishwashing and laundry sinks. Three washing machines and dryer. Shop (Easter - Sept). Drinks, sweets and ices machine in the TV room for all year use. Gas, bread and milk to order when shop closed. Refrigerator hire. Swimming pool (20 x 10 m.) and children's pool, heated and covered for winter use (closed mid Nov-mid Dec) with jacuzzi. Internet point. Table tennis, basketball and boule pitch. Games and competitions organised in July/Aug. Off site: Fishing 1 km, golf 2 km.

Open

All year.

At a glance

Welcome & Ambience	✓✓✓✓✓	Location	✓✓✓✓
Quality of Pitches	✓✓✓✓	Range of Facilities	✓✓✓✓✓

Directions

From west take Antibes exit from Esterel autoroute and turn left towards Nice when joining the N7 outside Antibes. After 3.5 km. on N7 turn left for site. From east take N7 towards Antibes and turn right after Villeneuve Loubet Plage. The turning off the N7, though signed, is not easy to see particularly at busy times but, coming from Antibes, it is on the left, more or less between the Marine Land and the Parc de Vaugrenier. Site is 150 m. on right. Avoid N98 Route du Bord de Mer. Site has prepared its own small, yellow site signs.

Charges 2006

Per unit incl. 2 persons and electricity (10A)	€ 23,76 - € 34,76

Reservations

Advised over a long season and made with 25% deposit and € 20 fee; Sat.-Sat. only in July/Aug and at Easter. Tel: 04 93 33 41 44. Email: vieilleferme@bigfoot.com

371

FR06030 Camping Caravaning Domaine de la Bergerie

Route de la Sine, F-06140 Vence (Alpes-Maritimes)

La Bergerie is a quiet, family owned site, situated in the hills about 3 km. from Vence and 10 km. from the sea at Cagnes-sur-Mer. This extensive, lightly wooded site has been left very natural and is in a secluded position about 300 m. above sea level. Because of the trees most of the pitches are shaded and all are of a good size. It is a large site but because it is so extensive it does not give that impression. There are 450 pitches, 300 with electricity (2/5A) and 65 also with water and drainage. Because of the nature of this site, some pitches are a little distance from the toilet blocks. There are no organised activities and definitely no groups allowed.

Facilities

Both toilet blocks have been refurbished and include washbasins in cabins and excellent provision for disabled people (pitches near the block are reserved for disabled people). Very good shop, small bar/restaurant with takeaway (all 1/5-30/9). Large swimming pool, paddling pool and spacious sunbathing area (5/6-30/9). Playground. Bicycle hire. Table tennis, tennis courts and 10 shaded boules pitches (lit at night) with competitions in season. Barbecues are not permitted. Off site: Riding 6 km. Fishing 10 km. Golf 12 km. Hourly bus service (excl. Sundays) from site to Vence.

Open

25 March - 15 October.

At a glance

Welcome & Ambience	✓✓✓✓	Location	✓✓✓✓
Quality of Pitches	✓✓✓	Range of Facilities	✓✓✓✓

Directions

From autoroute A8 exit 47 take Cagnes-sur-Mer road towards Vence. Site is west of Vence – follow 'toutes directions' signs around the town to join the D2210 Grasse road. Follow this to roundabout (2 km), turn left and follow site signs for 1 km. Site is on right in light woodland.

Charges 2005

Per unit incl. 2 persons	€ 14,00 - € 19,50
with electricity (2A)	€ 17,50 - € 23,50
with water, drainage, electricity (5A)	€ 22,50 - € 30,00
extra person	€ 4,80
child (under 5 yrs)	€ 3,10

Less 10-15% for longer stays.
Camping Cheques accepted.

Reservations

Necessary only in July/Aug. for the special pitches and made with 25% deposit and € 12.96 fee.
Tel: 04 93 58 09 36.
Email: info@camping-domainedelabergerie.com

FR06010 Camping Domaine Sainte Madeleine

Route de Moulinet, F-06380 Sospel (Alpes-Maritimes)

Domaine Sainte Madeleine is an attractive, peaceful site, with swimming pool, in spectacular mountain scenery. It is about 20 km. inland from Menton, and very near the Italian border. The approach to this site is not for the faint-hearted although having said that, when we visited in late July, the site was very busy with touring caravans so it cannot be too bad. The site itself makes the effort worthwhile – situated on a terraced hillside with mountain views towards Italy. On a fairly steep hillside, manoeuvring within the site presents no problem and the pitches themselves are on level, well drained grass. The lower ones have shade but those higher up on the hill have none. Electricity connections are available to 70 of the 90 pitches. There are way-marked walks for serious walkers in the surrounding hills. English is spoken.

Facilities

The single toilet block is of good quality, including washbasins in cabins and showers on payment. Hot water (often only warm) for dishwashing and laundry sinks drawn from single tap. Washing machines. Motorcaravan services. Gas supplies. Bread can be ordered. Swimming pool (140 sq.m. and heated in spring and autumn). Off site: The attractive small town of Sospel is only 4 km. with many restaurants, bars, cafés and shops. Tennis, riding and a centre for mountain biking. Fishing 1 km.

Open

25 March - 1 October.

At a glance

Welcome & Ambience	✓✓✓✓	Location	✓✓✓✓
Quality of Pitches	✓✓✓	Range of Facilities	✓✓✓

Directions

From the A8 autoroute take the Menton exit towards Sospel from where you turn onto the D2566 (route de Moulinet), Site is 4 km. north of Sospel on the left.

Charges 2006

Per unit incl. 2 persons	€ 19,00
extra person	€ 4,00
child (under 6 yrs)	€ 2,40
electricity (10A)	€ 2,90
animal	€ 1,40

Less 15% outside July/Aug. No credit cards.

Reservations

Necessary for July/Aug. and made with € 50 deposit.
Tel: 04 93 04 10 48.
Email: camp@camping-sainte-madeleine.com

FR06080 Camping Caravaning Les Cigales

Mobile homes ▶ page 444

505 avenue de la Mer, F-06210 Mandelieu-la-Napoule (Alpes-Maritimes)

It is hard to imagine that such a quiet, peaceful site could be in the middle of such a busy town and so near Cannes – we were delighted with it. The entrance (easily missed) with reception and parking has large electronic gates that ensure that the site is very secure. There are only 115 pitches (40 used for mobile homes) so this is really quite a small, personal site. There are three pitch sizes, from small ones for tents to pitches for larger units. All are level with much needed shade in summer, although the sun will get through in winter when it is needed, and all have electricity (6A), some also with water and waste water. The site is alongside the Canal de Siagne and for a fee, small boats can be launched at La Napoule, then moored outside the campsite's side gate. Les Cigales is open all year so it is useful for the Monte Carlo Rally, the Cannes Film Festival and the Mimosa Festival, all held out of the main season. English is spoken.

Facilities

Two well appointed unisex toilet blocks are kept very clean, one heated for the winter months. Washbasins in cabins and facilities for babies and disabled visitors. Dishwashing and laundry sinks. Washing machine. Motorcaravan service point. Restaurant at entrance also serves takeaways (April - 30 Sept). Swimming pool, quite new with large sunbathing area (March - Oct), heated mid-March - mid-Oct). Small play area. Table tennis and two games machines. Fishing possible in the canal (but not many fish!). Off site: Beach 800 m. The town is an easy walk. Two golf courses within 1 km. Railway station 1 km. for trains to Cannes, Nice, Antibes and Monte Carlo. Centre commercial (supermarket and 40 shops) 2 km. Riverside and canal walks. Bus stop 10 minutes.

Open

All year.

At a glance

Welcome & Ambience	✓✓✓✓✓	Location	✓✓✓✓✓
Quality of Pitches	✓✓✓✓✓	Range of Facilities	✓✓✓✓

Directions

From A8 take exit 40 and bear right. Remain in right hand lane and continue right signed Plages-Ports and Creche-Campings. Casino supermarket is on the right. Continue under motorway to T-junction. Turn left and site is 60 m. on left opposite Chinese restaurant.

Charges 2006

Per person	€ 5,50
child (under 5 yrs)	€ 2,75
tent	€ 11,00 - € 17,00
caravan	€ 13,50 - € 27,00
motorcaravan	€ 13,50 - € 27,00
dog	€ 1,00

Reservations

Made with deposit (€ 77). Tel: 04 93 49 23 53.
Email: campingcigales@wanadoo.fr

373

FR06090 Camping Caravaning Les Gorges du Loup

965 chemin des Vergers, F-06620 Le Bar-sur-Loup (Alpes-Maritimes)

In the hills above Grasse, Les Gorges du Loup is situated on a steep hillside. Some pitches are only suitable for tents and the site roads are quite steep. The one kilometre lane which leads to the site is narrow but there are many passing places. The 70 pitches are on level terrace areas, all with electricity, and many have quite stupendous views. A quiet family site, there is no organised entertainment. Bar-de-Loup with its few shops and restaurants is only a 500 m. walk. Grasse (9 km.) is surrounded by fields of lavender, mimosa and jasmine and has been famous for the manufacture of perfume since the 16th century. The Musée International de la Perfume has a garden of fragrant plants and the cathedral in the old town has three paintings by Reubens. The very friendly and enthusiastic owners will site your caravan with their 4x4 free of charge if required. They also speak a little English.

Facilities

Two tiled toilet blocks are kept very clean and include washbasins mostly in cubicles. More than half the WCs are British style. Dishwashing and laundry sinks have a single hot tap to draw from. Washing machine and iron. Reception has small shop with bread daily. Small bar/restaurant and takeaway (July/Aug). Swimming pool (no Bermuda style shorts), small slide and diving board, but no pool for small children. Boules pitches, table tennis, basketball, volleyball and skittles. TV room with tables and chairs for board games, plus a library. Children's climbing frame and slide. Charcoal barbecues are not allowed. Chalets and mobile homes for hire.

Open

1 April - 30 September.

At a glance

Welcome & Ambience	✓✓✓✓✓	Location		✓✓✓✓✓
Quality of Pitches	✓✓✓✓	Range of Facilities		✓✓✓✓

Directions

From Grasse take D2085 Nice road. Take D3 briefly and then at Châteauneuf Pré du Lac take D2210 to Pont-de-Loup and Vence. Site is signed on right. Pass village of Bar-sur-Loup on left and then, after a very tight right turn, take 0.75 km. narrow access road (a few passing places). From direction of Vence, site is well signed and straightforward.

Charges 2005

Per unit incl. 2 persons	€ 13,50 - € 23,70
extra person	€ 3,80
child (under 5 yrs)	€ 3,10
dog	€ 2,00
electricity (4/10A)	€ 2,50 - € 4,00

No credit cards.

Reservations

Advised in high season. Tel: 04 93 42 45 06.
Email: info@lesgorgesduloup.com

FR06070 Domaine Naturiste Club Origan

F-06260 Puget-Theniers (Alpes-Maritimes)

Origan is a naturist site set in the mountains behind Nice. Despite its rather spectacular location, it is easily accessible from the coast and you only discover that you are at a height of 500 m. when you arrive! The access road is single track and winding with a few passing places for about a mile, so arrival is not recommended until late afternoon. The terrain within the extensive confines of the site is fairly wild and the roads distinctly stony. The site is not suitable for caravans longer than six metres due to the steep slopes, although the site will assist with a 4x4 vehicle if requested. The scenery is impressive and footpaths in and around the site offer good, if fairly strenuous, walks up to a height of 1,000 m. The 100 touring pitches, in three different areas with many wild flowers, are of irregular size and shape and all have good views. Electricity connection (6A) is possible on most pitches (by long cable). Reservation is necessary in high season. Member 'France 4 Naturisme'.

Facilities

Sanitary facilities, exceptionally clean when we visited, are of a standard and type associated with most good naturist sites - mainly British type WCs, mostly open plan hot showers and ample washbasins with hot and cold water. Laundry facilities. Shop (1/5-21/8). Bar/restaurant (all season). Takeaway. Heated swimming pools, one for children (1/5-31/8). Jacuzzi and sauna. Disco in cellars. Tennis. Fishing. Bicycle hire. Organised activities for adults and children (high season). Only gas or electric barbecues are permitted. Torches advised. Off site: The nearby small town of Puget-Theniers is very pleasant and offers choice of bars, cafés, shops, etc. Steam train. Eco-museum of the Roudoule.

At a glance

Welcome & Ambience	✓✓✓✓	Location		✓✓✓✓
Quality of Pitches	✓✓✓✓	Range of Facilities		✓✓✓✓

Directions

Heading west on the N202, just past the town of Puget-Theniers, turn right at camp sign at level crossing; site is 1.5 km.

Charges 2005

Per unit incl. 2 persons	€ 14,00 - € 27,50
incl. electricity	€ 17,00 - € 31,50
extra peron	€ 4,50 - € 7,40
child (4-10 yrs)	€ 2,00 - € 5,79
dog	€ 1,00 - € 2,50

Camping Cheques accepted.

Reservations

Made with 25% deposit and fee (€ 30) - contact site. Tel: 04 93 05 06 00. Email: origan@wanadoo.fr

Open

12 April - 30 September.

FR06120 Camping Green Park

Mobile homes ▶ page 445

159 Vallon des Vaux, F-06800 Cagnes-sur-Mer (Alpes-Maritimes)

Green Park has many facilities of a high standard and the owning family are justifiably proud. Situated just over 4 km. from the beaches at Cagnes-sur-Mer, Green Park is at the centre of the Cote d'Azur. There are two parts to Green Park, one newly constructed and very active site to keep every member of the family occupied for most of the day and evening, with club activities for children, teenagers and even adults, while on the other side of the approach road there is a quieter and more traditional site, with limited facilities. Activities and facilities are interchangeable. There are 78 touring pitches mostly on the left or west side of the site, mainly on grass, all with electricity of which 24 are serviced, plus 67 mobile homes and chalets. The site has two swimming pools, one on each side of the road (this road is not busy and goes 'nowhere' further up the valley). Green Park is situated in an area which benefits from a 'micro climate', hot during the day but pleasantly cooler at night.

Facilities

All the toilets are modern and mostly British, with facilities for children and disabled visitors (the disabled facilities are superb). Showers and washbasins are modern and kept very clean. Dishwashing and laundry sinks and three washing machines. Bar, restaurant and takeaway (29/4-25/9). Two swimming pools - one heated. Internet point. Games room. Electronic barrier (€5 card deposit) and a gate keeper on duty all night. Off site: Golf 12 km. Riding 10 km.

Open

25 March - 16 October.

At a glance

Welcome & Ambience	✓✓✓✓✓	Location	✓✓✓✓
Quality of Pitches	✓✓✓✓	Range of Facilities	✓✓✓✓✓

Directions

Coming from Aix on the A8, take exit 47 onto the N7 towards Nice. Go straight on at traffic lights by the racecourse for 2 km. then turn left towards Val Fleuri on Av. du Val Fleuri. Go over roundabouts onto Chemin Vallon des Vaux to site on right in 2 km. From Nice on N98 coast road, turn right at Le Port du Cros de Cagnes and follow camping signs. It is important to avoid the town centre.

Charges 2005

Per unit incl. 2 persons	€ 14,00 - € 34,00
extra person	€ 4,50 - € 5,50
child (2-7 yrs)	€ 2,80 - € 5,00
electricity	€ 3,80 - € 5,00
dog	€ 2,50 - € 3,50

Camping Cheques accepted.

Reservations

Contact site. Tel: 04 93 07 09 96.
Email: info@greenpark.fr

FR06140 Ranch Camping

Chemin Saint Joseph, F-06110 Le Cannet (Alpes-Maritimes)

Ranch Camping is a well run 'French flavoured' site which will be celebrating its 50th anniversary in 2006. The ambience here is calm and there is relatively little by way of entertainment or leisure amenities. However, the site is very well located for the beaches of Cannes just 2 km. away; a regular bus service runs past the site entrance. Despite its urban setting the site enjoys a tranquil setting on a wooded hillside. There are 108 touring pitches which are generally level and well shaded. all with 6A electrical connections. The swimming pool is quite small and can be covered in low season. Other leisure facilities can be found nearby.

Facilities

The two toilet blocks are quite different – the principal block has been recently refurbished, whereas the second block is of 'portacabin' style. Both however were very clean and well maintained when we visited. Facilities for disabled people. Washing machines and dryers. Small shop. Swimming pool (covered in low season). Games room. Mobile homes and rooms for rent. Off site: Beach 2 km. Bus stop at site entrance (regular service to Cannes and beaches). Tennis 200 m. Fishing and bicycle hire 2 km. Golf 4 km.

At a glance

Welcome & Ambience	✓✓✓✓✓	Location	✓✓✓✓
Quality of Pitches	✓✓✓✓	Range of Facilities	✓✓✓

Directions

Leave A8 autoroute at exit 42 and follow signs to Le Cannet, and then L'Aubarède to the right (D809). Follow this road until you see signs for La Bocca and the site is signed from here.

Charges 2005

Per unit incl. 1 person	€ 10,00 - € 16,00
extra person	€ 5,00
child (5-10 yrs)	€ 2,00
electricity (6A)	€ 3,00

Reservations

Contact site; minimum 7 nights. Tel: 04 93 46 00 11.

Open

1 April - 30 October.

FR13010 Camping Municipal Les Romarins

F-13520 Maussane (Bouches du Rhône)

A well kept, neat municipal site, Les Romarins has been in the guide for several years and remains popular with readers. Tarmac access roads lead to 145 good sized grassy pitches separated by hedges and bushes, all with electrical connections (4A). The municipal swimming pool (with discounts) is near and shops and restaurants are in the pleasant little town. Les Baux and St Remy-de-Provence are tourist attractions not to be missed, especially St Remy's Roman ruins. Les Romarins is popular and becomes very busy from 1 July - late August.

Facilities

Three toilet blocks, two refurbished with adjustable, roomy showers (on payment)and washbasins in cubicles. Baby room, washing machine, laundry and dishwashing sinks and facilities for disabled visitors. An older block with some Turkish style WCs is open for July and August and there are plans for it to be refurbished. Motorhome service point. Municipal swimming pool (50 m. from site) is free to campers between 15 June and 31 Aug. Play area. Free tennis courts. Pleasant reading room for cooler days. Internet access in reception. Off site: Bicycle hire or golf 1 km. Fishing or riding 3 km.

Open

15 March - 15 October.

At a glance

Welcome & Ambience	✓✓✓✓	Location	✓✓✓
Quality of Pitches	✓✓✓✓	Range of Facilities	✓✓✓

Directions

Site is within the little town of Maussane on the eastern edge.

Charges 2005

Per unit incl. 1 or 2 adults and 1 child	€ 14,50 - € 16,00
extra person	€ 3,30 - € 3,70
child	€ 1,90 - € 2,30
dog	€ 2,20
electricity	€ 2,90
Less 10-20% for longer stays.	

Reservations

Made for any length with fee. Tel: 04 90 54 33 60. Email: camping_municipal_maussane.@wannadoo.fr

FR13030 Camping Le Nostradamus

Route d'Eyguières, F-13300 Salon-de-Provence (Bouches du Rhône)

Only some five kilometres from Salon-de-Provence, near the village of Eyguieres, this is a very pleasant campsite with grassy shaded pitches thanks to the many trees which have been preserved here as a result of the imaginative irrigation scheme developed by the owners in the 18th century. The campsite edging the canal was first opened 42 years ago as a farm site but has now been developed to offer 83 hedged pitches including 10 used for mobile homes. There are 20 with full services, the rest having electricity connections (4/6A). This is a family site but having said that the canal is unfenced. You can swim or fish in it or even paddle in the adjoining stream. However, there is also a swimming pool beside the entrance, along with a bar/restaurant. In the high season activities are organised for children in the afternoons and for adults in the evening. With the Alpilles Mountains as a backdrop and places like Les Baux and St Rémy to visit, Nostradamus makes a very good venue.

Facilities

One large block with showers and toilets upstairs, and one small toilet block both provide all modern facilities including an en-suite units for babies and children and another for disabled visitors (key). Washing machine (key). Motorcaravan service point. Shop (basic essentials) and bar (1/4-30/10) Takeaway/restaurant (limited in early season). Swimming and paddling pools (15/5-15/9). Play area outside entrance. Table tennis. Volleyball. Petanque. Fishing. Off site: Riding 4 km. Golf 5 km.

Open

1 May - end October.

At a glance

Welcome & Ambience	✓✓✓✓	Location	✓✓✓✓
Quality of Pitches	✓✓✓✓	Range of Facilities	✓✓✓✓

Directions

From A7 autoroute take exit 26 (Senas) and follow N538 south for 5 km. Then take D175 west and pick up the D17 going south to Salon. Site is at junction of the D17 and CD72 with the entrance off the CD72. From A54 exit 13 go north towards Eyguières and take first right on CD72 (site signed). Entrance is just before the T-junction with the D17.

Charges 2005

Per unit incl. 2 persons	€ 15,00
extra person	€ 5,00
child (1-7 yrs)	€ 2,50
electricity	€ 2,80 - € 5,00
dog	€ 2,50

Reservations

Made with deposit (€ 35) and fee (€15).
Tel: 04 90 56 08 36. Email: gilles.nostra@wanadoo.fr

FR13040 Camping Monplaisir

Chemin de Monplaisir, F-13210 St Rémy-de-Provence (Bouches du Rhône)

Only a kilometre from the centre of St Rémy, in the foothills of the Alpilles mountains, this is one of the most pleasant and well run sites we have come across. Everything about the site is of a high standard and quality. Interestingly enough, the owners have chosen to remain a two star site until now, although they are certainly of three, or even four star standard. The good impression created by the reception and shop continues through the rest of the site. In all there are 130 level grass pitches with 8 taken by smart mobile homes, with 6A electricity everywhere. Flowering shrubs and greenery abounds, roads are tarmac and all is neat and tidy. There are five toilet blocks strategically placed for all areas, two heated and one larger, but all unisex. The recreation area with a swimming pool (18 x 10 m.), jacuzzi and paddling pool is overlooked by the bar area. Open in July and August, it provides light meals and snacks and some entertainment. St Rémy is a very popular town and the site was full when we visited in mid June.

Facilities

Five good quality toilet blocks all have some washbasins in cabins. Family rooms and en-suite facilities for disabled people in two. Washing machines. Two motorcaravan service points. Shop with essentials (good cheese and cold meat counter), also providing takeaway pizzas. Bar with snacks (July/Aug). Swimming pool (1/5-31/10). Play area. Table tennis. Boules. Off site: St Rémy 1 km. Les Baux 5 km. Bicycle hire 1 km. Riding 2 km. Fishing 3 km. Golf 15 km.

Open

1 March - 10 November.

At a glance

Welcome & Ambience	✓✓✓✓✓	Location	✓✓✓✓✓
Quality of Pitches	✓✓✓✓	Range of Facilities	✓✓✓✓

Directions

From St Rémy town centre follow signs for Arles and Nîmes. At roundabout on western side of town take D5 signed Maillane and immediately left by a supermarket. Site is signed and is on the left a little further on.

Charges 2005

Per unit incl. 2 persons	€ 12,50 - € 16,80
extra person	€ 4,00 - € 5,60
child (2-7 yrs)	€ 2,00 - € 3,50
electricity	€ 1,50

Reservations

Necessary for June, July and August and made with fee (€ 16). Tel: 04 90 92 22 70.
Email: reception@camping-monplaisir.fr

FR13050 Camping Mas de Nicolas

Avenue Plaisance du Touch, F-13210 Saint Rémy-de-Provence (Bouches du Rhône)

Saint Rémy de Provence is a very popular town and this reflects on Mas de Nicolas, as this too is very popular and always reasonably busy. The site has a very spacious feel to it, due mainly to the central area of gently sloping grass, dotted with shrubs, that is kept clear of pitches and used for leisure and sunbathing. The 140 pitches are separated by hedges, 120 with electricity, water and drainage, and access roads are wide. Some pitches are an irregular shape and some are sloping, but many have views and they are mostly organised into groups of two and four. There is an attractive pool area with new 'Balneotherapie et Remise en form', or as we would call it a spa and gym.

Facilities

Two modern toilet blocks give good facilities including washbasins in cabins and a baby bathroom. There are plans to refurbish a third block. Dishwashing and laundry sinks, washing machines and drying lines. A small bar (May-Sept) has occasional paella evenings. Swimming pool (15/5-15/9). Sauna, steam room, spa bath and gym. Play area. Internet access at reception. Off site: Adjacent municipal gymnasium, tennis and volleyball courts. Bicycle hire or riding 1 km. Fishing 2 km. Golf 15 km. St Rémy has a wide selection of restaurants and a Wednesday market.

Open

1 March - 31 October.

At a glance

Welcome & Ambience	✓✓✓✓	Location	✓✓✓✓
Quality of Pitches	✓✓✓✓	Range of Facilities	✓✓✓✓

Directions

St Rémy de Provence is located where the D571 from Avignon connects with the D99 Tarascon - Cavaillon road. Site is signed from the village centre on the north side. Leave autoroute A7 at Cavaillon or Avignon-Sud.

Charges 2005

Per unit incl. 2 persons	€ 13,50 - € 15,10
extra person	€ 4,30 - € 4,60
child (under 10 yrs)	€ 2,20 - € 2,50
animal	€ 1,50
electricity (6A)	€ 3,00

Reservations

Necessary for main season and made with € 17 fee (non returnable). Tel: 04 90 92 27 05.
Email: camping-masdenicolas@nerim.fr

FR13060 Camping Les Micocouliers

445 route de Cassoulen, F-13690 Graveson-en-Provence (County)

M. et Mme. Riehl started work at Les Micocouliers in 1997 and they have worked hard to develop a comfortable site. On the outskirts of the town it only some 10 km. from St Remy and Avignan. A purpose built, terracotta 'house' in a raised position provides all the facilities. The 65 pitches radiate out from here with the pool and entrance to one side. The pitches are on level grass, separated by small bushes, and shade is developing. Electricity connections are possible (4-13A). There are also a few mobile homes. The popular swimming pool is a welcome addition. Bread can be ordered and in July and August a simple snack kiosk operates otherwise Mme. Riehl is most helpful in suggesting places to eat. She will also suggest places to visit with suggested itineraries for car tours. Each village in the area offers entertainment on different weeks so you are never short of experiencing the real France.

Facilities

Unisex facilities in one unit provide toilets and facilities for disabled visitors (by key), another showers and washbasins in cabins and another dishwashing and laundry facilities. Reception and limited shop (July/Aug) are in another. Swimming pool (12 x 8 m; 5/5-15/9). Paddling pool (1/7-31/8). Play area. Table tennis. Volleyball. Off site: Fishing and bicycle hire 1 km. Riding next door. Golf 8 km. Beach 60 km. at Ste Marie de la Mer.

Open

15 March - 15 October.

At a glance

Welcome & Ambience	✓✓✓✓	Location	✓✓✓✓
Quality of Pitches	✓✓✓	Range of Facilities	✓✓✓

Directions

Site is southeast of Graveson. From the N570 at new roundabout take D5 towards St Rémy and Maillane and site is 500 m. on the left.

Charges 2005

Per unit incl. 2 persons	€ 12,50 - € 15,00
extra person	€ 4,00 - € 4,80
child (7-12 yrs)	€ 3,00 - € 3,80
child (2-7 yrs)	€ 2,00 - € 2,30
electricity	€ 1.80 - € 5,20
animal	€ 1,60

Reservations

Made with booking fee of € 16. Tel: 04 90 95 81 49.
Email: micocou@free.fr

FR83030 Camping Caravaning Leï Suves

Mobile homes ▶ page 446

Quartier du Blavet, F-83520 Roquebrune-sur-Argens (Var)

This quiet, pretty site is a few kilometres inland from the coast, two kilometres north of the N7. Close to the unusual Roquebrune rock, it is within easy reach of resorts such as St Tropez, Ste Maxime, St Raphaël and Cannes. The site entrance is appealing – wide and spacious, with a large bank of well tended flowers. Mainly on a gently sloping hillside, the 310 pitches are terraced with shade provided by the many cork trees which give the site its name. All pitches have electricity and access to water. A good number of the pitches are used for mobile homes. A pleasant pool area is beside the bar/restaurant and entertainment area. It is possible to walk in the surrounding woods as long as there is no fire alert.

Facilities

Two modern, well kept toilet blocks include washbasins in cabins, external dishwashing sinks, laundry room with washing machines and ironing boards and facilities for disabled visitors. Shop. Good sized swimming pool and paddling pool. Bar and terrace, snack bar and takeaway (all 1/4-30/9). Outdoor stage near the bar for evening entertainment in high season. Excellent play area for all ages. Table tennis, tennis and sports area. Internet terminal. Only gas barbecues are permitted. Off site: Bus stop at site entrance. Riding 1 km. Fishing 3 km. Bicycle hire 5 km. Golf 7 km. Beach at St Aygulf 15 km.

Open

1 April - 15 October.

At a glance

Welcome & Ambience	✓✓✓✓✓	Location	✓✓✓✓
Quality of Pitches	✓✓✓✓	Range of Facilities	✓✓✓✓✓

Directions

Leave autoroute at Le Muy and take N7 towards St Raphaël. Turn left at roundabout onto D7 heading north signed La Boverie (site also signed). Site on right in 2 km. GPS: N43:28.677 E06:38.324

Charges 2005

Per unit incl. 2 persons	€ 19,00 - € 30,00
incl. 3 persons	€ 19,50 - € 31,00
extra person	€ 4,20 - € 5,25
child (under 7 yrs)	€ 2,80 - € 4,20
electricity	€ 6,00

Camping Cheques accepted.

Reservations

Contact site. Tel: 04 94 45 43 95.
Email: camping.lei.suves@wanadoo.fr

FR83010 Camping Caravaning Les Pins Parasols

Route de Bagnols, F-83600 Fréjus (Var)

Not everyone likes very big sites and Les Pins Parasols with its 189 pitches is of a size which is quite easy to walk around. It is family owned and run. Although on very slightly undulating ground, virtually all the pitches are levelled or terraced and separated by hedges or bushes with pine trees for shade. They are around 100 sq.m. and all have electricity. What is particularly interesting is that 48 of the pitches are equipped with their own fully enclosed, tiled sanitary unit, consisting of WC, washbasin, hot shower and dishwashing sink, all quite close together. These pitches naturally cost more but may well be of interest to those seeking extra comfort. The nearest beach is the once very long Fréjus-Plage (5.5 km) now reduced a little by the new marina, and adjoins St Raphaël. Used by tour operators (10%).

Facilities

Besides the individual units there are three toilet blocks of good average quality providing washbasins in cabins and facilities for disabled people. One block can be heated when necessary. Small shop with reasonable stocks and restaurant with takeaway (both 1/5-20/9). General room with TV. Swimming pool (200 sq.m) with attractive rock backdrop and separate long slide with landing pool and small paddling pool (heated). Half-court tennis. Off site: Bicycle hire or riding 2 km. Fishing 6 km. Golf 10 km. Bus from the gate into Fréjus 5 km. Beach 6 km.

Open

08 April - 30 September.

At a glance

Welcome & Ambience	✓✓✓✓	Location	✓✓✓✓
Quality of Pitches	✓✓✓✓	Range of Facilities	✓✓✓

Directions

From autoroute A8 take exit 38 for Fréjus Est. Turn right immediately on leaving pay booths on a small road which leads across to D4, where right again and under 1 km. to site.

Charges 2006

Per pitch incl. 2 persons	
and electricity	€ 17,40 - € 25,50
with sanitary unit	€ 22,00 - € 31,80
extra person	€ 4,40 - € 6,00
child (under 7 yrs)	€ 2,90 - € 3,65

Reservations

Necessary for July/Aug. only and made for min. 10 days for exact dates with deposit (€ 100) but no fee. Tel: 04 94 40 88 43. Email: lespinsparasols@wanadoo.fr

LES PINS PARASOLS

CAMPING CARAVANNING ★★★★NN
ROUTE DE BAGNOLS - F-83600 FRÉJUS
Telephone 0033 494.40.88.43

SWIMMING POOL
Supermarket - Snackbar - Individual washing cabins and hot water In all sanitary facilities - Separated pitches (80-100m2) all with electricity. Pitches with individual sanitary facilities (shower, washbasin, sink with hot water, WC) - Children's playground and solarium - Caravan pitches - Water points - Mini-tennis
SUN AND SHADE near the beaches
Fax : 0033 494.40.81.99
Email : lespinsparasols@wanadoo.fr
Internet : www.lespinsparasols.com

FR83100 Camping de la Plage

Route National 98, F-83310 Grimaud (Var)

A site actually on the beach is always in great demand, and Camping de la Plage is no exception and consequently it becomes very crowded. The site is divided into two parts by the N98 although a dangerous crossing is avoided by an underpass. All pitches are numbered and can be reserved – the pitches away from the beach will be the more peaceful. They are mostly of a decent size, with the ones over the road having more grass and more shade. There is some traffic noise on the pitches close to the busy road. All pitches have electricity but long leads may be required. Ste Maxime is 6 km.

Facilities

There are three toilet blocks on each side of the site. Of varying quality, but clean when we visited and, according to regulars, cleaned regularly. They are fully equipped, the majority of WCs of the British type. Baby bath. Large, well stocked supermarket (all season). Bar, restaurant and takeaway (from May). Beach volleyball. Tennis. Small play area. Off site: Bicycle hire 2 km. Golf and riding 3 km.

Open

Two weeks before Easter - 21 October.

At a glance

Welcome & Ambience	✓✓✓✓✓	Location	✓✓✓✓✓
Quality of Pitches	✓✓✓	Range of Facilities	✓✓✓✓

Directions

Site is on N98 main coast road about 6 km. southwest of Ste Maxime. Take care – this road is very busy in main season. GPS: N43:16.913 E06:35.159

Charges 2005

Per unit with 2 persons	€ 20,00 - € 24,00
extra person	€ 5,20 - € 6,20
child (under 7 yrs)	€ 2,60 - € 3,10
electricity (2-10A)	€ 3,70 - € 8,50

Reservations

Bookings taken for exact dates with booking fee from Oct.- March only. Tel: 04 94 56 31 15. Email: campingplagegrimaud@wanadoo.fr

FR83040 Camping Club La Bastiane

1056 chemin de Suvières, F-83480 Puget-sur-Argens (Var)

With a shady woodland setting, La Bastiane is a well established site with good amenities, well located for exploring the Côte d'Azur and with easy access to nearby beaches. There are 180 pitches here of which 100 are reserved for touring. They are generally of a good size and are all supplied with electrical connections (6A). The terrain is somewhat undulating but most of the pitches are on level terraces. There is a good swimming pool on site and a range of amenities including a shop, bar and restaurant. The site becomes lively in peak season with a range of activities including sports tournaments, discos, a childrens' club and excursions to nearby places of interest such as Monaco and the Gorges de Verdon.

Facilities

Four toilet blocks, three of which are of modern, with the remaining block having been refurbished. Facilities for disabled visitors. Washing machines and dryers. Shop. Bar. Takeaway food. Restaurant. Heated swimming pool. Tennis. Children's club. Play area. Games/TV room. Bicycle hire. Entertainment in peak season. Only electric barbecues are permitted. Only one dog per family accepted. Mobile homes and chalets for rent. Off site: Beach 7 km. Riding 500 m. Fishing 3 km. Golf 9 km.

Open

15 March - 21 October.

At a glance

Welcome & Ambience	✓✓✓✓	Location	✓✓✓✓
Quality of Pitches	✓✓✓✓	Range of Facilities	✓✓✓✓

Directions

Leave A8 autoroute at Puget (exit 37) and take a right turn at the first roundabout (signed Roquebrune) to join the N7. Turn right at first traffic lights (200 m.) and then left at T-junction. Site is signed from here and can be found on the right around 2.5 km. from the motorway.

Charges 2005

Per unit incl. 2 persons	
and electricity	€ 14,84 - € 29,84
extra person	€ 6,20
child (3-13 yrs)	€ 4,10

Reservations

Contact site. Tel: 04 94 55 55 94.
Email: info@labastiane.com

Sea Sun Smile

La Bastiane Camping Club ★★★★ Heated Swimming-pool 25°

Special Offer from 15,34 euros 9 nights = 8

Between Cannes and St Tropez - A few steps from the big blue
Book on line: www.labastiane.com - Tél.: 00.33.494.555.594

FR83130 Camping Le Beau Vezé

Route de la Moutonne, F-83320 Carqueiranne (Var)

Le Beau Vezé is a quiet site, some way inland from the busy resort of Hyères. The owner tries to keep it as a family site with its quiet position, although the superb beaches and hectic coastal areas are within easy reach. On a steep hillside it has terraced pitches and a plateau with more pitches on the top. The 150 pitches are well shaded but unfortunately some will be rather difficult to manoeuvre onto due to over-hanging trees and could be difficult for motorcaravans. There is some road noise on the lower pitches. The lovely old town of Hyères is only 8 km.

Facilities

Three sanitary blocks of a reasonable standard, two quite modern with heating, although maintenance may be variable in high season. All have hot showers and some cubicles have a washbasin also. Both British and Turkish style WCs. Baby room. Two washing machines. Bar/restaurant and takeaway. Bread to order. Medium sized pool and paddling pool. Play area. Minigolf, table tennis, volleyball, boule and tennis court. Bicycle hire. Jetski hire arranged. Evening entertainment in the restaurant. Off site: Fishing and bicycle hire 2 km. Riding 4 km.

Open

15 May - 15 September.

At a glance

Welcome & Ambience	✓✓✓✓✓	Location	✓✓✓✓
Quality of Pitches	✓✓✓✓	Range of Facilities	✓✓✓✓

Directions

From A57 autoroute take exit for Toulon Est and follow D559 between Carqueiranne and Le Pradet. Take D76 northwards signed La Moutonne and site is signed on right of D76.

Charges 2006

Per unit incl. 2 persons	€ 27,00
extra person	€ 6,30
child (under 10 yrs)	€ 4,60
electricity (6A)	€ 4,00
animal	€ 2,50
Camping Cheques accepted.	

Reservations

Made with deposit (€ 46) and fee (€ 15.24).
Tel: 04 94 57 65 30.
Email: info@camping-beauveze.com

381

FR83020 Castel Camping Caravaning Esterel

Mobile homes ▶ page 445

Avenue des Golf, F-83530 St Raphaël – Agay (Var)

For caravans only, Esterel is a quality site east of St Raphaël, set among the hills at the back of Agay. Developed by the Laroche family over the last 30 years, the site has an attractive quiet situation with good views of the Esterel mountains. The site is 3.5 km. from the sandy beach at Agay where parking is perhaps a little easier than at most places on this coast. In addition to a section for permanent caravans, it has some 230 pitches for tourists, on which caravans of any type are taken but not tents. Pitches are on shallow terraces, attractively landscaped with good shade and a variety of flowering plants, giving a feeling of spaciousness. Each pitch has an electricity connection and tap, and 18 special ones have their own individual en-suite washroom adjoining. Some 'maxi-pitches' from 110 to 160 sq.m. are available with 10A electricity. A pleasant courtyard area contains the shop and bar, with a terrace overlooking the attractively landscaped (floodlit at night) pool complex. Wild boar come to the perimeter fence each evening to be fed by visitors. This is a very good site, well run and organised in a deservedly popular area. A member of 'Les Castels' group.

Facilities

Toilet facilities in three blocks have been refurbished and are excellent. They can be heated and include washbasins mostly in cabins. Individual toilet units on 18 pitches. Facilities for disabled people. Laundry room. Motorcaravan service point. Shop. New souvenir and gift shop. Takeaway. Bar/restaurant. Five circular swimming pools (two heated), one large for adults, one smaller for children and three arranged as a waterfall (1/4-30/9). Disco. Archery, volleyball, minigolf, two tennis courts, pony rides, petanque and squash court. Playground. Nursery. Bicycle hire. Events and entertainment are organised in season. Barbecues of any type are forbidden. Off site: Good golf courses very close. Trekking by foot, bicycle or by pony in the surrounding natural environment of L'Esterel forest park. Fishing and beach 3 km.

Open

1 April - 1 October.

At a glance

Welcome & Ambience	✓✓✓✓✓	Location	✓✓✓✓✓
Quality of Pitches	✓✓✓✓	Range of Facilities	✓✓✓✓✓

Directions

You can approach from St Raphaël via Valescure but easiest way is to turn off the coast road at Agay where there are good signs. From Fréjus exit from autoroute A8, follow signs for Valescure throughout, then for Agay, and site is on left. (Reader's comment: If in doubt, follow golf complex signs, or Leclerc). The road from Agay is the easiest to follow.
GPS: N43:27.253 E06:49.945

Charges 2005

Per unit incl. 2 persons	€ 23,00 - € 40,00
'maxi' pitch	€ 26,00 - € 48,00
'deluxe' pitch	€ 30,00 - € 52,00
extra person	€ 8,00
child (1-7 yrs)	€ 6,00
animal	€ 2,00

Reservations

Necessary for high season and made for min. 1 week with deposit (€ 80) and fee (€ 30). CD brochure available from site. Tel: 04 94 82 03 28. Email: contact@esterel-caravaning.fr

FR83080 Au Paradis des Campeurs

La Gaillarde-Plage, F-83380 Les Issambres (Var)

Having direct access to a sandy beach (via an underpass) and being so well maintained are just two of the reasons which make Au Paradis so popular. Family owned and run, it now has 180 pitches, all with 6A electricity and 132 with water tap and drainaway. The original pitches vary in size and shape but all are satisfactory and most have some shade. The newer pitches are all large but at present have little shade although trees and bushes have been planted and shade is developing. There is no entertainment which gives peaceful nights. The gates are surveyed by TV (especially the beach gate) and a security man patrols all day. The site has become popular and it is essential to book for June, July and August.

Facilities

Two toilet blocks, refurbished to an excellent standard with high quality fittings and well maintained, include the majority of washbasins in cabins. Facilities for children are very good with baby baths and a shower at suitable height. En-suite unit for disabled visitors. Dishwashing, laundry sinks, two washing machines and dryer. Motorcaravan service point. Shop and restaurant (with takeaway service) front onto main road and open all season. TV room. Two excellent play areas, catering for the under and over 5s, both with top quality safety bases. Boules. Car wash area. Off site: Bicycle hire 2.5 km. Riding 3 km. Golf 6 km.

At a glance

Welcome & Ambience	✓✓✓✓✓	Location	✓✓✓✓✓
Quality of Pitches	✓✓✓✓	Range of Facilities	✓✓✓✓

Directions

Site is signed from N98 coast road at La Gaillarde, 2 km. south of St Aygulf.
GPS: N43:21.956 E06:42.738

Charges 2005

Per unit incl. 2 persons	€ 12,60 - € 19,50
with water and drainage	€ 14,50 - € 23,50
extra person	€ 5,00
child (under 4 yrs)	€ 2,80
electricity (6A)	€ 3,40

Reservations

Advised for main season. Tel: 04 94 96 93 55.

Open

28 March - 16 October.

FR83120 Camp du Domaine

La Favière, B.P. 207, F-83230 Bormes-les-Mimosas (Var)

Camp du Domaine, three kilometres south of Le Lavandou, is a large, attractive beach-side site with 1,200 pitches set in 45 hectares of pine woods, although surprisingly it does not give the impression of being so big. Most pitches are reasonably level and 800 have 10A electricity. The most popular pitches are at the beach, but the ones furthest away are, on the whole, larger and have more shade amongst the trees, although many of them are more suitable for tents. The beach is the attraction, however, and everyone tries to get as near it as they can. Despite its size, the site does not give the feeling of being busy, except perhaps around the supermarket. This is mainly because many pitches are hidden in the trees, the access roads are quite wide and it all covers quite a large area (some of the beach pitches are 600 m. from the entrance). Its popularity makes early reservation necessary over a long season (about mid June to mid Sept.) as regular clients book from season to season. English is spoken.

Facilities

Ten modern toilet blocks are kept clean but, due to high usage because of the popularity of the site, parts soon begin to show wear and tear. WCs are mostly of the Turkish type (management policy). All facilities have pre-mixed hot water with many washbasins in cabins (some with showers). Facilities for disabled visitors (but steep steps). Block for children and baby room. Washing machines in most blocks. Fridges to hire. Well stocked supermarket. Bars and a pizzeria. Excellent play area. Boats and pedaloes for hire. Wide range of watersports. Games and competitions arranged in July/Aug. Children's club. Six tennis courts, table tennis and minigolf. Multi-sports courts. American motorhomes not accepted. Barbecues are strictly forbidden. Dogs are not accepted 3/7-31/8. Off site: Bicycle hire 500 m. Riding or golf 15 km.

At a glance

Welcome & Ambience	✓✓✓✓	Location	✓✓✓✓✓
Quality of Pitches	✓✓✓✓	Range of Facilities	✓✓✓✓✓

Directions

Just outside and to west of Le Lavandou, at roundabout, turn off D559 towards the sea on road signed Favière. After some 2 km. turn left at camp signs. GPS: N43:07.080 E06:21.076

Charges 2005

Per unit incl. 2 persons	€ 17,00 - € 24,00
with electricity and water	€ 25,00 - € 30,50
extra person	€ 5,00 - € 6,50
child (under 7 yrs)	€ 2,80 - € 3,40

Reservations

Made with 30% deposit and fee (€ 22.87). Tel: 04 94 71 03 12. Email: mail@campdudomaine.com

Open

25 March - 31 October.

FR83140 Camping Les Lacs du Verdon

Domaine de Roquelande, F-83630 Régusse (Var)

In beautiful countryside and within easy reach of the Grand Canyon du Verdon and its nearby lakes (20 minutes drive), this site is only 90 minutes from Cannes. This bustling and possible noisy campsite is suitable for active families and teenagers. The 30 acre wooded park is divided in two by a minor road. The 480 very stony, but level pitches (rock pegs advised) are marked and separated by lines of stones and trees (watch for overhang). There are 130 pitches for tourists which are scattered amongst the trees and often have an irregular shape, although all are of average size. There are plenty of electricity boxes but long leads may be necessary. Water taps are few. The part across the road is used mainly for mobile homes but has some pitches for tourers, mostly at the far end. There are toilet blocks close by but the pitches are a long way from all the other site facilities. The main site is closer to all the activities. Tour operators and mobile homes, for hire and privately owned, take up nearly three quarters of this site.

Facilities

The toilet blocks are old and much of the equipment is looking very jaded, but they are just about acceptable. They mainly have British style WCs and some washbasins in cubicles with warm water only. The block we tried had fairly hot water but campers complained they were not so lucky. All blocks have sinks for laundry and dishes. Washing machines and dryers. At the end of May very little was open and the level of cleanliness was barely adequate. Motorcaravan service point (with charge). Shop. Bar. Restaurant and pizzeria (all 18/5-13/9). TV and teenage games. Discos, dances and theme nights. Excellent swimming pool/paddling pool complex (all season) and new artificial grass tennis courts - the highlight of this campsite. Volleyball, table tennis, archery and boules. Bicycle hire. Playground. Daily entertainment for all the family in May and June, with a more extensive programme in high season. Only electric barbecues are permitted. Off site: The village of Regusse is about 2.5 km. and the small town of Aups is 7 km. Fishing, beach, sailing and windsurfing at the site's club at Saint Croix (15 km). Riding 10 km.

At a glance

Welcome & Ambience	✓✓✓	Location	✓✓✓
Quality of Pitches	✓✓	Range of Facilities	✓✓✓✓

Directions

Leave the A8 motorway at St Maximin and take the D560 northeast to Barjols. At Barjols turn left on D71 to Montmeyan, turn right on D30 to Regusse and follow site signs.

Charges 2006

Per pitch incl. 1 or 2 persons	€ 18,00 - € 27,00
extra person	€ 5,00 - € 7,50
child (3-7 yrs)	€ 4,00 - € 6,00
electricity (10A)	€ 4,00
dog	€ 3,00

Camping Cheques accepted.

Reservations

Made with 25% deposit and fee (€ 20). Tel: 04 94 70 17 95. Email: info@lacs-verdon.com

Open

29 April - 23 September.

FR83170 Camping Domaine de la Bergerie Mobile homes ▶ page 447

Vallée du Fournel, route du Col du Bougnon, F-83520 Roquebrune-sur-Argens (Var)

This excellent site near the Côte d'Azur will take you away from all the bustle of the Mediterranean to total relaxation amongst the cork, oak, pine and mimosa. The 60 hectare site is quite spread out over terrain that varies from natural, rocky, semi-landscaped areas for mobile homes to flat, grassy avenues of 200 separated pitches for touring caravans and tents. All pitches average over 80 sq.m. and have electricity, with those in one area also having water and drainage. The restaurant/bar, a converted farm building, is surrounded by shady patios, whilst inside it oozes character with high beams and archways leading to intimate corners. Activities are organised daily and, in the evening, shows, cabarets, discos, cinema, karaoke and dancing at the amphitheatre prove popular (possibly until midnight). A superb new pool complex supplements the original pool adding more outdoor pools with slides and a river feature, an indoor pool and a fitness centre with jacuzzi, sauna, massage and gym.

Facilities
Four toilet blocks are kept clean and include washbasins in cubicles, facilities for disabled people and babies, plus dishwashing and laundry areas with washing machines. Well stocked supermarket. Bar/restaurant. Takeaway. New pool complex (1/4-30/9) with indoor pool and fitness centre (body building, sauna, gym, etc). Five tennis courts and two half courts. Archery, roller skating and minigolf. Volleyball and mini football. Mini-farm for children. Fishing. Only gas barbecues are permitted. Off site: Riding or golf 4 km. Bicycle hire 7 km. Beach, St Aygulf or Ste Maxime 7 km. Water skiing and rock climbing nearby.

Open
30 June - 17 September. Mobile homes 15 Feb - 15 Nov.

At a glance
Welcome & Ambience	✓✓✓✓✓	Location	✓✓✓✓✓
Quality of Pitches	✓✓✓✓	Range of Facilities	✓✓✓✓✓

Directions
Leave A8 at Le Muy exit on N7 towards Fréjus. Proceed for 9 km. then right onto D7 signed St Aygulf. Continue for 8 km. and then right at roundabout on D8; site is on the right.

Charges 2005
Per unit incl. 2 adults and electricity (5A)	€ 15,00 - € 28,50
3 persons and electricity, water and drainage	€ 22,00 - € 41,00
extra person	€ 4,00 - € 7,10
child (under 7 yrs)	€ 3,00 - € 5,50
electricity (10A)	€ 1,80 - € 2,70
dog	free - € 3,00

Reservations
Made with deposit (€ 200) and fee (€ 20). Tel: 04 98 11 45 45. Email: info@domainelabergerie.com

FR83060 Camping Caravaning de la Baume

Mobile homes ▶ page 446

Route de Bagnols, F-83618 Fréjus (Var)

La Baume is large, busy site that has been well developed with much investment. It is about 5.5 km. from the long sandy beach of Fréjus-Plage, but it has such a fine and varied selection of swimming pools on site that many people do not bother to make the trip. The pools with their palm trees are a feature of this site and are remarkable for their size and variety (water slides, etc.) – the very large 'feature' pool a highlight. An indoor pool and an aquatic play area. are planned. The site has nearly 250 pitches of varying but quite adequate size with electricity, water and drainage, with another 500 larger ones with mains sewerage to take mobile homes. Separators are being installed to divide the pitches and shade is available over most of the terrain. Although tents are accepted, the site concentrates mainly on caravaning. It is likely to become full in season, but one section with unmarked pitches is not reserved, and there is plenty of space off-peak. La Baume's convenient location has its 'downside' as there is some traffic noise from the nearby autoroute - somewhat obtrusive at first but we soon failed to notice it. A popular site with tour operators. Adjoining La Baume is its sister site La Palmeraie, containing self-catering accommodation, its own landscaped pool and providing some entertainment to supplement that at La Baume.

Facilities

The seven toilet blocks should be a satisfactory supply. Two have been enlarged recently, the others refurbished to provide mainly British style toilets with a few Turkish; washbasins in cabins and sinks for clothes and dishes with hot water. Supermarket and several other shops. Bar with external terrace overlooking pools and TV. Restaurant and takeaway. Five swimming pools (heated all season). Fitness centre. Tennis courts. Archery (July/Aug). Organised events - sports, competitions, etc. in daytime and some evening entertainment partly in English. Amphitheatre for shows. Discos daily in season. Children'a club (all season). Off site: Bus to Fréjus passes the gate. Riding 2 km. Fishing 3 km. Golf 5 km. Beach 5 km.

Open

1 April - 30 September, with full services.

At a glance

Welcome & Ambience	✓✓✓✓✓	Location		✓✓✓✓
Quality of Pitches	✓✓✓✓	Range of Facilities		✓✓✓✓✓

Directions

Site is 3 km. up the D4 road, which leads north from N7 just west of Fréjus. From west on autoroute A8 take exit for Fréjus/St Raphaël (junction 37), turn towards them and after 4 km. turn left on D4. From east take exit for Fréjus/St Raphaël (junction 38); after exit turn right immediately on small road marked 'Musée' etc. which leads you to D4 where right again. GPS: N43:27.992 E06:43.396

Charges 2005

Per unit incl. 2 persons, 6A electricity, water and drainage	€ 18,00 - € 37,00
extra person	€ 4,00 - € 8,00
child (under 7 yrs)	free - € 5,00
car	€ 3,50 - € 4,00

Min. stay for motorhomes 3 nights. Large units should book.

Reservations

Essential for high season, and made for exact dates with substantial deposit and fee (€ 31.25), from 1 Jan. Tel: 04 94 19 88 88. Email: reception@labaume-lapalmeraie.com

FR83600 Holiday Green Camping Caravanning

Route de Bagnols, F-83600 Fréjus (Var)

Holiday Green is seven kilometres inland from the busy resort of Fréjus. It is a large, modern campsite with a fantastic view of the red massif of Esterelle – very impressive as you arrive. The site has been developed on a hillside and by reception at the top of hill is a large Californian style heated swimming pool and a wide range of other facilities. This is where everything happens and it is said there are activities and entertainment from morning until closing. The rest of the site is terraced into the hillside and almost completely hidden in the 15 hectares of pine woods which absorbs about 500 mobile homes and some 135 touring pitches. Sloping in parts, there is plenty of shade and electricity connections (6/13A) available. The site provides a free daily bus (16/6-14/9) to go to the beach and to Aquatica, the biggest aqua park in the region with Europe's largest wave pool (open 7/6-14/9).

Facilities

Modern toilet facilities include good hot showers. Dishwashing and laundry sinks. Laundry. Shopping centre. Bar, restaurant and fast food. Sound proof disco. Swimming pool. Three tennis courts. Archery. Petanque. All facilities open all season. Excursions are organised on foot, on horse-back and on mountain bikes (to hire) offering the chance to explore the countryside. Entertainment programme of dances, concerts and festivals. Playground. Children's club (July/Aug). Charcoal barbecues are not permitted. Off site: Bus route outside entrance. Beach 8 km. Golf 8 km.

At a glance

Welcome & Ambience	✓✓✓✓	Location		✓✓✓✓
Quality of Pitches	✓✓✓✓	Range of Facilities		✓✓✓✓✓

Directions

From A8 autoroute exit 38 follow signs for Bagnols-en-Forêt about 2 km. back over the autoroute, and the site is clearly signed at roundabout. GPS: N43:29.138 E06:43.047

Charges 2005

Per unit incl. 2 persons	€ 21,00 - € 38,00
extra person	€ 6,00 - € 9,00
child (under 6 yrs)	€ 4,00 - € 6,00
animal	€ 2,00 - € 3,00

Reservations

Advanced booking necessary for high season. Tel: 04 94 19 88 30. Email: info@holiday-green.com

Open

30 March - 30 September.

LA BAUME ★★★★
Camping - Caravaning

LA PALMERAIE ★★
Tourist residence

Ongoing entertainment
Cabaret show disco

Fréjus Côte d'Azur

Heated sanitary blocks
Marked-out pitches
5 swimming pools
6 water-slides
5km from the beaches of
Frejus and St Raphael

Provencal chalets,
mobile homes and
apartments for
4 to 6 people for
hire

Special rates
in low season

Heated swimming pool

Route de Bagnols Rue des Combattants d'Afrique du Nord
83618 FREJUS Cedex
Tel: + 33 494 19 88 88 - Fax: + 33 494 19 83 50
www.labaume-lapalmeraie.com
E-mail : reception@labaume-lapalmeraie.com

FR83210 Camping Les Tournels

Route de Camarat, F-83350 Ramatuelle (Var)

Les Tournels is a large site set on a hillside and some of the pitches have wonderful panoramic views of the Gulf of St Tropez and Pampelonne beach. The whole hill is covered in parasol pines and old olive trees, so all pitches have some shade. Reasonably level, but varying in size, there is electricity on the majority (long electricity leads may be required). The rest are reserved for tents. Clean and well equipped toilet blocks are within reasonable distance of the pitches, but the swimming pool, play area, shop and bar could turn out to be quite some distance away. The large swimming pool is of an unusual shape, the circular paddling pool has a mushroom shaped fountain, and both are surrounded by sunbathing areas with sun-beds. Recent additions include a superb new spa centre with gym, sauna and jacuzzi with an excellent pool alongside, all reserved for people over 18 yrs, and a new restaurant with a large terrace. Competitions and shows are produced for adults and children in July/Aug. A shuttle bus runs the 500 m. to the local shopping centre and also to Pampelonne beach. Reception opens for long hours and English is spoken. The beaches are a big draw, but also who can resist a visit to St Tropez where perhaps you will see someone famous and the floating 'gin palaces' are a sight to behold.

Facilities

Two of the toilet blocks are of older design, the other six being very good. These include some washbasins in cubicles, mainly British style WCs (paper required), baby baths, children's WCs and facilities for disabled visitors. Three blocks are heated in low season. Washing and drying machines at five blocks, with refrigerators to rent outside all. Bar/restaurant (1/4-15/10). Takeaway. Another bar with disco at the furthest end of the site, well away from most pitches. New restaurant. Large swimming pool (600 sq.m, open 1/4-20/10 and heated in low season). Fitness centre and pool (over 18 yrs). Large fenced play area. Table tennis, volleyball, basketball and boules pitches. Archery. Mini-club for children over 5 years for sporting activities. Only gas barbecues are permitted. Off site: Shopping centre 500 m. from the site entrance (owned by the family) with shuttle bus service contains supermarket, tobacconist, launderette, rotisserie and a snack bar. Golf 6 km. Beach 1.5 km.

Directions

From A8 exit 36 take D25 to Ste Maxime, then D98 towards St Tropez. On outskirts of St Tropez, take D93 to Ramatuelle. Site is signed on left in 9 km. GPS: N43:12.315 E06:39.043

Charges 2005

Per unit incl. 2 persons	
with electricity and water	€ 23,00 - € 34,00
extra person	€ 5,50 - € 7,60
child (2-7 yrs)	€ 2,90 - € 3,80

Reservations

Contact site. Tel: 04 94 55 90 90. Email: info@tournels.com

Open

All year excl. 11 January - 28 February.

At a glance

Welcome & Ambience	✓✓✓✓	Location	✓✓✓✓
Quality of Pitches	✓✓✓✓	Range of Facilities	✓✓✓✓

FR83230 Domaine du Colombier

Route de Bagnols en Forêt, 1052 rue des Combattants D'AFN, F-83600 Fréjus (Var)

Domaine du Colombier is a busy site alongside a main road, so a few of the pitches will have some road noise. The majority however are down a hillside and pine trees help to deaden the noise. The pitches (268 for touring units out of 408) vary in size from 85 sq.m. to quite large ones, of which 40 are fully serviced. The hillside is terraced, with all pitches level and with electricity. The pool area with palm trees, a tiled surround and free sun beds is in a sunny location. There are also three slides and water polo nets for competitions. A disco is underground to deaden the noise. Like the cabarets and competitions all these facilities operate in high season. The only downside is that the swimming pool is at the bottom of the site, giving a long pull back up to the majority of pitches, although there is now a new snack bar beside the pool. Much new planting of attractive trees and shrubs has taken place with gazebos being provided on many pitches to provide shade.

Facilities

Well maintained and positioned toilet blocks are fully equipped, including baby rooms. Three blocks have en-suite units for people in wheelchairs. Two can be heated on cooler days. Well equipped laundry. Well stocked shop. Bar/restaurant with takeaway open at sometime during the day in low season and more often in busy periods. Snack bar (from 1/6). Disco. Large heated swimming pool (30 x 20 m) and paddling pool (all season). Internet terminal. Two play areas of excellent quality on rubber safety bases. Games room, mini-club room. Half court tennis, volleyball, basketball and boule. Tourist office with bookings to major attractions possible. Barbecues are not permitted on the pitches with communal areas provided. Off site: Bus passes the gate.

Directions

From A8 autoroute take 38 and follow D4 for Fréjus. Site is on left, well signed. GPS: N43:26.750 E06:43.636

Charges 2005

Per unit incl. 2 or 3 persons	€ 19,00 - € 37,00
large pitch incl. 2 or 3 persons and electricity	€ 25,00 - € 43,00
extra person	€ 6,00 - € 7,50
child (under 10 yrs)	€ 4,00 - € 5,50

Special low season offers. Camping Cheques accepted.

Reservations

Made with 25% deposit plus booking fee (€ 25). Tel: 04 94 51 56 01. Email: info@domaine-du-colombier.com

Open

8 March - 1 October.

At a glance

Welcome & Ambience	✓✓✓✓✓	Location	✓✓✓✓
Quality of Pitches	✓✓✓✓	Range of Facilities	✓✓✓✓✓

FR83190 Camping La Presqu'île de Giens

Mobile homes ▶ page 448

153 route de la Madraque-Giens, F-834000 Hyeres (Var)

La Presqu'île de Giens a good family campsite at the southern end of the Giens peninsula. Although there is no swimming pool, the site lies between two sandy beaches, and a free shuttle bus runs to the nearest, 800 metres away. The site is well maintained and extends over 17 acres of undulating terrain. Of the site's 460 pitches, 358 are reserved for touring. These are generally of a good size and well shaded – there is a separate area of smaller pitches reserved for tents. Electrical connections (6/0A) are available on all pitches. In high season this becomes a lively site with a well-run children's club (small charge) and an evening entertainment programme including discos, singers and dancers. Excursions are organised to the adjacent islands of Porquerolles, Port Cros and Le Levant.

Facilities

Five toilet blocks, two very good new ones which are heated in low season, and three refurbished blocks with a higher proportion of 'Turkish' style toilets. All blocks were very clean and well maintained when visited. Facilities for disabled visitors. Washing machines and dryers. Shop. Bar, restaurant, takeaway food. Play area. Children's club. Evening entertainment. Sports pitch. Diving classes. Sports tournaments. Excursion programme. Only electric barbecues are permitted. Mobile homes and chalets for rent. Off site: Beach 800 m. Fishing 1 km. Bicycle hire 3 km. Riding 10 km. Golf 15 km. 'Golden islands' excusions.

Open

1 April - 1 October.

At a glance

Welcome & Ambience	✓✓✓✓	Location	✓✓✓✓
Quality of Pitches	✓✓✓	Range of Facilities	✓✓✓

Directions

From the west, leave A57 motorway at Hyères and continue to Hyères on the A570. At Hyères follow signs to Giens - Les Iles (D97). The campsite can be found after about 11 km. on this road.

Charges 2005

Per unit incl. 2 persons	€ 12,80 - € 18,50
extra person	€ 3,90 - € 5,90
child (0-5 yrs)	free
electricity	€ 4,40 - € 5,00
pet	€ 2,50

Camping Cheques accepted.

Reservations

Contact site. Tel: 04 94 58 22 86.
Email: info@camping-giens.com

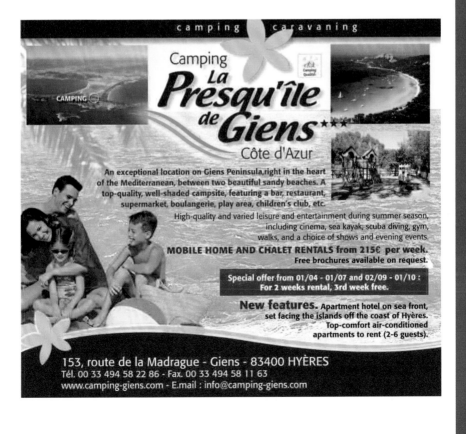

389

FR83070 Caravaning L'Etoile d'Argens

Mobile homes ▶ page 447

F-83370 Saint Aygulf (Var)

First impressions of L'Etoile d'Argens are of space, cleanliness and calm. Reception staff are very friendly and English is spoken (open 24 hrs). This is a site run with families in mind and many of the activities are free, making for a good value holiday. There are 493 level grass pitches (265 for touring units) laid out in typical French style, separated by hedges. There are five sizes of pitch, ranging from 50 sq.m. (for small tents) to 250 sq.m. These are exceptionally large and two families could easily fit two caravans and cars or one family could have a very spacious plot with a garden like atmosphere. All pitches are fully serviced with fresh and waste water and 10A electricity, with mainly good shade although the site is not overpowered by trees which leads to a spacious feeling. The pool and bar area is attractively landscaped with old olive and palm trees on beautifully kept grass. Heated pools have been added recently – both very much with families in mind, not teenagers as there are no big slides. The river runs along one side of the site and a free boat service (15/6-15/9) runs every 40 minutes to the beach. It is also possible to moor a boat or fish. This is a good family site for the summer but also good in low season for a quiet stay in a superb location with excellent pitches. Tour operators take 85 pitches and there are 175 mobile homes but for a large site it is unusually calm and peaceful even in July.

Facilities

Two new toilet blocks were added in 2000 adding to the 20 original small unisex blocks which have all been renovated. All are well kept and include some washbasins in cubicles. Laundry. Supermarket and gas supplies. Bar, restaurant, pizzeria, takeaway. Two adult pools (heated 1/4-20/6), paddling pool, jacuzzi and solarium. Tennis (two of the four courts are floodlit) with coaching and minigolf (both free in low season), aerobics, archery (July/Aug), football and swimming lessons. Volleyball, basketball, table tennis and boule. Play area. Children's entertainer in July/Aug. Activity programme includes games, dances for adults and escorted walking trips to the hills. Off site: Golf and riding 2 km. Beach 3.5 km.

Open

1 April - 30 September, with all services.

At a glance

Welcome & Ambience	✓✓✓✓✓	Location	✓✓✓✓✓
Quality of Pitches	✓✓✓✓✓	Range of Facilities	✓✓✓✓✓

Directions

Leave A8 at exit 36 and take N7 to Le Muy and Fréjus. After about 8 km. at roundabout take D7 signed Roquebrune and St Aygulf. In 9.5 km. (after roundabout) turn left signed Fréjus. Watch for site sign and ignore width and height limit signs as site is 500 m. to right. GPS: N43:24.947 E06:42.326

Charges 2005

Per tent pitch (100 sq.m.) with electricity and 2 persons	€ 20,00 - € 37,00
'comfort' pitch (100 sq.m.) incl. 3 persons	€ 28,00 - € 56,00
'luxury' pitch incl. 4 persons 180 sq.m	€ 39,00 - € 64,50
extra person	€ 5,50 - € 8,00
child (under 7 yrs)	€ 3,50 - € 6,00

Reservations

Made for any period with substantial deposit and fee. Tel: 04 94 81 01 41. Email: info@etoiledargens.com

FR83160 Parc Camping Les Cigales

721 chemin du Jas de la Paro, F-83490 Le Muy (Var)

Parc Les Cigales has been developed over the last 30 years by the same family to become a pleasant site benefiting from the shady environment of cork umbrella pines, further enhanced by olives, palm trees, sweet smelling mimosa and colourful shrubs. It has now undergone major rejuvenation. The entrance has been completely relocated which, in fact, turns the site round utilising the top of the site around the pretty pool area more. The 'piece de resistance' is the new 'survival area' with courses for all ages and a wide range of equipment including aerial runways. All the necessary safety equipment is in evidence and it is open to the public with costs varying according to the type of course used. A riding school, a vegetable garden and a small animal farm complete this unusual but environmentally thought out development. The terrain is typical of the area with rough, sloped and stony, dry ground but the pitches are of a good size, terraced where necessary and nestling amongst the trees. There are 163 pitches with 35 mobile homes to rent, nicely landscaped. The restaurant/bar area overlooks the attractive pool complex including a children's pool with sloping beach effect. Convenient for the autoroute, this is a spacious family site away from the hectic coast, to be enjoyed. A 'Sites et Paysages' member.

Facilities

Six modern sanitary blocks of varying size more than serve the site and include washbasins in cabins and facilities for disabled people. Dishwashing sinks outside but under cover. Laundry area with washing machines and ironing boards. Shop (1/5-30/8). Restaurant/bar with patio. Heated pool complex and sunbathing area. Adventure play area. Survival courses. Multi-sport area. Trampoline. Riding. Canoeing and hang-gliding are organised. Entertainment organised each evening in season, with a disco twice weekly and daytime activities for children and senior citizens. Internet terminal. Charcoal barbecues are not permitted. Off site: Le Muy (2 km.) has a Sunday market. Fishing 2 km. Golf 10 km.

At a glance

Welcome & Ambience	✓✓✓✓✓	Location	✓✓✓✓
Quality of Pitches	✓✓✓✓	Range of Facilities	✓✓✓✓

Directions

Site is signed off approach to autoroute péage on A8 at Le Muy exit and is 2 km. west of Le Muy on N7. It is necessary to cross the dual-carriageway as you approach the toll booth from Le Muy. Site entrance is well signed. GPS: N43:27.492 E06:32.728

Charges 2005

Per unit incl. 2 persons	€ 12,00 - € 22,00
extra person	€ 3,00 - € 5,50
child (under 7 yrs)	free - € 3,00
electricity (6-10A)	€ 3,00 - € 5,00

Reservations

Advised for July/Aug. Tel: 04 94 45 12 08. Email: contact@les-cigales.com

Open

1 April - 31 October.

L'Etoile d'Argens

2005

" 36 years experience with you "

ESE Communication - draguignan - tél : 04.94.67.06.00

www.etoiledargens.com

E-mail : info@etoiledargens.com

3370 St Aygulf - Tél. +33 4 94 81 01 41

FR83240 Camping Caravaning Moulin des Iscles

F-83520 Roquebrune-sur-Argens (Var)

A haven of peace and tranquillity, Moulin des Iscles is hidden down 500 metres of private, unmade road – an unusual find in this often quite hectic part of Provence. Based around a former mill, it is a small, pretty site beside the river Argens with access to the river in places for fishing, canoeing and swimming, with a concrete bank and fenced where deemed necessary (some sought after pitches overlook the river). The 90 grassy, level pitches with electricity (6A) and water to all, radiate out from M. Dumarcet's attractive, centrally situated home which is where the restaurant and shop are situated. A nice mixture of deciduous trees provide natural shade and colour and the old mill house rests comfortably near the entrance which has a security barrier closed at night. This is a quiet site with little on site entertainment, but with a nice little restaurant. A good effort has been made to welcome handicapped visitors. It is a real campsite not a 'camping village'.

Facilities

The toilet block is fully equipped, including ramped access for disabled visitors. Some Turkish style toilets. Washbasins have cold water, some in cubicles. Baby bath and changing facilities en-suite. Covered laundry and dishwashing sinks. Small separate unisex provision for pitches near the entrance. Washing machine. Restaurant with home cooked dish-of-the-day on a weekly rotation. Surprisingly well stocked shop. Library - some English books. TV room incl. satellite, Pool table, table tennis. Play area, minigolf and boules all outside the barrier for more peace and quiet on site. Internet terminal. Canoeing possible. Off site: Riding and golf 4 km. Bicycle hire 1 km. (cycle way to St Aygulf). Beach 9 km.

Open

1 April - 30 September.

At a glance

Welcome & Ambience	✓✓✓✓✓	Location	✓✓✓✓
Quality of Pitches	✓✓✓✓	Range of Facilities	✓✓✓✓

Directions

Follow as for site FR83200 Les Pecheurs, but continue past it through the village of Roquebrune towards St Aygulf for 1 km. Site signed on left. Follow private unmade road for approx. 500 m. to site entrance in front of you. GPS: N43:26.708 E06:39.470

Charges 2005

Per unit incl. 2 or 3 persons	€ 19,00
extra person	€ 3,20
child (over 10 yrs)	€ 2,20
electricity	€ 2,70

Prices are lower out of high season.
Camping Cheques accepted.

Reservations

Contact site. Tel: 04 94 45 70 74.
Email: moulin.iscles@wanadoo.fr

FR83250 Sunêlia Douce Quiétude

3435 boulevard Jacques Baudino, F-83700 St Raphaël (Var)

Douce Quiétude is only five kilometres from the beaches at Saint Raphaël and Agay but is quietly situated at the foot of the Estérel massif. There are 400 pitches, but only 70 of these are for touring units (around half are used for mobile homes) set in pleasant pine woodland or shaded, green areas. The pitches are of a comfortable size, separated by bushes and trees with electricity (6A), water, drainage and telephone/TV points provided. This mature site offers a wide range of services and facilities complete with a pool complex. It can be busy in the main season yet is relaxed and spacious. Security is good with the wearing of identity bracelets mandatory throughout your stay.

Facilities

Fully equipped modern toilet blocks have changing facilities for babies and provision for disabled visitors. Launderette. Bar and restaurant with takeaway and pizzeria (3/4-3/9). Shop. Three outdoor swimming pools (two heated), water slide and jacuzzi. Play area. Children's club and activities for teenagers (all July/Aug). Sports area for volleyball, basketball and petanque. Games room. Tennis. Table tennis. Minigolf. Archery. Fitness centre and sauna. Evening entertainment with shows, karaoke and discos (July/Aug). Mountain bike hire. Only gas barbecues are permitted. Off site: Bus route 1 km. Golf and riding 2 km. Windsurf hire and sea fishing 5 km.

Open

3 April - 2 October.

At a glance

Welcome & Ambience	✓✓✓	Location	✓✓✓✓
Quality of Pitches	✓✓✓✓	Range of Facilities	✓✓✓✓

Directions

Take exit 38 from A8 autoroute signed Fréjus and St Raphaël. Follow directions for Valescure then Agay on the D100, then site signs (takes you round the back of Fréjus/St Raphaël). The site can also be reached from the N98 coast road turning north at Agay on D100; continue past Esterel Camping to pick up site signs. GPS: N43:26.836 E06:48.360

Charges 2005

Per unit incl. 2 persons and electricity	€ 32,00 - € 45,00
extra person	€ 6,50 - € 8,50
child (3-13 yrs)	€ 5,50 - € 6,50
animal	€ 4,00

Camping Cheques accepted.

Reservations

Contact site. Tel: 04 94 44 30 00.
Email: sunelia@douce-quietude.com

Family campsite with warm atmosphere, situated at the foot of the Rock of Roquebrune, Côte d'Azur beaches at short distance, large and shady pitches, restaurant, mini tennis, river, swimming-pools. Mobile-home rental.

Les Pêcheurs

Camping ★★★★ Caravaning
Roquebrune sur Argens
Côte d'Azur

83520 Roquebrune sur Argens
Tél : +33 4 94 45 71 25
Fax : + 33 4 94 81 65 13
www.camping-les-pecheurs.com
E-mail:info@camping-les-pecheurs.com

FR83200 Camping Caravaning Les Pêcheurs

Mobile homes ▶ page 448

F-83520 Roquebrune-sur-Argens (Var)

Developed over three generations by the Simoncini family, this peaceful, friendly site is set in more than four hectares of mature, well shaded countryside at the foot of the Roquebrune Rock. It will appeal to families who appreciate natural surroundings together with many activities, cultural and sporting. Interspersed with a number of mobile homes, the 130 touring pitches are all of a good size with electricity (6/10A) and separated by trees or flowering bushes (there are 24 mobile homes and 75 pitches used by tour operators). The Provencal style buildings are delightful, especially the bar, restaurant and games room, with its terrace down to the river and the site's own canoe station (locked gate). Adjacent to the site, across the road, is a lake used exclusively for water skiing with a sandy beach, a restaurant and minigolf. Activities include climbing the 'Rock' with a guide. We became more and more intrigued with stories about the Rock and the Holy Hole, the Three Crosses and the Hermit all call for further exploration which reception staff are happy to arrange, likewise trips to Monte Carlo, Ventimigua (Italy) and the Gorges du Verdon, etc. The medieval village of Roquebrune is within walking distance.

Facilities

Modern, well designed toilet facilities are in three blocks, one new and attractively designed in the local style, the other two refurbished. Overall, it is a good provision, open as required, with washbasins in cabins (warm water only), baby baths and facilities for disabled visitors. Dishwashing and laundry sinks (H&C). Washing machines. Sheltered swimming pool (heated in low season) with separate paddling pool (child-proof gates, lifeguard in high season; closed lunch times in July/Aug.) with ice cream bar. Shop. Bar, restaurant and games room (all open all season). Play field with nets and play equipment. Fishing. Canoeing (free) and water skiing. Animation arranged in main season for children and adults, visits to local wine caves and sessions at rafting and diving schools. Only gas or electric barbecues are permitted. Off site: Bicycle hire 1 km. Riding 4 km. Golf 5 km. (reduced fees).

At a glance

Welcome & Ambience	✓✓✓✓✓	Location	✓✓✓✓
Quality of Pitches	✓✓✓✓	Range of Facilities	✓✓✓✓✓

Directions

From A8 autoroute take Le Muy exit and follow N7 towards Frèjus for approx. 13 km. bypassing Le Muy. After crossing over the A8, turn right at roundabout towards Roquebrune sur Argens. Site is on left after 1 km. just before bridge over river.

Charges 2005

Per unit incl. 2 persons	€ 18,00 - € 31,00
incl. 3 persons	€ 20,00 - € 33,00
extra person	€ 4,00 - € 6,00
child (under 7 yrs)	€ 3,00 - € 5,00
electricity (6/10A)	€ 4,00 - € 5,00
dog (max 1)	€ 3,00

Camping Cheques accepted.

Reservations

Made for touring pitches with deposit and fee.
Tel: 04 94 45 71 25.
Email: info@camping-les-pecheurs.com

Open

1 April - 30 September.

FR83260 Camping Château de l'Eouvière

Route de Tavernes, F-83670 Montmeyan (Var)

This spacious new site is in the grounds of an 18th century château, close to the magnificent hill village of Montmeyan. There are 30 hectares of grounds to explore and the swimming pool, bar, restaurant which are in front of the château, have lovely views over the valley and mountains beyond. The toilet block and children's play area are to one side. The 80 large pitches (all for tourers) are well marked and separated on terraces, mostly behind the château and many have magnificent views. The pitches are part grassy, part stony with varying amounts of shade from mostly mature trees. The majority have water and all have electricity points at the edge of the pitch. A log cabin toilet block is installed in the upper reaches for the high season. The owner will assist with his 4x4 vehicle any visitor experiencing difficulty in siting their unit on the higher pitches. This is a quieter site for those seeking the 'real' France.

Facilities

The main, refurbished toilet block includes all the necessary facilities. Facilities for disabled visitors are available with access from the lower pitches. Laundry and dishwashing sinks, washing machine and iron. Bar, restaurant and small shop (June - Sept). Swimming pool with large tiled sunbathing area. Small play area and paddling pool (some distance from the pool). Some entertainment and children's activities in high season. Virtually soundproof disco room in the cellars of the château. Off site: Montmeyan 1 km. Beach at Lake Quinson (7 km) and other lakes with a range of watersports. Gorges du Verdon. Many interesting towns with their markets and museums.

At a glance

Welcome & Ambience	✓✓✓✓✓	Location	✓✓✓✓✓
Quality of Pitches	✓✓✓✓	Range of Facilities	✓✓✓✓

Directions

Leave A8 autoroute at St Maximin and take D560 to Barjols and then D71 to Montmeyan. At roundabout on entering village, take D13 southeast signed Cotignac and site entrance is very shortly on the right.

Charges 2005

Per person	€ 5,00 - € 6,00
child (under 7 yrs)	€ 3,80 - € 4,50
pitch	€ 5,00 - € 8,00
electricity	€ 3,90

Reservations

Contact site. Tel: 04 94 80 75 54.
Email: contact@leouviere.com

Open

15 April - 15 October.

FR83280 Campasun Mas de Pierredon

652 chemin Paoul Coletta, F-83110 Sanary-sur-Mer (Var)

Situated on the outskirts of the pretty resort of Sanary, this small site is open from Easter through to October. Terraced under the traditional pines of the area, it provides 120 pitches of which a number are taken by mobile homes. The ground is fairly rocky but some sand and grass exists and trees and shrubs help to divide the pitches making it an attractive environment. All pitches have 10A electricity connections. The bar and restaurant overlook the heated pool at the entrance to the site and provide a comfortable family environment, all are open all season. The site is situated close to a fairly busy main road and the access is quite sharp and uphill. English is spoken at reception.

Facilities

Two toilet blocks with modern facilities include washbasins in cabins, controllable showers with a further 16 en-suite individual units on pitches. En-suite unit for disabled visitors. Washing machine in each block, plenty of laundry sinks and dishwashing sinks (H&C). Motorcaravan service point. Bar/restaurant with pizza oven. Bread to order from reception. Outdoor heated pool with new slide and paddling pool. Play equipment. Table tennis, minigolf, boules and tennis court. Pool table. Entertainment provided in July/Aug. for all ages. Barbecues are not permitted. Off site: Shop 800 m. Beach 3 km. Golf, bicycle hire and riding 10 km.

Open

1 April - 30 September.

At a glance

Welcome & Ambience	✓✓✓✓✓	Location	✓✓✓✓
Quality of Pitches	✓✓✓✓	Range of Facilities	✓✓✓✓✓

Directions

From A50 take exit for Bandol and follow directions for 'Jardin Exotique'. After Mercedes garage take first right and follow straight on for 5 km. (narrow road with lots of roads off) until a T-junction with a stop sign. Turn right and site is almost immediately on left. GPS: N43:07.908 E05:48.896

Charges 2006

Per unit incl. 3 persons and electricity	€ 24,00 - € 42,00
with own sanitary facility	€ 30,00 - € 50,00
extra person	€ 5,00
child (under 7 yrs)	€ 4,00
animal	€ 2,00 - € 4,00

Camping Cheques accepted.

Reservations

Made with deposit (€ 80) and booking fee (€ 23).
Tel: 04 94 74 25 02.
Email: pierredon@campasun.com

FR83220 Camping Caravaning Cros de Mouton

Mobile homes ▶ page 449

B.P. 116, F-83240 Cavalaire-sur-Mer (Var)

Cros de Mouton is a reasonably priced campsite in a popular area. High in the hills on a steep hillside, about 2 km. from Cavalaire and its popular beaches, the site is a calm oasis away from the hectic coast. There are stunning views of the bay but, unfortunately, due to the nature of the terrain, some of the site roads are very steep – the higher pitches with the best views are especially so. However, Olivier and Andre are happy to take your caravan up with their 4x4 Jeep if you are worried. There are 199 terraced pitches under cork trees which include 46 for mobile homes, 73 suitable only for tents with parking close by, and 80 for touring caravans. These are large and have electricity (10A), some also with water. The restaurant terrace and the pools share the wonderful view of Cavalaire and the bay. English is spoken by the welcoming and helpful owners.

Facilities

Two clean and well maintained toilet blocks have all the usual facilities including washbasins in cubicles. Washing machine at each and a fully fitted facility for disabled customers (although site is perhaps a little steep in places for wheelchairs). Bar/restaurant serving reasonably priced meals, plus takeaways. Swimming and paddling pools with lots of sun beds on the terrace and small bar for snacks and cold drinks. Small play area and games room. Off site: Beach 1.5 km. Bicycle hire 1.5 km. Riding 16 km. Golf 20 km.

Open

15 March - 1 November.

At a glance

Welcome & Ambience	✓✓✓✓✓	Location	✓✓✓✓
Quality of Pitches	✓✓✓✓	Range of Facilities	✓✓✓✓

Directions

Take the D559 to Cavalaire-su-Mer (not Cavalière 4 km. away). Site is about 1.5 km. north of the town, very well signed from the centre.

Charges 2005

Per person	€ 5,80 - € 7,10
child (under 7 yrs)	€ 4,00
pitch	€ 5,80 - € 7,10
electricity (10A)	€ 4,00
dog	free - € 2,00

Camping Cheques accepted.

Reservations

Made with deposit (€ 80) and fee (€ 20). Tel: 04 94 64 10 87. Email: campingcrosdemouton@wanadoo.fr

FR83290 Camping de Saint Aygulf Plage

270 avenue Salvarelli, F-83370 St Aygulf-Plage (Var)

This is a large, well run and self-sufficient campsite with a range of good facilities including a small supermarket and private bakery, two restaurants with takeaways and a long bar with an extensive patio and stage for discos and entertainment. It has direct access to the beach which is part of a long sandy bay which shelves gradually into the sea, suitable for children of all ages. The site is situated in Saint Aygulf which is a lively town with bars, restaurants and a popular market on Tuesdays. The theme parks of Aqatica and Luna Park are less than 2 km. away. The pitches here are well marked, flat and arranged in long rows, many with good shade from the pine trees. There are 1,100 in total, with 700 for touring units and the remainder used for mobile homes and chalets. Electricity is available on 500 touring pitches. Perhaps the only disappointment is the lack of a swimming pool on the site, but this is definitely offset by the direct access to the beach and overall this is a fine family holidaying campsite.

Facilities

Four large toilet blocks provide good, clean facilities in traditional style with British and Turkish style WCs, washbasins with warm water and free, pre-set showers. No facilities for disabled visitors. Washing machines in two blocks. Supermarket. Bakery. Two restaurants. Bar, pizzeria and takeaways. Play areas. Boules. First aid. Caravan storage. Entertainment. Beach. Only gas and electric barbecues are permitted. Off site: Bicycle hire 100 m. Riding 1 km. Golf 6 km. Restaurants, shops and bars nearby.

Open

1 May - 19 September.

At a glance

Welcome & Ambience	✓✓✓✓✓	Location	✓✓✓✓✓
Quality of Pitches	✓✓✓✓	Range of Facilities	✓✓✓✓

Directions

From A8 autoroute take exits for Puget or Fréjus and take RN7 to Fréjus town. Follow signs to seas front and join RN98. Saint Aygulf is 2 km. in direction of St Tropez and site is signed.

Charges 2005

Per unit incl. 2 persons	€ 9,30 - € 21,00
incl. electricity	€ 15,00 - € 28,00
extra person	€ 3,00 - € 7,50
child (0-7 yrs)	€ 2,00 - € 3,50
dog	€ 1,50 - € 3,50

Reservations

Made with deposit and fee; contact site.
Tel: 04 94 17 62 49.
Email: info@camping-cote-azur.com

FR83300 Camping Clos Sainte Thérèse

Route de Bandol, F-83270 Saint Cyr-sur-Mer (Var)

This is a very attractive, family run campsite set in hilly terrain four kilometres from the beaches of Saint Cyr. The terraced pitches are level, some with sea views, the friendly owners offering a tractor service to visitors who have difficulties in reaching their pitch. There is a good shade cover from pines, olives, almonds and evergreen oaks and all pitches have electricity (6/10A). There are 86 pitches for touring units and 26 used for chalets or mobile homes. The landscaped pool complex is pretty and well kept, with a small slide, jacuzzi and a separate paddling pool. Activities are organised in high season, for example, pool games, boules tournaments, bingo and karaoke. This is a friendly, small site, ideal for couples of families with younger children.

Facilities

Toilet facilities are clean and well maintained in two modern and two older blocks. British style WCs, open washbasins and controllable free showers. Fridge hire. Shop (from 1/5). Bar and restaurant (15/6-15/9). Swimming pools (one heated) and children's pool. Games room. Table tennis. TV room and library. Boules. Play area. Activities in high season. Off site: Golf course (9 and 18 holes, driving range) and tennis courts opposite site entrance. Bicycle hire 2 km. Fishing 4 km. Riding 8 km. Beach 4 km.

Open

1 April - 1 October.

At a glance

Welcome & Ambience	✓✓✓✓	Location	✓✓✓✓
Quality of Pitches	✓✓✓✓	Range of Facilities	✓✓✓✓

Directions

From A50 motorway take D559 to Saint Cyr. Continue towards Bandol and site is 3 km. on the left.

Charges 2005

Per unit incl. 2 persons	€ 13,70 - € 19,00
extra person	€ 3,10 - € 4,60
child (3-7 yrs)	€ 2,10 - € 3,10
electricity	€ 2,60 - € 4,70
dog	€ 1,60 - € 2,00

Camping Cheques accepted.

Reservations

Contact site. Tel: 00 33 4 94 32 1.
Email: camping@clos-therese.com

MAP 16

The island of Corsica is both dramatic and beautiful. The scenery is spectacular with bays of white sand lapped by the clear blue waters of the Mediterranean. At certain times of the year the entire island is ablaze with exotic flowers, aided by Corsica's excellent sunshine record.

Corsica

DÉPARTEMENTS: 2A CORSE-SUD; 2B HAUTE-CORSE

MAJOR CITIES: AJACCIO AND BASTIA

Corsica is regarded by some as the jewel of the Mediterranean islands and is made up of two départements: Haute Corse (upper Corsica) and Corse du Sud (southern Corsica). The island has endured a bloody history, having being much disputed the Greeks, Romans and Lombards. Five hundred years of Italian rule has influenced the look of the island with Italian-style hilltop hamlets and villages developed alongside mountain springs. Many of the villages feature rustic, unadorned churches and also a few Romanesque examples too.

The variety of scenery is spectacular. Across much of the island one can discover dramatic gorges, glacial lakes, gushing mountain torrents and magnificent pine and chestnut forests.You'll also experience the celebrated perfume of the Corsican maquis: a tangled undergrowth of fragrant herbs, flowers and bushes that fills the warm spring and summer air. The highest mountains lie to the west, while the gentler ranges, weathered to strange and often bizarre shapes, lie to the south and a continuous barrier forms the island's backbone.

Places of interest

Ajaccio: a dazzling white city full of Napoleonic memorabilia.

Bastia: historic citadel towering over the headland. The old town has preserved its streets in the form of steps connected by vaulted passages, converging on the Vieux port (the old port). The new port is the real commercial port of the island.

Cuisine of the region

Brocchui: sheeps' milk cheese is used much in cooking in both its soft form (savoury or sweet) or more mature and ripened.

Capone: local eels, cut up and grilled on a spit over a charcoal fire.

Dziminu: fish soup, like bouillabaise but much hotter. Made with peppers and pimentos.

Figatelli: a sausage made of dried and spiced pork with liver. Favourite between-meal snack.

Pibronata: a highly spiced local sauce

Prizzutu: a peppered smoked ham; resembles the Italian prosciutto, but with chestnut flavour added.

FR20000 Camping Pertamina U. Farniente

Pertamina Village, F-20169 Bonifacio (Corse-du-Sud)

Irrespective of whether or not you are using the ferry to Sardinia, Bonifacio deserves a visit and it would be difficult to find a more attractive or convenient site than this one at which to pitch for a night stop or longer stay. The 120 pitches, many with electricity (3A), are partially terraced and are hedged with trees and bushes, providing reasonable shade. They are reasonably flat and vary in size, many being well over 100 sq.m. A central feature of the site is the large attractive swimming pool.

Facilities
Two toilet blocks include washbasins in semi-private cubicles, British and Turkish style WCs. Washing machines plus drying and ironing facilities. Motorcaravan service point. Shop. Takeaway. Pizzeria/grill serving set meals and á la carte menu (shorter opening hours in May, June and Oct). Swimming pool. Tennis, table tennis. Play area. TV room. Off site: Bonifacio 4 km.

Open

Easter - 15 October.

At a glance

Welcome & Ambience	✓✓✓✓	Location	✓✓✓✓
Quality of Pitches	✓✓✓✓	Range of Facilities	✓✓✓✓

Directions

Site is on the RN198 road, 4 km. north of Bonifacio to the east. Watch for the sign – you come on it quite suddenly. GPS: N41:25.066 E09:10.803

Charges 2005

Per unit incl. 2 persons	
with electricity	€ 17,50 - € 27,00
extra person	€ 6,00 - € 8,00
child (under 8 yrs)	free - € 5,00

Camping Cheques accepted.

Reservations

Made with € 15.25 fee and 30% deposit.
Tel: 04 95 73 05 47. Email: pertamina@wanadoo.fr

FR20050 Camping Naturiste Club La Chiappa

Mobile homes ▶ page 450

F-20137 Porto-Vecchio (Corse-du-Sud)

This is a large naturist campsite on the Chiappa peninsula with 220 pitches for tourers and tents, plus 250 bungalows. These have the prime places, as do the seasonal pitches. A few touring pitches have sea views and are taken first in high season. The pitches are informally marked and are of a variety of shapes and sizes, some with difficult slopes and access, especially for large units. Cars are parked separately. Very long electricity leads are necessary for most pitches. Two beach restaurants and bars enjoy good views. There is high season amimation plus extensive watersports. When we visited a number of buildings appeared tired and several disused buildings could present hazards to children. The touring areas are some distance from the amenities - a bicycle would make life easier.

Facilities
The sanitary facilities were tired when we visitedand in need of refurbishment. Washing machines. Motorcaravan service point. Well stocked shop. Two bars and restaurants. Swimming pool. Play area. Riding. Tennis. Minigolf. Fishing. Diving, windsurfing and sailing schools. Keep fit, yoga, sauna. Internet access. Torches essential. Off site: Car rental. Excursions. Bus to La Chiappa once a week.

Open

14 May - 1 October.

At a glance

Welcome & Ambience	✓✓✓	Location	✓✓✓✓
Quality of Pitches	✓✓	Range of Facilities	✓✓✓✓

Directions

From Bastia on N198 heading south, take Porto-Vecchio bypass (signed Bonofaccio). At southern end, take first left (Pont de la Chiappa) ono unclassified road. After 8 km. turn left and follow rough track for 2 km. to site. GPS: N41:35 E09:21.40

Charges 2005

Per person	€ 7,50 - € 9,50
child (5-13 yrs)	€ 3,50 - € 4,50
pitch incl. electricity	€ 10,50 - € 13,00

Reservations

Contact site. Tel: 04 95 70 00 31.
Email: chiappa@wanadoo.fr

FR20070 Camping Caravaning Santa Lucia

Lieudit Mulindinu, F-20144 Ste Lucie-de Porto-Vecchio (Corse-du-Sud)

This is a small, friendly, family run site in a delightful southern Corsican setting, where little English is spoken. The entrance road encircles a huge palm tree. Behind the reception hut is an unsophisticated restaurant and bar which have a terrace which is pleasant in the evenings when ornamental lamps light up the area. There are 160 pitches, 60 with 6A electricity and 18 serviced pitches. Chalets and bungalow tents blend unobtrusively with the setting. We see this as a transit site, rather than for an extended stay, although the site is only minutes by car from Porto Vecchio which is surrounded by lovely beaches.

Facilities
Two toilet blocks include some washbasins in cubicles. Washing machine. Bread to order. Bar (15/6-15/9). Restaurant and takeaway (1/7-31/8). Swimming pool. Play area and high season miniclub for children. Table tennis, volleyball, and minigolf. Off site: Beach 5 km. Golf 20 km.

Open

15 May - 10 October.

At a glance

Welcome & Ambience	✓✓✓	Location	✓✓✓✓
Quality of Pitches	✓✓✓✓	Range of Facilities	✓✓✓✓

Directions

Site is at south end of Sainte-Lucie-de-Porto-Vecchio village, off N198 and well signed.

Charges 2005

Per person	€ 5,00 - € 7,10
pitch incl. electricity	€ 5,00 - € 6,90
car	€ 2,00 - € 2,90

Reservations

Contact site. Made with deposit and €15 fee.
Tel: 04 95 71 45 28.
Email: information@campingsantalucia.com

FR20010 Camping Arinella Bianca

Route de la Mer, F-20240 Ghisonaccia (Haute-Corse)

Arinella is a lively, family oriented site on Corsica's east coast. It is a tribute to its owner's design and development skills as it appears to be in entirely natural glades where, in fact, these have been created from former marshland with a fresh water lake. The 429 marked pitches (182 for touring units) are on flat grass among a variety of trees and shrubs providing ample shade. They are irregularly arranged but are all of a good size with 6A electricity (long leads may be necessary). The site is right beside a beach of soft sand that extends a long way either side of the attractive central complex which, together with the swimming pool, forms the hub of this site. A large range of sport and leisure facilities is available at or adjacent to the site. Evening entertainment starts at 10 pm. and continues until midnight and a local disco nearby unfortunately can go on until the early hours. Used by tour operators (76 pitches).

Facilities

Four open plan sanitary blocks provide showers in larger than average cubicles (some with dressing area), washbasins in cabins and mainly British, some Turkish style WCs. Open air dishwashing areas. Laundry with washing machines and ironing boards. Motorcaravan service point. Shop, bar, terraced restaurant, amphitheatre and snack bar (all 10/5-15/9). Swimming pool (from 1/5) free. Windsurfing, canoeing and fishing. Volleyball. Tennis. Riding. Children's mini-club and play area. Disco. Entertainment in the main season. Off site: Sailing 0.5 km. Boat launching 2 km.

Open

Mid April - 30 September.

At a glance

Welcome & Ambience	✓✓✓✓✓	Location	✓✓✓✓✓
Quality of Pitches	✓✓✓✓	Range of Facilities	✓✓✓✓✓

Directions

Site is 4 km. east of Ghisonaccia. From N198 after entering Ghisonaccia look for sign 'La Plage, Li Mare' (this road is easy to miss from south and difficult for caravans to turn, so go further and turn in garage forecourt to approach from north). Turn east on D144 and for 3.5 km. to roundabout. Turn right and site is on left in 500 m. GPS: N41:59.917 E09:26.523

Charges 2005

Per unit incl. 2 adults	€ 19,00 - € 33,00
extra person	€ 6,50 - € 9,00
electricity (6A)	€ 3,50

Camping Cheques accepted.

Reservations

Made with € 155 deposit and € 35 fee.
Tel: 04 95 56 04 78.
Email: arinella@arinellabianca.com

Camping Caravaning
20240 Ghisonaccia
Tel: 0033 495 56 04 78 - Fax: 0033 495 56 12 54
www.arinellabianca.com

FR20030 Camping Merendella

Moriani-Plage, F-20230 San-Nicolao (Haute-Corse)

This attractive family run site has the advantage of direct access to a pleasant, long sandy beach. It is peacefully situated on level grass with many well tended trees and shrubs providing shade and colour. Level green sites such as this are unusual in Corsica and are ideal for families or those with mobility problems. There are 133 pitches, all with electricity (long leads). The choice of placement is impressive with some hedged for privacy under the cool shade of mature trees, others with direct beach access with brilliant sea views and the sound of the waves. Merendella is 'old fashioned' camping in a natural setting. We found it delightful and relaxing but in high season there may be noise from local discos.

Facilities

Modern toilet facilities are in two main blocks, along with two individual cabin units near the beach. Washbasins in private cubicles. British and Turkish style WCs. Facilities for disabled campers. Two washing machines. Motorcaravan service area. Shop. Bar/restaurant and pizzeria. Late arrival area. Diving centre on site. Play area. Torches essential. Animals are not accepted. Off site: Town 800 m. with usual amenities. Tennis and riding 2 km. Bicycle hire 800 m.

At a glance

Welcome & Ambience	✓✓✓✓	Location	✓✓✓✓✓
Quality of Pitches	✓✓✓✓	Range of Facilities	✓✓✓

Directions

Site is to seaward side of the RN198, 800 m. south of Moriani Plage. GPS: N42:21 E09:31.78

Charges 2005

Per person	€ 5,80 - € 6,90
pitch incl. electricity (2/5A)	€ 8,00 - €10,55

Reservations

Are advisable; write to site. Tel: 04 95 38 53 47.
Email: merendel@club-internet.fr

Open

15 May - 15 October.

FR20060 Camping La Vetta

Route de Bastia, La Trinité, F-20137 Porto-Vecchio (Corse-du-Sud)

What an enjoyable experience we had at La Vetta! This is a site not to be missed in Corsica, the English/French owners Nick and Marieline Long having created a very friendly and peaceful country park setting for their campsite to the north of La Trinité village. Many of the delights of Corsica are only a short drive away and La Vetta is only 3 km. from Porto-Vecchio and its magnificent sandy beaches. The 8.5 hectares of well maintained campsite are part sloping, part terraced with an informal pitch allocation system. It seems to stretch endlessly. The abundance of tree varieties including many cork oaks give shade to 111 pitches which all have 16A electricity. The pool and bar area is delightful and for a campsite of this size, the restaurant is outstanding. The keen young chef takes a pride in the traditional and International dishes served at reasonable prices, sometimes to the accompaniment of live Corsican music.

Facilities

Spotless, modern and fully equipped toilet facilities have hot water throughout and include dishwashing, laundry sinks and a washing machine. Shop (July/Aug) with gas supplies. Excellent restaurant with patio and bar (July/Aug). Swimming pool (all season). Table tennis. Table football and snooker table. Play area. TV. Entertainment in high season. Off site: Beach 1.5 km. Fishing, watersports and boat launching 1.5 km. Riding 4 km. Bicycle hire 5 km. Golf 7 km. Public transport 800 m.

Open

1 June - 1 October.

At a glance

Welcome & Ambience	✓✓✓✓✓	Location	✓✓✓✓
Quality of Pitches	✓✓✓✓	Range of Facilities	✓✓✓✓

Directions

Site is in La Trinité village, off the RN198 (east side), north of Porto-Vecchio.

Charges 2005

Per person	€ 6,00 - € 7,00
child (under 7 yrs)	€ 3,00 - € 4,00
tent or caravan	€ 2,50 - € 3,00
car	€ 2,00
motorcaravan	€ 4,50 - € 5,00
electricity	€ 3,00

No credit cards.

Reservations

Made with 30% deposit. Tel: 04 95 70 09 86. Email: info@campinglavetta.com

FR20230 Camping Le Sagone

Route de Vico, F-20118 Sagone (Corse-du-Sud)

Situated just outside the bustling seaside resort of Sagone and surrounded by protective hills, this campsite, which used to be a fruit farm, is in a ideal location for exploring Corsica's wild and rocky west coast or its mountainous interior. The large site borders a pleasant river and has 300 marked, shaded pitches, 250 with electricity (6A). There are also 90 bungalows which are generally separate are offered for rent. The restaurant/bar and games room overlook the pool and are the focal point of this well managed site. Animation takes place in the central area by the pool during the high season. This peaceful, cheerful site is well suited to families and you will have the chance to practice your French or Corsican language skills.

Facilities

Four clean, fully equipped unisex toilet blocks include two with internal courtyard gardens. Washbasins in cubicles, washing up and laundry area (cold water only). Facilities for disabled people. Baby baths. An impressive battery of washing machines and dryers near the modern reception building. Motorcaravan service point. Large supermarket at entrance (all year). Restaurant, pizzeria, bar and games room. Swimming pool (May - Sept). Half court tennis. Volleyball. Table tennis. Basketball. Play area. Sub-aqua experience in pool. Communal barbecues. Satellite TV. Internet. Car wash. Off site: Riding 500 m. Diving, windsurfing, mountain biking, fishing, bicycle hire and climbing nearby. Tours to local places of interest.

Open

1 May - 30 September.

At a glance

Welcome & Ambience	✓✓✓✓	Location	✓✓✓✓
Quality of Pitches	✓✓✓✓	Range of Facilities	✓✓✓✓

Directions

From Ajaccio take the RD81 in direction of Cergése and Calvilby (by coast road). In Sagone take RD70 in direction of Vico, Sagone camping can be found on left after 1.5 km. next to Coccinelle supermarket. GPS: N42:07 E08:42.33

Charges 2005

Per unit incl. 2 persons	€ 14,50 - € 23,00
extra person	€ 4,50 - € 7,70
child (under 12 yrs)	€ 2,25 - € 3,90
electricity	€ 3,00
dog	€ 1,90 - € 2,00

Camping Cheques accepted.

Reservations

Made with 30% deposit and € 18.50 booking fee; write to site. Tel: 04 95 28 04 15. Email: sagone.camping@wanadoo.fr

FR20040 Riva Bella Nature Resort & Spa

Mobile homes ▶ page 449

B.P. 21, F-20270 Alèria (Haute-Corse)

This is a relaxed and informal naturist site alongside an extremely long and beautiful beach. If you enjoy spacious living, Riva Bella is naturist camping at its very best with great amenities. Although offering a large number and variety of pitches, they are situated in such a huge area of varied and beautiful countryside and seaside that it is difficult to believe it could ever become overcrowded. The site is divided into several distinct areas - pitches and bungalows, alongside the sandy beach, in a wooded glade with ample shade, behind the beach, or beside the lake/lagoon which is a feature of this site. The ground is undulating, so getting an absolutely level pitch could be a problem in the main season. Although electric hook-ups are available in most parts, a long cable is probably a necessity. There is an interesting evening entertainment programme. There is now a fabulous modern 'balneotherapy' centre where you can pamper yourself with the very latest beauty and relaxation treatments based on marine (men and women) – this really is very special. Noel Pasqual is justifiably proud of his site and the fairly unobtrusive rules are designed to ensure that everyone is able to relax, whilst preserving the natural beauty of the environment. There is, for example, a restriction on the movement of cars in certain areas (but ample free parking). Generally the ambience is relaxed and informal with nudity only obligatory on the beach itself. Member 'France 4 Naturisme'.

Facilities

Toilet facilities in most blocks have been refurbished. Whilst fairly typical in design for naturist sites, they are fitted and decorated to the highest standards facilities for disabled people and babies. Large well stocked shop (25/4-15/10). Fridge hire. Excellent restaurant (all season) with reasonable prices overlooks the lagoon. Snack bar beside the beach. Watersports including sailing school, fishing, sub-aqua etc. Therapy centre. Sauna. Volleyball, aerobics, table tennis, giant draughts and archery. Fishing. Mountain bike hire. Half-court tennis. Walk with llamas. The police/fire service ban barbecues during the summer. Off site: Riding 5 km.

Open

8 April - 1 November.

At a glance

Welcome & Ambience	✓✓✓	Location	✓✓✓✓✓
Quality of Pitches	✓✓✓✓	Range of Facilities	✓✓✓✓

Directions

Site is about 8 km. north of Aleria on N198 (Bastia) road. Watch for signs and unmade road to it and follow for 4 km GPS: N42:09.598 E09:32.64

Charges 2005

Per unit incl. 2 persons	€ 17,00 - € 31,00
extra person	€ 4,00 - € 8,50
child (3-8 yrs)	€ 2,00 - € 5,00
electricity	€ 3,80
dog	€ 3,00 - € 3,00

Special offers and half-board arrangements available. Camping Cheques accepted.

Reservations

Made with deposit and fee/cancellation insurance. Tel: 04 95 38 81 10. Email: riva-bella@wanadoo.fr

FR20100 Camping Caravaning Santa Barbara

RN 200 route d'Aleria, Aerodrome de Corte, F-20250 Corte (Haute-Corse)

Santa Barbara is a small, uncomplicated campsite in Corsica's mountainous interior. Corte, the historical capital of the island, stands at 396 m. altitude in the central mountains where you can experience Corsica of old. Originally established as a restaurant/bar, the campsite is an unambitious project with 25 level touring pitches and 15 mobile holiday homes. The pitches are separated by young shrubs and there is electricity (12A). A small, inviting swimming pool is alongside the pretty restaurant terrace and very welcome in this hot terrain with its impressive mountain views. The area outside the bar and restaurant has several functions and there is a quiet inside area which is good for cooling off and relaxing. The owners of the site are very friendly and helpful and you will have the opportunity to practice your French here. There is some noise from the road and on a runway behind the site you may see microlites and small aircraft having fun. A simple site with limited facilities but one where you will feel at home if you enjoy the French/Corsican way of life, little English is spoken.

Facilities

The toilet facilities are dated and tired but kept clean (unisex when seen). Dishwashing and laundry sinks (cold water) and washing machine. Restaurant/bar offers typical menu and snacks. Swimming pool. Basic play area. Table tennis. Pool table. Off site: Corte has all the usual town amenities. Bus 3 km. Bicycle hire 3 km. Riding 10 km. Golf 20 km.

Open

1 May - 30 September.

At a glance

Welcome & Ambience	✓✓✓✓	Location	✓✓✓
Quality of Pitches	✓✓✓	Range of Facilities	✓✓✓

Directions

Site is 3 km. southeast of Corte by the N200 Aléria road. GPS: N42:17 E09:11.42

Charges guide

Per person	€ 4,50
child (under 10 yrs)	€ 2,60
caravan	€ 3,70
car	€ 2,50
motorcaravan	€ 5,40
electricity	€ 3,70

Reservations

Write to site. Tel: 04 95 46 20 22.

FR20120 Camping Le Panoramic

Route de Lavatoggio, Lumio, F-20260 Calvi (Haute-Corse)

Le Panoramic, as its name suggests, enjoys magnificent views across the Golfe d'Ambroggio. It is a simple family run site with 100 pitches laid out in named terraces. The marked places are shaded by many trees and vegetation, with 15A electricity connections available to some (long leads required). The site is on a steep slope,some of the lower pitches have magnificent uninterrupted views. The pool is a pleasant area elevated on a concrete base. Sub-aqua diving introductions may be experienced in the high season. Snacks can be obtained from the single building which holds reception and the utilities. Larger units need to telephone ahead to ensure they can be accommodated but no English is spoken here. The tranquility of this country site will appeal to many who wish to savour the Corsican lifestyle whilst having the beach just 5 km away.

Facilities

Four unisex sanitary blocks are housed in typical rough-cast buildings with basic decor and fittings, but appear well maintained and fully equipped. Sinks for dishwashing and laundry (cold water only) and two washing machines. Chemical disposal can be arranged through reception. Small shop, takeaway and bar (1/6-15/9). Swimming pool. Table football, pool table. Play area. Caravan storage. No English spoken. Off site: A recommended scenic drive is the 5 km. climb to St Antonino, a mountain village on a rocky summit. Riding 3 km. Bicycle hire 4 km. Golf 5 km. Beach 5 km.

Open

1 June - 15 September.

At a glance

Welcome & Ambience	✓✓✓	Location	✓✓✓✓
Quality of Pitches	✓✓✓	Range of Facilities	✓✓✓

Directions

From Calvi take N197 towards L'Ile Rousse. Proceed for 10 km. to village of Lumio, then east on D71 and site is 2 km. on the left. GPS: N42:35 E08:50.84

Charges 2005

Per person	€ 6,00
child (2-7 yrs)	€ 2,90
pitch incl. car	€ 4,00 - € 6,00
electricity	€ 3,20

No credit cards.

Reservations

Phone or write. Tel: 04 95 60 73 13.
Email: panoramic@web-office.fr

FR20130 Camping San Damiano

Lido de la Marana-Pineto, F-20620 Biguglia-Bastia (Haute-Corse)

What we found pleasing about this site was the friendly reception we received and also its convenient situation only 9 km. from the port of Bastia. It makes an excellent night halt, or alternatively a suitable base for visiting Bastia, the northeast of the island or its mountainous interior. Despite being on the outskirts of a city, it enjoys an ideal location off the busy N193, situated between the Etang de Biguglia and the golden sands of Corsica's east coast. It is divided in two by a public access road to the beach and is a sprawling site with 280 pitches, all separated by shrubs and shaded by trees. There are 180 electricity connections (10A). A security guard patrols in high season and quiet is enforced after 11 pm.

Facilities

Two basic toilet blocks, but clean when we visited, include washing cabins and good provision for disabled visitors. Motorcaravan service point. Well-stocked shop (1/6-20/9). Bar and restaurant (from 1/5). Launderette. TV room. Minigolf. Play area for children. Fishing. Riding. Jet-ski and quad-bike hire. Off site: Golf 15 km.

Open

1 April - 15 October.

At a glance

Welcome & Ambience	✓✓✓✓	Location	✓✓✓✓
Quality of Pitches	✓✓✓✓	Range of Facilities	✓✓✓✓

Directions

From port of Bastia travel 5 km. on N193 then take D107 towards Lido de la Marana for 4 km. Site is signed on the left. GPS: N42:37.765 E09:28.089

Charges 2005

Per person	€ 5,00 - € 6,50
child (under 8 yrs)	€ 3,50 - € 4,50
pitch	€ 4,50 - € 6,50
electricity (6A)	€ 3,00
dog	€ 0,50

Reservations

Possible by phone. Tel: 04 95 33 68 02.
Email: l.pradier@wanadoo.fr

home
from home

Over recent years many of the campsites featured in this guide have added large numbers of high quality mobile homes and chalets. Many site owners believe that some former caravanners and motorcaravanners have been enticed by the extra comfort they can now provide, and that maybe this is the ideal solution to combine the freedom of camping with all the comforts of home.

Quality is consistently high and, although the exact size and inventory may vary from site to site, if you choose any of the sites detailed here, you can be sure that you're staying in some of the best quality and best value mobile homes available.

Home comforts are provided and typically these include a fridge with freezer compartment, gas hob, proper shower - often a microwave and radio/cassette hi-fi too but do check for details. All mobile homes and chalets come fully equipped with a good range of kitchen utensils, pots and pans, crockery, cutlery and outdoor furniture. Some even have an attractive wooden sundeck or paved terrace - a perfect spot for outdoors eating or relaxing with a book and watching the world go by.

Regardless of model, colourful soft furnishings are the norm and a generally breezy décor helps to provide a real holiday feel.

For your convenience and as a result of feedback from many of our readers, we have now included a distinct section on mobile homes and chalets.

Although some sites may have a large number of different accommodation types, we have restricted our choice to one or two of the most popular accommodation units (either mobile homes or chalets) for each of the sites listed.

The mobile homes here will be of modern design, and recent innovations, for example, often include pitched roofs which substantially improve their appearance.

Design will invariably include clever use of space and fittings/furniture to provide for comfortable holidays - usually light and airy, with big windows and patio-style doors, fully equipped kitchen areas, a shower room with shower, washbasin and WC, cleverly designed bedrooms and a comfortable lounge/dining area (often incorporating a sofa bed).

In general, modern campsite chalets incorporate all the best features of mobile homes in a more traditional structure, sometimes with the advantage of an upper mezzanine floor for an additional bedroom.

Our selected campsites offer a massive range of different types of mobile home and chalet, and it would be impractical to inspect every single accommodation unit. Our selection criteria, therefore, primarily takes account of the quality standards of the campsite itself. However, there are a couple of important ground rules

   Featured mobile homes must be no more than 5 years old, and chalets no more than 10 years old.

   All listed accommodation must, of course, fully conform with all applicable local, national and European safety legislation.

For each campsite we given details of the type, or types, of accommodation available to rent, but these details are necessarily quite brief. Sometimes internal layouts can differ quite substantially, particularly with regard to sleeping arrangements, where these include the flexible provision for 'extra persons' on sofa beds located in the living area. These arrangements may vary from accommodation to accommodation, and if you're planning a holiday which includes more people than are catered for by the main bedrooms you should check exactly how the extra sleeping arrangements are to be provided!

Charges

An indication of the tariff for each type of accommodation featured is also included, indicating the variance between the low and high season tariffs. However, given that many campsites have a large and often complex range of pricing options, incorporating special deals and various discounts, the charges we mention should be taken to be just an indication. We strongly recommend therefore that you confirm the actual cost when making a booking.

We also strongly recommend that you check with the campsite, when booking, what (if anything) will be provided by way of bed linen, blankets, pillows etc. Again, in our experience, this can vary widely from site to site.

On every campsite a fully refundable deposit (usually between 150 and 300 euros) is payable on arrival. There may also be an optional cleaning service for which a further charge is made. Other options may include sheet hire (typically 30 euros per unit) or baby pack hire (cot and high chair).

FR29000 Yelloh! Village Les Mouettes

La Grande Grève, F-29660 Carantec (Finistère)

For our full description of this campsite ▶ see page 30

The mobile homes and chalets are attractively located at the top of the site.

AR1 – COTTAGE BREHAT – Mobile Home

Sleeping:
2 bedrooms, sleeps 6: 1 double, 1 twin with 2 single beds, 1 double sofa bed; pillows & blankets provided

Living:
living/kitchen area, heating, shower & WC

Eating:
fitted kitchen with cooking hobs & fridge

Outside:
table & chairs, parasol

Pets:
not accepted

AR2 – CHALET 40 – Chalet

Sleeping:
2 bedrooms, sleeps 6: 1 double, 1 twin with 2 single beds, 1 double sofa bed; pillows & blankets provided

Living:
living/kitchen area, heating, shower & WC

Eating:
fitted kitchen with cooking hobs & fridge

Outside:
table & chairs, parasol

Pets:
not accepted

Weekly Charges

	AR1	AR2
Low Season *(from)*	€ 245	€ 406
High Season *(from)*	€ 791	€ 1183

FR29010 Castel Camping Le Ty-Nadan

Route d'Arzano, F-29310 Locunolé (Finistère)

For our full description of this campsite ▶ see page 33

The chalets are set amongst trees on a slope overlooking the river and woods beyond.

AR1 – IRM – Mobile Home

Sleeping:
2 bedrooms, sleeps 6: 1 double, 1 twin with 2 single beds, 1 double sofa bed; pillows & blankets provided

Living:
living/kitchen area, heating, shower & WC

Eating:
fitted kitchen with cooking hobs, oven & fridge

Outside:
table & chairs, sun loungers & parasol

Pets:
accepted

AR2 – Accommodation – Wooden Chalet

Sleeping:
2 bedrooms, sleeps 6: 1 double, 1 twin with 2 single beds, 1 double sofa bed; pillows & blankets provided

Living:
living/kitchen area, heating, shower & WC

Eating:
fitted kitchen with cooking hobs & fridge

Outside:
table & chairs, sun loungers & parasol

Pets:
accepted

Weekly Charges

	AR1	AR2
Low Season *(from)*	€ 270	€ 360
High Season *(from)*	€ 567	€ 840

FR29050 Castel Camping L'Orangerie de Lanniron

Château de Lanniron, F-29336 Quimper (Finistère)

For our full description of this campsite ▶ see page 35

The mobile homes are situated together on large (150 sq.m.) pitches at the top of the site in a peaceful area, all are fitted with wooden terraces.

AR1 – DELUXE – Mobile Home

Sleeping:
2 bedrooms, sleeps 4-6: 1 double, 1 twin with 2 single beds, 1 double sofa bed; pillows & blankets provided

Living:
living/kitchen area, heating, shower & WC

Eating:
fitted kitchen with cooking hobs, microwave & fridge-freezer

Outside:
table & chairs, sun loungers, parasol & BBQ

Pets:
not accepted

AR2 – COMFORT – Mobile Home

Sleeping:
2 bedrooms, sleeps 4-6: 1 double, 1 twin with 2 single beds, 1 double sofa bed,

Living:
living/kitchen area, heating, shower & WC

Eating:
fitted kitchen with cooking hobs, microwave & fridge-freezer

Outside:
table & chairs, sun loungers, parasol & BBQ

Pets:
not accepted

Weekly Charges	AR1	AR2
Low Season *(from)*	€ 371	€ 350
High Season *(from)*	€ 686	€ 665

FR29090 Camping Le Raguénés-Plage

19 rue des Iles, Raguénés, F-29920 Névez (Finistère)

For our full description of this campsite ▶ see page 38

The accommodation is located in the north part of the site in small groups, each mobile home is divided by hedges and trees to provide privacy.

AR1 – WILLERBY 2 – Mobile Home

Sleeping:
2 bedrooms, sleeps 5: 1 double, 1 twin with 2 single beds, 1 sofa bed; pillows & blankets provided

Living:
living/kitchen area, fan, heating, shower & WC

Eating:
fitted kitchen with cooking hobs, microwave & fridge-freezer

Outside:
table & chairs, sun loungers, parasol & BBQ

Pets:
not accepted

AR2 – WILLERBY 3 – Mobile Home

Sleeping:
2 bedrooms, sleeps 4: 1 double, 1 twin with 2 single beds; pillows & blankets provided

Living:
living/kitchen area, heating, fan, shower & WC

Eating:
fitted kitchen with cooking hobs microwave & fridge-freezer

Outside:
table & chairs, sun loungers, parasol & BBQ

Pets:
not accepted

Weekly Charges	AR1	AR2
Low Season *(from)*	€ 275	€ 340
High Season *(from)*	€ 660	€ 730

FR29130 Camping des Abers

Dunes de Sainte Marguerite, F-29870 Landéda (Finistère)

For our full description of this campsite ▶ see page 31

The accommodation is located in a quiet, high part of the site, each one is separated by hedges and some have sea views.

AR1 – IRM CONFORT – Mobile Home

Sleeping:
2 bedrooms, sleeps 4-5: 1 double, 1 twin with 2 single beds, 1 single sofa bed; pillows & blankets provided

Living:
living/kitchen area, heating, shower & WC

Eating:
fitted kitchen with cooking hobs & fridge

Outside:
table & chairs, sun loungers, parasol & BBQ

Pets:
accepted

AR2 – GRAND CONFORT – Mobile Home

Sleeping:
2 bedrooms, sleeps 4-6: 1 double, 1 twin with 2 single beds, 1 double sofa bed; pillows & blankets provided

Living:
living/kitchen area, heating, shower & WC

Eating:
fitted kitchen with cooking hobs & fridge

Outside:
table & chairs, sun loungers, parasol & BBQ

Pets:
accepted

Weekly Charges		
	AR1	AR2
Low Season (from)	€ 250	€ 270
High Season (from)	€ 470	€ 530

FR35040 Camping Le P'tit Bois

F-35430 St Jouan des Guerets (Ille-et-Vilaine)

For our full description of this campsite ▶ see page 48

The accommodation is dispersed throughout this attractive site.

AR1 – COTTAGE 5 – Mobile Home

Sleeping:
2 bedrooms, sleeps 6: 1 double, 1 twin with 2 single beds. Pillows & blankets provided

Living:
living/kitchen area, heating, shower & WC

Eating:
fitted kitchen with cooking hobs, microwave, fridge & indoor gas BBQ

Outside:
table & chairs, sun loungers & parasol.

Pets:
one small dog accepted

AR2 – COTTAGE 1 – Mobile Home

Sleeping:
2 bedrooms, sleeps 4: 1 double, 1 twin with 2 single beds, 1 sofa bed; pillows & blankets provided

Living:
living/kitchen area, heating, shower & WC

Eating:
fitted kitchen with cooking hobs, microwave, fridge & indoor gas BBQ

Outside:
table & chairs, sun loungers, parasol & BBQ

Pets:
one small dog accepted

Weekly Charges		
	AR1	AR2
Low Season (from)	€ 490	€ 315
High Season (from)	€ 910	€ 728

FR44090 Camping Château du Deffay

B.P. 18 Le Deffay, Ste Reine de Bretagne, F-44160 Pontchâteau (Loire-Atlantique)

For our full description of this campsite ▶ see page 51

The mobile homes are in areas surrounded with flowers and vegetation. Some of the chalets overlook the lake.

AR1 – Accommodation – Mobile Home

Sleeping:
2 bedrooms, sleeps 5: 1 double, 1 single bed, 2 bunk beds in living area, pillows & blankets provided

Living:
living/kitchen area, heating, shower & WC

Eating:
fitted kitchen with cooking hobs, microwave & fridge-freezer

Outside:
table & chairs, sun loungers, parasol & BBQ

Pets:
accepted (1 per mobile home)

AR2 – Accommodation – Chalet

Sleeping:
2 bedrooms, sleeps 6: 1 double, 2 bunk beds, 1 double sofa bed; pillows & blankets provided

Living:
living/kitchen area, heating, shower & WC

Eating:
fitted kitchen with cooking hobs, dishwasher, microwave & fridge-freezer

Outside:
table & chairs, sun loungers, parasol & BBQ

Pets:
accepted (1 per chalet)

Weekly Charges	AR1	AR2
Low Season (from)	€ 205	€ 225
High Season (from)	€ 569	€ 629

FR44100 Sunêlia Le Patisseau

29 rue du Patisseau, F-44210 Pornic (Loire-Atlantique)

For our full description of this campsite ▶ see page 52

Comfortable mobile homes and chalets on this site with superb amenities, including an all year heated swimming pool.

AR1 – CHALET 6

Sleeping:
2 bedrooms, sleeps 6: 1 double, 1 twin with 2 single beds, 1 double sofa bed; pillows & blankets provided

Living:
living/kitchen area, heating, shower & WC

Eating:
fitted kitchen with cooking hobs, microwave, pressure cooker & fridge

Outside:
table & chairs, parasol

Pets:
not accepted

AR2 – MOBILE HOME 6

Sleeping:
2 bedrooms, sleeps 6: 1 double, 2 single beds, 1 double sofa bed; pillows & blankets provided

Living:
living/kitchen area, heating, shower & WC

Eating:
fitted kitchen with cooking hobs, pressure cooker & fridge, microwave

Outside:
table & chairs, parasol

Pets:
not accepted

Weekly Charges	AR1	AR2
Low Season (from)	€ 430	€ 393
High Season (from)	€ 889	€ 840

409

FR44190 Camping Le Fief
57 chemin du Fief, F-44250 St Brévin-les-Pins (Loire-Atlantique)

For our full description of this campsite ▶ see page 54

Attractively located within this popular site.

AR1 – COTTAGES – Mobile home	**AR2 – COTTAGES – Mobile home**
Sleeping:	Sleeping:
3 bedrooms, sleeps 6: 1 double, 2 bedrooms with 2 twin beds	2 bedrooms, sleeps 6: 1 double, 1 twin with 2 single beds
Living:	Living:
living/kitchen area, shower & WC, sofa	living/kitchen area, shower & WC, sofabed
Eating:	Eating:
fitted kitchen with cooking hobs, fridge & microwave	fitted kitchen with cooking hobs, microwave & fridge
Outside:	Outside:
table & chairs, terrace	table & chairs, terrace
Pets:	Pets:
accepted	accepted

Weekly Charges	AR1	AR2
Low Season *(from)*	€ 340	€ 340
High Season *(from)*	€ 825	€ 770

FR80060 Camping Le Val de Trie
Bouillancourt-sous-Miannay, F-80870 Moyenneville (Somme)

For our full description of this campsite ▶ see page 91

The mobile homes are all grouped together on large pitches (120 sq.m.) in a dedicated area of the site, each one separated by hedges and flowers to provide privacy.

AR1 – MORÉVA – Mobile Home	**AR2 – ZEN – Mobile Home**
Sleeping:	Sleeping:
2 bedrooms, sleeps 6: 1 double, 1 twin with 2 single beds, 1 double sofa bed; pillows & blankets provided	3 bedrooms, sleeps 6: 1 double, 2 twin with 2 single beds
Living:	Living:
living/kitchen area, heating, shower & WC	living/kitchen area, cd player, shower & WC
Eating:	Eating:
fitted kitchen with cooking hobs, microwave & fridge-freezer	fitted kitchen with dishwasher, cooking hobs, microwave, fridge-freezer
Outside:	Outside:
terrace with table & chairs, parasol & BBQ	terrace with table & chairs, sun loungers, parasol & BBQ
Pets:	Pets:
not accepted	not accepted

Weekly Charges	AR1	AR2
Low Season *(from)*	€ 230	€ 305
High Season *(from)*	€ 580	€ 680

FR80070 Camping La Ferme des Aulnes

1 rue du Marais, Fresne-sur-Authie, F-80120 Nampont-St Martin (Somme)

For our full description of this campsite ● see page 89

Attractive locations within this beautiful site, with all amenities (swimming pool etc.) operating for the full season.

AR1 – CONFORT – Mobile Home

Sleeping:
2 bedrooms, sleeps 5: 1 double, 1 twin with 2 single beds, 1 sofa bed

Living:
living/kitchen area, heating, shower & WC, TV

Eating:
fitted kitchen with cooking hobs, microwave & fridge-freezer

Outside:
table & chairs, sun loungers, parasol & BBQ, terrace

Pets:
accepted (€ 50 per stay)

AR2 – PRIVILEGE – Mobile home

Sleeping:
3 bedrooms, sleeps 6: 1 double, 2 twin with 2 single beds

Living:
living/kitchen area, heating, shower & WC, TV (DVD player), safe

Eating:
fitted kitchen with cooking hobs, microwave, fridge-freezer, dishwasher

Outside:
terrace with table & chairs, sun loungers, parasol & BBQ

Pets:
accepted (€ 50 per stay)

Weekly Charges	AR1	AR2
Low Season (from)	€ 480	€ 580
High Season (from)	€ 680	€ 790

FR77020 Camping Le Chêne Gris

24 place de la Gare de Faremoutiers, F-77515 Pommeuse (Seine-et-Marne)

For our full description of this campsite ● see page 94

Mobile homes are centrally located on shady pitches.

AR1 – BALI – Mobile home

Sleeping:
2 bedrooms, sleeps 6: 1 double, 1 twin with 2 single beds, 1 double sofa bed

Living:
kitchen/living area, bathroom with shower & washbasin, separate toilet

Eating:
four burner gas hob, microwave & fridge-freezer

Outside:
covered wooden terrace

Pets:
Not accepted

AR2 – TAHITI – Mobile home

Sleeping:
2 bedrooms, sleeps 5: 1 double, 1 twin with 2 bunk beds & a single bed, 1 single sofa bed

Living:
kitchen/living area, 2 bathrooms each with shower, washbasin & toilet

Eating:
four burner gas hob & fridge-freezer

Outside:
wooden veranda enclosed by a wooden railing

Pets:
not accepted

Weekly Charges	AR1	AR2
Low Season (from)	€ 354	€ 384
High Season (from)	€ 693	€ 728

Mobile homes & chalets

FR77060 Le Parc de la Colline

Route de Lagny, F-77200 Torcy (Seine-et-Marne)

Pitches at this campsite are exclusively for mobile homes & chalets

Set in the heart of Marne-la-Vallée, with easy access to Paris and Disneyland, Parc de la Colline is in a relatively green area on the outskirts of the capital, situated on a fairly steep slope. There is a childrens' play area and a shop on site, with a supermarket and water park nearby. The site runs a minibus service to the nearest métro station at Torcy, for easy access to Paris or Disneyland, plus trips to Parc Asterix and group visits to central Paris. Reception will advise on the best value travel cards and these can be purchased on site. Reception staff speak good English. Note - you are close to a major city environment. Petty crime can be a problem and we recommend the use of the safety deposit boxes.

Facilities

Shop (all year). Snack bar (high season). Several children's play areas, minigolf, basketball and table tennis. Bus service (every 15 minutes between 0800 and 2400 with a pause at lunchtime). Off site: Disneyland 10 mins. (métro), central Paris 20 mins (métro), Parc Asterix 30 mins (car). Supermarket and restaurants nearby.

Open

All year.

Directions

From Paris and the Péripherique take A4 to the junction with the A104 (Charles de Gaulle - Lille). From A1 Paris - Lille take A104 (Marne la Vallée), leave at exit 10 and head west signed Parc de Loisirs de Torcy to campsite on left in 1 km.
GPS: N48:515.10 E02:39.219

Reservations

Contact site. Tel: 01 60 05 42 32
E-mail: camping.parc.de.la.colline@wanadoo.fr

AR1 – O'HARA – Mobile Home

Sleeping:
2 bedrooms, sleeps 6: 1 double, 1 twin with 2 single beds, 1 double sofa bed; pillows & blankets provided

Living:
living/kitchen area, heating, shower & WC

Eating:
fitted kitchen with cooking hobs & fridge

Outside:
table & chairs

Pets:
accepted (€ 4.50 per night)

AR2 – NEVA – Chalet

Sleeping:
2 bedrooms, sleeps 4: 1 double, 1 twin with 2 bunk beds; pillows & blankets provided

Living:
living/kitchen area, heating, shower & WC

Eating:
fitted kitchen with cooking hobs & fridge

Outside:
table & chairs

Pets:
accepted (€ 4.50 per night)

Weekly Charges

	AR1	AR2
Low Season (from)	€ 701	€ 687
High Season (from)	€ 701	€ 687

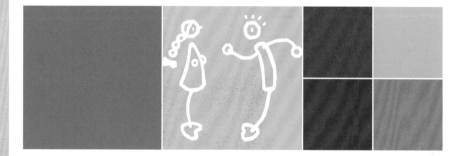

www.alanrogers.com for latest campsite news

FR52020 Castel Camping La Forge de Sainte Marie

F-52230 Thonnance-les-Moulins (Haute-Marne)

For our full description of this campsite ⊙ see page 105

Accommodation is set in the beautiful grounds of this family campsite.

AR1 – IRM – Mobile homes

Sleeping:
2 bedrooms, sleeps 6: 1 double, 1 twin with 2 single beds, 1 double sofa bed

Living:
kitchen/living/seating area, bathroom with shower & washbasin, toilet

Eating:
fitted kitchen.

Outside:
table & chairs

Pets:
accepted

AR2 – Accommodation – Gites

Sleeping:
2 bedrooms, sleeps 6: 1 double, 1 twin with 2 single beds, 1 double sofa bed

Living:
kitchen/living/seating area. Bathroom with shower & washbasin, toilet

Eating:
fitted kitchen, dishwasher

Outside:
covered terrace, table & chairs

Pets:
accepted

Weekly Charges

	AR1	AR2
Low Season *(from)*	€ 240	€ 250
High Season *(from)*	€ 570	€ 740

FR88040 Camping Club du Lac de Bouzey

19 rue du Lac, F-88390 Sanchey (Vosges)

For our full description of this campsite ⊙ see page 112

AR1 – ABI – Mobile Home

Sleeping:
2 bedrooms, sleeps 6: 1 double, 1 twin with 2 single beds, 1 double sofa bed; pillows & blankets provided

Living:
living/kitchen area, heating, shower & WC

Eating:
fitted kitchen with cooking hobs, microwave & fridge

Outside:
table & chairs, sun loungers, parasol & BBQ

Pets:
accepted

AR2 – ZEN – Mobile Home

Sleeping:
3 bedrooms, sleeps 6: 1 double, 2 twin with 2 single beds; pillows & blankets provided

Living:
living/kitchen area, heating, shower & WC

Eating:
fitted kitchen with cooking hobs microwave & fridge-freezer

Outside:
table & chairs, sun loungers, parasol & BBQ

Pets:
not accepted

Weekly Charges

	AR1	AR2
Low Season *(from)*	€ 300	€ 450
High Season *(from)*	€ 600	€ 850

FR88130 Camping La Vanne de Pierre

5 rue du camping, F-88100 St Dié-des-Vosges (Vosges)

For our full description of this campsite ▶ see page 114

Delightful location within this riverside campsite, ideal for a peaceful rural holiday.

AR1 – COUNTRY LODGE – Chalet	**AR2 – ZEN – Mobile Home**
Sleeping:	Sleeping:
2 bedrooms, sleeps 6: 1 double, 1 twin with 2 single beds, 1 double sofa bed	3 bedrooms, sleeps 6: 1 double, 2 twin with 2 single beds
Living:	Living:
living/kitchen area, heating, shower & WC	living/kitchen area, TV, heating, shower & WC
Eating:	Eating:
fitted kitchen with cooking hobs, microwave & fridge	fitted kitchen with cooking hobs, microwave & fridge
Outside:	Outside:
table & chairs, sun loungers & parasol	table & chairs, sun loungers & parasol
Pets:	Pets:
not accepted	not accepted

Weekly Charges	AR1	AR2
Low Season *(from)*	€ 500	€ 400
High Season *(from)*	€ 800	€ 700

FR17140 Castel Camping Sequoia Parc

La Josephtrie, F-17320 St Just-Luzac (Charente-Maritime)

For our full description of this campsite ▶ see page 121

The chalets are situated near the swimming pool or the tennis courts and the mobile homes (Cottages) are near to the château.

AR1 – GITOTEL – Chalet	**AR2 – COTTAGE 6 – Mobile Home**
Sleeping:	Sleeping:
3 bedrooms, sleeps 6: 2 double, 1 twin with 2 bunk beds; pillows & blankets provided	2 bedrooms, sleeps 6: 1 double, 1 twin with 2 single beds, 1 double sofa bed; pillows & blankets provided
Living:	Living:
living/kitchen area, heating (low season), shower & WC	living/kitchen area, heating (low season), shower & WC
Eating:	Eating:
fitted kitchen with cooking hobs, microwave & fridge	fitted kitchen with cooking hobs, microwave & fridge
Outside:	Outside:
table & chairs, sun loungers	table & chairs, sun loungers
Pets:	Pets:
not accepted	not accepted

Weekly Charges	AR1	AR2
Low Season *(from)*	€ 245	€ 210
High Season *(from)*	€ 931	€ 861

FR17230 Camping de L'Océan

La Passe, La Couarde sur Mer, F-17670 Ile de Ré (Charente-Maritime)

For our full description of this campsite ▶ see page 125

AR1 – SAVANAH – Mobile Home

Sleeping:
2 bedrooms, sleeps 6: 1 double, 1 twin with 1 single bed, 1 bunk bed, 1 double sofa bed; pillows & blankets provided

Living:
living/kitchen area, heating, shower & WC

Eating:
fitted kitchen

Outside:
table & chairs, parasol

Pets:
accepted

AR2 – CRL – Residence Mobile

Sleeping:
sleeps 4-7

Living:
living/kitchen area, heating, shower & WC

Eating:
fitted kitchen

Outside:
terrace, table, chairs, parasol & 2 sun loungers

Pets:
accepted

Weekly Charges	AR1	AR2
Low Season (from)	€ 317	€ 353
High Season (from)	€ 670	€ 721

FR85150 Camping La Yole

Chemin des Bosses, Orouet, F-85160 St Jean-de-Monts (Vendée)

For our full description of this campsite ▶ see page 133

The featured accommodation are situated in a wooded area within the campsite.

AR1 – LOUISIANE FLORÈS 2 – Mobile Home

Sleeping:
2 bedrooms, sleeps 4: 1 double, 1 twin with 2 single beds; pillows & blankets provided

Living:
living/kitchen area, heating, shower & WC

Eating:
fitted kitchen with cooking hobs, microwave & fridge-freezer

Outside:
table & chairs, sun loungers & parasol

Pets:
not accepted

AR2 – LOUISIANE FLORÈS 3 – Mobile Home

Sleeping:
3 bedrooms, sleeps 6: 1 double, 2 twin with 2 single beds; pillows & blankets provided

Living:
living/kitchen area, heating, safe, shower & WC

Eating:
fitted kitchen with cooking hobs, microwave & fridge-freezer

Outside:
table & chairs, sun loungers & parasol

Pets:
not accepted

Weekly Charges	AR1	AR2
Low Season (from)	€ 392	€ 420
High Season (from)	€ 740	€ 775

Mobile homes & chalets

415

FR17010 Camping Bois Soleil

2 avenue de Suzac, F-17110 St Georges-de-Didonne (Charente-Maritime)

For our full description of this campsite ● see page 116

The area of the site where mobile homes are situated is beside the sea and has direct access to the beach by steps.

AR1 – O'HARA COTTAGE CHARME – Mobile Home

Sleeping:
2 bedrooms, sleeps 4: 1 double, 1 twin with 2 single beds; pillows & blankets provided

Living:
living/kitchen area, heating, shower & WC

Eating:
fitted kitchen with cooking hobs, microwave & fridge

Outside:
table & chairs, parasol

Pets:
not accepted

AR2 – BÜRSTNER COTTAGE CONFORT – Mobile Home

Sleeping:
2 bedrooms, sleeps 5: 1 double, 1 twin with 2 single beds, 1 single sofa bed; pillows & blankets provided

Living:
living/kitchen area, heating, hair dryer, shower & WC

Eating:
fitted kitchen with cooking hobs, microwave & fridge

Outside:
table & chairs, parasol

Pets:
not accepted

Weekly Charges	AR1	AR2
Low Season (from)	€ 238	€ 218
High Season (from)	€ 860	€ 700

FR85300 Camping La Grand' Métairie

8 rue de la Vineuse en Plaine, F-85440 St Hilaire la Forêt (Vendée)

For our full description of this campsite ● see page 137

The mobile homes are situated in their own dedicated area close to the centre of the site, about five minutes from the swimming pool and main facilities. The chalets are on the edge of the site a little further away from the facilities.

AR1 – 4/7 PRESTIGE – Mobile Home

Sleeping:
2 bedrooms, sleeps 7: 1 double, 1 twin with 2 single beds, 2 bunk beds, 1 sofa bed; pillows & blankets provided

Living:
living/kitchen area, satellite TV, heating, shower & separate WC

Eating:
fitted kitchen with cooking hobs, microwave & fridge-freezer

Outside:
table & chairs, parasol, sun loungers & BBQ

Pets:
accepted

AR2 – COTTAGE LUXE – Mobile Home

Sleeping:
3 bedrooms, sleeps 6: 2 double, 1 twin with 2 bunk beds; pillows & blankets provided

Living:
living/kitchen area, satellite TV, heating, shower & separate WC

Eating:
fitted kitchen with cooking hobs, microwave & fridge-freezer

Outside:
table & chairs, parasol, sun loungers & BBQ

Pets:
accepted

Weekly Charges	AR1	AR2
Low Season (from)	€ 245	€ 215
High Season (from)	€ 750	€ 710

Bois Soleil

Camping ★★★★
Charente-Maritime

rrounded by pine trees and a sandy beach on the Atlantic
ast, with one direct access to the beach, Bois Soleil
pposes to you many attractions like tennis, tabletennis,
ildren playgrounds and entertainment.
ops, take-away and snack-bar with big TV screen.

Spring and Summer 2006

2, avenue de Suzac - 17110 ST GEORGES DE DIDONNE
Tel: 0033 546 05 05 94 - Fax: 0033 546 06 27 43
ww.bois-soleil.com / e-mail: camping.bois.soleil@wanadoo.fr

FR85330 Camping Naturiste Cap Natur'
151 avenue de la Faye, F-85270 St Hilaire-de-Riez (Vendée)

For our full description of this campsite ▶ see page 139

Attractive locations within this pretty naturist site.

AR1 – MOBILE HOME 4 – Chalet	AR2 – CONVIVES – Appartment
Sleeping:	**Sleeping:**
2 bedrooms, sleeps 4: 1 double, 1 twin with 2 single beds; all bed linen provided	2 bedrooms, sleeps 4: 1 double, 1 twin with 2 single beds; all bed linen provided
Living:	**Living:**
living/kitchen area, heating, shower & WC	living/kitchen area, heating, shower & WC
Eating:	**Eating:**
fitted kitchen with cooking hobs & fridge	fitted kitchen with cooking hobs, oven microwave & fridge
Outside:	**Outside:**
table & chairs, parasol	table & chairs, sun loungers & parasol
Pets:	**Pets:**
accepted	accepted

Weekly Charges

	AR1	AR2
Low Season *(from)*	€ 388	€ 240
High Season *(from)*	€ 675	€ 703

FR85400 Camping Bois Soleil
Chemin des Barres, F-85340 Olonne-sur-Mer (Vendée)

For our full description of this campsite ▶ see page 141

AR1 – Accommodation – Mobile home	AR2 – Accommodation – Chalet
Sleeping:	**Sleeping:**
2 bedrooms, sleeps 4: 1 double, 1 twin with 2 single beds.	2 bedrooms, sleeps 4: 1 double, 1 twin with 2 single beds.
Living:	**Living:**
living/kitchen area, heating, shower & WC	living/kitchen area, heating, shower & WC
Eating:	**Eating:**
fitted kitchen with cooking hobs & fridge	fitted kitchen with cooking hobs & fridge
Outside:	**Outside:**
table & chairs, parasol, sunloungers	table & chairs, parasol, sunloungers
Pets:	**Pets:**
accepted	accepted

Weekly Charges

	AR1	AR2
Low Season *(from)*	€ 235	€ 285
High Season *(from)*	€ 630	€ 660

FR37060 Camping L'Arada Parc

Rue de la Baratière, F-37360 Sonzay (Indre-et-Loire)

For our full description of this campsite ▶ see page 154

Chalets and mobile homes are separated by maturing trees, shrubs and flowers that provide some shade.

AR1 – SAMIBOIS – Chalet

Sleeping:
3 bedrooms, sleeps 6: 2 double, 2 bunk beds; pillows & blankets provided

Living:
living/kitchen area, heating, shower & WC

Eating:
fitted kitchen with cooking hobs, microwave & fridge

Outside:
table & chairs, parasol & BBQ

Pets:
accepted

AR2 – BÜRSTNER – Mobile Home

Sleeping:
2 bedrooms, sleeps 5: 1 double, 1 single bed, 1 bunk bed, 1 sofa bed; pillows & blankets provided

Living:
living/kitchen area, heating, shower & WC

Eating:
fitted kitchen with cooking hobs, microwave & fridge-freezer

Outside:
table & chairs, sun loungers, parasol & BBQ

Pets:
accepted

Weekly Charges

	AR1	AR2
Low Season *(from)*	€ 135	€ 270
High Season *(from)*	€ 465	€ 465

FR41020 Castel Camping Château de la Grenouillière

F-41500 Suèvres (Loir-et-Cher)

For our full description of this campsite ▶ see page 158

AR1 – O'HARA – Mobile Home

Sleeping:
2 bedrooms, sleeps 6: 1 double, 4 single beds

Living:
living/kitchen area, heating, shower & WC

Eating:
fitted kitchen with cooking hobs & fridge

Outside:
terrace with table & chairs, parasol, barbecue

Pets:
not accepted

AR2 – GITOTEL – Chalet

Sleeping:
2 bedrooms, sleeps 6: 2 double, 2 single beds, sofa bed

Living:
living/kitchen area, heating, shower & WC

Eating:
fitted kitchen with cooking hobs & fridge

Outside:
terrace with table & chairs, parasol, barbecue

Pets:
not accepted

Weekly Charges

	AR1	AR2
Low Season *(from)*	€ 400	€ 400
High Season *(from)*	€ 730	€ 730

Mobile homes & chalets

419

FR41070 Camping Caravanning La Grande Tortue

3 route de Pontlevoy, F-41120 Candé-sur-Beuvron (Loir-et-Cher)

For our full description of this campsite ▶ see page 159

The featured accommodation are situated amongst trees which provide welcome shade as well as some sunshine.

AR1 – IRM – Mobile Home

Sleeping:
2 bedrooms, sleeps 6: 1 double, 1 twin with 2 single beds, 1 double sofa bed; pillows & blankets provided

Living:
living/kitchen area, heating, shower & WC

Eating:
fitted kitchen with cooking hobs & fridge

Outside:
table & chairs, sun loungers & parasol

Pets:
accepted

AR2 – SHELBOX – Chalet

Sleeping:
2 bedrooms, sleeps 6: 1 double, 1 twin with 2 single beds, 1 double sofa bed; pillows & blankets provided

Living:
living/kitchen area, heating, shower & WC

Eating:
fitted kitchen with cooking hobs, microwave & fridge

Outside:
table & chairs, sun loungers & parasol

Pets:
accepted

Weekly Charges

	AR1	AR2
Low Season *(from)*	€ 257	€ 317
High Season *(from)*	€ 600	€ 650

FR45010 Sunêlia Les Bois du Bardelet

Route de Bourges, Poilly, F-45500 Gien (Loiret)

For our full description of this campsite ▶ see page 162

The mobile homes are situated in a group with paved terraces and the chalets are in a rural landscaped setting on the edge of the woods and fields.

AR1 – LOUISIANE – Mobile Home

Sleeping:
3 bedrooms, sleeps 6: 1 double, 1 twin with 2 single beds, 2 bunk beds; pillows & blankets provided (must be reserved)

Living:
living/kitchen area, heating, shower & WC

Eating:
fitted kitchen with cooking hobs, oven & fridge-freezer

Outside:
table & chairs, parasol & BBQ

Pets:
not accepted

AR2 – TITOM – Chalet

Sleeping:
2 bedrooms, sleeps 5: 1 double, 1 twin with 2 single beds & a bunk bed; pillows & blankets provided (must be reserved)

Living:
living/kitchen area, heating, shower & WC

Eating:
fitted kitchen with cooking hobs, oven & fridge

Outside:
table & chairs, parasol & BBQ

Pets:
accepted

Weekly Charges

	AR1	AR2
Low Season *(from)*	€ 351	€ 351
High Season *(from)*	€ 896	€ 721

FR49040 Camping de l'Etang

Route de St Mathurin, F-49320 Brissac (Maine-et-Loire)

For our full description of this campsite ▶ see page 165

Large pitches with gravel terraces. Free access to adjacent leisure park.

AR1 – WILLERBY – Mobile Home

Sleeping:
2 bedrooms, sleeps 6: 1 double, 1 twin with 2 single beds, 1 double sofa bed, disposable sheets for sale, blankets provided

Living:
living/kitchen area, heating, shower & WC

Eating:
fitted kitchen with cooking hobs & fridge

Outside:
table & chairs, sun loungers & BBQ

Pets:
accepted (€ 2.50 per night)

AR2 – CONCORDE – Mobile Home

Sleeping:
2 bedrooms, sleeps 6: 1 double, 1 twin with 2 single beds, 1 double sofa bed; blankets provided, disposable sheets for sale

Living:
living/kitchen area, heating, shower & WC

Eating:
fitted kitchen with cooking hobs & fridge

Outside:
table & chairs, BBQ

Pets:
accepted (€ 2.50 per night)

Weekly Charges

	AR1	AR2
Low Season *(from)*	€ 280	€ 280
High Season *(from)*	€ 650	€ 565

FR86030 Camping Le Relais du Miel

Route d'Antran, F-86100 Châtellerault (Vienne)

For our full description of this campsite ▶ see page 171

Attractive appartments in an old French house.

AR1 – FURNISHED FLAT – Apartment

Sleeping:
1 bedroom, sleeps 2 to 4

Living:
living/kitchen area, shower & W/C

Eating:
fitted kitchen with cooking hobs, microwave & fridge

Outside:
table & chairs

Pets:
not accepted

AR2 – FURNISHED FLAT – Apartment

Sleeping:
2 bedroom sleeps 4 - 6, 1 double, 2 single beds, 1 sofa bed

Living:
living/kitchen area, shower & WC

Eating:
fitted kitchen with cooking hobs, microwave & fridge

Outside:
table & chairs

Pets:
not accepted

Weekly Charges

	AR1	AR2
Low Season *(from)*	€ 250	€ 350
High Season *(from)*	€ 356	€ 495

421

FR86040 Camping Le Futuriste

F-86130 St Georges-les-Baillargeaux (Vienne)

For our full description of this campsite ▶ see page 173

All chalets are situated in the centre of the site and are accessed via neat, level and firmly rolled gravel roads.

AR1 – FABRE – Chalet

Sleeping:
2 bedrooms, sleeps 6: 1 double, 1 twin with 2 single beds, 1 double sofa bed; pillows & blankets provided

Living:
living/kitchen area, TV, heating, shower & WC

Eating:
fitted kitchen with cooking hobs, microwave & fridge-freezer

Outside:
table & chairs

Pets:
not accepted

AR2 – Accommodation – Chalet

Sleeping:
sleeps 4

Living:
living/kitchen area, TV, heating, shower & WC

Eating:
fitted kitchen with cooking hobs, microwave & fridge-freezer

Outside:
table & chairs

Pets:
not accepted

Weekly Charges	AR1	AR2
Low Season (from)	€ 344	€ 275
High Season (from)	€ 504	€ 353

FR86090 Camping du Parc de Saint Cyr

F-86130 St Cyr (Vienne)

For our full description of this campsite ▶ see page 174

A good modern site and a good place to relax.

AR1 – IRM – Mobile Home

Sleeping:
sleeps 4-6

Living:
living room

Eating:
fitted kitchen with oven

Outside:
table & chairs

Pets:
accepted

AR2 – WILLERBY – Mobile Home

Sleeping:
sleeps 4-6

Living:
living room

Eating:
fitted kitchen with oven

Outside:
table & chairs

Pets:
accepted

Weekly Charges	AR1	AR2
Low Season (from)	€ 290	€ 290
High Season (from)	€ 510	€ 510

FR58010 Camping des Bains

15 avenue Jean Mermoz, F-58360 St Honoré-les-Bains (Nièvre)

For our full description of this campsite ▶ see page 179

Gîtes are situated on the edge of the site in groups of two, three or four, separated from each other by hedges.

AR1 – Accommodation – Gîte

Sleeping:
2 bedrooms, sleeps 4: 1 double, 1 twin with 2 bunk beds; pillows & blankets provided

Living:
living/kitchen area, fan, heating, shower & WC

Eating:
fitted kitchen with cooking hobs, oven & fridge

Outside:
table & chairs, parasol

Pets:
accepted

Weekly Charges	
	AR1
Low Season (from)	€ 150
High Season (from)	€ 485

FR71020 Le Village des Meuniers

F-71520 Dompierre-les-Ormes (Saône-et-Loire)

For our full description of this campsite ▶ see page 182

Most of the 12 chalets/gîtes enjoy stunning views of the surrounding countryside - The Beaujolais, the Maconnais, the Charollais and the Clunysois.

AR1 – FRENE – Chalet

Sleeping:
3 bedrooms, sleeps 8: 1 double, 2 twin with 2 single beds, 1 double sofa bed; pillows & blankets provided

Living:
living/kitchen area, heating, shower & WC, TV, sofa

Eating:
fitted kitchen with cooking hobs, microwave & fridge

Outside:
table & chairs

Pets:
accepted

Weekly Charges	
	AR1
Low Season (from)	€ 260
High Season (from)	€ 560

Mobile homes & chalets

423

FR73030 Camping Les Lanchettes

F-73210 Peisey-Nancroix (Savoie)

For our full description of this campsite ▶ see page 201

AR1 – Accommodation – Chalet

Sleeping:
2 bedrooms, sleeps 4-5: 1 double bed, 1 twin with 2 single beds & a bunk bed

Living:
living/kitchen area shower & WC

Eating:
dishwasher, oven, fridge-freezer, cooking hobs

Outside:
table & chairs, parasol

Pets:
not accepted

AR2 – CHARLAY-BALLARIO – Chalet

Sleeping:
2 bedrooms, sleeps 4-6: 1double bed, 4 single beds

Living:
living/kitchen area, shower & WC

Eating:
fitted kitchen with dishwasher, oven, fridge-freezer & cooking hobs

Outside:
table & chairs, parasol

Pets:
not accepted

Weekly Charges	AR1	AR2
Low Season (from)	€ 250	€ 250
High Season (from)	€ 650	€ 650

FR33110 Airotel Camping de la Côte d'Argent

F-33990 Hourtin-Plage (Gironde)

For our full description of this campsite ▶ see page 214

Mobile homes are situated in the centre of the site, amongst the pine trees.

AR1 – LOUISIANE – Mobile Home

Sleeping:
2 bedrooms, sleeps 6: 1 double, 1 twin with 2 single beds, 1 double sofa bed; pillows & blankets provided

Living:
living/kitchen area, shower & WC

Eating:
fitted kitchen with cooking hobs & fridge

Outside:
picnic table & chairs, parasol

Pets:
not accepted

AR2 – O'HARA – Mobile Home

Sleeping:
2 bedrooms, sleeps 6: 1 double, 1 twin with 2 single beds, 1 double sofa bed; pillows & blankets provided

Living:
living/kitchen area, shower & WC

Eating:
fitted kitchen with cooking hobs & fridge

Outside:
picnic table & chairs, parasol

Pets:
not accepted

Weekly Charges	AR1	AR2
Low Season (from)	€ 399	€ 399
High Season (from)	€ 833	€ 833

FR40100 Camping du Domaine de la Rive

Route de Bordeaux, F-40600 Biscarosse (Landes)

For our full description of this campsite ▶ see page 224

AR1 – SAVANAH – Mobile Home

Sleeping:
2 bedrooms, sleeps 6: 1 double, 1 twin with 2 single beds, 1 double sofa bed; pillows & blankets provided

Living:
dining corner convertible into double bed, shower & WC

Eating:
fitted kitchen with cooking hobs & fridge, microwave

Outside:
table & chairs, parasol

Pets:
not accepted

AR2 – COTTAGE 3 – Mobile Home

Sleeping:
3 bedrooms, sleeps 6: 1 double, 4 single beds

Living:
living/kitchen area, shower & WC

Eating:
fitted kitchen with cooking hobs & fridge, microwave

Outside:
table & chairs

Pets:
not accepted

Weekly Charges	AR1	AR2
Low Season *(from)*	€ 329	€ 343
High Season *(from)*	€ 882	€ 917

FR40140 Camping Caravaning Lou P'tit Poun

110 avenue du Quartier Neuf, F-40390 St Martin de Seignanx (Landes)

For our full description of this campsite ▶ see page 229

Excellent locations within this beautiful, quiet campsite, ideal for a quiet holiday and close to Biarritz and the ocean.

AR1 – FABRE RÊVE – Chalet

Sleeping:
2 bedrooms, sleeps 5: 1 double, 1 twin with 2 single beds, 1 single bed,

Living:
living/kitchen area, shower & WC

Eating:
fitted kitchen with cooking hobs, & fridge

Outside:
table & chairs, sun loungers

Pets:
not accepted

AR2 – IRM MERCURE – Mobile Home

Sleeping:
2 bedrooms, sleeps 5: 1 double, 1 twin with 2 single beds, 1 single sofa bed

Living:
living/kitchen area, shower & WC

Eating:
fitted kitchen with cooking hobs & fridge

Outside:
table & chairs, sun loungers

Pets:
not accepted

Weekly Charges	AR1	AR2
Low Season *(from)*	€ 270	€ 260
High Season *(from)*	€ 690	€ 670

425

FR33300 Domaine Residentiel Naturiste La Jenny

F-33680 Le Porge (Gironde)

Pitches at this campsite are exclusively for chalet accommodation.

Situated at the heart of Europe's largest forest, yet within walking distance of the Atlantic beaches through the forest, La Jenny is a naturist site providing high quality chalets. There are 750 in total of which 600 are privately owned (many let on behalf of their owners) and 150 let by the site. This is an ideal spot for a quiet and peaceful holiday, yet with a great deal on offer for those seeking a more lively holiday. With four pools covering an area of 1,000 sq m, a wide range of sports amenities, including golf, tennis and archery, there is always something to do. There are many activities for children, including a special club in high season, as well as an extensive programme of evening entertainment. The site's 127 hectares stretches along 3 km. of shoreline.

Facilities

Supermarket, boulangerie and fish shop. Launderette. Restaurant and pizzeria. Bar and brasserie. Heated pool complex. Hairdresser. Newsagent. Body care centre. Fitness centre. Sauna. Yoga and aqua gym. Pony club. Tennis (10 full courts, 8 half-courts) with lessons. Short golf course with lessons and clubhouse. Archery. Bicycle hire. Pony club. Diving and instruction courses. Boomerang course. Fully fenced, staffed and gated play area (over 3 yrs).
Off site: Fishing and watersports 300 m. Riding 4 km.

Open

20 May - 9 September.

Directions

From the Bordeaux ring road take exit 8 signed Lacanau. Follow D107 to Lacanau via Le Temple and La Porge, then towards Lege/Cap Ferret on the D3 to La Jenny (on the right).

Reservations

Contact site. Tel: 05 56 26 56 90.
Email: info@lajenny.fr

AR1 – LOUISIANE – Chalet

Sleeping:

3 bedrooms, sleeps 8: 2 double, 2 bunk beds, 1 double sofa bed

Living:

living/kitchen area, shower & WC

Eating:

fitted kitchen with cooking hobs, oven, dishwasher & fridge

Outside:

table & chairs

Pets:

accepted (€ 28 per week)

AR2 – TOURTERELLE – Chalet

Sleeping:

1 bedroom, sleeps 6: 1 double, 2 single beds on mezzanine, 1 double sofa bed

Living:

living/kitchen area, shower & WC

Eating:

fitted kitchen with cooking hobs & fridge

Outside:

table & chairs

Pets:

accepted (€ 28 per week)

Weekly Charges

	AR1	AR2
Low Season *(from)*	€ 787	€ 525
High Season *(from)*	€ 1300	€ 800

FR40160 Camping Les Vignes

Route de la Plage du Cap de L'Homy, F-40170 Lit-et-Mixe (Landes)

For our full description of this campsite ● see page 230

The mobile homes and chalets have been arranged around the edge of the site.

AR1 – GITOTEL S3 – Chalet

Sleeping:
3 bedrooms, sleeps 5: 1 double, 1 single bed, 2 sofa beds,

Living:
living/kitchen area, heating, shower & WC

Eating:
fitted kitchen with cooking hobs, microwave & fridge

Outside:
table & chairs, sun loungers

Pets:
not accepted

AR2 – SELECTION – Mobile Home

Sleeping:
2 bedrooms, sleeps 4: 1 double, 1 twin with 2 single beds

Living:
living/kitchen area, shower & WC

Eating:
fitted kitchen with cooking hobs, microwave & fridge

Outside:
table & chairs, sun loungers

Pets:
not accepted

Weekly Charges

	AR1	AR2
Low Season *(from)*	€ 235	€ 235
High Season *(from)*	€ 798	€ 798

FR40180 Camping Le Vieux Port

Plage sud, F-40660 Messanges (Landes)

For our full description of this campsite ● see page 231

Mobile homes and chalets are dispersed around this site on large, shady pitches.

AR1 – Accommodation – Mobile Home

Sleeping:
2 bedrooms, sleeps 4: 1 double, 1 twin with 2 single beds; pillows & blankets provided

Living:
living/kitchen area, heating, shower & WC

Eating:
fitted kitchen with cooking hobs, oven, grill & fridge

Outside:
table & chairs, parasol

Pets:
not accepted

AR2 – Accommodation – Chalet

Sleeping:
3 bedrooms, sleeps 6: 2 double rooms, 1 twin with 2 single beds; pillows & blankets provided

Living:
living/kitchen area, heating, shower & WC

Eating:
fitted kitchen with cooking hobs, oven, toaster, grill & fridge-freezer

Outside:
covered terrace with table & chairs, sun loungers & parasol

Pets:
not accepted

Weekly Charges

	AR1	AR2
Low Season *(from)*	€ 265	€ 385
High Season *(from)*	€ 600	€ 900

427

FR40190 Le Saint Martin Airotel Camping

Avenue de l'Océan, F-40660 Moliets-Plage (Landes)

For our full description of this campsite ▶ see page 232

The chalets are attractively grouped on pitches separated by hedges, and surrounded by a variety of plane, pine and mulberry trees.

AR1 – COTTAGE – Chalet

Sleeping:
3 bedrooms, sleeps 6: sheets provided,

Living:
living/kitchen area, tables & chairs

Eating:
fitted kitchen with cooking hobs, fridge & dishwasher

Outside:
terrace, table & chairs

Pets:
accepted

AR2 – CLUB – Chalet

Sleeping:
2 bedrooms; sleeps 5; sheets provided

Living:
living/kitchen area, tables & chairs

Eating:
fitted kitchen with cooking hobs & fridge, microwave, electric coffee pot

Outside:
terrace, table & chairs

Pets:
accepted

Weekly Charges	AR1	AR2
Low Season *(from)*	€ 465	€ 330
High Season *(from)*	€ 1000	€ 890

FR64110 Camping du Col d'Ibardin

F-64122 Urrugne (Pyrénées-Atlantiques)

For our full description of this campsite ▶ see page 237

AR1 – O'HARA – Mobile Home

Sleeping:
2 bedrooms, sleeps 5: 1 double, 1 twin with 2 single beds, 1 single sofa bed; pillows & blankets provided

Living:
living/kitchen area, heating, shower & WC

Eating:
fitted kitchen with cooking hobs, microwave & fridge

Outside:
table & chairs, parasol

Pets:
not accepted

AR2 – WILLERBY – Mobile Home

Sleeping:
2 bedrooms, sleeps 5: 1 double, 1 twin with 2 single beds, 1 single sofa bed; pillows & blankets provided

Living:
living/kitchen area, heating, shower & WC

Eating:
fitted kitchen with cooking hobs & fridge

Outside:
table & chairs, parasol

Pets:
not accepted

Weekly Charges	AR1	AR2
Low Season *(from)*	€ 215	€ 195
High Season *(from)*	€ 550	€ 520

FR64140 Sunêlia Berrua

Rue Berrua, F-64210 Bidart (Pyrénées-Atlantiques)

For our full description of this campsite ▶ see page 236

Excellent locations within this beautiful family campsite, close to the beach and Pyrenees, and with a new swimming pool complex.

AR1 – CONFORT – Mobile Home	**AR2 – RÊVE – Chalet**
Sleeping:	**Sleeping:**
2 bedrooms, sleeps 6: 1 double, 1 twin with 2 single beds, 1 double sofa bed,	2 bedrooms, sleeps 6: 1 double, 1 twin with 2 single beds, 1 sofa bed,
Living:	**Living:**
living/kitchen area, heating, shower & WC	living/kitchen area, shower & WC
Eating:	**Eating:**
fitted kitchen with cooking hobs & fridge	fitted kitchen with cooking hobs & fridge
Outside:	**Outside:**
table & chairs, parasol	table & chairs, sun loungers
Pets:	**Pets:**
accepted (max. 6 kg)	accepted (max 6 kg.)

Weekly Charges	AR1	AR2
Low Season *(from)*	€ 392	€ 434
High Season *(from)*	€ 840	€ 882

FR12010 Castel Camping Le Val de Cantobre

F-12230 Nant-d'Aveyron (Aveyron)

For our full description of this campsite ▶ see page 239

AR1 – ABI – Mobile Home	**AR2 – FABRE 2012 – Chalet**
Sleeping:	**Sleeping:**
2 bedrooms, sleeps 4: 1 double, 1 twin with 2 single beds; blankets & pillows provided	2 bedrooms, sleeps 5: 1 double 1 single with 2 bunk beds; blankets & pillows provided
Living:	**Living:**
living/kitchen area, shower & WC	living/kitchen area, shower & WC
Eating:	**Eating:**
fitted kitchen with cooking hobs	fitted kitchen with cooking hobs, fridge, microwave
Outside:	**Outside:**
table & chairs, sun loungers, parasol & BBQ	table & chairs, sun loungers, parasol & BBQ
Pets:	**Pets:**
accepted	accepted

Weekly Charges	AR1	AR2
Low Season *(from)*	€ 259	€ 329
High Season *(from)*	€ 630	€ 798

FR12180 Le Hameau Saint Martial

Rue de la Calquière, F-12240 Rieupeyroux (Aveyron)

Pitches at this site are exclusively for chalets.

Le Hameau Saint Martial is a development lying on the edge of the pretty village of Rieupeyroux, capital of the Haut Ségala region. Originally the village was developed around a Benedictine monastery, but is now at the heart of a popular area for walking and cycling. The 47 chalets can each accommodate up to 5 people and are very attractively situated on large grassy pitches surrounded by flowering shrubs and hedges, some having views over the small lake or the surrounding countryside. Parking is away from the chalets, ensuring a safe pleasant, relaxed ambience. St Martial offers a number of good leisure facilities including a swimming pool, paddling pool, children's playground and volleyball court, and is situated alongside a small lake, suitable for fishing.

Facilities

Attractive bar (from mid june) with terrace overlooking pools. Laundry. Swimming pool and children's pool. Volleyball. Badminton. Play area. Fishing. Some family activities organised in July and August. English is spoken. Off site: Horse riding and bicycle hire (5 km). Rieupeyroux (various shops and restaurants). Discover the beautiful valley of the River Aveyron and the interesting ancient villages with their markets and châteaux.

Open

All year.

Directions

The site is just south of Rieupeyroux and on the D911 between Villefranche de Rouergue and Baraqueville. In the centre of Rieupeyroux turn south and follow signs Village Vacances. Descend to the entrance in a few hundred metres.

Reservations

Contact site Tel: 05 65 65 81 81.
Email: info@les-hameaux.fr

AR1 – RÊVE – Chalet

Sleeping:
2 bedrooms, sleeps 5: 1 double, 3 single beds

Living:
living/kitchen area, heating, shower & WC

Eating:
fitted kitchen with cooking hobs, microwave & fridge-freezer

Outside:
table & chairs

Pets:
accepted (€ 25 per week, I per unit)

AR2 – DÉTENTE – Chalet

Sleeping:
2 bedrooms, sleeps 5: 1 double, 3 single beds

Living:
living/kitchen area, heating, shower & WC

Eating:
fitted kitchen with cooking hobs, microwave & fridge-freezer

Outside:
table & chairs

Pets:
accepted (€ 25 per week, I per unit)

Weekly Charges

	AR1	AR2
Low Season (from)	€ 195	€ 195
High Season (from)	€ 530	€ 540

FR12020 Camping Caravaning Les Rivages

Avenue de l'Aigoual, Route de Nant, F-12100 Millau (Aveyron)

For our full description of this campsite ● see page 243

The IRM mobile homes are situated in a spacious area on the edge of the site and the O'Hara mobile homes are situated in a central area of the site. Both enjoy views of the cliffs and hills.

AR1 – IRM – Mobile Home

Sleeping:
2 bedrooms, sleeps 4: 1 double, 1 twin with 2 single beds; pillows & blankets provided

Living:
living/kitchen area, heating, shower & WC

Eating:
fitted kitchen with cooking hobs & fridge

Outside:
table & chairs, sun loungers & parasol

Pets:
accepted

AR2 – O'HARA – Mobile Home

Sleeping:
2 bedrooms, sleeps 4: 1 double, 1 twin with 2 single beds; pillows & blankets provided

Living:
living/kitchen area, heating, shower & WC

Eating:
fitted kitchen with cooking hobs, microwave & fridge

Outside:
table & chairs, sun loungers & parasol

Pets:
accepted

Weekly Charges	AR1	AR2
Low Season *(from)*	€ 318	€ 336
High Season *(from)*	€ 550	€ 580

FR12150 Camping Marmotel

F-12130 St Geniez-d'Olt (Aveyron)

For our full description of this campsite ● see page 246

AR1 – LOUISIANE – Mobile Home

Sleeping:
2 bedrooms, sleeps 5-6: 1 double, 1 twin with 2 single beds, 1 single bunk (for children 6-12 years), 1 double sofa bed; pillows & blankets provided

Living:
living/kitchen area, TV, heating, shower & WC

Eating:
fitted kitchen with cooking hobs, microwave & fridge

Outside:
table & chairs, sun loungers, parasol & BBQ

Pets:
accepted (low season only)

AR2 – FABRE – Chalet

Sleeping:
2 bedrooms, sleeps 2-4, 1 twin with 2 single beds, 1 single bunk (for children aged 6-12 years), 1 double sofa bed; pillows & blankets provided

Living:
living/kitchen area, TV, heating, shower & WC

Eating:
fitted kitchen with cooking hobs, microwave & fridge

Outside:
table & chairs, sun loungers, parasol & BBQ

Pets:
accepted (low season only)

Weekly Charges	AR1	AR2
Low Season *(from)*	€ 150	€ 200
High Season *(from)*	€ 624	€ 675

Mobile homes & chalets

FR12160 Camping Caravaning Les Peupliers

Route des Gorges du Tarn, F-12640 Rivière-sur-Tarn (Aveyron)

For our full description of this campsite ▶ see page 245

AR1 – Accommodation – Mobile Home

Sleeping:

2 bedrooms, sleeps 4: 1 double, 1 twin with 2 single beds

Living:

living/kitchen area shower & WC

Eating:

fitted kitchen with microwave, fridge

Outside:

wood terrace, table & chairs

Pets:

accepted

Weekly Charges	
	AR1
Low Season (from)	€ 250
High Season (from)	€ 550

FR24010 Castel Camping Château Le Verdoyer

Champs Romain, F-24470 St Pardoux (Dordogne)

For our full description of this campsite ▶ see page 251

AR1 – ATLAS – Mobile Home

Sleeping:

2 bedrooms, sleeps 6: 1 double, 1 twin with 2 single beds, 1 double sofa bed; pillows & blankets provided

Living:

living/kitchen area, heating, shower & WC

Eating:

fitted kitchen with cooking hobs, microwave & fridge

Outside:

table & chairs, sun loungers & parasol

Pets:

not accepted

AR2 – BÜRSTNER – Mobile Home

Sleeping:

2 bedrooms, sleeps 7: 1 double, 1 twin with 2 single beds, 1 bunk bed, 1 double sofa bed; pillows & blankets provided

Living:

living/kitchen area, heating, shower & WC

Eating:

fitted kitchen with cooking hobs, microwave & fridge

Outside:

table & chairs, sun loungers & parasol

Pets:

not accepted

Weekly Charges		
	AR1	**AR2**
Low Season (from)	€ 270	€ 270
High Season (from)	€ 630	€ 630

FR24080 Camping Caravaning Le Moulin de David

Gaugeac, F-24540 Monpazier (Dordogne)

For our full description of this campsite ▶ see page 255

AR1 – BLUE BIRD – Mobile Home

Sleeping:
2 bedrooms, sleeps 6: 1 double, 1 twin with 2 single beds, 1 double sofa bed; pillows & blankets provided

Living:
living/kitchen area, shower & WC

Eating:
fitted kitchen with cooking hobs, microwave & fridge

Outside:
table & chairs, sun loungers

Pets:
accepted

AR2 – PARADIS' – Mobile Home

Sleeping:
2 bedrooms, sleeps 6: 1 double, 1 twin with 2 single beds, 1 double sofa bed; pillows & blankets provided

Living:
living/kitchen area, shower & WC

Eating:
fitted kitchen with cooking hobs, microwave & fridge-freezer

Outside:
sun loungers & parasol

Pets:
accepted

Weekly Charges	AR1	AR2
Low Season *(from)*	€ 280	€ 308
High Season *(from)*	€ 650	€ 709

FR24090 Camping Soleil Plage

Caudon par Montfort, Vitrac, F-24200 Sarlat (Dordogne)

For our full description of this campsite ▶ see page 254

Excellent locations within this popular riverside site. Alternative models are also available.

AR1 – RÊVE – Chalet

Sleeping:
2 bedrooms, sleeps 5-7: 1 double & 3 single beds, 1 double sofa bed; blankets provided

Living:
living/kitchen area, TV, shower & WC

Eating:
fitted kitchen with cooking hobs & fridge

Outside:
table & chairs, sun loungers, parasol & BBQ, covered terrace

Pets:
accepted (€ 2.50 per day)

AR2 – SUPER MERCURE – Mobile Home

Sleeping:
2 bedrooms, sleeps 4-6: 1 double, 2 single beds, 1 sofa bed; blankets & pillows provided

Living:
living/kitchen area, shower & WC

Eating:
fitted kitchen with cooking hobs & fridge

Outside:
table & chairs, sun loungers, parasol & BBQ

Pets:
accepted (€ 2.50 per day)

Weekly Charges	AR1	AR2
Low Season *(from)*	€ 280	€ 250
High Season *(from)*	€ 690	€ 660

FR24310 Camping Caravaning La Bouquerie

F-24590 St Geniès-en-Périgord (Dordogne)

For our full description of this campsite ▶ see page 262

The mobile homes and chalets are settled on individually marked off pitches, in the shade or sun.

AR1 – MOREA – Chalet	**AR2 – O'HARA – Mobile Home**
Sleeping:	Sleeping:
2 bderooms, sleeps 5: 1 double, 1 single with bunk bed; blankets & pillows provided	2 bedrooms, sleeps 4-5: 1 double, 1 twin, 1 sofa bed; blankets & pillows provided
Living:	Living:
living/kitchen area, heating, shower & WC	living/kitchen area, heating, shower & WC
Eating:	Eating:
fitted kitchen with cooking hobs & fridge	fitted kitchen with hobs & fridge
Outside:	Outside:
table & chairs, sun loungers & BBQ	table & chairs, sun lounger, BBQ
Pets:	Pets:
accepted	accepted

Weekly Charges	AR1	AR2
Low Season *(from)*	€ 260	€ 250
High Season *(from)*	€ 690	€ 680

FR24320 Camping Les Peneyrals

Le Poujol, F-24590 St Crépin-Carlucet (Dordogne)

For our full description of this campsite ▶ see page 263

AR1 – ENEA – Mobile Home	**AR2 – RÊVE CONFORT – Chalet**
Sleeping:	Sleeping:
2 bedrooms, sleeps 6: 1 double, 1 twin with 2 single beds, sofa	2 bedrooms, sleeps 7: 1 double, bedroom with 3 single beds
Living:	Living:
living/kitchen area, shower & W/C	living/kitchen area, shower & WC
Eating:	Eating:
fitted kitchen with cooking hobs, fridge	fitted kitchen with cooking hobs & fridge
Outside:	Outside:
table & chairs, 2 sun loungers	garden furniture, table, 7 chairs & 2 sun loungers
Pets:	Pets:
accepted	accepted

Weekly Charges	AR1	AR2
Low Season *(from)*	€ 230	€ 330
High Season *(from)*	€ 690	€ 750

FR46010 Castel Camping Le Domaine de la Paille Basse
F-46200 Souillac-sur-Dordogne (Lot)

For our full description of this campsite ▶ see page 267

The mobile homes are situated in calm surroundings 300m from the centre of the site.

AR1 – OAKLEY LOUISIANE – Mobile Home

Sleeping:
2 bedrooms, sleeps 5: 1 double, 1 twin with 2 single beds & 3rd child bed

Living:
living/kitchen area, shower & WC

Eating:
fitted kitchen with cooking hobs, microwave & fridge

Outside:
table & chairs, BBQ

Pets:
not accepted

AR2 – ZEN LOUISIANE – Mobile Home

Sleeping:
3 bedrooms, sleeps 6: 1 double, 2 single beds, 2 bunk beds; bed linen provided

Living:
living/kitchen area, heating, cd player, shower & WC

Eating:
fitted kitchen with cooking hobs & fridge

Outside:
table & chairs, BBQ

Pets:
not accepted

Weekly Charges

	AR1	AR2
Low Season (from)	€ 265	€ 285
High Season (from)	€ 695	€ 795

FR47010 Camping Caravaning Moulin du Périé
F-47500 Sauveterre-la-Lemance (Lot-et-Garonne)

For our full description of this campsite ▶ see page 271

The mobile homes are situated in a quiet area on the edge of the site and the chalets are on the edge of a stream in a private and sunny setting.

AR1 – IRM SUPER MERCURE – Mobile Home

Sleeping:
2 bedrooms, sleeps 6: 2 double, 1 twin with 2 single beds; pillows & blankets provided

Living:
living/kitchen area, heating, shower & WC

Eating:
fitted kitchen with cooking hobs & fridge

Outside:
table & chairs, parasol

Pets:
not accepted

AR2 – HAVITAT RÊVE – Chalet

Sleeping:
2 bedrooms, sleeps 7: 2 double, 1 twin with 2 single beds, 1 bunk bed; pillows & blankets provided

Living:
living/kitchen area, heating, shower & WC

Eating:
fitted kitchen with cooking hobs & fridge

Outside:
table & chairs, parasol

Pets:
not accepted

Weekly Charges

	AR1	AR2
Low Season (from)	€ 330	€ 370
High Season (from)	€ 640	€ 690

Mobile homes & chalets

FR23010 Castel Camping Le Château de Poinsouze

Route de la Châtre, B.P. 12, F-23600 Boussac-Bourg (Creuse)

For our full description of this campsite ▶ see page 279

The mobile homes and chalets are grouped together in a quiet area of the campsite on the edge of the touring area, some facing the lake and Château. Very large pitches.

AR1 – BÜRSTNER NATUR'HOME – Mobile Home	**AR2 – SHELBOX COUNTRY LODGE – Chalet**
Sleeping:	Sleeping:
2 bedrooms, sleeps 5: 1 double, 1 twin with 2 single beds, 1 sofa bed; pillows & blankets provided	2 bedrooms, sleeps 5: 1 double, 2 twin with 2 single beds, sofa bed; pillows & blankets provided
Living:	Living:
living/kitchen area, heating, shower & WC	living/kitchen area, heating, shower & WC
Eating:	Eating:
fitted kitchen with cooking hobs, microwave & fridge-freezer	fitted kitchen with cooking hobs, microwave & fridge-freezer
Outside:	Outside:
table & chairs, sun loungers, parasol & BBQ	table & chairs, sun loungers, parasol & BBQ
Pets:	Pets:
not accepted	not accepted

Weekly Charges	AR1	AR2
Low Season *(from)*	€ 220	€ 285
High Season *(from)*	€ 520	€ 630

FR63030 Camping Caravaning de l'Europe

Route de Jassal, F-63790 Murol (Puy-de-Dôme)

For our full description of this campsite ▶ see page 283

Attractive locations within this family site in the 'Parc des Volcans d'Auvergne'.

AR1 – IRM – Mobile Home	**AR2 – IRM – Mobile Home**
Sleeping:	Sleeping:
2 bedrooms, sleeps 5: 1 double, 1 twin with 2 single beds, sofa bed	2 bedrooms, sleeps 4: 1 double, 1 twin with 2 single beds,
Living:	Living:
living/kitchen area, heating, shower & WC	living/kitchen area, heating, shower & WC
Eating:	Eating:
fitted kitchen with cooking hobs & fridge, microwave	fitted kitchen with cooking hobs & fridge, microwave
Outside:	Outside:
table & chairs, parasol	table & chairs, parasol
Pets:	Pets:
accepted (under 10 kg)	accepted (max 10 kg.)

Weekly Charges	AR1	AR2
Low Season *(from)*	€ 240	€ 220
High Season *(from)*	€ 710	€ 690

FR07120 Camping Nature Parc L'Ardéchois

Route touristique des Gorges, F-07150 Vallon-Pont-d`Arc (Ardèche)

For our full description of this campsite ▶ see page 292

The mobile homes are located between the swimming pool and the river, about 150 m. from the shop, bar and restaurant, in a particularly quiet part of the site. Each mobile home has a large, private pitch, and all are equipped with shaded terraces.

AR1 – LOUISIANE OAKLEY – Mobile Home

Sleeping:
2 bedrooms, sleeps 5: 1 double, 1 twin with 2 single beds, 1 bunk bed; pillows & blankets provided

Living:
living/kitchen area, heating, shower & WC

Eating:
fitted kitchen with cooking hobs & fridge

Outside:
table & chairs, sun loungers, parasol

Pets:
accepted (low season only)

AR2 – LOUISIANE PACIFIQUE – Mobile Home

Sleeping:
2 bedrooms, sleeps 5: 1 double, 1 twin with 2 single beds, 1 bunk bed; pillows & blankets provided

Living:
living/kitchen area, heating, shower & WC

Eating:
fitted kitchen with cooking hobs & fridge-freezer

Outside:
table & chairs, sun loungers & parasol

Pets:
accepted (low season only)

Weekly Charges	AR1	AR2
Low Season *(from)*	€ 360	€ 360
High Season *(from)*	€ 790	€ 790

FR07150 Camping Domaine de Gil

Route de Vals-les-Bains, Ucel, F-07200 Aubenas (Ardèche)

For our full description of this campsite ▶ see page 298

AR1 – IRM – Mobile Home

Sleeping:
2 bedrooms, sleeps 4-5: blankets & pillows provided

Living:
living/kitchen area, shower & WC

Eating:
fitted kitchen with cooking hobs & fridge

Outside:
terrace & garden furniture

Pets:
accepted

AR2 – IRM – Mobile Home

Sleeping:
2 bedrooms, sleeps 4-7: blankets, pillows & sheets provided

Living:
living/kitchen area, shower & WC

Eating:
fitted kitchen with cooking hobs & fridge

Outside:
terrace, garden furniture, 2 sun loungers

Pets:
accepted

Weekly Charges	AR1	AR2
Low Season *(from)*	€ 217	€ 266
High Season *(from)*	€ 595	€ 705

FR26120 Gervanne Camping

Bellevue, F-26400 Mirabel et Blacons (Drôme)

For our full description of this campsite ▶ see page 303

AR1 – O'HARA – Mobile Home

Sleeping:
2 bedrooms, sleeps 4: 1 double, 1 twin with 2 single beds; pillows & blankets provided

Living:
living/kitchen area, heating, shower & WC

Eating:
fitted kitchen with cooking hobs, oven & fridge

Outside:
table & chairs, parasol

Pets:
not accepted

AR2 – RÊVE – Chalet

Sleeping:
2 bedrooms, sleeps 6: 1 double, 1 twin with 2 single beds, 1 double sofa bed; pillows & blankets provided

Living:
living/kitchen area, heating, shower & WC

Eating:
fitted kitchen with cooking hobs, oven & fridge

Outside:
table & chairs, parasol

Pets:
not accepted

Weekly Charges	AR1	AR2
Low Season (from)	€ 250	€ 260
High Season (from)	€ 540	€ 580

FR04010 Sunêlia Hippocampe

Route de Napoléon, F-04290 Volonne (Alpes-de Haute-Provence)

For our full description of this campsite ▶ see page 311

Most mobile homes are situated away from the entrance and activities, though not far from the swimming pool. Some are attractively located near to the lake with good views.

AR1 – WATIPI COTTAGE/SUNÊLIA FAMILY – Mobile Home

Sleeping:
3 bedrooms, sleeps 6: 1 double, 2 twin with 2 single beds; pillows & blankets provided

Living:
living/kitchen area, heating, shower & WC (air conditioning on request)

Eating:
fitted kitchen with cooking hobs, microwave & fridge-freezer

Outside:
table & chairs, sun loungers & parasol

Pets:
accepted

AR2 – IRM – Mobile Home

Sleeping:
2 bedrooms, sleeps 4: 1 double, 1 twin with 2 single beds; pillows & blankets provided

Living:
living/kitchen area, heating, shower & WC

Eating:
fitted kitchen with cooking hobs & fridge

Outside:
table & chairs, parasol, sun loungers

Pets:
accepted

Weekly Charges	AR1	AR2
Low Season (from)	€ 273	€ 184
High Season (from)	€ 973	€ 756

FR04020 Castel Camping Le Camp du Verdon

Domaine du Verdon, F-04120 Castellane (Alpes-de Haute-Provence)

For our full description of this campsite ▶ see page 308

AR1 – WATIPI – Mobile Home

Sleeping:
2 bedrooms, sleeps 4: 1 double, 1 twin with 2 single beds; pillows & blankets provided

Living:
living/kitchen area, heating, shower & WC

Eating:
fitted kitchen with cooking hobs & fridge

Outside:
table & chairs, sun loungers

Pets:
accepted

AR2 – TITOM – Chalet

Sleeping:
2 bedrooms, sleeps 6: 1 double, 1 twin with 2 single beds, 2 bunk beds; pillows & blankets provided

Living:
living/kitchen area, heating, shower & WC

Eating:
fitted kitchen with cooking hobs & fridge

Outside:
table & chairs, sun loungers

Pets:
accepted

Weekly Charges

	AR1	AR2
Low Season (from)	€ 336	€ 364
High Season (from)	€ 630	€ 665

FR04100 Camping International

Route Napoleon, F-04120 Castellane (Alpes-de Haute-Provence)

For our full description of this campsite ▶ see page 308

AR1 – SHELBOX – Mobile Home

Sleeping:
2 bedrooms, sleeps 5: 1 double, 2 bunk beds, 1 single bed; pillows & blankets provided

Living:
living/kitchen area, heating, shower & WC

Eating:
fitted kitchen with cooking hobs, microwave & fridge-freezer

Outside:
table & chairs, sun loungers

Pets:
accepted

Weekly Charges

	AR1
Low Season (from)	€ 190
High Season (from)	€ 620

Mobile homes & chalets

(439)

FR84020 Domaine Naturiste de Bélézy
F-84410 Bédoin (Vaucluse)

For our full description of this campsite ▶ see page 318

The mobile homes have large, quiet pitches and each have a terrace and pergola. The wooden chalets are close to the swimming pool and the children's activity zone.

AR1 – IRM – Mobile Home

Sleeping:
2 bedrooms, sleeps 5: 1 double, 1 twin with 2 single beds, 1 single sofa bed,

Living:
large living/kitchen area, shower & WC, electric heating

Eating:
fitted kitchen with cooking hobs, microwave & fridge-freezer

Outside:
teak table & chairs, sun loungers

Pets:
not accepted

AR2 – FABRE – Chalet

Sleeping:
2 bedrooms, sleeps 5: 1 double, 2 single beds, 1 bunk bed

Living:
living/kitchen/dining area, shower & WC, heating

Eating:
fitted kitchen with cooking hobs & fridge-freezer

Outside:
teak table & chairs, sun loungers

Pets:
not accepted

Weekly Charges		
	AR1	AR2
Low Season *(from)*	€ 350	€ 336
High Season *(from)*	€ 840	€ 714

FR09020 Camping L'Arize
Lieu-dit Bourtol, F-09240 La Bastide-de-Sérou (Ariège)

For our full description of this campsite ▶ see page 320

AR1 – WILLERBY – Mobile Home

Sleeping:
2 bedrooms, sleeps 6: 1 double, 1 twin with 2 single beds, 1 double sofa bed; pillows & blankets provided

Living:
living/kitchen area, heating, shower & WC

Eating:
fitted kitchen with cooking hobs & fridge

Outside:
table & chairs, parasol & BBQ

Pets:
accepted

AR2 – FABRE – Chalet

Sleeping:
3 bedrooms, sleeps 8: 1 double, 2 single beds, 2 bunk beds,1 double sofa bed; pillows & blankets provided

Living:
living/kitchen area, heating, shower & WC

Eating:
fitted kitchen with cooking hobs, microwave & fridge-freezer

Outside:
wooden terrace with table & chairs, parasol & BBQ

Pets:
accepted

Weekly Charges		
	AR1	AR2
Low Season *(from)*	€ 279	€ 326
High Season *(from)*	€ 639	€ 739

440

FR32010 Le Camp de Florence

Route Astaffort, F-32480 La Romieu (Gers)

For our full description of this campsite ▶ see page 323

Type 1: spacious village of 10 cottages, Type 2: very large pitches on edge of campsite with magnificent views.

AR1 – WILLERBY/IRM – Mobile Home

Sleeping:
2 bedrooms, sleeps 6: 1 double, 1 twin with 2 single beds, sofabed

Living:
sitting area

Eating:
sitting/dining area

Outside:
table & chairs, covered terrace

Pets:
accepted

AR2 – IRM – Deluxe Mobile Home

Sleeping:
2 bedrooms, sleeps 6: 1 double, 1 twin with 2 single beds, sofabed

Living:
sitting area

Eating:
separate dining room

Outside:
table & chairs, covered terrace

Pets:
accepted

Weekly Charges		
	AR1	AR2
Low Season *(from)*	€ 250	€ 270
High Season *(from)*	€ 685	€ 730

FR65090 Camping Soleil du Pibeste

16 avenue du Lavedan, F-65400 Agos Vidalos (Haute-Pyrénées)

For our full description of this campsite ▶ see page 329

AR1 – Accommodation – Mobile Home

Sleeping:
2 bedrooms, sleeps 5: 1 double, 1 twin with 2 single beds, 1 bunk bed; pillows & blankets provided

Living:
living/kitchen area, TV, heating, shower & WC

Eating:
fitted kitchen with cooking hobs, microwave & fridge-freezer

Outside:
table & chairs, sun loungers, parasol & BBQ

Pets:
accepted

AR2 – RONDINS DE BOIS – Chalet

Sleeping:
2 bedrooms, sleeps 4-5: 1 double, 2 single beds, 1 bunk bed; pillows & blankets provided

Living:
living/kitchen area, TV, heating, shower & WC

Eating:
fitted kitchen with cooking hobs, oven, microwave & fridge-freezer

Outside:
table & chairs, sun loungers, parasol & BBQ

Pets:
accepted

Weekly Charges		
	AR1	AR2
Low Season *(from)*	€ 300	€ 300
High Season *(from)*	€ 696	€ 696

441

FR81060 Camping Les Clots
F-81190 Mirandol-Bourgnounac (Tarn)

For our full description of this campsite ⊙ see page 332

Each chalet has its own exclusive area.

AR1 – G44 – Gîte

Sleeping:
sleeps 4-6

Living:
living/kitchen area, sofa bed

Eating:
fitted kitchen with cooking hobs, fridge, microwave & dishwasher

Outside:
2 tables & chairs, parasol, seat

Pets:
accepted

AR2 – H15 – Chalet

Sleeping:
sleeps 4

Living:
living/kitchen area

Eating:
fitted kitchen with cooking hobs & fridge

Outside:
table & chairs

Pets:
accepted

Weekly Charges	AR1	AR2
Low Season (from)	€ 413	€ 390
High Season (from)	€ 550	€ 490

FR11060 Yelloh! Village Domaine d'Arnauteille
F-11250 Montclar (Aude)

For our full description of this campsite ⊙ see page 335

Chalets are located in the southeast part of the site on top of a hill and the mobile homes are on a terrace above the swimming pool with good views.

AR1 – GRAND CONFORT – Chalet

Sleeping:
2 bedrooms, sleeps 6: 1 double, 1 bedroom with 3 single beds, 1 sofa bed; pillows & blankets provided

Living:
living/kitchen area, heating, shower & WC

Eating:
fitted kitchen with cooking hobs, microwave & fridge-freezer

Outside:
table & chairs, sun loungers & parasol

Pets:
accepted

AR2 – LOUISIANE – Mobile Home

Sleeping:
3 bedrooms, sleeps 6: 1 double, 2 twin with 2 single beds, 1 sofa bed, all bedding provided

Living:
living/kitchen area, heating, shower & WC

Eating:
fitted kitchen with cooking hobs, microwave & fridge-freezer

Outside:
table & chairs, sun loungers & parasol

Pets:
accepted

Weekly Charges	AR1	AR2
Low Season (from)	€ 329	€ 441
High Season (from)	€ 763	€ 889

FR11070 Camping Les Mimosas

Chaussée de Mandirac, F-11100 Narbonne (Aude)

For our full description of this campsite see page 337

AR1 – Accommodation – Mobile Home

Sleeping:
2 bedrooms, sleeps 4: 1 double, 2 single beds; pillows & blankets provided

Living:
living/kitchen area, shower & WC

Eating:
fitted kitchen with cooking hobs, coffee maker & fridge

Outside:
table & chairs, sun loungers

Pets:
accepted

AR2 – Accommodation – Mobile Home

Sleeping:
2 bedrooms, sleeps 6: 1 double, 2 single beds, sofa bed; pillows & blankets provided

Living:
living/kitchen area, shower & WC

Eating:
fitted kitchen with cooking hobs, coffee maker & fridge

Outside:
table & chairs, sun loungers

Pets:
accepted

Weekly Charges	AR1	AR2
Low Season *(from)*	€ 251	€ 265
High Season *(from)*	€ 549	€ 619

FR34070 Yelloh! Village Le Sérignan Plage

Le Sérignan Plage, F-34410 Sérignan (Hérault)

For our full description of this campsite see page 348

Chalets and mobile homes are located beside the beach or in shady areas. All accommodation is separated by hedges to provide privacy.

AR1 – COTTAGE – Mobile home

Sleeping:
2 bedrooms, sleeps 6: 1 double, 1 twin with 2 single beds, 1 sofa bed

Living:
living/kitchen area, heating, shower & WC

Eating:
fitted kitchen with cooking hobs & fridge

Outside:
terrace with table & chairs, sun loungers

Pets:
not accepted

AR2 – VIP – Mobile Home

Sleeping:
2 bedrooms, sleeps 5: 1 double, 1 twin with 2 single beds, 1 single sofa bed,

Living:
living/kitchen area, fan, heating, shower & WC

Eating:
fitted kitchen with cooking hobs & fridge

Outside:
terrace with table & chairs, sun loungers

Pets:
not accepted

Weekly Charges	AR1	AR2
Low Season *(from)*	€ 245	€ 273
High Season *(from)*	€ 742	€ 833

FR66070 Yelloh! Village Le Brasilia

B.P. 204, F-66141 Canet-en-Roussillon (Pyrénées-Orientales)

For our full description of this campsite ▶ see page 364

AR1 – LOUISIANE – Mobile home

Sleeping:
2 bedrooms, sleeps 5: 1 double, 1 twin with 2 single beds. 1 single sofa bed; pillows & blankets provided, linen on request.

Living:
living area/kitchen, heating, shower & WC

Eating:
fitted kitchen with cooking hobs, oven & fridge

Outside:
table & chairs, sun loungers & parasol

Pets:
accepted

AR2 – OKAVANGO – Mobile home

Sleeping:
3 bedrooms, sleeps 6: 1double, 2 twins, pillows & blankets provided, sheets available on request.

Living:
living area/kitchen heating, shower & WC

Eating:
fitted kitchen with cooking hobs, oven or microwave & fridge-freezer

Outside:
table & chairs, sun loungers & parasol

Pets:
accepted

Weekly Charges	AR1	AR2
Low Season *(from)*	€ 245	€ 273
High Season *(from)*	€ 889	€ 994

FR06080 Camping Caravaning Les Cigales

505 avenue de la mer, F-06210 Mandelieu-la-Napoule (Alpes-Maritimes)

For our full description of this campsite ▶ see page 373

AR1 – O'HARA – Mobile Home

Sleeping:
2 bedrooms, sleeps 6: 1 double, 1 twin with 2 single beds, 1 double sofa bed; pillows & blankets provided

Living:
living/kitchen area, heating, shower & WC

Eating:
fitted kitchen with cooking hobs & fridge-freezer

Outside:
table & chairs, parasol

Pets:
accepted (max 10 kg)

AR2 – ROLLER – Mobile Home

Sleeping:
2 bedrooms, sleeps 6: 1 double, 1 twin with 2 single beds; pillows & blankets provided

Living:
living/kitchen area, heating, shower & WC

Eating:
fitted kitchen with cooking hobs & fridge-freezer

Outside:
table & chairs, parasol

Pets:
accepted

Weekly Charges	AR1	AR2
Low Season *(from)*	€ 385	€ 340
High Season *(from)*	€ 680	€ 635

FR06120 Camping Green Park

159 Vallon des Vaux, F-06800 Cagnes-sur-Mer (Alpes-Maritimes)

For our full description of this campsite ▶ see page 375

AR1 – LE LOFT – Mobile Home

Sleeping:
2 bedrooms, sleeps 6: 1 double, 1 twin with 2 single beds, sofabed

Living:
living/kitchen area, shower & WC

Eating:
fitted kitchen with cooking hobs, microwave, fridge-freezer

Outside:
garden furniture

Pets:
not accepted

AR2 – CLUB 5 – Chalet

Sleeping:
2 bedrooms, sleeps 4-5: 1 double, 3 single beds including bunk bed

Living:
living/kitchen area, shower & WC

Eating:
fitted kitchen with cooking hobs, microwave & fridge

Outside:
covered terrace, garden furniture

Pets:
accepted

Weekly Charges		
	AR1	AR2
Low Season *(from)*	€ 329	€ 322
High Season *(from)*	€ 595	€ 582

FR83020 Castel Camping Caravaning Esterel

Avenue des Golf, F-83530 St Raphaël - Agay (Var)

For our full description of this campsite ▶ see page 382

The mobile homes have terraces and panoramic views of the Estérel.

AR1 – LA SUITE – Mobile Home

Sleeping:
2 bedrooms, sleeps 6: 1 double, 1 twin with 2 single beds, 1 double sofa bed

Living:
living/kitchen area, heating, shower & WC

Eating:
fitted kitchen with cooking hobs, oven & fridge-freezer

Outside:
table & chairs, sun loungers & parasol

Pets:
accepted

AR2 – MINI LUXE – Mobile Home

Sleeping:
1 bedroom, sleeps 4: 1 twin with 2 single beds, sofa bed

Living:
living/kitchen area, shower & WC

Eating:
fitted kitchen with cooking hobs & fridge

Outside:
table & chairs, sun loungers & parasol

Pets:
accepted

Weekly Charges		
	AR1	AR2
Low Season *(from)*	€ 360	€ 220
High Season *(from)*	€ 810	€ 650

Mobile homes & chalets

445

FR83030 Camping Caravaning Leï Suves
Quartier du Blavet, F-83520 Roquebrune-sur-Argens (Var)

For our full description of this campsite ▶ see page 379

AR1 – TYPE D – Mobile home

Sleeping:
2 bedrooms, sleeps 6: 2 twin with 2 single beds, double sofa bed

Living:
living/kitchen area, shower & WC

Eating:
fitted kitchen with gas oven

Outside:
covered terrace with garden furniture

Pets:
not accepted

Weekly Charges	
	AR1
Low Season *(from)*	€ 280
High Season *(from)*	€ 660

FR83060 Camping Caravaning de la Baume
Route de Bagnols, F-83618 Fréjus (Var)

For our full description of this campsite ▶ see page 386

AR1 – BASTIDON – Chalet

Sleeping:
1 bedroom, sleeps 4-6: 1 double, 2 sofa beds

Living:
living/kitchen area, WC

Eating:
fitted kitchen with cooking hobs & fridge

Outside:
covered terrace, table & chairs, sunloungers

Pets:
accepted

AR2 – PHOENIX – Mobile Home

Sleeping:
2 or 3 bedrooms, sleeps 6: 1 double, 2 (or 4) single beds, 1 sofa bed

Living:
living/kitchen area, shower & WC

Eating:
fitted kitchen with cooking hobs & fridge

Outside:
table & chairs, sunloungers

Pets:
accepted

Weekly Charges		
	AR1	**AR2**
Low Season *(from)*	€ 280	€ 301
High Season *(from)*	€ 875	€ 900

FR83070 Caravaning L'Etoile d'Argens
F-83370 St Aygulf (Var)

For our full description of this campsite ▶ see page 390

Both types of mobile homes are in several different areas throughout the site.

AR1 – WATIPI – Mobile Home

Sleeping:
2 bedrooms, sleeps 6: 1 double, 1 twin with 2 single beds, 1 double sofa bed; pillows & blankets provided

Living:
living/kitchen area, heating, shower & WC

Eating:
fitted kitchen with cooking hobs, oven & fridge

Outside:
table & chairs, sun loungers & parasol

Pets:
accepted

AR2 – IRM – Mobile Home

Sleeping:
2 bedrooms, sleeps 6: 1 double, 1 twin with 2 single beds, 1 double sofa bed; pillows & blankets provided

Living:
living/kitchen area, heating, shower & WC

Eating:
fitted kitchen with cooking hobs, oven & fridge-freezer

Outside:
table & chairs, sun loungers & parasol

Pets:
accepted

Weekly Charges	AR1	AR2
Low Season (from)	€ 280	€ 250
High Season (from)	€ 820	€ 640

FR83170 Camping Domaine de la Bergerie
Vallée du Fournel, Route de Col du Bougnon, F-83520 Roquebrune-sur-Argens (Var)

For our full description of this campsite ▶ see page 385

All featured accommodation is situated in a natural, wooded park, 10 minutes from the coast. Large 200 sq.m. pitches with terraces and parking space.

AR1 – O'HARA 7.3m – Mobile Home

Sleeping:
2 bedrooms, sleeps 4: 1 double, 1 twin with 2 single beds

Living:
living/kitchen area, heating, shower & WC

Eating:
fitted kitchen with cooking hobs, microwave & fridge-freezer

Outside:
patio with table & chairs, sun loungers

Pets:
accepted (supplement in high season)

AR2 –O'HARA 8.3m – Mobile Home

Sleeping:
2 bedrooms, sleeps 5: 1 double, 1 twin with 2 single beds, 1 single sofa bed

Living:
living/kitchen area, heating, shower & WC

Eating:
fitted kitchen with cooking hobs, microwave & fridge-freezer

Outside:
table & chairs, sun loungers

Pets:
accepted (supplement in high season)

Weekly Charges	AR1	AR2
Low Season (from)	€ 343	€ 364
High Season (from)	€ 861	€ 917

Mobile homes & chalets

FR83190 Camping La Presqu'île de Giens
153 route de la Madraque-Giens, F-834000 Hyeres (Var)

For our full description of this campsite ▶ see page 389

AR1 – IRM – Mobile home

Sleeping:
2 bedrooms, sleeps 4: 1 double, 1 twin with 2 single beds: blankets & pillows provided

Living:
living/kitchen area, heating, shower & WC

Eating:
fitted kitchen with cooking hobs, microwave & fridge-freezer

Outside:
covered patio with table & chairs

Pets:
accepted

AR2 – GITOTEL – Chalet

Sleeping:
3 bedrooms, sleeps 6: 2 double, 1 twin with 2 single beds: blankets & pillows provided

Living:
living/kitchen area, heating, shower & WC

Eating:
fitted kitchen with cooking hobs, microwave & fridge-freezer

Outside:
covered patio with table, chairs & sunloungers

Pets:
accepted

Weekly Charges	AR1	AR2
Low Season (from)	€ 300	€ 350
High Season (from)	€ 630	€ 780

FR83200 Camping Caravaning Les Pêcheurs
F-83520 Roquebrune-sur-Argens (Var)

For our full description of this campsite ▶ see page 393

The mobile homes can be found on large pitches (100 sq.m.) in the quiet rear part of the site.

AR1 – SHELBOX PARADIS'HOME – Mobile Home

Sleeping:
2 bedrooms, sleeps 6: 1 double, 1 twin with 3 single beds, 1 single sofa bed; pillows & blankets but not sheets provided

Living:
living/kitchen area, fan, heating, shower & WC

Eating:
fitted kitchen with cooking hobs, microwave & fridge-freezer

Outside:
table & chairs, sun loungers & parasol

Pets:
accepted (supplement payable)

Weekly Charges	AR1
Low Season (from)	€ 330
High Season (from)	€ 710

FR83220 Camping Caravaning Cros de Mouton

B.P. 116, F-83240 Cavalaire-sur-Mer (Var)

For our full description of this campsite ▶ see page 385

Mobile homes are located at the lowest part of the site, each divided by hedges with plenty of shade provided by trees. The chalets are situated at the highest point of the site and some have panoramic views across the bay of Cavalaire.

AR1 – IRM – Mobile Home

Sleeping:
2 bedrooms, sleeps 6: 1 double, 1 twin with 2 single beds, 1 double sofa bed; pillows & blankets provided

Living:
living/kitchen area, heating, shower & WC

Eating:
fitted kitchen with cooking hobs, microwave & fridge

Outside:
table & chairs, parasol

Pets:
accepted

AR2 – GITOTEL – Chalet

Sleeping:
2 bedrooms, sleeps 6: 2 double, 1 twin with 2 bunk beds; pillows & blankets provided

Living:
living/kitchen area, heating, shower & WC

Eating:
fitted kitchen with cooking hobs, microwave & fridge

Outside:
table & chairs, parasol

Pets:
accepted

Weekly Charges	AR1	AR2
Low Season *(from)*	€ 360	€ 360
High Season *(from)*	€ 675	€ 675

FR20040 Riva Bella Nature Resort & Spa

B.P. 21, F-20270 Alèria (Haute-Corse)

For our full description of this campsite ▶ see page 401

AR1 – CHALET 4

Sleeping:
2 bedrooms, sleeps 5: 1 double, 1 single bed, 2 bunk beds, all bed linen provided

Living:
living/kitchen area, heating, shower & WC

Eating:
fitted kitchen with cooking hobs & fridge

Outside:
table & chairs, sun loungers & parasol

Pets:
accepted

AR2 – CHALET 2

Sleeping:
2 bedrooms, sleeps 4: 1 double, 2 bunk beds; all bed linen provided

Living:
living/kitchen area, heating, shower & WC

Eating:
fitted kitchen with cooking hobs & fridge

Outside:
table & chairs, sun loungers & parasol

Pets:
accepted

Weekly Charges	AR1	AR2
Low Season *(from)*	€ 329	€ 322
High Season *(from)*	€ 749	€ 728

FR20050 Camping Naturiste Club La Chiappa

F-20137 Porto-Vecchio (Corse-du-Sud)

For our full description of this campsite ▶ see page 398

AR1 – TYPE C – Bungalow	AR2 – TYPE B – Bungalow
Sleeping:	**Sleeping:**
2 bedrooms, sleeps 4: 2 twin with 2 single beds; pillows& blankets provided	1 bedroom, sleeps 2: 1 twin with 2 single beds; pillows & blankets provided
Living:	**Living:**
living/kitchen area, shower & WC	living/kitchen area, shower & WC
Eating:	**Eating:**
fitted kitchen with fridge	fitted kitchen with fridge
Outside:	**Outside:**
table & chairs	table & chairs
Pets:	**Pets:**
accepted	accepted

Weekly Charges	AR1	AR2
Low Season *(from)*	€ 588	€ 402
High Season *(from)*	€ 1015	€ 700

NATURIST SITES

We have had very favourable feedback from readers concerning our choice of naturist sites, which we first introduced several years ago.

Apart from the need to have a 'Naturist Licence' (see below), there is no need to be a practising naturist before visiting these sites. In fact, at least as far as British visitors are concerned, many are what might be described as 'holiday naturists' as distinct from the practice of naturism at other times. The emphasis in all the sites featured in this guide at least, is on naturism as 'life in harmony with nature', and respect for oneself and others and for the environment, rather than simply on nudity. In fact nudity is really only obligatory in the area of the swimming pools.

You may still be required to have a Naturist Licence. These can be obtained in advance from either the British or French national naturist associations, but are also available on arrival at any recognised naturist site (a passport sized photograph is required).

OPEN ALL YEAR

The following sites are understood to accept caravanners and campers all year round, although the list also includes some sites that are open for at least ten months. For sites marked with a star (*) – please refer to the site's individual entry for dates and other restrictions. In any case, it is always wise to phone as, for example, the facilities available may be reduced.

Brittany
FR22020 Fleur de Bretagne
FR56150 Du Haras

Normandy
FR76090 Etennemare

Northern France
FR59050 Mun. Clair de Lune

Paris & Ile de France
FR75020 Bois de Boulogne
FR78040 Etang d'Or*
FR91010 Le Beau Village
FR94000 Tremblay

Eastern France
FR88040 Lac de Bouzey
FR88090 Lac de la Moselotte
FR88130 Vanne de Pierre

Vendée & Charente
FR17070 Les Gros Joncs

Loire Valley
FR36050 Vieux Chênes
FR41060 De Dugny
FR86040 Le Futuriste

Burgundy
FR21060 Les Bouleaux

Savoy & Dauphiny Alps
FR38070 L'Oursière*
FR73020 Le Versoyen*
FR73030 Les Lanchettes*
FR74010 Deux Glaciers
FR74130 La Plage*

Atlantic Coast
FR33030 Club d'Arcachon
FR64040 Les Gaves

Dordogne & Aveyron
FR16040 Devezeau
FR24150 Deux Vallées
FR24280 Barnabé

Limousin & Auvergne
FR63060 Le Clos Auroy

Rhône Valley
FR26110 Les 4 Saisons
FR69010 Porte de Lyon

Provence
FR05030 Les Six Stations
FR84080 La Simioune*

Midi-Pyrénées
FR09080 Du Lac
FR09050 La Prade
FR65030 Pyrénées*
FR65080 Le Lavedan
FR65070 Le Rioumajou

Mediterranean West
FR11110 Val d'Aleth
FR34060 Oliveraie
FR34230 De Chênes
FR66130 Eau Vive*

Mediterranean East
FR06050 La Vieille Ferme
FR06080 Les Cigales
FR83210 Les Tournels*

DOGS

Since the introduction in 2000 of the Passports for Pets scheme many British campers and caravanners have been encouraged to take their pets with them on holiday. However, Pet Travel conditions are understandbly strict, the procedure is quite lengthy and complicated so we would advise you to check the current situation before travelling. The Passports for Pets website is: http://www.freespace.virgin.net/passports.forpets

For the benefit of those who want to take their dogs to France, we list here the sites which have indicated to us that they do not accept dogs or have certain restrictions. If you are planning to take your dog we do advise you to phone the park first to check – there my be limits on numbers, breeds, or times of the year when they are excluded.

FR14090	Brévedent	FR29140	Kerlann	FR46040	Moulin de Laborde
FR16020	Gorges du Chambon	FR30160	Le Boucanet	FR64060	Pavillon Royal
FR17010	Bois Soleil	FR34140	La Carabasse	FR66040	Le Soleil
FR17020	Puits de L'Auture	FR34250	Des Sources	FR81110	Saint Martin
FR17040	Bonne Anse Plage	FR40040	La Paillotte	FR84020	Bélézy
FR20030	Merendella	FR40170	La Réserve	FR85210	Les Ecureuils
FR24040	Moulin du Roch	FR40220	Les Acacias	FR85420	Bel

Sites that accept dogs but with certain restrictions:

FR12170	Le Caussanel	FR30070	Boisson	FR68080	Clair Vacances
FR23010	Poinsouze	FR34130	Le Neptune	FR74060	La Colombière
FR24100	Le Moulinal	FR49060	Montsabert	FR83040	La Bastiane
FR24290	Moulin du Bleufond	FR50030	Lez-Eaux	FR83120	Domaine
FR26030	Grand Lierne	FR66170	Mar I Sol	FR83200	Les Pêcheurs
FR29000	Les Mouettes	FR66210	Le Roussillon		

FISHING

We are pleased to include details of sites which provide facilities for fishing on site. Many others are near rivers or in popular fishing areas and have facilites within easy reach. Where we have been given details, we have included this information in our reports. It is always best to contact sites to check that they provide for your individual requirements.

Code	Name	Code	Name	Code	Name
FR01010	La Plaine Tonique	FR20100	Santa Barbara	FR33310	Panorama
FR01040	Lit Du Roi	FR21000	Lac de Panthier	FR33320	Talaris
FR02000	Vivier aux Carpes	FR21030	Savigny-les-Beaune	FR34030	Le Napoléon
FR02030	Croix du Vieux Pont	FR21040	De Fouché	FR34110	Le Club Farret
FR02060	Guignicourt	FR21070	Les Grèbes	FR34130	Le Neptune
FR03010	La Filature	FR22020	Fleur De Bretagne	FR34150	Nouvelle Floride
FR03050	La Petite Valette	FR22030	Nautic International	FR34160	Charlemagne
FR03170	Dompierre	FR22040	Le Châtelet	FR34170	Les Mimosas
FR04010	Hippocampe	FR22060	La Hallerais	FR34180	Borio de Roque
FR04020	Verdon	FR22090	Galinée	FR34240	Le Castellas
FR04030	Moulin de Ventre	FR22130	Port l'Epine	FR34250	Des Sources
FR04060	Haut-Verdon	FR22140	Port La Chaine	FR35000	Vieux Chêne
FR05030	Les Six Stations	FR22200	Le Bocage	FR35020	Des Ormes
FR06070	Origan	FR23010	Poinsouze	FR36050	Vieux Chênes
FR06100	Les Pinèdes	FR24010	Le Verdoyer	FR37030	Moulin Fort
FR07030	Soleil Vivarais	FR24040	Moulin du Roch	FR37050	La Citadelle
FR07070	Les Ranchisses	FR24060	Le Paradis	FR37070	L'Ile Auger
FR07080	La Bastide	FR24070	Lestaubière	FR37110	Bord du Cher
FR07090	Des Plantas	FR24090	Soleil Plage	FR37120	Fierbois
FR07110	Le Pommier	FR24100	Le Moulinal	FR38050	Temps Libre
FR07120	Ardéchois	FR24110	Aqua Viva	FR38070	L'Oursière
FR07130	Les Coudoulets	FR24140	Bel Ombrage	FR38110	Champ du Moulin
FR07150	Domaine de Gil	FR24150	Deux Vallées	FR38120	Bontemps
FR07170	Ludocamping	FR24170	Port de Limeuil	FR38140	Le Colporteur
FR07190	Chambourlas	FR24230	Moulin de Paulhiac	FR39010	Plage Blanche
FR07200	Oasis	FR24240	Les Bo-Bains	FR39030	Chalain
FR07210	L'Albanou	FR24280	Barnabé	FR39040	La Pergola
FR09020	Arize	FR24290	Moulin du Bleufond	FR39050	Fayolan
FR09060	Le Pré Lombard	FR24310	La Bouquerie	FR39080	L'Epinette
FR09080	Du Lac	FR24320	Les Peneyrals	FR39090	Les Bords De Loue
FR11070	Les Mimosas	FR24330	Etang Bleu	FR39110	Le Moulin
FR11110	Val d'Aleth	FR24340	Val de la Marquise	FR40040	La Paillotte
FR12000	Peyrelade	FR24350	Moulin de la Pique	FR40050	Le Col-Vert
FR12020	Les Rivages	FR24420	Les Valades	FR40070	Lous Seurrots
FR12050	Terrasses du Lac	FR25000	Val de Bonnal	FR40120	Arnaoutchot
FR12060	Beau Rivage	FR25050	Saint Point-Lac	FR40170	La Réserve
FR12150	Marmotel	FR26120	Gervanne	FR40190	Saint Martin
FR12160	Les Peupliers	FR27020	Catinière	FR40220	Les Acacias
FR12170	Le Caussanel	FR28110	Bonneval	FR41020	Grenouillière
FR12190	Les Calquières	FR29010	Ty-Nadan	FR41030	Alicourts
FR14060	Hautes Coutures	FR29020	Saint-Laurent	FR41040	Des Marais
FR14090	Brévedent	FR29030	Du Letty	FR41060	De Dugny
FR14100	Du Château	FR29040	Ar Kleguer	FR41090	de la Varenne
FR14130	Fanal	FR29050	Orangerie Lanniron	FR41100	Les Saules
FR14140	Pont Farcy	FR29060	Le Pil-Koad	FR42010	Charlieu
FR14150	Port'land	FR29090	Raguenès-Plage	FR43030	Vaubarlet
FR15030	Le Val Saint Jean	FR29110	La Plage	FR44020	Du Moulin
FR16030	Le Champion	FR29130	Des Abers	FR44040	Sainte-Brigitte
FR16050	Cognac	FR29240	Kéranterec	FR44090	Deffay
FR16060	Marco de Bignac	FR29290	Grand Large	FR45010	Bois du Bardelet
FR17060	Airotel Oléron	FR29340	Côte Des Légendes	FR46040	Moulin de Laborde
FR17200	Au Fil de l'Eau	FR30000	Gaujac	FR46110	Du Port
FR17210	Interlude	FR30060	Fumades	FR47030	Fonrives
FR17220	La Brande	FR30070	Boisson	FR47050	Moulin de Campech
FR17230	L'Océan	FR30100	La Sablière	FR48020	Capelan
FR19050	La Rivière	FR30120	Ile des Papes	FR48060	Lac de Naussac
FR19060	Le Mialaret	FR30160	Le Boucanet	FR49010	Etang de la Brèche
FR19070	Chateau de Gibanel	FR30170	La Sousta	FR49040	Etang
FR19080	Le Vianon	FR30180	Mas de la Cam	FR49090	Isle Verte
FR19090	Le Vaurette	FR30190	Gorges du Gardon	FR50000	Etang des Haizes
FR19100	Au Soleil d'Oc	FR32030	Verduzan	FR50050	Le Cormoran
FR20010	Arinella Bianca	FR32060	Trois Vallées	FR50060	Le Grand Large
FR20030	Merendella	FR33020	Fontaine-Vieille	FR50080	Haliotis
FR20040	Riva Bella	FR33080	Barbanne	FR50090	La Gerfleur
FR20050	La Chiappa	FR33220	Petit Nice	FR51020	Châlons-Champagne

FR52020	Forge de Ste Marie	FR71060	Montrouant	FR83100	La Plage
FR54010	Villey-le-Sec	FR71070	Epervière	FR83120	Domaine
FR55010	Les Breuils	FR71080	Etang Neuf	FR83170	La Bergerie
FR56010	Grande Métairie	FR71090	Lac de St-Point	FR83200	Les Pêcheurs
FR56080	Le Pâtis	FR71110	Du Lac	FR83240	Moulin des Iscles
FR56130	Mané Guernehué	FR72030	Chanteloup	FR83290	Saint Aygulf
FR56160	Vallée du Ninian	FR72060	Val de Sarthe	FR84050	La Sorguette
FR56180	Le Cénic	FR73020	Le Versoyen	FR85130	Pong
FR58030	Bezolle	FR73030	Les Lanchettes	FR85140	Colombier
FR58050	Château De Chigy	FR73040	Le Savoy	FR85200	Petite Boulogne
FR59010	La Chaumière	FR74070	Escale	FR85210	Les Ecureuils
FR59050	Mun. Clair de Lune	FR74170	Moulin de Dollay	FR85260	Guyonnière
FR61010	La Campière	FR76040	La Source	FR85350	La Ningle
FR62060	Orée du Bois	FR77030	Jablines	FR85510	Le Bois Joli
FR63040	La Grange Fort	FR77070	Belle Etoile	FR86030	Relais du Miel
FR63080	Le Moulin de Serre	FR77090	Etangs Fleuris	FR86040	Le Futuriste
FR63090	les Domes	FR78010	International	FR86080	Les Peupliers
FR63140	Les Loges	FR78040	Etang d'Or	FR86090	Saint Cyr
FR64040	Les Gaves	FR78050	Le Val de Seine	FR87020	Leychoisier
FR64060	Pavillon Royal	FR80030	Port de Plaisance	FR88040	Lac de Bouzey
FR64070	Le Ruisseau	FR80060	Val de Trie	FR88060	La Vologne
FR65060	Pyrenees Natura	FR80070	Ferme des Aulnes	FR88080	Des Bans
FR66030	Cala Gogo	FR80100	des Cygnes	FR88090	Lac de la Moselotte
FR66040	Le Soleil	FR81020	Moulin de Julien	FR89060	Les Ceriselles
FR66070	Le Brasilia	FR81030	Gourjade	FR90000	Etang des Forges
FR67030	Du Ried	FR81040	Auzerals	FR91010	Le Beau Village
FR68030	Masevaux	FR81060	Les Clots	FR94000	Tremblay
FR70020	Lac Vesoul	FR83070	Etoile d'Argens		
FR71050	Moulin de Collonge	FR83080	Au Paradis		

GOLF

We understand that the following sites have facilities for playing golf. However, we would recommend that you contact the site to check that the facility meets your requirements.

Brittany
FR35020 Des Ormes

Limousin & Auvergne
FR15030 Le Val Saint Jean

Midi-Pyrénées
FR81030 Gourjade

Mediterranean East
FR83300 Clos Sainte Thérèse

HORSE RIDING

We understand that the following sites offer riding on site for at least part of the year. However, we recommend that you contact the site to check that the facility meet your requirements. It is worth bearing in mind that French attitudes to safety may differ from your own (for example, you may be required to take your own hard hat).

Brittany
FR22140 Port La Chaine
FR29010 Ty-Nadan
FR29290 Grand Large
FR35020 Des Ormes

Normandy
FR50050 Le Cormoran

Paris & Ile de France
FR77030 Jablines
FR78050 Le Val de Seine

Eastern France
FR68070 Les Sources
FR88040 Lac de Bouzey
FR88080 Des Bans

Vendée & Charente
FR17060 Airotel Oléron
FR17210 Interlude
FR17230 L'Océan
FR85200 Petite Boulogne

Loire Valley
FR49010 Etang de la Brèche
FR86090 Saint Cyr

Burgundy
FR58030 Bezolle

Savoy & Dauphiny Alps
FR38110 Champ du Moulin
FR38120 Bontemps
FR73020 Le Versoyen

Atlantic Coast
FR33110 Côte d'Argent
FR33160 Euronat
FR33220 Petit Nice
FR40050 Le Col-Vert
FR40180 Le Vieux Port
FR40220 Les Acacias

Dordogne & Aveyron
FR12150 Marmotel
FR24100 Le Moulinal
FR24240 Les Bo-Bains
FR24250 Tourterelles
FR24310 La Bouquerie
FR46110 Du Port

Limousin & Auvergne
FR63050 La Ribeyre
FR63090 Les Domes

Rhône Valley
FR07030 Soleil Vivarais
FR07080 La Bastide

Provence
FR04020 Verdon
FR84080 La Simioune

Midi-Pyrénées
FR09020 Arize

Mediterranean West
FR11060 Arnauteille
FR30020 La Petite Camargue
FR34170 Les Mimosas
FR34190 Champs Blancs
FR66040 Le Soleil
FR66180 Mas Llinas
FR66200 Les Marsouins

Mediterranean East
FR83020 Esterel
FR83160 Les Cigales

Corsica
FR20010 Arinella Bianca
FR20030 Merendella
FR20050 La Chiappa

PUBLIC HOLIDAYS IN FRANCE 2006

1 January	New Year's Day	5 June	Whit Monday
14 April	Good Friday	14 July	Bastille Day
16 April	Easter	15 August	Assumption
17 April	Easter Monday	1 November	All Saint's Day
1 May	Labour Day	11 November	Armistice Day
8 May	Victory Day 1945	25 December	Christmas
25 May	Ascension	26 December	Boxing Day
4 June	Whit Sunday		(Alsace and Lorraine)

Note that when a holiday falls on a Tuesday or a Thursday, many French people may take the respective Monday or Friday off as well. This is not official and does not apply to institutions such as banks or government offices, but can cause difficulties on occasions.

When taking your car (and caravan, tent or trailer tent) or motorcaravan to the continent you do need to plan in advance and to find out as much as possible about driving in the countries you plan to visit. Whilst European harmonisation has eliminated many of the differences between one country and another, it is well worth reading the short notes we provide in the introduction to each country in this guide in addition to this more general summary.

Of course, the main difference from driving in the UK is that in mainland Europe you will need to drive on the right. Without taking extra time and care, especially at busy junctions and conversely when roads are empty, it is easy to forget to drive on the right. Remember that traffic approaching from the right usually has priority unless otherwise indicated by road markings and signs. Harmonisation also means that most (but not all) common road signs are the same in all countries.

Your vehicle

Book your vehicle in for a good service well before your intended departure date. This will lessen the chance of an expensive breakdown. Make sure your brakes are working efficiently and that your tyres have plenty of tread (3 mm. is recommended, particularly if you are undertaking a long journey).

Also make sure that your caravan or trailer is roadworthy and that its tyres are in good order and correctly inflated. Plan your packing and be careful not to overload your vehicle, caravan or trailer – this is unsafe and may well invalidate your insurance cover (it must not be more fully loaded than the kerb weight of the insured vehicle).

Check all the following:

☐ GB sticker. If you do not display a sticker, you may risk an on-the-spot fine as this identifier is compulsory in all countries. Euro-plates are an acceptable alternative within the EU (but not outside). Remember to attach another sticker (or Euro-plate) to caravans or trailers. Only GB stickers (not England, Scotland, Wales or N. Ireland) stickers are valid in the EU.

☐ Headlights. As you will be driving on the right you must adjust your headlights so that the dipped beam does not dazzle oncoming drivers. Converter kits are readily available for most vehicle, although if your car is fitted with high intensity headlights, you should check with your motor dealer. Check that any planned extra loading does not affect the beam height.

☐ Seatbelts. Rules for the fitting and wearing of seatbelts throughout Europe are similar to those in the UK, but it is worth checking before you go. Rules for carrying children in the front of vehicles vary from country to country. It is best to plan not to do this if possible.

☐ Door/wing mirrors. To help with driving on the right, if your vehicle is not fitted with a mirror on the left hand side, we recommend you have one fitted.

☐ Fuel. Leaded and Lead Replacement petrol is increasingly difficult to find in Northern Europe.

Compulsory additional equipment

The driving laws of the countries of Europe still vary in what you are required to carry in your vehicle, although the consequences of not carrying a required piece of equipment are almost always an on-the-spot fine.

To meet these requirements we suggest that you carry the following:

- ☐ Fire extinguisher
- ☐ Basic tool kit
- ☐ First aid kit
- ☐ Spare bulbs
- ☐ Two warning triangles – two are required in some countries at all times, and are compulsory in most countries when towing.
- ☐ High visibility vest – now compulsory in Spain, Italy and Austria (and likely to become compulsory throughout the EU) in case you need to walk on a motorway.

INSURANCE AND MOTORING DOCUMENTS

Vehicle insurance

Contact your insurer well before you depart to check that your car insurance policy covers driving outside the UK. Most do, but many policies only provide minimum cover (so if you have an accident your insurance may only cover the cost of damage to the other person's property, with no cover for fire and theft).

To maintain the same level of cover abroad as you enjoy at home you need to tell your vehicle insurer. Some will automatically cover you abroad with no extra cost and no extra paperwork. Some will say you need a Green Card (which is neither green nor on card) but won't charge for it. Some will charge extra for the Green Card. Ideally you should contact your vehicle insurer 3-4 weeks before you set off, and confirm your conversation with them in writing.

Breakdown insurance

Arrange breakdown cover for your trip in good time so that if your vehicle breaks down or is involved in an accident it (and your caravan or trailer) can be repaired or returned to this country. This cover can usually be arranged as part of your travel insurance policy (see below).

Documents you must take with you

You may be asked to show your documents at any time so make sure that they are in order, up-to-date and easily accessible while you travel. These are what you need to take:

- ☐ Passports (you may also need a visa in some countries if you hold either a UK passport not issued in the UK or a passport that was issued outside the EU).
- ☐ Motor Insurance Certificate, including Green Card (or Continental Cover clause)
- ☐ DVLC Vehicle Registration Document plus, if not your own vehicle, the owner's written authority to drive.
- ☐ A full valid Driving Licence (not provisional). The new photo style licence is now mandatory in most European countries).

Personal Holiday insurance

Even though you are just travelling within Europe you must take out travel insurance. Few EU countries pay the full cost of medical treatment even under reciprocal health service arrangements. The first part of a holiday insurance policy covers people. It will include the cost of doctor, ambulance and hospital treatment if needed. If needed the better companies will even pay for English language speaking doctors and nurses and will bring a sick or injured holidaymaker home by air ambulance.

The second part of a good policy covers things. If someone breaks into your motorhome and steals your passports and money, one phone call to the insurance company will have everything sorted out. If you manage to drive over your camera, it should be covered. NB – most policies have a maximum payment limit per item, do check that any valuables are adequately covered.

An important part of the insurance, often ignored, is cancellation (and curtailment) cover. Few things are as heartbreaking as having to cancel a holiday because a member of the family falls ill. Cancellation insurance can't take away the disappointment, but it makes sure you don't suffer financially as well. For this reason you should arrange your holiday insurance at least eight weeks before you set off.

Whichever insurance you choose we would advise reading very carefully the policies sold by the High Street travel trade. Whilst they may be good, they may not cover the specific needs of campers, caravanners and motorcaravanners.

Telephone 0870 405 4059 for a quote for our European Camping Holiday Insurance with cover arranged through Green Flag Motoring Assistance and Inter Group Assistance Services, one of the UK's largest assistance companies. Alternatively visit our website at www.insure4europe.com.

European Health Insurance Card (EHIC)

Important Changes since E111: Since September 2005 new European Health Insurance Cards have replaced the E111 forms .

Make sure you apply for your EHIC before travelling in Europe. Eligible travellers from the UK are entitled to receive free or reduced-cost medical care in many European countries on production of an EHIC. This free card is available by completing a form in the booklet 'Health Advice for Travellers' from local Post Offices. One should be completed for each family member. Alternatively visit www.dh.gov.uk/travellers and apply on-line. Please allow time to send your application off and have the EHIC returned to you.

The EHIC is valid in all European Community countries plus Iceland, Liechtenstein, Switzerland and Norway. If you or any of your dependants are suddenly taken ill or have an accident during a visit to any of these countries, free or reduced-cost emergency treatment is available - in most cases on production of a valid EHIC. Only state-provided emergency treatment is covered, and you will receive treatment on the same terms as nationals of the country you are visiting. Private treatment is generally not covered, and state-provided treatment may not cover all of the things that you would expect to receive free of charge from the NHS.

Remember an EHIC does not cover you for all the medical costs that you can incur or for repatriation - it is not an alternative to travel insurance. You will still need appropriate insurance to ensure you are fully covered for all eventualities.

The Law

You must be aged 18 or over to drive a car in France, but a UK national driving licence is sufficient. You should carry your Registration Document, and your Insurance (valid for use in Europe) and you must display a GB plate. Drive on the right-hand-side of the road, and remember to look left when turning onto another road.

Conditions and Conventions

'A' roads are Autoroutes, usually toll roads
'N' roads are Routes Nationale, the equivalent of our A roads
'D' roads are Routes Departemental, the equivalent of our B roads
'C' roads are Routes Communale, unclassified minor roads

'*Prioité à Droite*' means 'Give way to traffic coming from your right' (even if you think you are on a more main road and have the right of way – you don't, so give way. On roundabouts (rounded anti-clockwise of course) traffic already IN the roundabout has priority.

Traffic Lights

Lights in France turn from Red to Green without going through an amber period. Flashing amber means you can proceed with caution. Most traffic lights have small repeater lights at shoulder height adjacent to the line where you must stop. Watch for 'right filters' – a slowly flashing amber light/arrow which allows you to filter right, with care.

Autoroutes

Mostly these are toll roads, and you must pay to use them. You will either have to pay at the toll (*Péage*) where you join, or you must take a ticket from the machine at the Péage and surrender this, with your money or credit card, at the *Péage* where you leave the Autoroute. There are service areas (*Aires de Service*) with full facilities every 40 km, and rest areas (*Aires de Repos*) also at regular intervals. Both have warning signs well in advance, indicating the facilities and even the price of fuel.

Speed

Most of Europe has a bewildering range of speed limits, but in France it is simple and logical. One set of limits covers motorcaravans, solo cars and cars towing trailers or caravans. These are the limits:

In built-up areas 50 kph (31 mph)
Outside built-up areas 90 kph (56 mph)
Motorways 130 kph (81 mph)

There is also a requirement that no vehicle may use a French motorway unless it can cruise at 80 kph (50 mph). When it is raining the maximum speed outside built-up areas is automatically reduced to 80 kph (50 mph) and on motorways to 110 kph (68 mph). The definition of rain is any time you have to put wipers on, so reduce speed even if it has stopped raining but roads are wet.

The French do not tend to use a sign on the outskirts of a town or village to tell you a speed limit applies. A name post is sufficient to indicate that built-up area limits apply. On the exit from the town you will see the name post again, but with the name crossed out. That means the built-up area speed limits no longer apply.

Speed limits are rigidly enforced: 110 kph means exactly that, not 111 kph. The French have adopted the Gatso automatic speed recording and photographing machine and holidaymakers have returned home to find a speeding summons . Anyone caught exceeding the speed limit by more than 40kph will LOSE THEIR LICENCE ON THE SPOT – this means you won't be able to complete your journey without a substitute driver, to say nothing of the standard £900 fine! Anyone caught for a second offence faces a three month jail sentence plus a £2,200 fine.

www.insure④europe.com

Taking your own tent, caravan or motorhome abroad?
Looking for excellent cover at competitive rates?

Total Peace of Mind

To give you total peace of mind during your holiday our insurance policies have been specifically tailored to cover most potential eventualities on a self-drive camping holiday. Each is organised through Voyager Insurance Services Ltd who specialize in travel insurance for Europe and for camping in particular.

Leave your peace of mind to the specialists in camping insurance, not to chance.

24 Hour Assistance

Our personal insurance provides access to the services of Inter Group Assistant Services (IGAS), one of the UK's largest assistance companies. European vehicle assistance cover is provided by Green Flag who provide assistance to over 3 million people each year. With a Europe-wide network of over 7,500 garages and agents you know you're in very safe hands.

Both IGAS and Green Flag are very used to looking after the needs of campsite-based holidaymakers and are very familiar with the location of most European campsites, with contacts at garages, doctors and hospitals nearby.

SAVE with an Annual policy

If you are likely to make more than one trip to Europe over the next 12 months then our annual multi-trip policies could save you money. Personal cover for a couple starts at just £99 and the whole family can be covered for just £121. Cover for up to 17 days wintersports participation is included.

Low Cost Annual multi-trip insurance

Premier Annual Europe self-drive	Premier Annual Europe self-drive
including 17 days wintersports	including 17 days wintersports
£99.00 per couple	**£121.00** per family

Low Cost Combined Personal & Vehicle Assistance Insurance

Premier Couples Package	Premier Family Package
10 days cover for vehicle and 2 adults	10 days cover for vehicle, 2 adults plus dependent children under 16
£74.00*	**£91.00***

* Motorhomes, cars towing trailers and caravans, all vehicles over 4 years old and holidays longer than 10 days attract supplements – ask us for details. See leaflet for full terms and conditions.

One call and you're covered – ask us for a leaflet or no-obligation quote.

0870 405 4059   DELTA EUROCARD MasterCard VISA

Policies despatched within 24 hours insure4europe.com is a trading name of Mark Hammerton Travel Ltd.

A SHOW NEAR YOU, NORTH OR SOUTH...

MANCHESTER'S CARAVAN AND MOTORHOME SHOW
19-22 JANUARY 2006, G-MEX

CARAVAN &
MOTORHOME
SHOW 2006
G-MEX MANCHESTER
19–22 JANUARY

The Caravan and Motorhome Show held at G-Mex Manchester i the perfect place to come and view the latest products and top brands on the market. I the ideal opportunity to compare product specifications and do your market research. Thi year the show celebrates a successful 10 years with many dealers showcasing top brands, is a bargaining ground you could only dream of and a one stop shop for all your caravanning needs. Brands at the show include Adria, Timberland, Coachman, Compass, Fleetwood, Avondale, Swift, Crystal and many more. With everything all under one roof, ther is no need to travel from dealer to dealer, you can arrange your finance, set up your insurance, join clubs and even subscribe to your favourite magazines.

We have an array of awnings from various exhibitors. We even have a dedicated accessori hall with more caravanning accessories than ever before!

Tickets cost £8/£7 (Adult/Senior), however book in advance and pay just £6.50/£6 on 087 288 288 or at www.caravanshows.com.

SCOTTISH CARAVAN & OUTDOOR LEISURE SHOW 2006
SECC GLASGOW
2–5 FEBRUARY

SECC, GLASGOW
2–5 FEBRUARY 2006

Held at the SECC Glasgow the show provides visitors with the widest variety of outdoor leisure products in Scotland covering holid: homes, caravans, motorhomes, tents, camping accessories, parks, we even have an affordable boat show with prices ranging from £5,000 – £40,000. Discover all the latest products and brands for 2006. The line up includes: Adria, Hymer UK, Swift, Ace, Buccaneer Compass, Elddis, to name but a few!

Discover more UK destinations with Alan Rogers Guides. Towsure will have their Accessory Superstore, with up to 40% discount on all product

Tickets cost £8/£7 (Adult/Senior), however book in advance and pay just £6.50/£6 on 08701 288 288 or at www.caravanshows.com.

CARAVAN &
OUTDOOR
LEISURE
SHOW 2007

We have some brand new dates for our next Earls Court Show, 4-7 January 2007. Perfect for people looking for a caravan or motorhom or even a park or holiday home to get away more often. We will have many dealers showcasing many leading brands of models and accessories. All your outdoor holiday needs will be catered for at this great show.

EARLS COURT
4-7 JANUARY 2007

We will have plenty of entertainment with activities to suit both young and old. Visit our brand new website for further details
www.caravanshows.com

Driving to Holiday France?

Let us take the wheel...

...and save yourself miles

- Our routes **take you closer** to the popular holiday destinations
- Daily sailings from **Portsmouth**, **Poole** and **Plymouth**
- Choose from daytime and overnight cruise ferry, or high speed services
- Enjoy **award-winning service** with on-board shopping and dining
- Ask about our great value ferry-inclusive holidays

See how much driving we can save you
brittanyferries.com
0870 908 1282

PLYMOUTH
POOLE
PORTSMOUTH
CAEN
CHERBOURG
ST MALO
ROSCOFF
SANTANDER

You're better off booking with The Club

As a member of Europe's Premier Club for touring caravanners, motor caravanners and trailer tenters, you'll enjoy an unrivalled range of services and benefits to ensure you make the most of your holiday.

- **Channel Crossing Booking Service** with special offers, discounts and 'Members Only' ferry rates. You could 'save' more than your membership fee on your first trip.

- **European Site Booking Service** for around 200 inspected sites.

- **Camping Cheque and ACSI Card** '*go as you please*' schemes for freedom of choice.

- **Red Pennant Insurance** - competitive, 'tailor-made' cover.

- **Inclusive Holidays**, touring information and much more....

- **Caravan Club Magazine** free monthly and full of useful information and great holiday ideas.

To make sure you get the best deal when you book, call or visit our website to join or request an information pack.

0800 328 6635
www.caravanclub.co.uk

Quote ref. AR2006

SPECIAL SUBSCRIPTION OFFER

Save a massive 25% – for life!

1 year 12 issues ~~£47.40~~

YOU PAY JUST £34.95!

At last, a magazine for everyone who loves outdoor breaks in Europe's most camping-friendly country!

Whether you camp in a tent, a caravan or a motorhome, Destination France is the must-have guide to getting the best from your holiday. We do the research for you, putting together all the information you need to make the right choices for a great outdoor break. Where to go, how to get there, what to do when you get there, what to take with you (and what to leave behind!) – you'll find it all in Destination France.

Inside you'll find:

- All the travel information you need, from ferries, trains and planes to driving directions and advice
- The inside story on the best destinations – the local attractions, facilities and special activities that you want to know about
- Great places to go that would take years to discover
- Beginners' Guide – handle your first trip like an expert!
- Tests and reviews of all the gear you need to make your trip a breeze
- Regular competitions to win ferry tickets, camping equipment and complete camping holidays

...and much more!

As a founding subscriber, you will receive a huge **25% off** the price of Destination France – *and you will keep that discount every consecutive year that you renew, for life!*

Full price for 12 issues is £47.40 UK (£59.50 overseas), but you pay just **£34.95** UK (£44.60 overseas), plus your copies are delivered to your door at **no extra cost**.

This is a strictly limited offer, so **subscribe today** to enjoy Destination France at a great price!

www.bestfrancemagazine.co.uk ⬅ **SUBSCRIBE ONLINE**

call our hotline – 01795 412861* ⬅ **SUBSCRIBE BY PHONE**

*Quote code DF 100. Calls to this number may be recorded for training purposes

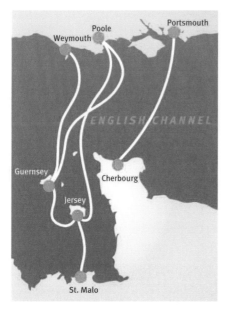

3 ISSUES FOR £1

Our practical titles are packed full of holiday tips, technical advice, reader reviews, superb photography...and much more!
So subscribe to Practical Caravan or Practical Motorhome for just £

YOU save 90% on the shop price with 3 issues for £1
YOU save 15% on the shop price after your trial
RISK-FREE offer*
FREE delivery, straight to your door!
EXCLUSIVE subscriber offers and discounts

CALL 08456 777 812 NOW!
OR VISIT www.haymarketsubs.com quote code PCM05

☐ **Please start my subscription to** *Practical Caravan*. I will pay £1 for the first 3 issues and £8.50 every 3 issues thereafter, saving 15% on the shop price.
☐ **Please start/renew my subscription to** *Practical Motorhome*. I will pay £1 for the first 3 issues and £7.90 every 3 issues thereafter, saving 15% on the shop price.

YOUR DETAILS BLOCK CAPITALS PLEASE (must be completed)

Mr/Mrs/Ms_____ Name_____ Surname_____

Address_____

_____

_____Postcode_____

Telephone_____

E-mail_____
We'd love to send you more great offers and information by email and SMS. Please tick this box to receive these. ☐

This offer is open to UK residents only and is a Direct Debit only offer. Details of the Direct Debit Guarantee are available on request. For International rates please call +44 (0)8456 777 823. Offer ends 31 December 2005. We'd like to send you great offers and information on other products from Haymarket Publishing. Please tick this box if you don't want to receive these offers ☐. Very occasionally we may pass your contact details to another company who's products we think you'd love to hear about. Please tick this box if you don't want to receive this information ☐

*If you're not completely satisfied , simply contact us at anytime and we'll cancel your subscription without further charge

DIRECT DEBIT DETAILS
Instructions to your Bank or Building Society to pay by Direct Debit
To The Manager: Bank/Building Society_____

Address_____
_____Postcode_____

Name(s) of Account Holder(s)_____

Branch Sort Code ☐☐☐☐☐☐ Bank/Building Society account number ☐☐☐☐☐☐☐☐
Reference Number (for office use only)_____

Signature(s)_____

Date_____ Originators ID No. 850899

Instruction to your Bank or Building Society
Please pay **Haymarket Publishing Services Ltd** Direct Debits from the account detailed in this instruction subject to the safeguards assured by the Direct Debit Guarantee. I understand that this instruction may stay with Haymarket Publishing Services Ltd and, if so, details will be passed electronically to my Bank/Building Society.

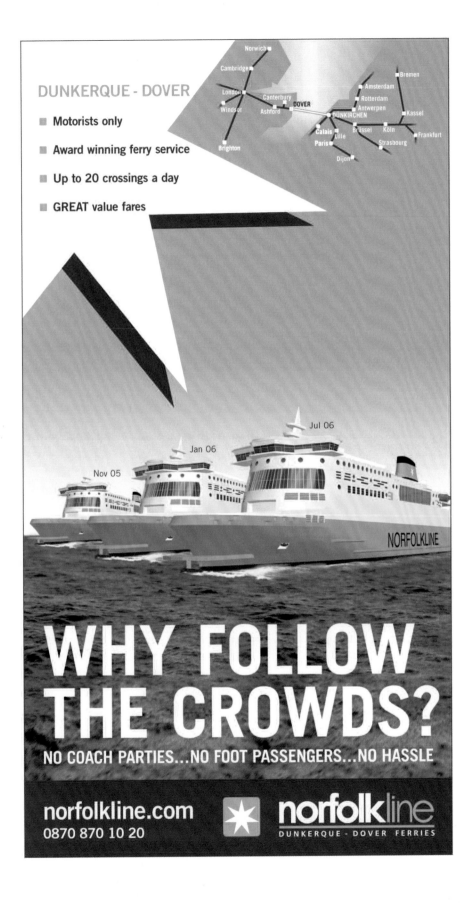

Walking & Cycling Holidays

Discover the easy going alternative

It's all on-line

The all-new website gives you all the details, visit

www.**bellefrance.co.uk**

Belle France offers leisurely holidays through the most beautiful and interesting parts of France.

On our walking and cycling holidays your luggage is moved for you whilst you find your own way, at your own pace with our detailed maps and notes.

Relax in the evening in charming family run hotels, offering a good standard of accommodation and a warm and friendly welcome.

Follow suggested routes, stopping where you choose and enjoy complete freedom.

Call now for a **FREE** brochure **0870 405 4056**

![Sites & Paysages de France logo and photos]

Fifty-eight good reasons for coming to France

SITES & LANSCAPES of FRANCE, 58 quality campsites covering the rich diversity of the French regions.

SITES & PAYSAGES of FRANCE offers campers and caravanners a carefully chosen selection of high quality, 3- and 4-star comfortable campsites across the country. Our 58 campsites are situated in attractively landscaped, tree-shaded environments, with all the amenities for tents, caravans, camping-cars, mobile homes or chalet accommodation. All are laid out with 'room to breathe' and located in areas of great natural beauty, with masses to do and see, from on-site sport and leisure activities, to nearby heritage visits... not forgetting the sublime joys of authentic local French cuisine.

information & booking office in England:
tel. **0870 873 34 11**
www.sites-et-paysages.com

Ask us for your FREE 2006 guide

E-mail us at: **setp@select-site.com**

inconito Photos : getty images

DOVER - DUNKERQUE FERRIES

Dover – Dunkirk

3 brand new ships will be operational for 2006, offering comfort, speed and efficiency.

Motorhomes **Priced as Cars*** Caravans from **£7** each way**

Travel **any time of day**, (including weekends for motorhomes). Popular times will book up fast, so don't delay to secure your first choice!

Weekends are Friday, Saturday, Sunday in each direction. Offer valid all year.

* Supplements for vehicles over 7m may apply. Please ask for details.

** Offer applies to all dates excluding crossings between 14/7-10/9 2006 (midweek and weekend).

P&O Ferries

Dover – Calais

Caravans **Go FREE***   Motorhomes **Priced as Cars****

* Between 23.30 – 07:15, all year except high season weekends.

** Any length, for off peak mid week-crossings all year.

SEAFRANCE
DOVER-CALAIS FERRIES

Dover – Calais

Caravans **Go FREE***   Motorhomes **Priced as Cars****

* Between 23:30 – 07:00, midweek and weekends all year.

** Up to 8m all year.

Brittany Ferries

Portsmouth – Caen
Portsmouth – Cherbourg
St Malo – Portsmouth
(low season only)

Plymouth – Roscoff

50% OFF Caravans

Off peak mid-week crossings.

Offer does not apply to certain Plymouth – Roscoff crossings.

P&O Ferries   Hull – Rotterdam/Zeebrugge

Caravans **Go FREE**   Motorhomes **Priced as Cars**

Any length, Sat/Sun crossings only.
Between 1st May - 31st October 2006.
Bookings must be made by 5th January 2006.

Condorferries   Poole/Weymouth – St Malo

Motorhomes Priced As Cars on all crossings direct to St Malo and via Channel Islands, travelling any day of the week.

Offer excludes high season (26-28/5 and 14/7-23/8 out, 2-4/6 and 21/7-3/9 in).

Don't delay –

these offers are strictly subject to availability and will be first come, first served.

Ferry offers only valid in conjunction with a Camping Cheque or Alan Rogers Travel Service holiday.

Just call us for
an instant quote
0870 405 4055

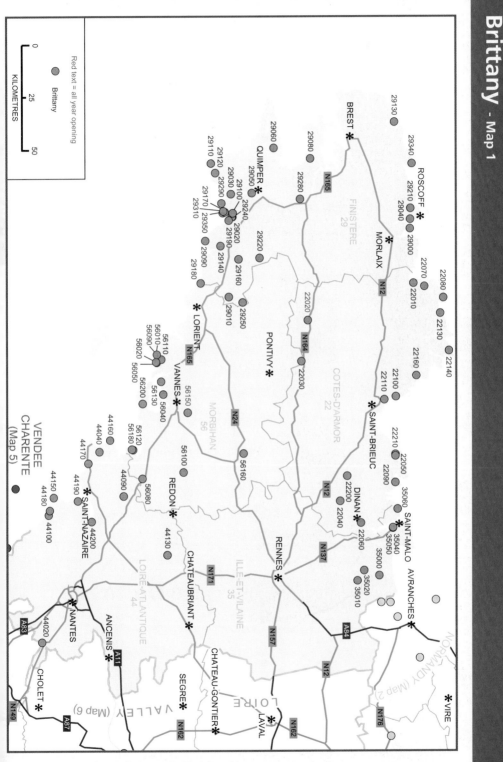

Red text = all year opening

● Brittany

KILOMETRES

0   25   50

BREST ✱

29130

ROSCOFF
29340
29210
29040
29000 ✱

29060

QUIMPER ✱
29080
29280

N165

FINISTERE 29

MORLAIX ✱
22070
22010
N12

22080
22130

22140

29110
29120
29290
29030
29170
29310   29350
29240
29100
29050
29020
29190
29140
29220
29090
29180
29160
29250
29010

22020
22030
22160

PONTIVY ✱

N64

COTES-D'ARMOR 22

22100
22110

22060

SAINT-BRIEUC ✱

LORIENT ✱

56110
56010
56090
56020
56050
56200
56130
56040

VANNES ✱
56150
56100

N165

MORBIHAN 56

N24

56120
56180
56160

56080

REDON ✱

44160
44040
44170

44190

44150
44180
44100

SAINT-NAZAIRE ✱
44200

44090

44130

CHATEAUBRIANT ✱

RENNES ✱

ILLE-ET-VILAINE 35

N171

N157

22210
22050
22090
35060
35050

DINAN ✱
22200
22040

35040
35000

SAINT-MALO ✱
35050

AVRANCHES ✱

35020
35010

N12

N137

A84

N12

VIRE ✱

NORMANDY (Map 2)

N176

VENDEE
CHARENTE
(Map 5)

NANTES ✱
44020
A83

ANCENIS ✱
A11

SEGRE ✱

CHATEAU-GONTIER ✱
N162

LAVAL ✱

LOIRE

LOIRE-ATLANTIQUE 44

CHOLET ✱
N149
A87

LOIRE VALLEY (Map 6)
N162

Sites on this map are featured on pages 21-63 of the guide.
Please refer to the numerical index (page 499) for exact campsite page references.

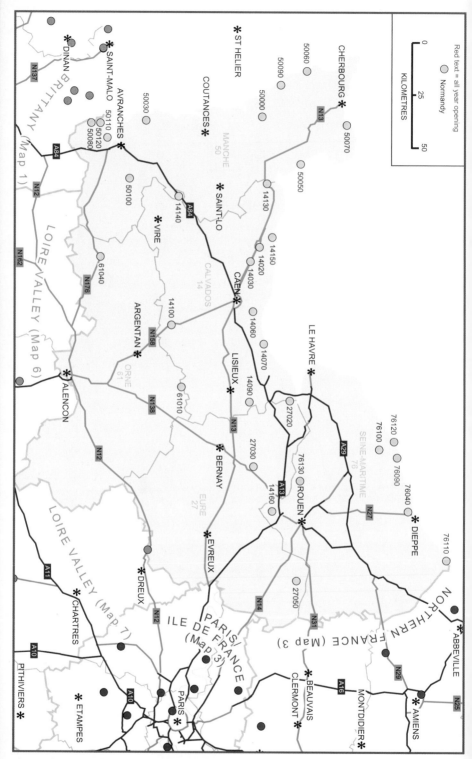

Red text = all year opening

○ Normandy

○ Normandy

KILOMETRES

0 25 50

N137

DINAN (BRITTANY (Map 1))

* SAINT-MALO

* ST HELIER

CHERBOURG

N13

50060

50090

50000

50070

COUTANCES *

* ST HELIER

MANCHE 50

50050

50030

AVRANCHES

50110
50120
50080

A84

N12

50100

14140 A84

* SAINT-LO

14130

50020

* VIRE

14150

14020

14030

CAEN

CALVADOS 14

LOIRE VALLEY (Map 1)

N162

61040

N176

ARGENTAN

14100

N158

ORNE 61

LISIEUX

14060

14070

LE HAVRE *

27020

* ALENCON

61010

N138

N13

14090

BERNAY *

27030

SEINE-MARITIME 76

76120

76100

76090

A29

* DREUX

A11

LOIRE VALLEY (Map 7)

EURE 27

14160 A13

76130 ROUEN

N27

76040

* DIEPPE

76110

EVREUX *

27050

N14

N31

NORTHERN FRANCE (Map 3)

* ABBEVILLE

N29

N25

* CHARTRES

N12

ILE DE FRANCE PARIS/ (Map 3)

BEAUVAIS *

CLERMONT *

MONTDIDIER *

A16

* AMIENS

A10

PITHIVIERS *

* ETAMPES

A10

PARIS

Sites on this map are featured on pages 64-80 of the guide.
Please refer to the numerical index (page 499) for exact campsite page references.

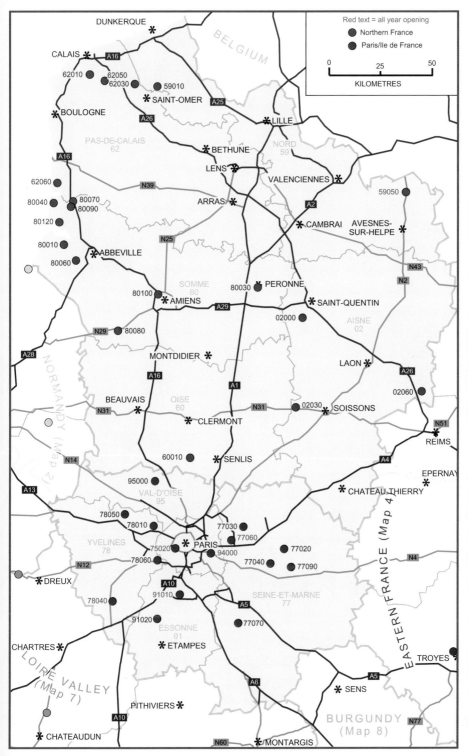

Sites on this map are featured on pages 81-100 of the guide.
Please refer to the numerical index (page 499) for exact campsite page references.

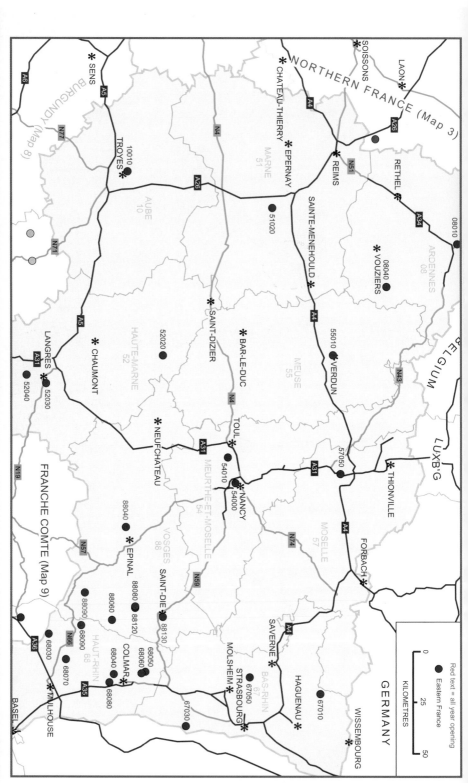

Sites on this map are featured on pages 101-114 of the guide.
Please refer to the numerical index (page 499) for exact campsite page references.

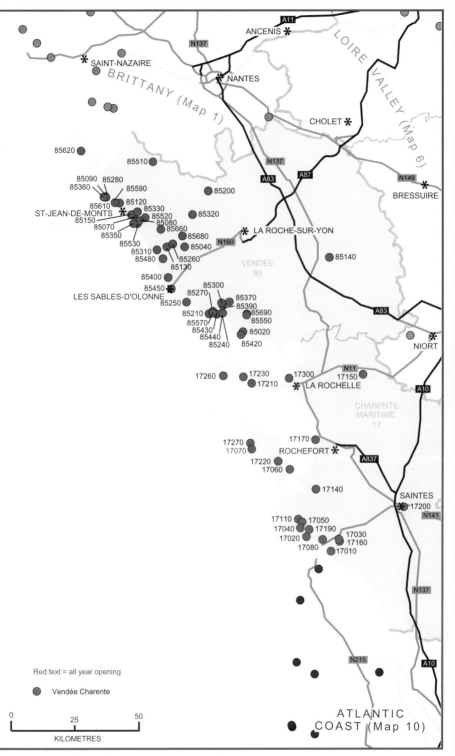

ANCENIS ✱

NANTES ✱

CHOLET ✱

SAINT-NAZAIRE ✱

BRITTANY (Map 1)

LOIRE VALLEY (Map 6)

BRESSUIRE ✱

N149

A11

N137

N137

A83

A87

85620

85510

85090 85280
85360 85590
85120
85610 85330
85150 85520 85320
85070 85080
85350 85660
85530 85680
85310 85040
85480 85260
85130
85400
85450
85270 85300
85250 85370
85210 85390
85570 85690
85430 85550
85440 85020
85240 85420

85200

ST-JEAN-DE-MONTS ✱

LES SABLES-D'OLONNE

LA ROCHE-SUR-YON ✱

N160

VENDÉE
85

85140

NIORT ✱

17260 17230 17300
17210 17150
N11
LA ROCHELLE ✱

A10

CHARENTE-
MARITIME
17

17270 17170
17070
17220
17060

17140

ROCHEFORT ✱

A837

SAINTES ✱
17200
N141

17110 17050
17040 17190
17020 17030
17080 17160
17010

N137

N215

A10

ATLANTIC
COAST (Map 10)

Red text = all year opening

● Vendée Charente

0   25   50

KILOMETRES

Sites on this map are featured on pages 115-149 of the guide.
Please refer to the numerical index (page 499) for exact campsite page references.

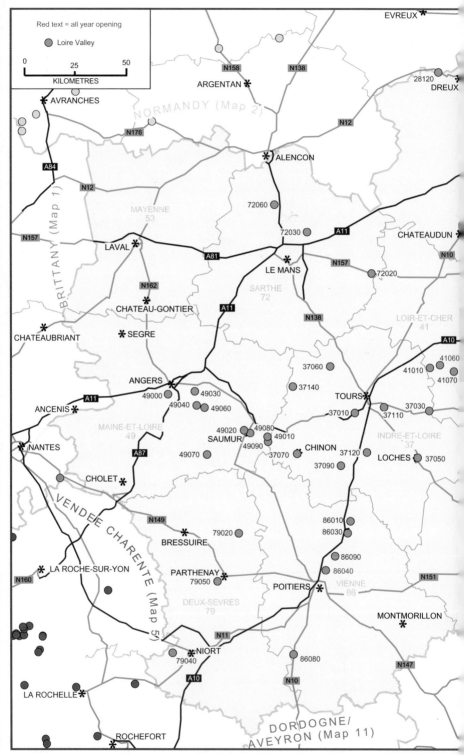

Red text = all year opening

◯ Loire Valley

0   25   50
KILOMETRES

EVREUX ✳

N158   N138

ARGENTAN ✳

28120 ◯
DREUX

N12

NORMANDY (Map 2)

✳ AVRANCHES

N176

A84

✳ ALENCON

N12

MAYENNE
53

CHATEAUDUN

72060 ◯

72030 ◯   A11

N157

N157   LAVAL ✳

A81

LE MANS ✳

72020 ◯

N10

N162

CHATEAU-GONTIER ✳

SARTHE
72

LOIR-ET-CHER
41

N138

A10

✳ CHATEAUBRIANT

✳ SEGRE

37060 ◯

41060 ◯
41010 ◯   41070 ◯

ANGERS ✳

49000 ◯   49030 ◯

49040 ◯   49060 ◯

37140 ◯

TOURS ✳

37030 ◯

37010 ◯   37110 ◯

ANCENIS ✳

A11

MAINE-ET-LOIRE
49

49020 ◯   49080 ◯

SAUMUR   49010 ◯

49090 ◯

INDRE-ET-LOIRE
37

✳ NANTES

A87

49070 ◯

CHINON ✳

37120 ◯

LOCHES ✳   37050 ◯

37070 ◯

37090 ◯

CHOLET ✳

N149

VENDEE

86010 ◯
86030 ◯

79020 ◯

BRESSUIRE ✳

86090 ◯
86040 ◯

CHARENTE (Map 5)

✳ LA ROCHE-SUR-YON

N160

PARTHENAY ✳

79050 ◯

POITIERS ✳

VIENNE
86

N151

DEUX-SEVRES
79

MONTMORILLON ✳

N11

✳ NIORT

79040 ◯

86080 ◯

N147

A10

N10

LA ROCHELLE ✳

DORDOGNE/
AVEYRON (Map 11)

ROCHEFORT ✳

Sites on these maps are featured on pages 151-174 of the guide.
Please refer to the numerical index (page 499) for exact campsite page references.

BRITTANY (Map 1)

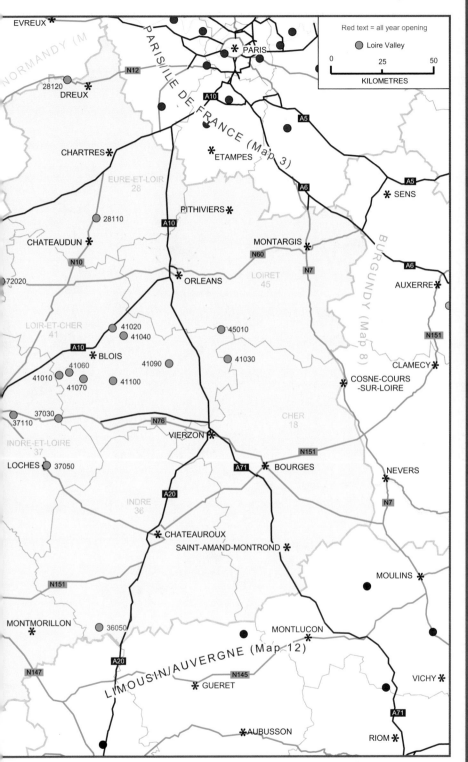

Sites on these maps are featured on pages 151-174 of the guide.
Please refer to the numerical index (page 499) for exact campsite page references.

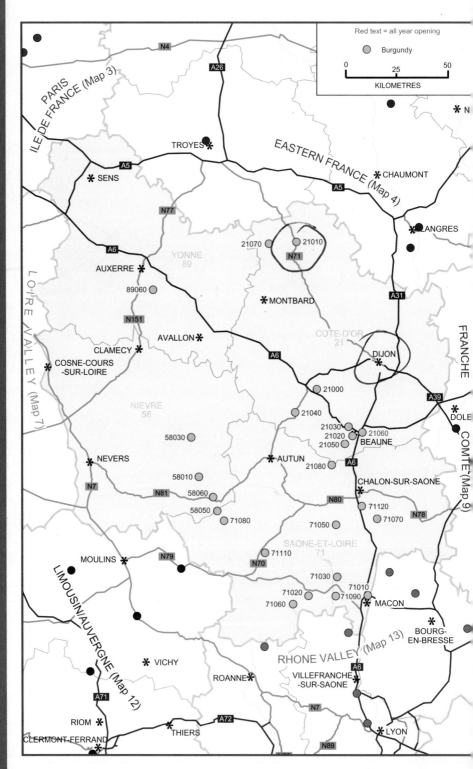

Red text = all year opening

◯ Burgundy

0   25   50
KILOMETRES

N4

A26

PARIS

ILE DE FRANCE (Map 3)

EASTERN FRANCE (Map 4)

✳ N

✳ CHAUMONT

TROYES ✳

A5

✳ SENS

A5

✳ LANGRES

N77

A6

AUXERRE ✳

YONNE
89

21070 ◯   ◯ 21010

N71

89060 ◯

✳ MONTBARD

A31

N151

COTE-D'OR
21

AVALLON ✳

LOIRE VALLEY (Map 7)

CLAMECY ✳

A6

DIJON
✳

FRANCHE

✳ COSNE-COURS
-SUR-LOIRE

◯ 21000

A39

NIEVRE
58

◯ 21040

✳ DOLE

58030 ◯

21030 ◯
21020 ◯   ◯ 21060
21050 ◯   BEAUNE

COMTE (Map 9)

✳ NEVERS

58010 ◯

✳ AUTUN   21080 ◯   A6

N7

N81   58060 ◯

CHALON-SUR-SAONE
✳

58050 ◯
◯ 71080

71050 ◯

N80   71120 ◯

◯ 71070   N78

SAONE-ET-LOIRE
71

MOULINS ✳

N79

71110 ◯

N70

71030 ◯

71020 ◯   71010 ◯
71060 ◯   ◯ 71090   ✳ MACON

✳ VICHY

✳ BOURG-
EN-BRESSE

LIMOUSIN/AUVERGNE (Map 12)

ROANNE ✳

RHONE VALLEY (Map 13)

A6

VILLEFRANCHE ✳
-SUR-SAONE

A71

N7

RIOM ✳

A72

✳ LYON

THIERS ✳

CLERMONT-FERRAND ✳

N89

Sites on these maps are featured on pages 175-186 of the guide.
Please refer to the numerical index (page 499) for exact campsite page references.

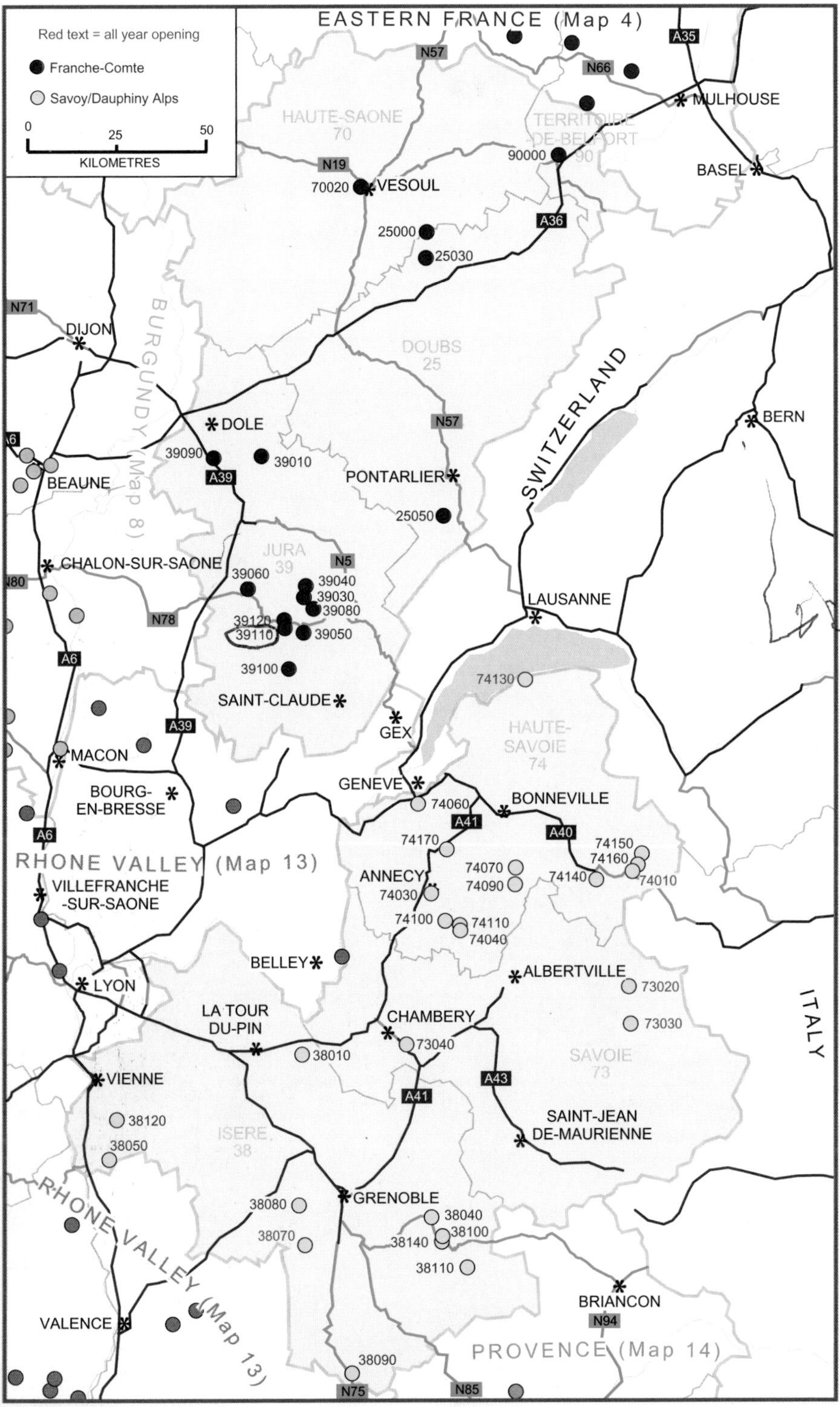

EASTERN FRANCE (Map 4)

Red text = all year opening
● Franche-Comte
○ Savoy/Dauphiny Alps

0   25   50
KILOMETRES

N57

A35

N66

MULHOUSE

HAUTE-SAONE
70

TERRITOIRE
DE BELFORT

90000

BASEL

N19

70020 VESOUL

A36

25000

25030

N71

DIJON

BURGUNDY (Map 8)

DOUBS
25

SWITZERLAND

BERN

DOLE

39090

39010

N57

PONTARLIER

25050

A39

BEAUNE

A6

CHALON-SUR-SAONE

JURA
39

N5

39060

39040
39030
39080

N78

39120
39110

39050

LAUSANNE

N80

A6

39100

SAINT-CLAUDE

GEX

HAUTE-
SAVOIE
74

74130

MACON

BOURG-
EN-BRESSE

GENEVE

74060

BONNEVILLE

74170

A41

74150
74160

A40

74140

74010

RHONE VALLEY (Map 13)

VILLEFRANCHE
-SUR-SAONE

ANNECY

74030

74070
74090

74100

74110
74040

A6

BELLEY

LYON

ALBERTVILLE

73020

ITALY

LA TOUR
DU-PIN

VIENNE

38010

CHAMBERY

73040

73030

SAVOIE
73

38120

38050

ISERE
38

A41

A43

SAINT-JEAN
DE-MAURIENNE

RHONE VALLEY (Map 13)

38080

38070

GRENOBLE

38040
38100

38140

38110

BRIANCON

N94

VALENCE

38090

N75

N85

PROVENCE (Map 14)

Sites on these maps are featured on pages 188-208 of the guide.
Please refer to the numerical index (page 499) for exact campsite page references.

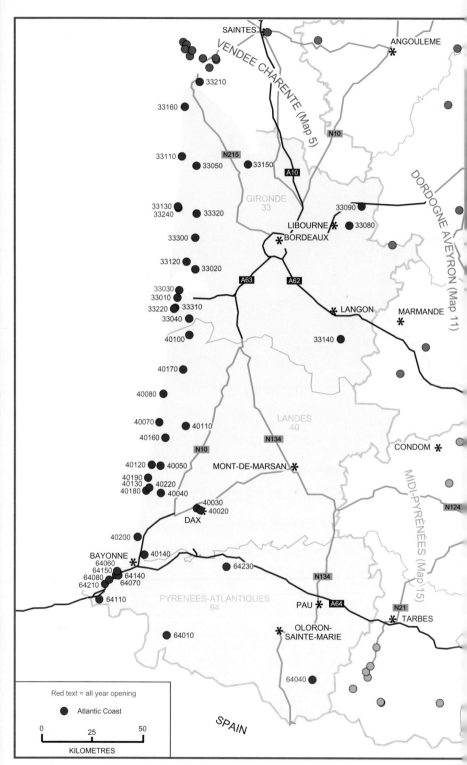

SAINTES

ANGOULEME

VENDEE CHARENTE (Map 5)

33210

33160

N10

33110

N215

33050

33150

A10

GIRONDE
33

33090

LIBOURNE

33080

33130
33240

33320

BORDEAUX

33300

33120

33020

A63

A62

33030
33010

LANGON

MARMANDE

33220

33310

33040

40100

33140

40170

40080

40070

40110

40160

LANDES
40

N134

N10

CONDOM

40120

40050

40190
40130
40180

40220

MONT-DE-MARSAN

40040

40030
40020

DAX

MIDI-PYRÉNÉES (Map 15)

N124

40200

BAYONNE

40140

64060
64150

64230

64080

64140

64210

64070

N134

64110

PYRENEES-ATLANTIQUES
64

PAU

A64

N21

TARBES

64010

OLORON-
SAINTE-MARIE

DORDOGNE AVEYRON (Map 11)

64040

SPAIN

Red text = all year opening

● Atlantic Coast

0   25   50

KILOMETRES

Sites on these maps are featured on pages 209-237 of the guide.
Please refer to the numerical index (page 499) for exact campsite page references.

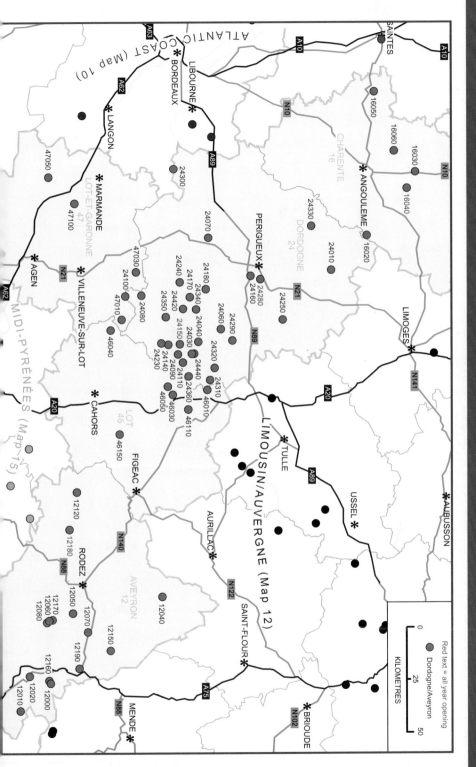

Sites on these maps are featured on pages 238-272 of the guide.
Please refer to the numerical index (page 499) for exact campsite page references.

Red text = all year opening

● Dordogne/Aveyron

KILOMETRES

0
25
50

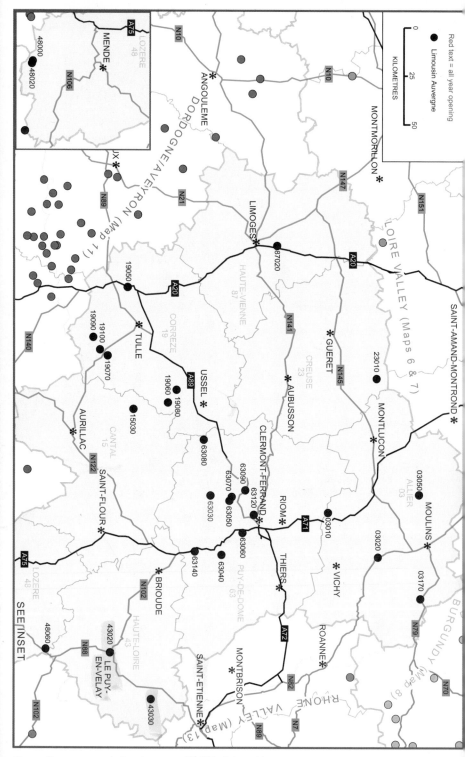

Sites on these maps are featured on pages 273-288 of the guide.
Please refer to the numerical index (page 499) for exact campsite page references.

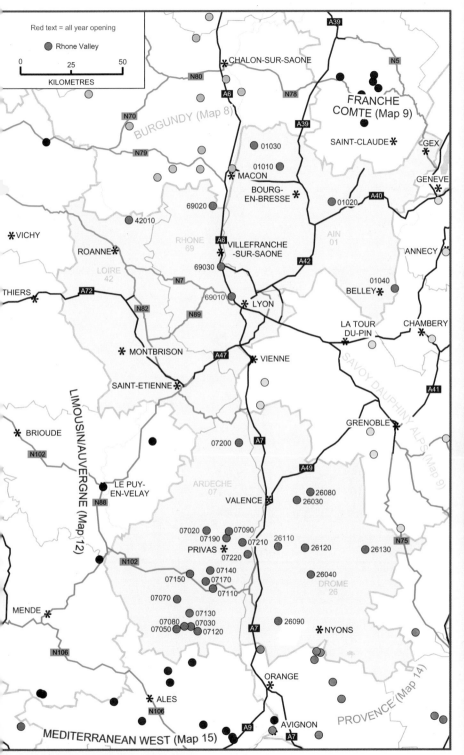

Red text = all year opening

● Rhone Valley

0   25   50
KILOMETRES

A39

CHALON-SUR-SAONE

N5

N80

A6

N78

N70

FRANCHE
COMTE (Map 9)

BURGUNDY (Map 8)

A39

N79

SAINT-CLAUDE ✱

GEX ✱

01030

GENEVE ✱

01010   MACON

BOURG-
EN-BRESSE ✱

01020   A40

69020

42010

RHONE
69

A6

VILLEFRANCHE
-SUR-SAONE

AIN
01

ANNECY

VICHY ✱

ROANNE ✱

69030

A42

01040

BELLEY ✱

LOIRE
42

N7

THIERS ✱

A72

N82

N89

69010   LYON ✱

LA TOUR
DU-PIN

CHAMBERY

MONTBRISON ✱

A47

VIENNE ✱

SAINT-ETIENNE ✱

SAVOY DAUPHINY ALPS (Map 9)

A41

BRIOUDE ✱

GRENOBLE ✱

N102

07200   A7

LE PUY-
EN-VELAY

A49

ARDECHE
07

26080

26030

VALENCE ✱

07020   07090

07190   07210   26110

07220   26120   26130

N75

PRIVAS ✱

07140

07150   07170

07110

07070

26040

DROME
26

MENDE ✱

07130

07080   07030

07050   07120

A7

26090

NYONS ✱

N106

ORANGE ✱

ALES ✱

N106

PROVENCE (Map 14)

MEDITERRANEAN WEST (Map 15)

A9

AVIGNON

A7

N102

N88

N106

LIMOUSIN/AUVERGNE (Map 12)

Sites on these maps are featured on pages 289-306 of the guide.
Please refer to the numerical index (page 499) for exact campsite page references.

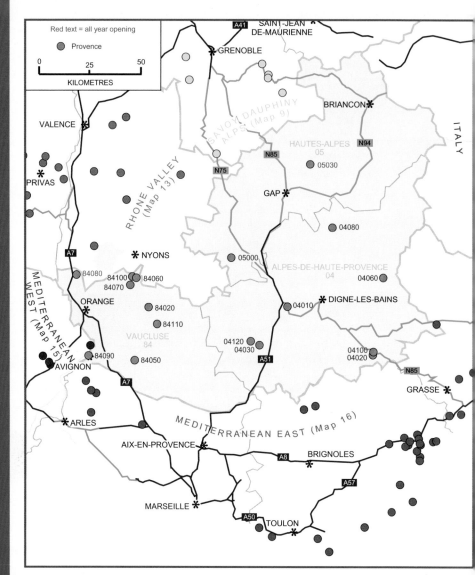

Red text = all year opening

● Provence

0   25   50
KILOMETRES

SAINT-JEAN ✱
DE-MAURIENNE

A41

✱ GRENOBLE

BRIANCON ✱

VALENCE ✱

RHONE VALLEY (Map 13)

SAVOY DAUPHINY ALPS (Map 9)

HAUTES-ALPES 05

N94

N85

05030

N75

PRIVAS ✱

GAP ✱

04080

✱ NYONS

05000

ALPES-DE-HAUTE-PROVENCE 04

04060

A7

84080

84100 84060
84070

04010   ✱ DIGNE-LES-BAINS

ORANGE ✱

84020

84110

VAUCLUSE 84

04120
04030

04100
04020

A51

N85

MEDITERRANEAN WEST (Map 15)

84090

84050

GRASSE ✱

AVIGNON

A7

✱ ARLES

MEDITERRANEAN EAST (Map 16)

AIX-EN-PROVENCE ✱

A8   BRIGNOLES ✱

A57

MARSEILLE ✱

A50

TOULON

ITALY

Sites on these maps are featured on pages 307-318 of the guide.
Please refer to the numerical index (page 499) for exact campsite page references.

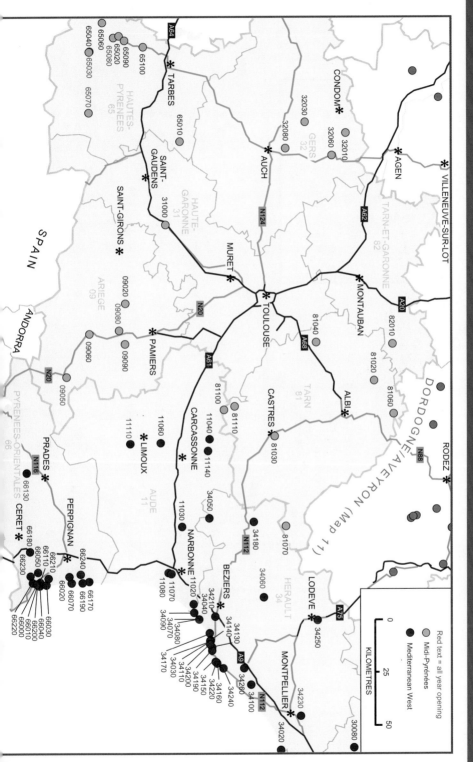

Sites on these maps are featured on pages 319-332 of the guide.
Please refer to the numerical index (page 499) for exact campsite page references.

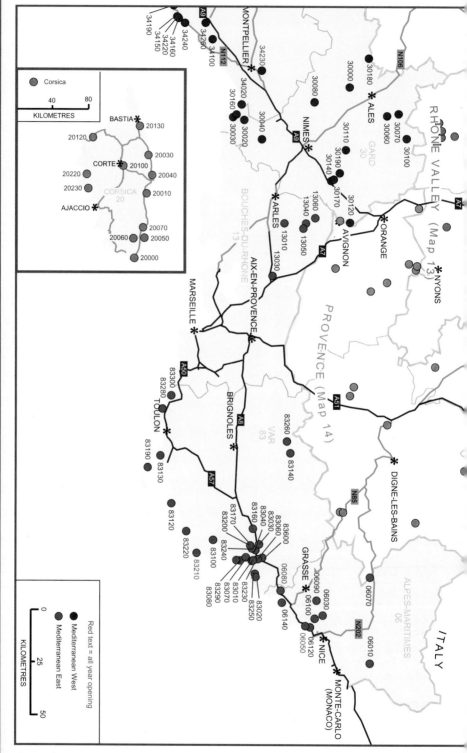

Corsica

40   80
KILOMETRES

Red text = all year opening

● Mediterranean West
● Mediterranean East

0
25
KILOMETRES
50

Sites on these maps are featured on pages 333-402 of the guide.
Please refer to the numerical index (page 499) for exact campsite page references.

For administrative purposes France is actually divided into 23 official Regions covering the 95 départements (similar to our counties).

However, theses do not always coincide with the needs of tourists (for example, the area we think of as the 'Dordogne' is split between two official regions. We have, therefore, opted to feature our campsites within unofficial 'tourist' regions.

We use the departement numbers as the first two digits of our campsite numbers so, for example, any site in the Manche departement will start with the number 50.

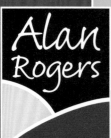